How to use your Connected Casebook

Step 1: Go to **www.CasebookConnect.com** and redeem your access code to get started.

Access Code: 

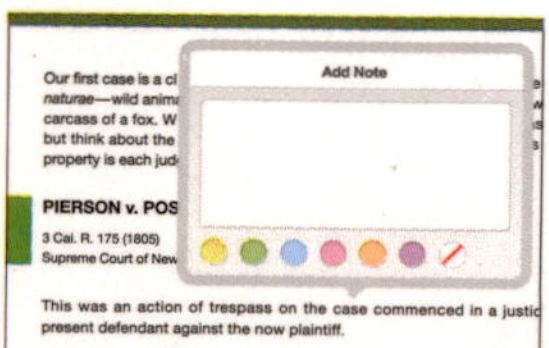

Step 2: Go to your **BOOKSHELF** and select your Connected Casebook to start reading, highlighting, and taking notes in the margins of your e-book.

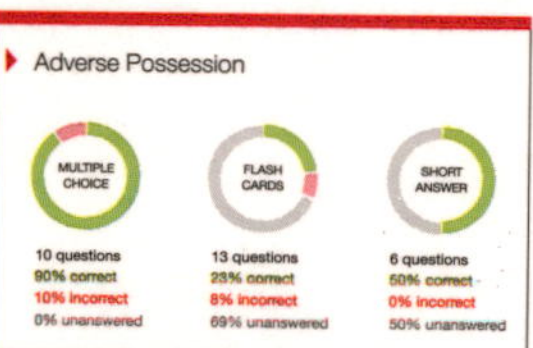

Step 3: Select the **STUDY** tab in your toolbar to access a variety of practice materials designed to help you master the course material. These materials may include explanations, videos, multiple-choice questions, flashcards, short answer, essays, and issue spotting.

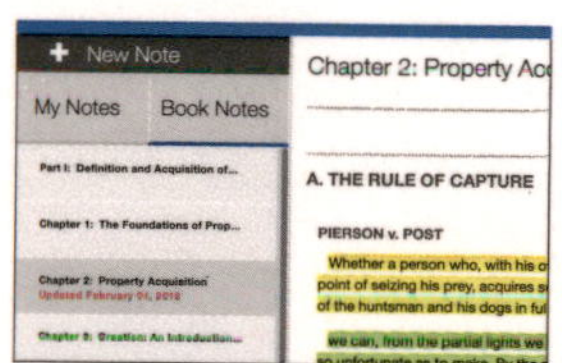

Step 4: Select the **OUTLINE** tab in your toolbar to access chapter outlines that automatically incorporate your highlights and annotations from the e-book. Use the My Notes area for copying, pasting, and editing your book notes or creating new notes.

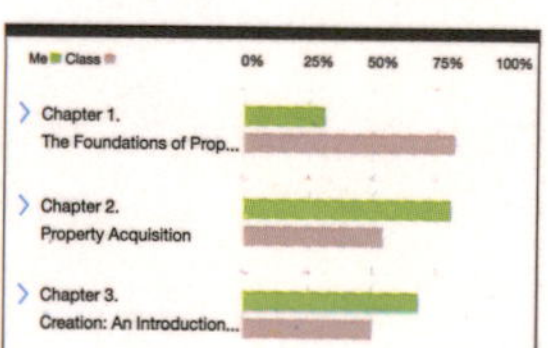

Step 5: If your professor has enrolled your class, you can select the **CLASS INSIGHTS** tab and compare your own study center results against the average of your classmates.

Is this a used casebook? Access code already scratched off?

You can purchase the Digital Version and still access all of the powerful tools listed above. Please visit CasebookConnect.com and select Catalog to learn more.

PLEASE NOTE: Each access code can only be used once. This access code will expire one year after the discontinuation of the corresponding print title and must be redeemed before then. CCH reserves the right to discontinue this program at any time for any business reason. For further details, please see the Casebook Connect End User Agreement.

PIN: 9111149532 HendTort9

88815

The Torts Process

Aspen Casebook Series

The Torts Process

Ninth Edition

James A. Henderson, Jr.

Frank B. Ingersoll Professor of Law, Emeritus
Cornell University Law School

Douglas A. Kysar

Joseph M. Field '55 Professor of Law
Yale University Law School

Richard N. Pearson

Cone, Wagner, Nugent, Johnson, Hasouri & Roth
Professor of Law Emeritus
Fredric G. Levin College of Law, University of Florida

Wolters Kluwer

Published by Wolters Kluwer in New York.

Wolters Kluwer Legal & Regulatory U.S. serves customers worldwide with CCH, Aspen Publishers, and Kluwer Law International products. (www.WKLegaledu.com)

To contact Customer Service, e-mail customer.service@wolterskluwer.com, call 1-800-234-1660, fax 1-800-901-9075, or mail correspondence to:

Wolters Kluwer
Attn: Order Department
PO Box 990
Frederick, MD 21705

Printed in the United States of America.

3 4 5 6 7 8 9 0

ISBN 978-1-4548-7569-7

Library of Congress Cataloging-in-Publication Data

Names: Henderson, James A., 1938- author. | Kysar, Douglas A., author. | Pearson, Richard N., author.
Title: The torts process / James A. Henderson Jr., Frank B. Ingersoll Professor of Law, Emeritus, Cornell University Law School; Douglas A. Kysar, Deputy Dean and Joseph M. Field '55 Professor of Law, Yale University Law School; Richard N. Pearson, Cone, Wagner, Nugent, Johnson, Hasouri & Roth, Professor of Law Emeritus, Fredric G. Levin College of Law, University of Florida.
Description: Ninth edition. | New York : Wolters Kluwer, 2017. | Series: Aspen casebook series
Identifiers: LCCN 2016056833 | ISBN 9781454875697
Subjects: LCSH: Torts—United States. | LCGFT: Casebooks.
Classification: LCC KF1250 .H46 2017 | DDC 346.7303—dc23
LC record available at https://lccn.loc.gov/2016056833

Certified Chain of Custody
Promoting Sustainable Forestry
www.sfiprogram.org
SFI-01681

SFI label applies to the text stock

About Wolters Kluwer Legal & Regulatory U.S.

Wolters Kluwer Legal & Regulatory U.S. delivers expert content and solutions in the areas of law, corporate compliance, health compliance, reimbursement, and legal education. Its practical solutions help customers successfully navigate the demands of a changing environment to drive their daily activities, enhance decision quality and inspire confident outcomes.

Serving customers worldwide, its legal and regulatory portfolio includes products under the Aspen Publishers, CCH Incorporated, Kluwer Law International, ftwilliam.com and MediRegs names. They are regarded as exceptional and trusted resources for general legal and practice-specific knowledge, compliance and risk management, dynamic workflow solutions, and expert commentary.

To Marcie, Chree, and Danella

Summary of Contents

Contents

Chapter 2. Actual Causation 115

Chapter 3. Negligence: Duty of Care and Proof of Breach 175

Chapter 5. Trespass to Land and Nuisance 439

Chapter 6. Strict Liability 481

Chapter 7. Products Liability 515

Table of Continuing Notes

Table of Problems

Preface

The Torts Process is premised on the view that tort law is more than a collection of doctrines and policies, and that it cannot realistically be understood apart from the processes by which tort disputes are resolved. It is as important for students to grasp the roles of the lawyer, the trial judge, the jury, and the appellate court in resolving a tort claim as it is to understand the doctrinal and policy elements that are at play. We find that providing students with this process perspective greatly enhances their appreciation for the actual nature, functions, and limits of tort law. To aid this effort to study tort law in motion, we have included a series of problems that challenge students to apply their understanding of doctrine to concrete circumstances. We have found that students, even in their first weeks of law study, benefit significantly from this effort and find it interesting and rewarding. There is no need, however, to assign all, or indeed any, of the problems, for the book is also designed to function as a traditional casebook. The book seeks to enrich and broaden students' understanding by providing integrated discussions of tort theory and policy issues and by raising important ethical and professional responsibility considerations.

For the ninth edition, we have updated the discussion material and added several new problems and lead cases. Specific topics such as governmental immunity and market share liability have been given added coverage. In addition, we have undertaken a comprehensive expansion throughout the book of the ''Law and Behavior'' notes, which summarize social scientific and empirical research on human behavior, legal decision making, and the tort system. We have also updated Chapter 11 significantly to reflect contemporary debates concerning race relations and the psychology of prejudice. Chapter 15, on comparative and international aspects of tort law, was new in the seventh edition, and we have made several changes for this edition in order to reflect major developments in Alien Tort Statute litigation. As with previous updates, however, this edition retains the book's original flavor. Those who have used the earlier editions will find this edition comfortably familiar.

James A. Henderson, Jr.
Douglas A. Kysar
Richard N. Pearson

February 2017

Acknowledgments

This book is now in its ninth edition, and the authors would like to thank all those who over the years have made significant contributions. Notably, Jylanda Diles helped assemble and prepare the manuscript for several editions and we remain deeply in her debt. We also would like to thank the student research assistants at the Yale Law School who helped with this edition: Cecilia Cheng, McKenna Cutler-Freese, Josh Handelsman, Scott Levy, Hyun-Soo Lim, David Miller, Conor Dwyer Reynolds, Bonnie Robinson, Aisha Saad, Javier Sinha, Roseanna Sommers, Beatrice Walton, and Jack Whiteley. We thank Deans Eduardo M. Peñalver and Robert C. Post for their support.

We also thank the authors and publishers of the following for permitting us to include excerpts from these works:

Kenneth S. Abraham, Insurance Law and Regulation: Cases and Materials (5th ed. 2010). Reprinted by permission of Thomson Reuters.

Kenneth S. Abraham, Twenty-First Century Insurance and Loss Distribution in Tort Law, in Exploring Tort Law (M. Stuart Madden, ed., 2005). Reprinted with the permission of Cambridge University Press.

American Bar Association, excerpts from the Model Rules of Professional Conduct, copyright © by the American Bar Association. Reprinted by permission.

American Law Institute, Restatement (Second) Agency, Volume 1. Copyright © 1958 by the American Law Institute. Reprinted with the permission of the American Law Institute. All right reserved.

American Law Institute, Restatement (Second) of Torts, Volumes 1 and 2. Copyright © 1965 by the American Law Institute. Reprinted with the permission of the American Law Institute. All right reserved.

American Law Institute, Restatement (Third) of Torts: Apportionment of Liability. Copyright © 2000 by the American Law Institute. Reprinted with the permission of the American Law Institute. All right reserved.

American Law Institute, Restatement (Third) of Torts: Liability for Physical and Emotional Harm, Volume 1. Copyright © 2009 by the American Law Institute. Reprinted with the permission of the American Law Institute. All right reserved.

American Law Institute, Restatement (Third) of Torts: Products Liability. Copyright © to the Sixth Edition 1998 by the American Law Institute. Reprinted with the permission of the American Law Institute. All right reserved.

Clarence Morris & C. Robert Morris, Jr., Morris on Torts 376-378 (2d ed. 1980) Foundation Press 1980. Reprinted by permission of Thomson Reuters.

National Conference of Commissioners on Uniform State Laws, Uniform Comparative Fault Act. This Act has been reprinted through the permission of the National Conference of Commissioners on Uniform State Laws, and copies of the Act may be ordered from them at a nominal cost at 676 North St. Clair Street, Suite 1700, Chicago, Illinois, 60611, (312) 915-0195.

National Conference of Commissioners on Uniform State Laws, Uniform Commercial Code. Sections of this Code reprinted through the permission of the National Conference of Commissioners on Uniform State Laws, and copies of the Act may be ordered from them at a nominal cost at 676 North St. Clair Street, Suite 1700, Chicago, Illinois, 60611, (312) 915-0195.

National Conference of Commissioners on Uniform State Laws, Uniform Contribution Among Tortfeasors Act. Copyright © 1955 by West Publishing Co. Sections 1 and 2 reprinted through the permission of the National Conference of Commissioners on Uniform State Laws, and copies of the Act may be ordered from them at a nominal cost at 676 North St. Clair Street, Suite 1700, Chicago, Illinois, 60611, (312) 915-0195.

The Torts Process

Chapter 1

Introduction to the Torts Process: Liability for Harmful and Offensive Battery

This chapter serves two functions. First, it provides an overview of the process of resolving torts disputes in our legal system. And second, it introduces one branch of the substantive law of torts — liability for harmful and offensive battery.

A. Some General Observations

The Lawyer as Part of the Legal Profession

One of the most important aspects of your undertaking the study of law is that you are joining a very special, time-honored profession.[1] We will be considering issues of professional responsibility throughout this course, with help from a series of continuing notes on the subject. But now is a good time for you to begin to understand what you are letting yourself in for. We begin by making three general points. First, the legal profession is largely self-governing in that the standards of professional responsibility are, for the most part, established by the legal community itself. Second, although one may speak generally of professional responsibility as embodying the requirement that a lawyer behave ethically, it is a significantly more nuanced topic over which bar associations and courts have long labored in order to formulate general rules.[2] Lastly, although bar associations have established an ethical floor below which the lawyer may not delve, many difficult decisions are left to the professional discretion of the lawyer.

Several reasons support the legal profession's self-governance. For one, because the average citizen finds the law a mysterious thing, the understanding necessary for external control of the profession is largely lacking. In addition, the formal agencies that might exercise control, such as legislatures and courts, are themselves controlled substantially, if not wholly, by lawyers. Finally, as noted in the preamble to the Model Rules of Professional Conduct, adopted by the American Bar Association (ABA) in 1983, "[s]elf-regulation also helps maintain the legal profession's independence from government domination. An independent legal profession is an important force in preserving government under law, for abuse of legal authority is more readily challenged by a profession whose members are not dependent on government for the right to practice."

1. As an enterprise separate from the church, the legal profession appeared in England in the thirteenth century. Once royal courts were established following the Norman Conquest, the clergy was not allowed to represent litigants in lay courts. Representation required not only expertise in legal technicalities but also a working fluency in Norman French, the language used in the oral proceedings in English courts after the Conquest, rendering professional advocacy indispensable. See generally J. H. Baker, An Introduction to English Legal History 178-179 (3d ed. 1990).

2. The element of professional regulation probably emerged late in the thirteenth century. Id.

A Bird's-Eye View of the Law of Torts

We begin the study of tort law with the intentional tort of battery, both harmful and offensive. It will help you to understand this important subject if you understand how it fits generally into the broader landscape of tort. Tort law is part of the *common law*, a body of court-made substantive law that developed gradually over many centuries in England and that stands in sharp contrast to the statute-based civil law that developed during the same period in continental Europe. England transferred the common law to her colonies, including North America. The common law of torts may be arranged analytically under three major headings: (1) intentional torts (of which battery is part), (2) negligence, and (3) strict liability. Historically, American tort law traces its lineage back to the writs of trespass in the King's Courts in England in the centuries following the Norman Conquest. Formally, the writs from which the law of torts developed were orders, backed by the authority of the Crown, that defendants appear in court. They were limited in number and scope, and plaintiffs had to adhere strictly to their predetermined elements. At the outset, the writ of trespass was essentially criminal in nature and sought to punish volitional acts committed with force and arms that had harmed persons or property and thus threatened the King's peace.[3] Gradually, along with the development of private causes of action, courts extended the basic writs of trespass to include what today are known as the intentional torts of battery, assault, and false imprisonment. Even later, the writ of trespass on the case developed and eventually evolved into negligence. Under the law of negligence, intentional wrongdoing is no longer necessary; acting without taking reasonable precautions for the safety of others supports liability for unintended harm caused by such conduct. And finally, relatively recently, common law courts began to identify categories of harmful conduct upon which strict liability is imposed without a showing of either wrongful intent or negligence. Of course, to the extent that the original writs of trespass stood ready to impose liability without any proof of negligence, these recent examples of strict liability may be viewed as a return, full circle, to the starting place of tort.

In addition to learning about tort law in this course, you will also be learning about the processes and procedures by which tort claims are resolved in our system. Indeed, this book is dedicated to the proposition that the substantive law can be understood only in relation to the processes by which it is applied.[4] Formal adjudication, which takes place in both state and federal trial courts, is the subject of a separate first-year law course, civil procedure. But it is sufficiently important to your study of the torts process that we provide a preliminary overview of the processes by which our legal system resolves torts disputes.

3. See generally id. [illegible]

4. This same interco[illegible] istory of the common law. In one author's des[illegible] bservations (id. at 63):

> Much of our l[illegible] on of law from procedure is put c[illegible] was fundamental to the common la[illegible] substantive law as now understo[illegible] stract, but grew around the forms [illegible]'s courts. There was a law of writ[illegible]

B. *A Preliminary Look at the Adjudicative Process*

Although the substance of this course involves the law of torts, that substance is created, defined, amended, and applied through many legal processes, including the process of adjudication. This section is designed to give you a preliminary look at adjudication in broad outline, so that later, when you study a particular problem or decision, you will know where the case has been and where it might be going.

The Investigation

Of all the potential tort claims that arise when one person harms another, only a few will be brought to a lawyer. See David M. Engel, Perception and Decision at the Threshold of Tort Law: Explaining the Infrequency of Claims, 62 DePaul L. Rev. 293 (2013). For someone to call upon a lawyer for help, he or she must be aware of possibly having a valid claim; must decide to pursue it; must be unwilling, or unable, to handle it alone; must know that a lawyer's help is available; and must be willing to incur the cost, both pecuniary and psychological, of invoking the torts process.

Once a claimant consults a lawyer, the next step in the process is for the lawyer to listen to the client's story to find out what happened from the client's viewpoint. Deciding to go to a lawyer is a major move, and a client typically will have already decided that he or she is right and that the other person is wrong. For this reason, it takes skill on the part of the lawyer to get a reasonably objective view of what happened without antagonizing the client. It may become readily apparent at this first interview that what the client thinks is a valid claim is clearly without legal merit and for that reason should be dropped. Letting the client down easily when the claim is without merit is a skill that is important both to the lawyer and to the legal profession.

Aside from assessing the potential merit of the claim, the lawyer will want to know when the claim arose. In every jurisdiction, *statutes of limitation* allow injured plaintiffs only a limited length of time to commence legal actions. These periods, which generally range from one to four years, typically begin to run when the plaintiff discovers or should have discovered the injury. Tort actions are usually subject to shorter limitation periods than contract actions, and battery actions are frequently subject to shorter periods than negligence actions. Plaintiffs who do not bring their actions within the time allowed are barred from recovery, although the statutes of limitation for persons under legal disabilities, such as minors, are suspended, or *tolled,* during the periods of disability.

Even if it appears that the claim has legal merit and is not time-barred, it may not be worth pursuing further if the harm suffered by the client is insubstantial. The clearest case of liability may be dropped if the amount of money damages likely to be recovered is insignificant. Of course, this effect of the size of the potential recovery upon the decision to go forward works both ways. If the client is severely harmed, a case in which liability is questionable may still be worth pursuing. For an in-depth empirical analysis of how in practice plaintiffs' lawyers determine which cases to pursue, see Stephen Daniels & Joanne Martin, Plaintiff's Lawyers: Dealing With the Possible But Not Certain, 60 DePaul L. Rev. 337 (2011).

Three categories of money damages may be available to the plaintiff in a torts case: nominal, compensatory, and punitive. Nominal damages, as the name implies, are small in amount, often a dollar. They are available only in intentional tort cases, and they are awarded to establish as a matter of public record that the defendant has wronged the plaintiff even if no actual harm occurred. The hope is that the plaintiff will seek satisfaction in the courtroom rather than resort to violent retaliation. Compensatory damages reflect the harm actually suffered. They include out-of-pocket expenses, such as hospital and doctors' bills, which ordinarily are specific and easy to compute, as well as more generalized elements of harm such as pain and suffering and impairment of earning capacity. Under the *collateral source rule*, amounts received from other sources such as medical insurance are not deducted from the plaintiff's tort recovery. Punitive damages are designed to punish the defendant for wrongdoing, and may be substantial in amount. They are ordinarily available only if the defendant is found to have acted with malice, or with reckless indifference to the rights of the plaintiff.

From the point of view of the plaintiff's lawyer, the amount of the potential recovery is of personal relevance. Ordinarily, the plaintiff's lawyer in torts cases works on a contingent fee basis — that is, the lawyer's compensation is a certain percentage of the plaintiff's recovery. (The defendant's lawyer is usually paid on an hourly basis regardless of the outcome in the case.) The lower the recovery, the less the compensation to the plaintiff's lawyer. The normal contingent fee for the plaintiff's lawyer if the case goes to trial is between 30 and 40 percent of the recovery and may be even higher if the case is appealed.

Even if the lawyer determines that the claim has legal merit and that the potential damages will be substantial, as a practical matter the defendant may be unable to pay. In torts cases, liability insurance is the source from which many claims are satisfied. However, the defendant may have no insurance, or the insurance may not cover intentional torts such as battery. In the absence of insurance, a claim must be satisfied, if at all, out of whatever personal assets the defendant may have. The difficulty of satisfying a claim under such circumstances often discourages litigation against uninsured defendants.

If the claim appears to be worth pursuing, the real work for the lawyer begins. The story told by the client is apt to be incomplete and one-sided, so that further investigation will be necessary. Witnesses to the events giving rise to the claim will have to be located and interviewed. Other sources of information include police reports and newspaper stories. The lawyer may also have to consult technical experts such as physicians, automobile mechanics, and engineers to develop a full understanding of the facts. In simpler cases, the law governing the claim may be clear, but with more complex cases, the lawyer is also likely to have to spend considerable time in the law library.

Once the lawyer feels that the facts and the law have been sufficiently mastered, an attempt will usually be made to settle the case. Most torts disputes are resolved by out-of-court settlement. Settlement may occur any time during litigation, but negotiations are almost always initiated well in advance of trying the case. The plaintiff's lawyer will make a tentative evaluation of the damages and of the probability of recovering any amount, and will determine a range within which the case should be settled. The evaluation will be discussed with the client, and the lawyer will then contact the defendant, or more likely the defendant's lawyer, to begin the bargaining process, although sometimes the initiative for settlement will come from the defendant's side. The fact that both sides can save the costs of going to trial pressures them to settle. If the assessments of likely recovery by both sides are in the same range, then the case is likely to be settled, especially if the plaintiff's harm is not serious.

The Pleadings

Formal court proceedings are instituted by the plaintiff with the filing of a *complaint*. The complaint is a document containing the plaintiff's claim for relief and a short statement of the facts upon which the claim is based. For example, in Vosburg v. Putney, the first case we shall examine, the plaintiff's complaint alleged that on February 20, 1889, the defendant "violently assaulted [the plaintiff] . . . kicked him and otherwise ill-treated him and that [he] was thereby made ill and lame and confined to his bed for a long time and suffered great physical pain and mental anguish and was permanently crippled." A complaint typically ends with a demand for damages; in *Vosburg,* for example, the plaintiff demanded what was then a considerable sum of $5,000.

The complaint both initiates the lawsuit and informs the defendant of the basis of the plaintiff's claim. In the early days of common law pleading, the writ (as the forerunner of the complaint was known) had to comply with many technical rules; a plaintiff who deviated from these rules might lose the cause of action entirely. Modern procedural rules, however, are more forgiving, typically requiring only "a short and plain statement of the claim showing that the pleader is entitled to relief."

After being served with the complaint, the defendant has a short period of time, typically 20 days, in which to file an answer in court. The *answer* must either admit or deny the allegations of fact contained in the complaint, or state that the defendant lacks sufficient knowledge of the facts to admit or deny them. In addition to challenging the plaintiff's version of the facts, the defendant may attack the legal theory upon which the complaint rests. This attack can either be included in the answer or be stated separately by a *motion to dismiss the complaint* asserting that the complaint fails to state a claim upon which relief can be granted. The test for whether such a motion should be granted is whether the plaintiff would be entitled to any recovery even if all the factual allegations in the complaint were proven true. A negative answer to this question requires the judge to grant the motion in favor of the defendant. In recent years, the United States Supreme Court has tinkered with this traditional pleading standard for purposes of federal civil litigation, arguably making it more difficult for plaintiffs to survive dismissal motions. See Arthur R. Miller, Are the Federal Courthouse Doors Closing? What Happened to the Federal Rules of Civil Procedure?, 43 Tex. Tech L. Rev. 587 (2011).

Even if the complaint states a cause of action, if the parties do not dispute the material facts of a case, the case may not need to go to trial. The method of testing in advance of trial whether a dispute as to material facts exists is the *motion for summary judgment.* This motion is available to both the plaintiff and the defendant, and the party making the motion has the burden of convincing the judge that no real and genuine dispute exists as to any material fact. When all the pleadings and any supporting affidavits have been filed, the judge determines whether any genuine factual disputes remain pertaining to the parties' claims and defenses, and grants or denies the motion accordingly. If a dispute remains as to some but not all the relevant facts, the scope of trial may be limited to the disputed facts. Summary judgment is infrequently used for avoiding trial in torts cases, because the resolution of torts claims so often depends upon an evaluation of the conduct of one or more of the parties.

The filing of the initial pleadings and motions does not end the lawyer's pretrial activities. Further investigation into both the law and the facts may be necessary, and in almost all cases negotiations for settlement will continue. If a significant delay is likely before the case is reached for trial, the plaintiff may feel considerable pressure to settle, particularly if the injuries are serious and the plaintiff needs money to pay medical expenses and to replace income lost because of the injuries.

The time period between the filing of the initial pleadings and the trial will depend on a number of factors, and in particular on the degree of congestion in the trial docket. Generally, a case to be tried with a jury will take longer to reach than one without a jury, which is one important reason why many cases that go to trial are tried without a jury. But a plaintiff with serious injuries is more likely to want a jury trial, so it is the serious injury cases that are most affected by crowded dockets. Attorneys for either side may also seek to postpone trial for a variety of tactical reasons.

The Trial

If the case is not settled, the next phase in the process is the trial. The Seventh Amendment to the United States Constitution provides for the right to trial by jury in federal courts in all "suits at common law." Thus, either party may, in a timely fashion, enter a request for a jury trial in a case that would have been heard "at law" at the time of the framing of the Constitution. The Seventh Amendment does not provide for a jury trial if the case would have been heard "at equity." Although the Supreme Court of the United States has never held that the Seventh Amendment applies to state proceedings, the constitutions of all states provide, with variations, for either party to elect a jury trial in civil cases. If the case is to be tried to a jury, the first important step in the trial process is the selection of jurors. In most states, jurors are selected from a larger panel chosen from citizens of the county in which the court is located. Attorneys for both parties, as well as the presiding judge, participate actively in the jury selection process. What each lawyer hopes for in a jury is not an unbiased cross section of the community, but a jury as many of whom as possible have biases that favor his or her client. Many lawyers believe that characteristics such as race, national origin, occupation, and education will influence the way a juror looks at the evidence and the people involved in the case, although the empirical validity of these intuitions is often open to doubt.

After the jury is selected, the trial itself begins with the plaintiff's lawyer's *opening statement.* The opening statement is an outline of the plaintiff's case and the evidence the lawyer expects to present. It is designed to predispose the jury to accept the plaintiff's view of the case and to enable the jury to relate the evidence as it comes in to the overall case. Following this statement, the plaintiff's lawyer presents the evidence. Typically this will consist of oral testimony of the witnesses, documentary evidence such as medical reports, and occasionally physical evidence. When the plaintiff's lawyer is finished with the direct examination of a witness, the defendant's lawyer has the opportunity to cross-examine. In the course of allowing evidence into the record, the judge rules on objections raised by both sides.

After all the plaintiff's evidence has been presented, the defendant may make a motion that the judge direct the jury to return a verdict in favor of the defendant. This *motion for a directed verdict* (referred to since 1991 as a *motion for judgment as a matter of law* in federal court) will be granted if the judge concludes that the plaintiff has failed to prove one or more of the elements of the case — that is, that a reasonable jury could not find other than for the defendant even if they were to believe all of the testimony favorable to the plaintiff, disbelieve all unfavorable testimony, and draw every reasonable inference favorable to the plaintiff from the testimony. When the plaintiff's proof fails in this manner, it is said that the plaintiff has failed to carry his or her *burden of proof.* If the judge grants the motion, the judge tells the jury that it must find for the defendant. In effect, granting the defendant's motion for directed verdict on the liability issue ends the trial for that defendant. Directed verdicts are granted in favor of defendants in a significant minority of torts trials, but similar motions by plaintiffs seldom prevail.

Assuming that the judge denies the defendant's motion for directed verdict, the defendant's lawyer then presents the defendant's case. If the defendant's lawyer feels that the plaintiff has not presented evidence that would justify recovery, no further evidence may be presented. But more typically, the defendant's lawyer will begin with an opening statement to the jury and follow up with witnesses and evidence for the defense.

When both sides have finished with the presentation of the evidence, motions for directed verdict by either party may be made again. Assuming such motions are denied by the judge, lawyers for both sides make their *closing arguments to the jury,* in which they review the evidence in the light most favorable to their case and indicate why, under the law as the judge will state it in the instructions, the jury ought to return a verdict one way or the other. At some point prior to the jury's deliberations — often just before or after closing arguments — the trial judge delivers *instructions to the jury* as to the applicable law and what the jury will have to find as facts to support a verdict for the plaintiff.

On most issues of fact in a torts case, the plaintiff has the *burden of persuasion,* often referred to as part of the *burden of proof*. What this means is that it is up to the plaintiff's lawyer to persuade the jury that his or her version of the events giving rise to the claim is true; it is not up to the defendant's lawyer to persuade the jury that the plaintiff's version is not true. In civil cases, disputes about the facts are resolved by the jury by assessing probabilities that either side's version is true. For example, in a battery case, the parties may dispute who struck the plaintiff. Putting the burden of persuasion on the plaintiff means that the plaintiff must persuade the jury that it was the defendant who caused the harm; it is not up to the defendant to persuade the jury that it was someone else. If, after analyzing the evidence, the jury believes that it was someone else, or concludes that there is no more reason to believe that it was the defendant than someone else, the plaintiff has not carried the burden of persuasion, and the jury should return its verdict for the defendant.

After the jury has been instructed on the law by the trial judge, it retires to determine its *verdict.* In a slight majority of jurisdictions, the verdict of a jury in a civil case must be unanimous, and if the jury cannot agree, the parties are entitled to a new trial by a different jury. The remaining jurisdictions allow verdicts by the concurrence of fewer than all the jurors, but typically require more than a bare majority of votes.

After the jury has determined its verdict, it reports that verdict to the trial judge. The verdict may be either "general" or "special." The former is a decision by the jury in favor of either the plaintiff or defendant. The latter contains the jury's specific findings of fact made in response to specific questions put to it by the trial judge, and furnishes the factual basis for the trial judge's decision in favor of either the plaintiff or the defendant. If the verdict is for the plaintiff, it will normally include the jury's determination of the damages the defendant is to pay to the plaintiff. The trial judge then enters *judgment* in accordance with the verdict. (If the case is tried without a jury, the judgment is based on the facts as determined by the judge.) The court's judgment in favor of a torts plaintiff is a written order, signed by the judge, directing the defendant to pay to the plaintiff the amount stated in the verdict. In contrast, a judgment for the defendant is not an order to anyone, but is simply a statement for the record that the defendant has won the trial.

Even after the jury verdict is returned, the losing party has an opportunity to make motions to the trial judge that may "save the day." If the losing party made a motion for a directed verdict earlier, that party may renew the motion by asking the judge to enter judgment for that party, notwithstanding the jury verdict for the other side. This is a motion for *judgment non obstante veridicto* (JNOV or judgment notwithstanding the verdict) (referred to since 1991 as a *renewed motion for judgment as a matter of law* in federal court). In addition, either side may make a *motion for a new trial.* The latter motion will be granted if the trial judge concludes that the verdict is against the clear weight of the evidence, that the damages awarded are excessive, that procedural errors damaging to the moving party were committed, or that entering judgment on the verdict would cause manifest injustice. The judge will order a new trial on the ground that the verdict is against the clear weight of the evidence only if the judge is convinced that the jury has reached a seriously erroneous result; the order will not issue merely because the judge, if cast in the role of a juror, would have reached a different result.

The Appeal

Few cases proceed past conclusion of the trial process. However, the losing party has one last chance at victory: *appeal.* In all states, there is one highest court to which a final appeal may be taken. In many states, and in the federal judicial system, a system of intermediate appellate courts considers appeals in the first instance, with the highest court hearing most tort cases only when it chooses to hear them.

One reason for the infrequency of appeals is that not all issues that come up at trial can be appealed. The only issues that can be appealed are decisions, explicit or implicit, about the law by the trial judge.[5] Thus, jury verdicts and judicial fact findings may be set aside because of errors of law committed by the trial judge, such as admitting (or refusing to admit) evidence, or erroneously instructing the jury. But absent such an error of law by the judge, the jury's verdict and the trial judge's findings of fact are binding on appeal.

Even if one or more appealable issues of law exist, the further delay and expense discourage the bringing of an appeal. Both sides must file briefs with the appellate court arguing why the result at the trial should or should not be overturned, and they must pay to have the relevant portions of the trial record printed. The trial record includes the pleadings, motions, the transcript of the testimony, if one is made, trial briefs, if any, and the orders of the trial judge. The appellate briefs are usually supplemented by oral arguments to the appellate court by the lawyers involved. Thus, the appellate process takes considerable time and money. And even if the party bringing the appeal is successful in having the results of the trial overturned, the victory may only be the right to a second trial.

In most cases, the appellate court announces the result of an appeal in a *written opinion.* This opinion serves a number of functions. It explains to the parties and their lawyers why the court decided the case the way it did, thereby providing some assurance to the parties that their claims and arguments were carefully considered. The opinion is of additional importance to the parties in cases where the result on appeal is the ordering of a new trial. The opinion functions as a lesson in the law to the judge who will preside at the new trial, spelling out the mistakes at the earlier trial that led to the necessity of a new trial.

However, an appellate opinion isn't only a source of psychic satisfaction to the parties and guidance to the trial judge. Appellate opinions are published and are made available to the general public. These appellate opinions are sources of law. As such, they are a part of the legal and moral environment, and consequently influence the way we conduct ourselves in society. And more particularly, and of greater immediate relevance to the lawyer, they are used in the resolution of subsequent legal disputes. Thus, the function of most opinions transcends the needs of the immediate parties in particular cases. Appellate opinions are part of our jurisprudence and have vitality even many years after they are written.

5. Appellate review of trial court decisions about the sufficiency of proof to support a given result, or whether a jury verdict is against the weight of the evidence, places the appellate court in a position that comes close to reviewing issues of fact. But strictly speaking the higher court, even in those instances, is reviewing the decisions of law reached by the court below concerning the sufficiency of the proof.

Mechanisms for Resolving Disputes: Adjudication

The foregoing text sketches only the general process by which torts cases are brought and decided. Yet even this brief description suggests a number of reasons why the torts process is currently undergoing critical analysis. It is thought by many to be too cumbersome, too time-consuming, and too expensive for both the immediate parties and society generally. It is also criticized on the ground that its outcomes are often unfair. Much of this criticism focuses on the use of adjudication as the primary means of resolving disputes and many reform efforts involve proposals to modify the adjudicative process or to replace it with alternative means of dispute resolution.

Although adjudication is undoubtedly central to the torts process, it is important not to overstate its function. To be sure, adjudication is the most formal method of resolving disputes in our legal system. But it is also the most ponderous and inefficient method, playing practically a far less important role in the day-to-day functioning of the torts process than most laypersons imagine. The truth is that very few torts disputes are resolved by the satisfaction of a judgment obtained in a court action.

Reflect for a moment upon the life cycle of a typical small tort claim. The parties probably would have to wait two years for their case to reach trial. Lawyers for both sides will in all likelihood have been connected with the case for more than three years before it is finally decided. There are expenses in connection with investigating and preparing the case, filing and serving the pleadings and other documents, assembling the witnesses, and providing a court stenographer to record and preserve the testimony, not to mention the judge's time and the use of the courthouse for which the parties are not directly charged but for which they and the rest of us pay out of general tax revenues. And the lawyers expect to be, and are, paid more if the case goes to trial. Moreover, their burdens are substantially increased if the case is tried before a jury. Justice may be blind, but when asked to adjudicate torts disputes it can also be frustratingly slow and expensive.

And yet for all of that, adjudication remains the epitome of the torts lawyer's craft. It is the cutting edge of the system of righting civil wrongs, the basic device against which all else is measured and to which all else is related. Throughout this course we will be encountering mechanisms other than adjudication whereby torts disputes are resolved in our system. Taken together, these other methods dispose of the overwhelming majority of torts claims. Yet all of these other mechanisms for resolving disputes rely for their continued existence on the availability of the adjudicative process, for it is largely in adjudication that the rules of liability undergo the process of adjustment and development so necessary to their continued vitality. And the threat of a trial is a powerful incentive to resolve the dispute in some other way.

It is appropriate, therefore, that the adjudicative process occupy center stage in this course. It is probably appropriate also that a great percentage of attention and effort during law school be directed toward gaining an understanding of the adjudicative process as it functions generally in our legal system. However, it is a premise upon which these materials are based that adjudication is only one of a number of dispute-resolving processes that constitute what is collectively referred to here as the torts process. It is no less appropriate, therefore, that the adjudicative process be put into its proper perspective. As far as the day-to-day process of resolving torts disputes is concerned, adjudication has its greatest impact as a ponderous potentiality rather than as an efficient, useful tool.

C. The Substantive Law Governing Liability for Battery

Several reasons support choosing battery as the place to begin the detailed study of the torts process. For one thing, battery is one of the easiest torts to understand. The facts of a battery case are likely to be simple. The law is also relatively uncomplicated, and yet there are enough wrinkles to make it interesting. Moreover, battery is one of the oldest concepts in our law. To study the origins of the common law concept of battery is to study the origins of the common law itself.

A simple and workable definition of the modern concept of battery is the intentional, unprivileged, and either harmful or offensive contact with the person of another. The basic parameters of the battery concept are best described by a hypothetical example. Assume that *A* is walking along the sidewalk and sees *B,* whom *A* dislikes intensely, approaching from the opposite direction. *A* punches *B* on the jaw, knocking out three of *B*'s teeth and rendering *B* unconscious. On these facts *A* has committed a battery upon *B* for which *A* may be held liable in tort. All of the elements of battery are present: *A* intentionally contacted *B*'s person in a harmful manner under circumstances that did not give rise to a privilege on *A*'s part. A battery would also result if *A* rudely tweaked *B*'s nose — a contact that reasonable persons would find offensive. It should be noted that the fact that *A* dislikes *B* explains *A*'s conduct, but is not a necessary element of the tort. Even if *B* were a stranger to *A, A*'s conduct would be tortious if the above-described elements are present. On the other hand, if we eliminate any of the elements — intent, harmful or offensive contact, or absence of privilege — there would be no battery. For example, if *A* had missed *B* or if *A* had acted out of sufficient necessity (e.g., in defense of a knife attack by *B*) to justify striking *B, A* would not have committed a *battery* upon *B* even if *A* in fact dislikes *B* intensely. (If *A* misses *B* but *B* is put in apprehension of imminent contact, *A* has committed an *assault* on *B*, a subject we discuss in Chapter 11.) But where, as in our hypothetical example, *A* intentionally and without justification strikes *B, A*'s liability in tort is clear from our preliminary definition of battery.

Although the informal definition of battery given above is satisfactory for most cases, the formal definitions contained in the Restatement (Second) of Torts are more suitable for detailed analysis:

> §13. Battery: Harmful Contact
>
> An actor is subject to liability to another for battery if
>
> (a) he acts intending to cause a harmful or offensive contact with the person of the other or a third person, or an imminent apprehension of such a contact, and
>
> (b) a harmful contact with the person of the other directly or indirectly results.
>
> §18. Battery: Offensive Contact
>
> (1) An actor is subject to liability to another for battery if
>
> (a) he acts intending to cause a harmful or offensive contact with the person of the other or a third person, or an imminent apprehension of such a contact, and
>
> (b) an offensive contact with the person of the other directly or indirectly results. . . .

Section 2 of the Restatement (Second) defines "act" as "an external manifestation of the actor's will and does not include any of its results, even the most direct, immediate, and intended."

The source of these rules, the Restatement (Second) of Torts, represents a revision of the original Restatement of Torts, which was first published by the American Law Institute from 1934 to 1939. The American Law Institute was created in 1923 by a distinguished group of judges, lawyers, and scholars. It is a nonprofit organization whose avowed purpose is improvement of the law. The Restatements of the law on a variety of topics, including Torts, have been the Institute's chief reason for being. Since its creation, its members have convened annually to review developments in the law and to consider changes in their formal summaries of what the law is in a majority of jurisdictions in this country. Professor Francis H. Bohlen of the University of Pennsylvania was put in charge of the original Restatement of Torts and given the title of Reporter for the project. Professor William L. Prosser, then of the University of California Law School at Berkeley, was appointed Reporter of the Restatement (Second) of Torts. From 1970 to 1981, Dean John Wade of Vanderbilt University Law School acted as Reporter. In 1992, the Institute undertook a Restatement (Third) of Torts. Rather than a single, comprehensive Restatement covering all tort topics, there will be several topical Restatements, each with its own Reporters. Three of these topical Restatements have been completed: Products Liability (1998), Apportionment of Liability (2000), and Liability for Physical and Emotional Harm (2009, 2012). Two additional projects — Liability for Economic Harm and Intentional Torts to Persons — are in progress.

It is important for the law student to appreciate what these Restatements are and what they are not. The original purpose of the American Law Institute was to restate the rules of tort law as recognized by most courts in this country. To some extent, the Second and Third Restatements have departed from this model, with the Reporters and the Institute adopting what was felt to be the "better" rule, even if not so recognized by a majority of states. Courts cite and rely upon the Restatements, but they are decidedly secondary authorities and give way to statutes and cases where the latter establish a different rule.

A further word is in order regarding the relative importance of the Second and Third Restatements in the materials in this book. Reliance herein will be mostly upon the Second Restatement of Torts, although the Third will be referenced when particularly relevant. Comment *a* to §5 of the Restatement, (Third) of Torts: Liability for Physical and Emotional Harm offers this explanation of why the Second Restatement remains authoritative:

> *a. An Umbrella Rule.* The rule of liability in this Section does not replace the doctrines for specific intentional torts, such as battery, assault, false imprisonment, and others. Rather, this Section provides a framework that encompasses many specific torts for intentionally caused physical harm. Restatement Second, Torts, remains authoritative in explaining the details of the specific torts encompassed by this Section and in specifying the elements and limits of the various affirmative defenses that might be available until the Third Restatement addresses the specific intentional torts.

1. The Prima Facie Case

Returning to the definitions of battery set forth in §§13 and 18 of the Restatement (Second), above, the elements of intent and harmful or offensive contact constitute what is known as the plaintiff's prima facie case. To win, the plaintiff must prove these elements, together with the necessary causal connection between the harm incurred and the defendant's conduct. If the defendant had a privilege to inflict harm upon the plaintiff it is up to the defendant to assert this privilege as a defense — it is not up to the plaintiff to assert the absence of privilege as a part of the prima facie case.

a. Intent

Beginning law students are often amazed at the extent to which lawyers can take common, everyday words and concepts and complicate their meanings. The concept of intent in the law of battery provides a good opportunity to test your own reactions in this regard. You have no doubt used the word *intent* for most of your life and never experienced any great difficulties with it — one intends a consequence of one's action when one subjectively desires that consequence to follow.[6] In what may be called the clear cases, the element of intent presents few difficulties even in the legal context of determining whether a battery has been committed. In the earlier hypothetical cases involving *A* and *B,* for example, it is clear that *A* intended to strike and harm *B. A* subjectively desired to achieve both of these consequences. And yet, there are other cases that are not so clear. The concept of intent can present difficulties regarding exactly what the defendant must intend in order to commit a battery. For example, what if *A* had tapped *B* lightly on the chin, intending merely to startle *B,* and *B* had fallen to the sidewalk, hit his head, and died from the resulting concussion, a result *A* did not expect and certainly did not desire?

The concept of intent can also present analytical difficulties regarding exactly what mental states suffice to conclude that an actor "intends" a consequence of her actions. For example, suppose that *A*, while intending to throw an empty soda bottle into a trash container, knows that there is a very good chance that the bottle will strike *B*. If the bottle strikes *B*, causing injury, did *A* "intend" that consequence and therefore commit a harmful battery on *B*? We take up these questions in the sections that follow.

(1) What Consequences Must the Defendant Intend to Commit a Battery?

Vosburg v. Putney

80 Wis. 523, 50 N.W. 403 (1891)

The action was brought to recover damages for [a] battery, alleged to have been committed by the defendant upon the plaintiff on February 20, 1889. The answer is a general denial. At the date of the alleged [battery] the plaintiff was a little more than fourteen years of age, and the defendant a little less than twelve years of age.

The injury complained of was caused by a kick inflicted by defendant upon the leg of the plaintiff, a little below the knee. The transaction occurred in a schoolroom in Waukesha, during school hours, both parties being pupils in the school. A former trial of the cause resulted in a verdict and judgment for the plaintiff for $2,800. The defendant appealed from such judgment to this court, and the same was reversed for error, and a new trial awarded. 78 Wis. 84.

The case has been again tried in the circuit court, and [the second trial from which the defendant brings the present appeal] resulted in a verdict for plaintiff for $2,500. The facts

6. Interestingly, in tort law one is not said to intend the act, as such. As indicated in §2 of the Restatement (Second), quoted on p. 10, "act" is defined as inherently volitional. Thus, the question in cases involving intentional torts, such as battery, is whether the actor intended the consequences of his act, not the act, itself. Of course, determining where to draw the line between an act and its consequence can sometimes be difficult.

of the case, as they appeared on both trials, are sufficiently stated in the opinion by Mr. Justice Orton on the former appeal. . . .

[The facts as stated in the first supreme court opinion referred to are: "The plaintiff was about fourteen years of age, and the defendant about eleven years of age. On the 20th day of February, 1889, they were sitting opposite to each other across an aisle in the high school of the village of Waukesha. The defendant reached across the aisle with his foot, and hit with his toe the shin of the right leg of the plaintiff. The touch was slight. The plaintiff did not feel it, either on account of its being so slight or of loss of sensation produced by the shock. In a few moments he felt a violent pain in that place, which caused him to cry out loudly. The next day he was sick, and had to be helped to school. On the fourth day he was vomiting, and Dr. Bacon was sent for, but could not come, and he sent medicine to stop the vomiting, and came to see him the next day, on the 25th. There was a slight discoloration of the skin entirely over the inner surface of the tibia an inch below the bend of the knee. The doctor applied fomentations, and gave him anodynes to quiet the pain. This treatment was continued, and the swelling so increased by the 5th day of March that counsel was called, and on the 8th of March an operation was performed on the limb by making an incision, and a moderate amount of pus escaped. A drainage tube was inserted, and an iodoform dressing put on. On the sixth day after this, another incision was made to the bone, and it was found that destruction was going on in the bone, and so it has continued exfoliating pieces of bone. He will never recover the use of his limb. There were black and blue spots on the shin bone, indicating that there had been a blow. On the 1st day of January before, the plaintiff received an injury just above the knee of the same leg by coasting, which appeared to be healing up and drying down at the time of the last injury. The theory of at least one of the medical witnesses was that the limb was in a diseased condition when this touch or kick was given, caused by microbes entering in through the wound above the knee, and which were revivified by the touch, and that the touch was the exciting or remote cause of the destruction of the bone, or of the plaintiff's injury. It does not appear that there was any visible mark made or left by this touch or kick of the defendant's foot, or any appearance of injury until the black and blue spots were discovered by the physician several days afterwards, and then there were more spots than one. There was no proof of any other hurt, and the medical testimony seems to have been agreed that this touch or kick was the exciting cause of the injury to the plaintiff. . . .

"The learned circuit judge [at the first trial], said to the jury: 'It is a peculiar case, an unfortunate case, a case, I think I am at liberty to say, that ought not to have come into court. The parents of these children ought, in some way, if possible, to have adjusted it between themselves.'"]

On the [second trial from the results of which the present appeal is taken,] the jury found a special verdict, as follows: "(1) Had the plaintiff during the month of January, 1889, received an injury just above the knee, which became inflamed, and produced pus? *Answer.* Yes. (2) Had such injury on the 20th day of February, 1889, nearly healed at the point of the injury? A. Yes. (3) Was the plaintiff, before said 20th of February, lame, as the result of such injury? A. No. (4) Had the *tibia* in the plaintiff's right leg become inflamed or diseased to some extent before he received the blow or kick from the defendant? A. No. (5) What was the exciting cause of the injury to the plaintiff's leg? A. Kick. (6) Did the defendant, in touching the plaintiff with his foot, intend to do him any harm? A. No. (7) At what sum do you assess the damages of the plaintiff? A. $2,500."

The defendant moved for judgment in his favor on the verdict, and also for a new trial. The plaintiff moved for judgment on the verdict in his favor. The motions of defendant were overruled, and that of the plaintiff granted. Thereupon judgment for plaintiff for

$2,500 damages and costs of suit was duly entered. The defendant appeals from the judgment.

LYON, J. Several errors are assigned, only three of which will be considered.

1. The jury having found that the defendant, in touching the plaintiff with his foot, did not intend to do him any harm, counsel for defendant maintain that the plaintiff has no cause of action, and that defendant's motion for judgment on the special verdict should have been granted. In support of this proposition counsel quote from 2 Greenl. Ev. §83, the rule that "the intention to do harm is of the essence of an assault." Such is the rule, no doubt, in actions or prosecutions for mere assaults. But this is an action to recover damages for an alleged assault and battery. In such case the rule is correctly stated, in many of the authorities cited by counsel, that plaintiff must show either that the intention was unlawful, or that the defendant is in fault. If the intended act is unlawful, the intention to commit it must necessarily be unlawful. Hence, as applied to this case, if the kicking of the plaintiff by the defendant was an unlawful act, the intention of defendant to kick him was also unlawful.

Had the parties been upon the play-grounds of the school, engaged in the usual boyish sports, the defendant being free from malice, wantonness, or negligence, and intending no harm to plaintiff in what he did, we should hesitate to hold the act of the defendant unlawful, or that he could be held liable in this action. Some consideration is due to the implied license of the play-grounds. But it appears that the injury was inflicted in the school, after it had been called to order by the teacher, and after the regular exercises of the school had commenced. Under these circumstances, no implied license to do the act complained of existed, and such act was a violation of the order and decorum of the school, and necessarily unlawful. Hence we are of the opinion that, under the evidence and verdict, the action may be sustained.

2. [At trial the plaintiff's medical expert was allowed to testify, over the defendant's objection, that in his opinion the exciting cause of the inflammation in the plaintiff's leg was the kick by the defendant. The Supreme Court of Wisconsin concluded that the defendant's objection to such testimony should have been sustained for a reason having more to do with the law of evidence than with the law of battery: the form of the question put to the expert witness was improper.]

3. Certain questions were proposed on behalf of defendant to be submitted to the jury, founded upon the theory that only such damages could be recovered as the defendant might reasonably be supposed to have contemplated as likely to result from his kicking the plaintiff. The court refused to submit such questions to the jury. The ruling was correct. The rule of damages in actions for torts was held in Brown v. C., M. & St. P.R. Co., 54 Wis. 342, to be that the wrong-doer is liable for all injuries resulting directly from the wrongful act, whether they could or could not have been foreseen by him. . . .

[The judgment for the plaintiff was reversed and the case remanded for yet another new trial on the basis of the evidentiary error described in part 2 of the opinion.]

The possibility of a third trial was precluded when, upon Putney's motion, the action was dismissed based on Vosburg's failure to pay court costs associated with the prior appeals and to reinstigate the action at the trial level in a timely fashion. This default is perhaps explained by the fact that the Vosburgs were pursuing legal remedies on multiple fronts, including a criminal complaint against Putney and an action by Vosburg's father against

Putney to recover his own out-of-pocket expenses and for the loss of his son's services. While the guilty verdict in the criminal action was overturned on appeal, the civil action brought by Vosburg's father was ultimately successful, with a trial judgment in favor of Mr. Vosburg for $1,200 that was affirmed on appeal in Vosburg v. Putney, 56 N.W. 480 (Wis. 1893).

Whether the four-year spate of litigation was actually a success for anyone involved is another matter. The Putneys originally offered to settle the suit for $250, while the Vosburgs insisted on $700. Neither party was willing to accept the other's offer or further compromise, and in all likelihood both suffered as a result. When court costs and attorneys' fees are considered, it is almost certain that the Vosburgs actually realized less than the Putneys' $250 settlement offer, if indeed they recovered anything at all. It is equally certain that the Putneys, in defending the actions, expended considerably more than the $700 the Vosburgs had originally requested. Thus, the first trial judge's observation that "[t]he parents of these children ought, in some way, if possible, to have adjusted it between themselves" rings true. For a detailed history of the litigation and its aftermath, see Zigurds L. Zile, *Vosburg v. Putney:* A Centennial Story, 1992 Wis. L. Rev. 877.

The central enigma of *Vosburg* involves the court's conclusion that the defendant could be held liable for a battery despite an express finding by the jury that he did not intend to harm the plaintiff. While a jury finding of intent to harm would clearly have sufficed to establish a battery, the court's opinion suggests that other, less malicious states of mind may support liability for a battery. The *Vosburg* court specifically refers to an intention to commit an unlawful act, yet this formulation seems circular — the intent necessary to make defendant's act an unlawful battery depends on whether the act was or was not unlawful. In the Wisconsin high court's view of *Vosburg,* what was the unlawful aspect of the defendant's act?

Another puzzling conclusion by the *Vosburg* court concerns the damages award. Once the defendant is determined to be liable, the court holds that all damages caused by the defendant's wrongdoing are recoverable, whether or not the damages were reasonably foreseeable and whether or not they flowed from an unusual trait or preexisting condition of the plaintiff. This rule — commonly referred to as the "thin skull" or "eggshell skull" rule — has remained a fixture of tort law despite frequent criticism from commentators. See, e.g., Steve P. Calandrillo & Dustin E. Buehlerd, Eggshell Economics: A Revolutionary Approach to the Eggshell Plaintiff Rule, 74 Ohio St. L.J. 375 (2013).

The Law-Fact Distinction: In General

A number of facts appear in and accompany the opinion in *Vosburg.* Which ones are essential to the decision? In attempting to analyze *Vosburg,* it is important to begin to understand one of the most basic concepts of the torts process — the distinction between law and fact.

Whenever the plaintiff brings a torts case before a court, as in Vosburg v. Putney, a legal remedy is being sought based on particular conduct of the defendant that harmed the plaintiff in some way. In deciding whether to grant the remedy asked for, the court performs three functions: (1) it finds the relevant facts, (2) it states the applicable rule of law, and (3) it applies the rule of law to the facts to reach the proper result. When the court finds the facts of a case, it determines what happened — in a torts case, the conduct of the parties, the circumstances surrounding the conduct, and the consequences of that conduct. If the court determines, after hearing the evidence, that the defendant kicked the plaintiff, it concludes that that event took place in time and space, much in the same sense that a scientist might conclude that a given object weighs three grams.

When the court states the law governing the case, it recognizes a generalized rule calling for certain legal consequences to follow from a particular set of facts. For example, the tribunal might declare the rule to be: "If any person shall intentionally kick another in school after the class is called to order, and if the kick causes harm, then that person shall pay damages to the one kicked." Observe that the description of facts appearing in the rule is general, in that it refers to generic kinds of behavior, and is not dependent on the specific identity of the parties. This characteristic of generality would be missing if the facts stated in the rule were: "If the defendant kicks the plaintiff on the right shin on February 20, 1889, in a school room in Waukesha, Wisconsin. . . ."

Observe also that the facts are connected to the legal consequences in the form of an *if-then* proposition. The portion of the rule following the *if* identifies the relevant facts, and the portion following the *then* describes the legal consequences. Thus, the substantive law of torts consists primarily of rules of conduct that match up generalized descriptions of fact patterns with appropriate legal consequences. In applying the rule of law to the facts of a particular case, the tribunal compares the facts, as it determines them to be, with the general description of the facts in the rule. If the particular facts of the case fit within this general description, the legal consequences described by the rule then follow.

So far we have spoken of the court as if it were composed of a single person who finds the facts, states the law, and applies the law to the facts. In *Vosburg,* however, the lower court consisted of two separate decisionmakers — the trial judge and the jury. When a jury is involved in a trial, the three functions of fact finding, law declaring, and law application are split between the judge and the jury, with the judge declaring the law and the jury finding the facts and, in most cases, applying the law to them.[7]

The means by which the allocation of functions between judge and jury is accomplished are the judge's instructions to the jury and the jury's verdict. The instructions to the jury contain a statement of the law governing the case — that is, a description of the facts that under the law must be found by the jury in order to support recovery for the plaintiff. If the facts found by the jury fit within the fact pattern described in the rules of law contained in the instructions, the jury should return its general verdict for the plaintiff. If the facts do not fit within the rules, the jury should return its general verdict for the defendant.

Occasionally, the trial judge may perform the ultimate law-applying function. The procedural device that permits this is the special verdict, which was used in *Vosburg*. In that case, the jury stated its findings of fact in the form of answers to questions, framed by the judge, about the facts. To determine the outcome, the judge then applied the law governing the case to the facts so stated.

The closest that a judge comes to invading the fact-finding province of the jury is when the judge decides whether or not to grant a motion for a new trial on the ground that the verdict is against the clear weight of the evidence. When reacting to a motion for a directed

7. The law-application function to which this discussion refers is the ultimate application that occurs after the trier of fact has resolved conflicts in the evidence relating to relevant factual issues. The judge performs a preliminary application of law to facts in reacting to motions to dismiss the complaint or to enter summary judgment because there is no substantial disagreement as to material facts. The facts to which the judge applies the law in these instances are not the facts ultimately found by the fact finder, however, but rather the facts as they are contained in the complaint or in supporting affidavits. In reacting to a motion for directed verdict or for a JNOV, the trial judge performs a similar function in reviewing the evidence introduced at the trial, viewing that evidence in the light most favorable to the nonmoving party.

verdict or for a JNOV (see p. 7, above), the judge may be said to be passing on the sufficiency of the proof itself, rather than on the reaction of the jury to that proof. In contrast, the "against the weight of the evidence" motion invites the trial judge to review the jury's reaction to the evidence, albeit on a standard weighted toward accepting that reaction. It is difficult to avoid the conclusion that in those cases, at least, the trial judge is to some extent acting as a "super-juror." Two constraints lessen the significance of this "non-judge-like" role: first, judges are admonished to grant such motions only in the rare cases when jurors appear grossly in error (some courts hold that the verdict must be against the "great weight of the evidence"); and second, the judge is limited to ordering a new trial — unlike the situation when reacting to motions for directed verdicts or JNOVs, the judge may not enter judgment for a party that was "robbed" by the jury. If the second jury reacts in the same fashion as the first, presumably the trial judge will conclude that jurors know best, and will deny the defendant's motion for new trial. The special quality of these motions for new trial is reflected in the fact that an appellate court will not overturn the trial judge's denial of such a motion unless the appellate court concludes that the trial judge has committed a clear abuse of discretion.

The division of functions between the judge and jury also has an impact on what issues may be appealed. Just as it is improper for the trial judge to invade the province of the jury and decide issues of fact (except on the rare occasions when an "against the weight of the evidence" motion is granted), it is also improper for an appellate court to review and set aside decisions made by the jury (except on the even rarer occasions when an appellate court decides that the denial of an "against the weight of the evidence" motion was reversible error). The right to a jury trial would be a hollow one if an appellate court were free to substitute its own conclusions of fact for those of the jury. The only issues an appellate court may decide for itself are issues of law — that is, the expressed or implied rulings of law made by the trial judge at the trial.

Note: Tort Liability of Minors and Their Parents

In *Vosburg,* the defendant was a minor. At common law, minors do not necessarily escape liability for intentionally causing harmful contacts. For example, in Bailey v. C.S., 12 S.W.3d 159 (Tex. Ct. App. 2000), the four-year-old defendant struck his baby-sitter in the throat, crushing her larynx. The baby-sitter sued, alleging battery. In reversing the lower court's grant of summary judgment for the young defendant, the appellate court held that under Texas law there is no specific age minimum at which children are deemed incapable of forming the intent necessary to commit a battery. However, some courts have held as matter of law that very young children may not be capable of having the requisite intent. See, e.g., Fromenthal v. Clark, 442 So. 2d 608 (La. Ct. App. 1983), *cert. denied,* 444 So. 2d 1242 (La. 1984), holding that the two-year-old defendant, who had severely bitten a newborn child, could not be held liable for an intentional tort. Courts also have reached inconsistent conclusions regarding the age at which children are capable of forming the mental state required to commit an intentional tort. While the court in *Bailey* held that a four-year-old child could potentially form intent, the court in DeLuca v. Bowden, 329 N.E.2d 109 (Ohio 1975), held that a child under seven years of age was incapable of committing an intentional tort.

Imposing liability on minors for intentionally causing harmful contact would not be remarkable if it were not for the fact that, in other areas of the law, minors receive special protection because of their age. One such area we will be dealing with later is negligence — children sometimes are not held to the same standard of care as adults, and young children are often held to be incapable of acting negligently even when they are deemed old enough to commit a battery. Thus, in many states, children under a certain age are incapable of negligence. See, e.g., Stark *ex rel.* Jacobsen v. Ford Motor Co., 693 S.E.2d 253 (N.C. Ct. App. 2010), *rev'd on other grounds*, 723 S.E.2d 753 (N.C. 2012), in which the appellate court reiterated the North Carolina rule that children under the age of seven are, as a matter of law, incapable of negligence. There are even more stringent rules for the protection of children in both contract and criminal law. As you develop your knowledge of these other areas of law, you should ask yourself whether these different rules represent inconsistencies, or whether different considerations of policy permit, if they do not require, different treatment.

Because children typically do not have the financial resources to satisfy tort claims, persons injured by young tortfeasors may try to collect from the youngster's parents. Parents may be liable for their own negligence in failing to supervise their minor children, but under the common law they were not held vicariously liable for their children's torts solely by virtue of the parent-child relationship. This has led all 50 states to enact statutes imposing some degree of liability on parents for the torts of their children. These statutes, which vary significantly in detail, often impose limitations on the amount of damages a parent can be required to pay for the tortious conduct of a child. Such statutes also typically require that the minor's conduct be willful or malicious before the parent can be held liable. Thus, for example, in Cogswell v. Holder, 2004 Ohio App. LEXIS 5085 (Ohio Ct. App. 2004), the court of appeals held that the parents of a minor child who drove the getaway car in a fatal shooting were not liable because the child did not personally harm the victims. Other statutes impose broader liability on parents. See, e.g., La. Civ. Code Ann. art. 2318 ("The father and the mother are responsible for the damage occasioned by their minor child . . . ."). The Louisiana statute imposes parental liability regardless of whether the parents could have prevented the act of the child and regardless of whether the child was too young to be capable of committing a tort. See Turner v. Bucher, 308 So. 2d 270 (La. 1975).

At the practical level, a potential source of recovery for plaintiffs is the homeowner's insurance that covers many American households against, among other contingencies, tort liability. Under such policies, the liability need not have any connection with the home, as such, and both the parents and their children are covered as insureds. The interesting wrinkle here is that the liability portion of most homeowner's policies excludes liability for intentional torts. See generally James L. Rigelhaupt, Annotation, Construction and Application of Provision of Liability Insurance Policy Expressly Excluding Injuries Intended or Expected by Insured, 31 A.L.R.4th 957 (1984). If the only tort for which a young child is likely to be held liable is the intentional tort of battery, homeowner's insurance is probably not available to cover the child's liability. However, if the child's parents are liable for their own negligent supervision, or are held vicariously liable without fault on their parts, homeowner's insurance covers the situation. See, e.g., Prudential Prop. & Cas. Ins. Co. v. Boylan, 704 A.2d 597 (N.J. Super. Ct. App. Div. 1998).

Statutory extensions of parental liability are generally recognized to be aimed at reducing juvenile delinquency. See generally Lisa Gentile, Parental Civil Liability for the Torts of Minors, 6 J. Contemp. Legal Issues 125 (2007). Under the threat of potential liability, parents are encouraged to supervise their children. As Professor Chapin notes, however, the assumption that parental control will reduce delinquency ignores other factors that influence the child's behavior. She cautions that in the absence of empirical evidence, parental liability should not be the primary focus in the effort to reduce juvenile delinquency, but acknowledges that an innocent victim will at least be partially compensated as a result of parental liability. Linda A. Chapin, Out of Control? Uses and Abuses of Parental Liability, 37 Santa Clara L. Rev. 621 (1997). See also Judith G. McMullen, "You Can't Make Me!": How Expectations of Parental Control over Adolescents Influence the Law, 35 Loy. U. Chi. L.J. 603 (2004). The author observes that authorities in the field of child-rearing contend that parents have only limited control over their children, and that children are motivated largely by peer influence and inborn personality traits.

(2) Which Mental States Constitute Intent to Cause a Harmful or Offensive Contact?

As observed at the outset, an actor intends a consequence when the actor subjectively desires that the consequence flow from her act. In *Vosburg*, the defendant conceded that he intended/desired to kick the plaintiff's shin, at least "ever so slightly." The argument in *Vosburg* was over what legal result followed from the jury findings that the kick caused the injury and that the defendant did not intend/desire to cause any harm by what he did. In this section we explore whether any mental state, other than a desire that one's act cause a particular consequence, will suffice legally to constitute an actor's intent to cause that consequence.

Garratt v. Dailey

46 Wash. 2d 197, 279 P.2d 1091 (1955)

HILL, J. The liability of an infant for an alleged battery is presented to this court for the first time. Brian Dailey (age five years, nine months) was visiting with Naomi Garratt, an adult and a sister of the plaintiff, Ruth Garratt, likewise an adult, in the backyard of the plaintiff's home, on July 16, 1951. It is plaintiff's contention that she came out into the backyard to talk with Naomi and that, as she started to sit down in a wood and canvas lawn chair, Brian deliberately pulled it out from under her. The only one of the three persons present so testifying was Naomi Garratt. (Ruth Garratt, the plaintiff, did not testify as to how or why she fell.) The trial court, unwilling to accept this testimony, adopted instead Brian Dailey's version of what happened, and made the following findings:

"III. . . . that while Naomi Garratt and Brian Dailey were in the back yard the plaintiff, Ruth Garratt, came out of her house into the back yard. Some time subsequent thereto defendant, Brian Dailey, picked up a lightly built wood and canvas lawn chair which was then and there located in the back yard of the above described premises, moved it sideways a few feet and seated himself therein, at which time he discovered the plaintiff, Ruth Garratt, about to sit down at the place where the lawn chair had formerly been, at which time he hurriedly got up from the chair and attempted to move it toward Ruth Garratt to aid her in sitting down in the chair; that due to the defendant's small size and lack of dexterity he was unable to get the lawn chair under the plaintiff in time to prevent her from falling to the ground. That plaintiff fell to the ground and sustained a fracture of her hip, and other injuries and damages as hereinafter set forth.

"IV. That the preponderance of the evidence in this case establishes that when the defendant, Brian Dailey, moved the chair in question *he did not have any wilful or unlawful purpose in doing so;* that *he did not have any intent to injure the plaintiff, or any intent to bring about any unauthorized or offensive contact with her person* or any objects appurtenant thereto; that the circumstances which immediately preceded the fall of the plaintiff established that the defendant, *Brian Dailey, did not have purpose, intent or design to perform a prank or to effect an assault and battery upon the person of the plaintiff.*" (Italics ours, for a purpose hereinafter indicated.)

It is conceded that Ruth Garratt's fall resulted in a fractured hip and other painful and serious injuries. To obviate the necessity of a retrial in the event this court determines that she was entitled to a judgment against Brian Dailey, the amount of her damage was found to be eleven thousand dollars. Plaintiff appeals from a judgment dismissing the action and asks for the entry of a judgment in that amount or a new trial.

The authorities generally, but with certain notable exceptions (see Bohlen, "Liability in Tort of Infants and Insane Persons," 23 Mich. L. Rev. 9), state that, when a minor has committed a tort with force, he is liable to be proceeded against as any other person would be.

In our analysis of the applicable law, we start with the basic premise that Brian, whether five or fifty-five, must have committed some wrongful act before he could be liable for appellant's injuries.

The trial court's finding that Brian was a visitor in the Garratt backyard is supported by the evidence and negatives appellant's assertion that Brian was a trespasser and had no right to touch, move, or sit in any chair in that yard, and that contention will not receive further consideration.

It is urged that Brian's action in moving the chair constituted a battery. A definition (not all-inclusive but sufficient for our purpose) of a battery is the intentional infliction of a harmful bodily contact upon another. The rule that determines liability for battery is given in 1 Restatement, Torts, 29, §13, as:

> An act which, directly or indirectly, is the legal cause of a harmful contact with another's person makes the actor liable to the other, if
>
> (a) the act is done with the intention of bringing about a harmful or offensive contact or an apprehension thereof to the other or a third person, and
>
> (b) the contact is not consented to by the other or the other's consent thereto is procured by fraud or duress, and
>
> (c) the contact is not otherwise privileged.

We have in this case no question of consent or privilege. We therefore proceed to an immediate consideration of intent and its place in the law of battery. In the comment on clause (a), the Restatement says:

> Character of actor's intention. In order that an act may be done with the intention of bringing about a harmful or offensive contact or an apprehension thereof to a particular person, either the other or a third person, the act must be done for the purpose of causing the contact or apprehension or with knowledge on the part of the actor that such contact or apprehension is substantially certain to be produced.

See also, Prosser on Torts 41, §8.

We have here the conceded volitional act of Brian, i.e., the moving of a chair. Had the plaintiff proved to the satisfaction of the trial court that Brian moved the chair while she was in the act of sitting down, Brian's action would patently have been for the purpose or with the intent of causing the plaintiff's bodily contact with the ground, and she would be entitled to a judgment against him for the resulting damages. Vosburg v. Putney (1891), 80 Wis. 523, 50 N.W. 403.

The plaintiff based her case on that theory, and the trial court held that she failed in her proof and accepted Brian's version of the facts rather than that given by the eyewitness who testified for the plaintiff. After the trial court determined that the plaintiff had not established her theory of a battery (i.e., that Brian had pulled the chair out from under the plaintiff while she was in the act of sitting down), it then became concerned with whether a battery was established under the facts as it found them to be.

In this connection, we quote another portion of the comment on the "Character of actor's intention," relating to clause (a) of the rule from the Restatement heretofore set forth:

> It is not enough that the act itself is intentionally done and this, even though the actor realizes or should realize that it contains a very grave risk of bringing about the contact or apprehension. Such realization may make the actor's conduct negligent or even reckless but unless he realizes that to a substantial certainty, the contact or apprehension will result, the actor has not that intention which is necessary to make him liable under the rule stated in this Section.

A battery would be established if, in addition to plaintiff's fall, it was proved that, when Brian moved the chair, he knew with substantial certainty that the plaintiff would attempt to sit down where the chair had been. If Brian had any of the intents which the trial court found, in the italicized portions of the findings of fact quoted above, that he did not have, he would of course have had the knowledge to which we have referred. The mere absence of any intent to injure the plaintiff or to play a prank on her or to embarrass her, or to commit an assault and battery on her would not absolve him from liability if in fact he had such knowledge. Without such knowledge, there would be nothing wrongful about Brian's act in moving the chair, and, there being no wrongful act, there would be no liability.

While a finding that Brian had no such knowledge can be inferred from the findings made, we believe that before the plaintiff's action in such a case should be dismissed there should be no question but that the trial court had passed upon that issue; hence, the case should be remanded for clarification of the findings to specifically cover the question of Brian's knowledge, because intent could be inferred therefrom. If the court finds that he had such knowledge, the necessary intent will be established and the plaintiff will be entitled to recover, even though there was no purpose to injure or embarrass the plaintiff. Vosburg v. Putney, supra. If Brian did not have such knowledge, there was no wrongful act by him, and the basic premise of liability on the theory of a battery was not established.

It will be noted that the law of battery as we have discussed it is the law applicable to adults, and no significance has been attached to the fact that Brian was a child less than six years of age when the alleged battery occurred. The only circumstance where Brian's age is of any consequence is in determining what he knew, and there his experience, capacity, and understanding are of course material.

From what has been said, it is clear that we find no merit in plaintiff's contention that we can direct the entry of a judgment for eleven thousand dollars in her favor on the record now before us.

Nor do we find any error in the record that warrants a new trial. . . .

The case is remanded for clarification, with instructions to make definite findings on the issue of whether Brian Dailey knew with substantial certainty that the plaintiff would attempt to sit down where the chair which he moved had been, and to change the judgment if the findings warrant it. . . .

Remanded for clarification.

SCHWELLENBACH, DONWORTH, and WEAVER, JJ., concur.

On remand, the trial court found for the plaintiff. On appeal, the Supreme Court of Washington affirmed, 304 P.2d 681 (Wash. 1956), disposing of the defendant's argument that the evidence did not support a finding of knowledge on the part of the defendant in the following manner:

> The record was carefully reviewed by this court in Garratt v. Dailey. Had there been no evidence to support a finding of knowledge on the part of the defendant, the remanding of the case for clarification on that issue would have been a futile gesture on the part of the court. As we stated in that opinion, the testimony of the two witnesses to the occurrence was in direct conflict. We assumed, since the trial court made a specific finding that the defendant did not intend to harm the plaintiff, that the court had accepted the testimony of the defendant and rejected that of the plaintiff's witness. However, on remand, the judge who heard the case stated that his findings had been made in the light of his understanding of the law, i.e., that the doctrine of constructive intent does not apply to infants, who are not chargeable with knowledge of the normal consequences of their acts. In order to determine whether the defendant knew that the plaintiff would sit in the place where the chair had been, it was necessary for him to consider carefully the time sequence, as he had not done before; and this resulted in his finding that the arthritic woman had begun the slow process of being seated when the defendant quickly removed the chair and seated himself upon it, and that he knew, with substantial certainty, at that time that she would attempt to sit in the place where the chair had been. Such a conclusion, he stated, was the only reasonable one possible. It finds ample support in the record. Such knowledge, we said in Garratt v. Dailey, is sufficient to charge the defendant with intent to commit a battery.

The defendant also argued on the second appeal that the findings on remand were technically inconsistent with the original findings. The Supreme Court refused to address this issue because the defendant had failed to preserve the issue on appeal.

Knowledge-based intent, which the Supreme Court of Washington in the preceding excerpt refers to as "the doctrine of constructive intent," is universally recognized by American courts. For an exposition of the doctrine, see generally James A. Henderson, Jr. & Aaron D. Twerski, Intent and Recklessness in Tort: The Practical Craft of Restating the Law, 54 Vand. L. Rev. 1133, 1138-43 (2001). See also §1(b) of the Restatement (Third) of Torts: Liability for Physical and Emotional Harm (2010). Constructive intent has played an important role in a number of different areas of tort law in recent years. One such area involves employment-related torts. Statutory workers' compensation systems offer exclusive no-fault remedies and bar tort claims by employees against the employer. Many courts have held that such statutes impliedly recognize an exception for intentional torts, typically on the ground that the limited remedies of the workers' compensation systems would provide inadequate compensation and deterrence incentives in the case of batteries and other intentional torts. See generally David B. Harrison, Annotation, What Conduct Is Willful, Intentional, or Deliberate Within Workmen's Compensation Act Provision Authorizing Tort Action for Such Conduct, 96 A.L.R.3d 1064 (1979). Thus, in Turner v. PCR, Inc., 754 So. 2d 683 (Fla. 2000), the plaintiff's decedent, an employee of PCR, was killed in an explosion that occurred in the company's chemical plant. The plaintiff brought a wrongful death action against PCR. The trial court granted summary judgment on the grounds of PCR's workers' compensation defense. On appeal, the Supreme Court of Florida reversed, recognizing an intentional tort exception to workers' compensation and finding that a triable issue of fact may have existed as to whether it was substantially certain that an employee would suffer injury or death while working in the chemical plant. This holding was based on the fact that at least three other uncontrolled explosions had occurred at the PCR plant in the two years prior to the fatal accident, thereby giving credence to the plaintiff's claim that the decedent's death in a plant explosion was substantially certain to occur. Compare with Batiste v. Bayou Steel Corp., 45 So. 3d 167 (La. 2010) (noting that an employer's mere awareness of prior similar accidents is insufficient to establish an employer's knowledge that an accident that injured the plaintiff was substantially certain to occur).

The Florida legislature codified the intentional tort exception in 2003. See Fla. Stat. §440.11(1). However, this codification modified the standard announced by the Supreme Court of Florida in *Turner*. The Florida statute requires that for an injured employee to recover in tort, he must prove by clear and convincing evidence either that his employer "deliberately intended to injure him" or that his employer engaged in conduct that the employer actually knew, based on prior similar accidents or on explicit warnings specifically identifying a known danger, was "virtually certain" to result in injury or death. The "virtually certain" standard has been adopted in other states, and clearly makes it more difficult for an employee to use the doctrine of constructive intent as a way of avoiding the exclusive, limited remedies of workers' compensation systems. See, e.g., List Indus., Inc. v. Dalien, 107 So. 3d 470, 471 (Fla. Dist. Ct. App. 2013) ("The change from 'substantial certainty' to 'virtually certain' is an extremely different and manifestly more difficult standard to meet. It would mean that a plaintiff must show that a given danger will result in an accident every — or almost every — time."). The Supreme Court of Florida in Travelers Indemnity Co. v. PCR Inc., 889 So. 2d 779 (Fla. 2004), considered whether liability insurance companies would be responsible for covering intentional torts based on the substantial certainty or virtual certainty standard. The liability insurance policy involved in the case specifically stated that the insurance company would cover all sums PCR must legally pay as damages because of bodily injuries to PCR's employees and that the policy applied only to claims of "bodily injury by accident . . . arising out of and in the course of . . . employment by [PCR]." The policy, however, enumerated several exclusions from coverage, one of which said that "this insurance does not cover . . . bodily injury intentionally caused or aggravated by [PCR]." The Florida Supreme Court held that, while the policy explicitly excluded coverage of intentionally-caused bodily injury, the insurance company was responsible for extending coverage to claims brought against the employer under the substantial certainty or virtual certainty standard. The court reasoned that the word "accident" in the liability policy should not be interpreted so narrowly as to cover only circumstances deemed accidental under workers' compensation and tort law. How can the court defend its view that harms caused with substantial or virtually certain knowledge can be both intentional for purposes of workers' compensation and tort law and accidental for purposes of construing the liability insurance contract?

Another case that turned on the issues of whether and in what situations a work-related hazard with substantial certainty of injury will fall into the intentional tort exception to workers' compensation is Laidlow v. Hariton Machinery Co., Inc., 790 A.2d 884 (N.J. 2002). In *Laidlow*, the plaintiff caught his hand in a rolling mill due to the lack of a safety guard on the machine. The high court of New Jersey formulated a test with two required prongs to determine whether the injury fell under the intentional tort exception to the workers' compensation exclusivity provision. First, similarly to *Garratt*, the court asked if the employer knew with substantial certainty that the injury would result. Second, the court formulated a "context" prong that examined whether the injury was simply the result of everyday industrial life, in which case workers' compensation was the exclusive remedy, or was plainly outside the legislative grant of immunity from tort under the workers' compensation statute, in which case the claimant could pursue a remedy in tort. Under this second prong, the court appeared to be inquiring into whether the injury was the type of injury that should be expected in a normal working environment and thus be compensated for exclusively under the workers' compensation statute. See also Price v. Howard, 236 P.3d 82 (Okla. 2010) (holding that even a willful and knowing violation of government safety standards by an employer did not rise to the level of an intentional tort against the decedent employee so as to subject the employer to liability beyond the workers' compensation act); Kerans v. Porter Paint Company, 575 N.E.2d 428 (Ohio 1991) (construing the definition of injury within the Ohio workers' compensation statute not to include "a non-physical injury with purely psychological consequences," such that a claim against an employer for sexual harassment could proceed outside the workers' compensation scheme).

Writers have argued for the use of battery as a basis for products liability. In 1980, Paul A. LeBel observed that the plaintiff could establish a battery claim based on the manufacturer's knowledge with substantial certainty that the product would injure unidentified persons. He concluded that the advantages of this strategy, such as recovery of punitive damages and avoidance of defenses based on the plaintiff's fault, encourage manufacturers to reevaluate their cost-benefit analysis, produce safer products, and better inform the consumer. See Paul A. LeBel, Intent and Recklessness as Bases of Products Liability: One Step Back, Two Steps Forward, 32 Ala. L. Rev. 31 (1980). More recently, the elements of battery have been applied to exposure to secondhand smoke. Such an analysis appears to suggest that the cigarette manufacturer acts voluntarily by placing its product on the market with the intent that the smoker smoke the cigarette. The manufacturer also manifests a constructive intent that contact with nonsmokers will be achieved. The force set in motion by the manufacturer thus results in a harmful/offensive contact. See generally Darren S. Rimer, Note, Secondhand Smoke Damages: Extending a Cause of Action for Battery Against a Tobacco Manufacturer, 24 Sw. U. L. Rev. 1237 (1995); Irene Scharf, Breathe Deeply: The Tort of Smokers' Battery, 32 Hous. L. Rev. 615 (1995).

Thus, in Shaw v. Brown & Williamson Tobacco Corp., 973 F. Supp. 539 (D. Md. 1997), the plaintiff brought an action for battery based on his exposure to secondhand smoke. The plaintiff was a long-distance trucker who, over an 11-year period, spent significant amounts of time in a truck cab with a co-worker who smoked. The plaintiff, himself, did not smoke, but he eventually developed lung cancer. He sued the defendant tobacco company alleging, inter alia, battery. The plaintiff claimed that it was substantially certain that Brown & Williamson's tobacco would contact nonsmokers, who, unlike smokers, did not consent to such contact. The trial court dismissed the battery count for failure to state a claim. The court concluded that the defendant did not know with substantial certainty that secondhand smoke from their cigarettes would contact any particular nonsmoker. The fact that the defendant knew that their products would impact some nonsmokers was, according to the court, too generalized to satisfy the knowledge-based intent requirement for battery. This approach has been more generally echoed in the Restatement (Third) of Torts: Liability for Physical and Emotional Harm (2010). Comment *e* of §1 limits applications of the substantial-certainty test to "situations in which the defendant has knowledge to a substantial certainty that the conduct will bring about harm to a particular victim, or to someone within a small class of potential victims within a localized area."

One major problem with arguments that the distribution of products by manufacturers should carry with it constructive intent on the part of the distributor that people suffer injury using and consuming products is that manufacturers would be liable in tort for all of the harm their products cause, regardless of whether those products are legally defective. Whenever a manufacturer distributes hundreds of thousands of units of any product, the manufacturer knows that a certain number of people will suffer product-related harm. If courts have chosen to impose liability on manufacturers when the products they market are defective — as they have, which we will find in Chapter 7 — then by what reasoning can they avoid the clear implications of the doctrine of constructive intent? The Third Restatement's blunt distinction between individualized and statistical knowledge has been viewed as promising but limited by commentators. One important qualification offered in the literature would place intentional tort liability for defendants back on the table when statistical knowledge exists of a risk that is "extremely unjustifiable." Kenneth W. Simons, Statistical Knowledge Deconstructed, 92 B.U. L. Rev. 1 (2012). What circumstances can you imagine in which a defendant holds merely "statistical knowledge" that its conduct poses a risk of harm, but the risk is "extremely unjustifiable"?

While you are pondering that question, remember that subjective intent may be present even when the probabilities of injury approach zero. Thus, *Garratt* describes a sufficient, but not an invariably necessary, basis for concluding that an actor intends a result. The *Garratt* rule governs situations where the actor does not subjectively desire the harmful or offensive contact. But when a defendant subjectively desires to harm the plaintiff, there is no requirement that success be highly probable. Instead, as long as the defendant desires to cause the harmful or offensive contact and the contact actually occurs as a result of the defendant's actions, a battery is established. Thus, if the defendant shoots at the plaintiff with a gun from a great distance, with minimal chances of success, a battery is committed as long as the desired result — the wounding of the plaintiff — actually occurs.

What happens when a defendant desires to strike one person, but misses the intended victim and instead strikes someone else? For example, in the leading case of Carnes v. Thompson, 48 S.W.2d 903 (Mo. 1932), the defendant had been quarrelling with the plaintiff's husband when the defendant struck at his adversary with a pair of pliers. The plaintiff's husband ducked and the pliers struck the plaintiff. Plaintiff brought a battery claim, but faced the seemingly impossible task of establishing the necessary intent, because the defendant neither desired to contact, nor believed he was substantially certain to contact, the plaintiff. Nonetheless, the court concluded that plaintiff could recover:

> If one person intentionally strikes at, throws at, or shoots at another, and unintentionally strikes a third person, he is not excused, on the ground that it was a mere accident, but it is [a] battery of the third person. Defendant's intention, in such a case, is to strike an unlawful blow, to injure some person by his act, and it is not essential that the injury be to the one intended.

Id. at 904.

The court's resolution illustrates what is commonly referred to as *transferred intent;* the ill intent that the defendant bore toward plaintiff's uninjured husband is applied to the conduct that harmed the plaintiff. Some regard the doctrine of transferred intent as a legal fiction, because rather than representing the true reality of defendant's state of mind, it imposes a legally constructed reality in order to achieve what courts perceive to be a just result.

The Law-Fact Distinction: Trials Without Juries

In the law-fact distinction note following *Vosburg,* we spoke of how the functions of fact finding, law declaring, and law applying are divided between the judge and jury. Frequently, however, torts cases are tried without a jury, as was done in Garratt v. Dailey. No constitutional provision requires that torts cases be tried to juries. The only requirement is that the parties be offered the opportunity to have a jury. In many torts cases the parties do not opt for a jury. The most important reason is that in many places, particularly urban areas, it takes much longer for a case which is to be tried by a jury to be reached for trial. Thus, although most lawyers believe, perhaps incorrectly, that juries are more sympathetic to plaintiffs than are trial judges, it may be in the plaintiff's best interests to get on with the trial. In most personal injury cases, defendants pay interest only after judgment is entered against them, so long delays in reaching trial tend to hurt plaintiffs more than defendants.

That a case is tried by a judge without a jury does not mean that the law-fact distinction loses its relevancy. It only means that the trial judge performs the functions of fact finding and law applying, as well as the function of law declaring. The distinction between law and fact is still important, because the findings of fact by the trial judge, like the findings of fact by a jury, are insulated from appellate review. Thus, the Supreme Court of Washington in Garratt v. Dailey could not properly have directed the trial judge to accept the testimony of the plaintiff's sister rather than that of the defendant.

The nonreviewability of the trial judge's factual findings rests on pragmatic considerations. Because the trial judge is present at the trial and can directly observe the testimony as it comes in, the trial judge is presumed to have a feel for the case that the appellate judges do not have. Thus, if the testimony of witnesses conflicts, the trial judge is better able to tell which witnesses are telling the truth. Further, appellate review of the facts is less needed than review of the law. Because a rule of law is applicable to more than one case, it is important that the law be uniform throughout a given jurisdiction. Review of questions of law by an appellate court that has the final word on what the law is does much to ensure that uniformity. In contrast to the law, the facts of a case are relevant only to that case. Were appellate review of a trial judge's findings of fact allowed, the appellate court would be duplicating the efforts of the trial judge, with no reason to believe that the appellate court would do a better job, and with some reason to believe it would not do as well.

Problem 1

A partner in the law firm in which you are an associate has asked for your help on a case she is handling. The client is Charlie Crowder, the 14-year-old son of a business acquaintance of the partner. Charlie suffered a gunshot wound in his left leg as the result of a game of Russian roulette engaged in by Charlie and another 14-year-old, Tim Rosen. According to Charlie, Tim challenged him to the game five months ago, after the two had been bragging to friends about who was braver. Tim produced a small-caliber revolver from his backpack and proposed that they place a loaded cartridge in one of the gun's six empty chambers and spin the cylinder. They would take turns, each pointing the revolver at the lower leg of the other and pulling the trigger. The cylinder would be spun again after each turn. At any time, either participant could call the game off ("chicken out") and the other would be the winner.

Responding to Tim's challenge, Charlie agreed to participate. Tim flipped a coin and Charlie went first. Charlie spun the cylinder, pointed the gun at Tim's leg, and pulled the trigger. The hammer clicked harmlessly on an empty chamber. Then Tim took a turn, with the same result. Then Charlie, Tim, and Charlie again with the same result. On Tim's next turn, the sixth in all, the revolver fired a bullet that struck Charlie in his left leg, below the knee. The injury was serious, though Charlie has recovered without permanent disability. Charlie's parents have asked the partner to represent Charlie in a tort action against Tim and his parents. (Tim's father owns the revolver and may have been negligent in failing to prevent Tim from gaining access to it.) The partner wants your advice on whether Tim committed a battery when he shot Charlie with the revolver. The partner wants you to concentrate on the element of intent. Someone else in the firm is looking at the issues of consent and negligence.

The partner explains that Charlie will, in any event, pursue claims based on negligence and recklessness, but the issue of intentional tort is important in several ways. If Charlie succeeds on a battery claim, his own contributory negligence, if any, will not reduce or defeat his recovery. And he may recover punitive damages if he can prove intent. On the other hand, to the extent that the Rosens' homeowner's insurance is an important source of funds out of which to satisfy a judgment against Tim (or his father), the insurance company is likely to raise the possibility that Tim intentionally injured Charlie as a way to escape responsibility under standard policy language excluding coverage for intentional torts. Whether the partner will pursue an intentional tort claim will depend on a consideration of all these issues. But her analysis must start with the question of whether Tim could be found to have committed a battery upon Charlie.

Making reasonable assumptions regarding facts not stated, and assuming the law in your jurisdiction is consistent with the general rules contained in the preceding materials in the casebook, advise the partner on the question of whether a trier of fact could find that Tim intended to shoot Charlie.

Mechanisms for Resolving Disputes: Judges vs. Juries as Triers of Fact

As mentioned in the preceding note on the law-fact distinction, lawyers generally perceive that a jury is more likely than a trial judge to find for the plaintiff and to award substantial monetary damages. Studies reveal that the general public also shares this notion of a pro-plaintiff bias on the part of juries.[8] Thus, it should come as no surprise that a study of federal court cases heard between 1979 and 1989 revealed that only 9.7 percent of medical malpractice cases and 12.1 percent of products liability cases were heard by a judge.[9] Plaintiffs, hoping to avail themselves of the jury's perceived sympathy, overwhelmingly opt for a jury trial in such cases. But are these plaintiffs really benefiting themselves when they choose a jury trial?

Researchers have conducted several empirical studies comparing the outcomes of judge and jury trials in an attempt to test the oft-held notions of pro-plaintiff jury bias. The University of Chicago Jury Project, conducted in the 1950s, studied verdicts in over 4,000 civil jury trials by inquiring of the trial judge how he or she would have decided

8. See generally Kevin M. Clermont & Theodore Eisenberg, Trial by Jury or Judge: Transcending Empiricism, 77 Cornell L. Rev. 1124 (1992).

9. Id. at 1141.

the case as the fact finder.[10] The study compared the actual verdicts with the judges' hypothetical outcomes and concluded that judge and jury agreed as to liability 78 percent of the time. Studies have also shown that judge-jury agreement rates are comparable to the agreement rates among judges and decisionmakers in other fields.[11] Those cases in which the judge disagreed with the jury verdict were about evenly split between verdicts for the defendant and verdicts for the plaintiff. Similarly, a study of Arizona civil juries found 77 percent agreement with jury verdicts in 46 cases in which the presiding judge expressed an opinion regarding the verdict he or she would have given.[12] These findings call into question the common perception that juries are more likely to find for plaintiffs than are their counterparts on the bench.

Professor Valerie Hans, who has done considerable research on civil juries, has found that "instead of rampant pro-plaintiff sympathy, many civil jurors were hostile to plaintiffs who brought civil lawsuits." [13] For example, studies of mock juries indicate that jurors are willing to hold plaintiffs partially responsible for their own injuries, even when the simulation is constructed so that the plaintiffs are legally without fault. Additionally, Hans's research calls into question the stereotype that jurors tend to be biased against business or corporate defendants. Her research indicates that juries do tend to be more likely to attribute responsibility for injuries to corporate defendants than to individual defendants.[14] This tendency, however, is not correlated with anti-business biases that might indicate the jurors' intent to punish businesses, but rather seems to stem from expectations that corporate conduct be held to a more rigorous standard, possibly because corporations have greater capacity to meet this standard than individual defendants.

Research has also undermined the assumption that juries tend to award significantly larger and more variable monetary damages than do judges. For example, a study of noneconomic damages (i.e., damages that compensate plaintiffs for their pain and suffering) conducted by Professor Vidmar reveals that twelve-person juries yield more consistent damage awards than do judges presiding over a bench trial.[15] That is, if five factually similar cases were to be heard by five separate judges, the judges would return monetary awards whose amounts varied to a greater degree than awards made by five juries hearing the same cases. The study also found that six-person juries produced more variable awards than did juries composed of more members, but that these smaller juries were still more consistent than individual judges. These findings fit with scientific assessments of group decisionmaking more broadly: as Professors Hans and Eisenberg note, "[a] host of studies comparing individual and group decision making finds that groups offer more stable and more accurate estimates of a population's preferences."[16] Concerning the size of jury verdicts, the University of Chicago Jury Project found that juries return

10. See Neil Vidmar, The Performance of the American Civil Jury: An Empirical Perspective, 40 Ariz. L. Rev. 849 (1998). Valerie P. Hans & Stephanie Albertson, Empirical Research and Civil Jury Reform, 78 Notre Dame L. Rev. 1497 (2003).

11. See Jennifer K. Robbennolt, Jury Decisionmaking: Evaluating Juries by Comparison to Judges: A Benchmark for Judging?, 32 Fla. St. U. L. Rev. 469, 479 (2005).

12. See Vidmar, supra note 10.

13. See Hans & Albertson, supra note 10 at 1507. See also Neil Vidmar & Valerie P. Hans, American Juries: The Verdict 267-279 (2007) (challenging perceptions that civil jurors are overly sympathetic toward plaintiffs); Scott Brister, The Decline in Jury Trials: What Would Wal-Mart Do?, 27 S. Tex. L. Rev. 191 (2005) (noting that a 2001 compilation of tort verdicts by the United States Bureau of Justice Statistics showed that plaintiffs prevailed in 65 percent of tort cases tried to a judge, but only 51 percent of those tried to a jury).

14. See Hans & Albertson, supra note 10, at 1508-1509. See generally Valerie P. Hans, Business on Trial: The Civil Jury and Corporate Responsibility (2000).

15. See Vidmar, supra note 10.

16. Valerie P. Hans & Theodore Eisenberg, The Predictability of Juries, 60 DePaul L. Rev. 375, 377 (2010-2011).

monetary awards that are, on average, 20 percent larger than what the judge presiding over the trial would have awarded. Although this finding corroborates the notion that juries award larger monetary damages than do judges, the existence of only a 20 percent differential is hardly consistent with the assertions commonly made by tort reformers that, compared with judges, juries are out of control and apt to award exorbitant damages for minor injuries. In fact, a study covering "one year of judge and jury trial outcomes from forty-five larger trial courts, comprising nearly nine thousand trials, yield[ed] no evidence that judges and juries differ significantly in their rates of awarding punitive damages, or in the relation between the size of punitive and compensatory awards."[17]

Another commonly held perception about juries is that they are poor fact finders in complex cases, such as patent litigation and antitrust lawsuits. Recent research lends credibility to this assertion. For example, a study of patent litigation found that judges are subtler at managing the complex nature of such cases and that juries are often distracted by tangential evidence that does not bear significantly on the merits of the case.[18] Moreover, another study of complex litigation reveals that judges agree with jury verdicts in only 63 percent of such cases.[19] When this figure is contrasted with the 78 percent agreement rate in the University of Chicago Jury Project, a study that included all categories of civil litigation, the results do tend to support the prevalent belief that judges are superior fact finders in complex cases.

Nevertheless, the fact that judges and juries tend to reach different outcomes in such cases does not necessarily mean that the judge's opinion as to the verdict is correct. While judges are better educated than most jurors, the deliberations of the six to twelve jurors, during which the individual members can pool their recollections and understanding of complex testimony, may result in a fuller comprehension of scientific evidence than that gleaned by the judge. In addition, studies indicate that a large percent of judges feel their legal educations did not prepare them to deal adequately with scientific evidence, and surveys indicate that some judges may lack expertise with basic scientific or statistical methods of analysis. With this in mind, it seems intuitively more likely that one of the twelve jurors, rather than the judge, would have some scientific training, with which she can enlighten her fellow fact finders during deliberations.[20] Thus, without further research into the subject of complex litigation, it is impossible to confirm the accuracy of the assumptions of juror incompetence that underpin the bias against utilizing juries to adjudicate complex cases.

In light of these recent studies, the jury's continued role in American court proceedings seems secure. Indeed, trial attorneys, tort reformers, and the general public would be well-advised to reevaluate their notions of juror bias and incompetence by heeding the words of Professor Vidmar, who concluded his study of juror behavior by stating that "There is no

17. See Theodore Eisenberg, Neil LaFountain, Brian Ostrum, David Rottman & Martin T. Wells, Juries, Judges and Punitive Damages: An Empirical Study, 87 Cornell L. Rev. 743, 746 (2002). Some research, however, has suggested judge-jury differences in awarding punitive damages based upon whether cases involve personal injury, with judges awarding such damages at a higher rate in personal injury cases, and juries awarding them at a higher rate in nonpersonal-injury cases. See Theodore Eisenberg & Michael Heise, Judge-Jury Difference in Punitive Damage Awards: Who Listens to the Supreme Court?, 8 J. Empirical Legal Stud. 325, 352 (2011).

18. See Kimberly A. Moore, Judges, Juries, and Patent Cases — An Empirical Peek Inside the Black Box, 99 Mich. L. Rev. 365 (2000). See also Eugene Morgulis, Note, Juror Reactions to Scientific Testimony: Unique Challenges in Complex Mass Torts, 15 B.U. J. Sci. & Tech. L. 252 (2009) (noting that jurors have particular difficulty assessing liability in complex mass tort cases).

19. See Vidmar, note 10 above.

20. See Robbennolt, note 11 above, at 488-492. See also Valerie P. Hans, Judges, Juries, and Scientific Evidence, 16 J.L. & Pol'y 19, 44 (2007) (presenting findings that college educated jurors possessed some advantages in assessing scientific evidence over both less educated jurors and, in some instances, judges).

evidence to support the claim that juries decide cases less competently than judges and some reason to suspect that the combined judgments of jurors, enhanced through the deliberation process, may be as good or better than those that would be rendered by a randomly selected judge."[21] For a recent symposium specifically addressing the civil jury as a "political institution," see National Center for State Courts, Center for Jury Studies, Institute of Bill of Rights Law, and William & Mary Law Review 2013 Symposium: The Civil Jury as a Political Institution, 55 Wm. & Mary L. Rev. (2014).

b. Contact

The preceding section considers two aspects of the element of intent: what consequences must the defendant intend in order to commit a battery (wrongful contact), and what states of mind constitute intent (desire or knowledge with substantial certainty). Now we focus attention on the element of contact, which also has two aspects: what constitutes contact, and what sorts of contacts are wrongful. In *Vosburg,* the defendant conceded the first aspect of contact — he admitted that he intentionally kicked the plaintiff's shin — and the court determined the second aspect of wrongfulness in reference to the defendant's breach of the order and decorum of the classroom. Now we take a closer look at both of these aspects of the element of contact.

(1) What Constitutes Contact?

In all of the cases we have considered thus far, the element of contact with the plaintiff's person was clear enough: the kick on the shin in *Vosburg*, the fall to the ground in *Garratt*, and the punch in the jaw in our hypothetical. But contact with the plaintiff can occur in less intuitively obvious ways, and cases occasionally test whether a particular contact suffices to establish a battery. As *Garratt* makes clear, the contact requirement does not mean that a part of the defendant's body must come into direct contact with a part of the plaintiff's body. Thus, in *Garratt* the defendant was exposed to liability because his act of moving the chair caused the plaintiff to come into harmful contact with the ground. What should the outcome be if the plaintiff were to eat a piece of fruit that the defendant had poisoned two hours earlier? Cf. Commonwealth v. Stratton, 114 Mass. 303 (1873) (defendant held criminally liable for assault and battery). Additionally, it is sufficient if the defendant causes contact with something very closely associated with the plaintiff's person, such as the clothing the plaintiff was wearing, the cane he was holding, the horse he was riding, or the car he was driving.

(2) Which Intended Contacts Are Wrongful?

Once the plaintiff shows that a contact with her person, or with something closely associated with her person, was intended by the defendant and has occurred, she still must satisfy the second aspect of contact: she must show that the intended contact was wrongful. In the more than 100 years since *Vosburg,* American courts have consistently deemed wrongful those intended contacts that are either harmful or offensive. The contacts in all of the cases considered thus far clearly satisfy the harmful branch of the disjunct. However, while the meaning of "harmful" may seem intuitively clear, it is, in fact, a rather nuanced element of

21. See generally Richard A. Posner, Economic Analysis of Law 204-208 (6th ed. 2003).

the law of battery. Just what sort of contact with the plaintiff's person is, at a minimum, "harmful"? Would a tiny, painless scratch on one's shin suffice? Would the successful surgical amputation of the plaintiff's life-threateningly gangrenous leg be harmful?

According to the Restatement (Third) of Torts: Liability for Physical and Emotional Harm, §4 (2010):

> "Physical harm" means the physical impairment of the human body ("bodily harm") or of real property or tangible personal property ("property damage"). Bodily harm includes physical injury, illness, disease, impairment of bodily function, and death.

Comment *c* to §4 states:

> [A]ny level of physical impairment is sufficient for liability; no minimum amount of physical harm is required. Thus, any detrimental change in the physical condition of a person's body or property counts as a harmful impairment; there is no requirement that the detriment be major.'

The Third Restatement definition of harm supplants the Second Restatement definition, which confusingly defines "harm" and "bodily harm" in two separate sections. Under the Second Restatement, "harm" implies a "loss or detriment to a person, and not a mere change or alteration, . . ." whereas any change or alteration in the body of another, even if not otherwise harmful, would constitute "bodily harm." The Third Restatement implicitly abolishes this distinction. The Reporters' Note to §4 indicates that in the absence of any detriment, alterations in the body do not count as physical harm or impairment. However, the reporters observe that even actions by others that are not ultimately detrimental, such as a physician successfully removing a wart from a non-consenting patient, can be violations of the right to bodily integrity and are thus tortious. Does the definition of physical harm provided in the Third Restatement suggest that this kind of contact would be classified as "offensive" rather than "harmful"?

Unlike harm, offensiveness appears on its face to elude precise definition. When a plaintiff claims that a defendant has intentionally caused an offensive contact, one might be tempted to ask: "Offensive to whom?" The Restatement (Second) takes the following position:

> §19. What Constitutes Offensive Contact
>
> A bodily contact is offensive if it offends a reasonable sense of personal dignity.
>
> COMMENT:
>
> a. In order that a contact be offensive to a reasonable sense of personal dignity, it must be one which would offend the ordinary person and as such one not unduly sensitive as to his personal dignity. It must, therefore, be a contact which is unwarranted by the social usages prevalent at the time and place at which it is inflicted.

Thus, the Restatement (Second) casts offensiveness in an objective light, using the hypothetical reaction of "the ordinary person" rather than the actual perception of either the defendant or the plaintiff. What are the justifications and consequences of this choice? How can a court determine what an "ordinary person" would find offensive?

Fisher v. Carrousel Motor Hotel

424 S.W.2d 627 (Tex. 1967)

GREENHILL, J. This is a suit for actual and exemplary damages growing out of an alleged assault and battery. The plaintiff Fisher was a mathematician with the Data Processing Division of the Manned Spacecraft Center, an agency of the National Aeronautics and Space Agency, commonly called NASA, near Houston. The defendants were the Carrousel Motor Hotel, Inc., located in Houston, the Brass Ring Club, which is located in the Carrousel, and Robert W. Flynn, who as an employee of the Carrousel was the manager of the Brass Ring Club. Flynn died before the trial, and the suit proceeded as to the Carrousel and the Brass Ring. Trial was to a jury which found for the plaintiff Fisher. The trial court rendered judgment for the defendants notwithstanding the verdict. The Court of Civil Appeals affirmed. 414 S.W.2d 774. The questions before this Court are whether there was evidence that an actionable battery was committed, and, if so, whether the two corporate defendants must respond in exemplary as well as actual damages for the malicious conduct of Flynn.

The plaintiff Fisher had been invited by Ampex Corporation and Defense Electronics to a one day's meeting regarding telemetry equipment at the Carrousel. The invitation included a luncheon. The guests were asked to reply by telephone whether they could attend the luncheon, and Fisher called in his acceptance. After the morning session, the group of 25 or 30 guests adjourned to the Brass Ring Club for lunch. The luncheon was buffet style, and Fisher stood in line with others and just ahead of a graduate student of Rice University who testified at the trial. As Fisher was about to be served, he was approached by Flynn, who snatched the plate from Fisher's hand and shouted that he, a Negro, could not be served in the club. Fisher testified that he was not actually touched, and did not testify that he suffered fear or apprehension of physical injury; but he did testify that he was highly embarrassed and hurt by Flynn's conduct in the presence of his associates.

The jury found that Flynn "forceably dispossessed plaintiff of his dinner plate" and "shouted in a loud and offensive manner" that Fisher could not be served there, thus subjecting Fisher to humiliation and indignity. It was stipulated that Flynn was an employee of the Carrousel Hotel and, as such, managed the Brass Ring Club. The jury also found that Flynn acted maliciously and awarded Fisher $400 actual damages for his humiliation and indignity and $500 exemplary damages for Flynn's malicious conduct.

The Court of Civil Appeals held that there was no assault because there was no physical contact and no evidence of fear or apprehension of physical contact. However, it has long been settled that there can be a battery without an assault, and that actual physical contact is not necessary to constitute a battery, so long as there is contact with clothing or an object closely identified with the body. . . .

Under the facts of this case, we have no difficulty in holding that the intentional grabbing of plaintiff's plate constituted a battery. The intentional snatching of an object from one's hand is as clearly an offensive invasion of his person as would be an actual contact with the body. . . .

. . . Damages for mental suffering are recoverable without the necessity for showing actual physical injury in a case of willful battery because the basis of that action is the unpermitted and intentional invasion of the plaintiff's person and not the actual harm done to the plaintiff's body. Personal indignity is the essence of an action for battery; and consequently the defendant is liable not only for contacts which do actual physical harm, but also for those which are offensive and insulting. We hold, therefore, that plaintiff was entitled to actual damages for mental suffering due to the willful battery, even in the absence of any physical injury. . . .

We now turn to the question of the liability of the corporations for exemplary damages. In this regard, the jury found that Flynn was acting within the course and scope of his employment on the occasion in question; that Flynn acted maliciously and with a wanton disregard of the rights and feelings of plaintiff on the occasion in question. There is no attack upon these jury findings. The jury further found that the defendant Carrousel did not authorize or approve the conduct of Flynn. It is argued that there is no evidence to support this finding. The jury verdict concluded with a finding that $500 would "reasonably compensate plaintiff for the malicious act and wanton disregard of plaintiff's feelings and rights. . . ."

The rule in Texas is that a principal or master is liable for exemplary or punitive damages because of the acts of his agent, but only if: (a) the principal authorized the doing and the manner of the act, or (b) the agent was unfit and the principal was reckless in employing him, or (c) the agent was employed in a managerial capacity and was acting in the scope of employment, or (d) the employer or a manager of the employer ratified or approved the act.

. . . At the trial of this case, the following stipulation was made in open court: "It is further stipulated and agreed to by all parties that as an employee of the Carrousel Motor Hotel the said Robert W. Flynn was manager of the Brass Ring Club." We think this stipulation brings the case squarely within part (c) of the rule. . . .

The judgment of the courts below are reversed, and judgment is here rendered for the plaintiff for $900 with interest. . . .

Leichtman v. WLW Jacor Communications, Inc.

634 N.E.2d 697 (Ohio Ct. App. 1994)

PER CURIAM.

The plaintiff-appellant, Ahron Leichtman, appeals from the trial court's order dismissing his complaint against the defendants-appellees, WLW Jacor Communications ("WLW"), William Cunningham and Andy Furman, for battery. . . . In his single assignment of error, Leichtman contends that his complaint was sufficient to state a claim upon which relief could be granted and, therefore, the trial court was in error when it granted the defendants' [motion to dismiss the complaint]. We agree in part.

In his complaint, Leichtman claims to be "a nationally known" antismoking advocate. Leichtman alleges that, on the date of the Great American Smokeout, he was invited to appear on the WLW Bill Cunningham radio talk show to discuss the harmful effects of smoking and breathing secondary smoke. He also alleges that, while he was in the studio, Furman, another WLW talk-show host, lit a cigar and repeatedly blew smoke in Leichtman's face "for the purpose of causing physical discomfort, humiliation and distress." . . .

Leichtman contends that Furman's intentional act constituted a battery. The Restatement of the Law 2d, Torts (1965), states:

> An actor is subject to liability to another for battery if
>
> (a) he acts intending to cause a harmful or offensive contact with the person of the other . . . , and
>
> (b) a harmful contact with the person of the other directly or indirectly results [; or]
>
> (c) an offensive contact with the person of the other directly or indirectly results.

In determining if a person is liable for a battery, the Supreme Court has adopted the rule that "[c]ontact which is offensive to a reasonable sense of personal dignity is offensive contact." Love v. Port Clinton (1988), 37 Ohio St. 3d 98, 99, 524 N.E.2d 166, 167. It has defined "offensive" to mean "disagreeable or nauseating or painful because of outrage to taste and sensibilities or affronting insultingness." State v. Phipps (1979), 58 Ohio St. 2d 271, 274, 12 O.O.3d 273, 275, 389 N.E.2d 1128, 1131. Furthermore, tobacco smoke, as "particulate matter," has the physical properties capable of making contact. R.C. 3704.01(B) and 5709.20(A); Ohio Adm. Code 3745-17.

As alleged in Leichtman's complaint, when Furman intentionally blew cigar smoke in Leichtman's face, under Ohio common law, he committed a battery. No matter how trivial the incident, a battery is actionable, even if damages are only one dollar. . . .

Other jurisdictions also have concluded that a person can commit a battery by intentionally directing tobacco smoke at another. Richardson v. Hennly (1993), 209 Ga. App. 868, 871, 434 S.E.2d 772, 774-775. We do not, however, adopt or lend credence to the theory of a "smoker's battery," which imposes liability if there is substantial certainty that exhaled smoke will predictably contact a nonsmoker. Ezra, Smoker Battery: An Antidote to Second-Hand Smoke (1990), 63 S. Cal. L. Rev. 1061, 1090. Also, whether the "substantial certainty" prong of intent from the Restatement of Torts translates to liability for secondary smoke via the intentional tort doctrine in employment cases . . . need not be decided here because Leichtman's claim for battery is based exclusively on Furman's commission of a deliberate act. Finally, because Leichtman alleges that Furman deliberately blew smoke into his face, we find it unnecessary to address offensive contact from passive or secondary smoke under the "glass cage" defense of McCracken v. Sloan (1979), 40 N.C. App. 214, 217, 252 S.E.2d 250, 252, relied on by the defendants. . . .

Arguably, trivial cases are responsible for an avalanche of lawsuits in the courts. They delay cases that are important to individuals and corporations and that involve important social issues. The result is justice denied to litigants and their counsel who must wait for their day in court. However, absent circumstances that warrant sanctions for frivolous appeals . . . we refuse to limit one's right to sue. Section 16, Article I, Ohio Constitution states, "All courts shall be open, and every person, for an injury done him in his land, goods, person, or reputation, shall have remedy by due course of law, and shall have justice administered without denial or delay."

This case emphasizes the need for some form of alternative dispute resolution operating totally outside the court system as a means to provide an attentive ear to the parties and a resolution of disputes in a nominal case. Some need a forum in which they can express corrosive contempt for another without dragging their antagonist through the expense inherent in a lawsuit. Until such an alternative forum is created, Leichtman's battery claim, previously knocked out by the trial judge in the first round, now survives round two to advance again through the courts into round three.

We . . . reverse that portion of the trial court's order that dismissed the battery claim. . . . This cause is remanded for further proceedings consistent with law on that claim only.

Judgment accordingly.

Doan, P.J., and Hildebrandt and Gorman, JJ., concur.

The court in *Leichtman* refers to the "glass cage" defense discussed in McCracken v. Sloan, 252 S.E.2d 250 (N.C. Ct. App. 1979). In *McCracken*, the plaintiff alleged that the defendant twice committed a battery upon him by smoking cigars in his presence. At a pretrial conference, the parties stipulated what the evidence most favorable to the plaintiff would be, and, based on that evidence, the trial court ordered the case dismissed on the ground "that plaintiff could not prove a sufficient case to carry his cause to the jury." The stipulated evidence showed that the plaintiff had been a postal employee in the City of Charlotte and the defendant was the postmaster in that city. The plaintiff had a documented medical history of being allergic to tobacco smoke. The plaintiff had made complaints and distributed literature within the post office building in regard to the dangers of smoking. He had requested and been denied sick leave for his allergic condition. On two occasions, the plaintiff attended meetings in the office of the defendant at which the plaintiff's application for sick leave was discussed. At both of these meetings, defendant smoked a cigar. At one of these meetings, the defendant said: "Bill, I know you claim to have an allergy to tobacco smoke and you have presented statements from your doctor stating this, but there is no law against smoking, so I'm going to smoke."

The court upheld the dismissal of the action, in part because the plaintiff did not allege any physical injury. The court quoted from William L. Prosser, The Law of Torts 37 (4th ed. 1971), that "it may be questioned whether any individual can be permitted, by his own fiat, to erect a glass cage around himself, and to announce that all physical contact with his person is at the expense of liability." For two more recent cases affirming dismissals of smokers' battery claims, see Golesorkhi v. Lufthansa German Airlines, 122 F.3d 1061 (4th Cir. 1997); and Wilson v. Johnson, 2003 Ohio App. LEXIS 891 (Ohio Ct. App. 2003).

The forthcoming Restatement (Third) of Torts: Intentional Torts to Persons (Am. Law Inst., Tentative Draft No. 1, April 8, 2015) deems a contact to be offensive if:

> (a) the contact offends a reasonable sense of personal dignity; or
> (b) the contact is highly offensive to the other's unusually sensitive sense of personal dignity, and the actor knows that the contact will be highly offensive to the other. [§103]

The section then further notes that "[l]iability under (b) shall not be imposed if the court determines that such liability would violate public policy or that requiring the actor to avoid the contact would be unduly burdensome." Would these provisions affect the outcome in *McCracken*?

Together, *Leichtman* and *McCracken* suggest that the tort of offensive battery is elastic — the tort has the ability to change in response to evolving social standards. The tort of offensive battery is also, in another sense, remarkably limited. What would have happened in *Fisher,* for example, if the defendant's employee had made the same remarks to the plaintiff, but had not grabbed the plaintiff's plate? The employee's remarks, rather than the plate snatching, may be seen as to be the primary source of the plaintiff's distress. What, then, is the value, if any, of the contact requirement?

Note: Returning (Briefly) to the Element of Intent

The text following the *Vosburg* case asks what it was that the Wisconsin court viewed as unlawful about the defendant's kicking the plaintiff's shin. Now that we have considered more fully what the term "offensive" means (see Restatement (Second) §19, above), we might respond that the defendant intended to cause an offensive contact. But that raises another question: Must the defendant intend to offend? The objectiveness of the definition in §19 — "unwarranted by the social usages" — seems to eliminate any requirement that the actor subjectively desire to offend the plaintiff. On that view, if *A* intentionally contacts

B in a socially unwarranted manner so as to offend a reasonable sense of personal dignity, *A* commits an offensive battery even if *A* convincingly argues that he did not know about the relevant social usages when he acted. In effect, *A* would be held strictly liable for having knowingly contacted another's person in a manner that, even if unknown to *A*, was socially unacceptable. Of course, one could argue that the objective definition of "offensive" does not necessarily eliminate the "intent to offend" requirement. Even if the test for offensiveness is objective, the intent element of battery is subjective in both the desire and the knowledge senses of the word "intent." In the end, the policy choice may be whether to impose strict liability on *A* to "get his social usage right" when he intentionally and physically contacts another person. In most instances, actors will know that what they are doing is offensive. In the truly rare instances when they don't know, should they be held to act at their peril?

Law and Policy: Preliminary Considerations

While the behavior of the motel manager in *Fisher* appears reprehensible on its face, the appropriateness of the outcomes in *Vosburg* and *Garratt,* involving young children, is not self-evident. One can easily imagine opinions construing the intent requirement for battery more narrowly, thereby precluding the possibility of recovery in both cases. Why, then, did these courts choose, or at least lend their approval to, those particular rules of tort law? What are the objectives sought to be served by those rules? Indeed, why do we maintain a system of tort liability at all? Our purpose here is not to try to answer these questions, but rather to stimulate thinking about possible answers.

One obvious explanation for the rules adopted by the courts in *Vosburg* and *Garratt* is that they increase the possibility that plaintiffs will succeed and thereby receive compensation for their injuries. This impulse to make victims financially whole undoubtedly influences tort law, but *compensation* as a policy goal fails to explain the precise configuration of rules that courts construct in the tort area. If the overriding objective of tort law is to compensate victims and their families, why do we require that the plaintiff must have been injured by someone's wrongful act? A broken jaw is not less painful, disabling, or expensive when suffered in an accidental fall in the backyard. If the objective of tort liability is to help people who need financial help, why not compensate all needy victims of accidents, irrespective of anyone's wrongdoing? Or why even limit our concern to victims of accidents — why not help the person who becomes ill, or who is the helpless victim of poverty? And couldn't the objective of helping people who need financial help be achieved more directly, equitably, and efficiently through other means, such as tax and welfare laws?

These questions reveal that the statement "tort law aims at compensating victims" begs the underlying question of why we choose to compensate *these particular victims,* rather than victims generally. The search for answers requires us to shift focus from victims to those who have caused the harm, and to ask whether it makes good sense to require them, through the vehicle of tort law, to pay compensation to injured victims.

Three general perspectives are available for analyzing whether particular harm-causing actors should be required to pay their victims under tort law. The first approach asks whether society as a whole will derive future benefits from a particular rule governing recovery. This "instrumental" perspective does not view the imposition of liability as an end in itself, but rather conceives of tort law as an instrument for achieving broader social goals. For most "instrumentalists," the central social goal to be furthered by tort law is to maximize total welfare in society by deterring wasteful injuries and accidents. With historical roots in the thought of John Stuart Mill and Jeremy Bentham, this approach was pioneered in the United States by Oliver Wendell Holmes, Jr. Today, the instrumentalist view is most closely associated with the law and economics movement. A prominent proponent of this view, scholar and Judge Richard Posner, argues that the law of battery, like all tort law, should deter persons from engaging in activities that a reasonable person would view ahead of time to be socially wasteful.[22] If the harm suffered by the victim exceeds the benefit enjoyed by the actor (in *Vosburg,* if Vosburg's pain and upset over being kicked in the shin exceeds in value Putney's enjoyment derived from doing the kicking), then society will be better off if such activities are deterred by threats of liability. Even if the actor benefits more than the victim suffers, activity such as unprovoked shin-kicking may nonetheless be wasteful if it generates higher transaction costs (in the form of the costs of bringing an expensive tort action to make the relevant cost-benefit determination) than would have been generated if the actor had simply gotten the victim's consent ahead of time, perhaps by means of a bribe. As Posner explains it:

> [B]ecause we want to channel resource allocation through the market as much as possible, we want to make sure that I am not allowed to be indifferent between stealing and buying my neighbor's car. We can do this by making the damages award greater than the value of the car so that I do not consider conversion an acceptable substitute for purchase. Punitive damages are one way of doing this. Another way, also common in intentional tort cases, is to make the tortfeasor pay the victim what the thing taken was worth to the tortfeasor . . . to try to make the tort worthless to the tortfeasor and thereby channel resource allocation through the market.[22]

Notice Posner's assumption that "we want to channel resource allocation through the market as much as possible." This assumption is widely held by instrumentalist thinkers, including especially legal economists. What arguments might be offered in favor of or against it?

In contrast to the foregoing view, a second, noninstrumental perspective argues that some harmful acts deserve to be punished simply because they are wrongs. Under this view, a legal response should issue regardless of its capacity to deter wasteful conduct and increase societal wealth. Arguments along these lines are often framed in terms of "fairness" or "corrective justice." They are easy to understand in cases in which one person deliberately and without justification inflicts physical harm on another. In these cases, tort liability may be imposed out of some shared sense that punishment, as an end in itself, is an appropriate societal response to these kinds of obvious wrongdoing. Although in its starker forms such a posture may be decried by some as uncivilized and barbaric, the psychological need for retribution runs deep and can be distinguished from brute revenge. Revenge is typically personal, disproportionate, and at least crudely pleasurable to the punisher; retribution is collective, proportionate, and dispassionate. From the retributive perspective, society as well as the plaintiff has been injured, and punishment helps to address the shared sense of loss generated by antisocial conduct.[23]

But, of course, the goal of retributive justice in this sense seems to be the province of criminal law, not torts. No doubt tort law does share important historical and intellectual connections to criminal law, but more will be necessary to account for tort as a distinctive

22. Id. at 206.

23. See generally Ronen Perry, The Role of Retributive Justice in the Common Law of Torts: A Descriptive Theory, 73 Tenn. L. Rev. 177 (2006); Emily Sherwin, Compensation and Revenge, 40 San Diego L. Rev. 1387 (2003).

practice. After all, if retributive justice were the only purpose served by the law of battery, what explains the results in *Vosburg* and *Garratt*? Levels of wrongfulness sufficient to justify retribution hardly seem to have been reached in those cases. To answer these sorts of questions, noninstrumentalist thinkers have been forced to develop more sophisticated visions of what concepts like "justice" and "fairness" require.[24] One influential view, advanced by Richard Epstein, is that the simple fact that *A* causes harm to *B* is enough to start the liability engine running.[25] *A* may be able to avoid liability by justifying or excusing his conduct in some way; but the fact that *A* caused *B*'s harm is the underlying source of *A*'s obligation to pay. It bears noting that Epstein developed this account of liability in connection with his overall libertarian approach to law. Thus, although mere causal connection is enough to make a prima facie case of liability for harmful invasions of a plaintiff's interests, this strict protection only applies for those "interests" that are recognized within a libertarian scheme, such as one's ownership of property or "self-possession" of one's body. Epstein would generally leave protection of other interests to the workings of the market and custom. In this sense, Epstein's noninstrumentalist account of tort law has much in common with market-favoring instrumentalists such as Posner.

A different and also influential version of noninstrumentalist thinking is offered by George Fletcher. Reacting to the efforts of Posner and other instrumental writers "to convert the [tort system] into a makeshift medium of accident insurance or into a mechanism for maximizing social utility," Professor Fletcher insists that achieving fairness between individuals is the important reason for shifting accident losses via rules of liability.[26] Fletcher's vision of fairness is fundamentally grounded in his paradigm of reciprocity, which holds that "a victim has a right to recover for injuries caused by a risk greater in degree and different in order from those created by the victim and imposed on the defendant — in short, for injuries resulting from nonreciprocal risks."[27] Professor Fletcher concludes that the intentional tort of harmful battery embodies the fairness principles reflected in the paradigm of reciprocity:

> To complete our account of the paradigm of reciprocity, we should turn to one of its primary expressions: intentional torts, particularly . . . battery. . . . An intentional . . . battery represents a rapid acceleration of risk, directed at a specific victim. These features readily distinguish the intentional blow from the background of risk. Perceiving intentional blows as a form of nonreciprocal risk helps us understand why the defendant's malice or animosity toward the victim eventually became unnecessary to ground intentional torts. The nonreciprocity of risk, and the deprivation of security it represents, render irrelevant the attitudes of the risk-creator.[28]

The author cites *Vosburg* and *Garratt* as support for his conclusions that the irrelevance of malevolence or actual desire to injure on the part of the defendant in a battery case can only be understood in terms of the fundamental fairness of allowing the injured plaintiff to recover as an innocent victim of unexcused nonreciprocal risks created by the defendant.

24. A significant amount of scholarship has been generated in this area. In addition to the ideas of Richard Epstein and George Fletcher, which are discussed in the text, major efforts to explain tort law at least partially from a corrective justice perspective have been undertaken by Jules Coleman, Gregory Keating, Stephen Perry, Arthur Ripstein, Ernest Weinrib, and Richard Wright, among others. For an excellent overview, see Benjamin C. Zipursky, Philosophy of Tort Law, in The Blackwell Guide to Philosophy of Law and Legal Theory 122 (Martin P. Golding & William A. Edmundson eds., 2004).

25. See Richard A. Epstein, A Theory of Strict Liability, 2 J. Legal Stud. 151 (1973).

26. See George P. Fletcher, Fairness and Utility in Tort Theory, 85 Harv. L. Rev. 537 (1972).

27. Id. at 542.

28. Id. at 550.

In Fletcher's view, liability is properly imposed in such cases irrespective of whether young children are likely to be deterred by the threat of liability.

In recent years, a number of scholars have built upon the work of corrective justice theorists to offer a significant third perspective on tort law, one that is being referred to as the "civil recourse" school. See, e.g., John C. P. Goldberg & Benjamin C. Zipursky, Torts as Wrongs, 88 Tex. L. Rev. 917 (2010); Benjamin C. Zipursky, Civil Recourse, Not Corrective Justice, 91 Geo. L.J. 695 (2003); Benjamin C. Zipursky, Rights, Wrongs, and Recourse in the Law of Torts, 51 Vand. L. Rev. 1 (1998). They begin with a central insight of corrective justice scholars, who had critiqued the instrumentalists for failing to explain why tort law focuses on rights and duties between particular parties. If tort law were concerned only with deterring socially wasteful conduct, then it might easily be replaced with criminal and regulatory law (and, in fact, many instrumentalist scholars have argued for the abandonment of tort law in just this fashion; see Chapter 10). Instead, as corrective justice theorists note, there is something distinctive about tort law's focus on the particular *relationship of wrongdoing* between a plaintiff and defendant. See, e.g., Jules Coleman, Doing Away with Tort Law, 41 Loy. L.A. L. Rev. 1149 (2008); Ernest J. Weinrib, The Idea of Private Law (1995). When a wrong has occurred, corrective justice requires that it be annulled, which is typically taken to mean that the specific parties involved be put back into the positions they held before the wrong occurred. Thus, if one person owes a duty to another and, in breaching that duty, injures a third, the third person generally may not recover unless she identifies an independent duty owed directly to her. See Sinram v. Pa. R.R. Co., 61 F.2d 767, 769-71 (2d Cir. 1932) (Hand, J.).

Much of tort law that appears mysterious from the instrumentalist viewpoint becomes quite understandable when this basic insight of corrective justice is kept in mind. It explains, for instance, why tort law generally requires actual causation of harm, rather than mere creation of a risk of harm (as discussed in the introduction to Chapter 2). It also explains why the defendant's level of punishment is tied to the plaintiff's level of harm, and why the damages award is paid directly to the plaintiff rather than to a public fund or other recipient.

Civil recourse theorists agree with many of the corrective justice school's arguments, but they still do not think that corrective justice gets to the heart of the tort system. After all, corrective justice might still be accomplished without tort law: A powerful "corrective justice agency" could be created with the ability to award compensation to victims from the general tax fund and the authority to fine or otherwise punish wrongdoers in an effort to annul wrongs. What, then, can be said on behalf of tort law as a distinctive practice? Civil recourse theorists emphasize the fact that tort law does not merely aim to address a carefully delineated set of wrongs done between specific parties; it does so specifically by empowering aggrieved individuals to seek redress against their wrongdoers. Thus understood, tort law is a form of *private law*, designed and intended to work within an overall system of limited government and a political culture of liberalism that are characteristic of the Anglo-American legal tradition.

For most of its history, a bedrock feature of this legal tradition has been the entitlement of injured parties to seek to persuade impartial courts that they hold a right of action against their wrongdoers. See John C. P. Goldberg, The Constitutional Status of Tort Law: Due Process and the Right to a Law for the Redress of Wrongs, 115 Yale L.J. 524 (2005). Chief Justice Marshall clearly embraced such a view in Marbury v. Madison, when he stated that "[t]he very essence of civil liberty . . . consists in the right of every individual to claim the protection of the laws, whenever he receives an injury. One of the first duties of government is to afford that protection." Marbury v. Madison, 5 U.S. (1 Cranch) 137, 163 (1803).

For centuries in the Anglo-American tradition, the manner in which government has fulfilled this duty to provide a venue for the airing of grievances has been through the common law of tort. Indeed, many states expressly confer a right of access to a civil justice system through "open courts" and "right to remedy" provisions in their constitutions. See, e.g., Jonathan M. Hoffman, By the Course of the Law: The Origins of the Open Courts Clause of State Constitutions, 74 Or. L. Rev. 1279 (1995); David Schuman, The Right to a Remedy, 65 Temple L. Rev. 1197 (1992). Such provisions are fairly routinely relied upon by state supreme courts in striking down tort reform measures. See, e.g., Wall v. Marouk, 302 P.3d 775 (Okla. 2013) (statute requiring an "affidavit of merit" from a medical professional in support of a claim for medical malpractice was unconstitutional).

Professors Goldberg and Zipursky, two leading proponents of the civil recourse view of tort law, summarize their approach to the field as follows:

> [B]y functioning as a law of responsibilities and redress, tort law contributes to the maintenance of social cohesion within a dynamic and generally individualistic culture. It also helps to legitimate our legal system and institutions of government in the eyes of citizens. It helps define and vindicate individual rights such as the rights to bodily integrity, to freedom of movement, and to property ownership. And it affirms the notion that each of us is equal in owing and being owed various obligations by others. Finally, by placing the power to seek legal redress in the hands of victims, tort law reinforces ideals of limited and accountable government. Our point is not that tort law as a feature of a liberal, egalitarian democracy is logically necessary or practically indispensable. Nor is it that negligence law or tort law is immune to improvement or revision. Rather, the point is that — not surprisingly, given its longstanding place in Anglo-American law — the institutions, practices, and rules of tort law tend to gibe well with many of the core ideals of our system of government . . . ." [64 Md. L. Rev. at 369]

John C. P. Goldberg & Benjamin C. Zipursky, Accidents of the Great Society, 64 Md. L. Rev. 364, 369 (2005).

As one can see, the civil recourse approach to tort law resonates with libertarianism and its focus on the self-reliance of individuals and the importance of "private" over "public" methods of social ordering. The general idea is that allowing individuals to press their grievances through the tort system furthers liberal goals by respecting litigants as agents who can assert rights, make arguments, and demand redress, rather than merely as passive beneficiaries of protective regulations imposed from above. See id. at 406 ("Although the existence of a private right of action relies upon the state's willingness to play its role, the state is not in the driver's seat."). Similarly, even defendants are afforded a form of respect through the torts process, in that they participate in a procedural mechanism that affirms the mutual answerability of private individuals within society. Such a mechanism of civil recourse "vindicates the notion of a community of equals who are answerable to one another and expected to treat one another with equal respect." Jason M. Solomon, Equal Accountability Through Tort Law, 103 Nw. U. L. Rev. 1765, 1771 (2009). See also Scott Hershovitz, Harry Potter and the Trouble with Tort Theory, 63 Stan. L. Rev. 67 (2010).

These ideas explain why it may not necessarily be problematic that studies find only one out of ten patients with viable medical malpractice claims actually brings suit. From the instrumentalist or corrective justice viewpoints, this finding might be taken to indicate that too little deterrence or corrective justice is being achieved. From the civil resource viewpoint, on the other hand, it might simply reflect the fact that individuals are voluntarily choosing to forgo a right of redress that is personal to them. See John C. P. Goldberg &

Benjamin C. Zipursky, Seeing Tort Law from the Internal Point of View: Holmes and Hart on Legal Duties, 75 Fordham L. Rev. 1563 (2006). To the civil recourse theorist, deterrence and corrective justice might be *effects* of the tort system, but they do not explain its fundamental purpose. Thus, if wronged individuals choose not to exercise their right of redress in a manner that maximizes deterrence or corrective justice or any other secondary effect of the tort system, then we should respect their decision.

To these brief descriptions of instrumentalist, corrective justice, and civil recourse perspectives on tort law should be added mention of those writers who are skeptical of all attempts to relate tort law to a set of basic normative principles. Richard Abel, for example, argues that while tort law purports to be made up of a set of preference-neutral rules that treat everyone alike, in reality it is designed to help maintain the dominance of the powerful and the wealthy over the weak and the poor.[29] In his Marxist critique of Anglo-American tort law,[30] Professor Abel observes that both the efficiency and corrective justice rationales avoid making any judgments regarding the traditional distributions of wealth and power in our society. Instead, the rightness of those distributions is assumed implicitly, without discussion, and attention focuses only on the changes in the status quo brought about by harm-causing conduct. These rationales are not to be faulted for having failed to relate their normative principles to questions of wealth distribution — such efforts are doomed to fail in any event in Abel's view. But given the relevance of distributions of wealth and power to an adequate assessment of any system of government and law and the irrelevance of normative principles to such distributions, attempts to justify tort law on normative grounds are unavoidably incoherent. What bothers Professor Abel is not that the efficiency and fairness rationales fail to justify traditional distributions of wealth and power, but that they skate over the issue as though it does not exist.[31]

Clearly, observers hold widely differing views on the underlying purposes served by tort law, and we do not intend to endorse any one above the others. To complicate matters further, debate centers not only on what tort law might be saying, but also on who, if anyone, is listening. In other words, even if one were to conclude that the purpose of tort law is, for example, to encourage socially efficient behavior, one might still question whether tort law is a proper tool to achieve this goal. Consideration of this question, which turns on an examination of the practical impact of tort rules on human behavior, is deferred until later in these materials. Even at this early junction, however, it should be clear that learning the law entails much more than memorizing a received set of rules. It involves, among many other things, both an effort to explore the purposes underlying the rules and an attempt to evaluate what impact, if any, the chosen rules are likely to have on actual human behavior. As a final note of reassurance, consider the view of the great torts scholar William Prosser, who once wrote, "I have never seen any reason why law should make any more sense than the rest of life." Quoted in John C. P. Goldberg, Ten Half Truths About Tort Law, 42 Val. U. L. Rev. 1221, 1223 (2008).

29. Similarly, feminist and critical race theorists have argued that tort law reproduces gendered and racialized hierarchies despite its employment of seemingly neutral doctrines and procedures. See, e.g., Martha Chamallas & Jennifer B. Wriggins, The Measure of Injury: Race, Gender, and Tort Law (2010).

30. See Richard L. Abel, Torts, in The Politics of Law: A Progressive Critique 445-470 (David Kairys ed., 3d ed. 1998).

31. See also Martin A. Kotler, The Myth of Individualism and the Appeal of Tort Reform, 59 Rutgers L. Rev. 779, 845 (2007) (arguing that a pervasive mythology of American self-sufficiency and personal responsibility permeates tort doctrine and favors those who have the means and resources to protect themselves from harmful conduct).

2. Privileges

Even if the plaintiff succeeds in proving the elements of the prima facie case, the defendant may escape liability by pleading and proving the existence of a privilege to inflict the harmful or offensive contact. Generally, then, the burdens of production and persuasion are on the defendant to establish an affirmative defense. To say that an act is "privileged" connotes that the actor owes no legal duty to refrain from such contact. The privileges identified in this section apply to intentional wrongs generally, not just to batteries. Thus, one may exercise the privilege of self-defense by locking another in a closet — an action that would ordinarily constitute actionable false imprisonment — if doing so is necessary to protect oneself from the other's potentially harmful attack. Privileges are generally divided into two types: *consensual privileges,* which depend on the plaintiff agreeing to the defendant's otherwise tortious act; and *nonconsensual privileges,* which shield the defendant from liability for otherwise tortious conduct even if the plaintiff objects to the defendant's conduct. We first turn to the privilege of consent, and then to a number of nonconsensual privileges.

a. Consent

What constitutes consent for purposes of barring a plaintiff's recovery in tort? The basic rule is consistent with the meaning of "consent" in everyday speech: "Consent is willingness in fact for conduct to occur. It . . . need not be communicated to the [defendant.]" Restatement (Second) of Torts §892(1). In addition to this general rule, which involves what we might call actual or subjective consent, there are other meanings of "consent" within the law of battery. The materials that follow consider some of these other meanings.

O'Brien v. Cunard Steamship Co.

154 Mass. 272, 28 N.E. 266 (1891)

[At trial, the plaintiff advanced counts in negligence and harmful battery. At the close of the evidence, the trial court directed verdicts for defendant on both counts, and plaintiff appealed. Only those portions of the opinion dealing with the battery count are reproduced below.]

KNOWLTON, J. This case presents [the question of] whether there was any evidence to warrant the jury in finding that the defendant, by any of its servants or agents, committed [a battery] on the plaintiff. . . . To sustain [this] count, which was for an alleged [battery,] the plaintiff relied on the fact that the surgeon who was employed by the defendant vaccinated her on shipboard, while she was on her passage from Queenstown to Boston. On this branch of the case the question is whether there was any evidence that the surgeon used force upon the plaintiff against her will. In determining whether the act was lawful or unlawful, the surgeon's conduct must be considered in connection with the circumstances. If the plaintiff's behavior was such as to indicate consent on her part, he was justified in his act, whatever her unexpressed feelings may have been. In determining whether she consented, he could be guided only by her overt acts and the manifestations of her feelings. It is undisputed that at Boston there are strict quarantine regulations in regard to the examination of immigrants, to see that they are protected from small-pox by vaccination, and that only those persons who hold a certificate from the medical officer of the steamship, stating that they are so protected, are permitted to land without detention in quarantine or vaccination by the port physician. It appears that the defendant is accustomed to have its surgeons vaccinate all immigrants who desire it, and who are not protected by previous vaccination, and give them a certificate which is accepted at quarantine as evidence of their protection. Notices of the regulations at quarantine, and of the willingness of the ship's medical officer to vaccinate such as needed vaccination, were posted about the ship, in various languages, and on the day when the operation was performed the surgeon had a right to presume that she and the other women who were vaccinated understood the importance and purpose of vaccination for those who bore no marks to show that they were protected. By the plaintiff's testimony, which in this particular is undisputed, it appears that about two hundred women passengers were assembled below, and she understood from conversation with them that they were to be vaccinated; that she stood about fifteen feet from the surgeon, and saw them form in a line and pass in turn before him; that he "examined their arms, and, passing some of them by, proceeded to vaccinate those that had no mark"; that she did not hear him say anything to any of them; that upon being passed by they each received a card and went on deck; that when her turn came she showed him her arm, and he looked at it and said there was no mark, and that she should be vaccinated; that she told him she had been vaccinated before and it left no mark; "that he then said nothing, that he should vaccinate her again"; that she held up her arm to be vaccinated; that no one touched her; that she did not tell him that she did not want to be vaccinated; and that she took the ticket which he gave her certifying that he had vaccinated her, and used it at quarantine. She was one of a large number of women who were vaccinated on that occasion, without, so far as appears, a word of objection from any of them. They all indicated by their conduct that they desired to avail themselves of the provisions made for their benefit. There was nothing in the conduct of the plaintiff to indicate to the surgeon that she did not wish to obtain a card which would save her from detention at quarantine, and to be vaccinated, if necessary, for that purpose. Viewing his conduct in the light of the circumstances, it was lawful; and there was no evidence tending to show that it was not. The ruling of the court on this part of the case was correct. . . .

[The court did not reach the substance of plaintiff's alternative allegation that the surgeon was negligent in performing the vaccination, concluding that such negligence, if it occurred, could not be legally attributed to the defendant steamship company. Judgment for the defendant affirmed.]

The Law-Fact Distinction: Sufficiency of the Evidence, Directed Verdicts, and Judgments Non Obstante Veredicto

Merely because a party to a lawsuit asserts that there is an issue of fact to be resolved by the jury does not mean that there is such an issue. It is up to the party with the burden of proving the existence of a fact to come forward with sufficient evidence to justify a reasonable person in believing that the fact occurred. Unless the trial judge determines that reasonable persons can disagree about the existence of a fact, the judge will not send the question of whether the fact existed to the jury.[32] Thus, in *O'Brien,* having concluded that no reasonable person could find otherwise than that the plaintiff had manifested consent to the vaccination, the trial judge directed the jury to return their verdict for the

32. This is not meant to imply that the trial judge will act on his or her own initiative. As the preliminary look at the process in Section A of this chapter makes clear, courts almost always act in response to requests and demands for action from the parties before them. This discussion of the sufficiency of the evidence proceeds on the assumption that the trial judge will take an issue of fact from the jury only when asked to do so by an appropriate motion for directed verdict.

defendant. If the judge had reached the same conclusion after the return of a plaintiff's verdict, a JNOV, or judgment notwithstanding the verdict, would have been in order. In either event, because the absence of consent was vital to the plaintiff's right to recover in that case, the judge's determination of the consent issue in favor of the defendant also determined the ultimate issue of liability. If the particular assertion of fact that lacks sufficient supporting evidence does not dispose of the ultimate issue of liability, the court will give the question of liability to the jury along with a binding instruction that as a matter of law the jury must decide the particular factual issue for the defendant. Logically, a binding instruction is equivalent to a directed verdict, but it is limited to an issue of fact other than the ultimate issue of the defendant's liability.

In reacting to a request for a binding instruction, a motion for a directed verdict, or a motion for a JNOV, courts in most jurisdictions look at the evidence in the light most favorable to the nonmoving party. For example, in deciding whether to grant the defendant's motion for a directed verdict in *O'Brien,* the trial judge resolved every conflict in the testimony in favor of the plaintiff. This does not mean that the court must accept the plaintiff's view of the law. In *O'Brien* it was appearances, not the plaintiff's subjective state of mind, that controlled. But in deciding whether to send the question of appearances to the jury, presumably the trial judge drew every reasonable inference from the record favorable to the plaintiff. The judge was authorized to direct a verdict for the defendant only after concluding that no reasonable juror, believing all of the plaintiff's witnesses and drawing every reasonable inference in favor of the plaintiff, could have found otherwise than for the defendant.

The plaintiff as well as the defendant may benefit from binding instructions, directed verdicts, and JNOVs. The trial judge may decide that the proof supporting a factual assertion by the plaintiff is so overwhelming that reasonable persons could only agree that the fact did occur. (Once again, in making this determination the trial judge draws all reasonable inferences and resolves all questions of credibility in favor of the nonmoving party, the defendant.) In that event, the court will either give the jury a binding instruction in favor of the plaintiff or direct the jury to return a verdict in favor of the plaintiff, depending on whether other facts remain to be decided relating to the question of the defendant's liability. In a battery case, if the trial judge were to decide that as a matter of law the plaintiff did not consent, the liability issue might still be sent to the jury for a determination of the elements in the plaintiff's prima facie case (i.e., intent, contact, and cause-in-fact). Even when the plaintiff wins a directed verdict on the issue of liability, the judge will almost always send the further question of damages to the jury.

But whether the directed verdict or other similar order favors the plaintiff or the defendant, the important point is that in rendering a decision about the sufficiency of the evidence the trial judge is not finding facts. Instead, the judge is making a ruling of law to the effect that a finding of fact by the jury is unnecessary. To be sure, it is a ruling of law that relates directly to the jury's responsibility as fact finder; but it is, nonetheless, a ruling of law. Thus, the trial judge's decision in *O'Brien* to direct a verdict on the consent issue was reviewable by the Supreme Judicial Court on appeal. In a case where the evidence of consent is such that reasonable persons may differ and the judge properly submits the consent issue to the jury, the decision of the jury on that issue is not reviewable on appeal.

In addition to the issue of whether the plaintiff manifested consent to being contacted, the issue sometimes arises concerning whether the plaintiff was legally capable of giving consent. For one effectively to surrender the right to be free from intentional interference by others, one must have the mental capacity to consent. Absent such capacity, courts hold the defendant legally responsible for the consequences of his tortious actions, despite the fact that the plaintiff was subjectively willing and communicated that willingness to the defendant. Frequently this issue is presented in the context of sexual relations with minors. Consider the following problem.

Problem 2

Alice Trudlow is seeking your advice regarding an action she wants to bring against William Jennings. Ms. Trudlow is 32 years old, unmarried, employed by the Postal Service, and the mother of one daughter, Samantha, who will be 15 years old in two months. William Jennings is 18 years old and lives nearby.

Your first interview with Alice Trudlow took place two weeks ago. She was upset over events that had occurred several months earlier. She explained that on the Saturday night on which the events had occurred, she had gone out to a movie and dinner with friends from work. She had, for about a year, been able to leave Samantha home without a baby-sitter; on that night Samantha had assured her mother that she would be busy working on a school paper. Early during the movie, Alice Trudlow developed a migraine headache and decided to return home early. When she opened the front door and walked through the hall to the living room, she saw Samantha and William Jennings on the sofa, both partially undressed, and obviously engaged in sexual intercourse. Jennings quickly left the house and Samantha locked herself in her room.

At the first interview, Alice Trudlow reported that, prior to the incident, she had become increasingly concerned with her daughter's interest in William Jennings. The two seemed to spend a lot of time together, even though prior to the incident Samantha claimed the two were "just friends." Alice Trudlow regarded Jennings as "the wrong type"; he reminded her of the teenage boyfriend who had abandoned her after finding out that she was pregnant with Samantha. Alice now deeply fears that Samantha may be heading down the same road. In her first interview, Alice told you, "I love Samantha, but having her so early was very hard and changed my life in ways that I couldn't possibly understand at the time. A girl that age just doesn't understand what sex is about. I can't let Sam make the same stupid mistakes I did, but she shuts me out when I try to talk to her about it. For all I know, Jennings tricked her or forced himself on her. I've forbidden her to see him, but I'm really afraid what happened will happen again, and I have to do something."

Specifically, Alice Trudlow wanted you to talk to the District Attorney and have Jennings criminally prosecuted, or bring a civil action against him if the District Attorney won't do anything. Asked whether Samantha had encountered any physical complications as a result of the sexual encounter, Alice Trudlow explained that her daughter had suffered a tubal pregnancy that had to be surgically terminated. Without treatment, tubal pregnancy is an extremely serious condition, and in fact is a leading cause of death of women during the first trimester of pregnancy. Thus, when Alice Trudlow learned of Samantha's unexplained abdominal pain and vaginal bleeding and insisted that Samantha go to the emergency room, she may well have saved her daughter's life. Even with treatment the condition can result in tubal scarring and impairment of the ability to conceive. Although Alice Trudlow had incurred significant expenses in connection with her daughter's medical care, her main interest in pursuing legal action against Jennings seemed to be to scare him from further involvements with Samantha.

At the end of the interview, Alice Trudlow agreed, somewhat reluctantly, to permit you to interview Samantha out of Alice's presence. When Samantha came to your office last week, she at first refused to talk about the matter at all. After your assurance that you were trying to help her, she admitted that she had intercourse with Jennings on the night in question and that she had done so willingly. When asked whether this was the first time, she answered that it was her business. But after a long conversation in which you gained her confidence and in which you explained that it was important for you to have the whole story, she said that it was. She said she had been "sort of going out" with Jennings for about six months, and that on several previous occasions he had suggested that they "go all the way." She had resisted, not knowing what was the right thing to do. When she later asked Bonnie Anderson, a 16-year-old girlfriend, what to do, Bonnie told her that "true love knows no limits." So, when her mother left for the movies, she invited Jennings over and did not resist his obvious moves toward having sexual intercourse.

At the interview, Samantha seemed unsure about her feelings about what had happened. She still wanted to be with Jennings, but reported that he had been decidedly cool toward her since the incident. She was, however, horrified at the thought of anything her mother might do that will make the incident public. She seemed to discount the significance of the physical complications she experienced, and seemed willing and eager to "drop the whole thing." As she left your office, she pleaded, "Can't you talk my mom out of making a big deal out of this?"

You have an appointment with Alice Trudlow to discuss the matter further with her. What advice will you give her? What, if anything, will you tell her if she asks what her daughter told you? Assume that Barton v. Bee Line, Inc., below, and the statutes referred to therein, are governing law in your jurisdiction.

Barton v. Bee Line, Inc.

238 App. Div. 501, 265 N.Y.S. 284 (1933)

LAZANSKY, J. Plaintiff appeals from an order setting aside the verdict of a jury in her favor and ordering a new trial. Plaintiff, who was fifteen years of age at the time, claimed that while a passenger of the defendant, a common carrier, she was forcibly raped by defendant's chauffeur. The chauffeur testified that she consented to their relations. It was conceded that if the chauffeur assaulted plaintiff while a passenger, defendant became liable in damages for failure to perform its duty as a common carrier to its passenger. The jury was charged that plaintiff was entitled to recover even if she consented, although consent might be considered in mitigation of damages. She had a verdict of $3,000. The court set the verdict aside on the ground that if plaintiff consented the verdict was excessive, while if she was outraged the verdict was inadequate. The court is not disposed to interfere with this exercise of discretion. The determination of the trial court was warranted for another reason which may be considered, since the verdict was set aside upon the other grounds set forth in section 549 of the Civil Practice Act as well as upon the ground that it was excessive.

It was error for the trial court to have instructed the jury that plaintiff was entitled to a verdict even if she consented to consort with the chauffeur. By the last paragraph of subdivision 5 of section 2010 of the Penal Law it is provided: "A person who perpetrates an act of sexual intercourse with a female, not his wife, under the age of eighteen years, under circumstances not amounting to rape in the first degree, is guilty of rape in the second degree, and punishable with imprisonment for not more than ten years." Under this subdivision a crime is committed even if the female consents. The effect of the charge of the court was that the provisions of the act are made the basis of a civil liability. The age limitation has been changed from time to time. At first it was ten years, then sixteen, now eighteen. There can be no doubt that the purpose of the legislative enactments was and is to protect the virtue of females and to save society from the ills of promiscuous intercourse. A female over eighteen who is ravished has a cause of action against her assailant. Should a consenting female under the age of eighteen have a cause of action if she has full understanding of the nature of her act? It is one thing to say that society will protect itself by punishing those who consort with females under the age of consent; it is another to hold that, knowing the nature of her act, such female shall be rewarded for her indiscretion. Surely public policy — to serve which the statute was adopted — will not be vindicated by recompensing her for willing participation in that against which the law sought to protect her. The very object of the statute will be frustrated if by a material return for her fall "we should unwarily put it in the power of the female sex to become seducers in their turn." (Smith v. Richards, 29 Conn. 232.) Instead of incapacity to consent being a shield to save, it might be a sword to desecrate. The court is of the opinion that a female under the age of eighteen has no cause of action against a male with whom she willingly consorts, if she knows the nature and quality of her act. . . .

Order setting aside verdict in favor of plaintiff unanimously affirmed, with costs.

Clients seldom come into a lawyer's office with problems involving one or perhaps two neatly identifiable legal issues. In addition to a range of legal issues of varying complexity, a case may involve even more difficult problems of professional responsibility and human relations. In this problem, the nonlegal aspects may actually be more difficult to resolve than the purely legal. Moreover, the skills called upon here are much more those of counselor and interviewer than of legal analyst. Indeed, a significant part of a lawyer's time is apt to be spent in one form or another of counseling.

Turning to the legal issues in the problem, Samantha appears to have manifested consent. Indeed, it appears that she subjectively consented as well. But under the *Barton* case, will proof of these facts, if the case does get to trial, be enough to defeat recovery? If not, what are the facts relevant to consent?

Although the facts as Samantha explains them appear to indicate that William Jennings did not trick her or coerce her into consenting, you should understand that conduct of either sort on his part would vitiate any consent given by Samantha regardless of her relative maturity or understanding.

Apart from the merits of the case on the law, there is the decision of whether to take the case at all. This case will not be a pleasant one to handle. The reaction of many lawyers to cases of this sort is, "I should have gone to business school." Is it proper for you to decline to take the case if this is your reaction? Even if you think the case has some legal merit, can you tell Alice Trudlow otherwise, or at least play down the chance of winning, in order to back out gracefully?

Other matters you may wish to think about and resolve before Alice Trudlow comes in are:

1. To what extent are Alice Trudlow's motives important? May you, or should you, decline to take what otherwise might be a meritorious case because your client is partly motivated by revenge?

2. In any event, should your own thoughts about the wisdom of taking legal action be relevant? Should your role as a lawyer be confined to advising Alice Trudlow of her legal rights? May you, or should you, decline to take her case just because you think that her legal rights ought not to be pursued?
3. To what extent should you be influenced by what Samantha wants? And should you reveal to Alice Trudlow what Samantha told you? Who is your client? Alice Trudlow? Samantha? Both?

The Lawyer's Professional Responsibility: Keeping Confidences

A lawyer's role in the legal system is multifaceted. In addition to acting as a legal analyst and advocate, a lawyer must often perform the role of a counselor. In fact, in a case like the one involving Alice and Samantha Trudlow, the nonlegal aspects may overshadow the purely legal ones. In such cases, a lawyer's experience in human relations is just as important as his or her legal training.

Before looking at the legal aspects of this case, you are faced with the decision whether to take the case at all. As you probably have already surmised, this will be a difficult case to handle. If you don't want to take the case, is it proper for you to decline to take it?

The place to begin to answer such a question is with the rules and standards that purport to guide lawyers in their professional dealings. The legal community, largely through the American Bar Association, has made several attempts at drafting formal regulations to guide an attorney's professional conduct. In 1908, the Association adopted the original Canons of Professional Ethics. The Canons were then amended from time to time until, in 1964, the House of Delegates of the American Bar Association created a Special Committee on Evaluation of Ethical Standards to determine whether changes should be made in the Canons. The Committee responded by producing the Model Code of Professional Responsibility (adopted by the ABA in 1969). The Model Code included both Disciplinary Rules and Ethical Considerations. A violation of the Disciplinary Rules provided grounds for sanctions; the Ethical Considerations, in contrast, were deemed "aspirational in character" only. Over time, simply amending the Model Code failed to reflect the continuing evolution of ethical thought. Thus, a comprehensive redrafting began in 1977, which culminated in the adoption by the ABA of the Model Rules of Professional Conduct in 1983. The Model Rules, themselves, have been subject to review with an eye to revision. In particular, the ABA Commission on Evaluation of the Rules of Professional Conduct issued a major report proposing changes to the Rules in 2000. The ABA House of Delegates adopted most of these changes as part of substantial revision efforts undertaken in 2002 and 2003. With the notable exception of California, all states have adopted the Model Rules as the basis for their attorney conduct codes, albeit with significant state-by-state modifications.

Returning to the question of whether you, as a practicing attorney, can properly decline to represent Alice Trudlow, according to the Model Rules, while a lawyer enjoys great latitude in deciding whom to represent, she does not have absolute discretion to decline to take cases. On this point, the Model Rules state:

> A lawyer ordinarily is not obliged to accept a client whose character or cause the lawyer regards as repugnant. The lawyer's freedom to select clients is, however, qualified. All lawyers have a responsibility to assist in providing pro bono publico service. See Rule 6.1. An individual lawyer fulfills this responsibility by accepting a fair share of unpopular matters or indigent or unpopular clients. A lawyer may also be subject to appointment by a court to serve unpopular clients or persons unable to afford legal services.

Model Rules of Prof'l Conduct R. 6.2 cmt. [1] (2016). Would you consider this case as merely "unattractive" or as a problem best left to a family counselor? Besides these general ethical concerns, to what extent are Alice Trudlow's motives relevant to your taking the case? Should you push for a prosecution of William Jennings if you suspect that Alice's primary motivation is to harass or maliciously injure Jennings? What if Samantha were 19 years old instead of 15 at the time of the incident and Alice still wanted to prosecute Jennings? There are no easy answers to these ethical questions and, in the end, the decision whether to take a particular case rests largely on the discretion of the lawyer.

Assume that you take the case and that you have scheduled a meeting with Alice Trudlow to discuss the matter. You know that she will want you to tell her about your conversation with Samantha. What and how much can you tell Alice? The American Bar Association has established strict standards for confidentiality for very legitimate reasons:

> A fundamental principle in the client-lawyer relationship is that, in the absence of the client's informed consent, the lawyer must not reveal information relating to the representation. . . . This contributes to the trust that is the hallmark of the client-lawyer relationship. The client is thereby encouraged to seek legal assistance and to communicate fully and frankly with the lawyer even as to embarrassing or legally damaging subject matter. The lawyer needs this information to represent the client effectively and, if necessary, to advise the client to refrain from wrongful conduct. Almost without exception, clients come to lawyers in order to determine their rights and what is, in the complex of laws and regulations, deemed to be legal and correct. Based upon experience, lawyers know that almost all clients follow the advice given, and the law is upheld.

Model Rules of Prof'l Conduct R. 1.6 cmt. [2] (2016). But who is your client in this case? Alice Trudlow? Samantha? Both? When does the attorney-client relationship begin? In DeVaux v. American Home Assurance Co., 444 N.E.2d 355 (Mass. 1983), the attorney-client relationship may have been formed when the client first wrote the firm asking for help. Additionally, the Supreme Court of Washington held in Bohn v. Cody, 832 P.2d 71 (Wash. 1992), that the existence of the attorney-client relationship was largely dependent on the client's subjective belief that the relationship exists. Under this standard, the relationship did not need to be contractual. Rather, the essence of the relationship, according to the court, was whether the client sought and received the attorney's advice. If the client's subjective belief was reasonable under the circumstances, the attorney-client relationship was formed. See also State *ex rel.* Bluestone Coal Corp. v. Mazzone, 697 S.E.2d 740 (W. Va. 2010) (holding that an attorney-client relationship can be implied from the conduct of parties). Would Alice's coming to you for help and your subsequent consultation pass this standard? Would Samantha's coming forward and divulging private information to you also qualify?

If Samantha and Alice are both clients, then a whole range of issues arises regarding confidentiality. Usually, the lawyer has no discretion to reveal confidences of one client to another, separate client unless the circumstances meet the general confidentiality exceptions outlined in Model Rule 1.6. By this reading, then, you shouldn't tell Alice anything about what Samantha told you in confidence unless you obtain Samantha's consent. However, if Samantha and Alice are considered joint clients (or the situation is one of "common representation," in the Model Rules' terminology), then the situation becomes much more complicated. Comments [30] and [31] to Model Rule 1.7 provide:

> A particularly important factor in determining the appropriateness of common representation is the effect on client-lawyer confidentiality and the attorney-client privilege. With regard to the attorney-client privilege, the prevailing rule is that, as between commonly represented clients, the privilege does not attach. Hence, it must be assumed that if litigation eventuates between the clients, the privilege will not protect any such communications, and the clients should be so advised.
>
> As to the duty of confidentiality, continued common representation will almost certainly be inadequate if one client asks the lawyer not to disclose to the other client information relevant to the common representation. This is so because the lawyer has an equal duty of loyalty to each client, and each client has the right to be informed of anything bearing on the representation that might affect that client's interests and the right to expect that the lawyer will use that information to that client's benefit. See Rule 1.4. The lawyer should, at the outset of the common representation and as part of the process of obtaining each client's informed consent, advise each client that information will be shared and that the lawyer will have to withdraw if one client decides that some matter material to the representation should be kept from the other. In limited circumstances, it may be appropriate for the lawyer to proceed with the representation when the clients have agreed, after being properly informed, that the lawyer will keep certain information confidential. For example, the lawyer may reasonably conclude that failure to disclose one client's trade secrets to another client will not adversely affect representation involving a joint venture between the clients and agree to keep that information confidential with the informed consent of both clients.

As you can see, a lawyer must face a number of controversial issues in every case. Not all of these issues are purely legal. In fact, in the case of Alice and Samantha Trudlow, you may find the legal issues surrounding the alleged rape easier to parse than the issues of confidentiality and lawyer discretion.

Note: Minors as Parties to Litigation

In the note on the tort liability of minors and their parents, p. 17, we indicated that in a number of areas the law has created special rules that take into account the immaturity of minors. One of these special rules of procedure is that minors usually may not be direct parties to litigation. Instead, two procedural devices allow minors to be represented in court: the guardian ad litem (guardian for the suit) and the next friend. There is little practical difference between the two. Both the guardian ad litem and the next friend are representatives who act on behalf of the minor party. The legal rights at stake in the litigation are not those of the representative but those of the minor. A risk exists, however, that because the representative has no direct interest in the outcome, the litigation will not be conducted in a way that best serves the minor's interest. One method by which the law protects minors from this risk is by giving older minors influence or control over who shall serve as the representative. For example, under §373 of the California Code of Civil Procedure, a minor 14 or over may nominate the guardian ad litem. A court may also dismiss an action brought by a next friend over the objections of a mature minor and his or her parents. But ordinarily, the consent of a minor, even a mature one, is not a prerequisite to the appointment of a representative, although the minor is, of course, entitled to be heard on the matter.

The most important basis for judicial control over the guardian ad litem or next friend is the theory that the minor is a ward of the court. Thus, although the representative has the primary responsibility for managing the litigation, the ultimate responsibility for protecting the rights of the minor is in the court. The court on its own motion can remove the representative if it determines that there is a conflict of interest, that the representative is mishandling the case, or that removal is otherwise necessary to protect the interests of the minor.

Note: The Effect of Criminal Statutes on Consent

One question not discussed in the *Barton* opinion is why the criminal statute proscribing sexual intercourse with a female under 18 was at all relevant to whether the consenting plaintiff can receive compensation in a private tort action for battery. The rule that makes criminal statutes relevant to civil battery cases may be traceable, in part, to the early relation between tort law and criminal law in England.

Indeed, tort law in its current manifestation is the product of many centuries of evolution and transformation, and it is therefore impossible to gain an effective understanding of the contemporary law without first gaining some appreciation of its ancient roots. Accordingly, we will touch on the origins of tort law in England throughout this book, so as to highlight the historical antecedents from which modern tort law has emerged and to shed light on the law in its contemporary form.

As mentioned at the outset of these materials, during the early period of the development of the King's Courts following the Norman Conquest, petitioners seeking redress were required to show themselves to be entitled to one of a limited number of writs by which defendants were ordered to appear in court. The main concern of the English monarchy during this early period appears to have been consolidating the power of the Crown at the head of the feudal hierarchy that had been introduced by the Norman invaders. The main function of the King's Courts was to reinforce the feudal land system and to maintain the King's peace. This royal court system, which would one day replace in importance the older Anglo-Saxon system of county and village courts, began modestly by hearing cases especially affecting the King's interests. The jurisdiction of these early King's Courts was limited, and they demonstrated no great willingness to expand on it. The writs, with which actions in these courts were commenced, outlined with rigid particularity the bases upon which relief might be granted. Most of the earlier writs concerned disputes over land. Gradually, a limited number were developed that concerned other matters of particular interest to the Crown. It was through the gradual revision and expansion of the writ system, in effect, that the common law grew and developed during the six or seven centuries following the Conquest. For further reading on the early development of the King's Courts and the origins of the common law action of trespass, see William L. Prosser and W. Page Keeton, Law of Torts 28-31 (5th ed. 1984); Theodore F. Plucknett, A Concise History of the Common Law 139-175, 353-378 (5th ed. 1956).

The writ of trespass, out of which the substantive law of battery eventually developed, began to be available in the King's Courts in the thirteenth century. It was originally issued at the commencement of a criminal action brought to punish volitional conduct, harmful to persons or property, that might otherwise provoke violent retaliation and thus threaten further breaches of the King's peace. In time, damages came to be awarded to the injured victims of such conduct as an adjunct to the criminal proceeding. By the sixteenth century, the civil trespass action had become fully separated procedurally from the criminal action, the term "misdemeanor" being employed to distinguish the latter from the former. Thus, in light of the early overlap between criminal law and tort law, it is not surprising that U.S.

courts today (which inherited the common law of England) would, in a civil case involving battery, look for guidance to a criminal statute establishing the minimum age of consent. Moreover, apart from the criminality aspects, the fact that the norms are embodied in statutes suggests that they should take precedence over the common law.

In addition to the historical reasons for deferring to a criminal statute in cases like *Barton,* there may be support for it in notions of public policy. One explanation typically given is that it is appropriate for the torts process to reinforce the criminal process. In effect, plaintiffs become private prosecutors in the fight against crime. How likely is it in Problem 2, for example, that Jennings will ever be prosecuted for statutory rape, even though his violation of the criminal law seems clear? Is it the kind of case that ought to be criminally prosecuted? Perhaps in response to policy questions of this sort, the rule in most states is more rigorous than that adopted in the *Barton* case. The weight of authority is that consent to a criminal act is totally irrelevant in civil cases — in such cases, consent does not constitute a privilege. In addition to statutory rape, these cases involve illegal abortions, illegal fights, illegal purveying of intoxicants, and the like. Thus, the majority rule may help expose and deter clandestine criminal activities by allowing the "willing" victims of such activities to sue for damages.

Critics of the majority rule argue that a consent-based privilege should be available even in cases where the underlying conduct is criminal in nature. The legal recognition of consent as a privilege that will defeat recovery stems from an ancient maxim that one who consents to being injured cannot later be heard to complain. To many persons, maxims of this sort do not lose their force simply because the act to which the plaintiff has consented happens to be criminal. Indeed, proponents of the minority rule argue that their position best deters this sort of illegal activity by denying a tort reward to those who are injured as a result of their voluntary participation in illegal activities.

Whichever argument you find more persuasive as a general proposition, special reasons may persuade you to honor the statutory scheme — and thereby refuse to recognize consent as a defense to a battery claim — when the statute in issue was intended to protect minors or others whose capacity for consent is legitimately open to question. Thus, for example, in Hudson v. Craft, 204 P.2d 1 (Cal. 1949), the court allowed an 18-year-old boy, who was injured while voluntarily participating in an illegal prize fight, to recover in battery on the ground that the statute prohibiting such fights was specifically intended to protect combatants, especially young ones such as plaintiff, "against their own ill-advised participation in an unregulated match." Consistent with this view, most courts have applied statutory rape statutes in civil cases regardless of proof that the individual plaintiff was able to understand the nature and consequences of her act. See, e.g., C.C.H. v. Philadelphia Phillies, Inc., 940 A.2d 336, 339 (Pa. 2008) ("[W]here the victim is a minor less than 13 years of age, evidence of the victim's consent to sexual contact, like in criminal proceedings, is not an available defense in determining civil liability for such contact"); Christensen v. Royal School Dist. No. 160, 124 P.3d 283, 284 (Wash. 2005) (holding that "as a matter of law, a child under the age of 16 may not have contributory fault assessed against her for her participation in a [sexual] relationship . . . because she lacks the capacity to consent and is under no legal duty to protect herself from the sexual abuse"). And yet, courts occasionally modify the legislative judgments with their own views of public policy. *Barton* took a middle-of-the-road approach and demanded an inquiry into whether the plaintiff really needed the law's protection.

It must be stressed that *Barton* represents the minority view regarding the effect of statutory rape statutes in battery cases. In fact, a concurring opinion from New York, Colon v. Jarvis, 742 N.Y.S.2d 304, 306 (N.Y. App. Div. 2002), notes that at the time

Barton was decided it was contrary to the contemporaneous weight of authority in New York and in other jurisdictions and that only one case in New York has since been determined on *Barton*'s authority. An approach similar to *Barton* was adopted, however, in a case involving the impact for tort law purposes of a criminal statute prohibiting sexual intercourse with prison inmates by those holding supervisory prison authority. See Grager v. Schudar, 770 N.W.2d 692 (N.D. 2009). The Supreme Court of North Dakota declined to hold that the statute precluded a defense of consent in a civil action premised on the prohibited sexual conduct:

> We conclude that when consent to a sexual act by a person in official custody or detained in a treatment facility, prison, or other institution is at issue in a situation where the actor has supervisory authority, disciplinary control or care over the detained person, the jury must be instructed that it must consider all of the factors limiting the detained person's ability to control the situation or to give consent in deciding whether the detained person effectively consented to the sexual act. Each case must be decided on its own factual circumstances, including the age, sex, mental capacity, and relative positions of the parties. [Id. at 698]

The challenge of respecting individual agency and responsibility while also displaying sensitivity to social pressure, power asymmetry, and other situational factors is powerfully represented by current efforts to reduce the incidence of sexual assault and harassment on college and university campuses. As federal agencies, state legislators, and educational leaders work to improve reporting and adjudicatory mechanisms, critics argue that reform efforts overly formalize the problem, creating "mini-bureaucracies" of campus sex regulators who overstep their bounds and ultimately trivialize the real harms they were supposed to prevent. See Jacob E. Gersen & Jeannie Suk Gersen, The Sex Bureaucracy, 104 Cal. L. Rev. 881 (2016). The following problem provides an opportunity to explore the interaction between tort law and this changing landscape of statutory law and campus policy.

Problem 3

In response to student protests and media attention regarding the prevalence of sexual assault on college campuses and the perceived lack of institutional response, the state of New Yornia recently passed legislation requiring all educational institutions in its jurisdiction to adopt an "affirmative consent" standard as part of the school's code of conduct. Specifically, the act in relevant portion states:

1. Every educational institution shall adopt the following definition of affirmative consent as part of its code of conduct: "Affirmative consent is a knowing, voluntary, and mutual decision among all participants to engage in sexual activity. Consent can be given by words or actions, as long as those words or actions create clear permission regarding willingness to engage in the sexual activity. Silence or lack of resistance, in and of itself, does not demonstrate consent. The definition of consent does not vary based upon a participant's sex, sexual orientation, gender identity, or gender expression."
2. Each institution's code of conduct shall reflect the following principles as guidance for the institution's community:
    a. Consent to any sexual act or prior consensual sexual activity between or with any party does not necessarily constitute consent to any other sexual act.

> b. Consent is required regardless of whether the person initiating the act is under the influence of drugs and/or alcohol.
>
> c. Consent may be initially given but withdrawn at any time.
>
> d. Consent cannot be given when a person is incapacitated, which occurs when an individual lacks the ability to knowingly choose to participate in sexual activity. Incapacitation may be caused by the lack of consciousness or being asleep, being involuntarily restrained, or if an individual otherwise cannot consent. Depending on the degree of intoxication, someone who is under the influence of alcohol, drugs, or other intoxicants may be incapacitated and therefore unable to consent.
>
> e. Consent cannot be given when it is the result of any coercion, intimidation, force, or threat of harm.
>
> f. When consent is withdrawn or can no longer be given, sexual activity must stop.

Educational institutions that fail to comply with the new law face a series of penalties, including withholding of government funding, withdrawal of tax exempt status, and potential revocation of operating licenses. The law does not provide for penalties against individuals who violate the new standard of affirmative consent.

Notwithstanding the clear requirements of the affirmative consent law, administrators at Crest College, a small liberal arts college in upstate New Yornia, have been unable to adopt the mandated policy changes. For the past several weeks, a group of students calling themselves Crest Grrls have occupied the school president's office in protest of the new law, arguing that its provisions continue a trend of "legal occupation" of women's bodies and "bureaucratization" of women's sexuality. They argue that the statute's language of gender neutrality cannot conceal the law's paternalistic motive to protect primarily female students and that it will inevitably be applied in ways that deny women's agency. They have called upon Crest College leadership to refuse to implement the new law and to challenge its provisions in court.

A different student group, the Women's Student Union, supports the new law and has begun organizing counter-protests to the Crest Grrls' sit-in. They argue that the prevalence of campus sexual assault against women remains shockingly high, and that female students cannot yet afford the luxury of the Crest Grrls' "post-gender utopian agenda." The campus LGBTQ community is similarly split, with some members applauding the new law's explicit gender and sexuality neutrality, and others arguing that such facially neutral language carries embedded heteronormative assumptions. With student views' fractured and polarized, the Crest College administration has failed to update its existing consent policy, which simply states that "sexual misconduct includes any act of a sexual nature that a reasonable individual would recognize is unwanted by the recipient of said act."

This policy was recently applied in a disciplinary hearing concerning a complaint brought by one Crest College sophomore student, Allie, against another, Sean. Allie and Sean were friends who had on occasion hooked up at parties since they met during freshman orientation. In the fall of their sophomore year, Allie and Sean both attended a party at a mutual friend's apartment. Sean was not sure how much Allie had been drinking, but he thought it was a lot. After the party, Sean walked Allie back to her dorm room. As he got ready to say goodnight, she pulled him near and began kissing him aggressively. Sean asked Allie whether she really felt up to having sex and she said "yes." Clothes quickly came off and the pair moved toward Allie's bed. Suddenly, Allie ran to the bathroom. When she came back, her face looked pale and Sean thought she may have vomited because she had brushed her teeth. Allie climbed into bed and they began having sex.

Sean felt good but he did notice that Allie seemed unusually passive and out of it. He wasn't sure because it was dark and he'd been drinking a lot himself, but he thought Allie may have passed out briefly during the sex. Still, he continued.

When Sean bumped into Allie on campus the next day, he thanked her for a fun night. Allie remembered nothing. She felt ashamed and taken advantage of, and she decided to make a complaint to college officials. Applying its existing sexual misconduct policy rather than the state's affirmative consent standard, the Crest College disciplinary board determined that a reasonable individual would not necessarily have recognized the sexual intercourse as unwanted by Allie. With encouragement from her family and supporters of the affirmative consent law, Allie decided to bring a tort suit against Sean alleging battery. The trial court awarded summary judgment to Sean, ruling that no reasonable jury could conclude that Allie had effectively withdrawn her consent to sex. An intermediate appeals court affirmed and the Supreme Court of New Yornia agreed to hear Allie's appeal.

You are a law clerk to one of the Justices of the Court. She has asked you to advise her on the following two questions:

1. As a matter of justice and sound policy, should the common law of New Yornia: (a) incorporate the state's affirmative consent standard for sexual battery cases involving students, (b) defer to the institutional rules and norms prevailing at Crest College, or (c) devise an independent standard of consent?
2. If the answer to the first question is (a), could Sean successfully counterclaim against Allie for sexual battery on the same facts?

Bang v. Charles T. Miller Hospital

251 Minn. 427, 88 N.W.2d 186 (1958)

Gallagher, J. Appeal from an order of the district court denying plaintiffs' alternative motion to vacate the dismissal of their action against Frederic E. B. Foley, herein referred to as defendant, or for a new trial.

This was an action for damages for alleged . . . unauthorized operation by the defendant on his patient, Helmer Bang, referred to herein as plaintiff. The latter contends that the question as to whether he expressly or impliedly consented to the operating procedures involved was one of fact for the jury. At the close of plaintiffs' case, the defendant moved for a directed verdict upon the grounds that plaintiffs had failed to prove any actionable negligence or any cause of action against him. This motion . . . was granted. A similar motion was granted with respect to the other defendant, Charles T. Miller Hospital, but that action is not questioned on appeal.

The sole issue raised by the plaintiff on appeal is: Should the question of whether or not there was an . . . unauthorized operation have been submitted to the jury as a fact issue? . . .

. . . [P]laintiff consulted with the defendant on April 6, 1953, at the latter's office in St. Paul. The defendant testified that at that time the patient complained of diminished size and force of the urinary stream and increased frequency of urination. He said that the plaintiff described various urinary symptoms and that a rectal examination of the prostate was performed. Not being certain at that time of the exact nature of the plaintiff's ailment, the defendant informed plaintiff that he wished to make a cystoscopic examination the following day and suggested that plaintiff be admitted to the Miller Hospital in St. Paul for further investigation, which was done. He said that he informed his patient "that the purpose of his going into the hospital was for further investigation with a view to making a prostate operation if the further examination showed that that was indicated."

The important question for determination of the matter presently before us is whether the evidence presented a fact question for the jury as to whether plaintiff consented to the severance of his spermatic cords when he submitted to the operation. Defendant testified on cross-examination under the rules that he did not tell plaintiff at the time of the office visit, April 6, that any examination defendant had made or was going to make had anything to do with the spermatic cords, nor did he recall explaining to his patient what a prostate-gland operation involved. He also said that plaintiff's life was in no immediate danger because of his condition on that day.

He was further questioned:

Q: Did you tell him in your office that if the later examination in the hospital the following day indicated prostate trouble it would be necessary for you as part of your operation to cut his spermatic cords?
A: I am not certain that particular detail of the operation was explained to him.
Q: Dr. Foley, is it not true that the only thing mentioned to Mr. Bang in your office was that a further examination was needed in order to confirm your diagnosis so that you would know what you were going to do next?
A: That is correct.

On the following day the operation was performed. When defendant was asked as to the procedure used, he replied:

A: . . . the cysto-urethroscopic examination was made; following that I went over to the head of the table and talked to Mr. Bang, told him what the findings were, and that in my opinion the transurethral prostatic resection should be done and I had his consent that we proceed with that operation.
Q: Did you at that time as I understand it now ask him for his consent?
A: Yes. . . .
Q: . . . did you at the time you talked to Mr. Bang on the table tell him anything about what you were going to do about his spermatic cords?
A: I do not recall definitely whether that particular detail of the operation was discussed with Mr. Bang or not.

The patient recalled the start of the operation and, when questioned on direct examination, stated:

Q: Did he at any time before the operation began tell you that he cut your spermatic cords?
A: No.
Q: Did he at any time before the operation began tell you that it was necessary to cut your cords?
A: No.

When being questioned on cross-examination with reference to consent, the plaintiff was asked:

Q: And you certainly did consent, didn't you, Mr. Bang, to Dr. Foley doing anything to correct your trouble which in his medical knowledge he felt should be corrected?
A: Not anything he wanted to, no.
Q: Did you put any limitation on his job as a surgeon?
A: No.
Q: When he said, if I find anything that needs correction I will do it at the same time and you said that was all right, that was all of the conversation there was, wasn't it?
A: That was all of the conversation there was.

It is plaintiff's claim that he thought he was discussing his bladder because he understood from his Austin physicians something about burning out the ulcers if there were any ulcers in there. He admitted, however, that defendant said nothing to him about ulcers. Plaintiff also admitted that he did not expect to tell the doctor what to do; that he had faith in him; and that he did not expect to tell him how to perform the operation. He said that he expected the doctor would operate to do what was necessary to right and cure his condition. He testified that he did not ask the doctor what he intended to do and left it up to him to do the right thing.

. . . It is our opinion that under the record here the question as to whether plaintiff consented to the severance of his spermatic cords was a fact question for the jury and that it was error for the trial court to dismiss the action. . . .

While we have no desire to hamper the medical profession in the outstanding progress it has made and continues to make in connection with the study and solution of health and disease problems, it is our opinion that a reasonable rule is that, where a physician or surgeon can ascertain in advance of an operation alternative situations and no immediate emergency exists, a patient should be informed of the alternative possibilities and given a chance to decide before the doctor proceeds with the operation. By that we mean that, in a situation such as the case before us where no immediate emergency exists, a patient should be informed before the operation that if his spermatic cords were severed it would result in his sterilization, but on the other hand if this were not done there would be a possibility of an infection which could result in serious consequences. Under such conditions the patient would at least have the opportunity of deciding whether he wanted to take the chance of a possible infection if the operation was performed in one manner or to become sterile if performed in another.

Reversed and a new trial granted.

Kennedy v. Parrott

243 N.C. 355, 90 S.E.2d 754 (1956)

Civil action to recover damages for personal injuries resulting from an alleged unauthorized operation performed by the defendant, a surgeon.

The plaintiff consulted the defendant as a surgeon. He diagnosed her ailment as appendicitis and recommended an operation to which she agreed. During the operation the doctor discovered some enlarged cysts on her left ovary, and he punctured them. After the operation the plaintiff developed phlebitis in her leg. She testified that Doctor Parrott told her "that while he was puncturing this cyst in my left ovary that he had cut a blood vessel and caused me to have phlebitis and that those blood clots were what was causing the trouble." She also testified that defendant told Dr. Tyndall, who was called in to examine her for her leg condition, "that while he was operating he punctured some cysts on my ovaries, and while puncturing the cyst on my left ovary he cut a blood vessel which caused me to bleed," to which Dr. Tyndall said, "Fountain [the defendant], you have played hell."

The defendant recommended that the plaintiff go to Duke Hospital, and there is evidence he promised he would pay the bill. She also saw Dr. I. Ridgeway Trimble at Johns Hopkins, Baltimore. Dr. Trimble operated on her left leg and side "to try to correct the damage that was done."

Plaintiff had to undergo considerable pain and suffering on account of the phlebitis. . . .

At the conclusion of the testimony, the court, on motion of the defendant, entered judgment of involuntary nonsuit. Plaintiff excepted and appealed.

BARNHILL, C.J. [The court first ruled that the plaintiff's evidence was not sufficient to support recovery in negligence. Although the defendant's conversation with Dr. Tyndall and his willingness to pay for her treatment at Duke Hospital suggest he may have been at fault, defendant's uncontradicted medical testimony (the plaintiff offered none) indicated that defendant had exercised due care.]

On the other hand, if her cause of action is for damages for personal injuries proximately resulting from [a] trespass on her person, as she now asserts, and such operation was neither expressly nor impliedly authorized, she is entitled at least to nominal damages. . . .

Prior to the advent of the modern hospital and before anesthesia had appeared on the horizon of the medical world, the courts formulated and applied a rule in respect to operations which may now be justly considered unreasonable and unrealistic. During the period when our common law was being formulated and applied, even a major operation was performed in the home of the patient, and the patient ordinarily was conscious, so that the physician could consult him in respect to conditions which required or made advisable an extension of the operation. And even if the shock of the operation rendered the patient unconscious, immediate members of his family were usually available. Hence the courts formulated the rule that any extension of the operation by the physician without the consent of the patient or someone authorized to speak for him constituted a battery or trespass upon the person of the patient for which the physician was liable in damages.

However, now that hospitals are available to most people in need of major surgery; anesthesia is in common use; operations are performed in the operating rooms of such hospitals while the patient is under the influence of an anesthetic; the surgeon is bedecked with operating gown, mask, and gloves; and the attending relatives, if any, are in some other part of the hospital, sometimes many floors away, the law is in a state of flux. More and more courts are beginning to realize that ordinarily a surgeon is employed to remedy conditions without any express limitation on his authority in respect thereto, and that in view of these conditions which make consent impractical, it is unreasonable to hold the physician to the exact operation — particularly when it is internal — that his preliminary examination indicated was necessary. We know that now complete diagnosis of an internal ailment is not effectuated until after the patient is under the influence of the anesthetic and the incision has been made.

These courts act upon the concept that the philosophy of the law is embodied in the ancient Latin maxim: Ratio est legis anima; mutata legis ratione mutatur et lex. Reason is the soul of the law; the reason of the law being changed, the law is also changed.

Some of the courts which realize that in view of modern conditions there should be some modification of the strict common law rule still limit the rights of surgeons to extend an operation without the express consent of the patient to cases where an emergency arises calling for immediate action for the preservation of the life or health of the patient, and it is impracticable to obtain his consent or the consent of someone authorized to speak for him.

Other courts, though adhering to the fetish of consent, express or implied, realize "that the law should encourage self-reliant surgeons to whom patients may safely entrust their bodies, and not men who may be tempted to shirk from duty for fear of a law suit." They recognize that "the law does not insist that a surgeon shall perform every operation according to plans and specifications approved in advance by the patient and carefully tucked away in his office-safe for courtroom purposes." . . .

In major internal operations, both the patient and the surgeon know that the exact condition of the patient cannot be finally and definitely diagnosed until after the patient is completely anesthetized and the incision has been made. In such case the consent — in the absence of proof to the contrary — will be construed as general in nature and the surgeon may extend the operation to remedy any abnormal or diseased condition in the area of the original incision whenever he, in the exercise of his sound professional judgment, determines that correct surgical procedure dictates and requires such an extension of the operation originally contemplated. This rule applies when the patient is at the time incapable of giving consent, and no one with authority to consent for him is immediately available.

In short, where an internal operation is indicated, a surgeon may lawfully perform, and it is his duty to perform, such operation as good surgery demands, even when it means an extension of the operation further than was originally contemplated, and for so doing he is not to be held in damages as for an unauthorized operation.

"Where one has voluntarily submitted himself to a physician or surgeon for diagnosis and treatment of an ailment it, in the absence of evidence to the contrary, will be presumed that what the doctor did was either expressly or by implication authorized to be done."

Unexpected things which arise in the course of an operation and incidental thereto must generally at least be met according to the best judgment and skill of the surgeon. And ordinarily a surgeon is justified in believing that his patient has assented to such operation as approved surgery demands to relieve the affliction with which he is suffering.

Here plaintiff submitted her body to the care of the defendant for an appendectomy. When the defendant made the necessary incision he discovered some enlarged follicle cysts on her ovaries. He, as a skilled surgeon, knew that when a cyst on an ovary grows beyond the normal size, it may continue to grow until it is large enough to hold six to eight quarts of liquid and become dangerous by reason of its size. The plaintiff does not say that the defendant exercised bad judgment or that the extended operation was not dictated by sound surgical procedure. She now asserts only that it was unauthorized, and she makes no real showing of resulting injury or damage.

In this connection it is not amiss to note that the expert witnesses testified that the puncture of the cysts was in accord with sound surgical procedure, and that if they had performed the appendectomy they would have also punctured any enlarged cysts found on the ovaries. "That is the accepted practice in the course of general surgery."

What was the surgeon to do when he found abnormal cysts on the ovaries of plaintiff that were potentially dangerous? Was it his duty to leave her unconscious on the operating table, doff his operating habiliments, and go forth to find someone with authority to consent to the extended operation, and then return, go through the process of disinfecting, don again his operating habiliments, and then puncture the cysts; or was he compelled, against his best judgment, to close the incision and then, after plaintiff had fully recovered from the effects of the anesthesia, inform her as to what he had found and advise her that these cysts might cause her serious trouble in the future? The operation was simple, the incision had been made, the potential danger was evident to a skilled surgeon. Reason and sound common sense dictated that he should do just what he did do. So all the expert witnesses testified.

Therefore, we are constrained to hold that the plaintiff's testimony fails to make out a . . . case for a jury on the theory she brings her appeal to this Court. The judgment entered in the court below is

Affirmed.

Problem 4

Your firm represents Dr. Carlos Somoza and Dr. James Park, two surgeons recently served with a complaint by a former patient, Tabitha Singh. Several months ago, Singh came to Dr. Somoza complaining of persistent migraines. A CT scan revealed the presence of a brain tumor, which Dr. Somoza advised must be removed. Surgery was scheduled and performed three weeks later, after which Singh suffered left-side paralysis and loss of peripheral vision. The complaint consists of two counts: first, that the surgery was negligently performed; and second, that Singh suffered a battery because she had granted permission only to Dr. Somoza to operate on her and — unbeknownst to Singh — Dr. Park performed the surgery instead.

The partner in charge of the case seeks your assistance with the battery count. (She is fairly confident that the plaintiff's negligence claim will fail on the facts.) Regarding the battery count, initial investigation largely confirms the factual allegations of the complaint. Drs. Somoza and Park work together in a practice unit at St. Francis Hospital. However, Singh never personally saw Dr. Park during her several preoperative consultations. All of those meetings were conducted by Dr. Somoza, and Singh will testify that she came to trust and depend on his judgment and skill during this time period. In fact, Singh sought and received oral assurances from Dr. Somoza during these meetings that he would personally be the one removing her tumor.

Two days before the scheduled procedure Dr. Somoza conducted an informed consent meeting with Singh, explaining the nature of the procedure and its various risks. She signed a consent form that stated, "I hereby authorize Dr. Somoza and/or other members of the Medical Staff of St. Francis Hospital of his choice, to perform those diagnostic or therapeutic medical and surgical procedures on me which in his or their judgment may be deemed necessary." After signing, she asked Dr. Somoza whether he would in fact be doing the procedure and he replied, "I can't imagine why I wouldn't."

Before driving to the hospital on the day of surgery, Singh called Dr. Somoza's office and again sought and received confirmation from his assistant that he was in the hospital and was scheduled to perform the surgery. When Singh arrived for surgery she immediately asked to see Dr. Somoza and was told by a desk nurse that he would be located. After checking in, Singh was taken to a holding room and was seen by an anesthesiologist, who began administering a general anesthetic. Before she lost consciousness, Singh remembers hearing a nurse say, "Somoza won't be able to make it but his partner is here." Singh attempted to object but could not as the anesthetic had already begun to affect her. Shortly thereafter, Dr. Park removed the tumor from her brain.

Following surgery, Singh suffered all of the expected scarring, pain, and discomfort that invariably accompanies a major invasive procedure. In addition, Singh experienced vision problems and an inability to move her left arm and leg. Follow-up analysis by Dr. Somoza confirmed that she had suffered an adverse side effect of the surgery that, although extremely rare, was known in the medical literature and had been explained to Singh during the informed consent process. In addition to her bodily impairments, Singh has experienced mental anguish stemming both from her reduced physical capacity and from her sense of betrayal over what happened.

Assess whether and for what your clients might be liable to Ms. Singh on the battery count. Assume that Kennedy v. Parrott is a decision of your jurisdiction.

The Relationship Between Tort and Contract: Medical Malpractice

Given the difficulties encountered by courts in trying to work out the limits of physicians' responsibilities in medical malpractice cases, it is not surprising that some commentators have urged that the problems be resolved, ahead of time, in contracts entered into by physicians and their patients. Indeed, many health care providers have already turned to contract law as a means of self-help. Consider the following consent form:[33]

Date: ______________

1. I, ______________, give my authorization and consent to an operation to be performed on me on or about ______________, by Dr. ______________. The purpose of the operation is to attempt to correct the following condition: ______________

2. I also consent that Dr. ______________, during, preceding, and following the operation, perform any other procedure that ______________ deems necessary or desirable in order to achieve the correction of the above-named condition, or any other unhealthy condition ______________ may encounter during the operation.

3. Realizing that an operation by modern methods requires the cooperation of numerous technicians, assistants, nurses, and other personnel, I give my further consent to ministrations and medical procedures on my body by all such qualified medical personnel working under the supervision of Dr. ______________ before, during and after the operation to be performed.

4. I consent also to the administration of ______________ anesthesia, to be applied by Dr. ______________.

5. I understand that this operation may not be successful in ______________ the condition named above, and also that there is a danger that certain unfavorable results may follow, namely, ______________.

____
Signature of Patient

I have read the above consent form, signed by my ______________ and join with ______________ in such consent. Paragraph 5 above has been specially pointed out to me and I am aware of the possible unfavorable consequences of the operation, namely, ______________.

____
Signature of Spouse

33. Taken from 15 Am. Jur. Legal Forms 2d §202:117 (2000).

The most interesting and important question presented by formal agreements of this sort is whether and to what extent courts will look behind them and review the facts of particular cases to see if the consent given by the patient was truly informed and uncoerced. At the extremes, courts could either give such contracts conclusive weight, inquiring only into whether, for example, the plaintiff actually signed the consent form; or give the agreement no weight, making the same full-blown inquiry into the surrounding facts as would be made if the contract never had been entered into. Few courts, if any, take either of these extreme approaches. All courts will allow the plaintiff to escape the contract if it can be shown to be the product of fraud or coercion on the part of the health care provider; all courts purport, at least, to give some weight to contracts to which patients freely agree. The problem most courts have with giving conclusive effect to such agreements is that they appear to be somewhat bootstrapping. Informed consent doctrines rest on the premise that patients lack knowledge of relevant risks and must be informed by the provider before their consent can be meaningful. How then, courts ask, can conclusive effect be given to a written agreement without inquiring into whether the patient did, in fact, understand the relevant risks of injury?

If the contract in question spells out the risks in elaborate, gory detail; if the patient admits signing it after reading it carefully; and if there are no elements suggesting lack of free consent; then we can assume most courts would end their inquiry. But contracts of consent are almost never written that way. Gory detail, spelled out ad nauseam (in the literal as well as the figurative sense) is thought to be counterproductive from the standpoint of the patient's welfare. What many physicians and patients would prefer, at least before the fact, is a contract indicating that the risks (identified in a more general way) were discussed and that consent was freely given. Such contracts, if given effect, would arguably benefit both physicians and patients in many cases. (Can you articulate how and why?) The problem, as courts see it, is that if such contracts are enforced they will also unavoidably insulate some physicians from the unpleasant consequences of their own overbearing conduct. (Again, do you see why?)

Viewed more generally, the possibility of contractually handling informed consent disputes before tort claims arise raises fundamental issues to which we shall return in these materials. In the present context, it will be recalled from an earlier law and policy note that the efficiency-based argument in favor of allowing recovery for harmful batteries is that the tortfeasors in these cases have improperly substituted forceful unilateral takings (that require later review under tort law) for peaceful bilateral agreements (that do not). (See pp. 36-37, above.) The appropriate judicial response in battery cases, according to efficiency analysis, is to allow recovery in tort in order to admonish the actors for having "bypassed the market." Interestingly, in the present context of informed consent contracts, the physicians seemingly have done just what they should have done — they have tried to substitute before-the-fact contractual agreements for after-the-fact review under tort law. When courts later set those agreements aside and impose liability on physicians notwithstanding the patients' earlier agreements, the courts are, in effect, admonishing those actors for having tried to rely on the market, rather than for trying to bypass it.

Is this an instance of "damned if you do, and damned if you don't"? Can you begin to work out a means of accommodating the sometimes conflicting objectives of contract and tort? Are some of the expectations regarding the nature and quality of medical care best policed by tort, while others are better handled through bargaining between the patient and the health care provider? For skepticism regarding whether these forms of doctor-patient "contracting out of tort liability" actually make patients better off, see Jennifer Arlen, Contracting over Liability: Medical Malpractice and the Cost of Choice, 158 U. Pa. L. Rev. 957 (2010).

The issue of informed consent involves two distinct situations. The first of these, illustrated by the *Kennedy* case, above, is presented when the physician is given consent to perform a certain medical operation or treatment and thereafter extends the operation or treatment beyond the boundaries of the consent given. On the issue of whether consent may be inferred, Kennedy v. Parrott is not universally followed. In some states, the consent is inferred only if there is an emergency that requires treatment not expressly authorized. The Restatement (Second) of Torts contains the following provision relevant to the question of the physician's (or any actor's, for that matter) privilege to act in an emergency, absent actual consent:

> §892D. Emergency Action Without Consent
>
> Conduct that injures another does not make the actor liable to the other, even though the other has not consented to it if
>
> (a) an emergency makes it necessary or apparently necessary, in order to prevent harm to the other, to act before there is opportunity to obtain consent from the other or one empowered to consent for him, and
>
> (b) the actor has no reason to believe that the other, if he had the opportunity to consent, would decline.

For an example of a case applying the §892D approach, see Estate of Allen v. Rockford Health Sys., 2006 Ill. App. LEXIS 367 (Ill. App. Ct. 2006) (reversing summary judgment for the defendant doctor because, even though the patient's consent was unnecessary due to the emergency situation and her intoxicated state, the doctor might have been able to get consent from some other authorized source). Cf. Curtis v. Jaskey, 759 N.E.2d 962 (Ill. App. Ct. 2001) (holding that a doctor could not use the emergency exception to override a patient's earlier-expressed wishes not to undergo a particular procedure).

If the contract set out in the note on the relationship between tort and contract above had been signed by the patient in a *Kennedy*-type situation, would it help to resolve the question of whether the surgeon had authority to extend the operation? In Washburn v. Klara, 561 S.E.2d 682 (Va. 2002), the patient-plaintiff signed a written consent form authorizing the surgical removal of a damaged intervertebral disc and fusion of the vertebrae at the "C6-7" level of her spine. The form also authorized the performance of such other procedures as the doctor "considers necessary or advisable in the exercise of his professional judgment in accordance with reasonable medical standards." The plaintiff allegedly suffered permanent damage to her spine as a result of the surgery. Her evidence indicated that the operation had resulted in the fusion of not only the vertebrae at the C6-7 level, but also fusion at the C7-T1 level. Plaintiff brought an action against the surgeon for battery and lack of informed consent, voluntarily withdrawing her claim of medical malpractice. The surgeon insisted that he had not intentionally extended the operation to the C7-T1 level, and that such an extension, if it occurred, had been inadvertent. He claimed that deliberate extension had not been proved. The trial court dismissed plaintiff's battery claim on the ground that there was no evidence that the defendant had intentionally exceeded the consent given to him. The Supreme Court of Virginia reversed and remanded for trial on the question of whether in fact the medical procedure had extended to the C7-T1 level. The Virginia high court held that, if such an extension occurred, then the defendant exceeded the consent given and committed a battery whether or not he realized what he was doing. See also Kaplan v. Mamelak, 75 Cal. Rptr. 3d 861 (Ct. App. 2008) (holding that where the patient gave signed permission for the defendant surgeon to operate only on his T8-9 spinal disk, it was up to the jury to find whether operation on both the T6-7 and T8-9 disks was a "substantially different procedure" that thereby constituted medical battery).

Similarly, in Massingale v. Lee, 2005 Tenn. App. LEXIS 250 (Ct. App. 2005), the court of appeals addressed a battery claim arising from a procedure that the plaintiff claimed was unauthorized. The plaintiff-patient had surgery to repair a bilateral hernia, and during the procedure the defendant-doctor also performed an orchiectomy and removed the plaintiff's left testicle. Prior to the surgery, plaintiff specifically asked the defendant if the surgery would "affect me in any way in my manhood," and the doctor replied in the negative. Even given the consent form the plaintiff signed, which provided consent to procedures "in addition or different than those contemplated," the court of appeals found that reasonable minds could disagree as to whether the plaintiff authorized this procedure and held that the trial court erred in granting a directed verdict for the defendant on the plaintiff's medical battery claim.

What if the patient or patient's guardians sign a blanket consent form but further qualify to doctors how they want the treatment administered? In Piedra v. Dugan, 21 Cal. Rptr. 3d 36 (Ct. App. 2004), an infant suffered severe brain damage as a result of medication a doctor administered to the infant in the hospital. The parents brought suit as guardians ad litem alleging that although the mother signed a conditions-of-admission form in which she consented to "the procedures which may be performed during this hospitalization" she also told the admitting person, two nurses, and the infant's attending physician, Dr. Magdalena Salcedo, not to give the infant any medication, specifically phenobarbital, without her knowledge. Subsequently, a doctor during treatment administered medication without seeking the consent of the parents. A pharmacological expert testified that the infant's respiratory depression and respiratory failure, which led to the infant lapsing into a permanent vegetative state, were caused by the combined effects of the drugs used. The court, while acknowledging that a cause of action for battery could exist if a doctor exceeds the terms or conditions of the consent, found that the doctor who administered the drugs did not have actual direct knowledge of the limitation on consent — the infant's mother had not directly informed the doctor either orally or by the relevant paperwork — and therefore did not commit the tort of battery because he did not intentionally violate the condition on the patient's consent.

Courts have also addressed situations in which plaintiffs' treating physicians did have actual knowledge of explicit limitations on consent. For example, Hoofnel v. Segal, 199 S.W.3d 147 (Ky. 2006), involved a medical battery claim arising out of a surgery to treat the plaintiff's colorectal cancer. Eva Hoofnel met with her surgeon, Dr. Galandiuk, to discuss the removal of a lesion in her lower colon. During this meeting, the parties agreed that Dr. Galandiuk would perform an appendectomy on Hoofnel. Dr. Galandiuk also recommended that Hoofnel undergo a hysterectomy to remove her uterus, but Hoofnel stated that she did not want her uterus removed. Subsequently, however, Hoofnel signed a "Consent to Operation" form authorizing the appendectomy as well as any "additional procedures that may be medically necessary." During the surgery, Dr. Galandiuk discovered an abnormally large uterus that impaired excision of the lesion in Hoofnel's colon. Because Dr. Galandiuk believed that the uterus may have been cancerous, she consulted with a gynecologist, Dr. Segal, who concurred with her assessment. Upon reviewing Hoofnel's consent form, Dr. Segal noticed that a hysterectomy was not a specifically listed procedure. Nevertheless, upon being advised by Dr. Galandiuk that Hoofnel had provided conditional consent for a hysterectomy, Dr. Segal removed Hoofnel's uterus. Although Hoofnel had explicitly informed Dr. Galandiuk that she did not wish to have her uterus removed, the court affirmed summary judgment for the doctors because Hoofnel had signed the consent form authorizing medically necessary procedures incident to her appendectomy. Compare with Orduno v. Mowry, 2001 Cal. App. Unpub. LEXIS 1432 (Ct. App. 2001) (reversing trial court's grant of nonsuit where plaintiff alleged that she told her physician "at least three times" that she wanted saline, not silicone, breast implants for her reconstruction surgery, but that her physician used silicone implants which led her to suffer myriad ailments).

The second type of informed consent problem involves cases in which the doctor fails to explain to the patient the risk of side effects of a treatment to which the patient has consented. In such cases, most courts determine the doctor's liability by the law of negligence. The court in Christman v. Davis, 889 A.2d 746 (Vt. 2005), clarified the distinction between cases sounding in battery and those sounding in negligence. Where treatment is unauthorized and performed without consent, the doctor has committed a battery. On the other hand, where the doctor obtains consent but has breached a duty to adequately inform the patient of risks, the patient has a cause of action in negligence. The distinction between the two causes of action is not purely academic. Under a battery theory, the only issue of fact is whether the defendant adequately explained the nature of the operation; but under negligence, the doctor may be able to avoid liability by proving that the failure to explain was reasonable. Furthermore, under negligence, the defendant can also avoid liability by proving that even if the collateral risks of the treatment had been fully explained, the plaintiff would have consented—that is, that the failure to inform did not cause the harm. Accordingly, in Mitchell v. Kayem, 54 S.W.3d 775 (Tenn. Ct. App. 2001), the court ordered summary judgment for the defendant-surgeon in a fault-based informed consent action because the plaintiff testified that she would have consented to the cancer surgery performed by the defendant even if the surgeon had appraised her of all the risks associated with the procedure. Under battery, whether or not the plaintiff would have consented is irrelevant. What reasons in policy support the distinction between failure to inform as to the nature and extent of the treatment and the failure to inform of collateral risks?

Quite apart from how the courts may treat informed consent claims, plaintiffs are free to allege that the physician acted negligently by failing to perform the treatment skillfully (as seen earlier in *O'Brien*). An interesting juxtaposition of the two types of claims was presented in Jandre v. Wisconsin Injured Patients and Families Compensation Fund, 813 N.W.2d 627 (Wis. 2012). Plaintiff suffered a physical breakdown that defendant physician determined was most consistent with Bell's palsy, but that might also have been a stroke caused by a blocked artery. Defendant failed to inform plaintiff of the availability of a carotid ultrasound—an alternative, non-invasive, and effective means of determining whether plaintiff had, in fact, suffered a stroke. Several days later plaintiff suffered another, significant stroke, which might have been prevented through a correct initial diagnosis. The jury held that defendant's diagnosis of Bell's palsy, though incorrect, was not negligent. The jury also held, however, that defendant's failure to inform plaintiff of the availability of a screening test for stroke had breached the physician's duty of informed consent. The Wisconsin Supreme Court narrowly affirmed, refusing to recognize "a bright-line rule that, once a physician makes a non-negligent final diagnosis, there is no duty to inform the patient about diagnostic tests for conditions unrelated to the condition that was included in the final diagnosis." Id. at 634. A vigorous dissent argued that the high court's ruling "imposed strict liability for missed diagnoses by expanding a patient's right of informed consent . . . from a right to be informed about the risks and benefits of treatments and procedures that *were recommended* by the physician into a right to be informed about all treatments and procedures that *were not recommended* by the physician, but which may be relevant to whether the correct diagnosis was made." Id. at 687.

Whatever the legal theory on which informed consent claims are based, plaintiffs are required to prove more than that the physician failed to mention some minor aspect of a pending treatment. Thus, in Henderson v. Milobsky, 595 F.2d 654 (D.C. Cir. 1978), the court of appeals held that a dentist did not owe his patient the duty to warn him of a one-in-20,000 chance that the patient would suffer some slight loss of sensation to a small section of his face as a result of a tooth extraction. Compare with Martin v. Richards, 531 N.W.2d 70 (Wis. 1995), in which the Supreme Court of Wisconsin held that a one to three percent chance of developing intracranial bleeding merits disclosure by a physician, especially in light of the possibly fatal consequences of the disorder.

What about giving percentages related to the surgeons themselves? See Johnson by Adler v. Kokemoor, 545 N.W.2d 495 (Wis. 1996), in which the Supreme Court of Wisconsin held that, besides informing the patient of potential risks directly related to the surgery, the doctrine of informed consent may require disclosure of the fact that different physicians may have substantially different success rates with the same procedure. See also Goldberg v. Boone, 912 A.2d 698 (Md. 2006) (holding that it was for the jury to decide whether the defendant surgeon, who had performed only one revisionary mastoidectomy in the past three years, had a duty to inform the patient that there were more experienced surgeons in the region who could have performed the procedure). Other jurisdictions, however, have been reluctant to impose such a duty to disclose on the physician but have held that an affirmative misrepresentation of the physician's credentials may allow a claim based on the doctrine of informed consent. See Willis v. Bender, 596 F.3d 1244 (10th Cir. 2010); Wissell v. Fletcher Allen Health Care, Inc., 2014 Vt. Super. LEXIS 89 (Super. Ct. May 22, 2014). The giving of surgeon-specific percentages is a relatively recent development in the area of informed consent. For an extensive discussion of the topic, see Aaron D. Twerski & Neil B. Cohen, The Second Revolution in Informed Consent: Comparing Physicians to Each Other, 94 Nw. U. L. Rev. 1 (1999).

Hackbart v. Cincinnati Bengals, Inc.

601 F.2d 516 (10th Cir. 1979)

DOYLE, Circuit Judge.

The question in this case is whether in a regular season professional football game an injury which is inflicted by one professional football player on an opposing player can give rise to liability in tort where the injury was inflicted by the intentional striking of a blow during the game.

The injury occurred in the course of a game between the Denver Broncos and the Cincinnati Bengals, which game was being played in Denver in 1973. The Broncos' defensive back, Dale Hackbart, was the recipient of the injury and the Bengals' offensive back, Charles "Booby" Clark, inflicted the blow which produced it.

By agreement the liability question was determined by the United States District Court for the District of Colorado without a jury. The judge resolved the liability issue in favor of the Cincinnati team and Charles Clark. Consistent with this result, final judgment was entered for Cincinnati and the appeal challenges this judgment. In essence the trial court's reasons for rejecting plaintiff's claim were that professional football is a species of warfare and that so much physical force is tolerated and the magnitude of the force exerted is so great that it renders injuries not actionable in court; that even intentional batteries are beyond the scope of the judicial process.

Clark was an offensive back and just before the injury he had run a pass pattern to the right side of the Denver Broncos' end zone. The injury flowed indirectly from this play. The pass was intercepted by Billy Thompson, a Denver free safety, who returned it to midfield. The subject injury occurred as an aftermath of the pass play. As a consequence of the interception, the roles of Hackbart and Clark suddenly changed. Hackbart, who had been defending, instantaneously became an offensive player. Clark, on the other hand, became a defensive player. Acting as an offensive player, Hackbart attempted to block Clark by throwing his body in front of him. He thereafter remained on the ground. He turned, and with one knee on the ground, watched the play following the interception.

The trial court's finding was that Charles Clark, "acting out of anger and frustration, but without specific intent to injure . . . stepped forward and struck a blow with his right forearm to the back of the kneeling plaintiff's head and neck with sufficient force to cause both players to fall forward to the ground." Both players, without complaining to the officials or to one another, returned to their respective sidelines since the ball had changed hands and the offensive and defensive teams of each had been substituted. Clark testified at trial that his frustration was brought about by the fact that his team was losing the game.

Due to the failure of the officials to view the incident, a foul was not called. However, the game film showed very clearly what had occurred. Plaintiff did not at the time report the happening to his coaches or to anyone else during the game. However, because of the pain which he experienced he was unable to play golf the next day. He did not seek medical attention, but the continued pain caused him to report this fact and the incident to the Bronco trainer who gave him treatment. Apparently he played on the specialty teams for two successive Sundays, but after that the Broncos released him on waivers. (He was in his thirteenth year as a player.) He sought medical help and it was then that it was discovered by the physician that he had a serious neck fracture injury.

Despite the fact that the defendant Charles Clark admitted that the blow which had been struck was not accidental, that it was intentionally administered, the trial court ruled as a matter of law that the game of professional football is basically a business which is violent in nature, and that the available sanctions are imposition of penalties and expulsion from the game. Notice was taken of the fact that many fouls are overlooked; that the game is played in an emotional and noisy environment; and that incidents such as that here complained of are not unusual.

The trial court spoke as well of the unreasonableness of applying the laws and rules which are part of injury law to the game of professional football, noting the unreasonableness of holding that one player has a duty of care for the safety of others. He also talked about the concept of assumption of risk and contributory fault as applying and concluded that Hackbart had to recognize that he accepted the risk that he would be injured by such an act. . . .

The evidence at the trial uniformly supported the proposition that the intentional striking of a player in the head from the rear is not an accepted part of either the playing rules or the general customs of the game of professional football. The trial court, however, believed that the unusual nature of the case called for the consideration of underlying policy which it defined as common law principles which have evolved as a result of the case to case process and which necessarily affect behavior in various contexts. From these considerations the belief was expressed that even intentional injuries incurred in football games should be outside the framework of the law. The court recognized that the potential threat of legal liability has a significant deterrent effect, and further said that private civil actions constitute an important mechanism for societal control of human conduct. Due to the increase in severity of human conflicts, a need existed to expand the body of governing law more rapidly and with more certainty, but that this had to be accomplished by legislation and administrative regulation. The judge compared football to coal mining and railroading insofar as all are inherently hazardous. Judge Matsch said that in the case of football it was questionable whether social values would be improved by limiting the violence. Thus the district court's assumption was that Clark had inflicted an intentional blow which would ordinarily generate civil liability and which might bring about a criminal sanction as well, but that since it had occurred in the course of a football game, it should not be subject to the restraints of the law; that if it were it would place unreasonable impediments and restraints on the activity. The judge also pointed out that courts are ill-suited to decide the different social questions and to administer conflicts on what is much like a battlefield where the restraints of civilization have been left on the sidelines. . . .

Plaintiff, of course, maintains that tort law applicable to the injury in this case applies on the football field as well as in other places. On the other hand, plaintiff does not rely on the theory of negligence being applicable. This is in recognition of the fact that subjecting another to unreasonable risk of harm, the essence of negligence, is inherent in the game of football, for admittedly it is violent. Plaintiff maintains that in the area of contributory fault, a vacuum exists in relationship to intentional infliction of injury. Since negligence does not apply, contributory negligence is inapplicable. Intentional or reckless contributory fault could theoretically at least apply to infliction of injuries in reckless disregard of the rights of others. This has some similarity to contributory negligence and undoubtedly it would apply if the evidence would justify it. But it is highly questionable whether a professional football player consents or submits to injuries caused by conduct not within the rules, and there is no evidence which we have seen which shows this. However, the trial court did not consider this question and we are not deciding it.

Contrary to the position of the court then, there are no principles of law which allow a court to rule out certain tortious conduct by reason of general roughness of the game or difficulty of administering it.

Indeed, the evidence shows that there are rules of the game which prohibit the intentional striking of blows. Thus, Article 1, Item 1, Subsection C, provides that:

> All players are prohibited from striking on the head, face or neck with the heel, back or side of the hand, wrist, forearm, elbow or clasped hands.

Thus the very conduct which was present here is expressly prohibited by the rule which is quoted above.

The general customs of football do not approve the intentional punching or striking of others. That this is prohibited was supported by the testimony of all of the witnesses. They testified that the intentional striking of a player in the face or from the rear is prohibited by the playing rules as well as the general customs of the game. Punching or hitting with the arms is prohibited. Undoubtedly these restraints are intended to establish reasonable boundaries so that one football player cannot intentionally inflict a serious injury on another. Therefore, the notion is not correct that all reason has been abandoned, whereby the only possible remedy for the person who has been the victim of an unlawful blow is retaliation. . . .

In sum, having concluded that the trial court did not limit the case to a trial of the evidence bearing on defendant's liability but rather determined that as a matter of social policy the game was so violent and unlawful that valid lines could not be drawn, we take the view that this was not a proper issue for determination and that plaintiff was entitled to have the case tried on an assessment of his rights and whether they had been violated.

The trial court has heard the evidence and has made findings. The findings of fact based on the evidence presented are not an issue on this appeal. Thus, it would not seem that the court would have to repeat the areas of evidence that have already been fully considered. The need is for a reconsideration of that evidence in the light of that which is taken up by this court in its opinion. We are not to be understood as limiting the trial court's consideration of supplemental evidence if it deems it necessary.

The cause is reversed and remanded for a new trial in accordance with the foregoing views.

As indicated in the decision of the court of appeals, the trial court in *Hackbart* had held that tort law should not regulate the on-the-field behavior of professional football players, given that violence is an integral part of the game to which players impliedly consent when they agree to participate. The trial judge held that players are conditioned so as to maximize their violent inclinations, noting that one witness had testified "that the pre-game psychological preparation should be designed to generate an emotion equivalent to that which would be experienced by a father whose family had been endangered by another driver who had attempted to force the family car off the edge of a mountain road. The precise pitch of motivation for players . . . should be the feeling of that father when . . . he is about to open the door to take revenge upon the person of the other driver." Acknowledging this tradition of violence, the trial court believed that it would be impossible for courts to distinguish between incidents that are "fair play" and those that merit legal liability. According to the trial judge, a player impliedly consents to all manner of violent contact that could be construed as part of "professional football."

The issue of implied consent plays a role not only in professional sports but also in the context of amateur sports activities. For example, should the rules and customs of the game control liability issues arising from injuries suffered in college sports? See generally Avila v. Citrus Comty. Coll. Dist., 131 P.3d 383 (Cal. 2006), holding that collegiate baseball players assume the risk that pitchers will intentionally throw pitches at them. What about high school sports? Athletes at these levels are often rewarded for their aggressiveness. At the end of the spectrum are games among friends. Should courts hold that participants in backyard sports impliedly consent to the range of violent contact that the players in *Hackbart* did? In Knight v. Jewett, 834 P.2d 696 (Cal. 1992), the Supreme Court of California held backyard games to the same standard as *Hackbart,* holding that participants in a touch football game impliedly consent to violent contact — but not to "conduct that is so reckless as to be totally outside the range of the ordinary activity involved in the sport." Id. at 712. *Knight* is reproduced at p. 427, below, in the section dealing with contributory negligence.

In Pfister v. Shusta, 657 N.E.2d 1013 (Ill. 1999), the Supreme Court of Illinois held that the implied consent doctrine also extends to games outside traditional sports. In that case the court found that a college student could not recover damages for injuries sustained during a game of "kick the can" — a game that involves kicking a crushed soda can around and attempting to gain control of the can by pushing other players out of the way. The court stressed that the relevant inquiry is whether the participants were involved in a contact sport, not whether the sport was formally organized or coached. See generally Erica K. Rosenthal, Inside the Lines: Basing Negligence Liability in Sports for Safety-Based Rule Violations on the Level of Play, 72 Fordham L. Rev. 2631 (2004).

Note: Consent Procured by Fraud or Duress

Notwithstanding that the plaintiff consents to what would otherwise be considered tortious conduct, such consent will not shield the defendant from liability if it is procured by means of fraud or duress. For example, in DeMay v. Roberts, 9 N.W. 146 (Mich. 1881), the plaintiff arranged for a doctor to attend to her while she was giving birth at her home. The doctor brought along a male companion to assist him. Although both men aided the plaintiff in the birthing process, neither informed the pregnant woman or her husband that the doctor's companion was not himself medically trained. Upon subsequently learning this fact, the woman sued both men. Affirming a jury's verdict in favor of the plaintiff, the appellate court held that the defendants, by failing to disclose the identity of the doctor's companion, had fraudulently procured the plaintiff's consent to the man's presence in the birthing room.

Although this nineteenth-century court's decision holding the doctor and his companion liable may strike you as unduly harsh, most examples of fraudulently induced consent are clear-cut. In Bowman v. Home Life Ins. Co., 243 F.2d 331 (2d Cir. 1957), an insurance company employee falsely represented himself to be a physician and conducted complete physical examinations of two women seeking to purchase life insurance. On appeal, the court determined that the women's consent to this examination was ineffective because the defendant had procured their acquiescence through fraudulent misrepresentations concerning his status as a doctor. See also Sanchez-Scott v. Alza Pharm., 86 Cal. App. 4th 365 (2001) (plaintiff brought an action after learning that the person assisting her doctor during a breast examination was, in fact, a pharmaceutical salesman). Would the same outcomes be justified if the defendants had not posed as physicians but had simply offered to pay the women to disrobe — and then had given them counterfeit money?

Not all misrepresentations will qualify as fraud. In Conley v. Romeri, 806 N.E.2d 933 (Mass. App. Ct. 2004), a woman filed a cause of action for battery after engaging in consensual sexual relations with a man. She claimed she consented because she wanted children and alleged the man induced her into having a sexual relationship by telling her that a fortune teller told him he would have six children and he currently had only four. In actuality, the man was sterile due to a vasectomy. The court held that the plaintiff's claim that she wasted time with the defendant because her biological clock was running did not support recovery for battery nor did his claims of fertility qualify as fraud which vitiated her consent.

That courts invalidate consent procured by duress is straightforward enough, certainly when defendants threaten their victims with physical harm. Consider a situation in which *A*, holding a gun to *B*, tells *B* that unless *B* kisses *A*, *A* will shoot her. *B* is a sober, reasonable adult who fully understands the consequences of consenting. Courts invalidate such consent, even though it is offered by an otherwise reliable, competent person. Indeed, courts also invalidate consent given in order to protect a loved one from physical harm. See Restatement (Second) of Torts §58 cmt. a, illus. 1 (1965) ("*A* points a revolver which *B* believes to be loaded at *C*, *B*'s child, and threatens to shoot *C* if *B* does not submit to degrading familiarities. *B* submits thereto to save her child. *A* is subject to liability to *B*.").

Determining whether a defendant's conduct amounts to duress can be difficult. As the above hypothetical illustrates, physical threats are relatively unproblematic. But what if the threat is not immediate? For example, in the above hypothetical, should *B* be able to maintain that her consent was invalid if she consented on the threat that, otherwise, *A* would come back in two days and shoot her?

Whether potentially coercive conduct will invalidate consent is more difficult to determine when the pressure does not take the form of a physical threat. One common example is economic pressure. An employer, for example, might threaten to fire a female employee unless she consents to sexual advances. If she consents, should a court disregard that consent by reason of duress? Generally, courts do not recognize pure "economic duress." But see Reavis v. Slominski, 551 N.W.2d 528, 546 (Neb. 1996) (Gerrard, J. dissenting) (refusing "to perpetuate the fiction that the threat from an employer of loss of future employment is never sufficient to invalidate apparent consent to sexual contact by an employee," particularly where the employee cannot file a sexual harassment claim). What if the employee consented, in the absence of a threat, because she *believed* that she would be fired if she did not accede to such demands?

Note: Patients' Consent to Lifesaving Medical Treatment

All of the foregoing materials on consent rest on the premise that, if a person with legal capacity and not under duress refuses to submit to physical contact with his or her person, the courts will honor that person's intentions and allow recovery against anyone who intentionally causes harmful or offensive contact. In some situations, however, a court may override an actor's refusal to give consent, a scenario that arises most often in medical settings. While a preceding note on tort and contract highlighted the use of express contract as a means of working out the reciprocal rights and duties between doctor and patient, at the other extreme is the method of imposing treatment on patients who have expressly refused to give consent. For example, *In re* Estate of Brooks, 205 N.E.2d 435 (Ill. 1965), embodies the ultimate clash of wills between doctor and patient when the patient expressly refuses treatment. In that case, a woman had refused a medically necessary blood transfusion, on religious grounds, prior to losing consciousness. The hospital brought a civil action to have a guardian appointed, and the guardian consented to the transfusion. The woman recovered and sued to have the guardianship decision reversed. The court agreed with her that the consent was invalid, and reversed the earlier order.

In Anderson v. St. Francis–St. George Hospital, Inc., 671 N.E.2d 225 (Ohio 1996), the defendant hospital administered life-prolonging treatment against the explicit instructions of the plaintiff's decedent, a competent adult. Having survived the life-threatening incident, the decedent subsequently suffered a severe stroke that plaintiff argued generated substantial treatment costs and ruined the decedent's quality of life. The stroke was not caused by the life-prolonging treatment except as that treatment caused the decedent to live long enough to suffer the stroke. Concluding that the defendant had committed a battery on the decedent, the court also concluded (671 N.E.2d at 229):

> The only damages that appellee may recover are those damages suffered by [decedent] due directly to the battery. Where the battery was physically harmless, however, the plaintiff is entitled to nominal damages only.

> We also observe that unwanted life-saving treatment does not go undeterred. Where a patient clearly delimits the medical measures he or she is willing to undergo, and a health care provider disregards such instructions, the consequences for that breach would include the damages arising from any battery inflicted on the patient, as well as appropriate licensing sanctions against the medical professionals.

For arguments in favor of tort recovery when individuals have been subjected to unwanted life-saving treatment, see Holly Fernandez Lynch et al., Compliance with Advance Directives: Wrongful Living and Tort Law Incentives, 29 J. Legal Med. 133 (2008); and Mark Strasser, A Jurisprudence in Disarray: On Battery, Wrongful Living, and the Right to Bodily Integrity, 36 San Diego L. Rev. 997 (1999).

The litigation of refusal-to-consent is not frequent and the results are diverse, so that any particular judicial response cannot be called typical. See generally Mark Strasser, A Jurisprudence in Disarray: On Battery, Wrongful Living, and the Right to Bodily Integrity, 36 San Diego L. Rev. 997 (1999). In *Estate of Brooks,* above, the court emphasized the religious basis of the patient's refusal to consent. Should it matter that the reasons given were religious? What if the operation promised survival, but a life of pain? Or immobility? Or what if the patient has just had enough of life? The court in *Estate of Brooks* also seemed to regard as important the fact that the patient had no minor children. What should the relevance of that fact be? See *In re* Maria Isabel Duran, 769 A.2d 497 (Pa. Super. Ct. 2001). The patient in that case, a woman in the process of receiving a liver transplant who was a devout Jehovah's Witness and a wife and mother of two children, executed a durable power of attorney for medical care, absolutely refusing any transfer of blood regardless of her medical condition. She further stressed in writing that her friends' and family's wishes were legally and ethically irrelevant to her decision and appointed another individual as her designated healthcare agent. During the transplant, her body rejected the liver and doctors estimated that without a blood transfusion she would die within 24 hours. Her husband, who was not a Jehovah's Witness, petitioned the court to be appointed her emergency guardian for the purpose of consenting to a blood transfusion. The court granted the petition, but the woman died shortly thereafter. Her designated healthcare agent asked the court to address the validity of the court's granting of the husband's petition. The court, while acknowledging the state's interest in protecting dependents who would be left emotionally and financially bereft because of the patient's refusal of medical treatment, held that, in light of the decedent's unequivocal and clear refusal of medical treatment, the trial court erred in granting her husband's petition. But see Application of the President and Directors of Georgetown College, Inc., 331 F.2d 1000 (D.C. Cir. 1964) (court should prevent the "ultimate abandonment" of a seven-month-old child by ordering blood transfusion for the mother).

In *In re* Fetus Brown, 689 N.E.2d 397 (Ill. App. Ct. 1997), the defendant was 34 weeks pregnant when she underwent surgery to remove a urethral mass. Although she lost a substantial amount of blood during the operation, she refused a blood transfusion because her Jehovah's Witness faith contravened such procedures. As Darlene and the fetus had only a 5 percent chance of survival without the transfusion, the hospital sought a court order permitting it to perform the procedure. In reversing the lower court's decision to grant the order, the appeals court held that the state lacks the authority to override a competent pregnant woman's decision to refuse medical treatment, even when that treatment is necessary to save the life of a viable fetus.

However, in HCA, Inc. v. Miller, 36 S.W.3d 187 (Tex. App. 2000), a court in Texas framed the issue differently. The parents in the case were informed that if their 23-week-old baby was born alive and survived it would suffer severe impairments. The parents requested that no heroic measures be performed on the baby after her birth. The doctors, however, instituted resuscitative measures after birth, and the child survived and subsequently suffered from severe physical and mental impairments. In reversing a trial court's judgment and significant damage award for the parents, the Texas Court of Appeals found that a health care provider is under no duty to follow a parent's instruction to withhold urgently-needed life sustaining medical treatment from their child if the child is born viable. While the baby in this case had actually been born, unlike the fetus in Fetus Brown v. Darlene Brown, in justifying its holding, the Texas court cited a case for the proposition that even an *unborn fetus* is a "patient" to whom a doctor treating the mother owes a duty of care. For a similar attempt to grapple with these intractable issues in the tort law context, see *Burgess*, infra p. 361.

The issue of consent becomes even more problematic when the patient is comatose or otherwise incompetent to make medical decisions. Consider the highly publicized case confronted by the Florida Court of Appeals in Schindler v. Schiavo (*In re* Schiavo), 851 So. 2d 182 (Fla. Dist. Ct. App. 2003). A young woman, Terry Schiavo, suffered cardiac arrest and lapsed into an apparently permanent vegetative state in 1990. The appellate court described Terry's condition as follows (Schindler v. Schiavo (*In re* Schiavo), 780 So. 2d 176, 177 (Fla. Dist. Ct. App. 2001)):

> Since 1990, Theresa has lived in nursing homes with constant care. She is fed and hydrated by tubes. The staff changes her diapers regularly. She has had numerous health problems, but none have been life threatening. The evidence is overwhelming that Theresa is in a permanent or persistent vegetative state. It is important to understand that a persistent vegetative state is not simply a coma. She is not asleep. She has cycles of apparent wakefulness and apparent sleep without any cognition or awareness. As she breathes, . . . she often makes moaning sounds. Theresa has severe contractures of her hands, elbows, knees, and feet. Over the span of this last decade, Theresa's brain has deteriorated because of the lack of oxygen it suffered at the time of the heart attack. By mid-1996, the CAT scans of her brain showed a severely abnormal structure. At this point, much of her cerebral cortex is simply gone and has been replaced by cerebral spinal fluid. Medicine cannot cure this condition. Unless an act of God, a true miracle, were to recreate her brain, Theresa would always remain in an unconscious, reflexive state, totally dependent upon others to feed her and care for her most private needs. She could remain in this state for many years.

Michael Schiavo, Terry's husband and guardian, successfully petitioned a Florida guardianship court for a discontinuance of artificial life support. Terry's parents appealed. The appellate court affirmed the trial court's order, reasserting the proposition that "when families cannot agree, the law has opened the doors of the circuit courts to permit trial judges to serve as surrogates or proxies to make decisions about life-prolonging procedures." 851 So. 2d at 186. In finding that there was clear and convincing evidence to support the determination that Terry Schiavo would choose to withdraw the life-prolonging procedures, the court stated that it believed Terry "would wish to permit a natural death process to take its course and for her family members and loved ones to be free to continue their lives." Id. at 187. For an examination of the subsequent history of the *Schiavo* decision and the ethical and political controversies surrounding the principles of patient autonomy and medical decisions, see Barbara A. Noah, Politicizing the End of Life: Lessons from the *Schiavo* Controversy, 59 U. Miami L. Rev. 107 (2004).

b. Pulling Some Strands Together: Intent, Consent, and Liability Insurance

Before proceeding to examine nonconsensual defenses to battery claims, it will be useful to pause briefly to consider how intent and consent play off each other. Both elements involve a "constructive" aspect — actors who do not desire certain consequences are deemed to have intended them, or to have consented to their taking place. Into the latter category fall actors who manifest consent to others (*O'Brien*) or who willingly engage with others in dangerous competitive activities (*Hackbart*). Moreover, consent sometimes works not only as an affirmative defense but also as a means of eliminating an element of the plaintiff's prima facie case — the wrongfulness of the intended contact with the plaintiff's person. For example, whether a contact is offensive may depend on whether it is consented to. If a person holds out his cheek to be kissed, it may be better to say that the actor who kisses him in response has committed an inoffensive contact, and thus no prima facie case is made out, rather than to say that the act is prima facie wrongful but the actor may invoke the defense of manifested consent. The decision set out in this section raises questions of this nature regarding exactly how intent and consent play off against each other in battery cases.

Another benefit of pausing at this juncture is to introduce the student to liability insurance. As the following decision demonstrates, the potential availability of liability insurance exerts significant influence over the behavior of litigants and judges. Indeed, it is impossible to understand the doctrinal workings and social impacts of tort law without also appreciating the role played by liability insurance. Under a liability insurance contract, the insurer promises to indemnify the insured against losses suffered as a result of the insured's legal liability to other parties, such as tort plaintiffs who claim to have been wrongfully injured by the insured. Liability insurance is often referred to as "third-party insurance," because the insurer's obligation to indemnify depends on the insured party's underlying legal liability to a third party; it could also be thought of as "injurer's insurance." This distinguishes it from "first-party insurance" such as fire, theft, collision, and medical insurance in which the insured is covered for losses suffered directly by her and in which the insurer's obligation depends solely on whether a loss falls within the coverage provisions of the insurance contract. First-party insurance could be thought of as "victim's insurance." Liability insurers sometimes have the option of denying an obligation to indemnify by arguing either that there is no underlying tort liability on the part of the insured, or that the insurance contract excludes coverage for the type of act or loss that gave rise to the insured's liability.

State Farm Fire & Casualty Co. v. S.S. & G.W.

858 S.W.2d 374 (Tex. 1993)

HIGHTOWER, Justice.

[S.S. contracted genital herpes after engaging in consensual sexual intercourse with G.W. at his home in November 1986. After consulting with her lawyer, S.S. filed suit against G.W. alleging that he negligently transmitted genital herpes to her. During the course of the litigation, S.S. offered to settle within the limits of G.W.'s liability policy, and State Farm, G.W.'s insurer, refused. Thereafter, the parties settled the tort suit and entered into an agreement providing for the entry of a $1 million judgment in favor of S.S., which S.S. agreed not to execute in exchange for the assignment of a one-third interest in any claim that G.W. might have against his insurance company, for bad faith settlement practices, deceptive trade practices, or state insurance code violations.] State Farm . . . brought suit against G.W. and S.S. seeking a declaratory judgment that G.W.'s homeowner's policy did not provide coverage for the claims asserted against him by S.S. The trial court rendered summary judgment in favor of State Farm. The court of appeals reversed and remanded holding that State Farm failed to meet its summary judgment burden because it did not produce conclusive evidence that G.W. intended to transmit herpes to S.S. 808 S.W.2d 668. For the reasons explained herein, we affirm the judgment of the court of appeals. . . .

State Farm argues that as a matter of law, the transmission of genital herpes is an intentional injury which comes within the "intentional injury exclusion" of G.W.'s homeowner's policy. Consequently, S.S.'s claim is not covered by G.W.'s homeowner's policy. We disagree. . . .

The homeowner's policy covering G.W. in November 1986 included the following "intentional injury exclusion" provision:

> EXCLUSIONS — Coverage D shall not apply:
> to bodily injury or property damage caused intentionally by or at the direction of the Insured[.]

. . . When considering whether G.W. intended to injure S.S. it is instructive to examine the meaning of intent. Ordinarily, whether an insured intended harm or injury to result from an intentional act is a question of fact. . . . [The Court next relies on the Restatement (Second) of Torts §8A (1965) to assert that an insured intends injury if he desires the consequences of his act, or believes they are substantially certain to result.] Prosser also provides insight on the nature of intent:

> [I]ntent is broader than a desire or purpose to bring about physical results. It extends not only to those consequences which are desired, but also to those which the actor believes are substantially certain to follow from what the actor does. . . . On the other hand, the mere knowledge and appreciation of a risk — something short of substantial certainly — is not intent. The defendant who acts in the belief or consciousness that the act is causing an appreciable risk of harm to another may be negligent, and if the risk is great the conduct may be characterized as reckless or wanton, but it is not an intentional wrong. In such cases the distinction between intent and negligence obviously is a matter of degree. The line has been drawn by the courts at the point where the known danger ceases to be only a foreseeable risk which a reasonable person would avoid, and becomes in the mind of the actor a substantial certainty.

W. Page Keeton et al., Prosser and Keeton on the Law of Torts §8, at 35-36 (5th ed. 1984).

Although it is undisputed that G.W. intentionally engaged in sexual intercourse without informing S.S. of his condition, the summary judgment evidence in this case does not indicate that G.W. acted with intent to cause S.S. bodily injury. The summary judgment evidence indicates that G.W. did not believe it was possible to transmit the disease without an active lesion and fails to demonstrate that G.W. knew that engaging in sexual intercourse with S.S. was substantially certain to result in transmission of the disease to S.S.

State Farm argues that G.W. committed the intentional tort of battery because S.S.'s consent to the sexual act was vitiated by the fact the G.W. did not inform her that he had herpes. The Restatement discusses when a person's consent is ineffective so that the person is entitled to maintain any tort action that would be available to him if the consent had not been given. Restatement (Second) of Torts §892B (1979). As an illustration of ineffective consent, the Restatement explains that when A consents to sexual intercourse with B, and B knows that A is ignorant of the fact that B has a venereal disease, B is subject to liability to A for battery, an intentional tort. *Id.* at cmt. e, illus. 5. However, the Restatement also explains that B's "own mistake may indeed prevent his conduct from amounting to an intentional tort, as when there is no knowledge that a touching will be harmful." *Id.* at cmt. c. Here, it appears to be undisputed, or at least there is a fact issue concerning whether G.W. was operating under the mistaken impression that he could not transmit herpes when he had no symptoms of the disease. Consequently, we conclude that an issue of material fact exists concerning whether G.W. knew at that time with substantial certainty that he would transmit herpes to S.S. Because an issue of material fact exists, we hold that the trial court improperly rendered summary judgment. . . .

State Farm also argues that even if G.W. did not intend to injure S.S. by his conduct, his intent to injure is inferred as a matter of law. We disagree.

Jurisdictions which infer intent in sexual misconduct cases usually do so only in instances of sexual misconduct with minors or forcible sex acts between adults. . . . Those jurisdictions reason that intent to injure may be inferred only when the character of an act is such that the "degree of certainty that the conduct will cause injury is sufficiently great to justify inferring intent to injure as a matter of law." *Loveridge v. Chartier,* 161 Wis. 2d 150, 468 N.W.2d 146, 151 (1991). . . . This case differs from the sexual misconduct cases inferring intent because G.W. and S.S. were consenting adults. California and Minnesota specifically refuse to infer intent to injure as a matter of law when the voluntary sexual acts of consenting adults result in the transmission of herpes. *See State Farm Fire & Casualty Co. v. Eddy,* 218 Cal. App. 3d 958, 267 Cal. Rptr. 379, 385 (1990) (refusing to infer intent because the sexual conduct between adults did not constitute rape); *North Star Mut. Ins. Co. v. R.W.,* 431 N.W.2d 138, 143 (Minn. Ct. App. 1988) (refusing to infer intent as a matter of law in a negligence case involving consenting adults). In this case involving intercourse between consenting adults, there is no evidence that G.W. knew with a high degree of certainty that he would transmit genital herpes to S.S. Consequently, we will not infer intent as a matter of law. . . .

For the reasons explained herein, we hold that an issue of material fact exists concerning whether G.W. knew at the time with substantial certainty that he would transmit herpes to S.S., that intent to injure is not inferred as a matter of law, and that the trial court improperly rendered summary judgment. Accordingly, we affirm the judgment of the court of appeals. . . .

HECHT, Justice, dissenting.

. . . When G.W. had sexual intercourse with S.S., he knew he had genital herpes, but he did not tell S.S. G.W. was a doctor of optometry, and he had read medical books on the disease. He recognized its symptoms and knew that he had suffered them for years. He knew that herpes is highly contagious and that it is transmitted by sexual contact. He knew he had experienced an outbreak of symptoms — open sores on his genitals — three to four weeks before the night of his thirtieth birthday when he met S.S. at a nightclub and took her to his house. He knew all of this, but he did not tell S.S. before he had sexual intercourse with her. He did not use a condom. The next morning, when he felt the symptoms of his disease coming on again, he told her. She was, in her words, "real upset." The next day G.W. told S.S. he wanted to continue to see her and "be her lover." When she declined, he said, "Well, you have to date me because I may have given you herpes." A week later she began experiencing the symptoms of herpes.

Had S.S. known G.W. had herpes, she would not have had intercourse with him. G.W. did not forget to tell her about his condition before they had intercourse; he intentionally did not tell her. His reason, he says, was that he believed he could not transmit the disease unless he was experiencing its symptoms, which did not begin to occur until the morning after their encounter. Assuming that this truthfully explains his motivation, it does not alter the fact that all G.W.'s actions were intentional.

I agree with the Court that a person is considered to have intended those consequences which are substantially certain to follow from his actions. The Court focuses on whether G.W. was substantially certain that his liaison with S.S. would cause her to contract herpes. This is not, in my view, the relevant inquiry. The question, rather, is whether G.W. was substantially certain that having sexual intercourse with S.S. without first disclosing his condition to her would *injure* her, even if she did not contract herpes. It was no surprise to G.W., nor could it have been, that S.S. was extremely upset at having been exposed to herpes without her knowledge. The exposure, and whatever injuries resulted, were caused intentionally.

The Court refers to encounters like this one as "the voluntary sexual acts of consenting adults". *Ante* at 379. This is a serious mischaracterization of S.S.'s behavior. S.S. did not consent to exposure to herpes. She was unaware of G.W.'s condition, and had she known, she would have avoided it. She volunteered and consented to their encounter in the sense that she was not coerced against her will. But she did not consent in any legally significant way. Restatement (Second) of Torts §892B (1979).

To conclude as the Court does that G.W.'s conduct may not have been intentional, in my view, defies common sense. He may have been mistaken about the nature of herpes, but he was very deliberate in his conduct toward S.S. I would hold that this conduct is not covered by G.W.'s homeowner's policy. . . . I believe the summary judgment that the trial court did grant was proper. Accordingly, I would reverse the judgment of the court of appeals and affirm the judgment of the trial court. I therefore dissent.

The court in *S.S. & G.W.* sometimes fails to separate two related, but distinct, questions: First, did G.W. commit the intentional tort of battery against S.S.? Second, is State Farm obligated to cover G.W.'s liability to S.S. under the terms of the homeowner's insurance contract between the two parties? The former question requires consulting the principles and precedents of tort law, while the latter question raises matters of contract interpretation that judges generally resolve according to the language of the contract and the presumed intent of the contracting parties. See Robert A. Hillman, Principles of Contract Law 242-243 (Thomson West 2004). See also Restatement (Third) of Torts: Liability for Physical and Emotional Harm §1 cmt. *f* (2010). The difficulty for the court in *S.S. & G.W.* is that, even though the judges seem eager to address the novel and challenging issues of battery law that are raised by consensual — though not fully informed — sexual relations, the first question is not really before the court. Instead, the only question squarely raised by State Farm's declaratory judgment suit is whether the language of the intentional injury exclusion in the contract ("Coverage . . . shall not apply: to bodily injury . . . caused intentionally by . . . the insured") is sufficient to relieve State Farm of the obligation to cover G.W.'s liability costs, irrespective of how G.W.'s underlying tort law liability to S.S. is resolved.

With respect to the contract interpretation question, the majority opinion in *S.S. & G.W.* makes a fairly straightforward argument that in order for G.W. to have intentionally caused bodily injury (as the contract exclusion provision requires), State Farm must show that G.W. was substantially certain at the time of the encounter that unprotected sex with S.S. would transmit herpes to her. Unlike the majority, the dissent is ready to conclude that G.W. acted with the requisite certainty. To reach that conclusion, however, the dissent first recharacterizes S.S.'s injury as one stemming primarily from G.W.'s failure to disclose rather than from the actual transmission of herpes. Thus, the dissent's position implicates several related aspects of battery law: Does effective "consent" in the context of voluntary sexual relations between adults require each party to understand the nature and quality of the act, as in *Barton*, or should a court construe the plaintiff's manifested willingness in favor of the defendant, as in *O'Brien*? Echoing *Vosburg*, does the "implied license" of the bedroom include permission to engage in unprotected sexual relations without disclosing known facts about one's sexually transmitted disease status? Assuming that sexual encounters frequently do include such nondisclosures, should that customary or prevalent behavior be enough to stop a court from condemning the behavior as tortious, or should a court follow *Hackbart* in trying to impose some judicially determined norms onto this realm of potentially harmful, "voluntary" relations? For an argument that tort law should require a heightened duty of disclosure between sexual partners, see Deanna Pollard Sacks, Intentional Sex Torts, 77 Fordham L. Rev. 1051 (2008).

Putting all of these tort law questions aside, however, does the dissent's argument about the nature of S.S.'s injury adequately consider the actual language of the insurance contract? What understanding of "bodily injury" in the intentional injury exclusion provision is necessary in order for the dissent's argument to hold up? At the behest of homeowner's insurance providers, the Texas State Board of Insurance approved an amendment to the state insurance code allowing providers explicitly to exclude coverage for sexually transmitted sickness or disease. See 12 Tex. Reg. 1031-32 (1987). Although not available to State Farm at the time that G.W.'s insurance policy was issued, such an exclusion obviously provides a more direct way to exclude coverage for the type of harm that S.S. suffered than do the undefined and contestable notions of intent, consent, and bodily injury that attracted the attention of the judges in *S.S. & G.W.*

Besides excluding intentionally caused injuries from insurance coverage, insurers often exclude criminal conduct from coverage. In Slayko v. Security Mut. Ins. Co., the insured accidentally shot the victim, his friend, while playing with a rifle he believed to be unloaded. 774 N.E.2d 208 (N.Y. 2002). Though he did not intend the victim's injury, he was convicted of second degree criminal assault. The victim brought a civil action against him. The Court of Appeals reversed an order of the appellate division declaring that exclusion of criminal acts in a liability insurance contract violated public policy, and permitted the insurer to enforce a provision denying coverage for liability "arising directly or indirectly out of instances, occurrences or allegations of criminal activity by the insured." For more on this topic, see 17 Williston on Contracts §49:115 (4th ed. 1990).

S.S. & G.W. also demonstrates the way in which liability insurance can affect the behavior of litigants and their attorneys. In *S.S. & G.W.*, the injured party not only seeks to describe G.W.'s actions as merely negligent rather than intentional, but she also agrees to waive her rights in the underlying tort claim against G.W. in exchange for a share of his perhaps quite speculative claim against State Farm. Why would S.S. agree to these maneuvers that seemingly go against her interest? The phenomenon of "underlitigation"—in which plaintiffs present their claims as sounding in negligence rather than intentional tort in order to stay within the coverage of the defendant's liability insurance contract—has been thoroughly explored by Ellen Pryor (The Stories We Tell:

Intentional Harm and the Quest for Insurance Funding, 75 Tex. L. Rev. 1721 (1997)). She describes several examples (75 Tex. L. Rev. at 1721-22):

> A forty-two-year-old man engages in a sexual relationship for a year and a half with a twelve-year-old boy. The boy and his mother sue the man in tort, alleging intentional infliction of emotional distress and negligence. At trial, the plaintiffs argue that the defendant intended the acts but did not intend to harm either the boy or the mother. The trial judge directs a verdict in favor of the defendant on the intentional tort theory and in favor of plaintiffs on the negligent tort theory.
>
> A man calls his neighbor into the street between their homes and, saying little else, shoots him in the face from a distance of five feet with a .357 Magnum pistol; the victim lives. In lawsuits arising from the injury, the victim sues on grounds of both negligence and intentional tort. Counsel for the victim questions the defendant about his alcoholism and irrationality, emphasizing the defendant's inability to form intent.
>
> A man is indicted for the murders of his wife and son and for the attempted murder of his daughter. While the defendant is awaiting trial, he is sued by the personal representative of the decedents. The complaint alleges only a theory of negligence in causing the deaths of the wife and son.
>
> A family is racially harassed by their next-door neighbor. The neighbor leaves racially offensive and threatening messages on the family's answering machine, sends his dog to chase the child and mother, drives his truck onto their lawn, throws firecrackers on their lawn, and spray-paints racially offensive words on their house. The family eventually argues in court that the neighbor did act purposefully, but did not intend to injure the family.

Underlitigation raises important questions about the purposes of tort law. Cf. City of Watauga v. Gordon, 434 S.W.3d 586 (Tex. 2014) (court holds plaintiff's complaint that police officers negligently injured his wrists with handcuffs during arrest—framed as such to stay within the government's waiver of sovereign immunity—was really a claim for battery for which the state retains immunity). From the instrumental perspective, the phenomenon may not seem especially problematic, given that liability insurance provides a mechanism for expanding the pool of funds available to compensate tort victims, and that insurers may engage in various practices to monitor the behavior of their insureds and deter harmful conduct. These functional goals of liability insurance, and the difficulty of achieving them, are discussed in Chapter 9. From the noninstrumental perspective, however, underlitigation seems to sacrifice an important expressive function of tort law: that of providing a symbolic or communicative message to the community about shared social norms, rather than of seeking simply to control or influence behavior. See Cass R. Sunstein, On the Expressive Function of Law, 144 U. Pa. L. Rev. 2021 (1996). Compensation to the victim may be gained as a result of underlitigation and the presence of liability insurance, but condemnation of the wrongdoer may be lost or diluted in the process. See Leslie Bender, Teaching Tort Law as if Gender Matters: Intentional Torts, 2 Va. J. Soc. Pol'y & L. 115 (1994).

c. Self-Defense

Of the nonconsensual privileges, the most important is self-defense. The general rules governing self-defense are set forth in the Restatement (Second) of Torts:

> §63. Self-Defense by Force not Threatening Death or Serious Bodily Harm
>
> (1) An actor is privileged to use reasonable force, not intended or likely to cause death or serious bodily harm, to defend himself against unprivileged harmful or offensive contact or

other bodily harm which he reasonably believes that another is about to inflict intentionally upon him.

(2) Self-defense is privileged under the conditions stated in Subsection (1), although the actor correctly or reasonably believes that he can avoid the necessity of so defending himself,

(a) by retreating or otherwise giving up a right or privilege, or

(b) by complying with a command with which the actor is under no duty to comply or which the other is not privileged to enforce by the means threatened.

64. Self-Defense Against Negligent Conduct

(1) Except as stated in Subsection (2), an actor is privileged to use reasonable force, not intended or likely to cause death or serious bodily harm, to defend himself against harmful or offensive contact or bodily harm which he reasonably believes to be threatened by the conduct of another, although he recognizes such conduct to be negligent.

(2) The actor is not privileged so to defend himself if he knows or should know that he can escape the necessity of doing so by retreating, or by giving up the exercise of a right or privilege which, under the circumstances, it is reasonable to require him to relinquish.

65. Self-Defense by Force Threatening Death or Serious Bodily Harm

(1) Subject to the statement in Subsection (3), an actor is privileged to defend himself against another by force intended or likely to cause death or serious bodily harm, when he reasonably believes that

(a) the other is about to inflict upon him an intentional contact or other bodily harm, and that

(b) he is thereby put in peril of death or serious bodily harm or ravishment, which can safely be prevented only by the immediate use of such force.

(2) The privilege stated in Subsection (1) exists although the actor correctly or reasonably believes that he can safely avoid the necessity of so defending himself by

(a) retreating if he is attacked within his dwelling place, which is not also the dwelling place of the other, or

(b) permitting the other to intrude upon or dispossess him of his dwelling place, or

(c) abandoning an attempt to effect a lawful arrest.

(3) The privilege stated in Subsection (1) does not exist if the actor correctly or reasonably believes that he can with complete safety avoid the necessity of so defending himself by

(a) retreating if attacked in any place other than his dwelling place, or in a place which is also the dwelling of the other, or

(b) relinquishing the exercise of any right or privilege other than his privilege to prevent intrusion upon or dispossession of his dwelling place or to effect a lawful arrest.

. . .

70. Character and Extent of Force Permissible

(1) The actor is not privileged to use any means of self-defense which is intended or likely to cause a bodily harm . . . in excess of that which the actor correctly or reasonably believes to be necessary for his protection. . . .

The Restatement (Second) goes on to provide, in §71, that an actor who uses excessive force in self-defense is liable "for only so much of the force . . . as is excessive."

Note: Rules vs. Standards as Means of Guiding and Judging Behavior

The Restatement provisions are noteworthy in their textual detail. They distinguish, for example, between deadly and nondeadly threats and between attacks against the actor that occur in the actor's dwelling and those that occur elsewhere. As such, the provisions might be characterized as *specific rules* in that they attempt to specify how an actor should behave under carefully defined circumstances. As a means of formulating legal commands, a rule-based approach has several advantages. Before the fact, rules tend to offer relatively unambiguous guidance to those seeking to comply with the law's commands. And after the fact, clear rules make it easier for the judicial process to determine whether an actor has in fact satisfied legal requirements. This, in turn, tends to promote consistency in adjudication. Under a perfectly detailed set of rules, application of the law should be error-proof, for the rules would specify the precise outcome for every conceivable set of facts the fact finder might determine.

Yet, using highly detailed rules to guide and judge human behavior also has its disadvantages. First, a rule-based approach invites ever more detailed rules. What for example, is a "dwelling place"? Does it include the hallway of an apartment building? What of a homeless person attacked under a highway overpass where he frequently sleeps? It is tempting to answer such questions by formulating more rules, either through judicial decision or legislation. But doing so risks encrusting the law with excessive detail. Moreover, as rules are further refined, their ability to guide human behavior prospectively may, paradoxically, diminish rather than increase; rather than being a beacon informing human conduct, the law may become a thicket through which only the professionally initiated—i.e., the lawyers—can safely pass. Finally, the limits of human foresight, the imprecision of language, and the corrosive effects of time make it highly improbable that any set of rules can anticipate and account for all possible cases. Thus, we are always left with the problem of the hard case, the one that falls between the rules.

In response to such problems, the law might rely less heavily on specific rules in favor of *general standards.* Rather than attempting to specify all possible sets of circumstances, such standards simply set a single, general rule of behavior and leave courts the task of determining, on a case by case basis, whether the standard was met. Thus, the law of negligence, which we take up in Chapter 3, essentially takes a standard-based approach; its basic command boils down to something like "be reasonable, or pay the consequences." Can the Restatement provisions regarding self-defense be replaced by such a unified standard? How about: "A defendant is privileged to fight back only as necessary"?

Generally speaking, standards tend to have benefits and drawbacks that are the mirror image of those of detailed rules. Thus, a standard is simple and accessible, and it applies to all cases. Yet, compared to a detailed set of rules, a general standard is of limited value in guiding behavior prospectively or ensuring consistent assessments of that behavior retrospectively. For instance, in the two examples of general standards given above, how will individuals, or the courts that will later assess their conduct, know when their behavior is "reasonable" or their actions in self-defense are "necessary"?

At this point, two things may become clear. First, rules and standards are not really distinct approaches, but rather represent ends of a spectrum along which we can formulate legal commands. Thus, a set of rules is simply a highly differentiated standard, or, put conversely, a standard is a highly aggregated and generalized rule. Many legal commands lie somewhere in the middle of the spectrum, offering some detail and some generality.

Thus, the Restatement's self-defense provisions, although quite detailed, don't define the circumstances that might lead an actor to "reasonably believe" that harm is imminent. Second, legal regimes are seldom static in their choice of approaches: Over time, very general standards tend toward differentiation, while overly detailed rules risk recapitulation into a general standard.

The rules-standards spectrum, as well as the dynamic process of movement along that spectrum, can be observed in many areas of law. For a classic critical account, see Duncan Kennedy, Form and Substance in Private Law Adjudication, 89 Harv. L. Rev. 1685 (1976). For a subsequent discussion in the context of behavioral economic analyses of law, see Russell B. Korobkin, Behavioral Analysis and Legal Form: Rules vs. Standards Revisited, 79 Or. L. Rev. 23 (2000). In the context of this course, it will often prove useful for you to consider where a particular legal command is situated on the spectrum, and why it might make sense for it to be framed in that manner.

Problem 5

The presentation of the evidence in Aman v. Diaz, a case tried before a jury in Hardwick County Superior Court, has been completed. Defendant has filed a motion for a directed verdict. There is some dispute as to the facts, but a fair summary of the evidence is as follows.

During the summer months prior to August 8, two years ago, there had been escalating tension in Central City following a series of violent attacks by individuals who proclaimed allegiance to an international terrorist organization known as the Islamic Fulfillment. The tension was particularly acute in the commercial section of the West End, a predominantly working-class, ethnically and racially diverse section of the city. West End was home to a significant population of recent Muslim immigrants as well as being the location of most of the recent attacks. The defendant, Oscar Diaz, owns and operates a small grocery store in the West End. The incident out of which the case arose occurred a few minutes after 10:00 P.M. on August 8. Khaled Aman, a 35-year-old Afghan American man, was shot by the defendant after he entered the store. On direct examination, the plaintiff described what happened in this way:

Q: Now, Mr. Aman, will you tell us what time you entered Diaz's store?
A: Several minutes after ten o'clock, probably two or three minutes after.
Q: That's ten P.M., at night?
A: Yes, I knew that it closes at ten, and I had run to get there before it closed.
Q: You went there to buy some groceries?
A: That's right — a carton of eggs.
Q: What was the weather that night?
A: It had been raining off and on; it was raining as I went in.
Q: Tell us about how you went into the store. Did you walk right in frontwards?
A: No. As I walked up to the front of the store, I had my umbrella up. I looked in the window to see if the store was open, and saw someone behind the counter. I tried the door and it was unlocked. Then I closed my umbrella and sort of pushed the door the rest of the way open with my shoulder and went in sort of backwards, with the umbrella behind me. When I got through the door, I stood there for a couple of seconds to shake the water off the umbrella. I didn't want to get water all over the floor of the store.

Q: What happened then?
A: Well, I turned around and saw someone behind the counter with a gun pointed at me. I shouted in fear, and next thing I know he shoots me. Hit me in the shoulder and I went down.
Q: How many times did he shoot? Was that in the left shoulder?
A: Yes, in the left shoulder. I don't know how many times he shot. I was terrified. It . . . It happened so fast I couldn't count.
Q: How were you dressed that night?
A: Well, I had on a raincoat, boots, and a pakol.
Q: What is a pakol Mr. Aman?
A: It's a soft wool cap traditionally worn by Afghan men.
Q: Were you carrying a gun — a rifle, shotgun, or anything like that?
A: No, I wasn't. I really don't like guns. I sure don't now.
Q: How were you holding your umbrella as you entered the store? After you shook the water off?
A: In my hand, or maybe under my arm. I don't know.
Q: Did you point it toward the counter?
A: I might have. I might have sort of held both hands and the umbrella up toward the counter to try and shield myself, you know? I don't remember exactly.

On cross-examination, the plaintiff admitted that he knew that the store usually closed at ten and that it was after ten when he arrived at the store that night. The plaintiff also testified that he had opened the door partway and left it ajar while he turned to close his umbrella. He characterized the length of time from when he first looked in the window until he was shot entering the store as "several seconds, maybe five or six."

On direct examination by his own attorney, the defendant testified in part as follows:

Q: So you were aware of the Islamic Fulfillment attacks that had been going on in the West End?
A: You bet I was. I bought the gun when I read about the shooting at Rubio's Market on Fourth Street.
Q: What type of gun did you buy?
A: A 38-caliber revolver.
Q: Did you register the gun?
A: Yes.
Q: Why did you stay open until ten, with all that happening?
A: I do a lot of business after supper. People always need something on the way home — bread, milk, eggs. There aren't so many places they can get it. So I stay open. It's good business.
Q: Tell us what happened on the night of August 8.
A: The shooting, you mean. I was about to close — to lock up, to count the cash, and put it in the safe. I usually have quite a bit of cash on hand at closing time. The store was empty. Then I see this guy looking in the window, and when I look up and see him, he ducks back behind the door.
Q: Did you get a good look at the person through the window?
A: No. The light isn't good outside, and the window was wet from the rain. Then the door opens, maybe a foot or so, and no one comes through the door. I'm getting pretty nervous at this point so I reach for my gun just in case.

Q: Where was your gun?
A: I kept it under the counter.
Q: So then what happened?
A: So then this guy pushes the door open and backs into the store. He just stands there for a minute, and I can see that he's got something in his hands. Then he spins around. He's this big guy with a beard and a funny hat on, and he points this thing at me and starts yelling. It looks like a shotgun or a rifle; so I shoot. I'm not taking any chances. I remember what happened to Marco Rubio, and it's not going to happen to me.
Q: Mr. Diaz, who is Marco Rubio?
A: A friend of mine who owns the grocery store I mentioned a minute ago. Got shot and killed by one of those Islamic terrorists right around the time he was closing up for the night.
Q: Prior to the incident in your store, did you know a lot about the other attacks that were carried out for the Islamic Fulfillment?
A: Not much. Just that the victims were taken by surprise and that they all seemed to be small business owners like me.
Q: All right, Mr. Diaz, returning to the night of August 8, two years ago, when Mr. Aman turned around in front of you, how many times did you shoot?
A: Once. One time.
Q: Did you pull your revolver out before he turned around?
A: Yes. It was right there, and I had it by the time he stuck that thing in my face.
Q: How long would you say it took from the time you first saw someone through the window until the plaintiff spun around and you shot him? How many seconds?
A: I would say 15 or 20 seconds, maybe more. Twenty at least.
Q: Did you have to shoot? Could you have ducked behind the counter, or made it back to the storage room?
A: Frankly, I didn't think about that. It was my store, and I thought there was a gun pointing at me. I just reacted to save myself.
Q: What happened after the shooting?
A: I ran around the counter and out the front door. I was yelling for help. I saw some people running toward me and then I went back inside. When I realized that the guy on the floor didn't have a gun, I did everything I could to help him. I'm sorry this ever happened, but I really thought my number was up.
Q: Getting back to your description of the store. How far is it from your counter to the front door?
A: Twenty feet.
Q: How was the lighting in your store?
A: Overhead fluorescents.
Q: How is your eyesight, Mr. Diaz?
A: I wear glasses. I was wearing them then and I could see all right.

Should the defendant's motion for a directed verdict be granted? If the judge sends the case to the jury, what would be the substance of your closing argument to the jury on behalf of the plaintiff? On behalf of the defendant? Assume that the Restatement provisions and the following opinion are governing law in the jurisdiction.

Courvoisier v. Raymond

23 Colo. 113, 47 P. 284 (1896)

Edwin S. Raymond, appellee, as plaintiff below, complains of Auguste Courvoisier, appellant, and alleges that on the 12th day of June, A.D. 1892, plaintiff was a regularly appointed and duly qualified acting special policeman in and for the city of Denver; that while engaged in the discharge of his duties as such special policeman, the defendant shot him in the abdomen, thereby causing a serious and painful wound; that in so doing the defendant acted wilfully, knowingly and maliciously, and without any reasonable cause. . . .

The defendant, answering the complaint, denies each allegation thereof, and, in addition to such denials, pleads five separate defenses. These defenses are all in effect a justification by reason of unavoidable necessity. A trial resulted in a verdict and judgment for plaintiff for the sum of three thousand, one hundred and forty-three (3,143) dollars. To reverse this judgment, the cause is brought here by appeal.

Chief Justice HAYT delivered the opinion of the court.

It is admitted or proven beyond controversy that appellee received a gunshot wound at the hands of the appellant at the time and place designated in the complaint, and that as the result of such wound the appellee was seriously injured. It is further shown that the shooting occurred under the following circumstances:

That Mr. Courvoisier, on the night in question, was asleep in his bed in the second story of a brick building, situate[d] at the corner of South Broadway and Dakota streets in South Denver; that he occupied a portion of the lower floor of this building as a jewelry store. He was aroused from his bed shortly after midnight by parties shaking or trying to open the door of the jewelry store. These parties, when asked by him as to what they wanted, insisted upon being admitted, and upon his refusal to comply with this request, they used profane and abusive epithets toward him. Being unable to gain admission, they broke some signs upon the front of the building, and then entered the building by another entrance, and passing upstairs commenced knocking upon the door of a room where defendant's sister was sleeping. Courvoisier partly dressed himself, and, taking his revolver, went upstairs and expelled the intruders from the building. In doing this he passed downstairs and out on the sidewalk as far as the entrance to his store, which was at the corner of the building. The parties expelled from the building, upon reaching the rear of the store, were joined by two or three others. In order to frighten these parties away, the defendant fired a shot in the air, but instead of retreating they passed around to the street in front, throwing stones and brickbats at the defendant, whereupon he fired a second and perhaps a third shot. The first shot fired attracted the attention of plaintiff Raymond and two deputy sheriffs, who were at the Tramway depot, across the street. These officers started toward Mr. Courvoisier, who still continued to shoot, but two of them stopped when they reached the men in the street, for the purpose of arresting them, Mr. Raymond alone proceeding towards the defendant, calling out to him that he was an officer and to stop shooting. Although the night was dark, the street was well lighted by electricity, and when the officer approached him defendant shaded his eyes, and, taking deliberate aim, fired, causing the injury complained of.

The plaintiff's theory of the case is that he was a duly authorized police officer, and in the discharge of his duties at the time; that the defendant was committing a breach of the peace, and that the defendant, knowing him to be a police officer, recklessly fired the shot in question.

The defendant claims that the plaintiff was approaching him at the time in a threatening attitude, and that the surrounding circumstances were such as to cause a reasonable man to believe that his life was in danger, and that it was necessary to shoot in self-defense, and that defendant did so believe at the time of firing the shot. . . .

The next error assigned relates to the instructions given by the court to the jury and to those requested by the defendant and refused by the court. The second instruction given by the court was clearly erroneous. The instruction is as follows: "The court instructs you that if you believe from the evidence, that, at the time the defendant shot the plaintiff, the plaintiff was not assaulting the defendant, then your verdict should be for the plaintiff."

The vice of this instruction is that it excluded from the jury a full consideration of the justification claimed by the defendant. The evidence for the plaintiff tends to show that the shooting, if not malicious, was wanton and reckless, but the evidence for the defendant tends to show that the circumstances surrounding him at the time of the shooting were such as to lead a reasonable man to believe that his life was in danger, or that he was in danger of receiving great bodily harm at the hands of the plaintiff, and the defendant testified that he did so believe.

He swears that his house was invaded shortly after midnight by two men, whom he supposed to be burglars; that when ejected, they were joined on the outside by three or four others; that the crowd so formed assaulted him with stones and other missiles, when, to frighten them away, he shot into the air; that instead of going away someone approached him from the direction of the crowd; that he supposed this person to be one of the rioters, and did not ascertain that it was the plaintiff until after the shooting. He says that he had had no previous acquaintance with plaintiff; that he did not know that he was a police officer, or that there were any police officers in the town of South Denver; that he heard nothing said at the time by the plaintiff or anyone else that caused him to think the plaintiff was an officer; that his eyesight was greatly impaired, so that he was obliged to use glasses, and that he was without glasses at the time of the shooting, and for this reason could not see distinctly. He then adds: "I saw a man come away from the bunch of men and come up towards me, and as I looked around I saw this man put his hand to his hip pocket. I didn't think I had time to jump aside, and therefore turned around and fired at him. I had no doubts but it was somebody that had come to rob me, because some weeks before Mr. Wilson's store was robbed. It is next door to mine."

By this evidence two phases of the transaction are presented for consideration: *First*, was the plaintiff assaulting the defendant at the time plaintiff was shot? *Second*, if not, was there sufficient evidence of justification for the consideration of the jury? The first question was properly submitted, but the second was excluded by the instruction under review. The defendant's justification did not rest entirely upon the proof of assault by the plaintiff. A riot was in progress, and the defendant swears that he was attacked with missiles, hit with stones, brickbats, etc.; that he shot plaintiff, supposing him to be one of the rioters. We must assume these facts as established in reviewing the instruction, as we cannot say what the jury might have found had this evidence been submitted to them under a proper charge.

By the second instruction the conduct of those who started the fracas was eliminated from the consideration of the jury. If the jury believed from the evidence that the defendant would have been justified in shooting one of the rioters had such person advanced towards him as did the plaintiff, then it became important to determine whether the defendant mistook plaintiff for one of the rioters, and if such a mistake was in fact made, was it excusable in the light of all the circumstances leading up to and surrounding the commission of the act? If these issues had been resolved by the jury in favor of the defendant, he would have been entitled to a judgment. . . .

Where a defendant in a civil action like the one before us attempts to justify on a plea of necessary self-defense, he must satisfy the jury not only that he acted honestly in using force, but that his fears were reasonable under the circumstances; and also as to the reasonableness of the means made use of. In this case perhaps the verdict would not have been different had the jury been properly instructed, but it might have been, and therefore the judgment must be reversed.

Reversed.

Focusing on the rules governing self-defense expressed by the Restatement (Second) and by *Courvoisier,* how many separate issues of fact do you see in this problem? What evidence is there in the case that would lead the jury to resolve these issues one way or the other? As to any of these issues, is the evidence so compelling that a reasonable jury could resolve them only one way — that is, in favor of the plaintiff or the defendant?

The Lawyer's Professional Responsibility: Playing to the Prejudices of the Jury

Were the defendant's motion for directed verdict to be denied in Problem 5, and the issue of self-defense to go to the jury, the lawyers would face a problem that, in a variety of forms, arises fairly frequently in trial practice: To what extent may, or should, a lawyer try to play to the prejudices of the jury? The question arises here in stark form: The plaintiff is an Afghan American (who may or may not be Muslim) at a time when certain individuals (who may or may not be of Arab or Afghan descent) have committed acts of violence in the name of an Islamic extremist organization; the possibility exists that some of the jurors will indulge in inappropriate assumptions based on underlying prejudices. At the outset of this chapter, in the introductory text in Section A, we observed in general terms that trial lawyers *want* jurors who are biased in their favor, and presumably couch their arguments to play to those biases. Do, or should, the biases to which lawyers play include socially harmful prejudices of the sort we are now considering?

These questions force lawyers into delicate balancing acts. On the one hand, playing to the socially reprehensible biases and prejudices of the jury strikes most lawyers as ethically underhanded when compared to their own personal senses of right and wrong. On the other hand, lawyers (and law students) often feel that they are ethically bound to zealously pursue every available lawful means of achieving their client's goals. In truth, however, the obligation to provide diligent representation is not nearly so blunt as lawyers often presume:

> A lawyer should pursue a matter on behalf of a client despite opposition, obstruction or personal inconvenience to the lawyer, and take whatever lawful and ethical measures are required to vindicate a client's cause or endeavor. A lawyer must also act with commitment and dedication to the interests of the client and with zeal in advocacy upon the client's behalf. A lawyer is not bound, however, to press for every advantage that might be realized for a client. For example, a lawyer may have authority to exercise professional discretion in determining the means by which a matter should be pursued. See Rule 1.2. The lawyer's duty to act with reasonable diligence does not require the use of offensive tactics or preclude the treating of all persons involved in the legal process with courtesy and respect.

Model Rule of Prof'l Conduct R. 1.3 cmt. [1] (2006). Of course, although this comment does not require the lawyer to engage in offensive or disrespectful tactics on behalf of a client, it does not seem to rule out the lawyer's discretion to use them.

Judges in tort cases have broad discretion in granting a new trial if they believe that a lawyer's tactics have inflamed the passions and prejudices of a jury. See generally, Tierco Md., Inc. v. Williams, 849 A.2d 504 (Md. 2004). The Model Rules of Professional Conduct ban the presentation of irrelevant matters and prohibit a lawyer from seeking to influence jurors by improper means. Rules 3.4(e) & 3.5(a). The American Bar Association Standards Relating to the Administration of Criminal Justice contain similarly worded provisions forbidding prosecutors and defense counsel from using "arguments calculated to appeal to improper prejudices" of the trier of fact. Standards 3-5.8(c) & 4-7.8(c).

More direct prohibitions on discriminatory conduct include Model Rule 8.4, which states that "[i]t is professional misconduct for a lawyer to: . . . (d) engage in conduct that is prejudicial to the administration of justice." Comment [3] to Rule 8.4 explains that "[a] lawyer who, in the course of representing a client, knowingly manifests by words or conduct bias or prejudice based upon race, sex, religion, national origin, disability, age, sexual orientation or socioeconomic status, violates paragraph (d) when such actions are prejudicial to the administration of justice." Numerous states have adopted rules similar to this one. For instance, the professional responsibility rules of Massachusetts state:

> In appearing in his professional capacity before a tribunal, a lawyer shall not . . . [e]ngage in conduct manifesting bias or prejudice based on race, sex, religion, national origin, disability, age, or sexual orientation against a party, witness, counsel or other person. This passage does not preclude legitimate advocacy when race, sex, national origin, disability, age, or sexual orientation, or other similar factor, is at issue in the proceeding.

Massachusetts Rules of Professional Conduct, Chapter 3.4(i). For further analysis of the impact of prejudices and biases on the trial process, see Justin D. Levinson, Forgotten Racial Equality: Implicit Bias, Decisionmaking and Misremembering, 57 Duke L.J. 345 (2007); and Gary Blasi, Critical Race Studies: Advocacy Against the Stereotype: Lessons from Cognitive Psychology, 49 UCLA L. Rev. 1241 (2002).

In considering the issue of whether to use bias or prejudice to influence a tribunal, you should test your own ethical limits in the context of the foregoing problem. What would you do if you decided that it would be in your client's best interest to play to the jury's biases? Where would you draw the line between zealous representation and bias-baiting?

The Law-Fact Distinction: Evaluation of Conduct

In the law-fact distinction note following *Vosburg*, conclusions of fact were described as "what happened," reached by the fact finder "much in the same sense that a scientist might conclude that a given object weighs three grams," and rules of law were defined as "generalized rules calling for certain legal consequences to follow from a particular set of facts." In many cases of harmful battery, these definitions suffice for whatever purpose is to be served by labeling a particular issue as one of fact or law. However, since that first note we have encountered issues that are not so easily classified according to these definitions. For example, one of the issues in a battery case may be whether the contact with the plaintiff is "offensive." (See §§13, 18, and 19 of the Restatement (Second) of Torts discussed in connection with *Vosburg,* above.) Scientists do not typically make scientific assertions as to the offensiveness of contacts. Or consider the question of the reasonableness of the defendant's belief in the preceding problem that he was being robbed — a scientist's function does not typically include answering questions of that sort. Obviously, the assertion that an actor's conduct is offensive, or unreasonable, conveys more than merely "what happened." And yet, if these issues of offensiveness and unreasonableness do not fit the classic definition of an issue of fact, it is equally clear that they do not fit the definition of an issue of law. The assertion that Petrangelo's conduct in the preceding problem was reasonable, or unreasonable, is not a declaration of a prospective, generalized rule to govern behavior. It is a retrospective evaluation of his conduct.

Because issues of this sort do not fit neatly into either of the standard definitions, some commentators have referred to them as "mixed questions of law and fact." See, e.g., Francis H. Bohlen, Mixed Questions of Law and Fact, 72 U. Pa. L. Rev. 111 (1924); Frederick Green, Mixed Questions of Law and Fact, 15 Harv. L. Rev. 271 (1901). See also Ronald J. Allen & Michael S. Pardo, The Myth of the Law-Fact Distinction, 97 Nw. U. L. Rev. 1769 (2003) (observing the difficulty of distinguishing between law and fact). Others prefer to talk instead in terms of the process of applying law to fact. See, e.g., Stephen A. Weiner, The Civil Jury Trial and the Law-Fact Distinction, 54 Cal. L. Rev. 1867, 1871-76 (1966). Regardless of the terminology employed, these issues are almost universally treated, in this country, as issues for the jury to resolve; if there is no jury, they will be the subject of findings of fact by the judge. On balance, this seems to be a commonsense solution. Recall that an offensive contact is one "that offends a reasonable sense of personal dignity." The experience of the ordinary citizen rather than the expertise of the lawyer would seem to be the better authority for gauging offensiveness. Furthermore, offensiveness and unreasonableness usually can be determined only on the facts and circumstances of each individual case. It is not the sort of determination that can have much value as precedent in later cases.

Problem 6

A partner in your firm has asked you for help with a difficult case. Your firm represents the parents of Jason Talco, a 12-year-old sixth-grader who seriously injured a classmate with a baseball bat. From interviews with Jason, his parents, and school officials, the following story emerges.

At the time of the incident, Jason was a student at Dearborn Middle School. Small for his age, shy, and bookish, Jason was an easy target for the school's bullies. Among them was an eighth-grade student named Louie Chevette, now the plaintiff in a battery action against Jason. Big and mean-spirited, Louie had picked on Jason and several other students from the beginning of the school year. Mostly, this consisted of shoving Jason into lockers, knocking his books loose, and the like. By mid-year, however, the harassment had escalated. Louie had begun using threats of violence to extort lunch money from other students, including Jason. He had also beaten up several students after school. Suspensions by the school had failed to temper Louie's behavior.

The incident in question occurred shortly after Jason told his father of the problem. Rather than contact school officials, Jason's father insisted that Jason resolve the conflict himself. He ordered Jason to stop paying Louie and encouraged his son to "get Louie before he can get you." Jason's father freely admits all this. Always disappointed by his son's timidity and small size, he believed this to be a situation where his son could "grow up and learn to handle his problems like a man."

Several days after his conversation with his father, Jason was again accosted by Louie. When Jason refused Louie's demand for money, Louie pinned Jason against a wall and told him: "You will pay. I will get you. I will get you today. I will cut you bad." Jason spent the remainder of the school day in terror. He did not go to school officials, both because of his father's prohibition and because he believed, based on Louie's past attacks on other students, that such officials would be powerless to protect him.

As Jason was returning from gym before the final period of school, he saw Louie bending over to retrieve something from his locker. Jason's rage and fear exploded, and he attacked the unsuspecting Louie with a baseball bat. Jason's attack took place with stunning speed and ferocity, and Louie was severely injured before several teachers intervened to restrain Jason.

Jason is now facing juvenile disciplinary proceedings and a civil suit by Louie. Under state law, parents are vicariously liable for the intentional wrongdoing of their children. Here, the evidence unequivocally establishes that Jason attacked Louie, and that Louie did not see the attack coming. Before approaching Louie's lawyer concerning settlement, however, the supervising partner wants to know whether any defenses to liability exist. In particular, the partner wonders to what extent the events surrounding the attack might bear on the question of liability.

In this regard, two other aspects of the case may be pertinent. First, Jason has consistently maintained that he remembers little of the attack. He remembers returning from gym class, and seeing Louie's back. He remembers feeling sweaty and "his head boiling." And he recalls several teachers holding him against the wall and shouting at him to calm down. But he claims no direct recollection of the actual attack.

Second, the psychologist for the school system has supplied a written evaluation of Jason that suggests that the nature of the attack may have been partly due to the way Jason was raised. The psychologist believes that in families like the Talcos, where the parents are strict, authoritarian, and reluctant to display emotion, children often have difficulty handling strong feelings. The report notes:

> Such a family system emphasizes controlling rather than processing emotions. The overconstrained range of acceptable behavior within the family unit forces children to suppress feelings that are incompatible with the parental insistence on order. The child eventually internalizes this demand for control and develops internal resources for suppressing emotions. However, when very strong emotions are stimulated by external events, the child's control system often breaks down catastrophically and without warning, resulting in a behavioral manifestation that is inappropriate to context. The events in this case are consistent with this hypothesis.

The partner who is handling this case wants your assessment of Jason's chances of raising a successful defense to Louie's battery claim, based on traditional self-defense principles. She also wants you to consider whether any other defenses may be available. The partner tells you that a few jurisdictions have recognized contributory negligence as a defense to battery claims, allowing juries to apportion fault between the parties on a percentage basis. The courts in your state have not faced the issue, but might be willing to listen to well-reasoned arguments in support of such an approach. The partner asks: "Why should the defenses to battery be limited to consent, self-defense, and the like? Why shouldn't courts let defendants argue that the plaintiff also acted badly, and had it coming?"

Law and Policy: Why All This Reliance on Reasonableness?

As the preceding law-fact distinction note suggests, tort law often requires the trier of fact to pass on the reasonableness of an actor's behavior. Indeed, even in this chapter, which focuses on intentional wrongdoing rather than negligence, issues of reasonableness abound. Would a reasonable person find a kick during class hours to be offensive? Would a reasonable doctor perceive the patient in *O'Brien* to have consented? Would a reasonable person have perceived a need to act in self-defense under the circumstances presented in *Courvoisier*? Such questions continue to percolate throughout the remainder of the materials on intentional torts, and when we reach negligence, they dominate the inquiry, requiring judges and juries constantly to decide whether the conduct in question was reasonable.

At that point, in Chapters 3 and 4, we will explore in greater detail the various tools courts use to resolve the reasonableness inquiry. At this juncture, however, it is useful to raise some preliminary concerns regarding tort law's reliance on shared notions of what is reasonable. First, why insist on reasonableness at all? In the self-defense context, for example, shouldn't it be sufficient that the defendant honestly believed that he was in imminent danger of bodily harm? What is gained by requiring, as a condition for escaping liability, that such belief and the attendant response by the defendant also be judged as reasonable by the trier of fact?

An instrumental response might be that the requirement of objective reasonableness inspires caution and reflection in an actor contemplating potentially harmful activity. One can imagine, for example, the doctor in *O'Brien* thinking: "She appears to consent to be vaccinated, but I'm not sure everyone would agree. Perhaps I should make sure." As a deterrent against imprudence, then, the reasonableness requirement obviously has some value.

Yet this deterrence rationale also has limitations. First, situations arise in which prudent deliberation is unlikely to occur. Self-defense is perhaps the best example. As Justice Holmes once noted: "Detached reflection cannot be demanded in the presence of an uplifted knife." Brown v. United States, 256 U.S. 335, 343 (1921). Modern psychological research tends to support this view by suggesting that under situations of extreme stress, the primitive limbic system of the brain, which is programmed to respond vigorously to perceived threats to an individual's survival, is capable of overwhelming the cerebral cortex wherein the capacities for reflection, judgment, and restraint are thought to reside. See R. Restak, The Fiction of the "Reasonable Man," Wash. Post, May 17, 1987, at C3. Under such circumstances, the law's announced preference for prudence is likely to go unheard. See also David J. Arkush, Situating Emotion: A Critical Realist View of Emotion and Nonconscious Processes for Law and Legal Theory, 2008 BYU L. Rev. 1275 (surveying evidence from psychology and neuroscience on the extensive role that emotion and unconscious cognitive processes play in human behavior).

Moreover, just as situations arise that preclude prudent deliberation, some individuals, by their very nature, have difficulty discerning and meeting the standard of reasonable behavior. For example, young children, such as those involved in *Vosburg* and *Garratt,* are unlikely to have any firm sense of ordinary adult standards of care. Similarly, some adults, because of physical or mental disabilities, will be unable to react to situations in the same manner as would the theoretical "reasonable person." Other individuals might have distinctive — but not necessarily unreasonable — reactions to situations based on their particular experiences or identities. For instance, those who have suffered from domestic abuse or childhood bullying might not necessarily be expected to engage in acts of self-defense or self-protection in the same manner as non-affected individuals. In Doe BF v.

Diocese of Gallup, 722011 WL 4048778 (2011), the Supreme Court of the Navajo Nation addressed such a possibility when assessing the "reasonableness" of plaintiff's diligence in pursuing a tort claim premised on childhood sexual abuse, for purposes of applying a statute of limitations:

> [Plaintiff-]Appellant asks that the Court use the "Objective person in Plaintiff's position" standard, taking into account a person's upbringing, culture and circumstances after having been subjected to the abuse. This Court agrees that such a standard is applicable on the Navajo Nation. Under this standard in this case, "reasonable diligence" . . . must be applied to a Navajo person, not a faceless individual whose "reasonable diligence" is measured by an objective standard applied by the dominant culture. We interpret justice through Diné eyes. We do not blindly accept what the phrases have been taken to mean by other societies. To determine what is reasonable for [a] member of the Navajo Nation, it is entirely appropriate to consider factors such as historical trauma and the deference expected of a people by authority figures of a colonizing culture.

Given the possibility of tailoring a reasonable person standard to take account of important determinants of an individual's perspective such as their identity or significant life experiences, why not go all the way to adopt a subjective standard? How, put differently, can we explain tort law's retention of a reasonableness requirement, particularly in cases like *Courvoisier,* where the circumstances conspire against careful deliberation? One answer may lie in noninstrumental considerations of corrective justice. In such situations, the reasonableness requirement helps courts fairly to resolve a "choice of innocents" dilemma. Consider, for example, a case like *Courvoisier* involving a mistaken use of self-defense. From a moral perspective, most would conclude that such a mistake is innocent as long as the defendant was honestly trying to make the best decision under the circumstances. But nonetheless, an equally innocent plaintiff was injured by the defendant's intentional conduct.

In deciding which of two innocent parties should bear the resulting loss, the law might sensibly focus on whether the defendant's honest mistake was reasonable. If it was, then the law can justify a privilege because the defendant only did what any "ordinary" person might have done under the circumstances. In short, the law rejects the claim of wrongdoing by noting that the same outcome might well have occurred had the plaintiff been in the defendant's shoes. But if the defendant's mistake was honest but unreasonable, the innocent plaintiff's claim for compensation arguably becomes more compelling because the plaintiff was exposed to the nonreciprocal risk of unreasonable behavior. Justice Holmes again voices the traditional sentiment:

> [W]hen men live in society, a certain average of conduct, a sacrifice of individual peculiarities going beyond a certain point, is necessary to the general welfare. If, for example, a man is born hasty and awkward, is always having accidents and hurting himself or his neighbors, no doubt his congenital defects will be allowed for in the courts of Heaven, but his slips are no less troublesome to his neighbors than if they sprang from guilty neglect. His neighbors accordingly require him, at his proper peril, to come up to their standard, and the courts which they establish decline to take his personal equation into account.

Oliver Wendell Holmes, The Common Law 108 (1881). As will be developed further in Chapter 3, on negligence, the law offers other justifications for its frequent decision to assess individual conduct against the behavior of the hypothetical reasonable person.

d. Defense of Others

Although at early common law the privilege to defend third persons against harmful contacts encompassed only one's family and household, it is now generally agreed that the privilege extends to protecting total strangers as well. The force that may be used by an intervenor to repel an attack on another is measured by the force that the other could lawfully use. Thus, if the attack imperils the life of the third person, the intervenor can use deadly force on behalf of that person.

The one exception to this general rule arises in the case of mistake. The intervenor may be mistaken as to which of two other persons is the aggressor, or mistaken as to the nature of the threat posed by the aggressor. In such cases, there is a split of authority as to whether the intervenor's privilege is derivative from, or independent of, the privilege of the person on whose behalf the actor intervenes. The weight of authority seems to be that the intervenor's privilege is derivative — that is, that the intervenor may use only the force that the person to be protected could legally use. If the intervenor is mistaken, even reasonably mistaken, as to the identity of the aggressor or the severity of the threat, the privilege is unavailable if it would not be available to the person to be protected.

In contrast, the Restatement (Second) of Torts, in §76, adopts the view that the intervenor's privilege is independent of that held by the person to be protected. Thus, an intervenor is entitled to use reasonable force to protect a third party as long as the intervenor reasonably believes that intervention is necessary and that the third party would be privileged to use self-defense if able to do so, even if the person to be protected would not be privileged to defend himself. Comment *c* to this section states: "The actor does not take the risk that the person for whose protection he interferes is actually privileged to defend himself. He may be guided by appearances which would lead a reasonable man in the actor's position to believe that the third person is privileged."

e. Defense of Property

In preceding sections we considered the privilege that sometimes arises to inflict bodily injury intentionally upon another in order to defend oneself or others from imminent threat of physical harm. We now consider the privilege to inflict bodily injury intentionally upon another in order to defend property from imminent threat of theft or destruction. The following sections of the Restatement (Second) of Torts reflect the lower priority afforded the privilege to act in defense of one's property:

§77. Defense of Possession by Force Not Threatening Death or Serious Bodily Harm

> An actor is privileged to use reasonable force, not intended or likely to cause death or serious bodily harm, to prevent or terminate another's intrusion upon the actor's land or chattels, if
>
> (a) the intrusion is not privileged . . . and
>
> (b) the actor reasonably believes that the intrusion can be prevented or terminated only by the force used, and
>
> (c) the actor has first requested the other to desist and the other has disregarded the request, or the actor reasonably believes that a request will be useless or that substantial harm will be done before it can be made.

§79. Defense of Possession by Force Threatening Death or Serious Bodily Harm

> The intentional infliction upon another of a harmful or offensive contact or other bodily harm by a means which is intended or likely to cause death or serious bodily harm, for the purpose of preventing or terminating the other's intrusion upon the actor's possession of land or chattels, is privileged if, but only if, the actor reasonably believes that the intruder, unless expelled or excluded, is likely to cause death or serious bodily harm to the actor or to a third person whom the actor is privileged to protect.

Subsection (c) of §77 is especially interesting in light of the policies underlying the law of battery which support legal recovery as a more civilized alternative to self-help in the form of physical retaliation. Notice that the actor must actually go through a more or less formal procedure of "asking first," in most cases, before the privilege to use reasonable force arises.

The following decision by the Supreme Court of Iowa affords an excellent opportunity to observe these rules in action. Rarely does a decision reflect so starkly the balancing of interests that underlies much of the law of torts. And rarely has a torts decision provoked the sort of public controversy that this one provoked following its publication.

Katko v. Briney

183 N.W.2d 657 (Iowa 1971)

Moore, C.J. . . . Plaintiff's action is for damages resulting from serious injury caused by a shot from a 20-gauge spring shotgun set by defendants in a bedroom of an old farm house which had been uninhabited for several years. Plaintiff and his companion, Marvin McDonough, had broken and entered the house to find and steal old bottles and dated fruit jars which they considered antiques.

At defendants' request plaintiff's action was tried to a jury consisting of residents of the community where defendants' property was located. The jury returned a verdict for plaintiff and against defendants for $20,000 actual and $10,000 punitive damages.

After careful consideration of defendants' motions for judgment notwithstanding the verdict and for new trial, the experienced and capable trial judge overruled them and entered judgment on the verdict. Thus we have this appeal by defendants. . . .

II. Most of the facts are not disputed. In 1957 defendant Bertha L. Briney inherited her parents' farmland in Mahaska and Monroe Counties. Included was an 80-acre tract in southwest Mahaska County where her grandparents and parents had lived. No one occupied the house thereafter. Her husband, Edward, attempted to care for the land. He kept no farm machinery thereon. The outbuildings became dilapidated.

For about 10 years, 1957 to 1967, there occurred a series of trespassing and housebreaking events with loss of some household items, the breaking of windows and "messing up of the property in general." The latest occurred June 8, 1967, prior to the event on July 16, 1967 herein involved.

Defendants through the years boarded up the windows and doors in an attempt to stop the intrusions. They had posted "no trespass" signs on the land several years before 1967. The nearest one was 35 feet from the house. On June 11, 1967 defendants set "a shotgun trap" in the north bedroom. After Mr. Briney cleaned and oiled his 20-gauge shotgun, the power of which he was well aware, defendants took it to the old house where they secured it to an iron bed with the barrel pointed at the bedroom door. It was rigged with wire from the doorknob to the gun's trigger so it would fire when the door was opened. Briney first pointed the gun so an intruder would be hit in the stomach but at Mrs. Briney's suggestion it was lowered to hit the legs. He admitted he did so "because I was mad and tired of being tormented" but "he did not intend to injure anyone." He gave no explanation of why he used a loaded shell and set it to hit a person already in the house. Tin was nailed over the bedroom window. The spring gun could not be seen from the outside. No warning of its presence was posted.

Plaintiff lived with his wife and worked regularly as a gasoline station attendant in Eddyville, seven miles from the old house. He had observed it for several years while hunting in the area and considered it as being abandoned. He knew it had been uninhabited. In 1967 the area around the house was covered with high weeds. Prior to July 16, 1967 plaintiff and McDonough had been to the premises and found several old bottles and fruit jars which they took and added to their collection of antiques. On the latter date about 9:30 P.M. they made a second trip to the Briney property. They entered the house by removing a board from a porch window which was without glass. While McDonough was looking around the kitchen area plaintiff went to another part of the house. As he started to open the north bedroom door the shotgun went off striking him in the right leg above the ankle bone. Much of his leg, including part of the tibia, was blown away. Only by McDonough's assistance was plaintiff able to get out of the house and after crawling some distance was put in his vehicle and rushed to a doctor and then to a hospital. He remained in the hospital 40 days. . . .

There was undenied medical testimony plaintiff had a permanent deformity, a loss of tissue, and a shortening of the leg.

The record discloses plaintiff to trial time had incurred $710 medical expense, $2056.85 for hospital service, $61.80 for orthopedic service and $750 as loss of earnings. In addition thereto the trial court submitted to the jury the question of damages for pain and suffering and for future disability.

III. Plaintiff testified he knew he had no right to break and enter the house with intent to steal bottles and fruit jars therefrom. He further testified he had entered a plea of guilty to larceny in the nighttime of property of less than $20 value from a private building. He stated he had been fined $50 and costs and paroled during good behavior from a 60-day jail sentence. Other than minor traffic charges this was plaintiff's first brush with the law. On this civil case appeal it is not our prerogative to review the disposition made of the criminal charge against him.

IV. The main thrust of defendants' defense in the trial court and on this appeal is that "the law permits use of a spring gun in a dwelling or warehouse for the purpose of preventing the unlawful entry of a burglar or thief." They repeated this contention in their exceptions to the trial court's instructions 2, 5, and 6. They took no exception to the trial court's statement of the issues or to other instructions.

In the statement of issues the trial court stated plaintiff and his companion committed a felony when they broke and entered defendants' house. In instruction 2 the court referred to the early case history of the use of spring guns and stated under the law their use was prohibited except to prevent the commission of felonies of violence and where human life is in danger. The instruction included a statement [that] breaking and entering is not a felony of violence.

Instruction 5 stated: "You are hereby instructed that one may use reasonable force in the protection of his property, but such right is subject to the qualification that one may not use such means of force as will take human life or inflict great bodily injury. Such is the rule even though the injured party is a trespasser and is in violation of the law himself."

Instruction 6 stated: "An owner of premises is prohibited from willfully or intentionally injuring a trespasser by means of force that either takes life or inflicts great bodily injury; and therefore a person owning a premise is prohibited from setting out 'spring guns' and like dangerous devices which will likely take life or inflict great bodily injury, for the purpose of harming trespassers. The fact that the trespasser may be acting in violation of the law does not change the rule. The only time when such conduct of setting a 'spring gun' or a like dangerous device is justified would be when the trespasser was committing a felony of violence or a felony punishable by death, or where the trespasser was endangering human life by his act."

Instruction 7, to which defendants made no objection or exception, stated: "To entitle the plaintiff to recover for compensatory damages, the burden of proof is upon him to establish by a preponderance of the evidence each and all of the following propositions:

> "1. That defendants erected a shotgun trap in a vacant house on land owned by defendant, Bertha L. Briney, on or about June 11, 1967, which fact was known only by them, to protect household goods from trespassers and thieves.
>
> "2. That the force used by defendants was in excess of that force reasonably necessary and which persons are entitled to use in the protection of their property.
>
> "3. That plaintiff was injured and damaged and the amount thereof.
>
> "4. That plaintiff's injuries and damages resulted directly from the discharge of the shotgun trap which was set and used by defendants."

The overwhelming weight of authority, both textbook and case law, supports the trial court's statement of the applicable principles of law.

Prosser on Torts, Third Edition, pages 116-118, states:

> ". . . the law has always placed a higher value upon human safety than upon mere rights in property, it is the accepted rule that there is no privilege to use any force calculated to cause death or serious bodily injury to repel the threat to land or chattels, unless there is also such a threat to the defendant's personal safety as to justify a self-defense. . . . Spring guns and other man-killing devices are not justifiable against a mere trespasser, or even a petty thief. They are privileged only against those upon whom the landowner, if he were present in person would be free to inflict injury of the same kind." . . .

In Hooker v. Miller, 37 Iowa 613, we held defendant vineyard owner liable for damages resulting from a spring gun shot although plaintiff was a trespasser and there to steal grapes. At pages 614, 615, this statement is made: "This court has held that a mere trespass against property other than a dwelling is not a sufficient justification to authorize the use of a deadly weapon by the owner in its defense; and that if death results in such a case it will be murder, though the killing be actually necessary to prevent the trespass. The State v. Vance, 17 Iowa 138." At page 617 this court said: "[T]respassers and other inconsiderable violators of the law are not to be visited by barbarous punishments or prevented by inhuman inflictions of bodily injuries."

The facts in Allison v. Fiscus, 156 Ohio 120, 100 N.E.2d 237, 44 A.L.R.2d 369, decided in 1951, are very similar to the case at bar. There plaintiff's right to damages was recognized for injuries received when he feloniously broke a door latch and started to enter defendant's warehouse with intent to steal. As he entered a trap of two sticks of dynamite buried under the doorway by defendant owner was set off and plaintiff seriously injured. The court held the question whether a particular trap was justified as a use of reasonable and necessary force against a trespasser engaged in the commission of a felony should have been submitted to the jury. The Ohio Supreme Court recognized plaintiff's right to recover punitive or exemplary damages in addition to compensatory damages. . . .

In Wisconsin, Oregon and England the use of spring guns and similar devices is specifically made unlawful by statute. 44 A.L.R., section 3, pages 386, 388.

The legal principles stated by the trial court in instructions 2, 5, and 6 are well established and supported by the authorities cited and quoted supra. There is no merit in defendants' objections and exceptions thereto. Defendants' various motions based on the same reasons stated in exceptions to instructions were properly overruled. . . .

Study and careful consideration of defendants' contentions on appeal reveal no reversible error.

Affirmed.

All Justices concur except LARSON, J., who dissents.

LARSON, J.

I respectfully dissent, first, because the majority wrongfully assumes that by installing a spring gun in the bedroom of their unoccupied house the defendants intended to shoot any intruder who attempted to enter the room. Under the record presented here, that was a fact question. Unless it is held that these property owners are liable for any injury to an intruder from such a device regardless of the intent with which it is installed, liability under these pleadings must rest upon two definite issues of fact, i.e., did the defendants intend to shoot the invader, and if so, did they employ unnecessary and unreasonable force against him?

It is my feeling that the majority oversimplifies the impact of this case on the law, not only in this but other jurisdictions, and that it has not thought through all the ramifications of this holding.

There being no statutory provisions governing the right of an owner to defend his property by the use of a spring gun or other like device, or of a criminal invader to recover punitive damages when injured by such an instrumentality while breaking into the building of another, our interest and attention are directed to what should be the court determination of public policy in these matters. On both issues we are faced with a case of first impression. We should accept the task and clearly establish the law in this jurisdiction hereafter. I would hold there is no absolute liability for injury to a criminal intruder by setting up such a device on his property, and unless done with an intent to kill or seriously injure the intruder, I would absolve the owner from liability other than for negligence. I would also hold the court had no jurisdiction to allow punitive damages when the intruder was engaged in a serious criminal offense such as breaking and entering with intent to steal.

It appears to me that the learned trial court was and the majority is now confused as to the basis of liability under the circumstances revealed. Certainly, the trial court's instructions did nothing to clarify the law in this jurisdiction for the jury. Timely objections to Instructions Nos. 2, 5, and 6 were made by the defendants, and thereafter the court should have been aware of the questions of liability left unresolved, i.e., whether in this jurisdiction we by judicial declaration bar the use in an unoccupied building of spring guns or other devices capable of inflicting serious injury or death on an intruder regardless of the intent with which they are installed, or whether such an intent is a vital element which must be proven in order to establish liability for an injury inflicted upon a criminal invader.

Although the court told the jury the plaintiff had the burden to prove "That the force used by defendants was in excess of that force reasonably necessary and which persons are entitled to use in the protection of their property," it utterly failed to tell the jury it could find the installation was not made with the intent or purpose of striking or injuring the plaintiff. There was considerable evidence to that effect. As I shall point out, both defendants stated the installation was made for the purpose of scaring or frightening away any intruder, not to seriously injure him. It may be that the evidence would support a finding of an intent to injure the intruder, but obviously that important issue was never adequately or clearly submitted to the jury.

Unless, then, we hold for the first time that liability for death or injury in such cases is absolute, the matter should be remanded for a jury determination of defendants' intent in installing the device under instructions usually given to a jury on the issue of intent. . . .

If, after proper instructions, the finder of fact determines that the gun was set with an intent and purpose to kill or inflict great bodily injury on an intruder, then and only then may it be said liability is established unless the property so protected is shown to be an occupied dwelling house. Of course, under this concept, if the finder of fact determines the gun set in an unoccupied house was intended to do no more than to frighten the intruder or sting him a bit, no liability would be incurred under such pleadings as are now presented. If such a concept of the law were adopted in Iowa, we would have here a question for the fact-finder or jury as to whether the gun was willfully and intentionally set so as to seriously injure the thief or merely scare him away.

I feel the better rule is that an owner of buildings housing valuable property may employ the use of spring guns or other devices intended to repel but not seriously injure an intruder who enters his secured premises with or without a criminal intent, but I do not advocate its general use, for there may also be liability for negligent installation of such a device. What I mean to say is that under such circumstances as we have here the issue as to whether the set was with an intent to seriously injure or kill an intruder is a question of fact that should be left to the jury under proper instructions, and that the mere setting of such a device with a resultant serious injury should not as a matter of law establish liability.

In the case of a mere trespass able authorities have reasoned that absolute liability may rightfully be fixed on the landowner for injuries to the trespasser because very little damage could be inflicted upon the property owner and the danger is great that a child or other innocent trespasser might be seriously injured by the device. In such matters they say no privilege to set up the device should be recognized by the courts regardless of the owner's intent. I agree.

On the other hand, where the intruder may pose a danger to the inhabitants of a dwelling, the privilege of using such a device to repel has been recognized by most authorities, and the mere setting thereof in the dwelling has not been held to create liability for an injury as a matter of law. In such cases intent and the reasonableness of the force would seem relevant to liability.

Although I am aware of the often-repeated statement that personal rights are more important than property rights, where the owner has stored his valuables representing his life's accumulations, his livelihood business, his tools and implements, and his treasured antiques as appears in the case at bar, and where the evidence is sufficient to sustain a finding that the installation was intended only as a warning to ward off thieves and criminals, I can see no compelling reason why the use of such a device alone would create liability as a matter of law. . . .

In the case at bar, as I have pointed out, there is a sharp conflict in the evidence. The physical facts and certain admissions as to how the gun was aimed would tend to support a finding of intent to injure, while the direct testimony of both defendants was that the gun was placed so it would "hit the floor eventually" and that it was set "low so it couldn't kill anybody." Mr. Briney testified, "My purpose in setting up the gun was not to injure somebody. I thought more or less that the gun would be at a distance of where anyone would grab the door, it would scare them," and in setting the angle of the gun to hit the lower part of the door, he said, "I didn't think it would go through quite that hard."

If the law in this jurisdiction permits, which I think it does, an explanation of the setting of a spring gun to repel invaders of certain private property, then the intent with which the set is made is a vital element in the liability issue.

In view of the failure to distinguish and clearly give the jury the basis upon which it should determine that liability issue, I would reverse and remand the entire case for a new trial. . . .

Being convinced that there was reversible error in the court's instructions, that the issue of intent in placing the spring gun was not clearly presented to the jury . . . I would reverse and remand the matter for a new trial. . . .

The problem of liability for harm caused by spring guns has been before courts and legislatures for many years. One of the earliest reported cases is Bird v. Holbrook, 4 Bing. 628, 130 Eng. Rep. 911 (C.P. 1828), which imposed liability on a defendant who used a spring gun to protect prize tulips grown in a walled garden. The plaintiff, a teenager seeking to impress the female servant of defendant's neighbor by retrieving a pea-hen that had escaped into the tulip garden, was injured by defendant's trap.

Only rarely have defendants escaped liability in the case of spring guns, in part because the use of such devices is so suggestive of an indiscriminate and malicious intent. A similar, but more problematic, set of cases involves the use of unmarked cables or chains to block off properties from access by motorcycles or similar vehicles. See, e.g., Commonwealth v. Guffey, 244 S.W.3d 79 (Ky. 2008); Humphrey v. Glenn, 167 S.W.3d 680 (Mo. 2005). As a means of protecting property from trespassers, such devices can prove as lethal as spring guns, but the success of plaintiffs has been considerably more limited.

The Louisiana legislature enacted the following statute (amended in 2006), apparently in reaction to a large number of carjackings that occurred in the 1990s:

> A. A homicide is justifiable: . . .
>
> (3) When committed against a person whom one reasonably believes to be likely to use any unlawful force against a person present in a dwelling or a place of business, or when committed against a person whom one reasonably believes is attempting to use any unlawful force against a person present in a motor vehicle as defined in R.S. 32:1(40), while committing or attempting to commit a burglary or robbery of such dwelling, business, or motor vehicle.
>
> (4)(a) When committed by a person lawfully inside a dwelling, a place of business, or a motor vehicle as defined in R.S. 32:1(40), against a person who is attempting to make an unlawful entry into the dwelling, place of business, or motor vehicle, or who has made an unlawful entry into the dwelling, place of business, or motor vehicle, and the person committing the homicide reasonably believes that the use of deadly force is necessary to prevent the entry or to compel the intruder to leave the premises or motor vehicle.

La. Rev. Stat. art.14 §20. Additional sections of the statute emphasize that the user of such force has no duty to retreat in the face of a threat:

> C. A person who is not engaged in unlawful activity and who is in a place where he or she has a right to be shall have no duty to retreat before using deadly force as provided for in this Section, and may stand his or her ground and meet force with force.

D. No finder of fact shall be permitted to consider the possibility of retreat as a factor in determining whether or not the person who used deadly force had a reasonable belief that deadly force was reasonable and apparently necessary to prevent a violent or forcible felony involving life or great bodily harm or to prevent the unlawful entry. [Id.]

The statute does not explicitly address civil liability, but one may reasonably assume that defendants will be allowed similar privileges in battery actions. R.S. 32:1(40) defines "motor vehicle" as "every vehicle which is self-propelled, and every vehicle which is propelled by electric power obtained from overhead trolley wires, but not operated upon rails, but excluding a motorized bicycle."

Law and Policy: Why Should We Care About Sneak Thieves?

Katko v. Briney provides an opportunity to develop and apply the ideas presented in the earlier law and policy note following *Garratt,* above. When the majority opinion quotes Prosser's statement that "the law has always placed a higher value upon human safety than upon mere rights in property," it appears that the noninstrumentalists have carried the day. Professor Fletcher would, presumably, conclude that when the Brineys retaliated against sneak thieves with life-threatening force, they were creating a nonreciprocal risk of injury, and thus in fairness should be liable to their victim. That would clearly be the case if the Brineys, angry at the world, had aimed their shotgun to shoot a passerby in the road. But what about a sneak thief who breaks and enters the Brineys' farmhouse? In a manner of speaking, the sneak thief is the one creating a nonreciprocal risk, inasmuch as he is the one who knowingly commits a wrong to the Brineys in the first instance, without any possible justification. Can you explain the rule in Katko v. Briney in noninstrumental/fairness terms, with or without using the concept of nonreciprocity?

In any event, instrumental/efficiency analysts would seem to have an especially hard time explaining why tort law should invariably favor human safety over property, without inquiring from case to case into the comparative costs of sacrificing one interest or the other. Professor (now Judge) Posner criticized the traditional rule in Katko v. Briney on exactly this basis:

> [N]either blanket permission nor blanket prohibition of spring guns and other methods of using deadly force to protect property interests is likely to be the rule of liability that minimizes the relevant costs. What is needed is a standard of reasonableness that permits the courts to weigh such considerations as the value of the property at stake, its location (which bears not only on the difficulty of protecting it by other means but also on the likelihood of innocent trespass), what kind of warning was given, the deadliness of the device (there is no reason to recognize a privilege to kill when adequate protection can be assured by a device that only wounds), the character of the conflicting activities, the trespasser's care or negligence, and the cost of avoiding interference by other means (including storing the property elsewhere). . . .
>
> All things considered, the approach to tort questions sketched here seems decidedly superior to the "method of maxims" — the pseudo-logical deduction of rules from essentially empty formulas such as "no man should be permitted to do indirectly what he would be forbidden to do directly" or "the interest in property can never outweigh the value of a human life" — that plays so large a role in certain kinds of legal scholarship. . . .

Are you comfortable with this instrumental/efficiency approach? Psychological studies suggest that many of us, in fact, are not comfortable with making explicit tradeoffs between categories that are considered "sacred" (e.g., human life) and those that are considered "profane" (e.g., money). See Alan Page Fiske & Philip E. Tetlock, Taboo Trade-offs: Reactions to Transactions that Transgress Spheres of Justice, 18 Pol. Psychol. 255, 256 (1997); Philip E. Tetlock et al., The Psychology of the Unthinkable: Taboo Trade-Offs, Forbidden Base Rates, and Heretical Counterfactuals, 78 J. Personality & Soc. Psychol. 853, 854 (2000). Observe that by implication the instrumental/efficiency approach would allow a life to be taken under circumstances where that was the least costly alternative from an overall social welfare perspective. Is it appropriate to place values on — and in a real sense "spend" — human lives in this manner? Consider the following excerpt from Professor Guido Calabresi, another prominent spokesperson for what we here describe as the *efficiency rationale* (The Cost of Accidents 17-18 (1970)):

> Our society is not committed to preserving life at any cost. In its broadest sense, the rather unpleasant notion that we are willing to destroy lives should be obvious. Wars are fought. The University of Mississippi is integrated at the risk of losing lives. But what is more pertinent to the study of accident law, though perhaps equally obvious, is that lives are spent not only when the *quid pro quo* is some great moral principle, but also when it is a matter of convenience. Ventures are undertaken that, statistically at least, are certain to cost lives. Thus we build a tunnel under Mont Blanc because it is essential to the Common Market and cuts down the traveling time from Rome to Paris, though we know that about one man per kilometer of tunnel will die. We take planes and cars rather than safer, slower means of travel. And perhaps most telling, we use relatively safe equipment rather than the safest imaginable because — and it is not a bad reason — the safest costs too much. It should be apparent that while some of these accident-causing activities also result in diminution of accidents — the Mont Blanc tunnel may well save more lives by diminishing traffic fatalities than it took to build it — this explanation does not come close to justifying most accident-causing activities. Railroad grade crossings are used because they are cheap, not because they save more lives than they take.

One interesting example of the lack of commitment "to preserving life at any cost" is the conclusion some years ago of the National Highway Traffic Safety Administration, a part of the U.S. Department of Transportation, not to require trucks to be equipped with "underride protection." If a truck were to stop short, a car immediately behind it might not be able to stop in time to avoid a collision. The front of the car might then go under the rear of a large truck, so that the first impact of the car with the truck would be by the car's windshield, which results in a high risk of death to the front seat occupants of the car. Underride protection in the form of a metal bar attached to the rear of the truck would prevent direct windshield-truck contacts. The NHTSA declined to require underride protection when it determined that underride protection on trucks would cost $5 million for each life saved, and that any cost over $200,000 per life saved would be societally unacceptable. Today, the monetary value of life for federal agency decisionmaking has gone up considerably, as agencies explicitly adopt a value of around $7 million per life saved when using cost-benefit analysis to justify their regulations. Still, whatever the number, its logical implication is that some lives are not "worth" saving.

Do the preceding examples of situations in which society refuses to "preserve life at all costs" convince you that there is no underlying validity to the maxim, recited in *Katko,* that tort law should not tolerate conduct that risks life to preserve property? Legal economist W. Kip Viscusi has argued that corporate actors should be given a safe harbor from tort liability when they use monetary valuations of life in corporate decisionmaking that are similar to those of federal agencies. See W. Kip Viscusi, Pricing Lives for Corporate Risk

Decisions, 68 Vand. L. Rev. 1117 (2015). Are situations like *Katko,* where a defendant deliberately seeks to injure another, fundamentally different from the kinds of general safety compromises that society makes concerning railroad crossings and truck bumpers? See John Finnis, Allocating Risks and Suffering: Some Hidden Traps, 38 Clev. St. L. Rev. 193 (1990). Even if it is not so clear, as between the noninstrumental/fairness and the instrumental/efficiency camps, who has the better of the debate over Prosser's "human life wins over property" assertion, is it not clear that the assertion is inconsistent with Professor Abel's "tort law as a capitalist tool" thesis (see p. 41, above)? Prosser's statement and the rule in *Katko* cut against, rather than support, the idea that tort law is designed to further the interests of the propertied classes, do they not?

f. Necessity

Ploof v. Putnam

81 Vt. 471, 71 A. 188 (1908)

Munson, J. It is alleged as the ground of recovery that on the 13th day of November, 1904, the defendant was the owner of a certain island in Lake Champlain, and of a certain dock attached thereto, which island and dock were then in charge of the defendant's servant; that the plaintiff was then possessed of and sailing upon said lake a certain loaded sloop, on which were the plaintiff and his wife and two minor children; that there then arose a sudden and violent tempest, whereby the sloop and the property and persons therein were placed in great danger of destruction; that to save these from destruction or injury the plaintiff was compelled to, and did, moor the sloop to defendant's dock; that the defendant by his servant unmoored the sloop, whereupon it was driven upon the shore by the tempest, without the plaintiff's fault; and that the sloop and its contents were thereby destroyed, and the plaintiff and his wife and children cast into the lake and upon the shore, receiving injuries.

This claim is set forth in two counts; one in trespass, charging that the defendant by his servant with force and arms wilfully and designedly unmoored the sloop; the other in case, alleging that it was the duty of the defendant by his servant to permit the plaintiff to moor his sloop to the dock, and to permit it to remain so moored during the continuance of the tempest, but that the defendant by his servant, in disregard of this duty, negligently, carelessly and wrongfully unmoored the sloop. Both counts are demurred to generally. [The demurrer was overruled and defendant appeals.]

There are many cases in the books which hold that necessity, and an inability to control movements inaugurated in the proper exercise of a strict right, will justify entries upon land and interferences with personal property that would otherwise have been trespasses. . . .

A traveller on a highway, who finds it obstructed from a sudden and temporary cause, may pass upon the adjoining land without becoming a trespasser, because of the necessity.

An entry upon land to save goods which are in danger of being lost or destroyed by water or fire is not a trespass. In Proctor v. Adams, 113 Mass. 376, 18 Am. Rep. 500, the defendant went upon the plaintiff's beach for the purpose of saving and restoring to the lawful owner a boat which had been driven ashore and was in danger of being carried off by the sea; and it was held no trespass.

This doctrine of necessity applies with special force to the preservation of human life. One assaulted and in peril of his life may run through the close of another to escape from his assailant. One may sacrifice the personal property of another to save his life or the lives of his fellows. In Mouse's Case, 12 Co. 63, the defendant was sued for taking and carrying away the plaintiff's casket and its contents. It appeared that the ferryman of Gravesend took forty-seven passengers into his barge to pass to London, among whom were the plaintiff and defendant; and the barge being upon the water a great tempest happened, and a strong wind, so that the barge and all the passengers were in danger of being lost if certain ponderous things were not cast out, and the defendant thereupon cast out the plaintiff's casket. It was resolved that in case of necessity, to save the lives of the passengers, it was lawful for the defendant, being a passenger, to cast the plaintiff's casket out of the barge; that if the ferryman surcharge the barge the owner shall have his remedy upon the surcharge against the ferryman, but that if there be no surcharge, and the danger accrue only by the act of God, as by tempest, without fault of the ferryman, every one ought to bear his loss, to safeguard the life of a man.

It is clear that an entry upon the land of another may be justified by necessity, and that the declaration before us discloses a necessity for mooring the sloop. But the defendant questions the sufficiency of the counts because they do not negative the existence of natural objects to which the plaintiff could have moored with equal safety. The allegations are, in substance, that the stress of a sudden and violent tempest compelled the plaintiff to moor to defendant's dock to save his sloop and the people in it. The averment of necessity is complete, for it covers not only the necessity of mooring, but the necessity of mooring to the dock; and the details of the situation which created this necessity, whatever the legal requirements regarding them, are matters of proof and need not be alleged. It is certain that the rule suggested cannot be held applicable irrespective of circumstance, and the question must be left for adjudication upon proceedings had with reference to the evidence or the charge. . . .

Judgment affirmed and case remanded.

Professor Vogel has conducted research into the social and cultural forces at work in Vermont at the time that Ploof v. Putnam was decided. See Joan Vogel, Cases in Context: Lake Champlain Wars, Gentrification and *Ploof v. Putnam,* 45 St. Louis U. L.J. 791 (2001). From a reading of the Vermont Supreme Court's decision, one might assume that the Ploofs were an average American family spending a day sailing on Lake Champlain, when an unexpected storm suddenly arose. When the Ploofs sought harmless refuge on a nearby island, a mean-spirited groundskeeper cast the family back into the storm. In fact, as Professor Vogel explains, the Ploofs were actually a poor family who lived on their boat, transporting firewood and other goods. The Ploofs were a constant irritation to the local gentry, of which Putnam was a member, and were regularly accused of stealing from the lavish summer homes that lined the shores of the lake. Indeed, the Ploofs were notoriously known as the "pirates of Lake Champlain." Thus, when Putnam's caretaker cast the Ploofs into the storm on that fateful November day, he may not have been acting out of unprovoked malice, as one might assume from reading the Vermont court's factually sparse decision. Seen through the caretaker's eyes, he may have been attempting to protect his master's property from a well-known band of ne'er-do-wells who, for all he knew, were coming ashore to do mischief (although it bears noting that Putnam's attorney never argued that the Ploofs actually threatened his client's property).

Seen through a sociologist's eyes, the case becomes richer still. The Ploofs' ill reputation among local elites may have been influenced by ethnic and class bias. Vermont, like much of the Northeast, was characterized by strong bigotry against French Canadians in the late nineteenth and early twentieth centuries, and the Ploofs, as descendants of French Canadian immigrants who spoke French and were Catholic, were likely stigmatized in this way. At the time, negative stereotypes and pseudo-scientific generalizations were used to justify the inferior social and economic status to which French Canadian descendants were relegated in the Northeast. Indeed, "[d]uring the 1920s, the Ploofs were the subject of a famous Vermont Eugenics survey that was designed to illustrate the social costs of allowing 'degenerate families' to reproduce." Id. at 799. Additionally, Lake Champlain during this time experienced significant class conflict between longtime residents, who were generally poor, and newer seasonal residents, who began building luxury vacation homes around the lake. "Gentrification of lakeshore properties made poorer Vermonters unwelcome in places where they may have worked for centuries." Id. The Ploofs' status as landless boat dwellers who scratched out a living through odd jobs likely contributed to the disdain with which they were viewed in well-off quarters. In short, the case implicates social disputes much larger than the dock spat that gave rise to it.

Vincent v. Lake Erie Transportation Co.

109 Minn. 456, 124 N.W. 221 (1910)

Action in the district court for St. Louis county to recover $1,200 for damage to plaintiffs' wharf, caused by defendant negligently keeping its vessel tied to it. The defendant in its answer alleged that a portion of the cargo was consigned to plaintiffs' dock and on November 27, 1905, its vessel was placed alongside at the place and in the manner designated by plaintiffs and the discharge of cargo continued until ten o'clock that night, that by the time the discharge of cargo was completed the wind had attained so great a velocity the master and crew were powerless to move the vessel. The case was tried before Ensign, J., who denied the defendant's motion to direct a verdict in its favor, and a jury which rendered a verdict in favor of plaintiffs for $500. From an order denying defendant's motion for judgment notwithstanding the verdict or for a new trial, it appealed. Affirmed.

O'Brien, J. The steamship Reynolds, owned by the defendant, was for the purpose of discharging her cargo on November 27, 1905, moored to plaintiff's dock in Duluth. While the unloading of the boat was taking place a storm from the northeast developed, which at about ten o'clock p.m., when the unloading was completed, had so grown in violence that the wind was then moving at fifty miles per hour and continued to increase during the night. There is some evidence that one, and perhaps two, boats were able to enter the harbor that night, but it is plain that navigation was practically suspended from the hour mentioned until the morning of the twenty-ninth, when the storm abated, and during that time no master would have been justified in attempting to navigate his vessel, if he could avoid doing so. After the discharge of the cargo the Reynolds signaled for a tug to tow her from the dock, but none could be obtained because of the severity of the storm. If the lines holding the ship to the dock had been cast off, she would doubtless have drifted away; but, instead, the lines were kept fast, and as soon as one parted or chafed it was replaced, sometimes with a larger one. The vessel lay upon the outside of the dock, her bow to the east, the wind and waves striking her starboard quarter with such force that she was constantly being lifted and thrown against the dock, resulting in its damage, as found by the jury, to the amount of $500.

We are satisfied that the character of the storm was such that it would have been highly imprudent for the master of the Reynolds to have attempted to leave the dock or to have permitted his vessel to drift away from it. One witness testified upon the trial that the vessel could have been warped into a slip, and that, if the attempt to bring the ship into the slip had failed, the worst that could have happened would be that the vessel would have been blown ashore upon a soft and muddy bank. The witness was not present in Duluth at the time of the storm, and, while he may have been right in his conclusions, those in charge of the dock and the vessel at the time of the storm were not required to use the highest human intelligence, nor were they required to resort to every possible experiment which could be suggested for the preservation of their property. Nothing more was demanded of them than ordinary prudence and care, and the record in this case fully sustains the contention of the appellant that, in holding the vessel fast to the dock, those in charge of her exercised good judgment and prudent seamanship.

It is claimed by the respondent that it was negligence to moor the boat at an exposed part of the wharf, and to continue in that position after it became apparent that the storm was to be more than usually severe. We do not agree with this position. The part of the wharf where the vessel was moored appears to have been commonly used for that purpose. It was situated within the harbor at Duluth, and must, we think, be considered a proper and safe place, and would undoubtedly have been such during what would be considered a very severe storm. The storm which made it unsafe was one which surpassed in violence any which might have reasonably been anticipated.

The appellant contends by ample assignments of error that, because its conduct during the storm was rendered necessary by prudence and good seamanship under conditions over which it had no control, it cannot be held liable for any injury resulting to the property of others, and claims that the jury should have been so instructed. An analysis of the charge given by the trial court is not necessary, as in our opinion the only question for the jury was the amount of damages which the plaintiffs were entitled to recover, and no complaint is made upon that score.

The situation was one in which the ordinary rules regulating property rights were suspended by forces beyond human control, and if, without the direct intervention of some act by the one sought to be held liable, the property of another was injured, such injury must be attributed to the act of God, and not to the wrongful act of the person sought to be charged. If during the storm the Reynolds had entered the harbor, and while there had become disabled and been thrown against the plaintiffs' dock, the plaintiffs could not have recovered. Again, if while attempting to hold fast to the dock the lines had parted, without any negligence, and the vessel carried against some other boat or dock in the harbor, there would be no liability upon her owner. But here those in charge of the vessel deliberately and by their direct efforts held her in such a position that the damage to the dock resulted, and having thus preserved the ship at the expense of the dock, it seems to us that her owners are responsible to the dock owners to the extent of the injury inflicted.

[Discussion of earlier cases, including Ploof v. Putnam, above, is omitted.] Theologians hold that a starving man may, without moral guilt, take what is necessary to sustain life; but it could hardly be said that the obligation would not be upon such person to pay the value of the property so taken when he became able to do so. And so public necessity, in times of war or peace, may require the taking of private property for public purposes; but under our system of jurisprudence compensation must be made.

Let us imagine in this case that for the better mooring of the vessel those in charge of her had appropriated a valuable cable lying upon the dock. No matter how justifiable such appropriation might have been, it would not be claimed that, because of the overwhelming necessity of the situation, the owner of the cable could not recover its value.

This is not a case where life or property was menaced by any object or thing belonging to the plaintiffs, the destruction of which became necessary to prevent the threatened disaster. Nor is it a case where, because of the act of God, or unavoidable accident, the infliction of the injury was beyond the control of the defendant, but is one where the defendant prudently and advisedly availed itself of the plaintiffs' property for the purpose of preserving its own more valuable property, and the plaintiffs are entitled to compensation for the injury done.

Order affirmed.

LEWIS, J. (dissenting). I dissent. . . .

In my judgment, if the boat was lawfully in position at the time the storm broke, and the master could not, in the exercise of due care, have left that position without subjecting his vessel to the hazards of the storm, then the damage to the dock, caused by the pounding of the boat, was the result of an inevitable accident. If the master was in the exercise of due care, he was not at fault. The reasoning of the opinion admits that if the ropes, or cables, first attached to the dock had not parted, or if, in the first instance, the master had used the stronger cables, there would be no liability. If the master could not, in the exercise of reasonable care, have anticipated the severity of the storm and sought a place of safety before it became impossible, why should he be required to anticipate the severity of the storm, and, in the first instance, use the stronger cables?

I am of the opinion that one who constructs a dock to the navigable line of waters, and enters into contractual relations with the owner of a vessel to moor the same, takes the risk of damage to his dock by a boat caught there by a storm, which event could not have been avoided in the exercise of due care, and further, that the legal status of the parties in such a case is not changed by renewal of cables to keep the boat from being cast adrift at the mercy of the tempest.

JAGGARD, J. I concur with Lewis, J.

The Restatement (Second) of Torts combines the principles of *Ploof* and *Vincent* in §197, recognizing a necessity-based privilege (often described as *qualified* or *incomplete*) to enter the land of another in order to avoid serious harm to one's person, land, or chattels, or to those of a third person. This privilege is coupled with an obligation on the part of the entrant to pay for whatever harm he causes. In the end, what turns on the characterization of the entry as privileged in cases of this sort, assuming that the entrant must pay for the harm he causes regardless of whether his entry is privileged?

Restatement §263 creates a similar privilege regarding chattels; that is, an actor is privileged to damage the chattels of another in order to avoid serious harm. Do you agree with the proposition that one person should be privileged to sacrifice the property of another merely to safeguard his own possessions? Professor George C. Christie has strongly criticized the Restatement's stance on this issue. He concludes that while the law should privilege an actor to harm another's property when such actions are necessary to save human life, it is both legally and morally wrong to permit one person to sacrifice the private property of another simply to safeguard his own belongings, even if the privileged party must later pay for the damage he has caused. See George C. Christie, The Defense of Necessity Considered from the Legal and Moral Points of View, 48 Duke L.J. 975 (1999).

A decision in the Ninth Circuit suggests the fact patterns involved in *Ploof* and *Vincent* are apt to recur today. In Protectus Alpha Navigation Co. v. North Pacific Grain Growers, Inc., 767 F.2d 1379 (9th Cir. 1985), the plaintiff's vessel was refueling at the defendant's dock when the vessel caught fire. Local fire fighters and the Coast Guard placed fire fighting equipment on the dock. The fire fighting efforts brought the flames under control, and the fire would have been extinguished within minutes. The defendant's dock manager, however, ordered the vessel cast off and, with the help of another of defendant's employees, did so contrary to the instructions of the fire fighters. The vessel drifted downstream with several fire fighters left on board, and the now unopposed fire destroyed it. Plaintiff sued defendant for negligence. The trial court found for the plaintiff and awarded \$7,045,000 in general damages, \$2,032,760 in prejudgment interest, and \$500,000 in punitive damages for a grand total of \$9,577,760. On appeal the Ninth Circuit affirmed, holding that the dock manager's conduct in disobeying the fire fighters had violated state law and was therefore negligence per se. What result if the dock manager had acted before the fire fighters arrived?

Problem 7

Mark Brown and two high school friends were deer hunting in a state forest when caught by a late November blizzard. Poorly dressed for the rapidly deteriorating conditions, Brown and his companions sought to return quickly to their car, but disagreed over the best route. Brown's friends wanted to retrace the arduous and winding trail they had already taken, while Brown argued that taking a straight line over two successive ridges should bring them directly to the trailhead.

Unable to agree, the group split up, and Brown headed toward the first ridge. In the driving snow and dwindling light, however, he became lost. After several hours, Brown emerged onto a plowed field, shivering and slightly disoriented from the onset of hypothermia. He stumbled toward a lighted farmhouse in the distance. When he arrived, he held his hunting rifle behind his back to avoid alarming whoever answered his knock. Sarah Ellman, a single mother of two young children, opened the door a crack without undoing the security chain. His speech slurred and disjointed because of his condition, Brown began explaining that he was lost and freezing and needed to come in. Ellman, however, felt immediately fearful. Brown seemed strange and appeared to be hiding something behind his back. Moreover, since recently divorcing her abusive husband, Ellman had been distrustful of men in general. Without fully understanding Brown's situation, she blurted out, "I'm sorry, I can't help," and quickly closed and locked the door.

Brown pounded on the door for several minutes, but to no avail. He then proceeded to a barn on the property, pried open the door, and huddled among some tarps stored in the barn. A search party, launched after his friends reported him missing, found him five hours later. He had suffered additional severe hypothermia and developed frostbite on several toes.

Brown subsequently sued Ellman for his injuries and medical care. Ellman counterclaimed for damage to the barn door and for the value of a pony that had to be destroyed after it wandered from the open door during the storm and was injured in a drainage ditch. What theories of recovery are the parties likely to advance? What defenses are available to Brown and Ellman? What is the likely outcome if the case goes to trial?

g. Miscellaneous Privileges

Some privileges to inflict harmful contacts arise primarily out of the status of the parties. The most notable examples are the privileges that, at least to some extent, protect parents and teachers from battery claims brought on behalf of children they have physically disciplined. The common law justifications for the disciplinary privilege are diverse, with the most dominant themes being the ones suggested by courts such as the Supreme Judicial Court of Maine in Patterson v. Nutter, 7 A. 273, 274 (Me. 1886):

> Free political institutions are possible only where the great body of the people are moral, intelligent, and habituated to self-control, and to obedience to lawful authority. The permanency of such institutions depends largely upon the efficient instruction and training of children in these virtues. It is to secure this permanency that the state provides schools and teachers. Schoolteachers, therefore, have important duties and functions. Much depends upon their ability, skill, and faithfulness. They must *train* as well as instruct their pupils. The acquiring of learning is not the only object of our public schools. To become good citizens, children must be taught self-restraint, obedience, and other civic virtues. To accomplish these desirable ends, the master of a school is necessarily invested with much discretionary power. He is placed in charge sometimes of large numbers of children, perhaps of both sexes, of various ages, temperaments, dispositions, and of various degrees of docility and intelligence. He must govern these pupils, quicken the slothful, spur the indolent, restrain the impetuous, and control the stubborn. He must make rules, give commands, and punish disobedience. What rules, what commands, and what punishments shall be imposed are necessarily largely within the discretion of the master, where none are defined by the school board.

While the underlying justifications of instilling discipline and enforcing order are easy enough to state, it is often difficult, in the context of a particular case, to determine whether the harm inflicted by a parent or a teacher was appropriately related to the social goals underlying the privilege. See, e.g., Peterson v. Baker, 504 F.3d 1331 (11th Cir. 2007) (holding that a teacher was immune from a student's battery claim under Georgia law, because it "was not entirely unreasonable" for the teacher to have grabbed and squeezed the student's neck while attempting to prevent the student from exiting the classroom without permission). The Supreme Court of Iowa, in the case of Tinkham v. Kole, 110 N.W.2d 258 (Iowa 1961), held that the reasonableness of a teacher's action was a question of fact for the jury and offered the following guidance as to the determination of reasonableness (110 N.W.2d at 261):

> But a teacher's right to use physical punishment is a limited one. His immunity from liability in damages requires that the evidence show that the punishment administered was reasonable, and such a showing requires consideration of the nature of the punishment itself, the nature of the pupil's misconduct which gave rise to the punishment, the age and physical condition of the pupil, and the teacher's motive in inflicting the punishment. If consideration of all of these factors indicates that the teacher violated none of the standards implicit in each of them, then he will be held free of liability; but it seems liability will result from proof that the teacher, in administering the punishment, violated any one of such standards. . . .

Cases like *Tinkham* point out that the privilege to impose reasonable discipline possessed by teachers is largely derivative of that held by parents. Teachers, in essence, stand *in loco parentis* during school hours. Yet it should be noted that parents traditionally enjoy additional immunity from liability based simply on the general reluctance of courts to adjudicate disputes between family members. Under this doctrine of intrafamily tort immunity, which also bars tort claims by one spouse against the other, courts decline to hear suits against parents even if the harm inflicted is unrelated to any disciplinary effort and, indeed, even if the conduct violates the criminal law. Growing recognition of the prevalence of violence within marriages has led almost all states to abandon intrafamily tort immunity in the context of claims of spousal abuse. See Sally F. Goldfarb, Violence Against Women and the Persistence of Privacy, 61 Ohio St. L.J. 1, 23 (2000). Parental immunity, however, raises somewhat different issues.

Statistics indicate that approximately 90 percent of American parents occasionally spank or hit their children. Recent research reflects that such punishment may be counterproductive in that it psychologically damages the child, increases social violence in general, leads to children's increased aggression and anger, and creates the propensity in children who receive such violence to treat their children similarly. Further, substantial evidence shows that corporal punishment is ineffective as a teaching method and can be adequately replaced by non-violent methods that do not lead to harmful social and psychological consequences. See generally Deana Pollard, Banning Child Corporal Punishment, 77 Tul. L. Rev. 575 (2003). See also Tamer Ezer, A Positive Right to Protection for Children, 7 Yale H.R. & Dev. L.J. 1 (2004) (noting that the tools of tort law are insufficient to prevent violence against children and have actually been used to promote violence; thus, the United States should recognize a positive right to protection for children, including freedom from corporal punishment).

Many courts in recent years have partially or wholly abrogated the near absolute tort immunity of parents at common law. While different courts have drawn the line in different places, a frequent reform has been to allow minors to sue their parents for intentional torts (not arising from an effort to impose reasonable discipline) but to continue to bar such claims if the injuries complained of are due to the negligence of the parent. Spears v. Spears, 3 S.W.3d 691 (Ark. 1999); Buono v. Scalia, 817 A.2d 400 (N.J. Super. Ct. 2003). Can you see why such a line might be reconcilable with the judicial concern that allowing tort suits between family members may permanently poison family relations? For another attempt to draw such a line, see Plumley v. Klein, 199 N.W.2d 169, 172-73 (Mich. 1972) (holding that children may sue their parents for injuries suffered as a result of ordinary negligence, provided the negligent acts do not involve the exercise of "reasonable parental authority" or "reasonable parental discretion with respect to the provision of food, clothing, housing . . . and other care"). Intrafamily tort immunities are treated more extensively in Section D of Chapter 4.

In addition to the defenses afforded to parents and teachers, tort law has traditionally recognized a number of other nonconsensual privileges that shield actors from liability for intentionally inflicting harm. Such privileges include those relating to the arrest of lawbreakers and the prevention of crime, the enforcement of military orders, and the recapture of land and possessions. The details of the rules vary, but they all tend to manifest a theme common to the privileges discussed above. The reasonableness of the actor's perception of the need to use force, as well as the reasonableness of the harm actually inflicted, are typically the touchstones upon which the availability of the privilege turns. See, e.g., District of Columbia v. Chinn, 839 A.2d 701 (D.C. 2003) ("Strictly speaking, a police officer effecting an arrest commits a battery. If the officer does not use force beyond that which the officer reasonably believes is necessary, given the conditions apparent to the officer at the time of the arrest, he is clothed with privilege. Otherwise, he has no defense to the battery, at least insofar as it involves the use of excessive force.").

Law and Behavior: Does the One Affect the Other?

As noted earlier, one common hope, especially for instrumentalists, is that the decision regarding liability in the context of a particular case can, aside from officially resolving that conflict, help establish rules of conduct that will deter unnecessary injuries in the future. This assumption regarding the prospective behavioral consequences of tort decisions merits further analysis.

At the outset, a distinction should be drawn between the direct and the indirect effects of legal rules upon primary behavior. Rules that proscribe specific patterns of conduct, as do the rules governing harmful battery, may be said to affect behavior directly when they induce individuals to refrain from engaging in the proscribed conduct. Rules may be said to affect behavior indirectly insofar as they help to reinforce the general moral climate in society which encourages primary actors, unconsciously perhaps, to avoid socially destructive conduct. The difference between direct and indirect effects of rules upon conduct is one of degree. However, as subsequent discussions in these materials will indicate, the distinction between direct and indirect effects is useful, and has been recognized by behavioral scientists and legal scholars investigating the effects of law upon behavior. See, e.g., Lawrence Lessig, The New Chicago School, 27 J. Legal Stud. 661 (1998) (arguing that the law-and-economics approach of the "Old Chicago School" failed to take adequate account of the law's indirect effects on behavior). Clearly, the assumptions in this book up to this point have concerned the direct effects of tort rules upon primary behavior, and it is upon these effects that the remainder of this note will focus.

For legal rules directly and prospectively to affect behavior, at least three conditions must be present: (1) the rules must be known and understood by the persons to whom they are addressed; (2) the addressees must desire, perhaps because of fear of sanctions that may be imposed, to follow the rules; and (3) the addressees must be capable of following, and be in a position to follow, the rules. All three conditions are open to question. First, empirical research suggests that decisionmakers are often unaware of the rules that govern them.[34] Second, people's behavior is influenced by myriad factors which may overwhelm or complicate the influence furnished by tort law. Decisionmakers are swayed by prevailing social norms, by their personal views of right and wrong, by their sense that the rules are legitimate and fair, and by nonmonetary goals such as avoiding social sanctions by peers.[35] In fact, the literature on "motivation crowding-out" has documented instances in which imposing monetary penalties for undesirable conduct can backfire, where monetary

34. See, e.g., Jennifer K. Robbennolt & Valerie P. Hans, The Psychology of Tort Law 2 (2016); Stephen D. Sugarman, Doing Away with Tort Law, 73 Calif. L. Rev. 554, 565 ("[M]any people seem to be ignorant of the threat of tort liability before the first sting"); Gary T. Schwartz, Reality in the Economic Analysis of Tort Law: Does Tort Law Really Deter? 42 UCLA L. Rev. 377, 383 (1994) ([I]ndividuals operate under cognitive and psychological limitations that can prevent them from acting rationally in the face of liability. For example, they may be simply ignorant of the legal rules (and the applications of those rules) that entail a liability threat; or they may psychologically discount the significance of a small chance of a major future liability.").

35. See Tom R. Tyler, Why People Obey the Law (2006); Harold Grasmick & Robert Bursik, Jr. Conscience, Significant Others, and Rational Choice: Extending the Deterrence Model, 24 Law & Soc'y Rev. 837 (1990); Herbert Jacob, Deterrent Effects of Formal and Informal Sanctions, 2 Law & Pol'y 61 (1980).

incentives supplant people's existing social or moral reasons for avoiding bad behavior.[36] Third, people's ability to comport themselves in accordance with law, even if they are aware of the rules and motivated to follow them, is limited by their human psychology. By and large, our emotional states and physiological arousal affect our judgments and behavior.[37] Our cognitive capacities for attention, memory, and self-control are limited.[38] Our natural modes of probabilistic reasoning tend to distort our impressions of risk.[39] Far from contemplating the costs and benefits of each action we take, most of us operate on autopilot most of the time, relying on habits, scripts, mental shortcuts called "heuristics," and other forms of automatic behavior.[40] In short, realists can point to numerous reasons why legal rules may be neither necessary nor sufficient to change behavior.[41]

The first two decisions considered in this chapter illustrate the precarious nature of the behavioral propositions presumed by a deterrence theory of tort law. In the *Vosburg* case, for example, one might argue that the 11-year-old defendant neither understood the law of battery applicable to his acts nor was he, in his capacity as a naturally rambunctious schoolboy, willing or able to conform his conduct to the law. The question might be asked: Do we really think that imposing liability on young Putney will make schoolchildren in Wisconsin behave any better, or any differently?

Before committing yourself to an answer, consider whether it is even relevant that schoolchildren's behavior will or will not be directly affected by this sort of decision. Are the schoolchildren of Wisconsin, after all, the only, or even the primary, addressees of the rules imposing tort liability upon them for their unlawful conduct? Even if schoolchildren are not likely to behave differently simply because liability is imposed in this manner, can the same thing be said of their parents? Might not the court be tacitly assuming that the behavior of schoolchildren will indirectly be affected to the extent that their parents will learn of the decision and be affected by it?

Implicit in this last question is the assumption that adults are more likely than children to be deterred from committing batteries by the threat of tort liability. Clearly, such an assumption seems sensible in most situations. The remote prohibitions of tort law probably offer little leverage over the pugnacious Putneys of the world. Indeed, the relative ineffectiveness of tort law as a deterrent in this context may explain, at least in part, why tort law privileges other actors, such as parents and teachers, to use decidedly more tangible and immediate deterrents, such as reasonable corporal punishment. These actors, of course, may conceivably abuse these privileges, but they are also more likely, as a general matter, to be deterred from doing so by the legal consequences of their conduct.

36. Uri Gneezy & Aldo Rustichini, A Fine is a Price, 29 J. Legal Stud. 1 (2000); Bruno S. Frey & Felix Oberholzer-Gee, The Cost of Price Incentives: An Empirical Analysis of Motivation Crowding-Out, 87 Am. Econ. Rev. 746 (1997); Yuval Feldman & Orly Lobel, The Incentives Matrix: The Comparative Effectiveness of Rewards, Liabilities, Duties, and Protections for Reporting Illegality, 88 Tex. L. Rev. 1151 (2010); Ernst Fehr & Bettina Rockenbach, Detrimental Effects of Sanctions on Human Altruism, 422 Nature 137 (2003).

37. See, e.g., George Loewenstein & Jennifer S. Lerner, The Role of Affect in Decision Making, in Handbook of Affective Sciences 619 (Davidson et al., eds., 2003); Jeremy A. Blumenthal, Law and the Emotions: The Problems of Affective Forecasting, 80 Indiana L.J. 155 (2005); George Loewenstein, Out of Control: Visceral Influences on Human Behavior, 65 Org. Behav. & Hum. Decision Processes 272 (1996).

38. See, e.g., Robbennolt & Hans, *supra* note 34, at 48-51.

39. See generally id., at 42-48 (summarizing the empirical literature demonstrating "a variety of reasons why people might not engage in perfect Hand Formula-style calculations when deciding how to act.").

40. See, e.g., Paul J. Heald & James E. Heald, Mindlessness and Law, 77 Va. L. Rev. 1127 (1991); John A. Bargh & Tonya L. Chartrand, The Unbearable Automaticity of Being, 54 Am. Psychol. 462 (1999).

41. See, e.g., Schwartz, *supra* note 34, at 422-423 (concluding that there is no "one-to-one relationship between the incentives afforded by tort liability rules and the resulting conduct of real-world actors").

However, even granting the existence of a differential in the sensitivity of minors and adults to tort law's commands, questions remain concerning the extent to which the conduct of adults may be directly affected. Clearly, the deterrence potential of tort law will vary according to the circumstances in which the defendant finds himself. An actor responding emotionally and spontaneously to outside stimuli — the defendant in *Courvoisier* who perceived he was being attacked by a street mob, for example — is probably unlikely to weigh potential tort liability in the balance before acting. On the other hand, individuals acting with conscious deliberation — the defendants in *Katko* who set the shotgun trap, for example — may be more likely to consider potential liability; and later would-be trap gun setters might be expected to weigh liability even more heavily, on the reasonable assumption (given the publicity that case received) that Iowans know about the trap gun liability rule. Moreover, within the broad category of deliberate actors, doctors, such as the defendants in *Bang* and *Kennedy,* are probably more likely to be aware of and be affected by the law of battery than are landowners such as the defendants in *Katko.* And perhaps even more than doctors, corporations, such as the defendants in *O'Brien, Barton,* and *Vincent,* are likely to know the law and to attempt to guide their employees' conduct accordingly.

Thus, it may be possible to generalize concerning the deterrence potential of the law of battery in relation to the various categories of actors to whom the rules are addressed. As we move up the scale from the schoolchild in *Vosburg* to the doctors in *Bang* and *Kennedy* to the corporations in *O'Brien, Barton,* and *Vincent,* we move from individuals acting on impulse to professionals and institutions acting with a certain amount of planning and deliberation. It seems safe to assume as a general proposition that the more institutional the actor to whom the rules are addressed, the more likely the actor's behavior is to be affected by those rules. Managers of corporations are more likely than are schoolchildren to know the legal rules governing liability, and are in a better position to ensure that their employees' conduct conforms to those rules. (As institutions, they face the same situations over and over again, and can train their employees regarding what to expect and how to behave.) Returning momentarily to the *Vosburg* case and applying these insights to the problem of trying to affect the behavior of schoolchildren in Wisconsin, consider these questions: If the court in that case were to resolve to hold responsible the person who is in the best position to act effectively to prevent schoolchildren from harming each other, who besides the children or their parents might be prime candidates for liability? How might we describe the basis of that liability?

Bear in mind that we have been speaking in terms of *assumptions* regarding the conditions that determine behavior effects of tort law. Later in these materials we will consider the extent to which these assumptions have been the subject of empirical study by behavioral scientists. From time to time in this book, we will refer to the published work of legal scholars and behavioral scientists for the purpose of testing and exploring basic assumptions regarding the relationship between law and behavior. In the years to come, lawyers will increasingly be required to be familiar with the methods of inquiry and analysis employed by behavioral scientists.

Law and Policy: Taking Stock

At the close of this chapter on the law of battery, it is useful to take stock of the cases and problems we have considered and how they may reflect various sets of underlying, unifying themes. Earlier, we identified several possible explanations of the objectives that lie behind tort law. Tort law may be seen to reflect noninstrumental values relating to fairness among individuals. It may be explained instrumentally as part of a broader effort to increase social welfare by eliminating unnecessary waste and achieving more efficient allocations of scarce (natural and human) resources. Or it may be viewed more skeptically as lacking any basis in underlying normative values, and thus be viewed as part of the existing American political system designed to promote capitalism and traditional liberalist ideology. For that matter, tort law may reflect some other set of values altogether, or be simply the product of random development. While it is a bit early to try to tie all of tort law into a neat package, what follow are brief observations aimed at stimulating your own thinking along these paths.

As observed earlier, the fairness perspective seems most strongly reflected in the "property never outweighs human life" dictum in connection with the use of deadly force to protect property. Neither the efficiency nor the radical critique perspectives appears able to do more than observe that this is an exception to their organizing principles. But what about the Vincent v. Lake Erie decision, in which someone who committed no wrong was forced to pay damages for harm caused to property? Here the efficiency perspective offers an explanation: Liability is imposed on the intruder (in *Vincent,* the boat owner) not because of any "wrong," but because the intruder is the one in the relatively better position to make the appropriate cost-benefit analysis to determine whether it is "worth it" to intrude and cause damage to the owner's property. Thus, the threat of liability will give that party the necessary incentives to avoid wasting scarce resources — the intruder will act in a manner that would be appropriate if the intruder owned all the property interests — boat and dock — threatened with injury. If the parties have contracted ahead of time, as they well might when they enter the contract concerning dockage of the boat, courts presumably will give effect to the contractual assignments of liability. But if they have not, or if before the event contracting is impossible, or too costly, then arguably tort law should impose liability on the one who appears to be the better minimizer of overall costs (total damage to dock and boat, in *Vincent*).

From the noninstrumental/fairness perspective, perhaps *Vincent* represents the view that whenever one person deliberately takes the property or welfare of another for the taker's own benefit, liability should be imposed in order to avoid unjustly enriching the taker. But this explanation may assume the result when it uses the phrase "takes the property or welfare of another." The words "property" and "welfare" imply legally protected entitlements in the victim, and the word "takes" implies violation of the entitlement. And yet the question of entitlement is the one we set out to answer in the first place. Thus, even the noninstrumental/fairness perspective, which *seems* to rely more on the inherent justness of imposing liability, must struggle to explain its underlying assumptions.

On its facts, *O'Brien* appears to support the view that tort law is biased against the lower classes. The rule of law established in that case — that manifestations of consent should count more than uncommunicated, subjective states of mind — seems neutral enough. But its application in that case seems to rest on a tacit assumption that steerage passengers deserve little in the way of a personalized explanation of the relevant risks and had better speak up quickly if they should be so brazen as to object to being treated like cattle at roundup time. Of course, that decision is over 100 years old. Would the case be decided the same way today, on the same facts?

In any event, the foregoing are meant only as suggestions. Can you explain these decisions, and the others considered in this chapter, more satisfactorily?

Chapter 2

Actual Causation

The causation issues considered in this chapter surpass all others with respect to their immediate significance to the parties in a tort action. Even before someone who has been injured by another person seeks legal advice — even before seeking medical attention — the victim is likely to want answers to the questions, "Who did this to me? Who is responsible?" Certainly for the plaintiff's lawyer these questions have top priority. Unless the one who caused the plaintiff's harm can be identified, even the clearest example of tortious wrongdoing will not support a legal claim. Thus it is appropriate to consider actual causation here, before going on to consider the most frequently relied on bases of tort liability. While solid factual evidence linking a seriously injured plaintiff's harm to the defendant's conduct does not guarantee success, without evidence of cause-in-fact the claim will almost certainly die aborning.

We have already encountered actual causation in this course. Thus, in all of the battery cases considered in Chapter 1, the plaintiffs sought to recover for physical harm or mental upset suffered as a consequence of the tortious conduct of others. Implicit in all of those cases was the requirement that the plaintiffs establish that the defendants' conduct actually caused the harm or upset for which they sought recovery. Indeed, in some of the cases, the fact question of actual causation was contested at trial and presented issues of law for decision on appeal. In *Vosburg* (p. 12, above), for example, involving serious injuries from a light kick on the shin, the causation issue on appeal related to the admissibility of medical expert testimony that the kick actually caused the plaintiff's injuries.

In this chapter, we examine the cause-in-fact issue more closely, often relying on cases involving negligence rather than battery. Negligence cases, like the harmful battery cases in Chapter 1, require the plaintiff to prove that the defendant's conduct caused the harm of which the plaintiff complains. In this chapter we will not focus on the question of what constitutes negligence; that will be deferred until Chapter 3. The focus here is on the issue of actual causation: Did the defendant cause the plaintiff's harm? To answer this question requires that another question be answered: "But for the defendant having acted at all, would the plaintiff nevertheless have suffered the same harm?" A negative answer to this question — "No, the plaintiff would not have suffered the same harm if the defendant had never acted at all" — establishes that defendant's conduct, being a necessary condition of plaintiff's harm, was an actual cause of that harm. An affirmative answer to the same question establishes, subject to a few important exceptions, that the defendant's conduct was not an actual cause.

This question is the reason cause-in-fact is often called "but for" causation. "But for" causation asks the fact finder, usually the jury, to imagine a hypothetical "what if" scenario. The fact finder must "know not only what happened, but what *might* have happened if the defendant's conduct had been other than what it actually was." Wex S. Malone, Ruminations on Cause-In-Fact, 9 Stan. L. Rev. 60, 60 (1954). The generic "but for" causation question exists in every tort case — irrespective of the theory of liability being pressed by the plaintiff — and requires the fact finder to determine whether the defendant's conduct was necessary in order for the plaintiff's harm to have occurred. At this point, we must also note that a second form of "but for" causation question exists, even though detailed discussion is deferred until Chapter 4. In brief, the second "but for" causation question asks: "But for the *wrongful quality* of defendant's conduct, would the plaintiff have suffered the same harm?" This question establishes not only that defendant's conduct in general was a necessary condition of plaintiff's harm, but that the wrongful aspect of defendant's conduct in particular was required for the harm to occur. We defer further discussion of this related "but for" causation question until after introduction of the negligence concept in Chapter 3, which will help readers understand what precisely is meant by the question's focus on the "wrongful quality" of a defendant's conduct.

Finally, before examining the actual causation issue in the courts, you should consider why the torts process should impose a causation requirement in the first place. What policy objectives does the causation requirement serve? After all, when two drivers engage in the same risky conduct — for instance, running a red light while texting on their phones — but only the second driver happens to collide with another vehicle, is the wrongfulness of the latter's behavior really distinct from that of the other driver? See John C. P. Goldberg & Benjamin C. Zipursky, Tort Law and Moral Luck, 92 Cornell L. Rev.1123, 1126 (2007) (introducing this curious feature of tort law and relating it to philosophical discussion on the problem of "moral luck"). This question cannot be answered once and for all here, at the outset of our inquiry. But it is a question you should consider as you work through this chapter. In developing your answer, the following observations may prove useful.

First, although the causation requirement is apt to be viewed as an impediment to plaintiff's recovery, bear in mind that for plaintiffs who succeed in satisfying it, together with the other prerequisites to recovery, the causation concept strongly suggests that they will recover for the full amount of their actual harm, however great that amount might prove to be. From this perspective, the concept of actual cause not only helps to sort out the worthy cases from the unworthy, but also helps to fix the size of the recoveries in worthy cases.

The second point to bear in mind is that the causation requirement may reflect a policy judgment that, in some cases, the strength of the signal sent to the defendant from a deterrence perspective should be proportional to the harm caused. In battery cases, "deterrence for its own sake," or even "quasi-criminal punishment" may seem appropriate in light of the intentionally wrongful nature of defendants' conduct. If the basis of liability is negligence, the attitude seems to be that so long as no harm is caused, the actor will not be exposed to liability.

Third, the requirement of causation may reflect a shared concern that practical limits be placed on an actor's exposure to liability. Without the actual causation requirement, a negligent factory operator might be held liable for all the harm, accidental or otherwise, suffered by anyone in his town, or in his state, for the period during which he acted negligently. Such potential exposure to liability might go a long way toward eliminating the negligent operation of factories, to be sure; but given the unavoidable vagueness of the negligence concept, it might eliminate properly managed factories as well.

Finally, the causation element helps to distinguish tort law from other areas of law that also concern potentially harmful behavior. By requiring a causal relationship between the defendant's wrongful conduct and the plaintiff's harm, tort law zeroes in on the essentially *private* wrong that occurs between specific parties. In contrast, *public* laws such as environmental, health, and safety laws typically reflect concern regarding the defendant's conduct in general — regulation may be justifiable even if no one is actually harmed, or the only harms are to public interests. Thus, a factory that operates with excessive risk of harm may be offensive to society at large whether or not harm actually results, and whether or not particular individuals are identified as the ultimate victims of harm. For tort law, on the other hand, it is the relationship of wrongdoing between particular parties that is arguably paramount — hence the requirement of actual causation between the doer and the deed. See Goldberg & Zipursky, supra.

A. *Did the Defendant Cause the Plaintiff's Harm?*

The actual causation issue presented in this section breaks down logically into two components. The first, sometimes referred to as "general," or "generic," causation, concerns whether defendant's alleged activity is inherently capable of causing the sort of harm suffered by the plaintiff. If it is not, the defendant wins on causation as a matter of law. In most tort cases, the general causation issue presents few problems for plaintiffs. When, for example, an automobile runs over the plaintiff and the issue is whether the defendant was driving the vehicle at the time, general causation is not an issue — no one questions that automobiles are inherently capable of harming people.

But what if the plaintiff claims that fumes from the automobile's exhaust caused his cattle to get sick? In that instance, the defendant may argue not only that he was not driving, but also that exhaust fumes from a single vehicle do not, as a general rule, cause cattle to get sick. Indeed, even if the defendant admits that he was driving the vehicle in question, he may still have the general causation argument that, in any event, his driving could not — and, therefore, did not — cause harm to the plaintiff's cattle. And the opposite is also true. Even if it were clear that the peculiarly toxic exhaust fumes from the vehicle in question can, and did, cause the cattle to get sick, the defendant may still introduce proof that he was not the driver of the automobile. This second actual causation issue in our hypothetical — whether the defendant was driving the vehicle that harmed the plaintiff — may be termed the issue of "specific causation."

Hoyt v. Jeffers

30 Mich. 181 (1874)

[Defendant owned and operated a steam saw mill located 233 feet from a hotel owned by plaintiff. On August 17, 1870, the hotel was damaged by fire. Plaintiff sued defendant claiming that the fire was caused by sparks emitted from the chimney of defendant's mill, and that defendant was negligent in permitting sparks to escape from the chimney. Judgment was entered upon a jury verdict for plaintiff, and defendant appeals.]

Christiancy, J. . . . The chimney was a square brick chimney, originally about seventy feet high, but in the spring of 1870 about twelve or twelve and one-half feet were added to the height; but neither before nor after the addition did it have any spark-catcher on it, nor what is called a butterfly valve, with wire netting, nor a hole behind the boiler for the sparks to fall into, so far as the evidence shows. The Sherman House was situated about two hundred and thirty-three feet to the northeast of the mill, and on the other side of the street from it.

There was evidence on the part of the plaintiff relating to the particular time of the fire, which tended to show that the plaintiff's buildings were set on fire and burned by a spark from the mill chimney, though the spark was not seen to fall, or the fire to start from there. But this evidence was greatly strengthened by, and to some extent consisted of, a large amount of testimony showing the action and operation of the chimney in throwing such sparks, endangering and setting fire to property, for a long time previous, and up to the time of the fire, and how the mill had been run, and what measures had been taken or omitted by those running the mill, to avoid such danger to surrounding property, a change made in the height of the chimney, and whether, and how far, that change affected the action of the chimney by increasing or diminishing the escape of, and danger from sparks or cinders.

The evidence on the part of the plaintiff (some of which was received under objection, which will be noticed hereafter) tended to show, *first*, as to the habit of the chimney to throw sparks and the danger to surrounding property: — that from 1862 down to and after the time of this fire, sparks of fire and burning cinders or fragments of fire were frequently and quite generally emitted from the chimney when the mill was running, and carried to considerable distance (as far, and often farther than the Sherman House), falling to the ground and on buildings and sidewalks while still on fire, and sometimes setting fire to buildings and other wooden material they fell upon; that when the wind was from the southwest (especially if strong), and the mill was running, live sparks were frequently seen to fly from the chimney and fall around the Sherman House and near to and upon other buildings, on sidewalks and the yards in and near the same direction; that in 1862 sparks from the chimney were seen to fall and set fire to sawdust near this house; that in 1863 or 1864, and again in 1869, this same Sherman House took fire on the outer south side, when the wind was in the southwest, and mill running, and sparks coming from that direction; that sparks were seen to fall on the sidewalk and set it on fire at one time; that sparks had been picked up on the platform of the Sherman House; that on one occasion clothes were set on fire when out drying on the line near the premises, and that clothes on the line drying in this neighborhood had holes burned in them, and were covered with black, dead sparks, and blackened, and that furniture set out at a cabinet shop about the same distance was rendered smutty in the same way; and that several houses near the Sherman House, and some further off, had to keep their windows shut to avoid injury of this kind to clothes, etc., inside, when the mill was running and the wind coming from the mill; that in 1873, after this fire, the Garvey House, somewhat near the mill, was set on fire under circumstances indicating that it came from such sparks; that fire had caught in several buildings similarly situated, and that all caught on the side towards the mill, and as far as known, when the mill was running, and the wind in the southwest, etc.

The first set of errors assigned [are] based upon exceptions to the admission of evidence tending to show how this chimney had been in the habit of throwing sparks, and setting fire to buildings, etc., for several years previous to the burning of this hotel. The court upon the objection of the defendant, refused to receive evidence extending back over so long a period, except upon the understanding and with the undertaking, on the part of the plaintiff, to follow it up with evidence to show that it was then in the same condition as at the time of the fire; and the plaintiff did produce a large amount of evidence tending to show this, and that the mode of using the mill, the throwing of sparks from the chimney, and the danger to other property in the vicinity, continued substantially the same, from the earliest period to which this evidence referred, down to the time of this fire, and that the raising of the chimney about twelve feet, in the spring prior to the fire, did not appreciably diminish the emission of sparks, or the danger therefrom.

Now, as the evidence of the burning of the plaintiff's property complained of, need not and did not consist of direct evidence, that in that particular instance a particular spark was seen to come from the mill, traced by the same eye through the air and seen to light upon the side of the house and set it on fire, but the plaintiff must be at liberty to show, as he did, circumstances tending to prove that the property was set on fire in this way on the occasion alluded to, I can see no sound reason why he should not be at liberty to show any circumstances fairly tending to prove, or calculated to produce a reasonable belief, that this fire originated in this way on the occasion in question. On principle, I think all such testimony is admissible, and its force or weight to be estimated by the jury. It does not, as is here objected, raise a multitude of distinct issues, any more than in all other cases of circumstantial evidence, where the circumstances are equally numerous. And to show, as was done here, that while the mill and chimney, and the mode of using them, remained the same in all essential respects, the wind in the same direction, and the other surrounding circumstances the same, sparks had been seen to issue from this chimney in large quantities, watched, and seen to fall upon buildings or sidewalks, or other wood material, and to set them on fire, and all the other facts which the evidence given tended to show, as already stated, would strongly tend to produce a reasonable belief of the particular fact of the burning being from this cause on the occasion in question. I therefore see no error in the admission of this evidence.

Upon the same principle, I think the evidence of the Garvey House taking fire, in May, 1873 (though after the burning of plaintiff's building) was admissible, together with all the circumstances tending to show that it was set on fire by sparks from this chimney. . . .

[Judgment affirmed.]

Smith v. Rapid Transit Inc.

317 Mass. 469, 58 N.E.2d 754 (1945)

SPALDING, J. The decisive question in this case is whether there was evidence for the jury that the plaintiff was injured by a bus of the defendant that was operated by one of its employees in the course of his employment. If there was, the defendant concedes that the evidence warranted the submission to the jury of the question of the operator's negligence in the management of the bus. The case is here on the plaintiff's exception to the direction of a verdict for the defendant.

These facts could have been found: While the plaintiff at about 1:00 A.M. on February 6, 1941, was driving an automobile on Main Street, Winthrop, in an easterly direction toward Winthrop Highlands, she observed a bus coming toward her which she described as a "great big, long, wide affair." The bus, which was proceeding at about forty miles an hour, "forced her to turn to the right," and her automobile collided with a "parked car." The plaintiff was coming from Dorchester. The department of public utilities had issued a certificate of public convenience or necessity to the defendant for three routes in Winthrop, one of which included Main Street, and this was in effect in February, 1941. "There was another bus line in operation in Winthrop at that time but not on Main Street." According to the defendant's time-table, buses were scheduled to leave Winthrop Highlands for Maverick Square via Main Street at 12:10 A.M., 12:45 A.M., 1:15 A.M., and 2:15 A.M. The running time for this trip at that time of night was thirty minutes.

The direction of a verdict for the defendant was right. The ownership of the bus was a matter of conjecture. While the defendant had the sole franchise for operating a bus line on Main Street, Winthrop, this did not preclude private or chartered buses from using this street; the bus in question could very well have been one operated by someone other than the defendant. It was said in Sargent v. Massachusetts Accident Co., 307 Mass. 246, at page 250, that it is "not enough that mathematically the chances somewhat favor a proposition to be proved; for example, the fact that colored automobiles made in the current year outnumber black ones would not warrant a finding that an undescribed automobile of the current year is colored and not black, nor would the fact that only a minority of men die of cancer warrant a finding that a particular man did not die of cancer." The most that can be said of the evidence in the instant case is that perhaps the mathematical chances somewhat favor the proposition that a bus of the defendant caused the accident. This was not enough. A "proposition is proved by a preponderance of the evidence if it is made to appear more likely or probable in the sense that actual belief in its truth, derived from the evidence, exists in the mind or minds of the tribunal notwithstanding any doubts that may still linger there." Sargent v. Massachusetts Accident Co., 307 Mass. 246, at page 250. . . .

Exceptions overruled.

Mock jurors in psychological experiments consistently agree with the *Smith* holding, displaying reluctance to rest judgments on naked probabilistic evidence alone. This finding — dubbed the "Wells Effect" after the researcher who first demonstrated it, see Gary L. Wells, Naked Statistical Evidence of Liability: Is Subjective Probability Enough?, 62 J. Personality & Soc. Psychol. 739 (1992) — is thought to be driven by the ease with which purely probabilistic evidence enables jurors to imagine alternative scenarios in which cause (or guilt) is not present. See Keith E. Niedermeier et al., Jurors' Use of Naked Statistical Evidence: Exploring Bases and Implications of the Wells Effect, 76 J. Personality & Soc. Psychol. 533 (1999). Eyewitness testimony and other qualitative evidence, in contrast, allows jurors to formulate a rich narrative in which essential elements of the story are supported by "actual belief," rather than mere statistical likelihood, however great. Of course, "actual belief" is not necessarily more accurate than probabilistic assessment; in fact, it may be far less accurate. But for jurors tasked with sometimes grave decisionmaking responsibilities in our legal system, "actual belief" offers cognitive comfort that "cold statistics" cannot. For an illuminating discussion of these studies and their implications, see Kevin Jon Heller, The Cognitive Psychology of Circumstantial Evidence, 105 Mich. L. Rev. 241 (2006).

One of the more interesting cases involving the use of statistics is People v. Collins, 438 P.2d 33 (Cal. 1968). In that case, the court overturned a robbery conviction because it had been obtained improperly through the use of testimony regarding mathematical probabilities. As in *Smith*, the issue was whether the evidence was sufficient to present a jury question as to the defendant identification issue, and it is a case study in the use and misuse of probability analysis. The defendants were convicted on the evidence that the robbery of the victim was committed by two people: a young white woman with blond hair and a ponytail, and a black man with a mustache and beard, who fled the scene in a yellow car. Four days later, the police arrested the defendants, who fit the general description and who owned a yellow car. At the trial, a mathematics instructor from a state college testified as to the *product rule*, which is that the probability of the joint occurrence of a number of mutually independent events is equal to the product of the individual probabilities that each of the events will occur. He was allowed to assume the following probability factors for each of the characteristics:

Yellow automobile	1/10
Man with mustache	1/4
Woman with ponytail	1/10
Woman with blond hair	1/3
Black man with beard	1/10
Interracial couple in car	1/1000

Under the product rule, the prosecutor argued to the jury that there was but one chance in 12 million that any given couple would possess all these distinctive characteristics; therefore, there was only one chance in 12 million that the defendants were innocent. In reversing the convictions, the court ruled that there was no evidence as to the accuracy of the probabilities, and that there was no basis for assuming that the factors were independent. As to the latter point, men with mustaches and men who are black with beards obviously represent overlapping categories. The court also observed that the evidence on its face did not exclude the possibility of at least one other couple in the Los Angeles area that would satisfy the characteristics, so there was no basis for concluding that it was the defendants who had committed the robbery.

Understandably, the *Collins* case generated a considerable amount of commentary in the law reviews, all of which seems to have been favorable to the decision reached in that case by the supreme court. See, e.g., Alan D. Cullison, Identification by Probabilities and Trial by Arithmetic (A Lesson for Beginners in How to Be Wrong with Greater Precision), 6 Hous. L. Rev. 471 (1969); Laurence H. Tribe, Trial by Mathematics: Precision and Ritual in the Legal Process, 84 Harv. L. Rev. 1329 (1971); Charles Nesson, The Evidence or the Event? On Judicial Proof and the Acceptability of Verdicts, 98 Harv. L. Rev. 1357, 1368-77 (1985); Saul Levmore, Conjunction and Aggregation, 99 Mich. L. Rev. 723 (2001). See also George Fisher, Green Felt Jungle: The Story of *People v. Collins*, in Evidence Stories 16 (Richard Lempert ed., 2006). However, although all of the commentators agree that the particular application of probability analysis in *Collins* was inappropriate, a number of writers insist that as a general proposition probability theory may serve as a useful tool in the fact-finding process.

An interesting application of the *Collins* decision is found in Jonathan J. Koehler, One in Millions, Billions, and Trillions: Lessons from People v. Collins (1968) for People v. Simpson (1995), 47 J. Legal Educ. 214 (1997). Koehler points to the analytic errors that occurred at trial in *Collins* and applies the same critique to the DNA evidence presented at the Simpson trial, concluding that (47 J. Legal Educ. at 222):

> [i]n both *Collins* and *Simpson*, prosecutors used very tiny statistical frequencies to link defendants with a crime. And, in both cases, the matching characteristics that lurked behind these frequencies (eyewitness characteristics in *Collins*, DNA characteristics in *Simpson*) did have probative value.
>
> But in both cases the probative value of this evidence, as suggested by the frequency statistics, was severely constrained by the possibility of error. This is not to say that error was likely in either case. But because the possibility of error was much more likely than 1 in 12,000,000 in *Collins*, and 1 in 57 billion in *Simpson*, the probative value of these figures might have been outweighed by the danger of unfair prejudice.

More recently, spurred by the creation of nationwide offender DNA databases, prosecutors in criminal cases have sought convictions based almost exclusively on the statistical unlikelihood of a "cold hit" between a defendant's preexisting DNA profile and evidence obtained at a crime scene. See David H. Kaye, Rounding Up the Usual Suspects: A Legal and Logical Analysis of DNA Trawling Cases, 87 N.C. L. Rev. 425 (2009). Consider the following example of such a case:

> In 1972, a young nurse was raped and murdered in her San Francisco home. The initial suspect, Robert Baker, had escaped from an asylum a month before, raped a woman less than a quarter-mile from the nurse's home, stalked a young mother and her child's nanny on the nurse's block, and left a parking ticket in his van with blood drops on it matching the nurse's type. But the case against Baker stalled, and the investigation went cold for over thirty years. In 2004, authorities reopened the case, comparing DNA found inside the victim to the 338,000 DNA profiles in California's offender database. The search yielded one match, or "cold hit," to then-seventy-one-year-old John Puckett, a wheelchair-bound man in Stockton. At Puckett's trial, the primary evidence against him was the DNA profile match, though jurors also heard that he lived in the Bay Area in 1972 and had a 1977 sexual assault conviction. The government's DNA expert reported that the chance that a random person from the population would match the profile (the "random match probability," or RMP) was 1 in 1.1 million. The judge allowed the defense to argue to the jury that "[t]here really is no other evidence against Mr. Puckett," but refused the defense's request to tell the jury that the chance of finding at least one match in California's database was one in three. The jury also never heard — and neither party volunteered or asked permission to state — that the chance that another prime-aged man living in the Bay Area in 1972 shared the matching profile was likely over fifty percent.

Andrea Roth, Safety in Numbers? Deciding When DNA Evidence Alone Is Enough to Convict, 85 N.Y.U. L. Rev. 1130 (2010). John Puckett was found guilty at trial, but did not live long enough to complete his appeal. The court held that Puckett's death rendered the case moot, and refused to issue an opinion on the question of DNA evidence. People v. Puckett, No. A121368 (Cal. Ct. App. Apr. 18, 2009).

For further support of the idea that jurors seek "actual belief" rather than "mere statistical knowledge," see Nicholas Scurich & Richard S. John, Mock Jurors' Use of Error Rates in DNA Database Trawls, 37 Law & Hum. Behav. 424 (2103). In this experiment, mock jurors were told that the police, investigating a rape, had found a DNA match between the defendant and some DNA samples recovered from the victim. Some of the jurors were told that there was a 1-in-10 error rate, and other jurors were told that the error rate was 1-in-1,000. Despite the fact that a match with a 1-in-1,000 error rate should be 100 times more probative than a match with a 1-in-10 error rate, both sets of jurors rated the defendant's likelihood of guilt almost equally. The study concluded that either jurors are not persuaded by error rates or they do not truly understand them.

The Law-Fact Distinction: Sufficiency of the Evidence and Circumstantial Proof of Causation

The preceding cases and the text on mathematical probabilities raise the issue of the sufficiency of the plaintiff's proof of causation in the absence of direct eyewitness testimony linking the defendant's conduct to the plaintiff's harm. In most cases, there will be direct evidence relating to causation. Direct evidence of a particular fact goes directly to the fact in question. It is evidence based on the senses of the witness — what the witness saw, or touched, or heard. In *Hoyt*, for example, if a witness had testified that he saw sparks from the defendant's chimney drift over to and start a fire on the plaintiff's property, the witness would have supplied direct evidence of the cause-in-fact connection between the defendant's conduct and the plaintiff's harm. But, as the preceding cases indicate, reliance on direct evidence is not the only way in which causation may be proved. Causation may also be proved indirectly, on the basis of circumstantial evidence. Where no direct evidence of cause-in-fact is available, as in *Hoyt*, where no eyewitness actually saw sparks from the defendant's chimney set fire to the plaintiff's hotel, the plaintiff may be able to prove facts from which an inference of causation may be drawn. Thus, the plaintiff in *Hoyt* was able to prove that sparks had on previous occasions flown from the defendant's mill and started fires. This fact, coupled with others, was considered sufficient to establish cause-in-fact circumstantially. Proving a fact circumstantially rather than directly should not necessarily be viewed as a handicap, at least in cases that reach the jury. Direct evidence is, after all, only as strong and convincing as the credibility of the witness who tenders it. In *Hoyt*, for example, the plaintiff was probably better off going to the jury with his circumstantial evidence of causation than he would have been if the only evidence of cause-in-fact had been direct, eyewitness testimony by the plaintiff's brother, a well-known liar.

To the extent that being forced to rely on circumstantial proof of causation is likely to be a handicap, it will be in the plaintiff's ability to get to the jury in the first place. Direct evidence of causation will almost always be sufficient to create a jury question, because it raises issues of credibility of the witnesses. Traditionally, it has been agreed that whenever the resolution of a question of fact depends upon the credibility of witnesses, it is up to the jury to decide whom they will believe. In other words, it is the jury's job to observe the expression on the witness's face, to discern the wringing of the witness's hands and the like, and finally to decide whether the witness is telling the truth. Only rarely will a trial judge rule that a witness's direct evidence is not believable as a matter of law. Thus, even where the only eyewitness is the plaintiff's untrustworthy brother, the defendant ordinarily will not win a directed verdict on the cause-in-fact issue. However, where direct evidence of causation, or of any other relevant fact, is not available, the plaintiff may encounter difficulties in overcoming the defendant's assertion that the circumstantial evidence is insufficient to warrant sending the case to the jury. Therefore, the cases involving circumstantial proof of causation afford an excellent opportunity to develop and refine your understanding of the law-fact distinction and the allocation of functions between judge and jury.

As was indicated in the law-fact distinction note following O'Brien v. Cunard Steamship Co., p. 42, above, the determination of whether there is evidence sufficient to create a jury issue is one of law, initially to be decided by the trial judge and subject to review on appeal. Whether there is sufficient evidence is a matter about which it is difficult to generalize. Each case tends to be unique and generally applicable rules for measuring sufficiency are difficult to formulate. (*Smith* involves one such rule of general applicability — a jury question is typically not created if the only evidence of cause is evidence of mathematical probabilities.) The judge's own experience and how he or she views reality are likely to be as important as any other factor in the resolution of close cases. The judge may also be influenced by more or less unarticulated notions of policy. Cf. Dan M. Kahan, David A. Hoffman, & Donald Braman, Whose Eyes Are You Going to Believe? Scott v. Harris and the Perils of Cognitive Illiberalism, 122 Harv. L. Rev. 837 (2009) (demonstrating that psychological dispositions and cultural beliefs influence the manner in which individuals evaluate video evidence).

The appealability of trial judges' rulings as to the sufficiency of the evidence ensures to some extent that these rulings are not entirely whimsical. Appellate review is also important as a way of ensuring that a proper balance is struck across a range of cases in the decisions relating to the sufficiency of evidence. If the power to give binding instructions or to direct verdicts were exercised to an extreme, judges would end up deciding the outcomes in most cases. There might remain a theoretical category of "issues of fact," but in effect most of them would be decided by judges as a matter of law, and this would effectively undermine the jury system. On the other hand, a system under which all cases were sent to the jury with no screening as to the sufficiency of the evidence would not be a system of law. As Justice Frankfurter once explained: "The easy but timid way out for a trial judge is to leave all cases tried to a jury for jury determination, but in so doing he fails in his duty . . . . A timid judge, like a biased judge, is intrinsically a lawless judge." Wilkerson v. McCarthy, 336 U.S. 53, 65 (1949). Thus, rulings about the sufficiency of the evidence are among the most important decisions that judges make.

The preceding material presents the issue of *specific causation*—whether the defendant's wrongful conduct specifically caused the plaintiff's injuries. As indicated at the outset of this chapter, courts occasionally confront the issue of *general causation*—whether the defendant's conduct is of the sort that is generally capable of causing injury of the type suffered by the plaintiff. In *Hoyt*, above, the general causation issue was easy: Of course a mill emitting showers of burning embers is capable of starting a hotel fire a few blocks downwind. But what if the plaintiff's injury had consisted of a herd of cattle getting sick? In that case the mill operator could well argue that burning embers do not, as a general matter, cause illness in cattle. Of course, even if the plaintiff could somehow establish the necessary general causal connection between embers and cattle illness, the defendant could nevertheless argue, as in *Hoyt*, "It wasn't *my* embers that caused the illness." But the plaintiff's first task in the embers-cattle context would be to establish the nonobvious general causation link between defendant's conduct and plaintiff's loss.

Although only a very small percentage of tort cases involve the general causation issue, it is important to understand how courts have reacted to it. Almost always, in cases where general causation is at issue, plaintiffs have been exposed to an allegedly toxic substance and claim to have been injured as a consequence. Invariably, the claims depend for their validity on the strength of the scientific evidence—typically in the form of epidemiological studies and laboratory research—supporting the plaintiffs' assertion of general causation. No area of tort litigation in recent years captures the essence of general causation analysis better than cases involving the widely used prescription drug Bendectin. Approved in 1956 by the Food and Drug Administration as a safe treatment for morning sickness during pregnancy, Bendectin had been used by more than 30 million women between 1957 and 1983, when Richardson-Merrell, Inc., the manufacturer, withdrew it from the market. Merrell withdrew the drug because of fears that it caused severe birth defects in children of the women who had ingested the drug while pregnant. A large number of tort claims had been filed based on scientific studies, including epidemiological studies, allegedly revealing the drug to be a teratogen, or birth-defect-causing agent. By the mid-1980s, Bendectin litigation appeared to be a growing area for plaintiffs' lawyers. One example of such a case is Oxendine v. Merrell Dow Pharm., 506 A.2d 1100 (D.C. 1986), in which a Bendectin manufacturer was held liable based on epidemiological proof of causation, *cert. denied*, 493 U.S. 1074 (1990).

Notwithstanding the optimism that reigned in the early to mid-1980s among plaintiffs' lawyers regarding the future of Bendectin litigation, the tide began turning against them as the established scientific community concluded in a number of research projects that the link between the drug and the birth defects had not been established at an adequate level of statistical significance — that is, observed correlations between ingestion and injury could have been the product of chance. Courts hearing these cases began to issue summary judgments for the defendant, Merrell, with increasing frequency. A good example is Richardson v. Richardson-Merrell, Inc., 857 F.2d 823 (D.C. Cir. 1988), *cert. denied*, 493 U.S. 882 (1989), in which the court of appeals affirmed a JNOV on behalf of defendant, holding that, given the great weight of scientific opinion to the contrary, plaintiff's expert's testimony on actual causation was insufficient. In fact, the *Oxendine* case mentioned above was eventually overturned after a ten-year legal battle because the court held that the state of scientific knowledge had changed too much during the appeals process to allow the earlier ruling to stand. Oxendine v. Merrell Dow Pharm., Inc., No. CIV. 82-1245, 1996 WL 680992, at *1 (D.C. Super. Ct. Oct. 24, 1996). Many of the courts that rejected plaintiffs' expert testimony in Bendectin cases relied on Frye v. United States, 293 F. 1013, 1014 (D.C. 1923), for the proposition that expert opinion based on a scientific technique is admissible only if the technique is "generally accepted" as reliable in the relevant scientific community. For more information on *Frye* and the important standard it developed, see Jill Lepore, On Evidence: Proving *Frye* as a Matter of Law, Science, and History, 124 Yale L.J. 1092 (2015).

In Daubert v. Merrell Dow Pharm., Inc., 509 U.S. 579 (1993), the Supreme Court vacated the judgment of the court of appeals in favor of the defendant in a Bendectin case. The Court held that "general acceptance" is not a necessary precondition to the admissibility of scientific evidence under the Federal Rules of Evidence:

> Faced with a proffer of expert scientific testimony . . . the trial judge must make a preliminary assessment of whether the testimony's underlying reasoning or methodology is scientifically valid and properly can be applied to the facts at issue. Many considerations will bear on the inquiry, including whether the theory or technique in question can be (and has been) tested, whether it has been subjected to peer review and publication, its known or potential error rate, the existence and maintenance of standards controlling its operation, and whether it has attracted widespread acceptance within a relevant scientific community. The inquiry is a flexible one, and its focus must be solely on principles and methodology, not on the conclusions that they generate. Throughout, the judge should also be mindful of other applicable Rules . . . . [C]ross examination, presentation of contrary evidence, and careful instruction on the burden of proof, rather than wholesale exclusion under an uncompromising "general acceptance" standard, is the appropriate means by which evidence based on valid principles may be challenged.

Excerpted from official Syllabus, 509 U.S. at 580. Rather than necessarily making it easier or more difficult for plaintiffs to get their scientific testimony admitted into evidence, the Supreme Court appears to have aimed at giving federal courts more control over the admissibility issue, rather than deferring under *Frye* to the scientific community. See, e.g., Milward v. Acuity Specialty Products Group., Inc., 639 F.3d 11 (1st Cir. 2011) (thoroughly reviewing the epistemological and evidentiary basis of plaintiffs' experts' use of a "weight of the evidence" methodology to infer general causation in a toxic tort case). Nevertheless, many commentators regard *Daubert* as having created a heightened bar for plaintiffs in environmental, toxic tort, and products liability suits, as judges have shown a willingness to utilize their gatekeeper role to hold plaintiffs' experts to a high standard of scientific veracity. See, e.g., Andrew Jurs & Scott DeVito, The Stricter Standard: An Empirical Assessment of *Daubert*'s Effect on Civil Defendants, 62 Cath. U. L. Rev. 675 (2013); Margaret A. Berger, Upsetting the Balance Between Adverse Interests: The Impact of the Supreme Court's Trilogy on Expert Testimony in Toxic Tort Litigation, 64 Law & Contemp. Probs., Spring/Summer 2001, at 289.

Several state courts have rejected *Daubert*'s reconsideration of the Federal Rules of Evidence, opting instead to continue following *Frye*'s "general acceptance" principle. For example, in Goeb v. Theraldson, 615 N.W.2d 800 (Minn. 2000), the Supreme Court of Minnesota declined to adopt the *Daubert* standard. The court stated that "[*Frye*] is more apt to ensure objective and uniform rulings as to particular scientific methods and techniques"; and that while "a key assumption to [*Daubert*] is that judges can . . . resolve disputes among qualified scientists who have spent years immersed in their field of study, . . . the *Frye* general acceptance standard ensures that the persons most qualified to assess scientific validity of a technique have the determinative vote." Id. at 813-14. See also Christian v. Gray, 595 P.3d 591 (Okla. 2003), adopting the *Daubert* standard for civil actions in Oklahoma state courts and ruling that the trial court abused its discretion by excluding plaintiff's expert testimony that airborne chemicals at a state fair allegedly caused severe and chronic respiratory problems.

The *Christian* case also provides a detailed synopsis of which states have adopted which standard. See id. at 595. Connecticut recognizes a fluid relationship between the *Frye* and *Daubert* standards. In State v. Porter, 698 A.2d 739 (Conn. 1997), the Supreme Court of Connecticut conducted a *Daubert* inquiry but stated that "general acceptance remains a part of the analysis, and in many cases its presence may alone be sufficient to admit the evidence." Id. at 754. For non-scientist expert witnesses, the Connecticut high court continues to apply a traditional common law inquiry into whether "(1) the witness has a special skill or knowledge directly applicable to a matter in issue, (2) that skill or knowledge is not common to the average person, and (3) the testimony would be helpful to the court or jury in considering the issues." Sullivan v. Metro-North Commuter R. Co., 971 A.2d 676 (Conn. 2009).

The U.S. Supreme Court has revisited the *Daubert* principle in several decisions. See General Elec. Co. v. Joiner, 522 U.S. 136 (1997) (holding that a court of appeals should utilize the "abuse of discretion" standard in reviewing a trial court's decision to exclude expert testimony under *Daubert*); Kumho Tire Co. v. Carmichael, 526 U.S. 137 (1999) (holding that a trial court correctly applied the *Daubert* standard when excluding the testimony of a witness who purported to be an expert in tire defects). Because these more recent cases did not involve the issue of actual causation, further discussion is beyond the scope of this chapter.

What is important to understand about general causation at this juncture may be briefly outlined: (1) the general causation issue arises with some frequency in cases involving exposure to hazardous substances and can be critical to the plaintiff's chances in those contexts; (2) American courts have begun to scrutinize technical expert testimony, much of which relates to general causation; and (3) even when the plaintiff's technical proof of general causation is solid and persuasive, specific causation — i.e., did exposure to the toxic substance cause *this plaintiff's* injury? — also must be established.

It is also important to recognize that evidentiary law on the admissibility of expert testimony interacts with substantive tort law on the standards for demonstrating causation. For instance, some courts have developed relaxed causation standards in the asbestos context in light of the long latency period and complex etiology of asbestos-related health effects. See Jane Stapleton, The Two Explosive Proof-of-Causation Doctrines Central to

Asbestos Claims, 74 Brook. L. Rev. 1011 (2009). Other courts retain traditional, more stringent standards. See, e.g., Borg-Warner Corp. v. Flores, 232 S.W.3d 765 (Tex. 2007). Whether an expert will be deemed qualified to testify and whether the expert's testimony will be deemed to create a triable issue of fact will therefore hinge on whether the expert's opinion speaks to the specific legal standard that governs the case. See id. at 773 (holding, under Texas law, that the expert must proffer "[d]efendant-specific evidence relating to the approximate dose [of toxin] to which the plaintiff was exposed"); Scapa Dryer Fabrics, Inc. v. Knight, (Ga. 2016) (reversing judgment for asbestos plaintiff because plaintiff's expert testimony regarding causal significance of *any* asbestos fiber exposure above ambient levels did not "'fit' the pertinent causation inquiry" under Georgia law which requires that exposure levels create a "meaningful contribution" to plaintiff's mesothelioma).

The following excerpt represents a significant attempt by the Co-Reporters of the Third Restatement to grapple with these issues and to remedy persistent areas of confusion in the field of toxic torts and causation. The discussion is notable because it reflects not only the ordinary rigors of the Restatement drafting process but also an additional review by a panel of scientific and medical experts assembled by the Science, Technology, and Law Program at the National Academy of Sciences. It has proven influential in the courts, see, e.g., Milward v. Acuity Specialty Prods. Grp., Inc., 969 F. Supp.2d 101 (D. Mass. 2013), and it will be helpful to your consideration of Problem 8, which immediately follows.

Restatement (Third) of Torts: Liability for Physical and Emotional Harm (2010)

§28 cmt. c. Toxic substances and disease

(1) Introduction . . . .

[Some courts rely] on a view that "science" presents an "objective" method of establishing that, in all cases, reasonable minds cannot differ on the issue of factual causation. Such a view is incorrect. First, scientific standards for the sufficiency of evidence to establish a proposition may be inappropriate for the law, which itself must decide the minimum amount of evidence permitting a reasonable (and, therefore, permissible) inference, as opposed to speculation that is not permitted. . . . Second, scientists report that an evaluation of data and scientific evidence to determine whether an inference of causation is appropriate requires judgment and interpretation. Scientists are subject to their own value judgments and preexisting biases that may affect their view of a body of evidence. There are instances in which although one scientist or group of scientists comes to one conclusion about factual causation, they recognize that another group that comes to a contrary conclusion might still be "reasonable." . . . Scientists' judgments about causation outside the legal context may also be affected by the comparative costs of errors, as when caution counsels in favor of declaring an uncertain agent toxic because the potential harm it may cause if toxic is so much greater than the benefit forgone if it were not introduced. Courts, thus, should be cautious about adopting specific "scientific" principles, taken out of context, to formulate bright-line legal rules or conclude that reasonable minds cannot differ about factual causation. . . .

(3) General causation.

"General causation" exists when a substance is capable of causing a given disease. The concept developed because a prominent form of scientific methodology investigates causation on a group basis and therefore addresses whether an agent causes an increased incidence of disease in the group being studied. These studies proceed by comparing the incidence of disease in a group that has been exposed to the agent with the incidence of disease in a group of unexposed persons. The latter group's disease, thus, is attributable to causes other than the agent being studied. Traumatic-injury cases, by contrast, do not require this form of evidence because other causes that might explain the injury are absent, and we have a reasonably good understanding of the causal mechanisms involved from trauma to injury.

Occasionally, biological-mechanism evidence is sufficiently developed to prove general causation. More frequently, however, the evidence consists of scientific studies comparing the incidence of disease in groups of individuals (epidemiologic evidence) or animals (toxicologic evidence) with different levels of exposure. When a study finds a difference in the incidence of disease in the exposed and unexposed groups, an "association" exists between exposure and disease. Another type of epidemiologic study compares the extent of exposure among those with and without the disease. These studies seek to identify toxic substances at the aggregate population level — by finding a higher incidence of a disease in a group exposed to the substance (an "association").

Even when epidemiologic studies find an association between a substance and a disease, further analysis is necessary before a causal conclusion can be drawn . . . . If an association is found, epidemiologists use a number of factors (commonly known as the "Hill guidelines") for evaluating whether that association is causal or spurious. A spurious association may be the result of study errors — such as biases (scientists use "bias" to mean a source of error rather than as a predisposition to testify or decide a matter in an improper way) and uncorrected confounding factors (alternative causes that are responsible for the association, rather than the agent under study) — or sampling error (the result of small numbers of subjects and random chance). Similarly, a study may incorrectly fail to find an association that exists, because of study errors, especially when the disease is rare and an insufficient number of subjects exist[s] to reveal any relationship. . . .

Whether an inference of causation based on an association is appropriate is a matter of informed judgment, not scientific methodology, as is a judgment whether a study that finds no association is exonerative or inconclusive. No algorithm exists for applying the Hill guidelines to determine whether an association truly reflects a causal relationship or is spurious . . . . Thus, in some cases, reasonable scientists can come to differing conclusions on whether a body of epidemiologic data justifies an inference of causation. Similarly, reasonable scientists may, in some instances, disagree on whether the absence of an association is exonerative of the agent or is merely inconclusive . . . .

Occasionally, courts have suggested or implied that a plaintiff cannot meet the burden of production on causation without epidemiologic evidence. Those cases often confronted a substantial body of epidemiologic evidence introduced by the defendant that tended to exonerate the agent as causal. Circumstances in individual cases, however, are sufficiently varied that almost all courts employ a more flexible approach to proof of causation — except in those cases with a substantial body of exonerative epidemiologic evidence. Epidemiologic studies are expensive and can take considerable time to design, conduct, and publish. For disease processes with long latency periods, valid studies cannot be performed until the disease has manifested itself. As a consequence, some plaintiffs may be forced to litigate long before epidemiologic research is available. Indeed, sometimes epidemiologic evidence is impossible to obtain, which may explain why neither the plaintiff nor the defendant is able to proffer supportive epidemiology. Thus, most courts have appropriately declined to impose a threshold requirement that a plaintiff always must prove causation with epidemiologic evidence . . . .

(4) Specific causation.

"Specific causation" exists when exposure to an agent caused a particular plaintiff's disease. Sometimes proof of specific causation is easy and collapses into proof of general causation, as when there are no alternative causal agents for a disease, and the disease is said to be a "signature" of the substance. In other cases, however, specific causation remains an issue even though general causation is established.

Scientists who conduct group studies do not examine specific causation in their research. No scientific methodology exists for assessing specific causation for an individual based on group studies. Nevertheless, courts have reasoned [that] . . . when there is group-based evidence finding that exposure to an agent causes an incidence of disease in the exposed group that is more than twice the incidence in the unexposed group, the evidence is sufficient to satisfy the burden of production and permit submission of specific causation to a jury . . . .

[T]he extent to which the group-study outcome reflects the increased risk to the plaintiff depends on the plaintiff's similarity to those included in the group study. Relevant differences include whether: (a) the plaintiff was exposed to a comparable dose; (b) the plaintiff was not differentially exposed to other potential causes of the disease; and (c) the plaintiff has individual characteristics that might also bear on the risk of disease, such as age, gender, or general health, comparable to those in the study group.

The likelihood that an agent caused an individual's disease may be refined when there are independent, alternative known causes of the disease. The underlying premise is that each of these known causes is independently responsible for some proportion of the disease in a given population. Eliminating one or more of these as a possible cause for a specific plaintiff's disease increases the probability that the agent in question was responsible for that plaintiff's disease. Courts frequently refer to the elimination of other known causes for a plaintiff by employing the medical terminology of "differential diagnosis." Assessing whether other causes can be ruled out (or in) as potential causes of a plaintiff's disease can provide probative evidence of specific causation. This technique is more accurately described as a "differential etiology.". . .

For all of these reasons, any judicial requirement that plaintiffs must show a threshold increase in risk or a doubling in incidence in a group study in order to satisfy the burden of proof of specific causation is usually inappropriate. . . .

Problem 8

Twenty-five years ago, a privately owned utility, Electricorp, erected transformers and high-voltage power lines in the northern region of your state. The power lines created a winding, 25-mile long, ¼-mile wide corridor from Carthage to Harrisville. The power lines passed very close to several hundred homes between the two towns. In order to maintain the transformers and power lines, Electricorp cleared the trees and vegetation from the corridor. In response to the public outcry this clearing process caused, Electricorp created and maintained a nature trail that ran along the corridor.

Last year, Adam Smith and Gil Vargo came upon each other while riding their mountain bikes on the nature trail. They hadn't met before and didn't seem to have much in common, so they began to talk about the high-voltage power lines. Both men live within close proximity to the power lines and both have children who had been born with severe birth defects. Each expressed to the other his strong suspicions that the power lines caused the defects. As they talked, they became more and more angry until Mr. Vargo suggested that they talk with a lawyer to "stick it to Electricorp for what it's done to our kids."

Two months ago, Mr. Smith and Mr. Vargo came to your office. You remembered having read an article in *Newsweek* speculating about a possible link between high-voltage power lines and birth defects. Electricorp strikes you as an attractive, deep-pocket defendant for which a jury would have little sympathy. Despite your gut sense that this case might be a winner, you did not think at your first meeting that you had enough evidence to file a lawsuit. You told Mr. Vargo and Mr. Smith that if they were able to identify other families similarly situated, you might be willing to take the case.

Shortly after your first meeting, Mr. Vargo and Mr. Smith returned to your office. They had biked the power line corridor and taken a crude survey of the families who live close to the power lines. They discovered that 8 out of 100 families or so they interviewed had at least one child with moderate or severe birth defects. These statistics seemed to reinforce your gut feeling, so you agreed to take the case and represent the Vargos and the Smiths against Electricorp. Two weeks ago you filed a complaint against Electricorp alleging several counts of negligence and strict liability and alleging that the defendant's activities caused your clients' injuries.

Electricorp has issued a public statement calling the lawsuit "preposterous" and saying that you are "just the kind of ambulance-chasing attorney that gives lawyers a bad name." In addition, Electricorp plans to file a motion for summary judgment. You have learned that it plans to use the testimony of Dr. Carolyn Harding, a respected scientist who specializes in genetics and epidemiological analysis, to defeat your claims. Dr. Harding will testify that Mr. Vargo possesses a rare flaw in one of his genes that, within a 93 percent certainty, caused the birth defects in his children. Although Dr. Harding has no similar genetic explanation for the birth defects in the other families, she will testify that the other incidents of birth defects, although somewhat high for such a small community, fall within broader statistical norms and could be the product of random chance.

Unfortunately, you are having a difficult time finding a scientist of Dr. Harding's caliber to refute her testimony and to offer a causal hypothesis that supports the actions you filed on behalf of the Vargo and Smith families. Three days ago you were approached by a Dr. Matthew Motley, a medical biologist who learned of the lawsuit through the newspapers. After a brief discussion, you determined that Dr. Motley has the paper credentials to be qualified as an expert witness, but that he also has somewhat radical views regarding the effects of electrical current on human genes. Essentially, Dr. Motley believes that being in proximity with any source of high-voltage electricity for any period of time dramatically increases a person's risk of cancer and the occurrence of birth defects. Given this view, he feels particularly strongly that people should not live within the vicinity of high-voltage power lines.

Dr. Motley tells you that he would be delighted to testify as to the negative effects of high-voltage power lines on fetal development. He states that he can back up his testimony with empirical data from a study he conducted five years ago that shows that the occurrence of birth defects in families living within a mile of high-voltage power lines is approximately twice the national average. He also acknowledges that he might be branded as an eccentric if his general views about electricity were known. Therefore, he offers to limit his condemnation to power lines.

You believe that if Dr. Motley were to testify as to his broader theory, he would lose credibility with the jury and you would most likely lose the case. However, if Dr. Motley were to limit his testimony to the effect of high-voltage power lines on fetal development and present the data from his study, your chances of surviving summary judgment and getting the claims to the jury would be significantly improved.

Had you known then what you know now, would you have filed this suit? If you proceed with the case, will you put Dr. Motley on the stand? How will you prepare him for cross-examination? How will you attack the statistical analysis embedded in Dr. Harding's testimony? What are your chances of reaching the jury?

The Lawyer's Professional Responsibility: The Partisan Expert Witness, Frivolous Lawsuits, and Perjury

Besides the substantive law problems this case presents, your representation of the Vargos and the Smiths also raises important ethical questions. Despite your sympathy for the two families and your instinctive belief in the validity of their claims, you must also determine whether you have done yourself and the legal system a disservice by filing this suit. For an entertaining and in-depth treatment of a real case that parallels this problem, see Jonathan Harr, A Civil Action (1996).

Of course, the first question you must ask yourself in this case is whether you should have filed the lawsuit at all. Yes, you have sympathy for the families and a gut feeling that the case has merit, but sympathy and gut feelings do not serve evidentiary functions. The Federal Rules of Civil Procedure forbid a lawyer from bringing an action lacking in evidentiary support and provide authority for judges to hand down severe sanctions in such an event. See Fed. R. Civ. P. 11(b)(3) & (c). The Model Rules of Professional Conduct similarly provide:

> A lawyer shall not bring or defend a proceeding, or assert or controvert an issue therein, unless there is a basis in law and fact for doing so that is not frivolous, which includes a good faith argument for an extension, modification or reversal of existing law.

Model Rules of Prof'l Conduct R. 3.1 (2016). Would you deem the Vargo-Smith suit in the preceding problem frivolous when it was filed? Comment 2 to Rule 3.1 provides: "The filing of an action or defense or similar action taken for a client is not frivolous merely because the facts have not first been fully substantiated or because the lawyer expects to develop vital evidence only by discovery." On the other hand, the comment also requires lawyers to "inform themselves about the facts of their clients' cases and the applicable law and determine that they can make good faith arguments in support of their clients' positions." Do you think that Dr. Motley's study is sufficient to satisfy these obligations? If not, what will you do now?

Another set of issues you must face in this case involve the proper use of expert witnesses. Several aspects regarding the use of the expert witnesses present such experts in the posture of "witnesses for hire," thereby placing significant professional strain on lawyers. First, the expert is not a witness to the events that give rise to the plaintiff's claim, thereby eliminating any pretense of "just telling it like it was." Moreover, experts will testify only if their opinions support particular positions favorable to their sides. And, the fee payable to an expert may be based on the reasonable value of the services, while the fee payable to the nonexpert is limited to the witness's expenses and income lost because of the testifying. Model Rules of Prof'l Conduct R. 3.4 cmt. [3] (2016).

One of the most contentious issues regarding expert witnesses is whether they may be paid on a contingent fee basis (i.e., they are only paid if the case is won). Many commentators argue that this method of payment gives the expert incentives to present false or exaggerated testimony. See, e.g., Logan Ford & James H. Holmes III, The Professional Medical Advocate, 17 Sw. L.J. 551 (1963). The Model Code took a stronger position on this issue than the Model Rules do. The Model Code stated that "in no event should a lawyer pay or agree to pay a contingent fee to any witness." Model Code of Prof'l Responsibility EC 7-28 (1980). The Model Rules defer this issue to local law and say that "[t]he common law rule in most jurisdictions is . . . that it is improper to pay an expert witness a contingent fee." Model Rules of Prof'l Conduct R. 3.4 cmt. [3] (2016). See also N.Y. Rules of Prof'l Conduct R. 3.4(b) (2009) (prohibiting any "offer to pay or acquiesce in the payment of compensation to a witness contingent upon the content of the witness's testimony or the outcome of the matter").

In the Vargo-Smith case, however, the issue of truthful testimony may not be related to the question of how the expert will be paid. Dr. Motley may be tempted to alter his testimony because of the motivation of supporting what he deems to be a just cause, rather than because of his pecuniary interest. In either case, the problem of perjury arises and must be addressed. This case is somewhat peculiar in that regard. Dr. Motley truly believes that the high-voltage power lines caused the birth defects, so he is not self-consciously lying on that point. However, by presenting only a portion of his views, he renders himself a vulnerable witness if the opposing attorney reads some of Dr. Motley's articles and is determined to make Dr. Motley's radical theories known through cross-examination. A lawyer has a duty not to suborn perjury, see Model Rules of Prof'l Conduct R. 3.4 (2016), but would questioning Dr. Motley in a manner that avoids his radical theories during direct examination constitute suborning a "false statement of fact"? Would counseling him to hide or obfuscate his view on cross-examination do so?

This problem presents a spectrum of ethical considerations. From the fundamental question of whether to file a suit in the first place to the ever-contentious question of how pristine a case must be, a lawyer must always enter a case with open eyes. Again, except for the rare exceptions, these areas of the law are policed almost exclusively by the lawyers themselves. A lawyer must always walk the fine line between zealous advocacy and professional responsibility. That line is particularly fuzzy in the context of this problem.

B. When One of Several Defendants Did It, But We Can't Tell Which One: Alternative Liability

Summers v. Tice

33 Cal. 2d 80, 199 P.2d 1 (1948)

CARTER, J. Each of the two defendants appeals from a judgment against them in an action for personal injuries. Pursuant to stipulation the appeals have been consolidated.

Plaintiff's action was against both defendants for an injury to his right eye and face as the result of being struck by birdshot discharged from a shotgun. The case was tried by the court without a jury and the court found that on November 20, 1945, plaintiff and the two defendants were hunting quail on the open range. Each of the defendants was armed with a 12-gauge shotgun loaded with shells containing 7½ size shot. Prior to going hunting plaintiff discussed the hunting procedure with defendants, indicating that they were to exercise care when shooting and to "keep in line." In the course of hunting plaintiff proceeded up a hill, thus placing the hunters at the points of a triangle. The view of defendants with reference to plaintiff was unobstructed and they knew his location. Defendant Tice flushed a quail which rose in flight to a 10-foot elevation and flew between plaintiff and defendants. Both defendants shot at the quail, shooting in the plaintiff's direction. At that time defendants were 75 yards from plaintiff. One shot struck plaintiff in his eye and another in his upper lip. Finally it was found by the court that as the direct result of the shooting by defendants the shots struck plaintiff as above mentioned and the defendants were negligent in so shooting and plaintiff was not contributorily negligent. . . .

The problem presented in this case is whether the judgment against both defendants may stand. It is argued by defendants that they are not joint tort feasors, and thus jointly and severally liable, as they were not acting in concert, and that there is not sufficient evidence to show which defendant was guilty of the negligence which caused the injuries — the shooting by Tice or that by Simonson. . . .

Considering [this argument], we believe it is clear that the court sufficiently found on the issue that defendants were jointly liable and that thus the negligence of both was the cause of the injury or to that legal effect. It found that both defendants were negligent and "That as a direct and proximate result of the shots fired by *defendants, and each of them*, a birdshot pellet was caused to and did lodge in plaintiff's right eye and that another birdshot pellet was caused to and did lodge in plaintiff's upper lip." . . . Implicit in such finding is the assumption that the court was unable to ascertain whether the shots were from the gun of one defendant or the other or one shot from each of them. The one shot that entered plaintiff's eye was the major factor in assessing damages and that shot could not have come from the gun of both defendants. It was from one or the other only. . . .

. . . Dean Wigmore has this to say: "When two or more persons by their acts are possibly the sole cause of a harm, or when two or more acts of the same person are possibly the sole cause, and the plaintiff has introduced evidence that the one of the two persons, or the one of the same person's two acts, is culpable, then the defendant has the burden of proving that the other person, or his other act, was the sole cause of the harm. . . . The real reason for the rule that each joint tortfeasor is responsible for the whole damage is the practical unfairness of denying the injured person redress simply because he cannot prove how much damage each did, when it is certain that between them they did all; let them be the ones to apportion it among themselves. Since, then, the difficulty of proof is the reason, the rule should apply whenever the harm has plural causes, and not merely when they acted in conscious concert. . . ." (Wigmore, Select Cases on the Law of Torts, §153.) . . .

When we consider the relative position of the parties and the results that would flow if plaintiff was required to pin the injury on one of the defendants only, a requirement that the burden of proof on that subject be shifted to defendants becomes manifest. They are both wrong doers — both negligent toward plaintiff. They brought about a situation where the negligence of one of them injured the plaintiff, hence it should rest with them each to absolve himself if he can. The injured party has been placed by defendants in the unfair position of pointing to which defendant caused the harm. If one can escape the other may also and plaintiff is remediless. Ordinarily defendants are in a far better position to offer evidence to determine which one caused the injury. . . .

Cases are cited for the proposition that where two or more tort feasors acting independently of each other cause an injury to plaintiff, they are not joint tort feasors and plaintiff must establish the portion of the damage caused by each, even though it is impossible to prove the portion of the injury caused by each. In view of the foregoing discussion it is apparent that defendants in cases like the present one may be treated as liable on the same basis as joint tort feasors, and hence the last-cited cases are distinguishable inasmuch as they involve independent tort feasors.

In addition to that, however, it should be pointed out that the same reasons of policy and justice shift the burden to each of defendants to absolve himself if he can — relieving the wronged person of the duty of apportioning the injury to a particular defendant, apply here where we are concerned with whether plaintiff is required to supply evidence for the apportionment of damages. If defendants are independent tort feasors and thus each liable for the damage caused by him alone, and, at least, where the matter of apportionment is incapable of proof, the innocent wronged party should not be deprived of his right to redress. The wrong doers should be left to work out between themselves any apportionment. Some of the cited cases refer to the difficulty of apportioning the burden of damages between the independent tort feasors, and say that where factually a correct division cannot be made, the trier of fact may make it the best it can, which would be more or less a guess, stressing the factor that the wrongdoers are not in a position to complain of uncertainty. . . .

The judgment is affirmed.

In Summers v. Tice, the court explains the reasoning behind its use of burden shifting, commonly known as alternative liability. In a situation where both defendants are culpable and it is unclear which caused a harm, it would be unfair to hold neither liable merely because direct causation could not be established. In this sense, alternative liability defies the general rule laid out at the beginning of the chapter: Tort liability is placed on a defendant only if that specific defendant's conduct caused the plaintiff's harm. Rather, in alternative liability, one defendant whose conduct may not have caused any harm at all may still be held liable for that harm. In addition to fairness concerns, courts also shift the burden to the defendants in cases like Summers v. Tice because defendants may be thought to be more capable of providing proof of causation regarding each other. For this reason, the Restatement (Third) of Torts states two requirements for alternative liability: First, every defendant joined must have acted tortiously. Second, the plaintiff must join all possible defendants whose conduct may have caused injury. These safeguards ensure that a court will not hold liable a defendant who had committed no wrongful behavior and that the person who is causally responsible will not evade liability. See Restatement (Third) of Torts: Apportionment of Liability §28 cmt. g-i (2000).

A recent variation on the Summers v. Tice scenario was presented in Burks v. Abbott Laboratories, 917 F. Supp. 2d 902 (D. Minn. 2013). Plaintiffs individually and on behalf of their minor child brought an action against two manufacturers of powdered infant formula. Plaintiffs alleged that both manufacturers failed to adequately warn of the risk that babies might contract meningitis from contaminated formula and that one of the two manufacturers — albeit with no proof available as to which one — had provided the tainted formula that injured plaintiffs' infant child. While invoking alternative liability to shift the burden of proof as to specific causation onto the defendant manufacturers, the court was careful to stress that plaintiffs still bore the burden of proving that the infant's injury resulted from one of the defendants' products as opposed to, say, environmental factors: "If a plaintiff establishes that both defendants engaged in tortious conduct, that the harm was more likely than not caused by one of the defendants' tortious conduct, and that all potentially liable defendants are joined in the action, the policies underlying alternative liability are served by applying the doctrine." Id. at 915.

Ybarra v. Spangard

25 Cal. 2d 486, 154 P.2d 687 (1944)

GIBSON, C.J. This is an action for damages for personal injuries alleged to have been inflicted on plaintiff by defendants during the course of a surgical operation. The trial court entered judgments of nonsuit as to all defendants and plaintiff appealed.

On October 28, 1939, plaintiff consulted defendant Dr. Tilley, who diagnosed his ailment as appendicitis, and made arrangements for an appendectomy to be performed by defendant Dr. Spangard at a hospital owned and managed by defendant Dr. Swift. Plaintiff entered the hospital, was given a hypodermic injection, slept, and later was awakened by Doctors Tilley and Spangard and wheeled into the operating room by a nurse whom he believed to be defendant Gisler, an employee of Dr. Swift. Defendant Dr. Reser, the anesthetist, also an employee of Dr. Swift, adjusted plaintiff for the operation, pulling his body to the head of the operating table and, according to plaintiff's testimony, laying him back against two hard objects at the top of his shoulders, about an inch below his neck. Dr. Reser then administered the anesthetic and plaintiff lost consciousness. When he awoke early the following morning he was in his hospital room attended by defendant Thompson, the special nurse, and another nurse, who was not made a defendant.

Plaintiff testified that prior to the operation he had never had any pain in, or injury to, his right arm or shoulder, but that when he awakened he felt a sharp pain about half way between the neck and the point of the right shoulder. He complained to the nurse, and then to Dr. Tilley, who gave him diathermy treatments while he remained in the hospital. The pain did not cease, but spread down to the lower part of his arm, and after his release from the hospital the condition grew worse. He was unable to rotate or lift his arm, and developed paralysis and atrophy of the muscles around the shoulder. He received further treatments from Dr. Tilley until March, 1940, and then returned to work, wearing his arm in a splint on the advice of Dr. Spangard.

Plaintiff also consulted Dr. Wilfred Sterling Clark, who had X-ray pictures taken which showed an area of diminished sensation below the shoulder and atrophy and wasting away of the muscles around the shoulder. In the opinion of Dr. Clark, plaintiff's condition was due to trauma or injury by pressure or strain, applied between his right shoulder and neck.

Plaintiff was also examined by Dr. Fernando Garduno, who expressed the opinion that plaintiff's injury was a paralysis of traumatic origin, not arising from pathological causes, and not systemic, and that the injury resulted in atrophy, loss of use and restriction of motion of the right arm and shoulder.

[Omitted here are several paragraphs in which the court recognizes that the plaintiff has not introduced any direct evidence of negligence on the part of any defendant, but concludes that on the record here established the jury might draw the inference that one or more of the defendants was negligent towards the plaintiff. That is, although the plaintiff is unable to point specifically to the person who harmed him, that person must have been negligent. The court invokes the notion that the plaintiff's injury "speaks for itself," employing a Latin phrase to that effect about which we shall have more to say in a later chapter. Referring to the rule of law that permits an inference of negligence as "the doctrine," the court continues:]

The present case is of a type which comes within the reason and spirit of the doctrine more fully than any other. The passenger sitting awake in a railroad car at the time of a collision, the pedestrian walking along the street and struck by a falling object or the debris of an explosion, are surely not more entitled to an explanation than the unconscious patient on the operating table. Viewed from this aspect, it is difficult to see how the doctrine can, with any justification, be so restricted in its statement as to become inapplicable to a patient who submits himself to the care and custody of doctors and nurses, is rendered unconscious, and receives some injury from instrumentalities used in his treatment. Without the aid of the doctrine a patient who received permanent injuries of a serious character, obviously the result of someone's negligence, would be entirely unable to recover unless the doctors and nurses in attendance voluntarily chose to disclose the identity of the negligent person and the facts establishing liability. If this were the state of the law of negligence, the courts, to avoid gross injustice, would be forced to invoke the principles of absolute liability, irrespective of negligence, in actions by persons suffering injuries during the course of treatment under anesthesia. But we think this juncture has not yet been reached, and that the doctrine . . . is properly applicable to the case before us. . . .

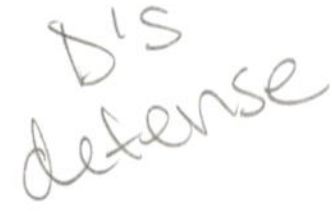

The argument of defendants is simply that plaintiff has not shown an injury caused by an instrumentality under a defendant's control, because he has not shown which of the several instrumentalities that he came in contact with while in the hospital caused the injury; and he has not shown that any one defendant or his servants had exclusive control over any particular instrumentality. Defendants assert that some of them were not the employees of other defendants, that some did not stand in any permanent relationship from which liability in tort would follow, and that in view of the nature of the injury, the number of defendants and the different functions performed by each, they could not all be liable for the wrong, if any.

We have no doubt that in a modern hospital a patient is quite likely to come under the care of a number of persons in different types of contractual and other relationships with each other. For example, in the present case it appears that Doctors Swift, Spangard and Tilley were physicians or surgeons commonly placed in the legal category of independent contractors; and Dr. Reser, the anesthetist, and defendant Thompson, the special nurse, were employees of Dr. Swift and not of the other doctors. But we do not believe that either the number or relationship of the defendants alone determines whether the [jury may draw an inference of negligence]. Every defendant in whose custody the plaintiff was placed for any period was bound to exercise ordinary care to see that no unnecessary harm came to him and each would be liable for failure in this regard. Any defendant who negligently injured him, and any defendant charged with his care who so neglected him as to allow injury to occur, would be liable. The defendant employers would be liable for the neglect of their employees; and the doctor in charge of the operation would be liable for the negligence of those who became his temporary servants for the purpose of assisting in the operation. . . .

It may appear at the trial that, consistent with the principles outlined above, one or more defendants will be found liable and others absolved, but this should not preclude the application of the [doctrine]. The control, at one time or another, of one or more of the various agencies or instrumentalities which might have harmed the plaintiff was in the hands of every defendant or of his employees or temporary servants. This, we think, places upon them the burden of initial explanation. Plaintiff was rendered unconscious for the purpose of undergoing surgical treatment by the defendants; it is manifestly unreasonable for them to insist that he identify any one of them as the person who did the alleged negligent act. . . .

The judgment is reversed.

On remand, a trial was held without a jury and the trial judge ruled in favor of the plaintiff against all defendants. All defendants, except the hospital's owner, testified that he or she did nothing and saw nothing that would cause the plaintiff's paralysis. The judgment for the plaintiff was affirmed in Ybarra v. Spangard, 208 P.2d 445 (Cal. 1949). There was a conflict in the medical testimony as to whether the paralysis was traumatic in origin or was caused by an infection. The court on appeal ruled that the conflict was up to the trial judge to resolve as an issue of fact.

Note: Joint and Several Liability

In Summers v. Tice, the court ruled that the defendants should "be treated as liable on the same basis as joint tortfeasors." In order to appreciate the implications of this ruling, it is necessary to have a basic understanding of what joint and several liability is, the circumstances under which such liability has traditionally been imposed, and the consequences that flow from such liability. What joint and several liability traditionally meant at common law can be quickly explained. Defendants who are jointly liable can be joined in a single suit, although they need not be. Defendants who are severally liable are each liable in full for the plaintiff's damages, although the plaintiff is entitled to only one total recovery.

At common law, two situations in which two or more defendants acted tortiously toward the plaintiff gave rise to what is now referred to as "joint and several liability": where the defendants acted in concert to cause the harm, and where the defendants acted independently but caused indivisible harm. Liability in the case of concerted action is a form of vicarious liability, in which all the defendants will be responsible for the harm actually caused by only one of them. An example of this is where *A* and *B* engage in an automobile race on a public street and *A* runs over the plaintiff. *B* will be liable to the plaintiff just as much as *A*, although *B* did not actually hit the plaintiff. Joint and several liability will also be imposed if the defendants act independently, each actually causing harm to the plaintiff but under circumstances in which it is impossible to allocate the harm to either defendant's conduct. Thus, if the plaintiff were a passenger in *A*'s automobile which collided with *B*'s automobile due to the fault of both drivers, *A* and *B* will be jointly and severally liable for the harm to the plaintiff.

Because of the procedural limitations relating to the circumstances under which two or more defendants could be joined in a single action, a distinction was made at common law between these two types of cases. Where the defendants acted in concert, they were joint tortfeasors and could be joined in one action. But where they acted independently to cause indivisible harm, they could not be joined. Thus, technically, only defendants acting in concert were called joint tortfeasors. However, modern rules of procedure permit joinder in indivisible harm cases (see Fleming James, Jr. & Geoffrey C. Hazard, Civil Procedure 473 (3d ed. 1985)), and defendants causing such harm are today commonly referred to as joint tortfeasors.

At common law, if the plaintiff sued just one of the joint tortfeasors and recovered, that defendant was without legal recourse against other tortfeasors to compel them to share the burden of liability. The harshness of this earlier rule has been ameliorated to some extent, and today most states provide for contribution among joint tortfeasors, either by statute or judicial decision. One early and influential reform effort was the Uniform Contribution Among Tortfeasors Act (1955), which was adopted in whole or in part by about 30 states. The Act was drafted at a time when plaintiffs' contributory negligence still served as an absolute bar to recovery rather than as a partial defense that merely reduced plaintiff's award proportionately according to comparative fault principles. Thus, the basic principles of contribution contained in the 1955 Act focus on defendants' pro rata shares of responsibility, rather than on proportionate shares of fault[1]:

> §1. [*Right to Contribution*]. (a) Except as otherwise provided in this Act, where two or more persons become jointly or severally liable in tort for the same injury to person or property or for the same wrongful death, there is a right of contribution among them even though judgment has not been recovered against all or any of them.
>
> (b) The right of contribution exists only in favor of a tortfeasor who has paid more than his pro rata share of the common liability, and his total recovery is limited to the amount paid by him in excess of his pro rata share. No tortfeasor is compelled to make contribution beyond his own pro rata share of the entire liability.
>
> (c) There is no right of contribution in favor of any tortfeasor who has intentionally [willfully or wantonly] caused or contributed to the injury or wrongful death.
>
> (d) A tortfeasor who enters into a settlement with a claimant is not entitled to recover contribution from another tortfeasor whose liability for the injury or wrongful death is not extinguished by the settlement nor in respect to any amount paid in a settlement which is in excess of what was reasonable. . . .
>
> §2. [*Pro Rata Shares*]. In determining the pro rata shares of tortfeasors in the entire liability (a) their relative degrees of fault shall not be considered, . . .
>
> §4. [*Release or Covenant Not to Sue*]. When a release or a covenant not to sue or not to enforce judgment is given in good faith to one of two or more persons liable in tort for the same injury or the same wrongful death:
>
> (a) It does not discharge any of the other tortfeasors from liability for the injury or wrongful death unless its terms so provide; but it reduces the claim against the others to the extent of any amount stipulated by the release or the covenant . . . ; and,
>
> (b) It discharges the tortfeasor to whom it is given from all liability for contribution to any other tortfeasor.

The Uniform Act recognizes the distinction between a general release and a covenant not to sue. Both are agreements between the plaintiff and the tortfeasor that formalize an out-of-court settlement. The early law was that any release of liability given by the plaintiff to one joint tortfeasor would also release the others from liability. More recently, some states now give effect to the release only with respect to the persons actually named in it. Even in states in which a general release of one joint tortfeasor releases all, most give legal effect to a covenant not to sue. Such an agreement affects only the legal rights between the particular tortfeasor and the plaintiff, and enables the plaintiff to proceed against the other joint tortfeasors.

One final note on terminology should be added: With the advent of so many — and so many different — versions of comparative fault and contribution statutes, the traditional meaning of the term "several liability" has shifted somewhat. As the Reporters to the Third Restatement note, while several liability used to mean that a defendant was responsible for all of the plaintiff's damages, it is now commonly used to mean "that a defendant is liable only for the proportionate share of plaintiff's indivisible injury determined by multiplying

1. To illustrate the difference between pro rata and proportionate shares, suppose that plaintiff suffers $100,000 worth of harm that is determined to have been caused 70 percent by defendant A's negligence and 30 percent by defendant B's negligence. Under a pro rata system, both defendants would be responsible for $50,000 of damages. Under a proportionate fault scheme, defendant A would be responsible for $70,000 and defendant B $30,000. The modern trend, reflected in the Restatement (Third) of Torts: Apportionment of Liability, is to determine the amount of contribution by considering each tortfeasor's proportionate degree of fault. See Restatement (Third) of Torts: Apportionment of Liability §23 cmt. *e* (2000).

the comparative responsibility assigned to any defendant by the amount of plaintiff's damages." Restatement (Third) of Torts: Apportionment of Liability §11 rptrs note cmt. a (2000).

More on joint and several liability appears in Chapter 4, in connection with comparative fault laws. As discussed there, the most important takeaway point regarding joint and several liability is that state legislatures have been extremely active in this area through tort reform statutes. Familiarity with the traditional common law principles remains essential to a proper understanding of tort law, but students must remember that those principles have almost certainly been altered in whatever jurisdiction becomes the students' eventual practice location.

C. Market Share Liability

The problem of "Which defendant did it?" presented by *Summers* and *Ybarra* has played out dramatically in the products liability area over the past two decades. In the classic example of such a defendant-identification case, a defectively designed product manufactured and distributed by many companies harms the plaintiff, under circumstances where the plaintiff cannot prove which company produced and distributed the harm-causing product unit.

Suffolk County Water Authority v. Dow Chemical Co.

44 Misc. 3d 569, 987 N.Y.S.2d 819 (Sup. Ct. 2014)

[The Suffolk County Water Authority (SCWA) brought suit against several defendants for manufacturing and distributing "perc," a toxic chemical that SCWA alleged had contaminated the Suffolk County water wells. The SCWA was unable to identify which of the many suppliers and manufacturers of perc caused the alleged contamination, and, as a result, sued multiple parties under the theory of market share liability. The defendants filed a motion to dismiss.]

Pines, J. As Defendants have aptly stated, the [market share] theory of recovery has been sanctioned in only one instance by the [New York] Court of Appeals in Hymowitz v. Eli Lilly, 539 N.E.2d 1069 (1989). In that case, claims based on market share liability were allowed to proceed in a litigation stemming from injuries caused by DES, a drug administered to pregnant women and later found to cause birth defects, in a situation where plaintiffs were unable, after many years had passed since the marketing of the drug and the appearance of the injuries, to identify the precise company that had manufactured the product giving rise thereto. In identifying the bases for its holding, the *Hymowitz* court set forth that victims of DES needed a "[r]ealistic avenue of relief for plaintiffs injured by DES who could not identify the actual manufacturer." However, the court made clear that this approach would be limited to those instances where manufacturers of a defective product produced an "[i]dentical, generically marketed product, which causes injury many years later." In addition, the liability of the DES manufacturers was held to be determined according to each producer's share of the national market . . . .

Since *Hymowitz*, the courts have been reluctant to apply market share liability in a series of other cases involving product liability and other tort claims. Thus, where the Court of

Appeals rejected application of the approach in Hamilton v. Beretta USA Corp., 750 N.E.2d 1055 (2001), it stressed that handguns were not identical, fungible items; [and] that the plaintiffs could often identify the manufacturer that caused a particular injury . . . . In Brenner v. American Cyanamid Co., 263 A.D.2d 165 (4th Dep't 1999), the [court] looked at all the reasons why market share liability was applied in *Hymowitz* and, finding none of them in a case involving injury arising from ingestion of lead-based paint pigment, rejected its use. [The *Brenner* court noted that, among other things, the national market for lead-paint was not easily defined, and that lead paint was not a generic or fungible product.]

The key case, in [this] Court's view is *Hymowitz v. Eli Lilly and Company.* After all is said and done, [the *Hymowitz* court] stressed that judicial action was necessitated in the DES arena in order to overcome the "[i]nordinately difficult problems of proof" caused by generically fungible products which were defective from their inception, where the harm caused by the same did not occur until substantial time had passed since ingestion. Under such circumstances, the court found that equity required that where the injury remained dormant for such a long period and where manufacturers contributed to the devastation, the "[e]ver-evolving dictates of justice and fairness, which are the heart of our common-law system, required formation of a remedy for injuries caused by [the defective product]."

In the case of perc . . . , the SCWA has set forth that perc is defective from the moment of its manufacture; that it is a generically fungible product, and that it takes many years from the point of its "ingestion" through seepage into the ground until it appears in one of the water purveyor's wells, causing extensive environmental harm, in the form of serious property damage. The allegations continue with excerpts from Defendants' witnesses to the effect that the fungible product of one manufacturer of perc becomes commingled with that of another over time and that it is essentially impossible to locate which manufacturer contributed to what extent to the contamination of which particular Water Authority well. In addition, the Plaintiff herein has asserted that without application of the market share theory for determining liability, it, like the DES plaintiffs, will be left without remedy for the harm assertedly caused by the chemical manufacturers herein. Plaintiff has further alleged that the product was not only dangerous from the point of manufacture; but, also, that it was reasonably foreseeable that it would cause harm to the groundwater system wherever it was ultimately used. It has assertedly named the entire chemical manufacturing market for the relevant time period and states that its experts are able to track the time periods from product use to resultant property damage.

[T]he Court believes that Plaintiff has set forth a proper claim for relief and that such is not dismissible as a matter of law. The Court, in so holding, does not ignore the cautionary language set forth in *Hymowitz*; but, rather, looks to the fact that what appear to be the major reasons for its holding are present in this matter. In contrast, those very same elements are found not to be present in both *Hamilton v. Beretta USA Corp.*, nor in *Brenner v. American Cyanamid Co* . . . . [T]he Court of Appeals in *Hamilton*, found the very bases for market share set forth in *Hymowitz* to be absent i.e., handguns are not identical fungible products and the manufacturers of the same are possible to identify. In addition, the assertion in the current complaint is that the product was defective the very moment it left the manufacturer's control and did not become dangerous, as in the case of handguns, only through the use of third parties. Similarly, in *Brenner*, there was again a finding that lead paint is not a fungible product remaining unchanged from manufacture to ingestion; it was not a generically marketed product; the identical nature of the injuries alleged were absent; and the Plaintiffs had not narrowed a national market to include only manufacturers that sold the product for interior use — the area from which the harm assertedly rose . . . .

[This] Court does not agree that if it is found that the product as designed was dangerous and that such danger arose from the point of manufacture, in conjunction with fungibility and the impossibility of designating chemical Defendants, all of whom are set forth in this action, as well as a lengthy latency period, that Plaintiff cannot utilize the market share theory in this case. Accordingly, Defendants' motion to dismiss the SCWA's . . . complaint is denied.

The Court in *Dow Chemical* discusses what is the most famous example of market share liability: personal injuries allegedly resulting from plaintiffs' prenatal exposure to the prescription drug diethylstilbestrol (DES). The plaintiffs in these cases are women whose mothers took DES many years earlier, while pregnant, to reduce the risk of miscarriage and pregnancy complications. Reliable expert testimony shows that the drug affected the plaintiffs while in their mothers' wombs, resulting in reproductive tract cancers in the plaintiffs many years later. Hundreds of thousands of women have been involved. Many of the plaintiffs cannot prove which drug company distributed the DES their mothers took. (As many as 300 companies may have produced the generic drug during the relevant period.) Some courts responded in ways that allow the injured plaintiffs to overcome otherwise fatal gaps in their proofs of actual causation by joining as defendants all, or most, of the companies manufacturing and distributing DES during the time periods relevant to their cases. The leading case is Sindell v. Abbott Labs., 607 P.2d 924 (Cal. 1980), *cert. denied*, 449 U.S. 912 (1980).

The California high court in *Sindell* considered and rejected the "alternative liability" theory from *Summers* and *Ybarra*. Not only did the companies lack any comparative advantage in determining which company's drug had caused the cancer, but the numbers of victims were much greater, and not all of the possible defendants could be joined in one legal action. And allocating liability pro rata among companies overlooked the reality that some companies produced many times the quantities of DES compared with other, smaller companies. To overcome these difficulties, the *Sindell* court adopted what has come to be known as the "market-share theory." According to the market-share approach, when a plaintiff joins the manufacturers of a substantial share of the relevant DES market, the burden shifts to each defendant to prove it did not produce the drug that her mother ingested. Those companies that do not carry this burden are held liable to the plaintiff for the percentage of damages approximating their individual share of the relevant DES market. The court reasoned that it was fair to shift the burden of proof on causation to the defendants in light of the fact that each defendant's market share, and therefore its share of the damages, would approximate the probability that it caused the plaintiff's injuries.

As discussed in *Dow Chemical*, the New York high court adopted the market-share approach, but based its assessment of defendants' proportionate responsibility on a national market. See Hymowitz v. Eli Lilly Co., 539 N.E.2d 1069 (N.Y. 1989). In *Hymowitz*, the New York court also refused to permit a defendant to exculpate itself by showing that its product could not have caused plaintiff's injury. Id. at 1078. Can you see why that ruling is consistent with the basic logic of market share liability?

One of the difficulties facing plaintiffs under *Sindell* — the necessity of joining companies that manufacture a "substantial share" of the DES that may have harmed the plaintiff—caused the Supreme Court of Wisconsin to modify the *Sindell* approach a few years after that landmark decision. Thus, in Collins v. Eli Lilly Co., 342 N.W.2d 37, 50-52 (Wis. 1984), the court outlined its more liberal approach:

> Thus, the plaintiff need commence suit against only one defendant and allege the following elements: that the plaintiff's mother took DES; that DES caused the plaintiff's subsequent injuries; that the defendant produced or marketed the type of DES taken by the plaintiff's mother; and that the defendant's conduct in producing or marketing the DES constituted a breach of a legally recognized duty to the plaintiff. In the situation where the plaintiff cannot allege and prove what type of DES the mother took, as to the third element the plaintiff need only allege and prove that the defendant drug company produced or marketed the drug DES for use in preventing miscarriages during pregnancy. . . .
>
> Once the plaintiff has proven a prima facie case . . . , the burden of proof shifts to the defendant to prove by a preponderance of the evidence that it did not produce or market the subject DES either during the time period the plaintiff was exposed to DES or in the relevant geographical market area in which the plaintiff's mother acquired the DES. In utilizing these defenses, the defendant must establish that the DES it produced or marketed could not have reached the plaintiff's mother. We conclude that it is appropriate to shift the burden of proof on time and geographic distribution to the defendant drug companies because they will have better access to relevant records than the plaintiff. Further, if relevant records do not exist, we believe that the equities of DES cases favor placing the consequences on the defendants.
>
> We believe that this procedure will result in a pool of defendants which it can reasonably be assumed could have caused the plaintiff's injuries. We note in this regard that, in cases where the plaintiff's mother took DES over a period of time and had the prescription refilled, it is possible that DES from several drug companies may have contributed to the plaintiff's injuries. This still could mean that some of the remaining defendants may be innocent, but we accept this as the price the defendants, and perhaps ultimately society, must pay to provide the plaintiff an adequate remedy under the law.

In a footnote to the above-quoted excerpt from *Collins*, the opinion refers to defendant's argument that the sort of remedy adopted by the court "should be fashioned by the legislature" (342 N.W.2d at 52, n.12). The court responds by saying: "We disagree with this argument. It is the function of this court to modify the existing common law if that becomes necessary to promote justice under the law."

Several other jurisdictions have adopted the *Sindell* market-share approach or some variation thereof in DES cases. See, e.g., Conley v. Boyle Drug Co., 570 So. 2d 275 (Fla. 1990); Martin v. Abbott Lab., 689 P.2d 368 (Wash. 1984). Other courts have rejected using market-share even in DES cases. See, e.g., Smith v. Eli Lilly & Co., 560 N.E.2d 324 (Ill. 1990); Gorman v. Abbott Lab, 599 A.2d 1364 (R.I. 1991); Mulcahy v. Eli Lilly & Co., 386 N.W.2d 67 (Iowa 1986); Bortell v. Eli Lilly & Co., 406 F. Supp. 2d 1 (D.D.C. 2005) (applying Pennsylvania law).

Attempts to extend the market-share approach beyond DES cases have been mostly rejected, often based on lack of fungibility. See, e.g., Becker v. Baron Bros., 649 A.2d 613 (N.J. 1994) (asbestos); Ferris v. Gatke Corp., 132 Cal. Rptr. 2d 819 (Ct. App. 2003) (asbestos brake pads); Hamilton v. Beretta, 750 N.E.2d 1055 (N.Y. 2001) (handguns); Santiago v. Sherwin Williams Co., 3 F.3d 546 (1st Cir. 1993) (lead paint); Doe v. Cutter, 380 F.3d 399 (8th Cir. 2004) (HIV-tainted blood products); S.F. v. Archer-Daniels-Midland Co., No. 13-CV-634S, 2014 WL 1600414, 2014 U.S. Dist. LEXIS 55195 (W.D.N.Y. Apr. 21, 2014) (high fructose corn syrup); George v. Hous. Auth., 906 So. 2d 1282 (La.

2005) (smoke alarms); Pooshs v. Philip Morris USA, Inc., 904 F. Supp. 2d 1009 (N.D. Cal. 2012) (cigarettes).

One context in which plaintiffs have had success invoking the market share theory of liability involves a widely-used fuel additive found to cause significant water contamination. See *In re* Methyl Tertiary Butyl Ether (MTBE), 175 F. Supp. 2d 593 (S.D.N.Y. 2001) (court permitted a market-share theory of liability to go forward for well owners who alleged that oil companies conspired to mislead the government and public that concentrations of MTBE were acceptable); *In re* Methyl Tertiary Butyl Ether (MTBE) Prods. Liab. Litig., 643 F. Supp. 2d 461 (S.D.N.Y. 2009) (holding that defendants bear the burden of proof to apportion their shares of responsibility). As you read the following decision, consider whether and to what extent courts should approach the market share liability theory differently when the plaintiff is a government entity.

State v. Exxon Mobil Corp.

126 A.3d 266 (N.H. 2015)

[The State of New Hampshire filed suit against Exxon Mobil Corporation and ExxonMobil Oil Corporation (collectively, either Exxon or ExxonMobil), as well as other gasoline suppliers, refiners, and chemical manufacturers. The State argued that these companies included an additive in their gasoline, methyl tertiary butyl ether (MTBE), which caused extensive groundwater contamination. The State could not definitively trace the additive back to the company that caused the contamination, but argued that all of the companies should be held liable according to their market share of products containing MTBE. The jury found for the State, awarding total damages of nearly eight hundred million dollars; because Exxon's market share for gasoline in New Hampshire during the applicable time period was around 30%, the final verdict against Exxon was close to two hundred and thirty million dollars. Exxon appealed.]

DALIANIS, C.J. As the trial court explained, the purpose behind market share liability is that

> [i]n our contemporary complex industrialized society, advances in science and technology create fungible goods which may harm consumers and which cannot be traced to any specific producer. The response of the courts can be either to adhere rigidly to prior doctrine, denying recovery to those injured by such products, or to fashion remedies to meet these changing needs. In an era of mass production and complex marketing methods the traditional standard of negligence is insufficient to govern the obligations of manufacturer to consumer, courts should acknowledge that some adaptation of the rules of causation and liability may be appropriate in these recurring circumstances.

The court noted that in determining whether market share liability applies in certain circumstances, the *Restatement (Third) of Torts: Products Liability* sets forth six factors that provide a general framework for analysis:

> (1) The generic nature of the product; (2) the long latency period of the harm; (3) the inability of plaintiffs to discover which defendant's product caused plaintiff's harm; (4) the clarity of the causal connection between the defective product and the harm suffered by plaintiffs; (5) the absence of other medical or environmental factors that could have caused or materially contributed to the harm; and (6) the availability of sufficient "market share" data to support a reasonable apportionment of liability.

See Restatement (Third) of Torts: Products Liability §15 comment *c* at 233 (1998).

Applying the six *Restatement* factors, the trial court determined that market share liability should be applied in this case. As to the first factor, the generic nature of the product, the court found that the State had alleged sufficient facts for the court to conclude that MTBE is fungible, *i.e.,* that it is interchangeable with other brands of the same product. As to the second factor, whether the harm caused by the product has a long latency period, the trial court found that the harm caused by MTBE was not latent because it travels faster and further than other chemicals. Thus, the court concluded that this factor weighs in favor of Exxon. As to the third factor, the plaintiff's inability to identify which defendant caused the harm, the trial court concluded this factor weighs in the State's favor because "retailers commingled gasoline in storage tanks at stations, so it would be impossible to determine which of the defendant[s'] MTBE gasoline was discharged into the environment."

The trial court found that the fourth factor, the clarity of the causal connection between the defective product and harm suffered by the State, favors the State. The court agreed with Exxon's general proposition that the gasoline market does not alone reflect the risk created and, thus, the court required the State "to introduce market share data as targeted as possible . . . ." Noting that it is impossible to determine market share with mathematical exactitude, the court concluded that the experts' market data was sufficient.

The trial court found the fifth and sixth factors favor the State. As to the fifth factor, whether other medical or environmental factors could have contributed to the harm, the court noted that Exxon had not asserted that other factors contributed. As to the sixth factor, the sufficiency of the market data, the court found that the State's experts had presented "enough market data to allow the State to proceed" on a market share liability theory.

Under market share liability, the burden of identification shifts to the defendants if the plaintiff establishes a *prima facie* case on every element of the claim except for identification of the actual tortfeasors, and the plaintiff has joined the manufacturers of a "substantial share" of the market. Once these elements are established, each defendant is . . . liable for the portion of the judgment that represents its share of the market at the time of the injury, unless it proves that it could not have made the [product] that caused the plaintiff's injuries.

We agree with the trial court that, based upon our willingness to construct judicial remedies for plaintiffs who would be left without recourse due to impossible burdens of proof, applying market share liability was justified in the circumstances presented by this case. In addition to finding that the State had proven all of the elements of its claims, the jury found: "MTBE gasoline is fungible"; the State "cannot trace MTBE gasoline found in groundwater and in drinking water back to the company that manufactured or supplied that MTBE gasoline"; and the State "has identified a substantial segment of the relevant market for gasoline containing MTBE." We have reviewed the record and conclude that it contains sufficient evidence to support the jury's findings. Given the evidence presented, the State faced an impossible burden of proving which of several MTBE gasoline producers caused New Hampshire's groundwater contamination. We hold that the trial court did not unsustainably exercise its discretion in allowing the State to use the theory of market share liability to determine the portion of the State's damages caused by Exxon's conduct.

In another relatively rare use of market-share liability outside the DES context, the high court of Wisconsin extended the doctrine to lead paint manufacturers on the basis of its controversial *Collins* decision. See Thomas v. Mallett, 701 N.W.2d 523 (Wis. 2005). Significantly, the Wisconsin high court did not limit its theory of market-share liability to physically identical products, but instead articulated a "risk contribution" theory according to which fungibility is assessed by a number of criteria such as functional interchangeability or uniformity of risk. Cf. Allen Rostron, Beyond Market Share Liability: A Theory of Proportional Share Liability for Nonfungible Products, 52 UCLA L. Rev. 151 (2004). The Wisconsin Legislature later passed a statute overruling *Thomas*, stating that the case "was an improperly expansive application of the risk contribution theory of liability announced in *Collins* . . . ." Wis. Stat. §895.046 (2015). Soon after the statute was passed, a federal court, in Gibson v. American Cyanamid Co., 760 F.3d 600 (2014) cert. denied, 135 S. Ct. 2311 (2015), found that retroactive application of the statute was barred by the Wisconsin Constitution. The same court rejected defendants' arguments that Wisconsin's risk contribution approach to market-share liability violated defendants' constitutional rights to property and substantive and procedural due process.

For an argument that market-share liability is not such a radical approach to causation after all, see Mark A. Geistfeld, The Doctrinal Unity of Alternative Liability and Market-Share Liability, 155 U. Pa. L. Rev. 447 (2006).

Problem 9

You have received the following memorandum from a partner in the firm in which you are an associate:

> We represent Bennett and Rachael Carrington, whose two-year-old son, Robert, was attacked and badly mauled by a dog in the side yard of their house while his mother was inside answering the telephone. The owner of the dog should be liable in damages, which in this case could be quite high. The potential defendants appear to be financially able to pay a fairly large judgment, and there is a good possibility that one or more of them have insurance covering this sort of liability.
>
> On the issue of liability, the difficulty is one of identifying the dog or dogs that attacked the Carrington boy. No one actually saw the attack take place. Mrs. Carrington came upon the scene immediately afterward and saw a German shepherd dog running from the yard. German shepherds appear to be popular in the Carrington neighborhood. Five have been located, and any one of them might have done it. Mrs. Carrington cannot identify any one of them as the attacker. None of the owners of the German shepherds leash or otherwise confine their dogs, and in light of an ordinance making failure to do so a misdemeanor, I am sure that we will get to the jury with the negligence issue if we can adequately identify the proper defendant in the case.
>
> I have been called out of town for a week, and this case won't wait until I get back. Therefore, I am handing the file over to you. Take whatever steps you think are reasonably necessary to complete the investigation, bearing in mind that we already have a considerable sum invested in the case to this point. Your main job will be to sift through the file, organize it, and decide whether we have enough as things stand to get to the jury re the identification issue. I note that the hospital lab technician mentions the possibility of DNA testing. I understand it is "iffy" and very expensive, and for now let's stick with what we've already got. When I get back, I will want to sit down with you to decide where to go with this thing. Have your conclusions ready for me when I return.

In preparing your response to the partner's memorandum, assume that *Hoyt, Summers,* and *Ybarra* are opinions of the highest court of your state.

File No. 427-6-708 Carrington

[The actual file in this case consists of correspondence, medical reports, signed statements, memoranda of investigations, and the like. What follows is a summary of the results of the investigation to date. Only material relating to the identification of the dogs has been included.]

GENERAL BACKGROUND

The Carrington family live in a rural farming area on Forest Road in Webster Township, approximately a quarter-mile north of the intersection of Forest Road and Long Pond Road, and approximately two miles south of the southern boundary of a state forest. Mr. Carrington is an architect, with an office in Central City. The area within approximately a four-mile radius of the Carrington house has been thoroughly checked, and five German shepherds have been discovered to have been living within that area. All are approximately the same size and color, and all wear collars. None is known to have bitten humans before. The names of the owners of these dogs, together with the dogs' names, age, sex, and the approximate distance of each from the Carrington house, are included in Table 2-1. A map showing the locations of the dog owners relative to the Carrington house is set out in Figure 2-1.

SUMMARY OF INTERVIEWS

Mrs. Carrington—At approximately 10 minutes after 12 o'clock noon last September 2, Mrs. Carrington was answering the telephone in their home in Webster Township. Robert was in his playpen in the side yard. The Carringtons have no other children and no pets. Mrs. Carrington could not see Robert from inside the house. She heard Robert cry out and heard what sounded like a dog growling. She ran through the kitchen and down the back steps shouting "Bobby! Bobby!" She missed a step and fell to the ground. When she got up she ran around the side of the house in time to see a German shepherd dog disappear into a cornfield across Forest Road in front of the Carrington house. The playpen was tipped over and Robert was on the ground, unconscious and severely mauled. She picked Robert up, put him in her car, and drove him to the Central City Hospital.

As far as the identity of the attacking dog is concerned, Mrs. Carrington is certain it was a German shepherd that she saw enter the cornfield. The dog was running quite fast and seemed to have just crossed the street in a line directly away from the Carrington house. She says the dog may have been limping but she cannot be sure, nor can she tell whether it had a

TABLE 2-1

Owner's Name	*Dog*	*Age*	*Sex*	*Distance from Carrington home (Miles)*
Ralph Wilson	Chief	5	M	½
	King Henry	4	M	½
	Dolly	7	F	½
Henry Jarvis	Butch	3	M	2
Larry Carson	Queenie	2	F	3

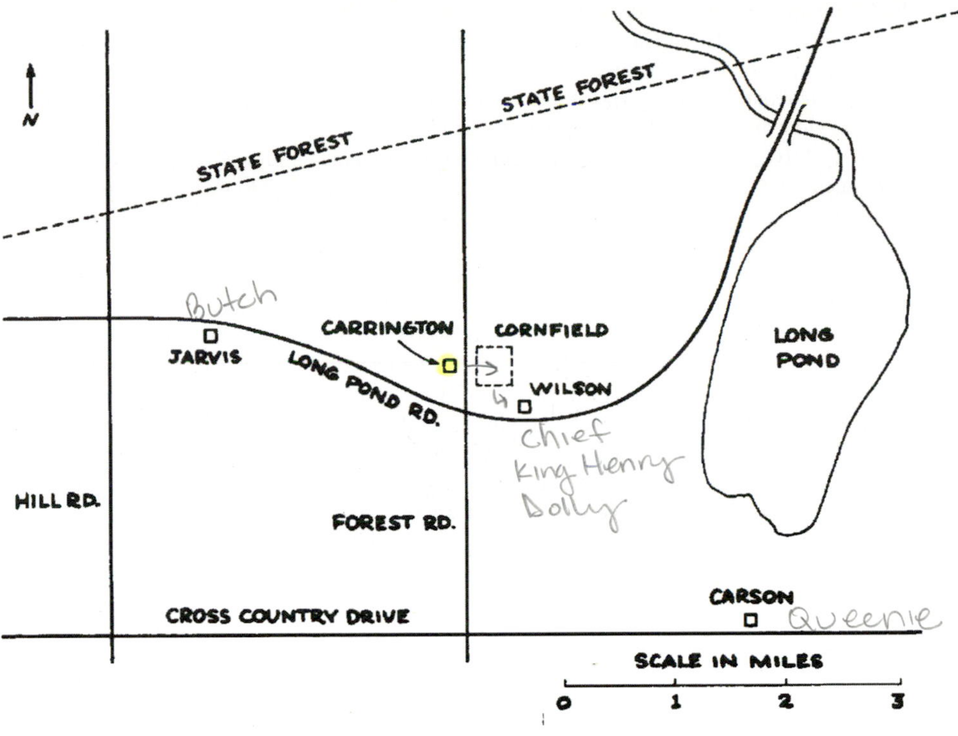

FIGURE 2-1

collar on or not. She has viewed the five suspect dogs, and cannot positively identify any one of them as the dog she saw on September 2, nor can she exclude any of the five. She is certain that the dogs owned by Wilson and Jarvis have visited the Carrington house at one time or other during the year prior to the incident, but she had not seen any dog near the house on the day in question. She does not know whether the Carson's dog had ever come by the Carrington house, as she would not have recognized it on sight. She thinks there may have been one or two times in the past few months when strange German shepherds came by the house, but she cannot be sure.

Mr. Carrington — A doctor called him from the Central City Hospital shortly after one o'clock in the afternoon of September 2, and he rushed to the hospital from his office. He took his wife home at 3:30 and went out into the yard to examine the playpen area. He found the playpen on its side, with the plastic-covered mattress several feet away. He found small amounts of blood on the mattress and more on the ground. Before washing the playpen and mattress, he collected about two dozen dog hairs from the mattress, which hairs he turned over to the police when they arrived in response to his call.

He explains that he and his wife knew the dogs owned by Wilson and Jarvis by name, and that the dogs visited their house periodically. All four dogs seem to have behaved themselves on such occasions. Neither Mr. Carrington nor his wife knew the Carson's dog by name.

Dr. Edmund Costa — Dr. Costa is the surgeon called in to treat Robert's injuries. He describes the injuries as severe, and he is certain that there will be some disfigurement even after extensive plastic surgery. In addition to describing the boy's injuries, he explains that in his judgment they were inflicted by the repeated bites of a fairly large dog. He cannot tell if Robert was bitten by more than one dog, nor can he identify the breed of dog from the nature of his patient's wounds. He found and collected samples of dog hair from Robert's body and clothing, which he gave to the hospital laboratory.

Ralph Wilson—He and his wife live approximately one-half mile from the Carringtons. They have no children. His three German shepherds run loose, and he cannot account for their whereabouts on the day and at the time of the accident. He was very uncooperative at the interview and refused to discuss the matter further.

Henry Jarvis—Mr. Jarvis, his wife, and their three young children live approximately two miles from the Carringtons. The Jarvis's German shepherd runs loose. Mr. Jarvis, who owns and operates a small grocery store in Webster Township, had arrived home from the veterinarian with their dog at 11 o'clock in the morning on September 2. The dog had a cut on its foot that had almost healed, and Mr. Jarvis had taken it to the vet for a final checkup. Upon arriving home, Mr. Jarvis explains that he turned the dog loose and observed it walk slowly in an easterly direction down Long Pond Road. After the dog walked 100 feet or so, he lay down and went to sleep. Mr. Jarvis does not know where the dog went after that, but he doesn't believe that it would have traveled very far on the injured foot. Mr. Jarvis and the children were in town until almost four o'clock, and the dog was in the backyard when they arrived home. His foot was tender and he appeared to have a slight limp, leading Jarvis to think that Butch might have wandered off some distance from home. But Jarvis noticed nothing about him to suggest he had attacked Bobby.

Larry Carson—Mr. Carson, his wife, and their two children live on and operate a fairly prosperous dairy farm approximately three miles from the Carringtons. Their dog is not confined, and the Carsons are unable to account for its whereabouts at the time of the attack on September 2.

Walter Palchek—Mr. Palchek is employed as a farmhand by a neighbor of the Carringtons, and was working in a field just south of the cornfield across from the Carrington house on September 2. Shortly after noon, he glanced up to see a large dog leave the southern end of the cornfield. He is sure that it was a German shepherd, but he cannot positively identify it. The dog was moving at a slow trot, southeasterly in the general direction of Wilson's house. Mr. Palchek thought he recognized the dog as King Henry. He called the dog by that name and it stopped for a moment and looked toward him, but then resumed its journey. The dog was never closer than 200 feet or so from Mr. Palchek, and he paid no further attention to it. He does not remember the dog to have been limping, but he cannot be certain due to the distance between him and the dog. He does not know if the dog was wearing a collar.

Other neighbors generally—Questioning of everyone known to live or work within the area surrounding the Carrington home tended generally to confirm the fact that the Wilson, Jarvis, and Carson dogs roam the area frequently. No one remembers having seen any German shepherds other than the five in question for several weeks surrounding the date of the attack on the Carrington boy.

Dr. James Thomas—Dr. Thomas is the veterinarian who treated the Jarvis's dog on September 2. He describes the dog as normally even-tempered, but likely to have been a bit more nervous and irritable on that date due to the foot injury. The dog had displayed no noticeable limp during the visit on September 2, but the paw was still tender enough so that a limp might have developed upon extended use of the injured foot. Dr. Thomas says that Jarvis's dog was physically capable of going to the Carrington house on September 2, although less likely to do so because of the residual soreness in the foot. If the dog were to have gone that far, he would have been more likely, once there, to attack a pestering child because of that soreness.

Jack Fagen, Chief of Police, Webster Township—Chief Fagen received a call from Mr. Carrington on the afternoon of September 2, and immediately took a deputy to go investigate. Inspection of the side yard area where the attack occurred produced no blood or skin samples usable in attempting to identify the attacker. Dog hairs were found at the scene, added to those received from Mr. Carrington, and later sent to the police lab in Central City.

A search of the area in cooperation with the County Health Officer revealed the five German shepherd dogs owned by Wilson, Jarvis, and Carson. Whenever there is an instance of a dog biting a person, an attempt is made to locate the dog to determine if it has rabies. In a case like this, where there is no positive identification, all dogs within the area of the attack generally fitting the description are apprehended for observation. How wide an area is searched depends on a number of factors. Because Webster Township is fairly rural, a somewhat more extensive search was made in this case than would have been made in a more congested area. Because rabies is a very serious disease, the police and public health officials try to be quite certain that the attacking dog is captured.

All five dogs were apprehended on September 3 and confined at the kennel of a local veterinarian in order to check them out for rabies. None showed any outward signs of having been involved in the attack. All five were released ten days later. Chief Fagen thinks that the guilty animal is King Henry. He bases his opinion on observations of the dog during its confinement at the veterinarian's kennel when the dog behaved more aggressively than the others. In addition, King Henry had been the subject of several minor complaints over the past three years. Once he chased a salesman, an incident that led to Mr. Wilson paying a $20 fine for violation of the dog leash ordinance. When asked why the ordinance is not more uniformly or rigorously enforced, Chief Fagen explained that the police department is small and overworked, and that it was customary to overlook violations of the leash law except when a formal complaint is made to the police.

Joseph Brown, technician in police lab, Central City— Mr. Brown examined microscopically the hair samples from the playpen area, and concluded that they are German shepherd hairs. He cannot determine the age or sex of the dog, and he feels that the hairs might even have come from two different dogs. He has compared the hair with samples from all five suspect dogs, and he cannot make any definite inclusionary or exclusionary determination.

Linda Balfours, technician in Central City Hospital lab— Ms. Balfours examined microscopically the hair samples from Robert's body and is reasonably certain that they came from the same German shepherd dog. She cannot determine the sex of the dog, and will only say that it must have been less than ten years of age. She has compared these hairs with the samples from the five suspect dogs and can make no definite inclusionary or exclusionary determination. One or two labs in the country might be able to shed light on the identity of the attacking dog via DNA testing. This would be very expensive and, at best, problematic. No lab in your state could perform such tests.

Dr. Martha Gilley, a lecturer on law-medicine at the state medical school— Dr. Gilley explains that the hair from an attacking dog presents problems in identification. Most authorities agree that the type of dog could probably be determined from a hair sample. However, even this determination could be confused according to where on the dog's body the hair comes from. Back hair is not the same as facial hair or the hair from the inside of the leg. Dr. Gilley concludes that very little can be determined from microscopic examination of the hair. There are other, newer techniques which sometimes allow much more precise identifications, but in her judgment they are not practical or possible in this case.

William Berger— Mr. Berger is the owner and operator of a large kennel in Central City. He has had 27 years of experience working with all breeds of dogs, including German shepherds. He explains that in terms of which breed or sex of dog is more likely to be vicious or to attack other dogs or humans, only the broadest of generalizations are possible. Generally, German shepherds have the reputation of being a slightly more, rather than less, aggressive breed of dog; but they are exceeded by many breeds, both small and large, with respect to their propensity to snap, bite, and attack humans. Generally, males are more aggressive than females, but even this is subject to exceptions — female dogs that have just whelped, for example, are likely to be nervous and overprotective, resulting in a belligerent attitude.

The difficulty in Problem 9 from the plaintiff's point of view is that a gap in the evidence as to the issue of causation may prevent the plaintiff from getting to the jury. The investigation so far does not reveal an eyewitness to the attack. Do you think that further investigation to locate such a witness would be worthwhile? Assuming that an eyewitness is not discovered, and that a sense of professional responsibility precludes the manufacturing of one, you are left to do the best you can with circumstantial evidence tending only inferentially to point to one or more defendants.

Circumstantially, there are at least two approaches to the problem of identifying the proper defendant in this case. Either the focus can be narrowed to a single dog, or rather dog owner, as the responsible party; or a limited group of persons whose dogs might have done it can be set up, with the attempt to hold them jointly and severally liable. The first of these approaches, if successful in bringing the case before the jury, ends up exposing a single defendant to liability for harm that he may not have caused. Which of the factual elements in this problem tend to narrow the field of potential defendants to a single individual? Do all of these elements point to the same person? If not, is this approach doomed to defeat, or will the court leave it to the jury?

The second approach suggested above — that of asserting the liability jointly and severally of a group of persons because any one of them might have been the person whose dog attacked the boy — is unique not only in the route taken but also in the conclusion reached. Unlike the first approach, which at most exposes a single dog owner to liability, the second could expose two innocent owners to liability for harm they did not cause. What are the legal theories that would support such an approach? Does this case fall into any of the traditional categories, outlined in the following Note, in which joint and several liability is imposed? Do the rules announced in *Summers* and *Ybarra* justify the multidefendant approach to this problem? If so, what factual showing must the plaintiff make to justify getting to the jury against each of the defendants on a joint and several liability theory? And what arguments are available to the defendants to avoid liability under this approach?

The Lawyer's Professional Responsibility: Interviewing Witnesses

In the preceding problem, if Mrs. Carrington could have given a positive identification of the dog that was running into the cornfield, the chances of getting to the jury on the cause issue would be substantially increased. A lawyer investigating the case should certainly appreciate this, but what could ethically be done in questioning Mrs. Carrington about the identity of the dog? Certainly, the lawyer ought not to ask her to lie. Not surprisingly, the Model Rules of Professional Conduct prohibit a lawyer from offering evidence to a tribunal that he or she knows to be false. See Rule 3.3(a)(3). But a layperson is often unaware of what facts are necessary to support a cause of action or defense. Is there a risk of subtle subornation of perjury if the lawyer explains in advance, or makes clear through skillful questioning, what facts must be established if the claim or defense is to be successful? Which of the following lines of inquiry, if any, would be improper in interviewing Mrs. Carrington?

1. Did you recognize the dog? Describe it to me to the best of your recollection.
2. Think for a minute. Was the dog limping? Were there any peculiar color markings? Was it wearing a collar? What size was it?

3. I'm sure you realize that it is important for you to remember as much as you can. Are you sure that the dog was not limping?
4. Unless we get a positive identification of the dog, we may very well not be able to collect against anyone. Think about it, and I will see you tomorrow.

These lines of inquiry are a progression from "Tell me what you know" to "Tell me what I want to hear." Is there a point on this progression beyond which the inquiry would violate the Rules of Professional Conduct? Your own sense of professional responsibility? For a classic depiction of this dilemma in the criminal defense context, see the 1959 film Anatomy of a Murder, in which James Stewart's character teeters precariously between witness coaching and suborning perjury.

In all of the materials in this section on "Which defendant did it?" — from *Summers* and *Ybarra* through the text on market-share liability and ending with the preceding problem, involving the dog that attacked a young boy in his backyard—courts seem to be trying to construct tort-based recovery mechanisms retroactively, after the fact of injury. Might not such recovery mechanisms be established before the fact of injury when problems of defendant identification are foreseeable? Consider the following problem.

Problem 10 skip

If you have already considered Problem 9, above, then its facts are incorporated by reference here. If you have not considered Problem 9, use the following summary to consider this problem. On September 2 of this year, an unidentified dog attacked and badly mauled a two-year-old boy, Robert Carrington, in his backyard in Webster Township. The Carringtons have asked your firm to represent them and their son in bringing an action against the owner of the dog that injured young Robert. Investigation reveals that the dog was almost certainly a German shepherd, but no eyewitness or other direct evidence is available to identify which, if any, of several German shepherds in Webster Township is the attacker. Your firm is considering the possibility of joining all the owners of German shepherds in a single action aimed at holding them jointly and severally liable. All such owners were arguably negligent in failing to restrain their animals in violation of a township leash law, but joint and several tort liability would result in at least one owner being held liable for harm that his dog did not cause. You have just received the following memorandum from the partner handling the case:

> As you know, the Carrington case presents some very difficult cause-in-fact issues, difficult enough to possibly cause our tort case against the German shepherd owners to fail as a matter of law. The parents are understandably upset over what happened and are frustrated over our inability to identify which dog attacked their son. Mr. Carrington has asked me some questions that I now pass on to you. Assuming for the sake of argument that our tort action does not succeed, he and his wife would feel better about the whole situation if *some* good, at least, could come of their ordeal. After researching the question of unidentified dog attacks statewide over the last five years, he found evidence of at least seven confirmed incidents. To his knowledge, none of the victims, who were all young children, received tort compensation. He assumes that the medical bills in such cases tend to be substantial —

> Mr. Carrington describes the medical bills for Robert as "already astronomical and going higher" — and he wants to know if some sort of fund could be set up to aid such victims in the future. He thinks maybe a statute at the state level, or an ordinance at the local level, might call for the creation of such a fund.
>
> Mr. Carrington's idea is to have the fund pay all victims of dog attacks "up front," with the fund being reimbursed out of tort proceeds, if any, recovered later on. He is unsure of how such a fund would be set up — that is, who would pay into it ahead of time to get it established. He is also unsure of how the fund would pay out to victims. Which victims? How much? He wants us to consider the problem and come up with recommendations regarding how he might proceed to support such a proposal. He will wait until our tort case is resolved to proceed further but however our case comes out, he intends to pursue his idea so his son's tragedy will not have been totally in vain.
>
> I want you to consider his idea and sketch the way(s) you think best to move forward with it. What are the major decision points and what are the pros and cons of different resolutions at each point?

The problem of dog attacks causing human injuries (and even deaths) is not trivial. Consider the following excerpts from Safia G. Hussain, Note, Attacking the Dog-Bite Epidemic: Why Breed-Specific Legislation Won't Solve the Dangerous-Dog Dilemma, 74 Fordham L. Rev. 2847, 2849-50 (2006) (footnotes omitted):

> There are approximately sixty-eight million dogs kept as pets in the United States. Every year, these dogs bite an estimated four to five million Americans, representing about two percent of the population, and that number is on the rise. The Center for Disease Control warns that, each year, Americans have a one in fifty chance of being bitten by a dog. Children are the most frequent bite victims, representing more than fifty percent of the total number of cases. Nearly half of all American children have been bitten before the age of twelve.
>
> Serious dog bites may also be on the rise. Notably, while the dog population increased only two percent between 1986 and 1996, the number of dog bites requiring medical attention rose thirty-seven percent. More than 350,000 victims per year, or nearly 960 per day, seek emergency room care for serious dog bites. In fact, dog bites now rank among the top causes of nonfatal injuries, and are responsible second only to baseball and softball injuries for emergency room visits.

The author describes the various statutes and ordinances that attempt to regulate the ownership and management of potentially dangerous dogs, and concludes that breed-specific regulations are less fair and effective than are regulations based on the demonstrated propensities of some individual dogs, regardless of the breed, to cause harm to humans.

D. When Two or More Causal Agents Would, Independent of Each Other, Have Caused Plaintiff's Harm: Concurrent and Successive Causation

Imagine a ship trying to get to port, but unable to reach its destination because a bridge has collapsed and is blocking the river. Further along the river, there is a second bridge that also has collapsed and would have blocked the ship's passage anyway, even if the first bridge had not obstructed the ship's path. Is the second bridge — a bridge that the ship did not and could not reach — a cause of the ship's delay? Would it matter if the second bridge collapsed first? Would it matter if the first bridge collapsed due to a small amount of negligence, while the second bridge collapsed due to gross negligence? Or vice versa — if the second bridge would have collapsed even though there was no negligence involved, but the first bridge collapsed due to it being unlawfully maintained?[2]

Dillon v. Twin State Gas & Electric Co.

85 N.H. 449, 163 A. 111 (1932)

The defendant maintained wires to carry electric current over a public bridge in Berlin.

The decedent [age 14] and other boys had been accustomed for a number of years to play on the bridge in the daytime, habitually climbing the sloping girders to the horizontal ones, on which they walked and sat and from which they sometimes dived into the river. No current passed through the wires in the daytime except by chance.

The decedent while sitting on a horizontal girder at a point where the wires from the post to the lamp were in front of him or at his side and while facing outwards from the side of the bridge, leaned over, lost his balance, instinctively threw out his arm and took hold of one of the wires with his right hand to save himself from falling. The wires happened to be charged with a high voltage current at the time and he was electrocuted.

Further facts appear in the opinion.

Transferred . . . on the defendant's exception to the denial of its motion for a directed verdict.

Allen, J. . . . The circumstances of the decedent's death give rise to an unusual issue of its cause. In leaning over from the girder and losing his balance he was entitled to no protection from the defendant to keep from falling. Its only liability was in exposing him to the danger of charged wires. If but for the current in the wires he would have fallen down on the floor of the bridge or into the river, he would without doubt have been either killed or seriously injured. Although he died from electrocution, yet if by reason of his preceding loss of balance he was bound to fall except for the intervention of the current, he either did not have long to live or was to be maimed. In such an outcome of his loss of balance the defendant deprived him, not of a life of normal expectancy, but of one too short to be given pecuniary allowance, in one alternative, and not of normal, but of limited, earning capacity, in the other.

If it were found that he would have thus fallen with death probably resulting, the defendant would not be liable unless for conscious suffering found to have been sustained from the shock. In that situation his life or earning capacity had no value. To constitute actionable negligence there must be damage, and damage is limited to those elements the [wrongful death] statute prescribes.

If it should be found that but for the current he would have fallen with serious injury, then the loss of life or earning capacity resulting from the electrocution would be measured by its value in such injured condition. Evidence that he would be crippled would be taken into account in the same manner as though he had already been crippled.

His probable future but for the current thus bears on liability as well as damages. Whether the shock from the current threw him back on the girder or whether he would

2. The case on which these scenarios are based, Douglas, Burt & Buchanan Co. v. Texas & Pacific R. Co., 91 So. 503 (La. 1922), is discussed in detail in H.L.A. Hart & Tony Honoré, Causation in the Law 250-51 (2d ed. 1985). See also Richard W. Wright, Causation in Tort Law, 73 Cal. L. Rev. 1735, 1796-97 (1985).

have recovered his balance, with or without the aid of the wire he took hold of if it had not been charged, are issues of fact, as to which the evidence as it stands may lead to different conclusions.

Exception overruled.

Kingston v. Chicago & Northwest Railway

191 Wis. 610, 211 N.W. 913 (1927)

OWEN, J. . . . We . . . have this situation: [A] fire [to the northeast of the plaintiff's property] was set by sparks emitted from defendant's locomotive. This fire, according to the finding of the jury, constituted a proximate cause of the destruction of plaintiff's property. This finding we find to be well supported by the evidence. We have the northwest fire, of unknown origin. This fire, according to the finding of the jury, also constituted a proximate cause of the destruction of the plaintiff's property. This finding we also find to be well supported by the evidence. We have a union of these two fires 940 feet north of plaintiff's property, from which point the united fire bore down upon and destroyed the property. We therefore have two separate, independent, and distinct agencies, each of which constituted the proximate cause of plaintiff's damage, and either of which, in the absence of the other, would have accomplished such result.

It is settled in the law of negligence that any one of two or more joint tortfeasors, or one of two or more wrongdoers whose concurring acts of negligence result in injury, are each individually responsible for the entire damage resulting from their joint or concurrent acts of negligence. This rule also obtains "where two causes, each attributable to the negligence of a responsible person, concur in producing an injury to another, either of which causes would produce it regardless of the other, . . . because, whether the concurrence be intentional, actual, or constructive, each wrongdoer, in effect, adopts the conduct of his co-actor, and for the further reason that it is impossible to apportion the damage or to say that either perpetrated any distinct injury that can be separated from the whole. The whole loss must necessarily be considered and treated as an entirety." Cook v. M., St. P. & S.S.M.R. Co., 98 Wis. 624 (74 N.W. 561), at p. 642. . . .

From our present consideration of the subject we are not disposed to criticise the doctrine which exempts from liability a wrongdoer who sets a fire which unites with a fire originating from natural causes, such as lightning, not attributable to any human agency, resulting in damage. It is also conceivable that a fire so set might unite with a fire of so much greater proportions, such as a raging forest fire, as to be enveloped or swallowed up by the greater holocaust, and its identity destroyed, so that the greater fire could be said to be an intervening or superseding cause. But we have no such situation here. These fires were of comparatively equal rank. If there was any difference in their magnitude or threatening aspect, the record indicates that the northeast fire was the larger fire and was really regarded as the menacing agency. At any rate there is no intimation or suggestion that the northeast fire was enveloped and swallowed up by the northwest fire. We will err on the side of the defendant if we regard the two fires as of equal rank.

According to well settled principles of negligence, it is undoubted that if the proof disclosed the origin of the northwest fire, even though its origin be attributed to a third person, the railroad company, as the originator of the northeast fire, would be liable for the entire damage. There is no reason to believe that the northwest fire originated from any other than human agency. It was a small fire. It had traveled over a limited area. It had been in existence but for a day. For a time it was thought to have been extinguished. It was not in the nature of a raging forest fire. The record discloses nothing of natural phenomena which could have given rise to the fire. It is morally certain that it was set by some human agency.

Now the question is whether the railroad company, which is found to have been responsible for the origin of the northeast fire, escapes liability because the origin of the northwest fire is not identified, although there is no reason to believe that it had any other than human origin. An affirmative answer to that question would certainly make a wrongdoer a favorite of the law at the expense of an innocent sufferer. The injustice of such a doctrine sufficiently impeaches the logic upon which it is founded. Where one who has suffered damage by fire proves the origin of a fire and the course of that fire up to the point of the destruction of his property, one has certainly established liability on the part of the originator of the fire. Granting that the union of that fire with another of natural origin, or with another of much greater proportions, is available as a defense, the burden is on the defendant to show that by reason of such union with a fire of such character the fire set by him was not the proximate cause of the damage. No principle of justice requires that the plaintiff be placed under the burden of specifically identifying the origin of both fires in order to recover the damages for which either or both fires are responsible. . . .

. . . There being no attempt on the part of the defendant to prove that the northwest fire was due to an irresponsible origin, that is, an origin not attributable to a human being, and the evidence in the case affording no reason to believe that it had an origin not attributable to a human being, and it appearing that the northeast fire, for the origin of which the defendant is responsible, was a proximate cause of plaintiff's loss, the defendant is responsible for the entire amount of that loss. While under some circumstances a wrongdoer is not responsible for damage which would have occurred in the absence of his wrongful act, even though such wrongful act was a proximate cause of the accident, that doctrine does not obtain "where two causes, each attributable to the negligence of a responsible person, concur in producing an injury to another, either of which causes would produce it regardless of the other." This is because "it is impossible to apportion the damage or to say that either perpetrated any distinct injury that can be separated from the whole," and to permit each of two wrongdoers to plead the wrong of the other as a defense to his own wrongdoing would permit both wrongdoers to escape and penalize the innocent party who has been damaged by their wrongful acts.

The fact that the northeast fire was set by the railroad company, which fire was a proximate cause of plaintiff's damage, is sufficient to affirm the judgment. This conclusion renders it unnecessary to consider other grounds of liability stressed in respondent's brief.

By the Court. Judgment affirmed.

Observe that in both *Dillon* and *Kingston*, above, the pair of destructive forces that threatened the plaintiff's well-being — in *Dillon*, the decedent's fall from the bridge toward the rocks below and the high tension wire maintained by the utility, and in *Kingston*, the northwest fire and the northeast fire — occurred more or less simultaneously. Even assuming that those cases were rightly decided, what should be the court's reaction when some length of time separates the two successive, destructive events? For example, what if the northeast fire in *Kingston*, started by the railroad, had burned plaintiff's property on July 1, cutting a narrow swath through the countryside; and then on September 1 a much larger fire, clearly caused by lightning, had swept through, burning a much larger area including that once occupied by the plaintiff? Would the September fire, which would have destroyed plaintiff's property had it not already been burned in July, affect plaintiff's rights against the railroad?

In Baker v. Willoughby, [1970] 2 W.L.R. 50, [1969] 3 All E.R. 1528 (H.L.), the defendant negligently struck the plaintiff with his automobile, causing severe injury to the plaintiff's left leg and ankle. Some time later, but before trial, the plaintiff was shot in the already-disabled left leg during a robbery at his place of employment. As a result of the gunshot wound, the already-disabled left leg had to be amputated. At trial, the defendant argued that he should be liable only for the plaintiff's damages up to the time of the shooting. The trial judge rejected this argument but the Court of Appeal accepted it. The House of Lords reversed, ruling that the plaintiff's recovery was not affected by the second injury because—in what amounts to a rather extreme legal fiction—"the *later* injuries merely become a *concurrent* cause of the disabilities caused by the injury inflected by the Defendant" (emphasis added). The case is discussed in Harvey McGregor, Successive Causes of Personal Injury, 33 Mod. L. Rev. 378 (1970), and D. M. A. Strachan, The Scope and Application of the "But For" Causal Test, 33 Mod. L. Rev. 386 (1970). See also David A. Fischer, Successive Causes and the Enigma of Duplicated Harm, 66 Tenn. L. Rev. 1127 (1999).

According to the court in *Kingston*, the outcome would have been different had the court found that the second fire resulted from natural forces and not a human actor. If both fires were the same size and either of them would have destroyed the property, but the second fire had a natural origin, the defendant would have escaped liability. Compare this result with the one reached under a similar fact pattern in Anderson v. Minneapolis, St. P. & S.S. M. Ry. Co., 179 N.W. 45, 49 (Minn. 1920), where the court ruled that defendant would be liable for harm caused by a fire originating from its locomotive even if a concurrent and independently sufficient fire originated from natural forces. The distinction that the *Kingston* court made between concurrent causes of natural and human origin is a distinction that only a minority of jurisdictions continue to make. See Restatement (Third) of Torts: Liability for Physical Harm §27 cmt. *d* (2005).

In *Kingston*, both of the fires were sufficient conditions of the plaintiff's harm; that is, either fire on its own would have been capable of destroying the property. But neither fire was a necessary condition in light of the existence of the alternative sufficient condition. What if a single actor's conduct is neither necessary nor sufficient to cause the plaintiff's harm? For instance, what if three individuals each independently and negligently lean against a car under circumstances where the combined force of any two of them together would be sufficient to cause the car to roll off a cliff, but the force of any one of them acting alone would not? See id. at §27 cmt. *f* (stating that all three individuals are a factual cause of the harm under such circumstances). This issue arises frequently in the pollution context, where numerous actors may emit pollution in combined amounts that exceed some safe or tolerable level. Courts have held that

> [e]ven if the amount of pollution caused by each party would be too slight to warrant a finding that any one of them had created a nuisance (the common law basis for treating pollution as a tort), "pollution of a stream to even a slight extent becomes unreasonable [and therefore a nuisance] when similar pollution by others makes the condition of the stream approach the danger point. The single act itself becomes wrongful because it is done in the context of what others are doing.

Boim v. Holy Land Foundation for Relief and Development, 549 F.3d 685, 697 (7th Cir. 2008) (quoting William L. Prosser & W. Page Keeton, Law of Torts 354 (5th ed. 1984)).

In thinking about these principles, should it matter whether the harm is caused by a threshold mechanism (e.g., if two or more actors lean against the car, it will roll off the cliff) or a cumulative mechanism (e.g., each individual's contribution adds to the harm and there is no threshold above or below which the contribution changes)? What if the number of actors involved is much larger than two or three? See Restatement (Second) of Torts §433B cmt. *e* (1965) ("[I]f a hundred factories each contribute a small, but still uncertain, amount of pollution to a stream, to hold each of them liable for the entire damage because he cannot show the amount of his contribution may perhaps be unjust.").

Some courts approach fact patterns such as these by applying an aggregated version of the traditional actual causation test. The court, after considering all of the individuals' conduct as a whole, applies a but-for test to determine if those actions collectively were the cause of the injury. In Spaur v. Owens-Corning Fiberglas Corp., 510 N.W.2d 854 (Iowa 1994), the Supreme Court of Iowa adopted this method, holding that "when the conduct of two or more persons 'is so related to an event that their combined conduct, viewed as a whole, is a but-for cause of the event, and application of the but-for rule to them individually would absolve all of them, the conduct of each is a cause in fact of the event.'" Id. at 858 (quoting W. Page Keeton, Prosser and Keeton on the Law of Torts §41, at 268 (5th ed. 1984). However, aggregation carries its own complications, most notably the requirement that the fact finder determine which causal factors are sufficiently related to be included in the aggregation. Consider the case mentioned above, where three actors lean against a car that rolls off a cliff. What if there had been an additional actor forcefully bouncing a large ball against the car. Should the force of the ball against the car be aggregated with the leaning of the other actors to test but-for causality?

Other courts in cases of concurrent causation utilize a "substantial factor" test. This test asks whether a defendant's actions were a substantial factor in causing the plaintiff's harm. In comparison to but-for causation, this test does not ask what *would* have happened, but what *did* happen. In Komlodi v. Picciano, 89 A.3d 1234, 1254-55 (N.J. 2014) the court explained:

> These two forms of causation — "but for" and "substantial factor" — are mutually exclusive. A "but for" charge is appropriate when there is only one potential cause of the injury or harm . . . . In contrast, the "substantial factor" test is given when there are concurrent causes potentially capable of producing the harm or injury . . . . Thus, a tortfeasor will be held answerable if its negligent conduct was a substantial factor in bringing about the injuries, even where there are other intervening causes which were foreseeable or were normal incidents of the risk created. (quotations and citations omitted)

One of the issues with the substantial factor test is that the very word "substantial" is vague. It requires the judge or jury to determine not only if the actor's conduct was a factor, but also whether it was a *substantial* factor. The New Jersey Supreme Court defines a substantial factor as a factor that is "not a remote, trivial or inconsequential cause." Id. at 1254-55 (citing Model Jury Charge (Civil) §6.13). Does this definition provide enough guidance to a fact finder? See also Section A.2 of Chapter 4, discussing the proposal of a similar "substantial factor" test for use in the context of proximate causation.

Concurrent or successive destructive causes are not always physical. Consider the case of Price Waterhouse v. Hopkins, 490 U.S. 228 (1989), where an employee of a large accounting firm was passed over for partnership, and brought a Civil Rights Act suit against her employer, claiming that the reasons for rejecting her candidacy were impermissibly based on gender. After a lower court found both discriminatory and non-discriminatory reasons for the employer's decision, the Supreme Court ruled on appeal that both reasons were the "cause" of the decision, but that the employer could defend itself from suit if it successfully proved that the non-discriminatory reasons alone would have yielded the same result. When the Civil Rights Act was amended in 1991, the issue of "mixed motives" was explicitly addressed: If an impermissibly discriminatory motive is a factor in an employment decision, a concurrent legitimate motive is no longer a defense. See 42 U.S.C. §2000e-2(m). Nevertheless, old tests die hard: In a 2013 decision, the Supreme Court held that retaliation claims brought under the Civil Rights Act, as opposed to other discriminatory employment actions, were not affected by the 1991 legislative amendments and thus plaintiffs pursuing retaliation claims must still succeed under traditional but-for causation principles. See Univ. of Texas Sw. Med. Ctr. v. Nassar, 133 S. Ct. 2517 (2013).

Problem 11

Earlier this past summer, Madolyn Hinkle retained your law firm to represent her in a claim against Vance & Weston Co., the manufacturer of Trophacin, a drug designed to relieve high blood pressure. Three years ago, Madolyn began taking the drug after it was prescribed by her doctor. Late last year, she was advised by her doctor that Trophacin can cause blindness. She stopped taking the drug, but later tests established that she had begun the irreversible process of losing her sight. Your investigation of the case has revealed that officials at Vance & Weston had been aware for some time that Trophacin causes blindness, but they failed to disclose that information to the medical profession. Madolyn's doctor is certain that had she ceased using the drug when the information first became known to Vance & Weston, her eyesight would not have been affected.

A month ago Madolyn was killed in an automobile accident. She was a passenger in a car driven by her husband, Arthur. They were driving in a sparsely populated part of the state when a severe windstorm arose. As Arthur was driving at a fairly high speed — he doesn't recall the exact rate — to get to a place of shelter, he ran into a large tree that had just fallen into the road. Arthur was unable to stop before hitting the tree, and a large branch crashed through the windshield on the passenger's side. Madolyn was killed in the accident. At the time of her death, Madolyn had over 90 percent of her normal vision. Had she lived, her vision would have started to deteriorate fairly rapidly, so that at the end of a year, she would have been almost totally blind.

The partner in your firm who is handling the case has asked you to help him with several aspects of it. In particular, he wants your thoughts as to what claims, if any, might be made against Vance & Weston Co. with respect to Madolyn's loss of vision. He suggests that you focus primarily on the issues of causation that may be presented.[3]

Assume that Dillon v. Twin State Gas & Electric Co., supra, is an opinion of the highest court in your state.

3. The fact of Madolyn's death does not terminate the cause of action against Vance & Weston in this case. All states have survival statutes that empower the representative of the decedent's estate to recover for causes of action the decedent had at the time of death, and for which the decedent himself could have recovered had he lived.

E. Relationship Between Actual Causation and Vicarious Liability

This section is concerned with the extent to which one person may be held liable for harm actually caused by the tortious conduct of another. The primary focus in this chapter has been on the extent of the actor's responsibility for the actor's own conduct. Here we assume that the causal connection between the actor's wrongful conduct and the plaintiff's harm has been established, and ask whether liability may be extended beyond the actor to include persons who have not committed a tortious act, but on whose behalf the wrongdoer acted. The primary focus here will be on masters' vicarious liability for the torts of their servants. When masters are held liable for the conduct of others, they are said to be "vicariously" liable under the doctrine of *respondeat superior*, which literally means "let the master answer."

The subject of vicarious liability fits comfortably in this chapter because it derives primarily from the cause-in-fact connection between the defendant's conduct and the plaintiff's harm. For vicarious liability to apply, the servant's conduct must be tortious; and the master must control, or have the right to control, the servant's harmful behavior. But the master need not be shown to have been at fault. Merely empowering the servant with the means and opportunity to cause harm suffices.

This concept of vicarious liability is one of considerable practical importance to the plaintiff because it is a most effective means of locating a financially responsible defendant, should the actual harm-causing actor be insolvent or otherwise incapable of satisfying a judgment. By far the largest class of persons to whom the rules in this chapter are applied is that of employers — typically, corporate employers held liable for the torts of their employees. From the plaintiff's viewpoint, employers make much more desirable defendants than do employees. Most important, employers are more likely than employees to be insured and to be financially able to satisfy a judgment when insurance does not cover the liability. Many observers also hold the view that juries are likely to be more sympathetic to holding an employer — especially a large, corporate employer — liable, and are more likely to be generous in their award of damages. Empirical support for these propositions about juror behavior is decidedly lacking. See generally Valerie P. Hans, Business on Trial: The Civil Jury and Corporate Responsibility (2000). Still, the beliefs persist among plaintiffs' lawyers as well as critics of the tort system. Thus, it is not surprising that, of the opinions reproduced in this book, a significant percentage involve large corporate defendants.

1. Masters, Servants, and Independent Contractors — Respondeat Superior

a. General Principles

The central principle establishing vicarious liability for the tortious conduct of another is this: Masters are vicariously liable for the torts of their servants committed while the latter are acting within the scope of their employment. See generally Restatement (Second) of Agency §219. The origins of the respondeat superior doctrine may be traced to ancient Greek and Roman law. Although early English law moved away from the imposition of vicarious liability, by the eighteenth century this trend had reversed itself and respondeat superior was well on its way to assuming its present position of importance.

The use of respondeat superior as a basis of imposing vicarious liability requires, as a threshold matter, the existence of a master-servant relationship. Whatever may be the connotations of the terms "master" and "servant" in a Charles Dickens novel, they do not legally connote menial or manual service slavishly performed. Simply stated, the master-servant relationship is a consensual relationship in which one person or legal entity, the servant, performs services on behalf of another person or legal entity, the master, and in which the master controls or has the right to control the conduct of the servant. Thus, even the highest-paid officers of multinational corporations are servants in the legal sense of the word. Moreover, although the concepts of servant and employee overlap considerably, strictly speaking a servant need not receive a wage in order to bind the master vicariously; someone can be the servant of another even if he is performing services out of a sense of friendship. As a practical matter, however, most servants are employees hired to perform services for their employers.

Indeed, the reach of master-servant vicarious liability outside employment contexts is limited. For instance, courts tend to shy away from finding a vicarious relationship where religious organizations and their non-employee members are involved. See, e.g., Gillet v. Watchtower Bible & Tract Society, 913 So. 2d 618 (Fla. Ct. App. 2005); Checkley v. Boyd, 107 P.3d 651 (Or. Ct. App. 2005); Nye v. Kemp, 646 N.E.2d 262 (Ohio Ct. App. 1994).

b. Distinguishing Servants from Independent Contractors

Not all persons hired to perform work for others are servants who thus expose their employers to vicarious tort liability. In contrast to servants, independent contractors are persons hired to do jobs under circumstances that, as a general rule, do not call for the application of the principle of respondeat superior. Basically, an *independent contractor* is one who contracts with another person to do something but who is not controlled by the other person nor subject to the other person's right to control. Where the tortfeasor is an independent contractor, the general rule is that the employer is not vicariously liable for the harm caused by the contractor's wrongful conduct. See Restatement (Second) of Torts §409. Thus, one of the major questions in cases involving respondeat superior concerns the status of the person acting on the defendant-employer's behalf. If the actor is a servant, the employer is, within limits, legally responsible for the actor's conduct; if the actor is an independent contractor, generally speaking the employer is not legally responsible. To the basic concept of control, the Restatement (Second) of Agency §220 adds a number of considerations in determining whether an actor falls into one category or the other, including whether or not the one employed is engaged in a distinct occupation or business, the skill required in the particular occupation, the length of time for which the person is employed, the method of payment (e.g., whether by the time or by the job), and whether the parties believe they are creating the relation of master and servant.

An example of a court applying a similar set of factors is D.A.R.E. American v. Rolling Stone Magazine, 101 F. Supp. 2d 1270 (C.D. Cal. 2000), *aff'd*, 270 F.3d 793 (9th Cir. 2001). In that case, the magazine *Rolling Stone* contacted Stephen Glass, a journalist working for *The New Republic* magazine, to write an article about the antidrug program D.A.R.E. Glass agreed, and submitted a piece that was highly critical of D.A.R.E. and its directors. D.A.R.E. sued *Rolling Stone* for defamation, claiming that Glass fabricated parts of the article. The plaintiffs alleged that Glass was an employee of *Rolling Stone* under the principles of respondeat superior. The court found that *Rolling Stone* exercised only minimal control over Glass because it could control only the result of the work, not the means by which it was accomplished; that is, *Rolling Stone* had editorial control only after Glass had submitted his draft to the magazine. Moreover, the fact that Glass provided his own instrumentalities and place of work, that he was not paid a regular salary, and that neither party considered their relationship to be that of employer-employee further supported the conclusion that Glass was an independent contractor. Therefore, the court held that *Rolling Stone* was not vicariously liable for Glass's fabrications.

Distinguishing between a servant and an independent contractor can be difficult. For example, in Throop v. F. E. Young & Co., 382 P.2d 560 (Ariz. 1963), the plaintiff was injured by the defendant's salesperson in an automobile accident. The central issue of the salesperson's status turned on whether the manufacturer had control over, or the right to control, the salesperson. The defendant was a small company that manufactured medical testing kits and sold them to wholesalers throughout the country. The salesperson involved in the accident with the plaintiff was the only individual who handled defendant's sales to wholesalers. He would come to the company office from time to time, pull cards on wholesale houses, and pick out the ones he desired to visit. He took care of his own hotel and traveling expenses out of his commissions. The salesperson owned the automobile in which he traveled but defendant compensated him one and one quarter cents per mile. Defendant fixed the prices, but the salesperson often gave greater discounts than were on the discount cards furnished to wholesalers, and the defendant accepted them. The salesperson also arranged his visits to wholesalers in accordance with the times he wished to visit relatives throughout the country. The amount of his commissions with the defendant company never exceeded $1,200 in any year since he did not wish to jeopardize his social security benefits. The company made deductions from payments to the salesperson for federal withholding tax and paid unemployment compensation premiums. The salesperson visited the defendant's office only four or five times a year.

The written contract between the defendant and the salesperson described the manner in which he was to call on his accounts; required him to file written reports; and described how he was to make collections, pick up stock from customers, put out display cards to dealers, and perform other duties. The contract, which was never signed, was apparently only used as a memorandum for computing commissions due to the salesperson. In fact, the salesperson never made any written reports and in other respects deviated from the written form of the contract.

The trial court granted the defendant's motion for a directed verdict. The Arizona Supreme Court affirmed. In concluding that the salesperson was an independent contractor as a matter of law, the court explained (382 P.2d at 565):

> [T]here is no evidence from which to reasonably infer the defendant had the right to control [the salesperson] in the operation of the automobile. The whole of the United States and anywhere he chose to go in it was [the salesperson's] territory. He visited prospects at whatever time he chose and he selected the prospects, visiting the office only four or five times a year. Clearly, no inference of control could stand the scrutiny of a judgment notwithstanding the verdict had the case been submitted to the jury.

Might the court in the *Throop* case have come out differently if the salesperson had dropped one of the medical testing kits on a customer's toe, injuring him? If it might have come out differently, would this be introducing a "scope of employment" limitation into the servant concept itself?

c. Relationship Between the Servant's Conduct and the Scope of Employment

Even if the plaintiff establishes that the tortfeasor was a servant at the time the harmful conduct occurred, courts do not impose vicarious liability unless the plaintiff also demonstrates that the servant was acting within the scope of employment. At first blush, this requirement would appear to offer employers a near universal defense, for they would typically be able to claim, quite justifiably, that they did not employ their servants to commit torts. Yet, with limited exceptions, the affirmative desire of employers that their servants act in a nontortious manner does not shield them from vicarious liability. Instead, as reflected in Restatement (Second) of Agency, §229, a court typically considers a number of factors in determining whether the scope of employment requirement is met, including whether or not the act that causes harm is one commonly done by servants of the sort involved in the particular case, the previous relations between the master and the servant, whether or not the master has reason to expect that such an act will be done, the similarity in quality of the act done to the act authorized, and whether or not the act is seriously criminal. See, e.g., Brown v. National Football League, 219 F. Supp. 2d 372 (S.D.N.Y. 2002) (the NFL could be held vicariously liable for the actions of a referee who allegedly threw a penalty flag into a player's eye, causing a career-ending injury).

In Richard v. Hall, 874 So. 2d 131 (La. 2004), the defendant company entered into a duck hunting lease and paid for hunting privileges for three of its executives. Two executives and another employee, the decedent, were hunting from a duck blind one morning, with the decedent sitting between the two executives. In the excitement and confusion of the hunt, one of the executives accidently shot and killed the decedent. Decedent's widow filed a wrongful death claim against the employer company under a theory of vicarious liability. The trial court granted summary judgment for the defendant. The appellate court affirmed, concluding that the executive who shot the decedent was not operating within the scope of employment. The Supreme Court of Louisiana reasoned that because the duck lease was never used by clients nor directly used to generate commercial profits, the tortious conduct of the executive was not so closely connected to his employment duties as to be regarded as a risk fairly attributable to the defendant employer.

The servant need not be performing precisely the activity for which he was hired in order to expose the master to liability. Thus, in Riviello v. Waldron, 391 N.E.2d 1278 (N.Y. 1979), a tavern owner was exposed to vicarious liability when one of the tavern's employees — who was employed as a cook, waiter, and bartender — negligently handled a pocketknife while exhibiting it to some patrons, causing the loss of the plaintiff's eye. And the tortious conduct for which the master will be held accountable need not involve physical injuries. In Orser v. State, 582 P.2d 1227 (Mont. 1978), the Supreme Court of Montana held that liability could be imposed on the state for claims of malicious prosecution by game wardens, who had brought suit against plaintiff for violations of state game laws.

Problem 12

A few days ago, Tammy Williams came to seek legal representation from your law firm after a terrible accident. The partner for whom you work, after speaking with Ms. Williams, has decided that the firm will take the case. She has asked you to listen to Ms. Williams's story and decide the best way of moving forward with the litigation. The partner wants a memo on her desk by the end of the week.

From speaking with Tammy, you've learned that five weeks earlier she was hit while walking across the street by a car driven by a City of Sterling police officer, Officer Mathew Taylor. Her injuries are extensive. At the emergency room, doctors worked to mend her leg and collarbone, both of which broke in several places. She also suffered severe internal bleeding and grave head injuries. She has admitted to you that she does not have health insurance and that the medical bills continue to pile up. She believes there is no way that she can pay them without a large award of money damages from this personal injury lawsuit. To ensure that she can get the money she needs for her medical care, she wants to sue the City of Sterling Police Department for Officer Taylor's tort, an approach that would require use of the doctrine of *respondeat superior*.

After hearing Tammy's side of the story, you begin to look more deeply into her case. Officer Taylor is a seasoned patrol officer with a string of high profile arrests in the last few years. These arrests were made during the course of his usual job, in which he is employed to patrol the streets in a Police Department squad car. Because of an injury, however, Officer Taylor was temporarily assigned to the Department's communications office, where he was responsible for sending out dispatch assignments, transmitting orders to officers in the field, and maintaining the radio-transmission equipment. Because of this transfer, his job did not generally involve driving and he was no longer assigned his usual squad car for official department business.

On the day of the accident, Officer Taylor was working a late shift — 4:00 p.m. to 11:00 p.m. His 12-year-old son was not feeling well that day, so Officer Taylor decided to go home during his meal break to check on his sick child. A few minutes before he was set to leave, Officer Taylor's commanding officer, Lieutenant Douglas, gave him an unusual assignment: One of the radios in a patrol car had malfunctioned. The car was near Officer Taylor's house, and the Lieutenant decided to send Officer Taylor over to fix the radio rather than order the car back to the station. The Lieutenant assured him that any time he spent working on the radio that cut into his break — even the time driving to the site — could be reported to the city for overtime pay.

Officer Taylor agreed to go fix the patrol car's radio during his break as well as visit his son. The Lieutenant, who understood the worry that a father might feel for a sick child, had given him discretion regarding the sequence in which to complete both tasks. At 8:00 p.m., Officer Taylor took his break and, still in uniform, began his commute. He was driving his personal car, and he was wearing his government issued firearm and his badge. He had not yet decided which to do first: go check on his son or go fix the radio. Because of his uncertainty, he picked a roundabout route that added time to his trip but allowed him to drive in the direction of both his house and the patrol car with the broken radio. As he was trying to decide which of the two tasks to complete first, his car struck your client, Tammy Williams, whom he had not seen crossing the street because of her dark clothing.

While your client is insistent that the City of Sterling Police Department should be held accountable for Office Taylor's actions, you are unsure that Officer Taylor was acting in the scope of his employment at the time of the accident. As you research the Police Department's rules, you've come across a few relevant sections of the Department's Employment Manual:

> §1 **Purpose**: This Manual defines the authority, duty, and code of conduct for every employee of the City of Sterling police department.
>
> . . . .

> §6 **Definitions**:
>
> §6(a) **Duty**: The requirements and responsibilities that a police officer must fulfill in order to uphold his sworn oath to serve and protect the people of Sterling.
>
> §6(b) **On duty**: The duty status of any Member of the department when he is engaged in performing his assigned tasks and duties or anytime during his designated work hours.
>
> §6(c) **Off duty**: The duty status of any Member of the department when he is on Department authorized leave or break and is not responsible for performing his assigned tasks or duties.
>
> §7 **Duty Status**: Sterling Police Department officers are always subject to duty when their intervention is required, even when relieved from regularly scheduled duty. If an off-duty police officer witnesses an event that requires police intervention, he will he held accountable for not acting.

The partner has made it clear that the Torts Claims Act that governs in the City of Sterling does not afford the Police Department, a public entity, any specialized immunity. She has also asked you to look over the Restatement (Second) of Agency (1958), upon which the judges in your district look favorably. Section 228 of the Restatement reads:

> (1) Conduct of a servant is within the scope of employment if, but only if:
>
> (a) it is of the kind he is employed to perform;
>
> (b) it occurs substantially within the authorized time and space limits;
>
> (c) it is actuated, at least in part, by a purpose to serve the master, and
>
> (d) if force is intentionally used by the servant against another, the use of force is not unexpectable by the master.
>
> (2) Conduct of a servant is not within the scope of employment if it is different in kind from that authorized, far beyond the authorized time or space limits, or too little actuated by a purpose to serve the master.

What will you write in the memo for the partner? What are the strongest arguments you can make that Officer Taylor's accident occurred within the scope of his employment? How much will the police department's rules covering when an officer is and is not considered "on duty" or "subject to duty" influence the court's analysis of whether a jury question has been presented?

Problem 12 poses an interesting variation on the "coming and going" rule, which "generally precludes an employer's liability for the torts of an employee committed during the employee's commute to and from work." Sharrock v. United States, 673 F.3d 1117, 1119 (9th Cir. 2012). Under the "coming and going" rule, torts caused during a worker's commute are not considered to have occurred within the scope of their employment. *See* Hopper v. Austin, 163 So. 3d 8 (La. Ct. App. 2015). A rationale for the rule is that the dangers to which employees are exposed while going and coming from work are not unique to the workplace, but are shared by society as a whole. See Evans v. III. Emp'rs Ins. of Wausau, 790 S.W.2d 302 (Tex. 1990). But courts have found an accident during a commute to be within the scope of employment when the employer provided the transportation, the employer paid wages or expenses for the employee's time traveling, or the traveling is somehow related to the job. See Woolard v. Atkinson, 988 So. 2d 836 (La. Ct. App. 2008). See also Restatement (Second) of Agency §§219, 220, 228, 229.

Related to the "coming and going" rule is the idea of a "frolic and detour." The phrase is often used to describe a type of conduct that falls outside of the scope of employment.

A frolic and detour typically arises when an employee is sent out to accomplish an objective of the employer and along the way the servant also runs an errand that is personal in nature. Then, while on the personal errand, the servant engages in tortious conduct. To determine if the servant has been on a frolic and detour, a court will normally determine whether the purpose of the trip is predominantly to serve the master's purposes. If so, the court must also determine whether the servant's detour deviated, to a significant degree, from the route strictly necessary to serve that purpose. If so, the master will not be vicariously liable. A slight to minor deviation, however, will not suffice. Unless it is manifestly clear that the purpose of the trip was personal or that there was a gross deviation from the contemplated route, such questions are generally resolved by the triers of fact. See, e.g., Nationwide Mut. Ins. Co. v. Liberatore, 408 F.3d 1158 (9th Cir. 2005) (holding that the defendant's "relevant personal conduct was not so foreseeable by his employer that his employer could fairly be held liable for damages resulting from . . . that conduct").

The limits of the scope of employment requirement are most severely pressed when the servant engages in intentional wrongdoing. While it may make sense to hold employers liable for the on-the-job negligence of their employees on the grounds that negligently caused accidents are a foreseeable part of many human activities, it is harder to explain why an employer should pay for an unauthorized, intentional tort committed by an employee. The early common law categorically barred vicarious liability for the intentional torts of servants unless the master in some way affirmatively solicited or encouraged such conduct. Similarly, modern courts are reluctant to hold employers liable for the intentional torts of their servants. In Maria D. v. Westec Residential Sec., Inc., 102 Cal. Rptr. 2d 326 (Ct. App. 2000), the plaintiff alleged that she was pulled over by a Westec security guard, who represented himself as a police officer and threatened to arrest her for driving under the influence (DUI). However, instead of taking her to the station, he drove her to another location and raped her. The plaintiff sued the security guard's employer, Westec, on the basis of respondeat superior. The trial court granted summary judgment for the defendant, on the grounds that the security guard was not acting within the scope of his employment when he allegedly raped the plaintiff. The appeals court affirmed, holding that "the security guard substantially deviated from his employment duties solely for personal purposes. . . . The assault was not motivated or triggered by anything in the employment activity but was the result of only . . . 'propinquity and lust.'"

Decisions in many jurisdictions, however, reflect an increased willingness to hold employers vicariously liable for the intentional torts of their employees. Although it is difficult to discern a common rationale for these decisions, in general courts focus on a cluster of factors, including whether the misconduct occurred within the time and space of employment, whether the employee was motivated, at least in part, by a concern for the employer's interests, and whether the potential for wrongdoing was foreseeable to the employer. Thus, in Mason v. Kenyon Zero Storage, 856 P.2d 410 (Wash. Ct. App. 1993), the Washington Court of Appeals remanded the case to determine whether the defendant employee was a supervisor and whether he acted within the scope of his employment. The trial court had granted summary judgment, refusing to impose liability on the employer when defendant employee rammed another employee, the plaintiff, in his back with a forklift, ostensibly to "enforc[e] discipline on the job." Courts may also bypass the difficulties of holding a master vicariously liable for the intentional torts of the servant and simply find the master directly liable for its own negligence in hiring, supervising, or monitoring the servant. See Avitia v. U.S., 24 F. App. 771, 2001 WL 1609833 (9th Cir. 2001) (federal government held liable in negligence where doctor at federally funded clinic sexually assaulted patient during exam, and clinic had failed to follow its own policy of providing a patient chaperone). For an argument that courts continue to shield employers and institutions from liability for the sexual misconduct of their employees and agents, notwithstanding the expansion of vicarious liability for other forms of intentional wrongdoing, see Martha Chamallas, Vicarious Liability in Torts: The Sex Exception, 48 Valp. U. L. Rev. 133 (2013).

d. Exceptions to the General Rule of Nonliability of Independent Contractors

The general rule imposing vicarious liability requires the plaintiff to show both that the employee was a servant rather than an independent contractor and that the employee's tortious behavior fell within the scope of employment. But courts have generally carved out three exceptions to the nonliability rule: (1) the employer is negligent in selecting, instructing, or supervising the independent contractor; (2) the duty of the employer, arising out of some relation to the public or to the particular plaintiff, is nondelegable; or (3) the work is specifically, peculiarly, or inherently dangerous.

In the first of these categories of exceptions, where the employer is negligent in selecting, instructing, or supervising the independent contractor, the employer is not held liable vicariously, but in its own right for its own acts of negligence. Thus, strictly speaking, these cases are not exceptions to the general rule that defendants are not vicariously liable for the torts of their independent contractors, but instead illustrate the potential availability of an alternative, direct remedy against the employer. It is also important to note that this first exception — holding employers directly responsible for their own negligence — applies equally well in the master-servant context. Thus, even though in a particular case a servant may be found to have acted beyond the scope of employment, the master may be held directly liable for negligence in selecting, instructing, supervising, or retaining the employee. In some circumstances, employers may even be held responsible for failing to exercise reasonable care to prevent a servant from committing an intentional tort. See Dragomir v. Spring Harbor Hospital, 970 A.2d 310 (Me. 2009) (grounding such a duty in the "special relationship" that exists between a hospital and its patient when the latter was sexually exploited by a hospital employee outside of work).

The second and third exceptions to the general rule encompass nondelegable duties and work that is especially dangerous. These exceptions are invoked by courts when confronted with defendants engaged in activities that expose the public to significant risks under circumstances where it seems appropriate to make those activities bear the accident costs they generate. Naturally, there is some variation in how different courts determine such exceptions. Compare Simmons v. Tuomey Reg'l Med. Ctr., 533 S.E.2d 312 (S.C. 2000) (holding that hospitals owe a nondelegable duty to provide competent emergency room care and thus cannot avoid liability for negligence of emergency room physicians by hiring them as independent contractors), with Renown Health v. Vanderford, 235 P.3d 614 (Nev. 2010) (rejecting nondelegable duty liability of hospital for its independent contractor physicians).

Nevertheless, defendants to whom these exceptions have been applied typically include common carriers and municipalities, but other extensions have reached hospitals, mental institutions, and security services. See, e.g., Wiggs v. City of Phoenix, 10 P.3d 625 (Ariz. 2000), holding that the city was vicariously liable for the death of a pedestrian who was struck by an automobile on a stretch of road where the street lights were not working. Although the city had hired an independent contractor to operate the street lights, Phoenix had a nondelegable duty to maintain the streets in a safe condition, and therefore was liable for the pedestrian's death. But see State v. Hicks, 198 P.3d 1200 (Ariz. 2009) (although state has an obligation to provide competent legal assistance to indigent criminal defendants, state cannot be held liable under nondelegable duty doctrine for court-appointed attorney's malpractice).

In addition to the above exceptions to the rule of nonliability of independent contractors, courts also recognize an exception when the party who caused the injury was an "ostensible agent" of the employer. Under this doctrine, when the acts or omissions of an employer induce a third party to reasonably believe that a person is the employer's agent, the employer is as vicariously liable as if a master-servant relationship existed. In such a situation, the actual status of the person as an independent contractor is irrelevant to the employer's liability. See Catherine Butler, Preferred Provider Organization Liability for Physician Malpractice, 11 Am. J. L. & Med. 345 (1985).

e. The Master's Right of Indemnity Against the Servant

Implicit in this summary of the rules governing the vicarious liability of a master for the torts of his servants is the principle that, regardless of whether the master is liable, the servant will be personally liable to the plaintiff for his (the servant's) tortious conduct. From the plaintiff's perspective, the master and servant will be jointly and severally liable when both are joined as defendants. But what about the rights between master and servant — how is the liability to be divided between them? At common law, the general rule was that the master enjoyed a right of full indemnification against the servant when the master (absent fault on his personal part) was held vicariously liable for the wrongs of the servant. This rule remains intact, although some courts and commentators have questioned whether allowing the employer to seek indemnification from the harm-causing employee defeats the social policies that underlie the general doctrine of vicarious liability. However, as a practical matter, this right is seldom exercised.

Law and Policy: Why Should Masters Be Liable for the Employment-Related Torts of Their Servants?

The somewhat complex and open-ended nature of the vicarious liability rules discussed above should not obscure the stark policy issue that they raise — specifically, what is the justification for imposing liability on an actor based not on any wrongdoing on that actor's part but *solely* because of that actor's relationship with the actual tortfeasor? Over time, courts and commentators have sought to justify vicarious liability by advancing some of the instrumental and noninstrumental rationales that underlie tort law. The nature and merits of these rationales deserve closer attention.

Some have insisted that masters are held liable on a *deep pocket theory*; that is, masters are held liable because they tend to be wealthier than servants and are thus more easily able to bear the costs of accidents. This argument clearly invokes a compensation rationale, but like all unadorned compensation arguments, it is quickly met with the question "Why me?" In other words, the deepness of a party's pockets, standing alone, can hardly explain the selection of that party as an appropriate defendant. Something else, in the form of a noninstrumental argument based on fairness or an instrumental argument tied to social welfare, is typically needed to justify forcing an otherwise faultless defendant to compensate the plaintiff.

Some have sought to supply this rationale by promoting vicarious liability as a means of allocating to business enterprises the costs of accidents caused by those enterprises, thus spreading those costs in the prices charged for the goods and services marketed by the enterprises. This argument has both instrumental and noninstrumental strands. From the noninstrumental fairness perspective, one might argue, in Epstein's terms (see p. 38, supra), that the employer "caused" the accident by engaging the servant in the first place. In this regard, the "scope of employment" requirement can be viewed as a means of testing whether the employer's activities "caused" the plaintiff's injuries. Alternately, one might attempt a noninstrumental rationale by asking whether, in Fletcher's terminology (see pp. 38-39 supra), liability is justified because the employer's activities have imposed a nonreciprocal risk on others.

In addition to these arguments, the cost-spreading argument suggests an instrumental justification: that accident losses are more detrimental to society when allowed to rest on individual injured plaintiffs than when borne generally by the consumers of the employer's products or services. However, even if one subscribes to the premise of this argument — that a spread loss is better than a concentrated loss — it is still necessary to justify the selection of the employer as the loss-spreading mechanism. Why not, for example, spread losses through the plaintiff's own personal insurance company or, alternatively, through government aid for accident victims? Again, we are back to the employer's "Why me?" question.

While a fuller exploration of these questions must wait until we confront similar problems in the strict and products liability areas, a partial answer to why tort law might, for instrumental reasons, choose to impose liability on a faultless employer can be gleaned by examining a third justification for vicarious liability. That argument centers on the long-standing claim that masters are held vicariously liable in order to create the strongest possible incentive for them to be appropriately careful in the selection and supervision of their servants. See Young B. Smith, Frolic and Detour, 23 Colum. L. Rev. 444 (1923); Gary T. Schwartz, The Hidden and Fundamental Issue of Vicarious Liability, 69 S. Cal. L. Rev. 1739, 1759-64 (1996). See also G. Edward White, The Unexpected Persistence of Negligence, 1980-2000, 54 Vand. L. Rev. 1337 (2001) (discussing how the deterrence aspect of vicarious liability is consistent with principles of negligence). Indeed, at first blush, this deterrence-based justification for vicarious liability seems powerful: Employers, faced with the knowledge that they will pay for the torts their servants commit within the scope of their employment, will exercise due care in hiring, training, supervising, and retaining employees. Indeed, the argument goes, without vicarious liability, employers may unfairly profit from the relatively judgment-proof nature of their employees. They will do so by bribing such employees to engage in high-risk, high-return behavior, knowing that as employers they will be shielded from any liability that such activities generate.

But on closer examination, this explanation proves too much because, as noted earlier, employers can be held *directly* liable to injured plaintiffs if they default on their own obligation to properly select, train, and supervise their employees. In other words, vicarious liability is not theoretically necessary to cause employers to adopt an appropriate level of care for their employees' conduct, since their failure to do so will provide an independent basis for liability.

In light of this apparent redundancy of remedies, does vicarious liability have any independent function in furthering the instrumental goal of deterrence? There are at least several arguments that it does. First, if plaintiffs systematically confront practical difficulties in establishing the employer's negligence at trial — perhaps because of their limited knowledge of the employer's methods of hiring, training, and supervising employees — employers may not experience a level of liability sufficient to force them to exercise appropriate care. Vicarious liability serves to redress this diminished incentive by eliminating altogether the plaintiff's need to show employer negligence. Of course, the plaintiff must still establish the employee's negligence, but that task is generally easier than proving a default by the employer.

Moreover, holding an employer strictly liable as a master not only helps ensure that the employer experiences sufficient incentives to monitor and control the manner in which the servant works, but it also creates incentives for the employer to make more socially responsible decisions regarding whether the work ought to be undertaken in the first place. Knowing that it will be liable for *all* the torts its servants cause within the scope of their employment, rather than simply those torts that can be attributed to the employer's own negligence in controlling its employees, the employer may decide against expanding its operations to areas where profitability (and therefore social usefulness) is questionable. Vicarious liability therefore pressures the master to optimize (from the broader social perspective) not only *how* servants act, but also *whether* and *to what extent* they act. This instrumental argument is similar to one that is often offered by law and economics scholars in favor of strict liability for abnormally dangerous activities. See Chapter 6, below.

This is an idea we have encountered before. The rules governing battery, for example, aim more at *whether* one acts than at *how*. A physician who fails to obtain a patient's informed consent is strictly liable regardless of the skill exercised in the operation. The message the physician receives is not that the operation should have been done differently, but that (absent informed consent) it should not have been done at all. And in the context of the dog-bite problems in this chapter, if a scheme combining a dog tax and a compensation fund were implemented in which the tax rate varied according to the relative riskiness of the breed of dog, such a scheme of strict liability based on dog ownership would presumably discourage some would-be owners from owning German shepherds rather than beagles, or goldfish.

Obviously, the policy questions raised by vicarious liability are quite complicated. In several subsequent areas of the course, including those dealing with res ipsa loquitur, strict liability, and products liability, you will have a chance to examine in more detail arguments similar to those discussed above. For further explorations of these questions within the context of vicarious liability, see generally Alan O. Sykes, The Boundaries of Vicarious Liability: An Economic Analysis of the Scope of Employment Rule and Related Legal Doctrines, 101 Harv. L. Rev. 563 (1988); Lewis A. Kornhauser, An Economic Analysis of the Choice Between Enterprise and Personal Liability for Accidents, 70 Cal. L. Rev. 1345 (1982); Timothy P. Glynn, Beyond "Unlimiting" Shareholder Liability: Vicarious Tort Liability for Corporate Officers, 57 Vand. L. Rev. 329 (2004); William L. Killion, Franchisor Vicarious Liability — The Proverbial Assault on the Citadel, 24 Franchise L.J. 162 (2005).

Problem 13

You have just received the following memorandum from a senior partner in your firm:

> Earlier this summer, Vernon Peeler retained our law firm to represent him in his suit against PetroTex, a major oil company. Mr. Peeler has alleged that Jeff Sorvino, an operator of one of PetroTex's many service stations, negligently injured him in an accident last year. At this

> point I am satisfied that Sorvino was both negligent and acting within the scope of his employment. However, I am concerned that the court in our jurisdiction may find that Sorvino is an independent contractor. I would like you to develop any policy and legal arguments that may support the contention that Mr. Sorvino is a servant, and to assess the evidence gathered at this point to see if there is enough here to get to the jury on this issue.
>
> I will be relying heavily on your conclusions when I decide whether to proceed any further. I will return to the office early next week. Please be prepared to discuss the case when I return.

Although pretrial discovery has not yet been completed, your preliminary investigations have revealed the following facts: Sorvino leased the premises from PetroTex, agreeing to pay $900 a month plus a percentage of the receipts from gasoline sold at the station. Sorvino paid all expenses of the operation; paid cash for all oil products purchased from PetroTex; sold those products at any price he determined; could hire and fire all employees; could sell his products on credit; and stood to gain or lose according to the profits or losses from the business. PetroTex had responsibility for making certain the building was properly maintained, and its representatives conducted inspections of the premises. Sorvino was encouraged to wear PetroTex uniforms and to identify with PetroTex products. The only pumps at the station bore the PetroTex trademark, and the sale of any products not bearing the PetroTex trademark was forbidden. The manner and nature of the delivery of PetroTex products to Sorvino was under PetroTex control, and it was customary for Sorvino to buy all items for sale from PetroTex. PetroTex had established criteria for obtaining operators for its stations; and the operators, including Sorvino, attended a school operated by PetroTex where they received instructions on marketing, operations, and safety. The accident in which Peeler was injured occurred at the service station operated by Sorvino. Peeler was helping Sorvino by pouring gasoline into the carburetor of a car Sorvino was trying to start. The car backfired, a flash fire broke out, and Peeler was badly burned. Since the accident, we have also learned that Sorvino and his operating company have filed for bankruptcy.

Assume for the purposes of your assessment that the supreme court of your state generally follows the principles summarized in this section.

2. Other Forms of Vicarious Liability

In addition to the master-servant rules, other, more limited forms of vicarious liability exist. Two such forms are considered in this section: joint enterprise and the family purpose doctrine.

a. Joint Enterprise

Quite often, two or more persons will join together in an enterprise in which each has an equal right to control the other's conduct. Under such circumstances, one might apply master-servant concepts and speak of each participant being both the master and the servant of all the other participants. However, instead of applying master-servant principles in such cases, the courts have developed a separate legal concept for the purpose, to which they apply the terms "joint enterprise" and "joint venture" interchangeably. Briefly stated, the negligent conduct of each participant in a joint enterprise is imputed to every other participant, assuming the negligent acts to have been committed in the course of the enterprise. The elements of a joint enterprise have been generally described as (1) an agreement, whether express or implied, to carry on an enterprise where (2) the parties manifest an intent to be associated as joint venturers, and have (3) a joint interest, shown by the contributions of the parties to the enterprise, (4) a degree of joint proprietorship or control over the enterprise, and (5) provisions for the sharing of profits and losses. See Trustmark Ins. Co. v. General & Cologne Life Re of America, 424 F.3d 542, 547 (7th Cir. 2005). The doctrine has its clearest application where a formal contract establishes a business enterprise calling for a sharing of profits and losses and mutual control over physical operations.

The doctrine of joint enterprise has also been applied in informal, nonbusiness contexts. Often such cases arise out of automobile collisions with the doctrine either being invoked by the injured plaintiff in an effort to hold the other car's passengers jointly responsible for its driver's negligence, or by the defendant in an effort to establish a contributory negligence defense against the other car's passengers by placing them in a joint enterprise with that car's negligent driver. For example, see Am. Family Mut. Ins. Co. v. AN/CF Acquisition Corp., 361 P.3d 1098 (Colo. Ct. App. 2015), in which a car dealer was held to be in a joint venture with a test driver who collided with another vehicle during a test drive. The court found that by placing one of the dealership's employees in the car with the customer, the dealership and the customer both had a common purpose and a right to control the vehicle. But see Hinson v. Jarvis, 660 S.E.2d 604 (N.C. Ct. App. 2008), where the court held that a wife could not be held to be in a joint venture with her husband. Although the court found a joint purpose in that they were going to dinner together, the wife did not have a right to control because she "was not responsible for [the car's] maintenance, did not own a vehicle, and never drove the vehicle or any other vehicle." Id. at 608.

b. The Family Purpose Doctrine

In many states, a special rule has been developed judicially which, under certain circumstances, imposes vicarious liability upon automobile owners for harm caused by persons to whom the automobiles have been loaned or made available. Briefly stated, the family purpose doctrine imposes liability upon the owner of a family automobile for harm negligently caused to others by a family member while operating the automobile on a family purpose. Thus, in a strong sense, the family purpose doctrine represents a domestic equivalent of the master-servant rule. See, e.g., Starr v. Hill, 353 S.W.3d 478, 482 (Tenn. 2011) (observing that "[t]he doctrine is a court-created legal fiction that employs agency principles to hold the owner of the vehicle vicariously liable" and that "[t]he doctrine is based on the theory that a family member who provides and maintains a vehicle for the pleasure or convenience of the family makes the vehicle's use his or her business, and that in using the vehicle, the family members are furthering the purpose for which it is maintained") (internal quotations omitted).

The elements of the doctrine are (1) ownership of the automobile by the defendant sought to be held liable vicariously; (2) designation of the automobile as a family automobile; (3) status of the driver as a family member; (4) use of the automobile for a family purpose; and (5) use of the automobile with the owner's permission. As might be expected, each of these elements has been the subject of extensive judicial review and refinement. For example, in Hurley v. Brown, 564 S.E.2d 558 (Ga. Ct. App. 2002), the court held that a father was not vicariously liable under the family purpose doctrine where the father was owner in title, but the son paid all the expenses, was not on any errand or mission for the father at the time of the accident, and did not reside at the father's household. In Griffith v. Kuester, 780 F. Supp. 2d 536 (E.D. Ky. 2011), the court was asked to apply the family purpose doctrine to hold a husband liable for the wife's negligence while piloting a boat that they co-owned. The court held that as co-owners of the boat, neither spouse could grant (or deny) the other permission to use of the boat, and thus the family purpose doctrine did not apply.

Some jurisdictions have gone so far as to sometimes allow the family purpose doctrine even when the driver is not a family member. For example, in Connecticut, the owner of a vehicle can be held liable when a family member with "general, unrestricted authority to use the vehicle" is a passenger in the car and the "the third party was operating the family car with the consent of that family member. In such cases, the negligent third party steps into the shoes of the family member for the purpose of applying the family car doctrine to the owner of the vehicle." Cima v. Sciaretta, 58 A.3d 345, 352 (Conn. App. Ct. 2013); see Dibble v. Wolff, 65 A.2d 479 (Conn. 1949) for the Connecticut Supreme Court case laying down this rule. Courts have even reviewed the very idea of what constitutes a family. In Hermosillo v. Leadingham, 13 P.3d 79 (N.M. Ct. App. 2000), the court held that a husband was not vicariously liable under the family purpose doctrine where his estranged wife, from whom he had been living apart for two months, was involved in a car accident with the plaintiff while driving a vehicle that both husband and wife had used during their marriage. The husband was not liable because he lacked control over the vehicle after separation from the wife (she had taken the car after the separation) and because the estranged couple was not a "household" as required by the family purpose doctrine. See also Alosi v. Hewitt, 276 P.3d 518 (Ariz. Ct. App. 2012) (rejecting the use of family purpose doctrine between two cohabitating adults).

c. Aiding and Encouraging

Courts have also been willing to hold a party liable for aiding or encouraging a tortfeasor, even if that party was not directly engaged in any tortious conduct. The Restatement (Second) of Torts states that a party that knowingly grants substantial encouragement or aid to another in committing a tort can be subject to liability. Restatement (Second) of Torts §876 (1979). Perhaps the prototypical example of this tortious aiding and abetting comes from Ayer v. Robinson, 329 P.2d 546 (Cal. Dist. Ct. App. 1958). In that case, a young man viciously attacked a truck driver. During the attack, the young man's father "egged him on," shouting "[h]it him . . . get him . . . ." Id. at 584. The court held that the father could be held liable because he had "aided and abetted" his son by encouraging the beating. Similarly, in Rael v. Cadena, 604 P.2d 822 (N.M. Ct. App. 1979), the court, citing the Restatement (Second), held that a defendant who was present during a battery and encouraged the assailant, was liable for providing "verbal encouragement" despite taking no physical part in the battery.

Some jurisdictions require a strong showing of intent for liability to attach. See, e.g., Taylor v. Am. Chemistry Council, 576 F.3d 16 (1st Cir. 2009) (noting that defendants did not have the "'unlawful intent' necessary for substantial assistance liability"). It is important to note, moreover, that almost all jurisdictions stress how vital it is that the aid or encouragement must be "substantial." See, e.g., Podias v. Mairs, 926 A.2d 859 (N.J. Super. Ct. App. Div. 2007) (analyzing in depth how much assistance is required to be classified as substantial). More recently, courts have applied this form of vicarious liability to a wider range of torts. Tensfeldt v. Haberman, 768 N.W.2d 641(Wis. 2009) involved a lawyer whose client violated a divorce judgment. While the client was supposed to leave two-thirds of his estate to his children, the client, with the help of his lawyer, decided to ignore this obligation. The children sued the lawyer under a theory of "tortious aiding and abetting," and the court found that the lawyer should be held liable for providing aid for his client's unlawful act.

Chapter 3

Negligence: Duty of Care and Proof of Breach

The subject of harmful and offensive battery, covered in Chapter 1, provides students with a useful introduction to central aspects of the law of torts. Yet it is important to note that the kind of intentional wrongdoing addressed by the law of battery is absent from the vast majority of tort claims. Put differently, most torts involve accidents.

What rules should govern liability for such cases of unintentionally caused harms? For a century and a half, the dominant regime in the United States for handling accidental harm has been the law of negligence. The basis of liability in negligence is the creation of an unreasonable risk of harm to another. Of course, there are few activities that do not involve some risk of harm. Driving an automobile, flying a plane, building a bridge — even mowing a lawn or riding a bicycle — involve risks that someone will be injured. We know with certainty that some accidents will happen, but we nonetheless accept them as a price of the kind of society we have. This is not to say that we accept them without regret or that we do not aspire to achieve a society in which such tragic tradeoffs are not so starkly or pervasively posed. However, an accident-free society is impossible to attain, and even reducing accidents as much as humanly possible would cost more than we would be willing to spend on safety. Therefore, an actor who causes harm is not held liable in negligence simply because the actor's conduct involves a risk of harm to others. For negligence to be found, the risk of harm must be unreasonable, which most typically means that the conduct involves a risk of harm greater than society is willing to accept in light of the benefits to be derived from that activity.

A. The Origins and Early Development of the Negligence Concept

Because the negligence concept dominates the torts process today, students understandably tend to assume that it has been an important part of our legal system from the beginning. Actually, it is a relative newcomer. In order to understand the law of negligence as it operates today, it will be necessary to know what preceded it, and to appreciate the social pressures in response to which it came into being in the mid-nineteenth century. According to some writers, the negligence concept for centuries competed with other, stricter conceptions of liability for accidental harm. See generally P.H. Winfield, The History of Negligence in the Law of Torts, 42 L. Q. Rev. 184 (1926); Wex S. Malone, Ruminations on the Role of Fault in the History of the Common Law of Torts, 31 La. L. Rev. 1 (1970-1971); G. Edward White, Tort Law in America: An Intellectual History (2003).

The most important such conception is represented by the writ of trespass, which eventually extended beyond intentionally caused invasions of person and property to reach invasions that were "direct," albeit unintentional. See generally Cornelius J. Peck, Negligence and Liability Without Fault in Tort Law, 46 Wash. L. Rev. 225, 225-26 (1971):

> The conclusion reached by most scholars is that until the 19th century a person whose actions caused harm to another was in most situations held responsible for that harm simply because he had acted. Holdsworth tells us that this was the case both with respect to early Anglo-Saxon law and the Mediaeval Common Law. Wigmore earlier summarized the primitive German doctrine that "The doer of a deed was responsible whether he acted innocently or inadvertently, because he was the doer. . . ." [John H. Wigmore, Responsibility for Tortious Acts: Its History, 7 Harv. L. Rev. 315, 317 (1894).] This absolute responsibility, without regard to blame, persisted until the early 1500s, when the primitive notion was abandoned in favor of permitting a defendant to exempt himself from liability by showing that he was without blame even though he had acted voluntarily. Street agreed that for several hundred years the conception of negligence was unknown to the law of trespass; a defendant was liable if it was shown that damage had been done by the direct or immediate application of force, without regard to whether or not he was negligent. Justice Holmes was persuaded that policy and consistency required rejection of the rule of strict liability, but recognized that the theory enjoyed the support of some lawyers of his time, and that the common law probably followed such a rule during what he called a period of dry precedent. Scholars today agree that a rule of strict liability prevailed at the early stages of development of the common law, usually rendering an actor liable if he in fact caused injury to another.

The author describes the development, over centuries, of "trespass on the case," in which the plaintiff might recover even if the harm followed *indirectly* from the defendant's conduct (as opposed to the kind of direct harm for which a traditional "trespass" action would lie). In such actions "in case," however, the defendant could escape liability by showing that he was free of fault, thus establishing an early form of liability premised on negligent conduct. The law remained this way both in England and the United States until the middle of the nineteenth century, when courts began to decide cases like the following.

Brown v. Kendall

60 Mass. 292 (1850)

This was an action of trespass for assault and battery. . . .

It appeared in evidence, on the trial, . . . that two dogs, belonging to the plaintiff and the defendant, respectively, were fighting in the presence of their masters; that the defendant took a stick about four feet long, and commenced beating the dogs in order to separate them; that the plaintiff was looking on, at the distance of about a rod, and that he advanced a step or two towards the dogs. In their struggle, the dogs approached the place where the plaintiff was standing. The defendant retreated backwards from before the dogs, striking them as he retreated; and as he approached the plaintiff, with his back towards him, in raising his stick over his shoulder, in order to strike the dogs, he accidentally hit the plaintiff in the eye, inflicting upon him a severe injury.

Whether it was necessary or proper for the defendant to interfere in the fight between the dogs; whether the interference, if called for, was in a proper manner, and what degree of care was exercised by each party on the occasion; were the subject of controversy between the parties, upon all the evidence in the case, of which the foregoing is an outline.

The defendant requested the judge to instruct the jury, that "if both the plaintiff and defendant at the time of the blow were using ordinary care, or if at that time the defendant was using ordinary care and the plaintiff was not, or if at that time both plaintiff and defendant were not using ordinary care, then the plaintiff could not recover."

The defendant further requested the judge to instruct the jury, that, "under the circumstances, if the plaintiff was using ordinary care and the defendant was not, the plaintiff [could] recover, and that the burden of proof on all these propositions was on the plaintiff."

The judge declined to give the instructions, as above requested, but left the case to the jury under the following instructions: "If the defendant, in beating the dogs, was doing a necessary act, or one which it was his duty under the circumstances of the case to do, and was doing it in a proper way; then he was not responsible in this action, provided he was using ordinary care at the time of the blow. If it was not a necessary act; if he was not in duty bound to attempt to part the dogs, but might with propriety interfere or not as he chose; the defendant was responsible for the consequences of the blow, unless it appeared that he was in the exercise of extraordinary care, so that the accident was inevitable, using the word inevitable not in a strict but a popular sense.

"If, however, the plaintiff, when he met with the injury, was not in the exercise of ordinary care, he cannot recover, and this rule applies, whether the interference of the defendant in the fight of the dogs was necessary or not. If the jury believe, that it was the duty of the defendant to interfere, then the burden of proving negligence on the part of the defendant, and ordinary care on the part of the plaintiff, is on the plaintiff. If the jury believe, that the act of interference in the fight was unnecessary, then the burden of proving extraordinary care on the part of the defendant, or want of ordinary care on the part of the plaintiff, is on defendant."

The jury under these instructions returned a verdict for the plaintiff; whereupon the defendant alleged exceptions. . . .

SHAW, C.J. The facts set forth in the bill of exceptions preclude the supposition, that the blow, inflicted by the hand of the defendant upon the person of the plaintiff, was intentional. The whole case proceeds on the assumption, that the damage sustained by the plaintiff, from the stick held by the defendant, was inadvertent and unintentional; and the case involves the question how far, and under what qualifications, the party by whose unconscious act the damage was done is responsible for it. We use the term "unintentional" rather than involuntary, because in some of the cases, it is stated, that the act of holding and using a weapon or instrument, the movement of which is the immediate cause of hurt to another, is a voluntary act, although its particular effect in hitting and hurting another is not within the purpose or intention of the party doing the act.

It appears to us, that some of the confusion in the cases on this subject has grown out of the long-vexed question, under the rule of the common law, whether a party's remedy, where he has one, should be sought in an action of the case, or of trespass. This is very distinguishable from the question, whether in a given case, any action will lie. The result of these cases is, that if the damage complained of is the immediate effect of the act of the defendant, trespass *vi et armis* lies; if consequential only, and not immediate, case is the proper remedy.

In these discussions, it is frequently stated by judges, that when one receives injury from the direct act of another, trespass will lie. But we think this is said in reference to the question, whether trespass and not case will lie, assuming that the facts are such, that some action will lie. These dicta are no authority, we think, for holding, that damage received by a direct act of force from another will be sufficient to maintain an action of trespass, whether the act was lawful or unlawful, and neither wilful, intentional, or careless. . . .

We think, as the result of all the authorities, the rule is correctly stated by Mr. Greenleaf, that the plaintiff must come prepared with evidence to show either that the *intention* was unlawful, or that the defendant was *in fault;* for if the injury was unavoidable, and the conduct of the defendant was free from blame, he will not be liable. If, in the prosecution of a lawful act, a casualty purely accidental arises, no action can be supported for an injury arising therefrom. In applying these rules to the present case, we can perceive no reason why the instructions asked for by the defendant ought not to have been given; to this effect, that if both plaintiff and defendant at the time of the blow were using ordinary care, or if at that time the defendant was using ordinary care, and the plaintiff was not, or if at that time, both the plaintiff and defendant were not using ordinary care, then the plaintiff could not recover.

In using this term, ordinary care, it may be proper to state, that what constitutes ordinary care will vary with the circumstances of cases. In general, it means that kind and degree of care, which prudent and cautious men would use, such as is required by the exigency of the case, and such as is necessary to guard against probable danger. A man, who should have occasion to discharge a gun, on an open and extensive marsh, or in a forest, would be required to use less circumspection and care, than if he were to do the same thing in an inhabited town, village, or city. To make an accident, or casualty, or as the law sometimes states it, inevitable accident, it must be such an accident as the defendant could not have avoided by the use of the kind and degree of care necessary to the exigency, and in the circumstances in which he was placed. . . .

The court instructed the jury, that if it was not a necessary act, and the defendant was not in duty bound to part the dogs, but might with propriety interfere or not as he chose, the defendant was responsible for the consequences of the blow, unless it appeared that he was in the exercise of extraordinary care, so that the accident was inevitable, using the word not in a strict but a popular sense. This is to be taken in connection with the charge afterwards given, that if the jury believed, that the act of interference in the fight was unnecessary (that is, as before explained, not a duty incumbent on the defendant), then the burden of proving extraordinary care on the part of the defendant, or want of ordinary care on the part of plaintiff, was on the defendant.

The court are of opinion that these directions were not conformable to law. If the act of hitting the plaintiff was unintentional, on the part of the defendant, and done in the doing of a lawful act, then the defendant was not liable, unless it was done in the want of exercise of due care adapted to the exigency of the case, and therefore such want of due care became part of the plaintiff's case, and the burden of proof was on the plaintiff to establish it.

Perhaps the learned judge, by the use of the term extraordinary care, in the above charge, explained as it is by the context, may have intended nothing more than that increased degree of care and diligence, which the exigency of particular circumstances might require, and which men of ordinary care and prudence would use under like circumstances, to guard against danger. If such was the meaning of this part of the charge, then it does not differ from our views, as above explained. But we are of opinion, that the other part of the charge, that the burden of proof was on the defendant, was incorrect. Those facts which are essential to enable the plaintiff to recover, he takes the burden of proving. The evidence may be offered by the plaintiff or by the defendant; the question of due care, or want of care, may be essentially connected with the main facts, and arise from the same proof; but the effect of the rule, as to the burden of proof, is this, that when the proof is all in, and before the jury, from whatever side it comes, and whether directly proved, or inferred from circumstances, if it appears that the defendant was doing a lawful act, and unintentionally hit and hurt the plaintiff, then unless it also appears to the satisfaction of the jury, that the defendant is chargeable with some fault, negligence, carelessness, or want of prudence, the plaintiff fails to sustain the burden of proof, and is not entitled to recover.

New trial ordered.

Scholars have long debated what social factors gave rise to the emergence of negligence as the dominant liability standard in American tort law in the nineteenth century. See, e.g., Cornelius J. Peck, Negligence and Liability Without Fault in Tort Law, 46 Wash. L. Rev. 225, 229-30 (1971):

> Why the change [from strict liability to negligence] took place must, of course, remain a matter of speculation. It has been suggested that Chief Justice Shaw may have been motivated by a desire to make the risk-creating enterprises of a developing industrial economy less vulnerable to liability than they had been under the earlier common law. This suggestion has been countered with the observation that Brown v. Kendall, which Shaw used as the vehicle for changing the law, involved not industry but instead the actions of private persons engaged in separating two fighting dogs. It seems unlikely that Chief Justice Shaw shrewdly selected the case in order to disguise the ends to be served by changing the law; but it seems equally unlikely that he could have written the decision without considering what the contemporary conditions of society suggested as appropriate standards for allocating responsibility for unintentionally caused harms. . . .
>
> The development of industry and transportation using steam and other sources of power, and the development of new products and devices, changed the situation. One need only read a description of the operation of steam locomotives prior to adoption of the air brake to realize what costs might have been imposed upon railroads if liability for harm were to be determined by the common law trespass rule. . . . [T]he reaction of the law was not strict condemnation of this activity which offered escape from the slow, uncomfortable, and jolting transport by stage over mud-filled roads, and which promised development of the nation's resources deposited over thousands of miles of virgin territory. The negligence standard provided a legal environment in which rail transportation could grow and prosper. It aided other branches of industry and commerce as well.

For more on the debate over whether nineteenth-century American courts utilized the concept of negligence in order to subsidize industry, compare Morton J. Horwitz, The Transformation of American Law, 1780-1860, at 85-101 (1977) (arguing that such subsidization was a primary goal of negligence jurisprudence), with Gary T. Schwartz, Tort Law and the Economy in Nineteenth-Century America: A Reinterpretation, 90 Yale L.J. 1717 (1981) (arguing that industry subsidization was not the driving force behind the rise of negligence, and, in fact, that nineteenth-century courts were quite willing to impose tort liability upon American industry), and G. Edward White, The Intellectual Origins of Torts in America, 86 Yale L.J. 671 (1976-1977) (arguing that more than industrial development, the evolution of tort law in nineteenth-century America owes itself to changes in jurisprudence, the collapse of the common law writ pleading system, and the evolution of the standard tort case from one involving parties acquainted with one another to one in which the parties are typically strangers).

Note: Legal Formalism vs. Legal Realism

Chief Justice Shaw may not consciously have intended to protect growing industries with his decision in *Brown,* but he and his colleagues could not have avoided being influenced in their decision by the social and political environment surrounding them. Suggestions of this sort raise interesting questions concerning the source and nature of influences upon judicial decisions — questions concerning why judges react the way they do in certain cases. The purpose of this note and the subsequent one (Law and Behavior:

Empirical Investigations on Legal Decisionmaking) is to raise these questions and to introduce you in a general way to some of the available literature on the subject of influences upon judicial behavior, both from theoretical and empirical perspectives.

Although some legal scholars have offered important alternative accounts that present classical legal thinkers in a more sophisticated, strategic, and self-aware light,[1] the conventional account of the development of modern jurisprudential thought is one in which naïve versions of legal formalism yield to hardnosed forms of legal realism. That is, until the beginning of the twentieth century, it was almost universally asserted and widely believed that the formal law itself was the *only* normative factor influencing judicial decisions. The notion was that by carefully searching their law books, judges could find answers to *all* of the questions brought to them, and that in deciding cases they performed the essentially ministerial functions of applying law to facts. Such mechanical legal formalism left little room for the possibility that judges might be influenced in their decisions by factors other than found facts and formally realized rules of law.

The movement away from this formalistic view began toward the end of the nineteenth century and may be said, at least in retrospect, to have culminated with the publication in 1921 of an important book in American jurisprudence — The Nature of the Judicial Process, by Benjamin Cardozo, then a judge on the New York Court of Appeals. In his book, Cardozo argued persuasively that in at least some cases judges do, and ought to, act not simply as law-finders but instead as law-givers and legislators. Although in the majority of instances, existing rules of law admit of but a single result, cases arise in which the rules are sufficiently ambiguous, or vague, or questionable, requiring the judge to perform a creative, and not strictly a mechanical, function. In performing this legislative function, Cardozo insisted, the judge should endeavor to suppress personal biases and prejudices and strive instead to be guided by "the accepted standards of the community, the *mores* of the times."[2]

As might have been expected, once legal formalism began to give way, many writers and scholars were attracted to questions relating to influences upon judicial behavior. Paramount in this intellectual movement were a number of lawyers, mostly law teachers, who came to be known as "legal realists." [3] These writers sought to expose the myths of traditional jurisprudence (chief among them the myth that judges never make law) to the "cynical acid of observed reality." One of the most famous of the legal realists was Jerome Frank, who published perhaps the best-known example of the realist approach, Law and the Modern Mind, in 1930. In his book, Frank asserted that the most important influence upon a judge's decision in a close case was not the judge's perception of community standards, but the judge's own personality.[4] Other legal realists ascribed judicial decisions in close cases to the judge's intuition,[5] or to the judge's emotional preferences.[6]

Reacting to the impact of what might be described as the extreme positions taken by some of the realists on the question of external influences upon judicial behavior, Karl Llewellyn (an early and influential legal realist himself) was moved in 1960 to publish

1. See, e.g., Duncan Kennedy, The Structure of Blackstone's Commentaries, 28 Buff. L. Rev. 209 (1979); Bernadette Meyler, Towards a Common Law Originalism, 59 Stan. L. Rev. 551 (2006).

2. Benjamin Cardozo, The Nature of the Judicial Process 108 (1921).

3. For a concise summary of the realist movement, see Jeffrey A. Segal & Harold J. Spaeth, The Supreme Court and the Attitudinal Model 65 (1993). For a recent discussion that outlines the parallel rise of American legal realism and the European "Free Law Movement" and contrasts mechanical, legal formalism with legal realism(s), see Douglas Lind, Logic, Intuition, and the Positivist Legacy of H.L.A. Hart, 52 SMU L. Rev. 135 (1999).

4. Jerome Frank, Law and the Modern Mind, ch. 12 (1930).

5. E.g., Joseph C. Hutcheson, Jr., The Judgment Intuitive: The Function of the "Hunch" in Judicial Decision, 14 Cornell L.Q. 274 (1929).

6. E.g., Samuel J. Stoljar, The Logical Status of a Legal Principle, 20 U. Chi. L. Rev. 181 (1953).

The Common Law Tradition: Deciding Appeals, in which he developed what he called "major steadying factors in our appellate courts." Contrary to what he described as the popular and unhappy tendency among legal realists to assume that judges are free to decide (and do decide) cases before them on personal whim, Llewellyn argued that a number of factors combine to minimize the arbitrary, personal element in appellate decisionmaking.[7] These factors include the existence of large areas of clear doctrine, the need in many cases for judges to produce a written opinion explaining their decisions, and an assorted array of stabilizing judicial traditions and techniques.[8] Still, strains of legal realism can be heard today. Several contemporary schools of thought revolve around the idea that extralegal factors tend to dominate judicial decisionmaking and that, in fact, attempts to distinguish "legal" from "extralegal" factors are themselves misguided endeavors. Some notable examples of contemporary legal realist approaches include critical legal studies,[9] feminist jurisprudence,[10] and critical race theory.[11]

Law and Behavior: Empirical Investigations of Legal Decisionmaking

In addition to the theoretical approaches just described, legal scholars and social scientists have begun exploring the complex underpinnings of legal decisionmaking using empirical methodologies. A considerable amount of research has been devoted to documenting the ways in which decisionmakers, whether judges or juries, are influenced by factors other than formal legal rules. Early work in this area focused on how decisionmakers' characteristics — their political leanings, policy preferences, and social backgrounds — seemed to affect their legal judgments.[12] More recently, behavioral scientists have begun examining more generalized aspects of decisionmaking, such as the ways in which human beings rely on a variety of mental shortcuts when presented with complicated decisions, which can introduce systematic biases into our legal judgments.[13] Much of the latter work as it relates to tort law is summarized in the note, Law and Behavior: What We Think About When We Think About Tort Law, infra pp. 229-232.

7. Legal philosopher and scholar H. L. A. Hart also weighed into the debate, attempting to show that *both* the legal realists and the legal formalists had taken untenably extreme positions. See H. L. A. Hart, The Concept of Law 124-54 (1961). See also Douglas Lind, Logic, Intuition, and the Positivist Legacy of H.L.A. Hart, 52 SMU L. Rev. 135 (1999).

8. Karl Llewellyn, The Common Law Tradition: Deciding Appeals 4 (1960).

9. See generally Allan C. Hutchinson, Critical Legal Studies (1989); Mark Kelman, A Guide to Critical Legal Studies (1987); Roberto Mangabeira Unger, The Critical Legal Studies Movement (1986).

10. See generally Nancy Levit & Robert R. M. Verchick, Feminist Legal Theory: A Primer (2006); Martha Chamallas, Introduction to Feminist Legal Theory 2 (2003); Feminist Legal Theory: An Anti-Essentialist Reader (Nancy E. Dowd & Michelle S. Jacobs eds., 2003); Feminist Legal Theory: Foundations and Outlooks (Frances E. Olsen ed., 1995); Feminist Legal Theory: Foundations (D. Kelly Weisberg ed., 1993); Feminist Legal Theory: Readings in Law and Gender (Katharine T. Bartlett & Rosanne Kennedy eds., 1991).

11. See generally Dorothy A. Brown, Critical Race Theory: Cases, Materials and Problems (2003); Richard Delgado & Jean Stefancic, Critical Race Theory: An Introduction (2001); Richard Delgado & Jean Stefancic, Critical Race Theory: The Cutting Edge (1995); Critical Race Theory: The Key Writings That Formed the Movement (Kimberle Crenshaw et al. eds., 1995).

12. For a useful overview of empirical work on juries, see Dennis J. Devine, Jury Decision Making: The State of the Science (2012) (summarizing fifty years of empirical studies of jury decisionmaking).

13. See, e.g., Jon D. Hanson & Douglas A. Kysar, Taking Behavioralism Seriously: The Problem of Market Manipulation, 74 N.Y.U. L. Rev. 630, 643-86 (1999) (cataloguing various cognitive biases and illusions that behavioral science has identified and arguing that profit-maximizing firms in consumer product markets will seek to manipulate those cognitive tendencies for gain).

In order to examine the relationship between decisionmakers' background characteristics and their legal judgments, researchers often study the records of trials that have been held or, where actual records are unavailable or inadequate for these purposes, conduct simulated trials with mock jurors. These research methodologies have enabled behavioral scientists to establish associations between decisionmakers' background characteristics and their typical responses to particular cases. For instance, researchers have found that juries composed entirely of men are less likely to decide in favor of tort plaintiffs, and more likely to decide in favor of litigants of superior status, than are juries composed of men and women.[14] Other research has demonstrated that jurors with higher education are more likely to place emphasis on procedure and the instructions in reaching their decisions than are jurors of lower education;[15] that jurors are likely to be prejudiced in favor of parties of their own sex and prejudiced against parties of the opposite sex;[16] and that depressed jurors may be more apt to award punitive damages.[17]

This list, by no means exhaustive, tends to support the beliefs traditionally held by trial lawyers regarding what may be expected from various types of jurors. The major practical application of these background studies, of course, is in the jury selection process. Trial lawyers working within the system have always wanted to know as much as possible about the prospective jurors whom they encounter in court.[18] Nevertheless, attorneys should be wary of placing too much emphasis upon the so-called science of jury selection. One researcher has concluded that the evidence presented at trial has a more significant impact upon the verdict than do the characteristics of the jurors themselves and that it is only where the evidence is ambiguous that individual differences among jurors become highly relevant.[19]

With respect to judicial decisionmaking, efforts have been made to correlate judges' characteristics with their decision patterns.[20] Early legal realists intuited that judges often

14. See Nancy S. Marder, Gender Dynamics and Jury Deliberations, 96 Yale L.J. 593 (1987). See also Sandra Benlevy, Venus and Mars in the Jury Deliberation Room: Exploring the Differences That Exist Among Male and Female Jurors During the Deliberation Process, 9 S. Cal. Rev. L. & Women's Stud. 445 (2000).

15. Laurence J. Severance et al., Toward Criminal Jury Instructions That Jurors Can Understand, 75 J. Crim. L. & Criminology 198 (1984).

16. For a discussion on the meaning and significance of gender in sociological research, see Carrie Mendel-Meadow & Shari Seidman Diamond, The Content, Method, and Epistemology of Gender in Sociological Studies, 25 Law & Soc'y Rev. 221 (1991).

17. See Debra Cassens Moss, Punitive-Damages Jurors: Study Suggests Selecting Depressed People, 74 A.B.A. J. 18 (1988).

18. For trial practice materials on jury selection, see, e.g., Lisa Blue & Jane Naida Saginaw, Jury Selection: Strategy and Science (1993); Arne Werchick, Civil Jury Selection (2d ed. 1993). Regarding the efficacy of social science data for jury selection, see Solomon M. Fulero & Steven D. Penrod, The Myths and Realities of Attorney Jury Selection Folklore and Scientific Jury Selection: What Works?, 17 Ohio N.U. L. Rev. 229 (1990). The extent to which lawyers can make use of gender and racial and ethnic characteristics in the jury selection process through peremptory challenges is limited by constitutional and ethical restrictions. See Karen M. Bray, Comment, Reaching the Final Chapter in the Story of Peremptory Challenges, 40 UCLA L. Rev. 517 (1992); David Everett Marko, The Case Against Gender-Based Peremptory Challenges, 4 Hastings Women's L.J. 109 (1993). For a discussion of the impact that racial diversity has on the deliberation process, see Kenneth S. Klein & Theodore D. Klastorin, Do Diverse Juries Aid or Impede Justice?, 1999 Wis. L. Rev. 553.

19. See Michael J. Saks, What Do Jury Experiments Tell Us About How Juries (Should) Make Decisions?, 6 S. Cal. Interdisc. L.J. 1 (1997).

20. See e.g., James L. Gibson, Judges' Role Orientations, Attitudes, and Decisions: An Interactive Model, 72 Am. Pol. Sci. Rev. 911 (1978); Melinda Gann Hall & Paul Brace, Toward an Integrated Model of Judicial Voting Behavior, 20 Am. Pol. Q. 147 (1992). Psychoanalytical theories have also been deployed in work attempting to generalize about how personality affects the decisionmaking process. See James L. Gibson, Personality and Elite Political Behavior: The Influence of Self-Esteem on Judicial Decision Making, 43 J. Pol. 104 (1981). Some studies also suggest that judicial status may strongly affect decisions. See, e.g., Richard B. Saphire & Michael E. Solimine, Diluting Justice on Appeal? An Examination of the Use of District Court Judges Sitting by Designation on the United States Courts of Appeals, 28 U. Mich. J.L. Ref. 351 (1995).

based their decisions on thoughtful, reflective "hunches," which they surmised were ultimately the product of the judges' social backgrounds[21] or political partisanship.[22] Empirical research in the late 1930s and 1940s examined non-unanimous Supreme Court opinions in order to assess whether justices' voting behavior could be explained in terms of their attitudes toward the public policy issues presented in the cases.[23] This approach — systematically examining sequences of judicial decisions to reveal voting patterns from which the influence of judicial attitudes may be deduced — has been developed and refined, and today constitutes a mainstay in the methodology of judicial behavioral research. For instance, modern researchers have examined Supreme Court decisions and have argued that the data show that although the justices purport to adhere to precedent, their decisions are largely guided by political and social preferences.[24] Insight into those preferences might be gleaned from associational studies demonstrating patterns such as the following: Judges with daughters are more likely to reach liberal decisions;[25] plaintiffs' claims of racial harassment are more likely to succeed when heard by African-American judges;[26] and the gender composition of a bench affects federal appellate court outcomes in Title VII sexual harassment and sex discrimination cases.[27]

It should be stressed that some research has concluded that neither the characteristics of federal judges nor the party affiliation of the appointing president significantly predict judicial decisions,[28] suggesting that the ideal of judicial independence and forthright decisionmaking is not as illusory as legal realists claim. Likewise, one recent study examined voting patterns of recess-appointed appeals court judges, finding significant differences in their pre- and post-confirmation voting behavior, a finding that the researchers take to indicate that the structural protections afforded for judges by Article III of the Constitution do support judicial independence.[29] Still, a significant amount of research seems to point in

21. See, e.g., Joel B. Grossman, Social Backgrounds and Judicial Decision-making, 79 Harv. L. Rev. 1551 (1966). See also Cassia Spohn, Decision Making in Sexual Assault Cases: Do Black and Female Judges Make a Difference?, 2 Women & Crim. Jus. 83 (1990) (finding no racial differences in sentencing patterns; finding that female judges imposed lengthier sentences than their male counterparts, and suggesting that socialization plays an influential role in judicial decisionmaking).

22. See, e.g., Jamie B. W. Stecher, Democratic and Republican Justice: Judicial Decision-Making on Five State Supreme Courts, 13 Colum. J.L. & Soc. Probs. 137 (1977); Stuart S. Nagel, Political Party Affiliation and Judges' Decisions, 55 Am. Pol. Sci. Rev. 843 (1961) (demonstrating that Democratic-appointed judges are more likely than their Republican colleagues to favor defendants in criminal cases, administrative agencies in business regulation cases, and employees in employee injury cases). See also Emerson H. Tiller & Frank B. Cross, A Modest Proposal for Improving American Justice, 99 Colum. L. Rev. 215 (1999) (arguing that no three-judge panel of the United States Courts of Appeal should be composed of three judges sharing the same political affiliation). More recent debate over political party influence on judicial decisions was sparked by Bush v. Gore, 531 U.S. 98 (2000). See generally The Vote: Bush, Gore and The Supreme Court (Cass R. Sunstein & Richard A. Epstein eds., 2001). For a pointed attack of the Supreme Court's decision in the case, see Alan M. Dershowitz, Supreme Injustice: How the High Court Hijacked Election 2000 (2001).

23. C. Herman Pritchett, The Roosevelt Court: A Study in Judicial Politics and Values, 1937-1947 (1948).

24. Jeffrey A. Segal & Harold J. Spaeth, Majority Rule or Minority Will: Adherence to Precedent on the U.S. Supreme Court (2001).

25. Adam N. Glynn & Maya Sen, Identifying Judicial Empathy: Does Having Daughters Cause Judges to Rule for Women's Issues?, 59 Am. J. Pol. Sci. Ass'n (2015).

26. Pat K. Chew & Robert E. Kelley, Unwrapping Racial Harassment Law, Berkeley J. Emp. & Lab. L. 49 (2006).

27. Jennifer Peresie, Female Judges Matter: Gender and Collegial Decisionmaking in the Federal Appellate Courts, Note, 114 Yale L.J. 1759 (2005).

28. Orley Ashenfelter et al., Politics and the Judiciary: The Influence of Judicial Background on Case Outcomes, 24 J. Legal Stud. 257 (1995).

29. Scott E. Graves, et al., Judicial Independence: Evidence from a Natural Experiment, 36 J.L. & Pol. 68 (2013). For additional recent modeling of judicial decisionmaking, see Alma Cohen et al., Judicial Decision Making: A Dynamic Reputational Approach, 44 J. Legal Stud. S133 (2015) (developing and testing a theoretical model suggesting that judges who are concerned about their reputation will tend to decide against their previous decisions as they approach elections), and Lee Epstein et al., The Behavior of Federal Judges: A Theoretical and

the other direction: that judges, like juries, behave according to patterns that seem hard to square with the supposition that judicial reasoning strictly follows precedent and principle.

In addition to associational studies, valuable work has been done employing an experimental methodology in which social scientists run multiple simulations of the same trial, tweaking certain aspects while holding the remaining aspects constant across all iterations. For instance, in Richard L. Cupp, Jr. & Danielle Polage, The Rhetoric of Strict Products Liability Versus Negligence: An Empirical Analysis, 77 N.Y.U. L. Rev. 874 (2002), the authors report on a hypothetical products liability claim that they presented to mock jurors, some of whom heard the claim argued by an attorney using negligence terminology and some of whom heard the claim argued using strict liability language. Surprisingly, the authors find that jurors awarded damages to plaintiffs at a lower rate and in lower amounts when strict liability language is used as opposed to negligence language, despite the arguably more plaintiff-friendly substance of the strict liability standard. The authors surmise that their findings "support the contention that, rather than serving as one of strict liability's remaining advantages, the doctrine's rhetoric is one of its weaknesses. . . . [J]urors prefer the 'hot' language of the more intuitive negligence approach over the 'cold' and technical language of strict liability." Id. at 937.

In a landmark study, the University of Chicago Jury Project created thirty different versions of the same trial involving an automobile accident, made tape recordings of each simulated trial, and asked thirty different mock juries to evaluate the tapes. The researchers recorded the mock juries' deliberations and interviewed individual jurors at various stages of the trial, including before and after group deliberations. The project, including the thirty variations and their effect on the juries' awards, is described below:

> In three treatments, defendant's liability was very clear; in three it was a little doubtful. These versions were then combined with three different treatments of defendant's liability insurance. In the first, defendant reveals he has no insurance but there is no objection or further attention paid to the disclosure; in the second, the defendant reveals that he has insurance, defense counsel objects and the court directs the jury to disregard; in the third treatment, the defendant again discloses insurance but there is no objection and no further notice is taken. The tapes were then played to sets of juries operating under the unanimity rule and to sets of juries operating under the three-fourths majority rule. In all, the experiment was given to thirty juries.
>
> Here briefly are some of the results. First, twenty-eight verdicts were for plaintiff, one jury hung on the damage issue and one jury found for the defendant. Second, the average award of all verdicts where liability was somewhat ambiguous was $34,000, $7,000 less. This, of course, supports the suspicion long entertained by the bar that the weaker the proof on liability the lower the verdict is apt to be. However, no significant difference in award level resulted between juries operating under the unanimity rule and juries operating under the three-fourths majority rule.
>
> Then there are the results of the three insurance treatments. Where the defendant disclosed that he had no insurance the average award of all verdicts was $33,000. Where defendant disclosed that he had insurance but there was no objection the average award rose to $37,000. Where, however, the defendant said he had insurance and there was an objection and an instruction to disregard, the average award rose to $46,000, $13,000 more than when the defendant said he was not insured, and $9,000 more than when he said he was insured but where there was no objection or instruction to disregard.

Empirical Study of Rational Choice (2013) (employing tools from labor economics, social science, and legal theory to evaluate the effects on judicial decisionmaking of judges' incentives within the legal marketplace, as well as the impact of their preexisting ideologies).

> The conclusion appears to be two-fold. First, that juries tend to award less when they know that an individual defendant is not insured; and, second, that where they know defendant is insured and a fuss is made over it the verdict will be higher than when no such fuss is made. The objection and the instruction to disregard, in other words, sensitize the jurors to the fact that defendant is insured and thereby increase the award. However, the instruction to disregard at least served the purpose of keeping the jurors from talking about insurance during the deliberations.[30]

Much of the focus of contemporary research into juror behavior was prompted by the Supreme Court's decision in Colgrove v. Battin, 413 U.S. 149 (1973) (see generally Jeffrey J. Rachlinski, The Story of *Colgrove*: Social Science on Trial, in Civil Procedure Stories 389 (Kevin M. Clermont ed., 2d ed. 2008)), upholding the constitutionality of six-person juries in federal civil trials. The case prompted researchers to study the effect that a jury's size has upon the deliberation process.[31] Several of these studies have called into question the efficacy of juries composed of less than twelve persons. For example, twelve-person juries deliberate longer than smaller juries and discuss trial testimony more accurately during their deliberations.[32] Moreover, researchers have observed that smaller juries return more unpredictable monetary awards than do larger juries.[33] In addition, social psychology research on group dynamics demonstrates that group members who dissent from the majority are more likely to conform to the group when they are the lone holdout than when they have a single other sympathizer. "Translating this finding into a jury scenario, the single minority vote in a 5-1 split will more likely acquiesce to the majority than if there were a 10-2 split in a 12-person jury," concludes a report by the National Center for State Courts.[34] Citing this body of research, as well as evidence that smaller juries do not produce significant reductions in court costs and trial duration — the impetus for size reduction — several commentators now advocate a universal return to the twelve-person jury.[35]

Other research has examined how juries evaluate defendants and plaintiffs of various social positions and backgrounds. Studies of civil cases find that plaintiffs' race, attractiveness, and socioeconomic status affect damages. Plaintiffs who are white, attractive, and come from high-status backgrounds tend to be awarded more in damages.[36] Unsurprisingly, social scientists have found corresponding biases in the way defendants are judged in the criminal context: defendants' race,[37] attractiveness,[38] and socioeconomic

30. Dale W. Broeder, The University of Chicago Jury Project, 38 Neb. L. Rev. 1, 753-54 (1959).

31. See, e.g., Michael J. Saks & Mollie Weighner Marti, A Meta-Analysis of the Effects of Jury Size, 21 Law & Hum. Behav. 451 (1997); N. L. Kerr & R. J. MacCoun, The Effects of Jury Size and Polling Method on the Process and Product of Jury Deliberation, 48 J. Personality & Soc. Psychol. 349 (1985).

32. See Saks & Marti, supra note 31.

33. See Michael J. Saks, What Do Jury Experiments Tell Us About How Juries (Should) Make Decisions?, 6 S. Cal. Interdisc. L.J. 1 (1997).

34. Nicole L. Waters, Does Jury Size Matter? A Review of the Literature, August 2004; Solomon Asch, Effects of Group Pressure Upon the Modification and Distortion of Judgments, in Group Dynamics 189 (2d ed. D. Cartwright & A. Zander, 1950).

35. See, e.g., Robert MacCoun, Inside the Black Box: What Empirical Research Tells Us about Decisionmaking by Civil Juries, in Verdict: Assessing the Civil Jury System 137 (Robert E. Litan ed., 1993).

36. Saks, supra note 31, at 27.

37. See David Abrams et al., 41 J. Legal Stud. 347, Do Judges Vary in Their Treatment of Race? (2013) (finding a statistically significant effect of race on incarceration decisions by judges); James D. Unnever, Direct and Organizational Discrimination in the Sentencing of Drug Offenders, 30 Soc. Probs. 212 (Dec. 1982); but see Steven Klein et al., Race and Imprisonment Decisions in California, 247 Sci. 812 (Feb. 16, 1990) (finding California courts' sentencing decisions racially equitable).

38. See, e.g., Robert J. MacCoun, The Emergence of Extralegal Bias During Jury Deliberation, 17 Crim. Just. & Behav. 303 (1990); Harold Sigall & Nancy Ostrove, Beautiful But Dangerous: Effects of Offender Attractiveness and Nature of the Crime on Juridic Judgment, 31 J. Personality & Soc. Psychol, 410 (1975). Defendant gender has also been found to affect sentencing. See Gayle S. Bickle & Ruth D. Peterson,

status[39] affect criminal sanctions. Even judges do not appear spared from such treatment: One recent study reports a substantial difference in the rate at which black federal district judges are overturned on appeal as compared to white district judges, a difference that is robust and persists after taking account of professional and judicial experience, educational qualifications, bar association judicial quality ratings, and appellate panel composition.[40]

A separate line of work examines how juries evaluate individual versus corporate defendants. Studies consistently find that juries award larger damages where the defendant is a corporate entity than where the defendant is an individual.[41] Some researchers have explained this finding by positing that jurors assume that corporate defendants have a greater capacity to pay damages than do individual defendants. However, not all of the relevant studies support this "deep pockets" hypothesis. One researcher presented separate groups of mock jurors with a fictitious case in which the defendant was described either as a corporation, a poor blue-collar individual, or an individual with personal wealth equivalent to that of the corporation.[42] While the "deep pockets" hypothesis suggests that the jurors would return equal monetary awards against both the corporation and the wealthy individual, the jurors in this study treated both individuals the same, while returning a larger award against the corporation. Thus, the explanation for jurors' disparate treatment of corporate entities may actually be that citizens hold corporations to a standard of care that is higher than the one which they apply to individual defendants. For an insightful analysis of these issues and a presentation of ground-breaking empirical research on juror attitudes toward business in civil litigation, see Valerie Hans, Business on Trial: The Civil Jury and Corporate Responsibility (2000).

As is always the case, important normative questions are intertwined with all of this empirical research. Consider: Increased knowledge and understanding of the influences upon jury decisions may present opportunities to affect the outcomes of trials by enabling attorneys to manipulate the juror-selection process and tailor courtroom arguments to the demographics of the jury. Given the extent to which the parties to civil litigation are afforded an opportunity to interview prospective jurors and within certain strict limits to eliminate those whom they believe on the basis of social science survey data and psychological screening will not react favorably to them, the traditional picture of the jury as a cross-section of the community will become outdated. Whether a system in which such sophisticated manipulations are commonplace is preferable to one in which jurors are selected essentially by lot is an open question, and one that may have to be answered in the years ahead as our understanding of law and behavior continues to deepen.

The Impact of Gender-Based Family Roles on Criminal Sentencing, 38 Soc. Probs. 372 (Aug. 1991) (including a literature review of past studies finding a correlation between marital status and gender and decisionmaking, and finding that familial criteria influence the sentencing of federal forgers).

39. See James M. Gleason & Victor A. Harris, Group Discussion and Defendant's Socio-Economic Status as Determinants of Judgments by Simulated Jurors, 2 J. Applied Soc. Psychol. 186 (1976); James D. Unnever, Direct and Organizational Discrimination in the Sentencing of Drug Offenders, 30 Soc. Probs. 212 (Dec. 1982). In contrast, another study found class position correlated to job loss, but not to incarceration. See Michael L. Benson, The Influence of Class Position on the Formal and Informal Sanctioning of White-Collar Offenders, 30 Soc. Q. 465 (Fall 1989).

40. Maya Sen, Is Justice Really Blind? Race and Reversal in U.S. Courts, 44 J. Legal Stud. (2015).

41. See, e.g., Audrey Chin & Mark A. Peterson, Deep Pockets, Empty Pockets (1985).

42. See MacCoun, supra note 38.

B. The General Standard

The general standard applicable in most negligence cases is one of reasonable care under the circumstances. Echoing Chief Justice Shaw's opinion in Brown v. Kendall, above, §283 of the Restatement (Second) of Torts states that "the standard of conduct to which [one] must conform to avoid being negligent is that of a reasonable man under like circumstances." Personifying the standard by the use of a hypothetical reasonable person serves at least two important purposes. For one thing, it makes the standard more comprehensible to the nonexperts who make up the juries and to whom the task of determining the defendant's negligence is often given. A description of the standard of care in terms of a flesh-and-blood image is more apt to be understood by persons of average experience and nonlegal background than some more precise but more abstract and legalistic description. It also serves to impress upon the jury that the standard can be met by something less than superhuman efforts. And second, putting the standard in the form of the reasonable person suggests the objective nature of the standard. In evaluating the defendant's conduct, the jury does not look to what might have been expected of this particular defendant — it is not enough that the defendant "did the best I could." Instead, the defendant is to be judged by what is to be expected of the reasonable person.

The basic objectivity of the standard appears to have been established very early in the development of the negligence concept in England. In Vaughan v. Menlove, 3 Bing. (N.C.) 468, 132 Eng. Rep. 490 (1837), the plaintiff obtained a verdict against the defendant who stacked hay so as to cause it to burn spontaneously and destroy the plaintiff's nearby property. On appeal to the Court of Common Pleas, the defendant argued that the trial judge had erred in instructing the jury to apply the reasonably prudent person standard and in denying the defendant's request that the jury should determine "whether he had acted bona fide to the best of his judgment." Affirming the verdict for plaintiff, Chief Justice Tindal explained (3 Bing. (N.C.) at 475, 132 Eng. Rep. at 493):

> [The subjective standard urged by the defendant] would leave so vague a line as to afford no rule at all, the degree of judgment belonging to each individual being infinitely various. . . . Instead, therefore, of saying that the liability for negligence should be co-extensive with the judgment of each individual, which would be as variable as the length of the foot of each individual, we ought rather to adhere to the rule which requires in all cases a regard to caution such as a man of ordinary prudence would observe.

The court in *Vaughan* was obviously concerned with the variability inherent in a subjective standard. But why? The court suggests that the standard offered by the defendant was too vague. But was the court right on that score? At least with respect to individual actors, the standard proposed by the defendant and rejected by the court may be less vague than the objective standard. The proposed standard tells defendants, in essence, to "do your best," a fairly straightforward command. The objective standard adopted by the court, in contrast, offers only the general instruction to "be reasonable." Perhaps it is useful to keep in mind that, however the standard is formulated, it must serve the joint functions of guiding prospective defendants' behavior, beforehand, and aiding courts in determining the liability of the defendant, after the fact. In that way, the "do your best" standard is not vague relative to a defendant before she acts, but that gain in clarity is later lost on a court when it must gauge the defendant's conduct. See generally James A. Henderson, Jr., Process Constraints in Tort, 67 Cornell L. Rev. 901, 904-11 (1982) ("The need for clarity, verifiability, and conformability in liability rules is just as important [as a guide to adjudicative behavior] as it is in the primary-behavior context.").

In any event, the adoption of an objective standard against which an actor's conduct is assessed raises the possibility that some individuals, by virtue of their unique characteristics, will not be able to meet the standard. The challenge for tort law, in this regard, is to determine when, if ever, the objective reasonable person standard should be modified to account for such characteristics. Note that the standard can, in theory, be modified without losing its basic objectivity. Although the court in *Vaughan* rejected the wholly subjective approach suggested by the plaintiff, it conceivably could have softened its objective approach by holding the defendant to the standard of care of a "reasonable not-so-smart person."

As a general matter, courts have balked at open-ended modifications of the reasonable person standard. The usual approach of courts is reflected in §283B of the Restatement (Second) of Torts, which follows *Vaughan* and refuses to consider mental deficiencies of actors in assessing conduct. See also Restatement (Third) of Torts: Liability for Physical and Emotional Harm §11(c) (2010). The only exception in the Second Restatement to this general rule appears in §283A, in which children are to be judged according to what might be expected of children of similar age and experience. Thus, in a case involving a ten-year-old defendant, the allegedly negligent conduct is not to be measured against the standard of what a reasonably prudent adult would have done, but rather is to be measured against the standard of a reasonably prudent child of similar age and maturity. See, e.g., Clay City Consol. Sch. Corp. v. Timberman, 918 N.E.2d 292, 295 (Ind. 2009) (judgment for parents in a wrongful death suit arising from the death of their 13-year-old-son during basketball practice; Supreme Court of Indiana affirmed the trial court's determination of no contributory fault, holding that the standard of care required of a child "is to be measured by that ordinarily exercised under similar circumstances by children of the same age, knowledge, judgment, and experience"). The Restatement (Third) of Torts follows this approach, but states additionally that children "engaging in a dangerous activity that is characteristically undertaken by adults" are to be judged by the standard of care applicable to adults, and that children under the age of five are incapable of negligence. See Restatement (Third) of Torts: Liability for Physical and Emotional Harm §10 (2010).

In contrast to the objectivity of their approach to the question of the mental capacity of defendants in negligence cases, the courts have adopted a more subjective, individualized approach to the question of defendants' physical disabilities. As Justice Holmes once observed:

> There are exceptions to the principle that every man is presumed to possess ordinary capacity to avoid harm to his neighbors, which illustrate the rule, and also the moral basis of liability in general. When a man has a distinct defect of such a nature that all can recognize it as making certain precautions impossible, he will not be held answerable for not taking them. A blind man is not required to see at his peril; and although he is, no doubt, bound to consider his infirmity in regulating his actions, yet if he properly finds himself in a certain situation, the neglect of precautions requiring eyesight would not prevent his recovering for an injury to himself, and, it may be presumed, would not make him liable for injuring another.

O. W. Holmes, The Common Law 109 (1881). Section 283C of the Restatement (Second) follows this view and requires that the individual defendant's physical disabilities be taken into consideration in judging whether the conduct has been negligent. Thus, if the defendant was blind at the time of the allegedly negligent conduct, the jury is to measure his conduct against that of a reasonably prudent blind person under similar circumstances. See also Restatement (Third) of Torts: Liability for Physical and Emotional Harm §11 (2010). (Are you able to articulate a rationale with which to explain the willingness of courts to take physical, but not mental, incapacities into account in negligence cases? For a critical perspective, see Johnny Chriscoe & Lisa Lukasik, Re-Examining Reasonableness: Negligence Liability in Adult Defendants with Cognitive Disabilities, 6 Ala. C.R. & C.L. L. Rev. 1 (2015) (arguing that modern negligence law creates something of a strict liability regime for defendants with cognitive disabilities)).

Thus far we have been considering essentially empirical characteristics, including mental and physical attributes. In the final analysis, the judgment that someone has been negligent is a value judgment — the pivotal concept of reasonableness is normative as well as empirical. See Alan D. Miller & Ronen Perry, The Reasonable Person, 87 N.Y.U. L. Rev. 323 (2012). Thus, even if we determine with precision which of the various empirical characteristics of mind and body to attribute to the hypothetical reasonable person, the negligence standard will remain vague and indeterminate as long as it relies on the general reasonableness concept. What does "reasonableness" look like? Justice Holmes once lamented that the general reasonableness concept was a "featureless generality." O. W. Holmes, The Common Law 111 (1881). One judge's subsequent attempt to render the concept of reasonableness more precise and manageable follows:

United States v. Carroll Towing Co.

159 F.2d 169 (2d Cir. 1947)

[The incident out of which this admiralty case arose was the sinking of a barge, along with its cargo, allegedly because of the defendant's negligence. A crucial issue in the case involved whether the person in charge of the barge, the bargee, was negligent in being ashore, away from the barge, during the period when the barge got into difficulties and sank. If the bargee's absence was negligence, and if it contributed substantially to the loss of the barge, then the bargee's employer, the owner of the barge, would not receive full recovery from the other parties whose negligence put the barge into difficulties in the first place.]

L. Hand, J. . . .

It appears . . . that there is no general rule to determine when the absence of a bargee or other attendant will make the owner of the barge liable for injuries to other vessels if she breaks away from her moorings. However, in any cases where he would be so liable for injuries to others, obviously he must reduce his damages proportionately, if the injury is to his own barge. It becomes apparent why there can be no such general rule, when we consider the grounds for such a liability. Since there are occasions when every vessel will break from her moorings, and since, if she does, she becomes a menace to those about her; the owner's duty, as in other similar situations, to provide against resulting injuries is a function of three variables: (1) The probability that she will break away; (2) the gravity of the resulting injury, if she does; (3) the burden of adequate precautions. Possibly it serves to bring this notion into relief to state it in algebraic terms: if the probability be called P; the injury L; and the burden, B; liability depends upon whether B is less than L multiplied by P: i.e., whether $B < PL$. Applied to the situation at bar, the likelihood that a barge will break from her fasts and the damage she will do, vary with the place and time; for example, if a storm threatens, the danger is greater; so it is, if she is in a crowded harbor where moored barges are constantly being shifted about. On the other hand, the barge must not be the bargee's prison, even though he lives aboard; he must go ashore at times. We need not say whether, even in such crowded waters as New York Harbor a bargee must be aboard at night at all; it may be that the custom is otherwise . . . and that, if so, the situation is one where custom should control. We leave that question open; but we hold that it is not in all cases a sufficient answer to a bargee's absence without excuse, during working hours, that he has properly made fast his barge to a pier, when he leaves her. In the case at bar the bargee left at five o'clock in the afternoon of January 3rd, and the flotilla broke away at about two o'clock in the afternoon of the following day, twenty-one hours afterwards. The bargee had been away all the time, and we hold that his fabricated story was affirmative evidence that he had no excuse for his absence. At the locus in quo — especially during the short January days and in the full tide of war activity — barges were being constantly "drilled" in and out. Certainly it was not beyond reasonable expectation that, with the inevitable haste and bustle, the work might not be done with adequate care. In such circumstances we hold — and it is all that we do hold — that it was a fair requirement that [the owner of the barge], should have a bargee aboard (unless he had some  excuse for his absence), during the working hours of daylight.

The proper balancing of social interests — both costs and benefits — has come to be recognized by many as the central inquiry in determining whether an actor has been negligent. The Restatement (Second) of Torts states the general rule thus:

§291. Unreasonableness: How Determined: Magnitude of Risk and Utility of Conduct

> Where an act is one which a reasonable man would recognize as involving a risk of harm to another, the risk is unreasonable and the act is negligent if the risk is of such magnitude as to outweigh what the law regards as the utility of the act or of the particular manner in which it is done.

Observe that the Restatement does not attempt to replicate Judge Hand's algebraic formula, opting instead to express the core idea in words, alone. Observe also that §291 is couched in terms of the threshold question of acting or not acting. In that context, what is the "B"? The "PL"?

The Restatement (Third) of Torts: Liability for Physical and Emotional Harm (2010) contains the following definition of negligence:

§3. Negligence

> A person acts negligently if the person does not exercise reasonable care under all the circumstances. Primary factors to consider in ascertaining whether the person's conduct lacks reasonable care are the foreseeable likelihood that the person's conduct will result in harm, the foreseeable severity of any harm that may ensue, and the burden of precautions to eliminate or reduce the risk of harm.

Comment *e* to §3 then "suggest[s] a 'risk-benefit test' for negligence, where the 'risk' is the overall level of the foreseeable risk created by the actor's conduct and the 'benefit' is the advantages that the actor or others gain if the actor refrains from taking precautions."

In any event, the ultimate question in a negligence case is not simply whether a reasonable person would have recognized the risk but whether, recognizing the risk, that person would have acted differently. Even reasonable persons engage in risk-creating conduct in some situations. Every car trip, for example, creates some foreseeable risk of harm. It is only when such risk-taking is unreasonable that the defendant's conduct is negligent. The essence of the bargee's argument in *Carroll Towing* was that even if a reasonable person in the bargee's position might recognize certain risks in leaving the barge unattended, such a person would nevertheless willingly and reasonably incur those risks in the interest of maintaining some freedom of movement.

It is in deciding what the reasonably prudent person would have done that the ultimate value judgment must be made. Thus, when Judge Hand decided that the bargee in the *Carroll Towing* case had taken an unreasonable amount of freedom, he made a value judgment that on these facts the social interest in security of the barge outweighed the social interest in freedom of the bargee. The critical question analytically, therefore, is this: What are the values to be ascribed to the reasonable person in order to judge the reasonableness of the defendant's conduct? The Restatement (Second) of Torts suggests the following formulation:

§292. Factors Considered in Determining Utility of Actor's Conduct

In determining what the law regards as the utility of the actor's conduct for the purpose of determining whether the actor is negligent, the following factors are important:

(a) The social value which the law attaches to the interest which is to be advanced or protected by the conduct;

(b) The extent of the chance that this interest will be advanced or protected by the particular course of conduct;

(c) The extent of the chance that such interest can be adequately advanced or protected by another and less dangerous course of conduct.

§293. Factors Considered in Determining Magnitude of Risk

In determining the magnitude of the risk for the purpose of determining whether the actor is negligent, the following factors are important:

(a) The social value which the law attaches to the interests which are imperiled;

(b) the extent of the chance that the actor's conduct will cause an invasion of any interest of the other or of one of a class of which the other is a member;

(c) the extent of the harm likely to be caused to the interests imperiled;

(d) the number of persons whose interests are likely to be invaded if the risk takes effect in harm.

Notice the care with which the drafters of the Second Restatement state that the valuation of interests for balancing purposes is to proceed from a societal or collective perspective. That is, rather than a purely private or market valuation of the interests at stake, factfinders are to identify the "social value that the law attaches to the interests." The Restatement (Third) of Torts: Liability for Physical and Emotional Harm appears to retreat somewhat from this position, stripping the chief negligence section of any "social value" language and endorsing instead a form of cost-benefit balancing that emphasizes the private or market valuation frame: "While negligence law is concerned with social interests, courts regularly consider private interests, both because society is the protector of private interests and because the general public good is promoted by the protection and advancement of private interests." Restatement (Third) of Torts: Liability for Physical and Emotional Harm §3 cmt. *h* (2010). Kenneth W. Simons criticizes this approach in his article, The Hand Formula in the Draft Restatement (Third) of Torts: Encompassing Fairness as Well as Efficiency Values, 54 Vand. L. Rev. 901, 925-26 (2001).

In most cases, courts conduct the negligence balancing process in an intuitive manner. That is, after all, how most of us behave much of the time — giving no conscious thought to the risk/utility calculus implicit in our conduct. See Ronen Perry, Re-Torts, 59 Ala. L Rev. 987, 993 (2008) (arguing that "the Hand formula is rarely cited and even more seldom applied"); Kenneth W. Simons, Tort Negligence, Cost-Benefit Analysis, and Tradeoffs: A Closer look at the Controversy, 41 Loy. L.A. L. Rev. 1171, 1182 (2008) (stating that "jury instructions . . . rarely refer to Hand balancing, and appellate decisions refer to such balancing only intermittently"). Sometimes, however, courts use Judge Hand's test quite explicitly. For example, in Davis v. Consolidated Rail Corp., 788 F.2d 1260 (7th Cir. 1986), the plaintiff railroad car inspector had climbed under a stationary train in order to inspect certain cars leased to the defendant railroad by his employer without setting up the customary blue flags to indicate that the train should not be moved. (He had earlier seen the locomotive decouple and move away.) Unbeknownst to him, a different crew, with orders to move the train, attached another locomotive at the other end. The crew moved the train without blowing the horn or ringing the bell. The plaintiff tried to scramble from under the train when it began to move but was not entirely successful. He lost one leg below the knee and most of his other foot. At trial, the plaintiff urged that the defendant's train crew should have blown the train's horn and rung its bell before moving or that a member of the defendant's crew should have walked the train's entire length and looked under each car. The jury returned a verdict for the plaintiff and defendant appealed.

The court of appeals, in an opinion by Judge Posner, held that requiring the inspection by defendant of the entire train was too burdensome, given the low probability of someone's being under the train and the high cost of the precaution. The court held, however, that the crew should have blown the train's horn and rung its bell, because in that case the B was relatively small and the PL significant, given the range of accidents such a precaution might prevent. "In determining the benefits of a precaution — and PL, the expected accident costs that the precaution would avert, is a measure of the benefits of the precaution — the trier of fact must consider not only the expected cost of this accident, but also the expected costs of any other, similar accidents that the precaution would have prevented." Id. at 1264.

In most cases, however, the court's assessment of the reasonableness of an actor's conduct occurs on a less formal level. Indeed, it is worth noting that in *Carroll Towing* itself, Judge Hand's announcement of his "B < PL" test, was followed by a much more intuitive analysis of the reasonableness of the defendant's conduct. Judge Hand himself later expressed doubt over the wisdom of trying to reduce the negligence concept to precise mathematical formulas. See Moisan v. Loftus, 178 F.2d 148, 149 (2d Cir. 1949) (stating that "all such attempts [to quantify the determinants of liability] are illusory; and, if serviceable at all, are so only to center attention upon which one of the factors may be determinative in any given situation"); Conway v. O'Brien, 111 F.2d 611, 612 (2d Cir. 1940), *rev'd,* 312 U.S. 492 (1941) (observing that the negligence determination "always involves some preference, or choice between incommensurables, and it is consigned to a jury because their decision is thought most likely to accord with commonly accepted standards, real or fancied").

Still, the basic idea that Hand tried to capture with his "B < PL" formulation has come to be recognized as one appropriate way of expressing the basis for liability for negligence. Although some judges prefer to express the negligence test in the more humanistic terms of "what a reasonable person would have done," even that formulation can be seen as consistent with the notion that reasonable persons weigh the costs of activities against their benefits in deciding upon courses of action. More broadly, hardly anyone would deem the consequences of action completely irrelevant to the moral and legal evaluation of that action. Thus, whether or not one believes that the consequences of action can be reduced to precise values and weighed quantitatively, *some* assessment of the risks and rewards of particular modes of conduct is unavoidable in the negligence context. To that extent, Hand's statement that negligence law always involves a "choice between incommensurables" does not mean that the different interests at stake in torts suits cannot be *compared*—only that they cannot be neatly aligned along a single numerical metric. See *In re* City of New York, 522 F.3d 279, 285 (2d Cir. 2008) (noting that the Hand formula is "really more of an analytic framework than an actual formula into which [the court] could plug rough numerical estimates of burdens and injuries").

Notwithstanding the foregoing caveats about the possible risks of taking the "B < PL" calculus too seriously, it is important that the student appreciate the underlying concept. Toward that end, consider the following problem.

Problem 14

Assume that you own a tug company that transports the barges and cargoes owned by others to different ports along the seacoast. Among other risks, your operation is chronically threatened by coastal storms that can sink the cargo barges. When that happens, the owners of the barges and cargoes may sue, claiming that their properties would not have been lost if your company had taken additional precautions against bad weather.

You might take a variety of precautions to reduce the risk of storm-related losses. For starters, you might try to make sure that each of your regular crews includes one of those legendary sailors who claims to predict storms by the twitches in his bum knee. But because this precaution might not always be effective, you might wish to take additional precautions. You could, for example, equip your fleet with radios capable of receiving the weather broadcasts available on the public airways. These radios might be useful in alerting you to general weather patterns and the potential risks posed by still distant storms. For an even more precise picture of the weather conditions directly affecting your fleet, you could begin equipping your tugs with individual weather radar systems, maritime satellite internet connections, GPS navigation instruments, and other even more advanced technologies. Tugs detecting bad weather could then warn your other tugs of the danger. The more of your tugs you equip with such equipment, the more precise picture you would have of overall weather risks.

Each of these additional precautions will help eliminate weather-related sinkings. And each supplements, rather than replaces, precautions adopted earlier. Yet, as these precautions become increasingly exotic, they also become increasingly expensive. You are aware that even with the best combination of precautions, some weather-related losses may occur. Therefore, rather than seeking complete safety, your goal is reasonable safety. In other words, you want to determine how many precautions you should purchase in order to maximize your profits and to help ensure that your operation will be judged to be reasonable in the event that you are sued in negligence by those whose barges and cargoes were lost in a storm.

Assume that the courts in your jurisdiction make such negligence assessments based on Judge Hand's "B < PL" test. Assume further that you have unusually good data about both precautions and potential losses. These data will tell you several things. First, without any precautions, you will on average lose $10,000 of barges and cargoes every 100 trips due to bad weather. As you begin to invest in precautions, you will reduce these losses. Specifically, for every additional precaution you take, you will on average drive down accident losses by an additional $1,000 per 100 trips (as shown in column 1 in Table 3-1). However, each additional precaution is more expensive than the previous one (see column 2). Given this information, how many precautions would you take in order to escape potential liability for negligence? Although you may reach your answer using only columns 1 and 2, fill in columns 5 and 6 to help you confirm its validity. To aid in completing column 6, note that column 3 is the equivalent of "liability costs under negligence" except that, once you have taken the reasonable number of precautions, liability costs go to zero because you are no longer negligent. At (and beyond) that point you incur only the costs of precautions.

The Law-Fact Distinction: The Negligence Issue

Despite Judge Hand's efforts in the *Carroll Towing* case to translate the test into algebraic symbols, the standard against which the conduct of the defendant is to be judged remains a very general standard, and the judgment about that conduct is the judgment of humans, not that of computers. Therefore, as important as the foregoing rules are to an understanding of the negligence concept, it is even more important to appreciate the process by which these rules are applied in concrete cases. Central to such an appreciation is an understanding of the roles played by the judge and the jury in negligence cases that actually are resolved by adjudication. Briefly stated, the determination of the applicable general standard of care is one of law for the judge, and the determination of whether the defendant failed to meet that standard — that is, whether the defendant was negligent — is a question of fact for the jury. See, e.g., Thompson v. Kaczinski, 774 N.W.2d 829 (Iowa 2009) (holding that plaintiff's negligence claim, arising out of injuries suffered in a motor vehicle accident after wind carried a disassembled trampoline from defendants' backyard onto a nearby highway, created an issue of fact for the jury). If the judge concludes that reasonable minds could not differ regarding the question of the reasonableness of the defendant's conduct, the judge will, upon a proper motion, take the negligence issue from the jury by directing a verdict on that issue for one side or the other. If the evidence warrants submission of the negligence issue to the jury, the judge will communicate the standard to the jury in the instructions at the end of the trial, and the jury will determine, on the basis of the evidence, whether the defendant's conduct measured up to that standard. 'Because in most cases the standard to be applied is very general, the judge's task in connection with the negligence issue is relatively simple. The large majority of negligence cases brought to trial are sent to the jury, on instructions that give the jury great latitude in its determination of the negligence issue. Actually, it is only a slight exaggeration to assert that negligence in most cases is whatever the jury says it is.

It warrants repeating here that this division of function between judge and jury is in no way dictated by the meaning inherent in the terms *law* and *fact*. The reasonableness concept on which the law of negligence is predicated is, strictly speaking, neither law nor fact but a conclusion calling for the application of the former to the latter. See the law-fact

TABLE 3-1

Number of Precautions Taken	(1) Amount Saved in Accident Costs for Each Additional Precaution Taken	(2) Cost of Each Additional Precaution Taken	(3) Total Remaining Accident Costs	(4) Total Costs of All Precautions Taken	(5) Total Social Costs (Sum of Total Remaining Accident Costs and Total Costs of All Precautions Taken)	(6) Actor's Total Costs (Sum of Total Precautions Costs and Liability Costs Under Negligence)
0	—	—	$10,000	$0		
1	$1,000	$100	9,000	100		
2	1,000	300	8,000	400		
3	1,000	700	7,000	1,100		
4	1,000	1,200	6,000	2,300		
5	1,000	1,900	5,000	4,200		
6	1,000	2,800	4,000	7,000		
7	1,000	5,400	3,000	12,400		
8	1,000	11,000	2,000	23,400		
No further precautions available						

distinction note, p. 88, above. The negligence issue is labeled *fact* because it is believed to be appropriate for the jury to play an important role in applying law to fact in these cases. If it were generally felt that judges should participate more directly in deciding the negligence issue, such an adjustment could be accomplished by changing the label. Were courts to label the negligence issue as one of law, and thus to begin to decide that issue themselves, some special verdict procedure could be developed as a means of allowing juries to continue to decide preliminary issues of historical fact that pertain to the negligence issue. See the note on verdicts and instructions, p. 227, below. As a middle ground short of deciding the negligence issue in every case, courts could simply begin to define the standard of care with much greater specificity in these subject matter areas in which greater judicial supervision and control was deemed necessary.

Washington v. Louisiana Power and Light Co.

555 So. 2d 1350 (La. 1990)

DENNIS, JUSTICE.

We granted certiorari in this power line accident case to review the Court of Appeal's judgment setting aside a jury award to the adult children of a man who was electrocuted when he accidentally allowed a citizens band radio antenna to come into contact with an uninsulated 8,000 volt electrical wire that spanned the backyard of his residence. We affirm. The jury verdict for the plaintiffs was manifestly erroneous. . . .

[The decedent was electrocuted when the antenna from his CB radio came into contact with the defendant's uninsulated 8,000 volt transmission line, which was about 21½ feet above the ground. Five years before the contact with the line that killed the decedent, the antenna came into contact with the line while the decedent was moving it, causing the decedent and his son, who was helping him move the antenna, to suffer burns on the hand. Several times after the earlier incident, the decedent requested the defendant to insulate the line, or move it underground. The defendant said that it would do so only at the decedent's expense.]

After a trial on the merits, a jury found LP & L at fault in the accident and awarded plaintiffs $500,000 for pain and suffering and the loss of life of the decedent and $75,000 for each plaintiff's loss of love, affection, and support. LP & L appealed suspensively. The Court of Appeal, noting that the decedent had five years earlier received an electrical shock when he touched the antenna to the same line, and had since that time been extremely careful to never move the antenna alone or toward the line until the day of the fatal accident, reversed, concluding that LP & L did not breach any duty owed to the decedent. . . .

When the evidence is clear, as in the present case, that the power company either knew or should have known of the possibility of an accident that materialized in the decedent's electrocution, the remaining negligence issue is whether the possibility of such injury or loss constituted an unreasonable risk of harm. Such a case invites "a sharp focus upon the essential balancing process that lies at the heart of negligence." Malone, Work of Appellate Courts, 29 La. L. Rev. 212, 212 (1969). In this regard, we recently held that the power company's duty to provide against resulting injuries, as in similar situations, is a function of three variables: (1) the possibility that the electricity will escape; (2) the gravity of the resulting injury, if it does; (3) the burden of taking adequate precautions that would avert the accident. When the product of the possibility of escape multiplied times the gravity of the harm, if it happens, exceeds the burden of precautions, the risk is unreasonable and the failure to take those precautions is negligence. [The court referred to other cases, including United States v. Carroll Towing Co., 159 F.2d 169, 173 (2d Cir. 1947).]

Applying the negligence balancing process, we conclude that although there was a cognizable risk that the antenna stationed in the corner of Mr. Washington's backyard could be lowered and moved to within a dangerous proximity of the power line, that possibility could not be characterized as an unreasonable risk and the power company's failure to take additional precautions against it was not negligence.

Under the circumstances, there was not a significant possibility before the accident that Mr. Washington or anyone acting for him would detach the antenna and attempt to carry it under or dangerously near the power line. Standing alone, Mr. Washington's 1980 accident might have caused an objective observer to increase his estimate of the chances that this particular antenna might be handled carelessly. The other surrounding circumstances, however, overwhelmingly erase any pre-accident enlargement of the risk at that site. Except for the single occasion of the 1980 accident, the antenna was stationed safely in the corner of the backyard for many years, one to three years before the 1980 mishap and five years afterwards. Most of that time it was maintained safely in the pipe receptacle which, by Mr. Washington's design, allowed it to be lowered only in a safe direction. Between his close call in 1980 and his fatal accident in 1985, Mr. Washington had never been known to handle the antenna carelessly. Indeed, after he and his son narrowly escaped death or serious injury in 1980, his remarks to friends and relatives indicated that the experience had convinced him to keep the antenna far away from the power line. That he continued to be aware of the danger and take exemplary precautions to avoid it until his fatal accident was further illustrated by the care that he and his friend took when they lowered and laid it next to the fence several days before the accident.

The likelihood that the antenna in this case would be brought into contact with the power line was not as great as the chances of an electrical accident in situations creating significant potential for injuries to victims who may contact or come into dangerous proximity with the power line due to their unawareness of or inadvertence to the charged wire.

Prior to the accident, the anticipated gravity of the loss if the risk were to take effect was, of course, of a very high degree. The deaths and serious injuries in this and other electrical accidents verify that the weight of the loss threatened by a power line accident is not trivial. While some accidents, such as Mr. Washington's 1980 mishap, do not lead to dire consequences, a consideration of all losses resulting from this type of risk indicates that the gravity of the loss if it occurs is usually extreme.

Yet when this high degree of gravity of loss is multiplied by the very small possibility of the accident occurring in this case, we think it is clear that the product does not outweigh the burdens or costs of the precautions of relocating or insulating the power line. This does not mean, of course, that it would not have been worth what it would have cost to place the line underground or to insulate it in order to save the decedent's life if it had been known that the accident would happen or even if the chance of it occurring had been greater. Nor does it mean, on the other hand, that we stop with a consideration of only the burden of an effective precaution in this single case. Common knowledge indicates that within any power company's territory there probably are a great number of situations involving antennas that have been safely installed, but which conceivably could be detached and carelessly moved about dangerously near a power line. In fairness, in this case, in which the coexistence of the power line and the safely installed antenna was no riskier than countless other similar coexistences not considered to involve negligence, the burden to the company of taking precautions against all such slight possibilities of harm should be balanced against the total magnitude of all these risks, including the relatively few losses resulting from the total of all those insignificant risks. Just as single case applications of the Hand formula can understate the benefits of accident prevention by overlooking all other accidents that could be avoided by the same safety expenditures, the burdens of taking precautions in all similar cases may be depreciated by single case consideration here.

The foregoing, of course, is merely a shorthand expression of the mental processes involved in such considerations. We cannot mathematically or mechanically quantify, multiply, or weigh risks, losses, and burdens of precautions. As many scholars have noted, the formula is primarily helpful in keeping in mind the relationship of the factors involved and in centering attention upon which of them may be determinative in any given situation. Nevertheless, the formula would seem to be of greater assistance in cases of the present type, in which the power company's ability to perceive risks is superior and its duty is utmost, than other notions, such as "reasonable man," "duty," or "foreseeability," for example, which must be little more than labels to be applied after some sort of balancing or weighing that the formula attempts to describe. In the present case, the balancing process focuses our attention on the fact that the possibility of an accident appeared to be slight beforehand and on the reality that precautions against such slight risks would be costly and burdensome because they exist in great number and have not usually been considered unreasonable or intolerable.

For the reasons assigned, the judgment of the court of appeals is affirmed.

Rodriguez v. Del Sol Shopping Center Associates, L.P.

326 P.3d 465 (N.M. 2014)

CHÁVEZ, Justice.

In this opinion we clarify and expressly hold that foreseeability is not a factor for courts to consider when determining the existence of a duty, or when deciding to limit or eliminate an existing duty in a particular class of cases. We reaffirm our adoption of Restatement (Third) of Torts: Liability for Physical and Emotional Harm §7 comment j (2010),[43] and require courts to articulate specific policy reasons, unrelated to foreseeability considerations, if deciding that a defendant does not have a duty or that an existing duty should be limited. Foreseeability is a fact-intensive inquiry relevant only to breach of duty and legal cause considerations. What may not be foreseeable under one set of facts may be foreseeable under a slightly different set of facts. Therefore, foreseeability cannot be a policy argument because foreseeability is not susceptible to a categorical analysis. We do not hold that courts may never consider foreseeability; however, when a court does so, it is to analyze no-breach-of-duty or no-legal-cause as a matter of law, not whether a duty exists.

BACKGROUND

In these consolidated cases, a truck crashed through the front glass of the Concentra Medical Clinic (Concentra) in the Del Sol Shopping Center (Del Sol) (collectively Defendants) in Santa Fe, killing three people and seriously injuring several others. Both groups of

43. Comment j addresses "The proper role for foreseeability" and states, in pertinent part: "Despite widespread use of foreseeability in no-duty determinations, this Restatement disapproves that practice and limits no-duty rulings to articulated policy or principle in order to facilitate more transparent explanations of the reasons for a no-duty ruling and to protect the traditional function of the jury as factfinder." [Eds.]

Plaintiffs (collectively Plaintiffs) sued Del Sol's owners and operators, alleging that Del Sol negligently contributed to the accident by, among other things, failing to adequately post signage; failing to install speed bumps; failing to erect barriers that would have protected buildings, employees, and visitors from errant vehicles; or failing to use other traffic control methods in the parking lot. [B]oth district courts granted summary judgment and found that this accident "was not foreseeable" as a matter of law, and therefore found that no duty existed.

On appeal, the Court of Appeals consolidated the two cases and affirmed the district courts' common ruling on summary judgment that Defendants "had no duty to protect Plaintiffs inside the building from criminally reckless drivers." After an exhaustive analysis of New Mexico precedent, the Court of Appeals correctly rejected the foreseeability-driven duty analysis relied upon by the district courts, stating that it was affirming both cases based on a "policy-driven duty analysis advanced by the Restatement (Third) of Torts. . . ." We agree with the Court of Appeals that New Mexico case law has created confusion regarding the extent to which foreseeability considerations are relevant to the legal determination of duty. . . . [W]e take this opportunity to explain why foreseeability should not be considered when determining duty, both generally and when considering the analysis of the Court of Appeals in these cases. We overrule prior cases insofar as they conflict with this opinion's clarification of the appropriate duty analysis in New Mexico. And because we conclude that the Court of Appeals analysis is a no-breach-of-duty analysis more than a policy-driven duty analysis, we reverse the Court of Appeals.

DISCUSSION

Foreseeability and breach are questions that a jury considers when it decides whether a defendant acted reasonably under the circumstances of a case or legally caused injury to a particular plaintiff. . . . The argument before the jury when it is determining whether breach occurred is whether the foreseeable likelihood and severity of injuries that might have occurred due to the defendant's conduct warranted the additional precautions argued by the plaintiff. These ordinary arguments relate to breach of duty and legal cause, and are not policy arguments that would justify a no-duty determination or modification of an existing duty.

In these cases, the Court of Appeals framed the issue as "[w]hat duty should owner/occupants of a shopping center in New Mexico have to protect business invitees within its buildings from vehicles that depart the confines of designated parking areas?" The Court of Appeals then correctly summarized the law [in New Mexico that an] owner/occupier owes a duty of ordinary care under the circumstances, including the duty to exercise ordinary care to prevent harmful conduct from a third person, even if the third person's conduct is intentional. The duty of ordinary care applies unless the owner/occupier can establish a policy reason, unrelated to foreseeability considerations, that compels a limitation on the duty or an exemption from the duty to exercise ordinary care. . . .

In the *Del Sol* cases, the Court of Appeals exempted owners/occupiers of shopping centers from the duty of ordinary care to protect invitees within its buildings from vehicles that departed the confines of designated parking areas. To arrive at its no-duty determination, the Court of Appeals considered (1) the nature of the activity, (2) the parties' relationship to the activity, and (3) public policy. Regarding the nature of the activity and the parties' relationship to the activity, the Court was persuaded by statistical evidence that there was a "sheer improbability and lack of inherent danger" of vehicle-pedestrian accidents within the related businesses. The flaw in the analysis is that it is a foreseeability-driven analysis, as evidenced by the authorities on which the Court of Appeals relied. See, e.g., Eckerd–Walton, Inc. v. Adams, 126 Ga. App. 210, 190 S.E.2d 490, 492 (1972) (finding that a merchant could not reasonably anticipate that a negligent motorist would attempt to drive through a store); Mack v. McGrath, 276 Minn. 419, 150 N.W.2d 681, 686 (1967) (concluding that liability cannot be predicated on the remote possibility that a vehicle would jump a curb and expose tenants to injury). . . .

A determination of no duty based upon the foreseeability, improbability, or remote nature of the risk is inconsistent with the Restatement approach, which provides that only "[i]n exceptional cases, when an articulated countervailing principle or policy warrants denying or limiting liability in a particular class of cases, a court may decide that the defendant has no duty or that the ordinary duty of reasonable care requires modification." Restatement (Third) of Torts, supra, §7(b). . . .

The Court of Appeals also concluded that there was not anything about Del Sol and its adjacent parking lot that "justifies a broadened standard of care owed to visitors." However, Plaintiffs are not seeking a broadened standard of care; they simply contend that Del Sol breached the duty of ordinary care. Implicit in the Court of Appeals' determination is that if there was something about the Del Sol parking lot — some significant difference in the fact pattern — the result may have been different. This also suggests a foreseeability-driven analysis. Once a court begins to rely on factual details in deciding whether to modify the duty of ordinary care or exempt a defendant from that duty, the court is really determining that there has been no breach of duty. Similarly, a court's concern that the plaintiffs are seeking a broader standard of care is a concern about whether the plaintiffs expect too much of the defendants — something more than what is reasonable — which is relevant to the issue of breach of duty, not whether a duty is owed, and breach of duty questions are usually reserved for the jury.

Regarding public policy considerations, the Court of Appeals began its analysis by stating that it would apply public policy as the primary barometer in ascertaining the "scope of ordinary care" owed by Defendants to Plaintiffs. As a preliminary matter, we note that Restatement (Third) of Torts, supra, §7 comment j is concerned with the scope of duty, and not with the scope of ordinary care. This distinction is more than semantic, because to be concerned about the scope of ordinary care is to be concerned about whether a defendant's conduct was reasonable — a breach of duty analysis. Restatement (Third) of Torts, supra, §7 cmt. i (discussing the mistake that courts sometimes make when they "inaptly express" a determination that there was no breach of duty as a matter of law in terms of no duty). On the other hand, concerns about the scope of duty require a judge to articulate policy considerations when modifying the duty of ordinary care or exempting a class of defendants from the duty of ordinary care in a class of cases. . . .

The Court of Appeals also rejected two categories of evidence tendered by Plaintiffs to prove that Defendants failed to act reasonably in order to conclude that Defendants were exempt from the duty of ordinary care. First, the Court rejected the affidavit of Plaintiffs' safety expert, which was supported by academic publications in safety engineering, that identified hazards on Defendants' property that contributed to the errant vehicle crashing into the building and methods to minimize the hazards. Second, the Court did not find persuasive several photographs of other local businesses that have installed safety features similar to those identified by Plaintiffs' safety engineer. The Court of Appeals was not persuaded that the proffered evidence "legally establishes a norm of professional safety giving rise to an expanded duty to protect." The Court also expressed the opinion that more safety precautions than those recommended by the safety engineer would be necessary to "have definitively prevented a runaway vehicle from crashing through Del Sol's storefronts" and "have prevented the injuries and loss of life." In summary, the Court of Appeals did not believe that the proffered evidence "indicate[d] that Del Sol's election not to employ such safety devices [fell] beneath professional norms of safety," nor did the evidence "establish a newly applicable safety norm, a building code-derived regulation, or a public policy" that would support "the heightened standards of safety advanced by Plaintiffs."

Weighing the evidence in this manner is not a proper policy consideration for departing from the duty of ordinary care. In these cases, Plaintiffs tendered the affidavit and photographs of other local businesses that have installed protective devices as evidence of what type of reasonable precautions should be taken and have been taken to avoid vehicle-building crashes. If a jury is persuaded that Plaintiffs are asking too much of Defendants, the jury will decline to hold Defendants liable, not because no duty of ordinary care was owed, but because even having the duty of ordinary care, Defendants either acted reasonably under the circumstances or their breach of duty did not legally cause the injuries and deaths at Concentra. Courts should not engage in weighing evidence to determine whether a duty of care exists or should be expanded or contracted — weighing evidence is the providence of the jury; instead, courts should focus on policy considerations when determining the scope or existence of a duty of care.

We also reject the notion [expressed by the Court of Appeals] that requiring owners/occupiers of buildings and land to exercise ordinary care makes them "absolute insurers of patron safety" from:

> remote mechanical and human fallibility . . . forcing businesses into one of three undesirable alternatives: (1) significantly revis[ing] the physical and aesthetic layout of buildings and parking lots at substantial expense, (2) retain[ing] the status quo and risk[ing] the enormous cost of catastrophic liability, or (3) clos[ing] down the business premises entirely.

First and foremost, the notion ignores our comparative fault system and the weight a jury will give to foreseeability considerations. Second, the presumptive undesirable alternatives identified by the Court of Appeals do not appear to be supported by any evidence. At a minimum, the affidavit of Plaintiffs' safety engineer and the photos of other businesses in the vicinity, which are apparently still in business, that have safety features the expert opines would be reasonable to minimize the danger of vehicle-building crashes, create a genuine issue of material fact.

The Court of Appeals also concluded that Del Sol could not have "anticipated, prevented, or even reacted to" the runaway truck, and the Court therefore could "discern no basis on the facts of these cases to legally extend a 'duty to protect' visitors from runaway vehicles into the responsibility of ordinary care applicable to Defendants." To say that Del Sol could not have "anticipated" is to say that the event was not foreseeable, an approach the Court of Appeals sought to avoid, and which we reject in determining the existence of a duty. To say that Del Sol could not have "prevented, or even reacted to" a runaway truck has no bearing on whether a duty exists; rather, it questions whether Del Sol acted reasonably and did not breach the duty of ordinary care.

In essence, the Court of Appeals' analysis is focused predominantly on foreseeability considerations and the reasonableness of Defendants' conduct. Foreseeability determinations are reserved for a jury because such determinations require the jury's common sense, common experience, and its consideration of community behavioral norms. . . .

Courts are not powerless to dismiss cases as a matter of law, despite our holding that a foreseeability-driven duty analysis is inappropriate. A court may still decide whether a defendant did or did not breach the duty of ordinary care as a matter of law, or that the breach of duty did not legally cause the damages alleged in the case. However, these determinations are materially different than a no-duty or modified-duty analysis. The court must determine that no reasonable jury would find that the defendant breached the duty of ordinary care or that the breach legally caused the plaintiff's damages. This determination requires judges to abandon their own personal thoughts regarding the merits of cases and to imagine the thoughts of twelve adult citizens from a variety of socioeconomic backgrounds — such as scientists, college faculty, laborers, uneducated, rich, poor, persons with different political persuasions — and what that diverse group might find regarding the merits of a case. The judge can enter judgment as a matter of law only if the judge concludes that no reasonable jury could decide the breach of duty or legal cause questions except one way. Because neither the Court of Appeals nor the district court judges engaged in this analysis, we reverse and remand to the district courts for proceedings consistent with this opinion.

CONCLUSION

Foreseeability is not a question for courts to consider when determining the existence of a duty, or whether to limit or eliminate an existing duty in a particular class of cases. Instead, courts must articulate specific policy reasons, unrelated to foreseeability considerations, when deciding whether a defendant does or does not have a duty or that an existing duty should be limited.

It Is So Ordered.

We Concur: Petra Jimenez Maes, Senior Justice, Richard C. Bosson, Justice, and Michael D. Bustamante, Judge Sitting By Designation.

Barbara J. Vigil, Chief Justice and Charles W. Daniels, Justice, Recused.

Note: The Duty Issue in Negligence Law

Professors Goldberg and Zipursky identify four different ways in which courts use "duty" in negligence cases. See John C. P. Goldberg & Benjamin C. Zipursky, The *Restatement (Third)* and the Place of Duty in Negligence Law, 54 Vand. L. Rev. 657, 698-723 (2001). First, they identify duty in its typical sense, which asks whether the defendant had a legal obligation to the plaintiff to conform his or her conduct to a particular standard of care. In cases using duty in this way, the issue is not whether the defendant's conduct conformed to a particular standard of care, but rather whether a standard of care was owed at all. See, e.g., Cabral v. Ralphs Grocery Co., 248 P.3d 1170 (Cal. 2011) (concluding that no "categorical exemption from the duty of ordinary care" exists to insulate motorists from potential liability for parking alongside freeways in emergency stopping lanes).

The second way in which courts use the word duty, according to Goldberg and Zipursky, could be called the "no-breach-as-matter-of-law" sense, in which the court uses the idea of duty to decide that no reasonable fact finder could conclude that the defendant failed to meet the applicable standard of care. In such cases, the court will claim that the defendant owed no duty to the plaintiff when the court more accurately should state that the risks the defendant imposed on the plaintiff did not, as a matter of law, breach the duty the defendant owed. Goldberg and Zipursky illustrate this second way of using duty through the case of Albert v. Hsu, 602 So. 2d 895 (Ala. 1992), where the plaintiff, a patron in defendant's restaurant, was struck and killed by a car that drove through the wall of the restaurant. The court held that there was no duty owed by defendant to plaintiff because the accident was too unforeseeable. As Goldberg and Zipursky note, however, "[c]learly . . . restaurant owners do owe a duty to patrons to ensure their premises are safe, including safe from the threat posed by forces outside the walls of the restaurant. What plaintiff failed to establish [was the breach of that duty]." 54 Vand. L. Rev. at 713.

The tendency to conflate the "obligation" and "no-breach-as-a-matter-of-law" senses of duty is addressed in Coburn v. City of Tucson, 691 P.2d 1078, 1079-81 (Ariz. 1984):

> Many tort decisions exhibit an unfortunate tendency to confuse the concepts of "duty" and standard of conduct and to argue that the city is, or is not, under a duty to post warning signs, remove obstructions from the road or sidewalks, install traffic control devices, fix potholes, and the like. We believe that an attempt to equate the concept of "duty" with such specific details of conduct is unwise. Attempting to define or evaluate conduct in terms of duty tends to rigidify the concept of negligence — a concept which, by definition, must vary from case to case, depending upon the relationship of the parties and the facts of each case. . . .
>
> . . . The true issue in this case, therefore, is not whether the city had a duty toward [plaintiffs' decedent]. It had a duty to keep the streets reasonably safe for travel by [him] and all others. The issue here is simply whether there is evidence sufficient to create a question of fact on the issue of whether the city's failure to remove the bush was conduct which fell below the standard of care and thus breached the duty.

The remaining ways that courts use duty, as identified by Goldberg and Zipursky, are the "nexus" and "exemption" senses. Briefly, the "nexus" sense refers to the requirement that the defendant's injury-causing breach of a duty must be the breach of a duty owed specifically to the plaintiff. Courts using this sense of duty employ the terminology as a shorthand way of addressing issues of foreseeability and connection that also are examined through the proximate cause doctrine (see Chapter 4).

Finally, through the "exemption" sense of duty, courts craft various policy-based limitations on liability by holding, as a matter of law, that certain classes of actors do not owe certain classes of victims the same general duty of reasonable care ordinarily owed by all to all. See Robert L. Rabin, The Historical Development of the Fault Principle: A Reinterpretation, 15 Ga. L. Rev. 925 (1981). Professor Stephen Sugarman has attempted to catalogue the circumstances in which courts feel motivated to adopt "no duty" holdings that exempt wrongdoers from tort liability. See Stephen D. Sugarman, Why No Duty?, 61 DePaul L. Rev. 669 (2012). His list includes the categories below, supplemented by representative examples in parentheses:

A. Tort Is the Wrong Regime to Deal with the Victim's Complaint (e.g., "fireman's rule")
B. The Judicial System Cannot Suitably Administer Claims like This (e.g., no general duty to avoid negligent infliction of emotional distress)
C. Permitting Tort Claims Will Induce Individuals to Respond in Socially Unacceptable (Perverse) Ways (e.g., relaxed duties between recreational sports participants, refusal to impose duties of care on providers of voluntary charitable services such as church

sexual abuse hotlines or anti-hazing initiatives on campus, the "baseball rule" which limits liability of baseball facilities to spectators injured by foul balls)

D. Trumping Social Values Override the Victim's Claim in Tort (e.g., no duty to rescue)
E. The Victims Are Morally Undeserving (e.g., relaxed duty toward trespassers)
F. Imposing a Duty of Care on This Defendant Would Result in an Unfairly Crushing Liability (e.g., extension of sovereign immunity principles to public utilities and other quasi-governmental actors)

See also Aaron D. Twerski, The Cleaver, the Violin, and the Scalpel: Duty and the *Restatement (Third) of Torts*, 60 Hastings L.J. 1 (2008) (arguing that "no duty" cases are always case-specific but that some significant factors can be identified). Some of the instances in which courts adopt exempting "no duty" rules are taken up in Sections D and E of this chapter. Others appear in Chapter 4. As you work through the materials in both chapters, it may be helpful to return to this list periodically to see how well it captures the case law.

As a general proposition, the taxonomy of duty proposed by Goldberg and Zipursky seems noncontroversial enough, and will prove useful as we work through the negligence materials in this chapter and the next. Controversy over the duty issue in negligence surfaced, however, in connection with the American Law Institute's Restatement (Third) of Torts: Liability for Physical Harm. In the first Tentative Draft of that project, dated March 28, 2001, and discussed at the annual meeting of the American Law Institute (ALI) in May 2001, the Restatement drafters eliminated "duty" in its obligation and no-breach-as-a-matter-of-law senses, and limited its use to the "exemption" sense. Thus, under the proposal the only function to be served by the duty concept was to relieve certain predetermined classes of actors from the obligation of due care.

Professors Goldberg and Zipursky adamantly disagreed with the Restatement drafters, insisting that the duty concept in all four traditional senses should be left as an integral part of the "duty-breach-cause-harm" approach in traditional negligence jurisprudence. See 54 Vand. L. Rev. at 736:

> The *Restatement (Third) of Torts: General Principles* has studiously avoided the concept of duty and the language expressing it. In doing so, it has disempowered itself from *restating* our actual law, from explaining the sense in which it is a *law* of torts and from capturing a plausible sense in which it is *general* or *principled*—all because of trepidation about the concept of duty. This hostility was a central feature in the work of the grandfather of American torts scholarship, Oliver Wendell Holmes, Jr., and it developed into a visceral distaste in the work of subsequent tort scholars such as William Prosser. . . .
>
> Alas, the Holmes-Prosser strategy of boiling down negligence to the concepts of unreasonableness, causation, and injury was never right, for their hostility toward duty was never intellectually or legally justified. Duty is not scary, mysterious, or empty, nor is it "grandiloquent quasi-philosophical rhetoric"; it is an aspect of legal doctrine that has conceptual content of its own, just as intent, causation, defect, and many other concepts do. Today's negligence law intermingles a primary sense of "duty" with other senses of the term. It is therefore something of a mess. That is no reason to walk away from duty, or to select one of these alternative senses of "duty" as its "true" meaning. It is a reason for academics charged with drafting a Restatement to roll up their sleeves and try to clean up the mess. That is what we have begun to do here.

At the ALI annual meeting in May 2001, Professors Goldberg and Zipursky moved to send the duty issue back to the reporters for further consideration. The motion carried by a solid majority. See Jordan K. Kolar, Note, Is This Really the End of Duty? The Evolution of the Third Restatement of Torts, 87 Minn. L. Rev. 233 (2002) (providing an account of these developments).

The final draft of the Restatement (Third) of Torts: Liability for Physical and Emotional Harm (2010) includes a section on duty that states explicitly that "an actor ordinarily has a duty to exercise reasonable care when that actor's conduct creates a risk of physical harm." Restatement (Third) of Torts: Liability for Physical and Emotional Harm §7(a) (2010). The section does not limit the duty of reasonable care to conduct that creates a risk of harm to foreseeable plaintiffs nor does it limit the duty to foreseeable risks of physical harm, such matters being exclusively relegated to other sections of the Third Restatement on proximate cause. Section 7(b), however, provides that "[i]n exceptional cases, when an articulated countervailing principle or policy warrants denying or limiting liability in a particular class of cases, a court may decide that the defendant has no duty or that the ordinary duty of reasonable care requires modification." In fact, a co-reporter of the Restatement (Third) of Torts: Liability for Physical and Emotional Harm, Michael Green, argues that the Third Restatement's basic duty provisions do not depart radically from those of the Restatement (Second) of Torts, especially in physical harm cases. See W. Jonathan Cardi & Michael D. Green, Duty Wars, 81 S. Cal. L. Rev. 671, 691–732 (2008) ("Third Restatement continues a long trend . . . in recognizing a default duty of reasonable care with regard to causing physical harm.").

Does the assumption, implicit in the negligence concept, that a defendant will weigh the costs and benefits of a given action, make sense in all cases? Should there be, for example, a different test for negligence in cases of sudden emergency? See Restatement (Third) of Torts: Liability for Physical and Emotional Harm §9 (2010) ("If an actor is confronted with an unexpected emergency requiring rapid response, this is a circumstance to be taken into account in determining whether the actor's resulting conduct is that of the reasonably careful person.") Consider the decision of the Supreme Court of Washington in Kappelman v. Lutz, 217 P.3d 286 (Wash. 2009), *aff'g* 170 P.3d 1189 (Wash. Ct. App. Div. 3, 2007), in which plaintiff, who was injured while riding as a passenger on defendant's motorcycle when the motorcycle struck a deer, brought a negligence action against defendant. Included in the trial court's instruction to the jury, over plaintiff's objection, was an explanation of the "sudden emergency" doctrine: "A person who is suddenly confronted by an emergency through no negligence of his or her own and who is compelled to decide instantly how to avoid injury and who makes such a choice as a reasonably careful person placed in such a position might make, is not negligent even though it is not the wisest choice." The jury found that the cause of the accident was not any negligence by the defendant, and the trial court entered judgment for defendant. The Supreme Court of Washington affirmed. But see Tidd v. Kroshus, 870 N.W.2d 181 (N.D. 2015) (holding that sudden emergency doctrine requires an external or intervening event and therefore cannot apply to a situation where a bicyclist collided with a vehicle and the driver of the vehicle did not see the bicyclist before the collision).

Even if one concedes that the suddenness with which the emergency arose is a factor to be considered, why call it a "doctrine" and give it special weight? See Bedor v. Johnson, 292 P.3d 924, 928 (Col. 2013) (en banc) (abolishing Colorado's sudden emergency doctrine on the grounds that it has "minimal utility weighed against its potential to mislead the jury"); Bjorndal v. Weitman, 184 P.3d 1115, 1116 (Or. 2008) (holding that sudden-emergency instruction, as used in vehicle negligence cases, is an erroneously "inaccurate and confusing supplement to the instructions on the law of negligence" because it introduces "additional concepts that are not part of the ordinary negligence standard"). Does the answer to this question relate in any way to Goldberg and Zipursky's "no-breach-as-a-matter-of-law" sense of the duty concept? Would recognizing discrete factors as "doctrines" survive as a method of allowing judges to control outcomes even under a regime that limited "duty" to its exemption sense?

Law and Policy: The Values Reflected in the Negligence Concept

In defining negligence in terms of costs and benefits, the courts in *Carroll Towing* and *Washington* clearly fall into the instrumentalist camp. See the note, Law and Policy: Preliminary Considerations, pp. 36-41, above. From that perspective, the goal of negligence law is to achieve the optimal level of accident prevention so that the total costs of accidents and accident prevention will be minimized.[44] But note that the net effect of the negligence rule is to force plaintiffs to bear the accident costs of a defendant's harm-causing activity as long as the defendant struck a reasonable balance between accident costs and the costs of precautions. Not surprisingly, this economic efficiency perspective of negligence law has been attacked as inadequately embodying the right social values. For important discussions of the moral implications — and limitations — of the "B < PL" formula, see Benjamin C. Zipursky, Sleight of Hand, 48 William & Mary L. Rev. 1999 (2007); Richard W. Wright, Hand, Posner, and the Myth of the "Hand Formula," 4 Theoretical Inquiries L. 145 (2003); Gregory C. Keating, Pressing Precaution Beyond the Point of Cost-Justification, 56 Vand. L. Rev. 653 (2003); Richard W. Wright, Justice and Reasonable Care in Negligence Law, 47 Am. J. Juris. 143 (2002); William E. Nelson, The Moral Perversity of the Hand Calculus, 45 St. Louis U. L.J. 759 (2001).

Consider, for example, the arguments in Steven Kelman, Cost-Benefit Analysis — An Ethical Critique, Regulation, Jan./Feb. 1981, at 33, 35-36. Kelman objects to the use of cost-benefit analysis in making decisions about environmental regulation, but his criticisms are relevant to cost-benefit analysis in other contexts as well, including negligence law. Justifying an act simply because its overall benefits outweigh its overall costs, Kelman argues, is not adequate as a "moral view":

> This does not mean that the question of whether benefits are greater than costs is morally irrelevant. Few would claim such. Indeed, for a broad range of individual and social decisions, whether an act's benefits outweigh its costs is a sufficient question to ask. But not for all such decisions. These may involve situations where certain duties — duties not to lie, break promises, or kill, for example — make an act wrong, even if it would result in an excess of benefits over costs. Or they may involve instances where people's rights are at stake. We would not permit rape even if it could be demonstrated that the rapist derived enormous happiness from his act, while the victim experiences only minor displeasure. We do not do cost-benefit analyses of freedom of speech or trial by jury. . . . The notion of human rights involves the idea that people may make certain claims to be allowed to act in

44. See Guido Calabresi, The Costs of Accidents 26 (1970) ("Apart from the requirements of justice, I take it as axiomatic that the principal function of accident law is to reduce the sum of the costs of accidents and the costs of avoiding accidents."); Richard A. Posner, A Theory of Negligence, 1 J. Legal Stud. 29, 33 (1972) ("Perhaps, then, the dominant function of the fault system is to generate rules of liability that if followed will bring about, at least approximately, the efficient — the cost-justified — level of accidents and safety.").

> certain ways, even if the sum of benefits does not outweigh the sum of costs. It is this view that underlies the statement that "workers have a right to a safe and healthy work place" and the expectation that OSHA's decisions will reflect that judgment.
>
> In the most convincing versions of nonutilitarian ethics, various duties or rights are not absolute. But each has a *prima facie* moral validity so that, if duties or rights do not conflict, the morally right act is the act that reflects a duty or respects a right. If duties or rights do conflict, a moral judgment, based on conscious deliberation, must be made. Since one of the duties nonutilitarian philosophers enumerate is the duty of beneficence (the duty to maximize happiness), which in effect incorporates all of utilitarianism by reference, a nonutilitarian who is faced with conflicts between the results of cost-benefit analysis and nonutility-based considerations will need to undertake such deliberation. But in that deliberation, additional elements, which cannot be reduced to a question of whether benefits outweigh costs, have been introduced. Indeed, depending on the moral importance we attach to the right or duty involved, cost-benefit questions may, within wide ranges, become irrelevant to the outcome of the moral judgment.
>
> . . . When officials are deciding what level of pollution will harm certain vulnerable people — such as asthmatics or the elderly — one issue involved may be the right of those people not to be sacrificed on the altar of somewhat higher living standards for the rest of us.

Id. at 35-36.

Kelman does not, in the course of his critique of cost-benefit analysis, indicate how regulators should decide how much to spend, for example, on clean air or safe workplaces. On the assumption that "absolutely clean" air and "absolutely safe" workplaces are neither attainable nor desirable, regulators must decide how much to spend. In deciding how safe workplaces, or flying, or driving, should be, should a dollar value be put on a human life? If so, how much? If not, *are* lives to be weighed in considering how much to spend on safety? There is a good bit of debate over these questions. As to the valuing of human lives question, various federal agencies have produced figures that range from $200,000 (see p. 101, above) to several million. A co-author of this book discusses and criticizes the studies from which these values are typically derived in Douglas A. Kysar, Climate Change, Cultural Transformation, and Comprehensive Rationality, 31 B.C. Envtl. Aff. L. Rev. 555, 573-78 (2004).

A noninstrumentalist view, somewhat similar to that of Kelman but aimed directly at tort law, is expressed in William H. Rodgers, Jr., Negligence Reconsidered: The Role of Rationality in Tort Theory, 54 So. Cal. L. Rev. 1 (1980). In marked contrast to the efficiency value that underlies the Learned Hand cost-benefit approach, Professor Rodgers asserts:

> The guiding assumption of this Article is that tort liability rules should reflect respect for people. This perception of fairness requires distribution of praise and blame, and the legal consequences of both, in accordance with what people deserve. . . .
>
> The ultimate goal of tort law assumed by the models presented in this Article is not to settle for a stand-off in a search for cost minimization of accidents and accident avoidance. . . . The goal is zero injury, however unattainable that aim may be; that goal follows from the natural duty people have "not to harm or injure others," and the natural right people have not to be harmed or injured.

Id. at 3, 5.

The first of the two models that Professor Rodgers discusses is that of "rational decisionmaking." In this model, actors make conscious choices about risk creation and prevention; actors would be strictly liable for harm caused by those choices, even if the choices are cost effective in the sense that benefits of the choices are greater than their costs. Professor Rodgers relies in part on Vincent v. Lake Erie Transp. Co. (p. 104), to support such a strict liability regime.

With respect to "nonrational actors"—those whose conduct is not the product of conscious choices about risk (an example is the defendant in Kappelman v. Lutz, the Washington decision discussed above, whose "nonrational" conduct was his response to the sudden and unpredictable change in road conditions)—the standard should not be that of a reasonable person under the circumstances, but a subjective "best efforts" standard:

> The decision to take wealth from anyone for the benefit of someone else is a moral decision rooted in the idea that the defendant failed to do what could be done and thus should be penalized for that failure. The offender should be judged as he would judge himself, *i.e.*, in light of his capacities and intentions. Ideally, the jury should discover a correct answer to the question of whether the defendant did his best to avoid the accident. The jury therefore would be permitted to take into account the person in all particulars and to make a judgment about whether the actor was able to avoid injury to another.

Id. at 19-20.

Under Professor Rodger's models, the electric utility in *Washington*, p. 196, very likely would have been liable, would it not? How the "nonrational" actor model would affect the outcome in *Young* is perhaps less clear.

Professor Bender advances a considerably different standard for negligence cases in Leslie Bender, A Lawyer's Primer on Feminist Theory and Tort, 38 J. Legal Educ. 3 (1988). The author asserts that the traditional objective standard of care was established from a gendered perspective in which conventionally "masculine" attributes and goals were privileged at the expense of more "feminine" alternatives. Indeed, as she correctly points out, the Restatement (Second) of Torts refers specifically to the "reasonable man." See, e.g., §291, p. 190.[45] She also asserts that the more gender-neutral "reasonable person" standard does not change the underlying value discriminations of the traditional standard. What is needed, she argues, is a fundamental change in the standard to reflect a feminist perspective:

> When the standard of care is equated with economic efficiency or levels of caution, decisions that assign dollar values to harms to human life and health and then balance those dollars against profit dollars and other evidences of benefit become commonplace. Such cost-benefit and risk-utility analyses turn losses, whether to property or to persons, into commodities in fungible dollar amounts. The standard of care is converted into a floor of unprofitability or inefficiency. People are abstracted from their suffering; they are dehumanized. The risk of their pain and loss becomes a potential debit to be weighed against the benefits or profits to others. The result has little to do with care or even with caution, if caution is understood as concern for safety.

45. Professor Bender cites the fictional case of Fardell v. Potts, one of the cases penned by A. P. Herbert in his collection of fictional cases called "Misleading Cases in the Uncommon Law." The opinion in *Fardell* held that a woman could not be held liable in negligence since the law did not recognize a "reasonable woman" standard; thus while the jury could have properly found that the defendant woman's conduct did not come up to the standard of the reasonable man, the judge should have told the jury that the defendant's conduct "was only what was expected of a woman, as such." See also Chapter 2, entitled "Reasonable Prudence and the Disadvantaged," in Guido Calabresi, Ideals, Beliefs, Attitudes, and the Law (1985).

> There is another possible understanding of "standard of care" . . . rooted in notions of interconnectedness, responsibility, and caring. What would happen if we understood the "reasonableness" of the standard of care to mean "responsibility" and the "standard of care" to mean the "standard of caring" or "consideration of another's safety and interests"? What if, instead of measuring carefulness or caution, we measured concern and responsibility for the well-being of others and their protection from harm? Negligence law could begin with [the] articulation of the feminine voice's ethic of care — a premise that no one should be hurt. We could convert the present standard of "care of a reasonable person under the same or similar circumstances" to a standard of "conscious care and concern of a responsible neighbor or social acquaintance for another under the same or similar circumstances." . . .
>
> The recognition that we are all interdependent and connected and that we are by nature social beings who must interact with one another should lead us to judge conduct as tortious when it does not evidence responsible care or concern for another's safety, welfare, or health. Tort law should begin with a premise of responsibility rather than rights, or interconnectedness rather than separation, and a priority of safety rather than profit or efficiency. The masculine voice of rights, autonomy, and abstraction has led to a standard that protects efficiency and profit; the feminine voice can design a tort system that encourages behavior that is caring about others' safety and responsive to others' needs or hurts, and that attends to human context and consequences. . . .
>
> Through a feminist focus on caring, context, and interconnectedness, we can move beyond measuring appropriate behavior by algebraic formulas to assessing behavior by its promotion of human safety and welfare. This approach will clearly lead to liability for some behaviors for which there was none before. If we do not act responsibly with care and concern for others, then we will be deemed negligent. Just as we can now evaluate behavior as negligent if its utility fails to outweigh its risks of harm, we could evaluate behavior as negligent if its care or concern for another's safety or health fails to outweigh its risk of harm. From a feminist perspective the duty of care required by negligence law might mean "acting responsibly toward others to avoid harm, with a concern about the human consequences of our acts or failure to act." It is tragic that our law has been insightful enough to use the language of care but has understood it as only carefulness or acting with caution. If the law imposed a duty of care and concern toward others' safety, orienting our behavior toward avoiding and preventing harms to others, and making it impossible for us to dismiss the consequences of our acts to people we do not directly know, our tort law would take on new dimensions.

Id. at 31-32.

The above writers seek to redefine the way tort law views the concept of negligence. But even if these critiques do not succeed in forcing a change in the negligence concept, they are important as potential arguments in favor of the main alternative to negligence — strict liability, taken up in Chapter 6.

C. Special Rules Governing the Proof of Negligence

The preceding section explored the nature of the concept of reasonableness that underlies negligence. However, most of the difficulties in a negligence regime arise not in the formulation of the general standard of care, but in the application of that standard to actual situations. To be sure, many cases exist where the jury can simply be told to judge the actor's conduct against that of a reasonable person, and the jury's own collective experience, judgment, and wisdom will suffice in applying the standard. Such cases tend to involve conduct that is commonly engaged in and which therefore presents risks and benefits that are easily understood by the fact finder. For example, in a negligence action brought by an injured pedestrian against a bicyclist, a jury can easily draw on its own collective experience and judgment in determining whether the bicyclist was riding in a reasonable manner.

In a number of situations, however, an intuitive application of the negligence standard may be difficult or problematic. What should courts do, for example, if the legislature has already announced governing rules of behavior? And how is the fact finder to determine the appropriate standard of care for complex activities that are beyond the experience of the ordinary person? In such cases, tort law has developed a series of devices, or rules, that either supplement or substitute for the fact finder's own resolution of the negligence issue.

1. Violation of Statutory and Regulatory Safety Standards

Martin v. Herzog

228 N.Y. 164, 126 N.E. 814 (1920)

CARDOZO, J. The action is one to recover damages for injuries resulting in death.

Plaintiff and her husband, while driving toward Tarrytown in a buggy on the night of August 21, 1915, were struck by the defendant's automobile coming in the opposite direction. They were thrown to the ground, and the man was killed. At the point of the collision the highway makes a curve. The car was rounding the curve when suddenly it came upon the buggy, emerging, the defendant tells us, from the gloom. Negligence is charged against the defendant, the driver of the car, in that he did not keep to the right of the center of the highway (Highway Law, sec. 286, subd. 3; sec. 332; Consol. Laws, ch. 25). Negligence is charged against the plaintiff's intestate, the driver of the wagon, in that he was traveling without lights (Highway Law, sec. 329a, as amended by L. 1915, ch. 367). There is no evidence that the defendant was moving at an excessive speed. There is none of any defect in the equipment of his car. The beam of light from his lamps pointed to the right as the wheels of his car turned along the curve toward the left; and looking in the direction of the plaintiff's approach, he was peering into the shadow. The case against him must stand, therefore, if at all, upon the divergence of his course from the center of the highway. The jury found him delinquent and his victim blameless. The Appellate Division reversed, and ordered a new trial.

We agree with the Appellate Division that the charge to the jury was erroneous and misleading. The case was tried on the assumption that the hour had arrived when lights were due. It was argued on the same assumption in this court. In such circumstances, it is not important whether the hour might have been made a question for the jury. A controversy put out of the case by the parties is not to be put into it by us. We say this by way of preface to our review of the contested rulings. In the body of the charge the trial judge said that the jury could consider the absence of light "in determining whether the plaintiff's intestate was guilty of contributory negligence in failing to have a light upon the buggy as provided by law. I do not mean to say that the absence of light necessarily makes him negligent, but it is a fact for your consideration." The defendant requested a ruling that the absence of a light on the plaintiff's vehicle was "*prima facie* evidence on contributory negligence." This request was refused, and the jury were again instructed that they might consider the absence of lights as some evidence of negligence, but that it was not conclusive evidence. The plaintiff then requested a charge that "the fact that the plaintiff's intestate was driving without a light is not negligence in itself," and to this the court acceded. The defendant saved his rights by appropriate exceptions.

We think the unexcused omission of the statutory signals is more than some evidence of negligence. It *is* negligence in itself. Lights are intended for the guidance and protection of other travelers on the highway (Highway Law, sec. 329a). By the very terms of the hypothesis, to omit, willfully or heedlessly, the safeguards prescribed by law for the benefit of another that he may be preserved in life or limb, is to fall short of the standard of diligence to which those who live in organized society are under a duty to conform. That, we think, is now the established rule in this state. . . . In the case at hand, we have an instance of the admitted violation of a statute intended for the protection of travelers on the highway, of whom the defendant at the time was one. Yet the jurors were instructed in effect that they were at liberty in their discretion to treat the omission of lights either as innocent or as culpable. They were allowed to "consider the default as lightly or gravely" as they would (Thomas, J., in the court below). They might as well have been told that they could use a like discretion in holding a master at fault for the omission of a safety appliance prescribed by positive law for the protection of a workman. Jurors have no dispensing power by which they may relax the duty that one traveler on the highway owes under the statute to another. It is error to tell them that they have. The omission of these lights was a wrong, and being wholly unexcused was also a negligent wrong. No license should have been conceded to the triers of the facts to find it anything else. . . .

We must be on our guard, however, against confusing the question of negligence with that of the causal connection between the negligence and the injury. A defendant who travels without lights is not to pay damages for his fault, unless the absence of lights is the cause of the disaster. A plaintiff who travels without them is not to forfeit the right to damages, unless the absence of lights is at least a contributing cause of the disaster. To say that conduct is negligence is not to say that it is always contributory negligence. "Proof of negligence in the air, so to speak, will not do." Pollock, Torts (10th ed.) p. 472. . . .

We are persuaded that the tendency of the charge, and of all the rulings following it, was to minimize unduly, in the minds of the triers of the facts, the gravity of the decedent's fault. Errors may not be ignored as unsubstantial, when they tend to such an outcome. A statute designed for the protection of human life is not to be brushed aside as a form of words, its commands reduced to the level of cautions, and the duty to obey attenuated into an option to conform.

The order of the Appellate Division should be affirmed, and judgment absolute directed on the stipulation in favor of the defendant, with costs in all courts.

[HOGAN, J., dissented.]

Tedla v. Ellman

280 N.Y. 124, 19 N.E.2d 987 (1939)

LEHMAN, J. While walking along a highway, Anna Tedla and her brother, John Bachek, were struck by a passing automobile, operated by the defendant Ellman. She was injured and Bachek was killed. Bachek was a deaf-mute. His occupation was collecting and selling junk. His sister, Mrs. Tedla, was engaged in the same occupation. They often picked up junk at the incinerator of the village of Islip. At the time of the accident they were walking along "Sunrise Highway" and wheeling baby carriages containing junk and wood which they had picked up at the incinerator. It was about six o'clock, or a little earlier, on a Sunday evening in December. Darkness had already set in. Bachek was carrying a lighted lantern, or, at least, there is testimony to that effect. The jury found that the accident was due solely to the negligence of the operator of the automobile. The defendants do not, upon this appeal, challenge the finding of negligence on the part of the operator. They maintain, however, that Mrs. Tedla and her brother were guilty of contributory negligence as matter of law.

Sunrise Highway, at the place of the accident, consists of two roadways, separated by a grass plot. There are no footpaths along the highway and the center grass plot was soft. It is not unlawful for a pedestrian, wheeling a baby carriage, to use the roadway under such circumstances, but a pedestrian using the roadway is bound to exercise such care for his safety as a reasonably prudent person would use. The Vehicle and Traffic Law (Cons. Laws, ch. 71) provides that "Pedestrians walking or remaining on the paved portion, or traveled part of a roadway shall be subject to, and comply with, the rules governing vehicles, with respect to meeting and turning out, except that such pedestrians shall keep to the left of the center line thereof, and turn to their left instead of right side thereof, so as to permit all vehicles passing them in either direction to pass on their right. Such pedestrians shall not be subject to the rules governing vehicles as to giving signals." (§85, subd. 6.) Mrs. Tedla and her brother did not observe the statutory rule and, at the time of the accident, were proceeding in easterly direction on the east-bound or right-hand roadway. The defendants moved to dismiss the complaint on the ground, among others, that violation of the statutory rule constitutes contributory negligence as matter of law. They did not, in the courts below, urge that any negligence in other respect of Mrs. Tedla or her brother bars a recovery. The trial judge left to the jury the question whether failure to observe the statutory rule was a proximate cause of the accident; he left to the jury no question of other fault or negligence on the part of Mrs. Tedla or her brother, and the defendants did not request that any other question be submitted. Upon this appeal, the only question presented is whether, as matter of law, disregard of the statutory rule that pedestrians shall keep to the left of the center line of a highway constitutes contributory negligence which bars any recovery by the plaintiff.

Vehicular traffic can proceed safely and without recurrent traffic tangles only if vehicles observe accepted rules of the road. Such rules, and especially the rule that all vehicles proceeding in one direction must keep to a designated part or side of the road — in this country the right-hand side — have been dictated by necessity and formulated by custom. The general use of automobiles has increased in unprecedented degree the number and speed of vehicles. Control of traffic becomes an increasingly difficult problem. Rules of the road, regulating the rights and duties of those who use highways, have, in consequence, become increasingly important. The Legislature no longer leaves to custom the formulation of such rules. Statutes now codify, define, supplement and, where changing conditions suggest change in rule, even change rules of the road which formerly rested on custom. Custom and common sense have always dictated that vehicles should have the right of way over pedestrians and that pedestrians should walk along the edge of a highway so that they might step aside for passing vehicles with least danger to themselves and least obstruction to vehicular traffic. Otherwise, perhaps, no customary rule of the road was observed by pedestrians with the same uniformity as by vehicles; though, in general, they probably followed, until recently, the same rules as vehicles.

Pedestrians are seldom a source of danger or serious obstruction to vehicles and when horse-drawn vehicles were common they seldom injured pedestrians, using a highway with reasonable care, unless the horse became unmanageable or the driver was grossly negligent or guilty of willful wrong. Swift-moving motor vehicles, it was soon recognized, do endanger the safety of pedestrians crossing highways, and it is imperative that there the relative rights and duties of pedestrians and of vehicles should be understood and observed. The Legislature in the first five subdivisions of section 85 of the Vehicle and Traffic Law has provided regulations to govern the conduct of pedestrians and of drivers of vehicles when a pedestrian is crossing a road. Until, by chapter 114 of the Laws of 1933, it adopted subdivision 6 of section 85, quoted above, there was no special statutory rule for pedestrians walking *along* a highway. Then for the first time it reversed, for pedestrians, the rule established for vehicles by immemorial custom, and provided that pedestrians shall keep to the left of the center line of a highway.

The plaintiffs showed by the testimony of a State policeman that "there were very few cars going east" at the time of the accident, but that going west there was "very heavy Sunday night traffic." Until the recent adoption of the new statutory rule for pedestrians, ordinary prudence would have dictated that pedestrians should not expose themselves to the danger of walking along the roadway upon which the "very heavy Sunday night traffic" was proceeding when they could walk in comparative safety along a roadway used by very few cars. It is said that now, by force of the statutory rule, pedestrians are guilty of contributory negligence as matter of law when they use the safer roadway, unless that roadway is left of the center of the road. Disregard of the statutory rule of the road and observance of a rule based on immemorial custom, it is said, is negligence which as matter of law is a proximate cause of the accident, though observance of the statutory rule might, under the circumstances of the particular case, expose a pedestrian to serious danger from which he would be free if he followed the rule that had been established by custom. If that be true, then the Legislature has decreed that pedestrians must observe the general rule of conduct which it has prescribed for their safety even under circumstances where observance would subject them to unusual risk; that pedestrians are to be charged with negligence as matter of law for acting as prudence dictates. It is unreasonable to ascribe to the Legislature an intention that the statute should have so extraordinary a result, and the courts may not give to a statute an effect not intended by the Legislature.

. . . The appellants lean heavily upon [Martin v. Herzog] and kindred cases and the principle established by them.

The analogy is, however, incomplete. The "established rule" should not be weakened either by subtle distinctions or by extension beyond its letter or spirit into a field where "by the very terms of the hypothesis" it can have no proper application. At times the indefinite and flexible standard of care of the traditional reasonably prudent man may be, in the opinion of the Legislature, an insufficient measure of the care which should be exercised to guard against a recognized danger; at times, the duty, imposed by custom, that no man shall use what is his to the harm of others provides insufficient safeguard for the preservation of the life or limb or property of others. Then the Legislature may by statute prescribe additional safeguards and may define duty and standard of care in rigid terms; and when the Legislature has spoken, the standard of the care required is no longer what the reasonably prudent man would do under the circumstances but what the Legislature has commanded. That is the rule established by the courts and "by the very terms of the hypothesis" the rule applies where the Legislature has prescribed safeguards "for the benefit of another that he may be preserved in life or limb." In that field debate as to whether the safeguards so prescribed are reasonably necessary is ended by the legislative fiat. Obedience to that fiat cannot add to the danger, even assuming that the prescribed safeguards are not reasonably necessary and where the legislative anticipation of dangers is realized and harm results through heedless or willful omission of the prescribed safeguard, injury flows from wrong and the wrongdoer is properly held responsible for the consequent damages.

The statute upon which the defendants rely is of different character. It does not prescribe additional safeguards which pedestrians must provide for the preservation of the life or limb or property of others, or even of themselves, nor does it impose upon pedestrians a higher standard of care. What the statute does provide is rules of the road to be observed by pedestrians and by vehicles, so that all those who use the road may know how they and others should proceed, at least under usual circumstances. A general rule of conduct — and, specifically, a rule of the road — may accomplish its intended purpose under usual conditions, but, when the unusual occurs, strict observance may defeat the purpose of the rule and produce catastrophic results.

Negligence is failure to exercise the care required by law. Where a statute defines the standard of care and the safeguards required to meet a recognized danger, then, as we have said, no other measure may be applied in determining whether a person has carried out the duty of care imposed by law. Failure to observe the standard imposed by statute is negligence, as matter of law. On the other hand, where a statutory general rule of conduct fixes no definite standard of care which would under all circumstances tend to protect life, limb or property but merely codifies or supplements a common-law rule, which has always been subject to limitations and exceptions; or where the statutory rule of conduct regulates conflicting rights and obligations in manner calculated to promote public convenience and safety, then the statute, in the absence of clear language to the contrary, should not be construed as intended to wipe out the limitations and exceptions which judicial decisions have attached to the common-law duty; nor should it be construed as an inflexible command that the general rule of conduct intended to prevent accidents must be followed even under conditions when observance might cause accidents. We may assume reasonably that the Legislature directed pedestrians to keep to the left of the center of the road because that would cause them to face traffic approaching in that lane and would enable them to care for their own safety better than if the traffic approached them from the rear. We cannot assume reasonably that the Legislature intended that a statute enacted for the preservation of the life and limb of pedestrians must be observed when observance would subject them to more imminent danger. . . .

The generally accepted rule and the reasons for it are set forth in the comment to section 286 of the Restatement of the Law of Torts: "Many statutes and ordinances are so worded as apparently to express a universally obligatory rule of conduct. Such enactments, however, may in view of their purpose and spirits be properly construed as intended to apply only to ordinary situations and to be subject to the qualification that the conduct prohibited thereby is not wrongful if, because of an emergency or the like, the circumstances justify an apparent disobedience to the letter of the enactment. . . . The provisions of statutes, intended to codify and supplement the rules of conduct which are established by a course of judicial decision or by custom, are often construed as subject to the same limitations and exceptions as the rules which they supersede. Thus, a statute or ordinance requiring all persons to drive on the right side of the road may be construed as subject to an exception permitting travellers to drive upon the other side, if so doing is likely to prevent rather than cause the accidents which it is the purpose of the statute or ordinance to prevent."

Even under that construction of the statute, a pedestrian is, of course, at fault if he fails without good reason to observe the statutory rule of conduct. The general duty is established by the statute, and deviation from it without good cause is a wrong and the wrongdoer is responsible for the damages resulting from his wrong. . . .

In each action, the judgment should be affirmed, with costs.

CRANE, C.J., HUBBS, LOUGHRAN and RIPPEY, JJ., concur; O'BRIEN and FINCH, JJ., dissent on the authority of Martin v. Herzog (228 N.Y. 164).

A violation of a statute may be excused if it was impossible for the defendant under the circumstances to comply with the statute. See, e.g., Bush v. Harvey Transfer Co., 67 N.E.2d 851 (Ohio 1946) (fuse on truck blew out, causing lights to fail). The impossibility defense and the "sudden emergency" exception discussed above may come into play in the same case. Consider, for example, James v. Greater Dayton RTA, 2010 Ohio 6343 (Ohio Ct. App., Montgomery County Dec. 2, 2010), in which a bus passenger brought a personal injury suit against the bus owner and operator after being thrown into a metal partition when the driver, in order to avoid a collision, suddenly slammed on the brakes. Consistent with the above discussion of the emergency doctrine, the court in *James* held that to invoke the emergency doctrine to avoid liability for injuries resulting from a failure to comply with a safety statute, a defendant must show: "(1) compliance with [the] specific safety statute was rendered impossible, (2) by a sudden emergency, (3) that arose without the fault of the party asserting the excuse, (4) because of circumstances over which the party asserting the excuse had no control, and (5) the party asserting the excuse exercises such care as a reasonably prudent person would have under the circumstances." Id. at 14.

For general discussion of statutory violations in negligence suits, see Clarence Morris, The Role of Criminal Statutes in Negligence Actions, 49 Colum. L. Rev. 21 (1949). For an argument that courts have begun to pull back from the negligence per se approach in cases involving violations of federal food and drug safety regulations, see Gwendolyn McKee, Injury Without Relief: The Increasing Reluctance of Courts to Allow Negligence Per Se Claims Based on Violations of FDA Regulations, 83 UMKC L. Rev. 161 (2014-2015).

Brown v. Shyne

242 N.Y. 176, 151 N.E. 197 (1926)

LEHMAN, J. The plaintiff employed the defendant to give chiropractic treatment to her for a disease or physical condition. The defendant had no license to practice medicine, yet he held himself out as being able to diagnose and treat disease, and under the provisions of the Public Health Law (Cons. Laws, ch. 45) he was guilty of a misdemeanor. The plaintiff became paralyzed after she had received nine treatments by the defendant. She claims, and upon this appeal we must assume, that the paralysis was caused by the treatment she received. She has recovered judgment in the sum of $10,000 for the damages caused by said injury. . . .

At the close of the plaintiff's case the plaintiff was permitted to amend the complaint to allege "that in so treating the plaintiff the defendant was engaged in the practice of medicine contrary to and in violation of the provisions of the Public Health Law of the State of New York in such case made and provided, he at the time of so treating plaintiff not being a duly licensed physician or surgeon of the State of New York." Thereafter the trial judge charged the jury that they might bring in a verdict in favor of the plaintiff if they found that the evidence established that the treatment given to the plaintiff was not in accordance with the standards of skill and care which prevail among those treating disease.

He then continued: "This is a little different from the ordinary malpractice case, and I am going to allow you, if you think proper under the evidence in the case, to predicate negligence upon another theory. The public health laws of this State prescribe that no person shall practice medicine unless he is licensed so to do by the Board of Regents of this State and registered pursuant to statute. . . . This statute to which I have referred is a general police regulation. Its violation, and it has been violated by the defendant, is some evidence, more or less cogent, of negligence which you may consider for what it is worth, along with all the other evidence in the case. If the defendant attempted to treat the plaintiff and to adjust the vertebrae in her spine when he did not possess the requisite knowledge and skill as prescribed by the statute to know what was proper and necessary to do under the circumstances, or how to do it, even if he did know what to do, you can find him negligent." In so charging the jury that from the violation of the statute the jury might infer negligence which produced injury to the plaintiff, the trial justice in my opinion erred.

The provisions of the Public Health Law prohibiting the practice of medicine without a license granted upon proof of preliminary training and after examination intended to show adequate knowledge, are of course intended for the protection of the general public against injury which unskilled and unlearned practitioners might cause. If violation of the statute by the defendant was the proximate cause of the plaintiff's injury, then the plaintiff may recover upon proof of violation; if violation of the statute has no direct bearing on the injury, proof of the violation becomes irrelevant. For injury caused by neglect of duty imposed by the penal law there is civil remedy; but of course the injury must follow from the neglect.

Proper formulation of general standards of preliminary education and proper examination of the particular applicant should serve to raise the standards of skill and care generally possessed by members of the profession in this State; but the license to practice medicine confers no additional skill upon the practitioner; nor does it confer immunity from physical injury upon a patient if the practitioner fails to exercise care. Here, injury may have been caused by lack of skill or care; it would not have been obviated if the defendant had possessed a license yet failed to exercise the skill and care required of one practicing medicine. True, if the defendant had not practiced medicine in this State, he could not have injured the plaintiff, but the protection which the statute was intended to provide was against risk of injury by the unskilled or careless practitioner, and unless the plaintiff's injury was caused by carelessness or lack of skill, the defendant's failure to obtain a license was not connected with the injury. The plaintiff's cause of action is for negligence or malpractice. The defendant undertook to treat the plaintiff for a physical condition which seemed to require remedy. Under our law such treatment may be given only by a duly qualified practitioner who has obtained a license.

The defendant in offering to treat the plaintiff held himself out as qualified to give treatment. He must meet the professional standards of skill and care prevailing among those who do offer treatment lawfully. If injury follows through failure to meet those standards, the plaintiff may recover. The provisions of the Public Health Law may result in the exclusion from practice of some who are unqualified. Even a skilled and learned practitioner who is not licensed commits an offense against the State; but against such practitioners the statute was not intended to protect, for no protection was needed, and neglect to obtain a license results in no injury to the patient and, therefore, no private wrong. The purpose of the statute is to protect the public against unfounded assumption of skill by one who undertakes to prescribe or treat for disease. In order to show that the plaintiff has been injured by defendant's breach of the statutory duty, proof must be given that defendant in such treatment did not exercise the care and skill which would have been exercised by qualified practitioners within the State, and that such lack of skill and care caused the injury. Failure to obtain a license as required by law gives rise to no remedy if it has caused no injury. . . .

It is said that the trial justice did not charge that plaintiff might recover for defendant's failure to obtain a license but only that failure to obtain a license might be considered "some evidence" of defendant's negligence. Argument is made that even if neglect of the statutory duty does not itself create liability, it tends to prove that injury was caused by lack of skill or care. That can be true only if logical inference may be drawn from defendant's failure to obtain or perhaps seek a license that he not only lacks the skill and learning which would enable him to diagnose and treat disease generally, but also that he lacks even the skill and learning necessary for the physical manipulation he gave to this plaintiff. Evidence of defendant's training, learning and skill and the method he used in giving the treatment was produced at the trial and upon such evidence the jury could base finding either of care or negligence, but the absence of a license does not seem to strengthen inference that might be drawn from such evidence, and a fortiori would not alone be a basis for such inference. Breach or neglect of duty imposed by statute or ordinance may be evidence of negligence only if there is logical connection between the proven neglect of statutory duty and the alleged negligence. . . .

For these reasons the judgments should be reversed and a new trial granted, with costs to abide the event.

Crane, J. (dissenting). . . . The judge fully and completely charged the jury that the defendant was not liable for any of the plaintiff's injuries unless they were the direct and proximate [result] of his acts. The evidence was abundant to prove that the plaintiff's paralysis and injuries resulted from the defendant's manipulation and treatment of her back, neck and head. The jury were justified in finding that whatever he did, whether it were proper or improper, resulted in the plaintiff's painful condition. We start, therefore, the consideration of this point with the fact that the defendant's acts were the direct and proximate cause of the injury. The next question arises as to whether or not the acts were negligent.

As I have stated, the judge charged the jury as if this were the ordinary malpractice case, furnishing for the defendant a standard of the legally authorized physician. It is difficult for me personally to follow this reasoning and the logic of the situation. I think this rule all too liberal to the defendant. What he did was prohibited by law. He could not practice medicine without violating the law. The law did not recognize him as a physician. How can the courts treat him as such? Provided his act, in violation of the law, is the direct and proximate cause of injury, in my judgment he is liable, irrespective of negligence. It seems somewhat strange that the courts, one branch of the law, can hold up for such a man the standards of the licensed physician, while the Legislature, another branch of the law, declares that he cannot practice at all as a physician. The courts thus afford the protection which the Legislature denies.

The judge in this case, however, did not go this far. He charged for the defendant's benefit the ordinary rules of negligence in malpractice cases, and then stated that the violation of the Public Health Law was some evidence of negligence, leaving the whole question to the jury. It is this much milder form of ruling which is challenged. The defendant must be treated, so the appellant claims, as if he were a duly licensed physician, and in this action for damages, resulting from his act, he is only liable if a duly licensed physician would have been liable. Such is the effect of excluding evidence of the defendant's practicing medicine without a license. . . .

The prohibition against practicing medicine without a license was for the very purpose of protecting the public from just what happened in this case. The violation of this statute has been the direct and proximate cause of the injury. The courts will not determine in face of this statute whether a faith healer, a patent medicine man, a chiropractor, or any other class of practitioner acted according to the standards of his own school, or according to the standards of a duly licensed physician. The law, to insure against ignorance and carelessness, has laid down a rule to be followed, namely, examinations to test qualifications, and a license to practice. If a man, in violation of this statute, takes his chances in trying to cure disease, and his acts result directly in injury, he should not complain if the law, in a suit for damages, says that his violation of the statute is some evidence of his incapacity. . . .

The ruling was correct, and the judgments below should be affirmed, with costs.

After *Brown* was decided, the New York legislature enacted the following statute (N.Y. Civ. Prac. L. & R. §4504(d)):

> Proof of negligence; unauthorized practice of medicine. In any action for damages for personal injuries or death against a person not authorized to practice medicine under article 131 of the education law for any act or acts constituting the practice of medicine, when such act or acts were a competent producing proximate or contributing cause of such injuries or death, the fact that such person practiced medicine without being so authorized shall be deemed prima facie evidence of negligence.

State legislatures have tended not to respond in this manner when courts refuse to attach negligence-per-se liability to violations of liquor licensing, sale, and use regulations that lead to injury or death. See, e.g., Bland v. Scott, 112 P.3d 941 (Kan. 2005) (observing longstanding failure of Kansas legislature to impose civil liability for violation of liquor regulations as reason for continuing to refuse to find negligence per se for such violations); Wakulich v. Mraz, 785 N.E.2d 843 (Ill. 2003) (noting failure of Illinois General Assembly to adopt civil liability for persons who supply alcoholic beverages to minors who are subsequently harmed).

Judge Cardozo's approach to the violation of safety statutes in the *Martin* case is clearly the majority position in this country. See generally Restatement (Second) of Torts §288B; Restatement (Third) of Torts: Liability for Physical and Emotional Harm §14 (2010); William L. Prosser & W. Page Keeton, Law of Torts 230 n.1 (5th ed. 1984). Judge Cardozo's description of the trial in that case suggests that other approaches have been taken. One alternative approach is that adopted in Sheehan v. Nims, 75 F.2d 293 (2d Cir. 1935), in which the court applied Vermont law in a diversity case arising out of a motor vehicle accident. The defendant had run out of gas and parked his truck at dusk on the edge of a highway. The plaintiff's decedent drove his automobile into the defendant's truck. A Vermont statute required a clearance lamp to be displayed by such trucks, and the defendant admittedly did not have one. However, the defendant had hung a lighted kerosene lantern near the left rear corner of the truck. The trial court ruled the defendant negligent as a matter of law, and the defendant appealed. Reversing for a new trial, the court of appeals explained (75 F.2d at 294):

> While it is true that in many states the violation of a standard of care prescribed by statute is held to be negligence per se, the law of Vermont is otherwise. On such a point the federal

> court will follow the state law. From the foregoing authorities relating to similar safety regulations it appears that a violation of the statute in question gives rise to a rebuttable presumption of negligence which may be overcome by proof of the attendant circumstances if they are sufficient to persuade the jury that a reasonable and prudent driver would have acted as did the person whose conduct is in question.
>
> Counsel for the appellee contends that this is so only when the delinquent party is in a position to substitute his own judgment of what is prudent for that of the Legislature. Since the truck was not equipped with clearance lights, it is argued that the appellants were never able to exercise their judgment as to when the lights should be displayed. This argument is specious. Admittedly, while on the highway the appellants had no choice other than to operate without lights; but they had the choice of not being on the highway at all, and their act in operating the truck at the particular time in question might well have involved a decision that to do so was not imprudent. The appellee further urges that not enough was shown to overcome the prima facie case made by proof of absence of a clearance light, and hence the peremptory instruction that negligence existed was justifiable. This contention we are unable to accept. Although it was more than thirty minutes after sunset, it was not yet dark. The truck was standing on a straight stretch of road where it could be expected to be seen from a considerable distance by any motorist approaching from the rear. According to the defendants' testimony, a lighted red lantern was hung near to the left rear corner. The driver intended to leave the truck standing only so long as it should take him to walk three hundred feet to a garage and back again with a borrowed tool with which he would change the gasoline feed pipe from one tank to another so that he could resume his journey. Whether under the same circumstance a reasonable and prudent driver would have done as he did, despite the prohibition of the statute, seems to us a jury question under the Vermont cases.

A somewhat different approach to the question of safety statute violations is the one adopted by the trial judge in the *Martin* case and expressly rejected by Judge Cardozo on appeal — that is, to allow the jury to accept the fact of the violation as some evidence of negligence. In Gill v. Whiteside-Hemby Drug Co., 122 S.W.2d 597 (Ark. 1938), the plaintiff was struck by the defendant's motorcycle. Although there was evidence that the defendant had violated several city ordinances by speeding and passing a streetcar at an intersection (the streetcar was moving toward the plaintiff and blocked the plaintiff's view of the defendant's motorcycle), the trial court instructed the jury that such violations would not of themselves conclusively establish negligence. Affirming a verdict and judgment for the defendant, the Supreme Court of Arkansas made it clear that violation of either state law or city ordinances is merely evidence of negligence, and not negligence per se. See also Orduna v. Total Const. Services, Inc., 713 N.W.2d 471, 479 (Neb. 2006) (violation of statute, regulation, or ordinance "is not negligence per se, but is evidence of negligence").

The decisions generally do not distinguish between statutes and ordinances in applying the rules described herein. See, e.g., Ferrell v. Baxter, 484 P.2d 250 (Alaska 1971); William L. Prosser & W. Page Keeton, Law of Torts 220 (5th ed. 1984); Clarence Morris, The Role of Administrative Safety Measures in Negligence Actions, 28 Tex. L. Rev. 143 (1949). However, violations of administrative regulations are sometimes treated as providing only some evidence of negligence, even by those states that accept negligence per se with respect to statutory violations. See, e.g., Allen v. Cloutier Construction Corp., 376 N.E.2d 1276, 1278 (N.Y. 1978) (commenting on "the well-recognized principle that there is a clear distinction between the effect of a violation of an administrative regulation promulgated pursuant to statute, and a violation of a substantive provision of the statute itself"). Why might a court draw this distinction? A tailored approach was adopted in Wiersgalla v. Garrett, 486 N.W.2d 290, 293 (Iowa 1992), in which the court held that violations of Occupational Safety and Health Administration regulations could constitute negligence per se in an action by an employee against an employer, but only evidence of negligence in suits by other parties likely to be harmed by the violations. With respect to even less formal government rules, Peterson v. City of Long Beach, 594 P.2d 477 (Cal. 1979), the Supreme Court of California held that a policeman's violation of an internal police department regulation gave rise to a rebuttable presumption of negligence. This decision is criticized in Recent Developments, 1979 Wash. U. L.Q. 1133, 1154, in part on the ground that it will discourage police departments from establishing rules of conduct for their personnel. Cf. Everitt v. General Elec. Co., 979 A.2d 760 (N.H. 2009) (holding that the "mere existence of an internal policy setting forth procedures to deal with an [alcohol] impaired employee does not, standing alone, create a duty of care to the public at large," in part because such a rule might discourage the adoption of internal policies). But see Scheffel v. Oregon Beta Chapter of Phi Kappa Psi Fraternity, 359 P.3d 436 (Or. Ct. App. 2015) (finding that administrative rules governing a fraternity chapter's alcohol policies were substantive and that repeal of these rules did not preclude a negligence per se claim).

The Law-Fact Distinction: The Effects of Safety Statute Violations upon the Division of Functions Between Judge and Jury

Perhaps the most significant general effect of safety statutes upon negligence cases is that upon the division of functions between judge and jury. Whenever violations of such statutes are held to be relevant to the issue of negligence, the ultimate task of evaluating conduct, usually performed by the jury, is taken over to some extent (perhaps entirely) by the judge. The manner in which this reallocation of functions occurs may be explained very simply. Safety statutes operate to particularize, rather than necessarily to raise, the applicable minimum standard of care. They tend to transform the general standard of reasonableness into a particular standard which can be stated in terms much more closely related to the actual conduct in question. The effect of this particularization is to allow issues to be resolved by the judge as a matter of law which would ordinarily be decided by the jury as issues of fact. This is especially true in cases in which violation of the statute is held to be negligence per se. If there is no dispute over whether the party violated the statute, the judge disposes of the negligence issue as a matter of law. Where the question of violation is disputed, the judge instructs the jury that the negligence issue has become the narrower issue of whether a violation occurred.

Even when statutory violation is only evidence of lack of due care, the judge will play a more influential role in the process of evaluating the defendant's conduct. If the case is close on its facts, the presence of the statute may tip the scales and cause the judge to dispose of the negligence issue as a matter of law. And even where the case goes to the jury, it is accompanied by a special instruction from the judge that the violation does bear upon the central issue of negligence. What has happened in these cases is that the legislature has to some extent performed the task of evaluation in advance; the judge, as interpreter of legislative intent, steps in to play a much more influential role in the evaluative process than would otherwise be the case in the absence of a statutory violation. For further discussion of the impact of safety statute violations upon the division of function between judge and jury, see Stephen A. Weiner, The Civil Jury Trial and the Law-Fact Distinction, 54 Cal. L. Rev. 1867, 1885-86 (1966).

Problem 15

Sandra Doherty, a partner in your law firm, has asked you for a memorandum discussing the liability issues in a case she is handling. Your client, Mildred Riley, was named as the defendant in a suit by Amanda Salazar. Reliance Insurance Company retained your firm to represent Riley. Specifically, Doherty wants to know if she should file a motion for summary judgment, and if so, what the chances are that it will be granted. The pleadings reveal the following facts, none of which seems to be the subject of any significant dispute:

At 10:00 P.M., on December 16, two years ago, Riley was driving on Route 83 when she witnessed an automobile accident. She stopped immediately and saw that occupants of both cars involved in the accident were seriously injured. She decided that she could better help the injured by reporting the accident, but no house or telephone was available from which to make the report. She then drove to a nearby shopping center. The only parking space near the first telephone she saw was in front of a drug store and was marked as reserved for the handicapped. She quickly looked around and saw no other open space, so she decided to park in that space in order to make the call. Checking her purse, she found that she did not have the correct change for the telephone, so she went into the drug store to get change. At the time that Riley entered the store, the plaintiff drove into the shopping center, intending to pick up a prescription at the drug store. She suffered from severe arthritis in both knees, and had a handicapped parking sticker for her automobile. She wrote down Riley's license plate number, intending to report the violation to the police. A parking space about one hundred yards from the drug store opened up, where she decided to park. She knew that she could walk that distance, although with considerable difficulty and pain. The lighting was not particularly good where she parked, and just as she got out of her car, she was attacked and robbed by a purse snatcher. As a result she suffered serious injuries, for which she brought suit against Riley.

The Uniform Traffic Control Law of your state contains the following statute:

> (1) Any commercial real estate property owner offering parking for the general public shall provide specially designed and marked motor vehicle parking spaces for the exclusive use of physically disabled persons who have been issued parking permits pursuant to subsection (5) of this statute.
>
> (2) Any person who parks a vehicle in any parking space designated with the international symbol of accessibility or the caption "PARKING BY DISABLED PERMIT ONLY," or with both such symbol and caption, is guilty of a traffic infraction, and shall be punished accordingly unless such vehicle displays a parking permit issued pursuant to subsection (5) of this statute, and such vehicle is occupied by a person eligible for such permit.

The parking space occupied by Riley had the sign required by the statute.

In preparing your memorandum, assume that Martin v. Herzog and Tedla v. Ellman are controlling precedent.

One final aspect of negligence per se deserves mention. The mere violation of a safety statute does not automatically trigger a negligence-per-se inquiry. Rather, the harm suffered by the plaintiff must be within the risks envisioned by the legislature when it passed the statute. Thus, if a legislature passed a leash law for the single purpose of preventing roaming dogs from biting people, the parents of a child who wandered in front of a car while chasing an unleashed dog typically could not rely on the leash law as the basis of a negligence claim against the dog owner. In Leizerman v. Kanous, 910 N.E.2d 26 (Ohio Ct. App. 2009), the plaintiff was riding a bicycle on a sidewalk in violation of an Ohio statute and suffered injury when he was struck by an automobile exiting a driveway. The plaintiff argued that the statute prohibiting adults from riding bicycles on sidewalks was intended to protect pedestrians, not bicyclists, and was therefore irrelevant in assessing plaintiff's contributory negligence. On appeal, the court held that the statute was also aimed at protecting bicyclists and the plaintiff was therefore contributorily negligent per se. This "harm within the risk" analysis is often treated as a matter of proximate cause, considered in Chapter 4.

2. Custom

Trimarco v. Klein

56 N.Y.2d 98, 436 N.E.2d 502 (1982)

FUCHSBERG, JUDGE.

[The plaintiff, a tenant in an apartment owned by the defendant, was severely injured when a glass shower door shattered as he stepped out of the shower. The plaintiff alleged that the defendant was negligent in failing to provide a door made of shatterproof safety glass. In support of this allegation, the plaintiff introduced evidence of a general practice among landlords to use safety glazing in showers. At the trial, the judge entered judgment for the plaintiff after a jury verdict for the plaintiff; the Appellate Division reversed and dismissed the complaint, on the ground that the defendant had no duty to replace the glass absent notice of the danger either from the plaintiff or from a similar accident in the building. The Court of Appeals reversed, and ordered a new trial.]

Which brings us to the well-recognized and pragmatic proposition that when "certain dangers have been removed by a customary way of doing things safely, this custom may be proved to show that [the one charged with the dereliction] has fallen below the required standard" (Garthe v. Ruppert, 264 N.Y. 290, 296, 190 N.E. 643). Such proof, of course, is not admitted in the abstract. It must bear on what is reasonable conduct under all the circumstances, the quintessential test of negligence.

It follows that, when proof of an accepted practice is accompanied by evidence that the defendant conformed to it, this may establish due care and, contrariwise, when proof of a customary practice is coupled with a showing that it was ignored and that this departure was a proximate cause of the accident, it may serve to establish liability. Put more conceptually, proof of a common practice aids in "formulat[ing] the general expectation of society as to how individuals will act in the course of their undertakings, and thus to guide the common sense or expert intuition of a jury or commission when called on to judge of particular conduct under particular circumstances" (Pound, Administrative Application of Legal Standards, 44 ABA Rep., 445, 456-457).

The source of the probative power of proof of custom and usage is described differently by various authorities, but all agree on its potency. Chief among the rationales offered is, of course, the fact that it reflects the judgment and experience and conduct of many. Support for its relevancy and reliability comes too from the direct bearing it has on feasibility, for its focusing is on the practicality of a precaution in actual operation and the readiness with which it can be employed. Following in the train of both of these boons is the custom's exemplification of the opportunities it provides to others to learn of the safe way, if that the customary one be.

From all this it is not to be assumed customary practice and usage need be universal. It suffices that it be fairly well defined and in the same calling or business so that "the actor may be charged with knowledge of it or negligent ignorance" (Prosser, Torts [4th ed.], §33, p.168; Restatement, Torts 2d, §295A, p.62, Comment *a*).

However, once its existence is credited, a common practice or usage is still not necessarily a conclusive or even a compelling test of negligence. Before it can be, the jury must be satisfied with its reasonableness, just as the jury must be satisfied with the reasonableness of the behavior which adhered to the custom or the unreasonableness of that which did not. After all, customs and usages run the gamut of merit like everything else. That is why the question in each instance is whether it meets the test of reasonableness. As Holmes' now classic statement on this subject expresses it, "[w]hat usually is done may be evidence of what ought to be done, but what ought to be done is fixed by a standard of reasonable prudence, whether it usually is complied with or not" (Texas & Pacific Ry. Co. v. Behymer, 189 U.S. 468, 470, 23 S. Ct. 622, 622-623, 47 L. Ed. 905).

So measured, the case the plaintiff presented . . . was enough to send it to the jury and to sustain the verdict reached. The expert testimony, the admissions of the defendant's manager, the data on which the professional and governmental bulletins were based, the evidence of how replacements were handled by at least the local building industry for the better part of two decades, these in the aggregate easily filled that bill. Moreover, it was also for the jury to decide whether, at the point in time when the accident occurred, the modest cost and ready availability of safety glass and the dynamics of the growing custom to use it for shower enclosures had transformed what once may have been considered a reasonably safe part of the apartment into one which, in the light of later developments, no longer could be so regarded.

[Nonetheless, the court reversed and remanded because the trial judge erroneously permitted the jury to consider a safety statute that was not applicable to defendant. The statute required that safety glazing material be used in all bathroom enclosures, but the requirement did not retroactively apply to installations existing at the effective date of the statute.]

Recall that violation of an applicable safety statute can be proof of negligence per se. In *Trimarco*, however, the trial judge decided to allow the jury to consider the inapplicable statute not as the controlling standard but merely as an element in assessing the negligence of defendant. The New York high court held that the statute should have been excluded because its inclusion was misleading. Regarding the admissibility into evidence of non-applicable safety statutes for purposes of assessing negligence, the Supreme Court of Virginia faced a similar issue in Norfolk and Portsmouth Belt Line R.R. Co. v. Wilson, 667 S.E.2d 735 (Va. 2008). Plaintiff brought a Federal Employers Liability Act (FELA) action against defendant railroad, alleging that defendant had been negligent in failing to provide him a safe workplace. Even though there was no Virginia safety statute applicable, the trial judge allowed the jury to consider safety statutes of other jurisdictions, and then entered judgment on the jury's verdict for plaintiff. The Supreme Court of Virginia reversed and remanded, stating that the out-of-state statutes were "likely to be both misleading to the jury and prejudicial to the opposing party." Id. at 738. Could defendant argue that the statutes should be admitted as proof of a nationwide custom, especially considering that FELA is a federal statute aiming at a uniform federal law of liability? (For background information about FELA, see Nordgren v. Burlington N. R.R. Co., 101 F.3d 1246, 1248-50 (8th Cir. 1996).) More generally, what is the proper geographical scope of custom?

The T. J. Hooper

60 F.2d 737 (2d Cir.), cert. denied, 287 U.S. 662 (1932)

[The operator of a tugboat was sued for the value of two barges and their cargoes, which were lost at sea during a coastal storm in March 1928. The basis of the claim was that the tug was negligently unseaworthy in that it was not equipped with a radio receiver, and thus could not receive reports of an impending storm. There was evidence that the master, had he heard the weather reports, would have turned back.]

L. Hand, J. . . . [A] master is not justified in putting his tow to every test which she will survive, if she be fit. There is a zone in which proper caution will avoid putting her capacity to the proof; a coefficient of prudence that he should not disregard. Taking the situation as a whole, it seems to us that these masters would have taken undue chances, had they got the broadcasts.

They did not, because their private radio receiving sets, which were on board, were not in working order. These belonged to them personally, and were partly a toy, partly a part of the equipment, but neither furnished by the owner, nor supervised by it. It is not fair to say that there was a general custom among coastwise carriers so to equip their tugs. One line alone did it; as for the rest, they relied upon their crews, so far as they can be said to have relied at all. An adequate receiving set suitable for a coastwise tug can now be got at small cost and is reasonably reliable if kept up; obviously it is a source of great protection to their tows. Twice every day they can receive these predictions, based upon the widest possible information, available to every vessel within two or three hundred miles and more. Such a set is the ears of the tug to catch the spoken word, just as the master's binoculars are her eyes to see a storm signal ashore. Whatever may be said as to other vessels, tugs towing heavy coal laden barges, strung out for half a mile, have little power to maneuver, and do not, as this case proves, expose themselves to weather which would not turn back stauncher craft. They can have at hand protection against dangers of which they can learn in no other way.

Is it then a final answer that the business had not yet generally adopted receiving sets? There are, no doubt, cases where courts seem to make the general practice of the calling the standard of proper diligence; we have indeed given some currency to the notion ourselves. Indeed in most cases reasonable prudence is in fact common prudence; but strictly it is never its measure; a whole calling may have unduly lagged in the adoption of new and available devices. It never may set its own tests, however persuasive be its usages. Courts must in the end say what is required; there are precautions so imperative that even their universal disregard will not excuse their omission. But here there was no custom at all as to receiving sets; some had them, some did not; the most that can be urged is that they had not yet become general. Certainly in such a case we need not pause; when some have thought a device necessary, at least we may say that they were right, and the others too slack. The statute (section 484, title 46, U.S. Code [46 USCA §484]) does not bear on this situation at all. It prescribes not a receiving, but a transmitting set, and for a very different purpose; to call for help, not to get news. We hold the tugs therefore because had they been properly equipped, they would have got the [weather] reports. The injury was a direct consequence of this unseaworthiness. Decree affirmed.

For a discussion of custom in general, and of *The T. J. Hooper* in particular, see Richard A. Epstein, The Path to *The T. J. Hooper*: The Theory and History of Custom in the Law of Tort, 21 J. Legal Stud. 1 (1992). Among other provocative claims, the article states that Judge Learned Hand's famous line rejecting industry custom as a decisive test for negligence — "a whole calling may have unduly lagged in the adoption of new and available devices" — constitutes "the most influential, and mischievous, sentence in the history of the law of torts." Id. at 38. From what perspective would Hand's assertion merit such a strong condemnation?[46]

Recall that Hand, who authored *The T. J. Hooper*, also wrote the opinion in *Carroll Towing*, above. In *Carroll Towing*, he suggested that a weighing of costs and benefits was inherent in the determination of negligence. He also noted, however, that if there had been a custom regarding the use of bargees on barges in the New York harbor, "the situation was one where custom should control." Thus, according to Hand, custom might, under some circumstances, represent the best practical evidence of how the "B < PL" calculus would play out in the real world.

Yet in *The T. J. Hooper*, Hand cautioned that custom may not always be a reliable proxy for reasonable care and that courts therefore must be cautious in their deference to custom. But why should a court respect custom in the *Carroll Towing* context, when another seagoing custom is rejected as unreasonable in *The T. J. Hooper*? Hand's opinion in the two cases provides little guidance as to what forces give rise to a custom and determine whether it is a reliable benchmark for reasonable care. In thinking about these deeper questions, consider the following observations about custom by Professors Henderson and Siliciano in Universal Health Care and the Continued Reliance on Custom in Determining Medical Malpractice, 79 Cornell. L. Rev. 1382, 1384-89 (1994):

> Judicial deference to professional custom spares the tort system the difficult and error-prone task of externally determining an appropriate standard of conduct. . . . We begin by defining "custom." In its simplest terms, custom is common practice. Custom develops over time when a group of actors, acting independently of, and often in competition with, each other, reach the same decisions regarding the manner in which their activity should be conducted. . . . Two questions need to be addressed: First, what conditions give rise to the formations of customs? Second, under what circumstances should a court, in the context of a tort suit, defer to such customs in determining what constitutes reasonable care? . . .

46. One implication of Hand's assertion is that to allow industry custom to control may lead to underinvestment in care. Is such underinvestment the only likely effect of adopting industry custom as a standard? Commentators have made the argument that judicial deference to industry custom may actually lead to overinvestment in care and underinvestment in socially beneficial, albeit risky, innovation. See Gideon Parchomovsky & Alex Stein, Torts and Innovation, 107 Mich. L. Rev. 285 (2008); James Gibson, Doctrinal Feedback and (Un)Reasonable Care, 94 Va. L. Rev. 1641 (2008).

> Let us suppose that a finite number of actors — barge operators, tug operators, dock operators, and cargo owners — operate collectively and competitively in a large harbor. One of the risks of life in the harbor is that of barges breaking loose from their moorings, threatening harm to themselves and other interests in the harbor. . . . Now, it stands to reason that any given barge operator will employ different . . . precautions, depending on the surrounding circumstances. Valuable cargoes during rough weather require a different response than do empty barges in a calm harbor. The question of interest here is whether, holding constant any given set of conditions, the various actors will respond uniformly with the same design. If they do, a careful observer of such response patterns could conceivably write a book "How to Operate in a Harbor." Moreover, a newcomer to the harbor could reasonably be advised, quite literally, to "go by the book."
>
> What, then, are the necessary conditions for custom to develop to the point that such a book, based upon observed behavior, could be written about any given activity? We submit that the relevant participants in an activity must be similar in three respects for discernible custom to develop. First, the actors who directly affect the levels of risk generated by an activity must possess roughly the same knowledge of the real world in which their activity plays out. This knowledge will pertain not only to risks, but also to ways of dealing effectively with risk. Absent such uniformity of knowledge, actors lack the coherence of outlook necessary to engage in the kind of parallel decisionmaking that generates custom. . . .
>
> [The authors identify the second condition for custom to develop — the actors must possess capacity to act effectively on their knowledge — and the third — they must share the same attitudes toward the relevant risks.]
>
> [W]hat should lead a court to decide that such customs are worthy of judicial adoption of legal standards of care? Homogeneity of knowledge, resources, and attitudes toward risk help generate custom, but these factors do not necessarily ensure that such customs will represent the kind of socially optimal responses to risk to which courts should defer.
>
> Rather, the justification for such deference would depend on the extent to which all, or nearly all, of the interests at risk of harm from harbor activities are linked with each other by a network of contractual bargaining through which all interests, including those least able to affect risks directly — here, the cargo owners — are adequately taken into account. In our harbor, on reasonable assumptions, that is almost certain to be the case. Every major actor need not be linked contractually with every other. It will suffice if every actor is linked to a sufficient number of other actors, including representatives from other interest groups, so that no actor's decision affecting risk of harm can afford to ignore, or undervalue, the interests of any other actor. Under such conditions, a court might readily conclude that the balance of risks and benefits reflected in the established custom represents the best approximation of reasonable care.

What about the admissibility of a common practice not sufficiently widespread to rise to the level of custom? There is not much case law on the question. In Kenneth S. Abraham, Custom, Noncustomary Practice, and Negligence, 109 Colum. L. Rev. 1784 (2009), the author explains that even though admitting evidence of noncustomary practice might complicate negligence trials, it would serve a beneficial jury-educating function.

Problem 16

You are the clerk to the judge presiding at the trial in the case of King v. Marina Costa Co., Inc. The evidence has been completed and the defendant has moved for a directed verdict. Both the plaintiff and the defendant have filed requests for jury instructions in the event that the motion is denied. The judge has asked you to review the record and to give your views as to whether the motion for the directed verdict should be granted and as to which of the requested instructions should be given.

Marina Costa manufactures motorboats for recreational use. The plaintiff bought a boat new from the defendant in 1988. Two years ago, he was operating the boat when it struck a submerged log, throwing him overboard. The motor continued to run and, as the boat circled around the plaintiff, the propeller struck him, causing severe injuries. The plaintiff's complaint alleges that the defendant was negligent in failing to equip the boat with a "kill switch" which would have stopped the motor as soon as the plaintiff was thrown from the seat.

The defendant presented evidence that when the plaintiff bought the boat in 1988, no manufacturer installed kill switches as standard equipment. They had been an optional feature with some manufacturers, including the defendant, beginning in 1970, but they proved to be unpopular. They occasionally malfunctioned, causing motors to be unstartable. In addition, users were apt to trigger the switches inadvertently when they moved away from the motor to perform some task toward the front of the boat. The few customers that bought boats equipped with kill switches from the defendant soon had them disabled, and the defendant stopped installing the switches in 1978.

The plaintiff introduced evidence that kill switches were relatively inexpensive. As public attention to the hazards of boating increased in the late 1980s, kill switches began to be installed and used more frequently. Today they are routinely included in all boat and motor designs. Their design has been significantly improved so that they avoid most of the problems associated with the first generation of kill switches.

In the event that the motion for directed verdict is denied, the defendant has requested that the jury be instructed that in determining whether the defendant was negligent it should give great weight to the custom in 1988 of not having kill switches as standard equipment on motorboats. The plaintiff has requested that the jury be instructed that, under the circumstances, little if any weight should be given to the custom upon which defendant relies, and that the jury should be free to make its own determination of whether the failure to include kill switches was negligent.

Mechanisms for Resolving Disputes: Special Verdicts, General Verdicts, and Instructions to the Jury

In most of the cases set out in this casebook that reached trial before a jury, the judge instructed the jury concerning the law governing liability and damages, often employing instructions the content of which is established by statute or rule of court,[47] and told the jury that they were bound to follow the law as contained in the instructions. The jury's deliberations may result in a general verdict for the defendant or the plaintiff, in the latter event with an assessment of the damages to which the plaintiff is entitled. This general verdict procedure is not followed in all negligence cases. Most states have by rule or statute authorized trial judges to request special verdicts from juries and to require them to answer special interrogatories.[48] Rule 49 of the Federal Rules of Civil Procedure authorizes similar

47. Uniform instructions established by statute or rule of court for either optional or mandatory use by judges are called pattern instructions. For an overview of pattern instructions, see Robert L. McBride, The Art of Instructing the Jury (1969).

48. See generally Edson R. Sunderland, Verdicts, General and Special, 29 Yale L.J. 253 (1920); William H. Wicker, Special Interrogatories to Juries in Civil Cases, 35 Yale L.J. 296 (1926).

procedures in federal district courts.[49] Essentially, these alternative procedures require the jury in varying degrees to supply findings of fact that are more specific and concrete than are findings relating merely to the ultimate issues of liability and damages. The first case in this book, *Vosburg,* employed the special verdict technique.

Historically, special verdicts may be traced to the earliest developments of juries, called inquests, in England before the Norman Conquest. Members of these ancient forerunners of our modern juries were chosen because they were presumed to have direct, prior knowledge of the facts, and in effect they acted as their own witnesses. If the King's minister responsible for calling such a jury was unhappy with the verdict reached, a second, or attainting, jury could be appointed to decide the case de novo. If the attainting jury reached a verdict different from that reached by the first jury, the second verdict controlled and the members of the first jury were punished. Because the greatest source of possible confusion and error lay in applying the law, these early juries, in order to minimize the risk of punishment, began refusing to return general verdicts and, instead, began merely finding the specific facts relevant to the case and leaving the application of the law to the judges.[50]

In spite of its historical antecedents in England, implementation of the special verdict in this country has met substantial resistance. Perhaps this resistance is due to a deep-rooted American attitude in favor of increasing the power of the jury system as a distinctly democratic institution. Allowing juries to reach general verdicts gives them wide latitude, especially in negligence cases, to apply their collective common sense, or popular prejudice, in reaching results. In contrast, under the special verdict procedure the judge exerts more control over the application of the law to the facts of the case — either by performing that application in the first instance, or by reviewing the final outcome reached by the jury in light of their more specific, preliminary findings.

As might be expected, the feature of the general jury verdict procedure in negligence cases that is viewed by many to be its major strength — the empowerment of the jury to reach commonsense, ad hoc results — is viewed by others as a serious weakness. For the last 50 years or more, legal commentators have questioned the extent to which the judge's instructions operate as a guide to the jury in reaching general verdicts. Professor James, in Functions of Judge and Jury in Negligence Cases, 58 Yale L.J. 667, 681-82 (1949), typifies the doubts about the effectiveness of jury instructions:

> Now it should be clear . . . that *the instruction is an effective device only to the extent that it is actually followed by the jury.* Moreover there is in many jurisdictions no real way (save through the jurors' own consciences) to make a jury follow instructions.[51]
>
> The question then arises whether juries, having the *power* to decide cases in violation of instructions, actually do so in a significant number of instances. A scientific answer to this question probably cannot be had. There is, however, good reason to believe that

49. See Robert Dudnik, Comment, Special Verdicts: Rule 49 of the Federal Rules of Civil Procedure, 74 Yale L.J. 483 (1965).

50. See generally Edmund M. Morgan, A Brief History of Special Verdicts and Special Interrogatories, 32 Yale L.J. 575 (1923).

51. If instructions or other rulings are erroneous, or the verdict is unsupported by a sufficiency of the credible evidence, a new trial may be granted. But in many states a new trial may not be granted, in the absence of such a situation, merely because the trial court believed that the jury failed to follow a perfectly proper set of instructions (e.g., where the jury might have found for the plaintiff under the evidence and instructions on one ground but where the court believes — on the basis of intuition, or the like — that the jury did find for the plaintiff on grounds which were properly "withdrawn" from their consideration by the charge). The situation may be different in those states where the trial court has real discretion to set aside a verdict rendered upon conflicting evidence. Franklin v. McGranahan, 241 P. 113 (Kan. 1925) (implies that in the judgment of the court the jury has failed to give proper weight to the instructions). [Eds.]

> instructions are not particularly effective in getting the jury to perform their theoretical function and in keeping them within the bounds charted out for them by the rules of law.[52]

Doubts of this sort have led a number of legal writers to the conclusion that universal implementation of the special verdict procedure, especially in negligence cases, is a much needed reform.[53] One of the earliest and most eloquent advocates of the special verdict was Professor Sunderland, who in a classic treatment of the subject, Verdicts, General and Special, 29 Yale L.J. 253, 262 (1919), asserted:

> The real objection to the special verdict is that it is an honest portrayal of the truth, and the truth is too awkward a thing to fit the technical demands of the record. The record must be absolutely flawless, but such a result is possible only by concealing, not by excluding, mistakes. This is the great technical merit of the general verdict. It covers up all the shortcomings which frail human nature is unable to eliminate from the trial of a case. In the abysmal abstraction of the general verdict concrete details are swallowed up, and the eye of the law, searching anxiously for the realization of logical perfection, is satisfied. In short, the general verdict is valued for what it does, not for what it is. It serves as the great procedural opiate, which draws the curtain upon human errors and soothes us with the assurance that we have attained the unattainable.

In recent years, the center of controversy concerning civil juries has shifted from the debate over whether to replace general verdicts with special verdicts to a debate over whether to replace the entire jury-fault system of liability with some type of nonfault system of compensation.[54] Some writers believe that a more sensible resolution of the first controversy would have eliminated the necessity of even considering the second.[55]

Law and Behavior: What We Think About When We Think About Tort Law

How can we know what affects a person's decisionmaking? How can we know whether, in any given instance, a judge or a juror is relying on mental shortcuts, implicit biases, unconscious motivations, or other "non-rational" influences? Social scientists seeking to study decision processes have their work cut out for them, especially when trying to quantify the degree to which a decision was influenced by psychological bias. Many of our mental shortcuts operate outside of conscious awareness, so it is unlikely that the decisionmakers themselves know when they are being swayed by extralegal influences.

52. Studies suggest that things have not improved much, if at all, in the years since Professor James wrote these words. See Walter W. Steele, Jr. & Elizabeth G. Thornburg, Jury Instructions: A Persistent Failure to Communicate, 67 N.C. L. Rev. 77 (1988), and Symposium, Making Jury Instructions Comprehensible, 8 U. Bridgeport L. Rev. 279 (1987). Both survey studies regarding the effectiveness, or lack thereof, of jury instructions, and suggest ways in which instructions could be made more effective. See also David Alan Slansky, Evidentiary Instructions and the Jury as Other, 65 Stan. L. Rev. 407 (2013) (arguing that academics should re-conceptualize evidentiary instructions based on the premises that juries are inherently flawed, but still capable of reason). [Eds.]

53. For a summary of the commentaries on the reform movement, see Robert Dudnik, Comment, Special Verdicts: Rule 49 of the Federal Rules of Civil Procedure, 74 Yale L.J. 483, 488-97 (1965). For an empirical assessment of jurors' ability to deal with complex civil cases, coupled with an appeal for greater use of jury decisionmaking aids and modified procedures (including special verdicts), see Matthew A. Reiber & Jill D. Weinberg, The Complexity of Complexity: An Empirical Study of Juror Competence in Civil Cases, 78 U. Cin. L. Rev. 929 (2010).

54. See Chapter 10, Section B, below.

55. See Leon Green & Allen E. Smith, Negligence Law, No-Fault, and Jury Trial, (I) 50 Tex. L. Rev. 1093 (1972); (II) 50 Tex. L. Rev. 1297 (1972); (III) 51 Tex. L. Rev. 207 (1973); (IV) 51 Tex. L. Rev. 825 (1973).

Reading a judge's opinion to trace their reasoning or interviewing jurors after a trial to ascertain their thought processes is unlikely to reveal the work of cognitive heuristics or biases, because most people cannot, even upon reflection, appreciate the extent to which their reasoning is biased, motivated, or otherwise psychologically naive. Self-reports are suspect, thanks to the pervasive "illusion of objectivity."[56]

As discussed in the law and behavior note above, p. 181, a wealth of social scientific insight has been developed regarding judge and jury decisionmaking that penetrates below the surface of a written judicial opinion or a juror's personal explanation. Much of that work demonstrates that demographic, social, or political characteristics seem to influence legal outcomes to a greater extent than can be explained by a model of pure judicial or juror "reasoning." More recently, scholars have begun setting aside the question of how individual characteristics of particular legal actors affect outcomes, focusing instead on more universal aspects of human psychology and how those aspects might influence legal decisionmaking in focused settings. In particular, behavioral scientists have used experimental methods to document the ways in which decisionmakers fall prey to predictable biases when determining legally important matters such as causation, foreseeability, intentionality, and responsibility. Here we offer a partial list of well-documented biases that affect decisionmaking and that carry clear relevance for tort law.

Legal decisionmakers are often asked to determine the causal relationship between a defendant's conduct and a plaintiff's injury. Researchers have discovered several quirks in how such decisions tend to be made. For instance, in general, people tend to over-perceive causation. We prefer to believe that everything happens for a reason rather than by coincidence or due to random chance.[57] This "illusory causation" phenomenon is compounded by our tendency to favor causal explanations that involve *human agency* rather than those that point to situational forces.[58] Our preference for internal, personal causes leads us to attribute too much responsibility to legal actors in cases in which situational factors strongly influenced their behaviors, a pattern known as the "fundamental attribution error."[59]

More generally, when selecting from an array of possible causes, we sometimes choose based on factors that are logically irrelevant to physical causation. For instance, Mark Alicke has demonstrated that people more readily believe that a speeding driver "caused" an accident when the driver is described as speeding for blameworthy reasons (rushing home to hide illegal drugs) than when he is described as speeding for praiseworthy reasons (rushing home to hide a surprise gift for his parents).[60] Whether we intend to or not, we often smuggle judgments of moral blame into our judgments of causation, even though the two are conceptually and legally distinct.

56. See, e.g., Ziva Kunda, The Case for Motivated Reasoning, 108 Psychol. Bull. 480, 482-483 (1990) ("[People] maintain an 'illusion of objectivity.' . . . [They] do not realize that the process is biased by their goals, that they are accessing only a subset of their relevant knowledge, that they would probably access different beliefs and rules in the presence of different directional goals . . . ."); Robert J. Robinson et al., Actual Versus Assumed Differences in Construal: "Naive Realism" in Intergroup Perception and Conflict, 68 J. Personality & Soc. Psychol. 404, 405 (1995) (describing "the individual's unshakable conviction that he or she is somehow privy to an invariant, knowable, objective reality — a reality that others will also perceive faithfully, provided that they are reasonable and rational, a reality that others are apt to misperceive only to the extent that they (in contrast to oneself) view the world through a prism of self-interest, ideological bias, or personal perversity").

57. G. Daniel Lassiter, et al., Illusory Causation: Why It Occurs, 13 Psychol. Sci. 299 (2002).

58. Lee Ross & Richard E. Nisbett, The Person and the Situation (1991); Edward E. Jones & Victor A. Harris, The Attribution of Attitudes, 3 J. Experimental & Soc. Psychol. 1 (1967).

59. Lee Ross, The Intuitive Scientist and His Shortcomings (1977).

60. Mark Alicke, Culpable Causation, 63 J. Personality & Soc. Psychol. 368 (1992).

Researchers have also studied what happens when legal decisionmakers are asked to determine whether harm was reasonably foreseeable at the time of the defendant's tortious conduct. A plethora of research demonstrates that people tasked with determining foreseeability fall prey to hindsight bias.[61] Possessed of the knowledge of how things turned out, we tend to overestimate the degree to which the consequences were foreseeable, believing the outcome to have been inevitable and easily anticipated. It is cognitively difficult — for experienced judges and novice jurors alike[62] — to take an ex ante perspective when asked to assess the reasonableness of the actors' conduct at the time. Several studies have documented the effects of hindsight bias in the context of tort litigation.[63] This body of research has generated debate about whether trials should be bifurcated such that the decisionmakers charged with deciding negligence can be insulated from information concerning outcomes, or whether the adversarial system is sufficient to counteract the effects of hindsight bias.[64]

Our judgments of intentionality, like our judgments of causation and foreseeability, can be influenced by factors that are logically and legally irrelevant. For instance, researchers have demonstrated that people who view a video recording of a physical altercation believe that the aggressor acted more intentionally and deserves more severe punishment when they view the video in slow motion than when the same footage is played at regular speed.[65] Experimental philosopher Joshua Knobe has found that people more readily attribute intentionality to actions that have negative consequences than actions that have positive consequences.[66] This asymmetry is generally regarded as evidence that our folk theory of intentionality is influenced by moral judgments of right and wrong.[67] More broadly, cognitive psychologists have found that we have a general bias toward interpreting human action as intentional, and outcomes as intended. This bias appears deeply engrained and has been demonstrated using reaction-time measures: People need additional time to process unintentional explanations for observed behavior, suggesting that our default cognitive orientation is to assume that actions are undertaken purposefully.[68]

61. See Baruch Fischhoff, Hindsight ≠ Foresight: The Effect of Outcome Knowledge on Judgment Under Uncertainty, 1 J. Experimental Psychol.: Hum. Perception & Performance 288 (1975); Jeffrey J. Rachlinski, A Positive Psychological Theory of Judging in Hindsight, 65 U. Chi. L. Rev. 571 (1998); John C. Anderson, D. Jordan Lowe & Philip M. J. Reckers, Evaluation of Auditor Decisions: Hindsight Bias Effects and the Expectation Gap, 14 J. Econ. Psychol. 711 (1993); D. Jordan Lowe & Philip M. J. Reckers, The Effects of Hindsight Bias on Jurors' Evaluations of Auditor Decisions, 25 Decision Sci. 401 (1994).

62. Rachlinksi, *supra* note 61, at 587 ("The bias is large enough to have an important impact on the legal system and has been shown to affect the two kinds of decisionmakers upon which the legal system relies — groups (juries) and experienced decisionmakers (judges).").

63. Susan J. LaBine & Gary LaBine, Determinations of Negligence and the Hindsight Bias, 20 Law & Hum. Behav. 501 (1996) (finding that mock jurors rate a therapist as being less reasonable, and the violence committed by the therapist's patient more foreseeable, when the therapist is judged in hindsight (knowing the patient became violent) as opposed to foresight (knowing nothing about the patient's behavior)); Kim A. Kamin & Jeffrey J. Rachlinski, Ex Post ≠ Ex Ante: Determining Liability in Hindsight, 19 Law & Hum. Behav. 89 (1995) (finding that 24% of mock jurors think a city should take precautionary measure to prevent flooding, while 57% of mock jurors who are told that the city did in fact flood think that the city's failure to take precautions was negligent).

64. E.g., James A. Henderson, Jr., Fred Bertram, & Michael J. Toke, Optimal Issue Separation in Modern Products Liability Legislation, 73 Tex. L. Rev. 1653 (1995) (delineating the types of issues that are best adjudicated in a bifurcated system); Christine Jolls, Cass R. Sunstein, & Richard Thaler, A Behavioral Approach to Law and Economics, 50 Stan. L. Rev. 1471, 1527-29 (1997); David B. Wexler & Robert F. Schopp, How and When to Correct for Juror Hindsight Bias in Mental Health Malpractice Litigation: Some Preliminary Observations, 7 Behav. Sci. & L. 485 (1989); Jennifer Robbenott & Valerie P. Hans, The Psycology of Tort Law 54 (2016).

65. Eugene M. Carusoa, Zachary C. Burns & Benjamin A. Converse, Slow Motion Increases Perceived Intent, Proc. Natl. Acad. Sci., August 1, 2016, available at http://www.pnas.org/content/early/2016/07/27/1603865113.

66. Joshua Knobe, Intentional Action and Side-Effects in Ordinary Language, 63 Analysis, 190 (2003).

67. Robbenolt & Hans, *supra* note 64, at 31.

68. Evelyn Rosset, It's No Accident: Our Bias for Intentional Explanations, 108 Cognition 771 (2008).

At the same time, our judgments of whether an action was undertaken intentionally can affect our judgments of the severity of the harm that resulted: intentionally caused harm is seen as more injurious than unintentionally caused harm, even when the amount of physical damage is held constant.[69] Judgments of harm, in turn, affect judgments of negligence. The negligence inquiry is supposed to focus on the harm that is *risked*, not the harm that results, yet mock jurors blame actors as more negligent when their actions result in more serious injuries.[70] In sum, whether they mean to or not, decisionmakers often let their judgments in one area bleed into their judgments in other areas that are supposed to be kept conceptually and legally distinct — an example of what psychologists call "motivated reasoning."[71] Motivated to punish a defendant for bad behavior, decisionmakers inflate judgments of intentionality, harm, negligence, and so on in order to achieve their desired results.

Relatedly, researchers have found that a plaintiff's comparative negligence diminishes the plaintiff's recovery beyond the degree contemplated by tort law. A "double discounting" phenomenon has been documented both in laboratory experiments and in real-world torts cases: Jurors punish comparatively negligent plaintiffs first when they make their initial valuation of the total damages, and again when they discount those damages to take account of the plaintiff's responsibility.[72] The determination of gross damages is not supposed to take into account the blameworthiness of the plaintiff, and yet researchers find that these initial valuations are significantly lowered for comparatively negligent plaintiffs — another instance of motivated reasoning.

To sum up, the crucial points of this new line of behavioral research are that (a) human beings regularly, indeed quite normally, make decisions via non-rational mechanisms that they themselves cannot perceive or control, (b) judges and jurors are human beings, and thus (c) judges and jurors tend to fall prey to the same sorts of errors, illusions, and quirks of perception, judgment, and reasoning that affect any decisionmaker faced with a hard choice.[73] In this respect, the conclusions of behavioral science may diverge from some of the more politically charged critiques of the legal realists, discussed above, Note: Legal Formalism vs. Legal Reaslism, pp. 179-181. Of course, social and political factors may play a role in influencing legal decisionmaking, but so too may cognitive influences lurking deep below conscious understanding and control. Thus, perhaps, one virtue of this new research is its ability to teach us that there is no simple, univocal answer to the question of why legal decisionmakers draw the conclusions they draw. It is instead far more messy and complicated than even the early legal realists recognized.

69. For instance, psychologists John Darley and Charles Huff gave mock jurors a description of a truck driver who backs his car into a homeowner's garage, damaging the garage. When asked to determine how damaged the garage was, the mock jurors calibrated their monetary assessments based on whether the truck driver was portrayed as acting intentionally versus unintentionally. John M. Darley & Charles W. Huff, Heightened Damage Assessment as a Result of the Intentionality of the Damage-Causing Act, 29 British J. Soc. Psychol. 181 (1990).

70. Edith Greene, Michael Johns & Jason Bowman, The Effects of Injury Severity on Jury Negligence Decisions, 23 Law & Hum. Behav. 675 (1999); Jennifer K. Robbennolt, Outcome Severity and Judgments of "Responsibility": A Meta-Analytic Review, 30 J. Applied Soc. Psychol. 2575 (2000).

71. See generally Avani Mehta Sood, Motivated Cognition in Legal Judgments — An Analytic Review, 9 Ann. Rev. L. Soc. Sci. 307 (2013); Ziva Kunda, The Case for Motivated Reasoning, 108 Psychol. Bull. 480 (1990).

72. See, e.g., Douglas J. Zickafoose & Brian H. Bornstein, Double Discounting: The Effects of Comparative Negligence on Mock Juror Decision Making, 3 Law & Hum. Behav. 577 (1999); James K. Hammitt et al., Tort Standards and Jury Decisions, 14 J. Legal Stud. 751 (1985).

73. For enlightening studies of how judges fall prey to heuristics and other cognitive illusions and errors, see Andrew J. Wistrich et al., Can Judges Ignore Inadmissible Information? The Difficulty of Deliberately Disregarding, 153 U. Pa. L. Rev. 1251 (2005); Chris Guthrie et al., Blinking on the Bench: How Judges Decide Cases, 93 Cornell L. Rev. 1 (2007).

Helling v. Carey

83 Wash. 2d 514, 519 P.2d 981 (1974)

[The plaintiff sued the defendant ophthalmologists in negligence. A trial was held, and the evidence was that the plaintiff suffered from glaucoma, which had seriously impaired her vision. The defendants had given the plaintiff routine eye examinations over a period of several years, but did not administer a test that would have revealed the glaucoma in time to treat it effectively. When her condition was diagnosed, the plaintiff was 32 years old. The uncontradicted expert testimony was that the test for glaucoma is not routinely given to persons under the age of 40, since the incidence of the disease in this age group is only 1 in 25,000. In keeping with precedent, the trial judge instructed the jury, in effect, that the standard to which the defendants must conform is the custom within their medical specialty. The jury returned its verdict for the defendants, upon which the trial judge entered judgment. An intermediate appellate court affirmed, and the plaintiff appealed.]

HUNTER, J. . . . In her petition for review, the plaintiff's primary contention is that under the facts of this case the trial judge erred in giving certain instructions to the jury and refusing her proposed instructions defining the standard of care which the law imposes upon an ophthalmologist. As a result, the plaintiff contends, in effect, that she was unable to argue her theory of the case to the jury that the standard of care for the specialty of ophthalmology was inadequate to protect the plaintiff from the incidence of glaucoma, and that the defendants, by reason of their special ability, knowledge and information, were negligent in failing to give the pressure test to the plaintiff at an earlier point in time which, if given, would have detected her condition and enabled the defendants to have averted the resulting substantial loss in her vision.

We find this to be a unique case. The testimony of the medical experts is undisputed concerning the standards of the profession for the specialty of ophthalmology. . . . The issue is whether the defendant's compliance with the standard of the profession of ophthalmology, which does not require the giving of a routine pressure test to persons under 40 years of age, should insulate them from liability under the facts in this case where the plaintiff has lost a substantial amount of her vision due to the failure of the defendants to timely give the pressure test to the plaintiff.

The defendants argue that the standard of the profession, which does not require the giving of a routine pressure test to persons under the age of 40, is adequate to insulate the defendants from liability for negligence because the risk of glaucoma is so rare in this age group. . . .

The incidence of glaucoma in one out of 25,000 persons under the age of 40 may appear quite minimal. However, that one person, the plaintiff in this instance, is entitled to the same protection, as afforded persons over 40, essential for timely detection of the evidence of glaucoma where it can be arrested to avoid the grave and devastating result of this disease. The test is a simple pressure test, relatively inexpensive. There is no judgment factor involved, and there is no doubt that by giving the test the evidence of glaucoma can be detected. The giving of the test is harmless if the physical condition of the eye permits. The testimony indicates that although the condition of the plaintiff's eyes might have at times prevented the defendants from administering the pressure test, there is an absence of evidence in the record that the test could not have been timely given.

Justice Holmes stated in Texas & P. Ry. v. Behymer, 189 U.S. 468, 470, 47 L. Ed. 905, 23 S. Ct. 622 (1903): "What usually is done may be evidence of what ought to be done, but

what ought to be done is fixed by a standard of reasonable prudence, whether it usually is complied with or not."

In The T. J. Hooper, 60 F.2d 737 (2d Cir. 1932), Justice Hand stated on page 740: "[I]n most cases reasonable prudence is in fact common prudence; but strictly it is never its measure; a whole calling may have unduly lagged in the adoption of new and available devices. It never may set its own tests, however persuasive be its usages. *Courts must in the end say what is required; there are precautions so imperative that even their universal disregard will not excuse their omission.*" (Italics ours.)

Under the facts of this case reasonable prudence required the timely giving of the pressure test to this plaintiff. The precaution of giving this test to detect the incidence of glaucoma to patients under 40 years of age is so imperative that irrespective of its disregard by the standards of the ophthalmology profession, it is the duty of the courts to say what is required to protect patients under 40 from the damaging results of glaucoma.

We therefore hold, as a matter of law, that the reasonable standard that should have been followed under the undisputed facts of this case was the timely giving of this simple, harmless pressure test to this plaintiff and that, in failing to do so, the defendants were negligent, which proximately resulted in the blindness sustained by the plaintiff for which the defendants are liable.

There are no disputed facts to submit to the jury on the issue of the defendants' liability. Hence, a discussion of the plaintiff's proposed instructions would be inconsequential in view of our disposition of the case.

The judgment of the trial court and the decision of the Court of Appeals is reversed, and the case is remanded for a new trial on the issue of damages only.

HALE, C.J., and ROSELLINI, STAFFORD, WRIGHT, and BRACHTENBACH, JJ., concur.

[In a concurring opinion, UTTER, J., urged that the liability of the defendants in this case be strict, rather than based upon negligence, in order to avoid "imposing a stigma of moral blame upon the doctors, who, in this case, used all the precautions commonly prescribed by their profession in diagnosis and treatment."]

At first glance, *Helling* appears to represent a routine application of *The T. J. Hooper*'s treatment of custom in the medical malpractice context. Yet, in terms of doctrine, *Helling* represents an aberration. For most courts in medical malpractice cases, professional custom is not just evidence of the standard of care, it *is* the standard of care. See Allan H. McCoid, The Care Required of Medical Practitioners, 12 Vand. L. Rev. 549 (1959); but see Philip G. Peters, Jr., The Quiet Demise of Deference to Custom: Malpractice Law at the Millennium, 57 Wash. & Lee L. Rev. 163 (2000) (arguing that there is no longer a judicial consensus favoring deference to custom in medical malpractice litigation). Shortly after the *Helling* decision, the Washington legislature passed a statute seemingly aimed at superseding *Helling*. The Supreme Court of Washington interpreted the statute such that the *Helling* rule still prevailed after the enactment of the statute. Gates v. Jensen, 595 P.2d 919 (Wash. 1979).With few exceptions, the plaintiff must establish the professional standard by the use of expert testimony. See Cardenas v. Muangman, 998 A.2d 303, 306 (D.C. 2010). Although some courts have suggested that conclusive effect will not be given to medical custom (Advincula v. United Blood Serv., 678 N.E.2d 1009 (Ill. 1996)), *Helling* is unique in that it not only permitted plaintiff to recover in the absence of any expert testimony supporting her claim that the defendants were negligent, but it also held that she was entitled to prevail on that issue as a matter of law. For somewhat differing explanations of the rule that makes medical custom dispositive of the standard of care, see Richard N. Pearson, The Role of Custom in Medical Malpractice Cases, 51 Ind. L.J. 528 (1976), and the article by McCoid cited above. Interestingly, the American Academy of Ophthalmologists continues to recommend routine glaucoma screening for patients beginning only at age 40. See http://www.aao.org/eye-health/tips-prevention/screening (last visited October 28, 2016).

At one time, the source to which courts turned to determine medical custom was the locality in which the defendant practiced, or one similar to it. The trend in recent years has been to depart from the "locality rule" and to turn to the country as a whole to determine medical custom, at least with respect to specialists. See, e.g., Brune v. Belinkoff, 235 N.E.2d 793 (Mass. 1968); Hawes v. Chua, 769 A.2d 797 (D.C. 2001). But see Hill v. Medlantic Health Care Group, 933 A.2d 314, 322 (D.C. 2007) (illustrating the difficulty of establishing a national standard of medical care). Even applying the broader national standards of practice, however, will not necessarily foreclose the relevance of more limited resources to physicians practicing in less populated areas. See Vergara v. Doan, 593 N.E.2d 185 (Ind. 1992). See also Jackson v. Graham, 753 N.E.2d 525 (Ill. App. Ct. 2001) (indicating that Illinois's "similar locality rule" should be read broadly so that evidence of the national standard of care is allowable on its own, but so too is evidence regarding the standard in the particular locality and those to which it is similar).

The rejection of the locality rule is based on the assumption that the quality of medical care ought not vary with the geographical area in which the defendant practices. The assumption has some empirical support: One recent study of physician behavior concludes that the switch has resulted in a 30-50 percent reduction in the gap between state and national utilization rates of various treatments and diagnostic procedures. See Michael Frakes, The Impact of Medical Liability Standards on Regional Variations in Physician Behavior: Evidence from Adoption of National-Standard Rules, 103 Amer. Econ. Rev. 257 (2013). Putting aside geography, should the quality of medical care vary with the ability of patients to pay? The traditional answer of tort law, at least at the level of dictum, is that the standard of care should not vary with a patient's resources. As one court explained, "[w]hether the patient be a pauper or a millionaire, whether he be treated gratuitously or for reward, the physician owes him precisely the same measure of duty, and the same degree of skill and care." Becker v. Janiski, 15 N.Y.S. 675, 677 (1891). This unitary standard of care appeals to the widespread sentiment that, in matters as important as one's health, an individual's wealth should not be a consideration. But as laudable as this sentiment is, is tort law really an effective instrument to achieve this end? In other areas directly related to individual health and welfare, such as the quality of housing or the safety of automobiles, tort law declines to mandate absolute equality. One reason is that doing so may actually disadvantage the poor by pricing such goods and services beyond their means. For a similar argument regarding medical care, see John A. Siliciano, Wealth, Equity, and the Unitary Medical Malpractice Standard, 77 Va. L. Rev. 439 (1991).

The standard of care applied in attorney malpractice cases is similar to that used in cases involving medical malpractice: The duty of attorneys is "to use such skill, prudence, and diligence as lawyers of ordinary skill and capacity commonly possess and exercise in the performance of tasks which they undertake." Lucas v. Hamm, 364 P.2d 685 (Cal. 1961); Janik v. Rudy, Exelrod & Zieff, 14 Cal. Rptr. 3d 751 (Ct. App. 2004); Byrne v. Grasso, 985 A.2d 1064 (Conn. App. Ct. 2009). See generally Charles W. Wolfram, Modern Legal Ethics 209-17 (1986).

The Relationship Between Tort and Contract: Breach of Promise to Cure as a Basis of Medical Malpractice Liability

As the note on tort and contract following *Bang* in Chapter 1, p. 61, indicates some commentators have urged greater reliance upon express contract between patient and doctor and lesser reliance upon tort in determining the liability of physicians for medical injuries. In some cases, plaintiffs have relied upon contract as a basis of recovery, although with mixed results.

The major difficulty with express contract as a basis of liability is in separating cases in which the physician has made an express promise to cure from those in which he or she has done no more than to express an opinion that the outcome will be satisfactory, or to make an assurance to a timid and cautious patient. Most courts faced with the issue have required something more than evidence to the effect that the doctor has expressed such opinions or assurances. See Vanhierden v. Swelstad, 779 N.W.2d 441 (Wis. Ct. App. 2009) (affirming summary judgment for defendant doctor, who told the plaintiff-patient: "We're going to get rid of your pain and we're going to get you back to work" when plaintiff signed a consent-to-surgery form recognizing that "no guarantees [had] been made to [him]"). While recognizing that Pennsylvania law does permit implied breach of contract claims against health care providers in rare circumstances, the court in Byrne v. Cleveland Clinic, 684 F. Supp. 2d 641 (E.D. Penn. 2010), held that a delay in treatment beyond a promised waiting period would not constitute such a circumstance. Thus, some courts have insisted that the plaintiff present "clear proof" that the defendant intended to guarantee a specific result. See, e.g., Clevinger v. Haling, 394 N.E.2d 1119 (Mass. 1979). Other courts have required that to be actionable a promise to achieve a particular result must be supported by separate consideration. See, e.g., Dorney v. Harris, 482 F. Supp. 323 (D. Colo. 1980).

A more receptive judicial approach to contract liability was taken in Guilmet v. Campbell, 188 N.W.2d 601 (Mich. 1971). The plaintiff had undergone an operation for a bleeding ulcer. He was unsatisfied with his postoperation condition, and sued the surgeons for negligence and breach of express contract to cure. The jury returned a verdict for the defendants on the negligence claim, and for the plaintiff on the contract claim. The Supreme Court of Michigan affirmed the judgment for the plaintiff on the latter claim, pointing to statements made by the defendants as related by the plaintiff (88 N.W.2d at 606):

> Once you have an operation it takes care of all your troubles. You can eat as you want to, you can drink as you want to, you can go as you please. Dr. Arena and I are specialists, there is nothing to it at all — it's a very simple operation. You'll be out of work three to four weeks at the most. There is no danger at all in this operation. After the operation you can throw away your pill box. In twenty years if you figure out what you spent for Maalox pills and doctor calls, you could buy an awful lot. Weigh it against an operation.

The court ruled that the effect of these statements was to create a jury issue as to whether a contract to cure had been formed. See also Coron v. Sandin, 2006 WL 1766841 (W.D. Mich. 2006) (holding that a jury question was created by a doctor's written and signed "Yes!" in response to plaintiff's query whether she would be able to work at her same position following surgery, because the evidence "reasonably could be interpreted as establishing an obligation to provide medical treatment sufficient to allow her to resume her employment without pain").

If *Guilmet* were a controlling case in your jurisdiction, what advice would you give a doctor who asks how to avoid exposure to contract liability? Would a prospective patient be well advised to consult a lawyer before seeing a doctor? What impact would you expect *Guilmet* to have upon doctor-patient relationships? Perhaps concerns of this sort led the Michigan legislature to substantially undercut *Guilmet* in Mich. Comp. Laws Ann. §566.132(g) (Supp. 1992), requiring that "an agreement, promise, contract, or warranty of cure relating to medical care or treatment" be in writing and signed by the doctor to be enforceable. Medical malpractice liability based upon contract is discussed in Richard N. Pearson, The Role of Custom in Medical Malpractice Cases, 51 Ind. L.J. 528, 545-50 (1976). Also recall that medical providers often try to contract out of medical malpractice liability. Proponents of contractual liability claim that it is the most efficient method of risk allocation. For an economic argument against the efficiency of contractual arrangements in the medical malpractice context, see Jennifer Arlen, Contracting over Liability: Medical Malpractice and the Cost of Choice, 158 U. Pa. L. Rev. 957 (2010).

Claims of legal malpractice are also sometimes brought in contract. Thus, in McComas v. Bocci, 996 P.2d 506 (Or. Ct. App. 2000), the Liquor Control Commission turned down the plaintiffs' request for a license; thereafter, the plaintiffs hired the defendant attorney to file a petition for judicial review of the Commission's decision. The plaintiffs alleged that after the defendant was hired he promised the review would be successful. However, the court in which the attorney sought review of the Commission's decision dismissed the petition as time-barred. The plaintiffs then sued the defendant, alleging both legal malpractice and breach of contract. The contract claim stemmed from the defendant's alleged assurances that the review would inevitably be successful. The trial court granted summary judgment for the defendant. The court of appeals affirmed, holding that, because the defendant made his alleged promises of success after being hired, such statements lacked new consideration on the part of the plaintiffs and, as a consequence, were nothing more than gratuitous, unenforceable promises.

3. Res Ipsa Loquitur

In most negligence cases, the plaintiff's evidence, if believed, will paint a fairly complete picture of what the defendant did. This will enable the plaintiff to make a detailed argument of how the defendant's conduct missed the mark. But often a serious gap in the evidence remains. We have already encountered such a gap in the case of *Ybarra* in Chapter 2, in which both the identity of the actor and the means by which the plaintiff was injured were not amenable to direct proof because the plaintiff was unconscious at the time of injury. In the cases that follow, the plaintiff similarly cannot make an adequately detailed argument as to how the defendant was negligent. One approach to these cases might be for courts to follow the oft-stated injunction that the trier of fact may never be left to speculate, and that every decision in favor of the plaintiff must be based solidly on evidence pointing to the specific manner in which the defendant was negligent. But common sense, and our experience in connection with the earlier dog-bite problem, suggest that such a hard-line approach is unlikely to appeal to very many judges. Our sense of justice would be offended if the plaintiff necessarily were to lose because it could not be established exactly what it was that the defendant did that was negligent. We may feel that, even with the evidentiary gap, the facts as we have them clearly indicate that the defendant was negligent. These feelings have been translated into the doctrine of res ipsa loquitur, which allows plaintiffs to win some of the cases in which a gap in the evidence prevents them from proving the specifics of the defendants' negligent conduct.

Literally translated, *res ipsa loquitur* means "the thing speaks for itself." Baron Pollock coined the phrase in Byrne v. Boadle, 2 H. & C. 722, 159 Eng. Rep. 299 (Ex. 1863), a case in which the plaintiff was injured by a barrel of flour that had fallen from a window in the defendant's warehouse. At the trial, the plaintiff introduced the only evidence put in by either party, and he made no attempt to show how the barrel fell from the window. On this state of the evidence, the trial judge granted the defendant's motion for a nonsuit. In the course of argument on appeal, the defendant's attorney made this point: "Surmise ought not to be substituted for strict proof. . . . The plaintiff should establish his case by affirmative evidence. . . . The plaintiff was bound to give affirmative proof of negligence." To which Pollock replied: "There are certain cases of which it may be said res ipsa loquitur and this seems one of them. In some cases the Court has held that the mere fact of the accident having occurred is evidence of negligence." Two years later, in a case involving bags of sugar that fell on the plaintiff, Chief Justice Erle, in Scott v. London & St. Katherine Docks Co., 3 H. & C. 596, 601, 159 Eng. Rep. 665, 667 (Ex. 1865), supplied what is generally recognized as the first formulation of the res ipsa loquitur doctrine:

> There must be reasonable evidence of negligence.
>
> But where the thing is shown to be under the management of the defendant or his servants, and the accident is such as in the ordinary course of things does not happen if those who have the management use proper care, it affords reasonable evidence, in the absence of explanation by the defendants, that the accident arose from want of care.

Although on the surface these judicial expressions seem relatively simple, few concepts in tort law have caused more confusion. Indeed, courts disagree over whether res ipsa loquitur is a distinct concept at all. As an American judge asserted in a case brought to his court on appeal (Bond, C.J., dissenting, in Potomac Edison Co. v. Johnson, 152 A. 633, 636 (Md. 1930)):

> In this case, as in similar cases, the expression res ipsa loquitur has been the basis of much of the argument, and I venture to urge upon the attention of the profession in the state an objection to the continued use of it. It adds nothing to the law, has no meaning which is not more clearly expressed for us in English, and brings confusion to our legal discussions. It does not represent a doctrine, is not a legal maxim, and is not a rule.
>
> It is merely a common argumentative expression of ancient Latin brought into the language of the law by men who were accustomed to its use in Latin writings. . . . It may just as appropriately be used in argument on any subject, legal or otherwise. Nowhere does it mean more than the colloquial English expression that the facts speak for themselves, that facts proved naturally afford ground for an inference of some fact inquired about, and so amount to some proof of it. The inference may be one of certainty, as when an excessive interest charge appeared on the face of an instrument, or one of more or less probability only, as when negligence in the care of a barrel of flour was found inferable from its fall out of a warehouse.

Judicial deprecations of this sort notwithstanding, in one sense, at least, cases involving res ipsa loquitur are different from other examples of the use of circumstantial evidence. Circumstantial evidence is normally directed at preliminary issues of fact such as, in the *Hoyt* case from Chapter 2, "Did sparks from the defendant's mill start the fire at the plaintiff's hotel?" In res ipsa loquitur cases, however, the circumstantial evidence is directed at the ultimate issue of the defendant's negligence, an issue that calls for a value judgment rather than simply an empirical judgment. (See the law-fact distinction note above.) Thus, in deciding whether the fact of the plaintiff's injury provides, in and of itself, a sufficient basis upon which to conclude that the defendant has been negligent, the court is necessarily required to assess the relationship between the parties and the nature of the duty owing by the defendant to the plaintiff. Much more than in other cases involving reliance upon circumstantial evidence, here the fact of the accident will "speak for itself" if the court (as the formulator of legal duties) and the jury (as appliers of those legal duties) want it to. See generally Mark F. Grady, Res Ipsa Loquitur and Compliance Error, 142 U. Pa. L. Rev. 887 (1994).

Res ipsa loquitur almost everywhere gives rise to a permissible inference of negligence — that is, it permits, but does not compel, the jury to find that the defendant acted negligently. See, e.g., Curtis v. Lein, 239 P.3d 1078 (Wash. 2010); Giles v. City of New Haven, 630 A.2d 1335 (Conn. 1994). See generally William L. Prosser, The Procedural Effect of Res Ipsa Loquitur, 20 Minn. L. Rev. 241 (1936). In some states, res ipsa gives rise to a rebuttable presumption of negligence. See, e.g., Chapman v. Harner, 339 P.3d 519 (Col. 2014); Szydel v. Markman, 117 P.3d 200 (Nev. 2005). The court in Morejon v. Rais Construction Co., 818 N.Y.S.2d 792 (2006), engaged in an extensive historical analysis of the doctrine to develop a far more complicated taxonomy of res ipsa loquitur formulations, including res ipsa as a "presumption of law," "presumption of fact," "conclusive presumption," "rebuttable presumption," "mandatory inference," "presumptive inference," and "permissive presumption." This "dizzying array of formulations" led the court to conclude that "things would be far less complicated if we viewed the res ipsa loquitur . . . issue without undue emphasis on labels and pigeonholes." Id. at 797-798. Regarding New York law, the court concluded that the res ipsa doctrine in appropriate circumstances creates an inference of negligence and that, in some exceedingly rare circumstances, a plaintiff may even obtain summary judgment in his or her favor through use of the doctrine. Id. at 798.

Whether the doctrine gives rise to an inference or a presumption, the preliminary factual elements upon which it rests must be proved by a preponderance of the evidence. In most states, if the defendant presents evidence explaining the occurrence, the case will still go to the jury unless the defendant's countervailing proof is so strong that no reasonable person could find the defendant negligent. See Brown v. Racquet Club of Bricktown, 471 A.2d 25 (N.J. 1984); Brown v. Baptist Mem'l Hosp., 806 So. 2d 1131 (Miss. 2002) (affirming summary judgment for defendant and refusing to apply res ipsa where expert testified that several factors other than negligence by the doctor could have caused the injury). On the other hand, in some states, where the elements of res ipsa include the additional requirement of "no evidence to the contrary," courts have held the doctrine inapplicable when the defendant presents evidence of nonnegligence. See, e.g., Schmidt v. Gibbs, 807 S.W.2d 928 (Ark. 1991); Aaron D. Twerski, Negligence Per Se and Res Ipsa Loquitur: Kissing Cousins, 44 Wake Forest L. Rev. 997, 1004 (2009) ("With a generalization on one side of the scale and hard evidence on the other, the generalization should lose."). In evidence law, such an approach is sometimes referred to as the "bursting bubble" theory of rebuttable presumptions.

If the judge determines that res ipsa applies, the jury will be advised that they may draw an inference of fault, but may not be told of the doctrine, as such. Thus, the court may instruct the jury that if they find on a preponderance of the evidence that the defendant had control of the instrumentality in question, and that the accident was one which would not ordinarily have occurred in the absence of defendant's negligence, they may find the endant to have acted negligently. See, e.g., Tierney v. St. Michael's Med. Ctr., 518 A.2d 2 (N.J. Super. Ct. App. Div. 1986).

The Restatement (Third) of Torts: Liability for Physical and Emotional Harm (2010) ontains a succinct statement of the res ipsa loquitur doctrine:

> §17. Res ipsa loquitur
>
> The factfinder may infer that the defendant has been negligent when the accident causing the plaintiff's physical harm is a type of accident that ordinarily happens as a result of the negligence of a class of actors of which the defendant is the relevant member.

Comments to §17 indicate that the drafters believe that the various two-step approaches adopted by many courts are clumsy and sometimes place the focus on the wrong factual element of the case. They use the element of defendant's control over the instrumentality as a good example of a commonsense idea that sometimes leads to confusion.

Boyer v. Iowa High School Athletic Ass'n

260 Iowa 1061, 152 N.W.2d 293 (1967)

Garfield, C.J. [The plaintiff, a spectator at a basketball game under the management of the defendant, was injured when the bleachers in which she sat collapsed. The bleachers were designed to fold against the gymnasium wall when not in use. As the game ended and the spectators began to leave, the section occupied by the plaintiff and others suddenly folded back toward the wall, throwing the plaintiff to the floor nine feet below. After verdict and judgment for plaintiff, the defendant appealed.]

I. Plaintiff pleaded her case in two counts or divisions, one charging specific acts of negligence, the other in reliance on the doctrine of res ipsa loquitur. We have frequently held this is permissible provided, of course, the doctrine is properly applicable.

The trial court ruled there was no evidence to support the charges of specific negligence and withdrew them from jury consideration. The case was submitted to the jury on the doctrine of res ipsa loquitur.

II. Defendant first assigns error in the court's refusal to withdraw from the jury the division based on res ipsa loquitur.

"'Under the doctrine referred to, where injury occurs by an instrumentality under the exclusive control and management of defendant and the occurrence is such as in the ordinary course of things would not happen if reasonable care had been used, the happening of the injury permits but does not compel an inference that defendant was negligent.' Shinofield v. Curtis," 245 Iowa 1352, 1360, 66 N.W.2d 465, 470, 50 A.L.R.2d 964, and citations.

"' . . . In considering the applicability of res ipsa loquitur, the question whether the particular occurrence is such as would not happen if reasonable care had been used rests on common experience and not at all on evidence in the particular case that tends in itself to show such occurrence was in fact the result of negligence.' Shinofield v. Curtis, supra." Smith v. Ullerich, 259 Iowa 797, 804, 145 N.W.2d 1, 5.

Thus the two foundation facts for application of the res ipsa doctrine, which permits an inference of defendant's negligence from happening of the injury, are: (1) exclusive control and management by defendant of the instrumentality which causes the injury, and (2) the occurrence is such as in the ordinary course of things would not happen if reasonable care had been used.

We think the jury could properly find these foundation facts existed and infer therefrom plaintiff's injury was caused by defendant's negligence. Bleachers designed for use by spectators at athletic events do not ordinarily collapse, when used as they normally are, without negligence of those having control and management thereof.

Defendant asserts the res ipsa doctrine does not apply, first, because it is said the evidence of the cause of the collapse was accessible to plaintiff and not peculiarly accessible to defendant. As plaintiff admits in argument, under our decisions the underlying reason for the res ipsa rule is that the chief evidence of the true cause of the injury is practically accessible to defendant but inaccessible to the injured person.

In these precedents one or both of the foundation facts above referred to were lacking and the absence of what we have said is the underlying reason for the rule was given as an added reason why it was not applicable to the particular case. We have never held presence of this "underlying reason" is an indispensable requirement for application of the doctrine.

Nor are we persuaded evidence of the true cause of the collapse or partial collapse of the bleachers was not peculiarly accessible to defendant rather than to plaintiff. The athletic director of the Mason City schools was acting manager of the tournament. He and the head custodian at Roosevelt Junior High School must be deemed, under the contract between the school and defendant, to have been acting under the management, supervision and direction of defendant. They had the exclusive control and management of the bleachers at least until game time and had the best opportunity to then discover any defect in them which may have caused the collapse.

We are told plaintiff had as much access to the bleachers immediately after the accident as defendant did and could discover any defect in them. A seriously injured person could hardly be expected to then examine the bleachers for defects rather than to be concerned with proper treatment of her injuries. . . .

The [defendant's] argument [that] the only permissible conclusion to be drawn from the evidence is that the movement of the spectators at the end of the game caused the bleachers to collapse cannot be accepted. Such a conclusion would rest wholly on speculation or conjecture. There is no evidence to support it. Assuming, but not deciding, this would be a defense to the res ipsa doctrine, it was defendant's burden to rebut the inference of negligence.

Such limited control of the bleachers as plaintiff and other spectators may have had during and immediately following the game did not, as a matter of law, render the doctrine of res ipsa loquitur inapplicable. The jury could find defendant and its agents were in control of the bleachers at the time of the negligent act, as failure to inspect, which subsequently resulted in injury to plaintiff and that she and the other spectators did nothing improper or unusual during their occupancy of them. . . .

We find no reversible error in any respect assigned and argued. Affirmed.

[The concurring opinion of Becker, J., is omitted.]

One source of confusion in the application of res ipsa is the requirement that the "event [be] of a kind which ordinarily does not occur in the absence of negligence." See Restatement (Second) of Torts, §328D. If this phrase is interpreted as meaning "an event which is more likely than not the result of negligence," the res ipsa loquitur doctrine constitutes a rule of circumstantial proof based upon probabilities. If the phrase is interpreted more broadly to impose liability for unfavorable negative outcomes simply because they rarely occur in the absence of negligence, however, the res ipsa doctrine can reach unusual, and probably improper, results. Assume, for example, that an unfavorable event occurs on the average of once in every 100 times that an activity is engaged in with reasonable care. Assume, further, that a particular actor is, on the average, negligent once in 200 times, resulting in the same unfavorable event. On these assumptions, if the actor engages in the activity 1,000 times, the unfavorable event can be expected to occur approximately 15 times — 10 times in spite of due care on the part of the actor and 5 times because of the actor's negligence. If all that is known is that the unfavorable event has occurred, the probabilities are 2 to 1 *against* the event being the result of negligence. And yet, the traditional formulation of the res ipsa loquitur rule that speaks of events that ordinarily do not occur when care is taken might support liability because of the remoteness (1 in 100) of the occurrence of the unfavorable event even when the actor uses due care — that is, the unfavorable event does not "ordinarily" happen when the actor is exercising care, in the sense that it only happens 1 percent of the time.[74]

A misapplication of this sort may have occurred in Younger v. Webster, 510 P.2d 1182 (Wash. Ct. App. 1973), in which the plaintiff, following an injection of spinal anesthesia, permanently lost all feeling from his navel to his knees. Medical testimony was unanimous to the effect that this consequence was "unusual," but there was no evidence that when it did occur it was usually produced by negligence. The court ruled that, on this evidence, res ipsa loquitur was applicable, and reversed the trial judge's dismissal of the action at the end of the plaintiff's evidence. In so doing, the court stated (id. at 94, 510 P.2d at 1186):

> The present case comes within the reason and spirit of the doctrine. It is difficult to justifiably disregard the application of the doctrine when a patient submits himself to the care and custody of medical personnel, is rendered unconscious, and receives some injury from instrumentalities used in his treatment. Without the aid of the doctrine, a patient who receives permanent injuries of a serious character, apparently the result of someone's negligence, would be unable to recover unless the doctors and nurses voluntarily chose to disclose the facts establishing liability.

Cf. Ybarra v. Spangard, p. 135, above.

In States v. Lourdes Hospital, 762 N.Y.S.2d 1 (2003), the Court of Appeals of New York determined that a medical malpractice plaintiff could rely on expert testimony to establish the predicate condition that an injury was unlikely to occur in the absence of medical negligence (762 N.Y.S.2d at 4):

> [E]xpert testimony may properly be used to help the jury bridge the gap between its own common knowledge, which does not encompass the specialized knowledge and experience necessary to reach a conclusion that the occurrence would not normally take place in the absence of negligence, and the common knowledge of physicians, which does. . . . Our conclusion not only is supported by a majority of courts that have considered the question,

74. Cognitive psychologists refer to this misapplication of statistics as the "inverse fallacy." It describes "the tendency to treat the probability of a hypothesis given the evidence (for example, the probability that a defendant was negligent given that a plaintiff was injured) as the same as, or close to, the probability of the evidence given the hypothesis (for example, the probability that the plaintiff would be injured if the defendant were negligent)." Chris Guthrie, Jeffrey J. Rachlinski & Andrew J. Wistrich, Inside the Judicial Mind, 86 Cornell L. Rev. 777, 807 (2001). The error tends, in general, to lead people to overestimate the likelihood that a defendant was negligent. It may have special significance in the res ipsa loquitor context. See David Kaye, Probability Theory Meets Res Ipsa Loquitur, 77 Mich. L. Rev. 1456 (1979).

> but also is the approach adopted by the Restatement of Torts. . . . In an increasingly sophisticated and specialized society such as ours, it is not at all surprising that matters entirely foreign to the general population are commonplace within a particular profession or specially trained segment of society. . . .
>
> Notwithstanding the availability of expert testimony to aid a jury in determining whether an event would normally occur in the absence of negligence, expert opinion of course does not negate the jury's ultimate responsibility as finder of fact to draw that necessary conclusion. The purpose of expert opinion in this context is to educate the jury, enlarging its understanding of the fact issues it must decide. However, the jury remains free to determine whether its newly-enlarged understanding supports the conclusion it is asked to accept.

See also Sides v. St. Anthony's Med. Ctr., 285 S.W.3d 811 (Mo. 2008) (citing authority in 28 other jurisdictions allowing the use of expert evidence in res ipsa loquitur medical malpractice cases).

Shutt v. Kaufman's, Inc.

165 Colo. 175, 438 P.2d 501 (1968)

En Banc. Mr. Justice Kelley delivered the opinion of the Court. . . .

[Plaintiff, a customer in defendant's shoe store, sat down on a chair which bumped a display table causing a metal shoe stand to topple and strike plaintiff on the head.]

. . . The questions of liability and damages were submitted to a jury which returned a verdict in favor of the defendant. From a denial of her motion for new trial the plaintiff sued out this writ of error.

Plaintiff's grounds for reversal all involve questions arising out of the application of the doctrine of res ipsa loquitur. One phase of alleged error relates to either instructions given or tendered and refused, while the second phase involves the failure of the trial court to direct a favorable verdict for the plaintiff as to liability.

In short, the plaintiff, although having convinced the court that the doctrine of res ipsa loquitur applied, now objects to the manner in which it was applied. On the other hand, the defendant maintains that under the circumstances of this case the doctrine of res ipsa loquitur is not applicable.

The threshold question, therefore, is whether under the circumstances there should have been any instructions given in reference to the doctrine of res ipsa loquitur. An examination of prior pronouncements of this court indicates that a careful analysis of the doctrine or rule and the evidence is necessary to determine that question. . . .

In considering the applicability of res ipsa, some other fundamental rules of law must be integrated into our thinking. We are here concerned with the relationship of a storekeeper and a business visitor. In such relationship the storekeeper owes a duty to one who enters upon the premises at his invitation, express or implied, to protect such visitor not only against known dangers, but also against those which, by the exercise of reasonable care, he might discover.

In short, although the storekeeper must exercise reasonable care for the safety of the business visitor, he is not an insurer of the safety of such visitor; thus, the mere happening of an accident raises no presumption of negligence, except under those circumstances where the doctrine of res ipsa loquitur is applicable.

There is no fundamental disagreement between the parties as to the law. The plaintiff would invoke res ipsa because she "could not possibly have foreseen that by merely sitting down in a proffered chair in a normal manner she would, in effect, spring a concealed trap resulting in a steel and plastic display rack striking her on the head from behind." We are inclined to agree that she probably could not "have foreseen" the accident. But this is not the res ipsa test.

The circumstances here were such that the plaintiff could have shown that the defendant was responsible for her injuries because of its negligence. By way of illustration, it could have been demonstrated, if such were the fact, that the display table was unstable; that it wobbled from a mere touch, and that by placing the shoe display stand on the top shelf the defendant negligently created a dangerous condition. Or it might have been demonstrated that the tripod-based shoe stand was so unstable that the mere use of it on a shelf high above the head of a customer was likely to topple off from the usual and customary bumps which a display table receives. In other words, the plaintiff had the means available to her to establish negligence on the part of the defendant, if any there was. As we pointed out above, the storekeeper is not an insurer.

Under the circumstances of this case, the court erred in submitting any instruction on res ipsa loquitur. Holding as we do, it is not necessary to discuss the correctness of either of the given or the tendered instructions.

No questions have been raised as to the other instructions which the court gave. It appears that, except for the improper res ipsa instruction, the instructions given fairly presented the issues of negligence and contributory negligence. Consequently, the plaintiff, by virtue of the improper instruction, had an unfair advantage, but, even so, failed to prevail. The defendant having won, despite the improper instruction, has therefore not been prejudiced.

The judgment of the trial court is affirmed.

In Marrero v. Goldsmith, 486 So. 2d 530 (Fla. 1986), the plaintiff suffered from numbness, weakness, and pain in her left arm following surgery that did not involve her left arm. She joined the three doctors who performed the surgery and the hospital in a negligence action. Her expert testified that her type of injury does not ordinarily occur in the absence of negligence and that it was probably caused by incorrect arm positioning during surgery. The doctors testified that nothing unusual had happened during the surgery. The trial court denied the plaintiff's request for a res ipsa loquitur jury instruction. The jury found for the defendant doctors. The intermediate appellate court affirmed, on the ruling that res ipsa loquitur was not applicable because the plaintiff had introduced expert testimony regarding specific acts of negligence.

The Supreme Court of Florida reversed and remanded for new trial, concluding (486 So. 2d at 532):

> If a case is a proper res ipsa case in other respects, the presence of some direct evidence of negligence should not deprive the plaintiff of the res ipsa inference. There comes a point, however, when a plaintiff can introduce enough direct evidence of negligence to dispel the need for the inference. According to Prosser:
>
> > Plaintiff is of course bound by his own evidence; but proof of some specific facts does not necessarily exclude inferences of others. When the plaintiff shows that the railway car in which he was a passenger was derailed, there is an inference that the defendant railroad has somehow been negligent. When the plaintiff goes further and shows that the derailment was caused by an open switch, the plaintiff destroys any

> inference of other causes; but the inference that the defendant has not used proper care in looking after its switches is not destroyed, but considerably strengthened. If the plaintiff goes further still and shows that the switch was left open by a drunken switchman on duty, there is nothing left to infer; and if the plaintiff shows that the switch was thrown by an escaped convict with a grudge against the railroad, the plaintiff has proven himself out of court. It is only in this sense that when the facts are known there is no inference, and res ipsa loquitur simply vanishes from the case. On the basis of reasoning such as this, it is quite generally agreed that the introduction of some evidence which tends to show specific acts of negligence on the part of the defendant, but which does not purport to furnish a full and complete explanation of the occurrence, does not destroy the inferences which are consistent with the evidence, and so does not deprive the plaintiff of the benefit of res ipsa loquitur.

Prosser and Keeton §40 (footnotes omitted).

See also Estate of Hall v. Akron Gen. Med. Ctr., 927 N.E.2d 1112 (Ohio 2010).

In *Marrero*, above, the defendant doctors also argued on appeal that res ipsa was inapplicable because no one of them had exclusive control for the entire period during which the plaintiff may have been injured. The Florida high court concluded that exclusive control by defendant doctors on these facts was not likely but, in fairness to the plaintiff, the case should go to the jury with an instruction on res ipsa (486 So. 2d at 532-33). Comment *g* to §17 of the Restatement (Third) of Torts: Liability for Physical and Emotional Harm (2010) addresses the issue of whether a plaintiff may combine res ipsa claims with claims of specific negligence:

> *g. Specific evidence of non-negligence or negligence.* The defendant may offer evidence showing that the defendant's own conduct was not negligent or that the accident happened for reasons unrelated to the defendant's negligence. If accepted by the jury, such evidence defeats the plaintiff's res ipsa claim. In such cases it can be said that the defendant's evidence prevents the application of res ipsa loquitur; alternatively, it can be said that res ipsa loquitur applies and permits an inference of negligence, but that the defendant's evidence sufficiently negates that inference.
>
> A more difficult question arises when the plaintiff relies on res ipsa loquitur, but seeks in the alternative to assert and prove specific negligence on the defendant's part. A number of courts still follow the traditional rule that the plaintiff, by professing to explain to the jury how the accident actually happened, cannot concurrently invite the jury to speculate about the causes of accidents in a res ipsa loquitur manner. But most modern courts find it inappropriate to penalize the plaintiff who seeks to prove specific negligence by preventing the plaintiff from developing and submitting to the jury a res ipsa loquitur argument in the alternative.
>
> In certain cases, the evidence offered by the plaintiff can be properly understood as displacing any res ipsa loquitur claim. For example, the plaintiff's evidence may conclusively establish the sequence of events leading up to the accident, as well as the circumstances of the defendant's conduct. At this point, the jury's responsibility is to determine whether this conduct is negligent; in such a case, there is no room for res ipsa reasoning. In other cases, both the plaintiff and the defendant provide at trial extensive but conflicting evidence as to how the accident happened: the case might be one, for example, in which the passenger sues the driver on account of a highway accident, and each is able to offer direct eye-witness testimony as to how the accident happened. In such a case, the evidence provided by the parties, though in conflict, provides the appropriate foundation for the jury's decision, and res ipsa loquitur should be regarded as an inappropriate distraction.

In other situations, however, a claim of specific negligence can coexist with a more general res ipsa claim. Consideration should be given as to how these two claims interrelate. When both claims go to the jury, the jury should be encouraged to consider first the plaintiff's claim of specific negligence. If this claim is accepted, the jury can avoid deciding the possibly difficult res ipsa issue. If the jury rejects the plaintiff's claim, the reason for this rejection affects how the jury evaluates the plaintiff's remaining res ipsa loquitur claim. For example, in a medical-malpractice case, there may be four possible causes of the type of adverse result the plaintiff has suffered, two of which — A and B — are associated with the negligence of the physician. If the plaintiff makes a specific claim that the physician was guilty of A, and if the jury, in considering that claim, ends up believing that the physician's conduct was in fact free of A, that removes A from the list of causal options the jury should consider for purposes of res ipsa loquitur. Another possibility, however, is that the jury rejects the plaintiff's claim of A only because the plaintiff's evidence relating to A, while suggestive, is not strong enough by itself to justify a more-likely-than-not finding that A was the cause of the plaintiff's injury. If so, the jury's inability to rule in favor of the plaintiff on the specific claim of A does not diminish the plaintiff's res ipsa loquitur claim, and may even enhance that claim, as suggested in Comment *d*.

City of Louisville v. Humphrey

461 S.W.2d 352 (Ky. Ct. App. 1970)

EDWARD P. HILL, JR., C.J. The appellee obtained judgment on a verdict of $56,534.34 against appellant for injuries, resulting in the death of her husband, which she claimed he received after his arrest or while he was confined in the city's jail. The city appeals. We reverse. Before stating the facts, we should emphasize the appellee's theory of the case that her husband's fatal injuries were inflicted by one or both of the two arresting officers, or by a jail employee, or by a fellow prisoner.

The deceased, Ruel McKinley Humphrey, a hard-working man about 59 years of age with some drinking problems, was highly intoxicated about 2:15 A.M., on the morning of November 21, 1966. He was wandering around in the vicinity of Frankfort and Hite Avenues, near his home, when a report was received by Louisville Police Headquarters that he was shaking doors in that neighborhood. The officers proceeded to arrest him and to deliver him to the booking clerk at the city jail at 2:35 A.M. He was retained in the holdover department in the basement of the city jail until 4:15 A.M., when he was taken by elevator to the third floor of the jail.

The two guards in charge of the third floor of the jail testified that immediately after the deceased stepped off the elevator on the third floor, he began to fall down or collapse. One of the guards caught him and lightened his fall. Shortly thereafter he was dragged by the two guards to the "drunk tank" and left lying on the floor with his feet toward the entrance of the tank. Two of the jail employees testified that no one else was in the "drunk tank" while the deceased was there. However, a third employee testified that he believed there was another prisoner in the "drunk tank" during that time.

At 7:15 A.M. a jail guard attempted to awaken deceased in order that he might appear in court that morning. The guard was unable to arouse him, concluding that Humphrey was in a high state of intoxication. At noon the guard again attempted to arouse him without success. He was then taken to Louisville General Hospital and found to be unconscious with a subdural hematoma from injuries apparently received around the left eye and forehead. He underwent brain surgery and died on December 13, 1966, without ever regaining consciousness. . . .

[The opinion here describes the evidence in the case, which was inconclusive on the question of the cause of the decedent's injuries. Referring to the conduct of the defendant in failing to investigate the incident, the court concludes:]

It would seem that this is a bad way to run a railroad, more especially in a situation where a man imprisoned in the city jail had been injured and dies within a very short period thereafter. Nevertheless, the issue is not the failure of the appellant and its representatives or employees to conduct a proper investigation into the injuries of the deceased, but is whether there was probative evidence that an employee of the city inflicted injuries on the deceased, or that a fellow prisoner did so, and if so, that the city was negligent with respect to the infliction of his injuries by a fellow prisoner.

We may safely say that there is no direct evidence that any of the prison employees inflicted the injuries on the deceased. Neither is there any direct evidence that those injuries were inflicted by a fellow prisoner. The appellee suggests that the proof in the case warrants the application of res ipsa loquitur. With this theory we cannot agree. Although the evidence and circumstances come pretty close to creating an inference that the deceased received his injuries after his arrest and while he was in the custody of the city's employees, yet they fall short of justifying res ipsa. If we assume his injuries were received after his arrest, we are still left to speculate as to whether the injuries were received at the hands of the city employees or whether they were inflicted by a fellow prisoner. We cannot assume either to be the case.

Admitting for the purpose of discussion that the deceased was injured by a fellow prisoner, it is still incumbent upon the appellee to prove negligence on the part of the city in permitting those injuries. The court has written in a similar case that the city will not be liable unless it had knowledge of the violent propensities of the fellow prisoner.

It would appear at first blush that when the officers of the law arrest and confine a highly intoxicated person, the arresting authorities should exercise a degree of care higher than ordinary care, for the simple reason that they are dealing with a helpless human being. Yet, in many prisons, especially large city prisons, large numbers of highly intoxicated persons may be arrested and imprisoned in the short space of a few hours. It would be difficult to provide each and every such prisoner with a padded, injury-proof, individual cell. After all, in a great majority of cases the helpless drunk is safer in prison than outside.

The court is mindful of the hardship placed upon the plaintiff in this class of case by the rule that the plaintiff must prove knowledge of violent propensities of a fellow prisoner before a recovery will be permitted. It is common knowledge that highly intoxicated persons are not given to exercising good judgment or restraint, that they are subject to becoming belligerent on the least provocation.

A majority of this court is of the opinion that to place on the prison keeper the burden of going forward with proof simply upon a showing that a prisoner was injured while in prison would amount to holding that the prison keeper is the absolute insurer of the safety and well-being of the prisoner, which may result in an unfair burden on him.

It is concluded that the appellee did not meet the burden of proof required in our case law above cited. The judgment is, therefore, reversed with directions to enter an order sustaining the appellant's motion for judgment notwithstanding the verdict.

Milliken, Neikirk, Osborne, Reed, and Steinfeld, JJ., concur.

For a successful res ipsa loquitur claim by an incarcerated prisoner, see Farra'd v. New Jersey Dep't of Corr., 2009 WL 3429681 (N.J. 2009). In this case, plaintiff inmate brought a res ipsa loquitur claim for property damage after his computer was shipped from one prison to another in connection with plaintiff's transfer. Plaintiff alleged that the computer was in proper working condition before the shipping, but did not work after. Final administrative decisions issued by the Department of Corrections denied plaintiff relief. In an unpublished opinion, the New Jersey Supreme Court reversed and remanded for payment of the claim.

Problem 17

You are an associate in a medium-sized Collegetown law firm. Your supervising attorney wants your evaluation of the applicability of res ipsa loquitur to the following case. The plaintiff, Helen Sims, was severely injured when an empty whiskey bottle struck her in the face. The incident occurred two months ago on the day of Columbia State University's homecoming game against Corning College in Collegetown. Helen was standing on the curb waiting to cross a fairly busy street just off campus when a taxi cab drove past and an empty bottle, apparently thrown from the cab, struck her in the face. Helen's boyfriend, Rob Westin, was standing next to her at the time. He is ready to testify that he saw a passenger in the cab move his hand toward them, releasing the bottle, and then roll up the window. The cab never slowed, proceeding around the corner and out of sight. The passenger who threw the bottle was wearing a red Columbia State scarf. Rob's blue sweatshirt resembled those worn by Corning College students. Rob did not notice the cab's number but is certain it was an Acme Taxicab Company cab. Helen's physician indicates that Helen's injuries were probably enhanced by the bottle's moving thirty to thirty-five miles per hour parallel to her in addition to the impetus imparted by the throw.

The cab company's policy is to require its drivers to report unusual incidents such as this at the end of the day. No report of the incident in question is on file. Your firm questioned several drivers and received no further information. It is quite possible that the driver of the cab could not see or hear what was happening in the back seat due to the thick plastic protective shield between the driver and passengers, included in all Acme cab designs. The cab company says that there is no way to identify the driver who was at that corner at that time.

Your firm has had no luck tracing the scarfed figure through Columbia State's alumni office. It appears that Acme Taxicab Company is the only possible defendant. Your supervising attorney wants to know whether res ipsa loquitur might be applicable. Advise him.

As the above materials suggest, modern courts have shown considerable flexibility in the use of res ipsa loquitur. Perhaps the most noteworthy of these efforts occurred as U.S. courts struggled to develop a workable strict liability regime for injuries caused by product defects.

Escola v. Coca Cola Bottling Co.

24 Cal. 2d 453, 150 P.2d 436 (1944)

GIBSON, C.J. Plaintiff, a waitress in a restaurant, was injured when a bottle of Coca Cola broke in her hand. She alleged that defendant company, which had bottled and delivered the alleged defective bottle to her employer, was negligent in selling "bottles containing said beverage which on account of excessive pressure of gas or by reason of some defect in the bottle was dangerous . . . and likely to explode." This appeal is from a judgment upon a jury verdict in favor of plaintiff. . . .

[B]eing unable to show any specific acts of negligence, [plaintiff] relied completely on the doctrine of res ipsa loquitur.

Defendant contends that the doctrine of res ipsa loquitur does not apply in this case, and that the evidence is insufficient to support the judgment. . . .

Res ipsa loquitur does not apply unless (1) defendant had exclusive control of the thing causing the injury and (2) the accident is of such a nature that it ordinarily would not occur in the absence of negligence by the defendant.

Many authorities state that the happening of the accident does not speak for itself where it took place some time after defendant had relinquished control of the instrumentality causing the injury. Under the more logical view, however, the doctrine may be applied upon the theory that defendant had control at the time of the alleged negligent act, although not at the time of the accident, *provided* plaintiff first proves that the condition of the instrumentality had not been changed after it left the defendant's possession. As said in Dunn v. Hoffman Beverage Co., 126 N.J. L. 556 [20 A.2d 352, 354], "defendant is not charged with the duty of showing affirmatively that something happened to the bottle after it left its control or management; . . . to get to the jury the plaintiff must show that there was due care during that period." Plaintiff must also prove that she handled the bottle carefully. The reason for this prerequisite is set forth in Prosser on Torts, [1st ed.] at page 300, where the author states: "Allied to the condition of exclusive control in the defendant is that of absence of any action on the part of the plaintiff contributing to the accident. Its purpose, of course, is to eliminate the possibility that it was the plaintiff who was responsible. If the boiler of a locomotive explodes while the plaintiff engineer is operating it, the inference of his own negligence is at least as great as that of the defendant and res ipsa loquitur will not apply until he has accounted for his own conduct." It is not necessary, of course, that plaintiff eliminate every remote possibility of injury to the bottle after defendant lost control, and the requirement is satisfied if there is evidence permitting a reasonable inference that it was not accessible to extraneous harmful forces and that it was carefully handled by plaintiff or any third person who may have moved or touched it. If such evidence is presented, the question becomes one for the trier of fact and, accordingly, the issue should be submitted to the jury under proper instructions.

In the present case no instructions were requested or given on this phase of the case, although general instructions upon res ipsa loquitur were given. Defendant, however, has made no claim of error with reference thereto on this appeal. Upon an examination of the record, the evidence appears sufficient to support a reasonable inference that the bottle here involved was not damaged by any extraneous force after delivery to the restaurant by defendant. It follows, therefore, that the bottle was in some manner defective at the time defendant relinquished control, because sound and properly prepared bottles of carbonated liquids do not ordinarily explode when carefully handled.

The next question, then, is whether plaintiff may rely upon the doctrine of res ipsa loquitur to supply an inference that defendant's negligence was responsible for the defective condition of the bottle at the time it was delivered to the restaurant. Under the general rules pertaining to the doctrine, as set forth above, it must appear that bottles of carbonated liquid are not ordinarily defective without negligence by the bottling company. An explosion such as took place here might have been caused by an excessive internal pressure in a sound bottle, by a defect in the glass of a bottle containing a safe pressure, or by a combination of these two possible causes. The question is whether under the evidence there was a probability that defendant was negligent in any of these respects. If so, the doctrine of res ipsa loquitur applies.

The bottle was admittedly charged with gas under pressure, and the charging of the bottle was within the exclusive control of defendant. As it is a matter of common knowledge that an overcharge would not ordinarily result without negligence, it follows under the doctrine of res ipsa loquitur that if the bottle was in fact excessively charged an inference of defendant's negligence would arise. If the explosion resulted from a defective bottle containing a safe pressure, the defendant would be liable if it negligently failed to discover such flaw. If the defect were visible, an inference of negligence would arise from the failure of defendant to discover it. Where defects are discoverable, it may be assumed that they will not ordinarily escape detection if a reasonable inspection is made, and if such a defect is overlooked an inference arises that a proper inspection was not made. A difficult problem is presented where the defect is unknown and consequently might have been one not discoverable by a reasonable, practicable inspection. In [an earlier] case we refused to take judicial notice of the technical practices and information available to the bottling industry for finding defects which cannot be seen. In the present case, however, we are supplied with evidence of the standard methods used for testing bottles.

A chemical engineer for the Owens-Illinois Glass Company and its Pacific Coast subsidiary, maker of Coca Cola bottles, explained how glass is manufactured and the methods used in testing and inspecting bottles. He testified that his company is the largest manufacturer of glass containers in the United States, and that it uses the standard methods for testing bottles recommended by the glass containers association. A pressure test is made by taking a sample from each mold every three hours — approximately one out of every 600 bottles — and subjecting the sample to an internal pressure of 450 pounds per square inch, which is sustained for one minute. (The normal pressure in Coca Cola bottles is less than 50 pounds per square inch.) The sample bottles are also subjected to the standard thermal shock test. The witness stated that these tests are "pretty near" infallible.

It thus appears that there is available to the industry a commonly-used method of testing bottles for defects not apparent to the eye, which is almost infallible. Since Coca Cola bottles are subjected to these tests by the manufacturer, it is not likely that they contain defects when delivered to the bottler which are not discoverable by visual inspection. Both new and used bottles are filled and distributed by defendant. The used bottles are not again subjected to the tests referred to above, and it may be inferred that defects not discoverable by visual inspection do not develop in bottles after they are manufactured. Obviously, if such defects do occur in used bottles there is a duty upon the bottler to make appropriate tests before they are refilled, and if such tests are not commercially practicable the bottles should not be re-used. This would seem to be particularly true where a charged liquid is placed in the bottle. It follows that a defect which would make the bottle unsound could be discovered by reasonable and practicable tests.

Although it is not clear in this case whether the explosion was caused by an excessive charge or a defect in the glass, there is a sufficient showing that neither cause would ordinarily have been present if due care had been used. Further, defendant had exclusive control over both the charging and inspection of the bottles. Accordingly, all the requirements necessary to entitle plaintiff to rely on the doctrine of res ipsa loquitur to supply an inference of negligence are present.

It is true that defendant presented evidence tending to show that it exercised considerable precaution by carefully regulating and checking the pressure in the bottles and by making visual inspections for defects in the glass at several stages during the bottling process. It is well settled, however, that when a defendant produces evidence to rebut the inference of negligence which arises upon application of the doctrine of res ipsa loquitur, it is ordinarily a question of fact for the jury to determine whether the inference has been dispelled.

The judgment is affirmed.

Shenk, J., Curtis, J., Carter, J., and Schauer, J., concurred.

Traynor, J. I concur in the judgment, but I believe the manufacturer's negligence should no longer be singled out as the basis of a plaintiff's right to recover in cases like the present one. In my opinion it should now be recognized that a manufacturer incurs an absolute liability when an article that he has placed on the market, knowing that it is to be used without inspection, proves to have a defect that causes injury to human beings. McPherson v. Buick Motor Co., 217 N.Y. 382 [111 N.E. 1050, Ann. Cas. 1916C 440, L.R.A. 1916F 696], established the principle, recognized by this court, that irrespective of privity of contract, the manufacturer is responsible for an injury caused by such an article to any person who comes in lawful contact with it.

. . . Even if there is no negligence, however, public policy demands that responsibility be fixed wherever it will most effectively reduce the hazards to life and health inherent in defective products that reach the market. It is evident that the manufacturer can anticipate some hazards and guard against the recurrence of others, as the public cannot. Those who suffer injury from defective products are unprepared to meet its consequences. The cost of an injury and the loss of time or health may be an overwhelming misfortune to the person injured, and a needless one, for the risk of injury can be insured by the manufacturer and distributed among the public as a cost of doing business. It is to the public interest to discourage the marketing of products having defects that are a menace to the public. If such products nevertheless find their way into the market it is to the public interest to place the responsibility for whatever injury they may cause upon the manufacturer, who, even if he is not negligent in the manufacture of the product, is responsible for its reaching the market. However intermittently such injuries may occur and however haphazardly they may strike, the risk of their occurrence is a constant risk and a general one. Against such a risk there should be general and constant protection and the manufacturer is best situated to afford such protection. . . .

As handicrafts have been replaced by mass production with its great markets and transportation facilities, the close relationship between the producer and consumer of a product has been altered. Manufacturing processes, frequently valuable secrets, are ordinarily either inaccessible to or beyond the ken of the general public. The consumer no longer has means or skill enough to investigate for himself the soundness of a product, even when it is not contained in a sealed package, and his erstwhile vigilance has been lulled by the steady efforts of manufacturers to build up confidence by advertising and marketing devices such as trademarks. Consumers no longer approach products warily but accept them on faith, relying on the reputation of the manufacturer or the trade-mark.

Manufacturers have sought to justify that faith by increasingly high standards of inspection and a readiness to make good on defective products by way of replacements and refunds. The manufacturer's obligation to the consumer must keep pace with the changing relationship between them. . . .

Eighteen years after *Escola*, Justice Traynor wrote the opinion for the court in Greenman v. Yuba Power Products, Inc., 377 P.2d 897 (Cal. 1962), in which California became the first jurisdiction to apply the rule of strict liability in tort to manufacturers of defective products. See Section C of Chapter 7.

D. Modification of the General Standard Arising out of Special Relationships Between the Parties

In a few situations, the general duty of reasonable care may be raised or lowered because of some special relationship existing between the parties. The most common relationships as to which the duty may be modified are those between a possessor of land and entrants on the land, between a common carrier and its passengers, and between a driver of an automobile and guest-passengers.

1. Responsibility of Possessors of Land for the Safety of Entrants

In theory, the tort system could treat possessors in the same manner as any other potential tortfeasor by simply requiring that they exercise reasonable care toward those who have entered their property. Instead of applying the general reasonableness standard, the duty owed by a possessor to entrants with respect to conditions on the land has traditionally depended upon a formal scheme of classification of the persons on the land as trespassers, licensees, or invitees. These traditional classifications often lower, but never raise, the normal duty of reasonable care, and therefore benefit landowners and possessors generally. Historically, the classifications and their attendant duties owe their existence to the high place that land has occupied in Anglo-American society. At one time, land was the primary source of wealth and social status, and thus the foundation of economic and political power. The importance of land ownership and possession have lessened through the years, and, as discussed below in this Section, recent cases indicate that we may be in a period of transition toward a single duty of reasonable care to all persons who enter the land of another.

a. Invitees and Licensees

Invitees and licensees share the common characteristic of being on the land with the permission of the possessor. Beyond that, there are significant differences.

Invitees are defined by the Restatement (Second) of Torts, §332:

§332. Invitee Defined

(1) An invitee is either a public invitee or a business visitor.

(2) A public invitee is a person who is invited to enter or remain on land as a member of the public for a purpose for which the land is held open to the public.

(3) A business visitor is a person who is invited to enter or remain on land for a purpose directly or indirectly connected with business dealings with the possessor of the land.

The "public invitee" concept is perhaps somewhat narrower than the black letter might indicate. According to Comment *d*:

> It is not enough, to hold land open to the public, that the public at large, or any considerable number of persons, are permitted to enter at will upon the land for their own purposes. As in other instances of invitation, there must be some inducement or encouragement to enter, some conduct indicating that the premises are provided and intended for public entry and use, and that the public will not merely be tolerated, but is expected and desired to come. When a landowner tacitly permits the boys of the town to play ball on his vacant lot they are licensees only; but if he installs playground equipment and posts a sign saying that the lot is open free to all children, there is then a public invitation, and those who enter in response to it are invitees.

The duty owed to an invitee is one of reasonable care under the circumstances. The duty is fleshed out in §343 of the Restatement (Second) of Torts:

§343. Dangerous Conditions Known to or Discoverable by Possessor

A possessor of land is subject to liability for physical harm caused to his invitees by a condition on the land if, but only if, he

(a) knows or by the exercise of reasonable care would discover the condition, and should realize that it involves an unreasonable risk of harm to such invitees, and

(b) should expect that they will not discover or realize the danger, or will fail to protect themselves against it, and

(c) fails to exercise reasonable care to protect them against the danger.

The definition of licensee is set out in §330 of the Restatement:

§330. Licensee Defined

A licensee is a person who is privileged to enter or remain on land only by virtue of the possessor's consent.

The duty to licensees is set out in §342:

§342. Dangerous Conditions Known to Possessor

A possessor of land is subject to liability for physical harm caused to licensees by a condition on the land if, but only if,

> (a) the possessor knows or has reason to know[75] of the condition and should realize that it involves an unreasonable risk of harm to such licensees, and should expect that they will not discover or realize the danger, and
>
> (b) he fails to exercise reasonable care to make the condition safe, or to warn the licensees of the condition and the risk involved, and
>
> (c) the licensees do not know or have reason to know of the condition and the risk involved.

As might be expected, considerable litigation has occurred over the issue of the status of the injured person. Courts usually characterize police officers and fire fighters acting in their official capacities as licensees. See, e.g., Levandoski v. Cone, 841 A.2d 208 (Conn. 2004), although some states limit firemen's rights under the so-called firemen's rule. See p. 320 below. Door-to-door solicitors are also generally held to be licensees. See, e.g., Singleton v. Jackson, 935 P.2d 644 (Wash. Ct. App. 1997). Mail carriers, on the other hand, are likely to be invitees (see, e.g., Jiminez v. Maisch, 748 A.2d 121 (N.J. Super. Ct. App. Div. 2000)), as are utility company meter readers (see, e.g., Sims v. Giles, 541 S.E.2d 857 (S.C. 2001)). Users of governmental property have been considered licensees. Thus, a title examiner who slipped while visiting a courthouse to check the names on her title report was a licensee and suffered summary judgment against her. See Estate of Enzweiler v. Clermont Cty. Bd. of Commrs., No. CA2010-11-085, 2011 WL 684570 at *3-4 (Ohio Ct. App. Feb. 28, 2011). Further, a person who provides services for the benefit of the landowner is generally held to be an invitee, even if that person does not enter for any explicit business purpose. See Hall v. Cagle, 773 So. 2d 928 (Miss. 2000) (plaintiff, who was invited to help defendants move into their new home, sustained injuries when she fell on the steps to defendants' back door). Persons who accompany invitees may be inferred to be invitees as well. Thus, a wife accompanying her husband to the doctor was an invitee. See Richardson v. Nwadiuko, 966 A.2d 972, 978 (Md. Ct. Spec. App. 2009).

b. Trespassers

The lowest duty is owed to a trespasser, who is defined by §329 of the Restatement (Second) as "a person who enters or remains upon land in the possession of another without a privilege to do so created by the possessor's consent or otherwise." In general, the duty of the possessor toward trespassers is to refrain from wanton and willful conduct. See, e.g., Wagner v. Doehring, 553 A.2d 684 (Md. 1989). However, if the trespasser is on the land for the purpose of committing a crime, the possessor may be liable only for intentionally injuring the trespasser. See, e.g., Ryals v. United States Steel Corp., 562 So. 2d 192 (Ala. 1990). The circumstances under which the possessor has a privilege to injure trespassers intentionally was the subject of Katko v. Briney, the spring gun case set out in Chapter 1, p. 94, above.

Two sections of the Restatement (Second) impose duties to use reasonable care to warn trespassers of hazardous conditions:

75. According to Comment *a* to §12, Restatement (Second) of Torts, *reason to know* means "that the actor has knowledge of facts from which a reasonable man of ordinary intelligence or one of the superior intelligence of the actor would either infer the existence of the fact in question or would regard its existence as so highly probable that his conduct would be predicated upon the assumption that the fact did exist." [Eds.]

§335. Artificial Conditions Highly Dangerous to Constant Trespassers on Limited Area

A possessor of land who knows, or from facts within his knowledge should know, that trespassers constantly intrude upon a limited area of the land, is subject to liability for bodily harm caused to them by an artificial condition on the land, if

(a) the condition

(i) is one which the possessor has created or maintains and

(ii) is, to his knowledge, likely to cause death or serious bodily harm to such trespassers and

(iii) is of such a nature that he has reason to believe that such trespassers will not discover it, and

(b) the possessor has failed to exercise reasonable care to warn such trespassers of the condition and the risk involved.

§337. Artificial Conditions Highly Dangerous to Known Trespassers

A possessor of land who maintains on the land an artificial condition which involves a risk of death or serious bodily harm to persons coming in contact with it, is subject to liability for bodily harm caused to trespassers by his failure to exercise reasonable care to warn them of the condition if

(a) the possessor knows or has reason to know of their presence in dangerous proximity to the condition, and

(b) the condition is of such a nature that he has reason to believe that the trespasser will not discover it or realize the risk.

Note that these sections do not apply to natural conditions on the land. If the trespasser stumbles into a quicksand bog on the possessor's land, there is no liability at all for failure to warn. Can you think of any reason why there should be a distinction between artificial and natural conditions in this respect? But also note that the sections do apply even if the possessor has done all that can reasonably be done to keep trespassers from the land. See, e.g., Grant v. City of Duluth, 672 F.2d 677 (8th Cir. 1982).

A higher duty may be owed to young trespassers under the "attractive nuisance doctrine," as set out in §339 of the Restatement (Second):

§339. Artificial Conditions Highly Dangerous to Trespassing Children

A possessor of land is subject to liability for physical harm to children trespassing thereon caused by an artificial condition upon the land if

(a) the place where the condition exists is one upon which the possessor knows or has reason to know that children are likely to trespass, and

(b) the condition is one of which the possessor knows or has reason to know and which he realizes or should realize will involve an unreasonable risk of death or serious bodily harm to such children, and

(c) the children because of their youth do not discover the condition or realize the risk involved in intermeddling with it or in coming within the area made dangerous by it, and

(d) the utility to the possessor of maintaining the condition and the burden of eliminating the danger are slight as compared with the risk to children involved, and

(e) the possessor fails to exercise reasonable care to eliminate the danger or otherwise to protect the children.

The attractive nuisance doctrine is sometimes referred to as the "turntable doctrine," after an early case involving a child injured while he was trespassing on a railroad turntable. See Sioux City & Pac. R.R. v. Stout, 84 U.S. (17 Wall) 657 (1873). Most states follow the attractive nuisance doctrine. See, e.g., S.W. v. Towers Boat Club, Inc., 315 P.3d 1257 (Col. 2013) (holding, as a matter of first impression, that all children can bring attractive nuisance claims regardless of whether they are classified as trespasser, licensee, or invitee); Laster *ex rel.* Laster v. Norfolk S. Ry. Co., 13 So. 3d 922, 927 (Ala. 2009) (applying the doctrine to a child who suffered injury while walking along privately owned train tracks).

An early Michigan case rejecting the attractive nuisance doctrine seemed to view unruly children as a threat to the entire industrial economy:

> There is no more lawless class than children, and none more annoyingly resent an attempt to prevent their trespasses. The average citizen has learned that the surest way to be overrun by children is to give them to understand that their presence is distasteful. The consequence is that they roam at will over private premises, and, as a rule this is tolerated so long as no damage is done. The remedy which the law affords for trifling trespasses of children is inadequate. No one ever thinks of suing them, and to attempt to remove a crowd of boys from private premises by gently laying on of hands, and using no more force than necessary to put them off, would be a roaring farce, with all honors to the juveniles. For a corporation with an empty treasury, and overwhelmed with debt, to be required to be to the expense of preventing children from going across its lots to school, lest it be said that it invited and licensed them to do so, is to our minds an unreasonable proposition.

Ryan v. Towar, 87 N.W. 644, 645 (Mich. 1901).

A much different attitude toward trespassing children — one that would be concurred in by most courts today — is expressed in a later Michigan case, Lyshak v. City of Detroit, 88 N.W.2d 596 (Mich. 1958). The plaintiff, together with other boys, went through a hole in a fence surrounding a golf course owned and operated by the defendant. He was injured when he was struck by a flying golf ball. The defendant's employees were aware that children sneaked onto the course, and chased them off whenever they were discovered. In holding that the defendant owed a duty of reasonable care to the plaintiff, even though he was a trespasser, the court said (88 N.W.2d at 598-99):

> This case, we are told, concerns merely a trespassing child. And, as all know, a trespasser has no rights. A licensee has a few, and an invitee more, but as to a mere trespasser there is no duty of care. There being no duty there can be no negligence, and there being no negligence there can be no recovery by a trespassing child, though grievously hurt.
>
> And yet, if a defendant baits traps with stinking meat and thus lures a trespassing dog to destruction, the defendant has been held liable. There seems to be here a valid (and perplexing) analogy. The theory is that one is liable if he lures something to its destruction. In the case before us, a great city maintained, in a densely populated residential section, a park-like area, a golf course, with ample lawn, trees, and "a little creek." Upon this area, in the summer, children entered daily. They were drawn to it for purposes of play as naturally as the dog to the bait. The city of Detroit knew this, knowing it the only way a "city" can know anything, through the knowledge of its employees, servants, and agents. The professional at [the course] knew it. The supervising greenskeeper, who had charge of all men working on the golf course, and the repair and control of the fence, knew it. The official in charge of the . . . course knew it. However, knowing of the daily entrance of children onto the course, for purposes of childish play, the city, it is asserted, nevertheless continued to conduct thereon an enterprise of such character as to subject these children to risk of grave bodily injury, resulting in infant plaintiff's loss of one eye.

> We will assume that the infant plaintiff, like the dog, was a trespasser. The dog's owner, nevertheless, recovered for his loss. The boy, according to the trial court, is to get nothing. What kind of law is this? . . . It takes great legal skill to distinguish the trespassing boy, having viewed the allurements of the park-like area across the crowded city street, where he had the right to be, from the trespassing dog that followed his instincts to his destruction, denying recovery to the trespassing boy, but granting it to the owner of the trespassing dog. We are not sure we possess the skill required.

Some courts have refused to extend the doctrine to children over 14, although most follow Comment *c* to §339 and reject any arbitrary age limitation in favor of a case-by-case determination of whether "the child is still too young to appreciate the danger." See Annotation, 16 A.L.R.3d 25 (1967). For instance, in Burton v. State, 80 A.3d 856 (R.I. 2013), plaintiff was a seventeen year old who trespassed on state property with friends after drinking beer. Plaintiff attempted to remove bottles containing clear liquid from the property, one of which broke and splashed plaintiff with sulfuric acid, causing severe burns. In light of plaintiff's awareness of the potential dangers of transporting unknown substances, the court held that the attractive nuisance doctrine was inapplicable. *Burton* is consistent with cases holding that, regardless of the age of the child, the attractive nuisance doctrine does not apply if the condition is obvious and the child recognizes its danger. See Ross v. U.S., 910 F.2d 1422 (7th Cir. 1990) (applying Illinois law); Wiles v. Metzger, 473 N.W.2d 113 (Neb. 1991).

Problem 18

The presentation of the evidence has been completed in the case of Toth v. Livingston, a case tried to a jury in the superior court. The defendant has filed a motion for a directed verdict. There is little dispute as to the facts, and a fair summary of the evidence as it relates to liability is:

The plaintiff, Allen Toth, was injured when he fell through a dock belonging to the defendant, Barry Livingston. The dock extends into Loon Lake from the defendant's property on Snake Island, where the defendant has a summer home. The plaintiff testified that at the time of the accident he was ten years old, and that he went onto the dock, without permission of the defendant, at about 8:30 P.M. on June 16, two and a half years ago, to fish from its end. The plaintiff was large for his age and when he got about 15 feet from the end, a plank gave way under his weight and he fell through and was injured.

The defendant testified that he had built the dock 11 years before the accident. It extended into the lake about 45 feet and was 8 feet wide. The pine planks forming the top of the dock ran the width of the dock, and were 9 ¾ inches wide and 1¾ inches thick. The broken plank was admitted into evidence. The plaintiff's expert testified that it had rotted from underneath in the area of two knots in the plank. The plank had become sufficiently dry so that the knots would contribute to the weakness caused by the rot. The expert also testified that an inspection of the underside of the dock in the spring before the accident, and probably the previous fall as well, would have revealed the deterioration of the plank. On cross-examination the expert testified that viewed from above the plank would have appeared normal.

The defendant testified that he casually inspected the topside of the dock from time to time and that he had replaced two planks two or three years before the accident. He could not recall if he had made any inspection since then. He knew that he had not looked the dock over during the spring just prior to the accident. He had opened the house around the first of June and had moved his family to the lake the weekend before the accident. He testified that he did not know that this particular plank was in any way defective. He further testified that he was aware that youngsters used his dock for fishing from time to time, that he chased them off whenever this happened, and that he did not see the plaintiff go onto the dock on the evening of June 16. The plaintiff was spending the summer with his family at the lake and did not know that other people had been chased from the dock.

Assuming that your state generally follows the rules set forth in the Restatement (Second) of Torts, how would you argue on behalf of the defendant in support of the motion for a directed verdict? On behalf of the plaintiff in opposition to the motion? If the motion is denied, what instructions should the judge give to the jury?

Problem 19

Assume that Rowland v. Christian, below, is an opinion of the supreme court of your state. Should the trial judge on the facts of Problem 18 grant the defendant's motion for a directed verdict? If not, what instructions should be given to the jury?

Rowland v. Christian

69 Cal. 2d 108, 443 P.2d 561, 70 Cal. Rptr. 97 (1968)

[This is an appeal from an order of the trial judge granting the defendant's motion for summary judgment. The facts, as they appeared in the complaint, the answer, and the affidavits supporting and opposing summary judgment, were these: The plaintiff was a social guest in defendant's apartment. The plaintiff asked to use the bathroom, and while he was in the bathroom, a cracked handle of a water faucet broke in his hand, causing severe injuries. The defendant was aware that the handle was cracked, and had so informed her landlord and had asked that the handle be replaced, but she did not warn the plaintiff of the condition of the handle. The pleadings did not indicate whether the condition was obvious, although the defendant alleged in her answer that the plaintiff had failed to use his "eyesight" and that he was aware of the condition.]

Peters, J. . . . Section 1714 of the Civil Code provides: "Every one is responsible, not only for the result of his willful acts, but also for an injury occasioned to another by his want of ordinary care or skill in the management of his property or person, except so far as the latter has, willfully or by want of ordinary care, brought the injury upon himself. . . ." This code section, which has been unchanged in our law since 1872, states a civil law and not a common law principle.

Nevertheless, some common law judges and commentators have urged that the principle embodied in this code section serves as the foundation of our negligence law. Thus in a concurring opinion, Brett, M. R. in Heaven v. Pender (1883) 11 Q.B.D. 503, 509, states: "whenever one person is by circumstances placed in such a position with regard to another that every one of ordinary sense who did think would at once recognize that if he did not use ordinary care and skill in his own conduct with regard to those circumstances he would cause danger of injury to the person or property of the other, a duty arises to use ordinary care and skill to avoid such danger."

California cases have occasionally stated a similar view: "All persons are required to use ordinary care to prevent others being injured as the result of their conduct." Although it is true that some exceptions have been made to the general principle that a person is liable for injuries caused by his failure to exercise reasonable care in the circumstances, it is clear that in the absence of statutory provision declaring an exception to the fundamental principle enunciated by section 1714 of the Civil Code, no such exception should be made unless clearly supported by public policy.

A departure from this fundamental principle involves the balancing of a number of considerations; the major ones are the foreseeability of harm to the plaintiff, the degree of certainty that the plaintiff suffered injury, the closeness of the connection between the defendant's conduct and the injury suffered, the moral blame attached to the defendant's conduct, the policy of preventing future harm, the extent of the burden to the defendant and consequences to the community of imposing a duty to exercise care with resulting liability for breach, and the availability, cost, and prevalence of insurance for the risk involved.

One of the areas where this court and other courts have departed from the fundamental concept that a man is liable for injuries caused by his carelessness is with regard to the liability of a possessor of land for injuries to persons who have entered upon that land. It has been suggested that the special rules regarding liability of the possessor of land are due to historical considerations stemming from the high place which land has traditionally held in English and American thought, the dominance and prestige of the landowning class in England during the formative period of the rules governing the possessor's liability, and the heritage of feudalism.

The departure from the fundamental rule of liability for negligence has been accomplished by classifying the plaintiff either as a trespasser, licensee, or invitee and then adopting special rules as to the duty owed by the possessor to each of the classifications. Generally speaking a trespasser is a person who enters or remains upon land of another without a privilege to do so; a licensee is a person like a social guest who is not an invitee and who is privileged to enter or remain upon land by virtue of the possessor's consent, and an invitee is a business visitor who is invited or permitted to enter or remain on the land for a purpose directly or indirectly connected with business dealings between them.

Although the invitor owes the invitee a duty to exercise ordinary care to avoid injuring him, the general rule is that a trespasser and licensee or social guest are obliged to take the premises as they find them insofar as any alleged defective condition thereon may exist, and that the possessor of the land owes them only the duty of refraining from wanton or willful injury. The ordinary justification for the general rule severely restricting the occupier's liability to social guests is based on the theory that the guest should not expect special precautions to be made on his account and that if the host does not inspect and maintain his property the guest should not expect this to be done on his account.

An increasing regard for human safety has led to a retreat from this position, and an exception to the general rule limiting liability has been made as to active operations where an obligation to exercise reasonable care for the protection of the licensee has been imposed on the occupier of land. In an apparent attempt to avoid the general rule limiting liability, courts have broadly defined active operations, sometimes giving the term a strained construction in cases involving dangers known to the occupier. . . .

Another exception to the general rule limiting liability has been recognized for cases where the occupier is aware of the dangerous condition, the condition amounts to a concealed trap, and the guest is unaware of the trap. . . .

The cases dealing with the active negligence and the trap exceptions are indicative of the subtleties and confusion which have resulted from application of the common law principles governing the liability of the possessor of land. Similar confusion and complexity exist as to the definitions of trespasser, licensee, and invitee.

In refusing to adopt the rules relating to the liability of a possessor of land for the law of admiralty, the United States Supreme Court stated: "The distinctions which the common law draws between licensee and invitee were inherited from a culture deeply rooted to the land, a culture which traced many of its standards to a heritage of feudalism. In an effort to do justice in an industrialized urban society, with its complex economic and individual relationships, modern common-law courts have found it necessary to formulate increasingly subtle verbal refinements, to create subclassifications among traditional common-law categories, and to delineate fine gradations in the standards of care which the landowner owes to each. Yet even within a single jurisdiction, the classifications and subclassifications bred by the common law have produced confusion and conflict. As new distinctions have been spawned, older ones have become obscured. Through this semantic morass the common law has moved, unevenly and with hesitation, towards imposing on owners and occupiers a single duty of reasonable care in all the circumstances." (Footnotes omitted.) (Kermarec v. CompagnieGenerale, 358 U.S. 625, 630-631 [79 S. Ct. 406, 3 L. Ed. 2d 550, 554-555]). . . .

There is another fundamental objection to the approach to the question of the possessor's liability on the basis of the common law distinctions based upon the status of the injured party as a trespasser, licensee, or invitee. Complexity can be borne and confusion remedied where the underlying principles governing liability are based upon proper considerations. Whatever may have been the historical justifications for the common law distinctions, it is clear that those distinctions are not justified in the light of our modern society and that the complexity and confusion which has arisen is not due to difficulty in applying the original common law rules — they are all too easy to apply in their original formulation — but is due to the attempts to apply just rules in our modern society within the ancient terminology.

Without attempting to labor all of the rules relating to the possessor's liability, it is apparent that the classifications of trespasser, licensee, and invitee, the immunities from liability predicated upon those classifications, and the exceptions to those immunities, often do not reflect the major factors which should determine whether immunity should be conferred upon the possessor of land. Some of those factors, including the closeness of the connection between the injury and the defendant's conduct, the moral blame attached to the defendant's conduct, the policy of preventing future harm, and the prevalence and availability of insurance, bear little, if any, relationship to the classifications of trespasser, licensee and invitee and the existing rules conferring immunity.

Although in general there may be a relationship between the remaining factors and the classifications of trespasser, licensee, and invitee, there are many cases in which no such relationship may exist. Thus, although the foreseeability of harm to an invitee would ordinarily seem greater than the foreseeability of harm to a trespasser, in a particular case the opposite may be true. The same may be said of the issue of certainty of injury. The burden to the defendant and consequences to the community of imposing a duty to exercise care with resulting liability for breach may often be greater with respect to trespassers than with respect to invitees, but it by no means follows that this is true in every case. In many situations, the burden will be the same, i.e., the conduct necessary upon the defendant's part to meet the burden of exercising due care as to invitees will also meet his burden with respect to licensees and trespassers. The last of the major factors, the cost of insurance, will, of course, vary depending upon the rules of liability adopted, but there is no persuasive evidence that applying ordinary principles of negligence law to the land occupier's liability will materially reduce the prevalence of insurance due to increased cost or even substantially increase the cost. . . .

A man's life or limb does not become less worthy of protection by the law nor a loss less worthy of compensation under the law because he has come upon the land of another without permission or with permission but without a business purpose. Reasonable people do not ordinarily vary their conduct depending upon such matters, and to focus upon the status of the injured party as a trespasser, licensee, or invitee in order to determine the question whether the landowner has a duty of care, is contrary to our modern social mores and humanitarian values. The common law rules obscure rather than illuminate the proper considerations which should govern determination of the question of duty.

It bears repetition that the basic policy of this state set forth by the Legislature in section 1714 of the Civil Code is that everyone is responsible for an injury caused to another by his want of ordinary care or skill in the management of his property. The factors which may in particular cases warrant departure from this fundamental principle do not warrant the wholesale immunities resulting from the common law classifications, and we are satisfied that continued adherence to the common law distinctions can only lead to injustice or, if we are to avoid injustice, further fictions with the resulting complexity and confusion. We decline to follow and perpetuate such rigid classifications. The proper test to be applied to the liability of the possessor of land in accordance with section 1714 of the Civil Code is whether in the management of his property he has acted as a reasonable man in view of the probability of injury to others, and, although the plaintiff's status as a trespasser, licensee, or invitee may in the light of the facts giving rise to such status have some bearing on the question of liability, the status is not determinative.

Once the ancient concepts as to the liability of the occupier of land are stripped away, the status of the plaintiff relegated to its proper place in determining such liability, and ordinary principles of negligence applied, the result in the instant case presents no substantial difficulties. As we have seen, when we view the matters presented on the motion for summary judgment as we must, we must assume defendant Miss Christian was aware that the faucet handle was defective and dangerous, that the defect was not obvious, and that plaintiff was about to come in contact with the defective condition, and under the undisputed facts she neither remedied the condition nor warned plaintiff of it. Where the occupier of land is aware of a concealed condition involving in the absence of precautions an unreasonable risk of harm to those coming in contact with it, the trier of fact can reasonably conclude that a failure to warn or to repair the condition constitutes negligence. Whether or not a guest has a right to expect that his host will remedy dangerous conditions on his account, he should reasonably be entitled to rely upon a warning of the dangerous condition so that he, like the host, will be in a position to take special precautions when he comes in contact with it. . . .

The judgment is reversed.

TRAYNOR, C.J., TOBRINER, J., MOSK, J., and SULLIVAN, J., concurred.

BURKE, J. I dissent. In determining the liability of the occupier or owner of land for injuries, the distinctions between trespassers, licensees and invitees have been developed and applied by the courts over a period of many years. They supply a reasonable and workable approach to the problems involved, and one which provides the degree of stability and predictability so highly prized in the law. The unfortunate alternative, it appears to me, is the route taken by the majority in their opinion in this case; that such issues are to be decided on a case by case basis under the application of the basic law of negligence, bereft of the guiding principles and precedent which the law has heretofore attached by virtue of the relationship of the parties to one another.

Liability for negligence turns upon whether a duty of care is owed, and if so, the extent thereof. Who can doubt that the corner grocery, the large department store, or the financial institution owes a greater duty of care to one whom it has invited to enter its premises as a prospective customer of its wares or services than it owes to a trespasser seeking to enter after the close of business hours and for a nonbusiness or even an antagonistic purpose? I do not think it unreasonable or unfair that a social guest (classified by the law as a licensee, as was plaintiff here) should be obliged to take the premises in the same condition as his host finds them or permits them to be. Surely a homeowner should not be obliged to hover over his guests with warnings of possible dangers to be found in the condition of the home (e.g., waxed floors, slipping rugs, toys in unexpected places, etc., etc.). Yet today's decision appears to open the door to potentially unlimited liability despite the purpose and circumstances motivating the plaintiff in entering the premises of another, and despite the caveat of the majority that the status of the parties may "have some bearing on the question of liability . . ." whatever the future may show that language to mean.

In my view, it is not a proper function of this court to overturn the learning, wisdom and experience of the past in this field. Sweeping modifications of tort liability law fall more suitably within the domain of the Legislature, before which all affected interests can be heard and which can enact statutes providing uniform standards and guidelines for the future.

I would affirm the judgment for defendant.

Rowland was the first reported case in which a state court abrogated the rules under which the duty of a landowner depends upon the status of the entrant. The reception given *Rowland* in other jurisdictions has been mixed. Some have rejected it entirely. For example, the Washington Supreme Court rejected *Rowland* in Younce v. Ferguson, 724 P.2d 991 (Wash. 1986). The court offered the following reasons for retaining the traditional rules:

> The reasons proffered for continuing the distinctions include that the distinctions have been applied and developed over the years, offering a degree of stability and predictability and that a unitary standard would not lessen the confusion. Furthermore, a slow, piecemeal development rather than a wholesale change has been advocated. Some courts fear a wholesale change will delegate social policy decisions to the jury with minimal guidance from the court. Also, it is feared that the landowner could be subjected to unlimited liability.
>
> We find these reasons to be compelling. . . . We are not ready to abandon [the traditional classifications and exceptions] for a standard with no contours. . . . We do not choose to erase our developed jurisprudence for a blank slate.

724 P.2d at 995.

Many courts to consider the matter have adopted a middle ground, abolishing the licensee/invitee distinction, while retaining the trespasser category. See, e.g., Demag v. Better Power Equipment Inc., 197 Vt. 176 (Vt. 2014); Mallet v. Pickens, 522 S.E.2d 436 (W. Va. 1999); Koenig v. Koenig, 766 N.W.2d 635 (Iowa 2009). The court in Mounsey v. Ellard, 297 N.E.2d 43, n.7 (Mass. 1973), explained its decision to retain the trespasser category this way:

> We feel that there is significant difference in the legal status of one who trespasses on another's land as opposed to one who is on the land under some color of right — such as a

> licensee or invitee. For this reason, among others, we do not believe they should be placed in the same legal category. For example, one who jumps over a six foot fence to make use of his neighbor's swimming pool in his absence does not logically belong in the same legal classification as a licensee or invitee. Frankly, we are not persuaded as to the logic and reasoning in Rowland v. Christian in placing trespassers in the same legal status as licensees and invitees. The possible difference in classes of trespassers is miniscule compared to the others. These differences can be considered when they arise in future cases.

Equally as many courts have followed *Rowland* and abolished entirely the licensee, invitee, and trespasser categories. See, e.g., Ouellette v. Blanchard, 364 A.2d 631 (N.H. 1976). However, even those rejecting the trespasser classification have difficulty accepting the full implications of that rejection. For instance, the court in *Ouelette* stated (364 A.2d at 634):

> The character of and circumstances surrounding the intrusion will be relevant and important in determining the standard of care applicable to the landowner. When the intrusion is not foreseeable or is against the will of the landowner many intruders will be denied recovery as a matter of law. In other words, a landowner cannot be expected to maintain his premises in a safe condition for a wandering tramp or a person who enters against the known wishes of the landowner. Essentially the traditional tort test of foreseeability determines the liability or nonliability of the landowner in these cases.

And a dissenting judge in Soule v. Massachusetts Elec. Co., 390 N.E.2d 716 (Mass. 1979), a case upholding the *Mounsey* rule, observed (390 N.E.2d at 722-33):

> The Chief Justice's concurrence, speaking of the inequity of "abolishing all distinctions among tort plaintiffs who are invitees, licensees, or trespassers," may conjure up in some minds the spectre of an armed robber recovering damages for injuries suffered by him in tripping over a rug while engaged in his criminal adventure. It can be predicted flatly that that would not occur if the court should adopt quite frankly the position I espouse. The robber would be denied recovery, but not for the reason that the common law called him a "trespasser"; rather it would be for good and sufficient functional reasons that appeal to common sense. To make that common law catchword, or any other such as "invitee" or "licensee," in itself determinative, is a gateway to errors, as the history of the problem shows.

The California legislature, uneasy over the full implications of *Rowland*'s abrogation of the trespasser classification, enacted Cal. Civil Code §847, which insulates a landowner from liability for injury to a person on the land who has been convicted of any one of 25 listed crimes or of lesser included offenses that stem from the trespass. See also Colo. Rev. Stat. §13-21-115 (2006) (restoring categories of trespasser, licensee, and invitee); Tantimonico v. Allendale Mut. Ins. Co., 637 A.2d 1056 (R.I. 1994) (restoring category of trespasser). The debate over the categories of entrants continues, although the overall trend seems to be in favor of at least partial adoption of the *Rowland* approach. For a summary of case law from 26 states abrogating the traditional categories in some fashion, see the concurring opinion in Benham v. King, 700 N.W.2d 314 (Iowa 2005). The Restatement (Third) of Torts: Liability for Physical and Emotional Harm (2010) embraces *Rowland* and purports to abolish the categorical distinction among trespassers, licensees, and invitees. Thus, §51 has a general rule that "a land possessor owes a duty of reasonable care to entrants with regard to: (a) conduct by the land possessor that creates risks to entrants on the land; (b) artificial conditions on the land that pose risks to entrants on the land; (c) natural conditions on the land that pose risks to entrants on the land; and (d) other risks to entrants on the land when any of the affirmative duties . . . [are] applicable." Comment *c* to §51 makes clear that the purpose of the integration is to reduce confusion related to status classification and to develop a general, unitary standard without imposing an additional "burden of precaution" on land possessors.

Interestingly, the Restatement (Third) does not fully abolish status differentiation; §52 provides that a lower standard of care is owed to "flagrant trespassers." Comment *a* to §52 describes flagrant as "egregious or atrocious rather than . . . conspicuous," although the drafters left the exact meaning to the determination of the individual jurisdiction:

> §52. Duty of Land Possessors to Flagrant Trespassers
>
> (a) The only duty a land possessor owes to flagrant trespassers is the duty not to act in an intentional, willful, or wanton manner to cause physical harm.
>
> (b) Notwithstanding Subsection (a), a land possessor has a duty to exercise reasonable care for flagrant trespassers who reasonably appear to be imperiled and
>
> (1) helpless; or
>
> (2) unable to protect him- or herself.

One of the authors of this book has criticized the new Restatement's concept of flagrant trespassers, observing that it allows triers of fact to exercise too much discretion. See James A. Henderson, Jr., Status of Trespassers on Land, 44 Wake Forest L. Rev. 1071, 1073 (2009). See also Keith N. Hylton, Tort Duties of Landowners: A Positive Theory, 44 Wake Forest L. Rev. 1049 (2009) (criticizing the Restatement (Third) and providing an economic justification for maintaining the common law categories of entrants).

2. Responsibility of Common Carriers for the Safety of Their Passengers

In most states, common carriers are held to a duty to their passengers higher than that of reasonable care. The verbalization of the higher standard of care varies somewhat from state to state, with some courts holding carriers to the "highest" degree of care, "extraordinary care," "utmost care," "great caution," or some similar formulation. See, e.g., Bayer v. Crested Butte Mountain Resort, Inc., 960 P.2d 70 (Colo. 1998). The common carrier might also face expansive vicarious liability on account of its special status. See, e.g., Doe v. Celebrity Cruises, Inc., 394 F.3d 891 (11th Cir. 2004) (applying admiralty law to hold cruise ship line strictly liable, as a common carrier, for a crew member's assault on a passenger).

A few states have adhered to the general standard of reasonableness in these cases. See, e.g., Bethel v. New York City Transit Auth., 703 N.E.2d 1214, 1217 (N.Y. 1998), in which the court observed:

> In addition to its inherent inconsistency with the underlying concept of negligence in common-law tort doctrine . . . , our contemporary negligence jurisprudence has essentially undermined both of the main policy justifications for exacting of common carriers a duty of extraordinary care. The two most often expressed rationales for duty of highest care were

> (1) the perceived ultrahazardous nature of the instrumentalities of public rapid transit, and (2) the status of passengers and their relationship to the carrier, notably their total dependency upon the latter for safety precautions.
>
> We, however, have . . . held that the single, reasonable person standard is sufficiently flexible by itself to permit courts and juries fully to take into account the ultrahazardous nature of a tortfeasor's activity. . . . There is no empirical or policy basis why, in the case of common carriers, the reasonable care standard is not . . . sufficient to permit triers of fact to take into account all of the hazardous aspects of public transportation in deciding whether due care was exercised in a particular case.

Accordingly, the court ruled that a jury instruction that the defendant owed "the highest degree of care that human prudence and foresight can suggest" was reversible error. See also Nunez v. Professional Transit Management of Tuscon, Inc., 271 P.3d 1104, 1109 (Ariz. 2012) (concluding that "the appropriate standard of care in negligence actions by passengers against common carriers is the objective, reasonable person standard in traditional negligence law").

The definition of a common carrier has also been the subject of some litigation. One early opinion defined a common carrier as "one who engages in the transportation of persons or things from place to place for hire, and who holds himself out to the public as ready and willing to serve the public, indifferently, in the particular line in which he is engaged." Burnett v. Riter, 276 S.W. 347, 349 (Tex. Civ. App. 1925). More recently, a ski lift has been characterized as a common carrier (see Bayer v. Crested Butte Mountain Resort, Inc., 960 P.2d 70 (Colo. 1998)), as has an elevator in a public building (see Pruneda v. Otis Elevator Co., 828 P.2d 642 (Wash. Ct. App. 1992)) and an ambulance (see Nazareth v. Herndon Ambulance Service, Inc., 467 So. 2d 1076 (Fla. App.), *review denied,* 478 So. 2d 53 (Fla. 1985)). However, a carriage for hire that takes people on pleasure rides has been held not to be a common carrier (see Friedli v. Kerr, 2001 WL 177184 (Tenn. 2001)). Similarly, a whitewater raft operator is not a common carrier. See, e.g., Nat'l Union Fire Ins. Co. v. McMurray, 342 Fed. App. 956 (5th Cir. 2009) (determining that a whitewater raft operator was not a common carrier for insurance purposes).

Many commentators believe that fleets of autonomous (i.e., self-driving) vehicles soon will be available for hire in major U.S. metropolitan areas. Should such robotic taxis be considered common carriers? See Dylan LeValley, Autonomous Vehicle Liability—Application of Common Carrier Liability, 36 Seattle U. L. Rev. supra 5 (2013).

3. Responsibility of Operators of Motor Vehicles for the Safety of Their Passengers

A few states have laws that lower the standard of care owed by operators of automobiles to their nonpaying guests. Most of these laws are in the form of so-called automobile guest statutes, although the initial development came about through judicial decision. The first state to adopt the lower standard was Massachusetts. In Massaletti v. Fitzroy, 118 N.E. 168 (Mass. 1917), the court analogized a nonpaying guest in a horse-drawn wagon to property in the hands of a gratuitous bailee, who is liable only for gross negligence. This rule was later applied to automobiles, and remained the law in Massachusetts until it was overturned in 1971 by legislation, Mass. Gen. L., ch. 231, §85L, imposing a general duty of care on drivers of automobiles toward their passengers. In states in which the lower standard was judicially created, only Georgia continues to adhere to it. See Bickford v. Nolen, 240 S.E.2d 24 (Ga. 1977).

By far, the most important source of the lowered duty to nonpaying passengers is automobile guest legislation. But most of that legislation has been repealed, and now only a handful of states retain the modified duty. See, e.g., Code of Ala. §32-1-2, which establishes a "willful or wanton misconduct" standard. The Oregon statute, Or. Rev. Stat. §30.115, applies to operators of aircraft and watercraft, but not to operators of automobiles.

E. The Absence of a General Duty to Rescue

Section 314 of the Restatement (Second) of Torts provides:

> [t]he fact that the actor realizes or should realize that action on his part is necessary for another's aid or protection does not of itself impose upon him a duty to take such action.

The Supreme Court of New Hampshire dramatically described the absence of a general duty to rescue in Buch v. Amory Mfg. Co., 44 A. 809, 811 (N.H. 1897):

> I see my neighbor's two-year-old babe in dangerous proximity to the machinery of his windmill in his yard, and easily might, but do not, rescue him. I am not liable in damages to the child for his injuries . . . because the child and I are strangers, and am under no legal duty to protect him.

Although the Restatement and *Buch* remain the law today, courts have recognized that special circumstances may call for the imposition of a duty to act affirmatively to prevent harm to another. Thus, §37 of the Restatement (Third) of Torts: Liability for Physical and Emotional Harm (2010) states that "[a]n actor whose conduct has not created a risk of physical harm or emotional harm to another has no duty of care to the other unless a court determines that one of the affirmative duties provided in [other sections of the Restatement] is applicable." Perhaps the most typical set of circumstances involves a preexisting relationship between the potential rescuer and the person in need of rescue. Section 40 of the Restatement (Third) of Torts: Liability for Physical and Emotional Harm (2010) sets out a number of such relationships. Thus, an innkeeper has a duty to act reasonably to protect guests from harm; a possessor of land held open to the public owes a similar duty to those who have been invited to enter upon the land. If the potential rescuer has voluntarily taken custody of the rescuee under circumstances where care to protect against harm is expected from that relationship, a duty to act affirmatively exists. An example would be the relationship between summer camp counselors and the campers under their charge.

Even absent a preexisting relationship, courts have been willing to imply an affirmative duty to act under certain conditions. Consider the following cases.

Erie Railroad Co. v. Stewart

40 F.2d 855 (6th Cir.), cert. denied, 282 U.S. 843 (1930)

Hickenlooper, C.J. Stewart, plaintiff below, was a passenger in an automobile truck, sitting on the front seat to the right of the driver, a fellow employee of the East Ohio Gas Company. He recovered a judgment in the District Court for injuries received when the truck was struck by one of the defendant's trains at the 123d street crossing in the city of

Cleveland. Defendant maintained a watchman at this crossing, which was admittedly heavily traveled, but the watchman was either within the shanty or just outside of it as the train approached, and he gave no warning until too late to avoid the accident. Two alleged errors are relied upon. . . .

The second contention of appellant presents the question whether the court erred in charging the jury that the absence of the watchman, where one had been maintained by the defendant company at a highway crossing over a long period of time to the knowledge of the plaintiff, would constitute negligence as a matter of law. In the present case it is conceded that the employment of the watchman by the defendant was voluntary upon its part, there being no statute or ordinance requiring the same, and that plaintiff had knowledge of this practice and relied upon the absence of the watchman as an assurance of safety and implied invitation to cross. We are not now concerned with the extent of the duty owing to one who had no notice of the prior practice. . . . The question is simply whether there was any positive duty owing to the plaintiff in respect to the maintenance of such watchman, and whether a breach of such duty is so conclusively shown as to justify a peremptory charge of negligence. The question whether such negligence was the proximate cause of the injury was properly submitted to the jury.

Where the employment of a watchman or other precaution is required by statute, existence of an absolute duty to the plaintiff is conclusively shown, and failure to observe the statutory requirement is negligence per se. . . . Conversely, where there is no duty prescribed by statute or ordinance, it is usually a question for the jury whether the circumstances made the employment of a watchman necessary in the exercise of due care. Where the voluntary employment of a watchman was unknown to the traveler upon the highway, the mere absence of such watchman could probably not be considered as negligence toward him as a matter of law, for in such case there is neither an established duty positively owing to such traveler as a member of the general public, nor had he been led into reliance upon the custom. The question would remain simply whether the circumstances demanded such employment. But where the practice is known to the traveler upon the highway, and such traveler has been educated into reliance upon it, some positive duty must rest upon the railway with reference thereto. The elements of invitation and assurance of safety exist in this connection no less than in connection with contributory negligence. The company has established for itself a standard of due care while operating its trains across the highway, and, having led the traveler into reliance upon such standard, it should not be permitted thereafter to say that no duty required, arose from or attached to these precautions.

This duty has been recognized as not only actual and positive, but as absolute, in the sense that the practice may not be discontinued without exercising reasonable care to give warning of such discontinuance, although the company may thereafter do all that would otherwise be reasonably necessary. Conceding for the purposes of this opinion that, in cases where a watchman is voluntarily employed by the railway in an abundance of precaution, the duty is not absolute, in the same sense as where it is imposed by statute, still, if there be some duty, it cannot be less than that the company must use reasonable care to see that reliance by members of the educated public upon its representation of safety is not converted into a trap. Responsibility for injury will arise if the service be negligently performed or abandoned without other notice of that fact. If this issue of negligent performance be disputed, the question would still be for the jury under the present concession. But if the evidence in the case justifies only the conclusion of lack of due care, or if the absence of the watchman or the failure to give other notice of his withdrawal be wholly unexplained, so that but one inference may be drawn therefrom, the court is warranted in instructing the jury that, in that particular case, negligence appears as a matter of law.

So, in the present case, the evidence conclusively establishes the voluntary employment of a watchman, knowledge of this fact and reliance upon it by the plaintiff, a duty, therefore, that the company, through the watchman, will exercise reasonable care in warning such travelers as plaintiff, the presence of the watchman thereabouts, and no explanation of the failure to warn. Therefore, even though the duty be considered as qualified, rather than absolute, a prima facie case was established by plaintiff, requiring the defendant to go forward with evidence to rebut the presumption of negligence thus raised, or else suffer a verdict against it on this point. . . .

The judgment of the District Court is affirmed.

A similar reliance-based duty was expressed by the court in Lacey v. United States, 98 F. Supp. 219, 220 (D. Mass. 1951):

> It is true that, while the common law imposes no duty to rescue, it does impose on the Good Samaritan the duty to act with due care *once he has undertaken rescue operations.* The rationale is that other would-be rescuers will rest on their oars in the expectation that effective aid is being rendered.

The rationale was applied in Cottam v. CVS Pharmacy, 764 N.E.2d 814 (Mass. 2002). The court held that although a pharmacist has no duty to warn customers of side effects of prescription drugs, if the pharmacist has provided a detailed warning, he or she must use care to make sure that the warnings are complete.

Section 42 of the Restatement (Third) of Torts: Liability for Physical and Emotional Harm (2010) recognizes a duty to render aid premised on a "voluntary undertaking" by the defendant:

> An actor who undertakes to render services to another and who knows or should know that the services will reduce the risk of physical harm to the other has a duty of reasonable care to the other in conducting the undertaking if:
>
> (a) the failure to exercise such care increases the risk of harm beyond that which existed without the undertaking, or
>
> (b) the person to whom the services are rendered or another relies on the actor's exercising reasonable care in the undertaking.

Observe that failing to follow through with an undertaking does not impose liability unless the above conditions are met. In Morgan v. Scott, 291 S.W.3d 622, 632 (Ky. 2009), the Supreme Court of Kentucky ruled that a car dealership was under no duty of care when it violated its own policy in allowing a customer to test-drive a truck unsupervised because "failure to observe its own in-house policy did not increase the risk of harm."

Suppose that a pharmaceutical company is the only manufacturer of injectable Vitamin A, which it knows is needed by some individuals who cannot absorb Vitamin A through diet and who will be at risk for blindness, infections, and other serious illnesses without the company's product. Could the reliance rationale be extended to prevent the company from stopping production of injectable Vitamin A? On these facts, the court in Lacognata v. Hospira, Inc., 2012 WL 6962884 at *2 (M.D. Fla. 2012), declined to adopt such a duty: "There is no authority that supports Plaintiff's argument that a drug manufacturer, like Hospira, has a duty to continue supplying a patient with a drug that it knows the patient relies upon for his or her medical health." Note that the court's decision is supported by the requirement in Section 42 that defendant's conduct must increase plaintiff's risk of harm "beyond that which existed without the [defendant's] undertaking."

Section 44 addresses the more particular situation in which the defendant has "taken charge" of a helpless plaintiff:

> (a) An actor who, despite no duty to do so, takes charge of another who reasonably appears to be:
>
> (1) imperiled; and
>
> (2) helpless or unable to protect himself or herself
>
> has a duty to exercise reasonable care while the other is within the actor's charge.
>
> (b) An actor who discontinues aid or protection is subject to a duty of reasonable care to refrain from putting the other in a worse position than existed before the actor took charge of the other and, if the other reasonably appears to be in imminent peril of serious bodily harm at the time of termination, to exercise reasonable care with regard to the peril before terminating the rescue.

The court in Wakulich v. Mraz, 785 N.E.2d 843 (Ill. 2003), applied the predecessors to these provisions, Sections 323 and 324 of the Restatement (Second) of Torts. In this case, plaintiff brought suit individually and as representative of the estate of her deceased 16-year-old daughter against the hosts of a party and their father. Plaintiff alleged that, after the hosts had applied intense social pressure to persuade her daughter to become intoxicated, they "placed her in the family room of their home, where they observed her "vomiting profusely and making gurgling sounds." They later removed her vomit-saturated blouse and placed a pillow under her head to prevent aspiration." Id. at 846. Beyond these measures, however, the hosts "allegedly refused to drive [plaintiff's daughter] home, did not contact her parents, did not seek medical attention, and actually prevented other individuals at the home from calling 911 or seeking other medical intervention." Id. at 846. The court held that these allegations validly stated a cause of action for negligent performance of a voluntary undertaking.

In Long v. Broadlawns Medical Center, 656 N.W.2d 71 (Iowa 2002), the court applied the "voluntary undertaking" concept to a hospital and mental health care provider based on a promise by the latter to the decedent, Jillene Long, that they would warn her before her husband was released from the hospital. Long's husband had physically abused her for years and, on July 19, 1996, fired a gun at her. After the initial shooting incident, Long's husband checked himself into a hospital to receive voluntary psychiatric care. A social worker at the hospital promised Long that she would be notified when her husband was discharged, but when he was released on July 25, 1996, no one at the hospital notified Long. Her husband murdered her later that evening. The Iowa Supreme Court first distinguished Tarasoff v. Regents of the University of California, 551 P.2d 334 (1976), set forth below at p. 279, in which the Supreme Court of California imposed a duty on psychotherapists to warn third parties of foreseeable acts of violence that might be perpetrated against them by the psychotherapists' patients. The *Long* court felt that it was unnecessary to address *Tarasoff*'s expansive duty principles because, in the case before it, an actual promise of notification had been made by the defendant hospital and mental health care provider. Thus, "the real issue [in the case] arises from whether [defendants] failed to exercise reasonable care in performing a promise to warn [Long] of [her husband's] discharge, thereby increasing the risk of harm to her or resulting in harm to her because of her reliance on the promised warning." Id. at 81. With respect to that issue, the court concluded that a triable question had been presented.

Tubbs v. Argus

140 Ind. App. 695, 225 N.E.2d 841 (1967)

PFAFF, J. This appeal arises as a result of demurrer to appellant's Second Amended Complaint which was sustained and judgment entered thereon upon the failure and refusal of the appellant to plead over.

The facts material to a determination of the issues raised on this appeal may be summarized as follows: . . .

. . . [T]he appellant was riding as a guest passenger in the right front seat of an automobile owned and operated by the appellee . . . [when it] was driven over the south curb of West Hampton Drive and into a tree, resulting in injury to the appellant. After the said collision, the appellee abandoned the automobile and did not render reasonable aid and assistance to the injured appellant. Appellant alleges that she suffered additional injuries as a result of appellee's failure to render reasonable aid and assistance and seeks to recover only for these additional injuries.

In her assignment of errors, the appellant avers that the trial court erred in sustaining the demurrer to appellant's Second Amended Complaint. More specifically, the appellant alleges that appellee's failure to render reasonable aid and assistance constituted a breach of a common law duty. . . .

The appellant herein is seeking recovery for additional injuries arising from the appellee's failure to render reasonable aid and assistance, and not for the initial injuries which resulted from the operation of the automobile [since she was precluded from recovering for ordinary negligence under Indiana's automobile guest law]. . . .

At common law, there is no general duty to aid a person who is in peril. L. S. Ayres & Company v. Hicks (1941), 220 Ind. 86, 40 N.E.2d 334. However, in *L. S. Ayres & Company*, the Supreme Court of Indiana held that "under some circumstances, moral and humanitarian considerations may require one to render assistance to another who has been injured, even though the injury was not due to negligence on his part and may have been caused by the negligence of the injured person. Failure to render assistance in such a situation may constitute actionable negligence if the injury is aggravated through lack of due care." Tippecanoe Loan, etc., Co. v. Cleveland, etc., R. Co. (1915), 57 Ind. App. 644, 104 N.E. 866, 106 N.E. 739.

In Tippecanoe Loan, etc., Co. v. Cleveland, etc. R. Co., this court held that a railroad company was liable for failing to provide medical assistance to an employee who was injured through no fault of the railroad company, but who was rendered helpless and by reason of which the employee's injuries were aggravated.

The Supreme Court of Indiana in *L. S. Ayres,* supra, found the appellant liable for aggravation of injuries when it failed to extricate the appellee, a six-year-old boy, whose fingers were caught in the moving parts of an escalator, even though the jury conclusively established that the appellant was not negligent with respect to the choice, construction, or manner of operating the elevator. In so holding, the Supreme Court stated that it may be deduced from Tippecanoe Loan, etc. Co. v. Cleveland, etc. R. Co., "that there may be a legal obligation to take positive or affirmative steps to effect the rescue of a person who is helpless and in a situation of peril, when the one proceeded against is a master or an invitor or when the injury resulted from use of an instrumentality under the control of the defendant."

The doctrine of law as set forth in Restatement (Second) of Torts, §322 adds credence to these two Indiana cases. ". . . If the actor knows or has reason to know that by his conduct,

whether tortious or innocent, he has caused such bodily harm to another as to make him helpless and in danger of future harm, the actor is under a duty to exercise reasonable care to prevent such further harm." . . .

In the case at bar, the appellant received her injuries from an instrumentality under the control of the appellee. Under the rule stated above and on the authority of the cases cited, this was a sufficient relationship to impose a duty to render reasonable aid and assistance, a duty for the breach of which the appellee is liable for the additional injuries suffered.

We are of the opinion that the court below erred in sustaining the demurrer to appellant's Second Amended Complaint.

This cause is reversed and remanded for proceedings not inconsistent with this opinion.

Judgment reversed.

Bierly and Smith, JJ., concur.

What level of "conduct, whether tortious or innocent," on the part of defendant is necessary to invoke the duty outlined in *Tubbs*? In Rasnick v. Krishna Hospitality, Inc., 713 S.E.2d 835 (Ga. 2011), plaintiff's 77-year-old husband died shortly after being found unresponsive by a housekeeper in his room at defendant's hotel. Plaintiff had called the hotel numerous times the evening prior to her husband's death, asking them to check on him since he could not be reached and she believed he might require medical aid. The hotel staff declined to do so and eventually stopped answering her phone calls. The court refused to recognize a duty to render aid on the part of defendant, reasoning that "any risk or problem stemming from a medical condition unrelated to and not caused by the guest's stay at the facility is not internal *to the premises* but rather internal *to the guest*." Id. at 838. The court also declined to adopt Section 314A of the Restatement (Second) of Torts (1965), which imposes upon a common carrier, innkeeper, or public premises invitor a duty to provide "first aid after it knows or has reason to know that [its guests] are ill or injured, and to care for them until they can be cared for by others." Three dissenting justices argued that "[t]he evidence in this case shows that the defendant motel was placed on notice of [plaintiff's husband's] medication, his likely presence in the hotel room due to his earlier departure from work, his failure to respond to phone calls, and his wife's great concern. Under this evidence, a jury could find that the motel had reason to know that [he] was ill or injured, thereby triggering its duty to protect him from further danger." Id. at 841.

Some courts have extended the rule in *Tubbs* to situations where the defendant acted in self-defense and caused injury to the plaintiff, but subsequently failed to notify authorities or otherwise rescue the plaintiff. In Kuntz v. Montana Thirteenth Judicial District, 995 P.2d 951 (Mont. 2000), the defendant faced criminal charges after failing to notify authorities or otherwise rescue her boyfriend. Defendant admitted that she stabbed her boyfriend, but claimed that she did so in self-defense after the victim attacked her by pulling her hair, shaking her, and slamming her into the stove. Defendant then left the victim and did not notify the authorities or otherwise attempt to help the bleeding victim. The prosecution argued that, even if the defendant was successful in her self-defense claim, she could be held criminally liable for her failure to rescue. The trial court denied defendant's motion to dismiss the criminal information and defendant appealed by writ. In denying defendant's writ, the Montana Supreme Court agreed with the prosecution, finding a duty to rescue. Although this was a criminal case, the court wrote broadly, suggesting that a duty to rescue exists in both criminal and tort law. The court ruled that the defendant may be held liable for a failure to rescue if she has full knowledge of the injuries, the failure to rescue is the cause-in-fact of the injuries, and the defendant has already exercised her right to seek and secure safety from physical harm. For a criticism of this case, see Penny Lee Merreot, Rescuing Your Attacker: State of Montana *ex rel.* Kuntz v. Montana Thirteenth Judicial District Court, 63 Mont. L. Rev. 229 (2002), in which the author argues that it is "absurd" to hold a person liable for failing to rescue a person that the self-defense doctrine permits her to kill. Compare Estate of Cilley v. Lane, 985 A.2d 481 (Me. 2009) (holding that defendant, an ex-girlfriend of plaintiff, was not liable for failing to rescue plaintiff, who was a trespasser in her house, after he accidentally shot himself).

The legislatures of a few states have enacted duty-to-rescue statutes. The Vermont statute, the Duty to Aid the Endangered Act (Vt. Stat. Ann. tit. 12, §519), which calls for a fine of up to $100 for its violation, provides:

> (a) A person who knows that another is exposed to grave physical harm shall, to the extent that the same can be rendered without danger or peril to himself or without interference with important duties owed to others, give reasonable assistance to the exposed person unless that assistance or care is being provided by others.

Minnesota and Rhode Island require individuals "at the scene of an emergency" to provide "reasonable assistance" to those who are exposed to or have suffered "grave physical harm." Minn. Stat. Ann. §604A.01; R.I. Gen. Laws §11-56-1. For discussion, see Marc A. Franklin, Vermont Requires Rescue: A Comment, 25 Stan. L. Rev. 51 (1972); A. D. Woozley, A Duty to Rescue: Some Thoughts on Criminal Liability, 69 Va. L. Rev. 1273 (1983). More common are statutes that impose duties on those involved in automobile accidents to render or seek medical assistance for others injured in the accident, see, e.g., Ky. Rev. Stat. §189.580(1), or that require hospital emergency rooms not to turn away patients in distress until their condition has been stabilized, see, e.g., Thomas v. Christ Hospital, 328 F.3d 890 (7th Cir. 2003) (construing federal Emergency Medical Treatment and Active Labor Act). Occasionally, civil suits have been brought for injuries resulting from the breaches of such statutes. See Annotation, 80 A.L.R.2d 299 (1961). Section 38 of the Restatement (Third) of Torts: Liability for Physical and Emotional Harm (2010) advises courts to consider the existence of affirmative duty statutes, such as those requiring health care professionals to report signs of suspected child abuse, when deciding whether to impose an affirmative tort law duty.

Despite these exceptions, the absence of a general duty to rescue remains one of the more controversial features of Anglo-American tort law. Perhaps compounding this problem is the fact that courts stand ready to impose negligence liability on rescuers if the job is botched. See, e.g., Dunson v. Friedlander Realty, 369 So. 2d 792 (Ala. 1979); Farwell v. Keaton, 240 N.W.2d 217 (Mich. 1976). This might leave an observer to conclude that the law has it backwards—first, by refusing to impose a general obligation to rescue and, second, by threatening with liability those noble souls who do come to the aid of others.

With respect to this second concern, all states have enacted "Good Samaritan" statutes designed to protect rescuers from claims arising out of the rendering of gratuitous assistance in an emergency. Some of the statutes protect only medical practitioners; others protect additional persons, such as fire fighters, rescue squad members, and police officers. At least one court distinguishes between individual rescuers and the "rescue squads" who employ them. See Murray v. Plainfield Rescue Squad, 46 A.3d 1262 (N.J. 2012) (holding that New Jersey immunity statute insulates individual members of rescue squad from liability but not squad as an entity). Many statutes specify that all persons who render aid are protected against liability for negligence, while others require that the aid be delivered voluntarily. See, e.g., Verdugo v. Target Corp., 327 P.3d 774 (Cal. 2014) ("No person who in good faith, and not for compensation, renders emergency medical or nonmedical care at the scene of an emergency shall be liable for any civil damages resulting from any act or omission.") (quoting Cal. Health & Saf. Code, §1799.102 (a)). For a complete listing of the statutes, see 3 David W. Louisell & Harold Williams, Medical Malpractice, §§21.01-21.05 (2002).

Few empirical studies have been undertaken to systematically examine the effects of these various legal regimes on the incidence of rescue, non-rescue, and other behavioral effects related to rescue. However, in David A. Hyman, Rescue Without Law: An Empirical Perspective on the Duty to Rescue, 84 Tex. L. Rev. 653 (2006), the author examined more than 20 independent data sources to compile what he termed a "law and reality" picture of the state of rescue in America. The findings are summarized as follows (id. at 656-57):

> [P]roven cases of non-rescues are extraordinarily rare, and proven cases of rescues are exceedingly common — often in hazardous circumstances, where a duty to rescue would not apply in the first instance. Controlled for population, the frequency of proven cases of rescue declined in the first forty years of the twentieth century, but has remained fairly stable or increased since then. Most rescuers are young males, particularly when strangers are rescued or the rescue is risky. States that have adopted a duty to rescue rule have not seen an increase or decrease in the number of non-risky rescues or in the number of accidental deaths. The rate of non-risky rescue in these states is also lower than that in comparable states that do not have a duty to rescue. There is no evidence that prosecutors are misusing these laws; indeed, after a combined total of almost eighty years of experience in three states, there have been no prosecutions for non-rescue — most likely because there were never any actionable non-rescues in those states to begin with.
>
> Finally, if the no-duty rule that prevails in forty-seven of the fifty states is "sending the wrong message" about the desirability of undertaking a rescue, it is doing a singularly poor job of it. Indeed, even in the absence of a statutory duty, Americans appear to be too willing to undertake rescue if one judges by the number of injuries and deaths among rescuers. Indeed, proven rescuer deaths outnumber proven deaths from non-rescue by approximately 70:1.
>
> These results suggest that both more and less is at stake in the debate over the duty to rescue than has been commonly appreciated. The handful of highly salient anecdotes of non-rescue that everyone knows about are extraordinarily unrepresentative of the real world. Simply stated, rescue is the rule — even if it is not the law.

Problem 20

You are the attorney of Thomas Potter, whom you have represented in a variety of matters over the years. Potter is the treasurer of The First National Bank of Canton, is married and the father of three children, and is actively engaged in the community. Potter called you last week after he received a letter from Mark Granger, who identified himself as the lawyer for George Harper. Potter read the letter to you over the telephone, and in substance it stated the following: George Harper is the father of Martha Harper, who was killed in an automobile accident. Martha was a passenger in an automobile driven by Peter Blake. Blake's automobile collided with a tree after being forced off the road by another automobile. Both Blake and Harper were seriously injured, and Harper later died in a local hospital. After the accident, the driver of the other automobile, a man now identified by Blake as Potter, came up to the Blake car. He looked into the window, and told Blake that he would send for help. When help did not arrive after an hour, Blake set out to look for a house from which he could call an ambulance. He was able to locate a telephone and call an ambulance, but too late for Harper who died from the substantial head injuries shortly after her arrival at the hospital. Granger said that he was preparing to sue Potter on behalf of Harper, claiming both that Potter negligently drove his automobile in a way that forced Blake off the road, and for failing to follow through on his promise to call for help.

According to Potter, the actual events leading up to Granger's letter are these: For a period of several months, Potter had an affair with Valerie Whitman, a vice president of the bank. Whitman is also married. About three months ago, Potter drove to a nearby city to confer with a lawyer about a real estate transaction. Whitman had driven to the same city, also on business. When they finished, they had a hurried dinner, and then drove in Potter's automobile to a seldom-used country road. After parking beside the road for about 30 minutes, he pulled back onto the road to return to where Whitman had left her car. But a few minutes later, a car came speeding from the opposite direction, half in Potter's lane. Potter slammed on his brakes and the other car swerved sharply to its right, narrowly avoiding a collision. The other car ran off the road and hit a tree. Potter stopped, got out of his car, and ran back to the other car. When he got there, he found two people in the car, a young man behind the wheel and a young woman next to him. The man was shaken but conscious; the woman was bleeding profusely about her head. Potter panicked, and fearing exposure of his affair, he ran to his car, while the driver was shouting to him to get help. Potter said nothing to Blake at any time. He returned to his car, drove Whitman to her car, and then returned home. Neither Potter nor Whitman reported the accident.

On the day following the accident, a police officer visited Potter at his office. The officer recounted in a general way the occurrence of the accident, and said that Blake stated in his report to the police that he thought that Potter was the driver of the other car and the person, who after the accident, looked into the window of his car and said he would get help. Blake said he was able to identify Potter as he has seen him on several occasions in the bank. In response to the officer's questions, Potter denied that he was there. He told the officer that he had returned home after completing his business by a route that was many miles from the scene of the accident. He explained to the officer that he often took the "back way" home when he wanted to sort out his thoughts about business matters. As the officer was leaving, he expressed outrage that anybody could be so indifferent as not to even call the police. The officer had spoken with the doctor attending Harper at the hospital, and she stated that she couldn't be sure that Harper would have survived even with prompt care. Potter told you that he felt better about the incident after hearing that Harper probably would have died anyway. "What I did can't be so bad, can it? After all, it didn't make any difference." In any event, Potter said that the police and his family have all apparently accepted his story without question.

The police file on the accident contains a statement by Charles Herzog. Just before the accident, Herzog was driving on the same road and a car of the same description as Blake's almost forced him off the road. According to Herzog, the car must have been going 50 to 60 miles an hour. The file also contains a diagram of the scene of the accident made by the investigating police officer showing skid marks leading to the Blake car, starting from a point well into the wrong side of the road. The police report indicated that Blake was arrested for vehicular homicide, reckless driving, speeding, and operating without an operator's license. The case is still pending in Superior Court.

At the time of the accident, Blake was 22 years old, and Harper was 16. Blake had been convicted on two earlier occasions for speeding and reckless driving. His operator's license had been suspended three weeks before the accident.

Granger is known as a lawyer who processes personal injury cases quickly and rarely takes cases to court. Potter is coming to your office tomorrow to discuss the matter. In deciding what advice to give him, assume that your state supreme court has adopted the Model Rules of Professional Conduct.

Model Rules of Professional Conduct

American Bar Association (2016)
Rule 1.2 Scope of Representation and Allocation of Authority Between Client and Lawyer

(a) Subject to paragraphs (c) and (d), a lawyer shall abide by a client's decisions concerning the objectives of representation and, as required by Rule 1.4, shall consult with the client as to the means by which they are to be pursued. . . .

(d) A lawyer shall not counsel a client to engage, or assist a client, in conduct that the lawyer knows is criminal or fraudulent, but a lawyer may discuss the legal consequences of any proposed course of conduct with a client and may counsel or assist a client to make a good faith effort to determine the validity, scope, meaning or application of the law.

Rule 1.6 Confidentiality of Information

(a) A lawyer shall not reveal information relating to the representation of a client unless the client gives informed consent, the disclosure is impliedly authorized in order to carry out the representation or the disclosure is permitted by paragraph (b).

(b) A lawyer may reveal information relating to the representation of a client to the extent the lawyer reasonably believes necessary:

(1) to prevent reasonably certain death or substantial bodily harm;

(2) to prevent the client from committing a crime or fraud that is reasonably certain to result in substantial injury to the financial interests or property of another and in furtherance of which the client has used or is using the lawyer's services;

(3) to prevent, mitigate or rectify substantial injury to the financial interests or property of another that is reasonably certain to result or has resulted from the client's commission of a crime or fraud in furtherance of which the client has used the lawyer's services; . . .

Rule 1.16 Declining or Terminating Representation

(a) [A] lawyer shall not represent a client or, where representation has commenced, shall withdraw from the representation of a client if:

(1) the representation will result in violation of the rules of professional conduct or other law; . . .

(b) [A] lawyer may withdraw from representing a client if:

(1) withdrawal can be accomplished without material adverse effect on the interests of the client;

(2) the client persists in a course of action involving the lawyer's services that the lawyer reasonably believes is criminal or fraudulent;

(3) the client has used the lawyer's services to perpetrate a crime or fraud;

(4) the client insists upon taking action that the lawyer considers repugnant or with which the lawyer has a fundamental disagreement; . . . or

(7) other good cause for withdrawal exists.

Rule 2.1 Advisor

In representing a client, a lawyer shall exercise independent professional judgment and render candid advice. In rendering advice, a lawyer may refer not only to law but to other considerations such as moral, economic, social and political factors, that may be relevant to the client's situation.

Rule 3.1 Meritorious Claims and Contentions

A lawyer shall not bring or defend a proceeding, or assert or controvert an issue therein, unless there is a basis for doing so that is not frivolous, which includes a good faith argument for an extension, modification or reversal of existing law. A lawyer for the defendant in a criminal proceeding, or the respondent in a proceeding that could result in incarceration, may nevertheless so defend the proceeding as to require that every element of the case be established.

Rule 3.3 Candor Toward the Tribunal

(a) A lawyer shall not knowingly:

(1) make a false statement of fact or law to a tribunal or fail to correct a false statement of material fact or law previously made to the tribunal by the lawyer;

(2) fail to disclose to the tribunal legal authority in the controlling jurisdiction known to the lawyer to be directly adverse to the position of the client and not disclosed by opposing counsel; or

(3) offer evidence that the lawyer knows to be false. If a lawyer, the lawyer's client, or a witness called by the lawyer, has offered material evidence and the lawyer comes to know of its falsity, the lawyer shall take reasonable remedial measures, including, if necessary, disclosure to the tribunal. A lawyer may refuse to offer evidence, other than the testimony of a defendant in a criminal matter, that the lawyer reasonably believes is false.

(b) A lawyer who represents a client in an adjudicative proceeding and who knows that a person intends to engage, is engaging or has engaged in criminal or fraudulent conduct related to the proceeding shall take reasonable remedial measures, including, if necessary, disclosure to the tribunal. . . .

Rule 4.1 Truthfulness in Statements to Others

In the course of representing a client a lawyer shall not knowingly:

(a) make a false statement of material fact or law to a third person; or

(b) fail to disclose a material fact to a third person when disclosure is necessary to avoid assisting a criminal or fraudulent act by a client, unless disclosure is prohibited by Rule 1.6.

Prior to the adoption of amendments in 2002, the Model Rules strictly limited the circumstances in which an attorney had discretion to reveal confidential client information. Under an earlier version of Rule 1.6, lawyers had discretion to reveal confidential information only "to prevent the client from committing a criminal act which the lawyer believes is likely to result in imminent death or substantial bodily harm." No discretion was granted to reveal confidential information in order to prevent or rectify criminal behavior that threatened or caused substantial financial injury. An ABA Commission Report, published in 2000, stated that the then-current version of Rule 1.6 was "out of step with public policy and the values of the legal profession." It also was out of step with the vast majority of states, whose bar associations and high courts had refused to go along with the Model Rules' earlier narrow recommendations on permissive disclosure. Thus, the Commission proposed a sweeping package of changes, the bulk of which were adopted by the American Bar Association's House of Delegates. If the amendments to the Model Rules had not been adopted, how would your handling of the Potter case have been affected?

The Lawyer's Professional Responsibility: The Relevance of Moral Considerations

It is clear in the preceding problem that the client, Thomas Potter, has committed a crime in lying to the police on the police report. But many might regard lying on a police report to be a venial sin at most — no harm, no foul. And everybody does it, don't they? But his fabricated story, if accepted by George Harper, also will have the effect of foreclosing any claim in tort Harper might have had against Potter. Should that have an impact on what advice you will give Potter when you talk to him tomorrow?

Not surprisingly, there is a good deal of controversy over the extent to which a lawyer in representing a client should be influenced by the lawyer's notions of right and wrong — of morality. Most of the debate has been in the context of a client whose goals are legal, but for some reason are repugnant to the lawyer, and perhaps to a large segment of society. One article that argues for a prominent role for the moral views of the lawyer is Richard Wasserstrom, Lawyers as Professionals: Some Moral Issues, 5 Human Rights 1 (1975). He poses a number of hypotheticals in which he suggests that the lawyer should not help a client achieve otherwise lawful aims: the client who wants to disinherit a child because of the child's opposition to the war in Vietnam; the client who wants to take advantage of a loophole in the tax laws available only to the rich; the client who wants to set up a corporation to manufacture a socially harmful product, such as cigarettes (military-style assault weapons might furnish an apt contemporary example.)

A different, and the more traditional, view is expressed in Pepper, The Lawyer's Amoral Ethical Role: A Defense, A Problem and Some Possibilities, 1986 Am. B. Found. Res. J. 613, 617-18:

> Our first premise is that law is intended to be a public good which increases autonomy. The second premise is that increasing individual autonomy is morally good. The third step is that in a highly legalized society such as ours, autonomy is often dependent upon access to the law. Put simply, first-class citizenship is dependent on access to the law. And while access to law — to the creation and use of a corporation, to knowledge of how much overtime one has to pay or is entitled to receive — is formally available to all, in reality it is available only through a lawyer. Our law is usually not simple, usually not self-executing. For most people most of the time, meaningful access to the law requires the assistance of a lawyer. Thus the resulting conclusion: First-class citizenship is frequently dependent upon the assistance of a lawyer. If the conduct which the lawyer facilitates is above the floor of the intolerable — is not unlawful — then this line of thought suggests that what the lawyer does is a social good. The lawyer is the means to first-class citizenship, to meaningful autonomy, for the client.
>
> For the lawyer to have moral responsibility for each act he or she facilitates, for the lawyer to have a moral obligation to refuse to facilitate that which the lawyer believes to be immoral, is to substitute lawyers' beliefs for individual autonomy and diversity. Such a screening submits each to the prior restraint of the judge/facilitator and to rule by an oligarchy of lawyers. (If, in the alternative, the suggestion is that the lawyer's screening should be based not on the lawyer's personal morality, but on the lawyer's assessment of society's moral views or on guidelines spelled out in a professional code of ethics, then one has substituted collective moral decision making for individual moral decision making, contrary to the principle of autonomy. Less room has been left for private decision making through a sub rosa form of lawmaking.) If the conduct is sufficiently "bad," it would seem that it ought to be made explicitly unlawful. If it is not that bad, why subject the citizenry to the happenstance of the moral judgment of the particular lawyer to whom each has access? If making the conduct unlawful is too onerous because the law would be too vague, or it is too difficult to identify the conduct in advance, or there is not sufficient social or political concern, do we intend to delegate to the individual lawyer the authority for case-by-case legislation and policing?

W. Bradley Wendel articulates a nuanced middle ground in Civil Obedience, 104 Colum. L. Rev. 363 (2004), where he proposes an "authority conception" of legal ethics in which lawyers advance the interests of their clients while maintaining awareness and respect for the "substantial social achievement" that is law (id. at 366):

> [L]awyers are duty-bound not to frustrate the achievement of law by reintroducing contested moral values into the domain of law, either in the guise of principles of interpretation or as the basis for an ethically motivated decision to act or not to act on behalf of a client. In other words, lawyers should not treat the law instrumentally, as an obstacle to furthering the autonomy of their clients, but instead should treat it as an inherently valuable achievement of a pluralistic democracy. Lawyers have an obligation to preserve the common framework of law and respect for legal institutions as public goods, rather than permit clients to free ride on trust, expectations of cooperation, and compliance by others. Lawyers may of course challenge the status quo and need not acquiesce in the continued vitality of an unjust rule, but they are obligated to seek to modify the law overtly, not through covert means, such as creating complex structures of entities to prevent the detection of a sham transaction or withholding relevant information in response to a legitimate discovery request in litigation.

The Model Rules of Professional Conduct, set out above, are tilted somewhat in favor of the traditional view of the lawyer-client relationship. Rule 2.1 does state that a lawyer may refer to considerations other than the law, such as moral factors. The Comments elaborate on this a bit:

> Advice couched in narrowly legal terms may be of little value to a client, especially where practical considerations, such as cost or effects on other people, are predominant. Purely technical legal advice, therefore, can sometimes be inadequate. It is proper for a lawyer to refer to relevant moral and ethical considerations in giving advice. Although a lawyer is not a moral advisor as such, moral and ethical considerations impinge upon most legal questions and may decisively influence how the law will be applied.

The moral issue you face in the preceding problem is somewhat different from that discussed so far in this Note. This Note has involved clients with lawful, but perhaps morally deficient, goals. In the Problem, what Potter seeks to achieve, the prevention of a claim against him in order to preserve his status in his family and the community, is not so clearly lawful, is it? Or at the least, his methods are questionable. Should that make a difference in how you would advise Potter? Would your advice depend on your assessment of the merits of Harper's case? Might you conclude that, even if Potter's involvement in the accident were made public, Harper ought not to be able to recover? That conclusion might be based on your conclusions about the law, or on your view of the facts. From what Potter has told you, Blake is lying in his statement that Potter said that he would get help. Would either of these conclusions be relevant to the ethical problem?

One of the things you might want to discuss with Potter is what the options would be if Harper were to follow through with a suit against Potter; that is something that you would also want to think out before your meeting with him.

Tarasoff v. Regents of University of California

17 Cal. 3d 425, 551 P.2d 334, 131 Cal. Rptr. 14 (1976)

TOBRINER, J. On October 27, 1969, Prosenjit Poddar killed Tatiana Tarasoff. Plaintiffs, Tatiana's parents, allege that two months earlier Poddar confided his intention to kill Tatiana to Dr. Lawrence Moore, a psychologist employed by the Cowell Memorial Hospital at the University of California at Berkeley. They allege that on Moore's request, the campus police briefly detained Poddar, but released him when he appeared rational. They further claim that Dr. Harvey Powelson, Moore's superior, then directed that no further action be taken to detain Poddar. No one warned plaintiffs of Tatiana's peril.

Concluding that these facts set forth causes of action against neither therapists and policemen involved, nor against the Regents of the University of California as their employer, the superior court sustained defendants' demurrers to plaintiffs' second amended complaints without leave to amend. This appeal ensued. . . .

[Plaintiffs' second amended complaints set forth four causes of action: (1) a claim that defendants negligently failed to detain a dangerous patient; (2) a claim that defendants negligently failed to warn Tatiana's parents; (3) a claim for punitive damages on the ground that defendants acted "maliciously and oppressively"; and (4) a claim that defendants breached their duty to their patient and the public. The court concludes that plaintiffs' first and fourth causes of action are barred by governmental immunity, and that plaintiffs' third cause of action is barred by a rule precluding exemplary damages in a wrongful death action. Therefore, the court addresses the question of whether plaintiffs' second cause of action can be amended to state a basis for recovery.]

The second cause of action can be amended to allege that Tatiana's death proximately resulted from defendants' negligent failure to warn Tatiana or others likely to apprise her of her danger. Plaintiffs contend that as amended, such allegations of negligence and proximate causation, with resulting damages, establish a cause of action. Defendants, however, contend that in the circumstances of the present case they owed no duty of care to Tatiana or her parents and that, in the absence of such duty, they were free to act in careless disregard of Tatiana's life and safety.

In analyzing this issue, we bear in mind that legal duties are not discoverable facts of nature, but merely conclusory expressions that, in cases of a particular type, liability should be imposed for damage done. As stated in Dillon v. Legg (1968) 68 Cal. 2d 728, 734, 69 Cal. Rptr. 72, 76, 441 P.2d 912, 916: "The assertion that liability must . . . be denied because defendant bears no 'duty' to plaintiff 'begs the essential question — whether the plaintiff's interests are entitled to legal protection against the defendant's conduct. . . . [Duty] is not sacrosanct in itself, but only an expression of the sum total of those considerations of policy which lead the law to say that the particular plaintiff is entitled to protection.' (Prosser, Law of Torts [3d ed. 1964] at pp. 332-333.)"

In the landmark case of Rowland v. Christian (1968) 69 Cal. 2d 108, 70 Cal. Rptr. 97, 443 P.2d 561, Justice Peters recognized that liability should be imposed "for an injury occasioned to another by his want of ordinary care or skill" as expressed in section 1714 of the Civil Code. Thus, Justice Peters, quoting from Heaven v. Pender (1883) 11 Q.B.D. 503, 509 stated: "'whenever one person is by circumstances placed in such a position with regard to another . . . that if he did not use ordinary care and skill in his own conduct . . . he would cause danger of injury to the person or property of the other, a duty arises to use ordinary care and skill to avoid such danger.'"

We depart from "this fundamental principle" only upon the "balancing of a number of considerations"; major ones "are the foreseeability of harm to the plaintiff, the degree of certainty that the plaintiff suffered injury, the closeness of the connection between the defendant's conduct and the injury suffered, the moral blame attached to the defendant's conduct, the policy of preventing future harm, the extent of the burden to the defendant and consequences to the community of imposing a duty to exercise care with resulting liability for breach, and the availability, cost and prevalence of insurance for the risk involved."

The most important of these considerations in establishing duty is foreseeability. As a general principle, a "defendant owes a duty of care to all persons who are foreseeably endangered by his conduct, with respect to all risks which make the conduct unreasonably dangerous." As we shall explain, however, when the avoidance of foreseeable harm requires a defendant to control the conduct of another person, or to warn of such conduct, the common law has traditionally imposed liability only if the defendant bears some special relationship to the dangerous person or to the potential victim. Since the relationship between a therapist and his patient satisfies this requirement, we need not here decide whether foreseeability alone is sufficient to create a duty to exercise reasonable care to protect a potential victim of another's conduct.

Although, as we have stated above, under the common law, as a general rule, one person owed no duty to control the conduct of another, nor to warn those endangered by such conduct, the courts have carved out an exception to this rule in cases in which the defendant stands in some special relationship to either the person whose conduct needs to be controlled or in a relationship to the foreseeable victim of that conduct. Applying this exception to the present case, we note that a relationship of defendant therapists to either Tatiana or Poddar will suffice to establish a duty of care; as explained in section 315 of the Restatement Second of Torts, a duty of care may arise from either "(a) a special relation . . . between the actor and the third person which imposes a duty upon the actor to control the third person's conduct, or (b) a special relation . . . between the actor and the other which gives to the other a right of protection."

Although plaintiffs' pleadings assert no special relation between Tatiana and defendant therapists, they establish as between Poddar and defendant therapists the special relation that arises between a patient and his doctor or psychotherapist. Such a relationship may support affirmative duties for the benefit of third persons. Thus, for example, a hospital must exercise reasonable care to control the behavior of a patient which may endanger other persons. A doctor must also warn a patient if the patient's condition or medication renders certain conduct, such as driving a car, dangerous to others.

Although the California decisions that recognize this duty have involved cases in which the defendant stood in a special relationship *both* to the victim and to the person whose conduct created the danger, we do not think that the duty should logically be constricted to such situations. Decisions of other jurisdictions hold that the single relationship of a doctor to his patient is sufficient to support the duty to exercise reasonable care to protect others against dangers emanating from the patient's illness. The courts hold that a doctor is liable to persons infected by his patient if he negligently fails to diagnose a contagious disease or, having diagnosed the illness, fails to warn members of the patient's family. . . .

Defendants contend, however, that imposition of a duty to exercise reasonable care to protect third persons is unworkable because therapists cannot accurately predict whether or not a patient will resort to violence. In support of this argument amicus representing the American Psychiatric Association and other professional societies cites numerous articles which indicate that therapists, in the present state of the art, are unable reliably to predict violent acts; their forecasts, amicus claims, tend consistently to overpredict violence, and indeed are more often wrong than right. Since predictions of violence are often erroneous, amicus concludes, the courts should not render rulings that predicate the liability of therapists upon the validity of such predictions.

The role of the psychiatrist, who is indeed a practitioner of medicine, and that of the psychologist who performs an allied function, are like that of the physician who must conform to the standards of the profession and who must often make diagnoses and predictions based upon such evaluations. Thus the judgment of the therapist in diagnosing emotional disorders and in predicting whether a patient presents a serious danger of violence is comparable to the judgment which doctors and professionals must regularly render under accepted rules of responsibility.

We recognize the difficulty that a therapist encounters in attempting to forecast whether a patient presents a serious danger of violence. Obviously we do not require that the therapist, in making that determination, render a perfect performance; the therapist need only exercise "that reasonable degree of skill, knowledge, and care ordinarily possessed and exercised by members of [that professional specialty] under similar circumstances." Within the broad range of reasonable practice and treatment in which professional opinion and judgment may differ, the therapist is free to exercise his or her own best judgment without liability; proof, aided by hindsight, that he or she judged wrongly is insufficient to establish negligence.

In the instant case, however, the pleadings do not raise any question as to failure of defendant therapists to predict that Poddar presented a serious danger of violence. On the contrary, the present complaints allege that defendant therapists did in fact predict that Poddar would kill, but were negligent in failing to warn.

Amicus contends, however, that even when a therapist does in fact predict that a patient poses a serious danger of violence to others, the therapist should be absolved of any responsibility for failing to act to protect the potential victim. In our view, however, once a therapist does in fact determine, or under applicable professional standards reasonably should have determined, that a patient poses a serious danger of violence to others, he bears a duty to exercise reasonable care to protect the foreseeable victim of that danger. While the discharge of this duty of due care will necessarily vary with the facts of each case, in each instance the adequacy of the therapist's conduct must be measured against the traditional negligence standard of the rendition of reasonable care under the circumstances. . . .

Contrary to the assertion of amicus, this conclusion is not inconsistent with our recent decision in People v. Burnick, supra, 14 Cal. 3d 306, 121 Cal. Rptr. 488, 535 P.2d 352. Taking note of the uncertain character of therapeutic prediction, we held in *Burnick* that a person cannot be committed as a mentally disordered sex offender unless found to be such by proof beyond a reasonable doubt. The issue in the present context, however, is not whether the patient should be incarcerated, but whether the therapist should take any steps at all to protect the threatened victim; some of the alternatives open to the therapist, such as warning the victim, will not result in the drastic consequences of depriving the patient of his liberty. Weighing the uncertain and conjectural character of the alleged damage done the patient by such a warning against the peril to the victim's life, we conclude that professional inaccuracy in predicting violence cannot negate the therapist's duty to protect the threatened victim.

The risk that unnecessary warnings may be given is a reasonable price to pay for the lives of possible victims that may be saved. We would hesitate to hold that the therapist who is aware that his patient expects to attempt to assassinate the President of the United States would not be obligated to warn the authorities because the therapist cannot predict with accuracy that his patient will commit the crime.

Defendants further argue that free and open communication is essential to psychotherapy; that "Unless a patient . . . is assured that . . . information [revealed by him] can and will be held in utmost confidence, he will be reluctant to make the full disclosure upon which diagnosis and treatment . . . depends." (Sen. Com. on Judiciary, comment on Evid. Code, §1014.) The giving of a warning, defendants contend, constitutes a breach of trust which entails the revelation of confidential communications. . . .

We realize that the open and confidential character of psychotherapeutic dialogue encourages patients to express threats of violence, few of which are ever executed. Certainly a therapist should not be encouraged routinely to reveal such threats; such disclosures could seriously disrupt the patient's relationship with his therapist and with the persons threatened. To the contrary, the therapist's obligations to his patient require that he not disclose a confidence unless such disclosure is necessary to avert danger to others, and even then that he do so discreetly, and in a fashion that would preserve the privacy of his patient to the fullest extent compatible with the prevention of the threatened danger.

The revelation of a communication under the above circumstances is not a breach of trust or a violation of professional ethics; as stated in the Principles of Medical Ethics of the American Medical Association (1957), section 9: "A physician may not reveal the confidence entrusted to him in the course of medical attendance . . . *unless he is required to do so by law or unless it becomes necessary in order to protect the welfare of the individual or of the community.*" (Emphasis added.) We conclude that the public policy favoring protection of the confidential character of patient-psychotherapist communications must yield to the extent to which disclosure is essential to avert danger to others. The protective privilege ends where the public peril begins.

Our current crowded and computerized society compels the interdependence of its members. In this risk-infested society we can hardly tolerate the further exposure to danger that would result from a concealed knowledge of the therapist that his patient was lethal. If the exercise of reasonable care to protect the threatened victim requires the therapist to warn the endangered party or those who can reasonably be expected to notify him, we see no sufficient societal interest that would protect and justify concealment. The containment of such risks lies in the public interest. For the foregoing reasons, we find that plaintiffs' complaints can be amended to state a cause of action against defendants Moore, Powelson, Gold, and Yandell and against the Regents as their employer, for breach of a duty to exercise reasonable care to protect Tatiana . . . .

[The majority concludes that the police defendants did not have a special relationship to either Tatiana or Poddar to impose upon them a duty to warn. The court also concludes that the defendant therapists are not protected by governmental immunity in connection with their failure to warn Tatiana's parents because their decisions were not "basic policy decisions" within the meaning of earlier precedent.]

For the reasons stated, we conclude that plaintiffs can amend their complaints to state a cause of action against defendant therapists by asserting that the therapists in fact determined that Poddar presented a serious danger of violence to Tatiana, or pursuant to the standards of their profession should have so determined, but nevertheless failed to exercise reasonable care to protect her from that danger. To the extent, however, that plaintiffs base their claim that defendant therapists breached that duty because they failed to procure Poddar's confinement, the therapists find immunity in Government Code section 856. Further, as to the police defendants we conclude that plaintiffs have failed to show that the trial court erred in sustaining their demurrer without leave to amend.

The judgment of the superior court in favor of defendants Atkinson, Beall, Brownrigg, Hallernan, and Teel is affirmed. The judgment of the superior court in favor of defendants Gold, Moore, Powelson, Yandell, and the Regents of the University of California is reversed, and the cause remanded for further proceedings consistent with the views expressed herein.

WRIGHT, C.J., and SULLIVAN and RICHARDSON, JJ., concur.

MOSK, J. (concurring and dissenting).

I concur in the result in this instance only because the complaints allege that defendant therapists did in fact predict that Poddar would kill and were therefore negligent in failing to warn of that danger. Thus the issue here is very narrow: we are not concerned with whether the therapists, pursuant to the standards of their profession, "should have" predicted potential violence; they allegedly did so in actuality. Under these limited circumstances I agree that a cause of action can be stated.

Whether plaintiffs can ultimately prevail is problematical at best. As the complaints admit, the therapist *did* notify the police that Poddar was planning to kill a girl identifiable as Tatiana. While I doubt that more should be required, this issue may be raised in defense and its determination is a question of fact.

I cannot concur, however, in the majority's rule that a therapist may be held liable for failing to predict his patient's tendency to violence if other practitioners, pursuant to the "standards of the profession," would have done so. The question is, what standards? Defendants and a responsible amicus curiae, supported by an impressive body of literature demonstrate that psychiatric predictions of violence are inherently unreliable. . . .

I would restructure the rule designed by the majority to eliminate all reference to conformity to standards of the profession in predicting violence. If a psychiatrist does in fact predict violence, then a duty to warn arises. The majority's expansion of that rule will take us from the world of reality into the wonderland of clairvoyance.

CLARK, J. (dissenting).

Until today's majority opinion, both legal and medical authorities have agreed that confidentiality is essential to effectively treat the mentally ill, and that imposing a duty on doctors to disclose patient threats to potential victims would greatly impair treatment. . . . Moreover, . . . imposing the majority's new duty is certain to result in a net increase in violence. . . .

Overwhelming policy considerations weigh against imposing a duty on psychotherapists to warn a potential victim against harm. While offering virtually no benefit to society, such a duty will frustrate psychiatric treatment, invade fundamental patient rights and increase violence.

The importance of psychiatric treatment and its need for confidentiality have been recognized by this court. . . .

Assurance of confidentiality is important for three reasons.

Deterrence from Treatment

First, without substantial assurance of confidentiality, those requiring treatment will be deterred from seeking assistance. It remains an unfortunate fact in our society that people seeking psychiatric guidance tend to become stigmatized. Apprehension of such stigma—apparently increased by the propensity of people considering treatment to see themselves in the worst possible light—creates a well-recognized reluctance to seek aid. This reluctance is alleviated by the psychiatrist's assurance of confidentiality.

Full Disclosure

Second, the guarantee of confidentiality is essential in eliciting the full disclosure necessary for effective treatment. The psychiatric patient approaches treatment with conscious and unconscious inhibitions against revealing his innermost thoughts. "Every person, however well-motivated, has to overcome resistances to therapeutic exploration. These resistances seek support from every possible source and the possibility of disclosure would easily be employed in the service of resistance." (Goldstein & Katz, supra, 36 Conn. Bar J. 175, 179; see also, 118 Am. J. Psych. 734, 735.) Until a patient can trust his psychiatrist not to violate their confidential relationship, "the unconscious psychological control mechanism of repression will prevent the recall of past experiences." (Butler, Psychotherapy and Griswold: Is Confidentiality a Privilege or a Right? (1971) 3 Conn. L. Rev. 599, 604.)

Successful Treatment

Third, even if the patient fully discloses his thoughts, assurance that the confidential relationship will not be breached is necessary to maintain his trust in his psychiatrist—

the very means by which treatment is effected. "[T]he essence of much psychotherapy is the contribution of trust in the external world and ultimately in the self, modelled upon the trusting relationship established during therapy." (Dawidoff, The Malpractice of Psychiatrists, 1966 Duke L.J. 696, 704.) Patients will be helped only if they can form a trusting relationship with the psychiatrist. All authorities appear to agree that if the trust relationship cannot be developed because of collusive communication between the psychiatrist and others, treatment will be frustrated.

Given the importance of confidentiality to the practice of psychiatry, it becomes clear the duty to warn imposed by the majority will cripple the use and effectiveness of psychiatry. Many people, potentially violent — yet susceptible to treatment — will be deterred from seeking it; those seeking it will be inhibited from making revelations necessary to effective treatment; and, forcing the psychiatrist to violate the patient's trust will destroy the interpersonal relationship by which treatment is effected.

Violence and Civil Commitment

By imposing a duty to warn, the majority contributes to the danger to society of violence by the mentally ill and greatly increases the risk of civil commitment — the total deprivation of liberty — and those who should not be confined. The impairment of treatment and risk of improper commitment resulting from the new duty to warn will not be limited to a few patients but will extend to a large number of the mentally ill. Although under existing psychiatric procedures only a relatively few receiving treatment will ever present a risk of violence, the number making threats is huge, and it is the latter group — not just the former — whose treatment will be impaired and whose risk of commitment will be increased. . . .

Neither alternative open to the psychiatrist seeking to protect himself is in the public interest. The warning itself is an impairment of the psychiatrist's ability to treat, depriving many patients of adequate treatment. It is to be expected that after disclosing their threats, a significant number of patients, who would not become violent if treated according to existing practices, will engage in violent conduct as a result of unsuccessful treatment. In short, the majority's duty to warn will not only impair treatment of many who would never become violent but worse, will result in a net increase in violence.

The second alternative open to the psychiatrist is to commit his patient rather than to warn. Even in the absence of threat of civil liability, the doubts of psychiatrists as to the seriousness of patient threats have led psychiatrists to overcommit to mental institutions. This overcommitment has been authoritatively documented in both legal and psychiatric studies. . . .

Given the incentive to commit created by the majority's duty, this already serious situation will be worsened, contrary to Chief Justice Wright's admonition "that liberty is no less precious because forfeited in a civil proceeding than when taken as a consequence of a criminal conviction." (*In re* Gary W. (1971) 5 Cal. 3d 296, 307, 96 Cal. Rptr. 1, 9, 486 P.2d 1201, 1209.) . . .

[T]he majority impedes medical treatment, resulting in increased violence from — and deprivation of liberty to — the mentally ill.

We should accept . . . medical judgment, relying upon effective treatment rather than on indiscriminate warning.

The judgment should be affirmed.
McComb, J., concurs.

In imposing a duty on the defendant psychologist to warn of Poddar's threats to kill Tatiana, the court in *Tarasoff* quoted from Heaven v. Pender, 11 Q.B. Div. 503 (1883):

> whenever one person is by circumstances placed in such a position with regard to another . . . that if he did not use ordinary care and skill in his own conduct . . . he would cause danger of injury to the person or property of the other, a duty arises to use ordinary care and skill to avoid such danger.

Would that principle have supported imposing liability on the defendant? In any event, the *Tarasoff* court passed on the question of "whether foreseeability alone is sufficient to create a duty to exercise reasonable care to protect a potential victim of another's conduct." Rather, the court relied on the relationship between the defendant and Poddar to impose the duty to warn. The court found support for this conclusion in cases involving three sets of circumstances: (1) "[A] hospital must exercise reasonable care to control the behavior of a patient which may endanger other persons"; (2) "A doctor must also warn a patient if the patient's condition or medication renders certain conduct, such as driving a car, dangerous to others"; (3) "[A] doctor is liable to persons infected by his patient if he negligently fails to diagnose a contagious disease or, having diagnosed the illness, fails to warn members of the patient's family." Are any of these circumstances sufficiently analogous to *Tarasoff* to justify the court's reliance on them?

Most courts that have addressed the issue have followed *Tarasoff.* Some courts have held that the psychotherapist's duty is triggered only if the patient threatens a particular, identified victim who can be warned. See, e.g., Estate of Morgan v. Fairfield Family Counseling Ctr., 673 N.E.2d 1311, *reconsideration denied*, 676 N.E.2d 534 (Ohio 1997). Some have held that no duty is triggered when the victim had prior knowledge of the patient-attacker's violent tendencies. See, e.g., Weitz v. Lovelace Health Systems, 214 F.3d 1175 (10th Cir. 2000). Other courts have rejected the "readily identifiable victim" requirements and imposed a more open-minded disclosure requirement. See, e.g., Shuster v. Altenberg, 424 N.W.2d 159 (Wis. 1988). See also Volk v. DeMeerleer, 337 P.3d 372 (Wash. Ct. App. 2015) (holding that fact question exists whether therapist owed a duty to "the general public" as foreseeable victims to warn of patient's violent tendencies), *review granted*, 183 Wash. 2d 1007 (2015). In addition, in recent years, legislatures have begun codifying the *Tarasoff* duty. See, e.g., N.J. Stat. Ann. §2A:62A-16b. Most such statutes are restricted to notification in cases where the potential victim is clearly identifiable.

Not all courts have accepted *Tarasoff.* Among those that have not are Nasser v. Parker, 455 S.E.2d 502 (Va. 1995), and Santana v. Rainbow Cleaners, 969 A.2d 653 (R.I. 2009) (using an on-the-facts approach to determine that a community mental health center did not owe a duty to exercise control over a violence-prone outpatient). Most of the cases imposing *Tarasoff* duties have involved the failure of medical or mental health professionals to warn. In Coombes v. Florio, 450 Mass. 182, 877 N.E.2d 567 (2007), for instance, the court held that physicians owe a duty of care to third parties to warn patients of the effects of treatment in some circumstances, such as when a prescribed medication may impair patients' ability to drive a motor vehicle. In Medina v. Hochberg, 987 N.E.2d 1206 (Mass. 2013), however, the court refused to extend *Coombes* to a context in which plaintiff was struck and injured by a vehicle driven by defendant's patient. The patient, who was under defendant's care for an inoperable brain tumor, suffered a grand mal seizure while driving and lost control of his vehicle. The court distinguished between risks posed by medicine prescribed by a physician and what the court viewed as natural, underlying medical conditions: "Taken to its logical end, [plaintiff's] proposed duty would require warning patients about the dangers associated with driving based on any number of pre-existing health conditions, none of which stems from the physician's affirmative treatment of the patient." Id. at 1212.

Outside of the medical or mental health professional contexts, *Tarasoff*-style duties to protect third parties are even more limited. In J.S. v. R.T.H., 714 A.2d 924 (N.J. 1998), the court ruled that a person who knows that his or her spouse is engaging in sexually abusive behavior toward another has a duty to use reasonable care to either warn of the harm or otherwise prevent it. More typical are cases such as Ross v. University of Tulsa, 2016 WL 1545138 (N.D. Okla. 2016) (appeal filed May 16, 2016), in which the court discussed *Tarasoff* and determined that defendant university did not have a duty to exercise reasonable care to prevent sexual assault by a school basketball player: "[I]s there any number of *allegations* of sexual assault against one student that gives rise to a college's duty to exercise reasonable care in preventing sexual assault by that student on campus? In this case, the Court holds that one report is not enough, at least where the victim expresses a desire not to proceed and the accused has no prior arrests or convictions for sexual assault." Id. at *22 (emphasis in original).

Is the duty to warn imposed by *Tarasoff* having the adverse effects that the dissenting judge predicted? The returns conflict. For support of the dissent on that score, see Alan A. Stone, The *Tarasoff* Decisions: Suing Psychotherapists to Safeguard Society, 90 Harv. L. Rev. 358 (1976); Toni Pryor Wise, Where the Public Peril Begins: A Survey of Psychotherapists to Determine the Effects of *Tarasoff,* Note, 31 Stan. L. Rev. 165 (1978). For a different view, see David B. Wexler, Victimology and Mental Health: An Agenda, 66 Va. L. Rev. 681 (1980); Daniel J. Givelber et al., *Tarasoff,* Myth and Reality: An Empirical Study of Private Law in Action, 1984 Wis. L. Rev. 443. For the conclusion that *Tarasoff* has not interfered with the psychotherapist-patient relationship, see Fillmore Buckner & Marvin Firestone, "Where the Public Peril Begins"—25 Years after Tarasoff, 21 J. Legal Med. 187 (2000). And for a suggestion that the issuance of a "*Tarasoff* warning" has become viewed by some psychiatric commentators as a valuable clinical tool, particularly when issued by the patient himself, see Brian Ginsberg, *Tarasoff* at Thirty: Victim's Knowledge Shrinks the Psychotherapist's Duty to Warn and Protect, 21 J. Contemp. Health L. & Pol'y 1 (2004).

Some states have enacted statutes that provide protection to therapists in *Tarasoff*-type cases. The California statute (Cal. Civ. Code §43.92) provides:

> (a) There shall be no monetary liability on the part of, and no cause of action shall arise against, any person who is a psychotherapist as defined in Section 1010 of the Evidence Code in failing to warn of and protect from a patient's threatened violent behavior or failing to predict and warn of and protect from a patient's violent behavior except where the patient has communicated to the psychotherapist a serious threat of physical violence against a reasonably identifiable victim or victims.
>
> (b) There shall be no monetary liability on the part of, and no cause of action shall arise against, a psychotherapist who, under the limited circumstances specified above, discharges his or her duty to warn and protect by making reasonable efforts to communicate the threat to the victim or victims and to a law enforcement agency.

Would this statute have benefited the defendant in *Tarasoff* had it been in force at that time?

Perhaps of more immediate concern to lawyers is whether the rule of *Tarasoff* will be extended to the legal profession. While there are no reported opinions involving lawyers, the exposure does exist. See Hawkins v. King County, 602 P.2d 361 (Wash. Ct. App. 1979) (refusing to adopt a *Tarasoff*-style duty of disclosure where court-appointed defense attorney failed to divulge information regarding client's mental state at bail hearing, and client later assaulted his mother and lost both legs in a failed suicide attempt). The 1980 draft of the ABA Model Rules of Professional Conduct (Rule 1.7(b)) made it mandatory for a lawyer to "disclose information about a client to the extent it appears necessary to prevent a crime that would result in death or serious bodily harm to another person. . . ." The current version is permissive in this regard, rather than mandatory. It states that a lawyer "may reveal" such information. See Rule 1.6(b). A similar delegation of discretion to the attorney is contained in the Restatement (Third) of the Law Governing Lawyers (2000), a project of the American Law Institute. Section 66(1) provides that a "lawyer may use or disclose confidential client information when the lawyer reasonably believes that its use or disclosure is necessary to prevent reasonably certain death or serious bodily harm to a person." Would the imposition of tort liability on a lawyer who has not disclosed the kind of information that the psychotherapist had in *Tarasoff* be appropriate?[76] Keep in mind that the rules of professional responsibility are usually enacted by the highest court of the state. The commitment by both sets of rules of the decision to disclose or not to the discretion of the lawyer is interesting — what considerations would be relevant to the lawyer's decision had Poddar confessed his intent to his lawyer, rather than to his psychotherapist?

Problem 21

Yesterday, you received a telephone call from Elizabeth Green, one of your clients. Green runs Insu-Screen Associates, a company that conducts medical exams on individuals applying for life insurance offered by commercial insurance companies. Upon the request of an insurer, Insu-Screen conducts a full medical exam on applicants for insurance. These exams include a lengthy physical exam, comprehensive blood tests and a detailed medical and family history. Some insurance companies pay Insu-Screen for the testing; others require the applicant to cover the costs of the screening exam.

Green is concerned because Insu-Screen is now finding that a small but growing number of applicants are testing positively for Zika — a virus that poses relatively mild health risks to affected individuals, but that can cause severe birth defects to the unborn children of pregnant women. Although mosquitoes are the primary transmitters of Zika, scientists have discovered that Zika also can be passed between sexual partners. In addition, an individual infected with Zika can transmit the virus to mosquitoes by being bitten, thereby expanding the virus's range of impact if, for instance, the individual has traveled from a Zika outbreak area to a previously unaffected area.

Under current company policy, Insu-Screen does not inform prospective insurance applicants of the outcome of the tests that it runs. Applicants are provided with a written form which indicates that the results of the medical exam are confidential and are the

76. Section 66(3) of the Restatement (Third) of the Law Governing Lawyers (2000) attempts to preempt any legal consequence flowing from the permission to disclose: "A lawyer who takes action or decides not to take action permitted under this Section is not, solely by reason of such action or inaction, subject to professional discipline, liable for damages to the lawyer's client or any third person, or barred from recovery against a client or third person."

property of the insurance company seeking the test. She notes that most insurers, confronted with a problematic medical report, simply deny the application for life insurance without informing the applicant of the reasons for the denial.

Green is particularly concerned about the legal implications of her company's nondisclosure policy. She notes that such individuals, if female and uninformed of their Zika-positive status, may become pregnant or fail to seek early medical attention if they already are pregnant. Moreover, such individuals may continue to engage in sexual practices that expose others to Zika infection, including perhaps women who are pregnant or about to become pregnant. Indeed, because of the detailed family histories that constitute part of Insu-Screen's medical exam, Green notes that it is often possible to identify by name the third parties — typically spouses — that are at risk of being infected by the applicant. Even absent such specifically identifiable at-risk third parties, Green is worried that failure to inform Zika-positive individuals contributes to a public health disaster by possibly allowing the virus to continue to spread its range.

Green has asked your advice concerning the outlines of an appropriate disclosure policy. Must she inform insurance applicants when they test positive for Zika? Must she inform known sexual partners of those individuals? Are there other medical findings she must disclose? Assume that there are no statutes on point.

Law and Policy: A Legal Duty to Rescue?

In the early morning of March 3, 1964, Kitty Genovese was stabbed to death outside an apartment house in New York City. When she was first attacked by her assailant, she screamed: "Oh, my God, he stabbed me! Please help me! Please help me!" Lights in the building went on, and a man called down, "Let that girl alone!" The assailant walked away, but after the lights went out, he returned and stabbed the young woman again. She again screamed, and again the lights went on. Once more, the assailant left, only to return and stab the dying victim a third and final time. The third attack took place 35 minutes after the first and 15 minutes before the police received the first call reporting the incident. The man who finally called the police said that he had given the matter much thought before he called. "I didn't want to get involved" was his explanation. In all, 38 people witnessed the attack. N.Y. Times, March 27, 1964, at 1, col. 4. For a more detailed report of this incident, see Abraham M. Rosenthal, Thirty-Eight Witnesses: The Kitty Genovese Case (1964).

This notorious incident provoked much legal and societal soul searching. Is something fundamentally wrong with a society in which 38 people can stand by and do nothing, not even call the police, to aid a woman under attack? The explanation of the Kitty Genovese incident may have less to do with collective morality than with the psychology of people in groups. One psychological study following the incident concluded that a bystander is less likely to come to the aid of a person in need of aid if the bystander is one of a group rather than being a lone observer. It is thus, according to the study, not so much a matter of apathy as it is a matter of each person in the group feeling that someone else is doing something. See Bibb Latané & John M. Darley, Group Inhibition of Bystander Intervention in Emergencies, 10 J. Personality & Soc. Psychol. 215 (1968). More generally, a vast literature on the so-called "omission bias" demonstrates that individuals feel less responsible for harm that is perceived to follow from inaction than action. See generally Robert A. Prenticed & Jonathan J. Koehler, A Normality Bias in Legal Decision Making, 88 Cornell L. Rev. 583 (2003).

A different explanation of the Kitty Genovese story might be that it did not happen . . . or at least, it did not happen in the stark terms reported by the *New York Times*:

> The *Times* story was inaccurate in a number of significant ways. There were two attacks, not three. Only a handful of people saw the first clearly and only one saw the second, because it took place indoors, within the vestibule. The reason there were two attacks was that Robert Mozer, far from being a "silent witness," yelled at Moseley when he heard Genovese's screams and drove him away. Two people called the police. When the ambulance arrived at the scene — precisely because neighbors had called for help — Genovese, still alive, lay in the arms of a neighbor named Sophia Farrar, who had courageously left her apartment to go to the crime scene, even though she had no way of knowing that the murderer had fled.

Nicholas Lemman, A Cry for Help: What the Kitty Genovese Story Really Means, New Yorker (March 10, 2014). This alternative account seems more consistent with the empirical information on the rescues presented by Professor David Hyman, supra, p. 273.

Still, more recent events have kept the "duty to rescue" issue and questions about the inherent goodness or evil of humanity alive. In May 1997, a young man witnessed a friend rape, and then murder, a seven-year-old girl in a casino bathroom in Las Vegas, without making any effort to prevent it. The young man did not even report this to the authorities after the event. He was quoted later to have said: "I'm not going to get upset over someone else's life. I just worry about myself first. I'm not going to lose sleep over somebody else's problems." Hugo Martin, Victim's Mother Begins Campaign, L.A. Times, Aug. 1 1998, at B-1. In late 2009, a chilling replay of the Kitty Genovese incident unfolded as numerous bystanders stood and watched while a 15-year-old girl was raped and beaten by multiple assailants outside a homecoming dance in Richmond, California. See Shoshana Walter, A Brutal Attack Outside a School Continues to Horrify One Year Later, N.Y. Times, Dec. 24, 2010, at A17. Some bystanders reportedly took photographs and video footage of the attack with their cell phones. Unlike the original Kitty Genovese incident, no evidence has surfaced to challenge the allegations of shocking bystander apathy in the Richmond attack.

Notwithstanding widespread public concern over such incidents, there has been relatively little legislative activity to establish a general duty to rescue. See p. 272, above. Nor have courts acted to fill the void. Judicial inaction led one leading treatise writer to bemoan that "[s]ome of the decisions have been shocking in the extreme. . . . Such decisions are revolting to any moral sense." William L. Prosser and W. Page Keeton, The Law of Torts 375-76 (5th ed. 1984).

If the legislatures and the courts have been largely silent, the commentators have not. A number of commentators over the years, reacting to their perceptions that the no-duty-to-rescue law lacks a moral foundation, have argued for a more general duty. One of the early advocates was Professor Ames in his well-known work Law and Morals, 22 Harv. L. Rev. 97 (1908). In this article, he urged that tort liability be imposed on those who, with "little or no inconvenience" to themselves, could have rescued another in danger but failed to do so. A similar proposal was advanced in Ernest J. Weinrib, The Case for a Duty to Rescue, 90 Yale L.J. 247 (1980). Here, Professor Weinrib advocated a judicially created tort duty of "easy rescue." While he did not elaborate much on the contours such a duty would have (for instance, he did not state whether the easiness of the rescue would be measured objectively — easy to a reasonable person — or subjectively — easy to this particular defendant), he did state that such a duty ought to be imposed only in "emergency situations where the rescue will not inconvenience the rescuer," and that the rescuer ought not to be compelled to "place himself in physical danger." Id. at 285. See also Saul Levmore, Waiting for Rescue: An Essay on the Evolution and Incentive Structure of the Law of Affirmative Obligations, 72 Va. L. Rev. 879 (1986); Daniel B. Yeager, A Radical Community of Aid: A Rejoinder to Opponents of Affirmative Duties to Help Strangers, 71 Wash. U. L.Q. 1 (1993); Kenneth W. Simons, Dworkin's Two Principles of Dignity: An Unsatisfactory Nonconsequentialist Account of Interpersonal Moral Duties, 90 B.U. L. Rev. 715 (2010).

The argument for requiring easy rescue and imposing criminal sanctions — albeit minor ones — for failure to do so appears in Liam Murphy, Beneficence, Law, and Liberty: The Case of the Required Rescue, 89 Geo. L.J. 605 (2001). The author doubts that tort liability is appropriate, based on the concern that the defendant would be exposed to liability for substantial damages. See also Ken Levy, Killing, Letting Die, and the Case for Mildly Punishing Bad Samaritanism, 44 Ga. L. Rev. 607 (2010) (advocating the imposition of heavy fines or short-term imprisonment for failure to rescue using moral and utilitarian arguments).

The existing law is not without its defenders. One is Richard A. Epstein, A Theory of Strict Liability, 2 J. Legal Stud. 151 (1973). Professor Epstein asserted that tort liability should be based on cause, rather than on fault. Since the nonrescuer would not have caused the harm, it would be inappropriate for the law to impose liability. "It may well be," Professor Epstein stated, "that the conduct of individuals who do not aid fellow men is under some circumstances outrageous, but it does not follow that a legal system that does not enforce a duty to aid is outrageous as well." Id. at 201. For an economic analysis of the efficiency implications of the law of rescue, see William M. Landes and Richard A. Posner, Salvors, Finders, Good Samaritans, and Other Rescuers: An Economic Study of Law and Altruism, 7 J. Legal Stud. 83 (1978). The authors conclude that a law imposing a general duty to rescue would not be more efficient than the existing no-duty law.

Writing from a broader philosophical perspective, though of relevance to the duty to rescue, Professor Lon L. Fuller in The Morality of Law (rev. ed. 1969) argues that not all goals of society can be accomplished through law. In distinguishing between societal concerns that ought, and those that ought not, to be the subject of legal compulsion, he discusses what he calls the "morality of aspiration" and the "morality of duty." He defines the two concepts as follows (pp. 5-6):

> The morality of aspiration is most plainly exemplified in Greek philosophy. It is the morality of the Good Life, of excellence, of the fullest realization of human powers. . . .
>
> Where the morality of aspiration starts at the top of human achievement, the morality of duty starts at the bottom. It lays down the basic rules without which an ordered society is impossible, or without which an ordered society directed toward certain specific goals must fail of its mark. It is the morality of the Old Testament and the Ten Commandments. It speaks in terms of "thou shalt not," and, less frequently, of "thou shalt." It does not condemn men for failing to embrace opportunities for the fullest realization of their powers. Instead, it condemns them for failing to respect the basic requirements of social living.

The importance of these concepts lies, according to Fuller, in the inability of the law to "compel a man to live up to the excellences of which he is capable." He makes the argument this way (pp. 9-10, 27-28):

> As we consider the whole range of moral issues, we may conveniently imagine a kind of scale or yardstick which begins at the bottom with most obvious demands of social living

> and extends upward to the highest reaches of human aspiration. Somewhere along this scale there is an invisible pointer that marks the dividing line where the pressure of duty leaves off and the challenge of excellence begins. The whole field of moral argument is dominated by a great undeclared war over the location of this pointer. There are those who struggle to push it upward; others work to pull it down. Those whom we regard as being unpleasantly—or at least, inconveniently—moralistic are forever trying to inch the pointer upward so as to expand the area of duty. Instead of inviting us to join them in realizing a pattern of life they consider worthy of human nature, they try to bludgeon us into a belief we are duty bound to embrace this pattern. . . .
>
> . . . If the morality of duty reaches upward beyond its proper sphere the iron hand of imposed obligation may stifle experiment, inspiration, and spontaneity. If the morality of aspiration invades the province of duty, men may begin to weigh and qualify their obligations by standards of their own and we may end with the poet tossing his wife into the river in the belief—perhaps quite justified—that he will be able to write better poetry in her absence.

Most of the preceding debate involving a general duty to rescue has involved a "stick" approach—the threat of legal sanctions for the failure to attempt a reasonable rescue effort. The law does not typically resort to "carrot" approaches, by which those attempting to rescue another would be affirmatively rewarded. There are carrots of that sort, but they ordinarily come from private organizations. The law on occasion, however, has used modified carrot approaches by removing what otherwise might be disincentives to rescue. The most common approach in this regard are "Good Samaritan" statutes, which insulate rescuers from liability for their negligence in the course of the rescue effort. Apart from such statutes, courts stand ready to impose negligence liability on the rescuer if the job is botched. See, e.g., Dunson v. Friedlander Realty, 369 So. 2d 792 (Ala. 1979); Farwell v. Keaton, 240 N.W.2d 217 (Mich. 1976). A number of states have enacted statutes designed to protect persons from claims arising out of the rendering of gratuitous assistance in an emergency. See supra, pp. 272-273. See also Gerrit De Geest & Giuseppe Dari-Mattiacci, The Rise of Carrots and the Decline of Sticks, 80 U. Chi. L. Rev. 3419 (2013) (discussing how and why incentives are used more frequently than punishments in a variety of policy and legal contexts, including the duty to rescue).

Another approach that the law might take to remove disincentives to rescue would be to permit the rescuer to recover the cost of rescue from the rescuee. The rescuer's right to recover, however, has been quite limited. There is no recovery, for example, if, among other things, the rescuer "acted unofficiously and with intent to charge. . . ." Restatement of Restitution §116. Recovery may be had in contract if, after the rescue, the rescuee promises to compensate the rescuer. See Restatement (Second) of Contracts §86. Hanoch Dagan, in In Defense of the Good Samaritan, 97 Mich. L. Rev. 1152 (1999), argues that the rescuer should be able to recover from the rescuee in restitution. Damages would be the cost of the rescue to the rescuer or the benefit to the rescuee, whichever is lower.

The arguments discussed so far over whether the law should impose a general tort duty to rescue have all involved the merits from a substantive perspective. In Process Constraints in Tort, 67 Cornell L. Rev. 901 (1982), Professor James Henderson, Jr., suggests that there are important process considerations which explain the reluctance of courts to adopt a general duty. According to Professor Henderson, to satisfy process requirements, tort law must adequately guide the behavior of two groups of persons: those "whose activities generate the accident costs upon which liability issues focus" (primary behavior); and "the lawyers, judges, and jurors who have responsibility for officially resolving liability disputes" (adjudicative behavior). Id. at 903. With respect to both groups, Professor

Henderson asserts that a general duty to rescue would fail to meet the following process criteria (id. at 905):

> First, their clarity must be such as to enable persons to distinguish between modes of conduct that will bring liability and modes that will not. Second, they must refer to factual circumstances that can be objectively verified, so that persons can apply the rules with some measure of confidence. Finally, to the extent that the rules describe patterns of behavior to which individuals are expected to conform, they must avoid calling for behavioral patterns that are not achievable by those to whom the rules are directed.

Many European legislatures have established a general duty to rescue, at least for criminal law purposes. These statutes are discussed in Alberto Cadoppi, Failure to Rescue and the Continental Law, in The Duty to Rescue 93 (Michael A. Menlove & Alexander McCall Smith eds., 1993).

Whether the rescuer can recover for his own personal injuries from the person, including the rescuee, whose negligence caused the need for the rescue is taken up in the section on proximate cause in Chapter 4.

Law and Behavior: The Effect of Legal Rules upon Individual Conduct

One of the questions suggested by the preceding note on law and policy is the extent to which the recognition of a general legal duty to be a Good Samaritan would actually affect behavior in a way that would lead to increased altruism. Earlier notes on law and behavior have considered the influences, including law, upon the behavior of two specialized actors in the torts process — the judge and the jury. In this note, we turn to a consideration of the effect that legal rules have upon the behavior of the person in the street[77] — a question first raised in the note on law and behavior at the end of Chapter 1.[78]

The empirical evidence concerning tort law's deterrent effect on behavior is decidedly mixed.[79] In 1994, Gary Schwartz undertook a comprehensive, sector-by-sector review of whether various tort laws — medical malpractice, products liability, workers' compensation, no-fault automobile laws — deter risky tortious conduct. Schwartz found little

77. Perhaps the high-water mark of optimism regarding the potential for influencing human conduct through legal rules is reflected in the following sign observed near a power station in Ireland: "To touch these overhead cables means instant death. Violators will be prosecuted." Quoted in N.Y. Times, Dec. 11, 1969, at 59, col. 2.

78. Much of the interest in this subject has been stimulated by the enactment into law in many states of no-fault automobile compensation plans. Although some writers have opposed these plans on the grounds that the system of fault-based liability in tort does serve as a deterrence to unreasonably dangerous automobile driving, their arguments appear to be based on the premise that in a general way the fault system reinforces the community's sense of moral and social responsibility, and therefore helps indirectly to curb tendencies on the part of drivers to behave negligently. See Elisabeth M. Landes, Insurance, Liability, and Accidents: A Theoretical and Empirical Investigation of the Effect of No-Fault Accidents, 25 J.L. & Econ. 49, 50 (1982).

79. Linda Sandstrom Simard, A View from Within the Fortune 500: An Empirical Study of Negative Value Class Actions and Deterrence, 47 Ind. L. Rev. 739, 744-45 (2014) ("Studies seeking to test the efficacy of the deterrence theory have reached mixed conclusions. . . . [O]ne study found no clear link between the threat of punitive damages and deterrence, another study found only 'thin' evidence of a correlation between liability for medical malpractice and a reduction in negligence rates, and several studies have reached mixed results on deterrence effects of tort reform."); W. Jonathan Cardi, Randall D. Penfield & Albert H. Yoon, Does Tort Law Deter Individuals? A Behavioral Science Study, 9 J. Empirical Stud. 567, 570 (2012) ("Results are mixed."). See also William J. Bowers, Daniel J. Givelber & Carolyn L. Blitch, How Did "Tarasoff" Affect Clinical Practice?, 484 Annals Am. Acad. Pol. & Soc. Sci. 70 (March 1986); William B. Schwartz & Neil K. Komesar, Doctors, Damages and Deterrence: An Economic View of Medical Malpractice, 23 New England J. Med. 1282 (1978).

evidence to support the "strong view" of deterrence theory proposed by law-and-economic scholars, which holds that tort liability systematically deters inefficient tortious behavior in accordance with rational actor models. Schwartz did find evidence in support of the "moderate view," however, which holds that tort law provides *some* amount of deterrence, but does not deter tortious behavior as thoroughly as economic models suggest.[80] More recent empirical work has arrived at similar conclusions. A 2012 review concluded, "To date, no study has found that tort law serves as a comprehensive deterrent, as William Landes, Richard Posner, and Steven Shavell have proposed. Some scholars have found limited evidence that tort acts as a weak deterrent with respect to certain behaviors. Still others have found no evidence of deterrence or even, in a few cases, negative associations."[81]

In seeking to gain traction on an issue as thorny as whether people are deterred by tort law, researchers have employed a variety of investigative techniques — each of which carries important limitations. One commonly used method involves comparing behavior patterns in two jurisdictions, only one of which imposes a particular tort liability regime. For instance, Michelle White compared states with comparative fault rules to states employing contributory negligence, and found that drivers take less care in states with comparative fault regimes, as revealed by jury verdicts in automobile accident cases.[82] A variation of this interjurisdictional comparative technique involves observing patterns of behavior in a single jurisdiction before and after tort reform. By comparing rates of accidents or deaths before and after the implementation of a new regime, researchers can assess whether tort liability is associated with a change in behavior.[83]

Note that neither of these two methods can establish that tort law *causes* people to change their behavior. In order to establish a deterrent effect, we would need to rule out that possibility that the jurisdictions being compared, or the time periods being compared, differ in other ways that correspond to the behavior being studied. This is a tall order, as social scientists have lamented: "An optimal study of tort law's efficacy as a deterrent would consist of an experiment involving two jurisdictions — identical with respect to demographics, economics, cultural norms, and criminal law — in which one jurisdiction was randomly chosen to impose liability for injuries cased by risky behavior, while the other would impose no such liability. Under this design, one could credibly identify whether common-law tort liability deterred risky behavior. Practical constraints, however, make such a study unlikely."[84]

80. Gary T. Schwartz, Reality in the Economic Analysis of Tort Law: Does Tort Law Really Deter?, 42 UCLA L. Rev. 377, 443 (1994) ("[B]etween the economists' strong claim that tort law systematically deters and the critics' response that tort law rarely if ever deters lies an intermediate position: tort law, while not as effective as economic models suggest, may still be somewhat successful in achieving its stated deterrence goals."). For discussion on the deterrence rationale of tort law, see Richard A. Posner, Instrumental and Noninstrumental Theories of Tort Law, 88 Ind. L.J. 469 (2013); Stephen F. Williams, Commentary, Second Best: The Soft Underbelly of Deterrence Theory in Tort, 106 Harv. L. Rev. 932 (1993).

81. Cardi et al., supra note 79, at 570.

82. Michelle J. White, An Empirical Test of the Comparative and Contributory Negligence Rules in Accident Law, 20 Rand J. Econ. 308 (1989).

83. For examples of this approach, see Paul Rubin & Joanna Shepherd, Tort Reform and Accidental Deaths, 50 J.L. & Econ. 221 (2007); Joanna Shepherd, Tort Reform's Winners and Losers: The Competing Effects of Care and Activity Levels, 55 UCLA L. Rev. 905 (2008).

84. Cardi et al., supra note 79, at 570. This research team attempted to conduct an experimental test of tort deterrence. They asked over 700 first-year law students to read vignettes describing conduct that might result in liability and to rate their willingness to engage in the risky conduct, given a description of the applicable law. The researchers found that people are much less deterred by the threat of potential tort liability than they are by the threat of potential criminal sanctions. Yet note that in order to deploy the features of a scientifically sound experiment — randomly assigning subjects to read different versions of the survey questions, controlling all features of the scenario except the treatment of interest — the researchers needed to concoct an artificial scenario and administer it to a group of research subjects that is likely unrepresentative of the population of interest.

Overall, measuring and evaluating the effects of legal rules on behavior is a complicated and difficult task, due largely to the following factors:

(a) "The law," the effects of which are sought to be measured, is often remarkably indeterminate. The realities of the processes by which legal rules are applied and enforced may be very different from what one might have expected from the rules taken at face value, and the effects upon behavior of legal rules will vary greatly depending upon the processes by which they are implemented.[85] Tort rules, especially those governing liability in negligence, tend to be somewhat open-ended and vague, and therefore would appear less likely to serve as guides to conduct. Further, empirical investigations into the way tort law is implemented suggests that fact finders often do not pursue optimal deterrence, preferring to vindicate other values such as corrective justice.[86]

(b) The law itself limits the extent to which scientists may manipulate variables in order to test experimentally the effects of law upon behavior. Rules of due process and equal protection prohibit selective and discriminatory applications of the law, and thus inhibit scientists from making full use of the experimental mode of inquiry.[87]

(c) It is extremely difficult to sort out the direct effects of law upon behavior from the direct effects of other, nonlegal influences. The complexity of the processes of human thought and action will probably forever frustrate attempts to explain exactly how and why any factors, such as legal rules, affect behavior.

(d) Even if the direct effects of legal rules could be separated from the effects of other factors, these other factors are themselves affected, on a more long-run basis, by the existence of the legal rules. Thus, even if it were possible in a particular instance to conclude that an individual's conduct is more likely to be affected in the short run by his sense of right and wrong than by the threat of tort liability, it nevertheless may be that the individual's moral values are significantly affected in the longer run by the fact that certain actions are publicly branded tortious.

Due to these challenges, it is difficult to draw conclusions about the deterrent effect of tort law. From a review of the literature, the following are offered as tentative factors that must be considered when predicting and evaluating the effects of a legal rule:

(a) The broader legal and social environment in which the particular rule is encountered. One important factor determining the effect of legal rules is what might be termed the overall morale of the addressees in the system of which the rules are a part. Apparently, people who have confidence in the basic fairness of the system are more likely than those who do not to conform their conduct to legal rules.[88]

85. See Samuel W. Buell, Good Faith and Law Evasion, 58 UCLA L. Rev. 611 (2011) (discussing how actors can modify their behavior to evade the law and providing suggestions to combat this phenomenon).

86. See Robbennolt & Hans, supra note 64, at 51 ("[W]e have seen that fact-finders have an array of motives and that they ultimately attempt to reach decisions that are 'just.' It seems clear that fact finders do not solely seek to accomplish economic efficiency or optimal deterrence, nor do they strictly apply a cost-benefit calculus in reaching decisions about whether someone is negligent.").

87. See generally Solutions to Ethical and Legal Problems in Social Research (Robert F. Boruch & Joe S. Cecil eds., 1983). See also Laurens Walker, Perfecting Federal Civil Rules: A Proposal for Restricted Field Experiments, 51 Law & Contemp. Probs. 67 (1988).

88. See generally Tom R. Tyler, Why People Obey the Law (1990).

(b) The type of behavior toward which the rule is directed. The more the conduct deemed unlawful is likely to be engaged in as a means of achieving a material objective of the actor, the more the actor is likely to be deterred by the threat of legal sanction; the more the conduct tends to be engaged in as a pleasurable end in itself, the less likely the actor is to be deterred by such a threat.[89]

(c) The nature of the rule itself and the accompanying implementation process. The more likely the deviant actor is to be apprehended and punished, and the more severe the punishment, the more likely the rule is to deter the actor's conduct.[90] Note that tort liability is very apt to be insured against, lessening its potential impact upon the individual upon whom liability is imposed.

(d) The psychological predispositions of the population of actors to whom the rule is addressed. It is generally agreed that every individual is possessed of certain psychological traits which affect the manner in which behavior is influenced by legal rules, and it is becoming increasingly possible to generalize about these traits. As some scholars have suggested, the deterrent potential of tort law on the behavior of what might be described as "quasi-institutional actors" — corporations, professionals, etc. — may be higher than the deterrent potential upon private individuals.[91]

89. See generally Neal K. Katyal, Deterrence's Difficulty, 95 Mich. L. Rev. 2385 (1997).

90. See generally David Klein & Julian A. Waller, Causation, Culpability and Deterrence in Highway Crashes 134-135; Samuel Kramer, An Economic Analysis of Criminal Attempt: Marginal Deterrence and the Optimal Structure of Sanctions, 81 J. Crim. L. & Criminology 398 (1990); Steven Shavell, Deterrence and the Punishment of Attempts, 19 J. Legal Stud. 435 (1990).

91. See the note on law and behavior at the end of Chapter 1, p. 110, above. See also David S. Cohen, Regulating Regulators: The Legal Environment of the State, 40 U. Toronto L.J. 213 (1990).

Chapter 4

Negligence: Proximate Cause, Special Instances of Nonliability, and Defenses

This chapter considers several doctrines that limit the scope of liability of negligent defendants who otherwise would be held responsible for plaintiff's harm. Although many of these legal concepts are also relevant in connection with claims based on intentional torts and strict liability, the cases and materials presented in this chapter mostly involve negligence claims. This focus on negligence is driven both by the fact that most observers regard negligence as the most significant area of American tort law, and by the fact that some conceptual aspects of proximate causation, contributory fault and other doctrines considered in this chapter become especially salient in the context of a negligence claim.

A. Proximate Cause

The rules of proximate cause sometimes allow a defendant to escape liability even if all other elements of the prima facie case — duty, breach, cause-in-fact, and harm — have been established. At first glance, this seems to be a remarkable assertion. Assume that *D*, the driver of an automobile, negligently speeds down a highway and collides with *P*, resulting in severe physical harm to *P*. Clearly, *D*'s driving is a cause-in-fact of *P*'s harm. However, *D* will escape liability if *P* cannot additionally establish that the negligent aspect of *D*'s driving — his speeding — caused the collision and that *P*'s harm is of the sort one would normally anticipate from such an accident. Why does the law impose these added burdens? An adequate answer must await consideration of the following material. But whatever the explanation, most people would probably agree that some outer limit must be placed on the liability of even clearly negligent actors. It may be true, as the poet said, that "for want of a nail, the kingdom was lost." But tort law is understandably reluctant to impose such a king-sized liability on the shoulders of the blacksmith, even if he were negligent in shoeing the horse.

In many circumstances proximate cause turns on *foreseeability* — the defendant may be liable for the foreseeable, but not the unforeseeable, consequences of her negligent conduct. This formulation requires evaluating the defendant's negligence in relation to the harm that a reasonably prudent person would have foreseen at the time the defendant acted. If the actual consequences of the defendant's conduct fall within the scope of the preliminarily defined risks, one essential element of the proximate cause requirement is satisfied. If the consequences fall outside these risks, a necessary link in the chain of proximate cause is missing, and the defendant is not liable.[1] The foreseeability of the consequences of the defendant's negligent conduct may refer either to the foreseeability of the plaintiff as a

1. The best and clearest explication of this approach is Robert E. Keeton, Legal Cause in the Law of Torts (1963).

possible victim of the defendant's negligent conduct, or to the foreseeability of the particular way in which the plaintiff became injured. We shall deal with each of these — foreseeable results and foreseeable plaintiffs — in the subsections that follow. As you will see, there is more to the proximate causation story than foreseeability. After all, almost anything that has ever happened before (and much that hasn't) is, in the literal sense, "foreseeable." But reasonable foreseeability is a good place to begin to think about proximate cause.

1. Liability Linked Logically to Defendant's Negligence and Limited to Foreseeable Consequences

a. Some Preliminary Considerations

Before we examine proximate causation in detail, some general points should be made. First, there was a time when courts flirted with the idea that the additional requirement of proximate causation was superfluous. Courts designed a loose test, the "direct consequences" test, best illustrated by three famous English cases. The first of these is *In re* Polemis & Furness, Withy & Co., [1921] 3 K.B. 560 (C.A.). Defendant's servant dropped a plank into the hold of plaintiff's ship. This caused a spark, which ignited highly flammable vapor that had escaped from broken cans of benzene. The resulting fire destroyed the ship. The claim was submitted to arbitration, and the arbitrators found that defendant's servant was negligent in dropping the plank, but that it was not foreseeable that the plank would cause a spark that would trigger a conflagration. In overturning the arbitrators and ruling that plaintiff was entitled to judgment, Scrutton L.J. said (3 K.B. at 577): "[T]he fact that the damage [the negligent act] in fact causes is not the exact kind of damage one would expect is immaterial, so long as the damage is in fact directly traceable to the negligent act." Is this a real-life example of king-size liability for the loss of a nail?

In Overseas Tankship (U.K.), Ltd. v. Morts Dock & Engineering Co., [1961] 1 All E.R. 404, commonly referred to as *Wagon Mound (No. 1),* the charterers of an oil-burning vessel, the Wagon Mound, spilled a quantity of oil into the harbor of Sydney, Australia. The oil ignited due to embers dropping from a wharf adjacent to the harbor, and the ensuing fire destroyed the entire wharf area. The wharf owners sued the charterers of the Wagon Mound. The trial court found that the fire was unforeseeable, but awarded damages to the plaintiffs for the destruction of the wharf. The English high court reversed the order of the trial court and entered judgment for the defendants based upon the finding that the ignitability of the oil was unforeseeable. The court said (1 All E.R. at 413): "[I]t does not seem consonant with current ideas of justice and morality that, for an act of negligence, however slight or venial, which results in some trivial foreseeable damage, the actor should be liable for all consequences, however unforeseeable and however grave, so long as they can be said to be 'direct.'" See also Overseas Tankship (U.K.), Ltd. v. Miller Steamship Co. Pty. Ltd., [1966] 2 All. E.R. 709, known as *Wagon Mound (No. 2),* arising out of the same occurrence that gave rise to *Wagon Mound (No. 1).*

This conflict between a king-size "direct consequences" approach and a more moderate "foreseeable consequences" approach is illustrated in the United States by the famous case of Kinsman (No. 1), 338 F.2d 708 (2d Cir.), *cert. denied*, 380 U.S. 944 (1964). A large grain barge broke loose from her moorings in the Buffalo River due to the negligence of her handlers. Drifting downstream, the barge broke a second vessel loose, and the two rammed into a drawbridge, knocking it down. Eventually, the two barges became stuck in the debris from the fallen bridge, effectively damming the river. Extensive flooding occurred upstream. On the issue of whether the negligent defendant could be held liable for the extensive flooding, the majority of the court of appeals held that the defendants were liable (338 F.2d at 724-26), stating: "The weight of authority in this country rejects the limitation of damages to consequences foreseeable at the time of the negligent conduct when the consequences are 'direct,' and the damage, although other and greater than expectable, is of the same general sort that was risked." Moore, J., dissented, emphasizing that reasonable foreseeability must be the guide to decision (338 F.2d at 728). As the materials that follow will make clear, the "direct consequences" test from earlier decisions has today largely been replaced by tests rooted in foreseeability.

Second, it is important to stress the distinction between the issue of proximate causation and the so-called "thin skull" rule or "eggshell skull" rule (often phrased: "the defendant takes the victim as found"), illustrated in *Vosburg*, the first case in this book. According to this rule, if the defendant wrongfully and foreseeably causes the plaintiff's person to be invaded, and if the initial invasion systemically leads to further injury, then the defendant is liable for all injuries to the plaintiff, even if the final extent of the plaintiff's injuries was unforeseeable at the time the initial invasion occurred. See generally Restatement (Third) of Torts: Liability for Physical and Emotional Harm §31 (2010). In *Kinsman*, above, the court contrasted the two issues, 338 F.2d at 725: "The oft encountered argument that failure to limit liability to foreseeable consequences may subject the defendant to a loss wholly out of proportion to his fault seems scarcely consistent with the universally accepted rule that the defendant takes the plaintiff as he finds him and will be responsible for the full extent of the injury even though a latent susceptibility of the plaintiff renders this far more serious than could reasonably have been anticipated." Do you see a problem with this argument? Given that the thin skull rule imposes liability for even unforeseen extents of injury to the plaintiff, can it be reconciled with proximate cause?

Finally, when we later deal with plaintiff's fault, you will see that contributory negligence has a comparative dimension, which can lead to percentage verdicts — a sharing of liability. Proximate causation, however, is an all-or-nothing inquiry: An act is either a proximate cause of the harm or it is not. One implication of this difference is that while comparisons of fault are, when called for, always for the trier of fact to decide, courts may use proximate causation to rule for defendants as a matter of law.

CSX Transp., Inc. v. McBride

564 U.S. 685 (2011)

[Respondent employee, McBride, won a verdict and judgment against his employer, CSX, in a Federal Employers Liability Act (FELA) negligence action. CSX had requested a proximate cause jury instruction, which the district court denied. After the Seventh Circuit affirmed, the Supreme Court of the United States granted certiorari to clarify the role of proximate cause in FELA cases.]

JUSTICE GINSBURG delivered the opinion of the Court.

[T]he Federal Employers Liability Act (FELA), 45 U.S.C. §51 et seq. . . . renders railroads liable for employees' injuries or deaths "resulting in whole or in part from [carrier] negligence." §51. In accord with the text and purpose of the Act, this Court's decision in Rogers v. Missouri Pacific R. Co., 352 U.S. 500 (1957), and the uniform view of federal appellate courts, we conclude that the Act does not incorporate "proximate cause" standards developed in nonstatutory common-law tort actions. The charge proper in FELA cases, we hold, simply tracks the language Congress employed, informing juries that a defendant railroad caused or contributed to a plaintiff employee's injury if the railroad's negligence played any part in bringing about the injury. . . .

Liability under FELA is limited in these key respects: Railroads are liable only to their employees, and only for injuries sustained in the course of employment. FELA's language on causation, however, "is as broad as could be framed." Urie v. Thompson, 337 U.S. 163, 181 (1949). . . . In our 1957 decision in *Rogers*, we described that relaxed standard as follows:

> "Under [FELA] the test of a jury case is simply whether the proofs justify with reason the conclusion that employer negligence played any part, even the slightest, in producing the injury or death for which damages are sought." 352 U.S., at 506.

As the Seventh Circuit emphasized, the instruction the District Court gave in this case, permitting a verdict for McBride if "[railroad] negligence played a part — no matter how small — in bringing about the injury," tracked the language of *Rogers*. If *Rogers* prescribes the definition of causation applicable under FELA, that instruction was plainly proper. . . .

Our subsequent decisions have confirmed that *Rogers* announced a general standard for causation in FELA cases. . . .

In reliance on *Rogers*, every Court of Appeals that reviews judgments in FELA cases has approved jury instructions on causation identical or substantively equivalent to the Seventh Circuit's instruction. Each appellate court has rejected common-law formulations of proximate cause of the kind CSX requested in this case. . . .

CSX nonetheless insists that proximate causation, as captured in the charge and definitions CSX requested, is a concept fundamental to actions sounding in negligence. The *Rogers* "any part" instruction opens the door to unlimited liability, CSX worries, inviting juries to impose liability on the basis of "but for" causation. The dissent shares these fears. But a half century's experience with *Rogers* gives us little cause for concern: CSX's briefs did not identify even one trial in which the instruction generated an absurd or untoward award. Nor has the dissent managed to uncover such a case. . . .

While some courts have said that Rogers eliminated the concept of proximate cause in FELA cases, we think it "more accurate . . . to recognize that *Rogers* describes the test for proximate causation applicable in FELA suits." *Sorrell*, 549 U.S., at 178 (Ginsburg, J., concurring in judgment). . . . Avoiding "dialectical subtleties" that confound attempts to convey intelligibly to juries just what "proximate cause" means, see *Coray*, 335 U.S., at 524, the *Rogers* instruction uses the everyday words contained in the statute itself. Jurors can comprehend those words and apply them in light of their experience and common sense. . . .

"[R]easonable foreseeability of harm," we clarified in *Gallick*, is indeed "an essential ingredient of [FELA] negligence." 372 U.S., at 117. . . . If negligence is proved, however, and is shown to have "played any part, even the slightest, in producing the injury," *Rogers*, 352 U.S., at 506, then the carrier is answerable in damages even if "the extent of the [injury] or the manner in which it occurred" was not "[p]robable" or "foreseeable." . . .

Properly instructed on negligence and causation, and told, as is standard practice in FELA cases, to use their "common sense" in reviewing the evidence, juries would have no warrant to award damages in far out "but for" scenarios. Indeed, judges would have no warrant to submit such cases to the jury. . . . In addition to the constraints of common sense, FELA's limitations on who may sue, and for what, reduce the risk of exorbitant liability. As earlier noted, the statute confines the universe of compensable injuries to those sustained by employees, during employment. Hence there are no unforeseeable plaintiffs in FELA cases. And the statute weeds out the injuries most likely to bear only a tenuous relationship to railroad negligence, namely, those occurring outside the workplace. . . .

For the reasons stated, it is not error in a FELA case to refuse a charge embracing stock proximate cause terminology. Juries in such cases are properly instructed that a defendant railroad "caused or contributed to" a railroad worker's injury "if [the railroad's] negligence played a part — no matter how small — in bringing about the injury." That, indeed, is the test Congress prescribed for proximate causation in FELA cases. As the courts below so held, the judgment of the U.S. Court of Appeals for the Seventh Circuit is

Affirmed.

CHIEF JUSTICE ROBERTS, with whom JUSTICE SCALIA, JUSTICE KENNEDY, and JUSTICE ALITO join, dissenting.

"It is a well established principle of [the common] law, that in all cases of loss we are to attribute it to the proximate cause, and not to any remote cause: *causa proxima non remota spectatur.*" Waters v. Merchants' Louisville Ins. Co., 36 U.S. 213 (1837) (Story, J.). The Court today holds that this principle does not apply to actions under the Federal Employers Liability Act (FELA), and that those suing under that statute may recover for injuries that were not proximately caused by the negligence of their employers. . . . The Court is wrong to dispense with that familiar element of an action seeking recovery for negligence, an element "generally thought to be a necessary limitation on liability," Exxon Co., U.S.A. v. Sofec, Inc., 517 U.S. 830 (1996). The test the Court would substitute — whether negligence played any part, even the slightest, in producing the injury — is no limit at all. It is simply "but for" causation. Nothing in FELA itself, or our decision in *Rogers*, supports such a boundless theory of liability. . . .

Recovery for negligence has always required a showing of proximate cause. "In a philosophical sense, the consequences of an act go forward to eternity." Holmes v. Securities Investor Protection Corporation, 503 U.S. 258, 266, n. 10 (1992) (quoting W. Keeton, D. Dobbs, R. Keeton, & D. Owen, Prosser and Keeton on Law of Torts §41, p. 264 (5th ed. 1984)). Law, however, is not philosophy, and the concept of proximate cause developed at common law in response to the perceived need to distinguish "but for" cause from those more direct causes of injury that can form the basis for liability at law. . . . Proximate cause refers to the basic requirement that before recovery is allowed in tort, there must be "some direct relation between the injury asserted and the injurious conduct alleged," *Holmes*, 503 U.S., at 268. . . . It limits liability at some point before the want of a nail leads to loss of the kingdom. . . .

The Court's theory seems to be that the words "in whole or in part" [in §51 of the Act] signal a departure from the historic requirement of proximate cause. But those words served a very different purpose. They did indeed mark an important departure from a common law principle, but it was the principle of contributory negligence — not proximate cause.

As noted, FELA abolished the defense of contributory negligence; the "in whole or in part" language simply reflected the fact that the railroad would remain liable even if its negligence was not the sole cause of injury. . . .

The Court today takes the "any part, even the slightest" language [from *Rogers*] out of context and views it as a rejection of proximate cause. But *Rogers* was talking about contributory negligence — it said so — and the language it chose confirms just that. "Slight" negligence was familiar usage in this context. . . . The use of the term "even the slightest" in *Rogers* makes perfect sense when the decision is understood to be about multiple causes — not about how direct any particular cause must be. . . .

The Court is correct that the federal courts of appeals have read *Rogers* to support the adoption of instructions like the one given here. But we do not resolve questions such as the one before us by a show of hands. . . . In addition, the Court discounts the views of those state courts of last resort that agree FELA did not relegate proximate cause to the dustbin. . . .

Even the Court seems to appreciate that it is creating a troubling gap in the FELA negligence action and ought to do something to patch it over. The something it proposes is "[r]easonable foreseeability of harm." Foreseeability as a test for proximate causation would be one thing; foreseeability has, after all, long been an aspect of proximate cause. But that is not the test the Court prescribes. It instead limits the foreseeability inquiry to whether the defendant was negligent in the first place. . . .

If courts must instruct juries on foreseeability as an aspect of negligence, why not instruct them on foreseeability as an aspect of causation? And if the jury is simply supposed to intuit that there should also be limits on the legal chain of causation — and that "but for" cause is not enough — why hide the ball? Why not simply tell the jury? Finally, if the Court intends "foreseeability of harm" to be a kind of poorman's proximate cause, then where does the Court find that requirement in the test *Rogers* — or FELA — prescribes? Could it be derived from the common law? . . .

Proximate cause supplies the vocabulary for answering such questions. It is useful to ask whether the injury that resulted was within the scope of the risk created by the defendant's negligent act; whether the injury was a natural or probable consequence of the negligence; whether there was a superseding or intervening cause; whether the negligence was anything more than an antecedent event without which the harm would not have occurred. . . . It is not necessary to accept every verbal formulation of proximate cause ever articulated to recognize that these standards provide useful guidance — and that juries should receive some instruction — on the type of link required between a railroad's negligence and an employee's injury.

Law has its limits. But no longer when it comes to the causal connection between negligence and a resulting injury covered by FELA. A new maxim has replaced the old: *Caelum terminus est* — the sky's the limit.

I respectfully dissent.

b. But For the Wrongful Quality of Defendant's Conduct, Would the Plaintiff Have Suffered the Same Harm?

It will be recalled from Chapter 2 that the actual causation issue is framed in the terms, "But for the defendant having acted at all, would the plaintiff nevertheless have suffered the same harm?" Here, it is assumed that the answer to this first causation question is negative — that the defendant's *conduct* was a necessary condition of the plaintiff's harm. A further question is then presented that seems to straddle the line between "actual" and "proximate" causation — namely, whether the *wrongful quality* of defendant's conduct was a necessary or "but-for" condition of plaintiff's harm. Because this second inquiry requires examination of the normative elements of defendant's wrongdoing, we have chosen to treat it as an aspect of the issue of "proximate," or "legal," causation rather than "actual" causation, even though both this issue and the actual causation issue in Chapter 2 involve "but-for" inquiries. In truth, the material presented in this subsection could well be considered part of "actual causation" doctrine; we present it here, however, because we believe it is easier to understand the "wrongful quality of defendant's conduct" inquiry after having first learned the basic principles of negligence in Chapter 3.

Ford v. Trident Fisheries Co.

232 Mass. 400, 122 N.E. 389 (1919)

Tort by the administratrix of the estate of Jerome Ford . . . against the Trident Fisheries Company . . . for negligently causing the death by drowning of the plaintiff's intestate on December 21, 1916, when he was employed as the mate of the defendant's steam trawler. . . .

. . . At the close of the plaintiff's evidence, which is described in the opinion, the judge, upon motion of the defendant, ordered a verdict for the defendant; and the plaintiff alleged exceptions.

CARROLL, J. The plaintiff's intestate was drowned while employed as mate of the defendant's steam trawler, the Long Island. This action is to recover damages for his death.

On December 21, 1916, about five o'clock in the afternoon, the vessel left T Wharf, Boston, bound for the "Georges," which are fishing banks in Massachusetts waters. About six o'clock, shortly after passing Boston Light, the plaintiff's intestate, Jerome Ford, came on deck to take charge of his watch as mate of the vessel. He came from the galley in the forecastle and walked aft on the starboard side. As he was ascending a flight of four steps leading from the deck to the pilot house, the vessel rolled and he was thrown overboard. At the time of the accident there was a fresh northwest breeze and the vessel was going before the wind; no cry was heard, no clothing was seen floating in the water, and Ford was not seen by any one from the time he fell overboard. . . .

The plaintiff . . . contends that the boat which was lowered to pick up the intestate was lashed to the deck instead of being suspended from davits and in order to launch it the lashings had to be cut; that McCue, who manned it, had only one oar and was obliged to scull, instead of rowing as he might have done if he had had two oars. Even if it be assumed that upon these facts it could have been found the defendant was negligent, there is nothing to show they in any way contributed to Ford's death. He disappeared when he fell from the trawler and it does not appear that if the boat had been suspended from davits and a different method of propelling it had been used he could have been rescued. . . .

Exceptions overruled.

Aegis Insurance Services, Inc. v. 7 World Trade Co., L.P.

737 F.3d 166 (2d Cir. 2013)

POOLER, C.J.:

The 7 World Trade Center Building ("7WTC") stood on the northern edge of the World Trade Center site. As the North Tower collapsed on September 11, 2001, it sent flaming debris spewing into the area around 7WTC. The fiery debris crashed into 7WTC, gouging chunks out of the building. Fires burned on multiple floors. Confident that the people inside had evacuated, grappling with the death of hundreds of firefighters and a non-existent supply of water, the New York City Fire Department made the decision to establish a collapse zone and walk away, rather than fight the fire. After burning for seven hours, 7WTC collapsed, destroying the electrical substation owned by Consolidated Edison Co. of New York, Inc. ("Con Ed") directly underneath the building.

Con Ed, along with its insurers, sued the defendants, who designed, built, operated and maintained 7WTC, alleging in relevant part that the defendants' negligence caused the building to collapse. The district court disposed of the claims against the defendants [by holding that no duty of care was owed to plaintiff]. . . . We affirm the grants of summary judgment, albeit on different grounds than those relied on by the district court. We hold that even assuming arguendo negligence on the part of the defendants, any such negligence was not the cause in fact of the collapse of 7WTC.

Background

I. 7 World Trade Center

The Con Ed substation in question was built in 1970 to provide electric power to the World Trade Center site, built on land owned by the Port Authority of New York and New Jersey. . . .

The substation was built on a trapezoidal parcel of land, and 7WTC was designed as a trapezoid to mimic the shape of the parcel. . . . The relevant building standards at the time 7WTC was constructed specified that:

> Through accident or misuse, structures capable of supporting safely all conventional design loads may suffer local damage, that is, the loss of load resistance in an element or small portion of the structure. In recognition of this, buildings and structural systems shall possess general structural integrity, which is the quality of being able to sustain local damage with the structure as a whole remaining stable and not being damaged to an extent disproportionate to the original local damage.

American National Standard: Minimum Design Loads for Buildings and Other Structures, §58.1, Section 1.3 (1982). Construction on 7WTC was completed in 1987.

II. Terrorism in Manhattan

In 1984, the Port Authority formed "The Office for Special Planning" (the "Office") to assess the vulnerability of the Authority's various facilities to terrorism. A report prepared by the Office examined the vulnerabilities of the World Trade Center Complex, noting a number of "Symbolic Bombing Incidents in New York City from 1980 to 1985," including:

- Three people injured in explosion at the Manhattan offices of the airline Aeroflot in 1980, with the Jewish Defense League claiming credit.
- A pipe bomb exploding the sub-basement of New York State Supreme Court in Manhattan in 1981 after warnings of a bomb blast by the Croatian Freedom Fighters.
- Four bombs at stock exchanges and banks in Manhattan in 1982, with Fuerzas Armadas de Liberacion Nacional ("FALN") claiming credit.

- A bomb at the Bankers Trust Company in Manhattan, also in 1982, with FALN again claiming credit.
- A bomb at 250 Broadway (apparently directed toward the New York City Police Benevolent Association) in 1985.

In 1993, a car bomb was detonated in the parking garage below One World Trade Center. See United States v. Yousef, 327 F.3d 56, 79 (2d Cir. 2003). Ramzi Yousef, along with several co-conspirators, "drove a bomb-laden van onto the B–2 level of the parking garage below the World Trade Center. They then set the bomb's timer to detonate minutes later. At approximately 12:18 p.m. that day, the bomb exploded, killing six people, injuring more than a thousand others, and causing widespread fear and more than $500 million in property damage." Id. Testifying at Yousef's trial, a U.S. Secret Service agent told the jury that Yousef's intent was to cause One World Trade Center to topple, killing tens of thousands of people.

III. September 11, 2001

The horrific events of September 11, 2001 are well known and need not be repeated here in great detail. . . .

When firefighters arrived to assess 7WTC, they found a building ravaged by the debris that careened through the air when the North Tower collapsed, with multiple active fires throughout the structure. . . .

The collapse of the Twin Towers destroyed the water main responsible for bringing water to 7WTC, resulting in "significant damage done to the water supply in the area". . . .

With no water, and no civilian lives at risk, and with their comrades buried in the Towers' debris, the fire department decided to create a collapse zone around 7WTC and allow the fire to burn, unchecked. Hayden explained:

> The decision not to attempt to extinguish the fire in that building was based on the fact that, number 1, the amount of fire that was occurring in the building, the fact that the buildings had been searched and evacuated, and thirdly, and most important I think at that point in time is we had already lost 400 firefighters. The building at this time we deemed to be vacant and we decided not to risk any more firefighters' lives that day.

Deputy Commissioner Cruthers, in command at the time, said:

> The idea was that we expected that this building would come down, my goal at that point was not to lose any more people.
>
> * * *
>
> I made up my mind when I assumed command that my primary responsibility was to the living, and . . . although we had a strong obligation to conduct searches and extinguishment operations where we could and those in any building are inherently dangerous.
>
> So it wasn't that we weren't going to do any things that involved danger, but there had to be a favorable risk/reward analysis to justify committing people — what was the upside, what were we going to get, and at that point, not only the firefighters, but the police officers, the Port Authority workers, [Office of Emergency Management] people, everyone was there.

> The first obligation is to the people who are alive, and then decide what is the likelihood of a successful effort compared to the risk of their lives.

The building collapsed roughly seven hours after the fire department decided to walk away, at 5:21 p.m., crushing the Con Ed substation. . . .

Discussion

. . . The parties agree that 7WTC collapsed as a result of fire ignited by burning debris from the collapse of One World Trade Center, but on little after that. Con Ed argues that its expert declarations and reports support the conclusion that "inadequate design and construction of 7WTC permitted office contents fires to cause the collapse of 7WTC." Con Ed posits that debris from Tower 1 hit 7WTC, setting off "office contents fires." In broad strokes, Con Ed argues one of the building's girders was not adequately connected to an appropriate column, and this inadequate connection set off a series of failures leading to the building's collapse. Defendants argue 7WTC was properly designed and constructed, but simply could not withstand the events of September 11.

For the purposes of this appeal, we need not delve into the mechanics behind the building's failure. While we conclude that the district court erred in finding the 7WTC defendants did not owe Con Ed a duty of care, we nevertheless affirm on the ground that the record before us establishes that, given the unprecedented nature and sheer magnitude of the events of September 11, the alleged negligence on the part of defendants was not the cause-in-fact of the collapse of 7WTC.

The district court erred in granting 7WTC summary judgment on the ground that the events of September 11 were not foreseeable, and thus defendants did not owe Con Ed a duty to protect against them . . . .The district court found that:

> It was not within 7WTC's . . . 'range of apprehension' that terrorists would slip through airport security, hijack an airplane, crash it suicidally into the one of the two tallest skyscrapers in New York City, set off falling debris that would ignite a building several hundred feet away, cause structural damage to it, destroy water mains causing an internal sprinkler system to become inoperable, kill 343 firemen, and paralyze the rest so that a fire within a building would not be put out and the building would be allowed to burn an entire day before it consumed itself and collapsed.

The district court's foreseeability analysis misses the mark. "Foreseeability, alone, does not define duty — it merely determines the scope of the duty once it is determined to exist." Hamilton v. Beretta U.S.A. Corp., 96 N.Y.2d 222, 231, 727 N.Y.S.2d 7, 750 N.E.2d 1055 (2001) (internal citations omitted). . . . New York law makes plain that Con Ed need not show 7WTC foresaw the precise risk of terrorists hijacking planes and flying them into Towers One and Two, setting off the chain of events leading to 7WTC's collapse. . . . The risk of massive fire at a high-rise building such as 7WTC is a foreseeable risk, and the district court erred in finding otherwise. How that fire started plays no part in the foreseeability analysis for the purposes of determining whether 7WTC owed Con Ed a duty.

Finding 7WTC owed Con Ed a duty, however, does not settle the matter of liability. Once a duty is established, to prevail Con Ed must prove a breach of that duty, and that the breach was the cause of Con Ed's injuries. There is an alternate ground for affirming the grant of summary judgment to defendants: even assuming arguendo negligence on the part of the defendants, any such negligence was not the cause-in-fact of the collapse of 7WTC. In New York:

> Causation incorporates at least two separate but related concepts: cause-in-fact and proximate cause. Cause-in-fact refers to those antecedent events, acts or omissions which have so far contributed to the result that without them it would not have occurred. . . . Proximate cause serves to limit, for legal or policy reason, the responsibility of an actor for the consequences of his conduct.

Monahan v. Weichert, 82 A.D.2d 102, 442 N.Y.S.2d 295, 298 (4th Dep't 1981) (internal alterations and citations omitted). The trend in New York cases is to focus analysis more on "substantial factor" or proximate cause analysis and less on cause-in-fact analysis. However, it remains "the general rule that in common-law negligence actions, [that] a plaintiff must prove that the defendant's conduct was a cause-in-fact of the injury." Hamilton, 96 N.Y.2d at 241, 727 N.Y.S.2d 7, 750 N.E.2d 1055. We find it especially difficult to shoehorn this extraordinary sequence of events into the "welter of confusion" that is proximate cause. See Prosser & Keeton, The Law of Torts (5th Ed.1984) §41 at 263. When faced with the unique constellation of events that comprised September 11, 2001, we find it most appropriate to return to a bedrock principle of tort law that for there to be a recovery for an injury, it must be established that defendant's act was a cause-in-fact of an injury if there is to be a recovery.

This principle requires a plaintiff to establish, beyond the point of speculation and conjecture, a factual, causal connection between its losses and a defendant's actions. . . .

Con Ed's primary argument is an unfought fire would not have caused 7WTC to collapse had the building been property designed and constructed. But Con Ed's focus on the fires that engulfed 7WTC carves what occurred at 7WTC out of the series of events that occurred on September 11, and this we cannot do. This failure to relate the constellation of events surrounding the collapse of 7WTC or to link the unprecedented nature of those events with the negligence at issue is fatal to Con Ed's claims. Under Con Ed's approach to liability, those who designed and constructed the building would presumably be liable if, for example, 7WTC collapsed as a result of a fire triggered by a nuclear attack on lower Manhattan. While the concepts underlying tort law must, by their nature, be fluid, at the end of the day they must engage with reality.

Although Con Ed proffered expert reports speculating how various design features of 7WTC could have been modified to withstand collapse, we find the reports too speculative to avoid summary judgment, even drawing all inferences in favor of Con Ed. Con Ed's experts opine that a properly designed building would have withstood "a local failure" as well as "complete combustion of its fuel load without collapsing and with no intervention by manual fire-fighting or automatic sprinkler combustion." In support of these assertions, the experts point to several "vulnerabilities" in 7WTC's design and construction based on their review of photographs of the scene and of computer modeling.

None of the expert reports, however, address in any substantive or adequate way the interaction between the identified "vulnerabilities" and the unprecedented etiology and severity of the cataclysm that engulfed lower Manhattan on September 11, 2001. The failure to connect the defendants' alleged negligence to the events of the day renders the proffered reports too speculative and conjectural to create triable issues of fact. . . . The crashing of airplanes into the Twin Towers, and the Towers' subsequent collapse, caused debris to cascade onto 7WTC, tearing off chunks of 7WTC's walls and floors. Falling, burning debris from the Towers also triggered multiple fires on multiple, noncontiguous floors of 7WTC, unusual in a high-rise building. The collapse of the Towers severed the water main responsible for bringing water to 7WTC, leaving the firefighters and 7WTC's sprinkler system without water. When the Towers collapsed, 343 firefighters were killed. Among their numbers were members of New York City Fire Department's special operations units, including its specially trained high rise units. Faced with this unprecedented constellation of events, fire department commanders chose to let the building burn rather than fight the fire. The fire raged unabated for roughly seven hours before the building collapsed. We have little trouble concluding that the confluence of these events demonstrates that 7WTC would have collapsed regardless of any negligence ascribed by plaintiffs' experts to the design and construction of 7WTC more than a decade earlier. It is simply incompatible with common sense and experience to hold that defendants were required to design and construct a building that would survive the events of September 11, 2001.

Conclusion

For the reasons given above, the judgment of the district court is AFFIRMED.

Judge WESLEY dissents by separate opinion.

WESLEY, Circuit Judge, dissenting:

Plaintiffs' experts have articulated a standard of care: high-rise buildings must be built to withstand a fire that cannot be extinguished by the efforts of firefighters. Plaintiffs' experts have also identified a deviation from that standard: the building was designed and erected in such a way that it was subject to failure if a fire broke out that could not be quelled. They have tied that standard and its deviation to the injury for which they seek recompense. Lastly, plaintiffs' experts have offered opinions that 7WTC did not collapse as a result of structural damage from falling debris.

One would think that, on this record, the majority would want to hear from defendants' experts on why 7WTC collapsed. It may well be that causation, be it proximate or in fact, can be decided as a matter of law in the district court after a careful review of all expert submissions or that a trial will result in a defendants' verdict, but that is not the path the majority has chosen for this case. I would remand the matter to the district court for trial. I, therefore, respectfully dissent.

In Texas & Pac. Ry. v. McCleery, 418 S.W.2d 494 (Tex. 1967), the plaintiff was injured when the truck in which he was a passenger collided with a train owned and operated by the defendant. The train had exceeded the speed limit, and one of the plaintiff's arguments was that if the train had not been speeding, the truck would have reached the intersection ahead of the train and passed over it without incident. In a second Texas case, Lear Siegler, Inc. v. Perez, 819 S.W.2d 470 (Tex. 1991), the decedent's job was to pull a truck with a flashing arrow sign, manufactured by the defendant, to alert drivers of sweeping operations on the road. The plaintiff alleged that the sign malfunctioned, and when the decedent got out of the truck to fix it, he was fatally injured when one Lerma, who had fallen asleep at the wheel of his van, drove into the sign. In the wrongful death action, the plaintiff argued that if the sign had not malfunctioned, the decedent would not have been in a position to be injured by Lerma's oncoming car. The Supreme Court of Texas rejected the plaintiffs' arguments in both cases, ruling that in neither could it be found that the defendant's negligence caused the harm. Did the court get both cases right? In *Perez,* the court stated (819 S.W.2d at 472):

> It is undisputed that Lerma was asleep, and proper operation of the flashing arrow sign would have had no effect on his conduct. Plaintiffs assert that, had the sign functioned properly, Perez would not have been at the place where the collision occurred at the time it occurred. We conclude that these particular circumstances are too remotely connected with Lear Siegler's conduct to constitute legal cause. If Perez had instead taken the sign back to the highway department office where the roof caved in on him, we likewise would not regard it as a legal cause.

See Restatement (Third) of Torts: Liability for Physical and Emotional Harm §30 Ills. 1 & 2 (2010) (considering similar *rendez-vous* issues).

Problem 22

A partner in the law firm in which you are an associate has asked for your help on a tort case she is handling. The client is Rose Miller, an 81-year-old woman who lives in the home of her son, Daniel. When his aging mother came three months earlier to live in his home, Daniel bought and had installed a special bathtub equipped with "no-slip" strips, specifically for Rose's safety. Rose fell and broke her hip while showering in the tub. Hearing her fall, Daniel ran into the bathroom and found her unconscious, lying on her side in the tub. After examination of the tub, it appeared that one of the strips had come loose, apparently due to a defect in the glue used to adhere the strips to the tub. Daniel and Natalie (Daniel's wife) are ready to swear that neither of them observed the strip being loose before the accident.

Rose has no recollection of the details of the accident. She remembers standing in the tub with the shower operating and then waking up in the ambulance that took her to the hospital. Prior to the accident, Rose had been subject to light-headedness, including one fainting spell. Rose's doctor maintains that it is possible that, on the day of the accident, the strip dislodged while Rose was standing on it, causing her to fall and only then become unconscious because of the intense pain caused by the injuries to her hip. Her doctor also explains that it is possible that Rose fainted in the shower, the strip having come loose earlier and having nothing to do with her fall. Nothing in the nature of her injuries suggests that one or the other scenario is more likely.

The partner wants your assessment of Rose's chances of reaching the jury on a claim against the bathtub manufacturer. You may assume that further investigation will support the conclusion that the strip was defective when Daniel bought the tub, although it had not yet become loosened. As you are about the leave the partner's office, she adds: "One more point — I know that Daniel and Natalie have a sizable homeowners insurance policy. You might consider the strength of a claim against them." Assuming that Ford v. Trident, above, is a decision by your jurisdiction's highest court, advise the partner.

Cahoon v. Cummings

734 N.E.2d 535 (Ind. 2000)

[This was a wrongful death action in which the plaintiff alleged that the defendant physicians negligently failed to diagnose and treat the decedent's esophageal cancer. A Medical Review Panel determined that the defendants "failed to follow the appropriate standard of care, but that their conduct 'was not a factor of the resultant damages.'" After a jury trial, the trial judge instructed the jury that the plaintiff could recover wrongful death damages in full if the jury determined that the defendants' negligence was a "substantial factor" in causing the decedent's death. From a judgment on a jury verdict for the plaintiff for the full amount of damages, the defendants appealed.]

BOEHM, JUSTICE.

In Mayhue v. Sparkman, 653 N.E.2d 1384, 1388-1389 (1995), this Court held that a plaintiff is not precluded from bringing a medical malpractice claim against a negligent doctor merely because the plaintiff is unable to prove by a preponderance of the evidence that the doctor's conduct was the proximate cause of the resulting injury. We adopted Section 323 of the Restatement of Torts, which reads:

> One who undertakes, gratuitously or for consideration, to render services to another which he should recognize as necessary for the protection of the other's person or things, is subject to liability to the other for physical harm resulting from his failure to exercise reasonable care to perform his undertaking, if:
>
> (a) his failure to exercise such care increases the risk of such harm, or;
>
> (b) the harm is suffered because of the other's reliance upon the undertaking.

This doctrine permits recovery from a defendant whose negligence significantly increases the probability of the ultimate harm, even if the likelihood of incurring that injury was greater than fifty percent in the absence of the defendant's negligence. Here, as in *Mayhue,* all experts agreed that [decedent] would probably not have survived even if he had been properly diagnosed and treated. . . . However, [decedent's] expert testified that [he] would have had a statistically significant chance, perhaps twenty-five to thirty percent, of surviving his esophageal cancer if it had been diagnosed at [his] first visit to [one of the defendants]. . . .

The trial court instructed that the defendants would be liable for full wrongful death damages if the jury determined that their actions were a substantial factor in Cummings' death.

Holding the defendant liable for the full value of the wrongful death claim . . . [i]n effect, . . . would hold doctors liable not only for their own negligence, but also for their patients' illnesses, which are not the product of the doctors' actions. To be sure, this rule might encourage doctors to be more vigilant, but compensation for injuries caused, not deterrence of future actions, is the basis of recovery the legislature has chosen for a wrongful death.

There is little support in other jurisdictions for the practice of awarding damages measured by the full value of the injury in a Section 323 or "loss of chance" case. . . .

In sum, we . . . hold that upon a showing of causation under *Mayhue,* damages are proportional to the increased risk attributable to the defendant's negligent act or omission. . . . [B]ecause the jury was instructed to award full wrongful death damages if a defendant's conduct was a "substantial factor" in Cummings' death, the degree of increased risk was not quantified and we have no basis to conclude that any specific dollar award is proper under that theory. In sum, the amount of any award for wrongful death is unknowable and it is equally unknowable whether the survivor theory supported the jury's award. As a result, remand for a new trial is required. . . .

We reverse the judgment of the trial court and remand for a new trial.

Cases embracing one or [illegible]e variations of the "loss of chance" theory of recovery adopted by the court in *Cal*[illegible] include Komlodi v. Picciano, 89 A.3d 1234 (N.J. 2014); Dickhoff v. Green, 836 N.[illegible] 321 (Minn. 2013); Matsuyama v. B[illegible]nbaum, 890 N.E.2d 819 (Mass. 2008); Boon[illegible]iam W. Backus Hosp., 864 A.2d 1 (Conn. 2005); McMackin v. Johnson County Healthcare Ctr., 73 P.3d 1094 (Wyo. 2003), *aff'd on reh'g*, 88 P.3d 491 (Wyo. 2004); Holton v. Memorial Hosp., 679 N.E.2d 1202 (Ill. 1997); Anderson v. Picciotti, 676 A.2d 127 (N.J. 1996); Wollen v. DePaul Health Ctr., 828 S.W.2d 681 (Mo. 1992); Smith v. State through Dep't of Health & Human Resources Admin., 523 So. 2d 815 (La. 1988); Aasheim v. Humberger, 695 P.2d 824 (Mont. 1985); Roberson v. Counselman, 686 P.2d 149 (Kan. 1984); Herskovits v. Group Health Co-op. of Puget Sound, 664 P.2d 474 (Wash. 1983). Other courts have rejected the "loss of a chance" approach. See, e.g., Kemper v. Gordon, 272 S.W.3d 146 (Ky. 2008); Smith v. Parrott, 833 A.2d 843 (Vt. 2003); Jones v. Owings, 456 S.E.2d 371 (S.C. 1995); Kramer v. Lewisville Mem'l Hosp., 858 S.W.2d 397 (Tex. 1993); Kilpatrick v. Bryant, 868 S.W.2d 594 (Tenn. 1993); Manning v. Twin Falls Clinic & Hosp., Inc., 830 P.2d 1185 (Idaho 1992). The Restatement (Third) is agnostic on the issue. Restatement (Third) of Torts: Liability for Physical and Emotional Harm §26 cmt. *n* (2010) ("Both because the lost-opportunity doctrine is one involving the definition of legally cognizable harm and because it has been confined to medical malpractice, a specialized area of negligence liability outside the scope of this Restatement, the Institute takes no position on this matter, leaving it for future developments and future Restatements.").

After the Supreme Court of Michigan adopted the "loss of a chance" rule in Falcon v. Memorial Hosp., 462 N.W.2d 44 (Mich. 1990), the Michigan legislature passed the following statute (Mich. Comp. Laws Ann. §600.2912(a)(2)):

> In an action alleging medical malpractice, the plaintiff has the burden of proving that he or she suffered an injury that more probably than not was proximately caused by the negligence of the defendant or defendants. In an action alleging medical malpractice, the plaintiff cannot recover for loss of an opportunity to survive or an opportunity to achieve a better result unless the opportunity was greater than 50%.

In Wickens v. Oakwood Healthcare System, 631 N.W.2d 686 (Mich. 2001), the Supreme Court of Michigan construed the statute to preclude recovery by a living person purely for a lost opportunity to survive, but to permit recovery for any injuries actually suffered that more likely than not were caused by defendant's negligence. Thus, damages caused by a negligent failure to timely diagnose plaintiff's breast cancer, including the need for a more invasive form of surgery and emotional suffering associated with the experience, could be pursued under the statute. Note that if plaintiff had a 50 percent or less chance of survival prior to the defendant's negligence, it would seemingly be impossible for plaintiff to prove by a preponderance of the evidence that defendant's conduct actually caused plaintiff's injury. The loss-of-a-chance theory is designed to address precisely this problem.

To what extent should courts permit recovery if the plaintiff had a 50 percent or less chance of survival prior to the defendant's negligence? Compare Pipe v. Hamilton, 56 P.3d 823 (Kan. 2002), in which the court held that a 5 to 10 percent chance of survival was sufficient to maintain a cause of action for loss of chance of survival, with Boone v. William W. Backus Hosp., 864 A.2d 1 (Conn. 2005), in which the court required a loss-of-a-chance plaintiff to show that the decedent had at least a 51 percent chance of survival prior to the defendant's negligence. Does the proportional damages rule adopted in *Cahoon* alleviate some of the concerns underlying cases like *Boone*?

In Grant v. American National Red Cross, 745 A.2d 316 (D.C. 2000), the court refused to adopt the loss-of-a-chance doctrine in a case in which the alleged negligence of the defendant was its failure to adequately screen blood for the hepatitis C virus. The trial judge entered summary judgment for the defendant because the plaintiff, who contracted hepatitis following a blood transfusion, could not establish that any testing system available at that time would have provided a greater than 50 percent chance of screening out all infected blood. The court wrote broadly in rejecting loss-of-a-chance liability, but also distinguished the case from cases like *Cahoon. Cahoon* involved the failure of the defendant to prevent harm from an existing cancerous condition. *Grant,* on the other hand, involved a claim that the defendant's negligence allowed the plaintiff to *contract* the condition — hepatitis — of which he complained. Another distinction the court pointed out was that *Grant* did not involve negligence of a physician, but of a supplier of a product used in medical treatment.

In McMullen v. Ohio State University Hospitals, 725 N.E.2d 1117 (Ohio 2000), the Ohio Supreme Court refused to apply the loss-of-a-chance doctrine to situations where the defendant's conduct independently causes death, as opposed to those situations where it hastens or aggravates a preexisting condition. In that case, the court found that the hospital workers' negligence in removing and then reinstalling an endotracheal tube did not combine with a preexisting condition, but instead directly caused the patient's death. The court therefore refused to use the loss-of-a-chance approach, treating it, instead, as a straightforward medical malpractice claim. See also Mead v. Adrian, 670 N.W.2d 174 (Iowa 2003) (refusing to reduce damages to be proportionate with loss of chance where jury could conclude from the evidence that defendant's negligence was the proximate cause of plaintiff's death).

If you are otherwise disposed to accept *Cahoon*'s loss-of-a-chance approach, do you think that the distinctions suggested by the courts in *Grant* or *McMullen* hold up?

Courts have been unwilling to extend loss-of-a-chance reasoning beyond cases of medical malpractice. See, e.g., Lyons v. Am. Coll. of Veterinary Sports Med. & Rehab., Inc., 997 F. Supp. 2d 92, 115 (D. Mass. 2014) ("Applying the loss of chance doctrine outside of the medical malpractice context . . . would be premature."); Shea v. Williams, 974 N.E.2d 1168 (Mass. App. Ct. 2012) ("[A] loss of chance claim must be supported by expert evidence supported by probability statistics grounded in medical data."). Why would applying loss-of-a-chance more broadly be "premature?" What distinguishes medical malpractice from other areas of tort law?

David A. Fischer offers one answer in Tort Recovery for Loss of a Chance, 36 Wake Forest L. Rev. 605 (2001). Noting that the rule "could be applied in virtually every case of questionable causation," Fischer nonetheless concludes that doing so would be "much more difficult" outside of medical malpractice. This is because "scientists have collected good statistical information concerning the chances of success of a wide variety of medical procedures," whereas "[i]n cases involving such issues as failure to warn, legal malpractice, and loss of business opportunity . . . the facts of each case are highly individualistic and there is no good body of statistics showing the likelihood of causation." Id. at 605-33. If the key distinction is the availability of good statistical information in the medical context, might the development of more comprehensive data collection justify expansion of the loss-of-a-chance doctrine to other domains? Some analysts outside of the legal profession suggest that systemic and transformative developments in data collection and analysis are presently occurring in a variety of fields. See, e.g., Viktor Mayer-Schönberger & Kenneth Cukier, Big Data: A Revolution That Will Transform How We Live, Work, and Think (2013). On this evidence, one could imagine a future in which the quality of medical statistics was no longer so differentiable from statistics in other significant areas addressed by tort law.

Perhaps other factors beyond confidence in statistics are in play. Discussing the same issue two years after Fischer's article, the Supreme Court of Iowa noted there was a "very real concern that expanded recognition of the loss of chance doctrine could threaten to swallow whole the equitable, established principles of causation and damages that have guided tort law for centuries." Mead v. Adrian, 670 N.W.2d 174, 185 (Iowa 2003). See also Tory A. Weigand, Lost Chances, Felt Necessities, and the Tale of Two Cities, 43 Suffolk U. L. Rev. 327 (2010); Lars Noah, An Inventory of Mathematical Blunders in Applying the Loss-of-Chance Doctrine, 24 Rev. Litig. 369 (2005); John C. P. Goldberg, What Clients Are Owed: Cautionary Observations on Lawyers and Loss of Chance, 52 Emory L.J. 1201 (2003); John C. P. Goldberg & Benjamin C. Zipursky, Unrealized Torts, 88 Va. L. Rev. 1625 (2002).

c. Was Any Harm at All to the Plaintiff Foreseeable When the Defendant Acted?

Palsgraf v. Long Island Railroad

248 N.Y. 339, 162 N.E. 99 (1928)

Appeal from a judgment of the Appellate Division of the Supreme Court in the second judicial department . . . affirming a judgment in favor of plaintiff entered upon a verdict.

CARDOZO, C.J. Plaintiff was standing on a platform of defendant's railroad after buying a ticket to go to Rockaway Beach. A train stopped at the station, bound for another place. Two men ran forward to catch it. One of the men reached the platform of the car without mishap, though the train was already moving. The other man, carrying a package, jumped aboard the car, but seemed unsteady as if about to fall. A guard on the car, who had held the door open, reached forward to help him in, and another guard on the platform pushed him from behind. In this act, the package was dislodged, and fell upon the rails. It was a package of small size, about fifteen inches long, and was covered by a newspaper. In fact it contained fireworks, but there was nothing in its appearance to give notice of its contents. The fireworks when they fell exploded. The shock of the explosion threw down some scales at the other end of the platform, many feet away. The scales struck the plaintiff, causing injuries for which she sues.

The conduct of the defendant's guard, if a wrong in its relation to the holder of the package, was not a wrong in its relation to the plaintiff, standing far away. Relative to her it was not negligence at all. Nothing in the situation gave notice that the falling package had in it the potency of peril to persons thus removed. Negligence is not actionable unless it involves the invasion of a legally protected interest, the violation of a right. "Proof of negligence in the air, so to speak, will not do" (Pollock, Torts [11th ed.], p. 455. . . .). The plaintiff as she stood upon the platform of the station might claim to be protected against intentional invasion of her bodily security. Such invasion is not charged. She might claim to be protected against unintentional invasion by conduct involving in the thought of reasonable men an unreasonable hazard that such invasion would ensue. These, from the point of view of law, were the bounds of her immunity, with perhaps some rare exceptions, survivals for the most part of ancient forms of liability, where conduct is held to be at the peril of the actor.

If no hazard was apparent to the eye of ordinary vigilance, an act innocent and harmless, at least to outward seeming, with reference to her, did not take to itself the quality of a tort because it happened to be a wrong, though apparently not one involving the risk of bodily insecurity, with reference to some one else. . . . The plaintiff sues in her own right for a wrong personal to her, and not as the vicarious beneficiary of a breach of duty to another.

A different conclusion will involve us, and swiftly too, in a maze of contradictions. A guard stumbles over a package which has been left upon a platform. It seems to be a bundle of newspapers. It turns out to be a can of dynamite. To the eye of ordinary vigilance, the bundle is abandoned waste, which may be kicked or trod on with impunity. Is a passenger at the other end of the platform protected by the law against the unsuspected hazard concealed beneath the waste? If not, is the result to be any different, so far as the distant passenger is concerned, when the guard stumbles over a valise which a truckman or a porter has left upon the walk? The passenger far away, if the victim of a wrong at all, has a cause of action, not derivative, but original and primary. His claim to be protected against invasion of his bodily security is neither greater nor less because the act resulting in the invasion is a wrong to another far removed. In this case, the rights that are said to have been violated, the interests said to have been invaded, are not even of the same order. The man was not injured in his person nor even put in danger. The purpose of the act, as well as its effect, was to make his person safe. If there was a wrong to him at all, which may very well be doubted, it was a wrong to a property interest only, the safety of his package. Out of this wrong to property, which threatened injury to nothing else, there has passed, we are told, to the plaintiff by derivation or succession a right of action for the invasion of an interest of another order, the right to bodily security. The diversity of interests emphasizes the futility of the effort to build the plaintiff's right upon the basis of a wrong to some one else. The gain is one of emphasis, for a like result would follow if the interests were the same. Even then, the orbit of the danger as disclosed to the eye of reasonable vigilance would be the orbit of the duty. One who jostles one's neighbor in a crowd does not invade the rights of others standing at the outer fringe when the unintended contact casts a bomb upon the ground. The wrongdoer as to them is the man who carries the bomb, not the one who explodes it without suspicion of the danger. Life will have to be made over, and human nature transformed, before prevision so extravagant can be accepted as the norm of conduct, the customary standard to which behavior must conform.

The argument for the plaintiff is built upon the shifting meanings of such words as "wrong" and "wrongful," and shares their instability. What the plaintiff must show is "a wrong" to herself, i.e., a violation of her own right, and not merely a wrong to some one else, nor conduct "wrongful" because unsocial, but not "a wrong" to any one. We are told that one who drives at reckless speed through a crowded city street is guilty of a negligent act and, therefore, of a wrongful one irrespective of the consequences. Negligent the act is, and wrongful in the sense that it is unsocial, but wrongful and unsocial in relation to other travelers, only because the eye of vigilance perceives the risk of damage. If the same act were to be committed on a speedway or a race course, it would lose its wrongful quality. The risk reasonably to be perceived defines the duty to be obeyed, and risk imports relation; it is risk to another or to others within the range of apprehension. . . . The range of reasonable apprehension is at times a question for the court, and at times, if varying inferences are possible, a question for the jury. Here, by concession, there was nothing in the situation to suggest to the most cautious mind that the parcel wrapped in newspaper would spread wreckage through the station. If the guard had thrown it down knowingly and willfully, he would not have threatened the plaintiff's safety, so far as appearances could warn him. His conduct would not have involved, even then, an unreasonable probability of invasion of her bodily security. Liability can be no greater where the act is inadvertent.

Negligence, like risk, is thus a term of relation. Negligence in the abstract, apart from things related, is surely not a tort, if indeed it is understandable at all. . . .

The law of causation, remote or proximate, is thus foreign to the case before us. The question of liability is always anterior to the question of the measure of the consequences that go with liability. If there is no tort to be redressed, there is no occasion to consider what damage might be recovered if there were a finding of a tort. We may assume, without deciding, that negligence, not at large or in the abstract, but in relation to the plaintiff, would entail liability for any and all consequences, however novel or extraordinary. There is room for argument that a distinction is to be drawn according to the diversity of interests invaded by the act, as where conduct negligent in that it threatens an insignificant invasion of an interest in property results in an unforeseeable invasion of an interest of another order, as, e.g., one of bodily security. Perhaps other distinctions may be necessary. We do not go into the question now. The consequences to be followed must first be rooted in a wrong.

The judgment of the Appellate Division and that of the Trial Term should be reversed, and the complaint dismissed, with costs in all courts.

ANDREWS, J. (dissenting). . . .

. . . The result we shall reach [in this case] depends upon our theory as to the nature of negligence. Is it a relative concept — the breach of some duty owing to a particular person or to particular persons? Or where there is an act which unreasonably threatens the safety of others, is the doer liable for all its proximate consequences, even where they result in injury to one who would generally be thought to be outside the radius of danger? This is not a mere dispute as to words. We might not believe that to the average mind the dropping of the bundle would seem to involve the probability of harm to the plaintiff standing many feet away whatever might be the case as to the owner or to one so near as to be likely to be struck by its fall. If, however, we adopt the second hypothesis we have to inquire only as to the relation between cause and effect. We deal in terms of proximate cause, not of negligence. . . .

But we are told that "there is no negligence unless there is in the particular case a legal duty to take care, and this duty must be one which is owed to the plaintiff himself and not merely to others." (Salmond, Torts [6th ed.], 24.) This, I think too narrow a conception. Where there is the unreasonable act, and some right that may be affected there is negligence whether damage does or does not result. That is immaterial. Should we drive down Broadway at a reckless speed, we are negligent whether we strike an approaching car or miss it by an inch. The act itself is wrongful. It is a wrong not only to those who happen to be within the radius of danger but to all who might have been there — a wrong to the public at large. Such is the language of the street. . . . Due care is a duty imposed on each one of us to protect society from unnecessary danger, not to protect A, B or C alone.

It may well be that there is no such thing as negligence in the abstract. "Proof of negligence in the air, so to speak, will not do." In an empty world negligence would not exist. It does involve a relationship between man and his fellows. But not merely a relationship between man and those whom he might reasonably expect his act would injure. Rather, a relationship between him and those whom he does in fact injure. If his act has a tendency to harm some one, it harms him a mile away as surely as it does those on the scene. . . .

In the well-known Polemis Case (1921, 3 K. B. 560), Scrutton, L. J., said that the dropping of a plank was negligent for it might injure "workman or cargo or ship." Because of either possibility the owner of the vessel was to be made good for his loss. The act being wrongful the doer was liable for its proximate results. Criticized and explained as this statement may have been, I think it states the law as it should be and as it is.

The proposition is this. Every one owes to the world at large the duty of refraining from those acts that may unreasonably threaten the safety of others. Such an act occurs. Not only is he wronged to whom harm might reasonably be expected to result, but he also who is in fact injured, even if he be outside what would generally be thought the danger zone. There needs be duty due the one complaining but this is not a duty to a particular individual because as to him harm might be expected. Harm to some one being the natural result of the act, not only that one alone, but all those in fact injured may complain. We have never, I think, held otherwise. . . . Unreasonable risk being taken, its consequences are not confined to those who might probably be hurt.

If this be so, we do not have a plaintiff suing by "derivation or succession." Her action is original and primary. Her claim is for a breach of duty to herself — not that she is subrogated to any right of action of the owner of the parcel or of a passenger standing at the scene of the explosion.

The right to recover damages rests on additional considerations. The plaintiff's rights must be injured, and this injury must be caused by the negligence. We build a dam, but are negligent as to its foundations. Breaking, it injures property down stream. We are not liable if all this happened because of some reason other than the insecure foundation. But when injuries do result from our unlawful act we are liable for the consequences. It does not matter that they are unusual, unexpected, unforeseen and unforeseeable. But there is one limitation. The damages must be so connected with the negligence that the latter may be said to be the proximate cause of the former.

These two words have never been given an inclusive definition. What is a cause in a legal sense, still more what is a proximate cause, depend in each case upon many considerations, as does the existence of negligence itself. Any philosophical doctrine of causation does not help us. A boy throws a stone into a pond. The ripples spread. The water level rises. The history of that pond is altered to all eternity. It will be altered by other causes also. Yet it will be forever the resultant of all causes combined. Each one will have an influence. How great only omniscience can say. You may speak of a chain, or if you please, a net. An analogy is of little aid. Each cause brings about future events. Without each the future would not be the same. Each is proximate in the sense it is essential. But that is not what we mean by the word. Nor on the other hand do we mean sole cause. There is no such thing. . . .

. . . What we do mean by the word "proximate" is, that because of convenience, of public policy, of a rough sense of justice, the law arbitrarily declines to trace a series of events beyond a certain point. This is not logic. It is practical politics. Take our rule as to fires. Sparks from my burning haystack set on fire my house and my neighbor's. I may recover from a negligent railroad. He may not. Yet the wrongful act as directly harmed the one as the other. We may regret that the line was drawn just where it was, but drawn somewhere it had to be. We said the act of the railroad was not the proximate cause of our neighbor's fire. Cause it surely was. The words we used were simply indicative of our notions of public policy. Other courts think differently. But somewhere they reach the point where they cannot say the stream comes from any one source.

Take the illustration given in an unpublished manuscript by a distinguished and helpful writer on the law of torts. A chauffeur negligently collides with another car which is filled with dynamite, although he could not know it. An explosion follows. A, walking on the sidewalk nearby, is killed. B, sitting in a window of a building opposite, is cut by flying glass. C, likewise sitting in a window a block away, is similarly injured. And a further illustration. A nursemaid, ten blocks away, startled by the noise, involuntarily drops a baby from her arms to the walk. We are told that C may not recover while A may. As to B it is a question for court or jury. We will all agree that the baby might not. Because, we are again told, the chauffeur had no reason to believe his conduct involved any risk of injuring either C or the baby. As to them he was not negligent.

But the chauffeur, being negligent in risking the collision, his belief that the scope of the harm he might do would be limited is immaterial. His act unreasonably jeopardized the safety of any one who might be affected by it. C's injury and that of the baby were directly traceable to the collision. Without that, the injury would not have happened. C had the right to sit in his office, secure from such dangers. The baby was entitled to use the sidewalk with reasonable safety.

The true theory is, it seems to me, that the injury to C, if in truth he is to be denied recovery, and the injury to the baby is that their several injuries were not the proximate result of the negligence. And here not what the chauffeur had reason to believe would be the result of his conduct, but what the prudent would foresee, may have a bearing. May have some bearing, for the problem of proximate cause is not to be solved by any one consideration.

It is all a question of expediency. There are no fixed rules to govern our judgment. There are simply matters of which we may take account. . . . There is in truth little to guide us other than common sense.

There are some hints that may help us. The proximate cause, involved as it may be with many other causes, must be, at the least, something without which the event would not happen. The court must ask itself whether there was a natural and continuous sequence between cause and effect. Was the one a substantial factor in producing the other? Was there a direct connection between them, without too many intervening causes? Is the effect of cause on result not too attenuated? Is the cause likely, in the usual judgment of mankind, to produce the result? Or by the exercise of prudent foresight could the result be foreseen? Is the result too remote from the cause, and here we consider remoteness in time and space. . . . Clearly we must so consider, for the greater the distance either in time or space, the more surely do other causes intervene to affect the result. . . .

Here another question must be answered. In the case supposed it is said, and said correctly, that the chauffeur is liable for the direct effect of the explosion although he had no reason to suppose it would follow a collision. "The fact that the injury occurred in a different manner than that which might have been expected does not prevent the chauffeur's negligence from being in law the cause of the injury." But the natural results of a negligent act — the results which a prudent man would or should foresee — do have a bearing upon the decision as to proximate cause. We have said so repeatedly. What should be foreseen? No human foresight would suggest that a collision itself might injure one a block away. On the contrary, given an explosion, such a possibility might be reasonably expected. I think the direct connection, the foresight of which the courts speak, assumes prevision of the explosion, for the immediate results of which, at least, the chauffeur is responsible.

It may be said this is unjust. Why? In fairness he should make good every injury flowing from his negligence. Not because of tenderness toward him we say he need not answer for all that follows his wrong. We look back to the catastrophe, the fire kindled by the spark, or the explosion. We trace the consequences — not indefinitely, but to a certain point. And to aid us in fixing that point we ask what might ordinarily be expected to follow the fire or the explosion.

This last suggestion is the factor which must determine the case before us. The act upon which defendant's liability rests is knocking an apparently harmless package onto the platform. The act was negligent. For its proximate consequences the defendant is liable. If its contents were broken, to the owner; if it fell upon and crushed a passenger's foot, then to him. If it exploded and injured one in the immediate vicinity, to him also as to A in the illustration. Mrs. Palsgraf was standing some distance away. How far cannot be told from the record — apparently twenty-five or thirty feet. Perhaps less. Except for the explosion, she would not have been injured. We are told by the appellant in his brief "it cannot be denied that the explosion was the direct cause of the plaintiff's injuries." So it was a substantial factor in producing the result — there was here a natural and continuous sequence — direct connection. The only intervening cause was that instead of blowing her to the ground the concussion smashed the weighing machine which in turn fell upon her. There was no remoteness in time, little in space. And surely, given such an explosion as here it needed no great foresight to predict that the natural result would be to injure one on the platform at no greater distance from its scene than was the plaintiff. Just how no one might be able to predict. Whether by flying fragments, by broken glass, by wreckage of machines or structures no one could say. But injury in some form was most probable.

Under these circumstances I cannot say as a matter of law that the plaintiff's injuries were not the proximate result of the negligence. That is all we have before us. The court refused to so charge. No request was made to submit the matter to the jury as a question of fact, even would that have been proper upon the record before us.

The judgment appealed from should be affirmed, with costs.

POUND, LEHMAN and KELLOGG, JJ., concur with CARDOZO, C.J.; ANDREWS, J., dissents in opinion in which CRANE and O'BRIEN, JJ., concur.

Judgment reversed, etc.

The range of different circumstances under which courts have been called upon to decide whether injured plaintiffs were within the scope of the risks foreseeably created by defendants' conduct is very wide. Thus, in Geyer v. City of Logansport, 346 N.E.2d 634 (Ind. Ct. App. 1976), the Indiana Court of Appeals reversed a dismissal by the trial court of a claim for damages arising out of the plaintiff's being shot accidentally by a police officer. A bull had been negligently allowed to escape, and the police officer shot his revolver at the bull to prevent it from injuring others. The plaintiff, who was not within the line of fire, was struck and injured when the bullet ricocheted off one of the bull's horns. The court of appeals held that the issue of the foreseeability of harm to the plaintiff should have been given to the jury. In contrast, consider Williams v. Cingular Wireless, 809 N.E.2d 4[illegible] 478 (Ind. Ct. App. 2004), in which the appeals court held that although it was [illegible] foreseeable that the misuse of a cell phone while driving would lead to an [illegible] insufficient to find it foreseeable "to a legally significant extent" tha[illegible] act of selling the cell phone in the first place would cause an acc[illegible] er Kubert v. Best, 75 A.3d 1214, 1219 (N.J. App. 2013), in whic[illegible] that the sender of a text message can potentially be liable if an accide[illegible] exting, but only if the sender knew or had special reason to know that the reci[illegible] ld view the text while driving and thus be distracted."

Another area in which the scope of foreseeability frequently arises is attempted rescue. In Solomon v. Shuell, 457 N.W.2d 669 (Mich. 1990), plainclothes police officers were in the process of arresting a robbery suspect. The suspect's father, not knowing the officers were police and intending to rescue his son, exited his house holding a gun that was pointed toward the ground, at which point one of the officers shot and killed him. At trial for his wrongful death, the jury, having been instructed that the rescue doctrine, which provided that "[a] person who goes to the rescue of another who is in imminent and serious peril caused by the negligence of someone else is not contributorily negligent, so long as the rescue attempt is not recklessly or rashly made," could only apply if the decedent's son had been in actual peril, found that the defendants and the plaintiff all were negligent. It thus reduced the plaintiff's recovery according to the Michigan comparative fault regime from $100,000 to $20,000 given that decedent was held to be 80 percent at fault. On appeal, the Michigan Supreme Court considered whether the rescue doctrine applied to cases in which the victim was not in actual danger. It rejected the trial court's instruction, concluding that "it is clear that the dispositive issue determining whether the rescue attempt itself is reasonable is whether the rescuer acted as a reasonable person under the same or similar circumstances. Because the inquiry as to whether the rescue attempt itself was reasonable also rests upon whether the utility of the rescue attempt outweighs the increased risk of harm the rescuer faces, the . . . rescue doctrine applies even if the victim never was in actual danger." Id. at 683.

Solomon follows the well nigh universal rule that a negligent defendant may be liable to someone who is injured in an effort to rescue another put at risk by the defendant's negligence. See Kimble v. Carey, 691 S.E.2d 790, 795 (Va. 2010) ("It makes no difference to rescue doctrine analysis whether the victim was guilty of simple negligence, gross negligence, or willful or wanton conduct in creating his or her peril, because the rescuer's right to recover for injuries sustained during the rescue attempt rises or falls with the determination whether the rescuer acted rashly or recklessly."); Restatement (Third) of Torts: Liability for Physical and Emotional Harm §32 (2010). Justice Cardozo, one of the most influential judges shaping American tort law (see, e.g., Martin v. Herzog, p. 210, above; Palsgraf v. Long Island R.R., p. 313, above; and MacPherson v. Buick Motor Co., p. 517, below) wrote an opinion on the subject, Wagner v. International Railway, 133 N.E. 437, 438 (N.Y. 1921), that begins with one of his famous epigrams:

> Danger invites rescue. The cry of distress is the summons to relief. The law does not ignore these reactions of the mind in tracing conduct to its consequences. It recognizes them as normal. It places their effects within the range of the natural and probable. The wrong that imperils life is a wrong to the imperilled victim; it is a wrong also to his rescuer. The state that leaves an opening in a bridge is liable to the child that falls into the stream, but liable also to the parent who plunges to its aid. . . . The risk of rescue, if only

> it be not wanton, is born of the occasion. The emergency begets the man. The wrongdoer may not have foreseen the coming of a deliverer. He is accountable as if he had.
>
> The defendant says that we must stop, in following the chain of causes, when action ceases to be "instinctive." By this, is meant, it seems, that rescue is at the peril of the rescuer, unless spontaneous and immediate. If there has been time to deliberate, if impulse has given way to judgment, one cause, it is said, has spent its force, and another has intervened. In this case, the plaintiff walked more than four hundred feet in going to Herbert's aid. He had time to reflect and weigh; impulse had been followed by choice; and choice, in the defendant's view, intercepts and breaks the sequence. We find no warrant for thus shortening the chain of jural causes. We may assume, though we are not required to decide, that peril and rescue must be in substance one transaction; that the sight of the one must have aroused the impulse to the other; in short, that there must be unbroken continuity between the commission of the wrong and the effort to avert its consequences. If all this be assumed, the defendant is not aided. Continuity in such circumstances is not broken by the exercise of volition. . . . The law does not discriminate between the rescuer oblivious of peril and the one who counts the cost. It is enough that the act, whether impulsive or deliberate, is the child of the occasion.

In an interesting twist, the court in Rasmussen v. State Farm Mut. Auto. Ins. Co., 770 N.W.2d 619 (Neb. 2009), applied the rescue doctrine against a rescuee, rather than against a third-party tortfeasor who created the situation necessitating a rescue. Plaintiff stopped on the highway to help defendant, who had negligently allowed her car to skid off the road. While plaintiff was searching for a tow rope, another car skidded off the road and injured plaintiff. The court ruled that the rescue doctrine could be applied against the imperiled victim herself: "We conclude that the facts in the case at bar lend themselves to application of the rescue doctrine. The rescuer who sustains injuries in reasonably undertaking a rescue may recover from the rescued person if such person's negligence created a situation which necessitated the rescue." Id. at 627.

One important exception to the general rule allowing recovery by rescuers is the "fire fighter's rule," which bars recovery by professional rescuers for injuries incurred in the course of their duties. The rule reflects the judgment that professional rescuers have been compensated ahead of time for the risks inherent in their work. See Babes Showclub Jaba, Inc. v. Lair, 918 N.E.2d 308, 313 (Ind. 2009) (stating that "the fireman's rule is best understood as reflecting a policy determination that emergency responders should not be able to sue for the negligence that created the emergency to which they respond in their official capacity"). Importantly, the rule generally does not bar emergency personnel from recovering based on unreasonable risks that are separate from the reason for their presence at an emergency scene. See Torchik v. Boyce, 905 N.E.2d 179 (Ohio 2009) (holding that the fire fighter's rule did not apply to action by deputy sheriff injured on a negligently built deck stair while responding to a burglar alarm). Just who is covered by the fire fighter's rule has been the subject of considerable litigation. Members of a volunteer fire department have been included, even though they are not monetarily compensated for their services. See Flowers v. Rock Creek Terrace Ltd. Partnership, 520 A.2d 361 (Md. 1987). Police officers also are included. See White v. State, 202 P.3d 507 (Ariz. Ct. App. 2008). An emergency medical technician was held to be covered by the rule in Pinter v. American Family Mutual Ins. Co., 613 N.W.2d 110 (Wis. 2000), as was a police officer responding to a disturbance call in Collins v. Flash Lube Oil, Inc., 2012 WL 4605562 (S.D. Miss. Sept. 30, 2012) (unpublished). The court in Ciervo v. City of New York, 715 N.E.2d 91 (N.Y. 1999), held that a city sanitation worker was not subject to the rule. One court has held that the rule does not apply to nongovernmental employees.

See Crews v. Hollenbach, 751 A.2d 481 (Md. 2000), involving a gas company worker injured while attempting to repair a gas leak. However, the court ruled that the plaintiff's recovery was barred because such an injury was within the foreseeable risks of his employment.

Although the fire fighter's rule is widely followed, it has occasionally been abrogated by judicial decision (see, e.g., Christensen v. Murphy, 678 P.2d 1210 (Or. 1984)) and by statute (see, e.g., N.J. Stat. Ann. §2A:62A-21). In Minnich v. Med-Waste, Inc., 564 S.E.2d 98, 103 (S.C. 2002), the South Carolina Supreme Court faced the issue and refused to apply the fire fighter exception. The court concluded that:

> South Carolina has never recognized the firefighter's rule, and we find it is not part of this state's common law. . . . In our view, the tort law of this state adequately addresses negligence claims brought against non-employer tortfeasors arising out of injuries incurred by firefighters and police officers during the discharge of their duties. We are not persuaded by any of the various rationales advanced by those courts that recognize the firefighter's rule. The more sound public policy — and the one we adopt — is to decline to promulgate a rule singling out police officers and firefighters for discriminatory treatment.

See also Bole v. Erie Ins. Exch., 967 A.2d 1017 (Pa. 2009). In Beaupre v. Pierce Cty., 166 P.3d 712, 716 (Wash. 2007), the Supreme Court of Washington held that the professional rescuer doctrine does not bar a plaintiff police officer's suit against a defendant county for injuries sustained when a fellow officer struck plaintiff with a patrol car during a hot pursuit. The court reasoned that the professional rescuer doctrine "does not apply to negligent or intentional acts of intervening parties not responsible for bringing the rescuer to the scene." Id. at 716.

d. Were the Nature and Circumstances of the Plaintiff's Particular Harm Foreseeable?

Marshall v. Nugent

222 F.2d 604 (1st Cir. 1955)

[Plaintiff Marshall was a passenger in an automobile driven by one Harriman in northern New Hampshire during the winter. The road on which they were driving was covered with hard packed snow and ice. As Harriman approached an uphill curve to his right, an oil truck owned by Socony-Vacuum and driven by Prince approached from the opposite direction, and intruded into Harriman's lane as it rounded the curve. To avoid a collision, Harriman cut to his right and went into a skid, coming to a stop completely off of and at right angles to the road. Neither Harriman nor plaintiff was hurt. Prince stopped his truck on the road, blocking his lane of traffic. He offered to help Harriman pull his car back onto the road, and suggested that someone ought to go back up the hill to warn oncoming traffic of the danger in the road. Plaintiff volunteered, and started walking up the hill. After he had walked about seventy-five feet, an automobile driven by Nugent came around the curve and over the hill. Nugent turned to his left to avoid hitting the truck, went into a skid and hit plaintiff.]

MAGRUDER, C.J. . . . Marshall filed his complaint in the court below against both Socony-Vacuum Oil Co., Inc., and Nugent, charging them as joint tortfeasors, each legally responsible for the plaintiff's personal injuries. . . . After a rather lengthy trial, the jury reported a verdict in favor of Marshall as against Socony in the sum of $25,000, and a verdict in favor of the defendant Nugent. The district court entered judgments against Socony and in favor of Nugent in accordance with the verdict.

No. 4867

This is an appeal by Socony from the judgment against it in favor of Marshall. Appellant has presented a great number of points, most of which do not merit extended discussion.

The most seriously pressed contentions are that the district court was in error in refusing Socony's motion for a directed verdict in its favor, made at the close of all the evidence. The motion was based on several grounds, chief of which were . . . (2) that if Socony's servant Prince were found to have been negligent in "cutting the corner" on the wrong side of the road, and thus forcing Harriman's car off the highway, Marshall suffered no hurt from this, and such negligent conduct, as a matter of law, was not the proximate cause of Marshall's subsequent injuries when he was run into by Nugent's car. . . .

Coming then to contention (2) above mentioned, this has to do with the doctrine of proximate causation, a doctrine which appellant's arguments tend to make out to be more complex and esoteric than it really is. To say that the situation created by the defendant's culpable acts constituted "merely a condition," not a cause of plaintiff's harm, is to indulge in mere verbiage, which does not solve the question at issue, but is simply a way of stating the conclusion, arrived at from other considerations, that the causal relation between the defendant's act and the plaintiff's injury is not strong enough to warrant holding the defendant legally responsible for the injury.

The adjective "proximate," as commonly used in this connection, is perhaps misleading, since to establish liability it is not necessarily true that the defendant's culpable act must be shown to have been the next or immediate cause of the plaintiff's injury. In many familiar instances, the defendant's act may be more remote in the chain of events; and the plaintiff's injury may more immediately have been caused by an intervening force of nature, or an intervening act of a third person whether culpable or not, or even an act by the plaintiff bringing himself in contact with the dangerous situation resulting from the defendant's negligence. . . .

Back of the requirement that the defendant's culpable act must have been a proximate cause of the plaintiff's harm is no doubt the widespread conviction that it would be disproportionately burdensome to hold a culpable actor potentially liable for all the injurious consequences that may flow from his act, i.e., that would not have been inflicted "but for" the occurrence of the act. This is especially so where the injurious consequence was the result of negligence merely. And so, speaking in general terms, the effort of the courts has been, in the development of this doctrine of proximate causation, to confine the liability of a negligent actor to those harmful consequences which result from the operation of the risk, or of a risk, the foreseeability of which rendered the defendant's conduct negligent.

Of course, putting the inquiry in these terms does not furnish a formula which automatically decides each of an infinite variety of cases. Flexibility is still preserved by the further need of defining the risk, or risks, either narrowly, or more broadly, as seems appropriate and just in the special type of case.

Regarding motor vehicle accidents in particular, one should contemplate a variety of risks which are created by negligent driving. There may be injuries resulting from a direct collision between the carelessly driven car and another vehicle. But such direct collision may be avoided, yet the plaintiff may fall and injure himself in frantically racing out of the way of the errant car. Or the plaintiff may be knocked down and injured by a human stampede as the car rushes toward a crowded safety zone. Or the plaintiff may faint from intense excitement stimulated by the near collision, and in falling sustain a fractured skull. Or the plaintiff may suffer a miscarriage or other physical illness as a result of intense nervous shock incident to a hair-raising escape. This bundle of risks could be enlarged indefinitely with a little imagination. In a traffic mix-up due to negligence, before the disturbed waters have become placid and normal again, the unfolding of events between the culpable act and the plaintiff's eventual injury may be bizarre indeed; yet the defendant may be liable for the result. In such a situation, it would be impossible for a person in the defendant's position to predict in advance just how his negligent act would work out to another's injury. Yet this in itself is no bar to recovery.

When an issue of proximate cause arises in a borderline case, as not infrequently happens, we leave it to the jury with appropriate instructions. We do this because it is deemed wise to obtain the judgment of the jury, reflecting as it does the earthy viewpoint of the common man — the prevalent sense of the community — as to whether the causal relation between the negligent act and the plaintiff's harm which in fact was a consequence of the tortious act is sufficiently close to make it just and expedient to hold the defendant answerable in damages. That is what the courts have in mind when they say the question of proximate causation is one of fact for the jury. It is similar to the issue of negligence, which is left to the jury as an issue of fact. Even where on the evidence the facts are undisputed, if fairminded men might honestly and reasonably draw contrary inferences as to whether the facts do or do not establish negligence, the court leaves such issue to the determination of the jury, who are required to decide as a matter of common-sense judgment, whether the defendant's course of conduct subjected others to a reasonable or unreasonable risk, i.e., whether under all the circumstances the defendant ought to be recognized as privileged to do the act in question or to pursue his course of conduct with immunity from liability for harm to others which might result.

In dealing with these issues of negligence and proximate causation, the trial judge has to make a preliminary decision whether the issues are such that reasonable men might differ on the inferences to be drawn. This preliminary decision is said to be a question of law, for it is one which the court has to decide, but it is nevertheless necessarily the exercise of a judgment on the facts, just as an appellate court may have to exercise a judgment on the facts, in reviewing whether the trial judge should or should not have left the issue to the jury.

Exercising that judgment on the facts in the case at bar, we have to conclude that the district court committed no error in refusing to direct a verdict for the defendant Socony on the issue of proximate cause. . . .

. . . Plaintiff Marshall was a passenger in the oncoming Chevrolet car, and thus was one of the persons whose bodily safety was primarily endangered by the negligence of Prince, as might have been found by the jury, in "cutting the corner" with the Socony truck in the circumstances above related. In that view, Prince's negligence constituted an irretrievable breach of duty to the plaintiff. Though this particular act of negligence was over and done with when the truck pulled up alongside of the stalled Chevrolet without having actually collided with it, still the consequences of such past negligence were in the bosom of time, as yet unrevealed.

If the Chevrolet had been pulled back onto the highway, and Harriman and Marshall, having got in it again, had resumed their journey and had had a collision with another car five miles down the road, in which Marshall suffered bodily injuries, it could truly be said that such subsequent injury to Marshall was a consequence in fact of the earlier delay caused by the defendant's negligence, in the sense that but for such delay the Chevrolet car would not have been at the fatal intersection at the moment the other car ran into it. But on such assumed state of facts, the courts would no doubt conclude, "as a matter of law," that Prince's earlier negligence in cutting the corner was not the "proximate cause" of this later injury received by the plaintiff. That would be because the extra risks to which such negligence by Prince had subjected the passengers in the Chevrolet car were obviously entirely over; the situation had been stabilized and become normal, and, so far as one could foresee, whatever subsequent risks the Chevrolet might have to encounter in its resumed journey were simply the inseparable risks, no more and no less, that were incident to the Chevrolet's being out on the highway at all. But in the case at bar, the circumstances under which Marshall received the personal injuries complained of presented no such clear-cut situation.

As we have indicated, the extra risks created by Prince's negligence were not all over at the moment the primary risk of collision between the truck and the Chevrolet was successfully surmounted. Many cases have held a defendant, whose negligence caused a traffic tie-up, legally liable for subsequent property damage or personal injuries more immediately caused by an oncoming motorist. This would particularly be so where, as in the present case, the negligent traffic tie-up and delay occurred in a dangerous blind spot, and where the occupants of the stalled Chevrolet, having got out onto the highway to assist in the operation of getting the Chevrolet going again, were necessarily subject to risks of injury from cars in the stream of northbound traffic coming over the crest of the hill. It is true, the Chevrolet car was not owned by the plaintiff Marshall, and no doubt, without violating any legal duty to Harriman, Marshall could have crawled up onto the snowbank at the side of the road out of harm's way and awaited there, passive and inert, until his journey was resumed. But the plaintiff, who as a passenger in the Chevrolet car had already been subjected to a collision risk by the negligent operation of the Socony truck, could reasonably be expected to get out onto the highway and lend a hand to his host in getting the Chevrolet started again, especially as Marshall himself had an interest in facilitating the resumption of the journey in order to keep his business appointment in North Stratford. Marshall was therefore certainly not an "officious intermeddler," and whether or not he was barred by contributory negligence in what he did was a question for the jury, as we have already held. The injury Marshall received by being struck by the Nugent car was not remote, either in time or place, from the negligent conduct of defendant Socony's servant, and it occurred while the traffic mix-up occasioned by defendant's negligence was still persisting, not after the traffic flow had become normal again. In the circumstances presented we conclude that the district court committed no error in leaving the issue of proximate cause to the jury for determination.

Of course, the essential notion of what is meant by "proximate cause" may be expressed to the jury in a variety of ways. We are satisfied in the present case that the charge to the jury accurately enough acquainted them with the nature of the factual judgment they were called upon to exercise in their determination of the issue of proximate cause. . . .

No. 4866

This is an appeal by plaintiff Marshall from the judgment entered in favor of codefendant Nugent pursuant to the jury verdict.

We find no substantial or prejudicial error at the trial which would necessitate our overturning of the verdict in favor of Nugent. . . .

In Socony-Vacuum Oil Co., Inc. v. Marshall, No. 4867, the judgment of the District Court is affirmed.

In Marshall v. Nugent, No. 4866, the judgment of the District Court is affirmed.

In Lodge v. Arett Sales Corporation, 717 A.2d 215 (Conn. 1998), the court overturned a jury verdict in favor of plaintiff firefighters against defendant alarm companies, where plaintiffs had shown that the companies negligently transmitted a false fire alarm to which the firefighters responded, suffering an accident en route. The accident occurred after a failure of the brakes in a fire engine that had been negligently maintained by the city. The parties' positions on appeal were described by the court as follows (717 A.2d at 220-21):

> Both the plaintiffs and the defendants agree that to meet the test of foreseeability, the *exact* nature of the harm suffered need not have been foreseeable, only the "general nature" of the harm. They diverge, however, with respect to the proper interpretation of the permissible level of the generality of the harm. The plaintiffs assert that the general nature of the harm at issue is the possibility of a collision of a fire engine occurring while it is responding to an alarm. They would have us conclude that the brake failure is essentially irrelevant to the determination of foreseeability and should be viewed as no more than one of many possible contributing factors.
>
> The defendants, on the other hand, assert that the general nature of the harm is a collision precipitated by the brake failure of the engine owing to negligent maintenance by the city. . . . The defendants argue that by employing a foreseeability test that incorporates such a high level of generality to the harm in this case, the plaintiffs have essentially created a strict liability standard. That is, under the plaintiffs' argument, any accident involving a fire engine responding to a negligently transmitted false alarm would be a basis for imposing liability on the initiator of the alarm, irrespective of the direct cause of the accident.

Although the plaintiffs argued that such a wide scope of liability is desirable to encourage due care on the part of alarm companies in the installation and servicing of their products, the court found the plaintiffs' reasoning unpersuasive (717 A.2d at 222-23):

> We conclude that the brake failure of a negligently maintained fire engine is beyond the scope of the reasonably foreseeable risks created by the transmission of a false alarm and that legal responsibility for the resulting accident should not extend to these defendants. Negligent transmission of a false alarm, by unnecessarily causing an emergency response, does increase the usual road hazards attendant on the operation of an emergency vehicle on the public roadways. Such increased road hazards might include the danger that the driver of the fire engine or the operators of other vehicles might cause accidents as a result of high rates of speed and congested streets. It might be reasonable in some such circumstances to impose liability on the initiator of the false alarm. It cannot reasonably be said, however, that liability for negligently causing a false alarm should include the risk that the emergency vehicle will be negligently maintained and utilized, causing it to experience brake failure. Imposing liability on these defendants for a harm that they reasonably could not be expected to anticipate and over which they had no control would serve no legitimate objective of the law.

The problem of intervening conduct by third parties, such as the negligent brake maintenance at issue in *Lodge*, becomes especially salient in the case of intervening criminal behavior. In Kush v. City of Buffalo, 449 N.E.2d 725 (N.Y. 1983), the plaintiff was injured by chemicals which she claimed were negligently stored by the defendant, and which were stolen by two 15-year-olds. In affirming a judgment for the plaintiff, the court stated (449 N.E.2d at 729):

> Defendant argues that the student employees' stealing of the chemicals was an intentional act and, hence, a superseding cause of plaintiff's injury, relieving it of liability. Defendant is correct that an intervening intentional or criminal act will generally sever the liability of the original tort-feasor, but, on the facts here, it may not rely on this doctrine.
>
> That doctrine has no application when the intentional or criminal intervention of a third party or parties is reasonably foreseeable. Defendant's duty was to take reasonable steps to secure the dangerous chemicals from unsupervised access by children. By its very definition, any breach of this duty that leads to injury will involve an intentional, unauthorized taking of chemicals by a child. When the intervening, intentional act of another is itself the foreseeable harm that shapes the duty imposed, the defendant who fails to guard against such conduct will not be relieved of liability when that act occurs.

See also Wilkins v. Dist. Of Columbia, 879 F. Supp. 2d 35 (D.D.C. 2012) (holding that whether a jail staff's failure to comply with standards of care for inmate access to storage closets was the proximate cause of a pre-trial detainee's stabbing by another inmate should go to a jury); Bd. of Trustees of Univ. of Dist. of Columbia v. DiSalvo, 974 A.2d 868 (D.C. 2009) (trial court's denial of defendant university's motion for judgment as a matter of law reversed on appeal; plaintiff was attacked in a parking garage on defendant university's campus).

These concepts were applied by a unanimous jury to find the owner and manager of the World Trade Center negligent for failing to guard against the first terrorist attack on the iconic buildings, the 1993 garage bombing that resulted in the deaths of six people and scores of injuries. The jury apportioned 68 percent of the responsibility for the bombing to the defendant, implying a responsibility of 32 percent at most for the terrorists themselves. See Anemona Hartocollis, Port Authority Found Negligent in 1993 Bombing, N.Y. Times, Oct. 27, 2005, at A1. Putting aside questions of moral blame, how might you defend the jury's allocation of legal responsibility? Cf. Restatement (Third) of Torts: Apportionment of Liability §14 (2000) ("A person who is liable to another based on a failure to protect the other from the specific risk of an intentional tort is jointly and severally liable for the share of comparative responsibility assigned to the intentional tortfeasor in addition to the share of comparative responsibility assigned to the person."). On appeal the defendant argued that the duty to guard against foreseeable criminal activity should attach only after an actual incident has previously occurred at the same site. The court rejected this argument, reasoning that "[t]he obligation to avoid a potentially catastrophic event may not sensibly be made to depend upon a precedent catastrophe at the same premises." Nash v. Port Authority of N.Y. & N.J., 856 N.Y.S.2d 583, 589 (App. Div. 2008). Despite these rulings, the defendant Port Authority was later found to be protected by governmental immunity. See In re World Trade Ctr. Bombing Litig., 957 N.E.2d 733 (N.Y. 2011).

Herrera v. Quality Pontiac

134 N.M. 43, 73 P.3d 181 (2003)

Serna, Justice. . . . Plaintiffs-Appellants Kenneth Herrera, personal representative of Octavio Ruiz, and Jose Encinias filed a complaint for wrongful death and personal injury against Defendant-Appellee Quality Pontiac, a corporation doing business in Albuquerque,

New Mexico, following a traffic accident caused by a thief who stole a car from Defendant's lot. The district court dismissed the case with prejudice for failure to state a claim for which relief can be granted. . . .

Plaintiffs alleged the following facts in their complaint. On May 27, 1996, an individual took his car to Defendant for repairs. At Defendant's direction, the owner left the keys in the car and the doors unlocked. The lot was fenced, and the gate was unlocked. After 9:00 p.m., Billy Garcia entered the lot, apparently looking inside the cars for something to steal. Garcia stole the vehicle in question. The following day, at approximately 11:00 a.m., a Bernalillo County deputy sheriff observed Garcia driving quickly through a school zone and pursued him, engaging his emergency lights and sirens. Garcia drove at a speed of up to ninety miles per hour and collided head on with Plaintiffs' car, which had pulled over onto the shoulder after hearing the sirens. One occupant was killed and the other seriously injured.

Plaintiffs presented an affidavit of a sociologist to the district court that asserted that "[t]he Albuquerque metropolitan area's motor vehicle theft rate of 1,345.5 per 100,000 residents was the second highest rate in the nation in 1997." The expert estimated that between forty-five and eighty percent of stolen cars had been left unlocked and that between nineteen and forty-seven percent of stolen cars had the ignition keys left inside. The expert claimed that a high proportion of thefts were for the purpose of joyriding and short term transportation. The expert estimated that there is a high probability that a stolen car will be involved in traffic accidents, relying on a study which "found that nearly [seventeen percent] of all stolen cars are involved in accidents in a matter of hours or days after their theft," and another study which found "the accident rate for stolen cars [to be] approximately 200 times the accident rate for cars that have not been stolen." The expert relied on a study which found that "police pursuit was involved in [thirty-seven] percent of the motor vehicle theft cases examined [in a] national sample." . . .

II. Discussion

A. Duty

1. Introduction

Generally, a negligence claim requires the existence of a duty from a defendant to a plaintiff, breach of that duty, which is typically based upon a standard of reasonable care, and the breach being a proximate cause and cause in fact of the plaintiff's damages. . . . "Negligence is generally a question of fact for the jury. A finding of negligence, however, is dependent upon the existence of a duty on the part of the defendant. Whether a duty exists is a question of law for the courts to decide." Schear v. Bd. of County Comm'rs, 101 N.M. 671, 672, 687 P.2d 728, 729 (1984) (citations omitted). . . .

As this Court has frequently noted, questions of both proximate cause and duty are related to the concept of foreseeability. . . . "Both questions of foreseeability are distinct; the first must be decided as a matter of law by the judge, using established legal policy in determining whether a duty was owed petitioner, and the second, proximate cause, is a question of fact." [Calkins v. Cox Estates, 110 N.M. 59, 61, 792 P.2d 36, 38 (1990)]. "Duty and foreseeability have been closely integrated concepts in tort law since the court in Palsgraf v. Long Island Railroad Co., 248 N.Y. 339, 162 N.E. 99 (1928) stated the issue of foreseeability in terms of duty." [Ramirez v. Armstrong, 100 N.M. 538, 541, 673 P.2d 822, 825 (1983)].

> The duty element of negligence focuses on whether the defendant's conduct foreseeably created a broader "zone of risk" that poses a general threat of harm to others. The proximate causation element, on the other hand, is concerned with whether and to what extent the defendant's conduct foreseeably and substantially caused the specific injury that actually occurred. In other words, the former is a minimal threshold legal requirement for opening the courthouse doors, whereas the latter is part of the much more specific factual requirement that must be proved to win the case once the courthouse doors are open.

McCain v. Fla. Power Corp., 593 So. 2d 500, 502 (Fla. 1992) (citation and footnote omitted); see Calkins, 110 N.M. at 61, 792 P.2d at 38.

. . . In the present case, we determine whether, as a threshold question of law, one who leaves an unattended and unlocked vehicle with its ignition keys inside foreseeably creates a zone of risk and a general unreasonable threat of harm and thus owes a duty of ordinary care to others injured in a resulting automobile accident caused by the criminal or negligent actions of a third party. For our duty analysis, "it must be determined that the injured party was a foreseeable plaintiff—that he [or she] was within the zone of danger created by [the defendant's] actions[—] . . . as a matter of law by the judge, using established legal policy. . . ." Calkins, 110 N.M. at 61, 792 P.2d at 38. We must analyze whether, as a matter of policy as well as foreseeability, one in such circumstances has an obligation to the injured party for which we will give legal effect and recognition. . . .

3. *Whether Defendant Owed Plaintiffs a Common Law Duty*

. . .

(c) The Foreseeability Component of Duty

. . . New Mexico has adopted and applied for decades the majority view of *Palsgraf*, that a negligent actor only owes a duty to those whose injuries are a foreseeable result of the negligence, rather than the dissenting *Palsgraf* view, that one owes a duty to the world, even if the plaintiff is outside of the zone of danger. . . . This Court has consistently relied on the principle of foreseeability, along with policy concerns, to determine whether a defendant owed a duty to a particular plaintiff or class of plaintiffs. . . .

The present case is complicated by the fact that Plaintiffs' injuries were directly caused by Garcia's criminal operation of the stolen vehicle. As Defendant notes, "[a]s a general rule, a person does not have a duty to protect another from harm caused by the criminal acts of third persons unless the person has a special relationship with the other giving rise to a duty." . . . However, "the criminal acts of a third person will not relieve a negligent defendant of liability if the defendant should have recognized that his or her actions were likely to lead to that criminal activity." Sarracino v. Martinez, 117 N.M. 193, 195-96, 870 P.2d 155, 157-58 (Ct. App. 1994).

> The act of a third person in committing an intentional tort or crime is a superseding cause of harm to another resulting therefrom, although the actor's negligent conduct created a situation which afforded an opportunity to the third person to commit such a tort or

> crime, unless the actor at the time of his [or her] negligent conduct realized or should have realized the likelihood that such a situation might be created, and that a third person might avail himself [or herself] of the opportunity to commit such a tort or crime.

Id. at 195, 870 P.2d at 157 (quoted authority and emphasis omitted). Thus, the lack of a special relationship does not end our inquiry. Rather, under the facts of this case as alleged, we find persuasive an exception to the general rule other than a special relationship: whether Defendant realized or should have realized the likelihood that leaving an ignition key in an unlocked and unattended vehicle created a situation in which a third person might avail himself or herself of the opportunity to commit criminal acts such that Defendant reasonably could be said to have created or increased a risk of harm to Plaintiffs through the criminal conduct of the thief.

The present case presents a claim whereby Defendant, arguably, knew or should have known that a theft was likely to occur, and Defendant's actions may have enhanced or increased the risk of such criminal conduct. According to Plaintiffs' affidavit, Albuquerque has a high auto theft rate, and thieves are much more likely to steal vehicles to which they have ready access, as when the cars are left unlocked and unattended with the key in the ignition. Stolen cars are much more likely to be involved in automobile accidents. In this context, Defendant's alleged conduct leaving the keys in the ignition of an unlocked and unattended vehicle arguably increased the likelihood that criminal acts would occur, which ultimately led to the accident in which Plaintiffs were injured, so that we impose a duty of ordinary care. . . .

(d) The Policy Component of Duty: Adoption of Comparative Fault

The recognition of a legal duty is dependent upon considerations of both foreseeability and policy. In addition to our conclusion that leaving an ignition key in an unlocked and unattended vehicle creates a foreseeable zone of danger which supports a duty, we must now decide whether, as a matter of policy, we should impose a duty. We conclude that a change in our law warrants the recognition of a legal duty. [The court noted that its decision in Bouldin v. Sategna, 71 N.M. 329, 378 P.2d 370 (1963), which concluded that the court did "not perceive theft of a car as a natural event to be foreseen by a person who is negligent in leaving his [or her] car unattended with the key in the ignition," 71 N.M. at 333, 378 P.2d at 373, had been rendered prior to the court's adoption of comparative fault.] The implicit fear in *Bouldin* may very well have been the clearly troublesome notion of holding a car owner completely responsible for the negligent or criminal actions of a third party because of joint and several liability; in other words, the defendant in *Bouldin* could have been liable for all of the injuries suffered by the plaintiffs, rather than in proportion to his fault. . . . However, this fear is alleviated by principles of comparative fault.

B. Other Issues

. . .

2. *Proximate Cause*

Defendant argues that its actions did not proximately cause Plaintiffs' injuries. The issue of proximate cause is also for the jury or factfinder. . . . While we agree with Defendant that there is not great closeness in the connection between Defendant's wrongful acts and the resulting injuries, especially considering a gap in time of approximately fourteen hours and a distance of many miles, we do not believe that the connection is so tenuous that we must conclude, as a matter of law, that there is no proximate cause. We leave the fact that the accident occurred approximately fourteen hours after Garcia stole the car from Defendant's lot and the fact that the accident took place several miles away from its property for the jury's consideration on the issue of proximate cause. See Calkins, 110 N.M. at 65-66 & n. 6, 792 P.2d at 42-43 & n. 6. Thus, the finder of fact must determine whether Defendant's acts, which occurred many hours prior to the accident and many miles away, were a proximate cause of Plaintiffs' injuries. . . .

III. Conclusion

We reverse the district court. We conclude that an owner or one in possession of a vehicle who leaves a key in the ignition of an unattended and unlocked car owes a duty of ordinary care to those individuals injured in an automobile accident involving the vehicle when a thief steals the car and negligently or criminally causes the accident. The jury or finder of fact must decide whether Defendant's actions breached this duty of ordinary care and are a proximate cause and cause in fact of injuries which Plaintiffs prove.

It is so ordered.

We concur: Petra Jimenez Maes, Chief Justice, Pamela B. Minzner, and Richard C. Bosson, Justices (specially concurring) [The concurring opinion of Justice Bosson is omitted.]

Stahlecker v. Ford Motor Co.

266 Neb. 601, 667 N.W.2d 244 (2003)

Stephan, J.

This is a civil action for damages resulting from the injury and wrongful death of Amy M. Stahlecker (Amy). Appellants, Susan Stahlecker and Dale Stahlecker, parents of the deceased and special administrators of her estate, alleged that during the early morning hours of April 29, 2000, Amy was driving a 1997 Ford Explorer equipped with Firestone Wilderness AT radial tires in a remote area of western Douglas County, Nebraska, when one of the tires failed, rendering the vehicle inoperable. They further alleged that Richard Cook encountered Amy "alone and stranded" as a direct result of the tire failure and that he assaulted and murdered her. The Stahleckers brought this action against Ford Motor Company (Ford), the manufacturer of the vehicle; Bridgestone/Firestone, Inc. (Firestone), the manufacturer of the tire; and Cook. The district court for Dodge County sustained demurrers filed on behalf of Ford and Firestone and dismissed the action as to those parties.

We affirm.

Background

. . . The Stahleckers . . . alleged that "long before April 29, 2000," Ford and Firestone had actual knowledge of "the defective nature of the Ford Explorer's Firestone tires and their propensity to unexpectedly blow out causing wide-ranging results that included stranding and rollovers." The Stahleckers alleged that Ford and Firestone withheld this knowledge from consumers and the general public and advertised the Ford Explorer equipped with Firestone tires as "dependable when used under similar circumstances as Amy was using them during the early morning hours of April 29, 2000." They alleged:

> [I]t was further promoted and generally understood that the vehicle and tires would help protect its consumers, such as Amy, from encountering dangerous situations which could invite criminal behavior, such as might be encountered in dark parking lots at night or during breakdowns in remote areas and from weather related acts of God, such as blizzards, heavy rain or extreme heat in arid country.

. . . They further alleged:

> [The Stahleckers] have reason to believe that at all times material hereto Defendant Ford and Defendant Firestone knew, or, in the exercise of sound safety engineering and marketing of its products knew or should have known that people similarly situated to Amy would rely upon the Ford Explorer and its Firestone tires dependability when those consumers and users would make decisions regarding encountering circumstances of travel in incl[ement] weather or other dangerous circumstances and locations such as those locations and circumstances encountered by Amy Stahlecker on April 29, 2000. Further, [the Stahleckers] have reason to believe that Defendant Ford and Defendant Firestone had or should have had knowledge, to include statistical information, regarding the likelihood of criminal conduct and/or sexual assault against auto and tire industry consumers as a result of unexpected auto and/or tire failures in general. . . .

Negligence

. . . In order to prevail in a negligence action, a plaintiff must establish the defendant's duty to protect the plaintiff from injury, a failure to discharge that duty, and damages proximately caused by the failure to discharge that duty. Sharkey v. Board of Regents, 260 Neb. 166, 615 N.W.2d 889 (2000). . . . [B]y alleging that Ford and Firestone failed to exercise reasonable care in designing and manufacturing their tires, and failed to warn users of potential tire defects, the Stahleckers have alleged the existence of a legal duty and a breach thereof by both Ford and Firestone. The remaining issue is whether the breach of this duty was the proximate cause of Amy's harm.

The proximate cause of an injury is "that cause which, in a natural and continuous sequence, without any efficient, intervening cause, produces the injury, and without which the injury would not have occurred." Haselhorst v. State, 240 Neb. 891, 899, 485 N.W.2d 180, 187 (1992). Stated another way, a plaintiff must meet three basic requirements in establishing proximate cause: (1) that without the negligent action, the injury would not have occurred, commonly known as the "but for" rule; (2) that the injury was a natural and probable result of the negligence; and (3) that there was no efficient intervening cause. World Radio Labs. v. Coopers & Lybrand, 251 Neb. 261, 557 N.W.2d 1 (1996); Anderson ex rel. Anderson/Couvillon v. Nebraska Dept. of Soc. Servs., 248 Neb. 651, 538 N.W.2d 732 (1995); Merrick v. Thomas, 246 Neb. 658, 522 N.W.2d 402 (1994).

As to the first requirement, a defendant's conduct is the cause of the event if "the event would not have occurred but for that conduct; conversely, the defendant's conduct is not a cause of the event if the event would have occurred without it." Haselhorst v. State, 240 Neb. at 899, 485 N.W.2d at 187. In this case, accepting as true the allegations of the operative amended petition, the first element of proximate causation is established. The petition alleges that Cook "found Amy alone and stranded as a direct result of the failure of the Firestone Wilderness AT Radial Tire and proceeded to abduct, terrorize, rape and murder Amy." Firestone concedes that under the factual allegations of the Stahleckers' petition, that "'but for'" the failure of its tire, Amy would not have been at the place where she was assaulted and murdered. Brief for appellee Firestone at 21.

The second and third components of proximate causation are somewhat interrelated. Was the criminal assault and murder the "natural and probable" result of the failure to warn of potential tire failure, or did the criminal acts constitute an effective intervening cause which would preclude any causal link between the failure to warn and the injuries and wrongful death for which damages are claimed in this action? An efficient intervening cause is a new, independent force intervening between the defendant's negligent act and the plaintiff's injury. Fuhrman v. State, 265 Neb. 176, 655 N.W.2d 866 (2003). This force may be the conduct of a third person who had full control of the situation, whose conduct the defendant could not anticipate or contemplate, and whose conduct resulted directly in the plaintiff's injury. See *id.* An efficient intervening cause must break the causal connection between the original wrong and the injury. *Id.;* Sacco v. Carothers, 253 Neb. 9, 567 N.W.2d 299 (1997). In Shelton v. Board of Regents, 211 Neb. 820, 320 N.W.2d 748 (1982), we considered whether criminal conduct constituted an intervening cause. *Shelton* involved wrongful death claims brought on behalf of persons who were poisoned by a former employee of the Eugene C. Eppley Institute for Research in Cancer and Allied Diseases (the Institute). In their actions against the Institute and related entities, the plaintiffs alleged that despite the fact that the former employee had a prior criminal conviction involving an attempted homicide, the Institute hired him as a research technologist and gave him access to the poisonous substance which he subsequently used to commit the murders. The plaintiffs alleged that the Institute was negligent in hiring the employee, in allowing him to have access to the poisonous substance, and in failing to monitor its inventory of the substance. The plaintiffs further alleged that the Institute's negligence was the proximate cause of the injuries and deaths of the victims. The district court sustained a demurrer filed by the Institute and dismissed the actions. This court affirmed, holding as a matter of law that the criminal acts of stealing the drug and administering it to the victims "were of such nature as to constitute an efficient intervening cause which destroys any claim that the alleged negligence of the [Institute] was the proximate cause of the appellants' injuries and damage." *Id.* at 826, 320 N.W.2d at 752. . . .

We have, however, determined in certain premises liability cases and in cases involving negligent custodial entrustment that the criminal act of a third person does not constitute an efficient intervening cause. For example, in Sacco v. Carothers, 253 Neb. 9, 567 N.W.2d 299 (1997), a patron of a bar was seriously injured by another patron in the parking lot after the two were instructed by the bartender to take their argument "outside." The injured patron sued the owner of the bar, alleging that the owner negligently failed to contact law enforcement, maintain proper security on the premises, and properly train his personnel. We reversed a judgment on a jury verdict in favor of the owner because of error in giving an intervening cause instruction. We reasoned that

> [b]ecause the harm resulting from a fight is precisely the harm against which [the owner] is alleged to have had a duty to protect [the patron], the "intervention" of [the other patron] cannot be said to be an independent act that would break the causal connection between [the owner's] negligence and [the patron's] injuries.

Id. at 15, 567 N.W.2d at 305. We employed similar reasoning in Anderson ex rel. Anderson/Couvillon v. Nebraska Dept. of Soc. Servs., 248 Neb. 651, 538 N.W.2d 732 (1995), and Haselhorst v. State, 240 Neb. 891, 485 N.W.2d 180 (1992), both of which involved negligent placement of juvenile wards of the state in foster homes without disclosure of their known histories of violent acts. In each of those cases, we held that criminal acts of foster children perpetrated upon members of the foster parents' households could not be asserted as intervening causes to defeat liability for the negligent placement. Similarly, we recently held that a psychiatric patient's criminal assault upon a nurse was not an intervening cause as to the negligence of a state agency which breached its duty to disclose the violent propensities of the patient at the time of his admission to the hospital where the assault occurred. Fuhrman v. State, 265 Neb. 176, 655 N.W.2d 866 (2003). These decisions were based upon the principle articulated in *Anderson/Couvillon* that "[o]nce it is shown that a defendant had a duty to anticipate an intervening criminal act and guard against it, the criminal act cannot supersede the defendant's liability." 248 Neb. at 660, 538 N.W.2d at 739.

This principle requires that we determine whether the duty owed to Amy by Ford and Firestone, as manufacturers and sellers of the allegedly defective tires, included a duty to anticipate and guard against criminal acts perpetrated against the users of such tires. . . . Generally, we have recognized a duty to anticipate and protect another against criminal acts where the party charged with the duty has some right of control over the perpetrator of such acts or the physical premises upon which the crime occurs. In Anderson/Couvillon v. Nebraska Dept. of Soc. Servs., *supra,* and Haselhorst v. State, *supra,* the state agency responsible for foster placement of the juvenile wards had a duty to warn foster parents of the wards' known histories of violent and abusive behavior. Similarly, in Fuhrman v. State, *supra,* a state agency which placed a ward in a psychiatric hospital had a duty to make disclosures regarding the ward's known violent and dangerous propensities for the benefit of the hospital's employees. In Doe v. Gunny's Ltd. Partnership, 256 Neb. 653, 593 N.W.2d 284 (1999), we recognized a duty on the part of the owner of business premises to protect invitees from criminal assault where there had been documented criminal activity in the immediate vicinity of the premises. In Knoll v. Board of Regents, 258 Neb. 1, 601 N.W.2d 757 (1999), we held that a university had a duty to protect a student from physical hazing conducted in a fraternity house where similar incidents were known to have occurred previously. Similarly, in Sharkey v. Board of Regents, 260 Neb. 166, 182, 615 N.W.2d 889, 902 (2000), we held that a university "owes a landowner-invitee duty to its students to take reasonable steps to protect against foreseeable acts of violence on its campus and the harm that naturally flows therefrom." . . .

We have found no authority recognizing a duty on the part of the manufacturer of a product to protect a consumer from criminal activity at the scene of a product failure where no physical harm is caused by the product itself. . . . The Stahleckers argue that a duty to anticipate criminal acts associated with product failure arises from their allegations that Ford and Firestone knew or should have known of "the potential for similar dangerous situations arising as a result of a breakdown of a Ford Explorer and/or its tires resulting in danger to its consumers and users from criminal activity, adverse weather conditions, inability to communicate with others or any combination thereof." They also allege that Ford and Firestone had or should have had "knowledge, to include statistical information, regarding the likelihood of criminal conduct and/or sexual assault against auto and tire industry consumers as a result of unexpected auto and/or tire failures in general." Assuming the truth of these allegations, the most that can be inferred is that Ford and Firestone had general knowledge that criminal assaults can occur at the scene of a vehicular product failure. However, it is generally known that violent crime can and does occur in a variety of settings, including the relative safety of a victim's home. The facts alleged do not present the type of knowledge concerning a specific individual's criminal propensity, or right of control over premises known to have been the scene of prior criminal activity, upon which we have recognized a tort duty to protect another from criminal acts. The Stahleckers have not and could not allege any special relationship between Ford and Firestone and the criminal actor (Cook) or the victim of his crime (Amy) which would extend their duty, as manufacturers and sellers of products, to protect a consumer from harm caused by a criminal act perpetrated at the scene of a product failure. In the absence of such a duty, Shelton v. Board of Regents, 211 Neb. 820, 320 N.W.2d 748 (1982), controls and requires us to conclude as a matter of law that the criminal assault constituted an efficient intervening cause which precludes a determination that negligence on the part of Ford and Firestone was the proximate cause of the harm which occurred. . . .

Conclusion

Although the operative amended petition alleges sufficient facts to establish that Ford and Firestone negligently placed defective products on the market which caused Amy to become stranded at night in a remote location, it alleges no facts upon which either Ford or Firestone would have a legal duty to anticipate and guard against the criminal acts which were committed at that location by another party. Therefore, the criminal acts constitute an efficient intervening cause which necessarily defeats proof of the essential element of proximate cause.

Although the determination of causation is ordinarily a question of fact, where only one inference can be drawn, it is for the court to decide whether a given act or series of acts is the proximate cause of the injury. Tapp v. Blackmore Ranch, 254 Neb. 40, 575 N.W.2d 341 (1998); Shelton v. Board of Regents, 211 Neb. 820, 320 N.W.2d 748 (1982). Because the only reasonable inference which can be drawn from the facts alleged in this case is that Cook's criminal acts constituted an efficient intervening cause, the district court did not err in sustaining the demurrers of Ford and Firestone without leave to amend and in dismissing the action as to them.

Affirmed.

In Lucero v. Holbrook, 288 P.3d 1228 (Wyo. 2012), defendant left her car running in her driveway with the keys in the ignition while she went inside her home to retrieve her pocketbook. A methamphetamine user stole the car while defendant was inside and later got into a high-speed chase with police. The thief crashed into plaintiff's vehicle during the chase, injuring plaintiff and her children. Plaintiff alleged that defendant breached a duty of care by leaving her car unguarded with the keys in the ignition. The Supreme Court of Wyoming affirmed summary judgment for defendant, reasoning that "[i]t must be remembered that the imposition of a duty not to leave the motor running in a vehicle in one's driveway would apply across the board, and would create potential liability for every person in Wyoming who, on a cold winter day, starts his or her car to warm it up and defrost the windshield before driving upon the public highways." Id. at 1235. Are the facts in *Lucero* sufficiently distinct from *Herrera*, supra, to justify the different outcomes?

An issue that arises fairly frequently is whether a negligent defendant who causes an injury to another will be held liable for the harm that subsequently results from an accident that occurs in the course of the plaintiff's treatment for his original injuries. Courts in this country have traditionally included a rather broad range of such subsequent accidental injuries within the scope of the risks for which the original tortfeasor will be held liable. See generally Restatement (Third) of Torts: Liability for Physical and Emotional Harm §35 (2010); Restatement (Second) of Torts §457, cmts. *a-c,* illus. 1-3 (1965). In Anaya v. Superior Court, 93 Cal. Rptr. 2d 228 (Ct. App. 2000), the court ruled that a jury could find it foreseeable that a person injured in an automobile accident would be killed in the crash of a helicopter taking the injured person to a hospital, even though the crash was caused by negligent maintenance of the helicopter. And in Weber v. Charity Hosp., 475 So. 2d 1047 (La. 1985), the plaintiff contracted hepatitis from blood transfusions necessitated by the injuries she received in an automobile accident. The negligent driver who caused the accident was held liable for the hepatitis as well as for the initial injuries. But this reasoning was later superseded by the legislature. La. C.C. art. 2324 (1996) (limiting such follow-on liability to cases of intentional tort). For a case considering the intervention of two successive medical providers, and the interaction between intervening cause and comparative negligence, see Puckett v. Mt. Carmel Reg'l Med. Ctr., 228 P.3d 1048 (Kan. 2010) (reversing jury verdict and remanding for a new trial; the trial court improperly instructed the jury on intervening cause when there was no evidence that the behavior of the second medical provider was unforeseeable).

Should the defendant be liable in a wrongful death action if the decedent committed suicide as a consequence of the defendant's negligence? "Yes," ruled the court in Porter v. Murphy, 792 A.2d 1009, 1011 (Del. 2001), if the defendant's negligence causes "an uncontrollable impulse to commit suicide." But not if the decedent realizes "the nature of the act, and has the power to control it if he so desires." See also Walsh v. Tehachapi Unified Sch. Dist., 997 F. Supp. 2d 1071 (E.D. Cal. 2014) (holding that whether action or inaction of school employees caused a student to have an uncontrollable suicidal impulse, after being bullied and harassed by fellow students for being gay, was a proper question of fact); McKnight v. South Carolina Dep't of Corr., 684 S.E.2d 566 (S.C. Ct. App. 2009) (affirming summary judgment for defendant Department of Corrections; plaintiff's decedent, a prison inmate, committed suicide 13 months after prison doctor negligently administered anti-psychotic medication).

Lawyers who are sued for legal malpractice have been able to keep suicide cases from the jury. See, e.g., Snyder v. Baumecker, 708 F. Supp. 1451 (D.N.J. 1989), and McPeake v. Cannon, 553 A.2d 439 (Pa. Super. 1989), both involving alleged negligence in defending criminal cases. In the latter case, the court stated (553 A.2d at 443):

> Because an attorney does not possess the ability either to perceive that a client is likely to commit suicide, or to prevent the suicide, we will not impose liability upon him for failing to prevent a harm that is not a foreseeable result of prior negligent conduct.

See also Estate of Robinson v. Continental Casualty Co., 31 So. 3d 1194 (La. Ct. App. 2010) (reversing district court's denial of defendant's motion for summary judgment, when defendant, a lawyer representing plaintiff's decedent, failed to file a lawsuit and decedent, upset over such failure, committed suicide several months later).

One of the more unusual suicide cases not involving a health care provider or a lawyer is Zygmaniak v. Kawasaki Motors Corp., 330 A.2d 56 (N.J. Super.), *appeal dismissed,* 343 A.2d 97 (N.J. 1975), in which a motorcyclist who had been severely injured in an accident allegedly caused by a defect in his motorcycle manufactured by the defendant was shotgunned to death by his brother at his own request. Given that the macabre request was prompted by the injuries suffered at the hands of the defendant, the court held that the issue of proximate cause was for the jury.

Problem 23

You are clerk to Judge Robert Cohen of the United States Court of Appeals for the circuit in which your state is located, that has before it for decision the appeal of the defendant in Barnett v. Clinton Lumber Co. Clinton Lumber has appealed from decisions of the district judge refusing to grant its motion for a directed verdict and refusing to give certain instructions to the jury. Judge Cohen wants a memorandum concerning the correctness of these decisions.

The following is from the plaintiff's brief. (The jurisdictional statement and references to the record have been omitted.)

Statement of the Case

This is an action for negligence brought by the plaintiff, Gordon Barnett, against the defendant, Clinton Lumber Co., for personal injuries arising out of an accident on Route 102 in Clinton. Trial was held which resulted in a jury verdict for plaintiff in the amount of $53,528.28. Judgment was entered on the verdict.

Statement of Facts

There is little dispute as to the facts of this case. The accident giving rise to plaintiff's claim for damages occurred on Route 102 in Clinton at a point 682 feet south of the intersection with Messenger Road. Route 102, at the portions relevant to this case, is a two-lane highway, the traveled portion of which is 45 feet wide. The posted speed limit is 45 miles an hour.

Just prior to the accident plaintiff was proceeding alone in his automobile at about 40 miles an hour in a northerly direction on Route 102. A truck owned by defendant and being operated by its employee, William Mosely, was traveling in a southerly direction at a speed estimated by different witnesses from 40 to 50 miles an hour. The truck was loaded with logs 12 feet in length. The logs were not secured to the truck by means of a rope or chain.

As the defendant's truck approached the automobile driven by plaintiff, several logs fell from the truck and into plaintiff's path. Plaintiff immediately applied the brakes, but was unable to stop in time to avoid colliding with four of the logs. Plaintiff's automobile came to a stop near the easterly edge of the traveled portion of Route 102, and substantially blocking the east lane. There was extensive damage to the front end of plaintiff's automobile, which resulted in both front fenders being crumpled tightly against the front wheels, preventing plaintiff from immediately driving his automobile off the road. It was apparent that it would take some time to remove plaintiff's automobile so that it would not block traffic.

Route 102 curves to the west 280 feet south of the point of the accident. Barry Cook, a passenger in defendant's truck, walked to the curve to warn oncoming traffic of the hazard in the road. Plaintiff and Mosely then worked to pull the fenders back so plaintiff's automobile could be moved. This done, they discovered that the automobile could not be started, so plaintiff and Mosely attempted to push it off the road. While trying to push the automobile off the road, an automobile driven by Harold Craig came around the curve to the south of the accident at a great rate of speed, estimated by Cook to be at least 70 miles an hour. Craig ignored Cook's waves to slow down, and did not apply his brakes until he was 98 feet from where plaintiff and Mosely were trying to push plaintiff's automobile from the road, as indicated by the brake marks left by the Craig automobile. Upon hearing the squealing of Craig's brakes, plaintiff looked back and immediately jumped to the side of the road. Craig's automobile hit plaintiff's, and spun to the right and hit plaintiff, causing the injuries complained of in this suit.

Craig had been drinking heavily at his home for about two hours until he left his home about a half an hour before the accident. A blood test taken less than an hour after the accident showed an alcohol content in Craig's blood of .16 percent. Under General Laws, ch. 86, §27, one who has a blood alcohol content of .10 percent or more is presumed to be under the influence of intoxicating liquor.

Statement of the Issues

The issues presented on this appeal are whether:

1. The district court properly refused to grant defendant's motion for a directed verdict at the close of the evidence.
2. The district court correctly charged the jury on the issue of proximate cause.

The statements of the facts and issues in the defendant's brief are somewhat different from those in the plaintiff's brief in that they are phrased more favorably to the defendant. But because there is no real dispute as to the primary facts, in essence these statements are the same in both briefs.

The defendant's motion for a directed verdict is as follows:

United States District Court

Gordon Barnett, Plaintiff

v.

Clinton Lumber Co., Defendant

No. 5,738

Defendant's Motion for a Directed Verdict

Comes now the defendant in the above entitled action and moves that the Court direct a verdict for defendant on the grounds that as a matter of law any injuries of plaintiff were not the proximate result of the negligence of defendant, if any.

/s/Stanley Winthrop
Attorney for Defendant

The requests for instructions, and the judge's charge to the jury, insofar as relevant to the appeal, are as follows:

Plaintiff's Request for Instructions

8. The defendant is responsible for plaintiff's injuries if the negligence of defendant was the proximate cause of those injuries. The negligence of defendant is a proximate cause of the injuries if the negligence was a substantial factor in producing those injuries.

The negligence is a substantial factor in producing the injuries if plaintiff would not have been injured if defendant had not been negligent.

9. The fact that the negligence of some third party also helped to cause the plaintiff's injuries does not excuse the responsibility of defendant. If the negligence of defendant created a situation whereby plaintiff was exposed to harm from the wrongful conduct of a third person, defendant's negligence is the proximate cause of the harm that results from the situation.

10. If the defendant's negligence placed plaintiff in a position of increased danger, it is not necessary that defendant foresee the exact way by which the plaintiff was injured. It is enough that the wrongful conduct of a third person is of the same general kind as should have been foreseen by defendant.

DEFENDANT'S REQUEST FOR INSTRUCTIONS

13. Defendant is responsible for plaintiff's injuries only if its negligence is the proximate cause of those injuries.

14. Defendant's negligence may be a condition or circumstance of plaintiff's injuries, but it is not the proximate cause of those injuries if the independent wrongful act of a third person intervenes and causes the injuries. Defendant is responsible only for the consequences of his own acts, and not for the independent, intervening wrongful conduct of another.

15. If you find that the conduct of the third party in this case, Harold Craig, amounted to gross negligence or willful and wanton misconduct, you will return a verdict for defendant.

16. Notwithstanding the negligence of defendant, if you find that defendant exercised reasonable care to alleviate the effects of that negligence, and some intervening and independent negligence nonetheless caused harm to the plaintiff, the original negligence of the defendant is not the proximate cause of those injuries. In this case, should you find that the stationing of Barry Cook as a road guard was reasonably designed to prevent further injury to the plaintiff, you will return your verdict for defendant.

17. Notwithstanding the negligence of the defendant, if you find that by the time the plaintiff was injured, the risk created originally by any negligence of the defendant had terminated and that it was unforeseeable that a person operating under the influence of alcohol would drive at 70 miles an hour and ignore the warning of the road guard posted by the defendant, you will return your verdict for the defendant.

THE DISTRICT COURT'S CHARGE TO THE JURY

If you find that the driver of the defendant's truck was negligent, and that negligence caused plaintiff's car to block the road, then you have to consider the principle of the chain of causation.

You are instructed that in many cases, after an act of negligence has occurred, another force may intervene and become the sole proximate cause of the accident; in such an event, if you find such to be the fact in the present case, there could be no recovery against the defendant.

On the other hand, it is the law that whoever does an unlawful act is answerable for all the consequences that may ensue in the ordinary course of events, even though such consequences are brought about by an intervening cause. If, in fact, such intervening cause was set in motion or made probable by the act of the original wrongdoer, and if the consequences are such as might with reasonable diligence be foreseen, the test is whether or not there was an unbroken connection between the wrongful act and the injury. Did the acts constitute a succession of events so linked together as to make a natural whole, or was there some other new, independent cause intervening between the wrong and the injury?

> You are instructed that the driver of the truck which is negligently operated by him in such a manner as to place others in a position where they are struck and injured by an automobile operated by a third person may be held liable therefor, where it is established that such negligence was the proximate cause of the resulting injuries. The fact that the driver of a third car was also negligent is not a defense, provided it is established by the evidence that both drivers were negligent, and that their concurrent negligence was the proximate cause of the resulting injury. It is, of course, essential to a recovery against the first wrongdoer that it be established by the evidence that there was a causal connection between his negligent conduct and the final resulting injury. The ultimate test is whether it appears from all the evidence that the negligence of the first wrongdoer was such that it could have been properly said that it could have been the proximate cause of the later injury; in other words, whether in all the circumstances surrounding the situation he ought reasonably to have foreseen that the later consequences might occur as a result of his negligence.
>
> In negligence cases, the law recognizes that there may be more than one proximate cause of the same injury, and where a chain of events has once been started, due to the negligence of the driver of an automobile, he may be liable for all the mishaps which are, in fact, the proximate results of his unlawful conduct.
>
> The chain of causation is not broken by an intervening act, even if wrongful, which is a normal reaction to the stimulus of a situation created by negligence.

In preparing the memorandum for Judge Cohen, you are to assume that Herrera v. Quality Pontiac is an opinion by your state's supreme court, and that Marshall v. Nugent is an opinion of the United States Court of Appeals for the circuit in which your state is located. Under the circumstances of this case, the substantive law of negligence to be determined and applied is that of your state. Because of this, the opinion in *Marshall* does not have the binding effect of an opinion of your state's supreme court, but it is an authoritative interpretation of your state's law at the time the opinion was written.

Recall from Section C.1. of Chapter 3 that violations of criminal safety statutes may give rise to causes of action in negligence. Proximate cause problems can arise in this context as well.

Gorris v. Scott

[1874] 9 L.R. (Exch.) 125

KELLY, C.B. This is an action to recover damages for the loss of a number of sheep which the defendant, a shipowner, had contracted to carry, and which were washed overboard and lost by reason (as we must take it to be truly alleged) of the neglect to comply with a certain order made by the Privy Council, in pursuance of the Contagious Diseases (Animals) Act, 1869. The Act was passed merely for sanitary purposes, in order to prevent animals in a state of infectious disease from communicating it to other animals with which they might come in contact. Under the authority of that Act, certain orders were made; amongst others, an order by which any ship bringing sheep or cattle from any foreign port to ports in Great Britain is to have the place occupied by such animals divided into pens of certain dimensions, and the floor of such pens furnished with battens or foot-holds. The object of this order is to prevent animals from being overcrowded, and so brought into a condition in which the disease guarded against would be likely to be developed. This regulation has been neglected, and the question is, whether the loss, which we must assume to have been caused by that neglect, entitles the plaintiffs to maintain an action.

. . . And if we could see that it was the object, or among the objects of this Act, that the owners of sheep and cattle coming from a foreign port should be protected by the means described against the danger of their property being washed overboard, or lost by the perils of the sea, the present action would be within the principle.

But, looking at the Act, it is perfectly clear that its provisions were all enacted with a totally different view; there was no purpose, direct or indirect, to protect against such damage; but, as is recited in the preamble, the Act is directed against the possibility of sheep or cattle being exposed to disease on their way to this country. The preamble recites that "it is expedient to confer on Her Majesty's most honourable Privy Council power to take such measures as may appear from time to time necessary to prevent the introduction into Great Britain of contagious or infectious diseases among cattle, sheep, or other animals, by prohibiting or regulating the importation of foreign animals," and also to provide against the "spreading" of such diseases in Great Britain. Then follow numerous sections directed entirely to this object. Then comes s. 75, which enacts that "the Privy Council may from time to time make such orders as they think expedient for all or any of the following purposes." What, then, are these purposes? They are "for securing for animals brought by sea to ports in Great Britain a proper supply of food and water during the passage and on landing," "for protecting such animals from unnecessary suffering during the passage and on landing," and so forth; all the purposes enumerated being calculated and directed to the prevention of disease, and none of them having any relation whatever to the danger of loss by the perils of the sea. That being so, if by reason of the default in question the plaintiffs' sheep had been overcrowded, or had been caused unnecessary suffering, and so had arrived in this country in a state of disease, I do not say that they might not have maintained this action. But the damage complained of here is something totally apart from the object of the Act of Parliament, and it is in accordance with all the authorities to say that the action is not maintainable.

How should the court rule on the defendants' motions for summary judgment in the following fact patterns, which are based on real cases?

1. A gasoline station attendant sold gasoline in a plastic milk container to a person who used the gasoline to burn a building. Actions in negligence for wrongful death and property damage were brought against the station based on its violation of a statute that made it illegal to sell gasoline in unapproved containers; plastic milk containers were not approved by the statute.

2. A minor bought cigarettes and gave one to another minor, who began smoking it. The latter dropped the lighted cigarette, resulting in a fire that destroyed a pile of telephone poles. The owner of the poles brought an action against the minor who supplied the cigarette, alleging negligence based on a statute that prohibited furnishing cigarettes to a minor.

Some courts, and the Restatement (Second) of Torts §286, combine the negligence per se and proximate cause aspects into a single rule. This fusion is carried forward into the Restatement (Third) of Torts: Liability for Physical and Emotional Harm §14 (2010):

> An actor is negligent if, without excuse, the actor violates a statute that is designed to protect against the type of accident the actor's conduct causes, and if the accident victim is within the class of persons the statute is designed to protect.

This departs from the conceptual approach to nonstatutory negligence, under which the defendant's negligence is treated separately from the issue of whether the defendant's negligence was the proximate cause of the plaintiff's injury.

Problem 24

A partner in your law firm has asked you for a memorandum of law on an issue raised in a case she is handling. The firm represents Thomas and Phillip Hagen, brothers who have been joined as defendants in a personal injury action. Both Thomas and Phillip live in Wayland. Thomas is married, with three children, and owns and operates a gasoline service station. Phillip is single and is a draftsman with a local engineering firm.

The complaint in the case was filed by Roger Baptiste in Tyler County Superior Court on January 20 of this year. The plaintiff alleges that on June 24 of last year, while walking through woods on the outskirts of Wayland, he was shot and injured with a 22-caliber rifle negligently fired by Phillip Hagen. The complaint further alleges that the rifle was owned by Thomas Hagen, who was with Phillip at the time and who had moments before the accident loaned the rifle to Phillip for the purpose of shooting at some targets the men had erected. The complaint charges the defendants with knowledge that there might be persons in the vicinity, and their conduct in its particulars is described as negligent. In addition, the plaintiff alleges that at the time of the shooting Phillip Hagen was unlicensed to possess a firearm and could not have obtained a license had he applied for one. The complaint alleges that the conduct of the defendants violated Chapter 36, Sections 1, 2, and 6 of the General Laws (the gun registration statute), and was therefore negligent as a matter of law. The complaint prays judgment of $25,000 against the defendants. The relevant portions of the statute follow.

General Laws, Chapter 36, §§1-3, 6, 9

1. *Registration and licensing.* It shall be unlawful for any person to own a firearm unless the same has been registered in accordance herewith and a license issued to the owner thereof. No license shall be issued to any person (a) who is not of good moral character; (b) who has been convicted anywhere of a felony; or (c) who has ever suffered any mental illness or has been confined to any hospital or institution, public or private, for mental illness. Nor shall any license be issued to any person under the age of 21 years.

2. *Possession.* It shall be unlawful for any person to possess a firearm which has not been registered in accordance herewith. It shall further be unlawful for any person to possess a firearm who for the reasons stated in §1 hereof is ineligible to receive a license for a firearm.

3. *Applications.* Applications for licenses shall be made to the clerk of the town or city in which the applicant resides, and shall be on a form prepared by the Commissioner of Public Safety. The application shall be on oath, and if the clerk is satisfied that the applicant is qualified, he shall register the firearm in a book kept for the purpose, and shall issue to the applicant a license therefor. . . .

6. *Transfer of ownership or possession.* It shall be unlawful for any person to transfer the ownership or possession of a firearm to any person who for the reasons stated in §1 hereof is ineligible to receive a license for a firearm. . . .

9. *Violations.* Any person who violates any provision of this Act shall be punished by a fine of not exceeding five hundred dollars and imprisonment for not more than six months. . . .

The partner wants your advice as to the effect that the gun registration statute is likely to have in this case. There is no question in her mind that both men violated the statute. The gun was properly registered to Thomas, who had a license. However, Phillip did not have a gun license, nor could he have obtained one because of his conviction 12 years ago, at the age of 20, of the felony of unarmed robbery. As a result of his conviction, he was sentenced to 5 years, and served 14 months, in state prison. Phillip explains that he was "associating with the wrong crowd" at the time and that he has not been in trouble since.

Assuming that Martin v. Herzog, Tedla v. Ellman, and Brown v. Shyne, in Chapter 3, above, are opinions of your state's supreme court, advise the partner on this issue.

2. The Restatements' Approaches to the Proximate Cause Issue

Numerous commentators have bemoaned the lack of consistency and coherence in proximate cause decisions. See, e.g., Leon Green, Rationale of Proximate Cause 4-5 (1927), in which the author states: "The deplorable expenditure and stupendous waste of judicial energy which has been employed in converting this simple problem [of causation] into an insoluble riddle beggars description. Only by the patient process of eliminative analysis can the rubbish of literally thousands of cases be cleared away." Nevertheless, the preceding material suggests that foreseeability of the consequences of conduct provides a critical focal point for the proximate cause analysis. The foreseeability concept might be criticized on two grounds:

1. *It is not workable.* It lacks sufficient substantive content to be capable of rational application across a range of cases.
2. *It is wrong in policy.* The defendant should sometimes be liable for consequences that are not foreseeable.

To what extent, if any, do the following sections of the Restatement (Second) address these concerns?

RESTATEMENT (SECOND) OF TORTS

§431. WHAT CONSTITUTES LEGAL CAUSE

The actor's negligent conduct is a legal cause of harm to another if

(a) his conduct is a substantial factor in bringing about the harm, and

(b) there is no rule of law relieving the actor from liability because of the manner in which his negligence has resulted in the harm.

COMMENT:

a. *Distinction between substantial cause and cause in the philosophic sense.* In order to be a legal cause of another's harm, it is not enough that the harm would not have occurred had the actor not been negligent. . . . The negligence must also be a substantial factor in bringing about the plaintiff's harm. The word "substantial" is used to denote the fact that the defendant's conduct has such an effect in producing the harm as to lead reasonable men to regard it as a cause, using that word in the popular sense, in which there always lurks the idea of responsibility, rather than in the so-called "philosophic sense," which includes every one of the great number of events without which any happening would not have occurred. Each of these events is a cause in the so-called "philosophic sense," yet the effect of many of them is so insignificant that no ordinary mind would think of them as causes.

§433. CONSIDERATIONS IMPORTANT IN DETERMINING WHETHER NEGLIGENT CONDUCT IS SUBSTANTIAL FACTOR IN PRODUCING HARM

The following considerations are in themselves or in combination with one another important in determining whether the actor's conduct is a substantial factor in bringing about harm to another:

(a) the number of other factors which contribute in producing the harm and the extent of the effect which they have in producing it;

(b) whether the actor's conduct has created a force or series of forces which are in continuous and active operation up to the time of the harm, or has created a situation harmless unless acted upon by other forces for which the actor is not responsible;

(c) lapse of time.

For criticism of the "substantial factor" test, see Peter Zablotsky, Mixing Oil and Water: Reconciling the Substantial Factor and Result-Within-the-Risk Approaches to Proximate Cause, 56 Clev. St. L. Rev. 1003, 1018-20 (2008); Joseph Sanders et al., The Insubstantiality of the "Substantial Factor" Test for Causation, 73 Mo. L. Rev. 399 (2008).

The Restatement (Third) of Torts: Liability for Physical and Emotional Harm §29 (2010) abandons the "legal cause" terminology in favor of more straightforward language:

§29. LIMITATIONS ON LIABILITY FOR TORTIOUS CONDUCT

An actor's liability is limited to those harms that result from the risks that made the actor's conduct tortious.

Comment *j* to this section makes clear that the drafters intend the proximate causation analysis to be applied independently of the foreseeability analysis that is undertaken to determine whether an actor's conduct is negligent. The comment argues that "factfinders can apply the [new Third Restatement approach] with more sensitivity to the underlying rationale than they might muster with an unadorned foreseeable-harm standard." Are you persuaded by this reasoning? In Michael L. Wells, Proximate Cause and the American Law Institute: The False Choice Between the "Direct Consequences" Test and the "Risk Standard," 37 U. Rich. L. Rev. 389 (2003), the author argues that the primary aim of "scope of liability" limitations such as proximate causation is to avoid imposing large financial burdens on defendants for small departures from ordinary care. With that aim in mind, the author contends that a superior approach to the Third Restatement's "risk standard" approach would be one that focuses directly on the magnitude of the harm and the fairness of imposing liability for it on defendant. For another critical appraisal of the causation issue in the Restatement (Third), see David W. Robertson, Causation in the Restatement (Third) of Torts: Three Arguable Mistakes, 44 Wake Forest L. Rev. 1007 (2009).

B. Special Instances of Nonliability for Harmful Consequences that Are Both Foreseeable and of the Sort that Made Defendant's Conduct Negligent

As the preceding materials on proximate cause illustrate, courts often invoke notions of reasonable foreseeability and results within the risk as means of restricting actual causation. The scope of negligence liability, both in terms of duty and causation, is therefore generally coterminous with the scope of reasonably foreseeable consequences likely to flow from the defendants' actions. But just as foreseeability-based proximate cause serves to limit a defendant's liability for harms that were actually caused by the defendant, courts have identified a number of situations where foreseeability itself may be too expansive a test for the limits of liability. In reviewing the materials that follow, consider whether the rules and justifications developed by courts for cutting off liability short of foreseeability make sense.

1. Mental and Emotional Upset

Recovery for mental and emotional upset resulting from tortiously caused physical injury is not controversial. That subject is taken up in Chapter 8 under the heading of Damages. The mental and emotional upset explored here occurs as a result of the defendant's negligent conduct, but with no physical injury predicate. In these cases, plaintiffs are upset by the prospect of themselves being physically injured, or from having experienced other victims suffering physical injury.

One legal approach to such cases would be a pure "liability based on foreseeability" rule, under which the plaintiff may recover for mental and emotional upset whenever it is determined that the psychological harm to the plaintiff was foreseeable. Courts have, by and large, rejected such a pure rule in favor of a variety of liability-limiting approaches. We consider several such approaches in the sections that follow.

a. The Impact and Zone of Danger Rules

The first liability-limiting rule was the "impact" rule of Mitchell v. Rochester Ry., 45 N.E. 354 (N.Y. 1896). The defendant's driver negligently drove a wagon pulled by two horses up to the plaintiff. When the horses stopped, the plaintiff was standing between them, although they did not come into contact with her. The plaintiff was frightened and later suffered a miscarriage, which medical testimony indicated was caused by the fright. In ordering judgment for the defendant notwithstanding a verdict for the plaintiff, the court ruled that there could be no recovery for fright alone without impact. In the court's view, it followed from that ruling that there could be no recovery for any resulting physical manifestations of the fright, such as "nervous disease, blindness, insanity or even a miscarriage." This became known as the impact rule, which at one time was the clear weight of authority. However, the rule announced in the following case has largely replaced it.

Waube v. Warrington

216 Wis. 603, 258 N.W. 497 (1935)

WICKHEM, J. In the statement of facts in both briefs it is said that deceased was looking out the window of her house watching her child cross the highway, and witnessed the negligent killing of the child by defendant. . . .

The question presented is whether . . . the mother of a child who, although not put in peril or fear of physical impact, sustains the shock of witnessing the negligent killing of her child, may recover for physical injuries caused by such fright or shock.

The problem must be approached at the outset from the viewpoint of the duty of defendant and the right of plaintiff, and not from the viewpoint of proximate cause. The right of the mother to recover must be based, first, upon the establishment of a duty on the part of defendant so to conduct herself with respect to the child as not to subject the mother to an unreasonable risk of shock or fright, and, second, upon the recognition of a legally protected right or interest on the part of the mother to be free from shock or fright occasioned by the peril of her child. It is not enough to find a breach of duty to the child, follow the consequences of such breach as far as the law of proximate cause will permit them to go, and then sustain a recovery for the mother if a physical injury to her by reason of shock or fright is held not too remote.

Upon this point we adopt and follow the doctrine of Palsgraf v. Long Island R.R. Co., 248 N.Y. 339, 162 N.E. 99. . . .

The right of a plaintiff to recover damages for nervous shock caused by negligence without actual impact has had an interesting history. In Victoria Railways Commissioners v. Coultas (1888), 13 A.C. 222, 226, it was held that plaintiff was not entitled to recover such damages. This became the prevailing doctrine in this country. This doctrine, however, was repudiated in a number of jurisdictions, including Wisconsin, in situations where fright without impact produced physical injuries. . . . The rule followed in Wisconsin appears to represent the modern tendency. . . . In jurisdictions following the liberal rule it has been held consistently . . . that in order to give rise to a right of action grounded on negligent conduct, the emotional distress or shock must be occasioned by fear of personal injury to the person sustaining the shock, and not fear of injury to his property or to the person of another.

Thus it may be said that the doctrine most favorable to plaintiff is not sufficiently broad to entitle [her] to recover. The question presented is whether there should be an extension of the rule to cases where defendant's conduct involves merely an unreasonable risk of causing harm to the child or spouse of the person sustaining injuries through fright or shock. . . .

The only case squarely dealing with this problem is Hambrook v. Stokes Bros. (1925), 1 K.B. 141. In this case a servant of defendants was in charge of a motor-truck belonging to defendants, and parked it at the top of a hill on Dover Street in Folkestone, leaving it unattended, with the motor running, and without taking proper precautions to prevent it from moving. During his absence the truck started to run down the hill. . . . On the day in question Mrs. Hambrook, whose house was at the bottom of Dover Street, accompanied her three children, a girl and two boys, part of the distance on their way to school. She walked with them to a point a little below the curve in Dover Street, and then left them. Shortly afterwards she saw the truck coming rapidly around the curve in her direction. She was not in any personal danger, as the truck stopped some distance short of where she was standing, and in any case she would have had ample opportunity to step into a position of safety. She immediately became fearful for the safety of her children. A crowd collected and there were rumors of an accident. She inquired who had been injured, and a friend stated that it was a little girl with glasses. It appeared that her little girl wore glasses. She went to the hospital and found that her daughter had been injured. She sustained a severe shock and consequent physical injuries from which she died. The trial court directed the jury that if the nervous shock was caused by fear of her child's safety, as distinguished from her own, plaintiff could not recover. From a verdict in favor of defendants, plaintiff appealed. The judgment was set aside and a new trial granted for misdirection. . . . Viewing the matter from the standpoint of proximate cause rather than duty, the court held that there should be no distinction between shock sustained by a mother as a result of fear for her own safety, and that sustained by reason of peril to her child. The court considered that defendant ought to have anticipated that if the unattended truck ran down this narrow street it might terrify some woman to such an extent, through fear of some immediate bodily injury to herself, that she would receive a mental shock with resultant physical injuries, and that defendant ought also to have anticipated that such a shock might result from the peril to the child of such a woman. While the majority mistakenly, as it seems to us, approach this problem from the standpoint of proximate cause, the dissenting opinion of SARGANT, L.J., approaches it from the standpoint of duty. . . .

With due deference to the learned judges who concurred in the decision, we cannot escape the conclusion that the determination in the *Hambrook* case is incorrect, both in its initial approach and in its conclusion, and that the doctrine contended for by plaintiff, and there approved, would constitute an unwarranted enlargement of the duties of users of the highway. Fundamentally, defendant's duty was to use ordinary care to avoid physical injury to those who would be put in physical peril, as that term is commonly understood, by conduct on his part falling short of that standard. It is one thing to say that as to those who are put in peril of physical impact, impact is immaterial if physical injury is caused by shock arising from the peril. It is the foundation of cases holding to this liberal ruling, that the person affrighted or sustaining shock was actually put in peril of physical impact, and under these conditions it was considered immaterial that the physical impact did not materialize. It is quite another thing to say that those who are out of the field of physical danger through impact shall have a legally protected right to be free from emotional distress occasioned by the peril of others, when that distress results in physical impairment. The answer to this question cannot be reached solely by logic, nor is it clear that it can be entirely disposed of by a consideration of what the defendant ought reasonably to have anticipated as a consequence of his wrong. The answer must be reached by balancing the social interests involved in order to ascertain how far defendant's duty and plaintiff's right may justly and expediently be extended. It is our conclusion that they can neither justly nor expediently be extended to any recovery for physical injuries sustained by one out of the range of ordinary physical peril as a result of the shock of witnessing another's danger. Such consequences are so unusual and extraordinary, viewed after the event, that a user of the highway may be said not to subject others to an unreasonable risk of them by the careless management of his vehicle. Furthermore, the liability imposed by such a doctrine is wholly out of proportion to the culpability of the negligent tortfeasor, would put an unreasonable burden upon users of the highway, open the way to fraudulent claims, and enter a field that has no sensible or just stopping point.

It was recognized by the court in the *Hambrook* case that had the mother there merely been told of the injury to her child, instead of having been virtually a witness to the transaction, there would have been no liability. The court thus selected at least one arbitrary boundary for the extension. . . . It was suggested in the dissenting opinion in the *Hambrook* case that if the mother may recover, why not a child whose shock was occasioned by the peril of the mother? It is not necessary to multiply these illustrations. They can be made as numerous as the varying degrees of human relationship, and they shade into each other in such a way as to leave no definite or clear-cut stopping place for the suggested doctrine, short of a recovery for every person who has sustained physical injuries as a result of shock or emotional distress by reason of seeing or hearing of the peril or injury of another. No court has gone this far, and we think no court should go this far. It is our view that fairness and justice, as well as expediency, require the defendant's duty to be defined as heretofore stated. . . . Human wrong-doing is seldom limited in its injurious effects to the immediate actors in a particular event. More frequently than not, a chain of results is set up that visits evil consequences far and wide. While from the standpoint of good morals and good citizenship the wrong-doer may be said to violate a duty to those who suffer from the wrong, the law finds it necessary, for reasons heretofore considered, to attach practical and just limits to the legal consequences of the wrongful act. . . .

By the Court Order reversed, and cause remanded with directions to sustain the demurrer.

In the relatively few earlier cases in which the issue arose, the zone of danger rule mostly carried the day. The Supreme Court of the United States signed on to the rule in Consolidated Rail Corp. v. Gottshall, 512 U.S. 532 (1994), a case arising under the Federal Employers Liability Act (FELA).[3] In Engler v. Illinois Farmers Ins. Co., 706 N.W.2d 764 (Minn. 2005), the Minnesota Supreme Court reaffirmed its adherence to the rule. The court did, however, indicate a willingness to expand emotional distress recovery by permitting the plaintiff to claim damages resulting not only from fear for her own safety, but also from fear for the safety of a loved one who also was in the zone of danger created by defendant's negligence. See also Chaparro v. Carnival Corp., 693 F.3d 1333 (11th Cir. 2012) (applying zone of danger rule to maritime law). Furthermore, the Restatement (Third) of Torts: Liability for Physical and Emotional Harm (2010) incorporates the zone of danger rule in §46: "An actor whose negligent conduct causes serious emotional disturbance to another is subject to liability to the other if the conduct: (a) places the other in immediate danger of bodily harm and the emotional disturbance results from the danger; or (b) occurs in the course of specified categories of activities, undertakings, or relationships in which negligent conduct is especially likely to cause serious emotional disturbance." Section 46(b) refers to special cases involving death telegrams, the handling of corpses, and other contexts deemed especially likely to lead to emotional distress. These somewhat anomalous categories of emotional distress recovery are discussed below in Subsection c.

Note: The Impact and Zone of Danger Rules in the Age of Toxics

The classic fact patterns arising under the impact and zone of danger rules involved traumatic accidents — a horse-drawn wagon in *Mitchell* and a motor vehicle in *Waube*. In these cases, the rules placed natural boundaries on the exposure of defendants to "excessive" liability that courts, such as the Wisconsin Supreme Court, feared would result from liability for emotional upset based only on foreseeability.

But with the coming of an era in which people are more frequently exposed to contact with toxic substances — asbestos, smoke, harmful chemicals in air and water — the traditional excessive liability limiting boundaries of the impact and zone of danger rules are being tested. Once scientists came to understand these exposures as involving "impact," although on a molecular scale often invisible to the eye, the same concerns about limitless liability returned. The view that small particles can constitute an impact has caused

3. Recall that in CSX Transp., Inc. v. McBride, p. 299, above, the Supreme Court confirmed that proximate causation is not a requirement in a negligence action against an employer under FELA. *McBride* cites *Gottshall* with approval regarding the historical background of the statute, impliedly supporting *Gottshall*'s holding on the zone of danger rule. See 564 U.S. at 692. Can you reconcile *McBride*'s holding regarding proximate cause with *Gottshall*'s holding regarding recovery for mental upset?

problems for the law in contexts other than those considered here. Recall from Chapter 1 (see pp. 33-35, above) the issue of whether tobacco smoke blown in the plaintiff's face might be a contact sufficient to support a battery claim. And looking ahead to Chapter 5, Trespass to Land and Nuisance, courts have been called on to determine if invasions of land by small particles constitute a trespass.

In these more modern factual contexts, courts have generally held that impact is, on its own, not sufficient to trigger liability for ensuing emotional upset. In cases involving exposure to asbestos, for example, courts have not imposed emotional upset liability when all the plaintiff has been able to allege is contact with asbestos fibers; courts have insisted on proof that the contact has caused present physical injury. It is not enough that there is a fear, even a reasonable fear, that some future physical harm will result. See Metro-North Commuter R.R. Co. v. Buckley, 521 U.S. 424 (1997) (requiring physical manifestation of disease as a prerequisite to recovery for emotional distress damages under FELA), and Temple-Inland Forest Products Corp. v. Carter, 993 S.W.2d 88 (Tex. 1999) (holding that presently non-afflicted asbestos workers could not recover for fear of contracting asbestos-related disease in the future). Even in contexts in which the impact is of the more conventional type, some courts have held that something more is required for emotional harm recovery. In Hamilton v. Nestor, 659 N.W.2d 321 (Neb. 2003), for example, the plaintiff, Christopher Hamilton, sought recovery for emotional injuries suffered following a motor vehicle accident that he was involved in and that was caused by the negligent driving of the decedent, DiAnn Nestor. In the accident, both Nestor and her daughter were killed. Hamilton testified that he suffered repeated nightmares and flashbacks, accompanied by feelings of guilt that he was unable to prevent their deaths. He also testified that he once blacked out while driving near the location where the accident occurred. On a motion for summary judgment brought by the representative of Nestor's estate, the court evaluated whether Hamilton's emotional distress rose to the level of severity required in order to recover under a "zone of danger" theory (659 N.W.2d at 329-30):

> The record includes the expert opinion of Moore, a psychiatrist, that Hamilton suffers from posttraumatic stress disorder as a result of the 1997 accident. Moore testified that Hamilton exhibits symptoms of this disorder, including dreams and flashbacks, which warrant treatment. Moore referred to these symptoms as "clinically significant distress." . . . While the evidence viewed in the light most favorable to Hamilton shows that he did experience diagnosable and clinically significant emotional distress resulting from the accident, it was not of sufficient severity to be actionable under our case law. Moore testified that post-traumatic stress disorder may range in severity from mild to severe. According to Moore, the posttraumatic stress disorder experienced by Hamilton falls within the lower half of the range, "[b]etween mild and moderate." On the basis of information obtained from Hamilton, Moore described him as "pretty well beat up emotionally for a short period of time, but before too long he went on with his life." Viewing this medical testimony, as well as Hamilton's testimony describing his symptoms, in a light most favorable to Hamilton, we conclude that the emotional injury so described cannot, as matter of law, be considered so severe that no reasonable person could be expected to endure it.

Other courts continue to require some physical manifestation of plaintiff's emotional distress as a limitation on recovery. In Palmer v. Nan King Restaurant, Inc., 798 A.2d 583 (N.H. 2002), for example, the court ruled that plaintiff could not recover for emotional harm suffered after biting into a used bandage in food served by defendant. While acknowledging that plaintiff suffered actual contact with the offensive item, the court stated that "regardless of physical impact, in order to recover for emotional distress under a traditional negligence theory, the plaintiff must demonstrate physical symptoms of her distress." Id. at 586. In Hagan v. Coca Cola bottling Co., 804 So. 2d 1234 (Fla. 2001), on the other hand, the court abandoned the physical manifestation rule in a case involving plaintiffs' fear of contracting AIDS after they drank from a bottle which appeared to contain a used condom. The court reasoned that "those who market foodstuffs should foresee and expect to bear responsibility for the emotional and physical harm caused by someone consuming a food product that is contaminated by a foreign substance." Id. at 1241. Earlier fear-of-AIDS cases had sometimes made recovery contingent on plaintiff's demonstrating that an actual chance of contracting AIDS existed. See, e.g., Burk v. Sage Products, 747 F. Supp. 285 (E.D. Pa. 1990) (plaintiff, who was pricked with a needle that had been available to patients with AIDS, could not recover for fear of contracting AIDS absent proof that the needle had actually come into contact with such a patient); Roes v. FHP, Inc., 985 P.2d 661 (Haw. 1999) (plaintiffs could recover for emotional distress after HIV-infected blood leaked from bags that plaintiffs were handling for defendants). For an argument that fear-of-AIDS claims require a different standard that is more favorable to plaintiffs, see Alexander Santee, More Than Just Bad Blood: Reasonably Assessing Fear of AIDS Claims, 46 Vill. L. Rev. 207 (2001). For a contrary perspective, see James A. Henderson, Jr. & Aaron D. Twerski, Asbestos Litigation Gone Mad: Exposure-Based Recovery for Increased Risk, Mental Distress, and Medical Monitoring, 53 S.C. L. Rev. 815 (2002).

b. Liability to Bystanders

Dillon v. Legg

68 Cal. 2d 728, 441 P.2d 912, 69 Cal. Rptr. 72 (1968)

Tobriner, Justice.

That the courts should allow recovery to a mother who suffers emotional trauma and physical injury from witnessing the infliction of death or injury to her child for which the tort-feasor is liable in negligence would appear to be a compelling proposition. As Prosser points out, "All ordinary human feelings are in favor of her (the mother's) action against the negligent defendant. If a duty to her requires that she herself be in some recognizable danger, then it has properly been said that when a child is endangered, it is not beyond contemplation that its mother will be somewhere in the vicinity, and will suffer serious shock." (Prosser, Law of Torts (3d ed. 1964), p. 353.)

Nevertheless, past American decisions have barred the mother's recovery. Refusing the mother the right to take her case to the jury, these courts ground their position on an alleged absence of a required "duty" of due care of the tortfeasor to the mother. Duty, in turn, they state, must express public policy; the imposition of duty here would work disaster because it would invite fraudulent claims and it would involve the courts in the hopeless task of defining the extent of the tortfeasor's liability. In substance, they say, definition of liability being impossible, denial of liability is the only realistic alternative.

We have concluded that neither of the feared dangers excuses the frustration of the natural justice upon which the mother's claim rests. We shall point out that in the past we have rejected the argument that we should deny recovery upon a legitimate claim because other fraudulent ones may be urged. We shall further explain that the alleged inability to fix definitions for recovery on the different facts of future cases does not justify the denial of recovery on the specific facts of the instant case; in any event, proper guidelines can indicate the extent of liability for such future cases.

[The plaintiffs were the mother and sister of the young primary victim injured by the defendant's alleged negligent operation of an automobile. Both were at the scene of and witnessed the accident, and both sued the defendant alleging emotional harm as a result of witnessing the accident. The trial judge granted the defendant's motion for judgment on the pleadings in the mother's action.]

We . . . note, at the outset, that defendant has interposed the defense that the contributory negligence of the mother, the sister, and the child contributed to the accident. If any such defense is sustained and defendant found not liable for the death of the child because of the contributory negligence of the mother, sister or child, we do not believe that the mother or sister should recover for the emotional trauma which they allegedly suffered. In the absence of the primary liability of the tort-feasor for the death of the child, we see no ground for an independent and secondary liability for claims for injuries by third parties. The basis for such claims must be adjudicated liability and fault of defendant; that liability and fault must be the foundation for the tort-feasor's duty of due care to third parties who, as a consequence of such negligence, sustain emotional trauma. . . .

2. The alleged inability to fix definitions for recovery on the different facts of future cases does not justify the denial of recovery on the specific facts of the instant case; in any event, proper guidelines can indicate the extent of liability for such future cases.

In order to limit the otherwise potential infinite liability which would follow every negligent act, the law of torts holds defendant amenable only for injuries to others which to defendant at the time were reasonably foreseeable.

Since the chief element in determining whether defendant owes a duty or an obligation to plaintiff is the foreseeability of the risk, that factor will be of prime concern in every case. Because it is inherently intertwined with foreseeability such duty or obligation must necessarily be adjudicated only upon a case-by-case basis. We cannot now predetermine defendant's obligation in every situation by a fixed category; no immutable rule can establish the extent of that obligation for every circumstance of the future. We can, however, define guidelines which will aid in the resolution of such an issue as the instant one.

We note, first, that we deal here with a case in which plaintiff suffered a shock which resulted in physical injury and we confine our ruling to that case. In determining, in such a case, whether defendant should reasonably foresee the injury to plaintiff, or, in other terminology, whether defendant owes plaintiff a duty of due care, the courts will take into account such factors as the following: (1) Whether plaintiff was located near the scene of the accident as contrasted with one who was a distance away from it. (2) Whether the shock resulted from a direct emotional impact upon plaintiff from the sensory and contemporaneous observance of the accident, as contrasted with learning of the accident from others after its occurrence. (3) Whether plaintiff and the victim were closely related, as contrasted with an absence of any relationship or the presence of only a distant relationship.

The evaluation of these factors will indicate the *degree* of the defendant's foreseeability: obviously defendant is more likely to foresee that a mother who observes an accident affecting her child will suffer harm than to foretell that a stranger witness will do so. Similarly, the degree of foreseeability of the third person's injury is far greater in the case of his contemporaneous observance of the accident than that in which he subsequently learns of it. The defendant is more likely to foresee that shock to the nearby, witnessing mother will cause physical harm than to anticipate that someone distant from the accident will suffer more than a temporary emotional reaction. All these elements, of course, shade into each other; the fixing of obligation, intimately tied into the facts, depends upon each case.

In light of these factors the court will determine whether the accident and harm was reasonably foreseeable. Such reasonable foreseeability does not turn on whether the particular defendant as an individual would have in actuality foreseen the exact accident and loss; it contemplates that courts, on a case-to-case basis, analyzing all the circumstances, will decide what the ordinary man under such circumstances should reasonably have foreseen. The courts thus mark out the areas of liability, excluding the remote and unexpected.

In the instant case, the presence of all the above factors indicates that plaintiff has alleged a sufficient prima facie case. Surely the negligent driver who causes the death of a young child may reasonably expect that the mother will not be far distant and will upon witnessing the accident suffer emotional trauma. . . .

We are not now called upon to decide whether, in the absence or reduced weight of some of the above factors, we would conclude that the accident and injury were not reasonably foreseeable and that therefore defendant owed no duty of due care to plaintiff. In future cases the courts will draw lines of demarcation upon facts more subtle than the compelling ones alleged in the complaint before us. . . .

We have explained that recovery here will not expose the courts to false claims or a flood of litigation. The test that we have set forth will aid in the proper resolution of future cases. Indeed, the general principles of tort law are acknowledged to work successfully in all other cases of emotional trauma.

Yet for some artificial reason this delimitation of liability is alleged to be unworkable in the most egregious case of them all: the mother's emotional trauma at the witnessed death of her child. If we stop at this point, however, we must necessarily question and reject not merely recovery here, but the viability of the judicial process for ascertaining liability for tortious conduct itself. . . .

To deny recovery would be to chain this state to an outmoded rule of the 19th century which can claim no current credence. No good reason compels our captivity to an indefensible orthodoxy.

The judgment is reversed.

The Restatement (Third) of Torts: Liability for Physical and Emotional Harm (2010) adopts the *Dillon* approach. Section 47 states that "[a]n actor who negligently causes serious bodily injury to a third person is subject to liability for serious emotional disturbance thereby caused to a person who: (a) perceives the event contemporaneously, and (b) is a close family member of the person suffering the bodily injury." *Dillon* opened the door to liability to bystanders — persons not in danger of immediate physical impact — for emotional upset resulting from concern over the safety of someone else. Most courts, though not all,[4] considering the matter went through that door. But what lay beyond

4. The Supreme Court of Georgia adhered to its long-standing impact rule in Lee v. State Farm Mutual Ins. Co., 533 S.E.2d 82 (Ga. 2000), but did hold that a parent injured in the same accident as a child could recover for emotional distress resulting from the parent's witnessing of the injury to the child. See also Engler v. Illinois Farmers Ins. Co., 706 N.W.2d 764 (Minn. 2005), discussed above; Straub v. Fisher & Paykel Health Care, 990 P.2d 384 (Utah 1999). And the Supreme Court of the United States rejected bystander liability in favor of the zone of danger rule in Consolidated Rail Corp. v. Gottshall, cited at p. 347 and footnote 3, above.

that door varied considerably from state to state, and even within California. At issue has been just what doctrinal significance should be attached to the three factors discussed by the court in *Dillon.* Did *Dillon* adopt a "pure" liability rule, under which liability would be measured by foreseeability? Most courts have concluded that it did not, or at least they have refused to adopt such a rule for their own states.

Some courts have insisted that the bystander be at the scene of the accident involving the primary victim (see, e.g., Nielson v. AT & T Corp., 597 N.W.2d 434 (S.D. 1997)),[5] while other courts have not so required (see, e.g., Squeo v. Norwalk Hosp. Ass'n, 113 A.3d 932 (Conn. 2015); Masake v. General Motors Corp., 780 P.2d 566, *reconsideration denied,* 833 P.2d 899 (Haw. 1989)). The bystander who comes onto the scene shortly after the accident has a better chance of recovering (see, e.g., Rodriguez v. Cambridge Hous. Auth., 823 N.E.2d 1249 (Mass. 2005)) than one who sees the primary victim later at the hospital (see, e.g., Wilder v. City of Keene, 557 A.2d 636 (N.H. 1989)). In Finnegan v. Wisconsin Patients Compensation Fund, 666 N.W.2d 797 (Wis. 2003), the court held that an improper diagnosis of an infant's bacterial infection that ultimately led to the infant's death did not satisfy the requirements for bystander recovery:

> The parent's experiences were horrific. The mother witnessed a prolonged and unsuccessful attempt to save their baby's life. . . . [H]owever, the compensable serious emotional distress of a bystander is not measured by the acute emotional distress of the loss of a family member. Rather, the damages arise from the bystander's observation of an extraordinary event. The hallmark of negligent infliction of emotional distress is a contemporaneous or nearly contemporaneous perception of a sudden, traumatic, injury-producing event. . . . In the present case, as in many cases, the failure to make the proper medical diagnosis is not an event that itself is perceived by a family member. To extend [bystander claims] to an injury caused by an improper diagnosis when the plaintiff observes the suffering of the victim and not the event that causes the suffering conflicts with the historical foundations for negligent infliction of emotional distress and would be a significant broadening of the [traditional] rule.

The dissent in *Finnegan* questioned how the court could distinguish the present case from those in which the court had permitted recovery by family members who arrive at the scene of an accident shortly after it occurred. See id. at 812-14. Nevertheless, a result similar to *Finnegan* obtained in Vedros v. Northrop Grumman Shipbuilding, Inc., 2014 WL 1093678 (E.D. La. 2014). Family members of a worker who suffered an excruciating death from mesothelioma caused by occupational asbestos exposure could not recover for emotional distress damages given that they did not directly witness the acts giving rise to the worker's illness.

The nature of the required relationship between the bystander and the primary victim also varies. Strangers to the primary victim typically cannot recover, no matter how severe or traumatic the observed event. See Pizarro v. 421 Port Associates, 739 N.Y.S.2d 152 (A.D.2d 2002) (plaintiff could not recover for emotional distress suffered after elevator accident left victim's decapitated head beside plaintiff's feet). In Catron v. Lewis, 712 N.W.2d 245 (Neb. 2006), the Nebraska Supreme Court affirmed summary judgment against a plaintiff who had suffered distress from witnessing his daughter's friend—who was riding on an inner tube attached to the plaintiff's boat—killed when the defendant jet-skied into the friend. Because the plaintiff was not related to the victim,

5. The court in *Nielson* also ruled that the bystander had to be in the zone of danger of physical impact, a ruling that no other court had made.

the court held that he could not recover. Similarly, in Grotts v. Zahner, 989 P.2d 415 (Nev. 1999), the court held that the relationship must be one of blood or marriage, so the fiancée of the primary victim could not recover. Other courts have held that less formal relationships will do. See, e.g., Binns v. Fredendall, 513 N.E.2d 278 (Ohio 1987) (plaintiff who was unmarried cohabitant with primary victim could recover). An open-ended approach to this issue was adopted by the court in Dunphy v. Gregor, 642 A.2d 372, 378 (N.J. 1994), involving engaged persons living together:

> [T]his critical determination must be guided as much as possible by a standard that focuses on those factors that identify and define the intimacy and familial nature of such a relationship. That standard must take into account the duration of the relationship, the degree of mutual dependence, the extent of common contributions to a life together, the extent and quality of shared experience, and . . . "whether the plaintiff and the injured person were members of the same household, their emotional reliance on each other, the particulars of their day to day relationship, and the manner in which they related to each other in attending to life's mundane requirements."

See also Graves v. Estabrook, 818 A.2d 1255 (N.H. 2003) (endorsing the *Dunphy* test and holding that plaintiff, who for seven years was an unmarried cohabitant of the motorcyclist killed in collision, could state a claim for bystander liability against motorist). What if the bystander reasonably but mistakenly believes that the primary victim is her daughter? No recovery, according to Barnes v. Geiger, 446 N.E.2d 78 (Mass. App. Ct.), *appeal denied*, 448 N.E.2d 767 (Mass. 1983).

Will the relationship between the bystander and the family pet be enough to trigger liability for emotional upset caused by the death of the pet? In Kondaurov v. Kerdasha, 629 S.E.2d 181 (Va. 2006), the court refused to permit such recovery, observing that the majority of courts to consider the issue have viewed pets as personal property, such that their loss is not tantamount to the loss of a family member or other loved one. See also McDougall v. Lamm, 48 A.3d 312 (N.J. 2012) (declining to allow recovery for loss of one's pet dog); Sheele v. Dustin, 998 A.2d 697 (Vt. 2010) (allowing recovery for only the property loss of the pet). But see Campbell v. Animal Quarantine Station, 632 P.2d 1066 (Haw. 1981) (permitting recovery for emotional upset despite personal property nature of pet).

Disagreement over the role that the factors from *Dillon* should play continued for 20 years in the lower courts in California, culminating in the following decision:

Thing v. La Chusa

48 Cal. 3d 644, 771 P.2d 814, 257 Cal. Rptr. 865 (1989)

[The plaintiff's son was injured in an automobile accident that the plaintiff did not witness. She was near the scene, and, on being informed of the accident, she "rushed to the scene where she saw her bloody and unconscious child, whom she believed was dead, lying in the roadway." She brought suit against the defendants for emotional harm she suffered as a result of witnessing her son in his injured condition. The trial judge granted the defendants' motion for summary judgment, which was reversed by the court of appeal.]

EAGLESON, JUSTICE. The narrow issue presented by the parties in this case is whether the Court of Appeal correctly held that a mother who did not witness an accident in which an automobile struck and injured her child may recover damages from the negligent driver for the emotional distress she suffered when she arrived at the accident scene. The more important question this issue poses for the court, however, is whether the "guidelines" enunciated by this court in Dillon v. Legg (1968) 68 Cal. 2d 728, 69 Cal. Rptr. 72, 441 P.2d 912, are adequate, or if they should be refined to create greater certainty in this area of the law.

. . . [W]e shall conclude that the societal benefits of certainty in the law, as well as traditional concepts of tort law, dictate limitation of bystander recovery of damages for emotional distress. In the absence of physical injury or impact to the plaintiff himself, damages for emotional distress should be recoverable only if the plaintiff: (1) is closely related to the injury victim; (2) is present at the scene of the injury-producing event at the time it occurs and is then aware that it is causing injury to the victim and, (3) as a result suffers emotional distress beyond that which would be anticipated in a disinterested witness. . . .

[The court surveyed the law leading up to Dillon v. Legg.] . . . In the ensuing 20 years, like the pebble cast into the pond, *Dillon*'s progeny have created ever widening circles of liability. Post-*Dillon* decisions have now permitted plaintiffs who suffer emotional distress, but no resultant physical injury, and who were not at the scene of and thus did not witness the event that injured another, to recover damages on grounds that a duty was owed to them solely because it was foreseeable that they would suffer that distress on learning of injury to a close relative. . . .

[W]hile the court [in *Dillon*] indicated that foreseeability of the injury was to be the primary consideration in finding duty, it simultaneously recognized that policy considerations mandated that infinite liability be avoided by restrictions that would somehow narrow the class of potential plaintiffs. But the test limiting liability was itself amorphous. . . .

The *Dillon* court anticipated and accepted uncertainty in the short term in application of its holding, but was confident that the boundaries of this NIED [negligent infliction of emotional distress] action could be drawn in future cases. In sum, as former Justice Potter Stewart once suggested with reference to that undefinable category of materials that are obscene, the *Dillon* court was satisfied that trial and appellate courts would be able to determine the existence of a duty because the court would know it when it saw it. (See Jacobellis v. Ohio (1964) 378 U.S. 184, 197, 84 S. Ct. 1676, 1683, 12 L. Ed. 2d 793 (conc. opn. of Stewart, J.).) Underscoring the questionable validity of that assumption, however, was the obvious and unaddressed problem that the injured party, the negligent tortfeasor, their insurers, and their attorneys had no means short of suit by which to determine if a duty such as to impose liability for damages would be found in cases other than those that were "on all fours" with *Dillon*. Thus, the only thing that was foreseeable from the *Dillon* decision was the uncertainty that continues to this time as to the parameters of the third-party NIED action. . . .

The expectation of the *Dillon* majority that the parameters of the tort would be further defined in future cases has not been fulfilled. Instead, subsequent decisions of the Courts of Appeal and this court, have created more uncertainty. And, just as the "zone of danger" limitation was abandoned in *Dillon* as an arbitrary restriction on recovery, the *Dillon* guidelines have been relaxed on grounds that they, too, created arbitrary limitations on recovery. Little consideration has been given in post-*Dillon* decisions to the importance of avoiding the limitless exposure to liability that the pure foreseeability test of "duty" would create and towards which these decisions have moved.

[The court's discussion of the post-*Dillon* California cases is omitted.]

. . . Not surprisingly, this "case-to-case" or ad hoc approach to development of the law that misled the Court of Appeal in this case has not only produced inconsistent rulings in the lower courts, but has provoked considerable critical comment by scholars who attempt to reconcile the cases. . . .

Our own prior decisions identify factors that will appropriately circumscribe the right to damages, but do not deny recovery to plaintiffs whose emotional injury is real even if not accompanied by out-of-pocket expense. Notwithstanding the broad language in some of those decisions, it is clear that foreseeability of the injury alone is not a useful "guideline" or a meaningful restriction on the scope of the NIED action. . . . It is apparent that reliance on foreseeability of injury alone in finding a duty, and thus a right to recover, is not adequate when the damages sought are for an intangible injury. In order to avoid limitless liability out of all proportion to the degree of a defendant's negligence, and against which it is impossible to insure without imposing unacceptable costs on those among whom the risk is spread, the right to recover for negligently caused emotional distress must be limited.

[The court's discussion of the *Dillon* factor involving the relationship of the plaintiff to the primary victim is omitted. The court discussed a variety of contexts in which that issue can arise, including claims for loss of consortium (see Borer v. American Airlines, p. 368) and for wrongful life (see Turpin v. Sortini, p. 384).]

Similar reasoning justifies limiting recovery to persons closely related by blood or marriage since, in common experience, it is more likely that they will suffer a greater degree of emotional distress than a disinterested witness to negligently caused pain and suffering or death. Such limitations are indisputably arbitrary since it is foreseeable that in some cases unrelated persons have a relationship to the victim or are so affected by the traumatic event that they suffer equivalent emotional distress. As we have observed, however, drawing arbitrary lines is unavoidable if we are to limit liability and establish meaningful rules for application by litigants and lower courts.

No policy supports extension of the right to recover for NIED to a larger class of plaintiffs. Emotional distress is an intangible condition experienced by most persons, even absent negligence, at some time during their lives. Close relatives suffer serious, even debilitating, emotional reactions to the injury, death, serious illness, and evident suffering of loved ones. These reactions occur regardless of the cause of the loved one's illness, injury, or death. That relatives will have severe emotional distress is an unavoidable aspect of the "human condition." The emotional distress for which monetary damages may be recovered, however, ought not to be that form of acute emotional distress or the transient emotional reaction to the occasional gruesome or horrible incident to which every person may potentially be exposed in an industrial and sometimes violent society. Regardless of the depth of feeling or the resultant physical or mental illness that results from witnessing violent events, persons unrelated to those injured or killed may not now recover for such emotional upheaval even if negligently caused. Close relatives who witness the accidental injury or death of a loved one and suffer emotional trauma may not recover when the loved one's conduct was the cause of that emotional trauma. The overwhelming majority of "emotional distress" which we endure, therefore, is not compensable.

Unlike an award of damages for intentionally caused emotional distress which is punitive, the award for NIED simply reflects society's belief that a negligent actor bears some responsibility for the effect of his conduct on persons other than those who suffer physical injury. In identifying those persons and the circumstances in which the defendant will be held to redress the injury, it is appropriate to restrict recovery to those persons who will suffer an emotional impact beyond the impact that can be anticipated whenever one learns that a relative is injured, or dies, or the emotion felt by a "disinterested" witness. The class of potential plaintiffs should be limited to those who because of their relationship suffer the greatest emotional distress. When the right to recover is limited in this manner, the liability bears a reasonable relationship to the culpability of the negligent defendant.

The elements which justify and simultaneously limit an award of damages for emotional distress caused by awareness of the negligent infliction of injury to a close relative are . . . the traumatic emotional effect on the plaintiff who contemporaneously observes both the event or conduct that causes serious injury to a close relative and the injury itself. Even if it is "foreseeable" that persons other than closely related percipient witnesses may suffer emotional distress, this fact does not justify the imposition of what threatens to become unlimited liability for emotional distress on a defendant whose conduct is simply negligent. Nor does such abstract "foreseeability" warrant continued reliance on the assumption that the limits of liability will become any clearer if lower courts are permitted to continue approaching the issue on a "case-to-case" basis some 20 years after *Dillon*.

We conclude, therefore, that a plaintiff may recover damages for emotional distress caused by observing the negligently inflicted injury of a third person if, but only if, said plaintiff: (1) is closely related to the injury victim; (2) is present at the scene of the injury producing event at the time it occurs and is then aware that it is causing injury to the victim; and (3) as a result suffers serious emotional distress — a reaction beyond that which would be anticipated in a disinterested witness and which is not an abnormal response to the circumstances. These factors were present in *Ochoa* and each of this court's prior decisions upholding recovery for NIED.

The undisputed facts establish that plaintiff was not present at the scene of the accident in which her son was injured. She did not observe defendant's conduct and was not aware that her son was being injured. She could not, therefore, establish a right to recover for the emotional distress she suffered when she subsequently learned of the accident and observed its consequences. The order granting summary judgment was proper.

The judgment of the Court of Appeal is reversed.

KAUFMAN, JUSTICE, concurring.

We granted review in this case because of the obvious and continuing difficulties that have plagued trial courts and litigants in the area of negligent infliction of emotional distress. Of course, any meaningful review of the issue necessarily entails reappraising, in the light of 20 years of experience, our landmark holding in Dillon v. Legg (1968) 68 Cal. 2d 728, 69 Cal. Rptr. 72, 441 P.2d 912, that a plaintiff may recover for the emotional distress induced by the apprehension of negligently caused injury to a third person. Two such "reappraisals" have now been suggested.

The majority opinion by Justice Eagleson proposes to convert *Dillon*'s flexible "guidelines" for determining whether the risk of emotional injury was foreseeable or within the defendant's duty of care, into strict "elements" necessary to recovery. While conceding that such a doctrinaire approach will necessarily lead to "arbitrary" results, Justice Eagleson nevertheless concludes that "[g]reater certainty and a more reasonable limit on the exposure to liability for negligent conduct" require strict limitations. (Maj. opn., p. 879 of 257 Cal. Rptr., p. 828 of 771 P.2d.)

Justice Broussard, in dissent, opposes the effort to rigidify the *Dillon* guidelines. He urges, instead, that the court remain faithful to the guidelines as originally conceived — as specific but "flexible" limitations on liability — and adhere to *Dillon*'s original reliance on "foreseeability as a general limit on tort liability." (Dis. opn. of Broussard, J., p. 868 of 257 Cal. Rptr., p. 817 of 771 P.2d.) Justice Broussard denies that *Dillon* has failed to afford adequate guidance to the lower courts or to confine liability within reasonable limits. On the contrary, the *Dillon* approach, in the dissent's view, has provided — and continues to provide — a workable and "*principled* basis for determining liability. . . ." (Id., at p. 895 of 257 Cal. Rptr., p. 844 of 771 P.2d, italics added.)

With all due respect, I do not believe that either the majority opinion or the dissent has articulated a genuinely "principled" rule of law. On the one hand, experience has shown that rigid doctrinal limitations on bystander liability, such as that suggested by Justice Eagleson, result inevitably in disparate treatment of plaintiffs in substantially the same position. To be sure, the majority freely — one might say almost cheerfully — acknowledges that its position is arbitrary; yet nowhere does it consider the cost of such institutionalized caprice, not only to the individuals involved, but to the integrity of the judiciary as a whole.

On the other hand, two decades of adjudication under the inexact guidelines created by *Dillon* and touted by the dissent, has, if anything, created a body of case law marked by even greater confusion and inconsistency of result.

The situation, therefore, calls for a wholesale reappraisal of the wisdom of permitting recovery for emotional distress resulting from injury to others. . . .

While the courts rejecting bystander liability have cited a number of reasons, one argument in particular has been considered dispositive: *Dillon*'s confident prediction that future courts would be able to fix just and sensible boundaries on bystander liability has been found to be wholly illusory — both in theory and in practice. . . .

Twenty-five years ago, this court posed a series of rhetorical questions concerning the guidelines later adopted in *Dillon:* "[H]ow soon is 'fairly contemporaneous?' What is the magic in the plaintiff's being 'present'? Is the shock any less immediate if the mother does not know of the accident until the injured child is brought home? And what if the plaintiff is present at the scene but is nevertheless unaware of the danger or injury to the third person until shortly after the accident has occurred . . . ?" (Amaya v. Home Ice, Fuel & Supply Co., supra, 59 Cal. 2d at p. 313, 29 Cal. Rptr. 33, 379 P.2d 513.) As the foregoing sampling of *Dillon*'s progeny vividly demonstrates, we are no closer to answers today than we were then. The questions, however, are no longer hypothetical; they are real: Is there any rational basis to infer that Mrs. Arauz was any less traumatized than Mrs. Dillon because she saw her bloody infant five minutes after it was struck by defendant's car? Was the Hathaways' suffering mitigated by the fact that they witnessed their child literally in death's throes, but failed to witness the precipitating event? Could it be argued that the emotional distress is even more traumatic, more foreseeable, for parents such as the Hathaways who fail to witness the accident and later blame themselves for allowing it to occur?

Clearly, to apply the *Dillon* guidelines strictly and deny recovery for emotional distress because the plaintiff was not a contemporaneous eye-witness of the accident but viewed the immediate consequences, ill serves the policy of compensating foreseeable victims of emotional trauma. Yet once it is admitted that temporal and spatial limitations bear no rational relationship to the likelihood of psychic injury, it becomes impossible to define, as the *Amaya* court well understood, any "sensible or just stopping point." (59 Cal. 2d at p. 311, 29 Cal. Rptr. 33, 379 P.2d 513.) By what humane and principled standard might a court decide, as a matter of law, that witnessing the bloody and chaotic aftermath of an accident involving a loved one is compensable if viewed within 1 minute of impact but noncompensable after 15 or 30? Is the shock of standing by while others undertake frantic efforts to save the life of one's child any less real or foreseeable when it occurs in an ambulance or emergency room rather than at the "scene"?

Obviously, a "flexible" construction of the *Dillon* guidelines cannot, ultimately, avoid drawing arbitrary and irrational distinctions any more than a strict construction. Justice Burke was right when he observed of the *Dillon* guidelines, "Upon analysis, their seeming certainty evaporates into arbitrariness, and inexplicable distinctions appear." (Dillon v. Legg, supra, 68 Cal. 2d at p. 749, 69 Cal. Rptr. 72, 441 P.2d 912, dis. opn. of Burke, J.) . . .

Of course, it could be argued that recovery — not rationality — is the essential thing; that ultimately justice is better served by arbitrarily denying recovery to some, than by absolutely denying recovery to all. I find this argument to be unpersuasive, however, for two reasons.

First, the cost of the institutionalized caprice which *Dillon* has wrought should not be underestimated. The foremost duty of the courts in a free society is the principled declaration of public norms. The legitimacy, prestige and effectiveness of the judiciary — the "least dangerous branch" — ultimately depend on public confidence in our unwavering commitment to this ideal. Any breakdown in principled decisionmaking, any rule for which no principled basis can be found and clearly articulated, subverts and discredits the institution as a whole.

It is not always easy, of course, to accommodate the desire for individual justice with the need for reasoned, well-grounded, general principles. We sacrifice the latter for the sake of the former, however, only at our peril. For the "power-base" of the courts, as noted above, is rather fragile; it consists of the perception of our role in the structure of American government as the voice of reason, and the faith that the laws we make today, we ourselves will be bound by tomorrow. Any "rule" — such as *Dillon*'s — which permits and even encourages judgments based not on universal standards but individual expediency, erodes the public trust which we serve, and on which we ultimately depend.

There is a second reason, apart from the inherently corrosive effect of arbitrary rules, that points to the conclusion that "bystander" liability should not be retained. The interest in freedom from emotional distress caused by negligent injury to a third party is simply not, in my view, an interest which the law can or should protect. It is not that the interest is less than compelling. The suffering of a parent from the death or injury of a child is terribly poignant, and has always been so. It is the very universality of such injury, however, which renders it inherently unsuitable to legal protection. . . .

A final argument against overruling *Dillon* is, of course, the simple fact that it has been the law for 20 years. Stare decisis should not be lightly dismissed in any thoughtful reconsideration of the law. History and experience, however, are the final judge of whether a decision was right or wrong, whether it should be retained, modified or abandoned.

Adherence to precedent cannot justify the perpetuation of a policy ill-conceived in theory and unfair in practice. . . .

For the foregoing reasons, therefore, I would overrule Dillon v. Legg, supra, 68 Cal. 2d 728, 69 Cal. Rptr. 72, 441 P.2d 912, and reinstate [the zone of danger rule] as the law of this state. Since the plaintiff was indisputably not within the zone of danger and could not assert a claim for emotional distress as the result of fear for her own safety, she could not establish a right to recover. Accordingly, I concur in the majority's conclusion that the order granting summary judgment in this case was proper.

[The dissenting opinion of MOSK, J., is omitted.]

BROUSSARD, JUSTICE, dissenting.

I dissent. . . .

The majority grope for a "bright line" rule for negligent infliction of emotional distress actions, only to grasp an admittedly arbitrary line which will deny recovery to victims whose injuries from the negligent acts of others are very real. In so doing, the majority reveal a myopic reading of Dillon v. Legg, supra, 68 Cal. 2d 728, 69 Cal. Rptr. 72, 441 P.2d 912. They impose a strict requirement that plaintiff be present at the scene of the injury-producing event at the time it occurs and is aware that it is causing injury to the victim. This strict requirement rigidifies what *Dillon* forcefully told us should be a flexible rule, and will lead to arbitrary results. I would follow the mandate of *Dillon* and maintain that foreseeability and duty determine liability, with a view toward a policy favoring reasonable limitations on liability. There is no reason why these general rules of tort law should not apply to negligent infliction of emotional distress actions. . . .

The Supreme Court of Wisconsin was not concerned with the difficulties presented by the variations among the states and in the lower California courts; in overruling *Waube* in Bowen v. Lumbermens Mutual Casualty Co., 517 N.W.2d 432, 443-44 (Wis. 1994), the court took a stand in favor of deciding each case "on its own merits":

> Historically, the tort of negligent infliction of emotional distress has raised two concerns: (1) establishing authenticity of the claim and (2) ensuring fairness of the financial burden placed upon a defendant whose conduct was negligent. A court deals with these concerns by exploring in each case such public policy considerations as: (1) whether the injury is too remote from the negligence; (2) whether the injury is wholly out of proportion to the culpability of the negligent tortfeasor; (3) whether in retrospect it appears too extraordinary that the negligence should have brought about the harm; (4) whether allowance of recovery would place an unreasonable burden on the negligent tortfeasor; (5) whether allowance of recovery would be too likely to open the way to fraudulent claims; or (6) whether allowance of recovery would enter a field that has no sensible or just stopping point. The court has stated these public policy considerations that may preclude liability in capsule form as follows: When it would shock the conscience of society to impose liability, the courts may hold as a matter of law that there is no liability.

Does this appear to be a pure "liability based on foreseeability" rule?

How narrowly the courts interpret contemporaneous perception depends on the jurisdiction. The Supreme Court of Iowa in Moore v. Eckman, 762 N.W.2d 459 (Iowa 2009), denied recovery to a mother who, although first on the scene, did not witness her son's fatal car injury. In contrast, the Supreme Court of Tennessee in Eskin v. Bartee, 262 S.W.3d 727 (Tenn. 2008), permitted recovery for the victim's mother and brother, arriving moments after the child was in a car accident.

The commentators, like the judges, disagree regarding the circumstances under which the bystander-plaintiff should be able to recover for emotional harm. An argument for a full-recovery rule based on foreseeability is Peter A. Bell, The Bell Tolls: Toward Full Tort Recovery for Psychic Injury, 36 Fla. L. Rev. 333 (1984). An argument for the zone of danger rule is advanced in Richard N. Pearson, Liability to Bystanders for Negligently Inflicted Emotional Harm — A Comment on the Nature of Arbitrary Rules, 34 Fla. L. Rev. 477 (1982). One commentator has argued that liability should be based on foreseeability, but that damages be limited to economic loss. See Richard S. Miller, The Scope of Liability for Negligent Infliction of Emotional Distress: Making "The Punishment Fit the Crime," 1 U. Haw. L. Rev. 1 (1979). For a feminist perspective, see Martha Chamallas & Linda K. Kerber, Women, Mothers, and the Law of Fright: A History, 88 Mich. L. Rev. 814 (1990). In their introduction, the authors first comment that the "law of torts values physical security and property more highly than emotional security and human relationships . . . [an] apparently gender-neutral hierarchy of values [that] has privileged men, as the traditional owners and managers of property, and has burdened women, to whom the emotional work of maintaining human relationships has commonly been assigned." 88 Mich. L. Rev. at 814. They then preview the historical analysis that they offer in the remainder of the article in support of this description and outline the normative implications that follow from it (88 Mich. L. Rev. at 815-16):

> This examination of the history of the law of fright shows that gendered thinking has influenced the law, but has remained unexamined. We make three basic observations. First, we claim that the legal categories of "physical" and "emotional" harm are not unrelated to the gender of the victims. Women who have suffered fright-induced physical injuries have been disadvantaged by the legal classification of their injuries as emotional harm. Second, we demonstrate how the legal system has placed women's fright-based injuries at the margins of the law by describing women's suffering for the injury and death of their unborn and born children as remote, unforeseeable, and unreasonable. Finally, we raise the possibility that the claims of female plaintiffs in these fright cases — plaintiffs such as Margery Dillon — should be viewed as women's rights claims, as attempts to pressure the legal system to recognize and value the interests of women. By constructing a gendered history of this legal claim, we aspire to reclaim *Dillon* for women and to contribute to a feminist reconstruction of tort law.

See also Martha Chamallas, The Architecture of Bias: Deep Structures in Tort Law, 146 U. Pa. L. Rev. 463 (1998) (arguing that such implicit dichotomies pervade tort law and work to subtly disadvantage women); Martha Chamallas, Removing Emotional Harm from the Core of Tort Law, 54 Vand. L. Rev. 751 (2001) (criticizing the decision of the American Law Institute to exclude emotional harm and relational injuries from the "core" of tort law in its Restatement (Third) of Torts: Liability for Physical Harm project); Martha Chamallas, Unpacking Emotional Distress: Sexual Exploitation, Reproductive Harm, and Fundamental Rights, 44 Wake Forest L. Rev. 1109 (2009) (advocating for enhanced protection of gender-based emotional distress).

Does the zone of danger test survive as an independent basis of liability for emotional upset caused by fear for one's own safety? Perhaps not, or at least not without some modification in the eyes of the court in Lawson v. Management Activities, Inc., 81 Cal. Rptr. 2d 745 (Ct. App. 1999). The plaintiffs alleged that they were frightened by witnessing an airplane fall out of the sky, fearing that they would be injured if the plane were to crash where they were standing. The trial court dismissed the complaint. Affirming the dismissal, the court on appeal suggested that only two categories of plaintiffs may recover emotional distress — bystanders and direct victims. (As to the "direct victim" category in California, see the discussion in the following section.) The traditional "zone of danger" category of compensable emotional distress was rejected by the court as being too broad: "A moment's reflection should reveal that there are too many situations in modern life when one can reasonably be scared for one's own safety. Permitting a lawsuit for just that fright would clog the courts and make transportation and commerce impossible." Id. at 751. The court did, however, suggest that plaintiffs in particular cases could attempt to satisfy the multi-factor test that California courts generally have used to determine the existence of a duty.

Another California appellate court ruled that the plaintiff, who suffered emotional upset when the defendant drove his car into the plaintiff's home, nearly hitting her, could recover, reasoning that because plaintiff "complains of being placed in fear of injury or death to herself personally . . . [she] claims to be a direct victim of defendant's negligence" rather than a victim who would need to proceed under a zone of danger theory. Wooden v. Raveling, 71 Cal. Rptr. 2d 891, 893 (Ct. App. 1998). Are these two California cases inconsistent? Still another approach was suggested in Bro v. Glaser, 27 Cal. Rptr. 2d

894 (App. 4th 1994), in which the court stated that plaintiffs whose close relatives suffered "outrageous" conduct on the part of the defendant could recover for emotional distress. In Steven F. v. Anaheim Union High School District, 6 Cal. Rptr. 3d 105 (App. 4th 2004), the court refused to deem "outrageous" an alleged pattern by school officials and employees of ignorance and neglect of a teacher's sexual relationship with a student, thereby foreclosing recovery for emotional distress by the student's parents.

Problem 25

Your investigation of the Carrington case (Problem 9 above) reveals that shortly after Mrs. Carrington left Robert at the emergency ward of the hospital she became extremely distraught. She spent that night at the hospital under sedation, and was released the next day. She still suffers from nervousness, sleeplessness, frequent nausea, and has lost weight. Assuming that it has been decided to bring suit against one or more of the dog owners for Robert's injuries, would you recommend filing a separate complaint seeking to recover damages to compensate Mrs. Carrington for the consequences to her resulting from the attack on Robert? If you would so recommend, prepare a draft of the complaint which maximizes the chances of defeating a motion to dismiss for failure to state a cause of action. Assume that the supreme court of your state has not yet had occasion to resolve the issues generated by the preceding cases.

c. Liability to Direct Victims

Burgess v. Superior Court

2 Cal. 4th 1064, 831 P.2d 1197, 9 Cal. Rptr. 2d 615 (1992)

PANELLI, ASSOCIATE JUSTICE.

Can a mother recover damages for negligently inflicted emotional distress against a physician who entered into a physician-patient relationship with her for care during labor and delivery if her child is injured during the course of the delivery? Because the professional malpractice alleged in this case breached a duty owed to the mother as well as the child, we hold that the mother can be compensated for emotional distress resulting from the breach of the duty. . . .

[The plaintiff underwent a cesarean section, during which she was under a general anesthetic. As she left the recovery room, she was told that something was wrong with her baby, and was given additional sedatives. The baby suffered permanent brain and nervous system damage as a result of oxygen deprivation. The plaintiff felt distress about the condition of the baby for the first time several hours later when she awoke from the sedative. Gupta, the defendant, moved for summary judgment, arguing that the plaintiff did not meet the requirements for recovery of damages for emotional harm established by Thing v. La Chusa. The trial court granted the motion. The intermediate appellate court reversed, ruling that *Thing* was not applicable because the plaintiff was a "direct victim" of the defendant's negligence rather than a "bystander."]

The law of negligent infliction of emotional distress in California is typically analyzed, as it was in this case, by reference to two "theories" of recovery: the "bystander" theory and the "direct victim" theory. In cases involving family relationships and medical treatment, confusion has reigned as to whether and under which "theory" plaintiffs may seek damages for negligently inflicted emotional distress.

Because the use of the "direct victim" designation has tended to obscure, rather than illuminate the relevant inquiry in cases such as the one at hand, we briefly turn our attention to the present state of the law in this area before proceeding to apply this law to the facts that confront us. . . .

Much of the confusion in applying rules for bystander and direct victim recovery to the facts of specific cases can be traced to this court's decision in [Molien v. Kaiser Found. Hosps., 27 Cal. 3d 916, 616 P.2d 813, 167 Cal. Rptr. 831 (1980)], which first used the "direct victim" label. In that case, we answered in the affirmative the question of whether, in the context of a negligence action, damages may be recovered for serious emotional distress unaccompanied by physical injury. In so holding, we found that a hospital and a doctor owed a duty directly to the husband of a patient, who had been diagnosed incorrectly by the doctor as having syphilis and had been told to so advise her husband in order that he could receive testing and, if necessary, treatment. We reasoned that the risk of harm to the husband was reasonably foreseeable and that the "alleged tortious conduct of the defendant was directed to him as well as to his wife." (Id. at pp. 922-923, 167 Cal. Rptr. 831, 616 P.2d 813.) Under such circumstances we deemed the husband to be a "direct victim" and found the criteria for bystander recovery not to be controlling. (Id. at p. 923, 167 Cal. Rptr. 831, 616 P.2d 813.)

The broad language of the *Molien* decision coupled with its perceived failure to establish criteria for characterizing a plaintiff as a "direct victim" rather than a "bystander," has subjected *Molien* to criticism from various sources, including this court. [Citation omitted.] The great weight of this criticism has centered upon the perception that *Molien* introduced a new method for determining the existence of a duty, limited only by the concept of foreseeability. To the extent that *Molien* stands for this proposition, it should not be relied upon and its discussion of duty is limited to its facts. . . .

Nevertheless, other principles derived from *Molien* are sound: (1) damages for negligently inflicted emotional distress may be recovered in the absence of physical injury or impact, and (2) a cause of action to recover damages for negligently inflicted emotional distress will lie, notwithstanding the criteria imposed upon recovery by bystanders, in cases where a duty arising from a preexisting relationship is negligently breached. In fact, it is this later principle which defines the phrase "direct victim." That label signifies nothing more.

Gupta, however, has succumbed to the confusion in this area by failing to recognize that the distinction between bystander and direct victim cases is found in the source of the duty owed by the defendant to the plaintiff. Gupta argues, relying upon Ochoa v. Superior Court, (1985) 39 Cal. 3d 159, 172-173, 216 Cal. Rptr. 661, 703 P.2d 1 (hereafter *Ochoa*), that, when the emotional distress for which damages are claimed is "purely derivative" of the injury of another, the plaintiff may only recover such damages by satisfying the criteria for bystander recovery. Gupta claims that Burgess's damages are "derivative" because he owed no duty of care to Burgess to avoid injuring her child. Therefore, she may recover for her emotional distress, if at all, only as a bystander. We disagree.

In *Ochoa,* the parents sought damages for the emotional distress that they suffered from witnessing the defendants' failure to provide adequate medical care to their son, who was incarcerated. We held that the parents could state a claim for such damages, but only as bystanders, not as direct victims. In so holding we stated, "the defendants' negligence . . . was directed primarily at the decedent, with Mrs. Ochoa looking on as a helpless bystander as the tragedy of her son's demise unfolded before her." (*Ochoa,* supra, 39 Cal. 3d at pp.

172-173, 216 Cal. Rptr. 661, 703 P.2d 1.) In *Ochoa* the defendants had no preexisting relationship with the parents upon which to premise a duty of care; therefore, Mrs. Ochoa was necessarily in the position of a bystander with respect to her son's health care. The source of the duty, rather than the "derivative nature" of the injuries suffered by Mrs. Ochoa, was determinative.

In contrast to the facts of *Ochoa* and *Molien,* we are presented in this case with a "traditional" plaintiff with a professional negligence cause of action. Gupta cannot and does not dispute that he owed a duty of care to Burgess arising from their physician-patient relationship. Rather, Gupta contends that, while his alleged negligence resulting in injury to Joseph breached a duty of care owed to Joseph, it did not breach a duty of care owed to Burgess. In other words, Gupta claims that the scope of the duty of care owed to Burgess was limited to avoiding physical injury to her during her prenatal care and labor; it did not extend to avoiding injury to her fetus and the emotional distress that would result from such an injury. The origin of these mutually exclusive duties to Burgess and Joseph is apparently Gupta's unsupported assertion that Burgess and Joseph were two separate patients, because his actions could physically injure one and not the other.

To accept Gupta's argument would require us to ignore the realities of pregnancy and childbirth. Burgess established a physician-patient relationship with Gupta for medical care which was directed not only to her, but also to her fetus. The end purpose of this medical care may fairly be said to have been to provide treatment consistent with the applicable standard of care in order to maximize the possibility that Burgess's baby would be delivered in the condition in which he had been created and nurtured without avoidable injury to the baby or to Burgess. Moreover, during pregnancy and delivery it is axiomatic that any treatment for Joseph necessarily implicated Burgess's participation since access to Joseph could only be accomplished with Burgess's consent and with impact to her body.

In addition to the physical connection between a woman and her fetus, there is an emotional relationship as well. The birth of a child is a miraculous occasion which is almost always eagerly anticipated and which is invested with hopes, dreams, anxiety, and fears. In our society a woman often elects to forego general anesthesia or even any anesthesia, which could ease or erase the pain of labor, because she is concerned for the well-being of her child and she anticipates that her conscious participation in and observance of the birth of her child will be a wonderful and joyous occasion. An obstetrician, who must discuss the decision regarding the use of anesthesia with the patient, surely recognizes the emotionally charged nature of pregnancy and childbirth and the concern of the pregnant woman for her future child's well-being. The obstetrician certainly knows that even when a woman chooses to or must undergo general anesthesia during delivery, the receiving of her child into her arms for the first time is eagerly anticipated as one of the most joyous occasions of the patient's lifetime. It is apparent to us, as it must be to an obstetrician, that for these reasons, the mother's emotional well-being and the health of the child are inextricably intertwined.

It is in light of both these physical and emotional realities that the obstetrician and the pregnant woman enter into a physician-patient relationship. It cannot be gainsaid that both parties understand that the physician owes a duty to the pregnant woman with respect to the medical treatment provided to her fetus. Any negligence during delivery which causes injury to the fetus and resultant emotional anguish to the mother, therefore, breaches a duty owed directly anguish to the mother.

Thus, as the Court of Appeal correctly determined in this case, the failure by Burgess to satisfy the criteria for recovery under *Thing* does not end the inquiry. The alleged negligent actions resulting in physical harm to Joseph breached a duty owed to both Joseph and Burgess. Burgess was unavoidably and unquestionably harmed by this negligent conduct. . . .

[The court affirmed the intermediate court of appeals decision reversing summary judgment for the defendant.

[The concurring opinion of Mosk, A.J., is omitted.]

The distinction between "direct victims" and "bystanders" is discussed in Julie A. Davies, Direct Actions for Emotional Harm: Is Compromise Possible?, 67 Wash. L. Rev. 1 (1992). Are you persuaded by the direct victim/bystander dichotomy of *Burgess*? Did the court in *Burgess* conclude that the plaintiff in *Molien,* discussed in *Burgess,* was, or was not, a direct victim? Into which category would you place the plaintiff in *Molien*?

Other courts have also permitted an action for negligent infliction of emotional distress by the mother as a direct victim where tortious activity results in harm to the infant during delivery. See, e.g., Pierce v. Physicians Ins. Co. of Wisc., Inc., 692 N.W.2d 558 (Wis. 2005); Broadnax v. Gonzalez, 809 N.E.2d 645 (N.Y. 2004). The emotional significance of child-bearing, referenced by the court in *Burgess*, seems to explain the case of Toney v. Chester County Hosp., 36 A.3d 83, 84 (Pa. 2011), in which an equally divided court held that a mother may recover for emotional distress if her child is born with "profound physical abnormalities" after medical staff negligently misrepresented the results of a prior ultrasound in a way that made the pregnancy appear "normal." See also Perry-Rogers v. Obasaju, 723 N.Y.S.2d 28, 29 (App. Div. 2001), *leave to appeal dismissed,* 760 N.E.2d 1290 (N.Y. 2001) (husband and wife stated a cause of action against their physician who mistakenly implanted the plaintiff wife's embryo in another woman, given the "emotional harm caused by their having been deprived of the opportunity of experiencing pregnancy, prenatal bonding and the birth of their child"). In Cohen v. Cabrini Medical Center, 730 N.E.2d 949 (N.Y. 2000), on the other hand, the plaintiff was not permitted to proceed as a direct victim with an action for emotional distress when the defendant's negligent medical treatment of the plaintiff's husband, undertaken to increase his fertility, actually reduced it and thereby lessened the chance that she could have a child by him.

In Larsen v. Banner Health System, 81 P.3d 196 (Wyo. 2003), a mother and daughter brought a negligence action against a hospital that had negligently switched two newborn babies at birth, leading the mother and daughter to be unknowingly separated for forty-three years. The court observed that many previous cases in Wyoming and other states have allowed recovery for mental distress in cases involving "the mishandling of corpses" or "the negligent transmission of telegraph messages, especially those messages announcing death or indicating a potential for mental distress." Id. at 203. Generalizing from these cases, the court concluded that an exception to the general rule of non-recovery for negligently inflicted emotional distress exists "in circumstances involving contractual services that carry with them deeply emotional responses in the event of breach." Id. Thus, although the plaintiffs had not been bystanders to, or within the zone of danger of, a negligent act threatening physical harm, they could nevertheless recover for their emotional distress given the great potential for psychological harm that exists in the context of negligent handling of newborns.

A similar line of reasoning was applied by the court in Miranda v. Said, 836 N.W.2d 8 (Iowa 2013), in which defendant immigration attorney negligently advised his clients, undocumented aliens, that they could travel to Ecuador and apply for readmission to the United States due to the U.S. citizenship status of their children. Based on defendant's advice, plaintiff parents left the country only to learn later that children are not eligible to serve as sponsoring relatives for U.S. immigration purposes. As a result, the family became separated for years. In determining that plaintiffs had stated a valid claim for negligent infliction of emotional distress, the court explained:

> This is not a case that requires us to reconsider the rule we have developed over the years to determine if damages for emotional harm are recoverable in an action for negligence. The exception to the rule, applied to the facts presented to the jury in this case, support emotional distress damages. The relationship involved a transaction charged with emotions in which negligent conduct by the attorney was very likely to cause severe emotional distress. Of course, it is not necessary to go further to decide just where the line between duty and no duty may be drawn. Here, we can draw the line at the nature of this attorney–client relationship and the likelihood that serious emotional harm would result from negligently undertaking the illegitimate course of action. While the relationship was formed for the purpose of establishing a path to citizenship and a means to keeping the family united, Said only pursued an illegitimate course of conduct that had no chance of success if the independent decision-maker followed the law. The negligent conduct was doomed to directly result in a separation of the family for a decade. In this light, it was the type of relationship in which negligent conduct was especially likely to cause severe emotional distress, supporting a duty of care to protect against such harm. [Id. at 33]

See also Hedgepeth v. Whitman Walker Clinic, 22 A.3d 789 (D.C. 2011) (plaintiff who was misdiagnosed as HIV positive could state a claim for negligent infliction of emotional distress against doctor because "the plaintiff's emotional well-being is necessarily implicated by the nature of the defendant's undertaking to or relationship with the plaintiff, and serious emotional distress is especially likely to be caused by the defendant's negligence"); S. Alaska Carpenters Health & Sec. Trust Fund v. Jones, 177 P.3d 844 (Alaska 2008) (when an employer negligently misrepresented that an employee was eligible for medical coverage, the employer was liable for the emotional distress to the employee because of their special relationship); Loudin v. Radiology & Imaging Servs., Inc., 924 N.E.2d 433 (Ohio Ct. App. 2009) (holding that a doctor's negligent diagnosis that a patient is cancer-free, resulting in upset when the truth is later revealed, justifies a claim for emotional distress precluding summary judgment); In re E. I. du Pont de Nemours & Co. C-8 Pers. Injury Litig., No. 2:13-md-2433, 2016 U.S. Dist. LEXIS 19880 (S.D. Ohio Feb. 17, 2016) (plaintiff can claim negligent infliction of serious emotional distress after drinking water negligently contaminated by defendant with chemicals known to increase the risk of cancer).

In Marlene F. v. Affiliated Psychiatric Medical Clinic, Inc., 770 P.2d 278 (Cal. 1989), the plaintiffs were mothers who had taken their children to the defendant clinic for family counseling. The psychologist assigned to the cases treated the mothers as well as the children, believing that the problems of the children stemmed in part from the mother-child relationships. The psychologist sexually molested the children, and the mothers brought suit against the defendant for their own emotional distress. The court held that the plaintiffs were direct victims rather than bystanders (770 P.2d at 282-83):

> In these circumstances, the therapist, as a professional psychologist, clearly knew or should have known in each case that his sexual molestation of the child would directly injure and cause severe emotional distress to his other patient, the mother, as well as to the parent-child relationship that was also under his care. His abuse of the therapeutic

relationship and molestation of the boys breached his duty of care to the mothers as well as to the children. . . .

It bears repeating that the mothers here were the patients of the therapist along with their sons, and the therapist's tortious conduct was accordingly directed against both. They sought treatment for their children — as they had the right, and perhaps even the obligation, to do — and agreed to be treated themselves to further the purposes of the therapy. They were plainly entitled to recover for the emotional distress they suffered.

One context in which the "direct victim" issue has generated litigation involves psychological therapists and diagnosis of "suppressed memory syndrome." In Doe v. McKay, 700 N.E.2d 1018 (Ill. 1998), plaintiff alleged that defendant therapist falsely suggested to plaintiff's daughter that plaintiff had sexually molested her during childhood. What would be the result in California? In New York? In Illinois, the court in *Doe* held, the plaintiff father had no cause of action — the therapist owed no duty to him. Compare Sawyer v. Midelfort, 595 N.W.2d 423 (Wis. 1999), in which the court reversed summary judgment in favor of defendant mental health professionals, given evidence that the defendants had caused plaintiffs' adult child to develop false memories of sexual abuse.

Finally, plaintiffs have occasionally pursued emotional distress damages under products liability claims in the absence of a physical injury. For instance, in Bylsma v. Burger King Corp., 293 P.3d 1168 (Wash. 2013), a deputy sheriff was allowed to seek recovery when defendant's franchise served him a hamburger with phlegm inside the bun. Likening the situation to those involving mishandling of human remains, the court reasoned, "Common sense tells us that food consumption is a personal matter and contaminated food is closely associated with disgust and other kinds of emotional turmoil. Thus, when a food manufacturer serves a contaminated food product, it is well within the scope of foreseeable harmful consequences that the individual served will suffer emotional distress." Id. at 1171.

Similarly, the court in Bray v. Marathon Corp., 588 S.E.2d 93 (S.C. 2003), held that plaintiffs may pursue strict products liability claims without regard to the limitations imposed on bystander recovery under negligent infliction of emotional distress doctrine. In *Bray*, the plaintiff alleged that she suffered emotional and physical harm after witnessing her co-worker crushed to death in a trash compactor that she was operating. In holding that the plaintiff's claim could proceed, the court stated: "It is not unreasonable to conclude the user of a defective product might suffer physical harm from emotional damage if the use of the product results in death or serious injury to a third person, irrespective of the relationship between the user and third person." Id. at 96. Compare with Kennedy v. McKesson Co., 448 N.E.2d 1332 (N.Y. 1983) (a dentist could not recover for his emotional upset when his anesthetic machine was miscoded and a patient died in his care), and Kallstrom v. U.S., 43 P.3d 162 (Alaska 2002) (emotional distress damages could not be recovered by a plaintiff whose mental upset arose from being made "an unwitting instrument" of defendant's negligence which, in turn, harmed a third party).

2. Injury to Personal Relationships

The earliest cases involving recovery for intangible harm arising out of negligent injury to personal relationships occurred in the husband-wife context; recovery was permitted by a husband whose wife was injured. The history of the action is set out in Diaz v. Eli Lilly & Co., 302 N.E.2d 555 (Mass. 1973), and in Chamallas and Kerber, cited at p. 359, above.

The latter authors quote from the famous English case of Lynch v. Knight, 11 Eng. Rep. 854 (1861), which established a hierarchy between physical or property interests, on the one hand, and emotional or relational interests, on the other. As the court's account of the loss of consortium claim reveals, this hierarchy was understood in explicitly gendered terms (11 Eng. Rep. at 863):

> [T]he benefit which the husband has in the consortium of the wife[] is of a different character from that which the wife has in the consortium of the husband. The relation of the husband to the wife is in most respects entirely dissimilar from that of the master to the servant, yet in one respect it has a similar character. The assistance of the wife in the conduct of the household of the husband, and in the education of his children, resembles the service of a hired domestic, tutor or governess; is of material value, capable of being estimated in money; and the loss of it may form the proper subject of an action, the amount of compensation varying with the position in society of the parties. This property is wanting in none. It is to the protection of such material interests that the law chiefly attends.
>
> Mental pain or anxiety the law cannot value, and does not pretend to redress, when the unlawful act complained of causes that alone. . . . The loss of such service of the wife, the husband, who alone has all the property of the married parties, may repair by hiring another servant; but the wife sustains only the loss of the comfort of her husband's society and affectionate attention, which the law cannot estimate or remedy. She does not lose her maintenance, which he is bound still to supply. . . .

The first American decision according a wife the right to recover is Hitaffer v. Argonne Co., 183 F.2d 811 (D.C. Cir.), *cert. denied,* 340 U.S. 852 (1950). Since then, a clear majority of states have permitted the wife to recover. The court in Montgomery v. Stephan, 101 N.W.2d 227, 234 (Mich. 1960), offered a justification for the gender-neutral approach that only marginally improved on the *Lynch* court's language:

> The gist of the matter is that in today's society the wife's position is analogous to that of a partner, neither kitchen slattern nor upstairs maid. Her duties and responsibilities in respect of the family unit complement those of the husband, extending only to another sphere. In the good times she lights the hearth with her own inimitable glow. But when tragedy strikes it is a part of her unique glory that, forsaking the shelter, the comfort, the warmth of the home, she puts her arm and shoulder to the plow. We are now at the heart of the issue. In such circumstances, when her husband's love is denied her, his strength sapped, and his protection destroyed, in short, when she has been forced by the defendant to exchange a heart for a husk, we are urged to rule that she has suffered no loss compensable at the law. But let some scoundrel dent a dishpan in the family kitchen and the law, in all its majesty, will convene the court, will march with measured tread to the halls of justice, and will there suffer a jury of her peers to assess the damages. Why are we asked, then, in the case before us, to look the other way? Is this what is meant when it is said that justice is blind?

Although extending actions for loss of consortium to wives was an obvious step for the common law to take, the two cases that follow illustrate the more difficult line-drawing issues that arose as plaintiffs sought to raise such claims in other contexts. In particular, once the conceptual basis of the action was not limited to the (now-disapproved) property interest theory of recovery, courts were forced to address directly the question of what kinds of emotional relationships are worthy of legal protection.

Feliciano v. Rosemar Silver Co.

401 Mass. 141, 514 N.E.2d 1095 (1987)

O'Connor, Justice. Marcial Feliciano and the plaintiff Dolores Feliciano commenced an action in the Superior Court against Miguel Costa and Rosemar Silver Company (Rosemar) claiming that Marcial sustained personal injuries and the plaintiff sustained loss of consortium due to Costa's wrongful conduct in the course of his employment by Rosemar. Rosemar moved for summary judgment on the loss of consortium claim. That motion was allowed, and the plaintiff appealed. . . . We now affirm the judgment.

According to the plaintiff's deposition and affidavit submitted in connection with Rosemar's summary judgment motion, Marcial and the plaintiff had lived together as husband and wife for approximately twenty years before Marcial's injuries in 1981 "as a de facto married couple," although they were not legally married until 1983. During those years, the plaintiff used Marcial's surname, and the plaintiff and Marcial held themselves out as husband and wife, had joint savings accounts, filed joint tax returns, jointly owned their home, depended on each other for companionship, comfort, love and guidance, and maintained a sexual relationship to the exclusion of all others. The question on appeal is whether, in those circumstances, the plaintiff may recover for loss of consortium. We answer that question in the negative.

"Marriage is not merely a contract between the parties. It is the foundation of the family. It is a social institution of the highest importance. The Commonwealth has a deep interest that its integrity is not jeopardized." French v. McAnarney, 290 Mass. 544, 546, 195 N.E. 714 (1935). Our recognition of a right of recovery for the loss of a spouse's consortium, see Diaz v. Eli Lilly & Co., 364 Mass. 153, 302 N.E.2d 555 (1973), promotes that value. Conversely, that value would be subverted by our recognition of a right to recover for loss of consortium by a person who has not accepted the correlative responsibilities of marriage. This we are unwilling to do.

Furthermore, as a matter of policy, it must be recognized that tort liability cannot be extended without limit. Distinguishing between the marriage relationship and the myriad relationships that may exist between mere cohabitants serves the purpose of limiting protection to interests and values that are reasonably ascertainable. That cohabitants must have a "stable and significant" relationship to qualify for loss of consortium recovery, a standard relied on in the case of Butcher v. Superior Court of Orange County, 139 Cal. App. 3d 58, 70, 188 Cal. Rptr. 503 (1983), is an unsatisfactorily vague and indefinite standard. . . .

Judgment affirmed.

Borer v. American Airlines, Inc.

19 Cal. 3d 441, 563 P.2d 858, 138 Cal. Rptr. 302 (1977)

Tobriner, Acting Chief Justice. In Rodriguez v. Bethlehem Steel Corp. (1974) 12 Cal. 3d 382, 115 Cal. Rptr. 765, 525 P.2d 669 we held that a married person whose spouse had been injured by the negligence of a third party may maintain a cause of action for loss of "consortium." We defined loss of "consortium" as the "loss of conjugal fellowship and sexual relations" (12 Cal. 3d at p. 385, 115 Cal. Rptr. at p. 766, 525 P.2d at p. 670), but ruled that the term included the loss of love, companionship, society, sexual relations, and household services. Our decision carefully avoided resolution of the question whether anyone other than the spouse of a negligently injured person, such as a child or a parent, could maintain a cause of action analogous to that upheld in *Rodriguez.* We face that issue today: the present case presents a claim by nine children for the loss of the services, companionship, affection and guidance of their mother; the companion case of Baxter v. Superior Court, Cal., 138 Cal. Rptr. 315, 563 P.2d 871 presents the claim of a mother and father for the loss of the companionship and affection of their 16-year-old son.

Judicial recognition of a cause of action for loss of consortium, we believe, must be narrowly circumscribed. Loss of consortium is an intangible injury for which money damages do not afford an accurate measure or suitable recompense; recognition of a right to recover for such losses in the present context, moreover, may substantially increase the number of claims asserted in ordinary accident cases, the expense of settling or resolving such claims, and the ultimate liability of the defendants. Taking these considerations into account, we shall explain why we have concluded that the payment of damages to persons for the lost affection and society of a parent or child neither truly compensates for such loss nor justifies the social cost in attempting to do so. We perceive significant differences between the marital relationship and the parent-child relationship that support the limitation of a cause of action for loss of consortium to the marital situation; we shall therefore further elaborate our reasons for concluding that a child cannot maintain a cause of action for loss of parental consortium. In similar fashion we conclude in the companion case of Baxter v. Superior Court that a parent cannot maintain a cause of action for loss of a child's consortium. . . .

. . . Plaintiffs, the nine children of Patricia Borer, allege that on March 21, 1972, the cover on a lighting fixture at the American Airlines Terminal at Kennedy Airport fell and struck Patricia. Plaintiffs further assert that as a result of the physical injuries sustained by Patricia, each of them has been "deprived of the services, society, companionship, affection, tutelage, direction, guidance, instruction and aid in personality development, all with its accompanying psychological, educational and emotional detriment, by reason of Patricia Borer being unable to carry on her usual duties of a mother." . . . Each plaintiff seeks damages of $100,000.

Defendant American Airlines demurred to the complaint for failure to state a cause of action. The trial court sustained the demurrer without leave to amend, and entered judgment dismissing the suit as to defendant American Airlines. Plaintiffs appealed from that judgment.

Our analysis of plaintiffs' appeal begins with our decision in Rodriguez v. Bethlehem Steel Corp., supra, 12 Cal. 3d 382, 115 Cal. Rptr. 765, 525 P.2d 669. In holding that a spouse has a cause of action for loss of consortium, we considered the proffered argument that such a holding would logically require us to uphold an analogous cause of action in the parent-child context or in even more distant relationships; we rejected that contention. . . .

Rodriguez, thus, does not compel the conclusion that foreseeable injury to a legally recognized relationship necessarily postulates a cause of action; instead it clearly warns that social policy must at some point intervene to delimit liability. Patricia Borer, for example, foreseeably has not only a husband (who has a cause of action under *Rodriguez*) and the children who sue here, but also parents whose right of action depends upon our decision in the companion case of Baxter v. Superior Court; foreseeably, likewise, she has brothers, sisters, cousins, inlaws, friends, colleagues, and other acquaintances who will be deprived of her companionship. No one suggests that all such persons possess a right of action for loss of Patricia's consortium; all agree that somewhere a line must be drawn. As stated by Judge Breitel in Tobin v. Grossman (1969) 24 N.Y.2d 609, 619, 301 N.Y.S.2d 554, 561, 249 N.E.2d 419, 424; "Every injury has ramifying consequences, like the ripplings of the waters, without end. The problem for the law is to limit the legal consequences of wrongs to a controllable degree."

The decision whether to limit liability for loss of consortium by denying a cause of action in the parent-child context, or to permit that action but deny any claim based upon more remote relationships, is thus a question of policy. . . .

In the first instance, strong policy reasons argue against extension of liability to loss of consortium of the parent-child relationship. Loss of consortium is an intangible, nonpecuniary loss; monetary compensation will not enable plaintiffs to regain the companionship and guidance of a mother, it will simply establish a fund so that upon reaching adulthood, when plaintiffs will be less in need of maternal guidance, they will be unusually wealthy men and women. To say that plaintiffs have been "compensated" for their loss is superficial; in reality they have suffered a loss for which they can never be compensated; they have obtained, instead, a future benefit essentially unrelated to that loss.

We cannot ignore the social burden of providing damages for loss of parental consortium merely because the money to pay such awards comes initially from the "negligent" defendant or his insurer. Realistically the burden of payment of awards for loss of consortium must be borne by the public generally in increased insurance premiums or, otherwise, in the enhanced danger that accrues from the greater number of people who may choose to go without any insurance. We must also take into account the cost of administration of a system to determine and pay consortium awards; since virtually every serious injury to a parent would engender a claim for loss of consortium on behalf of each of his or her children, the expense of settling or litigating such claims would be sizable.

Plaintiffs point out that courts have permitted recovery of monetary damages for intangible loss in allowing awards for pain and suffering in negligence cases and in sanctioning recovery for loss of marital consortium. The question before us in this case, however, pivots on whether we should recognize a wholly new cause of action, unsupported by statute or precedent; in this context the inadequacy of monetary damages to make whole the loss suffered, considered in light of the social cost of paying such awards, constitutes a strong reason for refusing to recognize the asserted claim. To avoid misunderstanding, we point out that our decision to refuse to recognize a cause of action for parental consortium does not remotely suggest the rejection of recovery for intangible loss; each claim must be judged on its own merits, and in many cases the involved statutes, precedents, or policy will induce acceptance of the asserted cause of action.

A second reason for rejecting a cause of action for loss of parental consortium is that, because of its intangible character, damages for such a loss are very difficult to measure. Plaintiffs here have prayed for $100,000 each; yet by what standard could we determine that an award of $10,000 was inadequate, or one of $500,000 excessive? Difficulty in defining and quantifying damages leads in turn to risk of double recovery: to ask the jury, even under carefully drafted instructions, to distinguish the loss to the mother from her inability to care for her children from the loss to the children from the mother's inability to care for them may be asking too much. . . .

Plaintiffs point out that similar policy arguments could be, and to some extent were, raised in *Rodriguez,* and that our decision to uphold the wife's action for loss of consortium rejected those arguments. We do not, however, read *Rodriguez* as holding that arguments based upon the intangible character of damages and the difficulty of measuring such damages do not merit consideration. Such a holding would imply an indefinite extension of liability for loss of consortium to all foreseeable relationships, a proposition *Rodriguez* plainly repudiates.

Rodriguez, then, holds no more than that in the context of a spousal relationship, the policy arguments against liability do not suffice to justify a holding denying a cause of action. Plaintiffs contend, however, that no adequate ground exists to distinguish a cause of action for loss of spousal consortium from one for loss of parental consortium. We reject the contention for three reasons.

First, as *Rodriguez* pointed out, the spousal action for loss of consortium rests in large part on the "impairment or destruction of the sexual life of the couple." (12 Cal. 3d 382, 405, 115 Cal. Rptr. 765, 780, 525 P.2d 669, 684.) No similar element of damage appears in a child's suit for loss of consortium.

Second, actions by children for loss of parental consortium create problems of multiplication of actions and damages not present in the spousal context. . . .

The instant case illustrates the point. Patricia Borer has nine children, each of whom would possess his own independent right of action for loss of consortium. Even in the context of a consolidated action, the assertion of nine independent causes of action for the children in addition to the father's claim for loss of consortium and the mother's suit for ordinary tort damages, demonstrates the extent to which recognition of plaintiffs' asserted cause of action will multiply the tort liability of the defendant.

Finally, the proposition that a spouse has a cause of action for loss of consortium, but that a child does not, finds overwhelming approval in the decisions of other jurisdictions. Over 30 states, a clear majority of those who have decided the question, now permit a *spousal* suit for loss of consortium. No state permits a child to sue for loss of parental consortium. That claim has been presented, at latest count, to 18 jurisdictions, and rejected by all of them. . . .

In summary, we do not doubt the reality or the magnitude of the injury suffered by plaintiffs. We are keenly aware of the need of children for the love, affection, society and guidance of their parents; any injury which diminishes the ability of a parent to meet these needs is plainly a family tragedy, harming all members of that community. We conclude, however, that taking into account all considerations which bear on this question, including the inadequacy of monetary compensation to alleviate that tragedy, the difficulty of measuring damages, and the danger of imposing extended and disproportionate liability, we should not recognize a nonstatutory cause of action for the loss of parental consortium.

The judgment is affirmed.

Clark, Richardson, Sullivan, Wright, JJ., concur.

Mosk, Justice, dissenting.

I dissent.

Each of the policy arguments which the majority marshal against recognizing the cause of action for loss of consortium in the parent-child relationship was expressly considered and rejected by this court in Rodriguez v. Bethlehem Steel Corp. (1974) 12 Cal. 3d 382, 115 Cal. Rptr. 765, 525 P.2d 669.

First, the majority assert that because deprivation of consortium is an "intangible, nonpecuniary" loss, it is an injury which "can never be compensated." (Ante, p. 306 of 138 Cal. Rptr., p. 862 of 563 P.2d.) In *Rodriguez,* however, we held that loss of consortium is principally a form of mental suffering, and like all such subjective disabilities, it is compensable in damages. (Id. 12 Cal. 3d at p. 401, 115 Cal. Rptr. 765, 525 P.2d 669.) . . .

The majority reject plaintiffs' claim for a second reason, i.e., that "because of its intangible character, damages for such a loss are very difficult to measure." (Ante, p. 138 of 307 Cal. Rptr., p. 863 of 563 P.2d.) This merely restates the first reason, and was likewise rejected in *Rodriguez.* The loss here is no more and no less "intangible" than that experienced by Mrs. Rodriguez, whose husband became permanently incapacitated, and yet we held the valuation problem to be difficult but manageable. . . .

The majority next reason that the asserted difficulty in measuring damages "leads in turn to risk of double recovery." (Ante, p. 307 of 138 Cal. Rptr., p. 863 of 563 P.2d.) Again we dismissed the identical argument in *Rodriguez,* explaining that the alleged "risk" can be avoided by the use of such well-known procedural devices as joinder of actions and appropriate instructions to the jury. (12 Cal. 3d at pp. 404-407, 115 Cal. Rptr. 765, 525 P.2d 669.)

The majority concede that we rejected the foregoing arguments in *Rodriguez,* but now claim they do not "read" — i.e., interpret — *Rodriguez* as holding that the arguments, "do not merit consideration." (Ante, p. 307 of 138 Cal. Rptr., p. 863 of 563 P.2d.) On this point, however, *Rodriguez* is crystal clear and requires no interpretation: far from implying that the double recovery argument might have some merit in another context, we characterized it in *Rodriguez* as wholly "without substance," and quoted with approval decisions which derided it as "fallacious," "fictional," and a "bogey" that is "merely a convenient cliche" for denying liability. (Id. 12 Cal. 3d at p. 404, 115 Cal. Rptr. 765, 525 P.2d 669.)

The majority next seek to distinguish *Rodriguez* on three grounds, but none is convincing. First, the majority claim *Rodriguez* "pointed out" that the spousal action for loss of consortium rests "in large part" on the impairment of the sexual life of the couple. (Ante, p. 307 of 138 Cal. Rptr., p. 863 of 563 P.2d.) *Rodriguez* "pointed out" no such thing; on the contrary, we there reasoned that the nonsexual loss suffered by a spouse is at least as great as the sexual loss: "Nor is the wife's personal loss limited to her sexual rights. As we recognized in *Deshotel* (v. Atchison, T. & S. F. Ry. Co., 50 Cal. 2d 664, at p. 665, 328 P.2d 449), consortium includes 'conjugal society, comfort, affection and companionship.' An important aspect of consortium is thus the *moral* support each spouse gives the other through the triumph and despair of life. A severely disabled husband may well need all the emotional strength he has just to survive the shock of his injury, make the agonizing adjustment to his new and drastically restricted world, and preserve his mental health through the long years of frustration ahead. He will often turn inwards, demanding more solace for himself than he can give to others. Accordingly, the spouse of such a man cannot expect him to share the same concern for *her* problems that she experienced before his accident. As several of the cases have put it, she is transformed from a happy wife into a lonely nurse. Yet she is entitled to enjoy the companionship and moral support that marriage provides *no less than its sexual side,* and in both cases no less than her husband." (Final italics added; 12 Cal. 3d at pp. 405-406, 115 Cal. Rptr. at p. 780, 525 P.2d at p. 684.)

Precisely the same reasoning can be invoked in the case at bar: a severely disabled mother may well need all her emotional strength to survive the shock of her injury, to adjust to her newly restricted life, and to prepare her mental health through the ensuing years of frustration; and she will therefore often turn inwards, demanding more solace and comfort from her children than she can give to them in return. By its terms, *Rodriguez* applies to such a situation.

Two further points must be made in this connection, however obvious they may seem. *Rodriguez* cannot fairly be limited, as the majority imply, to sexually active couples: surely a husband or wife of advanced years suffers a no less compensable loss of conjugal society when his or her lifetime companion is grievously injured by the negligence of another. And even if *Rodriguez* were to be subjected to such a harsh restriction, surely the majority do not mean to hold that sexual activity is more worthy of the law's concern than the affection, comfort, and guidance which loving parents bestow on their children.

The majority's second purported ground of distinction may conveniently be reduced to syllogistic form: (1) if loss of parental consortium were actionable, a single accident would give rise to as many claims as the victim had minor children; (2) in our society the victim is likely to have several such children but can have only one spouse; therefore (3) to recognize the cause of action for loss of parental consortium would result in a much larger liability for individual defendants and a much larger total cost to the insured community than flow from *Rodriguez*. (Ante, pp. 307-308 of 138 Cal. Rptr., pp. 863-864 of 563 P.2d.)

The minor premise of the majority's argument—that an accident victim is likely to have several children under age 18—is, however, demonstrably inaccurate. In *Rodriguez* we observed that "In our society the likelihood that an injured adult will be a married man or woman is substantial," and supported that statement by a reference to the Statistical Abstract of the United States published annually by the Bureau of the Census. (12 Cal. 3d at p. 400 & fn. 19, 115 Cal. Rptr. at p. 776, 525 P.2d at p. 680.) That document showed, for example, that during the peak working years of ages 25 to 65, the proportion of all men who were married ranged between 77.8 percent and 89.7 percent. (Ibid.) Contrary to the majority's supposition, the same source reveals that the proportion of families with several minor children is very low: as of 1974, 46 percent of the families in the United States had no minor children and an additional 19.2 percent had only 1 such child, making over 65 percent of the total; conversely, only 9.5 percent of families had 3 minor children, and the entire class of "4 or more" such children comprised a mere 7.4 percent.

The last of the quoted figures establishes that, contrary to the majority's implication, the case at bar is completely atypical of American society in the second half of the 20th century. If all the families with 4 or more minor children constitute only 7.4 percent of the total, the proportion of families with, as here, the extremely large number of 9 children—8 of whom were minors at the time the complaint was filed—must be a minute fraction of 1 percent. In these circumstances it is manifestly misleading for the majority to assert that the fact the victim has nine children "illustrates" this ground of distinction. (Ante, p. 307 of 138 Cal. Rptr., p. 863 of 563 P.2d.) . . .

Not only do the statistics show the majority's concern to be unwarranted, they also confirm the verdict of common sense in this matter, i.e., that plaintiffs actually ask us to take a smaller, not a larger, step than we took in *Rodriguez*. Inasmuch as adult, emancipated children who are no longer living in the family home could prove little if any damage from loss of parental consortium, I assume the majority are most troubled by the prospect of claims by minor children. (See ante, p. 307 of 138 Cal. Rptr., p. 863 of 563 P.2d.) Upon reflection, it will be seen that such children inevitably comprise a much more limited class than spouses, for two reasons: not all married persons have children; and of those who do, they are parents of *minor* children for a far shorter period of time than they are spouses. It is therefore not surprising that although more than three-quarters of the adult population is married, almost half of such households—46 percent—have no minor children whatever. It follows that recognition of the cause of action for loss of parental consortium will result in a lesser rather than a greater effect on individual liability and overall insurance costs than our approval of the corresponding action by a spouse in *Rodriguez*.

The majority's third proposed ground of distinction (ante, pp. 307-308 of 138 Cal. Rptr., pp. 863-864 of 563 P.2d) deserves little comment. Emphasis is placed on the fact that no state has recognized the cause of action for loss of parental consortium, while a substantial number had permitted a spousal consortium action by the time we decided *Rodriguez*. (12 Cal. 3d at pp. 389-390, 115 Cal. Rptr. 765, 525 P.2d 669.) But the latter fact was invoked in *Rodriguez* to justify our departure from a directly contrary decision of this court — a hurdle we do not face here. Even while emphasizing the out-of-state authorities, moreover, we expressly warned that although we should be mindful of the trend "our decision is not reached by a process of following the crowd." (Id. at p. 392, 115 Cal. Rptr. at p. 771, 525 P.2d at p. 675.)

When that crowd is marching in the wrong direction, we have not heretofore hesitated to break ranks and strike out on our own. . . .

I conclude that there is no escaping the conflict between the reasoning of the majority herein and the letter and spirit of *Rodriguez.* Yet the majority repeatedly reaffirm the holding of that decision. One can only infer that the majority's true motivation is neither the claimed inadequacy of monetary compensation for this loss, nor the difficulty of measuring damages, nor the danger of disproportionate liability. These are mere window-dressing, designed to lend an appearance of logic and objectivity to what is in fact a purely discretionary exercise of the judicial power to limit the potential liability of common law tortfeasors. The majority suggest their actual incentive earlier in the opinion, when they reason that the victim foreseeably has not only a husband, children, and parents, but also "brothers, sisters, cousins, inlaws, friends, colleagues, and other acquaintances who will be deprived of her companionship. No one suggests that all such persons possess a right of action for loss of [the victim's] consortium; all agree that somewhere a line must be drawn." (Ante, p. 306 of 138 Cal. Rptr., p. 862 of 563 P.2d.) . . .

I agree that it must, but I cannot subscribe to the majority's ad terrorem argument for determining the proper place to draw such a line. The majority raise the spectre of liability not only to the victim's spouse but also to a Gilbert and Sullivan parade of "his sisters and his cousins, whom he reckons up by dozens," then dismiss that possibility with the unimpeachable observation that no one is suggesting the latter be compensated. The implication lingers, however, that such demands will become irresistible if the rights of the victim's children are recognized in the case at bar. . . .

There is, in short, no valid excuse for denying these children their day in court. Justice, compassion, and respect for our humanitarian values require that the "line" in this matter be drawn elsewhere.

I would reverse the judgment.

Most courts that have considered the matter have, like the Supreme Court of California, denied loss of consortium recovery to both parents and children. But some courts do permit recovery. See, e.g., Campos v. Coleman, 123 A.3d 854 (Conn. 2015) (minor child may recover for loss of parental consortium resulting from a parent's injury during the parent's life); Rolf v. Tri State Motor Transit Co., 745 N.E.2d 424 (Ohio 2001) (adult child can recover for injury to parent); Cruz v. Broward County Sch. Bd., 800 So. 2d 213 (Fla. 2001) (parents can recover for injury to minor child). The Texas Supreme Court in Roberts v. Williamson, 111 S.W.3d 113 (Tex. 2003), held that parents could not recover loss of consortium damages for nonfatal injuries to their child, but a consortium claim would remain available in the case of death. Can you imagine why the court would adopt this distinction? See also Vitor v. Mihelcic, 806 N.E.2d 632 (Ill. 2004). The extent to which recovery can be had outside of the husband-wife and parent-child relationships varies from state to state. In Ford Motor Co. v. Miles, 967 S.W.2d 377 (Tex. 1998), the court ruled that neither siblings nor stepparents can recover. But in Fernandez v. Walgreen Hastings Co.,

968 P.2d 774 (N.M. 1998), the court held that the plaintiff grandmother could recover for loss of consortium with her granddaughter, because the plaintiff was "a family caretaker and provider of parental affection." A subsequent New Mexico case, however, held that a relationship between siblings did not support a loss of consortium claim. Wachocki v. Bernalillo County Sheriff's Dep't, 265 P.3d 701 (N.M. 2011).

Somewhat surprisingly, the Supreme Judicial Court of Massachusetts has held fast to *Feliciano*, refusing to extend the loss of consortium claim to nonmarried intimate couples, even when the claim is brought by a same-sex partner who was not legally permitted to marry at the time of her partner's injury. See Charron v. Amaral, 889 N.E.2d 946 (Mass. 2008). The court had previously ruled that the state's ban on same-sex marriage violated the Massachusetts constitution in Goodridge v. Dep't of Pub. Health, 798 N.E.2d 941 (Mass. 2003). The plaintiff in *Charron* had married her partner only four days after the state ban was lifted but more than a year after the plaintiff's partner had suffered the injury giving rise to the consortium claim. A concurrence explains that *Goodridge* had not held that cohabiting same-sex couples were legally married but that they could thereafter legally marry. The marriage in *Charron* occurred after the plaintiff's partner had suffered injury, and *Feliciano* barred recovery for consortium.

3. Liability for Prenatal Harm

The issues presented by the cases in this subsection are to a considerable extent conceptually diverse, and thus could have appeared in other places in the book. However, the cases are linked factually in that they all involve negligent actions that adversely affect children prior to birth. And, as is true with the other materials in this section, they all involve situations in which courts fear that a foreseeability-based definition of the scope of liability may sweep too broadly.

a. Actions by Parents for Their Own Harm

Werling v. Sandy

17 Ohio St. 3d 45, 476 N.E.2d 1053 (1985)

[This is an action for wrongful death alleging that because of the negligence of the defendants, the plaintiff's child was stillborn. The trial court dismissed the complaint, ruling that there is no action for the wrongful death of a fetus.]

HOLMES, J. Today, this court is confronted with the certified issue of whether an action for wrongful death exists under R.C. 2125.01 where the decedent was a stillborn fetus. More specifically, we are asked to determine whether the statutory beneficiaries of an unborn fetus are entitled to damages for the wrongful death of the fetus where both the alleged negligently inflicted injury and death of the child occurred before birth. To resolve this issue necessarily requires an answer to the question of whether an unborn fetus which dies *en ventre sa mere* may be considered a "person" for the purposes of the statute under consideration. For the reasons which follow, we answer each of the above queries affirmatively as long as it is established that the fetus was viable at the time of its injury. . . .

R.C. 2125.01 provides in pertinent part:

> When the death of a person is caused by wrongful act, neglect, or default which would have entitled the party injured to maintain an action and recover damages if death had not ensued, the person who would have been liable if death had not ensued, or the administrator or executor of the estate of such person, as such administrator or executor, shall be liable to an action for damages. . . .

The clear purpose of the wrongful death statute is to provide a remedy whenever there would have been an action in damages had death not ensued. The provision is remedial in nature and was designed to alleviate the inequity perceived in the common law.

In addition, an action for wrongful death is for the exclusive benefit of the statutory beneficiaries. It is rebuttably presumed within the statute that each beneficiary has suffered damages by reason of the wrongful death. R.C. 2125.02. In the present situation, it is the parents who suffer mental anguish and the loss of society *inter alia* due to the death of their child. Our decision is directed to justly compensate those parents for the loss of parenthood.

The rights of an unborn child are no strangers to our law, even though this precise question is one of first impression. The intestate rights of a posthumous child are recognized in R.C. 2105.14. A child in gestation who is subsequently born alive may be considered a life in being throughout the gestation period for purposes of the now statutory rule against perpetuities. R.C. 2131.08(A); Phillips v. Herron (1896), 55 Ohio St. 478, 45 N.E. 720. The definition of "decedent" within the Uniform Anatomical Gift Act includes a stillborn infant or fetus. R.C. 2108.01(B). And, finally, under the Uniform Parentage Act, the personal representative of an unborn child may bring an action on behalf of the infant to establish a father-child relationship. R.C. 3111.04.

While the cause of action herein is statutory, certain common-law decisions of this court assist our resolution of the issue presented. In Williams v. Marion Rapid Transit, Inc. (1949), 152 Ohio St. 114, 87 N.E.2d 334 [39 O.O. 433], the issue before the court was whether a living child injured *en ventre sa mere* was entitled to be heard as a "person" within Section 16, Article I of the Ohio Constitution. In recognizing that the child possessed an action for injuries negligently inflicted during gestation, Judge Matthias, writing for a unanimous court, stated at 128-129, 87 N.E.2d 334:

> To hold that the plaintiff [child] in the instant case did not suffer an injury in her person would require this court to announce that as a matter of law the infant is a part of the mother until birth and has no existence in law until that time. In our view such a ruling would deprive the infant of the right conferred by the Constitution upon all persons, by the application of a time-worn fiction not founded on fact and within common knowledge untrue and unjustified.

This court has also recognized the validity of a wrongful death action on behalf of a child who was born alive but died shortly thereafter as a result of prenatal injuries. . . .

Using these past decisions as a foundation, we are of the opinion that a cause of action may arise under the wrongful death statute when a viable fetus is stillborn since a life capable of independent existence has expired. It is logically indefensible as well as unjust to deny an action where the child is stillborn, and yet permit the action where the child survives birth but only for a short period of time. The requirement of birth in this respect is an artificial demarcation. As hypothetically stated by the court of appeals in *Stidam* [v. Ashmore] (109 Ohio App. 431, 167 N.E.2d 106), at 434:

> . . . Suppose, for example, viable unborn twins suffered simultaneously the same prenatal injury of which one died before and the other after birth. Shall there be a cause of action for death of one and not for that of the other? Surely logic requires recognition of causes of action for the deaths of both, or for neither.

To allow a cause of action where it is established that the fetus was viable certainly furthers the remedial nature of the wrongful death statute. To hold otherwise would only serve to reward the tortfeasor by allowing him to escape liability upon an increase in the severity of the harm, if such harm results in death to the child. In other words, the greater the harm inflicted, the better the opportunity that a defendant will be exonerated. This result is clearly not acceptable under the statute.

We recognize that our adoption of the viability test will present some practical problems. The term "viability" is an elusive one since not all fetuses arrive at this stage of their development at an identical chronological point in their gestation. The concept may also become increasingly difficult to apply with further developments surrounding the sophisticated medical techniques which allow a child to be conceived outside the mother's womb. Indeed, some commentators have questioned the standard and suggest the adoption of a causation test which permits recovery for an injury sustained by a child at any time prior to his birth if it can be proven that the injury was the proximate result of a wrongful act. However, for the purposes of this appeal, we believe the better reasoned view is to recognize the viable child as a person under the statute rather than to designate the same status to a fetus incapable of independently surviving a premature birth. . . .

We are also cognizant that the United States Supreme Court has held that a fetus is not a person for the purpose of the Fourteenth Amendment, and that states may not enact statutes which prohibit abortions during the first trimester of pregnancy. Roe v. Wade (1973), 410 U.S. 113, 93 S. Ct. 705, 35 L. Ed. 2d 147. However, the court recognized in *Roe* that once a fetus becomes viable, a state may prohibit all abortions except those necessary to preserve the life or health of the mother and that ". . . [s]tate regulation protective of fetal life after viability . . . has both logical and biological justifications." Id. at 163, 93 S. Ct. at 732. The court found the compelling point in the state's legitimate interest of protecting potential life to be at viability, as the fetus, at that time, has the capability of meaningful life outside the mother's womb. It follows, therefore, that our decision is entirely consistent with *Roe* to the effect that a viable fetus is a person entitled to protection and may be a basis for recovery under the wrongful death statute.

Finally, appellees contend that State v. Dickinson (1971), 28 Ohio St. 2d 65, 275 N.E.2d 599 [57 O.O.2d 255], is dispositive of this appeal. We disagree.

In *Dickinson,* it was held in paragraph two of the syllabus that a viable unborn fetus is not a person within the meaning of this state's former vehicular homicide statute, R.C. 4511.181. It is undisputed, however, that criminal statutes are strictly construed against the state and liberally interpreted in favor of the accused. R.C. 2901.-04; Harrison v. State (1925), 112 Ohio St. 429, 442, 147 N.E. 650, *affirmed* (1926), 270 U.S. 632, 46 S. Ct. 350, 70 L. Ed. 771. In fact, *Dickinson* recognizes ". . . that the definition of a word in a civil statute does not necessarily import the same meaning to the same word in interpreting a criminal statute." Id. 28 Ohio St. 2d at 70, 275 N.E.2d 599. Therefore, we find the *Dickinson* case not to be controlling under the facts as presented herein.

Accordingly, we hold that a viable fetus which is negligently injured *en ventre sa mere,* and subsequently stillborn, may be the basis for a wrongful death action pursuant to R.C. 2125.01.

The judgment of the court of appeals is hereby reversed and the cause is remanded to the trial court for further proceedings consistent with this opinion.

Judgment reversed and cause remanded.

CELEBREZZE, C.J., and SWEENEY, FORD, CLIFFORD F. BROWN, and WRIGHT, JJ., concur.

DOUGLAS, J., concurs separately.

FORD, J., of the Eleventh Appellate District, sitting for LOCHER, J.

DOUGLAS, J., concurring.

While I agree with the holding of the majority, I am troubled with what appears to be the open-endedness of the decision. In my judgment it would be the better policy of this court to say that for purposes of suit in Ohio, under the wrongful death statute, viability of an unborn child occurs at a time certain during pregnancy. I deem it important that we be precise in our decision and thereby send to the bench and bar under our jurisdiction a clear message. To do otherwise, it seems to me, will be to encourage the filing of multifarious actions to determine, in a descending manner, what this court means as to when viability occurs. Today's case says a full-term pregnancy. Tomorrow's case could be a pregnancy of seven months, then six months and, after that, five months, and so forth.

In addition, I find that the breadth of today's decision will present some very difficult questions, not only for lawyers who advise their clients, but for doctors, organizations and individuals who are concerned with the question in relationship to Roe v. Wade (1973), 410 U.S. 113.

On the question of whether a fetus is a person for purposes of a wrongful death action, consider the following excerpt from the dissenting opinion of Haynsworth, J., in Todd v. Sandidge Construction Co., 341 F.2d 75, 80-81 (4th Cir. 1964), a case arising under South Carolina law:

> Little can be said in favor of allowance of a cause of action for personal injury to a child en ventre sa mere, which thereafter is stillborn for some unrelated reason. When the stillbirth is unrelated to the prenatal injury, the child suffers no economic loss, and it is, at least, highly dubious that it will have endured conscious pain and suffering. The majority here, of course, make no suggestion that a cause of action for personal injury in such circumstances should be recognized or allowed. Yet, and this is where I think they go awry, it is only if an action for personal injury under such circumstances would be allowed that, under their construction of the wrongful death statute, an action for wrongful death would be allowed if the death before birth resulted from the injury rather than from an unrelated cause. Live birth is a prerequisite if we follow the statute's relation of the right to maintain an action for wrongful death to the right to maintain an action for personal injury. There is no right of action for personal injury if the child is stillborn for an unrelated or a related reason, and there is no action for wrongful death if it is stillborn for a related reason. If viability has any usefulness in discovering reasonable answers to the problem — live birth is crucial.
>
> In its social aspects, if a line is to be drawn anywhere, there is much more to be said for placing it at the point of live birth than at any other point after conception.
>
> As noted above, when the child is born alive there are compelling reasons for allowing him to maintain an action for personal injury by him when en ventre sa mere. Those reasons, legal and practical, are unaffected by his viability at the time of injury. Once the cause of action for personal injury matures with the live birth, it, of course, will survive

a subsequent death of the child. In the event of a subsequent death after birth, too, if the result of prenatal injury, the wrongful death statute literally and unequivocally applies, and such an action may be maintained.

There are no comparable reasons for allowance of a cause of action for personal injury of a child en ventre sa mere which is later stillborn. If a live birth is a prerequisite to a cause of action for personal injury, it is a prerequisite to a cause of action for wrongful death, for the wrongful death statute is expressly conditioned upon the existence of a cause of action for personal injury. If the need for recognition of a cause of action for wrongful death of a stillborn child were great, then it might be said without too much illogic that the substantive right of action for personal injury of a child later stillborn exists, but may not be maintained solely because of the absence of recoverable damages. It may be interpolated here that the South Carolina cases contain no shred of a suggestion of recognition of such a need. If such a need exists, however, it exists regardless of the child's maturity at the time of injury or at the time of the stillbirth.

The longer the pregnancy, the greater the parent's expectation and the deeper the sense of loss if there is a miscarriage or the child is stillborn. The potential personal loss the parents may suffer does not spring from nothingness the moment the child becomes viable. It is a progressive thing. The progress is unmarked by the attainment of viability, but it is tremendously enlarged when the child born alive is seen and embraced by its mother and, perhaps, by its father. In some circumstances, the loss of a month-old fetus may be a crushing disappointment to the prospective parents, but the loss of a child born alive and loved, even for a little while, is a cause of much greater grief.

When the child is stillborn, of course, the mother in an action for her injuries can recover the major items of damage, including compensation for her grief. If loss of the child's anticipated companionship is not technically compensable in her action, juries usually take care of the situation. The father is unlikely to have any net recoverable damages. The inevitable consequence of allowance of an action for wrongful death in these circumstances will be multiple recovery for the same items of damage.

This, then is not a particularly deserving plaintiff. Neither reason, analogy nor social considerations dictate allowance of a recovery. Allowance of recovery here, however, by enthroning viability at the time of injury as the touchstone of decision may gravely embarrass recovery by highly deserving plaintiffs, living children crippled by prenatal injuries sustained before they became viable.

Generalizations about whether a fetus is a person for wrongful death purposes should be made cautiously because wrongful death actions are governed by statutes that vary considerably from state to state. The court in Castro v. Melchor, 366 P.3d 1058 (Haw. Ct. App. 2016), held, as a matter of first impression, that an unborn viable fetus was a "person" under the state's wrongful death statute, such that a cause of action could be brought for death of such fetus. See also Aka v. Jefferson Hosp. Ass'n, Inc., 42 S.W.3d 508 (Ark. 2001). For those states that recognize the legal standing of a fetus for wrongful death actions, a further question becomes whether viability should be a requisite for recovery. Yes, according to Ladu v. Oregon Clinic, 998 P.2d 733 (Or. Ct. App.), *review denied*, 18 P.3d 1099 (Or. 2000); Kandel v. White, 663 A.2d 1264 (Md. 1995); Coveleski v. Bubnis, 634 A.2d 608 (Pa. 1993). No, according to Mack v. Carmack, 79 So. 3d 597 (Ala. 2011); Pino v. United States, 183 P.3d 1001 (Okla. 2008); Wiersma v. Maple Leaf Farms, 543 N.W.2d 787 (S.D. 1996); Connor v. Monkem Co., 898 S.W.2d 89 (Mo. 1995); Farley v. Sartin, 466 S.E.2d 522 (W. Va. 1995); Danos v. St. Pierre, 402 So. 2d 633 (La. 1981).

Fassoulas v. Ramey

450 So. 2d 822 (Fla. 1984)

Per Curiam. . . .

Plaintiffs, Edith and John Fassoulas, were married and had two children, both of whom had been born with severe congenital abnormalities. After much consideration, they decided not to have any more children due to the fear of having another physically deformed child and the attendant high cost of medical care. They then decided that John would undergo a vasectomy. This medical procedure was performed in January 1974 by defendant, Dr. Ramey. However, due to the negligence of the defendant in performing the operation, in giving medical advice concerning residual pockets of sperm, and in examining and judging the viability of sperm samples, Edith twice became pregnant and gave birth to two children. The first of these, Maria, was born in November 1974 and had many congenital deformities. Roussi, the second of the post-vasectomy children and the fourth Fassoulas child, was born in September 1976 with a slight physical deformity which was corrected at birth; he is now a normal, healthy child.

The plaintiffs sued Dr. Ramey and his clinic in tort based on medical malpractice for the two "wrongful births." They sought as damages Edith's past and future lost wages, her anguish and emotional distress at twice becoming pregnant, her loss of the society, companionship and consortium of her husband, John's mental anguish and emotional distress, his loss of the society, companionship and consortium of his wife, medical and hospital expenses and the expenses for the care and upbringing of the two new children until the age of twenty-one.

At trial, the jury found in favor of the plaintiffs, finding the defendants 100% negligent with reference to Maria and 50% negligent with reference to Roussi. The plaintiffs were found to be comparatively negligent as to the birth of Roussi. Damages were assessed in the amount of $250,000 for the birth of Maria and $100,000 for the birth of Roussi, the latter sum being reduced to $50,000 because of the plaintiff's comparative negligence. . . .

The rule in Florida is that "a parent cannot be said to have been damaged by the birth and rearing of a normal, healthy child." Public Health Trust v. Brown, 388 So. 2d 1084, 1085 (Fla. 3d DCA 1980), *petition denied,* 399 So. 2d 1140 (Fla. 1981) (footnote omitted). "[I]t has been imbedded in our law for centuries that the father and now both parents or legal guardians of a child have the sole obligation of providing the necessaries in raising the child, whether the child be wanted or unwanted." Ramey v. Fassoulas, 414 So. 2d at 200. "The child is still the child of the parents, not the physician, and it is the parents' legal obligation, not the physician's, to support the child." Id. For public policy reasons, we decline to allow rearing damages for the birth of a healthy child. As stated by the Supreme Court of Wisconsin:

> To permit the parents to keep their child and shift the entire cost of its upbringing to a physician who failed to determine or inform them of the fact of pregnancy would be to create a new category of surrogate parent. Every child's smile, every bond of love and affection, every reason for parental pride in a child's achievements, every contribution by the child to the welfare and well-being of the family and parents, is to remain with the mother and father. For the most part, these are intangible benefits but they are nonetheless real. On the other hand, every financial cost or detriment — what the complaint terms "hard money damages" — including the cost of food, clothing and education, would be shifted to the physician. . . . We hold that such result would be wholly out of proportion to the culpability involved. . . .

Rieck v. Medical Protective Co., 64 Wis. 2d 514, 518, 219 N.W.2d 242, 244-245 (1974) (footnote omitted). We agree with this reasoning and hold that, as a matter of law, the "benefits to the parents outweigh their economic loss in rearing and educating a healthy, normal child." Terrell v. Garcia, 496 S.W.2d 124, 128 (Tex. Civ. App. 1973), *cert. denied,* 415 U.S. 927, 94 S. Ct. 1434, 39 L. Ed. 2d 484 (1974); Public Health Trust v. Brown.

The same reasoning forcefully and correctly applies to the ordinary, everyday expenses associated with the care and upbringing of a physically or mentally deformed child. We likewise hold as a matter of law that ordinary rearing expenses for a defective child are not recoverable as damages in Florida.

We agree with the district court below that an exception exists in the case of special upbringing expenses associated with a deformed child. Special medical and educational expenses, beyond normal rearing costs, are often staggering and quite debilitating to a family's financial and social health; "indeed the financial and emotional drain associated with raising such a child is often overwhelming to the affected parents." Ramey v. Fassoulas, 414 So. 2d at 201. There is no valid policy argument against parents being recompensed for these costs of extraordinary care in raising a deformed child to majority. We hold these special upbringing costs associated with a deformed child to be recoverable. . . .

ALDERMAN, C.J., and BOYD, OVERTON, and MCDONALD, JJ., concur.

EHRLICH, J., dissents with an opinion with which ADKINS and SHAW, JJ., concur.

EHRLICH, JUDGE, dissenting. . . . It has often been said that hard cases make bad law. I am afraid that the majority opinion does just that. A look at the instant facts supports this conclusion. John and Edith Fassoulas already had two children and both were born with severe medical problems. They could not afford the medical bills arising out of the treatments required. This was partly a function of the high cost of the medical bills and partly a function of the unemployment of John himself because of ill health. The two decided upon the solution of a vasectomy, both for the stated economic reason and for the reason of their fear that any further children might also be born with defects. They went to Dr. Ramey for the vasectomy but the operation was negligently performed. Thereupon occurred what can only be described as a comedy of errors. The fact that the operation was not successful was not apparent to anyone at the time. Edith soon became pregnant but all concerned thought that the cause was Dr. Ramey's negligent instructions to the couple about how long to wait before resuming intercourse and how long to use birth control because of the presence of residual pockets of sperm. In any event, Maria made her appearance nine months later and was congenitally deformed. She had a short neck, an abnormal shaping of the skull, a skin irregularity that was described as fish-like and scaly in appearance, a heart murmur, hypertension, and malformations of the hands. The very result that John and Edith wished to avoid by having the vasectomy was thus visited upon them, clearly a foreseeable consequence of Dr. Ramey's negligence. Time passed. Dr. Ramey once again erred in his professional conduct, this time by negligently confusing sperm viability with sperm motility in his examination of John's sperm samples. John and Edith were told that John was sterile when in fact he was not. Believing that Maria was born because of the residual sperm pockets extant after the initial operation and that John was now sterile, the couple resumed sexual relations. Again, there resulted a surprise, this time Roussi's birth. Though born with minor infirmities, these were corrected and Roussi can be considered a normal child. But now, instead of having only two children with physical infirmities, John and Edith have a total of four children, three with infirmities and one without. There are now medical bills for three deformed children; John is still out of work; and Edith has to quit work in order to care for the four children. All are now on welfare. While Edith and John testified that they love their two unplanned children greatly (and what parent would not?), they have clearly been wronged by the negligent physician. Can it fairly be said as a matter of law that they have not been damaged by Roussi's birth? Is it fair to say as a matter of law that the nonextraordinary expenses associated with rearing Maria are not recoverable? I think not.

"It is no answer to say that a result which claimant specifically sought to avoid, *might be regarded as a blessing by someone else.*" Rivera v. State, 94 Misc. 2d 157, 162, 404 N.Y.S.2d 950, 954 (Ct. Cl. 1978) (emphasis supplied). "The doctor whose negligence brings about . . . an undesired birth should not be allowed to say, 'I did you a favor,' secure in the knowledge that the courts will give to this claim the effect of an irrebuttable presumption." Terrell v. Garcia at 131 [496 S.W.2d 124 (Tex. C.U. App. 1973, *cert. denied,* 415 U.S. 927 (1974)] (Cadena, J., dissenting).

Dr. Ramey did not do Edith and John a favor. That is what this Court should hold. Since it did not, I must dissent.

ADKINS and SHAW, JJ., concur.

Although a few courts refuse to recognize "wrongful birth" as a theory of recovery at all, see, e.g., Willis v. Wu, 607 S.E.2d 63 (S.C. 2004), most courts have accepted such claims at least with respect to pregnancy-related economic loss, such as lost wages and medical expenses. See Chaffee v. Seslar, 786 N.E.2d 705 (Ind. 2003) (stating that the "vast majority of jurisdictions" accept this approach to "wrongful birth" claims). With respect to children born with birth defects, most courts agree with the Florida Supreme Court in *Fassoulas* and permit recovery for out-of-the-ordinary expenses generated by the birth defect. See, e.g., Foote v. Albany Med. Ctr. Hosp., 16 N.Y.3d 211 (N.Y. 2011); Schirmer v. Mt. Auburn Obstetrics & Gynecologic Assocs., Inc., 844 N.E.2d 1160 (Ohio 2006). But some courts reject the idea that children with birth defects should be treated differently from healthy children. In Taylor v. Kurapati, 600 N.W.2d 670, 681 (Mich. Ct. App. 1999), the court, after stating the rule that there can be no recovery for the costs of raising a healthy child, said:

> We do not concede, however, that an intermediate appellate court of this state should implicitly endorse the view that the life of a disabled child is worth less than the life of a healthy child. If all life is presumptively valuable, how can we say that what we really mean is that all lives except for the lives of the disabled are presumptively valuable? . . . If we conclude that in a proper hierarchy of values, the expense of supporting life should not outweigh the benefit of that life, how can we say that what we really mean is that such expense should not outweigh the benefit of lives of healthy children, but can outweigh the benefit of lives of disabled children? If we say that a court "has no business declaring that among the living are people who never should have been born," how can we continue to say — and here virtually explicitly through the device of compensating the parents for the expenses of that "wrongful birth" — that courts can go about the business of declaring that living, but disabled, children should never have been born?

For those courts that permit recovery for expenses related to raising a child with severe birth defects, some also permit recovery by the parents for the emotional distress caused by the birth defects. See McAllister v. Ha, 496 S.E.2d 577 (N.C. 1998). The court in Viccaro v. Milunsky, 551 N.E.2d 8 (Mass. 1990), adjusted the plaintiffs' recovery for emotional harm caused by the birth defects by reducing the recovery by any emotional benefit the parents would receive from the child. The court also ruled that the damages should be reduced by the emotional benefit the parents derived from a healthy child born to them previously, apparently on the ground that had the defendant not been negligent in the genetic counseling, the healthy child, like the child with birth defects, would not have been born.

A number of courts follow this "netting out" approach with respect to the birth of an unwanted but healthy child, permitting recovery of the full expenses associated with raising the child but offsetting by an amount equal to the emotional benefits of having a healthy child. See, e.g., Reed v. Campagnolo, 630 A.2d 1145 (Md. 1993); Univ. of Arizona Health Sciences Ctr. v. Superior Court, 667 P.2d 1294 (Ariz. 1983); Ochs v. Borrelli, 445 A.2d 883 (Conn. 1982); Sherlock v. Stillwater Clinic, 260 N.W.2d 169 (Minn. 1977). Some courts have, however, permitted recovery in full for the costs of raising a healthy child. See, e.g., Custodio v. Bauer, 59 Cal. Rptr. 463 (Ct. App. 1967); Lovelace Med. Ctr. v. Mendez, 805 P.2d 603 (N.M. 1991); Zehr v. Haugen, 871 P.2d 1006 (Or. 1994); Dotson v. Bernstein, 207 P.3d 911 (Colo. App. 2009); Marciniak v. Lundborg, 450 N.W.2d 243 (Wis. 1990). As the court in *Marciniak* put it (450 N.W.2d at 247):

> We do not consider it reasonable to expect parents to essentially choose between the child and the cause of action. That would truly be a "Hobson's choice." In addition, the decisions concerning abortion or adoption are highly personal matters and involve deeply held moral or religious convictions.

Some courts and statutes distinguish between "wrongful conception" and "wrongful birth." The former category includes cases with preconception negligence, such as that involved in *Fassoulas* and *Williams.* Thus, in Molloy v. Meier, 679 N.W.2d 711 (Minn. 2004), the Minnesota high court ruled that doctors who failed to detect a genetic disorder in a patient breached a duty of care to the patient's biological parents when the parents conceived another child with the same genetic disorder. For an argument that courts should permit recovery under a negligent infliction of emotional distress theory when alternative reproductive technology malpractice leads to healthy but somehow "erroneous" babies (e.g., through negligent switching of embryos), see Ingrid H. Heidi, Negligence in the Creation of Healthy Babies, 9 J. Med. & L. 55 (2005). The latter category involves post-conception negligence, such as the failure of the plaintiff's doctor to diagnose the possibility that a fetus, if carried to term, will have severe birth defects. The plaintiff's claim in this type of case is that if the doctor had made a correct diagnosis she would have had an abortion. Some statutes bar recovery in cases where the plaintiff would have used abortion to avoid the costs associated with a child born with birth defects. See, e.g., Minn. Stat. Ann. §145.424.

Actions for wrongful birth, at least involving preconception wrongs, have been largely limited to actions against medical care providers. Thus, in Hegyes v. Unjian Enterprises, 286 Cal. Rptr. 85 (Ct. App. 1991), the court held that a motorist could not be held liable for a preconception tort. See also Williams v. Manchester, 888 N.E.2d 1 (Ill. 2008) (holding that a negligent motorist was not liable for wrongful death of a fetus when its mother terminated the pregnancy because the fetus, uninjured in the car accident, complicated the mother's medical recovery from injuries caused by the car accident). In C.A.M. v. R.A.W., 568 A.2d 556 (N.J. Super.), *appeal dismissed,* 604 A.2d 109 (N.J. 1990), the court held that a false representation by the father of the plaintiff's child that he had had a vasectomy could not be the basis of a wrongful birth of a healthy, normal child.

b. Actions on Behalf of Children for Their Own Harm

If a child is born alive, recovery is universally permitted for negligently caused injuries to the fetus occurring between conception and birth, without regard to viability at the time of the injury. See William L. Prosser & W. Page Keeton, The Law of Torts 367-70 (5th ed. 1984).

A number of cases have involved harm to the fetus stemming from treatment to the mother before conception. In Renslow v. Mennonite Hosp., 367 N.E.2d 1250 (Ill. 1977), the court upheld a complaint alleging that nine years before the plaintiff's birth, the defendant had negligently transfused incompatible blood to the plaintiff's mother, as a result of which she was born prematurely, with permanent brain and nervous system damage. What if the parents are aware that the defendant's prior treatment of the mother has caused a high risk that any child subsequently conceived will have severe birth defects? The court in Lynch v. Scheininger, 744 A.2d 113 (N.J. 2000), ruled that such knowledge might constitute an "intervening cause" that would preclude liability. However, if the parents were aware of a substantial, but otherwise unquantifiable risk, the avoidable consequences doctrine could limit, but not eliminate, the child's recovery. The court did "acknowledge that permitting the parents' willingness to bear the risk of conception to bear on [the child's] recovery stretches the contours of traditional applications of comparative fault" but that "[o]ur conclusion that such an apportionment of responsibility for [the child's] injuries is appropriate reflects our pragmatic evaluation of the respective alleged causes of those injuries." 744 A.2d at 130-31.

Some courts refuse to recognize a cause of action for preconception injury. See, e.g., Albala v. City of New York, 429 N.E.2d 786 (N.Y. 1981). The complaint alleged that the defendant negligently damaged the plaintiff's mother's uterus during the course of an abortion, as a result of which the later-conceived plaintiff was injured.

Most of the preconception injury cases involve injuries to the mother in the course of medical care. In Taylor v. Cutler, 703 A.2d 294 (N.J. Super. 1997), *aff'd in part,* 724 A.2d 793 (N.J. 1999), the plaintiff alleged that his preconception injuries were caused by an automobile accident involving his mother seven years before his birth. The court ruled that the defendant motorist could not reasonably have foreseen that her negligence would cause the injuries to the plaintiff.

Turpin v. Sortini

31 Cal. 3d 220, 643 P.2d 954, 182 Cal. Rptr. 337 (1982)

KAUS, J. This case presents the question of whether a child born with an hereditary affliction may maintain a tort action against a medical care provider who — before the child's conception — negligently failed to advise the child's parents of the possibility of the hereditary condition, depriving them of the opportunity to choose not to conceive the child. Although the overwhelming majority of decisions in other jurisdictions recognize the right of *the parents* to maintain an action under these circumstances, the out-of-state cases have uniformly denied *the child's* right to bring what has been commonly termed a "wrongful life" action. In Curlender v. Bio-Science Laboratories (1980) 106 Cal. App. 3d 811, 165 Cal. Rptr. 477, however, the Court of Appeal, 119 Cal. App. 3d 690, 174 Cal. Rptr. 128, concluded that under California common law tort principles, an afflicted child could maintain such an action and could "recover damages for the pain and suffering to be endured during the limited life span available to such a child and any special pecuniary loss resulting from the impaired condition" (id., at p. 831, 165 Cal. Rptr. 489), including the costs of medical care to the extent such costs were not recovered by the child's parents. In the case at bar, a different panel of the Court of Appeal disagreed with the conclusion in *Curlender* and affirmed a trial court judgment dismissing the child's cause of action on demurrer. We granted a hearing to resolve the conflict.

[The Turpins, husband and wife, brought suit on behalf of themselves and their two children against their physician and a hospital for negligence for failing to inform them that their offspring would very likely be totally deaf. Subsequent to this alleged negligence, a daughter, Joy, was conceived and was born totally deaf. Four causes of action were alleged. The only one involved in this appeal was brought on behalf of Joy, who sought damages for being "deprived of the fundamental right of a child to be born as a whole, functional human being without total deafness," and for expenses for "specialized teaching, training and hearing equipment."]

[D]efendants' basic position — supported by the numerous out-of-state authorities — is that Joy has suffered no legally cognizable injury or rationally ascertainable damages as a result of their alleged negligence. Although the issues of "legally cognizable injury" and "damages" are intimately related and in some sense inseparable, past cases have generally treated the two as distinct matters and, for purposes of analysis, it seems useful to follow that approach. . . .

Joy's complaint [asserts] that as a result of defendants' negligence she was "deprived of the fundamental right of a child to be born as a whole, functional human being without total deafness. . . ." While the *Curlender* decision did not embrace this approach to "injury" completely — refusing to permit the plaintiff to recover for a reduced lifespan — it too maintained that the proper point of reference for measuring defendant's liability was simply plaintiff's condition after birth, insisting that "[w]e need not be concerned with the fact that had defendants not been negligent, the plaintiff might not have come into existence at all" (106 Cal. App. 3d at p. 829), and rejecting "the notion that a 'wrongful life' cause of action involves any attempted evaluation of a claimed right *not* to be born." (Original italics.) (Id., at pp. 830-831, 165 Cal. Rptr. 477.)

The basic fallacy of the *Curlender* analysis is that it ignores the essential nature of the defendants' alleged wrong and obscures a critical difference between wrongful life actions and the ordinary prenatal injury cases noted above. In an ordinary prenatal injury case, if the defendant had not been negligent, the child would have been born healthy; thus, as in a typical personal injury case, the defendant in such a case has interfered with the child's basic right to be free from physical injury caused by the negligence of others. In this case, by contrast, the obvious tragic fact is that plaintiff never had a chance "to be born as a whole, functional human being without total deafness"; if defendants had performed their jobs properly, she would not have been born with hearing intact, but — according to the complaint — would not have been born at all.

A plaintiff's remedy in tort is compensatory in nature and damages are generally intended not to punish a negligent defendant but to restore an injured person as nearly as possible to the position he or she would have been in had the wrong not been done. . . . Because nothing defendants could have done would have given plaintiff an unimpaired life, it appears inconsistent with basic tort principles to view the injury for which defendants are legally responsible solely by reference to plaintiff's present condition without taking into consideration the fact that if defendants had not been negligent she would not have been born at all. . . .

If the relevant injury in this case is the change in the plaintiff's position attributable to the tortfeasor's actions, then the injury which plaintiff has suffered is that, as a result of defendants' negligence, she has been born with an hereditary ailment rather than not being born at all. Although plaintiff has not phrased her claim for general damages in these terms, most courts and commentators have recognized that the basic claim of "injury" in wrongful life cases is "[i]n essence . . . that [defendants], through their negligence, [have] forced upon [the child] the worse of . . . two alternatives[,] . . . that nonexistence — never being born — would have been preferable to existence in [the] diseased state." (Speck v. Finegold (1979) 268 Pa. Super. 342, 408 A.2d 496, 511-512 (conc. & dis. opn. by Spaeth, J.), *aff'd* (1981) 439 A.2d 110.)

Given this view of the relevant injury which the plaintiff has sustained at the defendant's hands, some courts have concluded that the plaintiff has suffered no legally cognizable injury on the ground that considerations of public policy dictate a conclusion that life — even with the most severe of impairments — is, as a matter of law, always preferable to nonlife. The decisions frequently suggest that a contrary conclusion would "disavow" the sanctity and value of less-than-perfect human life. . . .

Although it is easy to understand and to endorse these decisions' desire to affirm the worth and sanctity of less-than-perfect life, we question whether these considerations alone provide a sound basis for rejecting the child's tort action. To begin with, it is hard to see how an award of damages to a severely handicapped or suffering child would "disavow" the value of life or in any way suggest that the child is not entitled to the full measure of legal and nonlegal rights and privileges accorded to all members of society.

Moreover, while our society and our legal system unquestionably place the highest value on all human life, we do not think that it is accurate to suggest that this state's public policy establishes — as a matter of law — that under all circumstances "impaired life" is "preferable" to "nonlife." For example, Health and Safety Code section 7186, enacted in 1976, provides in part:

> The Legislature finds that adult persons have the fundamental right to control the decisions relating to the rendering of their own medical care, including the decision to have life-sustaining procedures withheld or withdrawn in instances of a terminal condition.
>
> . . . The Legislature further finds that, in the interest of protecting individual autonomy, such prolongation of life for persons with a terminal condition may cause loss of patient dignity and unnecessary pain and suffering, while providing nothing medically necessary or beneficial to the patient.

This statute recognizes that — at least in some situations — public policy supports the right of each individual to make his or her own determination as to the relative value of life and death. (Cf. Matter of Quinlan (1976) 70 N.J. 10 [355 A.2d 647, 662-664]; Superintendent of Belchertown v. Saikewicz (1977) 373 Mass. 728 [370 N.E.2d 417, 423-427].)

Of course, in the wrongful life context, the unborn child cannot personally make any choice as to the relative value of life or death. At that stage, however, just as in the case of an infant after birth, the law generally accords the parents the right to act to protect the child's interest. As the wrongful birth decisions recognize, when a doctor or other medical care provider negligently fails to diagnose an hereditary problem, parents are deprived of the opportunity to make an informed and meaningful decision whether to conceive and bear a handicapped child. . . . Although in deciding whether or not to bear such a child parents may properly, and undoubtedly do, take into account their own interests, parents also presumptively consider the interests of their future child. Thus, when a defendant negligently fails to diagnose an hereditary ailment, he harms the potential child as well as the parents by depriving the parents of information which may be necessary to determine whether it is in the child's own interest to be born with defects or not to be born at all.

In this case, in which the plaintiff's only affliction is deafness, it seems quite unlikely that a jury would ever conclude that life with such a condition is worse than not being born at all. Other wrongful life cases, however, have involved children with much more serious, debilitating and painful conditions, and the academic literature refers to still other, extremely severe hereditary diseases. Considering the short life span of many of these children and their frequently very limited ability to perceive or enjoy the benefits of life, we cannot assert with confidence that in every situation there would be a societal consensus that life is preferable to never having been born at all.

While it thus seems doubtful that a child's claim for general damages should properly be denied on the rationale that the value of impaired life, as a matter of law, always exceeds the value of nonlife, we believe that out-of-state decisions are on sounder grounds in holding that — with respect to the child's claim for pain and suffering or other general damages — recovery should be denied because (1) it is simply impossible to determine in any rational or reasoned fashion whether the plaintiff has in fact suffered an injury in being born impaired rather than not being born, and (2) even if it were possible to overcome the first hurdle, it would be impossible to assess general damages in any fair, nonspeculative manner. . . .

[T]he practical problems are exacerbated when it comes to the matter of arriving at an appropriate award of damages. [I]n fixing damages in a tort case the jury generally compares the condition plaintiff would have been in but for the tort, with the position the plaintiff is in now, compensating the plaintiff for what has been lost as a result of the wrong. Although the valuation of pain and suffering or emotional distress in terms of dollars and cents is unquestionably difficult in an ordinary personal injury action, jurors at least have some frame of reference in their own general experience to appreciate what the plaintiff has lost — normal life without pain and suffering. In a wrongful life action, that simply is not the case, for what the plaintiff has "lost" is not life without pain and suffering but rather the unknowable status of never having been born. In this context, a rational, nonspeculative determination of a specific monetary award in accordance with normal tort principles appears to be outside the realm of human competence.

The difficulty in ascertaining or measuring an appropriate award of general damages in this type of case is also reflected in the application of what is sometimes referred to as the "benefit" doctrine in tort damages. Section 920 of the Restatement Second of Torts . . . provides that "[w]hen the defendant's tortious conduct has caused harm to the plaintiff . . . and in so doing has conferred a special benefit to the interest of the plaintiff that was harmed, the value of the benefit conferred is considered in mitigation of damages, to the extent that this is equitable."

In requesting general damages in a wrongful life case, the plaintiff seeks monetary compensation for the pain and suffering he or she will endure because of his or her hereditary affliction. Under section 920's benefit doctrine, however, such damages must be offset by the benefits incidentally conferred by the defendant's conduct "to the interest of the plaintiff that was harmed." With respect to general damages, the harmed interest is the child's general physical, emotional and psychological well-being, and in considering the benefit to this interest which defendant's negligence has conferred, it must be recognized that as an incident of defendant's negligence the plaintiff has in fact obtained a physical existence with the capacity both to receive and give love and pleasure as well as to experience pain and suffering. Because of the incalculable nature of both elements of this harm-benefit equation, we believe that a reasoned, nonarbitrary award of general damage is simply not obtainable. . . .

Although we have determined that the trial court properly rejected plaintiff's claim for general damages, we conclude that her claim for the "extraordinary expenses for specialized teaching, training and hearing equipment" that she will incur during her lifetime because of her deafness stands on a different footing.[11]

As we have already noted, in the corresponding "wrongful birth" actions parents have regularly been permitted to recover the medical expenses incurred on behalf of such a child. . . . In authorizing this recovery by the parents, courts have recognized (1) that these are expenses that would not have been incurred "but for" the defendants' negligence and (2) that they are the kind of pecuniary losses which are readily ascertainable and regularly awarded as damages in professional malpractice actions.

Although the parents and child cannot, of course, both recover for the same medical expenses, we believe it would be illogical and anomalous to permit only parents, and not the child, to recover for the cost of the child's own medical care. If such a distinction were established, the afflicted child's receipt of necessary medical expenses might well depend on the wholly fortuitous circumstance of whether the parents are available to sue and recover such damages or whether the medical expenses are incurred at a time when the parents remain legally responsible for providing such care.

Realistically, a defendant's negligence in failing to diagnose an hereditary ailment places a significant medical and financial burden on the whole family unit. Unlike the child's claim for general damages, the damage here is both certain and readily measurable. Furthermore, in many instances these expenses will be vital not only to the child's well-being but to his or her very survival. . . . If, as alleged, defendant's negligence was in fact a proximate cause of the child's present and continuing need for such special, extraordinary medical care and training, we believe that it is consistent with the basic liability principles of Civil Code section 1714 to hold defendant liable for the cost of such care, whether the expense is to be borne by the parents or by the child. As Justice Jacobs of the New Jersey Supreme Court observed in his dissenting opinion in Gleitman v. Cosgrove, supra, 227 A.2d at page 703: "While the law cannot remove the heartache or undo the harm, it can afford some reasonable measure of compensation toward alleviating the financial burdens."

Moreover, permitting plaintiff to recover the extraordinary, additional medical expenses that are occasioned by the hereditary ailment is also consistent with the established parameters of the general tort "benefit" doctrine discussed above. As we have seen, under that doctrine an offset is appropriate only insofar as the defendant's conduct has conferred a special benefit "to the interest of the plaintiff that was harmed." Here, the harm for which plaintiff seeks recompense is an economic loss, the extraordinary, out-of-pocket expenses that she will have to bear because of her hereditary ailment. Unlike the claim for general damages, defendants' negligence has conferred no incidental, offsetting benefit to this interest of plaintiff. . . . Accordingly, assessment of these special damages should pose no unusual or insoluble problems. . . .

The judgment is reversed and the case is remanded to the trial court for further proceedings consistent with this opinion.

11. As noted, in a separate cause of action Joy's parents seek to recover, inter alia, for the medical expenses which they will incur on Joy's behalf during her minority. Since both Joy and her parents obviously cannot both recover the same expenses, Joy's separate claim applies as a practical matter only to medical expenses to be incurred after the age of majority.

RICHARDSON and BROUSSARD, JJ., concur. [The concurring opinion of NEWMAN, J., and the dissenting opinion of MOSK, J., are omitted.]

Justice Mosk's dissent consists largely of a quotation from the opinion in *Curlender,* discussed by the majority opinion in *Turpin.* In upholding the complaint in *Curlender,* the court in that case stated (165 Cal. Rptr. at 488-89):

> We have no difficulty in ascertaining and finding the existence of a duty owed by medical laboratories engaged in genetic testing to parents and their as yet unborn children to use ordinary care in administration of available tests for the purpose of providing information concerning potential genetic defects in the unborn. The public policy considerations with respect to the individuals involved and to society as a whole dictate recognition of such a duty, and it is of significance that in no decision that has come to our attention which has dealt with the "wrongful-life" concept has it been suggested that public policy considerations negate the existence of such a duty. Nor have other jurisdictions had any difficulty in finding a breach of duty under appropriate circumstances or in finding the existence of the requisite proximate causal link between the breach and the claimed injury; we find no bar to a holding that the defendants owed a duty to the child plaintiff before us and breached that duty.
>
> The real crux of the problem is whether the breach of duty was the proximate cause of an *injury cognizable at law.* The injury, of course, is not the particular defect with which a plaintiff is afflicted — considered in the abstract — but it is the birth of plaintiff with such defect.
>
> The circumstance that the birth and injury have come hand in hand has caused other courts to deal with the problem by barring recovery. The reality of the "wrongful-life" concept is that such a plaintiff both *exists* and *suffers,* due to the negligence of others. It is neither necessary nor just to retreat into meditation on the mysteries of life. We need not be concerned with the fact that had defendants not been negligent, the plaintiff might not have come into existence at all. The certainty of genetic impairment is no longer a mystery. In addition, a reverent appreciation of life compels recognition that plaintiff, however impaired she may be, has come into existence as a living person with certain rights.
>
> One of the fears expressed in the decisional law is that, once it is determined that such infants have rights cognizable at law, nothing would prevent such a plaintiff from bringing suit against its own parents for allowing plaintiff to be born. In our view, the fear is groundless. The "wrongful-life" cause of action with which we are concerned is based upon negligently caused failure by someone under a duty to do so to inform the prospective parents of facts needed by them to make a conscious choice *not* to become parents. If a case arose where, despite due care by the medical profession in transmitting the necessary warnings, parents made a conscious choice to proceed with a pregnancy, with full knowledge that a seriously impaired infant would be born, that conscious choice would provide an intervening act of proximate cause to preclude liability insofar as defendants other than the parents were concerned. Under such circumstances, we see no sound public policy which should protect those parents from being answerable for the pain, suffering and misery which they have wrought upon their offspring. . . .
>
> The extent of recovery, however, is subject to certain limitations due to the nature of the tort involved. While ordinarily a defendant is liable for all consequences flowing from the injury, it is appropriate in the case before us to tailor the elements of recovery, taking into account particular circumstances involved. . . .
>
> The complaint seeks damages based upon an actuarial life expectancy of plaintiff of more than 70 years — the life expectancy if plaintiff had been born without the Tay-Sachs

> disease. The complaint sets forth that plaintiff's actual life expectancy, because of the disease, is only four years. We reject as untenable the claim that plaintiff is entitled to damages as if plaintiff had been born without defects and would have had a normal life expectancy. Plaintiff's right to damages must be considered on the basis of plaintiff's mental and physical condition at birth and her expected condition during the short life span (four years according to the complaint) anticipated for one with her impaired condition. In similar fashion, we reject the notion that a "wrongful-life" cause of action involves any attempted evaluation of a claimed right *not* to be born. In essence, we construe the "wrongful-life" cause of action by the defective child as the right of such child to recover damages for the pain and suffering to be endured during the limited life span available to such a child and any special pecuniary loss resulting from the impaired condition.

The early "wrongful life" claims in America involved children who were born illegitimate and who sought to recover for that allegedly unfortunate circumstance. All such claims were unsuccessful. See, e.g., Slawek v. Stroh, 215 N.W.2d 9 (Wis. 1974). The recent cases have involved children with severe birth defects, and some have permitted, as did the court in *Turpin,* recovery by the child for living expenses attributable to the defect the child is projected to incur after she reaches majority. See, e.g., Kush v. Lloyd, 616 So. 2d 415 (Fla. 1992). Other courts, however, refuse to permit any recovery in "wrongful life" cases. See, e.g., Clark v. Children's Mem'l Hosp., 955 N.E.2d 1065, 1084 (Ill. 2011) ("In the wrongful-life context, there is no cause of action because the child, while burdened, cannot be said to have suffered a legal wrong."); Tomlinson v. Metro. Pediatrics, LLC, 366 P.3d 370, 389 (Or. Ct. App. 2015) ("As applied to [child's] claim, a trier of fact would be required to compare the value of nonexistence — the state that [child] would have been in but for defendants' alleged negligence — and the value of his life with [a genetic defect]. Simply put, as a matter of law, that comparison is impossible to make.").

The commentators have generally been more receptive to the cause of action for wrongful life than have the courts. See, e.g., Deana A. Pollard, Wrongful Analysis in Wrongful Life Jurisprudence, 55 Ala. L. Rev. 327 (2004); Thomas A. Burns, Note, When Life Is an Injury: An Economic Approach to Wrongful Life Lawsuits, 52 Duke L.J. 807 (2003); Mark Strasser, Wrongful Life, Wrongful Birth, Wrongful Death, and the Right to Refuse Treatment: Can Reasonable Jurisdictions Recognize All but One?, 64 Mo. L. Rev. 29 (1999); Michael B. Kelly, The Rightful Position in "Wrongful Life" Actions, 42 Hastings L.J. 505 (1991). However, commentators have not been as receptive when the suit is brought against the parents, as the court in *Curlender* suggested it might be. See Joan Waters, Wrongful Life: The Implications of Suits in Wrongful Life Brought by Children Against Their Parents, 31 Drake L. Rev. 411 (1981-1982). As an alternative to a wrongful life claim in tort by a disabled child, what about a contract claim by the child against his parents' doctor for warranting to his parents that he would be born free of disability? For arguments supporting such a contract claim, see Ronen Perry, It's a Wonderful Life, 93 Cornell L. Rev. 329 (2008).

An issue similar to that involved in *Turpin*, but at the other end of the age scale, arose in Anderson v. St. Francis–St. George Hosp., Inc., 671 N.E.2d 225 (Ohio 1995). The defendant administered life-preserving treatment to the plaintiff against his explicit instructions, thus prolonging his painful life. The court held that there is no cause of action for "wrongful living."

4. Purely Consequential Economic Loss

Barber Lines A/S v. M/V Donau Maru

764 F.2d 50 (1st Cir. 1985)

BREYER, C.J. In December 1979 the ship Donau Maru spilled fuel oil into Boston Harbor. The spill prevented a different ship, the Tamara, from docking at a nearby berth. The Tamara had to discharge her cargo at another pier. In doing so, she incurred significant extra labor, fuel, transport and docking costs. The Tamara, her owners, and her charterers sued the Donau Maru and her owners in admiralty. Insofar as is here relevant, they claimed negligence and sought recovery of the extra expenses as damages. The district court denied recovery on the basis of the pleadings. . . . The plaintiffs have appealed. We believe the district court was correct, and we affirm its judgment, for three related sets of reasons.

1. Plaintiffs-appellants seek recovery for a financial injury caused by defendant's negligence. We assume that the injury was foreseeable. Nonetheless controlling case law denies that a plaintiff can recover damages for negligently caused financial harm, even when foreseeable, except in special circumstances. There is present here neither the most common such special circumstance — physical injury to the plaintiffs or to their property — nor any other special feature that would permit recovery. . . .

2. Before affirming the district court on the basis of existing precedent, we have asked ourselves whether that precedent remains good law. After all, courts have sometimes departed from past legal precedent where changing circumstances viewed in light of underlying legal policy deprived that precedent of sound support. Here, however, precedent seems, at least in general, to rest on a firm policy foundation. . . . Much written commentary, which for a time in the 1940's attacked the limitation, has more recently supported it, while offering a variety of refinements. . . .

The cases and commentaries, in making a plausible argument that existing precedent rests on sound considerations of policy, also reveal that these considerations are highly general and abstract. Judges lack the empirical information that would allow measurement of their force or magnitude; and, in particular, judges cannot apply these considerations on a case by case basis.

We have concluded that we could not find for appellants here without ignoring these policy considerations, or at a minimum, applying them case by case, a practice that we believe would be unwise. A brief description of the kinds of policy considerations typically advanced as supporting existing law (perhaps with a few modifications) will show why these considerations have led us to conclude that we must adhere to prior precedent.

First, cases and commentators point to pragmatic or practical administrative considerations which, *when taken together,* offer support for a rule limiting recovery for negligently caused pure financial harm. The number of persons suffering foreseeable financial harm in a typical accident is likely to be far greater than those who suffer traditional (recoverable) physical harm. The typical downtown auto accident, that harms a few persons physically and physically damages the property of several others, may well cause financial harm (e.g., through delay) to a vast number of potential plaintiffs. The less usual, negligently caused, oil spill foreseeably harms not only ships, docks, piers, beaches, wildlife, and the like, that are covered with oil, but also harms blockaded ships, marina merchants, suppliers of those firms, the employees of marina businesses and suppliers, the suppliers' suppliers, and so forth. To use the notion of "foreseeability" that courts use in physical injury cases to separate the financially injured allowed to sue from the financially injured not allowed to sue would draw vast numbers of injured persons within the class of potential plaintiffs in even the most simple accident cases (unless it leads courts, unwarrantedly, to narrow the scope of "foreseeability" as applied to persons suffering physical harm). That possibility — a large number of different plaintiffs each with somewhat different claims — in turn threatens to raise significantly the cost of even relatively simple tort actions. Yet the tort action is already a very expensive administrative device for compensating victims of accidents. Indeed, the legal time, the legal resources, the delay appurtenant to the tort action apparently mean that on average the victim recovers only between 28 and 44 cents of every dollar paid by actual or potential defendants, while victims who insure themselves directly recover at least between 55 and 66 cents of each premium dollar earned by insurance companies and between 85 and 90 cents of every dollar actually paid out to investigate and satisfy claims. The added cost of the increased complexity, while unknowable with precision, seems likely significant.

At the same time many of the "financially injured" will find it easier than the "physically injured" to arrange for cheaper, alternative compensation. The typical "financial" plaintiff is likely to be a business firm that, in any event, buys insurance, and which may well be able to arrange for "first party" loss compensation for foreseeable financial harm. Other such victims will be able to sue under tort principles, for they will suffer at least some physical harm to their property. Still others may have contracts with, or be able to contract with, persons who can themselves recover from the negligent defendant. A shipowner, for example, might contract with a dock owner for "inaccessibility" compensation; and the dock owner (whose pier is physically covered with oil) might recover this compensation as part of its tort damages. Of course, such a tort suit, embodying a "contract-defined" injury, may still raise difficult foreseeability questions, cf. Hadley v. Baxendale, 9 Exch. 341 (1854). But the bringing of one suit, instead of several, still makes the litigation as a whole a less costly compensation device. Finally, some of the "financially injured" will have suffered harm that is, in any event, noncompensable because it is not sufficiently distinguishable from minor harms typical of ordinary living. The law does not compensate, for example, the cost of unused baseball tickets or flowers needed for apology regardless of the cause of delay that foreseeably led to the added expense. Insofar as these considerations, taken as a whole, support recovery limitations, they reflect a fear of creating victim compensation costs that, from an administrative point of view, are unnecessarily high. See Stevenson v. East Ohio Gas Co., 73 N.E.2d 200, 202 (Ohio 1946).

A second set of considerations focuses on the "disproportionality" between liability and fault. Those who argue "disproportionality" are not reiterating the discredited nineteenth century view that tort liability would destroy industry, investment, or capitalism. Rather, they recognize that tort liability provides a powerful set of economic incentives and disincentives to engage in economic activity or to make it safer, see generally G. Calabresi, The Costs of Accidents (1970). And, liability for pure financial harm, insofar as it proved vast, cumulative and inherently unknowable in amount, could create incentives that are perverse.

Might not unbounded liability for foreseeable financial damage, for example, make auto insurance premiums too expensive for the average driver? Is such a result desirable? After all, the high premiums would reflect not *only* the costs of the harm inflicted; they would also reflect administrative costs of law suits, jury verdicts in uncertain amounts, some percentage of unbounded or inflated economic claims, and lessened incentive for financial victims to avoid harm or to mitigate damage. Given the existing liability for physical injury (and for accompanying financial injury), can one say that still higher premiums are needed to make the public realize that driving is socially expensive or to provide greater incentive to drive safely (an incentive that risk spreading through insurance dilutes in any event, see Shavell, On Liability and Insurance, 13 Bell J. of Econ. 120 [1982])?

These considerations, of administrability and disproportionality, offer plausible, though highly abstract, "policy" support for the reluctance of the courts to impose tort liability for purely financial harm. While they seem unlikely to apply with equal strength to every sort of "financial harm" claim, their abstraction and generality, along with the comparative inaccessibility of the empirical information needed to confirm or to invalidate them, mean that courts cannot weigh or apply them case by case. What, for example, in cases like this one, are the added administrative costs involved in allowing all persons suffering pure financial harm to sue the shipowner instead of "channeling" suits (perhaps via contract) through traditionally injured plaintiffs? Is there a problem of "disproportionality"? How far, for example, would additional, unbounded, pure financial loss liability for negligently caused oil spills, when added to the already large potential traditional liability, affect the type of insurance carried, the incentive to mitigate losses, the incentive to transport oil safely, the likelihood that shippers will use pipelines and domestic wells instead of ships and foreign wells, and the consequences of these and other related changes? We do not know the answers to these questions, nor can judges readily answer them in particular cases.

It does not surprise us then that, under these circumstances, courts have neither enforced one clear rule nor considered the matter case by case. Rather they have spoken of a general principle against liability for negligently caused financial harm, while creating many exceptions. (See, e.g., 1) Newlin v. New England Telephone & Telegraph Co., 316 Mass. 234, 54 N.E.2d 929 (1944) (accompanying physical harm); 2) Lumley v. Gye, 2 El. & Bl. 216, 118 Eng. Rep. 749 (1853); Beekman v. Marsters, 195 Mass. 205, 80 N.E. 817 (1907) (intentionally caused harm); 3) Dalton v. Meister, 52 Wis. 2d 173, 188 N.W.2d 494 (defamation), *cert. denied,* 405 U.S. 934, 92 S. Ct. 947, 30 L. Ed. 2d 810 (1971); Systems Operations, Inc. v. Scientific Games Development Corp., 555 F.2d 1131 (3d Cir. 1977) (injurious falsehood); 4) Hitaffer v. Argonne Co., 183 F.2d 811 (D.C. Cir.) (loss of consortium), *cert. denied,* 340 U.S. 852, 71 S. Ct. 80, 95 L. Ed. 624 (1950); 5) Chicago, Duluth & Georgia Bay Transit Co. v. Moore, 259 Fed. 490 (6th Cir.) (medical costs of injured plaintiff paid by a different family member), *cert. denied,* 251 U.S. 553, 40 S. Ct. 118, 64 L. Ed. 411 (1919); 6) Hedley Byrne Co. Ltd. v. Heller & Partners Ltd., A.C. 465 (1964) (negligent misstatements about financial matters); 7) Jones v. Waterman S.S. Corp., 155 F.2d 992 (3d Cir. 1946) (master-servant); 8) Western Union Telegraph Co. v. Mathis, 215 Ala. 282, 110 So. 399 (1926) (telegraph-addressee); 9) Union Oil Co. v. Oppen, 501 F.2d 558 (9th Cir. 1974) (commercial fishermen as special "favorites of admiralty").) These exceptions seem designed to pick out broad categories of cases where the "administrative" and "disproportionality" problems intuitively seem insignificant or where some strong countervailing consideration militates in favor of liability. Thus an award of financial damages to one *also* caused physical harm does not threaten proliferation of law suits, for the plaintiff could sue anyway (for physical damages). Financial harm awards to family members carry with them an obvious self-limiting principle (as perhaps does awarding such damages to fishermen, as "favorites" of admiralty). Awarding damages for financial harm caused by negligent misrepresentation is special in that, without such liability, tort law would not exert significant financial pressure to avoid negligence; a negligent accountant lacks physically harmed victims as potential plaintiffs.

We need not explore the exceptions in detail. Rather, we here simply point to the existence of plausible reasons underlying the judicial hesitance to award damages in a case like this one, and the need to consider exceptions by class rather than case by case.

The existence of these factors, together with our comparative inability to evaluate their empirical significance, cautions us against departing from prior law. . . .

We conclude that we should follow existing precedent that requires us, as a matter of law, to deny recovery. That precedent is reasonably consistent. It is supported by plausible considerations of tort policy. Appellants have failed to bring themselves within any recognized class or category in which financial damages are already allowed, and appellants have failed to provide convincing reasons for the creation of any new exception or class that would work to their legal benefit.

For these reasons, the judgment of the district court is affirmed.

In *Barber Lines*, then-judge Breyer adopts a broad version of the economic loss rule which might be restated as follows: "[T]he doctrine holds that, in the absence of a specific duty, no general duty exists to avoid negligently causing economic loss." Schaefer v. Indymac Mortg. Servs., 731 F.3d 98, 103 (1st Cir. 2013). On this broad account, specific duties permitting economic loss recovery include only certain exceptions to the rule of no liability such as those catalogued in the *Barber Lines* opinion. A narrower version of the economic loss rule holds that "parties bound by a contract may not pursue tort recovery for purely economic or commercial losses associated with the contract relationship." Id. (quotations omitted). On this narrow account, noncontractual parties may seek to establish tort claims for purely economic losses against their alleged wrongdoers, as the purpose of the economic loss rule is merely "to prevent tort law's unreasonable interference with principles of contract law." Id. (quotations omitted).

An early landmark case denying recovery for purely consequential economic loss is Robins Dry Dock & Repair Co. v. Flint, 275 U.S. 303 (1927), in which the Court held that plaintiff, a time-charterer of a boat that was owned by another and that was negligently damaged by defendant, could not recover in tort for pecuniary losses against defendant based solely on the fact of plaintiff's contractual relationship with the boat's owner. Justice Holmes wrote for the Court, "[A]s a general rule, at least, a tort to the person or property of one man does not make the tort-feasor liable to another merely because the injured person was under a contract with that other unknown to the doer of the wrong. The law does not spread its protection so far." Id. at 309. As noted by Judge Jon Newman in a recent opinion, "Nowhere in the text of *Robins Dry Dock* is there a broad statement that economic losses for an unintentional maritime tort are not recoverable in the absence of physical damage to the claimant's property." American Petroleum & Transport, Inc. v. City of New York, 737 F.3d 185 (2d. Cir 2013). Nevertheless, the broader reading of *Robins Dry Dock* has tended to prevail in the federal courts for purposes of maritime law. The *Barber Lines* opinion is notable for its forthright attempt to justify that expansive version of the doctrine.

Many state courts also favor the broader reading of the economic loss rule. In 532 Madison Avenue Gourmet Foods, Inc. v. Finlandia Center, Inc., 750 N.E.2d 1098 (N.Y. 2001), for instance, two consolidated cases presented the pure economic loss issue in terrestrial contexts. One involved the collapse of an office building's 39-story wall, and the other involved the collapse of a construction elevator tower. The plaintiffs, individually and as members of a class action, were merchants whose businesses were adversely affected by the closing of streets following the collapses. The suits against the owners, lessees, and managing agents of the collapsed office structures were for negligence. In denying recovery as a matter of law, the court expressed concern over the problems of imposing potentially unlimited liability and knowing just where to draw the liability line in instances in which the plaintiffs suffered no property damage.

Tying recovery for economic loss to the occurrence of some physical harm raises the same concerns about arbitrariness that have plagued courts dealing with liability for mental and emotional harm. In *Barber Lines*, for example, should the outcome really turn on whether the plaintiff's ship was smudged by the oil spilled by the defendant? In considering the validity of the physical harm requirement, consider the following argument in Harvey S. Perlman, Interference with Contract and Other Economic Expectancies: A Clash of Tort and Contract Theory, 49 U. Chi. L. Rev. 61, 71-72 (1982), dealing with the differences between physical and economic harms:

> In cases of physical injury to persons or property, the task of defining liability limits is eased, but not eliminated, by the operation of the laws of physics. Friction and gravity dictate that physical objects eventually come to rest. The amount of physical damage that can be inflicted by a speeding automobile or a thrown fist has a self-defining limit. Even in chain reaction cases, intervening forces generally are necessary to restore the velocity of the harm-creating object. These intervening forces offer a natural limit to liability.
>
> The laws of physics do not provide the same restraints for economic loss. Economic relationships are intertwined so intimately that disruption of one may have far-reaching consequences. Furthermore, the chain reaction of economic harm flows from one person to another without the intervention of other forces. Courts facing a case of pure economic loss thus confront the potential for liability of enormous scope, with no easily marked intermediate points and no ready recourse to traditional liability-limiting devices such as intervening cause.

Rather than limit recovery through a requirement of physical harm, the court in Sullivan v. Pulte Home Corp., 306 P.3d 1 (Ariz. 2013), chose to limit application of the economic loss rule by requiring parties to be in contractual privity with one another for the doctrine to apply and prevent tort adjudication. In that case, which exemplifies the narrow reading of the rule, subsequent purchasers of a home sued the builder for monetary losses arising from a construction defect. The court held that the economic loss rule was not a bar to the suit: "In Arizona, the doctrine bars only the recovery of pecuniary or commercial damage, including any decreased value or repair costs for a product or property that is itself the subject of a contract between the plaintiff and defendant, and consequential damages such as lost profits. We decline to extend the doctrine to non-contracting parties." Id. at 3 (citations and quotations omitted). Would the Arizona approach permit a negligence claim to proceed on the facts of *532 Madison*? See also Tiara Condo. Ass'n, Inc. v. Marsh & McLennan Cos., Inc., 110 So. 3d 399 (Fla. 2013) (holding that the economic loss rule in Florida only applies in the context of products liability claims involving no personal injury or separate property damage).

As the *Sullivan* and *Tiara Condominium Ass'n* holdings suggest, cases involving pure economic loss raise the potential for overlap and conflict between contract and tort law. Judge Frank Easterbrook highlighted the problem through the following hypothetical:

> Defendant sells 1,000 widgets for $10,000 apiece. If 1% of the widgets fail as the result of an avoidable defect, and each injury creates a loss of $50,000, then the group will experience 10 failures, and the injured buyers will be entitled to $500,000 in tort damages. That is full compensation for the entire loss; a manufacturer should not spend more than $500,000 to make the widgets safer. . . . Suppose, however, that uninjured buyers could collect damages on the theory that the risk of failure made each widget less valuable; had

> they known of the risk of injury, these buyers contend, they would have paid only $9,500 per widget — for the expected per-widget cost of injury is $500, and each buyer could have used the difference in price to purchase insurance (or to self-insure, bearing the risk in exchange for the lower price). On this theory the 990 uninjured buyers would collect a total of $495,000. The manufacturer's full outlay of $995,000 ($500,000 to the 10 injured buyers + $495,000 to the 990 uninjured buyers) would be nearly double the total loss created by the product's defect. This would both overcompensate buyers as a class and induce manufacturers to spend inefficiently much to reduce the risks of defects. A consistent system — $500 in damages to every buyer, or $50,000 in damages to every injured buyer — creates both the right compensation and the right incentives. A mixed system overcompensates buyers and leads to excess precautions.

In the Matter of Bridgestone/Firestone, Inc., Tires Products Liability Litigation, 288 F.3d 1012, 1017 (7th Cir. 2002). See also Vincent R. Johnson, The Boundary-Line Function of the Economic Loss Rule, 66 Wash. & Lee L. Rev. 523 (2009).

Do the following cases provide adequate solutions to the tensions between the desire for rules that are not arbitrary and the perceived need, expressed by Professor Perlman, to limit liability in some clear fashion? Do they sufficiently consider the potential for complicating interactions between tort and contract law, as suggested by Judge Easterbrook's example?

J'Aire Corp. v. Gregory

24 Cal. 3d 799, 598 P.2d 60, 157 Cal. Rptr. 407 (1979)

BIRD, C.J. Appellant, a lessee, sued respondent, a general contractor, for damages resulting from the delay in completion of a construction project at the premises where appellant operated a restaurant. Respondent demurred successfully and the complaint was dismissed. This court must decide whether a contractor who undertakes construction work pursuant to a contract with the owner of premises may be held liable in tort for business losses suffered by a lessee when the contractor negligently fails to complete the project with due diligence.

I

The facts as pleaded are as follows. Appellant, J'Aire Corporation, operates a restaurant . . . in premises leased from the County of Sonoma. Under the terms of the lease the county was to provide heat and air conditioning. In 1975 the county entered into a contract with respondent for improvements to the restaurant premises, including renovation of the heating and air conditioning systems and installation of insulation.

As the contract did not specify any date for completion of the work, appellant alleged the work was to have been completed within a reasonable time as defined by custom and usage. . . . Despite requests that respondent complete the construction promptly, the work was not completed within a reasonable time. Because the restaurant could not operate during part of the construction and was without heat and air conditioning for a longer period, appellant suffered loss of business and resulting loss of profits.

Appellant alleged two causes of action in its third amended complaint. The first cause of action was based upon the theory that it was a third party beneficiary of the contract between the county and respondent. The second cause of action sounded in tort and was based upon negligence in completing the work within a reasonable time. Damages of $50,000 were claimed.

Respondent demurred on the ground that the complaint did not state facts sufficient to constitute a cause of action. . . . The trial court sustained the demurrer without leave to amend and the complaint was dismissed. On appeal only the sustaining of the demurrer to the second cause of action is challenged.

II

. . . The only question before this court is whether a cause of action for negligent loss of expected economic advantage may be maintained under these facts.

Liability for negligent conduct may only be imposed where there is a duty of care owed by the defendant to the plaintiff or to a class of which the plaintiff is a member. . . . A duty of care may arise through statute or by contract. Alternatively, a duty may be premised upon the general character of the activity in which the defendant engaged, the relationship between the parties or even the interdependent nature of human society. . . . Whether a duty is owed is simply a shorthand way of phrasing what is "'the essential question—whether the plaintiff's interests are entitled to legal protection against the defendant's conduct.'" (Dillon v. Legg (1968) 68 Cal. 2d 728, 734, 69 Cal. Rptr. 72, 76, 441 P.2d 912, 916, quoting from Prosser, Law of Torts (3d ed. 1964) pp. 332-333. . . .)

This court has held that a plaintiff's interest in prospective economic advantage may be protected against injury occasioned by negligent as well as intentional conduct. For example, economic losses such as lost earnings or profits are recoverable as part of general damages in a suit for personal injury based on negligence. . . . Where negligent conduct causes injury to real or personal property, the plaintiff may recover damages for profits lost during the time necessary to repair or replace the property. . . .

Even when only injury to prospective economic advantage is claimed, recovery is not foreclosed. Where a special relationship exists between the parties, a plaintiff may recover for loss of expected economic advantage through the negligent performance of a contract although the parties were not in contractual privity. . . .

In each of the [other] cases, the court determined that defendants owed plaintiffs a duty of care by applying [certain] criteria. . . . Those criteria are (1) the extent to which the transaction was intended to affect the plaintiff, (2) the foreseeability of harm to the plaintiff, (3) the degree of certainty that the plaintiff suffered injury, (4) the closeness of the connection between the defendant's conduct and the injury suffered, (5) the moral blame attached to the defendant's conduct and (6) the policy of preventing future harm. . . .

Applying these criteria to the facts as pleaded, it is evident that a duty was owed by respondent to appellant in the present case. (1) The contract entered into between respondent and the county was for the renovation of the premises in which appellant maintained its business. The contract could not have been performed without impinging on that business. Thus respondent's performance was intended to, and did, directly affect appellant. (2) Accordingly, it was clearly foreseeable that any significant delay in completing the construction would adversely affect appellant's business beyond the normal disruption associated with such construction. Appellant alleges this fact was repeatedly drawn to respondent's attention. (3) Further, appellant's complaint leaves no doubt that appellant suffered harm since it was unable to operate its business for one month and suffered additional loss of business while the premises were without heat and air conditioning. (4) Appellant has also alleged that delays occasioned by the respondent's conduct were closely connected to, indeed directly caused its injury. (5) In addition, respondent's lack of diligence in the present case was particularly blameworthy since it continued after the probability of damage was drawn directly to respondent's attention. (6) Finally, public policy supports finding a duty of care in the present case. The wilful failure or refusal of a contractor to prosecute a construction project with diligence, where another is injured as a result, has been made grounds for disciplining a licensed contractor [by the state legislature]. . . . Although [the statute] does not provide a basis for imposing liability where the delay in completing construction is due merely to negligence, it does indicate the seriousness with which the Legislature views unnecessary delays in the completion of construction. . . .

To hold under these facts that a cause of action has been stated for negligent interference with prospective economic advantage is consistent with the recent trend in tort cases. This court has repeatedly eschewed overly rigid common law formulations of duty in favor of allowing compensation for foreseeable injuries caused by a defendant's want of ordinary care. (See, e.g., Dillon v. Legg, supra, 68 Cal. 2d at p. 746, 69 Cal. Rptr. 72, 441 P.2d 912 [liability for mother's emotional distress when child killed by defendant's negligence]; Rowland v. Christian (1968) 69 Cal. 2d 108, 119, 70 Cal. Rptr. 97, 443 P.2d 561 [liability of host for injury to social guest on premises]; cf. Brown v. Merlo (1973) 8 Cal. 3d 855, 106 Cal. Rptr. 388, 506 P.2d 212 [liability of automobile driver for injury to nonpaying passenger]; Rodriguez v. Bethlehem Steel Corp. (1974) 12 Cal. 3d 382, 115 Cal. Rptr. 765, 525 P.2d 669 [liability for loss of consortium].) Rather than traditional notions of duty, this court has focused on foreseeability as the key component necessary to establish liability:

> While the question whether one owes a duty to another must be decided on a case-by-case basis, every case is governed by the rule of general application that all persons are required to use ordinary care to prevent others from being injured as a result of their conduct. . . . [F]oreseeability of the risk is a primary consideration in establishing the element of duty.

(Weirum v. RKO General, Inc. (1975) 15 Cal. 3d 40, 46, 123 Cal. Rptr. 468, 471, 539 P.2d 36, 39, fn. omitted.) Similarly, respondent is liable if his lack of ordinary care caused foreseeable injury to the economic interests of appellant. . . .

The chief dangers which have been cited in allowing recovery for negligent interference with prospective economic advantage are the possibility of excessive liability, the creation of an undue burden on freedom of action, the possibility of fraudulent or collusive claims and the often speculative nature of damages. . . . Central to these fears is the possibility that liability will be imposed for remote consequences, out of proportion to the magnitude of the defendant's wrongful conduct.

However, the factors [discussed above] place a limit on recovery by focusing judicial attention on the foreseeability of the injury and the nexus between the defendant's conduct and the plaintiff's injury. These factors and ordinary principles of tort law such as proximate cause are fully adequate to limit recovery without the drastic consequence of an absolute rule which bars recovery in all such cases. (See Dillon v. Legg, supra, 68 Cal. 2d at p. 746, 69 Cal. Rptr. 72, 441 P.2d 912.) Following these principles, recovery for negligent interference with prospective economic advantage will be limited to instances where the risk of harm is  foreseeable and is closely connected with the defendant's conduct, where damages are not wholly speculative and the injury is not part of the plaintiff's ordinary business risk.

III

Accordingly, this court holds that a contractor owes a duty of care to the tenant of a building undergoing construction work to prosecute that work in a manner which does not cause undue injury to the tenant's business, where such injury is reasonably foreseeable. The demurrer to appellant's second cause of action should not have been sustained. The judgment of dismissal is reversed.

TOBRINER, MOSK, MANUEL, and NEWMAN, JJ., concur.

CLARK and RICHARDSON, JJ., concur in the judgment.

Notwithstanding the inherently economic nature of lost employment, courts have held that an employee who is terminated based on a false-positive drug test result may recover against the third party that negligently performed the test on behalf of the plaintiff's employer. Such liability generally arises from a special duty of reasonable care owed to employees due to the career-impacting nature of the test results. See, e.g., Berry v. National Med. Servs., Inc., 257 P.3d 287 (Kan. 2011) (alcohol-testing facility owed a duty of care to nurse participating in a substance abuse assistance program, given foreseeability of harm to her from false positive reports); Duncan v. Afton, Inc., 991 P.2d 739, 745 (Wyo. 1999) ("[A] company contracting with an employer to collect and handle specimens for employee alcohol testing . . . is aware that the likely effect of a false positive result is significant and devastating; employment will likely be terminated and future prospects of employment adversely impacted.").

What if a defendant's negligence foreseeably leads to layoffs for employees by disrupting their opportunities to work? In Lawrence v. O and G Industries, Inc., 126 A.3d 569 (Conn. 2015), individuals employed on a construction site sought recovery for lost wages after defendant's negligence caused an explosion at the site and termination of work. The court held that plaintiffs' claims were precluded by the economic loss rule.

J'Aire Corp. is analyzed in Robert L. Rabin, Tort Recovery for Negligently Inflicted Economic Loss: A Reassessment, 37 Stan. L. Rev. 1513 (1985), and Gary T. Schwartz, Economic Loss in American Tort Law: The Examples of *J'Aire* and of Products Liability, 23 San Diego L. Rev. 37 (1986). Professor Rabin's article is generally favorable to *J'Aire Corp.,* while Professor Schwartz's is critical. Both authors' contributions are assessed in Anthony J. Sebok, The Failed Promise of a General Theory of Pure Economic Loss: An Accident of History?, 61 DePaul L. Rev. 615 (2012).

People Express Airlines, Inc. v. Consolidated Rail Corp.

100 N.J. 246, 495 A.2d 107 (1985)

HANDLER, J. This appeal presents a question that has not previously been directly considered: whether a defendant's negligent conduct that interferes with a plaintiff's business resulting in purely economic losses, unaccompanied by property damage or personal injury, is compensable in tort. The appeal poses this issue in the context of the defendants' alleged negligence that caused a dangerous chemical to escape from a railway tank car, resulting in the evacuation from the surrounding area of persons whose safety and health were threatened. The plaintiff, a commercial airline, was forced to evacuate its premises and suffered an interruption of its business operations with resultant economic losses.

[The trial court entered summary judgment for the defendant. The appellate division reversed. Defendant appeals.]

II

The single characteristic that distinguishes parties in negligence suits whose claims for economic losses have been regularly denied by American and English courts from those who have recovered economic losses is, with respect to the successful claimants, the fortuitous occurrence of physical harm or property damage, however slight. It is well-accepted that a defendant who negligently injures a plaintiff or his property may be liable for all proximately caused harm, including economic losses. Nevertheless, a virtually *per se* rule barring recovery for economic loss unless the negligent conduct also caused physical harm has evolved throughout this century. . . .

The reasons that have been advanced to explain the divergent results for litigants seeking economic losses are varied. Some courts have viewed the general rule against recovery as necessary to limit damages to reasonably foreseeable consequences of negligent conduct. This concern in a given case is often manifested as an issue of causation and has led to the requirement of physical harm as an element of proximate cause. In this context, the physical harm requirement functions as part of the definition of the causal relationship between the defendant's negligent act and the plaintiff's economic damages; it acts as a convenient clamp on otherwise boundless liability. The physical harm rule also reflects certain deep-seated concerns that underlie courts' denial of recovery for purely economic losses occasioned by a defendant's negligence. These concerns include the fear of fraudulent claims, mass litigation, and limitless liability, or liability out of proportion to the defendant's fault.

The assertion of unbounded liability is not unique to cases involving negligently caused economic loss without physical harm. Even in negligence suits in which plaintiffs have sustained physical harm, the courts have recognized that a tortfeasor is not necessarily liable for *all* consequences of his conduct. While a lone act can cause a finite amount of physical harm, that harm may be great and very remote in its final consequences. A single overturned lantern may burn Chicago. Some limitation is required; that limitation is the rule that a tortfeasor is liable only for that harm that he proximately caused. Proximate or legal cause has traditionally functioned to limit liability for negligent conduct. Duty has also been narrowly defined to limit liability. Compare the majority and dissenting opinions in Palsgraf v. Long Island R.R., . . . 248 N.Y. 339, 162 N.E. 99. Thus, we proceed from the premise that principles of duty and proximate cause are instrumental in limiting the amount of litigation and extent of liability in cases in which no physical harm occurs just as they are in cases involving physical injury.

Countervailing considerations of fairness and public policy have led courts to discard the requirement of physical harm as an element in defining proximate cause to overcome the problem of fraudulent or indefinite claims. . . . In this context, we have subordinated the threat of potential baseless claims to the right of an aggrieved individual to pursue a just and fair claim for redress attributable to the wrongdoing of another. The asserted inability to define damages in cases arising under the cause of action for negligent infliction of emotional distress absent impact or near-impact has not hindered adjudication of those claims. Nor is there any indication that unfair awards have resulted.

The troublesome concern reflected in cases denying recovery for negligently-caused economic loss is the alleged potential for infinite liability, or liability out of all proportion to the defendant's fault. . . .

It is understandable that courts, fearing that if even one deserving plaintiff suffering purely economic loss were allowed to recover, all such plaintiffs could recover, have anchored their rulings to the physical harm requirement. While the rationale is understandable, it supports only a limitation on, not a denial of, liability. The physical harm requirement capriciously showers compensation along the path of physical destruction, regardless of the status or circumstances of individual claimants. Purely economic losses are borne by innocent victims, who may not be able to absorb their losses. In the end, the challenge is to fashion a rule that limits liability but permits adjudication of meritorious claims. The asserted inability to fix chrystalline formulae for recovery on the differing facts of future cases simply does not justify the wholesale rejection of recovery in all cases.

Further, judicial reluctance to allow recovery for purely economic losses is discordant with contemporary tort doctrine. The torts process, like the law itself, is a human institution designed to accomplish certain social objectives. One objective is to ensure that innocent victims have avenues of legal redress, absent a contrary, overriding public policy. This reflects the overarching purpose of tort law: that wronged persons should be compensated for their injuries and that those responsible for the wrong should bear the cost of the tortious conduct.

Other policies underlie this fundamental purpose. Imposing liability on defendants for their negligent conduct discourages others from similar tortious behavior, fosters safer products to aid our daily tasks, vindicates reasonable conduct that has regard for the safety of others, and, ultimately, shifts the risk of loss and associated costs of dangerous activities to those who should be and are best able to bear them. Although these policies may be unevenly reflected or imperfectly articulated in any particular case, we strive to ensure that the application of negligence doctrine advances the fundamental purpose of tort law and does not unnecessarily or arbitrarily foreclose redress based on formalisms or technicalisms. Whatever the original common law justifications for the physical harm rule, contemporary tort and negligence doctrine allow — indeed, impel — a more thorough consideration and searching analysis of underlying policies to determine whether a particular defendant may be liable for a plaintiff's economic losses despite the absence of any attendant physical harm. . . .

III

We may appropriately consider two relevant avenues of analysis in defining a cause of action for negligently-caused economic loss. The first examines the evolution of various exceptions to the rule of nonrecovery for purely economic losses, and suggests that the exceptions have cast considerable doubt on the validity of the current rule and, indeed, have laid the foundation for a rule that would allow recovery. The second explores the elements of a suitable rule and adopts the traditional approach of foreseeability as it relates to duty and proximate cause molded to circumstances involving a claim only for negligently-caused economic injury.

A

Judicial discomfiture with the rule of nonrecovery for purely economic loss throughout the last several decades has led to numerous exceptions in the general rule. Although the rationalizations for these exceptions differ among courts and cases, two common threads run throughout the exceptions. The first is that the element of foreseeability emerges as a more appropriate analytical standard to determine the question of liability than a *per se* prohibitory rule. The second is that the extent to which the defendant knew or should have known the particular consequences of his negligence, including the economic loss of a particularly foreseeable plaintiff, is dispositive of the issues of duty and fault. . . .

We hold therefore that a defendant owes a duty of care to take reasonable measures to avoid the risk of causing economic damages, aside from physical injury, to particular plaintiffs or plaintiffs comprising an identifiable class with respect to whom defendant knows or has reason to know are likely to suffer such damages from its conduct. A defendant failing to adhere to this duty of care may be found liable for such economic damages proximately caused by its breach of duty.

We stress that an identifiable class of plaintiffs is not simply a foreseeable class of plaintiffs. For example, members of the general public, or invitees such as sales and service persons at a particular plaintiff's business premises, or persons travelling on a highway near the scene of a negligently-caused accident, such as the one at bar, who are delayed in the conduct of their affairs and suffer varied economic losses, are certainly a foreseeable class of plaintiffs. Yet their presence within the area would be fortuitous, and the particular type of economic injury that could be suffered by such persons would be hopelessly unpredictable and not realistically foreseeable. Thus, the class itself would not be sufficiently ascertainable. An identifiable class of plaintiffs must be particularly foreseeable in terms of the type of persons or entities comprising the class, the certainty or predictability of their presence, the approximate numbers of those in the class, as well as the type of economic expectations disrupted. . . .

We recognize that some cases will present circumstances that defy the categorization here devised to circumscribe a defendant's orbit of duty, limit otherwise boundless liability and define an identifiable class of plaintiffs that may recover. In these cases, the courts will be required to draw upon notions of fairness, common sense and morality to fix the line limiting liability as a matter of public policy, rather than an uncritical application of the principle of particular foreseeability.

B

Liability depends not only on the breach of a standard of care but also on a proximate causal relationship between the breach of the duty of care and resultant losses. Proximate or legal causation is that combination of "logic, common sense, justice, policy and precedent" that fixes a point in a chain of events, some foreseeable and some unforeseeable, beyond which the law will bar recovery. The standard of particular foreseeability may be successfully employed to determine whether the economic injury was proximately caused, *i.e.,* whether the particular harm that occurred is compensable, just as it informs the question whether a duty exists.

Although not expressly eschewing the general rule against recovery for purely economic losses, our courts have employed a traditional proximate cause analysis in order to decide whether particular claimants may survive motions for summary judgment. These cases embody a distinction between those economic losses that are only generally foreseeable, and thus noncompensable, and those losses the defendant is in a position particularly to foresee. . . .

The particular-general foreseeability axis is also accordant with the policies underlying tort law. For good reason, tortfeasors are liable only for the results falling within the foreseeable risks of their negligent conduct. Assigning liability for harm that fortuitously extends beyond the foreseeable risk of negligent conduct unfairly punishes the tortfeasor for harm that he could not have anticipated and taken precautions to avoid. This comports with an underlying policy of the negligence doctrine: the imposition of liability should deter negligent conduct by creating incentives to minimize the risks and costs of accidents. The imposition of liability for unforeseeable risks cannot serve to deter the conduct that has eventuated in attenuated results, but instead arbitrarily assigns liability unrelated or out of proportion to the defendant's fault. If negligence is the failure to take precautions that cost less than the damage wrought by the ensuing accident, see United States v. Carroll Towing Co., 159 F.2d 169, 173, *reh. den.,* 160 F.2d 482 (2d Cir. 1947), it would be unfair and socially inefficient to assign liability for harm that no reasonably-undertaken precaution could have avoided.

We conclude therefore that a defendant who has breached his duty of care to avoid the risk of economic injury to particularly foreseeable plaintiffs may be held liable for actual economic losses that are proximately caused by its breach of duty. In this context, those economic losses are recoverable as damages when they are the natural and probable consequence of a defendant's negligence in the sense that they are reasonably to be anticipated in view of defendant's capacity to have foreseen that the particular plaintiff or identifiable class of plaintiffs, is demonstrably within the risk created by defendant's negligence.

IV

We are satisfied that our holding today is fully applicable to the facts that we have considered on this appeal. Plaintiff has set forth a cause of action under our decision, and it is entitled to have the matter proceed to a plenary trial. Among the facts that persuade us that a cause of action has been established is the close proximity of the North Terminal and People Express Airlines to the Conrail freight yard; the obvious nature of the plaintiff's operations and particular foreseeability of economic losses resulting from an accident and evacuation; the defendants' actual or constructive knowledge of the volatile properties of ethylene oxide; and the existence of an emergency response plan prepared by some of the defendants (alluded to in the course of oral argument), which apparently called for the nearby area to be evacuated to avoid the risk of harm in case of an explosion. We do not mean to suggest by our recitation of these facts that actual knowledge of the eventual economic losses is necessary to the cause of action; rather, particular foreseeability will suffice. The plaintiff still faces a difficult task in proving damages, particularly lost profits, to the degree of certainty required in other negligence cases. The trial court's examination of these proofs must be exacting to ensure that damages recovered are those reasonably to have been anticipated in view of the defendant's capacity to have foreseen that this particular plaintiff was within the risk created by their negligence.

We appreciate that there will arise many similar cases that cannot be resolved by our decision today. The cause of action we recognize, however, is one that most appropriately should be allowed to evolve on a case-by-case basis in the context of actual adjudications. We perceive no reason, however, why our decision today should be applied only prospectively. Our holdings are well grounded in traditional tort principles and flow from well-established exceptional cases that are philosophically compatible with this decision.

Accordingly, the judgment of the Appellate Division is modified, and, as modified, affirmed. The case is remanded for proceedings consistent with this opinion.

Of the courts that have recently considered the issue, it is probably fair to say that a majority have retreated from the no-liability rule of *Barber Lines*. It is also fair to say that among the courts that have moved away from the traditional rule, no consensus has emerged as to what is the appropriate rule of liability. The court in Aikens v. Debow, 541 S.E.2d 576 (W. Va. 2000), adopted a rule similar to that of *People Express Airlines*. In so doing, however, the court denied recovery to the plaintiff, the owner of a motel and restaurant, who alleged loss of business after the defendant's truck struck and damaged a bridge near the plaintiff's location because there was no special relationship or privity of contract between the defendant and the plaintiff.

The issue was also presented in Petitions of Kinsman Transit Co. (*Kinsman No. 2*), 388 F.2d 821 (2d Cir. 1968), which arose out of the same events as *Kinsman* (*No. 1*), discussed at pp. 298-299, above. *Kinsman* (*No. 2*) involved claims for extra expenses the petitioners incurred in filling contracts for the delivery of grain and in unloading cargo. The court denied recovery on the facts of the claims presented because the harm for which recovery was sought was "too remote or 'indirect' a consequence of defendants' negligence." 388 F.2d at 824. The court did agree, however, that tested by the usual rules of foreseeability, the consequences could be found to have been foreseeable. In denying recovery, the court relied heavily on Judge Andrews' view in the *Palsgraf* decision (388 F.2d at 824-25):

> On the previous appeal we stated aptly: "somewhere a point will be reached when courts will agree that the link has become too tenuous — that what is claimed to be consequence is only fortuity." 338 F.2d at 725. We believe that this point has been reached with the Cargill and Cargo Carriers claims. Neither the Gillies nor the Farr suffered any direct or immediate damage for which recovery is sought. The instant claims occurred only because the downed bridge made it impossible to move traffic along the river. Under all the circumstances of this case, we hold that the connection between the defendants' negligence and the claimants' damages is too tenuous and remote to permit recovery. "The law does not spread its protection so far." Holmes, J., in *Robins Dry Dock*, . . . 275 U.S. at 309, 48 S. Ct. at 135.
>
> In the final analysis, the circumlocution whether posed in terms of "foreseeability," "duty," "proximate cause," "remoteness," etc. seems unavoidable. As we have previously noted, 338 F.2d at 725, we return to Judge Andrews' frequently quoted statement in Palsgraf v. Long Island R.R., 248 N.Y. 339, 354-355, 162 N.E. 99, 104, 59 A.L.R. 1253 (1928) (dissenting opinion): "It is all a question of expediency . . . of fair judgment, always keeping in mind the fact that we endeavor to make a rule in each case that will be practical and in keeping with the general understanding of mankind."

In Union Oil Co. v. Oppen, 501 F.2d 558 (9th Cir. 1974), the claims arose out of the escape of oil from one of the defendant's offshore drilling platforms. The plaintiffs were commercial fishermen, and they sought to recover for the resulting reduction of the fishing potential in the waters affected by the spill. In ruling that the trial court properly permitted recovery, the court stated (501 F.2d at 570-71):

> Finally, it must be understood that our holding in this case does not open the door to claims that may be asserted by those, other than commercial fishermen, whose economic or personal affairs were discommoded by the oil spill of January 28, 1969. The general rule urged upon us by defendants has a legitimate sphere within which to operate. Nothing said in this opinion is intended to suggest, for example, that every decline in the general commercial activity of every business in the Santa Barbara area following the occurrences of 1969 constitutes a legally cognizable injury for which the defendants may be responsible. The plaintiffs in the present action lawfully and directly make use of a resource of the

> sea, viz. its fish, in the ordinary course of their business. This type of use is entitled to protection from negligent conduct by the defendants in their drilling operations. Both the plaintiffs and defendants conduct their business operations away from land and in, on and under the sea. Both must carry on their commercial enterprises in a reasonably prudent manner. Neither should be permitted negligently to inflict commercial injury on the other. We decide no more than this.

In State of Louisiana *ex rel.* Guste v. M/V Testbank, 752 F.2d 1019 (5th Cir. 1985), *cert. denied,* 477 U.S. 903 (1986), suit was brought by several plaintiffs arising out of a spill of PCP, a highly toxic substance, in the waters out of which the plaintiffs made their living. After the spill, the area was closed to all navigation. The court upheld summary judgment in favor of the defendants against the "shipping interests, marina and boat rental operators, wholesale and retail seafood enterprises not actually engaged in fishing, seafood restaurants, tackle and bait shops, and recreational fishermen." The trial judge did not grant summary judgment against the plaintiffs who were "commercial oystermen, shrimpers, crabbers and fishermen who had been making a commercial use" of the area, so the legitimacy of their claims was not involved in the appeal.

In Curd v. Mosaic Fertilizer, LLC, 39 So. 3d 1216 (Fla. 2010), commercial fishermen brought a class action against the owner of a fertilizer storage facility for economic loss resulting from the latter's spilling of pollutants into Tampa Bay. The fishermen, while not claiming ownership of the damaged marine and plant life, alleged that the spilled pollutants resulted in damage to the reputation of the products they are able to catch and sell, leading to lost income and profits. At trial, the court held that the fishermen's claims of strict liability and negligence were barred by the economic loss rule. On appeal, the intermediate appeals court affirmed the judgment, holding that the claims were unrelated to any damage to the fishermen's property and therefore purely economic. Nevertheless, the court found the question of whether there was a common law theory under which the fishermen could recover for economic loss caused by the negligent release of pollutants to be of great public importance and certified the issue to the Supreme Court of Florida. Answering the certification affirmatively, the Florida high court found that the economic loss rule did not prevent the fishermen from recovering. It reasoned that the defendant owed a duty to the fishermen arising out of the "nature of [defendant's] business and the special interest of the commercial fishermen in the use of the public waters." Id. at 1228. Furthermore, the court explained that the defendant's business of storing pollutants "created an appreciable zone of risk within which [it] was obligated to protect those who were exposed to harm" and that commercial fishermen in particular had a "special interest within that zone of risk, an interest not shared by the general community." Id. Thus, defendant's breach of its duty gave rise to a cause of action in negligence.

For a survey of how courts have reacted to consequential economic loss issues, see Herbert Bernstein, Civil Liability for Pure Economic Loss under American Tort Law, 46 Am. J. Comp. L. 111 (1998). For an analysis of the economic loss rule in common law jurisdictions outside of the United States, see Jane Stapleton, Comparative Economic Loss: Lessons from Case-Law-Focused "Middle Theory," 50 UCLA L. Rev. 531 (2002). For a discussion of alternative means of addressing losses from major oil spills, see Chapter 10, Section C.3 of this book. And for recent scholarly discussion of the economic loss rule in general, see Peter Benson, The Problem with Pure Economic Loss, 60 S.C. L. Rev. 823 (2009).

Problem 26

Your firm represents Reliance Insurance Company, the liability insurer of Willy Reston. Last year, Reston was involved in an accident with a truck owned by Capitol City Refrigeration Company. Reston was driving his car in excess of the speed limit and ran through a stop sign, so there is no issue as to his negligence. At the time of the accident, the Capitol City truck was on its way to the Red Arrow Restaurant. Red Arrow's air conditioning system had broken down, and the manager called Capitol City to make the repairs. The two men in the truck were the only employees of Capitol City who had the know-how to repair the system, but they were both injured, and were unable to get to the restaurant. The manager of Red Arrow was unable to locate another repair company in time to repair the system by noon of the next day. As a result, Red Arrow was forced to cancel an all-afternoon and evening reception for Caroline Saunders, who was running for the United States Senate.

Reliance concedes its liability for the damage to the Capitol City truck and for the injuries to the occupants of the truck. Also making claims against Reston are: Capitol City Refrigeration for the profit it lost on the repair contract with Red Arrow; Red Arrow for the profit it lost because it could not hold the reception at its restaurant; and the Committee to Elect Saunders, for the increase in the cost of holding the reception at another restaurant.

In advising Reliance of its exposure to these claims, assume that no opinion of the supreme court of your state has dealt with the issue of liability for negligently caused, purely consequential economic loss.

C. Contributory Fault

1. Contributory Negligence

Butterfield v. Forrester

11 East. 60, 103 Eng. Rep. 926 (K.B. 1809)

This was an action on the case for obstructing a highway, by means of which obstruction the plaintiff, who was riding along the road, was thrown down with his horse, and injured, &c. At the trial before Bayley J. at Derby, it appeared that the defendant, for the purpose of making some repairs to his house, which was close by the road side at one end of the town, had put up a pole across this part of the road, a free passage being left by another branch or street in the same direction. That the plaintiff left a public house not far distant from the place in question at 8 o'clock in the evening in August, when they were just beginning to light candles, but while there was light enough left to discern the obstruction at 100 yards distance: and the witness, who proved this, said that if the plaintiff had not been riding very hard he might have observed and avoided it: the plaintiff however, who was riding violently, did not observe it, but rode against it, and fell with his horse and was much hurt in consequence of the accident; and there was no evidence of his being intoxicated at the time. On this evidence Bayley J. directed the jury, that if a person riding with reasonable and ordinary care could have seen and avoided the obstruction; and if they were satisfied that the plaintiff was riding along the street extremely hard, and without ordinary care, they should find a verdict for the defendant: which they accordingly did. . . .

Lord Ellenborough, C.J. A party is not to cast himself upon an obstruction which has been made by the fault of another, and avail himself of it, if he do not himself use common and ordinary caution to be in the right. In cases of persons riding upon what is considered to be the wrong side of the road, that would not authorise another purposely to ride up against them. One person being in fault will not dispense with another's using ordinary care for himself. Two things must concur to support this action, an obstruction in the road by the fault of the defendant, and no want of ordinary care to avoid it on the part of the plaintiff.

Per Curiam. Rule refused.

Butterfield is generally considered to be the first case in which the plaintiff's negligence was held to bar recovery. The doctrine was soon introduced into the United States in Smith v. Smith, 19 Mass. (2 Pick.) 621 (1824).

The Restatement (Third) of Torts: Apportionment of Liability §3 (2000) defines the plaintiff's negligence as "conduct that falls below the standard to which the plaintiff should conform." Comment *a* states that the plaintiff's conduct is to be judged by "the same standard of negligence employed to evaluate a defendant's conduct." And that standard is one of reasonableness.

Proximate causation — although not typically as significant in the context of analyzing plaintiff's conduct as opposed to defendant's — still must be satisfied in order to hold that a plaintiff's contributory negligence bars recovery. In DeMoss v. Hamilton, 644 N.W.2d 302 (Iowa 2002), the court addressed the causal role of plaintiff's contributory negligence in the context of a medical malpractice action (644 N.W.2d at 306):

> [T]o be considered as and constitute contributory negligence in a medical malpractice action, a patient's negligence must have been an active and efficient contributing cause of the injury, must have cooperated with the negligence of the malpractitioner, must have entered into proximate causation of the injury, and must have been an element in the transaction on which the malpractice is based. Accordingly, in a medical malpractice action, the defense of contributory negligence is inapplicable when a patient's conduct provides the occasion for medical attention, care, or treatment which later is the subject of a medical malpractice claim or when the patient's conduct contributes to an illness or condition for which the patient seeks the medical attention, care, or treatment on which a subsequent medical malpractice claim is based.

Applying these principles, the court concluded that it was error for the trial court to have allowed the jury to consider plaintiff's contributory fault in failing to improve his exercise regimen and to quit smoking following a heart attack some two years prior to defendant's allegedly negligent failure to detect plaintiff's cardiac distress.

Davies v. Mann

152 Eng. Rep. 588 (1842)

At the trial, before Erskine, J., at the last Summer Assizes for the county of Worcester, it appeared that the plaintiff, having fettered the fore feet of an ass belonging to him, turned it into a public highway, and at the time in question the ass was grazing on the off side of a road about eight yards wide, when the defendant's wagon, with a team of three horses, coming down a slight descent, at what the witness termed a smartish pace, ran against the ass, knocked it down, and the wheels passing over it, it died soon after. The ass was fettered at the time, and it was proved that the driver of the wagon was some little distance behind the horses. The learned Judge told the jury, that though the act of the plaintiff, in leaving the donkey on the highway so fettered as to prevent his getting out of the way of carriages travelling along it, might be illegal, still, if the proximate cause of the injury was attributable to the want of proper conduct on the part of the driver of the wagon, the action was maintainable against the defendant; and his Lordship directed them, if they thought that the accident might have been avoided by the exercise of ordinary care on the part of the driver, to find for the plaintiff. The jury found their verdict for the plaintiff, damages 40s.

[The defendant's attorney moved for a new trial based on the plaintiff's contributory negligence.]

LORD ABINGER, C.B. I am of opinion that there ought to be no [new trial] in this case. The defendant has not denied that the ass was lawfully in the highway, and therefore we must assume it to have been lawfully there; but even were it otherwise, it would have made no difference, for as the defendant might, by proper care, have avoided injuring the animal, and did not, he is liable for the consequences of his negligence, though the animal may have been improperly there.

PARKE, B. This subject was fully considered by this Court in the case of Bridge v. The Grand Junction Railway Company, 3 M. & W. 246 [(Exch. 1838)], where, as appears to me, the correct rule is laid down concerning negligence, namely, that the negligence which is to preclude a plaintiff from recovering in an action of this nature, must be such as that he could, by ordinary care, have avoided the consequences of the defendant's negligence. I am reported to have said in that case, and I believe quite correctly, that "the rule of law is laid down with perfect correctness in the case of *Butterfield v. Forrester*, that, although there might have been negligence on the part of the plaintiff, yet unless he might, by the exercise of ordinary care, have avoided the consequences of the defendant's negligence, he is entitled to recover; if by ordinary care he might have avoided them, he is the author of his own wrong." In that case of *Bridge v. Grand Junction Railway Company*, there was a plea imputing negligence on both sides; here it is otherwise; and the Judge simply told the jury, that the mere fact of negligence on the part of the plaintiff in leaving his donkey on the public highway, was no answer to the action, unless the donkey's being there was the immediate cause of the injury; and that, if they were of opinion that it was caused by the fault of the defendant's servant in driving too fast or, which is the same thing, at a smartish pace, the mere fact of putting the ass upon the road would not bar the plaintiff of his action. All that is perfectly correct; for although the ass may have been wrongfully there, still the defendant was bound to go along the road at such a pace as would be likely to prevent mischief. Were this not so, a man might justify the driving over goods left on a public highway, or even over a man lying asleep there, or the purposely running against a carriage going on the wrong side of the road.

[The other judges concurred in denying a new trial.]

The rule in *Davies* is now generally known as the last clear chance doctrine. The Restatement (Second) of Torts provisions relating to last clear chance state:

§479. Last Clear Chance: Helpless Plaintiff

A plaintiff who has negligently subjected himself to a risk of harm from the defendant's subsequent negligence may recover for harm caused thereby if, immediately preceding the harm,

(a) the plaintiff is unable to avoid it by the exercise of reasonable vigilance and care, and

(b) the defendant is negligent in failing to utilize with reasonable care and competence his then existing opportunity to avoid the harm, when he

(i) knows of the plaintiff's situation and realizes or has reason to realize the peril involved in it or

(ii) would discover the situation and thus have reason to realize the peril, if he were to exercise the vigilance which it is then his duty to the plaintiff to exercise.

§480. Last Clear Chance: Inattentive Plaintiff

A plaintiff who, by the exercise of reasonable vigilance, could discover the danger created by the defendant's negligence in time to avoid the harm to him, can recover if, but only if, the defendant

(a) knows of the plaintiff's situation, and

(b) realizes or has reason to realize that the plaintiff is inattentive and therefore unlikely to discover his peril in time to avoid the harm, and

(c) thereafter is negligent in failing to utilize with reasonable care and competence his then existing opportunity to avoid the harm.

The last clear chance doctrine is generally recognized in this country in the circumstances set out in the Restatement (Second) of Torts, although there are a number of variations among the jurisdictions. One of the most unusual variations from outside of this country is that applied in British Columbia Elec. Ry. v. Loach, 1 A.C. 719 (P.C. 1916). In this case, the defendant's train left the station with defective brakes, and for that reason the engineer was unable to stop the train in time to avoid hitting the plaintiff, who had negligently stalled his wagon on the railroad tracks. The Privy Council ruled that the plaintiff could recover, even though his negligence occurred *after* the defendant had negligently dispatched its train. Adopting what is called the "antecedent last clear chance" rule, the Council observed (1 A.C. at 727) that the defendant was still liable, for otherwise it "would be in a better position, when they supplied a bad brake but a good motorman, than when the motorman was careless but the brake efficient." This variation of the last clear chance doctrine was rejected in Andersen v. Bingham & Garfield Ry., 214 P.2d 607 (Utah 1950).

Judge Richard Posner has recently characterized the last clear chance doctrine as an exception to the general common law rule rejecting a duty to rescue, stating that "[t]he last clear chance cases are a subset of the peril-caused-by-rescuer cases." Stockberger v. U.S., 332 F.3d 479, 482 (7th Cir. 2003). Just as non-negligent actors have a duty of reasonable care to aid those who are injured and rendered vulnerable by the actors' actions, see *Tubbs*, reproduced above, negligent actors with a potential defense of contributory negligence have an additional duty to avoid harm to the plaintiff, if they have the last clear chance to do so. Is Judge Posner's conceptual synthesis of the doctrines persuasive?

2. Assumption of the Risk

Meistrich v. Casino Arena Attractions, Inc.

31 N.J. 44, 155 A.2d 90 (1959)

WEINTRAUB, C.J. Plaintiff was injured by a fall while ice-skating on a rink operated by defendant. The jury found for defendant. The Appellate Division reversed, 54 N.J. Super. 25 (1959), and we granted defendant's petition for certification. 29 N.J. 582 (1959). . . .

The Appellate Division found error in the charge of assumption of the risk. It also concluded there was no evidence of contributory negligence and hence that issue should not have been submitted to the jury.

Defendant urges there was no negligence and therefore the alleged errors were harmless. We think there was sufficient proof to take the case to the jury. There was evidence that defendant departed from the usual procedure in preparing the ice, with the result that it became too hard and hence too slippery for the patron of average ability using skates sharpened for the usual surface. . . .

We however agree with defendant that the issue of contributory negligence was properly left to the trier of the facts. Plaintiff had noted that his skates slipped on turns. A jury could permissibly find he carelessly contributed to his injury when, with that knowledge, he remained on the ice and skated cross-hand with another.

The remaining question is whether the trial court's charge with respect to assumption of risk was erroneous. . . .

The Appellate Division . . . found the trial court failed to differentiate between assumption of risk and contributory negligence. The Appellate Division added:

> We note that contributory negligence involves some breach of duty on the part of the plaintiff. His actions are such as to constitute a failure to use such care for his safety as the ordinarily prudent man in similar circumstances would use. On the other hand, assumption of risk may involve no fault or negligence, but rather entails the undertaking of a risk or a known danger. Hendrikson v. Koppers Co., Inc., 11 N.J. 600, 607 (1953).

As we read the charge, the trial court expressed essentially the same thought, i.e., that assumption of risk may be found if plaintiff knew or reasonably should have known of the risk, notwithstanding that a reasonably prudent man would have continued in the face of the risk. We think an instruction to that effect is erroneous in the respect hereinafter delineated. The error is traceable to confusion in the opinions in our State.

Assumption of risk is a term of several meanings. For present purposes, we may place to one side certain situations which sometimes are brought within the sweeping term but which are readily differentiated from the troublesome area. Specifically we place beyond present discussion the problem raised by an express contract not to sue for injury or loss which may thereafter be occasioned by the covenantee's negligence, and also situations in which actual consent exists, as, for example, participation in a contact sport.

We here speak solely of the area in which injury or damage was neither intended nor expressly contracted to be non-actionable. In this area, assumption of risk has two distinct meanings. In one sense (sometimes called its "primary" sense), it is an alternate expression for the proposition that defendant was not negligent, i.e., either owed no duty or did not breach the duty owed. In its other sense (sometimes called "secondary"), assumption of risk is an affirmative defense to an established breach of duty. In its primary sense, it is accurate to say plaintiff assumed the risk whether or not he was "at fault," for the truth thereby expressed in alternate terminology is that defendant was not negligent. But in its secondary sense, i.e., as an affirmative defense to an established breach of defendant's duty, it is incorrect to say plaintiff assumed the risk whether or not he was at fault. . . .

Hence we think it clear that assumption of risk in its secondary sense is a mere phase of contributory negligence, the total issue being whether a reasonably prudent man in the exercise of due care (a) would have incurred the known risk and (b) if he would, whether such a person in the light of all of the circumstances including the appreciated risk would have conducted himself in the manner in which plaintiff acted.

Thus in the area under discussion there are but two basic issues: (1) defendant's negligence, and (2) plaintiff's contributory negligence. In view of the considerations discussed above, it has been urged that assumption of risk in both its primary and secondary senses serves merely to confuse and should be eliminated. . . .

In short, each case must be analyzed to determine whether the pivotal question goes to defendant's negligence or to plaintiff's contributory negligence. If the former, then what has been called assumption of risk is only a denial of breach of duty and the burden of proof is plaintiff's. If on the other hand assumption of risk is advanced to defeat a recovery despite a demonstrated breach of defendant's duty, then it constitutes the affirmative defense of contributory negligence and the burden of proof is upon defendant.

With the modification expressed above, the judgment of the Appellate Division is affirmed.

For modification — CHIEF JUSTICE WEINTRAUB, and JUSTICES BURLING, JACOBS, FRANCIS, and PROCTOR — 5.

Opposed — None.

As indicated in *Meistrich*, the principal issue involving assumption of the risk today is the extent to which it should constitute a separate defense in negligence actions. *Meistrich* represents the view that, except in instances of express agreement by the plaintiff to assume the risk involved in the defendant's conduct, the doctrine has no independent legal vitality, and that the plaintiff's conduct is to be gauged by the rules of contributory negligence.

The Restatement (Second) of Torts adopts the view that assumption of the risk constitutes an independent defense.[6] Section 496B provides:

> A plaintiff who by contract or otherwise expressly agrees to accept a risk of harm arising from the defendant's negligent or reckless conduct cannot recover for such harm, unless the agreement is invalid as contrary to public policy.

6. The Restatement (Third) of Torts: Apportionment of Liability §2 (2000) largely adopts the *Meistrich* rule, as does the Restatement (Third) of Torts: Liability for Physical and Emotional Harm §25 (2010). It is too early to tell whether those states that have essentially followed the Restatement (Second) (see, e.g., ADM Partnership v. Martin, 702 A.2d 730 (Md. 1997)) will adopt the new Restatement rules.

Section 496C provides:

> (1) Except as stated in Subsection (2), a plaintiff who fully understands a risk of harm to himself or his things caused by the defendant's conduct or by the condition of the defendant's land or chattels, and who nevertheless voluntarily chooses to enter or remain, or to permit his things to enter or remain within the area of that risk, under circumstances that manifest his willingness to accept it, is not entitled to recover for harm within that risk. (2) The rule stated in Subsection (1) does not apply in any situation in which an express agreement to accept the risk would be invalid as contrary to public policy.

Section 496C embodies what is known as "secondary" or "implied" assumption of the risk, and it is that aspect of the doctrine that was rejected in *Meistrich.* Under §496D, "[e]xcept where he expressly so agrees, a plaintiff does not assume a risk of harm arising from the defendant's conduct unless he then knows of the existence of the risk and appreciates its unreasonable character." (How does this provision differ from the *Meistrich* court's focus on unreasonableness?). Finally, under §496E, the plaintiff does not assume a risk if, as a result of the defendant's tortious conduct, the plaintiff has no reasonable alternative to avoid the harm.

Problem 27

Your client is Security Casualty Insurance Company. The claims manager has sought your advice with respect to an automobile liability claim made against its insured, Robert Dooley. Late one winter night Dooley was driving home on a lightly traveled country road after a party. He admits that he had had a bit too much to drink at the party and that he had difficulty controlling his car. He saw the claimant, Shirley DeVrees, standing at the roadside waving to him to stop. Dooley did stop, and DeVrees told him that her car had run out of gas and that she needed a ride into town. Dooley told her that given his intoxicated condition, she might be better off waiting for someone else to come along. DeVrees said that she could drive the car, but Dooley insisted that he drive. It was a cold night and DeVrees had only a lightweight coat on over her dress. She said that it was too cold to wait for who knows how long for another car, and she then got into the car. Shortly thereafter, Dooley passed out. The car ran off the road and into a tree. DeVrees was seriously injured.

Assume that your state supreme court has not had occasion to choose between *Meistrich* and the Restatement (Second) rules set out above. The claims manager would like your opinion as to whether DeVrees would be barred from recovery under either set of rules.

The Relationship Between Tort and Contract: Exculpatory Clauses

The court in *Meistrich*, in analyzing the circumstances under which the plaintiff may be barred from recovery by his assumption of the risks presented by the defendant's conduct, put to one side the problems raised by express provisions in contracts that by their terms purport to relieve one of the contracting parties from liability in negligence. One might assume that express provisions in contracts allocating losses would be routinely enforced; after all, it is commonly argued that the parties are in a better position than courts to make loss allocation decisions. But some courts have held that preinjury releases of liability, often called "exculpatory clauses," for personal injuries are void as against public policy. See, e.g., Hiett v. Lake Barcroft Cmty. Ass'n, 418 S.E.2d 894 (1992). Several courts expressly apply a stricter standard of scrutiny to anticipatory releases of liability than ordinary contract terms. See, e.g., Sweeney v. City of Bettendorf, 762 N.W.2d 873 (Iowa 2009); Provoncha v. Vermont Motocross Ass'n, Inc., 974 A.2d 1261 (Vt. 2009); Brown v. Soh, 909 A.2d 43 (Conn. 2006).

Most courts enforce preinjury releases of liability unless the releases violate judicial notions of public policy. See, e.g., Berlangieri v. Running Elk Corp., 76 P.3d 1098 (N.M. 2003). At least one jurisdiction places the burden of proof on defendants to prove that the release does not contravene public policy. See McGrath v. SNH Dev., Inc., 969 A.2d 392 (N.H. 2009). Not surprisingly, a repeatedly litigated issue is whether participation in recreational sports constitutes a public interest sufficient to void preinjury liability releases. Compare Pearce v. Utah Athletic Found., 179 P.3d 760, 767 (Utah 2008) (holding, in the context of a bobsledding accident, that "preinjury releases for recreational activities are not invalid under the public interest exception"), with Hanks v. Powder Ridge Rest. Corp., 885 A.2d 734 (Conn. 2005) (holding, in the context of a snowtubing accident, that a preinjury release for commercial recreational activities "affects the public interest adversely and, therefore, is unenforceable because it violates public policy") and Bagley v. Mt. Bachelor, Inc., 340 P.3d 27 (Or. 2014) (holding that enforcement of an anticipatory negligence release would be unconscionable in the case of a snowboarding accident). Judicial screening through the lens of public policy is consistent with both the Restatement (Second) of Torts §496B and the Restatement (Third) of Torts: Apportionment of Liability §2 (2000). Comment *e* to the latter states:

> Some contracts for assumption of risk are unenforceable as a matter of public policy. Whether an exculpatory contract is unenforceable depends on the nature of the parties and their relationship to each other, including whether one party is in a position of dependency; the nature of the conduct or service provided by the party seeking exculpation, including whether the conduct or service is laden with "public interest"; the extent of the exculpation; the economic setting of the transaction; whether the document is a standardized contract of adhesion; and whether the party seeking exculpation was willing to provide greater protection against negligence for a reasonable, additional fee. Exculpatory contracts may be unenforceable on contract principles, such as fraud, misrepresentation, duress, undue influence, or mistake.

Courts often examine exculpatory clauses to determine if they involve some larger public interest. For example, in Henrioulle v. Marin Ventures, Inc., 573 P.2d 465 (Cal. 1978), the court refused to enforce an exculpatory clause in a residential lease, emphasizing that residential shelter is a necessity, and that there is an inequality of bargaining power between the landlord and tenant. Perhaps reflecting the greater availability of residential rental properties, courts today seem more willing to enforce exculpatory clauses in leases, if they otherwise meet the specificity requirements. See Warren v. Paragon Techns. Grp., Inc., 950 S.W.2d 844 (Mo. 1997).

The court in *Henrioulle* gave as one reason for setting the clause aside that the landlord performed an important service, which was of "practical necessity" to the public. Similar reasoning was employed by the court in Kopischke v. First Cont'l Corp., 610 P.2d 688 (Mont. 1980). A clause in a contract for the sale of a used car provided that "All used cars are sold on an as is basis with no guarantee either express or implied except as noted above." In refusing to enforce the clause, the court stated that liability cannot be disclaimed by "one performing an act in the public interest," and that inspecting used cars before sale is such an act. But the operation of a recreation program for seniors at a community center does not involve the public interest, or at least the court in YMCA of Metropolitan Los Angeles v. Superior Court, 63 Cal. Rptr. 2d 612 (Ct. App. 1997), so held in enforcing a release of liability.

Stelluti v. Casapenn Enterprises, LLC

1 A.3d 678 (N.J. 2010)

JUSTICE LAVECCHIA delivered the opinion of the Court.

On January 13, 2004, while participating in a spinning class at a private fitness center, the handlebars on plaintiff Gina Stelluti's spin bike dislodged from the bike, causing her to fall and suffer injuries. Stelluti brought a negligence action against the fitness center. The trial court granted summary judgment for the fitness center and the intermediate appellate court affirmed. Stelluti appealed. In this appeal we must determine whether plaintiff should be bound to a preinjury waiver of liability that she executed in connection with her membership application and agreement. We conclude, for the reasons expressed herein, that the exculpatory agreement between the fitness center and Stelluti is enforceable as to the injury Stelluti sustained when riding the spin bike.

I

Stelluti entered into an agreement with defendant Powerhouse Gym for membership at its Brick, New Jersey facility. To do so, she filled out [several forms].

[Among the forms she signed was a Waiver & Release form, which read in part:

> This waiver and release of liability includes, without limitation, all injuries which may occur as a result of (a) your use of all amenities and equipment in the facility and your participation in any activity, class, program, personal training or instruction, (b) the sudden and unforeseen malfunctioning of any equipment, (c) our instruction, training, supervision, or dietary recommendations, and (d) your slipping and/or falling while in the club, or on the club premises, including adjacent sidewalks and parking areas.
>
> You acknowledge that you have carefully read this "waiver and release" and fully understand that it is a **release of liability.** You expressly agree to release and discharge the health club, and all affiliates, employees, agents, representatives, successors, or assigns, from any and all claims or causes of action and you agree to voluntarily give up or waive any right that you may otherwise have to bring a legal action against the club for personal injury or property damage.
>
> To the extent that statute or case law does not prohibit releases for negligence, this release is also for negligence on the part of the Club, its agents, and employees.
>
> If any portion of this release from liability shall be deemed by a Court of competent jurisdiction to be invalid, then the remainder of this release from liability shall remain in full force and effect and the offending provision or provisions severed here from.
>
> By signing this release, I acknowledge that I understand its content and that this release cannot be modified orally.
>
> Signed: /s/ Gina Stelluti Names of family members (if applicable):]

Any patron who declined to sign the waiver was not permitted to use the Powerhouse Gym.

Stelluti's injury occurred at the gym the day that she joined. After signing the requisite paperwork to become a member, she went to participate in a spinning class. She advised the instructor of her inexperience and the instructor helped her to adjust the bike seat for height and showed her how to strap her feet to the pedals. The instructor then told Stelluti to watch and imitate her during the class.

As the class began, the participants started out pedaling in a seated position. Shortly afterward, the instructor told the participants to change from a seated to a standing position on their bikes. When Stelluti rose to a standing position, the handlebars dislodged from the bike. As a result, Stelluti fell forward while her feet remained strapped to the pedals. With assistance, she succeeded in detaching herself from the bike. When she tried to resume participation after resting for fifteen minutes, she soon had to quit, finding herself in too much pain to continue.

Stelluti's injuries included pain in her neck and shoulders, soreness in her thighs and back, a cracked tooth, and bruises on her legs. After a hospital visit, she was diagnosed with back and neck strain, prescribed medication, and discharged with a recommendation for a follow-up appointment with a doctor. She claims also to experience persistent pain as a result of the incident. Her medical expert has stated that three years after her accident Stelluti suffers from chronic pain associated with myofascial pain syndrome . . . .

III

As a general and long-standing matter, contracting parties are afforded the liberty to bind themselves as they see fit. *See* Twin City Pipe Line Co. v. Harding Glass Co., 283 U.S. 353, 356, 51 S. Ct. 476, 477, 75 L. Ed. 1112, 1116 (1931) ("The general rule is that competent persons shall have the utmost liberty of contracting and that their agreements voluntarily and fairly made shall be held valid and enforced in the courts."). Out of respect for that very basic freedom, courts are hesitant to interfere with purely private agreements.

However, certain categories of substantive contracts, including those that contain exculpatory clauses, have historically been disfavored in law and thus have been subjected to close judicial scrutiny.

In that consideration, it has been held contrary to the public interest to sanction the contracting-away of a statutorily imposed duty. An agreement containing a pre-injury release from liability for intentional or reckless conduct also is plainly inconsistent with public policy. . . . Beyond those clear parameters to inviolate public policy principles, the weighing process becomes opaque. The Appellate Division identified four considerations, pertinent to the enforcement of an exculpatory agreement. . . .

> [Such an agreement] will be enforced if (1) it does not adversely affect the public interest; (2) the exculpated party is not under a legal duty to perform; (3) it does not involve a public utility or common carrier; or (4) the contract does not grow out of unequal bargaining power or is otherwise unconscionable.

The . . . test, used by the panel below, captures the essential features to be explored when considering whether enforcement of an exculpatory agreement would be contrary to public policy. Other courts in sister jurisdictions have developed similar tests. One, which originated with the Supreme Court of California in Tunkl v. Regents of the University of California, 60 Cal. 2d 92, 32 Cal. Rptr. 33, 383 P.2d 441, 445-46 (1963), uses six inquiries[11] and it also has been identified as helpful. Although slightly more nuanced, *Tunkl*'s considerations . . . can provide additional guidance when applying the test that has been employed by our appellate courts and that we find acceptable also in the resolution of the instant exculpatory agreement. We thus turn to consider the specifics of the agreement.

IV

A

As a threshold matter, to be enforceable an exculpatory agreement must "reflect the unequivocal expression of the party giving up his or her legal rights that this decision was made voluntarily, intelligently and with the full knowledge of its legal consequences." . . . When a party enters into a signed, written contract, that party is presumed to understand and assent to its terms, unless fraudulent conduct is suspected. . . .

The agreement in question explicitly stated that it covered "the sudden and unforeseen malfunctioning of any equipment, . . . use of all amenities and equipment in the facility and . . . participation in any activity, class, program, personal training or instruction." In addition, the agreement explicitly covered negligence: "this release is also for negligence on the part of the Club, its agents, and employees." Further, terms that limited Powerhouse's liability — "entirely at your own risk," "assume all risks," and "release of liability" — were set forth prominently in the written document that Stelluti signed and from which she now seeks to be excused. Although Stelluti argues that she did not know what she was signing, she does not claim that she signed the waiver form as the result of fraud, deceit, or misrepresentation. Therefore, the trial court was well within reason to presume that she understood the terms of the agreement, *see ibid.,* and the finding to that effect is unassailable . . . .

B

When considering whether enforcement of the instant exculpatory agreement would adversely affect the public interest, the inquiry naturally blends into an examination of whether the exculpated party is under a legal duty to perform. Exculpatory agreements that attempt to release liability for statutorily imposed duties have been held invalid. When the subject of an exculpatory agreement is not governed by statute, we also have considered common law duties in weighing relevant public policy considerations. To a certain extent, we cannot view [the] public-interest inquiry separate from the question of whether there is a legal duty owed that is inviolate and non-waivable. In performing the weighing of public policy interests, then, we must take into account, in this private setting, both the extant common law duties and the right to freely agree to a waiver of a right to sue, which is part

11. *Tunkl* references the following inquiries as pertinent when determining whether to enforce an exculpatory agreement: 1) whether the agreement involves a business generally suitable for public regulation; 2) whether the exculpated party provides a service important and necessary to the public; 3) whether the exculpated party offers services to any person of the public seeking those services; 4) whether the exculpated party possesses a stronger bargaining power relative to the member of the public seeking services; 5) whether the exculpated party presents the member of the public with a contract of adhesion; and 6) whether the member of the public is under the control of the exculpated party and thus is subject to the careless risks of the more powerful party. *Tunkl, supra,* 32 Cal. Rptr. 33, 383 P.2d at 445-446.

and parcel to the freedom to contract to which we earlier adverted. The mere existence of a common law duty does not mean that there is no room for an exculpatory agreement. In other words, our analysis begins from the starting point that public policy does not demand a per se ban against enforcement of an exculpatory agreement based on the mere existence of a duty recognized in the common law in respect of premises liability. . . .

To properly balance the public-policy interests implicated in the instant matter one must consider the nature of the activity and the inherent risks involved.[13] Engaging in physical activity, particularly in private gyms and health clubs, is commonplace in today's society. The United States Bureau of Labor estimates that over the next decade jobs for physical fitness workers will increase faster than other occupations due to the increasing recognition of health benefits associated with physical activity and, consequently, increase the amount of time and money spent on fitness.

By its nature, exercising entails vigorous physical exertion. Injuries from exercise are common; indeed minor injuries can be expected — for example, sore muscles following completion of a tough exercise or workout may be indicative of building or toning muscles. Those injuries and others may result from faulty equipment, improper use of equipment, inadequate instruction, inexperience or poor physical condition of the user, or excessive exertion. . . .

Although there is public interest in holding a health club to its general common law duty to business invitees — to maintain its premises in a condition safe from defects that the business is charged with knowing or discovering — it need not ensure the safety of its patrons who voluntarily assume some risk by engaging in strenuous physical activities that have a potential to result in injuries. Any requirement to so guarantee a patron's safety from *all* risk in using equipment, which understandably is passed from patron to patron, could chill the establishment of health clubs. Health clubs perform a salutary purpose by offering activities and equipment so that patrons can enjoy challenging physical exercise. There has been recognized a "positive social value" in allowing gyms to limit their liability in respect of patrons who wish to assume the risk of participation in activities that could cause an injury. And, further, it is not unreasonable to encourage patrons of a fitness center to take proper steps to prepare, such as identifying their own physical limitations and learning about the activity, before engaging in a foreign activity for the first time.

However, just as we held in *Crawn, supra,* that there remains a standard for liability even in contact recreational sports, albeit a heightened one, there is also a limit to the protections that a private fitness center reasonably may exact from its patrons through the mechanism of an exculpatory agreement. Although it would be unreasonable to demand that a fitness center inspect each individual piece of equipment after every patron's use, it would be unreasonable, and contrary to the public interest, to condone willful blindness to problems that arise with the equipment provided for patrons' use. Thus, had Powerhouse's management or employees been aware of a piece of defective exercise equipment and failed to remedy the condition or to warn adequately of the dangerous condition, or if it had dangerously or improperly maintained equipment, Powerhouse could not exculpate itself from such reckless or gross negligence. That showing was not made on this record.

13. Our focus here substantially contemplates one of *Tunkl*'s inquiries, specifically whether the member of the public is under the control of the exculpated party and thus subject to the careless risks by the more powerful party. *See Tunkl, supra,* 32 Cal. Rptr. 33, 383 P.2d at 445-46. That question takes into account the patron's opportunity for self-protection, which removes the possibility that the injury could only be prevented by the operator. *See* Robert Heidt, The Avid Sportsman and the Scope for Self-Protection: When Exculpatory Clauses Should Be Enforced, 38 U. Rich. L. Rev. 381, 460-73 (2004).

As previously noted, the Appellate Division specifically found that the record was barren of evidence that Powerhouse had neglected over time to maintain its equipment. *Stelluti, supra,* 408 N.J. Super. at 460-61, 975 A.2d 494 (finding absence of any "chronic or repetitive patterns of inattention to the safety of the equipment"). There simply was no evidence in this record rising to such reckless or gross negligence in respect of Powerhouse's duty to inspect and maintain its equipment. Thus, we do not share the concern voiced by the dissent. Our decision cannot reasonably be read to signal that health clubs will be free to engage in "chronic or repetitive patterns of inattention to the safety of the[ir] equipment." *Ibid.* Nor do we share the dissent's view that today's holding gives a green light to permit widespread use of exculpatory agreements in restaurants, malls, and supermarkets. That extrapolation fails to account for our careful examination into the relevant nature of the type of activity that takes place in a private health club.

In sum, the standard we apply here places in fair and proper balance the respective public-policy interests in permitting parties to freely contract in this context (i.e., private fitness center memberships) and requires private gyms and fitness centers to adhere to a standard of conduct in respect of their business. Specifically, we hold such business owners to a standard of care congruent with the nature of their business, which is to make available the specialized equipment and facility to their invitees who are there to exercise, train, and to push their physical limits. That is, we impose a duty not to engage in reckless or gross negligence. We glean such prohibition as a fair sharing of risk in this setting, which is also consistent with the analogous assumption-of-risk approach used by the Legislature to allocate risks in other recreational settings with limited retained-liability imposed on operators.

V

For the foregoing reasons, we affirm the judgment of the Appellate Division that sustained the award of summary judgment to defendant.

JUSTICE ALBIN, dissenting.

Today the Court has abandoned its traditional role as the steward of the common law. For the first time in its modern history, the Court upholds a contract of adhesion with an exculpatory clause that will allow a commercial, profit-making company to operate negligently — injuring, maiming, and perhaps killing one of its consumer-patrons — without consequence. Under the Court's ruling, a health club will have no obligation to maintain its equipment in a reasonably safe manner or to require its employees to act with due care toward its patrons. That is because, the Court says, a health club patron has the *right* to contract not only for unsafe conditions at a health club, but also for careless conduct by its employees. The Court's decision will ensure that these contracts of adhesion will become an industry-wide practice and that membership in health clubs will be conditioned on powerless consumers signing a waiver immunizing clubs from their own negligence. The Court's ruling undermines the common-law duty of care that every commercial operator owes to a person invited onto its premises.

Without the incentive to place safety over profits, the cost to the public will be an increase in the number of avoidable accidents in health clubs. And like the plaintiff in this case, the victims of the clubs' negligence will suffer the ultimate injustice — they will have no legal remedy.

Tens of thousands of New Jersey citizens join health clubs to stay healthy — to reduce the prospect of suffering from heart disease or a stroke, to battle obesity, and to improve the likelihood of living a longer life. The irony is that those who seek to live a better lifestyle through membership at a health club, now, will have a greater likelihood of having their well-being impaired through the careless acts of a club employee.

The ruling today is not in the public interest, not consistent with this Court's long-standing, progressive common-law jurisprudence protecting vulnerable consumers, and not in step with the enlightened approaches taken by courts of other jurisdictions that have barred the very type of exculpatory clause to which this Court gives its imprimatur.

Because in upholding the exculpatory agreement the Court wrongly dismisses the case of plaintiff, Gina Stelluti, I respectfully dissent. . . .

3. Comparative Negligence

Contributory negligence as a complete bar to recovery by the plaintiff has been replaced in almost every jurisdiction by a variety of comparative fault regimes, under which the recovery may be reduced, but not necessarily eliminated, by the plaintiff's own fault. The impetus for this shift came primarily from the perceived unfairness of the contributory fault regime. See, e.g., Fleming James, Jr., Contributory Negligence, 62 Yale L.J. 691 (1953). While cases like *Butterfield* seemed comfortable with the notion that recovery had to be all or nothing, courts and legislatures ultimately rejected this simplistic approach to fault. Even before the switch to comparative fault occurred, it was often assumed that juries apply a rough and ready comparative negligence of their own, in violation of the instructions they received from the judges, by entering a judgment against a negligent defendant while simultaneously decreasing a plaintiff's recovery because of the plaintiff's own negligence. See, e.g., Jack B. Weinstein, Routine Bifurcation of Jury Negligence Trials: An Example of the Questionable Use of Rule Making Power, 14 Vand. L. Rev. 831 (1961). The role of plaintiff fault has been examined under the lens of economic analysis, and most of the commentary comes down on the side of comparative fault. See, e.g., Daniel Orr, The Superiority of Comparative Negligence: Another Vote, 20 J. Legal. Stud. 119 (1991).

The comparative negligence concept is not new. The first state to enact a general comparative negligence statute was Mississippi in 1910. Miss. Code Ann. §1454. The Federal Employers Liability Act, enacted in 1906, incorporates the principle of comparative negligence. 45 U.S.C.A. §53. Comparative negligence has long been a rule of admiralty law (see A. Chalmers Mole & Lyman P. Wilson, A Study of Comparative Negligence, 17 Cornell L.Q. 333 (1932)), and its origins have been traced to ancient Roman and medieval sea law (see Ernest A. Turk, Comparative Negligence on the March, 28 Chi.-Kent L. Rev. 189 (1950)).

Although the core concept of comparative fault — that the plaintiff's recovery should not necessarily be barred completely by contributory negligence — is easily agreed upon, there are substantial state-by-state variations in the implementation of that concept, as the following illustrates.

1. Bases of Liability. As a general matter, comparative fault regimes compare the negligence of the parties. But how should comparative fault work out if there are different bases of liability? In products liability cases, for example, the defendant may be subject to strict liability. How can the plaintiff's negligence be compared to the defendant's strict liability? That issue is addressed in Chapter 7. And what if the defendant is guilty of some sort of aggravated fault, such as willful, wanton, or intentional conduct? The court in Burke v. 12 Rothchild's Liquor Mart, Inc., 593 N.E.2d 522 (Ill. 1992), held that a defendant guilty of that sort of conduct is not entitled to a reduction in damages based on the plaintiff's fault. See also Murray v. Chicago Youth Ctr., 864 N.E.2d 176 (Ill. 2007); Specialized Commercial Lending, Inc. v. Murphy-Blossman Appraisal Servs. LLC, 978 So. 2d 927 (La. Ct. App. 2007) (comparative negligence is not a defense to willful or intentional conduct). The court in Blazovic v. Andrich, 590 A.2d 222 (N.J. 1991), took the opposite view, and ruled that the comparative fault statute does apply in cases in which the defendant acted intentionally. See also Frugis v. Bracigliano, 827 A.2d 1040 (N.J. 2003). In general, see Gail D. Hollister, Using Comparative Fault to Replace the All-or-Nothing Lottery Imposed in Intentional Tort Suits in Which Both Plaintiff and Defendant Are at Fault, 46 Vand. L. Rev. 121 (1993).

2. Intentional Wrongdoing of Third Persons. How should the law handle the case where the plaintiff has been injured by the negligence of the defendant and the intentional or willful wrongdoing of another person? The Restatement (Third) of Torts:

Apportionment of Liability §14 (2000) covers this type of case:

> A person who is liable to another based on a failure to protect the other from the specific risk of an intentional tort is jointly and severally liable for the share of comparative responsibility assigned to the intentional tortfeasor in addition to the share of comparative responsibility assigned to the person.

The Restatement uses as an illustration a case in which a hotel operated by the defendant has inadequate security devices, and as a result of the inadequacy the plaintiff is injured by an intruder. See also Ellen M. Bublick, Citizen No-Duty Rules: Rape Victims and Comparative Fault, 99 Colum. L. Rev. 1413 (1999).

If the intentional tortfeasor's conduct is not the precise conduct that the defendant is obligated to guard against, this rule does not apply. See, e.g., Board of County Commissioners v. Bassett, 8 P.3d 1079 (Wyo. 2000), in which a suspect fleeing police in a high-speed chase intentionally rammed into the plaintiff's automobile, injuring her. The court held that a portion of the total fault, for which the police would not be liable, should be assigned to the suspect.

3. Type of Plaintiff Fault. There is disagreement among the courts as to whether all forms of plaintiff fault should reduce recovery. What if the fault is the failure of the plaintiff to mitigate damages after the accident? The court in Ostrowski v. Azzara, 545 A.2d 148 (N.J. 1988), held that the failure to mitigate damages reduces, but not necessarily eliminates, recovery for the damages the plaintiff could have avoided. But see Weston v. Dun Transp., 695 S.E.2d 279, 282 (Ga. Ct. App. 2010) (holding that the plaintiff's failure to mitigate damages caused by the defendant's negligence was a complete bar to recovery, and stating: "The plaintiff must exercise ordinary care for [her] own safety, and must by the same degree of care avoid the effect of the defendants' negligence after it becomes apparent to [her] or in the exercise of ordinary care [she] should have learned of it" (citing Ga. Code Ann. §51-11-7 (2000)). Some courts have held that when the pre-accident conduct by the plaintiff is the failure to use an available seat belt, recovery for the increment of harm caused by that failure should preclude recovery altogether. See, e.g., Foley v. City of West Allis, 335 N.W.2d 824 (Wis. 1983). Other courts have ruled that comparative negligence principles apply in these cases. See, e.g., Davis v. Knippling, 576 N.W.2d 525 (S.D. 1998). Finally, in a number of states, failure of the plaintiff to wear a seat belt is entirely ignored in calculating damages, either by judicial decision (see, e.g., Thomas v. Henson, 695 P.2d 476 (N.M. 1985)) or by statute (see, e.g., Minn. Stat. Ann. ch. 169.685).

4. The Basis of Allocation of Damages Between Plaintiff and Defendant. There are two main approaches to the allocation of the plaintiff's damages between the plaintiff and the defendant. One is "pure" comparative fault, under which the plaintiff's recovery is reduced, but never eliminated, solely because of the plaintiff's negligence. If the plaintiff were allocated 100 percent of the negligence, the defendant, of course, would not be negligent at all. The other approach, or rather set of approaches, is "modified" comparative fault. Under one rule, the plaintiff whose negligence equals or exceeds that of the defendant cannot recover at all. Under the other rule, the plaintiff's negligence bars recovery only if it exceeds that of the defendant. Under both, if the plaintiff's negligence has not reached the cut-off point, the recovery is reduced proportionately.

5. Calculating the Shares of Fault. The statutes and cases are singularly unhelpful in determining just how the trier of fact should go about allocating the total fault between and among the parties. The Uniform Comparative Fault Act, which is set out after Problem 28, below, simply refers to "the nature of the conduct of each party at fault and the extent of the causal relation between the conduct and the damages claimed." Section 8 of the Restatement (Third) of Torts: Apportionment of Liability (2000) is set out at p. 425 n. 8, below. Would this section make the jury's job easier? Through whatever method, some juries have allocated fault with considerable precision. For example, in Falgoust v. Richardson Indus., Inc., 552 So. 2d 1348 (La. Ct. App. 1989), *writ denied*, 558 So. 2d 1126 (La. 1990), the jury's allocation of fault among the four parties was 60 percent, 37 percent, 1.5 percent, and 1.5 percent. For suggestions as to how the calculation could be approached, see Richard N. Pearson, Apportionment of Losses under Comparative Fault Laws — An Analysis of the Alternatives, 40 La. L. Rev. 343 (1980); and David W. Robertson, Eschewing Ersatz Percentages: A Simplified Vocabulary of Comparative Fault, 45 St. Louis U. L.J. 831 (2001). In Wassell v. Adams, 865 F.2d 849 (7th Cir. 1989), Judge Posner suggested that a useful heuristic for allocating shares of responsibility under comparative fault is to use the ratio of the plaintiff's and defendant's relative costs of avoiding the injury: "If each could have avoided it at the same cost, they are each 50 percent responsible for it." Id. at 854.

6. Joint and Several Liability. While the purpose of comparative fault laws is to reduce, but not necessarily eliminate, recovery by the at-fault plaintiff from at-fault defendants, comparative fault also has implications on how the plaintiff's damages should be divided among multiple defendants. At issue is whether a defendant should be exposed to liability greater than that defendant's proportionate share of the fault. Under the pre–comparative fault law, multiple defendants at fault were jointly and severally liable to the plaintiff — each defendant was liable to the plaintiff for the full amount of the plaintiff's damages, although the plaintiff could not recover from all defendants more than whatever damages were assessed. Some states have abrogated joint and several liability, and gear the liability of the defendants to their proportionate share of the fault.[7] See, e.g., Utah Code Ann. tit. 78B-5-818. Other states have fully retained joint and several liability. See, e.g., Ill. Comp. Stat. Ann. ch. 735 §5/2-1117 (2010). The more common legislative reaction has been to modify, but neither retain nor eliminate, joint and several liability. No two statutes modifying joint and several liability are exactly the same. Many statutes retain joint and several liability with respect to economic loss, but not with respect to intangible harm. Some statutes make the applicability of joint and several liability hinge on the ratio

7. Some statutes use the expression *several liability* to describe what we call *proportional liability*. See, e.g., Or. Rev. Stat. §31.610, which provides that liability for noneconomic damages "shall be several only and shall not be joint." The new Restatement (Third) of Torts: Apportionment of Liability (2000) uses "several liability" in the same way. Historically, however, *several liability* meant that each defendant was liable for the full amount of the plaintiff's damages, and not for just some lesser proportionate share. *Joint liability* traditionally meant that the defendants could be joined in the same suit, and not that each was liable for the plaintiff's full damages. See the note on joint and several liability, p. 137, above.

of the plaintiff's share of the fault to the defendants': joint and several liability applies only to defendants whose share of the fault exceeds that of the plaintiff.

7. Contribution. In states that have retained, in whole or in part, joint and several liability and also permit contribution between joint tortfeasors, should contribution be geared to the defendants' share of fault? Yes, according to the court in Owens v. Truckstops of America, 915 S.W.2d 420 (Tenn. 1996). This proportionate approach based on shares of assigned fault replaces the earlier method of straight pro rata apportionment among defendants that had prevailed prior to the advent of comparative fault. See supra p. 138.

8. Last Clear Chance. Most courts addressing the issue have held that the doctrine of last clear chance (see pp. 378-80, above) does not survive comparative fault as a basis for imposing the full loss on the defendant. See, e.g., Spahn v. Town of Port Royal, 499 S.E.2d 205 (S.C. 1998); Hale v. Beckstead, 116 P.3d 263, 265 (Utah 2005) ("Under Utah's comparative fault system for negligence, the last clear chance doctrine is no longer recognized as a total bar to a plaintiff's recovery; rather, the doctrine is used as just one of many factors juries can look to in apportioning fault under the comparative fault scheme.").

9. Assumption of the Risk. For courts that have eliminated implied or secondary assumption of risk as a defense separate from contributory negligence, incorporating assumption of the risk into comparative fault involves no conceptual problem. A reasonable assumption of the risk will not affect the plaintiff's recovery, while an unreasonable assumption will be treated as any other form of contributory negligence for comparison purposes. This approach is endorsed by the Restatement (Third) of Torts: Apportionment of Liability §2 cmt. *i*, §3 cmt. *c* (2000). But assumption of the risk seems to have a life of its own, as Knight v. Jewett, p. 427, below, illustrates. See also Kenneth W. Simons, Reflections on Assumption of Risk, 50 UCLA L. Rev. 481, 528 (2002) ("Despite calls for the abolition of [assumption of risk], and for its merger into comparative fault, the doctrine survives in some jurisdictions, and its spirit endures in most, if not all.").

10. Punitive Damages. Punitive damages are not generally subject to apportionment since the purpose of such damages is not to compensate the plaintiff, but to punish the defendant for his egregious conduct. See, e.g., Clark v. Cantrell, 529 S.E.2d 528 (S.C. 2000).

11. Allocation of Liability to Nonparties. A person whose fault has contributed to the plaintiff's injuries may, for a variety of reasons, be immune from liability. The immunity may be governmental, charitable, or intrafamily. In such a case, the issue arises as to whether the plaintiff's recovery should be reduced by the immune person's share of the comparative responsibility. A reduction would impose the risk of immunity on the plaintiff. Or the risk could fall on the defendants, making them jointly and severally liable for the immune person's share of the responsibility. The Restatement (Third) of Torts: Apportionment of Liability (2000) imposes the immune person's share of the responsibility on the defendants, not the plaintiff, to allow full recovery. See §29A, cmt. *e*. Not all courts follow the Restatement (Third) in this regard. See, e.g., Dotson v. Blake, 29 S.W.3d 26 (Tenn. 2000) (trier of fact could allocate a percentage of fault to a defendant whose liability to plaintiff was time-barred by a statute of repose).

The most comprehensive effort at finding a way out of what may be viewed as the morass of comparative fault is the Restatement (Third) of Torts: Apportionment of Liability (2000). This Restatement leaves some issues open — for example, it sets out five options for implementing joint and several liability. Judicial acceptance of the Restatement will be impeded in those states that have statutory comparative fault regimes. Furthermore, the American Law Institute's resolution of the issues has met with some academic criticism. See, e.g., Mark M. Hager, What's (Not!) in a Restatement? ALI Issue-Dodging on Liability Apportionment, 33 Conn. L. Rev. 77 (2000). Professor Hager accuses the ALI of siding with defendants with respect to several important issues and argues that the resolution of these issues by the ALI is "poorly supported." A more sympathetic treatment, focusing specifically on the way in which the Restatement project handles problems associated with comparing across negligent and intentional culpability standards, is provided in Ellen M. Bublick, The End Game of Tort Reform: Comparative Apportionment and Intentional Torts, 78 Notre Dame L. Rev. 355 (2003).

Problem 28

You represent Walter Geyer in connection with claims arising out of an automobile accident occurring on December 15 of last year. Your investigation of the accident has revealed the following:

The accident occurred about noon as Geyer was driving home in a northerly direction on School Street. He had been driving at about 40 mph as he approached the intersection of School with Wilson Avenue. The weather was clear and the road was dry. He saw an automobile to his right on Wilson Avenue stopped at the intersection. There are stop signs at Wilson directing traffic on Wilson to stop at the intersection. Geyer knew the stop signs were there. Suddenly the other car pulled into the intersection and started to cross it. Geyer slammed on his brakes and sounded his horn. Geyer had intended to turn sharply to his right and pass behind the other car, but when he applied the brakes, the car pulled sharply to the left and hit the other car in its left rear. As a result of the impact, Geyer was thrown forward onto the steering wheel, as he was not wearing the seat belt and shoulder harness. He felt a sharp pain in his chest.

After the accident Everett Moreland, the other driver, told Geyer that he had not seen Geyer before he, Moreland, entered the intersection. Moreland did not appear to be hurt. Geyer then called the Oxford police from a nearby house.

Geyer was driving his six-year-old Ford sedan at the time of the accident. There was considerable front end damage to his car, and he was told by the local Ford dealer that the cost of repairs would exceed the fair retail value of the car, which was $3,000 before the accident. Moreland was driving a two-year-old Ford station wagon. The damage that Geyer could see was to the left rear fender and door.

Three days prior to the accident, Geyer had noticed that his car was pulling to the left when the brakes were suddenly applied. Two weeks earlier, he had had the braking system reconditioned and the brake linings replaced at South End Ford, the local Ford dealership. He had intended to take the car back to South End to have the brakes checked, but had not gotten around to it before the accident. You have had a mechanic look at the car. He thinks that the South End mechanic who worked on the brakes did an inadequate job, and as a result brake fluid leaked into the right front brake drum. This resulted in uneven braking capability in the front wheel, causing the car to pull to the left when the brakes were applied.

On December 17, Geyer saw Dr. Margaret Inman, his personal physician, about the pain in his chest. He was referred to Dr. Carl Shanklin, an orthopedic surgeon, who told him he had a fractured rib. The pain was quite severe for three or four days after the accident, but had disappeared after about a week. On Dr. Shanklin's advice, he stayed away from work, which required a lot of lifting, for five weeks. He took two weeks of paid sick leave, and was unpaid for the other three weeks except for Christmas and New Year's Day, which were paid holidays. His take-home pay at that time was $600 a week. Mr. Geyer's medical expenses totaled $1,250, of which $1,000 was covered by his employer-financed medical insurance.

The accident report prepared by Albert Vose, an Oxford police officer, shows that the Geyer automobile left skid marks 89 feet long. When asked about this later, Officer Vose stated that in his opinion, the length of the skid marks indicates that Geyer was going about 40 mph when he applied his brakes. The posted speed limit for this portion of School Street is 30 mph.

Everett Moreland has refused to give a statement. His explanation of the accident appearing on his report to the Oxford police was: "I was driving on Wilson Avenue. Stopped at School and looked both ways. Saw no one coming. Proceeded into intersection when car #2 came at high rate of speed around curve on School. I accelerated to get through intersection so #2 could pass behind me, but #2 turned left and ran into #1." He stated on the report that he was not injured, and that the cost of repairing his automobile was $2,650.

Your examination of the scene of the accident reveals that the intersection of School Street and Wilson Avenue is in a moderately populated residential area of Oxford. School Street is a main road, and although it has a posted speed of 30 mph, your investigation shows that cars frequently travel at 45 mph on School Street in the vicinity of the intersection. A state criminal statute requires drivers to travel "at a reasonable speed," having in mind such things as the traffic conditions, weather, and the condition of the road. A speed in excess of the posted speed is, according to the statute, prima facie unreasonable. School Street, as it approaches Wilson from the south, is a flat asphalt road 33 feet wide. South of the intersection, the road curves to the west. A driver traveling north would get his first view of a car heading west on Wilson at the intersection at a distance of about 200 feet from the intersection.

Mr. Geyer will be in to see you next week to get your assessment of his claims against Moreland and the South End Garage. Assume that the legislature of your state has enacted the Uniform Comparative Fault Act.

Uniform Comparative Fault Act

12 Uniform Laws Ann. 43 (1996)

Section 1. [Effect of Contributory Fault]

(a) In an action based on fault seeking to recover damages for injury or death to person or harm to property, any contributory fault chargeable to the claimant diminishes proportionately the amount awarded as compensatory damages for an injury attributable to the claimant's contributory fault, but does not bar recovery. This rule applies whether or not under prior law the claimant's contributory fault constituted a defense or was disregarded under applicable legal doctrines, such as last clear chance.

(b) "Fault" includes acts or omissions that are in any measure negligent or reckless toward the person or property of the actor or others, or that subject a person to strict tort liability. The term also includes breach of warranty, unreasonable assumption of risk not constituting an enforceable express consent, misuse of a product for which the defendant otherwise would be liable, and unreasonable failure to avoid an injury or to mitigate damages. Legal requirements of causal relation apply both to fault as the basis for liability and to contributory fault.

Section 2. [Apportionment of Damages]

(a) In all actions involving fault of more than one party to the action, including third-party defendants and persons who have been released under Section 6, the court, unless otherwise agreed by all parties, shall instruct the jury to answer special interrogatories or, if there is no jury, shall make findings, indicating:

(1) The amount of damages each claimant would be entitled to recover if contributory fault is disregarded; and

(2) the percentage of the total fault of all of the parties to each claim that is allocated to each claimant, defendant, third-party defendant, and person who has been released from liability under Section 6. For this purpose the court may determine that two or more persons are to be treated as a single party.

(b) In determining the percentages of fault, the trier of fact shall consider both the nature of the conduct of each party at fault and the extent of the causal relation between the conduct and the damages claimed.[8]

(c) The court shall determine the award of damages to each claimant in accordance with the findings, subject to any reduction under Section 6, and enter judgment against each party liable on the basis of rules of joint-and-several liability. For the purposes of contribution under Sections 4 and 5, the court also shall determine and state in the judgment each party's equitable share of the obligation to each claimant in accordance with the respective percentages of fault.

(d) Upon motion made not later than one year after judgment is entered, the court shall determine whether all or part of a party's equitable share of the obligation is uncollectible from that party, and shall reallocate any uncollectible amount among the other parties, including a claimant at fault, according to their respective percentages of fault. The party whose liability is reallocated is nonetheless subject to contribution and to any continuing liability to the claimant on the judgment.

Section 3. [Set-off]

A claim and counterclaim shall not be set off against each other except by agreement of both parties. On motion, however, the court, if it finds that the obligation of either party is

8. Section 8 of the Restatement (Third) of Torts: Apportionment of Liability provides:

> Factors for assigning percentages of responsibility to each person whose legal responsibility has been established include
>
> (a) the nature of the person's risk-creating conduct, including any awareness or indifference with respect to the risks created by the conduct and any intent with respect to the harm created by the conduct; and
>
> (b) the strength of the causal connection between the person's risk-creating conduct and the harm.

Do you find this provision more helpful than §1(b) of the Uniform Laws in handling Problem 28? How, if at all, would your calculations differ were your court to adopt this section of the Restatement?

likely to be uncollectible, may order that both parties make payment into court for distribution. The court shall distribute the funds received and declare obligations discharged as if the payment into court by either party had been a payment to the other party and any distribution of those funds back to the party making payment had been a payment to him by the other party.

Section 4. [Right of Contribution]

(a) A right of contribution exists between or among two or more persons who are jointly and severally liable upon the same indivisible claim for the same injury, death, or harm, whether or not judgment has been recovered against all or any of them. It may be enforced either in the original action or by a separate action brought for that purpose. The basis for contribution is each person's equitable share of the obligation, including the equitable share of a claimant at fault, as determined in accordance with the provisions of Section 2.

(b) Contribution is available to a person who enters into a settlement with a claimant only (1) if the liability of the person against whom contribution is sought has been extinguished and (2) to the extent that the amount paid in settlement was reasonable.

Section 5. [Enforcement of Contribution]

(a) If the proportionate fault of the parties to a claim for contribution has been established previously by the court, as provided by Section 2, a party paying more than his equitable share of the obligation, upon motion, may recover judgment for contribution.

(b) If the proportionate fault of the parties to the claim for contribution has not been established by the court, contribution may be enforced in a separate action, whether or not a judgment has been rendered against either the person seeking contribution or the person from whom contribution is being sought.

(c) If a judgment has been rendered, the action for contribution must be commenced within [one year] after the judgment becomes final. If no judgment has been rendered, the person bringing the action for contribution either must have (1) discharged by payment the common liability within the period of the statute of limitations applicable to the claimant's right of action against him and commenced the action for contribution within [one year] after payment, or (2) agreed while action was pending to discharge the common liability and, within [one year] after the agreement, have paid the liability and commenced an action for contribution.

Section 6. [Effect of Release]

A release, covenant not to sue, or similar agreement entered into by a claimant and a person liable discharges that person from all liability for contribution, but it does not discharge any other persons liable upon the same claim unless it so provides. However, the claim of the releasing person against other persons is reduced by the amount of the released person's equitable share of the obligation, determined in accordance with the provisions of Section 2.

[Sections 7 through 11 are housekeeping sections, and do not add to the substantive features of the act.]

The Uniform Comparative Fault Act has received only limited endorsement by states, in substantial part because the Act reflects a "pure" comparative negligence standard while most states have instead adopted a "modified" standard. In 2002, the Uniform Law Commissioners promulgated the Uniform Apportionment of Tort Responsibility Act (UATRA) in an effort to accommodate this preference and to reflect various developments regarding the curtailing of joint and several liability among co-defendants that have been occurring in many states. It is too early to tell whether the UATRA will fare better than its predecessor. So far, no state has adopted it. The National Conference of Commissioners on Uniform State Laws tracks the legislative progress of the UATRA at http://www.uniformlaws.org/LegislativeFactSheet.aspx?title=Apportionment%20of%20Tort%20Responsibility%20Act.

Problem 29

In what way, if at all, would your analysis of Problem 27 be different under the Uniform Comparative Fault Act?

Knight v. Jewett

3 Cal. 4th 296, 834 P.2d 696, 11 Cal. Rptr. 2d 2 (1992)

George, Justice.

[The plaintiff sued the defendant for personal injuries arising out of a touch football game. There was some dispute as to the defendant's conduct which caused the plaintiff's injury. According to the plaintiff, after the plaintiff caught a pass, the defendant ran into her from the rear, knocking her down, and stepping on her hand. The defendant's version was that he collided with the plaintiff in an unsuccessful attempt to intercept the pass. The defendant moved for summary judgment, arguing that the plaintiff assumed the risk of injury by participating in the game. The trial judge granted the motion, and that decision was affirmed by the Court of Appeal.

The Court stated that the issue is the extent to which assumption of the risk has survived as a defense after the decision in Li v. Yellow Cab, 13 Cal. 3d 804, 532 P.2d 1226, 119 Cal. Rptr. 858 (1975), in which the Supreme Court of California adopted comparative fault.]

II

A number of appellate decisions, focusing on the language in *Li* indicating that assumption of risk is in reality a form of contributory negligence "where a plaintiff unreasonably undertakes to encounter a specific known risk imposed by a defendant's negligence"

(13 Cal. 3d at p. 824, 119 Cal. Rptr. 858, 532 P.2d 1226), have concluded that *Li* properly should be interpreted as drawing a distinction between those assumption of risk cases in which a plaintiff "unreasonably" encounters a known risk imposed by a defendant's negligence and those assumption of risk cases in which a plaintiff "reasonably" encounters a known risk imposed by a defendant's negligence. These decisions interpret *Li* as subsuming into the comparative fault scheme those cases in which the plaintiff acts unreasonably in encountering a specific known risk, but retaining the assumption of risk doctrine as a complete bar to recovery in those cases in which the plaintiff acts reasonably in encountering such a risk. Although aware of the apparent anomaly of a rule under which a plaintiff who acts reasonably is completely barred from recovery while a plaintiff who acts unreasonably only has his or her recovery reduced, these decisions nonetheless have concluded that this distinction and consequence were intended by the *Li* court.

In our view, these decisions — regardless whether they reached the correct result on the facts at issue — have misinterpreted *Li* by suggesting that our decision contemplated less favorable legal treatment for a plaintiff who reasonably encounters a known risk than for a plaintiff who unreasonably encounters such a risk. Although the relevant passage in *Li* indicates that the assumption of risk doctrine would be merged into the comparative fault scheme in instances in which a plaintiff "'unreasonably undertakes to encounter a specific known risk imposed by a defendant's negligence'" (13 Cal. 3d at p. 824, 119 Cal. Rptr. 858, 532 P.2d 1226), nothing in this passage suggests that the assumption of risk doctrine should survive as a total bar to the plaintiff's recovery whenever a plaintiff acts reasonably in encountering such a risk. Instead, this portion of our opinion expressly contrasts the category of assumption of risk cases which "'involve contributory negligence'" (and which therefore should be merged into the comparative fault scheme) with those assumption of risk cases which involve "'a reduction of defendant's duty of care.'" (Id. at p. 825, 119 Cal. Rptr. 858, 532 P.2d 1226.)

Indeed, particularly when the relevant passage in *Li*, supra, 13 Cal. 3d at pp. 824-825, 119 Cal. Rptr. 858, 532 P.2d 1226, is read as a whole *and in conjunction with the authorities it cites*, we believe it becomes clear that the distinction in assumption of risk cases to which the *Li* court referred in this passage was not a distinction between instances in which a plaintiff unreasonably encounters a known risk imposed by a defendant's negligence and instances in which a plaintiff reasonably encounters such a risk. Rather, the distinction to which the *Li* court referred was between (1) those instances in which the assumption of risk doctrine embodies a legal conclusion that there is "no duty" on the part of the defendant to protect the plaintiff from a particular risk — the category of assumption of risk that the legal commentators generally refer to as "primary assumption of risk" — and (2) those instances in which the defendant does owe a duty of care to the plaintiff but the plaintiff knowingly encounters a risk of injury caused by the defendant's breach of that duty — what most commentators have termed "secondary assumption of risk." Properly interpreted, the relevant passage in *Li* provides that the category of assumption of risk cases that is not merged into the comparative negligence system and in which the plaintiff's recovery continues to be completely barred involves those cases in which the defendant's conduct did not breach a legal duty of care to the plaintiff, i.e., "primary assumption of risk" cases, whereas cases involving "secondary assumption of risk" properly are merged into the comprehensive comparative fault system adopted in *Li*. . . .

An amicus curiae in the companion case has questioned, on a separate ground, the duty approach to the post-*Li* assumption of risk doctrine, suggesting that if a plaintiff's action may go forward whenever a defendant's breach of duty has played some role, however minor, in a plaintiff's injury, a plaintiff who voluntarily engages in a highly dangerous sport — for example, skydiving or mountain climbing — will escape *any* responsibility for the injury so long as a jury finds that the plaintiff was not "unreasonable" in engaging in the sport. This argument rests on the premise that, under comparative fault principles, a jury may assign some portion of the responsibility for an injury to a plaintiff only if the jury finds that the plaintiff acted *unreasonably*, but not if the jury finds that the plaintiff knowingly and voluntarily, but reasonably, chose to engage in a dangerous activity. Amicus curiae contends that such a rule frequently would permit voluntary risk takers to avoid all responsibility for their own actions, and would impose an improper and undue burden on other participants.

Although we agree with the general thesis of amicus curiae's argument that persons generally should bear personal responsibility for their own actions, the suggestion that a duty approach to the doctrine of assumption of risk is inconsistent with this thesis rests on a mistaken premise. Past California cases have made it clear that the "comparative fault" doctrine is a flexible, commonsense concept, under which a jury properly may consider and evaluate the relative responsibility of various parties for an injury (whether their responsibility for the injury rests on negligence, strict liability, or other theories of responsibility), in order to arrive at an "equitable apportionment or allocation of loss."

Accordingly, contrary to amicus curiae's assumption, we believe that under California's comparative fault doctrine, a jury in a "secondary assumption of risk" case would be entitled to take into consideration a plaintiff's voluntary action in choosing to engage in an unusually risky sport, whether or not the plaintiff's decision to encounter the risk should be characterized as unreasonable, in determining whether the plaintiff properly should bear some share of responsibility for the injuries he or she suffered. Thus, in a case in which an injury has been caused by both a defendant's breach of a legal duty to the plaintiff and the plaintiff's voluntary decision to engage in an unusually risky sport, application of comparative fault principles will not operate to relieve either individual of responsibility for his or her actions, but rather will ensure that neither party will escape such responsibility. . . .

Accordingly, in determining the propriety of the trial court's grant of summary judgment in favor of the defendant in this case, our inquiry does not turn on the reasonableness or unreasonableness of plaintiff's conduct in choosing to subject herself to the risks of touch football or in continuing to participate in the game after she became aware of defendant's allegedly rough play. Nor do we focus upon whether there is a factual dispute with regard to whether plaintiff subjectively knew of, and voluntarily chose to encounter, the risk of defendant's conduct, or impliedly consented to relieve or excuse defendant from any duty of care to her. Instead, our resolution of this issue turns on whether, in light of the nature of the sporting activity in which defendant and plaintiff were engaged, defendant's conduct breached a legal duty of care to plaintiff. We now turn to that question.

III . . .

. . . [W]e conclude that a participant in an active sport breaches a legal duty of care to other participants — i.e., engages in conduct that properly may subject him or her to financial liability — only if the participant intentionally injures another player or engages in conduct that is so reckless as to be totally outside the range of the ordinary activity involved in the sport. . . .

Therefore, we conclude that defendant's conduct in the course of the touch football game did not breach any legal duty of care owed to plaintiff. Accordingly, this case falls within the primary assumption of risk doctrine, and thus the trial court properly granted summary judgment in favor of defendant. Because plaintiff's action is barred under the primary assumption of risk doctrine, comparative fault principles do not come into play. The judgment of the Court of Appeal, upholding the summary judgment entered by the trial court, is affirmed.

In Nalwa v. Cedar Fair, L.P., 290 P.3d 1158 (Cal. 2012), the California Supreme Court extended the *Knight* holding to include participation in a bumper car ride at an amusement park:

> [T]he primary assumption of risk doctrine is not limited to activities classified as sports, but applies as well to other recreational activities involving an inherent risk of injury to voluntary participants where the risk cannot be eliminated without altering the fundamental nature of the activity.
>
> The primary assumption of risk doctrine rests on a straightforward policy foundation: the need to avoid chilling vigorous participation in or sponsorship of recreational activities by imposing a tort duty to eliminate or reduce the risks of harm inherent in those activities. It operates on the premise that imposing such a legal duty would work a basic alteration — or cause abandonment of the activity. [Id. at 1163 (internal quotations and citations omitted).]

Why is the court certain that liability would cause bumper car operators to alter or abandon their activity, rather than raise ticket prices to cover costs for the few cases of serious injury that do arise?

For an extensive analysis of *Knight* as part of an argument that California courts have been employing assumption of risk and related "no duty" doctrines in a way that transfers power from legislators and jurors to judges and that upsets the certainty and predictability of tort law, see Dilan A. Esper & Gregory C. Keating, Abusing "Duty," 79 S. Cal. L. Rev. 265 (2006).

D. Immunities

1. Governmental Immunity

The rule that a government may not be sued without its consent stems from the ancient English maxim "the King can do no wrong." The governmental immunity rule was incorporated into American law at an early date, apparently without much thought as to whether this assumption about royal rectitude was appropriate in a democracy. Ultimately, the statement that came to be more or less accepted in this country is that offered by Justice Holmes in Kawananakoa v. Polyblank, 205 U.S. 349, 353 (1907): "A sovereign is exempt from suit, not because of any formal conception or obsolete theory, but on the logical and practical ground that there can be no legal right as against the authority that makes the law on which the right depends."

The tort liability of the U.S. government is now controlled by the Federal Torts Claims Act (FTCA), enacted in 1946.[9] The FTCA is not a general consent by the United States to be sued in tort, as there are several types of claims which are specifically excluded. Under one exclusion, certain types of tort actions, such as assault, battery, defamation, and interference with contract, may not be brought. 28 U.S.C.A. §2680(h) (2006). A more important exclusion under the FTCA is that which precludes liability for a claim based on the "exercise or performance the failure to exercise or perform a discretionary function or duty. . . ." 28 U.S.C.A. §2680(a). The Supreme Court has developed a two-part test for determining the applicability of the discretionary function exception. See United States v. Gaubert, 499 U.S. 315, 322-25 (1991); Berkovitz v. United States, 486 U.S. 531, 536-37 (1988). Under this test, courts first ask whether the challenged action is governed by a mandatory statute, policy, or regulation, or whether it instead is "discretionary" in nature. See, e.g., Hinsley v. Standing Rock Child Protective Servs., 516 F.3d 668 (8th Cir. 2008) (negligent failure of the Bureau of Indian Affairs to warn plaintiff that her half-brother was a sexual abuser before placing him in plaintiff's home was a discretionary function because the agency had to balance confidentiality of the brother's past actions against the safety concerns of the children in the placement home). If the action is discretionary, courts then ask whether the challenged action involves a decision that is susceptible to social, economic, or political policy analysis, since that is the type of government action that the Court has held Congress intended to protect under the FTCA.

The court of appeals in Whisnant v. United States, 400 F.3d 1177, 1181 (9th Cir. 2005), noted that courts tend to hold "that the design of a course of governmental action is shielded by the discretionary function exception, whereas the implementation of that course of action is not," and that "matters of scientific and professional judgment—particularly judgments concerning safety—are rarely considered to be susceptible to social, economic, or political policy." Applying these principles to the context of government safety regulation, the court observed that "[t]he decision to adopt safety precautions may be based in policy considerations, but the implementation of those precautions is not. . . . [S]afety measures, once undertaken, cannot be shortchanged in the name of policy." Id. at 1182 (quoting Bear Medicine v. United States *ex rel.* Sec'y of the Dep't of the Interior, 241 F.3d 1208, 1216-17 (9th Cir. 2001)). Thus, the plaintiff in *Whisnant* could proceed against the government with his claim that he suffered illness as a result of the government's negligence in allowing toxic mold to persist in the meat department of a naval base commissary: "If [plaintiff] were claiming that the government was negligent in electing to employ contractors rather than doing the work itself, or in designing its safety regulations, then his claim would most likely be barred; instead, he is claiming that the government negligently ignored health hazards that were called to its attention, and so his claim is not barred." *Whisnant,* 400 F.3d at 1185. See generally Stephen P. Nelson, The King's Wrongs and the Federal District Courts: Understanding the Discretionary Function Exception to the Federal Torts Claims Act, 51 S. Tex. L. Rev. 259 (2009) (statistical survey of how courts apply the discretionary function exception).

One significant aspect of governmental immunity doctrine is the extension of liability protection to government contractors. In Yearsley v. W.A. Ross Constr. Co., 309 U.S. 18 (1940), the Supreme Court first established that private actors might be protected from

9. See 79 Cong. Ch. 753, August 2, 1946, 60 Stat. 812. The provisions of the act appear in various sections of the United States Code. Appendix 1 of 3 Lester S. Jayson, Handling Federal Torts Claims (1992), sets out the locations in the United States Code of the provisions of the act.

liability through a form of derivative sovereign immunity based on their contractual arrangements with the federal government. In *Yearsley*, two landowners lost 95 acres of their property when a government contractor's effort to maintain navigation on the Missouri river intentionally accelerated riverbank erosion. The contractor was held to be immune from suit by the Court, which reasoned that when the "authority to carry out the project was validly conferred . . . there is no liability on the part of the contractor for executing [Congress'] will." Id. at 20-21. Many lower courts minimized the impact of *Yearsley* by interpreting it to apply only in the context of property damage caused in connection with public works projects. Later, in Boyle v. United Techs. Corp., 487 U.S. 500, 108 S. Ct. 2510 (1988), the Court more explicitly laid out a "government contractor defense," relying on principles from the Federal Tort Claims Act (FTCA) — which by its terms applies to government employees and agencies but not government contractors — to establish a three-factor test for discerning whether the government exercised its policy discretion in establishing contract specifications that led to the alleged harm by the contractor. *Boyle* involved a product liability suit against a military helicopter manufacturer in which the alleged design defect had been specifically mandated by the government in its agreement with the manufacturer.

Lower courts subsequently struggled to interpret the breadth of *Yearsley* in light of the specificity of *Boyle*. See, e.g., Adkisson v. Jacobs Eng'g Grp., Inc., 790 F.3d 641, 646 (6th Cir. 2015), *cert. denied*, 136 S. Ct. 980 (2016) ("[If] *Yearsley* really does stretch as broadly as its language suggests, the Supreme Court in *Boyle* would presumably not have invented a new test to govern the liability of military procurement contractors; it could have simply cited *Yearsley* and called it a day."). Government contractors tended to rely on *Boyle* on the assumption that *Yearsley* had been displaced by a more rigorous framework. Their efforts were not fruitless. For instance, at least one lower court plumbed the FTCA to create a new contractor defense in an analogous fashion to *Boyle*. See, e.g., Saleh v. Titan Corp., 580 F.3d 1 (D.C. Cir. 2009) (relying on the "combatant activities" exception to sovereign immunity waiver in FTCA to shield contractors from liability for alleged torture and other human rights abuses at the Abu Ghraib military prison). Some clarity may or may not have been provided in Campbell-Ewald Co. v. Gomez, 136 S. Ct. 663, 673 n.7 (2016), which noted in a footnote that "[c]ritical in *Yearsley* was not the involvement of public works, but the contractor's performance in compliance with all federal directions." Such language is likely to be picked up by government contractor defendants, who will now argue that the broad immunizing language of *Yearsley* should prevail over the strained statutory construction of *Boyle*.

Sovereign immunity also applies to state and local governments, although there has been a long-term trend toward cutting back how far it extends. The change in the immunity rules has been accomplished both by statute (see, e.g., Wash. Rev. Code Ann. §§4.92.090 and 4.96.010) and by judicial decision (see Bulman v. Hulstrand Constr. Co., Inc., 521 N.W.2d 632 (N.D. 1994)). In Koffman v. Garnett, 574 S.E.2d 258 (Va. 2003), the court held that "gross negligence" is not protected by sovereign immunity and that plaintiff, a middle school student, stated a claim for "gross negligence" by alleging that the school football coach lifted him off his feet and slammed him to the ground to demonstrate proper tackling technique. Although judicial hostility to sovereign immunity is widespread, some courts have preserved it. See, e.g., McIntosh v. Sullivan, 875 A.2d 459 (Conn. 2005). And in states that have abrogated the immunity to some extent, it still remains with respect to discretionary or governmental functions. See, e.g., State *ex rel.* St. Louis Hous. Auth. v. Gaertner, 695 S.W.2d 460 (Mo. 1985) (operation of public housing project); City of Daytona

Beach v. Palmer, 469 So. 2d 121 (Fla. 1985) (fire fighting decisions); Hobrla v. Glass, 372 N.W.2d 630 (Mich. Ct. App. 1985) (issuance of automobile operators' licenses).[10]

Even assuming the absence of sovereign immunity barriers, plaintiffs still may face difficulty establishing a duty of care in light of the general nature of many government activities. For instance, in Valdez v. City of New York, 960 N.E.2d 356 (N.Y. 2011), plaintiff obtained an order of protection against her ex-boyfriend who later threatened to kill her. Plaintiff phoned officers in the domestic violence unit of her local police precinct to report the threat. She was told by those officers that the ex-boyfriend would be arrested "immediately" and that she should return to her apartment. Plaintiff did so and only emerged from her apartment 28 hours later to take out her garbage, whereupon she was surprised and shot by the ex-boyfriend. The New York Court of Appeals held that plaintiff failed to establish a "special relationship" with police sufficient to create a duty of care: "Under the public duty rule, although a municipality owes a general duty to the public at large to furnish police protection, this does not create a duty of care running to a specific individual sufficient to support a negligence claim, unless the facts demonstrate that a special duty was created." Id. at 361. The court in particular noted that plaintiff had not alleged facts sufficient to establish that her reliance on the officers' assurances was "justifiable," a "critical" factor in establishing the existence of a special relationship. Id. at 365. A strong dissent argued that under the majority's ruling, orders of protection seem incapable ever of being "reasonably" relied upon.

Statutory attempts to preserve sovereign immunity, in whole or in part, have been subject to constitutional attack. The court in City of Dover v. Imperial Cas. & Indem. Co., 575 A.2d 1280 (N.H. 1990), struck down a broad statutory grant of immunity to municipalities for injuries caused by the operation and maintenance of highways and sidewalks. The court held that the immunity could extend only to legislative, judicial, and other functions involving a high level of judgment or discretion. Other courts have been kinder to legislation preserving the immunity. See, e.g., Brown v. Wichita State Univ., 547 P.2d 1015 (Kan.), *appeal dismissed*, 429 U.S. 806 (1976). More limited preservations of sovereign immunity in the form of caps on the amount of damages that can be awarded have generally been upheld. See, e.g., State v. DeFoor, 824 P.2d 783 (Colo.), *cert. denied*, 506 U.S. 981 (1992).

2. Charitable Immunity

The rule that charitable organizations are not liable in tort stems from an early English case, Feoffees of Heriot's Hospital v. Ross, 12 C. & F. 507, 8 Eng. Rep. 1508 (1846), in which the court reasoned that the payment of tort claims would be inconsistent with the purposes of the donors in contributing to the hospital. Charitable immunity eventually gained almost universal acceptance in the United States. However, the doctrine has now been abolished or

10. Some courts have held that the purchase of liability insurance by a governmental agency does not waive the immunity. See Powell v. Clay County Bd. of Sup'rs, 924 So. 2d 523 (Miss. 2006). Other courts, perhaps a majority, have ruled that the purchase of liability insurance does constitute a waiver of the immunity. See, e.g., Crowell v. School District, 805 P.2d 522 (Mont. 1991). The Montana legislature responded to this case by passing a statute that provided that the purchase of liability insurance does not constitute a waiver of sovereign immunity. See Hyde v. Evergreen Volunteer Rural Fire Dept., 828 P.2d 1377 (Mont. 1992). The Supreme Court of Georgia held that a similar legislative attempt to reverse the immunity-waiving effect of liability insurance was unconstitutional (see Hiers v. City of Barwick, 414 S.E.2d 647 (Ga. 1992)), which then prompted an amendment of the Georgia state constitution (see City of Thomaston v. Bridges, 439 S.E.2d 906 (Ga. 1994); the Supreme Court of West Virginia held that such a statute is constitutional (see Pritchard v. Arvon, 413 S.E.2d 100 (W. Va. 1991)).

significantly limited in all but a handful of states. See Picher v. Roman Catholic Bishop of Portland, 974 A.2d 286 (Me. 2009) (thoroughly reviewing the history and status of charitable immunity in the United States and describing it as "a doctrine that has generally been acknowledged as bankrupt"). Most states have abolished the immunity by judicial decision (see, e.g., Davis v. Church of Jesus Christ of Latter Day Saints, 852 P.2d 640 (Mont. 1993), *overruled on other grounds*, Gliko v. Permann, 130 P.3d 155 (Mont. 2006)), although a few have done so by statute (see, e.g., N.C. Gen. Stat. §1-539.9).

The policies behind charitable immunity still have currency, however, and have led to frequent statutory preservation of the immunity. There are two concerns with regard to permitting tort suits against charities. One is the deterrent effect the abrogation might have on persons who engage in charitable activities without compensation. Imposing liability on such persons may not have the effect of internalizing the cost of injuries; rather, the costs of the abrogation may be externalized to the very people that the charity is intended to benefit due to the abandonment of charitable activities by those subject to liability. Some legislatures have responded to this concern by insulating charitable organization volunteers from negligence liability under some circumstances. See, e.g., Ohio Rev. Code Ann. 2305.38. A second concern is beneficiaries who might "bite the hand that feeds them" by suing the charities that help them. In some states, negligence liability to beneficiaries is limited, sometimes by statute (see, e.g., N.J. Stat. Ann. §2A:53A-7), and sometimes by judicial decision (see, e.g., Cowan v. Hospice Support Care, Inc., 603 S.E.2d 916 (Va. 2004)).

3. Intrafamily Immunities

The immunities arising out of family relationships are those barring tort claims between husband and wife and between parent and child.

The husband-wife immunity comes from the old English concept that the two spouses are in legal contemplation one person. Out of this concept there developed a number of legal disabilities that attached to married women and the broader tort immunity that attached to both spouses. Beginning in the middle of the nineteenth century, state legislatures enacted Married Women's Property Acts to remove some of the disabilities of married women. While these statutes were interpreted to permit interspousal tort suits with respect to property, most courts did not extend them to allow tort actions based on injuries to the person. Most states now have either completely or partially abrogated the immunity. See, e.g., Waite v. Waite, 618 So. 2d 1360 (Fla. 1993) (total abrogation); Boblitz v. Boblitz, 462 A.2d 506 (Md. 1983) (abrogated in negligence cases); Fernandez v. Romo, 646 P.2d 878 (Ariz. 1982) (abrogated in automobile accident cases); Townsend v. Townsend, 708 S.W.2d 646 (Mo. 1986) (abrogated in intentional tort cases). A minority of states continue to recognize interspousal immunity. Cf. Zellmer v. Zellmer, 188 P.3d 497 (Wash. 2008) (doctrine of parental immunity precludes liability of former spouse to plaintiff mother for negligent parental supervision that lead to drowning death of the ex-couple's child). However, even the minority jurisdictions have carved out exceptions to the general standard. In Robeson v. International Indem. Co., 282 S.E.2d 896 (Ga. 1981), the Georgia Supreme Court adhered to the immunity, but in Harris v. Harris, 313 S.E.2d 88 (Ga. 1984), it carved out an exception for cases in which there is no "marital harmony" to be protected by the immunity. In this case, the parties had been separated for ten years, and the defendant husband was living with another woman at the time of the accident. Still, the Georgia Supreme Court reaffirmed the general standard of interspousal immunity in 2003. See Gates v. Gates, 587 S.E.2d 32 (Ga. 2003).

The abrogation of the immunity does not necessarily mean that for tort purposes spouses will always be treated as strangers. In Weicker v. Weicker, 237 N.E.2d 876 (N.Y. 1968), the court stated that it would not recognize a cause of action for intentional infliction of emotional harm if the dispute arises out of marital differences. In this case, the defendant husband had gotten what the wife alleged was an invalid Mexican divorce and then purported to remarry. The court ruled that her action based on the resulting embarrassment and emotional upset was properly dismissed. The Restatement (Second) of Torts §895F provides that there is no "liability for an act or omission that, because of the marital relationship, is otherwise privileged or is not tortious." The scope of this rule is not made much clearer by Comment *h*, which states:

> The intimacy of the family relationship may also involve some relaxation in the application of the concept of reasonable care, particularly in the confines of the home. Thus, if one spouse in undressing leaves shoes out where the other stumbles over them in the dark, or if one spouse spills coffee on the other while they are both still sleepy, this may well be treated as not negligence. An analogy to the principle of assumption of risk is sometimes drawn.

With the Restatement's "shoes in the dark" hypothetical, compare Brown v. Brown, 409 N.E.2d 717 (Mass. 1980), in which the court ruled that the wife stated a cause of action for injuries she received from falling on the slippery driveway of their home.

Unlike the other immunities considered in this section, the parent-child immunity rule is homegrown. It originated in Hewellette v. George, 9 So. 885 (Miss. 1891), which involved a claim for false imprisonment brought by a minor child against her mother. A common justification for the immunity is that allowing recovery by children against their parents would promote family discord and interfere with parental control. See, e.g., Frye v. Frye, 505 A.2d 826, 831 (Md. 1986):

> It is clear that for over half a century this Court has recorded its belief in the importance of keeping the family relationship free and unfettered. Our primary concern with regard to matters involving the parent-child relationship was the protection of family integrity and harmony and the protection of parental discretion in the discipline and care of the child. We have steadfastly recognized the authority of parents and their need to fulfill the functions devolved upon them by that position. The parental status should be held inviolate so that there be no undue interference with the dependence of the minor unemancipated child on the parents for such judgment and care needed during the child's minority or with the dependence of the law on the parent for fulfillment of the necessary legal and social functions associated with the office of parent. This Court has declared it to be the public policy that discipline in the family not be impaired and that tranquility of the home be preserved. Matters which tend to disrupt or destroy the peace and harmony of family or home are not to be condoned.

Notwithstanding this plea for parental autonomy, the parent-child immunity, like the spousal immunity, has fallen on hard times. For instance, as the court observed in Allstate Ins. Co. v. Kim, 829 A.2d 611 (Md. 2003), the *Frye* immunity decision has been abrogated by statute in Maryland. A few courts have abrogated parent-child immunity entirely. See, e.g., Broadbent v. Northbrook Indem. Co., 907 P.2d 43 (Ariz. 1995). Other courts have abrogated the immunity only in certain circumstances. See, e.g., Newman v. Cole, 872 So.

2d 138 (Ala. 2003) (no parent-child immunity in a wrongful death action brought against a parent for allegedly intentionally causing the child's death). In Gibson v. Gibson, 479 P.2d 648 (Cal. 1971), the court, in responding to the argument that parents should be given legal leeway in bringing up their children, stated (479 P.2d at 653):

> In short, although a parent has the prerogative and the duty to exercise authority over his minor child, this prerogative must be exercised within reasonable limits. The standard to be applied is the traditional one of reasonableness, but viewed in light of the parental role. Thus, we think that the proper test of a parent's conduct is this: what would an ordinarily reasonable and prudent *parent* have done in similar circumstances?

The court did not indicate, however, whether it thought that the parental standard of reasonableness is the same as, higher than, or lower than the standard that would be applicable in cases of persons who are legal strangers to the child.

The abrogation of the parent-child immunity presents an interesting problem when coupled with the law that permits recovery on behalf of a child for prenatal injuries. (As to the latter law, see pp. 384-390, above.) Can an action be brought on behalf of a child against his mother based on injuries resulting from inadequate prenatal care? In Stallman v. Youngquist, 531 N.E.2d 355 (Ill. 1988), the court ruled that no such action could be brought in a case based on the claim that the defendant mother was negligent in the operation of an automobile while pregnant, and that as a result an accident occurred which injured the fetus. In rejecting the cause of action, the court stated (531 N.E.2d at 359-60):

> It is clear that the recognition of a legal right to begin life with a sound mind and body on the part of a fetus which is assertable after birth against its mother would have serious ramifications for all women and their families, and for the way in which society views women and women's reproductive abilities. The recognition of such a right by a fetus would necessitate the recognition of a legal duty on the part of the woman who is the mother; a legal duty, as opposed to a moral duty, to effectuate the best prenatal environment possible. The recognition of such a legal duty would create a new tort: a cause of action assertable by a fetus, subsequently born alive, against its mother for the unintentional infliction of prenatal injuries.
>
> It is the firmly held belief of some that a woman should subordinate her right to control her life when she decides to become pregnant or does become pregnant: anything which might possibly harm the developing fetus should be prohibited and all things which might positively affect the developing fetus should be mandated under penalty of law, be it criminal or civil. Since anything which a pregnant woman does or does not do may have an impact, either positive or negative, on her developing fetus, any act or omission on her part could render her liable to her subsequently born child. While such a view is consistent with the recognition of a fetus' having rights which are superior to those of its mother, such is not and cannot be the law of this State.
>
> A legal right of a fetus to begin life with a sound mind and body assertable against a mother would make a pregnant woman the guarantor of the mind and body of her child at birth. A legal duty to guarantee the mental and physical health of another has never before been recognized in law. Any action which negatively impacted on fetal development would be a breach of the pregnant woman's duty to her developing fetus. Mother and child would be legal adversaries from the moment of conception until birth. The error that a fetus cannot be harmed in a legally cognizable way when the woman who is its mother is injured has been corrected; the law will no longer treat the fetus as only a part of its mother. The law will not now make an error of a different sort, one with enormous implications for all women who have been, are, may be, or might become pregnant: the law will not treat a fetus as an entity which is entirely separate from its mother. . . .

> If a legally cognizable duty on the part of mothers were recognized, then a judicially defined standard of conduct would have to be met. It must be asked, By what judicially defined standard would a mother have her every act or omission while pregnant subjected to State scrutiny? By what objective standard could a jury be guided in determining whether a pregnant woman did all that was necessary in order not to breach a legal duty to not interfere with her fetus' separate and independent right to be born whole? In what way would prejudicial and stereotypical beliefs about the reproductive abilities of women be kept from interfering with a jury's determination of whether a particular woman was negligent at any point during her pregnancy?

The Supreme Court of Canada in Dobson v. Dobson, 174 D.L.R. 1 (1999), came to the same conclusion, as did the Supreme Judicial Court of Massachusetts in Remy v. MacDonald, 801 N.E.2d 260 (Mass. 2004).

The court in Bonte v. Bonte, 616 A.2d 464, 466 (N.H. 1992), recognized the cause of action:

> The defendant urges us to immunize the mother from tort liability based upon public policy reasons grounded in the unique relationship of the pregnant woman to her fetus. While we recognize that the relationship between mother and fetus is unique, we are not persuaded that based upon this relationship, a mother's duty to her fetus should not be legally recognized. If a child has a cause of action against his or her mother for negligence that occurred after birth and that caused injury to the child, it is neither logical, nor in accord with our precedent, to disallow that child's claim against the mother for negligent conduct that caused injury to the child months, days, or mere hours before the child's birth.
>
> The defendant further argues that public policy dictates against the plaintiff's cause of action because allowing this matter to proceed "deprives women of the right to control their lives during pregnancy . . . [and] unfairly subjects them to unlimited liability for unintended and often unforeseen consequences of every day living." We disagree that our decision today deprives a mother of her right to control her life during pregnancy; rather, she is required to act with the appropriate duty of care, as we have consistently held other persons are required to act, with respect to the fetus. The mother will be held to the same standard of care as that required of her once the child is born. Whether her actions are negligent is a determination for the finder of fact, considering the facts and circumstances of the particular case. Moreover, if a determination based upon public policy can be made denying a cause of action logically recognized by our case law, that determination should be made by the legislature.

If the cause of action against the mother is recognized, is the possibility opened up for actions based upon harm caused by smoking, drinking, drug use, and perhaps even dieting? In Chenault v. Huie, 989 S.W.2d 474 (Tex. App. 1999), the court refused to recognize such a cause of action against a plaintiff's mother who used cocaine throughout her pregnancy, causing injury to the plaintiff.

Some courts have retained the parent-child immunity (see, e.g., Ascuitto v. Farricielli, 711 A.2d 708 (Conn. 1998)), while others have partially abrogated it, reflecting the notion that family integrity is not always at stake when children sue their parents. Some courts, for example, have abrogated the immunity when the parents are covered by liability insurance. See, e.g., Unah v. Martin, 676 P.2d 1366 (Okla. 1984). But the presence of liability insurance did not lead the court in Terror Mining Co. v. Roter, 866 P.2d 929 (Colo. 1994), to dispense with the immunity. Many courts have ruled that there is no parental immunity when the suit involves an intentional tort, but have retained it in negligence actions. See, e.g., Pavlick v. Pavlick, 491 S.E.2d 602 (Va. 1997). In Herzfeld v. Herzfeld,

781 So. 2d 1070 (Fla. 2001), the court held that the immunity does not apply in a case involving intentional sexual abuse by the parent. In Broadwell v. Holmes, 871 S.W.2d 471, 471 (Tenn. 1994), the court ruled that the immunity only applies to the "exercise of parental authority, the performance of parental supervision, and the provision of parental care and custody." Whatever that may include, it does not include, according to the court, a mother's operation of an automobile.

The question of who is protected by the immunity has arisen in a number of cases. In Mitchell v. Davis, 598 So. 2d 801 (Ala. 1992), the court ruled that the immunity extended to foster parents and to state and local child care officials. The court in Mayberry v. Pryor, 374 N.W.2d 683 (Mich. 1985), refused to extend the immunity to foster parents with whom the child was placed for temporary care by the state Department of Social Services, although the court recognized that the result might be different if there were a more permanent, family-type, relationship. In Lawber v. Doil, 547 N.E.2d 752 (Ill. App. Ct. 1989), *appeal denied*, 553 N.E.2d 396 (Ill. 1990), the court held that the immunity applies to the plaintiff's stepfather. The court in Warren v. Warren, 650 A.2d 252 (Md. 1994), however, ruled that stepparents are not entitled to the immunity, a result that was later affected by Maryland's passage of legislation reforming intrafamily immunity doctrine for motor vehicle accidents. See Allstate Ins. Co. v. Kim, 829 A.2d 611 (Md. 2003).

Chapter 5

Trespass to Land and Nuisance

Trespass to land and nuisance are the traditional common law doctrines that have protected an owner's interests in the possession and enjoyment of land. Much of this legal territory is now occupied by modern environmental law, consisting largely of statutes and regulations. But the traditional common law retains much of its vitality and is a frequent recourse for advocates who believe that they face political obstacles in the legislative and regulatory branches too great to overcome.

Trespass and nuisance originally developed as separate bodies of law protecting different interests in land. Historically, trespass protected the right to exclusive possession; nuisance protected the possessor's right to enjoyment. Even though some recent cases suggest that these two doctrines have been fused into a single tort, it is important to understand the law of each one separate from the other.

A. Trespass to Land

Most non-lawyers associate the word *trespass* with a deliberate intrusion upon another's land by someone "up to no good." Trespassers tend to be thought of as fence-breaking, chicken-stealing good-for-nothings. However, the legal concept of trespass is much broader, more technical, and largely devoid of moralistic overtones. The legal interest of the plaintiff protected by the action is the interest in the exclusive possession of the land in question. At early common law, an action for trespass would lie for any unauthorized entry, either by person or thing, upon another's land directly resulting from a volitional act. For example, in the famous "Thorns Case" of 1466, an English court held that a man was guilty of trespass for going onto his neighbor's land to retrieve some thorns he had trimmed that had fallen onto the other's land. Hull v. Orange, YB 6 Edw. 4, fol. 7, pl. 18 (1466). If the defendant were to be bodily picked up and thrown upon the plaintiff's land against the defendant's will, no action for trespass would lie against the defendant because the entry did not result from a volitional act by the defendant. But it was no defense that the defendant had stumbled and fallen upon the land, or had entered the land mistakenly believing that the entry was authorized or that no such entry had occurred. In Dougherty v. Stepp, 18 N.C. (1 Dev. & Bat. Eq.) 371 (1835), the Supreme Court of North Carolina held that an action for trespass could lie against a defendant who had entered the plaintiff's land in order to survey it, even though the defendant had done no damage to the land and claimed that based upon the survey the land actually belonged to him, which if true would have made his entry authorized. Furthermore, under common law, unauthorized entry was a trespass even if the defendant had entered the plaintiff's land in reasonable response to physical threats from a third person. Having committed a trespass, the defendant was liable for all harm resulting from the entry, however unforeseeable. Moreover, because land was deemed to be inherently unique, threatened acts of continuous trespass were enjoinable in equity irrespective of the reasons given by the defendant to justify the entry.

Thus, trespass at early common law had very little, if anything, necessarily to do with moral culpability. To the contrary, it was one of the earliest and most stringent forms of strict liability. The main reason for this strictness lay in the fact that an action in trespass was an important legal means by which lawful possessors of land could maintain the integrity of their possessory interests. Even in the absence of substantial harm, the law allowed the plaintiff to establish legally the right to exclude others from the plaintiff's land. Thus, even the innocently motivated but unauthorized entrant would be liable for at least nominal damages, and for compensatory damages if actual harm resulted from the trespass.

To some extent, the strictness of the early common law of trespass has been ameliorated. In the fourteenth, fifteenth, and sixteenth centuries, English courts developed an important distinction between entries resulting *directly* and those resulting *indirectly* from the defendant's conduct. For entries resulting directly from defendant's conduct, trespass would lie; for entries resulting indirectly from defendant's conduct, the proper form of action was "trespass on the case."[1] The major difference between these two forms of action was the requirement in connection with the latter, but not the former, that the plaintiff show that the entry was committed either intentionally or negligently and that it caused actual harm.

These differences based upon the directness or indirectness of the entry have largely disappeared, and the forms of action themselves have been abolished. However, the impact of the earlier distinction between trespass and trespass on the case survives in the important distinction drawn by courts today between intentional and unintentional intrusions upon land. With respect to intentional intrusions, much of the earlier strictness remains. One who intentionally enters another's land, or causes a thing or a third person to enter, is liable in trespass irrespective of whether the actor causes actual harm and irrespective of any mistake, however reasonable, not induced by the possessor. However, with respect to unintentional intrusions, the earlier strictness has been almost entirely eliminated. One who unintentionally enters land in the possession of another is liable only for intrusions caused by recklessness, by negligence, or while engaging in an ultrahazardous activity. Moreover, an unintentional intruder is liable only for harm actually caused by the entry. Thus, the modern system of liability for unintentional entries, which has been freed from responsibility for protecting the possessor's legal title to land, has developed into a flexible system of liability for actual harm to the plaintiff's property. One modern case summarizes the position taken by most courts today: "Every unauthorized entry upon land is a trespass even if no damage is done. However, to determine what damages, if any, are recoverable for a trespass, the type of conduct or nature of an activity that causes the entry must be identified. While a trespass is a trespass, different recoveries are available, depending on whether the trespass was committed intentionally, negligently, accidentally, or by an abnormally dangerous activity." Watson v. Brazos Electric Power Coop., Inc., 918 S.W.2d 639, 645 (Tex. App. 1996).

The rules governing liability for intentional invasions, which continue to bear major responsibility for maintaining the legal integrity of possessory interests in land, retain a substantial measure of the earlier strictness and inflexibility. Yet, even here, trespass law has been rendered more flexible by the development and expansion of nonconsensual privileges which, in a variety of circumstances, excuse intentional entries upon the land

1. For two somewhat different analyses of the origins of the action of trespass on the case, see Theodore F. T. Plucknett, Case and the Statute of Westminster II, 31 Colum. L. Rev. 778 (1931), and Elizabeth Jean Dix, The Origins of the Action of Trespass on the Case, 46 Yale L.J. 1142 (1937).

of another. We have already encountered one such privilege — that of private necessity — in the earlier treatment of the duties owed by possessors of land to refrain from committing batteries upon would-be trespassers. See Ploof v. Putnam, p. 102 in Chapter 1. Sections 176-211 of the Restatement (Second) of Torts recognize no fewer than twenty separate privileges of this sort.

There is much more to the subject of trespass to land than is contained in these few paragraphs, and students interested in exploring this subject further are urged to make use of the sources readily available. Before proceeding to the subject of nuisance, it will be useful to summarize briefly the unique characteristics of trespass so that it can be more easily contrasted with nuisance in the next section:

(1) The interest sought to be protected by trespass actions for intentional entries is the plaintiff's interest in the exclusive possession of land.
(2) To constitute a trespass, the defendant must accomplish an entry on the plaintiff's land by means of some physical, tangible agency. The entry must be unauthorized, and (a) intended by the defendant, or (b) caused by defendant's recklessness or negligence, or (c) the result of defendant's carrying on an ultrahazardous activity.
(3) The circumstances in which a defendant may be privileged to commit an unauthorized, intentional entry are carefully limited by judicial decisions, and there exists no broadly based privilege deliberately to enter the land of another simply because, on balance, the social benefit of doing so appears to outweigh the risks of harm to the land or to the plaintiff's possessory interests.
(4) Once the defendant is found to have committed an intentional trespass, in the absence of circumstances giving rise to a privilege, the plaintiff is entitled to at least nominal damages and to injunctive relief if further acts by the defendant threaten similar entries upon his land.

As this summary reveals, trespass remains a relatively inflexible concept. No matter how bothersome the defendant's conduct may have been, it is not trespass unless an unauthorized entry upon the plaintiff's land has occurred. And whenever an intentional entry is found to have taken place, there is relatively little opportunity for the defendant to talk of justification apart from the specifically recognized privileges. Moreover, once a trespass is found to have occurred, the plaintiff may have threatened repetitions enjoined regardless of arguments that to do so would impose a greater hardship on the defendant than would otherwise be suffered by the plaintiff.

B. Nuisance

The first thing to know about the subject of nuisance is that two very different legal concepts — public nuisance and private nuisance — are embraced by the single word *nuisance. Public nuisance* is defined in §821B of the Restatement (Second) of Torts as "an unreasonable interference with a right common to the general public." Under modern law, it is a very broad concept. From its origins in criminal interferences with the rights of the Crown, public nuisance has expanded to include a variety of harms that could be suffered by the public at large or even, as discussed below, by individuals. Additionally, a public nuisance need not necessarily involve interference with interests in land. An illegal lottery or other gambling operation, for instance, might well constitute a public nuisance. See, e.g.,

Engle v. State, 90 P.2d 988 (Ariz. 1939). Such an operation might be a public nuisance even if its activities are conducted in a quiet, unobtrusive manner. As the phrase itself suggests, public nuisances are traditionally enjoined or abated in legal proceedings brought by public officials in the name of the state.

Private nuisance, on the other hand, is defined in §821D of the Restatement (Second) as "a nontrespassory invasion of another's interest in the private use and enjoyment of land." The law of private nuisance began and was developed entirely independently of the law of public nuisance, and tends to complement the tort of trespass, which as discussed earlier involves interference with the owner's possession of land. See, e.g., Martin v. Artis, 290 P.3d 687 (Mont. 2012) (upholding dismissal of nuisance claim challenging defendant's naturally growing tree which had blocked plaintiff's view, but reversing dismissal of trespass claim premised on root growth from the same tree underneath plaintiff's land). Private nuisance is a narrower concept than public nuisance and, as the Restatement definition indicates, necessarily involves interferences with private interests in land. Traditionally, private nuisances are enjoined in actions brought by individuals whose private interests are affected by them.

Although the main concern in this chapter is private nuisance, it is necessary at this point to pursue the subject of public nuisance further because private actions for damages based upon public nuisances are sometimes available to individual plaintiffs. The Restatement (Second) establishes the parameters of the concept of public nuisance in two sections:

§821B. PUBLIC NUISANCE

(1) A public nuisance is an unreasonable interference with a right common to the general public.

(2) Circumstances that may sustain a holding that an interference with a public right is unreasonable include the following:

(a) Whether the conduct involves a significant interference with the public health, the public safety, the public peace, the public comfort or the public convenience, or

(b) whether the conduct is proscribed by a statute, ordinance or administrative regulation, or

(c) whether the conduct is of a continuing nature or has produced a permanent or long-lasting effect, and, as the actor knows or has reason to know, has a significant effect upon the public right.

§821C. WHO CAN RECOVER FOR PUBLIC NUISANCE

(1) In order to recover damages in an individual action for a public nuisance, one must have suffered harm of a kind different from that suffered by other members of the public exercising the right common to the general public that was the subject of interference.

(2) In order to maintain a proceeding to enjoin to abate a public nuisance, one must

(a) have the right to recover damages, as indicated in Subsection (1), or

(b) have authority as a public official or public agency to represent the state or a political subdivision in the matter, or

(c) have standing to sue as a representative of the general public, as a citizen in a citizen's action or as a member of a class in a class action.

The provisions of greatest relevance to the subject of present concern are subsections (1) and (2)(a) of §821C, which provide for individual actions based upon a public nuisance. It is important to note that these subsections are not necessarily limited to interferences with individual plaintiffs' interests in the possession, enjoyment, and use of land, as actions for private nuisance or trespass would be. However, the cases in which subsections (1) and (2)(a) apply very often do involve conduct by the defendant that interferes substantially and uniquely with the interests of individual owners and possessors of land. In the case of an illegal lottery, for example, an individual land owner adjacent to the defendant's operation might be uniquely bothered by the coming and going of boisterous participants, and would, in that event, have a private cause of action under subsections (1) and (2)(a) of §821C based upon the public nuisance.

In recent years, state and local officials have turned to public nuisance doctrine in an effort to address a variety of complex and pervasive social harms, a phenomenon referred to as "regulation through litigation" in a prominent article by former U.S. Labor Secretary Robert Reich. See Robert B. Reich, Regulation Is Out, Litigation Is In, Am. Prospect (Dec. 19, 2001). These efforts have met with some success. For instance, the Ohio Supreme Court, in City of Cincinnati v. Beretta, 768 N.E.2d 1136 (Ohio 2002), held that a city could claim public nuisance against fifteen handgun manufacturers, three trade associations, and one handgun distributor for allegedly manufacturing, marketing, and distributing guns to prohibited users, namely children and criminals. See also City of Gary v. Smith & Wesson Corp., 801 N.E.2d 1222 (Ind. 2003) (city's allegations that defendants intentionally and willingly supplied the demand for illegal purchase of handguns were sufficient to state a claim of public nuisance). Although Congress blocked most such gun-related public nuisance actions through legislation passed in 2005,[2] state and local officials have not abandoned their attempts to use public nuisance doctrine to address concerns other than handgun violence. For instance, several governmental entities have sued lead pigment distributors for creating public nuisances by selling hazardous lead paint, which has caused extensive childhood injuries and necessitated massive and expensive abatement programs. Their suits, however, have been largely unsuccessful. See, e.g., State v. Lead Indus. Ass'n, Inc., 951 A.2d 428 (R.I. 2008); *In re* Lead Paint Litig., 924 A.2d 484 (N.J. 2007) (government's claims constituted products liability claims, not public nuisance).

Additionally, as discussed in Chapter 15 below, groups of public and private plaintiffs have brought public nuisance suits against electric utilities, fossil fuel companies, automobile manufacturers, and other entities that the plaintiffs claim are responsible for substantial, ongoing contributions to climate change. Most dramatically, in Connecticut v. American Electric Power Co., 406 F. Supp. 2d 265 (S.D.N.Y. 2005), a group of plaintiffs, including eight states, the City of New York, and several private organizations, brought suit against the five largest emitters of carbon dioxide in the country. Relying on a public nuisance theory, the plaintiffs sought injunctive relief to gradually abate the defendants' ongoing contributions to global warming. The district court dismissed the complaint on the ground that it raised non-justiciable political questions better reserved for the other branches of government. The Second Circuit reversed, stating that it was a justiciable issue and that the Clean Air Act, which authorizes federal regulation of carbon dioxide emissions, did not displace the federal common law public nuisance claim because the Environmental Protection Agency (EPA) had not yet established standards for emissions

2. *See* Protection of Lawful Commerce in Arms Act, Pub. L. No. 109-92, 119 Stat. 2095 (2005) (codified at 15 U.S.C. §§7901-7903 (2012)) (immunizing gun manufacturers and sellers and their trade associations from liability for most civil actions that are based on harm caused by the "criminal or unlawful misuse" of firearms). One of the few exceptions to immunity allowed under the Act, for negligent entrustment of firearms, is being tested in a lawsuit brought by relatives of victims of the mass shooting at Sandy Hook Elementary School. See Rick Rojas, Suit Against Maker of Gun in Newtown Massacre Can Proceed, Court Rules, N.Y. Times, April 14, 2016.

from the defendants' plants. See Connecticut v. American Electric Power Co., 582 F.3d 309 (2d Cir. 2009). The U.S. Supreme Court reversed the displacement decision, holding that the mere authorization of greenhouse gas regulations under the Clean Air Act was enough to displace federal common law, irrespective of whether and how the EPA decides to use the authority. American Electric Power Co. v. Connecticut, 564 U.S. 410 (2011). Although the Supreme Court foreclosed the possibility of a federal nuisance claim, it did not decide whether state nuisance law claims could proceed. For a discussion of public nuisance claims after American Electric Power Co. v. Connecticut, see Scott Gallisdorfer, Clean Air Act Preemption of State Common Law: Greenhouse Gas Nuisance Claims After AEP v. Connecticut, 99 Va. L. Rev. 131 (2013). For an argument that climate change nuisance suits — despite failing on the merits — offer an important catalyst for political and cultural conversation regarding an intractable policy problem, see Laura King, Narrative, Nuisance, and Environmental Law, 29 J. Envtl. L. & Litig. 331 (2014).

According to the Restatement (Second) §821C(1), to maintain a private action for public nuisance, the individual plaintiff must suffer harm that is *different in kind* from that suffered by the public at large. A mere difference in degree of the harm is generally not sufficient. For example, where the defendant without authority digs a ditch across a public highway, obstructing its use as a thoroughfare, an individual thereby inconvenienced will not have a private cause of action based upon the public nuisance simply because by traveling the highway twice as often in the course of a day as do other members of the highway-using public the individual is arguably twice as inconvenienced by defendant's conduct. However, were the plaintiff to fall into the unlighted ditch at night and be injured, a private action for damages would lie. For an argument that courts should reject the special injury rule as both historically unfounded and normatively undesirable, see Denise E. Antolini, Modernizing Public Nuisance: Solving the Paradox of the Special Injury Rule, 28 Ecology L.Q. 755 (2001). Observe also that subsection (1) of §821C speaks of an action to recover damages, while subsection (2) speaks of a proceeding to enjoin or abate a public nuisance. Just as courts have been willing to enjoin intentional trespasses to land, so they have traditionally been willing to enjoin continuing nuisances, both public and private. The important question of the nature of the remedy available to the plaintiff will be raised throughout the materials which follow.

Private nuisance is by far a more important body of law than public nuisance for the protection of private interests in land. As mentioned above, §821D of the Restatement (Second) defines a private nuisance as an invasion other than a trespass — although there may be an accompanying trespass — of the owner's "interest in the private use and enjoyment of land." Thus, private nuisance is different from, but not necessarily inconsistent with, the concept of trespass described in the preceding section. The basic difference may be expressed in terms of the different interests protected. A successful action in trespass serves to protect the plaintiff's interest in the exclusive possession of land; an action in private nuisance protects the plaintiff's interest in the use and enjoyment of land. Trespass requires a physical entry; private nuisance does not.

An early English decision illustrates clearly the function served by the law of private nuisance in our legal system. In William Aldred's Case, 9 Co. Rep. 57, 77 Eng. Rep. 816 (1611), the plaintiff brought an action on the case against the defendant alleging that the stench from defendant's hog sty next door constituted a nuisance substantially interfering with the plaintiff's use and enjoyment of his land. Clearly, if the defendant had driven his hogs onto the plaintiff's land without permission, the plaintiff's action would have been in trespass. However, here the defendant kept his hogs at home and sent, instead, their heady smell on the summer breezes to the plaintiff's land. On appeal from a judgment in favor of the plaintiff, the defendant argued "that the building of the house for hogs was necessary for the sustenance of man: and one ought not to have so delicate a nose, that he cannot bear the smell of hogs. . . ." No doubt moved by the plaintiff's appeal to the court's sense of smell as well as to its sense of justice, the King's Bench affirmed the judgment against the defendant. The plaintiff's nuisance action here was brought on the case and it therefore was necessary for the plaintiff to show that harm actually was suffered as a result of the defendant's operating his hog sty. This requirement of harm, reminiscent of a similar requirement in connection with actions for unintentional trespass that also developed out of the common law action on the case, has been carried over into the modern law of nuisance.

In addition to invading the plaintiff's interest in the private use and enjoyment of land and causing substantial harm in the process, the invasion must also be wrongful before it can constitute a private nuisance. The Restatement (Second) of Torts sets forth the general rule governing the establishment of the wrongfulness of the defendant's invasion as follows:

§822. General Rule

> One is subject to liability for a private nuisance if, but only if, his conduct is a legal cause of an invasion of another's interest in the private use and enjoyment of land, and the invasion is either
>
> (a) intentional and unreasonable, or
>
> (b) unintentional and otherwise actionable under the rules controlling liability for negligent or reckless conduct, or for abnormally dangerous conditions or activities.

It is interesting to note the extent to which this formulation of the general rule governing private nuisance parallels the formulation advanced earlier of the rules governing liability for trespass to land. The same distinction is here drawn between invasions that are intentional and those that are unintentional. As for the latter, they are subjected to the same requirements earlier observed in connection with unintentional trespass; that is, the plaintiff must show the defendant to have been negligent or reckless, or to have either engaged in some abnormally dangerous activity or allowed an abnormally dangerous condition to exist. See, e.g., Pesaturo v. Kinne, 20 A.3d 284 (N.H. 2011) (holding that "a landowner who knows or should know that his tree is decayed or defective and fails to maintain the tree reasonably is liable for injuries proximately caused by the tree, even when the harm occurs outside of his property lines").

For intentional invasions, §822 requires that they be "unreasonable" in order for them to be sufficient to establish liability. For example, in Bansbach v. Harbin, 728 S.E.2d 533 (W. Va. 2012), two homeowners sued their neighbors in a nuisance action for creating a junkyard and posting harassing signs directed at the plaintiffs. The court held that while the behavior was intentional, it was not unreasonable, and therefore the plaintiffs could not seek remedy through private nuisance. But see Apple Hill Farms Dev., LLP v. Price, 816 N.W.2d 914, 918-19 (Wis. Ct. App. 2012) (holding that "unsightly spite fences can constitute a private nuisance").

Recall that no such additional unreasonableness requirement is imposed in connection with intentional trespass, and that further questions regarding whether the defendant's intentional entry upon the plaintiff's land might have been justified are left to be handled by the various specific categories of privilege. In effect, the additional requirement that the plaintiff in a nuisance action show the invasion to have been unreasonable brings the question of possible justification of the defendant's conduct into the prima facie case and makes it part of the plaintiff's burden. In general, though, courts tend to focus on the consequences of the defendant's conduct rather than the nature of the conduct itself. As one venerable treatise notes, "[c]onfusion has resulted from the fact that the intentional interference with the plaintiff's use of his property can be unreasonable even when the defendant's conduct is reasonable." W. Page Keeton et al., Prosser and Keeton on the Law of Torts 629 (5th ed. 1984). The general rule governing this question of unreasonableness is contained in §826 of the Restatement (Second):

§826. Unreasonableness of Intentional Invasion

An intentional invasion of another's interest in the use and enjoyment of land is unreasonable if

(a) the gravity of the harm outweighs the utility of the actor's conduct, or

(b) the harm caused by the conduct is serious and the financial burden of compensating for this and similar harm to others would not make the continuation of the conduct not feasible.

The concepts of the gravity of the harm to the plaintiff and the utility of the defendant's conduct are developed in subsequent sections of the Restatement (Second):

§827. Gravity of Harm—Factors Involved

In determining the gravity of the harm from an intentional invasion of another's interest in the use and enjoyment of land, the following factors are important:

(a) The extent of the harm involved;

(b) the character of the harm involved;

(c) the social value that the law attaches to the type of use or enjoyment invaded;

(d) the suitability of the particular use or enjoyment invaded to the character of the locality; and

(e) the burden on the person harmed of avoiding the harm.

§828. Utility of Conduct—Factors Involved

In determining the utility of conduct that causes an intentional invasion of another's interest in the use and enjoyment of land, the following factors are important:

(a) the social value that the law attaches to the primary purpose of the conduct;

(b) the suitability of the conduct to the character of the locality; and

(c) the impracticability of preventing or avoiding the invasion.

These three sections deserve careful consideration. The lists of factors to be considered do not purport to be exhaustive, nor do they appear to be listed in any particular sequence of relative significance. Taken together, these three sections afford great latitude to courts in determining the reasonableness of the defendant's invasion of the plaintiff's interest in use and enjoyment of land. Drawing upon past judicial decisions that applied these principles of gravity versus utility, the Restatement (Second) provides some specific examples of "unreasonable" behavior. The invasion of the plaintiff's interest will be found to be unreasonable where the defendant's conduct is malicious or indecent (§829); where the resulting harm is severe and more than the plaintiff ought to have to bear without compensation (§829A); where the resulting invasion could have been avoided by the defendant relatively easily ("without undue hardship") (§830); or where the plaintiff's use of his land is, and the defendant's conduct is not, suited to the locality in which the invasion occurred (§831).

Section 829A is of particular interest. The exact language of the section states that the invasion is unreasonable "if the harm resulting from the invasion is severe and greater than the other should be required to bear without compensation." If §829A is to serve its function of supplying an illustrative example of the application of the rules contained in §§826-828, the quoted portion must refer to something more specific than the plaintiff's being entitled to compensation under the general rules comprising the law of private nuisance. As the history of this section makes clear, §829A was intended to assert that, quite apart from the traditional considerations of reasonableness reflected in the earlier sections, courts may base a finding of unreasonableness and impose liability upon the independent ground that the plaintiff cannot afford financially to go without a remedy. Thus, even if the utility of the defendant's conduct outweighs the gravity of the harm it is causing, it would appear that the invasion of the plaintiff's interest may be found to be unreasonable based solely upon the magnitude of the harm to the plaintiff and the accompanying financial burden. Interpreted in this manner, §829A is not so much an illustrative application of the rules contained in §§826-828 as it is a remarkable exception to them.

Any doubt that §829A was intended to make relevant the plaintiff's financial needs is eliminated by turning to an even more explicit recognition that the concomitant consideration — the defendant's ability to pay — is a sufficient, independent basis upon which to impose liability. In subsection (b) of §826, the defendant's intentional invasion of the plaintiff's interest is unreasonable, notwithstanding the fact that the utility of the defendant's conduct outweighs the gravity of the harm, if "the harm caused by the conduct is serious and the financial burden of compensating for this and similar harm to others would not make continuation of the conduct not feasible." Clearly, subsection (b) authorizes the imposition of liability for damages against an otherwise reasonable defendant based solely upon the judgment that the defendant is able to pay and still remain in operation — that is, that the defendant can financially afford to compensate for the harm. Admittedly, questions of the relative solvency of the parties to a tort action have been in the background of much of what we have considered in this book. However, they have never before been recognized as legitimate independent bases upon which to impose liability on a case-by-case basis.

In sum, the drafters inserted into the private nuisance sections of the Restatement (Second) unique recognitions that both the plaintiff's need to be paid and the defendant's ability to pay may serve as independent bases upon which to impose liability. The sections that accomplish this acknowledgment, §§829A and 826(b) respectively, are unquestionably the most intriguing and provocative provisions in the entire Restatement treatment of the subject of private nuisance. They raise questions regarding the interplay between deterrence and compensation, or efficiency and equity, that are at the very core of tort law and theory.

Up to this point, we have been concerned primarily with defining the nuisance concept and with describing the elements that must be proved for the plaintiff to succeed in placing the nuisance label upon the defendant's interference with his interest in the enjoyment and use of land. It is also important to consider the question of the remedies available to the plaintiff once the existence of a private nuisance has been shown. It will be recalled that once a trespass is proved, equity has traditionally purported to be willing, based upon the uniqueness of real property and the inadequacy of the legal remedy of damages, to enjoin threatened repetitions. One might have reasonably expected the same underlying recognition of the uniqueness of land to lead courts to enjoin nuisances whenever a substantial and unreasonable interference with the plaintiff's enjoyment and use of his land has been proved. In fact, courts have been willing to adopt this approach when the interference is found to be unreasonable in the sense that the harm to the plaintiff's interest outweighs the utility of the defendant's conduct.

However, this is not always true in cases in which judges have concluded that the utility of the defendant's conduct outweighs the gravity of the resulting harm, and yet have found a nuisance to exist based upon the substantiality of the harm and the feasibility of the defendant's enterprise compensating the plaintiff. In such cases, they have occasionally refused to enjoin the defendant's conduct but have, instead, ordered the defendant to pay damages. These are, of course, precisely the cases covered by §§829A and 826(b), in which the plaintiff's need to be paid and the defendant's ability to pay are made independent bases for concluding the defendant's intrusion to be unreasonable. In both of these provisions, the clear implication is that the only remedy available to the plaintiff in such cases will be monetary damages, and that injunctive relief will not be forthcoming.

C. Judicial Applications of the Substantive Law

It is one thing to arrive at a set of internally consistent rules purporting to solve the problems presented by our traditional commitment to protecting private interests in the possession, enjoyment, and use of land. It is quite another for the courts to develop socially acceptable and judicially manageable solutions when confronted, piecemeal, by these problems in real cases. One of the advantages enjoyed by the American Law Institute — and at the same time, perhaps, one of its weaknesses — is that it need not actually decide difficult cases. It should come as no surprise, therefore, that the rules of law developed in actual cases often lack the conceptual consistency and internal logic of the preceding Restatement summaries of the common law. Consistency and logic are often among the first victims when courts are called upon to struggle with major social problems. What follows is a collection of opinions indicating how a number of courts have attempted to harmonize the competing values in difficult cases, and how they have handled the interplay between trespass and nuisance. As you read these cases, try to map precisely how — as a doctrinal matter — the cases are resolved, both in terms of liability and remedy, in order to gain an understanding of what options are available and what forces might be motivating the courts' decisions.

Peters v. Archambault

361 Mass. 91, 278 N.E.2d 729 (1972)

CUTTER, J.

The plaintiffs by this bill seek to compel the defendants (the Archambaults) to remove a portion of the Archambault house which encroaches on the plaintiffs' land in Marshfield. The plaintiffs and the Archambaults own adjoining ocean-front lots. Both lots are registered (G.L. c. 185). Neither certificate of title shows the Archambault lot to have any rights in the plaintiffs' lot.

The Archambaults' predecessor in title obtained a building permit in 1946 and built a house partly on their own lot and partly on the plaintiffs' lot, of which the total area is about 4,900 square feet. Each lot had a frontage of only fifty feet on the adjacent way. The encroachment contains 465 square feet, and the building extends fifteen feet, three inches, onto the plaintiffs' lot, to a depth of thirty-one feet, four inches. The trial judge found that it will be expensive to remove the encroaching portion of the Archambaults' building. He ruled (correctly, so far as appears from his subsidiary findings and from the small portion of the evidence which has been reported) that there had been established no estoppel of, or laches on the part of, the plaintiffs in seeking to have the encroachment removed. It appears from the evidence that the Archambaults bought their lot from one vendor and the plaintiffs on June 14, 1966, bought their lot from another vendor. The judge found no evidence of any permission by the owners of the plaintiffs' lot for the encroachment. The encroachment was discovered on July 14, 1966, when the plaintiffs had a survey of their land made.[1]

A final decree ordered the removal of the encroachment. The Archambaults appealed. The judge adopted as his report of material facts the findings already summarized.

1. In Massachusetts a landowner is ordinarily entitled to mandatory equitable relief to compel removal of a structure significantly encroaching on his land, even though the encroachment was unintentional or negligent and the cost of removal is substantial in comparison to any injury suffered by the owner of the lot upon which the encroachment has taken place. [Citations omitted.] In rare cases, referred to in our decisions as "exceptional" [citation omitted], courts of equity have refused to grant a mandatory injunction and have left the plaintiff to his remedy of damages, "where the unlawful encroachment has been made innocently, and the cost of removal by the defendant would be greatly disproportionate to the injury to the plaintiff from its continuation, or where the substantial rights of the owner may be protected without recourse to an injunction, or where an injunction would be oppressive and inequitable.["] . . .

2. We here are considering the remedies to be applied with respect to registered land. Such land is protected to a greater extent than other land from unrecorded and unregistered liens, prescriptive rights, encumbrances, and other burdens. [Citations omitted.] Adverse possession (c. 185, §53) does not run against such land. . . .

3. The present record discloses no circumstances which would justify denial of a mandatory injunction for removal of an encroachment taking away over nine per cent (465/4900) of the plaintiffs' lot. . . . The invasion of the plaintiffs' lot is substantial and not de minimis. Photographs and maps in evidence, portraying the encroachment, show that the intrusion of the Archambaults' building on the plaintiffs' small lot greatly increases the congestion of that lot. The plaintiffs were entitled to receive whatever was shown by the land registration certificate as belonging to their grantor, unencumbered by any unregistered prescriptive easement or encroachment. . . .

Decree affirmed with costs of appeal.

TAURO, C.J. (dissenting).

The plaintiffs and defendants are owners of adjoining lots, with dwellings, both registered under G.L. c. 185. The defendants acquired title to their lot on June 18, 1954, and the plaintiffs acquired their title on June 14, 1966. The plaintiffs seek removal

1. The brief findings and the limited evidence designated for report to this court leave it wholly uncertain (a) what, if any, inspection the plaintiffs made before purchasing their present house and lot, and (b) how much, if at all, the location of the Archambaults' building affected the price paid by the plaintiffs.

of a portion of the defendants' dwelling which encroaches on their land. This encroachment existed in full view from June, 1946, when the defendants' predecessor in title erected the dwelling, until July 14, 1966, when the plaintiffs had their property surveyed for the purpose of erecting a retaining wall. During this period, neither the plaintiffs' predecessor in title nor the plaintiffs raised any objection to the location of the defendants' dwelling. It is reasonable to infer that prior to taking title, the plaintiffs viewed the property. Thus they had actual notice of the location of the defendants' dwelling and its relative position to their own dwelling.

The plaintiffs do not seek money damages but rather a decree for the removal of the encroachment on their land which, in effect, would result in the destruction of the defendants' dwelling. The Superior Court made, and the majority today affirm, such a decree. I cannot agree with the opinion of the majority that, in the property exercise of the court's discretion, "[t]he present record discloses no circumstances which would justify denial of a mandatory injunction" compelling the removal of the encroaching structure. To the contrary, I believe that the record before us sets forth unusual circumstances which would justify this court in denying a mandatory injunction and leaving the plaintiffs to seek their remedy at law for damages. Moreover, the granting of injunctive relief in the circumstances of this case would be "oppressive and inequitable."

To conclude, as does the majority opinion, that this court must grant a mandatory injunction because the facts in the instant case do not precisely fit the factual pattern adjudged to be "exceptional" in prior Massachusetts cases is illogical and untenable. Courts, especially courts of equity, should not be restricted to so fossilized a concept of what the law is or should be. The cause of justice deserves a better fate. . . .

As stated above, the defendants occupied their dwelling for over twelve years peacefully and without complaint prior to the present lawsuit. They bought their property in June, 1954, apparently without knowledge that, in 1946, their predecessor in title had mistakenly built partially upon an adjoining lot.[4] The defendants' house was in plain view when the plaintiffs acquired title to the adjoining lot in June, 1966. It seems likely that, before the plaintiffs took title, they viewed the property and were aware of the location of the defendants' house and its proximity (by approximately six feet) to the house they might purchase. It is reasonable to infer, either that they inquired and were told that the space between the dwellings marked the property line, or that they made this assumption. The plaintiffs have disclosed that they discovered the encroachment one month after taking title as the result of a survey undertaken by them for the purpose of constructing a retaining wall. Apparently there was nothing about the defendants' dwelling which was offensive to the plaintiffs or even aroused their suspicions at the time of purchase. It appears therefore that the plaintiffs were satisfied with their purchase and the proximity of the defendants' dwelling to their own until the survey and that, but for the fortuity of the survey, the encroachment might have continued undiscovered indefinitely as it had during the entire period 1946 to 1966.

The discovery of the encroachment in these circumstances is best characterized as an unexpected windfall[6] rather than an intentional injury. The defendants are innocent of any wrongdoing and are at most guilty of unknowingly continuing a longstanding

4. While the trial judge found no evidence that the plaintiffs' predecessor in title gave his permission in 1946 to the building of a house partially on his lot, neither did the judge find any evidence that the then owner protested during construction or in later years. It is clear therefore that the dwelling now owned by the defendants remained in plain view for a period of two decades apparently without objection from anyone.

6. The close proximity of the defendants' dwelling to the plaintiffs' dwelling was necessarily a factor in the purchase price. As a corollary, the plaintiffs' property would have been worth more, and the plaintiffs would have

encroachment. Nor can it be said that the defendants have deprived the plaintiffs of something which they believed they were entitled to at the time of their purchase. On the contrary, the plaintiffs could only have believed that they were acquiring exactly what they contemplated when they inspected the property. Subsequently, by virtue of the survey which they had made, the plaintiffs discovered they had purchased more than they had bargained for. At the same time, the defendants learned that what they had purchased in 1954 was less than they had bargained for. These circumstances should not pass unnoticed.

Moreover, removal would be a severe burden upon the defendant. As the trial judge indicated, it would "cost a lot of money, and [involve] a lot of inconvenience, and . . . reduce . . . [the defendants'] property value to a great extent." The judge does not appear to have considered whether removal might require the razing of a substantial portion of the defendants' house, but from the exhibits, we should not be unaware of this possibility. The judge made no finding of irreparable injury to the plaintiffs. Under the other facts which he did find, however, I conclude to the contrary that the injury to the plaintiffs, if any, is not of great significance compared with the defendants' loss and that money damages should be a sufficient remedy.

In the totality of circumstances, I conclude that equity does not, in the exercise of our sound discretion, require us to grant injunctive relief. Removal imposes upon the defendants substantial cost and inconvenience which are entirely disproportionate to the injury to the plaintiffs. Where, as here, it appears that the plaintiffs were content with the status quo until fortuitous discovery of the encroachment, it would be oppressive and inequitable for this court to grant a mandatory injunction against the defendants who have acted in good faith, albeit their predecessor in title made a mistake which remained undiscovered for some twenty years. Hardship alone is of course not a ground for denial of injunctive relief [citation omitted], but this court should take relative hardship into account, if, as in the instant case, the owner of the encroaching structure is not guilty of an intentional trespass. . . . Here, it appears not only that the defendants have always acted in good faith but that the initial trespass was committed many years before they acquired title to their lot. . . .

If we were to refuse injunctive relief, common sense suggests that, in all probability, this dispute would be settled eventually without the need for the destruction of the defendants' dwelling. This could be accomplished through an agreement by the plaintiffs to voluntarily relocate their boundary line in return for payment by the defendants of an amount negotiated between them. The parties would then have their certificates of title reformed to reflect the agreement. In the alternative, the plaintiffs could bring an action at law and the court would make an impartial assessment of damages. The placing of the potent weapon of injunctive relief in the hands of the plaintiffs is hardly conducive to a fair and just settlement. . . . I would dismiss the bill and relegate the plaintiffs to their remedy at law.

In Renaissance Development Corp. v. Universal Properties Group, Inc., 821 A.2d 233, 238 (R.I. 2003), the court ordered the removal of defendant's retaining wall, which encroached on a portion of plaintiff's property, observing that "where the encroachment was intentional, in that defendant proceeded despite notice or warning, or where he failed to take proper precautions to ascertain the boundary . . . the courts . . . have refused to

had to pay more, if the distance between the two dwellings had been greater. It would seem therefore that, because of the mistake of both parties and of their predecessors in title, the plaintiffs stand to obtain a windfall at the defendant's expense.

balance the equities, and have issued the mandatory injunction without regard to the relative convenience or hardship involved." Other courts have refused to enjoin clear encroachments when they have resulted from innocent mistakes. In Urban Site Venture II Ltd. Partnership v. Levering Associates Ltd. Partnership, 665 A.2d 1062 (Md. 1995), the defendant built a parking garage that encroached upon the plaintiff's property by 1.3 square feet. The trial court determined that the encroached-upon property had a value of $200, that it would cost the defendant about $500,000 to remove the encroachment, and that the defendant was "innocent" in creating the encroachment. The innocence of the defendant triggered a "balancing of the hardships" approach, and the trial court denied the plaintiff's request for an injunction. The Maryland Court of Appeals affirmed, notwithstanding the fact that the plaintiff had alerted the defendant of the encroachment shortly after construction began. There were conflicting surveys, and the defendant chose to rely on the conclusion that there was no encroachment. Nevertheless, the court of appeals ruled that the trial judge could properly find that the defendant was innocent: "We do not think it was necessary at that point for Urban Site to stop construction and await the outcome of the pending litigation." Id. at 1067.

In Parry v. Murphy, 913 N.Y.S.2d 285 (N.Y. App. Div. 2010), a hydroelectric facility installed an underground pipeline that encroached upon the plaintiffs' land. The trial court granted permanent injunctive relief. The intermediate court of appeals reversed and remanded for the determination of an appropriate award of damages, describing the injunction as an excessively drastic remedy. See also Fancher v. Fagella, 650 S.E.2d 519 (Va. 2007) (holding that courts must weigh benefits and burdens to both parties and to the public in deciding whether to enjoin continuing trespass). For an exposition of the "balancing of the hardships" approach, see Restatement (Second) of Torts, §941 "Relative Hardship—'Balancing of Equities.'"

Davis v. Georgia-Pacific Corp.

251 Or. 239, 445 P.2d 481 (1968)

HOLMAN, J.

Plaintiff Veva Davis owns a residence in the city of Toledo. Subsequent to her occupation of the premises defendant commenced the operation of a pulp and paper plant in close proximity thereto. The plaintiffs, Mrs. Davis and her husband, testified the premises was rendered uninhabitable by the operation of defendant's plant because of the emanation therefrom of vibrations, offensive odors, fumes, gases, smoke and particulates which damage the residence and plant life. Plaintiffs secured a judgment against defendant for both compensatory and punitive damages for trespass. Defendant appealed.

Defendant's first four assignments of error relate to the admission of evidence and an instruction to the jury which allowed the jury to consider whether the intrusion of fumes, gases, and odors upon the property in question constituted a trespass. Defendant contends such intrusions constitute a nuisance rather than a trespass because there was no direct physical invasion of the property. The traditional concept that a trespass must be a direct intrusion by a tangible and visible object . . . has been abandoned in this state. . . . In Martin et ux. v. Reynolds Metals Co., 221 Or. 86, 342 P.2d 790 (1960), we decided that the deposit of airborne particulates upon another's land constituted a trespass even though the particulates were so small as to be invisible in the atmosphere. . . . Error was not committed by allowing the jury to consider an intrusion of fumes, gases, smoke and odors as a trespass.

The next five assignments of error relate to the refusal of the trial court to admit evidence and give instructions relevant [to] weighing the utility of defendant's conduct of its business and its efforts to prevent harm, against the seriousness of the harm, if any, suffered by plaintiffs. Traditionally, such a weighing process by the jury is one which is permitted in nuisance cases but not in those of trespass. In a trespass case the social value of defendant's conduct, its efforts to prevent the harm and other circumstances that tend to justify an intrusion cannot be considered by the trier of the facts.

This does not mean, however, that a weighing process does not take place when a court decides whether a particular kind of an intrusion, if found by the jury to exist, is of such a nature that it should be classified as a trespass. [A common example of such a weighing process] is the decision of courts that the normal operation of airplanes high in a property's airspace does not constitute a trespass. A similar kind of weighing process takes place when a court decides whether a trespass is privileged. Such classifications, however, are ones that are made by courts and not by juries. If the jury finds that intrusion occurred which is of a kind that courts hold to be an unprivileged trespass, strict liability results. The jury is not allowed to consider the utility of the use to which defendant is putting his land or his efforts to prevent harm to plaintiff in deciding plaintiff's recovery. Therefore, it was proper in this case for the trial court not to allow the jury to consider the evidence and instructions in question in deciding whether defendant should be responsible for *compensatory* damages.

We wish to make clear that no conclusion should be drawn from the above language that such a weighing process is inappropriate in a court's consideration whether an injunction should issue to restrain a continuing unprivileged trespass or whether a plaintiff should be left to his remedy at law for damages. . . .

We have found [no] prejudicial error relevant to . . . compensatory damages. Therefore, the judgment for compensatory damages is affirmed. . . . [The judgment for punitive damages is reversed.]

[The concurring opinions of O'Connell and Denecke, JJ., are omitted.]

Johnson v. Paynesville Farmers Union Cooperative Oil Co.

817 N.W.2d 693 (Minn. 2012)

Gildea, C.J.

This action involves alleged pesticide contamination of organic farm fields in central Minnesota. Appellant Paynesville Farmers Union Cooperative Oil Company ("Cooperative") is a member owned farm products and services provider that, among other things, applies pesticides to farm fields. Respondents Oluf and Debra Johnson ("Johnsons") are organic farmers. The Johnsons claim that while the Cooperative was spraying pesticide onto conventionally farmed fields adjacent to the Johnsons' fields, some pesticide drifted onto and contaminated the Johnsons' organic fields. . . .

Based on the presence of pesticides in their fields, the Johnsons filed this lawsuit against the Cooperative, alleging trespass, nuisance, negligence per se, and battery. They sought damages and a permanent injunction prohibiting the Cooperative from spraying pesticides within a half mile of the Johnsons' fields. The Johnsons claimed the following types of damages: (1) loss of profits because they had to take the fields onto which pesticide drifted out of organic production for 3 years [under the Johnsons' interpretation of applicable government and private organic certification standards]; (2) loss of profits because they had to destroy approximately 10 acres of soybeans; (3) inconvenience due to increased weeding, pollution remediation, and [regulatory] reporting responsibilities; and (4) adverse health effects. . . .

[The district court granted summary judgment to the Cooperative and dismissed all of the Johnsons' claims. The court of appeals reversed and the Supreme Court of Minnesota granted the Cooperative's petition for review.]

We begin with a discussion of the tort of trespass. In Minnesota, a trespass is committed where a plaintiff has the "right of possession" to the land at issue and there is a "wrongful and unlawful entry upon such possession by defendant." All Am. Foods, Inc. v. Cnty. of Aitkin, 266 N.W.2d 704, 705 (Minn.1978) (citation omitted). . . . Actual damages are not an element of the tort of trespass. In the absence of actual damages, the trespasser is liable for nominal damages. Finally, because trespass is an intentional tort, reasonableness on the part of the defendant is not a defense to trespass liability.

We have not specifically considered the question of whether particulate matter can result in a trespass. The "gist of the tort" of trespass, however, is the "intentional interference with rights of exclusive possession." Dan B. Dobbs, The Law of Torts §50 at 95 (2000). In other words, the tort of trespass is committed when a person "intentionally enters or causes direct and tangible entry upon the land in possession of another." Dobbs, supra, §50 at 95 (footnotes omitted). And the defendant's entry must be done "by means of some physical, tangible agency" in order to constitute a trespass. James A. Henderson, Jr. et al., The Torts Process 386 (7th ed. 2007). Our case law is consistent with this traditional formulation of trespass because we have recognized that a trespass can occur when a person or tangible object enters the plaintiff's land. . . .

When people or tangible objects enter the plaintiff's land without permission, these entries disturb the landowner's right to exclusively possess her land. W. Page Keeton et al., Prosser & Keeton on the Law of Torts, §13, at 70 (5th ed.1984). But the disruption to the landowner's exclusive possessory interest is not the same when the invasion is committed by an intangible agency, such as the particulate matter at issue here. Id. §13, at 71. Such invasions may interfere with the landowner's use and enjoyment of her land, but those invasions do not require that the landowner share possession of her land in the way that invasions by physical objects do. See Adams v. Cleveland–Cliffs Iron Co., 237 Mich. App. 51, 602 N.W.2d 215, 218-19 (1999) ("[P]ossessory rights to real property include as distinct interests the right to exclude and the right to enjoy, violations of which give rise to the distinct causes of action respectively of trespass and nuisance." (citing Keeton, supra, §87)); John Larkin, Inc. v. Marceau, 184 Vt. 207, 959 A.2d 551, 555 (2008) (holding that landowner who sprayed pesticide on his land that drifted onto plaintiff's land did not commit trespass because there was no evidence that the pesticide interfered with the plaintiff's right to exclusive possession of his land).

The court of appeals forged new ground in this case and extended Minnesota trespass jurisprudence when it held that a trespass could occur through the entry of intangible objects, such as the particulate matter at issue here. The court looked outside Minnesota to support the holding it reached [by relying on Borland v. Sanders Lead Co., 369 So. 2d 523 (Ala. 1979) and Bradley v. Am. Smelting & Ref. Co., 104 Wash. 2d 677, 709 P.2d 782 (1985)].

In *Bradley*, the Washington Supreme Court held that particulate matter deposited on the plaintiff's land from the defendant's copper smelter could constitute a trespass. 709 P.2d at 784, 790. And in *Borland*, the Alabama Supreme Court upheld a trespass claim based on the defendant's "emission of lead particulates and sulfoxide gases" that the plaintiffs alleged accumulated on their property. 369 So. 2d at 525-26. These cases go beyond our precedent because they conclude that intangible objects can support a claim for trespass to land.

In addition, given that "the ambient environment always contains particulate matter from many sources," the expansion of the tort of trespass in cases such as *Bradley* and *Borland* to include invasions by intangible matter potentially "subject[s] countless persons and entities to automatic liability for trespass absent any demonstrated injury." John Larkin, Inc., 959 A.2d at 555; see also Borland, 369 So. 2d at 529 ("It might appear, at first blush, from our holding today that every property owner in this State would have a cause of action against any neighboring industry which emitted particulate matter into the atmosphere, or even a passing motorist, whose exhaust emissions come to rest upon another's property."). To guard against that result, the courts in both *Bradley* and *Borland* required that it be reasonably foreseeable that the intangible matter "result in an invasion of plaintiff's possessory interest," and that the invasion caused "substantial damages" to the plaintiff's property. Borland, 369 So. 2d at 529; accord Bradley, 709 P.2d at 791. This formulation of trespass, however, conflicts with our precedent defining the elements of trespass. Under Minnesota trespass law, entry upon the land that interferes with the landowner's right to exclusive possession results in trespass whether that interference was reasonably foreseeable or whether it caused damages.

Not only is the rule from the *Bradley* and *Borland* courts inconsistent with our trespass precedent, but the rule in those cases also blurs the line between trespass and nuisance. Traditionally, trespasses are distinct from nuisances: "[t]he law of nuisance deals with indirect or intangible interference with an owner's use and enjoyment of land, while trespass deals with direct and tangible interferences with the right to exclusive possession of land." Dobbs, supra, §50 at 96. But in cases like *Bradley* and *Borland*, the courts "call[ ] the intrusion of harmful microscopic particles" a trespass and not a nuisance, and then "us[e] some of the techniques of nuisance law to weigh the amount and reasonableness of the intrusion." Dobbs, supra, §50 at 96. Because *Bradley* and *Borland* require a showing of reasonable foreseeability and substantial damages, they essentially disregard the traditional understanding of trespass under Minnesota law, and they are "in reality, examples of either the tort of private nuisance or liability for harm resulting from negligence" and not trespass cases at all. Keeton, supra, §13 at 71-72.

But the Johnsons argue that *Bradley* and *Borland* reflect the modern view of trespass and urge us to likewise abandon the traditional distinctions between trespass and nuisance when considering invasions by particulate matter. We decline the Johnsons' invitation to abandon the traditional distinctions between trespass and nuisance law. Our trespass jurisprudence recognizes the unconditional right of property owners to exclude others through the ability to maintain an action in trespass even when no damages are provable. The rule the Johnsons advocate, and that the court of appeals adopted, erodes this right because it imposes on the property owner the obligation to demonstrate that the invasion causes some consequence. Imposing this restriction on a trespass claim is inconsistent with our precedent that provides a remedy to a property owner "for any trivial trespass" [Romans v. Nadler, 217 Minn. 174, 180, 14 N.W.2d 482, 486 (1944)]. And requiring that a property owner prove that she suffered some consequence from the trespasser's invasion before she is able to seek redress for that invasion "offends traditional principles of ownership" by "endanger[ing] the right of exclusion itself." Adams, 602 N.W.2d at 217, 221 (declining to recognize a trespass claim for dust, noise, and vibrations emanating from defendant's mining operation) . . . .[9]

9. The dissent would have us conclude that intangible objects can (but only sometimes) cause a trespass. The dissent argues that a trespass might occur "when [an] intangible object is actually a substance that settles on the land and damages it." (Emphasis added). But, as discussed above, the presence of actual damages is not relevant to a discussion of trespass law because damages are not an element of a trespass claim in Minnesota.

In summary, trespass claims address tangible invasions of the right to exclusive possession of land, and nuisance claims address invasions of the right to use and enjoyment of land. The Johnsons do not allege that a tangible object invaded their land. The Johnsons' claim is that the Cooperative's actions have prevented them from using their land as an organic farm, not that any action of the Cooperative has prevented the Johnsons from possessing any part of their land. The Johnsons' claim is one for nuisance, not trespass. We therefore hold that the district court did not err in concluding that the Johnsons' trespass claim failed as a matter of law.

[The remainder of the court's opinion discusses the Johnsons' nuisance and negligence per se claims, concluding that the bulk of those claims are unsupported by allegations of actual damage. In brief, the court concludes that the sacrificial measures taken by the Johnsons in destroying crops and removing cropland from production were not actually required under applicable federal organic regulations and private certification standards. The case was remanded to permit the Johnsons an opportunity to allege other grounds of actual damage stemming from the pesticide drift incidents.]

PAGE, J. (dissenting).

I respectfully dissent.

. . .

The court holds that Minnesota does not recognize claims for trespass by particulate matter. I disagree with the breadth of the court's holding. The term "particulate matter" encompasses a variety of substances, but the court's one-size-fits-all holding that particulate matter can never cause a trespass fails to take into account the differences between these various substances. The Environmental Protection Agency defines "particulate matter" as "a complex mixture of extremely small particles and liquid droplets" "made up of a number of components, including acids (such as nitrates and sulfates), organic chemicals, metals, and soil or dust particles." United States Envtl. Prot. Agency, http://www.epa.gov/pm/ (last updated June 28, 2012). Some particles are sufficiently large or dark to be observable, "such as dust, dirt, soot, or smoke." United States Envtl. Prot. Agency, http://www.epa. gov/pm/basic.html (last updated June 15, 2012). In terms of size, the largest "inhalable coarse particles" are 10 micrometers in diameter; that is one-seventh the diameter of a strand of human hair. Id. It seems to me that differences in size, quantity, and harmfulness of varying types of particulate matter will have an effect on whether the invasion by the substance causes a trespass. For example, if someone causes harmful dust to enter a person's land and that dust settles on the person's land and interferes with the owner's possession of the land, it would seem that a trespass has occurred. However, if that person were to cause car exhaust, which presumably dissipates quickly in the air, to enter a person's land, it would seem that a trespass would not occur.

Greenwood, 220 Minn. at 312, 19 N.W.2d at 734-35. Adding an element of damages to trespass, as the dissent would have us do, would also put our courts in the unenviable position of having to decide how much damage caused by what kind of actual substance is enough to support a trespass. Making these razor thin distinctions would inevitably lead to inconsistency and confusion in Minnesota trespass jurisprudence. Moreover, nothing would be gained by forcing Minnesota's courts into making such fine distinctions because, as we have said, in the event that an intangible object does cause actual damage to property, nuisance and negligence law provide a property owner with adequate remedies.

The distinction between trespass and nuisance should not be based on whether the object invading the land is tangible or intangible. Whereas that distinction may have been logical at times when science was not as precise as it is now, that distinction is not sound today. We have previously held that invasion by water constitutes a trespass and invasion by a bullet constitutes a trespass. Greenwood v. Evergreen Mines Co., 220 Minn. 296, 311-12, 19 N.W.2d 726, 734-35 (1945) (water); Whittaker v. Stangvick, 100 Minn. 386, 391, 111 N.W. 295, 297 (1907) (bullets and fallen game). It is a small extension, if any, of those holdings to conclude that invasion by pesticide can constitute a trespass, especially because pesticides are designed to affect the land, unlike an invasion by a bullet, which creates no such risk.

The proper distinction between trespass and nuisance should be the nature of the property interest affected. See Borland v. Sanders Lead Co., 369 So. 2d 523, 529 (Ala.1979) ("Whether an invasion of a property interest is a trespass or a nuisance does not depend upon whether the intruding agent is 'tangible' or 'intangible.' Instead, an analysis must be made to determine the interest interfered with. If the intrusion interferes with the right to exclusive possession of property, the law of trespass applies. If the intrusion is to the interest in use and enjoyment of property, the law of nuisance applies."); see also J.D. Lee & Barry A. Lindahl, 4 Modern Tort Law: Liability and Litigation §38:1 (2d ed. 2006) ("The distinction between nuisance and trespass is in the difference in the interest interfered with: in a nuisance action it is the use and enjoyment of land, while the interest in a trespass action is the exclusive possession of land."). As other courts have suggested, the same conduct may constitute both trespass and nuisance. See Borland, 369 So. 2d at 527 (noting, "the same conduct on the part of a defendant may, and often does, result in the actionable invasion of" exclusive possession of the property and use and enjoyment). Thus, while the court concludes that invasion by an intangible object never interferes with a property owner's possessory rights, I conclude that in some circumstances it may, particularly when that intangible object is actually a substance that settles on the land and damages it.

Rather than adopt a categorical conclusion that particulate matter can never cause a trespass, I conclude, as discussed above, that it may constitute a trespass under some circumstances. Here, on the record presented at this stage in the litigation, it is not clear to me whether the pesticides in this case constituted a trespass. Therefore, I would allow the suit to go forward and permit the record to be developed to resolve that question. . . .

Adams v. Cleveland-Cliffs Iron Col, 602 N.W.2d 215 (Mich. Ct. App. 1999), cited by the court in *Johnson*, vacated a trespass judgment against one of the largest iron ore mines in the United States, rejecting the "modern view" of cases like *Davis* that particulate pollution and other intangible invasions can interfere with a plaintiff's right of exclusive possession:

> To summarize, the effects of recent trends in the law of trespass have included eliminating the requirements of a direct invasion by a tangible object, requiring proof of actual and substantial damages, and weighing the plaintiff's damages against the social utility of the operation causing them. This so-called "modern view of trespass" appears, with all its nuances and add-ons, merely to replicate traditional nuisance doctrine as recognized in Michigan. Indeed, the trends . . . have conflated nuisance with trespass to the point of rendering it difficult to delineate the difference between the two theories of recovery.

> With all of these modern adjustments to traditional trespass law, it is little wonder that it has become difficult to differentiate between trespass and nuisance. . . . We prefer to preserve the separate identities of trespass and nuisance. . . .

Many jurisdictions adhere to this "traditional view" of trespass. See, e.g., Babb v. Lee County Landfill SC, 747 S.E.2d 468 (S.C. 2013) (stating that trespass is an inappropriate cause of action for claims premised on noxious odors, notwithstanding "modern science's understanding of microscopic and atomic particles").

On the other hand, like the Oregon Supreme Court in *Davis*, other courts have retreated from the rule that invasions by small chemicals or particles, such as smoke, gases, and odors, can only constitute a nuisance and not a trespass. In Stevenson v. E.I. DuPont De Nemours & Co., 327 F.3d 400 (5th Cir. 2003), for instance, the appeals court rejected *Adams* and instead ruled that under Texas law, heavy metal particulates could effect a "trespass" on plaintiffs' property. See also Nieman v. NLO, Inc., 108 F.3d 1546 (6th Cir. 1997) (release of uranium and radiation from nuclear processing facility constitutes trespass); Scribner v. Summers, 84 F.3d 554 (2d Cir. 1996) (barium leaching onto plaintiff's property held to be a trespass); Maddy v. Vulcan Materials Co., 737 F. Supp. 1528 (D. Kan. 1990) (airborne pollution constitutes trespass where the plaintiff can show that his property was physically damaged); Smith v. Carbide & Chems. Corp., 226 S.W.3d 52 (Ky. 2007) (intentional intrusion by means of visually imperceptible particles constitutes trespass); Gallagher v. Grant-Lafayette Elec. Coop., 637 N.W.2d 80 (Wis. Ct. App. 2001) (herbicide drift could constitute trespass); Ream v. Keen, 838 P.2d 1073 (Or. 1992) (following *Davis*, smoke from neighboring burning field held to be a trespass); Maryland Heights Leasing, Inc. v. Mallinckrodt, Inc., 706 S.W.2d 218 (Mo. Ct. App. 1985) (radioactive emissions may constitute trespass); Bradley v. American Smelting & Ref. Co., 709 P.2d 782, 786 (Wash. 1985) (permitting intentional trespass claim for microscopic airborne particles because the defendant "had to appreciate with substantial certainty that the law of gravity would visit the effluence upon someone, somewhere"); Sanders v. Beckwith, 283 P.2d 235 (Ariz. 1955) (use of DDT and other pesticides treated as negligent trespass).

What if, instead of intruding onto the land of another, a harmful chemical makes land harmful to animals that come onto the affected land? Consider Anderson v. State, Department of Natural Resources, 693 N.W.2d 181 (Minn. 2005), in which the court addressed an action by commercial beekeepers whose bees had been killed by the spraying of pesticides on land owned by defendants. Plaintiffs maintained beehives on neighboring land that they did not own. As the court noted, "[m]ost pesticide-related litigation involves actions . . . against applicators who allow pesticide to drift to neighboring land," but "[i]n this case, . . . it is the bees — not the chemicals — that have traveled to the neighboring land." Id. at 188. Nevertheless, the court held that defendants owed a duty to use their land in a manner that was reasonably careful toward the foraging bees, and that the evidence presented by plaintiffs of pesticide over-spraying suggested that this duty may have been breached. Compare Bennett v. Larsen Co., 348 N.W.2d 540 (Wis. 1984) (no common law duty to protect foraging bees on one's own property, except to avoid intentional or wanton harm). For a discussion of *Anderson* and *Bennett*, see Alexandra B. Klass, Bees, Trees, Preemption, and Nuisance: A New Path to Resolving Pesticide Land Use Disputes, 32 Ecology L.Q. 763 (2005).

Underground contamination of neighboring lands may give rise to liability under either nuisance or trespass. See Hoery v. United States, 64 P.3d 214 (Colo. 2003) (subterranean leakages of trichloroethylene, a toxic chemical, from defendants' military facility into water sources beneath plaintiffs' land constituted a physical intrusion subject to the ordinary principles of trespass); Shockley v. Hoechst Celanese Corp., 793 F. Supp. 670 (D.S.C. 1992) (barrels leaking hazardous chemicals as basis for action based on nuisance and trespass); Gulf Park Water Co. v. First Ocean Springs Dev. Co., 530 So. 2d 1325 (Miss. 1988) (discharge of waste from sewage plant into lagoon constitutes trespass). Some courts require a demonstration that defendant had substantially certain knowledge that contamination would result before finding an intentional trespass in the case of underground contamination. See Martin v. Amoco Oil Co., 679 N.E.2d 139 (Ind. 1997); United Proteins v. Farmland Indus., 915 P.2d 80 (Kan. 1996); Rushing v. Hooper-McDonald, Inc., 300 So. 2d 94 (Ala. 1974).

One challenging context in which plaintiffs invoke trespass and nuisance claims concerns activities by the defendant that cause genuine fear among plaintiffs or real diminutions in the market value of their property, but that are not regarded as actually harmful according to the existing scientific evidence. See Mehlenbacher v. Akzo Nobel Salt, Inc., 216 F.3d 291, 300 (2d Cir. 2000) (referring to the split of authority regarding whether "stigma damages are available in a tort action"). In San Diego Gas & Electric Co. v. Superior Court, 920 P.2d 669 (Cal. 1996), for instance, the plaintiffs, Martin and Joyce Covalt, brought an action for damages and injunctive relief against the defendant power company, claiming that electric and magnetic fields (EMF) emitted from the defendant's electric power lines had caused the Covalts to suffer emotional distress and, by making their home uninhabitable, had destroyed its market value. The trial court overruled the power company's demurrer, and the power company appealed. The Supreme Court of California held that the Covalts could maintain neither a trespass nor a nuisance claim. Their trespass claim failed because, on the one hand, the energy level of the suspect EMF was too low to cause physical property damage and, on the other, the Covalts' claim of "diminution in property *value* . . . is not a type of physical damage to the property itself" recoverable under trespass law. Id. at 695. As for the nuisance claim, for which "proof of interference with the plaintiff's use and enjoyment of that property is sufficient," the court noted that even if the Covalts could establish that the physical harm they feared outweighed the power company's social utility, such feared harm would be inconsistent with the California Public Utilities Commission's legislatively sanctioned conclusion that "the available evidence does *not* support a reasonable belief that [EMF] present[s] a substantial risk of physical harm." Id. at 696-97.

Another case illustrating the challenge posed by nuisance claims that do not appear supported by the scientific record is Adkins v. Thomas Solvent Co., 487 N.W.2d 715 (Mich. 1992). The plaintiffs were a group of landowners whose properties dropped in value as a result of the defendant Thomas Solvent Company's underground contamination of the local ground water. According to the allegations, negative publicity surrounding the contamination caused the diminution in property values. Although the plaintiffs' properties were not, nor ever would be, subject to the contamination, the plaintiffs nevertheless claimed a right to recover damages in nuisance. Not finding any cognizable claim for recovery under Michigan's nuisance law, the trial court dismissed the action. The court of appeals reversed on the grounds that a "physical intrusion or physical effect" is not necessary to sustain a claim for nuisance. Id. at 719. While the state supreme court did not disagree with the court of appeals' statement of the Michigan law, the high court nevertheless reinstated the trial court's judgment, holding that "the trial court properly found that the plaintiffs failed to trace any significant interference with the use and enjoyment of land to an action of the defendants." Id. at 721. The supreme court concluded that expanding Michigan's nuisance law to allow recovery in this case would be a move more appropriately undertaken by the legislature (id. at 717):

> We are persuaded that the boundaries of a traditional nuisance claim should not be relaxed to permit recovery on these facts. Compensation for a decline in property value caused by unfounded perception of underground contamination is inextricably entwined with complex policy questions regarding environmental protection that are more suitably resolved through the legislative process.

Much scholarship has addressed the related questions of how expert and lay observers tend to perceive environmental, health, and safety risks in different ways, whether lay risk perceptions generally are as "unfounded" as courts such as *Adkins* conclude, and how the law should respond to often life-impacting fears that are genuine, but scientifically ungrounded. For a sampling of this analysis, see Howard Margolis, Dealing with Risk: Why the Public and the Experts Disagree on Environmental Issues (1996); Paul Slovic, The Perception of Risk (2000); Cass R. Sunstein, Laws of Fear: Beyond the Precautionary Principle (2005); Matthew D. Adler, Fear Assessment: Cost-Benefit Analysis and the Pricing of Fear and Anxiety, 79 Chi.-Kent L. Rev. 977 (2004); Dan M. Kahan, Two Conceptions of Emotion in Risk Regulation, 156 U. Pa. L. Rev. 741 (2008); Dan M. Kahan & Donald Braman, More Statistics, Less Persuasion: A Cultural Theory of Gun-Risk Perceptions, 151 U. Pa. L. Rev. 1291 (2003); Dan M. Kahan et al., Fear of Democracy: A Cultural Evaluation of Sunstein on Risk, 119 Harv. L. Rev. 1071 (2006); Douglas A. Kysar, The Expectations of Consumers, 103 Colum. L. Rev. 1700 (2003).

Waschak v. Moffat

379 Pa. 441, 109 A.2d 310 (1954)

Stearne, J.

The appeal is from a judgment of the Superior Court refusing to enter judgment *non obstante veredicto* for defendants in an action in trespass and affirming the judgment of the Court of Common Pleas of Lackawanna County in favor of plaintiffs.

Gas or fumes from culm banks, the refuse of a coal breaker, damaged the paint on plaintiffs' dwelling. In this action for damages the applicable legal principles are technical and controversial. Considerable confusion appears in the many cases. The field is that of *liability without fault for escape of substances from land.*

Plaintiffs are owners of a dwelling in the Borough of Taylor which is in the center of Pennsylvania's anthracite coal lands. An action in trespass was instituted against two partners, operators of a coal breaker in that Borough. Without fault on the part of defendants, gas known as *hydrogen sulfide* was emitted from two of defendants' culm banks. This caused discoloration of the white paint (with lead base) which had been used in painting plaintiffs' dwelling. The painted surface became dark or black. The sole proven damage was the cost of restoring the surface with a white paint, having a titanium and zinc base, which will not discolor. There was no other injury either to the building or occupants. The verdict was for $1,250.

While the verdict is in a relatively modest amount, the principles of law involved, and their application, are extremely important and far reaching. Twenty-five other cases are at issue awaiting the decision in this case. The impact of this decision will affect the entire coal interests — anthracite and bituminous — as well as other industries. Application of appropriate legal principles is of vital concern to coal miners and to other labor. . . .

In the court below the case was tried on the theory of *absolute liability* for the maintenance of a nuisance. The jury was instructed that it should determine, as a *matter of fact*, whether or not what the defendants did and the conditions resulting therefrom constituted a "reasonable and natural use" of defendants' land. . . .

[The court concludes that the utility of the defendants' conduct clearly outweighed the gravity of the harm thereby caused.]

Even if the reasonableness of the defendants' use of their property had been the *sole* consideration, there could be no recovery here. . . .

In Versailles Borough v. McKeesport Coal & Coke Co., 83 Pittsb.Leg.J. 379, Mr. Justice Musmanno, when a county judge, accurately encompassed the problem when he said:

"The plaintiffs are subject to an annoyance. This we accept, but it is an annoyance they have freely assumed. Because they desired and needed a residential proximity to their places of employment, they chose to found their abode here. It is not for them to repine; and it is probable that upon reflection they will, in spite of the annoyance which they suffer, still conclude that, after all, one's bread is more important than landscape or clear skies.

"Without smoke, Pittsburgh would have remained a very pretty *village*." . . .

In applying [the law of nuisance], it is evident the invasion of plaintiffs' land was clearly *not intentional*. And even if it were, for the reasons above stated, it was not unreasonable. On the contrary, since the emission of gases was not caused by any act of defendants and arose merely from the normal and customary use of their land without negligence, recklessness or ultrahazardous conduct, it was wholly *unintentional*, and no liability may therefore be imposed upon defendants.

The judgment is reversed and is here entered in favor of defendants *non obstante veredicto*.

[The dissenting opinion of Jones, J., is omitted.]

Musmanno, J. (dissenting).

. . . .

In 1948 the plaintiffs painted their house with a white paint. Some time later the paint began to turn to a light colored brown, then it changed to a grayish tint, once it burst into a silvery sheen, and then, as if this were its last dying gasp, the house suddenly assumed a blackish cast, the blackness deepened and intensified until now it is a "scorched black." The plaintiffs attribute this chameleon performance of their house to the hydrogen sulfide emanating from the defendants' culm deposits in the town — all in residential areas. The hydrogen sulfide, according to the plaintiffs, not only assaults the paint of the house but it snipes at the silverware, bath tub fixtures and the bronze handles of the doors, forcing them, respectively, into black, yellowish-brown and "tarnished-looking" tints. . . .

The evidence here does not show any *necessity* on the part of the defendants to locate the culm banks in the very midst of the residential areas of Taylor.

The Majority Opinion explores the law of nuisance ably but does not indicate whether the circumstances here make out a case of nuisance, although it does say that the lower Court erred in ruling that this case was one of absolute nuisance. My opinion is that there can be no doubt that the defendants were operating an actionable nuisance. The record[,] which consists of 600 printed pages, overwhelmingly establishes this fact. The poisonous gases lifting from the defendants' culm banks were destructive of property, detrimental to health and disruptive of the social life of the town.

There was evidence that the poisonous hydrogen sulfide was of such intensity that the inhabitants compelled to breathe it suffered from headaches, throat irritation, inability to sleep, coughing, lightheadedness, nausea and stomach ailments. These grave effects of the escaping gas reached such proportions that the citizens of Taylor held protest meetings and demanded that the municipal authorities take positive action to curb the gaseous invasion. . . .

It must always be kept in mind that these culm banks were not mole hills. The Main Street dump measured 1,100 feet in length, 650 feet in width and 40 feet in height. If these dimensions were applied to a ship, one can visualize the size of the vessel and what would be the state of its odoriferousness if it was loaded stem to stern with rotten eggs. And that is only one of the dumps. There is another dump at Washington Street and, consequently, another ship of rotten eggs. Its dimensions are 800 feet by 750 feet by 50 feet. A third dump measures 500 feet by 500 feet by 40 feet. Then the defendants constructed a silt dam with the same rotten-egg-smelling materials.

I do not think that there can be any doubt that the constant smell of rotten eggs constitutes a nuisance. If such a condition is not recognized by the law, then the law is the only body that does not so recognize it. . . .

The Majority states that the "emission of offensive odors, noises, fumes, violations, etc., must be weighed against the utility of the operation." In this respect, the Majority Opinion does me the honor of quoting from an Opinion I wrote when I was a member of the distinguished Court of Common Pleas of Allegheny County. Versailles Borough v. McKeesport Coal & Coke Co., 83 Pittsb.Leg.J. 379. That was an equity case where the plaintiffs sought an injunction against the defendant coal company for maintaining a burning gob pile which emitted smoke. The coal mine was located in the very heart of an industrialized area which contained factories, mills, garbage dumps, incinerators and railroads, all producing their own individualized smoke and vapors so that it could not be said that the discomforts of the inhabitants were due exclusively to the operation of the coal mine. Furthermore, after hearings lasting one month I found that the operation of the mine in no way jeopardized the health of the inhabitants:

"Of course, if the continued operation of this mine were a serious menace to the health or lives of those who reside in its vicinity, there would be another question before us, but there is no evidence in this case to warrant the assumption that the health of anyone is being imperiled."

In the instant case the exact contrary is true. The health of the town of Taylor *is* being imperiled. And then also, as well stated by the lower Court in the present litigation, "Many factors may lead a chancellor to grant or deny injunctive relief which are not properly involved in an action brought to recompense one for injury to his land. . . . A denial of relief by a court of equity is not always precedent for denying redress by way of damages."

Even so, there is a vast difference between smoke which beclouds the skies and gas which is so strong that it peels the paint from houses. I did say in the Versailles case, "One's bread is more important than landscape or clear skies." But in the preservation of human life, even bread is preceded by water, and even water must give way to breathable air. Experimentation and observation reveal that one can live as long as 60 or 70 days without food; one can keep the lamp of life burning 3 or 4 days without water, but the wick is snuffed out in a minute or two in the absence of breathable air. For decades Pittsburgh was known as the "Smoky City" and without that smoke in its early days Pittsburgh indeed would have remained a "pretty village." But with scientific progress in the development of smoke-consuming devices, added to the use of smokeless fuel, Pittsburgh's skies have cleared, its progress has been phenomenal and the bread of its workers is whiter, cleaner, and sweeter.

On September 8, 1939, this Court, speaking through Chief Justice Kephart, handed down the monumental decision in the case of Summit Hotel Co. v. National Broadcasting Co., 336 Pa. 182, 8 A.2d 302, 124 A.L.R. 968. Chief Justice Kephart there said: 336 Pa. at page 189, 8 A.2d at page 305.

"In cases of trespass for nuisance, the person responsible may be unable, no matter how careful, to avoid injury to the lands of another, but, again, he knows that injury may result from the nature of his activities regardless of care. *Under such circumstances he also assumes the risk.* The responsibility for injury lies in creating or maintaining the harmful condition.

"In all of these illustrations, the person responsible has, or should have, *prior knowledge of the probable consequences, where the act done, or the instrumentality employed, possesses potentialities of serious harm.*"

There can be no doubt that the defendants were thoroughly aware of the probable consequences of their discarding operations before the plaintiffs suffered the damage of which they complain in this litigation. . . .

Even if the rights of the plaintiffs were to be considered by Restatement Rules they would still be entitled to recover under the proposition that the defendants were so well informed of the probable harmful effects of their operation that their actions could only be regarded as an intentional invasion of the rights of the plaintiff. . . .

If there were *no* other way of disposing of the coal refuse, a different question might have been presented here, but the defendants produced no evidence that they could not have deposited the debris in places removed from the residential districts in Taylor. Certainly, many of the strip-mining craters which uglify the countryside in the areas close to Taylor could have been utilized by the defendants. They chose, however, to use the residential sections of Taylor because it was cheaper to pile the culm there than to haul it away into less populous territory.

This was certainly an unreasonable and selfish act in no way indispensably associated with the operation of the breaker. It brought greater profits to the defendants but at the expense of the health and the comfort of the other landowners in the town who are also entitled to the pursuit of happiness. . . .

I would affirm the decision of the Superior Court.

Jost v. Dairyland Power Cooperative

45 Wis. 2d 164, 172 N.W.2d 647 (1969)

The action is one for damages for injury to crops and loss of market value of farm lands. The plaintiffs are farmers living within, or near, the city limits of Alma, Wisconsin. Their farms are located on the bluffs overlooking the Mississippi River. In 1947 the Dairyland Power Cooperative erected a coal burning electric generating plant at Alma. It is the contention of the farmers that consumption of high-sulfur-content coal at this plant has increased from 300 tons per day in 1948 to 1,670 tons per day in 1967. There was testimony that the 1967 coal consumption resulted in discharging approximately 90 tons of sulphur-dioxide gas into the atmosphere each day. There was substantial evidence to show that the sulphur-dioxide gas, under certain atmospheric conditions, settled on the fields, causing a whitening of the alfalfa leaves and a dropping off of some of the vegetation. There was also testimony to show that the sulphur compounds resulting from the industrial pollution killed pine trees, caused screens to rust through rapidly, and made flower raising difficult or impossible. There was some testimony to show that some of the sulphur came from locomotives or from river barges, but there was testimony that the power plant was the source of most of the contamination. Defendant's witness, a farmer who was "hit" less frequently by the sulphurous fumes, estimated his crop damage at 5 percent. There was also evidence of damage to apple trees, sumac, and wild grape, in addition to the alfalfa damage.

Each of the plaintiff farmers testified that his land had diminished in value as the result of the continuing crop loss. . . .

The trial judge . . . entered [judgment] upon the verdict [for the plaintiffs]. Defendant has appealed from the whole of the judgment, and plaintiffs have filed for a review of the judgment which sustained the jury's finding in regard to loss of market value . . . .

Heffernan, J . . . . [After stating that the evidence compelled the conclusion, as a matter of law, that the harm to the plaintiffs' land was substantial, the court continues:]

Defendant strenuously argues that it was prejudiced by the court's refusal to permit certain testimony, particularly testimony that tended to show that defendant had used due care in the construction and operation of its plant, and to show that the social and economic utility of the Alma plant outweighed the gravity of damage to the plaintiffs.

Defendant's contention that the evidence should have been admitted rests on two theories; one, that due care, if shown, defeats a claim for nuisance, and, two, that, if the social utility of the offending industry substantially outweighs the gravity of the harm, the plaintiffs cannot recover damages.

We can agree with neither proposition. . . .

In any event it is apparent that a continued invasion of a plaintiff's interests by non-negligent conduct, when the actor knows of the nature of the injury inflicted, is an intentional tort, and the fact the hurt is administered non-negligently is not a defense to liability.

It is thus apparent that the facts tending to show freedom from negligence would not have constituted a defense to plaintiffs' nuisance action. It was therefore proper that such evidence was excluded (the nominal character of plaintiffs' proof as to negligence has been commented on above).

While there are some jurisdictions that permit the balancing of the utility of the offending conduct against the gravity of the injury inflicted, it is clear that the rule, permitting such balancing, is not approved in Wisconsin where the action is for damages. . . .

We therefore conclude that the court properly excluded all evidence that tended to show the utility of the Dairyland Cooperative's enterprise. Whether its economic or social importance dwarfed the claim of a small farmer is of no consequence in this lawsuit. It will not be said that, because a great and socially useful enterprise will be liable in damages, an injury small by comparison should go unredressed. We know of no acceptable rule of jurisprudence that permits those who are engaged in important and desirable enterprises to injure with impunity those who are engaged in enterprises of lesser economic significance. Even the government or other entities, including public utilities, endowed with the power of eminent domain — the power to take private property in order to devote it to a purpose beneficial to the public good — are obliged to pay a fair market value for what is taken or damaged. To contend that a public utility, in the pursuit of its praiseworthy and legitimate enterprise, can, in effect, deprive others of the full use of their property without compensation, poses a theory unknown to the law of Wisconsin, and in our opinion would constitute the taking of property without due process of law. . . .

Judgment affirmed in part and reversed in part consistent with this opinion.

As in *Jost*, some courts grant relief for nuisance even without conducting a cost-benefit analysis. In *Waschak*, however, the court held that where the balance tipped in favor of the defendants, they would not be liable in the absence of a showing of intent to injure the plaintiff.

Numerous authorities and courts side with the *Waschak* court. See, e.g., Williams v. Amoco Prods. Co., 734 P.2d 1113 (Kan. 1987); W. Page Keeton et al., Prosser and Keeton on the Law of Torts 622 (5th ed. 1984). However, others side with *Jost*, holding that a knowing infliction of injury is sufficient to satisfy the intent requirement, even in the absence of negligence or an ultrahazardous activity. See, e.g., Morgan v. Quailbrook Condo. Co., 704 P.2d 573, 577 (Utah 1985) ("[It] is sufficient to demonstrate that the actor maintained the condition after he knew that it was causing an invasion of another's interest in the use and enjoyment of land."); Bradley v. American Smelting & Refining Co., 709 P.2d 782 (Wash. 1985). Still other courts eliminate the intent prong entirely, focusing instead on the reasonableness of the defendant's conduct. See, e.g., Mathis v. Barnes, 316 S.W.3d 795, 801 (Tex. App. 2010) ("'Nuisance' refers to a kind of damage done, rather than to any particular type of conduct."); Davis v. J.C. Nichols Co., 714 S.W.2d 679, 684 (Mo. Ct. App. 1986) ("Nuisance is a condition, not an act or failure to act and it is therefore immaterial in determining liability to inquire whether defendant was negligent and what his intention, design or motive may have been."). If intent is present, some courts have held that punitive damages are also available. See, e.g., Goff v. Elmo Greer & Sons Constr. Co., 297 S.W.3d 175, 187 (Tenn. 2009) (holding that where evidence is sufficient to establish that defendant's intentional or reckless conduct created the nuisance, punitive damages may be granted); Maryland Heights Leasing, Inc. v. Mallinckrodt, Inc., 706 S.W.2d 218 (Mo. Ct. App. 1985).

The majority approach to determining whether a nuisance exists is the "reasonableness" test. See generally Jeff L. Lewin, Boomer and the American Law of Nuisance: Past, Present, and Future, 54 Alb. L. Rev. 189, 234 (1990) (survey of nuisance law shows thirty-six jurisdictions have adopted some form of the reasonableness test). Thus, in Coty v. Ramsey Associates, Inc., 546 A.2d 196 (Vt. 1988), defendant built a pig farm on property abutting plaintiffs' land. Defendant accumulated excessive manure, junked automobiles, and dozens of sickly and dead animals on the farm. The court stated that a nuisance arises when the interference to the use and enjoyment of another's property is "unreasonable and substantial." Id. at 201. Without citing any single factor as having particular importance, the court concluded that the construction of the pig farm, which created strong odors and attracted flies, was unreasonable and constituted a substantial interference with the use and enjoyment of plaintiff's land. See also Peters v. ContiGroup, 292 S.W.3d 380, 385 (Mo. Ct. App. 2009) (explaining that "[t]he focus is on the defendant's unreasonable interference with the plaintiff's use and enjoyment of his land," the court noted that "[t]he law of nuisance recognizes the inherent conflict between the rights of neighboring property owners" and that "[t]he unreasonable use element seeks to balance those rights"); Pestey v. Cushman, 788 A.2d 496 (Conn. 2002) (defendant's 42,000-square-foot barn, housing a herd of dairy cows, unreasonably interfered with plaintiffs' use of their land because it produced a terrible smell causing, among other things, plaintiffs to lose sleep); Blanks v. Rawson, 370 S.E.2d 890 (S.C. Ct. App. 1988) (improperly maintained dog pen was an unreasonable nuisance).

The next case should be read with even more than your customary level of care and attention. As Professor Daniel Farber noted in his history of the case, it "has become an established part of the legal canon. It looms large, not just in environmental law, but also in property, remedies, and torts." Daniel A. Farber, The Story of Boomer: Pollution and the Common Law, 32 Ecology L.Q. 113, 113 (2005). Indeed, the following opinion has been described as "the great fertile crescent of the first year curriculum," such that "it seems that the whole first semester of law school could be taught out of that one case." Joel C. Dobris, Boomer Twenty Years Later: An Introduction, with Some Footnotes About "Theory," 54 Alb. L. Rev. 171, 171 (1990).

Boomer v. Atlantic Cement Co.

26 N.Y.2d 219, 257 N.E.2d 870, 309 N.Y.S.2d 312 (1970)

BERGAN, J.

Defendant operates a large cement plant near Albany. These are actions for injunction and damages by neighboring land owners alleging injury to property from dirt, smoke and vibration emanating from the plant. A nuisance has been found after trial, temporary damages have been allowed; but an injunction has been denied.

The public concern with air pollution arising from many sources in industry and in transportation is currently accorded ever wider recognition accompanied by a growing sense of responsibility in State and Federal Governments to control it. Cement plants are obvious sources of air pollution in the neighborhoods where they operate.

But there is now before the court private litigation in which individual property owners have sought specific relief from a single plant operation. The threshold question raised by the division of view on this appeal is whether the court should resolve the litigation between the parties now before it as equitably as seems possible; or whether, seeking promotion of the general public welfare, it should channel private litigation into broad public objectives.

A court performs its essential function when it decides the rights of parties before it. Its decision of private controversies may sometimes greatly affect public issues. Large questions of law are often resolved by the manner in which private litigation is decided. But this is normally an incident to the court's main function to settle controversy. It is a rare exercise of judicial power to use a decision in private litigation as a purposeful mechanism to achieve direct public objectives greatly beyond the rights and interests before the court.

Effective control of air pollution is a problem presently far from solution even with the full public and financial powers of government. In large measure adequate technical procedures are yet to be developed and some that appear possible may be economically impracticable.

It seems apparent that the amelioration of air pollution will depend on technical research in great depth; on a carefully balanced consideration of the economic impact of close regulation; and of the actual effect on public health. It is likely to require massive public expenditure and to demand more than any local community can accomplish and to depend on regional and interstate controls.

A court should not try to do this on its own as a by-product of private litigation and it seems manifest that the judicial establishment is neither equipped in the limited nature of any judgment it can pronounce nor prepared to lay down and implement an effective policy for the elimination of air pollution. This is an area beyond the circumference of one private lawsuit. It is a direct responsibility for government and should not thus be undertaken as an incident to solving a dispute between property owners and a single cement plant — one of many — in the Hudson River valley.

The cement making operations of defendant have been found by the court at Special Term to have damaged the nearby properties of plaintiffs in these two actions. That court, as it has been noted, accordingly found defendant maintained a nuisance and this has been affirmed at the Appellate Division. The total damage to plaintiffs' properties is, however, relatively small in comparison with the value of defendant's operation and with the consequences of the injunction which plaintiffs seek.

The ground for the denial of injunction, notwithstanding the finding both that there is a nuisance and that plaintiffs have been damaged substantially, is the large disparity in economic consequences of the nuisance and of the injunction. This theory cannot, however, be sustained without overruling a doctrine which has been consistently reaffirmed in several leading cases in this court and which has never been disavowed here, namely that where a nuisance has been found and where there has been any substantial damage shown by the party complaining an injunction will be granted.

The rule in New York has been that such a nuisance will be enjoined although marked disparity be shown in economic consequence between the effect of the injunction and the effect of the nuisance.

The problem of disparity in economic consequence was sharply in focus in Whalen v. Union Bag & Paper Co., 208 N.Y. 1, 101 N.E. 805. A pulp mill entailing an investment of more than a million dollars polluted a stream in which plaintiff, who owned a farm, was "a lower riparian owner[."] The economic loss to plaintiff from this pollution was small. This court, reversing the Appellate Division, reinstated the injunction granted by the Special Term against the argument of the mill owner that in view of "the slight advantage to plaintiff and the great loss that will be inflicted on defendant" an injunction should not be granted (p. 2, 101 N.E. p. 805). "Such a balancing of injuries cannot be justified by the circumstances of this case[,"] Judge Werner noted (p. 4, 101 N.E. p. 805). He continued: "Although the damage to the plaintiff may be slight as compared with the defendant's expense of abating the condition, that is not a good reason for refusing an injunction" (p. 5, 101 N.E. p. 806).

Thus the unconditional injunction granted at Special Term was reinstated. The rule laid down in that case, then, is that whenever the damage resulting from a nuisance is found not "unsubstantial[,"] viz., $100 a year, injunction would follow. This states a rule that had been followed in this court with marked consistency . . . .

[The court refers to several cases where injunctions have been denied, but explains that the damage shown by plaintiffs in those cases "was not only insubstantial, it was nonexistent."]

Although the court at Special Term and the Appellate Division held that injunction should be denied, it was found that plaintiffs had been damaged in various specific amounts up to the time of the trial and damages to the respective plaintiffs were awarded for those amounts. The effect of this was, injunction having been denied, plaintiffs could maintain successive actions at law for damages thereafter as further damage was incurred.

The court at Special Term also found the amount of permanent damage attributable to each plaintiff, for the guidance of the parties in the event both sides stipulated to the payment and acceptance of such permanent damage as a settlement of all the controversies among the parties. The total of permanent damages to all plaintiffs thus found was $185,000. This basis of adjustment has not resulted in any stipulation by the parties.

This result at Special Term and at the Appellate Division is a departure from a rule that has become settled; but to follow the rule literally in these cases would be to close down the plant at once. This court is fully agreed to avoid that immediately drastic remedy; the difference in view is how best to avoid it.*

One alternative is to grant the injunction but postpone its effect to a specified future date to give opportunity for technical advances to permit defendant to eliminate the nuisance; another is to grant the injunction conditioned on the payment of permanent damages to plaintiffs which would compensate them for the total economic loss to their property present and future caused by defendant's operations. For reasons which will be developed the court chooses the latter alternative.

If the injunction were to be granted unless within a short period — e.g., 18 months — the nuisance be abated by improved methods, there would be no assurance that any significant technical improvement would occur.

The parties could settle this private litigation at any time if defendant paid enough money and the imminent threat of closing the plant would build up the pressure on defendant. If there were no improved techniques found, there would inevitably be applications to the court at Special Term for extensions of time to perform on showing of good faith efforts to find such techniques.

Moreover, techniques to eliminate dust and other annoying by-products of cement making are unlikely to be developed by any research the defendant can undertake within any short period, but will depend on the total resources of the cement industry nationwide and throughout the world. The problem is universal wherever cement is made.

For obvious reasons the rate of the research is beyond control of defendant. If at the end of 18 months the whole industry has not found a technical solution a court would be hard put to close down this one cement plant if due regard be given to equitable principles.

On the other hand, to grant the injunction unless defendant pays plaintiffs such permanent damages as may be fixed by the court seems to do justice between the contending parties. All of the attributions of economic loss to the properties on which plaintiffs' complaints are based will have been redressed.

The nuisance complained of by these plaintiffs may have other public or private consequences, but these particular parties are the only ones who have sought remedies and the judgment proposed will fully redress them. The limitation of relief granted is a limitation only within the four corners of these actions and does not foreclose public health or other public agencies from seeking proper relief in a proper court.

It seems reasonable to think that the risk of being required to pay permanent damages to injured property owners by cement plant owners would itself be a reasonably effective spur to research for improved techniques to minimize nuisance.

The power of the court to condition on equitable grounds the continuance of an injunction on the payment of permanent damages seems undoubted.

[The discussion of authority for permanent damages is omitted.]

Thus it seems fair to both sides to grant permanent damages to plaintiffs which will terminate this private litigation. The theory of damage is the "servitude on land" of plaintiffs imposed by defendant's nuisance. (See United States v. Causby, 328 U.S. 256, 261, 262, 267, 66 S. Ct. 1062, 90 L. Ed. 1206, where the term "servitude" addressed to the land was used by Justice Douglas relating to the effect of airplane noise on property near an airport.)

* Respondent's investment in the plant is in excess of $45,000,000. There are over 300 people employed there.

The judgment, by allowance of permanent damages imposing a servitude on land, which is the basis of the actions, would preclude future recovery by plaintiffs or their grantees.

This should be placed beyond debate by a provision of the judgment that the payment by defendant and the acceptance by plaintiffs of permanent damages found by the court shall be in compensation for a servitude on the land.

Although the Trial Term has found permanent damages as a possible basis of settlement of the litigation, on remission the court should be entirely free to re-examine this subject. It may again find the permanent damage already found; or make new findings.

The orders should be reversed, without costs, and the cases remitted to Supreme Court, Albany County to grant an injunction which shall be vacated upon payment by defendant of such amounts of permanent damage to the respective plaintiffs as shall for this purpose be determined by the court.

Jasen, J (dissenting).

I agree with the majority that a reversal is required here, but I do not subscribe to the newly enunciated doctrine of assessment of permanent damages, in lieu of an injunction, where substantial property rights have been impaired by the creation of a nuisance.

It has long been the rule in this State, as the majority acknowledges, that a nuisance which results in substantial continuing damage to neighbors must be enjoined. To now change the rule to permit the cement company to continue polluting the air indefinitely upon the payment of permanent damages is, in my opinion, compounding the magnitude of a very serious problem in our State and Nation today.

In recognition of this problem, the Legislature of this State has enacted the Air Pollution Control Act (Public Health Law, Consol.Laws, c. 45, §§1264 to 1299-m) declaring that it is the State policy to require the use of all available and reasonable methods to prevent and control air pollution (Public Health Law §1265).

The harmful nature and widespread occurrence of air pollution have been extensively documented. Congressional hearings have revealed that air pollution causes substantial property damage, as well as being a contributing factor to a rising incidence of lung cancer, emphysema, bronchitis and asthma.

The specific problem faced here is known as particulate contamination because of the fine dust particles emanating from defendant's cement plant. The particular type of nuisance is not new, having appeared in many cases for at least the past 60 years. It is interesting to note that cement production has recently been identified as a significant source of particulate contamination in the Hudson Valley. This type of pollution, wherein very small particles escape and stay in the atmosphere, has been denominated as the type of air pollution which produces the greatest hazard to human health. We have thus a nuisance which not only is damaging to the plaintiffs, but also is decidedly harmful to the general public.

I see grave dangers in overruling our long-established rule of granting an injunction where a nuisance results in substantial continuing damage. In permitting the injunction to become inoperative upon the payment of permanent damages, the majority is, in effect, licensing a continuing wrong. It is the same as saying to the cement company, you may continue to do harm to your neighbors so long as you pay a fee for it. Furthermore, once such permanent damages are assessed and paid, the incentive to alleviate the wrong would be eliminated, thereby continuing air pollution of an area without abatement.

It is true that some courts have sanctioned the remedy here proposed by the majority in a number of cases, but none of the authorities relied upon by the majority are analogous to the situation before us. In those cases, the courts, in denying an injunction and awarding money damages, grounded their decision on a showing that the use to which the property was intended to be put was primarily for the public benefit. Here, on the other hand, it is clearly established that the cement company is creating a continuing air pollution nuisance primarily for its own private interest with no public benefit.

This kind of inverse condemnation may not be invoked by a private person or corporation for private gain or advantage. Inverse condemnation should only be permitted when the public is primarily served in the taking or impairment of property. The promotion of the interests of the polluting cement company has, in my opinion, no public use or benefit.

Nor is it constitutionally permissible to impose servitude on land, without consent of the owner, by payment of permanent damages where the continuing impairment of the land is for a private use. This is made clear by the State Constitution (art. I, §7, subd. [a]) which provides that "[p]rivate property shall not be taken for *public use* without just compensation" (emphasis added). It is, of course, significant that the section makes no mention of taking for a *private* use.

In sum, then, by constitutional mandate as well as by judicial pronouncement, the permanent impairment of private property for private purposes is not authorized in the absence of clearly demonstrated public benefit and use.

I would enjoin the defendant cement company from continuing the discharge of dust particles upon its neighbors' properties unless, within 18 months, the cement company abated this nuisance.

It is not my intention to cause the removal of the cement plant from the Albany area, but to recognize the urgency of the problem stemming from this stationary source of air pollution, and to allow the company a specified period of time to develop a means to alleviate this nuisance.

I am aware that the trial court found that the most modern dust control devices available have been installed in defendant's plant, but, I submit, this does not mean that *better* and more effective dust control devices could not be developed within the time allowed to abate the pollution.

Moreover, I believe it is incumbent upon the defendant to develop such devices, since the cement company, at the time the plant commenced production (1962), was well aware of the plaintiffs' presence in the area, as well as the probable consequences of its contemplated operation. Yet, it still chose to build and operate the plant at this site.

In a day when there is a growing concern for clean air, highly developed industry should not expect acquiescence by the courts, but should, instead, plan its operations to eliminate contamination of our air and damage to its neighbors.

Accordingly, the orders of the Appellate Division, insofar as they denied the injunction, should be reversed, and the actions remitted to Supreme Court, Albany County to grant an injunction to take effect 18 months hence, unless the nuisance is abated by improved techniques prior to said date.

FULD, C. J., and BURKE and SCILEPPI, JJ., concur with BERGAN, J.

JASEN, J., dissents in part and votes to reverse in a separate opinion.

BREITEL and GIBSON, JJ., taking no part.

In each action: Order reversed, without costs, and the case remitted to Supreme Court, Albany County, for further proceedings in accordance with the opinion herein.

The flexibility of nuisance doctrine, as demonstrated in *Boomer*, allows courts to tailor the remedy once they have determined the respective rights of the parties. In a famous law review article, Guido Calabresi & A. Douglas Melamed, Property Rules, Liability Rules, and Inalienability: One View of the Cathedral, 85 Harv. L. Rev. 1089 (1972), the authors explain that legal interests—entitlements—can be protected by "property rules," "liability rules," or a third type of rule ("inalienability rules") not relevant here. As the authors explain, "[a]n entitlement is protected by a property rule to the extent that someone who wishes to remove the entitlement from its holder must buy it from him in a voluntary transaction in which the value of the entitlement [the sale price] is agreed [to] by the seller." Id. at 1092. On the other hand, "[w]henever someone may destroy the initial entitlement if he is willing to pay [a judicially] determined value for it, an entitlement is protected by a liability rule." Id. We can use this framework to conceptualize the trespass and nuisance cases that we have read so far.

Assume that *A* is a polluter and *B* is an injured neighbor. If *B* may enjoin *A* from polluting, *B* has an entitlement protected by a property rule (*A* must buy from *B* the right to pollute). If *A* may pollute at will, *A* has an entitlement protected by a property rule (*B* must buy from *A* the right not to be polluted). An entitlement protected by a property rule is thought to be efficient because it enables parties to bargain for market exchanges of entitlements rather than requiring courts to determine the entitlements' value. In theory, the actor who values the entitlement more will, given the opportunity for negotiation, get it in the end.

However, when the transaction costs associated with bargaining (e.g., search and negotiation costs) are very high, a transfer of entitlement might not occur, even though it would benefit all of the actors involved. For instance, when numerous plaintiffs must all agree to waive their right to enjoin a nuisance in exchange for compensation, the temptation by any individual plaintiff to hold out for the highest compensation possible might cause bargaining to collapse. In that circumstance, or in any circumstance when transactions costs are so great that bargaining becomes infeasible, a liability rule may be preferred. If *A* may pollute and harm *B*, but must in return, as in *Boomer*, pay a judicially determined value to *B* for the harm caused to *B*'s property, then *B* has an entitlement protected by a liability rule (*A* must compensate *B* for polluting). Might *A* ever have an entitlement to pollute that is protected by a liability rule?

The *Boomer* court believed that the plaintiffs deserved relief, but that the defendant's factory should continue operating for the overall benefit of society. Because of the many individual landowners involved, a traditional injunctive award might have led to the shutting down of the factory. See Ward Farnsworth, Do Parties to Nuisance Cases Bargain After Judgment? A Glimpse Inside the Cathedral, 66 U. Chi. L. Rev. 373 (1999) (demonstrating that parties rarely, if ever, bargain for reallocation of nuisance remedies after judgment). Thus, the court shifted to a conception of plaintiffs' entitlement to be free from pollution as one that is protected only by a liability rule, not a property rule. On the standard law and economics account, if one assumes, as in *Boomer*, that negotiations involving a number of landowners would be difficult, then the court's awarding of damages avoided an inefficiency that would have resulted from the traditional injunctive remedy.

The psychological account of *Boomer*, however, is less enthusiastic. See Jeffrey J. Rachlinski & Forest Jourden, Remedies and the Psychology of Ownership, 51 Vand. L. Rev. 1541 (1998). In this article, the authors describe the fact that "people appear to value a commodity that they own much more than an identical commodity that they do not own," a cognitive heuristic that psychologists have termed the "endowment effect." Id. at 1551. People appear to ascribe meaning and value to the fact of ownership itself, separate and apart from whatever use or exchange values they derive from the particular item or resource that is owned. The implications of the endowment effect for the standard law and economics account of *Boomer* are dramatic. On the standard account, awarding the homeowners damages rather than an injunction was economically appropriate to overcome holdout problems and other strategic behaviors that would have prevented an efficient allocation of the legal entitlement to use the air. As Rachlinski and Jourden point out, however, "[t]he trial court's novel remedy, while economically sound, was a psychological insult." Id. at 1576. In the authors' view, an essential component of the value that the homeowners felt in their property was the ability to refuse to compromise that property except upon terms and conditions agreed to by the homeowners. The court removed that right from the plaintiffs' "bundle" of property rights, leaving them feeling poorer than before, irrespective of the monetary relief that they were afforded by order of the court.

One decision in which the court opted to enjoin a nuisance activity, rather than simply award damages, is Armory Park Neighborhood Ass'n v. Episcopal Community Services in Arizona, 712 P.2d 914 (Ariz. 1985), in which a residents' association sued to stop the community center from providing free meals to indigent persons, alleging that the indigent individuals frequently trespassed, urinated, defecated, drank, and littered on residents' property. Acknowledging the social utility of the center, the court nevertheless noted that "even admirable ventures may cause unreasonable interferences." Id. at 921. The court therefore affirmed the trial court's order granting a preliminary injunction. Similarly, in Mayes v. Tabor, 334 S.E.2d 489, 490 (N.C. Ct. App. 1985), the court stated its view that "[t]he degree of unreasonableness of the defendants' conduct determines whether damages or permanent injunctive relief is the appropriate remedy for an intentional private nuisance." According to the court, "injunctive relief requires proof that the defendant's conduct itself is unreasonable," whereas this is not necessary in order to award damages.

Professor Lewin has suggested a "comparative nuisance" theory that sees nuisance as a problem for both parties, as opposed to traditional doctrine that singles out one actor as the wrongdoer. His argument recalls the view of Nobel Laureate Ronald Coase, who, in his classic article *The Problem of Social Cost*, emphasized that many land use conflicts and other disputes should be seen as reciprocal problems involving competing claims on scarce resources, rather than as more overtly moralized problems involving "polluters" and "victims." See R.H. Coase, The Problem of Social Cost, 3 J.L. & Econ. 1 (1960). Similarly, under Professor Lewin's comparative nuisance approach, the allocation of costs should be based on the "comparative responsibility" of each party, rather than on an all-or-nothing decision to privilege one party's use of a resource. See Jeff L. Lewin, Comparative Nuisance, 50 U. Pitt. L. Rev. 1009 (1989). The power of Lewin's analysis rests in its acknowledgment that courts in nuisance contexts often must balance multiple, conflicting considerations. For instance, efficiency concerns, such as those that motivate law and economics scholars, might counsel in favor of a liability determination and a choice of remedy that are quite different from those that would be supported by fairness or psychological concerns. In that regard, consider the balancing act achieved by the following case, which is almost as pedagogically storied as *Boomer*.

Spur Industries, Inc. v. Del E. Webb Development Co.

108 Ariz. 178, 494 P.2d 700 (1972)

Cameron, Vice C.J.

From a judgment permanently enjoining the defendant, Spur Industries, Inc., from operating a cattle feedlot near the plaintiff Del E. Webb Development Company's Sun

City, Spur appeals. Webb cross-appeals. Although numerous issues are raised, we feel that it is necessary to answer only two questions. They are:

1. Where the operation of a business, such as a cattle feedlot is lawful in the first instance, but becomes a nuisance by reason of a nearby residential area, may the feedlot operation be enjoined in an action brought by the developer of the residential area?

2. Assuming that the nuisance may be enjoined, may the developer of a completely new town or urban area in a previously agricultural area be required to indemnify the operator of the feedlot who must move or cease operation because of the presence of the residential area created by the developer?

[The area involved in this suit is located 15 miles from Phoenix. It began to be used for farming around 1911. It was particularly well suited for cattle feeding, and in 1959 about 8,000 head of cattle were being fed on 35 acres. The defendant purchased these feedlots in 1960, and began expanding its feeding operations. By 1962, the defendant had expanded its holdings to a total of 114 acres. In May of 1959, the plaintiff began to plan a housing development known as Sun City, and acquired 20,000 acres of ranch land near the cattle feedlots.]

Del Webb's suit complained that the Spur feeding operation was a public nuisance because of the flies and the odor which were drifting or being blown by the prevailing south to north wind over the southern portion of Sun City. At the time of the suit, Spur was feeding between 20,000 and 30,000 head of cattle, and the facts amply support the finding of the trial court that the feed pens had become a nuisance to the people who resided in the southern part of Del Webb's development. The testimony indicated that cattle in a commercial feedlot will produce 35 to 40 pounds of wet manure per day, per head, or over a million pounds of wet manure per day for 30,000 head of cattle, and that despite the admittedly good feedlot management and good housekeeping practices by Spur, the resulting odor and flies produced an annoying if not unhealthy situation as far as the senior citizens of southern Sun City were concerned. There is no doubt that some of the citizens of Sun City were unable to enjoy the outdoor living which Del Webb had advertised and that Del Webb was faced with sales resistance from prospective purchasers as well as strong and persistent complaints from the people who had purchased homes in that area. . . .

May Spur Be Enjoined?

. . . .

It is clear that as to the citizens of Sun City, the operation of Spur's feedlot was both a public and a private nuisance. They could have successfully maintained an action to abate the nuisance. Del Webb, having shown a special injury in the loss of sales, had . . . standing to bring suit to enjoin the nuisance. The judgment of the trial court permanently enjoining the operation of the feedlot is affirmed.

Must Del Webb Indemnify Spur?

A suit to enjoin a nuisance sounds in equity and the courts have long recognized a special responsibility to the public when acting as a court of equity. . . .

In addition to protecting the public interest, however, courts of equity are concerned with protecting the operator of a lawful, albeit noxious, business from the result of a knowing and willful encroachment by others near his business.

In the so-called "coming to the nuisance" cases, the courts have held that the residential landowner may not have relief if he knowingly came into a neighborhood reserved for industrial or agricultural endeavors and has been damaged thereby. . . .

Were Webb the only party injured, we would feel justified in holding that the doctrine of "coming to the nuisance" would have been a bar to the relief asked by Webb, and, on the other hand, had Spur located the feedlot near the outskirts of a city and had the city grown toward the feedlot, Spur would have to suffer the cost of abating the nuisance as to those people locating within the growth pattern of the expanding city:

"The case affords, perhaps, an example where a business established at a place remote from population is gradually surrounded and becomes part of a populous center, so that a business which formerly was not an interference with the rights of others has become so by the encroachment of the population. . . ." City of Ft. Smith v. Western Hide & Fur Co., 153 Ark. 99, 103, 239 S.W. 724, 726 (1922).

We agree, however, with the Massachusetts court that:

"The law of nuisance affords no rigid rule to be applied in all instances. It is elastic. It undertakes to require only that which is fair and reasonable under all the circumstances. In a commonwealth like this, which depends for its material prosperity so largely on the continued growth and enlargement of manufacturing of diverse varieties, 'extreme rights' cannot be enforced. . . ." Stevens v. Rockport Granite Co., 216 Mass. 486, 488, 104 N.E. 371, 373 (1914).

There was no indication in the instant case at the time Spur and its predecessors located in western Maricopa County that a new city would spring up, full-blown, alongside the feeding operation and that the developer of that city would ask the court to order Spur to move because of the new city. Spur is required to move not because of any wrongdoing on the part of Spur, but because of a proper and legitimate regard of the courts for the rights and interests of the public.

Del Webb, on the other hand, is entitled to the relief prayed for (a permanent injunction), not because Webb is blameless, but because of the damage to the people who have been encouraged to purchase homes in Sun City. It does not equitably or legally follow, however, that Webb being entitled to the injunction, is then free of any liability to Spur if Webb has in fact been the cause of the damage Spur has sustained. It does not seem harsh to require a developer, who has taken advantage of the lesser land values in a rural area as well as the availability of large tracts of land on which to build and develop a new town or city in the area, to indemnify those who are forced to leave as a result.

Having brought people to the nuisance to the foreseeable detriment of Spur, Webb must indemnify Spur for a reasonable amount of the cost of moving or shutting down. It should be noted that this relief to Spur is limited to a case wherein a developer has, with foreseeability, brought into a previously agricultural or industrial area the population which makes necessary the granting of an injunction against a lawful business and for which the business has no adequate relief.

It is therefore the decision of this court that the matter be remanded to the trial court for a hearing upon the damages sustained by the defendant Spur as a reasonable and direct result of the granting of the permanent injunction. Since the result of the appeal may appear novel and both sides have obtained a measure of relief, it is ordered that each side will bear its own costs.

Affirmed in part, reversed in part, and remanded for further proceedings consistent with this opinion.

HAYS, C. J., STRUCKMEYER and LOCKWOOD, JJ., and UDALL, Retired Justice.

Recall the Calabresi and Melamed framework. *Spur* represents the possibility mentioned at the end of that discussion: an entitlement to pollute protected by a liability rule (*B* can prevent *A* from polluting, but only if *B* is willing to pay a judicially determined value for that benefit). Calabresi and Melamed anticipated *Spur* in these words: "Missing is a fourth rule representing an entitlement in [defendant] to pollute, but an entitlement which is protected only by a liability rule. The fourth rule, really a kind of partial eminent domain coupled with a benefits tax, can be stated as follows: [plaintiff] may stop [defendant] from polluting, but if he does he must compensate [defendant]." 85 Harv. L. Rev. at 1116. Judge Calabresi recently recalled: "When Spur came out . . . , I wrote Spur's author, Vice Chief Justice James Cameron, and said, 'Darn it, I wish that your opinion had come out a little bit sooner so that I could have cited it.' He wrote back, 'Nonsense, I wish your article had come out a little bit sooner, so I would have had something to rely on.'" Guido Calabresi, Neologisms Revisited, 64 Md. L. Rev. 736, 736-37 (2005).

Despite the great scholarly interest in *Spur* and its innovative approach, few courts have actually followed the case. Perhaps the possibilities for innovation are simply too overwhelming. In another important article, Professors James Krier and Stewart Schwab observed that the *Spur* court had overlooked a different potential remedy (which they termed the "double reverse twist") that would have set Spur's damages according to the residents' level of harm, rather than Spur's cost of moving. See James E. Krier & Stewart J. Schwab, Property Rules and Liability Rules: The Cathedral in Another Light, 70 N.Y.U. L. Rev. 440, 471 (1995). And in Saul Levmore, Unifying Remedies: Property Rules, Liability Rules, and Startling Rules, 106 Yale L.J. 2149 (1997), the author builds on the framework developed by Calabresi, Melamed, Krier, and Schwab to identify no fewer than fifteen different combinations of rights and remedies. More recently, scholars have incorporated insights from the economic literature on financial options to develop new legal forms that are capable of capturing some of the advantages of both property rules and liability rules. See Ronen Avraham, Modular Liability Rules, 24 Int'l Rev. L. & Econ. 269 (2004); Lee Anne Fennell, Revealing Options, 118 Harv. L. Rev. 1399 (2005); Richard A. Nagareda, Autonomy, Peace, and Put Options in the Mass Tort Class Action, 115 Harv. L. Rev. 747 (2002).

The *Spur* court's dictum that the plaintiff might have been barred by the doctrine of "coming to the nuisance," had its interests been at stake to the exclusion of those of the residents of Sun City, suggests a "first come, first served" approach to nuisance law. Most courts have held that, although the question of who got there first is relevant to whether the defendant's use is a nuisance, it is not dispositive. See, e.g., Merino v. Salem Hunting Club, No. 07-CO-16, 2008 WL 5124549, at *4 (Ohio Ct. App. Dec. 4, 2008) (noting that "[t]he prevailing American view" is that this question "is just one of several factors to be considered"); Crushed Stone Co. v. Moore, 369 P.2d 811, 816 (Okla. 1962) (holding that the fact that plaintiffs came to the nuisance was not "sufficient to render the trial court's judgment [for plaintiffs] erroneous"). The Restatement (Second) of Torts also agrees with this approach. Comment *g* to §827(d) of the Restatement, set out on p. 446 above, states:

> The character of a particular locality is, of course, subject to change over a period of time and therefore the suitability of a particular use of land to the locality will also vary with the passage of time. A use of land ideally suited to the character of a particular locality at a particular time may be wholly unsuited to that locality twenty years later. Hence the

suitability of the particular use or enjoyment invaded must be determined as of the time of the invasion rather than the time when the use or enjoyment began.

"Coming to the nuisance" is dealt with specifically in §840D of the Restatement:

§840D. Coming to the Nuisance

The fact that the plaintiff has acquired or improved his land after a nuisance interfering with it has come into existence is not in itself sufficient to bar his action, but it is a factor to be considered in determining whether the nuisance is actionable.

COMMENT:

. . . .

b. The rule generally accepted by the courts is that in itself and without other factors, the "coming to the nuisance" will not bar the plaintiff's recovery. Otherwise the defendant by setting up an activity or a condition that results in the nuisance could condemn all the land in his vicinity to a servitude without paying any compensation, and so could arrogate to himself a good deal of the value of the adjoining land. The defendant is required to contemplate and expect the possibility that the adjoining land may be settled, sold or otherwise transferred and that a condition originally harmless may result in an actionable nuisance when there is later development.

. . . .

c. Although it is not conclusive in itself, the fact that the plaintiff has "come to the nuisance" is still a factor of importance to be considered in cases where other factors are involved.

Two illustrations to Comment *c* further elaborate the doctrine set out in this section:

2. A operates a copper smelter near the land of B. Smoke, fumes and gases from the smelter create a private nuisance interfering with the use and enjoyment of the land of B. For the sole purpose of bringing a lawsuit and forcing A to buy him out at a high price, C buys the land from B and moves in upon it. In his action for the private nuisance, the fact that C has acquired the land with the nuisance in existence, together with his purpose, will prevent his recovery.

3. A operates a brewery in a former residential area in which industrial plants are beginning to appear. The brewery noises, odors and smoke interfere with the use and enjoyment of the land of B adjoining it. C buys the land from B, moves in upon it and brings an action for the private nuisance. The fact that C has come to the nuisance, together with the changing character of the locality, may be sufficient to prevent recovery.

The "coming to the nuisance" doctrine is discussed in Edward Rabin, Nuisance Law: Rethinking Fundamental Assumptions, 63 Va. L. Rev. 1299 (1977). Professor Rabin's principal concern in this article is with the range of remedies available in nuisance actions, and he approves of the unique approach taken by the court in *Spur Industries* in this respect. See also A. Mitchell Polinsky, Resolving Nuisance Disputes: The Simple Economics of Injunctive and Damage Remedies, 32 Stan. L. Rev. 1075 (1980); Donald Wittman, First Come, First Served: An Economic Analysis of "Coming to the Nuisance," 9 J. Legal Stud. 557 (1980).

Problem 30

You have been approached by a representative of the Inuit Circumpolar Conference (ICC), a federation of Native nations representing approximately 150,000 indigenous peoples in Canada, Greenland, Russia, and the United States. The ICC seeks your advice in regard to possible common law actions the organization might be able to bring on behalf of its members in response to the adverse effects of climate change.

Since the beginnings of the Industrial Revolution, atmospheric concentrations of carbon dioxide, methane, and other heat-trapping substances known as greenhouse gases have steadily increased. Indeed, according to a 2014 scientific assessment by the Intergovernmental Panel on Climate Change, an international scientific consensus body, concentrations of greenhouse gases in the earth's atmosphere have risen to levels not seen for at least 800,000 years. Scientists believe that the last time greenhouse gas concentrations were this high, the oceans were as much as 100 feet higher and global average surface temperatures as much as 11 degrees Fahrenheit warmer than today.

The consensus of the global scientific community is that most of the warming of the planet's surface that has occurred over the past fifty years is attributable to human activities, including fossil fuel combustion and deforestation, that have increased the concentration of greenhouse gases in the atmosphere. Although the most severe adverse effects of the resulting climate change are yet to be felt, scientists agree that the more recent process of human-induced warming has already begun in earnest and may be linked to such adverse events as droughts, heat waves, forest fires, flooding, and severe storms. Moreover, according to the Arctic Climate Impact Assessment, a substantial report issued in 2004 by the high-level intergovernmental forum known as the Arctic Council, in conjunction with the International Arctic Science Committee, the Arctic region that is home to the ICC's members is experiencing "some of the most rapid and severe climate changes on earth," including widespread glacier melting and sea ice loss, rising surface and permafrost temperatures, and dramatic shifts in flora and fauna composition. Susan Joy Hassol, Arctic Council, Impacts of a Warming Arctic: Arctic Climate Impact Assessment 10 (2004). These changes have already adversely impacted the lives of ICC members in a variety of ways, as detailed in the 2004 report.

The ICC would like you to consider what common law theories of liability might be available to its members, what parties might be sued under such theories, what remedies would be available to them, what the likelihood of success would be, and, for that matter, how you would define "success" under these circumstances. Assume that any tort suit would be brought at least initially only by Native Alaskans, so that the court is not necessarily required to address issues regarding the availability of tort remedies to foreign citizens. As background reading for your assignment, consider the following "key findings" from the Arctic Climate Impact Assessment:

Key Findings

The Arctic is extremely vulnerable to observed and projected climate change and its impacts. The Arctic is now experiencing some of the most rapid and severe climate change on earth. Over the next 100 years, climate change is expected to accelerate, contributing to major physical, ecological, social, and economic changes, many of which have already begun. Changes in arctic climate will also affect the rest of the world through increased global warming and rising sea levels.

1. Arctic climate is now warming rapidly and much larger changes are projected.
   - Annual average arctic temperature has increased at almost twice the rate as that of the rest of the world over the past few decades, with some variations across the region.
   - Additional evidence of arctic warming comes from widespread melting of glaciers and sea ice, and a shortening of the snow season.
   - Increasing global concentrations of carbon dioxide and other greenhouse gases due to human activities, primarily fossil fuel burning, are projected to contribute to additional arctic warming of about 4-7°C over the next 100 years.
   - Increasing precipitation, shorter and warmer winters, and substantial decreases in snow cover and ice cover are among the projected changes that are very likely to persist for centuries.
   - Unexpected and even larger shifts and fluctuations in climate are also possible.
2. Arctic warming and its consequences have worldwide implications.
   - Melting of highly reflective arctic snow and ice reveals darker land and ocean surfaces, increasing absorption of the sun's heat and further warming the planet.
   - Increases in glacial melt and river runoff add more freshwater to the ocean, raising global sea level and possibly slowing the ocean circulation that brings heat from the tropics to the poles, affecting global and regional climate.
   - Warming is very likely to alter the release and uptake of greenhouse gases from soils, vegetation, and coastal oceans.
   - Impacts of arctic climate change will have implications for biodiversity around the world because migratory species depend on breeding and feeding grounds in the Arctic.
3. Arctic vegetation zones are very likely to shift, causing wide-ranging impacts.
   - Treeline is expected to move northward and to higher elevations, with forests replacing a significant fraction of existing tundra, and tundra vegetation moving into polar deserts.
   - More-productive vegetation is likely to increase carbon uptake, although reduced reflectivity of the land surface is likely to outweigh this, causing further warming.
   - Disturbances such as insect outbreaks and forest fires are very likely to increase in frequency, severity, and duration, facilitating invasions by non-native species.
   - Where suitable soils are present, agriculture will have the potential to expand northward due to a longer and warmer growing season.
4. Animal species' diversity, ranges, and distribution will change.
   - Reductions in sea ice will drastically shrink marine habitat for polar bears, ice-inhabiting seals, and some seabirds, pushing some species toward extinction.
   - Caribou/reindeer and other land animals are likely to be increasingly stressed as climate change alters their access to food sources, breeding grounds, and historic migration routes.
   - Species ranges are projected to shift northward on both land and sea, bringing new species into the Arctic while severely limiting some species currently present.
   - As new species move in, animal diseases that can be transmitted to humans, such as West Nile virus, are likely to pose increasing health risks.

—Some arctic marine fisheries, which are of global importance as well as providing major contributions to the region's economy, are likely to become more productive. Northern freshwater fisheries that are mainstays of local diets are likely to suffer.

5. Many coastal communities and facilities face increasing exposure to storms.

   —Severe coastal erosion will be a growing problem as rising sea level and a reduction in sea ice allow higher waves and storm surges to reach the shore.

   —Along some arctic coastlines, thawing permafrost weakens coastal lands, adding to their vulnerability.

   —The risk of flooding in coastal wetlands is projected to increase, with impacts on society and natural ecosystems.

   —In some cases, communities and industrial facilities in coastal zones are already threatened or being forced to relocate, while others face increasing risks and costs.

6. Reduced sea ice is very likely to increase marine transport and access to resources.

   —The continuing reduction of sea ice is very likely to lengthen the navigation season and increase marine access to the Arctic's natural resources.

   —Seasonal opening of the Northern Sea Route is likely to make trans-arctic shipping during summer feasible within several decades. Increasing ice movement in some channels of the Northwest Passage could initially make shipping more difficult.

   —Reduced sea ice is likely to allow increased offshore extraction of oil and gas, although increasing ice movement could hinder some operations.

   —Sovereignty, security, and safety issues, as well as social, cultural, and environmental concerns are likely to arise as marine access increases.

7. Thawing ground will disrupt transportation, buildings, and other infrastructure.

   —Transportation and industry on land, including oil and gas extraction and forestry, will increasingly be disrupted by the shortening of the periods during which ice roads and tundra are frozen sufficiently to permit travel.

   —As frozen ground thaws, many existing buildings, roads, pipelines, airports, and industrial facilities are likely to be destabilized, requiring substantial rebuilding, maintenance, and investment.

   —Future development will require new design elements to account for ongoing warming that will add to construction and maintenance costs.

   —Permafrost degradation will also impact natural ecosystems through collapsing of the ground surface, draining of lakes, wetland development, and toppling of trees in susceptible areas.

8. Indigenous communities are facing major economic and cultural impacts.

   —Many Indigenous Peoples depend on hunting polar bear, walrus, seals, and caribou, herding reindeer, fishing, and gathering, not only for food and to support the local economy, but also as the basis for cultural and social identity.

   —Changes in species' ranges and availability, access to these species, a perceived reduction in weather predictability, and travel safety in changing ice and weather conditions present serious challenges to human health and food security, and possibly even the survival of some cultures.

   —Indigenous knowledge and observations provide an important source of information about climate change. This knowledge, consistent with complementary information from scientific research, indicates that substantial changes have already occurred.

9. Elevated ultraviolet radiation levels will affect people, plants, and animals.

—The stratospheric ozone layer over the Arctic is not expected to improve significantly for at least a few decades, largely due to the effect of greenhouse gases on stratospheric temperatures. Ultraviolet radiation (UV) in the Arctic is thus projected to remain elevated in the coming decades.

—As a result, the current generation of arctic young people is likely to receive a lifetime dose of UV that is about 30% higher than any prior generation. Increased UV is known to cause skin cancer, cataracts, and immune system disorders in humans.

—Elevated UV can disrupt photosynthesis in plants and have detrimental effects on the early life stages of fish and amphibians.

—Risks to some arctic ecosystems are likely as the largest increases in UV occur in spring, when sensitive species are most vulnerable, and warming-related declines in snow and ice cover increase exposure for living things normally protected by such cover.

10. Multiple influences interact to cause impacts to people and ecosystems.

—Changes in climate are occurring in the context of many other stresses including chemical pollution, overfishing, land use changes, habitat fragmentation, human population increases, and cultural and economic changes.

—These multiple stresses can combine to amplify impacts on human and ecosystem health and well-being. In many cases, the total impact is greater than the sum of its parts, such as the combined impacts of contaminants, excess ultraviolet radiation, and climatic warming.

—Unique circumstances in arctic sub-regions determine which are the most important stresses and how they interact.

Chapter 6

Strict Liability

As we saw in Chapter 3, a defendant is liable under negligence for causing another to suffer harm only if the defendant's conduct is determined to be unreasonably dangerous. If, however, the defendant behaves reasonably and harm to another nevertheless results, recovery is denied. In such cases, the *residual accident costs* generated by the defendant's harmful activities remain with the injured plaintiff who, absent casualty insurance, charity, or some other outside (collateral) source of relief, must bear those losses personally. In contrast to negligence, strict liability makes no distinction based on the presence or absence of fault on the part of the defendant. Instead, under strict liability, an actor whose conduct proximately causes harm to another is liable regardless of whether reasonable care, or, indeed, even extraordinary care, was exercised. Thus, as used in this chapter, strict liability equals *liability without fault* for harm proximately caused by certain categories of conduct.[1]

At English common law, negligence and strict liability co-existed for decades and competed for acceptance as the general standard of liability for physical harms. This struggle carried over to American courts, where numerous states in the late nineteenth and early twentieth centuries adopted the strict liability standard announced by the House of Lords in the famous case of Rylands v. Fletcher, which appears in Section B, below. See Jed Handelsman Shugerman, Note, The Floodgates of Strict Liability: Bursting Reservoirs and the Adoption of Strict Liability in the Gilded Age, 110 Yale L.J. 333 (2000) (documenting acceptance of *Rylands* by American courts). Ultimately, however, the prevailing American standard of liability for physical harm in tort became one of negligence, such that today the role of strict liability is limited to certain exceptional categories of activity. As Section A, below, details, one such longstanding "pocket" of strict liability in tort law concerns the ownership and possession of animals. While reading about this and other categories of strict liability, consider the reasons for and against the standard as a measure of responsibility for potentially harmful conduct.

A. Maintaining Custody of Animals

The common law developed a complex set of rules dealing with custodians' liability for harm caused by animals. These rules distinguished, among other things, between property damage caused by the trespass of livestock and other harms caused by animals. With respect to the former, the common law held livestock owners strictly liable for harm caused

1. Courts and commentators sometimes use the phrase *absolute liability*, and distinguish it from *strict liability*. The former phrase has several different meanings, depending on the context. Sometimes it means that the defendant is liable for certain bad outcomes even if the actor did not proximately cause them. When used in this way, *absolute liability* is synonymous with *insurer's liability*. In products liability, which is dealt with in Chapter 7, *absolute liability* is sometimes used to suggest liability caused by defendant's products whether or not defective.

to real property by their wandering livestock. Section 504 of the Restatement (Second) of Torts essentially adopts the common law position, providing that "a possessor of livestock which intrude upon the land of another is liable for their intrusion and for any harm done while upon the land . . . although the possessor of the livestock exercised the utmost care to prevent them from intruding." Section 21 of the Restatement (Third) of Torts: Liability for Physical and Emotional Harm (2010) applies this rule of strict liability for damage caused by trespass or intrusion not only to livestock, but to all other owned or possessed animals other than dogs and cats. In some states, the rules on intrusion are modified to the extent that landowners cannot recover for harm caused by wandering livestock unless the landowners have protected their property with appropriate fencing. See, e.g., SaBell's, Inc. v. Flens, 627 P.2d 750 (Colo. 1981).

With respect to both wild animals and domesticated animals other than livestock, the common law rules are somewhat more complicated, but they retain strong elements of strict liability. The leading English decision imposing strict liability upon the owners and possessors of wild animals for harm, including personal injuries, caused by their animals is Filburn v. People's Palace and Aquarium, Ltd., 25 Q.B. Div. 258 (1890). The plaintiff in that case had been attacked by an elephant owned and exhibited publicly by the defendants. Although the jury specifically found that the defendants did not know that the elephant was dangerous, the trial court entered judgment for the plaintiff. The Court of Appeal affirmed, Lord Esher explaining in his opinion (25 Q.B. Div. at 260):

> Unless an animal . . . is shown to be either harmless by its very nature, or to belong to a class that has become so by what may be called cultivation—it falls within the class of animals as to which the rule is that a man who keeps one must take the responsibility of keeping it safe. It cannot possibly be said that an elephant comes within the class of animals known to be harmless by nature, or within that shown by experience to be harmless in this country, and consequently it falls within the class of animals that a man keeps at his peril, and which he must prevent from doing injury under any circumstances, unless the person to whom the injury is done brings it on himself. It was, therefore, immaterial in this case whether the particular animal was a dangerous one, or whether the defendants had any knowledge that it was so.

The strict liability rule in the *Filburn* case is widely followed in the United States today and is set forth in §22 of the Third Restatement. Section 22(b) defines a wild animal as "an animal that belongs to a category of animals that have not been generally domesticated and that are likely, unless restrained, to cause personal injury." This category is harder in practice to delimit than one might imagine. See Oak Creek Whitetail Ranch v. Lange, 326 S.W.3d 549 (Mo. Ct. App. 2010) (breeder deer that has never been in the wild is a domestic animal, even though it is not a traditional domestic animal). Gallick v. Barto, 828 F. Supp. 1168 (M.D. Pa. 1993) involved a pet ferret that attacked a seven-month-old child. The court imposed strict liability on the defendants, the landlords of the ferret owner, holding that ferrets were wild animals even though, at the time, such animals were kept as pets by over one million people in the United States. The court concluded (828 F. Supp. at 1174):

> In sum, we are of the view that ferrets are an inverse of the types of dogs [e.g., pit bulls] we have noted above. A pit bull may be considered a domestic animal because dogs generally are considered domestic animals. Therefore, a pit bull is a domestic animal with dangerous propensities. A ferret, on the other hand, is a wild animal which people

> may, to a point, be successful in keeping at their home. Therefore, a ferret is a wild animal with domestic propensities. However, those propensities do not change its essential character as a wild animal. We hold that a ferret is a wild animal.

For an argument that *Gallick* was wrongly decided and that ferrets are not wild animals, see David L. Herman, California Law and Ferrets: Are They Truly "Wild Weasels"?, 23 Envtl. L. & Pol'y 37 (2000).

Not only must the plaintiff show the animal is wild, the plaintiff must also establish ownership or possession in order to recover. *Gallick*, for instance, involved not only the question of whether a pet ferret should be deemed wild or domesticated, but also whether the landlords of the ferret owner should be deemed "in possession" of the ferret, a question the court resolved by examining the landlords' authority under the lease agreement to control or remove the dangerous animal after learning of its existence. 828 F. Supp. at 1174-75. While in general rules of possession and ownership are more appropriately addressed in a property course, Leber v. Hyatt Hotels of Puerto Rico, Inc., 124 F.3d 47 (1st Cir. 1997) provides a straightforward example of what does *not* constitute ownership or possession. The plaintiff, a hotel guest, was sunbathing near the pool when she was attacked and bitten by a rabid mongoose, which suddenly appeared out of a swamp area that bordered the hotel. The plaintiff sued the hotel for her injuries, claiming, inter alia, that the hotel was strictly liable for the harm caused by wild animals on its property. However, since the hotel did not own the swamp area upon which the mongoose resided, the court of appeals held that it did not exercise the requisite control over the animal, and thus was not subject to strict liability.

The major exception to the strict liability rule in *Filburn* is for public zookeepers, who are generally liable only for their negligence in keeping wild animals. Thus, a Colorado court applied negligence principles instead of strict liability in a case brought by a plaintiff whose finger had been bitten off by a zebra at the Denver Zoo. See Kennedy v. City and County of Denver, 506 P.2d 764 (Colo. Ct. App. 1972). When the zoo is privately owned and operated for profit, however, strict liability may be imposed. See Isaacs v. Powell, 267 So. 2d 864 (Fla. Dist. Ct. App. 1972), *overruled on other grounds by* Donner v. Arkwright-Boston Mfrs. Mut. Ins. Co., 358 So. 2d 21 (Fla. 1978), in which the two-year-old plaintiff was injured when a chimpanzee attacked him through the bars of its cage at defendants' monkey farm, a well-known tourist attraction. The court of appeals reversed a verdict and judgment for the defendant on the grounds that the trial court erred in limiting the defendant's liability to negligence (267 So. 2d at 865-66):

> [W]e are of the view that the older and general rule of strict liability, which obviates the issue of the owner's negligence, is more suited to the fast growing populous and activity-oriented society of Florida. Indeed, our society imposes more than enough risks upon its members now, and we are reluctant to encourage the addition of one more, particularly when that one more is increasingly contributed by those who, for profit, would exercise their "right" to harbor wild animals and increase exposure to the dangers thereof by alluring advertising.

What if, instead of a vicious zebra, chimpanzee, or other exotic animal, the defendant owns a vicious dog that bites off the finger of a visitor? The general rule in this country has been that the owner of a domestic animal is strictly liable to injured persons if, but only if, the owner knows of the vicious tendencies of the animal. Section 23 of the Third Restatement dispenses with the distinctions between livestock, wild, and domestic animals, and instead applies strict liability according to the owner's actual or constructive knowledge of the animal's abnormal dangerousness alone:[2]

§23. Abnormally Dangerous Animals

> An owner or possessor of an animal that the owner or possessor knows or has reason to know has dangerous tendencies abnormal for the animal's category is subject to strict liability for physical harm caused by the animal if the harm ensues from that dangerous tendency.

In cases to which this section applies, the most important issue is likely to be the one of knowledge — that is, did the defendant know or have reason to know that the animal was vicious? The greatest percentage of such cases involve dogs. When the defendant's dog bites the plaintiff, must the plaintiff show that the dog has previously bitten others? Some courts have held that the plaintiff must show prior attacks in order to establish liability. Cf. Wilson *ex rel.* Wilson v. Simmons, 103 S.W.3d 211, 217 (Mo. Ct. App. 2003) (requiring "somewhat stringent proof" of the owner's prior knowledge because dogs "have earned and merited acceptance as man's best friend" and "the dog's social utility justifies permitting the owner a degree of freedom from potential liability"). See also Poznanski v. Horvath, 788 N.E.2d 1255 (Ind. 2003). But are there not some situations in which, even absent a first bite, a dog's owner should be aware of the dog's dangerous propensities? For example, should a harmed plaintiff be able to invoke strict liability against the owner of a dog that has been trained to attack others, or that belongs to a notoriously vicious breed? Compare Tucker v. Duke, 873 N.E.2d 664 (Ind. Ct. App. 2007) (judgment for plaintiff affirmed; trier of fact's finding that defendant dog owner should have known of pit bull's dangerous propensities was not clearly erroneous, even though the individual dog had not exhibited dangerous tendencies before), with Blackstone v. Hayward, 304 A.D.2d 941 (N.Y. App. Div. 2003) (entry of the word "nasty" in veterinary record, by itself, not sufficient to raise an issue with respect to owner's constructive knowledge of a dog's vicious propensity); Knapton ex rel. E.K. v. Monk, 347 P.3d 1257 (Mont. 2015) (landlord not strictly liable for injuries caused by tenants' pit bulls because plaintiff did not demonstrate that harboring purebred pit bulls is inherently dangerous), and Maura v. Randall, 705 A.2d 334 (Md. Ct. Spec. App. 1998) (absent evidence the particular dog was violent, the mere fact that owner's dog, a Rottweiler, belonged to breed with an unsavory reputation was insufficient to charge the owner with knowledge).

The question of knowledge also extends to whether a non-owner of a dog can be held strictly liable for injuries. In Tracey v. Solesky, 50 A.3d 1075, 1080 (Md. 2012), the court held that purebred pit bulls are "inherently dangerous." As a result, the court found that a landlord does not need actual knowledge of a tenant's pit bull's dangerous propensities to be held strictly liable for injuries caused by the dog. This expansive liability holding was quickly overturned by the Maryland state legislature. Md. Code Ann., Cts. & Jud. Proc. §3-1901 (West).

In many states, the liability of dog owners is expressly covered by statute. See, e.g., Cook v. Whitsell-Sherman, 796 N.E.2d 271 (Ind. 2003) (construing Indiana strict liability dog bite statute for letter carriers and other public servants). Many of these statutes change

2. Recall, though, that §22 of the Third Restatement additionally applies strict liability to wild animals irrespective of the owner's actual or constructive knowledge of the animal's dangerousness.

the common law rule and impose liability irrespective of the owner's prior knowledge of the dog's viciousness. The Michigan statute, Mich. Comp. Laws Ann. §287.351 (West 2003), is fairly typical:

> If a dog bites a person, without provocation while the person is on public property, or lawfully on private property, including the property of the owner of the dog, the owner of the dog shall be liable for any damages suffered by the person bitten, regardless of the former viciousness of the dog or the owner's knowledge of such viciousness.

Some statutes are written broadly to impose liability, irrespective of the owner's prior knowledge of the dog's viciousness, for any injuries of which the dog is a but-for cause. For example, the Wisconsin statute states that, "[w]ithout notice, . . . the owner of a dog is liable for the full amount of damages caused by the dog injuring or causing injury to a person, domestic animal or property." Wis. Stat. Ann. §174.02(1)(a) (West 2006). If the dog owner knew or was notified of a previous attack, the owner is liable for two times the full amount of damages. Id. at §174.02(1)(b). Based on this broad statute, a Wisconsin court of appeals held in an unpublished opinion that a dog owner could be held strictly liable for injuries to his neighbor, where the neighbor was bitten and then hit by a car after he went into the street to rescue the escaped dog. See Helmeid v. American Family Mut. Ins. Co., 640 N.W.2d 565 (Wis. Ct. App. 2002). However, this statute is not without limits. See Fandray *ex rel.* Connell v. American Family Mut. Ins. Co., 680 N.W.2d 345 (Wis. 2003) (refusing, on grounds of an implicit "public policy" exception, to apply statute to a homeowner whose best friend entered home when owner was away to deliver Christmas cookies, whereupon friend's daughter was attacked by homeowner's dog); Alwin v. State Farm Fire & Cas. Casualty Co., 610 N.W.2d 218 (Wis. Ct. App. 2000) (the defendant's mother, who sustained injuries after tripping over defendant's dog, could theoretically recover based on the broad language of the statute, but public policy precluded application).

These statutes holding dog owners strictly liable are reminiscent of the statutes considered in Chapter 1, holding parents strictly liable for the wrongful actions of their minor children. In this context, of course, owners are not being held "vicariously" liable because their animals are incapable of performing legal acts. In substance, however, both types of statutes impose strict liability in the sense that the defendants are held liable irrespective of fault on their parts. Based on the overwhelming legislative action across the country in this area, some courts have refused, without a statute authorizing it, to impose strict liability on dog owners for the harm caused by their dogs. See, e.g., Gerhtz v. Batteen, 620 N.W.2d 775 (S.D. 2001) (refusing to afford plaintiff, who was bitten by defendant's eight-month-old German shepherd, a strict liability remedy in the absence of a statute, although recognizing that South Dakota did offer a statutory strict liability remedy to owners of poultry and other livestock harmed by dogs). It is important to recall, though, that even in situations where neither common law nor statute imposes strict liability, owners of domestic animals can still be held liable in negligence for failing to exercise reasonable control over their animals. See, e.g., Ryman v. Alt, 266 N.W.2d 504 (Minn. 1978); Westberry v. Blackwell, 577 P.2d 75 (Or. 1978). In fact, the flexible contours of the reasonableness analysis under negligence law might even afford plaintiffs an advantage over strict liability in certain factual settings. See, e.g., Borns *ex rel.* Gannon v. Voss, 70 P.3d 262 (Wyo. 2003) (observing that dog bites can give rise to both strict liability and negligence causes of action, and that knowledge of a dog's vicious propensity is not necessarily a prerequisite to the latter action).

B. Abnormally Dangerous Activities

Fletcher v. Rylands

L.R. 1 Exch. 265 (1866)

[This action was originally tried at the Liverpool Summer Assizes in 1862, and resulted in a verdict for the plaintiff. An arbitrator, appointed to assess damages, was later empowered by court order to state a special case in the Exchequer for the purpose of obtaining that court's opinion on the novel question of law presented. In the Exchequer, two judges voted for the defendants and one for the plaintiff, and judgment was entered for the defendants. The plaintiff appealed to the next higher court, the Exchequer Chamber, the decision of which follows.]

BLACKBURN, J. This was a special case stated by an arbitrator, under an order of nisi prius, in which the question for the Court is stated to be, whether the plaintiff is entitled to recover any, and, if any, what damages from the defendants, by reason of the matters thereinbefore stated.

In the Court of Exchequer, the Chief Baron and Martin, B., were of opinion that the plaintiff was not entitled to recover at all, Bramwell, B., being of a different opinion. The judgment in the Exchequer was consequently given for the defendants, in conformity with the opinion of the majority of the court. The only question argued before us was, whether this judgment was right, nothing being said about the measure of damages in case the plaintiff should be held entitled to recover. We have come to the conclusion that the opinion of Bramwell, B., was right, and that the answer to the question should be that the plaintiff was entitled to recover damages from the defendants, by reason of the matters stated in the case, and consequently, that the judgment below should be reversed, but we cannot at present say to what damages the plaintiff is entitled.

It appears from the statement in the case, that the plaintiff was damaged by his property being flooded by water, which, without any fault on his part, broke out of a reservoir constructed on the defendants' land by the defendants' orders, and maintained by the defendants.

It appears from the statement in the case that the coal under the defendants' land had, at some remote period, been worked out; but this was unknown at the time when the defendants gave directions to erect the reservoir, and the water in the reservoir would not have escaped from the defendants' land, and no mischief would have been done to the plaintiff, but for this latent defect in the defendants' subsoil. And it further appears, that the defendants selected competent engineers and contractors to make their reservoir, and themselves personally continued in total ignorance of what we have called the latent defect in the subsoil; but that these persons employed by them in the course of the work became aware of the existence of the ancient shafts filled up with soil, though they did not know or suspect that they were shafts communicating with old workings.

It is found that the defendants, personally, were free from all blame, but that in fact proper care and skill was not used by the persons employed by them, to provide for the sufficiency of the reservoir with reference to these shafts. The consequence was, that the reservoir when filled with water burst into the shafts, the water flowed down through them into the old workings, and thence into the plaintiff's mine, and there did the mischief.

The plaintiff, though free from all blame on his part, must bear the loss, unless he can establish that it was the consequence of some default for which the defendants are responsible. The question of law therefore arises, what is the obligation which the law casts on a person who, like the defendants, lawfully brings on his land something which, though harmless whilst it remains there, will naturally do mischief if it escape[s] out of his land. It is agreed on all hands that he must take care to keep in that which he has brought on the land and keeps there, in order that it may not escape and damage his neighbours, but the question arises whether the duty which the law casts upon him, under such circumstances, is an absolute duty to keep it in at his peril, or is, as the majority of the Court of Exchequer have thought, merely a duty to take all reasonable and prudent precautions, in order to keep it in, but no more. If the first be the law, the person who has brought on his land and kept there something dangerous, and failed to keep it in, is responsible for all the natural consequences of its escape. If the second be the limit of his duty, he would not be answerable except on proof of negligence, and consequently would not be answerable for escape arising from any latent defect which ordinary prudence and skill could not detect.

Supposing the second to be the correct view of the law, a further question arises subsidiary to the first, viz., whether the defendants are not so far identified with the contractors whom they employed, as to be responsible for the consequences of their want of care and skill in making the reservoir in fact insufficient with reference to the old shafts, or the existence of which they were aware, though they had not ascertained where the shafts went to.

We think that the true rule of law is, that the person who for his own purposes brings on his lands and collects and keeps there anything likely to do mischief if it escapes, must keep it in at his peril, and, if he does not do so, is prima facie answerable for all the damage which is the natural consequence of its escape. He can excuse himself by showing that the escape was owing to the plaintiff's default; or perhaps that the escape was the consequence of vis major, or the act of God; but as nothing of this sort exists here, it is unnecessary to inquire what excuse would be sufficient. The general rule, as above stated, seems on principle just. The person whose grass or corn is eaten down by the escaping cattle of his neighbour, or whose mine is flooded by the water from his neighbour's reservoir, or whose cellar is invaded by the filth of his neighbour's privy, or whose habitation is made unhealthy by the fumes and noisome vapours of his neighbour's alkali works, is damnified without any fault of his own; and it seems but reasonable and just that the neighbour, who has brought something on his own property which was not naturally there, harmless to others so long as it is confined to his own property, but which he knows to be mischievous if it gets on his neighbour's, should be obliged to make good the damage which ensues if he does not succeed in confining it to his own property. But for his act in bringing it there no mischief could have accrued, and it seems but just that he should at his peril keep it there so that no mischief may accrue, or answer for the natural and anticipated consequences. And upon authority, this we think is established to be the law whether the things so brought be beasts, or water, or filth, or stenches.

The case that has most commonly occurred, and which is most frequently to be found in the books, is as to the obligation of the owner of cattle which he has brought on his land, to prevent their escaping and doing mischief. The law as to them seems to be perfectly settled from early times; the owner must keep them in at his peril, or he will be answerable for the natural consequences of their escape; that is with regard to tame beasts, for the grass they eat and trample upon, though not for any injury to the person of others, for our ancestors have settled that it is not the general nature of horses to kick, or bulls to gore; but if the owner knows that the beast has a vicious propensity to attack man, he will be answerable for that too. . . .

. . . But it was further said by Martin, B., [a majority judge in the Court of Exchequer], that when damage is done to personal property, or even to the person, by collision, either upon land or at sea, there must be negligence in the party doing the damage to render him legally responsible; and this is no doubt true, and as was pointed out by Mr. Mellish during his argument before us, this is not confined to cases of collision, for there are many cases in which proof of negligence is essential, as for instance, where an unruly horse gets on the footpath of a public street and kills a passenger; or where a person in a dock is struck by the falling of a bale of cotton which the defendant's servants are lowering; and many other similar cases may be found. But we think these cases distinguishable from the present. Traffic on the highways, whether by land or sea, cannot be conducted without exposing those whose persons or property are near it to some inevitable risk; and that being so, those who go on the highway, or have their property adjacent to it, may well be held to do so subject to their taking upon themselves the risk of injury from that inevitable danger; and persons who by the license of the owner pass near to warehouses where goods are being raised or lowered, certainly do so subject to the inevitable risk of accident. In neither case, therefore, can they recover without proof of want of care or skill occasioning the accident; and it is believed that all the cases in which inevitable accident has been held an excuse for what prima facie was a trespass, can be explained on the same principle, viz., that the circumstances were such as to shew that the plaintiff had taken that risk upon himself. But there is no ground for saying that the plaintiff here took upon himself any risk arising from the uses to which the defendants should choose to apply their land. He neither knew what these might be, nor could he in any way control the defendants, or hinder their building what reservoirs they liked, and storing up in them what water they pleased, so long as the defendants succeeded in preventing the water which they there brought from interfering with the plaintiff's property.

The view which we take of the first point renders it unnecessary to consider whether the defendants would or would not be responsible for the want of care and skill in the persons employed by them, under the circumstances stated in the case.

We are of the opinion that the plaintiff is entitled to recover, but as we have not heard any argument as to the amount, we are not able to give judgment for what damages. The parties probably will empower their counsel to agree on the amount of damages; should they differ on the principle, the case may be mentioned again.

Judgment for the plaintiff.

Rylands v. Fletcher

L.R. 3 H.L. 330 (1868)

The Lord Chancellor (Lord Cairns): . . . My lords, the principles on which this case must be determined appear to me to be extremely simple. The Defendants, treating them as the owners or occupiers of the close on which the reservoir was constructed, might lawfully have used that close for any purpose for which it might in the ordinary course of the enjoyment of land be used; and if, in what I may term the natural use of that land, there had been any accumulation of water, either on the surface or underground, and if, by the operation of the laws of nature, that accumulation of water had passed off into the close occupied by the Plaintiff, the Plaintiff could not have complained. . . .

On the other hand if the Defendants, not stopping at the natural use of their close, had desired to use it for any purpose which I may term a nonnatural use, for the purpose of introducing into the close that which in its natural condition was not in or upon it, for the purpose of introducing water either above or below ground in quantities and in a manner not the result of any work or operation on or under the land, — and if in the consequence of their doing so, or in consequence of any imperfection in the mode of their doing so, the water came to escape and to pass off into the close of the Plaintiff, then it appears to me that that which the Defendants were doing they were doing at their own peril; and, if in the course of their doing it, the evil arose to which I have referred, the evil, namely, of the escape of the water and its passing away to the close of the Plaintiff and injuring the Plaintiff, then for the consequence of that, in my opinion, the Defendants would be liable. . . .

My Lords, these simple principles, if they are well founded, as it appears to me they are, really dispose of this case. . . .

Judgment of the Court of Exchequer Chamber affirmed.

Turner v. Big Lake Oil Co.

128 Tex. 155, 96 S.W.2d 221 (1936)

MR. CHIEF JUSTICE CURETON delivered the opinion of the court.

The primary question for determination here is whether or not the defendants in error, without negligence on their part, may be held liable in damages for the destruction or injury to property occasioned by the escape of salt water from ponds constructed and used by them in the operation of their oil wells. . . .

The defendants in error in the operation of certain oil wells in Reagan County constructed large artificial earthen ponds or pools into which they ran the polluted waters from the wells. On the occasion complained of, water escaped from one or more of these ponds, and, passing over the grass lands of the plaintiffs in error, injured the turf, and after entering Garrison draw flowed down the same into Centralia draw. In Garrison draw there were natural water holes, which supplied water for the livestock of plaintiffs in error. The pond, or ponds, of water from which the salt water escaped were, we judge from the map, some six miles from the stockwater holes to which we refer. The plaintiffs in error brought suit, basing their action on alleged neglect on the part of the defendants in error in permitting the levees and dams, etc., of their artificial ponds to break and overflow the land of plaintiffs in error, and thereby pollute the waters to which we have above referred and injure the turf in the pasture of plaintiffs in error. The question was submitted to a jury on special issues, and the jury answered that the defendants in error did permit salt water to overflow from their salt ponds and lakes down Garrison draw and on to the land of the plaintiffs in error. *However, the jury acquitted the defendants in error of negligence in the premises.* . . .

[T]he immediate question presented is whether or not defendants in error are to be held liable as insurers, or whether the cause of action against them must be predicated upon negligence. We believe the question is one of first impression in this Court, and so we shall endeavor to discuss it in a manner in keeping with its importance.

Upon both reason and authority we believe that the conclusion of the Court of Civil Appeals that negligence is a prerequisite to recovery in a case of this character is a correct one. There is some difference of opinion on the subject in American jurisprudence brought about by differing views as to the correctness or applicability of the decision of the English courts in Rylands v. Fletcher, L.R. 3 H.L. 330. . . .

In Rylands v. Fletcher the Court predicated the absolute liability of the defendants on the proposition that the use of land for the artificial storage of water was not a natural use, and that, therefore, the land owner was bound at his peril to keep the waters on his own land. This basis of the English rule is to be found in the meteorological conditions which obtain there. England is a pluvial country, where constant streams and abundant rains make the storage of water unnecessary for ordinary or general purposes. When the Court said in Rylands v. Fletcher that the use of land for storage of water was an unnatural use, it meant such use was not a general or an ordinary one; not one within the contemplation of the parties to the original grant of the land involved, nor of the grantor and grantees of adjacent lands, but was a special or extraordinary use, and for that reason applied the rule of absolute liability. This conclusion is supported by the fact that those jurisdictions which adhere to the rule in Rylands v. Fletcher do not apply that rule to dams or reservoirs constructed in rivers and streams, which they say is a natural use, but apply the principle of negligence. In other words, the impounding of water in streamways, being an obvious and natural use, was necessarily within the contemplation of the parties to the original and adjacent grants, and damages must be predicated upon negligent use of a granted right and power; while things not within the contemplation of the parties to the original grants, such as unnatural uses of the land, the land owner may do only at his peril. As to what use of land is or may be a natural use, one within the contemplation of the parties to the original grant of land, necessarily depends upon the attendant circumstances and conditions which obtain in the territory of the original grants, or the initial terms of those grants.

In Texas we have conditions very different from those which obtain in England. A large portion of Texas is an arid or semi-arid region. West of the 98th meridian of longitude, where the rainfall is approximately 30 inches, the rainfall decreases until finally, in the extreme western part of the State, it is only about 10 inches. This land of decreasing rainfall is the great ranch or livestock region of the State, water for which is stored in thousands of ponds, tanks, and lakes on the surface of the ground. The country is almost without streams; and without the storage of water from rainfall in basins constructed for the purpose, or to hold waters pumped from the earth, the great livestock industry of West Texas must perish. No such condition obtains in England. With us the storage of water is a natural or necessary and common use of the land, necessarily within the contemplation of the State and its grantees when grants were made, and obviously the rule announced in Rylands v. Fletcher, predicated upon different conditions, can have no application here.

Again, in England there are no oil wells, no necessity for using surface storage facilities for impounding and evaporating salt waters therefrom. In Texas the situation is different. Texas has many great oil fields, tens of thousands of wells in almost every part of the State. Producing oil is one of our major industries. One of the by-products of oil production is salt water, which must be disposed of without injury to property or the pollution of streams. The construction of basins or ponds to hold this salt water is a necessary part of the oil business. In Texas much of our land was granted without mineral reservation to the State, and where minerals were reserved, provision has usually been made for leasing and operating. It follows, therefore, that as to these grants and leases the right to mine in the usual and appropriate way, as, for example, by the construction and maintenance of salt water pools such as here involved, incident to the production of oil, were contemplated by the State and all its grantees and mineral lessees, that being a use of the surface incident and necessary to the right to produce oil. . . .

The judgments of the Court of Civil Appeals and of the District Court are affirmed.

In Atlas Chem. Indus., Inc. v. Anderson, 514 S.W.2d 309 (Tex. Civ. App. 1974), *aff'd*, 524 S.W.2d 681 (Tex. 1975), the Texas Court of Appeals reviewed a verdict and judgment for the plaintiff in a case involving the deliberate dumping by the defendant of industrial wastes on 60 acres of the plaintiff's land. The defendant conceded that the discharge was intentional, but claimed that it was not done with the intent to harm the plaintiff. The court of appeals affirmed the judgment for the plaintiff, concluding that strict liability will attach under Texas law whenever pollutants are intentionally discharged. The court explained (514 S.W.2d at 315-16):

> We recognize that the rule of law hereinabove set out by this court may be a departure from the rules heretofore established by our courts and may be in conflict with some of those decisions. However, we believe that the common law rules of tort liability in pollution cases arising out of the intentional discharge of pollutants should be in conformity with the public policy of this state as declared by the Legislature in the Texas Water Code (1971). . . . Basically, the public policy is that the quality of water in this State shall be maintained free of pollution. . . . Texas Water Code, Sec. 21.003(11) states that "'Pollution' means the alteration of the physical, thermal, chemical, or biological quality of, or the contamination of, any water in the state that renders the water harmful, detrimental, or injurious to humans, animal life, vegetation, or property, or to public health, safety, or welfare, or impairs the usefulness or the public enjoyment of the water for any lawful or reasonable purpose." . . .
>
> We further believe the public policy of this State to be that however laudable an industry may be, its owners or managers are still subject to the rule that its industry or its property cannot be so used as to inflict injury to the property of its neighbors. To allow industry to inflict injury to the property of its neighbors without just compensation amounts to inverse condemnation which is not permitted under our law. We know of no acceptable rule of jurisprudence which permits those engaged in important and desirable enterprises to injure with impunity those who are engaged in enterprises of lesser economic significance. The costs of injuries resulting from pollution must be internalized by industry as a cost of production and borne by consumers or shareholders, or both, and not by the injured individual.

Is the Texas court correct in its claim that "no acceptable rule of jurisprudence" allows actors to impose accident costs on others? What about the rule of negligence? In any event, liability for the discharge or release of hazardous substances is not always covered by strict liability. In Indiana Harbor Belt Co. v. American Cyanamid Co., 916 F.2d 1174 (7th Cir. 1990), the court rejected an effort to apply strict liability to the manufacturer and shipper of acrylonitrile, a flammable, highly toxic, and possibly carcinogenic chemical used in many manufacturing processes. The plaintiff, a company operating a railroad switching yard, brought suit against the defendant to recover almost a million dollars in decontamination costs it incurred when the acrylonitrile leaked from a railroad tank car. In rejecting the plaintiff's strict liability claim, the court noted (916 F.2d at 1178):

> Acrylonitrile is one of a large number of chemicals that are hazardous in the sense of being flammable, toxic, or both; acrylonitrile is both, as are many others. A table in the record . . . contains a list of the 125 hazardous materials that are shipped in highest volume on the nation's railroads. Acrylonitrile is the fifty-third most hazardous on the list. Number 1 is phosphorus (white or yellow), and among the other materials that rank higher than acrylonitrile on the hazard scale are anhydrous ammonia, liquified petroleum gas, vinyl chloride, gasoline, crude petroleum, motor fuel antiknock compound, methyl and ethyl chloride, sulphuric acid, sodium metal, and chloroform. The plaintiff's lawyer acknowledged at argument that the logic of [recognizing strict liability for acrylonitrile] dictated

> strict liability for all 52 materials that rank higher than acrylonitrile on the list, and quite possibly for the 72 that rank lower as well, since all are hazardous if spilled in quantity while being shipped by rail. Every shipper of any of these materials would therefore be strictly liable for the consequences of a spill or other accident that occurred while the material was being shipped. . . . No cases recognize so sweeping a liability. Several reject it, though none has facts much like those of the present case.

Finding precedent unhelpful, the court concluded that the application of strict liability was inappropriate, in part because there was "no reason . . . for believing that a negligence regime is not perfectly adequate to remedy and deter, at reasonable cost, the accidental spillage of acrylonitrile from railroad cars." Id. at 1179.

Siegler v. Kuhlman

81 Wash. 2d 448, 502 P.2d 1181 (1972)

HALE, J. Seventeen-year-old Carol J. House died in the flames of a gasoline explosion when her car encountered a pool of thousands of gallons of spilled gasoline. She was driving home from her after-school job in the early evening of November 22, 1967, along Capitol Lake Drive in Olympia; it was dark but dry; her car's headlamps were burning. There was a slight impact with some object, a muffled explosion, and then searing flames from gasoline pouring out of an overturned trailer tank engulfed her car. The result of the explosion is clear, but the real cause of what happened will remain something of an eternal mystery.

[Testimony revealed that on the night in question defendant Aaron Kuhlman was driving a gasoline truck and trailer unit, owned by co-defendant Pacific Inter-Mountain Express and fully loaded with gasoline, along a freeway in Olympia, Washington. Without warning, the trailer came loose from the truck, catapulted off the freeway and through a chain link fence, and landed upside down on Capitol Lake Drive. Moments later, the plaintiff's decedent drove into the gasoline, somehow ignited it, and perished in the flames. What caused the trailer to come loose, and the gasoline to ignite, is not revealed in the record. Plaintiff joined the driver, the owner and the manufacturer of the truck and trailer, seeking recovery on the bases of negligence and strict liability. The trial court refused the plaintiff's request for an instruction on res ipsa loquitur and strict liability, and the jury returned a verdict for defendants. From a judgment for defendants entered on the verdict, the plaintiff appealed. The intermediate court of appeals affirmed, 3 Wash. App. 231, 473 P.2d 445 (1970).]

In the Court of Appeals, the principal claim of error was directed to the trial court's refusal to give an instruction on res ipsa loquitur, and we think that claim of error well taken. Our reasons for ruling that an instruction on res ipsa loquitur should have been given and that an inference of negligence could have been drawn from the event are found, we believe, in our statements on the subject. . . . We think, therefore, that plaintiff was entitled to an instruction permitting the jury to infer negligence from the occurrence.

But there exists here an even more impelling basis for liability in this case than its derivation by allowable inference of fact under the res ipsa loquitur doctrine, and that is the proposition of strict liability arising as a matter of law from all of the circumstances of the event.

Strict liability is not a novel concept; it is at least as old as Fletcher v. Rylands, L.R. 1 Ex. 265, 278 (1866), *aff'd*, House of Lords, 3 H.L. 330 (1868). . . . The basic principles supporting the *Fletcher* doctrine, we think, control the transportation of gasoline as freight along the public highways the same as it does the impounding of waters and for largely the same reasons.

In many respects, hauling gasoline as freight is no more unusual, but more dangerous, than collecting water. When gasoline is carried as cargo — as distinguished from fuel for the carrier vehicle — it takes on uniquely hazardous characteristics, as does water impounded in large quantities. Dangerous in itself, gasoline develops even greater potential for harm when carried as freight — extraordinary dangers deriving from sheer quantity, bulk and weight, which enormously multiply its hazardous properties. And the very hazards inhering from the size of the load, its bulk or quantity and its movement along the highways presents another reason for application of the Fletcher v. Rylands, supra, rule not present in the impounding of large quantities of water — the likely destruction of cogent evidence from which negligence or want of it may be proved or disapproved. It is quite probable that the most important ingredients of proof will be lost in a gasoline explosion and fire. Gasoline is always dangerous whether kept in large or small quantities because of its volatility, inflammability and explosiveness. But when several thousand gallons of it are allowed to spill across a public highway — that is, if, while in transit as freight, it is not kept impounded — the hazards to third persons are so great as to be almost beyond calculation. As a consequence of its escape from impoundment and subsequent explosion and ignition, the evidence in a very high percentage of instances will be destroyed, and the reason for and causes contributing to its escape will quite likely be lost in the searing flames and explosions. . . .

Thus, the reasons for applying a rule of strict liability obtain in this case. We have a situation where a highly flammable, volatile and explosive substance is being carried at a comparatively high rate of speed, in great and dangerous quantities as cargo upon the public highways, subject to all of the hazards of high-speed traffic, multiplied by the great dangers inherent in the volatile and explosive nature of the substance, and multiplied again by the quantity and size of the load. Then we have the added dangers of ignition and explosion generated when a load of this size, that is, about 5,000 gallons of gasoline, breaks its container and, cascading from it, spreads over the highway so as to release an invisible but highly volatile and explosive vapor above it. . . .

The rule of strict liability, when applied to an abnormally dangerous activity, as stated in the Restatement (Second) of Torts §519 (Tent. Draft No. 10, 1964), was adopted as the rule of decision in this state in Pacific Northwest Bell Tel. Co. v. Port of Seattle, 80 Wash. 2d 59, 64, 491 P.2d 1037, 1039-1040 (1971), as follows:

> (1) One who carries on an abnormally dangerous activity is subject to liability for harm to the person, land or chattels of another resulting from the activity, although he has exercised the utmost care to prevent such harm.
>
> (2) Such strict liability is limited to the kind of harm, the risk of which makes the activity abnormally dangerous.

As to what constitutes an abnormal activity, section 520 states:

> In determining whether an activity is abnormally dangerous, the following factors are to be considered:
>
> (a) Whether the activity involves a high degree of risk of some harm to the person, land or chattels of others;
>
> (b) Whether the gravity of the harm which may result from it is likely to be great;
>
> (c) Whether the risk cannot be eliminated by the exercise of reasonable care;
>
> (d) Whether the activity is not a matter of common usage;
>
> (e) Whether the activity is inappropriate to the place where it is carried on; and
>
> (f) The value of the activity to the community.

. . . Transporting gasoline as freight by truck along the public highways and streets is obviously an activity involving a high degree of risk; it is a risk of great harm and injury; it creates dangers that cannot be eliminated by the exercise of reasonable care. That gasoline cannot be practicably transported except upon the public highways does not decrease the abnormally high risk arising from its transportation. Nor will the exercise of due and reasonable care assure protection to the public from the disastrous consequences of concealed or latent mechanical or metallurgical defects in the carrier's equipment, from the negligence of third parties, from latent defects in the highways and streets, and from all of the other hazards not generally disclosed or guarded against by reasonable care, prudence and foresight. Hauling gasoline in great quantities as freight, we think, is an activity that calls for the application of principles of strict liability.

The case is therefore reversed and remanded to the trial court for trial to the jury on the sole issue of damages.

HAMILTON, C.J., FINLEY, ROSELLINI, and HUNTER, JJ., and RYAN, J. PRO TEM., concur.

ROSELLINI, J. (concurring). I agree with the majority that the transporting of highly volatile and flammable substances upon the public highways in commercial quantities and for commercial purposes is an activity which carries with it such a great risk of harm to defenseless users of the highway, if it is not kept contained, that the common-law principles of strict liability should apply. In my opinion, a good reason to apply these principles, which is not mentioned in the majority opinion, is that the commercial transporter can spread the loss among his customers — who benefit from this extrahazardous use of the highways. Also, if the defect which caused the substance to escape was one of manufacture, the owner is in the best position to hold the manufacturer to account.

I think the opinion should make clear, however, that the owner of the vehicle will be held strictly liable only for damages caused when the flammable or explosive substance is allowed to escape without the apparent intervention of any outside force beyond the control of the manufacturer, the owner, or the operator of the vehicle hauling it. I do not think the majority means to suggest that if another vehicle, negligently driven, collided with the truck in question, the truck owner would be held liable for the damage. But where, as here, there was no outside force which caused the trailer to become detached from the truck, the rule of strict liability should apply. . . .

HAMILTON, C.J., FINLEY, J., and RYAN, J. PRO TEM., concur with ROSELLINI, J.

[The dissenting opinion of NEILL, J., is omitted.]

Most states, but not all, have endorsed using the Restatement (Second) of Torts §520 factors to gauge what activities are abnormally dangerous and to determine whether strict liability should be applied. See, e.g., In re Chicago Flood Litig., 680 N.E.2d 265, 279 (Ill. 1997); Klein v. Pyrodyne Corp., 810 P.2d 917, 920, amended, 817 P.2d 1359 (Wash. 1991); Bridges v. Kentucky Stone Co., 425 N.E.2d 125, 126 (Ind. 1981); Harper v. Regency Dev. Co., 399 So. 2d 248, 253 (Ala. 1981); City of Neodesha v. BP Corp. N. Am., 287 P.3d 214, 217 (Kan. 2012). But see Lowder v. Slawson Expl. Co., 2014 WL 4352182, at *1 (D.N.D. Sept. 2, 2014) (North Dakota "does not recognize a claim for strict liability for abnormally dangerous activities").

In certain cases, identifying the activity itself can be of some importance. For example, in City of Neodesha v. BP Corp. N. Am., 287 P.3d 214, 228 (Kan. 2012), due to a statute of repose barring most tort actions after a period of ten years from the date of an activity, plaintiffs had to challenge the adequacy of defendant corporations' remediation efforts after their oil refinery operations had contaminated local groundwater, rather than directly challenge defendants' actions in operating the oil refinery and causing the contamination in the first place. The plaintiffs were therefore in the "unenviable position of pursuing a strict liability theory related to [defendants'] conduct *after* the refinery closed," which added an additional layer of complexity. Id. at 229. See also Machado-Avilla v. Doris Duke Found. for Islamic Art, No., 2013 WL 1817085, at *6 (D. Haw. Apr. 26, 2013) (teenager broke his neck after diving at defendant's boat harbor, but plaintiffs did not "adequately identify an 'activity' of [d]efendant's that is abnormally dangerous").

In recent years, courts have recognized that many activities are economically important despite their dangers and have begun to engage in more transparent forms of weighing when considering factor (f) of the Restatement (Second) §520: "The value of the activity to the community." For example, a court in Maine refused to apply strict liability against a cement manufacturing plant, holding that its blasting operations were "common and appropriate" to the location and stressing the company's "substantial value to the surrounding community." Darney v. Dragon Products Co., LLC, 771 F. Supp. 2d 91, 120 (D. Me. 2011). In its opinion, the court noted that the defendant company brought various economic benefits to the city, including paying $1.2 million of annual property taxes to the town and employing 97 employees who received wages and benefits of approximately $5 million. Id. Some courts also recognize a "public function" exception that exempts activities from the scope of strict liability if they bring public value to the community. See, e.g. Modern Holdings, LLC v. Corning Inc., No. CIV. 13-405-GFVT, 2015 WL 1481457, at *7 (E.D. Ky. Mar. 31, 2015) (noting Kentucky's "public function" exception applies broadly to exempt public service activities such as electricity transmission, and transportation of flammable or dangerous chemicals). See also Kirk v. Schaeffler Grp. USA, Inc., 2016 WL 928721, at *2 (W.D. Mo. Mar. 9, 2016) (considering the extent to which the challenged activity's "value to the community is outweighed by its danger"). In evaluating the potential dangers of an activity, some courts appear to consider not only the dangers of the activity itself, but also whether the activity helps reduce risks that would otherwise exist. For example, in an unpublished opinion, the Appeals Court of Massachusetts upheld the demolition of a building in an active state of collapse because the "value of removal of this building, which presented a great risk to the community, could not be underestimated." Silva v. Associated Bldg. Wreckers, Inc., 970 N.E.2d 814, 814 (Mass. App. Ct. 2012).

Courts and commentators have also begun to streamline the various Restatement (Second) factors to a more narrow focus on whether the risks associated with the activity can be reduced through the exercise of due care. See, e.g., Collins v. Olin Corp., 418 F. Supp. 2d 34 (D. Conn. 2006) (dismissing strict liability claim against the town of Hamden, Connecticut for damages caused by hazardous waste disposal in substantial part because "there is no claim [by plaintiffs] that the landfills could not have been managed in a safe way"). Reflecting these developments, the Restatement (Third) of Torts: Liability for Physical and Emotional Harm (2010) includes a truncated version of the Section 520 test:

§20. Abnormally Dangerous Activities

(a) An actor who carries on an abnormally dangerous activity is subject to strict liability for physical harm resulting from the activity.

(b) An activity is abnormally dangerous if:

(1) the activity creates a foreseeable and highly significant risk of physical harm even when reasonable care is exercised by all actors; and

(2) the activity is not one of common usage.

Despite these attempts to simplify the abnormally dangerous activity analysis, much of the case law retains an unsatisfactory, ad hoc quality. For instance, the court in Biniek v. Exxon Mobil Corp., 818 A.2d 330 (N.J. Super. Ct. Law Div. 2002) rejected *Siegler*'s imposition of strict liability, opining only that "the overwhelming strength of authority and a common sense application of the Restatement mandate the conclusion that the storage and transportation of gasoline does not qualify as an ultrahazardous activity." Id. at 339. See also Henke v. Arco Midcon, L.L.C., 750 F. Supp. 2d 1052, 1059 (E.D. Mo. 2010) (holding that "operation of a petroleum pipeline is not an abnormally dangerous activity as a matter of law"). Courts have also disagreed regarding whether pile driving is an ultrahazardous activity. For instance, in Oja & Assocs. v. Washington Park Towers, Inc., 569 P.2d 1141 (Wash. 1977), the Supreme Court of Washington affirmed a strict liability judgment based on property damage caused by pile driving activities, while in *In re* Chicago Flood Litig., 680 N.E.2d 265 (Ill. 1997), the Supreme Court of Illinois held that pile driving and freight tunnel maintenance activities that caused a major flood in downtown Chicago were not abnormally dangerous activities. See also Gallagher v. H.V. Pierhomes, LLC, 957 A.2d 628 (Md. Ct. Spec. App. 2008) (refusing to extend strict liability for abnormally dangerous activities to pile driving). Contrasting outcomes along these lines can be identified for numerous categories of activity. Compare, e.g., Klein v. Pyrodyne Corp., 810 P.2d 917 (Wash. 1991) (fireworks company is strictly liable for injuries caused by fireworks display), with Cadena v. Chicago Fireworks Mfg., 697 N.E.2d 802 (Ill. App. Ct. 1998) (holding that the display of fireworks is not ultrahazardous), and Beddingfield v. Linam, 127 So. 3d 1178 (Ala. 2013) (the use of ordinary consumer fireworks, unlike commercial public fireworks, is not an abnormally dangerous activity). See also Lipka v. DiLungo, 26 Conn. L. Rptr. 654 (Conn. Super. Ct. March 8, 2000) (holding that illegal fireworks displays are an ultrahazardous activity).

Still, a few specific kinds of dangerous activity have over time become especially likely to be subjected to strict liability. For instance, at least 41 states have adopted some form of strict liability for blasting activities. See Dyer v. Maine Drilling & Blasting, Inc., 984 A.2d 210, 216 (Me. 2009). But see Crouch v. N. Alabama Sand & Gravel, LLC, 177 So. 3d 200, 207 (Ala. 2015) (remanding to determine whether blasting activity can be considered abnormally dangerous if its accompanying vibrations led to damage in nearby house). The use of toxic agricultural chemicals is also frequently regarded as a procedure that is appropriately held to the strict liability standard. See Roberts v. Cardinal Servs., Inc., 266 F.3d 368 (5th Cir. 2001) (aerial crop dusting in Louisiana is classified as an ultrahazardous activity as a matter of law); Bella v. Aurora Air, Inc., 566 P.2d 489 (Or. 1997) (aerial chemical spraying deemed an abnormally dangerous activity); Kell v. Appalachian Power Co., 289 S.E.2d 450, 454 (W.V. 1982) (power company held strictly liable for use of toxic herbicides to clear right-of-way that inflicted damage upon nearby property); Langan v. Valicopters, Inc., 567 P.2d 218 (Wash. 1977) (aerial spraying of agricultural pesticides adjacent to a certified organic farm incurs strict liability for damages caused to organic farm due to loss of its certification). But see Bennett v. Larsen Co., 348 N.W.2d 540 (Wis. 1984) (spraying pesticide with a helicopter was not an ultrahazardous activity); Wilson v. Greg Williams Farm, Inc., 436 S.W.3d 485, 488 (Ark. Ct. App. 2014), reh'g denied (July 23, 2014) (aerial application of herbicide is not an inherently dangerous activity).

Not surprisingly, transporters and storers of explosives are generally held strictly liable for harm caused by accidental explosions. Thus, in Chevez v. South Pac. Transp. Co., 413 F. Supp. 1203 (E.D. Cal. 1976), a railroad was held strictly liable for the harm caused when 18 bomb-loaded boxcars exploded in the railroad's yard. The court refused to recognize an exception to the general rule of strict liability for ultrahazardous activities based on the fact that the railroad was authorized by law to transport the explosives. And in Yukon Equip., Inc. v. Fireman's Fund Ins. Co., 585 P.2d 1206 (Alaska 1978), the Supreme Court of Alaska imposed strict liability on the storers of explosives even when it was proved that the harmful explosion was deliberately caused by thieves who were attempting to prevent discovery of the fact that they had stolen some explosives. See also Alexandra B. Klass, From Reservoirs to Remediation: The Impact of CERCLA on Common Law Strict Liability Claims, 39 Wake Forest L. Rev. 903 (2004) (surveying use of strict liability in cases of environmental harm).

In recent years, a dramatic increase in the use of hydraulic fracturing techniques for oil and gas recovery has been accompanied by adverse publicity and concern over potential negative environmental, health, and safety effects. See generally Grace Heusner, Allison Sloto & Joshua Ulan Galperin, Defining and Closing the Hydraulic Fracturing Governance Gap, 41 Harv. Envtl. L. Rev. (2017). In addition to appeals for greater regulation, plaintiffs have filed lawsuits claiming that "fracking" should be considered an abnormally dangerous activity. Results in the suits have not been promising for plaintiffs thus far. See, e.g., Ely v. Cabot Oil & Gas Corp., 38 F. Supp. 3d 518 (M.D. Pa. 2014) (holding natural gas drilling activities, including hydraulic fracturing, are not abnormally dangerous); Kamuck v. Shell Energy Holdings GP, LLC., No. 4:11-CV-1425, 2015 WL 1345235, at *6 (M.D. Pa. Mar. 25, 2015) (natural gas extraction is "not an abnormally dangerous activity of the type that would give rise to strict tort liability"). But see Berish v. Sw. Energy Prod. Co., 763 F. Supp. 2d 702, 705 (M.D. Pa. 2011) (refusing to hold as a matter of law, in context of motion to dismiss, that underground natural gas drilling is not an abnormally dangerous activity).

Courts have also been reluctant to classify the marketing of products as ultrahazardous, even if those products subsequently cause harm when placed in the hands of consumers. See, e.g., Thompson v. Mindis Metals, 692 So. 2d 805 (Ala. 1997) (holding that the sale of batteries is not an ultrahazardous activity, even though the batteries eventually leaked harmful lead into the environment when processed by the recycling facility that had purchased them); Gaines-Tabb v. Ici Explosives USA, Inc., 995 F. Supp. 1304 (W.D. Okla. 1996) (holding that the marketing of explosive-grade ammonium nitrate fertilizer, which Timothy McVeigh utilized in the Oklahoma City bombing, is not an ultrahazardous activity).

In Kelley v. R. G. Indus., Inc., 497 A.2d 1143 (Md. 1985), however, the Maryland Court of Appeals became the first court of last resort to recognize a cause of action in products liability against the manufacturer of a small, inexpensive handgun, commonly known as a Saturday night special, when the victim was shot by a criminal who made use of this particular type of handgun. The court reasoned that those who market Saturday night specials know that they have no likely function other than to be used for the commission of a crime. The court was careful to point out that it was not finding that Saturday night specials were "unreasonably dangerous" within §402A, the products liability provision in the Restatement (Second). Nor was the marketing of handguns an abnormally dangerous activity under Restatement (Second) §§519-520. Rather, the court said it was drawing on basic common law principles to impose liability for the sale of this particular product, which was manufactured and marketed for the sole purpose of facilitating crime.

The Maryland legislature has since exempted firearms from strict liability. See Md. Code Ann., Pub. Safety §5-402 (LexisNexis 2003). Moreover, other courts that have faced the question have refused to impose strict liability on firearm manufacturers. See Copier v. Smith & Wesson Corp., 138 F.3d 833 at 836-37 (10th Cir. 1998) (collecting cases rejecting application of abnormally dangerous activity doctrine to sale of firearms). The U.S. Congress in late 2005 passed the Protection of Lawful Commerce in Arms Act, Pub. L. No. 109-92, 119 Stat. 2095 (2005), a statute that immunizes gun manufacturers, sellers, and their trade associations from most state tort liability actions arising out of the "criminal or unlawful misuse" of firearms.

Determination of the appropriateness of the strict liability standard for particular activities is made by the court as matter of law. Unless it appears plain beyond doubt that the category of activity at issue could never be characterized as an abnormally dangerous activity, courts generally allow plaintiffs an opportunity to develop through discovery the factual record necessary to support the abnormally dangerous activity determination. See, e.g., Muniz v. Rexnord Corp., 2006 WL 1430553, at *1 (N.D. Ill. May 17, 2006) (refusing to dismiss strict liability claim against defendants charged with "dump[ing] cancer-causing chemicals . . . into the ground in a densely populated area of DuPage County, close to private drinking wells" because "a more complete record is necessary to properly analyze and apply the factual considerations set out above"). Nevertheless, plaintiffs ultimately carry the burden of persuasion on the issue, an allocation that becomes of great practical significance, especially if the plaintiff's resources are limited. In *Kamuck*, cited above, the Pennsylvania district court dismissed plaintiff's complaint after holding that hydraulic fracturing is not an abnormally dangerous activity. There, the plaintiff, a disabled war veteran, was proceeding pro se after he had become estranged from his counsel. The plaintiff had not responded to numerous discovery requests and other litigation obligations and was ultimately unable to produce any "evidence to support many of the allegations which he initially made in this case." Id. at *5. Although the plaintiff tried to submit affidavits and other materials, the court rejected them because they were procedurally flawed. Id. at *7. In finding that hydraulic fracturing is not abnormally dangerous, the court stressed the practice's positive economic impact for the county and noted that "[n]one of these matters have been addressed or rebutted in any way" by the plaintiff. Id at *6.

The plaintiff's burden is particularly significant once it is understood that the abnormally dangerous activity doctrine is frequently invoked in litigation contexts that involve scientific uncertainty. For instance, in Cobos v. Stillwater Min. Co., No. CV 11-18-BLG-RFC, 2012 WL 6018147, at *8 (D. Mont. Dec. 3, 2012), the court rejected plaintiffs' strict liability claim after noting that plaintiffs had failed to present evidence showing that there is significant risk of nasal carcinoma from the airborne carcinogens in mining operations:

> Plaintiffs narrowly define the abnormally dangerous activity as the exposure that a miner allegedly suffers from the release of [a] "colorless, invisible airborne carcinogen" into the air. When considering §519(2), it is of note that Plaintiffs do not argue, nor does the evidence support, that this kind of harm is normally associated with underground mining operations and is what makes the activity abnormally dangerous. Specifically, Plaintiffs present no evidence to support cases of significant risk from mining operations of airborne carcinogens that cause nasal carcinoma . . . . Therefore, this Court concludes that Plaintiffs have not presented sufficient evidentiary materials to establish a genuine dispute that Defendant Stillwater's alleged activity of exposing miners to airborne contaminants was abnormally dangerous.

Would a burden-shifting doctrine akin to res ipsa loquitur from the negligence context be appropriate for uncertain but potentially ultrahazardous activities? Consider this question in the context of the following case.

PSI Energy, Inc. v. Roberts

829 N.E.2d 943 (Ind. 2005)

[Plaintiff William Roberts contracted mesothelioma as a result of working with asbestos-containing insulation as an employee of Armstrong Contracting and Supply Company (ACandS). ACandS was the nation's largest insulation contractor during the time Roberts worked for the company. In the course of his employment, Roberts frequently installed, handled, removed, and otherwise worked with asbestos-containing insulation at power generation facilities owned by PSI Energy, Inc. (PSI), one of ACandS's industrial customers. Roberts sued PSI for damages, alleging that the company should be held vicariously liable for the negligence of its independent contractor, ACandS. Alternatively, Roberts sought recovery against PSI for failing its responsibilities as an owner of premises on which dangerous conditions existed. The jury returned a general verdict in favor of Roberts and PSI appealed.

In the process of evaluating Roberts's vicarious liability claim, the Indiana Supreme Court examined whether vicarious liability should attach to PSI under an "intrinsically dangerous" activity exception to the general rule of nonliability for the torts of independent contractors. (This exception is discussed in detail in Chapter 2, Section D.) As both the majority and the dissenting opinions point out, this "intrinsically dangerous" activity analysis bears a strong resemblance to the more general "abnormally dangerous" activity analysis used by courts when considering the application of strict liability.]

BOEHM, JUSTICE. . . . [T]he "inherently dangerous" exception is normally associated with strict liability and does not require negligence on the part of the contractor. . . . It imposes liability for activities that are dangerous by nature, not merely because they are carried out in a risky manner. For example, if the enterprise hires an independent contractor to dust crops with poison, it is liable for damage to neighbors' crops without regard to negligence. . . .

Roberts asserts that asbestos itself is intrinsically dangerous and "any work that causes inherently dangerous fibers to enter the breathing space of humans is intrinsically dangerous work." He points to Covalt v. Carey Canada, Inc., 543 N.E.2d 382 (Ind. 1989), in which this Court described asbestos fibers as "an inherently dangerous substance . . . a toxic foreign substance . . . an inherently dangerous product . . . and a hazardous foreign substance." Id. at 384-86. Roberts asserts that there is nothing that can make asbestos fibers safe. PSI responds that although asbestos may be an inherently dangerous substance, it does not follow that working with material containing asbestos is intrinsically dangerous work. PSI asserts that the evidence at trial demonstrates that the dangers of working with asbestos could have been minimized if Roberts had taken proper precautions. . . .

We agree that working with asbestos can be perilous, but that is not enough to render it intrinsically dangerous as that term is used to establish liability for actions of an independent contractor. For example in McDaniel v. Business Investment Group, Ltd., 709 N.E.2d 17 (Ind. Ct. App. 1999), *trans. denied*, an employee working on a sewer line in a 9 foot deep trench was killed when the sides of the trench caved in. The Indiana Court of Appeals held that trenching is not intrinsically dangerous work because "although it can be dangerous, the use of proper procedures . . . renders the work relatively safe." Id. at 21. . . . [The court then asserted that "[h]ere, it seems agreed by all that precautions could have minimized Roberts's exposure to asbestos," and that Roberts's alternative theory of liability based on negligence principles seems to concede that due care could have significantly reduced his exposure.] Therefore, we conclude that working with asbestos is not intrinsically dangerous such that anyone hiring a contractor to address it incurs strict liability for injuries sustained from exposure to it. . . . We also recognize, as the dissent points out, that the consequences of mesothelioma can be horrific. But that does not render asbestos intrinsically dangerous. The same is true of electricity and a number of other substances that, if mishandled, can be dangerous. . . .

[The court goes on to conclude that the general verdict against PSI can be upheld under plaintiff's alternate, "premises liability" theory of recovery:]

The record includes evidence that at least by the 1960s hazards from asbestos exposure were identified and known to PSI. ACandS employees were nevertheless unprotected on the site. On this record, the jury could find that PSI met all of the conditions: PSI had knowledge of the hazard, knew ACandS employees were taking no action to protect themselves, and did nothing . . . . Because the jury returned a general verdict, and the evidence most favorable to the verdict support[s] one of the two counts, the judgment of the trial court is affirmed.

SHEPARD, C.J., and SULLIVAN, J., concur.

DICKSON, J., concurs in result and dissents with separate opinion in which RUCKER, J., concurs.

DICKSON, JUSTICE, dissenting. I dissent from the majority's general discussion regarding the responsibility of a principal or landowner for injuries suffered by workers employed by an independent contractor hired by the landowner or principal. In an apparent effort to provide protection for landowners and other entities that employ independent contractors to eliminate or ameliorate dangerous conditions, the Court's opinion, in my judgment, goes too far. . . .

[T]he Court concludes that "working with asbestos is not intrinsically dangerous such that anyone hiring a contractor to address it incurs strict liability for injuries sustained from exposure to it." Id. at 955. I strongly disagree with this assertion, believing that asbestos is precisely the sort of danger to which the intrinsically dangerous exception should apply.

This principle is expressed in Restatement of Torts, Second §427A: "One who employs an independent contractor to do work which the employer knows or has reason to know to involve an abnormally dangerous activity, is subject to liability to the same extent as the contractor for physical harm to others caused by the activity." The underlying purpose of this rule is that:

> [O]ne who employs an independent contractor to do work which the employer knows or has reason to know to involve an abnormally dangerous activity cannot be permitted to escape the responsibility for the abnormal danger created by the activity which he has set in motion, and so cannot delegate the responsibility for harm resulting to others to the contractor.

Comment b to §427A. The illustrations following §427 refer to injuries resulting from the non-negligent escape of lions and urban blasting operations as examples of abnormally dangerous activities. . . .

Dr. David Mares, who diagnosed the plaintiff's peritoneal mesothelioma, stated that, without a doubt, "it was caused by asbestos exposure." Trans. at 1208. Dr. Mares also provided vivid testimony describing the disease's deadly nature. He declared that malignant mesothelioma is a fatal disease process. "It is not curable." Trans. at 1196. The time from the date of diagnosis to the date of death in a person with malignant peritoneal mesothelioma is usually "a year or less." Trans. at 1206. . . .

Dr. Mares pointed out that Mr. Roberts's pain will be "uncontrollable" and "unbearable" and that the "best medications will not provide pain relief." Trans. at 1220.

Describing the nature of mesothelioma, pathologist Arnold R. Brody, Ph.D., explained: "Our peritoneal cavity is where some of our organs are, like the stomach and the liver and the spleen sit in the peritoneal cavity. And that is lined by a single layer of cells, the mesothelium. . . . And when there is cancer of those cells, those mesothelial cells, it is mesothelioma." Trans. at 1383. Professor Brody stated, "[A]ll of the asbestos fiber types can cause mesothelioma . . . they all are perfectly good carcinogens." Trans. at 1384. He observed that no safe level of asbestos exposure has ever been established and that "[t]here is no level below which we know it to be absolutely safe and will not cause mesothelioma." Trans. at 1429.

One of the more insidious aspects of this fatal disease is the fact that its symptoms suddenly appear often decades after a worker is exposed to asbestos. Regarding this latency period between the exposure to asbestos and the first appearance of symptoms of malignant mesotheliomas, Dr. Brody testified that the probability for the latency period to be less than 10 years is about zero; for latency periods of 10 to 14 years about 0.5%; for 15 to 19 years, still just about 3%; and for 20 years or more, 96%. Dr. Brody agreed with an estimate that the average period in these cases from initial exposure to death is about 32 years. Trans. at 1480-82.

The Court specifically notes the testimony of Dr. Michael Ellenbecker emphasizing that "when we're talking about mesothelioma, I think it's difficult to do any activities with asbestos where you completely eliminate the hazard." Op. at 954, quoting Tr. at 2538. Asked whether there is any safe level of exposure to asbestos in the context of the risk of developing mesothelioma, Dr. Eugene Mark answered, "I don't think there is any safe level." Tr. at 2021. Likewise, Dr. Edwin Holstein testified that there is no recognized safe level of exposure to asbestos insulation such that no mesothelioma would occur in insulation workers. He explained, "There may be such a level at very, very, very low levels, but we don't know what it is. What we do know is that even very small exposures have caused mesothelioma in some people." Tr. at 1559. In fact, the Court itself acknowledges that "it is clear that working with any level of asbestos can be associated with mesothelioma." Op. at 956.

Thus we see that asbestos workers are extraordinarily susceptible to this insidious and virulent disease that will usually go undetected for decades but then suddenly erupt with devastating and almost inevitably fatal consequences. Elimination of this enormous risk is virtually impossible because it requires preventing every possibility of asbestos workers inhaling any asbestos fibers.

Conceding that working with asbestos can be perilous, the Court nevertheless concludes that the work does not qualify for the intrinsically dangerous exception to the rule of subcontractor nonliability because, although dangerous, "proper precautions can minimize the risk of injury." Id. at 955. . . .

An intrinsically dangerous activity, also referred to as an "abnormally dangerous activity" in the Restatement of Torts, Second §520 . . . requires the full inability to eliminate the risk, not merely to significantly reduce it. In my view, this is preferable to the prevailing Indiana appellate view that prohibits resort to the intrinsically dangerous exception wherever risks can be "significantly reduced," rather than requiring that they be eliminated.

Even applying the view that the intrinsically dangerous exception is applicable where risks either cannot be eliminated, or significantly reduced by due precaution, it appears clear that the risk of contracting mesothelioma demands that working with asbestos still be deemed intrinsically dangerous. As noted above, the Restatement cites the escape of lions and urban blasting as examples of abnormally dangerous activities. Obviously, such risks can be somewhat reduced with due precaution, but they cannot be eliminated or even significantly reduced. So it is with asbestos.

The Court today asserts only that "precautions could have minimized Roberts's exposure to asbestos" to justify its conclusion that "working with asbestos is not intrinsically dangerous." Op. at 955. But minimizing is not enough. Not only must due precautions have "minimized" the risk; they must have been able to eliminate or significantly reduce it. The risk of asbestos workers contracting mesothelioma cannot be eliminated nor significantly reduced. It is the quintessential example of an intrinsically dangerous activity. . . .

Notwithstanding my disagreements with much of the Court's discussion today regarding liability for injuries to employees of independent contractors, I concur with its conclusion that the evidence in this case was sufficient under the instructions to sustain the jury's verdict and the trial court's judgment. For these reasons, I concur in result.

RUCKER, J., concurs.

Law and Policy: Why Strict Liability?

As described in Chapter 3, the early common law flirted with both fault-based and strict liability concepts before adopting negligence as the dominant regime for American tort law. This choice was applauded by observers of tort law like O. W. Holmes, who felt that in the absence of some aspect of carelessness to defendant's conduct, "loss from accident must lie where it falls." See Oliver Wendell Holmes, The Common Law 77-96 (Mark DeWolfe Howe ed., Little, Brown 1963). In Holmes's view, a rule of liability without fault would tend to discourage behavior by individuals and other actors in society that, although potentially harmful to others, was still desirable from the overall perspective: "A man need not, it is true, do this or that act, — the term *act* implies a choice, — but he must act somehow. Furthermore, the public generally profits from industrial activity. As action cannot be avoided, and tends to the public good, there is obviously no policy in throwing the hazard of what is at once desirable and inevitable upon the actor." Id. at 77.

Given the supposed superiority of a negligence system, why have courts (and to some extent legislatures) embraced strict liability in scattered areas of tort law? More specifically, is strict liability in some sense "fairer," from a noninstrumental perspective, than negligence, at least in certain contexts? And from an instrumental, efficiency-oriented viewpoint, does strict liability offer advantages — in terms of minimizing socially wasteful accidents — over a negligence rule?

Beginning with the noninstrumental perspective, it is useful to reflect on the *Rylands* court's emphasis on the fact that the defendants had exposed the plaintiff to risks due to the defendants' "nonnatural use" of their land. Although the scope of the court's conception of "nonnatural uses" is far from clear, if we assume that the court was referring to activities that create unusual or uncommon risks to others, the outlines of a fairness argument for strict liability emerge. Recall that the first "law and policy" note in Chapter 1 offered an analysis by Professor George Fletcher in which tort liability is justified on fairness grounds when the defendant imposes unusual or nonreciprocal risks on the plaintiff. As Fletcher observes, the concept of nonreciprocal risks is especially relevant to the justification of strict liability (85 Harv. L. Rev. at 547-48):

> Expressing the standard of strict liability as unexcused, nonreciprocal risk-taking provides an account not only of the *Rylands* . . . decision, but of strict liability in general. It is apparent, for example, that . . . uncommon, ultrahazardous activities . . . are readily subsumed under the rationale of nonreciprocal risk-taking. If uncommon activities are those with few participants, they are likely to be activities generating nonreciprocal risks. Similarly, dangerous activities like blasting, fumigating, and crop dusting stand out as distinct, nonreciprocal risks in the community. They represent threats of harm that exceed the level of risk to which all members of the community contribute in roughly equal shares.
>
> The rationale of nonreciprocal risk-taking accounts as well for [other] pockets of strict liability. . . . For example, an individual is strictly liable for damage done by a wild animal in his charge, but not for damage committed by his domesticated pet. Most people have pets, children, or friends whose presence creates some risk to neighbors and their property. These are risks that offset each other; they are, as a class, reciprocal risks. Yet bringing an unruly horse into the city goes beyond the accepted and shared level of risks in having pets, children, and friends in one's household. If the defendant creates a risk that exceeds those to which he is reciprocally subject, it seems fair to hold him liable for the results of his aberrant indulgence. Similarly, according to the latest version of the Restatement, airplane owners and pilots are strictly liable for ground damage, but not for mid-air collisions. Risk of ground damage is nonreciprocal; homeowners do not create risks to airplanes flying overhead. The risks of mid-air collisions, on the other hand, are generated reciprocally by all those who fly the air lanes. Accordingly, the threshold of liability for damage resulting from mid-air collisions is higher than mere involvement in the activity of flying. To be liable for collision damage to another flyer, the pilot must fly negligently or the owner must maintain the plane negligently; they must generate abnormal risks of collision to the other planes aflight.

Fletcher's focus on the unusual or imbalanced risk is useful in identifying some situations in which courts have and have not imposed strict liability. For instance, strict liability has been opposed in instances where the plaintiff actively seeks to benefit from the allegedly ultrahazardous activity. See, e.g, Restatement (Third) of Torts: Liability for Physical and Emotional Harm §24(a) (2010) (precluding strict liability for injuries caused by animals "if the person suffers physical harm as a result of making contact with or coming into proximity to the defendant's animal or abnormally dangerous activity for the purpose of securing some benefit from that contact or that proximity"); Pullen v. West, 92 P.3d 584 (Kan. 2004) (holding that plaintiff could not avail himself of strict liability for injuries suffered during illegal fireworks display because he participated in the activity). Nevertheless, the strength of Fletcher's nonreciprocity principle as a fairness justification for strict liability is more open to question. Why, for example, should a plaintiff be able to invoke strict liability simply because the plaintiff's injury occurred through the operation of an unusual risk? Fletcher's analysis suggests a variation on the Golden Rule: "I didn't expose the defendant to such risks; the defendant shouldn't have exposed me to them." Indeed, Fletcher characterizes the creation of nonreciprocal risks as an "aberrant indulgence" that justifies strict liability on fairness grounds. While this may be true with respect to the keeping of panthers and pit bulls, many activities that are subject to strict liability—such as the gasoline transportation involved in *Siegler*—are economically important. Despite the fact that such activities generate asymmetrical risks in society, they are arguably more socially valuable than other risk-generating activities — such as dog owning or Sunday driving — that are typically governed by negligence rules. In such cases, it is hard to see why the nonreciprocity of the risk, standing alone, should trigger strict liability.

Perhaps because of these problems, most theorists have sought to justify strict liability on instrumental rather than noninstrumental grounds. Indeed, the instinctive reaction of many beginning law students is that strict liability is better at deterring accident-producing behavior than negligence because, simply put, it is "more strict." But is this common assumption — that a rational actor will invest more in care under a strict liability rule than under a negligence rule — really true? To answer this question, it will be useful to return to Problem 14, p. 193 in Chapter 3. It will be recalled that, on the assumptions stated in that problem, a rational actor under a negligence regime would invest up to, but not beyond, the third level of care. At that point, the actor's total costs (costs of care plus liability costs) are \$1,100. If the actor invests only up to the second level of care, the actor's costs are \$8,400; and if the actor invests up to the fourth level, the actor's costs are \$2,300. So a rational actor under negligence would invest up to level 3 but not beyond.

What would be the same actor's costs under a regime of strict liability? The key to answering this question is to understand that the actor's costs under strict liability would be the same as the costs indicated in column (5) in Table 3-1, p. 195, the "total social costs of care and accidents" column. This is so because, under strict liability, the actor bears not only costs of care, but also the residual costs of accidents not worth avoiding. At what level of care would the actor's costs be least? Observe that at level 3, the actor's (and society's) total costs are \$8,100. Observe also that this is the lowest level — at level 2 the actor's costs are \$8,400 and at level 4, \$8,300. So the actor would invest up to level 3 under strict liability — exactly the same level to which the actor would invest under negligence.

Thus, even if actors are held strictly liable for all accident losses, including such residual accident costs, they will not, at least in theory, increase their investment in care beyond the level at which they would invest under negligence. Instead, because the residual losses are, by hypothesis, cheaper to incur than to prevent, actors under strict liability will simply pay for such losses (through insurance, perhaps) rather than make the additional investments in safety necessary to avoid them. It is a common mistake of students, lawyers, and even judges to assume that the imposition of strict liability is tantamount to an injunctive order for defendants to alter their behavior in specific ways, up to and including complete cessation of the activity that is subjected to strict liability. Assuming that damages are calculated appropriately, however, defendants will only cease their activity if the liability costs internalized through strict liability exceed whatever private benefits the activity is generating. In other words, defendants retain the option of simply paying strict liability damages as a cost of their activities.

If strict liability and negligence give actors identical incentives to invest in socially optimal levels of care, is there any reason, from an instrumental perspective, to prefer strict liability over negligence? There are several possible responses. First, despite their ability in theory to encourage the same optimal level of care, strict liability and negligence may vary in practice in the incentives they impose on harm-causing actors. Under negligence, a plaintiff must show not only that the defendant caused the harm, but also that the defendant's behavior was unreasonable. As the materials in Chapter 3 illustrate, this additional showing can be messy and costly. If plaintiffs experience systematic problems in their efforts to establish fault on the part of defendants — perhaps because of the loss, destruction, or other unavailability of evidence — defendants as a class will experience insufficient levels of liability. In *Siegler*, for example, the court noted that the explosive nature of gasoline created a risk of "the likely destruction of cogent evidence from which negligence . . . may be proved or disproved." Strict liability redresses this potential deficiency in the process of proof by removing the issue of fault from the test for liability. In this sense, strict liability functions similarly to res ipsa in correcting perceived imbalances in the trial process.[3]

More important, from an instrumental perspective, holding an actor strictly liable for the residual losses caused by his activity may affect variables that a negligence standard cannot affect, such as long-term, dynamic efficiency gains that come from technological innovations or other market changes not foreseen by a court applying the negligence calculus. See James A. Anderson, The Missing Theory of Variable Selection in the Economic Analysis of Tort Law, 2007 Utah L. Rev. 255 (2007). In a related fashion, strict liability may affect the actor's threshold decision of *whether*, and to what extent, to engage in the activity in the first place. As noted above, the actor's investment in care and the overall social costs of the activity do not in theory change when the liability regime changes from negligence to strict liability. But the residual costs borne by accident victims under negligence will now be borne under strict liability by the ones making the decisions on whether and how to engage in the particular activity. Some of these actors, who may have found the activity marginally profitable when victims bore the residual losses, presumably will conclude that the activity is no longer economically feasible now that they must bear those losses. Those decisions, of course, will depend on the aggregate, "all costs considered" profitability of the activity.

This "activity level" effect of strict liability is described by Judge Posner in Indiana Belt Harbor R.R. Co. v. American Cyanamid Co., 916 F.2d 1174, 1177 (7th Cir. 1990):

> The baseline common law regime of tort liability is negligence. When it is a workable regime, because the hazards of an activity can be avoided by being careful (which is to say, nonnegligent), there is no need to switch to strict liability. Sometimes, however, a particular type of accident cannot be prevented by taking care but can be avoided, or its consequences minimized, by shifting the activity in which the accident occurs to another locale, where the risk or harm of an accident will be less . . . , or by reducing the scale of the activity in order to minimize the number of accidents caused by it. . . . Shavell, Strict Liability versus Negligence, 9 J. Legal Stud. 1 (1980). By making the actor strictly liable — by denying him in other words an excuse based on his inability to avoid accidents by being more careful — we give him an incentive, missing in a negligence regime, to experiment with methods of preventing accidents that involve not greater exertions of care, assumed to be futile, but instead relocating, changing, or reducing (perhaps to the vanishing point) the activity giving rise to the accident. . . . The greater the risk of an accident . . . and the costs of an accident if one occurs . . . , the more we want the actor to consider the possibility of making accident-reducing activity changes; the stronger, therefore, is the case for strict liability. Finally, if an activity is extremely common, . . .

3. Of course, this analysis assumes that a negligence system is prone to systematic errors that favor defendants over plaintiffs, and therefore exposes defendants to levels of liability that are insufficient to encourage optimal investments in accident prevention. This assumption, however, is quite speculative. Some have argued that the opposite situation, in which the practical operation of the negligence system forces defendants to *overinvest* in accident avoidance, may be more descriptively accurate. For example, if defendants under a negligence regime experience systematic difficulties in determining ahead of time what amount of precaution constitutes reasonable care, they will tend to "err on the side of caution," that is, to overinvest in care. They will do so because, under negligence, a slight shortfall below what a court later determines to be adequate care will make the defendant liable for all accident losses, while overinvestment in care will help to ensure that the defendant pays no accident losses. Under strict liability, in contrast, the defendant faces no tactical incentive to spend excessively on precaution because the defendant's costs rise only slightly if underinvestment in care occurs. For more extensive analysis of this and related issues, see Eric A. Posner, Probability Errors: Some Positive and Normative Implications for Tort and Contract Law, 11 Sup. Ct. Econ. Rev. 125 (2004); Richard Coffee & John E. Craswell, Some Effects of Uncertainty on Compliance with Legal Standards, 70 Va. L. Rev. 965 (1984).

> like driving an automobile, it is unlikely either that its hazards are perceived as great or that there is no technology of care available to minimize them; so the case for strict liability is weakened.

To be sure, the negligence system itself, at least in theory, could have accommodated such a result by labeling as "negligent" the decision to engage in an activity at a level whose residual losses exceed its gains-net-of-all-other-costs. But for reasons we will not go into here, the negligence system has never chosen to grapple with such "macroefficiency" questions. See generally Steven Shavell, Strict Liability Versus Negligence, 9 J. Legal Stud. 1 (1985). See also David Gilo & Ehud Guttel, Negligence and Insufficient Activity: The Missing Paradigm in Torts, 108 Mich. L. Rev. 277 (2009) (arguing that courts have unduly neglected the problem of insufficient activity levels and that they should take it into account when considering whether to apply strict liability). Thus, the conventional wisdom has become that strict liability is the appropriate standard of liability to apply to activities that impose a significant threat of harm even after the actor has taken all reasonable precautions. With that understanding in mind, is the transportation of hazardous acrylonitrile the kind of activity that might be well disciplined by a strict liability standard, despite the *Indiana Belt Harbor* court's conclusion to the contrary?

Of course, if one accepts either of these arguments — that strict liability improves the clarity of the deterrent signal actually produced by the torts process or that strict liability encourages actors to adopt optimal levels of activity — the title of this note may seem to require rewriting. Rather than asking what explains the adoption of strict liability, perhaps the more appropriate question is what justifies the retention of negligence in many areas of the law. It is unlikely that the practical problems inherent in proving negligence are restricted only to those areas where courts already have invoked strict liability. Moreover, controlling excessive levels of harm-causing activity would surely be beneficial in some areas, such as driving, that are often governed by negligence principles.

Not surprisingly, then, the perceived advantages of strict liability over negligence have led to calls for its application to practically every area of tort law. Yet, the widescale adoption of strict liability has not occurred. See Gerald W. Boston, Strict Liability for Abnormally Dangerous Activity: The Negligence Barrier, 36 San Diego L. Rev. 597 (1999) (arguing that courts have increasingly relied on negligence, rather than strict liability, in deciding cases of "abnormally dangerous activity"); James A. Henderson, Jr., Why Negligence Dominates Tort, 50 UCLA L. Rev. 337 (2002). The reasons for the limited spread of strict liability are complex and their detailed examination lies beyond the scope of this note. Briefly, however, they include the noninstrumental argument that it is generally unfair to impose liability on those who are acting in a manner that is deemed to be socially reasonable; the problems of high administrative costs and possibly excessive liability that arise in some areas if the test for liability is too simple; and the arguable advantages of a negligence system in monitoring plaintiff behavior. Others contend, from a more historically contextualized perspective, that the reasons enthusiasm for strict liability has slowed in American jurisprudence arise from political and cultural factors, such as the desire to promote industrialization observed in the Holmes excerpt or the more recent effort by business interests to highlight perceived "crises" in tort litigation and insurance markets. For a sampling of the extensive writings on this question, see William M. Landes & Richard A. Posner, The Economic Structure of Tort Law 54-84 (1987); James A. Henderson, Jr. & Aaron D. Twerski, Closing the American Products Liability Frontier: The Rejection of Liability without Defect, 66 N.Y.U. L. Rev. 1263 (1991); William K. Jones, Strict Liability for Hazardous Enterprises, 92 Colum. L. Rev. 1705 (1992); Steven

P. Croley & Jon D. Hanson, Rescuing the Revolution: The Revived Case for Enterprise Liability, 91 Mich. L. Rev. 683 (1993); Gregory C. Keating, The Theory of Enterprise Liability and Common Law Strict Liability, 54 Vand. L. Rev. 1285 (2001); Richard A. Epstein, Toward a General Theory of Tort Law: Strict Liability in Context, 3 J. Tort L. 6 (2010).

In sum, the border between the two liability systems is not clearly established, and probably never will be. Each system offers an array of appealing justifications, both in instrumental and noninstrumental terms. The challenging and perhaps unending task of the torts system is to determine whether, in any given set of cases, one rule is preferable to the other. As the next two cases demonstrate, moreover, many of the same normative and jurisprudential considerations that go into choosing between strict liability and negligence as the standard of liability "reemerge" in the context of deciding whether the particular harmful consequence at issue belongs to the class of harms that rendered the activity appropriate for strict liability.

Toms v. Calvary Assembly of God, Inc.

446 Md. 543, 132 A.3d 866 (2016)

Greene, J. In this case, we address whether noise emanating from the discharge of a fireworks display constitutes an abnormally dangerous activity, which would warrant the imposition of strict liability.

Petitioner, Andrew David Toms ("Toms"), operates a dairy farm in Frederick County, Maryland, and maintains a herd of approximately 90 head of cattle. On September 9, 2012, a church-sponsored fireworks display took place on property adjacent to Toms' dairy operation. A permit to discharge fireworks had been obtained, and the event was supervised by a deputy fire marshal. No misfires or malfunctions took place. According to Toms, the fireworks display was so loud that it startled his cattle, and caused a stampede inside his dairy barn. The stampede resulted in the death of four dairy cows, property damage, disposal costs, and lost milk revenue . . . .

Maryland has long recognized the doctrine of strict liability, which does not require a finding of fault in order to impose liability on a party . . . . The doctrine is derived from the famous 1868 English case of Rylands v. Fletcher, which recognized that, under certain circumstances, no-fault liability could be imposed . . .

The modern formulation of the strict liability doctrine is found in the Restatement (Second) of Torts §§519-520 (1977). . . . In Rosenblatt v. Exxon Co., U.S.A., we discussed the evolution of the doctrine: "Unlike the rule first enunciated in *Rylands,* this definition does not limit applicable activities to those causing an 'escape' of something onto the land of another; it requires only that there be harm to the person or property of another resulting from the abnormally dangerous activity." 335 Md. 58, 70, 642 A.2d 180, 185 (1994).

. . . Whether fireworks discharge constitutes an abnormally dangerous activity is a case of first impression in Maryland, because fireworks liability normally arises in the context of nuisance and negligence litigation. Some jurisdictions, however, have addressed the issue of whether fireworks are abnormally dangerous. As evidenced by the cases below, litigation often came to fruition due to a malfunction or misfire at a fireworks display, which resulted in spectator injuries. Although fireworks liability cases often share similar facts, jurisdictions disagree on whether discharging fireworks is an abnormally dangerous activity, as evident by the split of legal authority on the matter.

[The court then discusses various states' holdings on whether fireworks shows and displays are inherently dangerous.]

. . . Maryland defines fireworks as "combustible, implosive or explosive compositions, substances, combinations of substances, or articles that are prepared to produce a visible or audible effect by combustion, explosion, implosion, deflagration, or detonation." Md. Code (2003, 2011 Repl. Vol.), §10–101(f) of the Public Safety Article. We disagree with Toms that our analysis should be so narrow as to focus solely on the audible component — the noise produced — by a fireworks display. In the petition for writ of certiorari, Toms refers to the "noise of a fireworks discharge," but the noise itself is a by-product of the activity of discharging fireworks. By definition, under §10–101(f) of the Public Safety Article, fireworks "are prepared to produce a visible or audible effect. . . ." Therefore, when applying the multi-factor test from §520 of the Restatement (Second) of Torts, we will consider all the characteristics and the nature of the risks associated with discharging fireworks . . . . We apply the Restatement factors to the instant case:

(a) *existence of a high degree of risk of some harm to the person, land or chattels of others*. Special events requiring the use of large, professional "display fireworks" are heavily regulated in Maryland pursuant to §§10–101 *et seq.* of the Public Safety Article . . . .

[The Court discusses the Maryland statute which authorizes the State Fire Marshal to issue permits only if the fireworks will (1) "not endanger the health or safety or damage property" and (2) "be supervised by an experienced and qualified person who has previously secured written authority from the State Fire Marshal to discharge fireworks." The application for a permit requires event information, as well as the size and number of fireworks shells. Prior to submitting the application, the site must be inspected and approved by an authority having jurisdiction. Here, the location was approved.]

We hold that a lawful fireworks display does not pose a high degree of risk, because the statutory scheme in place is designed to significantly reduce the risks associated with fireworks, namely mishandling, misfires, and malfunctions. Furthermore, the required firing radius of 250 feet was voluntarily extended by Mr. Lindberg [an employee of the fireworks manufacturing company] to 300 feet. Critically, in enacting the Public Safety Article, the General Assembly did not regulate the audible effects of display fireworks, which indicates that any risk associated with the decibel level of a fireworks discharge is minimal or non-existent.

Lawful fireworks displays do not pose a significant risk because "[a] person who possesses or discharges fireworks in violation" of the permitting process "is guilty of a misdemeanor and on conviction is subject to a fine not exceeding $250 for each offense." Md. Code (2003, 2011 Repl. Vol.), §10–111(a) of the Public Safety Article. To impose a relatively light penalty for an unlawful fireworks display is telling. If an unlawful fireworks display is only a misdemeanor offense with no possibility of incarceration, why then should strict liability be imposed for risks associated with a lawful fireworks display?

(b) *likelihood that the harm that results from it will be great*. This factor also weighs in favor of not imposing strict liability, because the purpose of a 300 foot perimeter surrounding the firing location is to mitigate the likelihood of harm. [The court notes that the application instructions specify that owners of properties within the fall out zone must give permission that their property be used in the fall out zone. Structures outside of the zone "shall be deemed as being unimportant."]

. . . Because Toms' dairy barn, and therefore his cows, were not located within the fall out zone, the likelihood of harm to the public and property was significantly reduced.

The 300 foot firing radius was effective because no shells fired that night malfunctioned, and no debris littered Toms' property.

(c) *inability to eliminate the risk by the exercise of reasonable care*. . . . The 300 foot firing radius is sufficient. Furthermore, notice to Toms was not necessary, because his dairy barn was located beyond the firing radius. In our view, the Restatement does not require the elimination of all risk, and because the risks inherent with a fireworks discharge can be reduced to acceptable levels, this factor does not support a conclusion of an abnormally dangerous activity.

(d) *extent to which the activity is not a matter of common usage*. "An activity is a matter of common usage if it is customarily carried on by the great mass of mankind, or by many people in the community." [Yommer v. McKenzie, 255 Md. 220, 225 n.2, 257 A.2d 138, 140 (1969)] (citation omitted). We recognize that the discharging of lawful fireworks displays is a matter of common usage. In a letter dated July 3, 1776, John Adams wrote about the pomp and circumstance that should surround the celebration of our Nation's independence: "I am apt to believe that it will be celebrated, by succeeding Generations. . . . It ought to be solemnized with . . . Bonfires and Illuminations from one End of this Continent to the other from this Time forward forever more." As stated in §10–101 of the Public Safety Article, fireworks are designed "to produce a visible or audible effect" for the benefit of spectators. Therefore, we define "common usage," as it pertains to this case, broadly to include not only the professionals who discharge fireworks, but also the spectators who partake in the fireworks display. . . .

(e) *inappropriateness of the activity to the place where it is carried on*. When this Court adopted the Restatement (Second) of Torts' multi-factor test for abnormally dangerous activities, this particular factor was identified as being the most crucial. . . . Implicit in the granting of a permit to discharge fireworks, is the lawfulness of that proposed fireworks display. [The court describes the testimony of deputy fire marshals that showed the event was properly supervised and executed.] Notably, Frederick County does not have a noise ordinance regulating the decibel level of fireworks. . . . In sum, we do agree that a lawful fireworks display does not fall within the context of "the unusual, the excessive, the extravagant, the bizarre . . . non-natural uses which lead to strict liability." *Yommer*, 255 Md. at 226, 257 A.2d at 141.

(f) *extent to which its value to the community is outweighed by its dangerous attributes*. Here, a church-sponsored fireworks display celebrated a youth crusade, and the event was open to the public. As a symbol of celebration, fireworks play an important role in our society, and are often met with much fanfare. The statutory scheme regulating its use minimizes the risk of accidents, thus, reinforcing the popularity of these displays. This Court recognizes that not all segments of the population may enjoy fireworks displays, especially those with noise sensitivities, however, we conclude that the social desirability of fireworks appear to outweigh their dangerous attributes.

Policy considerations. We are mindful that the doctrine of strict liability for abnormally dangerous activities is narrowly applied in order to avoid imposing "grievous burdens" on landowners and occupiers of land. . . . Toms argues that we should expand the factual application of this doctrine, however, the Restatement factors do not support such a position. The use of fireworks, especially in public fireworks displays, is heavily regulated pursuant to §§10–101 *et seq.* of the Public Safety Article. . . .

At issue in this case is a lawful fireworks display that was implemented pursuant to the requirements of the Public Safety Article. At trial, Toms did not present any evidence concerning what noise levels should be appropriate for public fireworks display[s]. Sufficient evidence was not presented to the trier of fact that a lawful fireworks display was abnormally dangerous to livestock. Thus, as a matter of law and on a case-by-case basis, we do not extend the doctrine of strict liability for abnormally dangerous activities under the circumstances. . . .

Accordingly, we affirm the judgment of the Circuit Court. Lawful fireworks displays are not an abnormally dangerous activity, because the statutory scheme regulating the use of fireworks significantly reduces the risk of harm associated with the discharge of fireworks. Furthermore, it is not the province of the Judiciary, but rather, the Legislature to determine zoning classifications and enact noise ordinances that would further regulate the use of fireworks.

HARRELL, J., joins in judgment only.

Foster v. Preston Mill Co.

44 Wash. 2d 440, 268 P.2d 645 (1954)

HAMLEY, J. Blasting operations conducted by Preston Mill Company frightened mother mink owned by B. W. Foster, and caused the mink to kill their kittens. Foster brought this action against the company to recover damages. His second amended complaint, upon which the case was tried, sets forth a cause of action on the theory of absolute liability, and, in the alternative, a cause of action on the theory of nuisance.

After a trial to the court without a jury, judgment was rendered for plaintiff in the sum of $1,953.68. The theory adopted by the court was that, after defendant received notice of the effect which its blasting operations were having upon the mink, it was absolutely liable for all damages of that nature thereafter sustained. The trial court concluded that defendant's blasting did not constitute a public nuisance, but did not expressly rule on the question of private nuisance. Plaintiff concedes, however, that, in effect, the trial court decided in defendant's favor on the question of nuisance. Defendant appeals.

[The court describes the operation of the plaintiff's mink ranch, explaining that during the whelping season, which lasts several weeks, female mink are very excitable. The defendant had been engaged in a logging operation adjacent to the plaintiff's land for more than 50 years. They began the blasting in order to clear a path for a road, approximately two and one-quarter miles away from the ranch. The vibrations at the ranch excited the mother mink, who began killing their young. After the plaintiff told the defendant about the loss of mink kittens, the defendant reduced the strength of the dynamite charges, but continued blasting throughout the remainder of the whelping season. Defendant's experts testified that unless the road had been cleared, the logging operation would have been delayed and the company's log production disrupted, with attendant costs to the defendant company.]

In this action, respondent sought and recovered judgment only for such damages as were claimed to have been sustained as a result of blasting operations conducted after appellant received notice that its activity was causing loss of mink kittens.

The primary question presented by appellant's assignments of error is whether, on these facts, the judgment against appellant is sustainable on the theory of absolute liability.

The modern doctrine of strict liability for dangerous substances and activities stems from Justice Blackburn's decision in Rylands v. Fletcher. As applied to blasting operations, the doctrine has quite uniformly been held to establish liability, irrespective of negligence, for property damage sustained as result of casting rocks or other debris on adjoining or neighboring premises.

There is a division of judicial opinion as to whether the doctrine of absolute liability should apply where the damage from blasting is caused, not by the casting of rocks and debris, but by concussion, vibration, or jarring. This court has adopted the view that the doctrine applies in such cases. . . .

However the authorities may be divided on the point just discussed, they appear to be agreed that strict liability should be confined to consequences which lie within the extraordinary risk whose existence calls for such responsibility. This limitation on the doctrine is indicated in the italicized portion of the rule as set forth in Restatement of Torts [§519]:

> Except as stated in §§521-4, one who carries on an ultra-hazardous activity is liable to another whose person, land or chattels the actor should recognize as likely to be harmed by the unpreventable miscarriage of the activity for harm resulting thereto *from that which makes the activity ultra-hazardous*, although the utmost care is exercised to prevent the harm. (Italics ours.)

This restriction which has been placed upon the application of the doctrine of absolute liability is based upon considerations of policy. As Professor Prosser has said:

> It is one thing to say that a dangerous enterprise must pay its way within reasonable limits, and quite another to say that it must bear responsibility for every extreme of harm that it may cause. The same practical necessity for the restriction of liability within some reasonable bounds, which arises in connection with problems of "proximate cause" in negligence cases, demands here that some limit be set. . . . This limitation has been expressed by saying that the defendant's duty to insure safety extends only to certain consequences. More commonly, it is said that the defendant's conduct is not the "proximate cause" of the damage. But ordinarily in such cases no question of causation is involved, and the limitation is one of the policy underlying liability. Prosser on Torts, 457, §60.

Applying this principle to the case before us, the question comes down to this: Is the risk that any unusual vibration or noise may cause wild animals, which are being raised for commercial purposes, to kill their young, one of the things which make the activity of blasting ultrahazardous?

We have found nothing in the decisional law which would support an affirmative answer to this question. The decided cases, as well as common experience, indicate that the thing which makes blasting ultrahazardous is the risk that property or persons may be damaged or injured by coming into direct contact with flying debris, or by being directly affected by vibrations of the earth or concussions of the air. . . .

The relatively moderate vibration and noise which appellant's blasting produced at a distance of two and a quarter miles was no more than a usual incident of the ordinary life of the community. The trial court specifically found that the blasting did not unreasonably interfere with the enjoyment of their property by nearby landowners, except in the case of the respondent's mink ranch.

It is the exceedingly nervous disposition of mink, rather than the normal risks inherent in blasting operations, which therefore must, as a matter of sound policy, bear the responsibility for the loss here sustained. We subscribe to the view . . . that the policy of the law does not impose the rule of strict liability to protect against harms incident to the plaintiff's extraordinary and unusual use of land. This is perhaps but an application of the principle that the extent to which one man in the lawful conduct of his business is liable for injuries to another involves an adjustment of conflicting interests.

It is our conclusion that the risk of causing harm of the kind here experienced, as a result of the relatively minor vibration, concussion, and noise from distant blasting, is not the kind of risk which makes the activity of blasting ultrahazardous. The doctrine of absolute liability is therefore inapplicable under the facts of this case, and respondent is not entitled to recover damages.

The judgment is reversed.

Grady, C.J., Mallery, Finley, and Olson, JJ., concur.

Would the court in *Toms* have been on surer ground to follow *Foster* in holding that, whether or not fireworks displays constitute an abnormally dangerous activity, the particular harm suffered by plaintiff in that case was not the kind of risk that would make fireworks displays abnormally dangerous? The outcomes in *Toms* and *Foster* are supported by §524A of the Restatement (Second) of Torts, which bars the application of strict liability to harms that "would not have resulted but for the abnormally sensitive character of the plaintiff's activity." One rationale for the imposition of strict liability is that it is inequitable for the harmful externalities of a publicly desirable activity to be borne disproportionately by a few individuals. Why doesn't that rationale extend to the contexts addressed in *Foster* and *Toms*?

Other defenses based on the plaintiff's actions or activity can sometimes defeat the application of strict liability. The Restatement (Second), for example, recognizes an assumption of risk defense in §523. It also precludes liability based on the plaintiff's contributory negligence, but only if the plaintiff "knowingly and unreasonably subject[ed] himself to the risk of harm."§524(2).

Problem 31

Your firm has been retained by Midvalle Grass Seed Company to handle a spate of litigation arising from a runaway grass fire. Midvalle owns a large grass farm in the central region of the state. It grows special grasses that produce grass seed for sale. Late each summer, after the seed is harvested but before the rainy season begins, Midvalle follows the long-standing tradition of grass seed farmers by "firing" its fields. Specifically, Midvalle intentionally sets fire to the dried grasses in its fields so that they burn completely. This process returns nutrients to the soil and sterilizes the top layer of soil, thereby killing all leftover seeds so that any grasses planted the next year will "run true" and not cross-breed with seeds from previous years.

Midvalle controls grass fires using a standard method used by seed farmers in the state. A 20-foot-wide swath is tilled around the perimeter of its farm. This bare soil acts as a firebreak, making it difficult for the burning grass to ignite grass on the other side. Midvalle also waits for a day with light winds. Using handheld torches, employees light the upwind portion of the field, and monitor the fire as it burns across its fields. A water truck is kept on hand as an extra precaution.

Last summer, when Midvalle lit its fields, things went badly. An unusually dry summer had left the grasses with a very low moisture content. When lit, the fields burned with near explosive speed and intensity despite the fact that Midvalle deliberately picked a day with almost no wind. The shear heat of the grass fire soon created its own wind, which generated a small firestorm that raced across the farm. Although the water truck was dispatched, it was unable to contain the quickly spreading fire. When the fire reached the downwind edge of the farm, burning stalks and grasses were blown well over the firebreak and ignited grasses on the other side.

This portion of Midvalle's farm adjoins a 2,000-acre forested hillside owned by Western Timber Co. When the fire escaped the farm, Midvalle quickly alerted both Western and the National Forest Service, which dispatched a fire fighting crew to the fire. Normally, a fire on Western's land would not pose a terrible risk, since most forest fires simply burn the undergrowth without igniting or killing the trees. In fact, the subsequent release of nutrients is believed to be beneficial to the forest ecosystem, and hence the Forest Service often lets such fires burn under careful supervision.

Unfortunately, many of the trees in the central section of Western's land were killed the year before by an infestation of the Western Pine Weevil. The dead trees, while still saleable as lumber, were extremely dry and flammable. The Forest Service had issued an advisory, urging timber companies to harvest any large stands of dead timber to reduce fire risk, but Western had held off harvesting the trees in the hopes that lumber prices would improve.

The fire fighting team dispatched to the fire was unaware of the special fire danger presented by the section of dead trees, and hence did not aggressively attack the fire while it was still confined to the underbrush in the nondamaged part of Western's land. When the team realized the risk, it was too late to take effective action. The fire reached the dead trees, and again exploded into a firestorm, destroying most of the trees, both alive and dead, on Western's property. The value of the destroyed timber was over $1 million. In the process of fighting the fire, a fire fighter from the Forest Service was seriously injured when burning debris from the firestorm struck him.

A heavy rainstorm two weeks later washed great amounts of ash from the burned forest into a tributary of the Rogue River. The runoff temporarily fouled the water, killing large numbers of game fish. As a result, High Country Expeditions, a commercial enterprise that runs fishing trips on the river, lost a significant amount of business.

Midvalle has already received a complaint from Western, and is anticipating litigation from the injured fire fighter and from High Country Expeditions. The supervising partner has asked you to assess the likely outcome of a strict liability claim brought by any of the potential plaintiffs. Assume that there is no controlling precedent in your jurisdiction, but that courts follow the general approach suggested by the materials in this chapter.

Chapter 7

Products Liability

Some of the most dramatic developments in tort law in the last 50 years have occurred in connection with manufacturers' and suppliers' liability for harm caused by defective products. These changes in the law have produced confusion, much of which may be traced to two sources: first, the development of no fewer than three distinct but overlapping legal theories of liability; second, a tendency for courts and commentators to insist upon applying the same rules of decision in all products liability cases, notwithstanding the fact that different categories of cases require significantly different solutions.

The bedrock principles of American products liability law find expression in §402A of the Restatement (Second) of Torts, published in 1965. We will consider this provision and its ramifications at length in this chapter. In 1998, the American Law Institute (ALI) committed itself to helping to reduce the confusion surrounding products liability by publishing a Restatement (Third) of Torts: Products Liability. One of the authors of this book, Professor Henderson, served as co-reporter on the project. Sections from the Restatement (Third) are excerpted in this chapter. The chapter is organized in the same manner as the Restatement (Third): on the basis of the different types of defects for which products liability is imposed. *Manufacturing defects* (sometimes referred to as *construction defects* or *production defects*) are features in a few product units that make those few units different from, and inferior to, the vast majority of units in the same product line. Some manufacturing defects are merely cosmetic and do not interfere with the product's intended function. Others interfere with the functioning, but in ways that are not particularly dangerous. The defects with which we shall be concerned are those that dangerously interfere with product function and are likely to cause personal injury or property damage. These defects are usually hidden from users and consumers, and may be said to "disappoint consumer expectations" when they cause product malfunction. In contrast to manufacturing defects, *design defects* are shared by every unit in the product line, causing the products to be generically dangerous. *Marketing defects,* which also produce generic defectiveness affecting an entire product line, include failures to instruct regarding proper product use and to warn of hidden dangers.

A. *Liability for Manufacturing Defects*

Manufacturing defects are imperfections that cause products to fail to perform their manifestly intended functions. The Restatement (Third) defines them as departures from intended product designs (§2(a)). These defects find their source in the fallibility of the manufacturing and distribution processes, and in the fact that the social costs of zero defect rates would be unacceptably high. Usually, only a small percentage of the total number of products in any product run turn out to be defective in a way posing unreasonable risks of harm, and only relatively few defective products actually cause injuries that become the subject of the sorts of actions considered in this section. Manufacturing defect cases do not present theoretical problems relating to the determination of defectiveness. As Professor Keith Hylton notes, the logic in favor of strict liability for manufacturing defects is straightforward: "In a market in which the vast majority of products are not dangerous due to manufacturing glitches, a paradox of safety will hold: consumers will not search for defects due to glitches for the same reason that they do not search for zebras in Central Park; they are unlikely to find any. In light of this safety paradox, strict liability enables the market to distinguish (and ultimately usher out of circulation) products generated from low-quality manufacturing processes." Keith N. Hylton, The Law and Economics of Products Liability, 88 Notre Dame L. Rev. 2457, 2460 (2013). Nevertheless, as this section illustrates, there are a few difficult issues involving the circumstances under which liability for harm caused by a manufacturing defect should be imposed. For a scholarly treatment of liability for manufacturing defects, see generally David G. Owen, Manufacturing Defects, 53 S.C. L. Rev. 851 (2002).

1. The Plaintiff's Prima Facie Case: Doctrinal Theories of Liability

In the subsections that follow we consider the three basic doctrinal theories upon which products liability is based: negligence, warranty, and strict liability. Although they are distinct theories of liability, each has influenced the development of the others, and they are often combined in the plaintiff's claim for relief.

a. Negligence

Although the basic concept of negligence as it is applied in products liability cases is the same as that developed in Chapter 3, the early law distinguished products liability cases from other negligence cases, affording substantial insulation from liability to manufacturers and suppliers of defective goods. The most significant early decision was Winterbottom v. Wright, 10 M. & W. 109 (Exch. 1842). The plaintiff was a mail coach driver who was injured when the coach broke down. The defendant had contracted with the Postmaster General to supply a number of coaches, including the coach in question, for the transport of mail. Under the terms of the contract, the defendant had promised the Postmaster General to keep the coaches in good repair. The plaintiff was employed by one Atkinson who, with knowledge of the defendant's contract, had contracted with the Postmaster General to supply horses and coachmen to operate the coaches. The plaintiff's declaration alleged that the defendant negligently failed to carry out his duties of maintenance and repair under the contract, and that as a consequence the coach had become weakened and dangerous, causing the plaintiff's injuries. Lord Abinger, writing for a unanimous court, denied liability as a matter of law, concluding (10 M. & W. at 114):

> There is no privity of contract between these parties; and if the plaintiff can sue, every passenger, or even any person passing along the road, who was injured by the upsetting of the coach, might bring a similar action. Unless we confine the operation of such contracts as this to the parties who entered into them, the most absurd and outrageous consequences, to which I can see no limit, would ensue.

The rule in the *Winterbottom* case came generally to be recognized in this country by the second half of the nineteenth century. See Lebourdais v. Vitrified Wheel Co., 80 N.E. 482 (Mass. 1907); Burkett v. Studebaker Bros. Mfg. Co., 150 S.W. 421 (Tenn. 1912). A number of exceptions to the privity requirement were judicially developed, the most interesting of which occurred in New York, commencing with the decision of the court of appeals in Thomas v. Winchester, 6 N.Y. 397 (1852). The injured plaintiff in *Thomas* was a woman who had purchased from a retail druggist a bottle of poison falsely labeled as a mild medicine. She took the poison believing it to be medicine and was injured. She brought a negligence action against both the retail druggist and the chemist who had erroneously labeled the bottle and sold it to the druggist. The jury returned a verdict in favor of the druggist and against the chemist, and judgments were entered accordingly. The defendant chemist appealed. Citing the *Winterbottom* decision for the general rule, the court of appeals nevertheless affirmed the judgment, concluding that the falsely labeled poison, unlike the defective mail coach, was "imminently dangerous to the lives of others."

In the years following Thomas v. Winchester, the New York Court of Appeals refined and extended the concept of "imminently dangerous products." These extensions culminated in one of the most famous American products liability decisions.

MacPherson v. Buick Motor Co.

217 N.Y. 382, 111 N.E. 1050 (1916)

CARDOZO, J. The defendant is a manufacturer of automobiles. It sold an automobile to a retail dealer. The retail dealer resold to the plaintiff. While the plaintiff was in the car, it suddenly collapsed. He was thrown out and injured. One of the wheels was made of defective wood, and its spokes crumbled into fragments. The wheel was not made by the defendant; it was bought from another manufacturer. There is evidence, however, that its defects could have been discovered by reasonable inspection, and that inspection was omitted. There is no claim that the defendant knew of the defect and willfully concealed it. . . . The charge is one, not of fraud, but of negligence. The question to be determined is whether the defendant owed a duty of care and vigilance to any one but the immediate purchaser.

[At the first trial, the court granted the defendant's motion for nonsuit at the close of the plaintiff's case, on the ground that there was no privity of contract between the plaintiff and the defendant. The Appellate Division reversed and granted a new trial on the ground that lack of privity no longer barred tort claims. On remand, the jury returned a verdict for the plaintiff and the court entered a judgment thereon. The defendant moved for a new trial, which was denied. The defendant appealed and the Appellate Division affirmed the trial court. On appeal to the New York Court of Appeals, Justice Cardozo begins his opinion by reviewing New York decisions, starting with Thomas v. Winchester, supra, and then proceeds to formulate a general rule of liability.]

We hold, then, that the principle of Thomas v. Winchester is not limited to poisons, explosives, and things of like nature, to things which in their normal operation are implements of destruction. If the nature of a thing is such that it is reasonably certain to place life and limb in peril when negligently made, it is then a thing of danger. Its nature gives warning of the consequences to be expected. If to the element of danger there is added knowledge that the thing will be used by persons other than the purchaser, and used without new tests, then, irrespective of contract, the manufacturer of this thing of danger is under a duty to make it carefully. That is as far as we are required to go for the decision of this case. There must be knowledge of a danger, not merely possible, but probable. It is *possible* to use almost anything in a way that will make it dangerous if defective. That is not enough to charge the manufacturer with a duty independent of his contract. Whether a given thing is dangerous may be sometimes a question for the court and sometimes a question for the jury. There must also be knowledge that in the usual course of events the danger will be shared by others than the buyer. Such knowledge may often be inferred from the nature of the transaction. But it is possible that even knowledge of the danger and of the use will not always be enough. The proximity or remoteness of the relation is a factor to be considered. We are dealing now with the liability of the manufacturer of the finished product, who puts it on the market to be used without inspection by his customers. If he is negligent, where danger is to be foreseen, a liability will follow. We are not required at this time to say that it is legitimate to go back of the manufacturer of the finished product and hold the manufacturers of the component parts. To make their negligence a cause of imminent danger, an independent cause must often intervene; the manufacturer of the finished product must also fail in *his* duty of inspection. It may be that in those circumstances the negligence of the earlier members of the series is too remote to constitute, as to the ultimate user, an actionable wrong. We leave that question open. We shall have to deal with it when it arises. The difficulty which it suggests is not present in this case. There is here no break in the chain of cause and effect. In such circumstances, the presence of a known danger, attendant upon a known use, makes vigilance a duty. We have put aside the notion that the duty to safeguard life and limb, when the consequences of negligence may be foreseen, grows out of the contract and nothing else. We have put the source of the obligation where it ought to be. We have put its source in the law.

From this survey of the decisions, there thus emerges a definition of the duty of a manufacturer which enables us to measure this defendant's liability. Beyond all question, the nature of an automobile gives warning of probable danger if its construction is defective. This automobile was designed to go fifty miles an hour. Unless its wheels were sound and strong, injury was almost certain. It was as much a thing of danger as a defective engine for a railroad. The defendant knew the danger. It knew also that the car would be used by persons other than the buyer. This was apparent from its size; there were seats for three persons. It was apparent also from the fact that the buyer was a dealer in cars, who bought to resell. The maker of this car supplied it for the use of purchasers from the dealer just as plainly as the contractor in Devlin v. Smith supplied the scaffold for use by the servants of the owner. The dealer was indeed the one person of whom it might be said with some approach to certainty that by him the car would not be used. Yet the defendant would have us say that he was the one person whom it was under a legal duty to protect. The law does not lead us to so inconsequent a conclusion. Precedents drawn from the days of travel by stage coach do not fit the conditions of travel to-day. The principle that the danger must be imminent does not change, but the things subject to the principle do change. They are whatever the needs of life in a developing civilization require them to be. . . .

We think the defendant was not absolved from a duty of inspection because it bought the wheels from a reputable manufacturer. It was not merely a dealer in automobiles. It was a manufacturer of automobiles. It was responsible for the finished product. It was not at liberty to put the finished product on the market without subjecting the component parts to ordinary and simple tests. Under the charge of the trial judge nothing more was required of it. The obligation to inspect must vary with the nature of the thing to be inspected. The more probable the danger, the greater the need of caution. . . .

[The dissenting opinion of CHIEF JUSTICE BARTLETT is omitted.]

HISCOCK, CHASE, and CUDDEBACK, JJ., concur with CARDOZO, J., and HOGAN, J., concurs in result; WILLARD BARTLETT, C.J., reads dissenting opinion; POUND, J., not voting.

Judgment affirmed.

The plain language with which Justice Cardozo describes the accident conceals the true circumstances under which the allegedly defective wheel collapsed. Contrary to what the language implies, the automobile the plaintiff was driving was not new. The plaintiff had owned the car for over a year and had used it without incident, in his business as a stone carver, hauling heavy tombstones from place to place over rough roads in rural New York State. Moreover, when the collapse occurred, MacPherson was not driving at a slow pace, nor did the wheel spontaneously collapse. Rather, he was driving upwards of 50 miles an hour when the car hit a stretch of deep gravel in the road, slid out of control, collided with a telephone pole, spun 180 degrees, and fell into a three-foot ditch. The wheel collapsed under the impact of the car landing in the ditch. On the whole, the odds that the wheel was mechanically defective when MacPherson purchased the car were very low. See James A. Henderson, Jr., *MacPherson v. Buick Motor Co.*: Simplifying the Facts While Reshaping the Law, Tort Stories 41 (Robert L. Rabin & Stephen D. Sugarman eds., 2003). Should appellate judges exercise this kind of license to manipulate and simplify the relevant facts? Justice Cardozo later defended the simplification of facts by appellate courts as necessary to ensure that the law being established is not diluted or distorted by the inconvenient particulars of the case. See Benjamin N. Cardozo, Law and Literature, in Selected Writings of Benjamin Nathan Cardozo 341 (Margaret E. Hall ed., 1947).

The basic holding in *MacPherson* — abrogating the privity requirement in negligence cases — gained rapid and widespread acceptance and is today universally recognized. See William L. Prosser & W. Page Keeton, Law of Torts 683 (5th ed. 1984); Restatement (Third) of Torts: Products Liability §2(a) (1998). Because the requirement of privity derived from the idea that the duty to use care existed only when a close contractual relationship between the parties demanded it, some writers have viewed Cardozo's recognition of liability without privity to represent a rejection of a relational duty concept in favor of a general duty of care owed to all the world. Is this interpretation sound, particularly in light of other Cardozo decisions that you have considered in this course? See, e.g., Palsgraf v. Long Island R.R., 162 N.E.99 (N.Y. 1928), p. 313, above. Professors Goldberg and Zipursky assert that, rather than rejecting the relational concept of duty that runs throughout Cardozo's writings, *MacPherson* simply expanded the scope of the relational duty concept beyond the limitations of contract. See John C. P. Goldberg & Benjamin C. Zipursky, The Moral of *MacPherson*, 146 U. Pa. L. Rev. 1733 (1998).

Whatever it may have done to the concept of duty, the *MacPherson* decision clearly did not eliminate the necessity of the plaintiff's proving negligence on the part of the manufacturer. Thus, the injured plaintiff was still required to prove not only that the product's breakdown and resulting injuries were proximately caused by a product defect but also that negligence attributable to the manufacturer caused the defect to be present. (You can review how one court coped with the problem of proving negligence in a manufacturing case by rereading Escola v. Coca Cola Bottling Co., p. 249, above.)

b. Breach of Warranty

Centuries ago, a body of law developed in England regulating commercial dealings between and among merchants. The substance of this specialized *law merchant* drew heavily from the customs of the marketplace and reflected a shared desire to give effect to commercial agreements and to uphold the reasonable expectations of participants when the market broke down. Among the features of this complex body of law were *warranties*—obligations imposed by law on sellers of goods requiring them to stand behind the quality of their goods and to make buyers whole when the quality fell short of promised performance levels or reasonable expectations.

Given the practical significance of the law merchant and the accompanying need for uniformity and predictability, the rules tended through time to be codified by statute. In the United States, the first great statute governing sales warranties was the Uniform Sales Act, which controlled commercial practices dealing with the sale of goods until the late 1950s and early 1960s. Beginning in 1954, state legislatures replaced the Sales Act and other commercial law statutes with the Uniform Commercial Code (U.C.C.), Article 2 of which governs sale-of-goods transactions. Today, the law of commercial sales warranties in this country is governed largely by the U.C.C. In 1991, the National Conference of Commissioners on Uniform State Laws began a revision of Article 2, which eventually was completed and received the approval of both the National Conference and the ALI. For an overview of the drafting process and its accompanying controversies, see Richard E. Speidel, Revising UCC Article 2: A View from the Trenches, 52 Hastings L.J. 607 (2001). Courts in recent years, as we shall see, have developed special warranty rules to cover sellers' liabilities for personal injuries caused by defective products. But the place to begin to understand sales warranties is Article 2.

Article 2 of the Uniform Commercial Code establishes three types of sales warranties: (1) *express warranties* (§2-313), which are promises by the seller that the product will perform in a certain manner; (2) *implied warranties of merchantability* (§2-314), which are implied-in-law obligations of the seller that his products are free of defects and meet generalized standards of acceptability; and (3) *implied warranties of fitness for a particular purpose* (§2-315), which are implied-in-law obligations that a product recommended by a knowledgeable seller will meet special needs of the purchaser communicated to the seller at the time of sale.

Implied warranties of merchantability were in the forefront of the movement to achieve strict, fault-free tort liability for harm caused by defective products. One product area that developed more rapidly than others involved goods for human consumption and intimate bodily use. An interesting subset of these cases involved food served in restaurants. The earliest rule was that restaurants dispensed services rather than goods. Thus, the implied-in-law warranties that imposed liability without fault on commercial sellers of food generally and on retail food sellers (grocers, and the like), did not apply to restaurants, against whom plaintiffs had to prove negligence. Cushing v. Rodman, 82 F.2d 864 (D.C. Cir. 1936), is typical of the decisions that began extending sales warranties to restaurants. In that case, the plaintiff was injured when he bit into a breakfast roll and broke his tooth on a hidden pebble. He sought to recover against the lunch counter at which he had ordered the roll on the basis of breach of implied warranty of wholesomeness. Judgment at trial was for the defendant, but the court of appeals reversed, holding that a warranty of wholesomeness ran from defendant to plaintiff under those circumstances. The plaintiff had not proven negligence—the breakfast rolls had been purchased by defendant from a reputable bakery, and the pebble could not have been discovered by reasonable inspection. But the implied warranty meant the restaurant operator was strictly liable to his customer.

The warranty law applied by the court in Cushing v. Rodman came from the Uniform Sales Act, then in effect in most American jurisdictions. Today, as mentioned earlier, the dominating influence is the Uniform Commercial Code. The implied warranty in the *Cushing* case was the equivalent of the implied warranty of merchantability under §2-314 of the Code:

§2-314. IMPLIED WARRANTY: MERCHANTABILITY; USAGE OF TRADE

(1) Unless excluded or modified,[1] a warranty that the goods[2] shall be merchantable is implied in a contract for their sale[3] if the seller is a merchant[4] with respect to goods of that kind. Under this section the serving for value of food or drink to be consumed either on the premises or elsewhere is a sale.

(2) Goods to be merchantable must be at least such as

(a) pass without objection in the trade under the contract description; and

(b) in the case of fungible goods, are of fair average quality within the description; and

(c) are fit for the ordinary purposes for which such goods are used; and

(d) run, within the variations permitted by the agreement, of even kind, quality and quantity within each unit and among all units involved; and

(e) are adequately contained, packaged, and labeled as the agreement may require; and

(f) conform to the promises or affirmations of fact made on the container or label if any.

(3) Unless excluded or modified other implied warranties may arise from course of dealing or usage of trade.

OFFICIAL COMMENT

13. In an action based on breach of warranty, it is of course necessary to show not only the existence of the warranty but the fact that the warranty was broken and that the breach of the warranty was the proximate cause of the loss sustained. In such an action an affirmative showing by the seller that the loss resulted from some action or event following his own delivery of the goods can operate as a defense. Equally, evidence indicating that the seller exercised care in the manufacture, processing or selection of the goods is relevant to

1. Section 2-316 of the Code explicitly allows for the exclusion or modification of implied warranties. When the seller disclaims in writing, it must be conspicuous. Section 2-316(3)(a) provides:

> Unless the circumstances indicate otherwise, all implied warranties are excluded by expressions like "as is," "with all faults" or other language which in common understanding calls the buyer's attention to the exclusion of warranties and makes plain that there is no implied warranty. . . .

Section 2-719 of the Code deals with the effect to be given contractual modification or limitation of remedy. It includes the following language: "Consequential damages may be limited or excluded unless the limitation or exclusion is unconscionable. Limitation of consequential damages for injury to the person in the case of consumer goods is prima facie unconscionable but limitation of damages where the loss is commercial is not." The Code also contains a general provision dealing with unconscionable contracts or clauses.

2. The term *goods* is defined in §2-105(1): "'Goods' means all things (including specially manufactured goods) which are movable at the time of identification to the contract for sale other than the money in which the price is to be paid, investment securities and things in action, 'Goods' also includes the unborn young of animals and growing crops and other identified things attached to realty. . . ."

3. The term *sale* is defined in §2-106(1): "A 'sale' consists of the passing of title from the seller to the buyer for a price."

4. The term *merchant* is defined in §2-104(1): "'Merchant' means a person who deals in goods of the kind or otherwise by his occupation holds himself out as having knowledge or skill peculiar to the practices or goods involved in the transaction or to whom such knowledge or skill may be attributed by his employment of an agent or broker or other intermediary who by his occupation holds himself out as having such knowledge or skill. . . ."

> the issue of whether the warranty was in fact broken. Action by the buyer following an examination of the goods which ought to have indicated the defect complained of can be shown as matter bearing on whether the breach itself was the cause of the injury.

Observe that §2-314 expressly resolves the primary issue presented for decision in the *Cushing* case.

One issue not presented by the facts in *Cushing* is whether implied warranties run from food suppliers who are not in privity of contract with the plaintiff. Privity was not a problem in the plaintiff's action against the remote manufacturer in *Escola,* you will remember, because the plaintiff sought to recover in negligence. But in a case such as *Cushing,* in which the plaintiff relies on implied warranty, can the plaintiff succeed against a remote food supplier with whom the plaintiff is not in privity? Section 2-314 suggests that such warranties run only between sellers and their purchasers, and it should not surprise you to learn that the privity requirement survived in warranty actions long after MacPherson v. Buick Motor Co. had eliminated that requirement in negligence cases. Indeed, the privity requirement in warranty cases involving personal injuries survived for quite a while, as the following landmark products liability decision indicates.

Henningsen v. Bloomfield Motors, Inc.

32 N.J. 358, 161 A.2d 69 (1960)

Francis, J. Plaintiff Claus H. Henningsen purchased a Plymouth automobile, manufactured by defendant Chrysler Corporation, from defendant Bloomfield Motors, Inc. His wife, plaintiff Helen Henningsen, was injured while driving it and instituted suit against both defendants to recover damages on account of her injuries. Her husband joined in the action seeking compensation for his consequential losses. The complaint was predicated upon breach of express and implied warranties and upon negligence. At the trial the negligence counts were dismissed by the court and the cause was submitted to the jury for determination solely on the issues of implied warranty of merchantability. Verdicts were returned against both defendants and in favor of the plaintiffs. Defendants appealed and plaintiffs cross-appealed from the dismissal of their negligence claim. The matter was certified by this court prior to consideration in the Appellate Division.

The facts are not complicated, but a general outline of them is necessary to an understanding of the case.

On May 7, 1955 Mr. and Mrs. Henningsen visited the place of business of Bloomfield Motors, Inc., an authorized De Soto and Plymouth dealer, to look at a Plymouth. They wanted to buy a car and were considering a Ford or a Chevrolet as well as a Plymouth. They were shown a Plymouth which appealed to them and the purchase followed. The record indicates that Mr. Henningsen intended the car as a Mother's Day gift to his wife. He said the intention was communicated to the dealer. When the purchase order or contract was prepared and presented, the husband executed it alone. His wife did not join as a party.

[The court describes the purchase order form as consisting of a single sheet, with print of various sizes appearing on the front and back. The two most important paragraphs on the front were in very fine type:

> The front and back of this Order comprise the entire agreement affecting this purchase and no other agreement or understanding of any nature concerning same has been made or entered into, or will be recognized. I hereby certify that no credit has been extended to me

for the purchase of this motor vehicle except as appears in writing on the face of this agreement.

I have read the matter printed on the back hereof and agree to it as a part of this order the same as if it were printed above my signature. I certify that I am 21 years of age, or older, and hereby acknowledge receipt of a copy of this order.

On the back of the form, also in fine type, appeared ten "conditions" numbered consecutively. The warranty was contained in paragraph seven:

7. It is expressly agreed that there are no warranties, express or implied, made by either the dealer or the manufacturer on the motor vehicle, chassis, or parts furnished hereunder except as follows:

The manufacturer warrants each new motor vehicle (including original equipment placed thereon by the manufacturer except tires), chassis or parts manufactured by it to be free from defects in material or workmanship under normal use and service. Its obligation under this warranty being limited to making good at its factory any part or parts thereof which shall, within ninety (90) days after delivery of such vehicle to the original purchaser or before such vehicle has been driven 4,000 miles, whichever event shall first occur, be returned to it with transportation charges prepaid and which its examination shall disclose to its satisfaction to have been thus defective; this warranty being expressly in lieu of all other warranties expressed or implied, and all other obligations or liabilities on its part, and it neither assumes nor authorizes any other person to assume for it any other liability in connection with the sale of its vehicle. . . .

Mr. Henningsen testified that he did not read the foregoing provisions of the contract before signing it, nor were they called to his attention.]

The new Plymouth was turned over to the Henningsens on May 9, 1955. No proof was adduced by the dealer to show precisely what was done in the way of mechanical or road testing beyond testimony that the manufacturer's instructions were probably followed. Mr. Henningsen drove it from the dealer's place of business in Bloomfield to their home in Keansburg. On the trip nothing unusual appeared in the way in which it operated. Thereafter, it was used for short trips on paved streets about the town. It had no servicing and no mishaps of any kind before the event of May 19. That day, Mrs. Henningsen drove to Asbury Park. On the way down and in returning the car performed in normal fashion until the accident occurred. She was proceeding north on Route 36 in Highlands, New Jersey, at 20-22 miles per hour. The highway was paved and smooth, and contained two lanes for northbound travel. She was riding in the right-hand lane. Suddenly she heard a loud noise "from the bottom, by the hood." It "felt as if something cracked." The steering wheel spun in her hands; the car veered sharply to the right and crashed into a highway sign and a brick wall. No other vehicle was in any way involved. A bus operator driving in the left-hand lane testified that he observed plaintiff's car approaching in normal fashion in the opposite direction; "all of a sudden [it] veered at 90 degrees . . . and right into this wall." As a result of the impact, the front of the car was so badly damaged that it was impossible to determine if any of the parts of the steering wheel mechanism or workmanship or assembly were defective or improper prior to the accident. The condition was such that the collision insurance carrier, after inspection, declared the vehicle a total loss. It had 468 miles on the speedometer at the time.

The insurance carrier's inspector and appraiser of damaged cars, with 11 years of experience, advanced the opinion, based on the history and his examination, that something definitely went "wrong from the steering wheel down to the front wheels" and that the untoward happening must have been due to mechanical defect or failure: "something down there had to drop off or break loose to cause the car" to act in the manner described.

As has been indicated, the trial court felt that the proof was not sufficient to make out a prima facie case as to the negligence of either the manufacturer or the dealer. The case was given to the jury, therefore, solely on the warranty theory, with results favorable to the plaintiffs against both defendants.

I. The Claim of Implied Warranty Against the Manufacturer

[The court begins its analysis with a review of the nature of common law warranties, both express and implied, and their fairly recent codification and liberalization by the Uniform Sales Act, which was in effect when Mr. Henningsen purchased his new automobile. The court proceeds to criticize the terms of the warranty in this case, calling them "a sad commentary upon the automobile manufacturers' marketing practices."]

Putting aside for the time being the problem of the efficacy of the disclaimer provisions contained in the express warranty, a question of first importance to be decided is whether an implied warranty of merchantability by Chrysler Corporation accompanied the sale of the automobile to Claus Henningsen. . . .

Chrysler points out that an implied warranty of merchantability is an incident of a contract of sale. It concedes, of course, the making of the original sale to Bloomfield Motors, Inc., but maintains that this transaction marked the terminal point of its contractual connection with the car. Then Chrysler urges that since it was not a party to the sale by the dealer to Henningsen, there is no privity of contract between it and the plaintiffs, and the absence of this privity eliminates any such implied warranty.

There is no doubt that under early common-law concepts of contractual liability only those persons who were parties to the bargain could sue for a breach of it. In more recent times a noticeable disposition has appeared in a number of jurisdictions to break through the narrow barrier of privity when dealing with sales of goods in order to give realistic recognition to a universally accepted fact. The fact is that the dealer and the ordinary buyer do not, and are not expected to, buy goods, whether they be foodstuffs or automobiles, exclusively for their own consumption or use. Makers and manufacturers know this and advertise and market their products on that assumption; witness, the "family" car, the baby foods, etc. The limitations of privity in contracts for the sale of goods developed their place in the law when marketing conditions were simple, when maker and buyer frequently met face to face on an equal bargaining plane and when many of the products were relatively uncomplicated and conducive to inspection by a buyer competent to evaluate their quality. With the advent of mass marketing, the manufacturer became remote from the purchaser, sales were accomplished through intermediaries, and the demand for the product was created by advertising media. In such an economy it became obvious that the consumer was the person being cultivated. Manifestly, the connotation of "consumer" was broader than that of "buyer." He signified such a person who, in the reasonable contemplation of the parties to the sale, might be expected to use the product. Thus, where the commodities sold are such that if defectively manufactured they will be dangerous to life and limb, then society's interests can only be protected by eliminating the requirement of privity between the maker and his dealers and the reasonably expected ultimate consumer. In that way the burden of losses consequent upon use of defective articles is borne by those who are in a position to either control the danger or make an equitable distribution of the losses when they do occur. . . .

Although only a minority of jurisdictions have thus far departed from the requirement of privity, the movement in that direction is most certainly gathering momentum. Liability to the ultimate consumer in the absence of direct contractual connection has been predicated upon a variety of theories. Some courts hold that the warranty runs with the article like a covenant running with land; others recognize a third-party beneficiary thesis; still others rest their decision on the ground that public policy requires recognition of a warranty made directly to the consumer. . . .

Most of the cases where lack of privity has not been permitted to interfere with recovery have involved food and drugs. In fact, the rule as to such products has been characterized as an exception to the general doctrine. But more recently courts, sensing the inequity of such limitation, have moved into broader fields. . . .

We see no rational doctrinal basis for differentiating between a fly in a bottle of beverage and a defective automobile. The unwholesome beverage may bring illness to one person, the defective car, with its great potentiality for harm to the driver, occupants, and others, demands even less adherence to the narrow barrier of privity. . . .

Under modern conditions the ordinary layman, on responding to the importuning of colorful advertising, has neither the opportunity nor the capacity to inspect or to determine the fitness of an automobile for use; he must rely on the manufacturer who has control of its construction, and to some degree on the dealer who, to the limited extent called for by the manufacturer's instructions, inspects and services it before delivery. In such a marketing milieu his remedies and those of persons who properly claim through him should not depend "upon the intricacies of the law of sales. The obligation of the manufacturer should not be based alone on privity of contract. It should rest, as was once said, upon 'the demands of social justice.'" . . .

Accordingly, we hold that under modern marketing conditions, when a manufacturer puts a new automobile in the stream of trade and promotes its purchase by the public, an implied warranty that it is reasonably suitable for use as such accompanies it into the hands of the ultimate purchaser. Absence of agency between the manufacturer and the dealer who makes the ultimate sale is immaterial.

II. The Effect of the Disclaimer and Limitation of Liability Clauses on the Implied Warranty of Merchantability

[The court takes judicial notice of the extensive advertising programs undertaken by automobile manufacturers, and the increasing willingness of courts to find express and implied warranties based upon that advertising.]

In the light of these matters, what effect should be given to the express warranty in question which seeks to limit the manufacturer's liability to replacement of defective parts, and which disclaims all other warranties, express or implied? In assessing its significance we must keep in mind the general principle that, in the absence of fraud, one who does not choose to read a contract before signing it, cannot later relieve himself of its burdens. And in applying that principle, the basic tenet of freedom of competent parties to contract is a factor of importance. But in the framework of modern commercial life and business practices, such rules cannot be applied on a strict, doctrinal basis. The conflicting interests of the buyer and seller must be evaluated realistically and justly, giving due weight to the social policy evinced by the Uniform Sales Act, the progressive decisions of the courts engaged in administering it, the mass production methods of manufacture and distribution to the public, and the bargaining position occupied by the ordinary consumer in such an economy. The history of the law shows that legal doctrines, as first expounded, often prove to be inadequate under the impact of later experience. In such case, the need for justice has stimulated the necessary qualifications or adjustments. . . .

The warranty before us is a standardized form designed for mass use. It is imposed upon the automobile consumer. He takes it or leaves it, and he must take it to buy an automobile. No bargaining is engaged in with respect to it. In fact, the dealer through whom it comes to the buyer is without authority to alter it; his function is ministerial—simply to deliver it. The form warranty is not only standard with Chrysler but, as mentioned above, it is the uniform warranty of the Automobile Manufacturers Association. Members of the Association are: General Motors, Inc., Ford, Chrysler, Studebaker-Packard, American Motors (Rambler), Willys Motors, Checker Motors Corp., and International Harvester Company. Of these companies, the "Big Three" (General Motors, Ford, and Chrysler) represented 93.5% of the passenger-car production for 1958 and the independents 6.5%. And for the same year the "Big Three" had 86.72% of the total passenger vehicle registrations.

The gross inequality of bargaining position occupied by the consumer in the automobile industry is thus apparent. There is no competition among the car makers in the area of the express warranty. Where can the buyer go to negotiate for better protection? Such control and limitation of his remedies are inimical to the public welfare and, at the very least, call for great care by the courts to avoid injustice through application of strict common-law principles of freedom of contract. Because there is no competition among the motor vehicle manufacturers with respect to the scope of protection guaranteed to the buyer, there is no incentive on their part to stimulate good will in that field of public relations. Thus, there is lacking a factor existing in more competitive fields, one which tends to guarantee the safe construction of the article sold. Since all competitors operate in the same way, the urge to be careful is not so pressing. . . .

Public policy at a given time finds expression in the Constitution, the statutory law and in judicial decisions. In the area of sale of goods, the legislative will has imposed an implied warranty of merchantability as a general incident of sale of an automobile by description. The warranty does not depend upon the affirmative intention of the parties. It is a child of the law; it annexes itself to the contract because of the very nature of the transaction. . . . True, the Sales Act authorizes agreements between buyer and seller qualifying the warranty obligations. But quite obviously the Legislature contemplated lawful stipulations (which are determined by the circumstances of a particular case) arrived at freely by parties of relatively equal bargaining strength. The lawmakers did not authorize the automobile manufacturer to use its grossly disproportionate bargaining power to relieve itself from liability and to impose on the ordinary buyer, who in effect has no real freedom of choice, the grave danger of injury to himself and others that attends the sale of such a dangerous instrumentality as a defectively made automobile. In the framework of this case, illuminated as it is by the facts and the many decisions noted, we are of the opinion that Chrysler's attempted disclaimer of an implied warranty of merchantability and of the obligations arising therefrom is so inimical to the public good as to compel an adjudication of its invalidity.

III. The Dealer's Implied Warranty

The principles that have been expounded as to the obligation of the manufacturer apply with equal force to the separate express warranty of the dealer. This is so, irrespective of the absence of the relationship of principal and agent between these defendants, because the manufacturer and the Association establish the warranty policy for the industry. The bargaining position of the dealer is inextricably bound by practice to that of the maker and the purchaser must take or leave the automobile, accompanied and encumbered as it is by the uniform warranty. . . .

For the reasons set forth in Part 1 hereof, we conclude that the disclaimer of an implied warranty of merchantability by the dealer, as well as the attempted elimination of all obligations other than replacement of defective parts, are violative of public policy and void. . . .

IV. Proof of Breach of the Implied Warranty of Merchantability

Both defendants argue that the proof adduced by plaintiffs as to the happening of the accident was not sufficient to demonstrate a breach of warranty. Consequently, they claim that their motion for judgment should have been granted by the trial court. We cannot agree. In our view, the total effect of the circumstances shown from purchase to accident is adequate to raise an inference that the car was defective and that such condition was causally related to the mishap. Thus, determination by the jury was required. . . .

V. The Defense of Lack of Privity Against Mrs. Henningsen

Both defendants contend that since there was no privity of contract between them and Mrs. Henningsen, she cannot recover for breach of any warranty made by either of them. On the facts, as they were developed, we agree that she was not a party to the purchase agreement. Her right to maintain the action, therefore, depends upon whether she occupies such legal status thereunder as to permit her to take advantage of a breach of defendant's implied warranties.

[The court concludes that "the cause of justice . . . can be served only by" allowing Mrs. Henningsen to recover.]

It is important to express the right of Mrs. Henningsen to maintain her action in terms of a general principle. To what extent may lack of privity be disregarded in suits on such warranties? In that regard, [precedent] points the way. By a parity of reasoning, it is our opinion that an implied warranty of merchantability chargeable to either an automobile manufacturer or a dealer extends to the purchaser of the car, members of his family, and to other persons occupying or using it with his consent. It would be wholly opposed to reality to say that use by such persons is not within the anticipation of parties to such a warranty of reasonable suitability of an automobile for ordinary highway operation. Those persons must be considered within the distributive chain. . . .

For affirmance — Chief Justice Weintraub, and Justices Burling, Jacobs, Francis, Proctor, and Schettino — 6.

For reversal — None.

The warranty materials in this section provide an opportunity to observe the interplay between tort and contract doctrines in the working out of the rules of decision in a significant area of private law. During the period following the *MacPherson* decision in

New York, American courts gradually moved the traditional tort concepts of negligence closer to strict liability by increasingly generous applications of the doctrine of res ipsa loquitur. This development of a fault-free negligence rule culminated in the *Escola* decision in California, p. 249, above, with Traynor urging his colleagues to take the last step of breaking free from negligence traditions. We will consider the rise of strict products liability in the next section. Over the same period, courts were heading in essentially the same direction by gradually stripping implied warranty concepts of their contract trappings in products liability cases. This evolution of a contract-free warranty rule culminated in the *Henningsen* decision, in which the court retained what it liked in warranties (negligence-free strict liability) and rejected what it did not like (the privity requirement and disclaimers.) By the time courts had eliminated the elements of contract from warranty, it was but a short step to embrace strict liability in tort.

At least from a tort/contract perspective, it would appear that tort has won the day, albeit with a helpful boost along the way from the contract warranties. Simply stated, tort concepts dominate present-day products liability. However, lest the erroneous impression be created that contract warranties have no continuing role to play in products liability, two important caveats are necessary. First, some jurisdictions have decided to retain implied warranty as the primary conceptual vehicle for imposing strict liability. Thus, the Supreme Judicial Court of Massachusetts in Back v. Wickes Corp., 378 N.E.2d 964 (Mass. 1978), retained §2-314(2)(c) of the U.C.C. as the basis for strict manufacturers' liability in that state, although the court readily admitted that "the duty which the plaintiff sues to enforce in a 'warranty' action for personal injuries is one imposed by law as a matter of social policy, and not necessarily one which the defendant has acquired by contract." (Id. at 969.) More recently, the court reiterated that its theory of "[w]arranty liability is fully as comprehensive as the strict liability theory of recovery that has been adopted by a great many other jurisdictions, and congruent in nearly all respects with the principles expressed in Restatement (Second) of Torts." Haglund v. Philip Morris, Inc., 847 N.E.2d 315, 321 (Mass. 2006) (quoting *Back*).

Second, even in those jurisdictions that recognize strict tort as their primary conceptual vehicle, two types of warranties — express warranties and implied warranties of fitness for a particular purpose — continue to serve unique and useful purposes in products liability cases. For example, if a product seller promises that a product will perform in a certain manner, a disappointed or injured plaintiff will have rights based on express warranty that might not otherwise be available under strict tort liability. And when a seller recommends a particular product as appropriate to the plaintiff's particular purpose, knowing that the buyer is relying on the seller's expertise, the seller will be liable if the product fails dangerously to serve the buyer's purpose, resulting in injury.

c. Strict Liability in Tort

The decision generally recognized to have been the first to avoid reliance on warranty terminology and to explicitly apply the rule of privity-free strict liability in tort to manufacturers of defective products is Greenman v. Yuba Power Products, Inc., 377 P.2d 897 (Cal. 1962). The plaintiff was using a power lathe in his basement to turn a piece of wood when a wrong-sized set screw caused the wood to fly free, imparting physical injury. Citing Henningsen v. Bloomfield Motors, Inc., above, the California court in *Greenman* concluded that the manufacturer's liability for defective products "is not one governed by the law of contract warranties but by the law of strict liability in tort." (377 P.2d at 901). The court concluded (377 P.2d at 901):

> Implicit in the machine's presence on the market, however, was a representation that it would safely do the jobs for which it was built. Under these circumstances, it should not be controlling whether plaintiff selected the machine because of the statements in the brochure, or because of the machine's own appearance of excellence that belied the defect lurking beneath the surface, or because he merely assumed that it would safely do the jobs it was built to do. It should not be controlling whether the details of the sales from manufacturer to retailer and from retailer to plaintiff's wife were such that one or more of the implied warranties of the sales act arose. . . . To establish the manufacturer's liability it was sufficient that plaintiff proved that he was injured while using the Shopsmith in a way it was intended to be used as a result of a defect in design and manufacture of which plaintiff was not aware that made the Shopsmith unsafe for its intended use.

Vandermark v. Ford Motor Co.

391 P.2d 168 (Cal. 1964)

TRAYNOR, JUSTICE.

In October 1958 plaintiff Chester Vandermark bought a new Ford automobile from defendant Lorimer Diesel Engine Company, an authorized Ford dealer doing business as Maywood Bell Ford. About six weeks later, while driving on the San Bernardino Freeway, he lost control of the car. It went off the highway to the right and collided with a light post. He and his sister, plaintiff Mary Tresham, suffered serious injuries. They brought this action for damages against Maywood Bell Ford and the Ford Motor Company, which manufactured and assembled the car. They pleaded causes of action for breach of warranty and negligence. The trial court granted Ford's motion for a nonsuit on all causes of action and directed a verdict in favor of Maywood Bell on the warranty causes of action. The jury returned a verdict for Maywood Bell on the negligence causes of action, and the trial court entered judgment on the verdict. Plaintiffs appeal.

Vandermark had driven the car approximately 1500 miles before the accident. He used it primarily in town, but drove it on two occasions from his home in Huntington Park to Joshua Tree in San Bernardino County. He testified that the car operated normally before the accident except once when he was driving home from Joshua Tree. He was in the left-hand west-bound lane of the San Bernardino Freeway when traffic ahead slowed. He applied the brakes and the car "started to make a little dive to the right and continued on across the two lanes of traffic till she hit the shoulder. Whatever it was then let go and I was able to then pull her back into the road." He drove home without further difficulty, but before using the car again, he took it to Maywood Bell for the regular 1000-mile new car servicing. He testified that he described the freeway incident to Maywood Bell's service attendant, but Maywood Bell's records do not indicate that any complaint was made.

After the car was serviced, Vandermark drove it in town on short trips totaling approximately 300 miles. He and his sister then set out on another trip to Joshua Tree. He testified that while driving in the right-hand lane of the freeway at about 45 to 50 miles per hour, "the car started to make a little shimmy or weave and started pulling to the right. . . . I tried to pull back, but it didn't seem to come, so I applied my brakes gently to see if I could straighten her up, but I couldn't seem to pull on the brakes and she wouldn't come back, and all of a sudden this pole was in front of me and we smashed into it." Plaintiff Tresham testified to a substantially similar version of the accident. A witness for plaintiffs, who was driving about 200 feet behind them, testified that plaintiff's car was in the right-hand lane when he saw its taillights come on. The car started to swerve and finally skidded into the light post. An investigating officer testified that there were skid marks leading from the highway to the car.

Plaintiffs called an expert on the operation of hydraulic automobile brakes. In answer to hypothetical questions based on evidence in the record and his own knowledge of the braking system of the car, the expert testified as to the cause of the accident. It was his opinion that the brakes applied themselves owing to a failure of the piston in the master cylinder to retract far enough when the brake pedal was released to uncover a bypass port through which hydraulic fluid should have been able to escape into a reservoir above the master cylinder. Failure of the piston to uncover the bypass port led to a closed system and a partial application of the brakes, which in turn led to heating that expanded the brake fluid until the brakes applied themselves with such force that Vandermark lost control of the car. The expert also testified that the failure of the piston to retract sufficiently to uncover the bypass port could have been caused by dirt in the master cylinder, a defective or wrong-sized part, distortion of the fire wall, or improper assembly or adjustment. The trial court struck the testimony of the possible causes to the failure of the piston to retract, on the ground that there was no direct evidence that any one or more of the causes existed, and it rejected plaintiffs' offer to prove that all of the possible causes were attributable to defendants. These rulings were erroneous, for plaintiffs were entitled to establish the existence of a defect and defendants' responsibility therefor by circumstantial evidence, particularly when, as in this case, the damage to the car in the collision precluded determining whether or not the master cylinder assembly had been properly installed and adjusted before the accident.

Accordingly, for the purposes of reviewing the nonsuit in favor of Ford and the directed verdict in favor of Maywood Bell on the warranty causes of action, it must be taken as established that when the car was delivered to Vandermark, the master cylinder assembly had a defect that caused the accident. Moreover, since it could reasonably be inferred from the description of the braking system in evidence and the offer of proof of all possible causes of defects that the defect was owing to negligence in design, manufacture, assembly, or adjustment, it must be taken as established that the defect was caused by some such negligence.

Ford contends, however, that it may not be held liable for negligence in manufacturing the car or strictly liable in tort for placing it on the market without proof that the car was defective when Ford relinquished control over it. Ford points out that in this case the car passed through two other authorized Ford dealers before it was sold to Maywood Bell and that Maywood Bell removed the power steering unit before selling the car to Vandermark.

In Greenman v. Yuba Power Products, Inc., 59 Cal.2d 57, 62, 27 Cal. Rptr. 697, 700, 377 P.2d 897, 900, we held that "A manufacturer is strictly liable in tort when an article he places on the market, knowing that it is to be used without inspection for defects, proves to have a defect that causes injury to a human being." Since the liability is strict it encompasses defects regardless of their source, and therefore a manufacturer of a completed product cannot escape liability by tracing the defect to a component part supplied by another. (Goldberg v. Kollman Instrument Corp., 12 N.Y.2d 432, 437, 240 N.Y.S.2d 592, 191 N.E.2d 81.) Moreover, even before such strict liability was recognized, the manufacturer of a completed product was subject to vicarious liability for the negligence of his suppliers or subcontractors that resulted in defects in the completed product. (Dow v. Holly Manufacturing Co., 49 Cal.2d 720, 726-727, 321 P.2d 736; Ford Motor Co. v.

Mathis, 5 Cir., 322 F.2d 267, 273; Boeing Airplane Co. v. Brown, 9 Cir., 291 F.2d 310, 313; see Rest., Torts, §400.) These rules focus responsibility for defects, whether negligently or nonnegligently caused, on the manufacturer of the completed product, and they apply regardless of what part of the manufacturing process the manufacturer chooses to delegate to third parties. It appears in the present case that Ford delegates the final steps in that process to its authorized dealers. It does not deliver cars to its dealers that are ready to be driven away by the ultimate purchasers but relies on its dealers to make the final inspections, corrections, and adjustments necessary to make the cars ready for use. Since Ford, as the manufacturer of the completed product, cannot delegate its duty to have its cars delivered to the ultimate purchaser free from dangerous defects, it cannot escape liability on the ground that the defect in Vandermark's car may have been caused by something one of its authorized dealers did or failed to do.

Since plaintiffs introduced or offered substantial evidence that they were injured as a result of a defect that was present in the car when Ford's authorized dealer delivered it to Vandermark, the trial court erred in granting a nonsuit on the causes of action by which plaintiff sought to establish that Ford was strictly liable to them. Since plaintiffs also introduced or offered substantial evidence that the defect was caused by some negligent conduct for which Ford was responsible, the trial court also erred in granting a nonsuit on the causes of action by which plaintiffs sought to establish that Ford was liable for negligence.

Plaintiffs contend that Maywood Bell is also strictly liable in tort for the injuries caused by the defect in the car and that therefore the trial court erred in directing a verdict for Maywood Bell on the warranty causes of action. Maywood Bell contends that the rule of strict liability in the Greenman case applies only to actions against manufacturers brought by injured parties with whom the manufacturers did not deal. . . .

Retailers like manufacturers are engaged in the business of distributing goods to the public. They are an integral part of the overall producing and marketing enterprise that should bear the cost of injuries resulting from defective products. (See Greenman v. Yuba Power Products, Inc., 59 Cal.2d 57, 63, 27 Cal. Rptr. 697, 377 P.2d 897.) In some cases the retailer may be the only member of that enterprise reasonably available to the injured plaintiff. In other cases the retailer himself may play a substantial part in insuring that the product is safe or may be in a position to exert pressure on the manufacturer to that end; the retailer's strict liability thus serves as an added incentive to safety. Strict liability on the manufacturer and retailer alike affords maximum protection to the injured plaintiff and works no injustice to the defendants, for they can adjust the costs of such protection between them in the course of their continuing business relationship. Accordingly, as a retailer engaged in the business of distributing goods to the public, Maywood Bell is strictly liable in tort for personal injuries caused by defects in cars sold by it. . . . [Citations omitted.]

Although plaintiffs sought to impose strict liability on Maywood Bell on the theory of sales-act warranties, they pleaded and introduced substantial evidence of all of the facts necessary to establish strict liability in tort. Accordingly, the trial court erred in directing a verdict for Maywood Bell on the so-called warranty causes of action. . . .

The judgment of nonsuit in favor of Ford Motor Company is reversed. The judgment in favor of Maywood Bell Ford on the negligence causes of action is affirmed and in all other respects the judgment in favor of Maywood Bell Ford is reversed.

GIBSON, C.J., and SCHAUER, McCOMB, PETERS, TOBRINER, and PEEK, JJ., concur.

Three years after *Greenman* was decided and one year after *Vandermark,* the American Law Institute, relying on *Greenman* and inspired by the scholarly work of the Reporter for the Restatement (Second) of Torts, William Prosser, published its well-known strict products liability rule:

RESTATEMENT (SECOND) OF TORTS (1965)

§402A. SPECIAL LIABILITY OF SELLER OF PRODUCT FOR PHYSICAL HARM TO USER OR CONSUMER

(1) One who sells any product in a defective condition unreasonably dangerous to the user or consumer or to his property is subject to liability for physical harm thereby caused to the ultimate user or consumer, or to his property, if

(a) the seller is engaged in the business of selling such a product, and

(b) it is expected to and does reach the user or consumer without substantial change in the condition in which it is sold.

(2) The rule stated in Subsection (1) applies although

(a) the seller has exercised all possible care in the preparation and sale of his product, and

(b) the user or consumer has not bought the product from or entered into any contractual relation with the seller.

COMMENT

g. Defective condition. The rule stated in this Section applies only where the product is, at the time it leaves the seller's hands, in a condition not contemplated by the ultimate consumer, which will be unreasonably dangerous to him. The seller is not liable when he delivers the product in a safe condition, and subsequent mishandling or other causes make it harmful by the time it is consumed. The burden of proof that the product was in a defective condition at the time that it left the hands of the particular seller is upon the injured plaintiff; and unless evidence can be produced which will support the conclusion that it was then defective, the burden is not sustained.

Safe condition at the time of delivery by the seller will, however, include proper packaging, necessary sterilization, and other precautions required to permit the product to remain safe for a normal length of time when handled in a normal manner.

i. Unreasonably dangerous. The rule stated in this Section applies only where the defective condition of the product makes it unreasonably dangerous to the user or consumer. Many products cannot possibly be made entirely safe for all consumption, and any food or drug necessarily involves some risk of harm, if only from over-consumption. Ordinary sugar is a deadly poison to diabetics, and castor oil found use under Mussolini as an instrument of torture. That is not what is meant by "unreasonably dangerous" in this Section. The article sold must be dangerous to an extent beyond that which would be contemplated by the ordinary consumer who purchases it, with the ordinary knowledge common to the community as to its characteristics. Good whiskey is not unreasonably dangerous merely because it will make some people drunk, and is especially dangerous to alcoholics; but bad whiskey, containing a dangerous amount of fusel oil, is unreasonably dangerous. Good tobacco is not unreasonably dangerous merely because the effects of smoking may be harmful; but tobacco containing something like marijuana may be unreasonably dangerous. Good butter is not unreasonably dangerous merely because, if such be the case, it deposits cholesterol in the arteries and leads to heart attacks; but bad butter, contaminated with poisonous fish oil, is unreasonably dangerous.

m. "Warranty." "[W]arranty" must be given a . . . different meaning if it is used in connection with this section. It is much simpler to regard the liability here stated as merely one of strict liability in tort.

Since 1965, all jurisdictions in this country have recognized the rule of privity-free strict products liability in manufacturing defect cases, although as noted above a few employ "implied warranty" language instead of "strict liability in tort" language.

The Restatement (Third) codifies these developments in §§1 and 2(a) and Comments thereto:

> §1. LIABILITY OF COMMERCIAL SELLER OR DISTRIBUTOR FOR HARM CAUSED BY DEFECTIVE PRODUCTS
>
> One engaged in the business of selling or otherwise distributing products who sells or distributes a defective product is subject to liability for harm to persons or property caused by the defect.
>
> §2. CATEGORIES OF PRODUCT DEFECT
>
> A product is defective when, at the time of sale or distribution, it contains a manufacturing defect, is defective in design, or is defective because of inadequate instructions or warnings. A product:
>
> (a) contains a manufacturing defect when the product departs from its intended design even though all possible care was exercised in the preparation and marketing of the product; . . .
>
> COMMENT
>
> *n. Relationship of definitions of defect to traditional doctrinal categories.* The rules in this Section and in other provisions of this Chapter define the bases of tort liability for harm caused by product defects existing at time of sale or other distribution. The rules are stated functionally rather than in terms of traditional doctrinal categories. Claims based on product defect at time of sale or other distribution must meet the requisites set forth in Subsections (a), (b), or (c), or the other provisions in this Chapter. As long as these requisites are met, doctrinal tort categories such as negligence or strict liability may be utilized in bringing the claim.
>
> Similarly, a product defect claim satisfying the requisites of Subsections (a), (b), or (c), or other provisions in this Chapter, may be brought under the implied warranty of merchantability provisions of the Uniform Commercial Code. It is recognized that some courts have adopted a consumer expectations definition for design and failure-to-warn defects in implied warranty cases involving harm to persons or property. This Restatement contemplates that a well-coordinated body of law governing liability for harm to persons or property arising out of the sale of defective products requires a consistent definition of defect, and that the definition properly should come from tort law, whether the claim carries a tort label or one of implied warranty of merchantability.

On the subject of coordinating warranty and strict tort liability, see generally James J. White, Reverberations from the Collision of Tort and Warranty, 53 S.C. L. Rev. 1067 (2002).

Observe that §1 of the new Restatement imposes duties on *all* commercial sellers. Thus, in most jurisdictions, all commercial entities in the vertical chain of distribution are held jointly and severally liable to injured plaintiffs for harm caused by defects attributable to the manufacturer. Some jurisdictions even impose liability on successor corporations that acquire rights to a product line, even if the particular product at issue was manufactured prior to the acquisition. See, e.g., Schmidt v. Boardman Co., 11 A.3d 924 (Pa. 2011).

Moreover, although generalizations are difficult in this area, as a general rule each seller in the chain has a right of indemnity against those sellers higher up the chain.

One of the interesting developments in recent years has been the movement to let retailers and wholesalers off (or at least partway off) the strict liability hook when the manufacturer is identified, amenable to suit, and financially able to pay a judgment. See Frances E. Zollers et al., Looking Backward, Looking Forward: Reflections on Twenty Years of Product Liability Reform, 50 Syracuse L. Rev. 1019, 1033 (2000). Under traditional rules governing contribution and indemnity among the members of the distributive chain, the tendency is for the liability to be passed up the chain from retailers and wholesalers to the manufacturer by means of implied rights of indemnity. Although this tendency reduces the ultimate exposures to liability of retailers and wholesalers, those categories of sellers are routinely joined as defendants and, even if eventually they escape liability to the plaintiff, they incur substantial costs defending against liability and otherwise protecting their interests.

Note: Circumstantial Proof of Defect

It will be recalled that the *Henningsen* decision, *supra*, one of the most famous American products liability decisions, involved circumstantial proof of defect. The automobile in that case was practically new when the steering suddenly failed and caused a collision. The Supreme Court of New Jersey concluded that (161 A.2d at 97): "[T]he total effect of the circumstances shown from purchase to accident is adequate to raise an inference that the car was defective and that such condition was causally related to the mishap." Courts have continued to recognize the sufficiency of such circumstantial evidence. For instance, in Stanley v. Lennox Industries, Inc., 102 P.3d 1104 (Idaho 2004), a furnace overheated a home, damaging its contents. The purchaser-owner of the home brought action against the manufacturer of the furnace and the manufacturer of the separate thermostat that sent signals to the furnace. Plaintiff's expert testified in an affidavit that the only two possible causes for the overheating were the thermostat and the controller in the furnace. The expert opined that the furnace was to blame because the thermostat worked properly in tests after the incident, and was displaying a "turn-off" signal when the problem was discovered. (Plaintiff argued that the defect in the controller caused it to ignore the "turn-off" signal sent by the thermostat.) The Supreme Court of Idaho reversed summary judgment for the furnace manufacturer, holding that the claim that the controller was defective was for the jury.

In Bennett v. Asco Services, Inc., 621 S.E.2d 710 (W. Va. 2005), plaintiffs brought action against an automobile manufacturer and a fire alarm manufacturer, alleging that a defect in the auto caused a garage fire and that a defect in the alarm allowed the fire to destroy their home. The West Virginia high court reversed summary judgments for defendants, concluding (621 S.E.2d at 718-19):

> After examining the record, we find sufficient evidence such that a reasonable juror could infer that the fire started in the Toyota Camry as a result of a malfunction, and that the fire would not have ordinarily happened in the absence of a defect. The Bennetts' expert testified that it was his opinion that a defect in the wiring system existed in the Camry, a defect which was the ultimate cause of the fire. Due to the destruction of the Camry, the expert was not able to identify the precise defect in question. Still, the record indicates that the Bennetts introduced sufficient evidence for jurors to conclude that the Camry was

> regularly maintained and serviced, was not previously exposed to neglect, abuse or abnormal use, and, most importantly, was not being misused at the time the fire started. Sufficient evidence was also offered such that jurors could exclude other reasonable secondary causes for the fire. For instance, an expert hired by Ohio Farmers and Westfield acknowledged that items such as a gasoline can and gasoline-powered equipment located in the garage lacked an ignition source and could not have been an independent cause of the fire. Expert testimony in the record also permits an inference that other reasonable alternative causes for the fire could be ruled out: the fact that Mrs. Bennett turned on the lights in the garage suggested that the electrical wiring was not a source, photographs of the fire scene ruled out other items or vehicles in the garage as the source of the fire, and the burn pattern and main collapse of the garage support the location of the Camry as being the origin of the fire. Accordingly, a genuine issue of material fact clearly exists regarding whether or not a defect in the wiring system caused the Camry to catch on fire. . . .
>
> After careful consideration of the record, we [also] find that material questions of fact exist regarding whether the Honeywell alarm system malfunctioned as a result of a defect, and was therefore not reasonably safe for its intended use. The record suggests that the fire was burning in the garage for at least twenty to thirty minutes before the Bennetts woke up. The Bennetts' expert testified that the alarm system should have offered immediate detection of either smoke or heat from the fire, and alerted the Bennetts to the fire in less than one minute based upon the proximity of the heat detectors to where the fire started. . . .

The Restatement (Third) recognizes the legitimacy of drawing an inference of defect from the fact that a relatively new, well-cared-for product malfunctions under normal condition of use:

> §3. Circumstantial Evidence Supporting Inference of Product Defect
>
> It may be inferred that the harm sustained by the plaintiff was caused by a product defect existing at the time of sale or distribution, without proof of a specific defect, when the incident that harmed the plaintiff:
>
> (a) was of a kind that ordinarily occurs as a result of product defect; and
>
> (b) was not, in the particular case, solely the result of causes other than product defect existing at the time of sale or distribution.
>
> COMMENT
>
> *b. Requirement that the harm be of a kind that ordinarily occurs as a result of product defect.* The most frequent application of this Section is to cases involving manufacturing defects. When a product unit contains such a defect, and the defect affects product performance so as to cause a harmful incident, in most instances it will cause the product to malfunction in such a way that the inference of product defect is clear. From this perspective, manufacturing defects cause products to fail to perform their manifestly intended functions. Frequently, the plaintiff is able to establish specifically the nature and identity of the defect and may proceed directly under §2(a). But when the product unit involved in the harm-causing incident is lost or destroyed in the accident, direct evidence of specific defect may not be available. Under that circumstance, this Section may offer the plaintiff the only fair opportunity to recover. . . .

One of the first applications of §3 was in Myrlak v. Port Authority of N.Y. and N.J., 723 A.2d 45 (N.J. 1999). The plaintiff in *Myrlak* sued the defendant chair manufacturer after the plaintiff fell from his chair at work when the back of the five-week-old chair unexpectedly cracked and gave way. The trial judge refused an instruction on res ipsa loquitur, and the jury found the plaintiff failed to establish a manufacturing defect. The court of appeals reversed and held that the trial judge should have given instruction on res ipsa. The New Jersey Supreme Court reversed in part and adopted §3 in place of res ipsa, noting that "Section 3 . . . permits the jury to draw two inferences: that the harmful incident was caused by a product defect, and that the defect was present when the product left the manufacturer's control. The res ipsa loquitur doctrine, on the other hand, creates the single inference of negligence." 723 A.2d at 55.

In Cooper Tire & Rubber Co. v. Mendez, 204 S.W.3d 797 (Tex. 2006), the court considered whether §3 could be invoked by plaintiffs who suffered injuries after a tire's tread separated and caused their vehicle to wreck. Because plaintiffs presented no competent direct evidence of the cause of the tire failure, they sought to use expert testimony to eliminate other potential causes. The court rejected this approach, reasoning that in the context of a tire with 30,000 miles of use behind it "[t]he universe of possible causes for the tire failure is simply too large and too uncertain to allow an expert to prove a manufacturing defect merely by the process of elimination." Id. at 807-08. Interestingly, the court stated that a presumption of defectiveness would be inappropriate even if the plaintiff's expert "eliminated every conceivable reason for the tire failure other than a product defect existing when the tire left Cooper Tire's plant." Id. at 808. The court argued that such evidence would not distinguish between manufacturing and design defect possibilities and, under Texas law, design defect claims require actual proof of a safer, alternative design. In contrast, Comment *b* to §3 notes that the section "allows the trier of fact to draw the inference that the product was defective whether due to a manufacturing defect or a design defect."

The Relationship Between Tort and Contract: Products Liability and Recovery for Pure Economic Loss

Perhaps the most significant caveat to the earlier pronouncement that tort law has won out over contract law in the products liability area concerns the limits of what is here referred to as "products liability." By their terms, §402A and §1 of the Restatement (Third) apply only to actions to recover for personal injuries and property damage caused by defective, unreasonably dangerous products. What of purely consequential economic loss caused by disappointment in the quality and performance of the product itself? Consistent with the general rules applicable in nonproducts cases, a clear majority of courts deny recovery based on tort and relegate plaintiffs to contract. See, e.g., JMB Mfg., Inc. v. Child Craft, LLC, 799 F.3d 780, 782 (7th Cir. 2015) (rejecting through use of the economic loss rule "a merchant's creative effort to avoid the limited remedies that contract law provides for a seller's delivery of non-conforming goods"); Wilson v. Style Crest Products, Inc., 627 S.E.2d 733, 736 (S.C. 2006) (observing that "the no-injury approach to product litigation has been rejected in most decisions"). In Pennsylvania Glass Sand Corp. v. Caterpillar Tractor Co., 652 F.2d 1165, 1172-73 (3d Cir. 1981), the court supported this position by the following reasoning:

> Although strict liability in tort developed out of the law of warranties, the courts of most states have recognized that the principles of warranty law remain the appropriate vehicle to redress a purchaser's disappointed expectations when a defect renders a product inferior or unable adequately to perform its intended function. These courts have classified the

> damages consequent to qualitative defects, such as reduced value, return of purchase price, repair and replacement, or lost profits, as economic loss, and have relegated those who suffer such commercial loss to the remedies of contract law.
>
> On the other hand, almost all courts have adopted the view that the benefit-of-the-bargain approach of warranty law is ill-suited to correct problems of hazardous products that cause physical injury. Manufacturers are better able to bear the risk or to take action to correct flaws that pose a danger. Accordingly, tort law imposes a duty on manufacturers to produce safe items, regardless of whether the ultimate impact of the hazard is on people, other property, or the product itself.

See also Grams v. Milk Prods., 699 N.W.2d 167 (Wis. 2005), in which the plaintiffs sought to recover against the defendant for a "milk replacer" intended for livestock nourishment. The plaintiffs claimed that it did not adequately nourish the cows and some died from malnutrition. The court held that the claim was based on disappointed expectations and fell within the rule barring recovery in tort for pure economic loss. Query: If the "milk replacer" had poisoned the cows, same result?

When courts send plaintiffs to the contract warranties side of the aisle, plaintiffs often run into difficulties with doctrines such as privity of contract, which present no difficulties in tort actions. In Limestone Farms, Inc. v. Deer & Co., 29 P.3d 457 (Kan. Ct. App. 2001), a lessee farmer bought a seed planter from his landlord. The planter did not work properly, allegedly due to manufacturing defects, and the plaintiff farmer brought a breach-of-warranty action against the manufacturer of the planter, seeking to recover for economic losses that flowed from crop failures. The trial court granted summary judgment for the defendant on the ground of lack of privity. The court of appeals affirmed, concluding (29 P.3d at 460): "Implied warranties . . . are not extended to a remote seller . . . for only economic loss suffered by a buyer who is not in contractual privity with the remote seller." But see Hyundai Motor America, Inc. v. Goodin, 822 N.E.2d 947 (Ind. 2005), in which the court held that a buyer of an automobile could recover for breach of implied warranty against the manufacturer for loss of the value of the auto notwithstanding lack of privity between plaintiff and defendant. For more on the distinction between tort law and contract law in product defect cases and an argument that courts should eliminate any overlapping, duplicative claims in economic loss cases, see Richard A. Mann & Barry S. Roberts, The Applicability of Tort Law to Commercial Buyers, 79 Neb. L. Rev. 215 (2000).

For a time, the Supreme Court of New Jersey extended strict tort liability even for pure economic loss. In Santor v. A & M Karagheusian, Inc., 207 A.2d 305 (N.J. 1965), the plaintiff purchased carpeting manufactured by the defendant from a third-party seller. After several months, unsightly lines began to appear on the surface of the carpet. The trial court determined that there was an implied warranty of merchantability and concluded that the defendant breached that warranty. The Supreme Court of New Jersey affirmed and held that the plaintiff could maintain a breach of implied warranty claim directly against the manufacturer despite the lack of privity between them. In dicta, the court stated that the plaintiff also possessed a cause of action in strict tort liability. As with cases involving personal injuries and property damage caused by defective products, said the court, a manufacturer of an unsatisfactory product is better able to insure against and to spread the risk of economic losses than are individual customers. (Id. at 311-12.) The court observed:

> [W]hen the manufacturer presents his goods to the public for sale he accompanies them with a representation that they are suitable and safe for the intended use. . . . The obligation of the manufacturer thus becomes what in justice it ought to be — an enterprise liability,

> and one which should not depend upon the intricacies of the law of sales. The purpose of such liability is to insure that the cost of injuries or damage, either to the goods sold or to other property, resulting from defective products, is borne by the makers of the products who put them in the channels of trade, rather than by the injured or damaged persons who ordinarily are powerless to protect themselves.

The court overturned this rule in Alloway v. General Marine Industries, L.P., 695 A.2d 264, 268 (N.J. 1997), reasoning that when a "product fails to fulfill a purchaser's economic expectations, contract principles, particularly as implemented by the U.C.C., provide a more appropriate analytical framework." The court relied heavily on East River Steamship Corp. v. Transamerica Delaval Inc., 476 U.S. 858 (1986), a case in which the Supreme Court, in admiralty, confronted the question of whether the plaintiff could recover in tort when the defect injured only the product itself. (A turbine engine failed in an oil supertanker, necessitating costly repairs.) After carefully reviewing the case law, the Court sided with the clear majority of jurisdictions and denied tort recovery. The Restatement (Third) of Torts: Products Liability, in §21(c), also adopts the *East River* majority rule.

The Supreme Court subsequently clarified what constitutes "the product itself" in Saratoga Fishing Co. v. J. M. Martinac & Co., 520 U.S. 875 (1997). An individual purchased a boat from the defendant-manufacturer and subsequently added certain equipment to the boat. The individual then sold the boat to the plaintiff. Sometime thereafter the boat sank due to an engine room fire that resulted from a defectively designed hydraulic system supplied to the defendant-manufacturer by a component supplier. The Court held that the plaintiff could recover for the physical damage to the equipment added by the initial purchaser, as this constituted "other property" and not the "product itself." In concluding that the term "other property" encompassed the equipment added by the initial purchaser, the Supreme Court explained:

> When a Manufacturer places an item in the stream of commerce by selling it to an Initial User, that item is the "product itself" under *East River*. Items added to the product by the Initial User are therefore "other property," and the Initial User's sale of the product to a Subsequent User does not change these characterizations.

Id. at 1786.

What if the "product itself" is clearly expected by the parties at the time of contracting to come into contact with or be incorporated into "other property"? Compare Dean v. Barrett Homes, Inc., 8 A.3d 766 (N.J. 2010) (holding that manufactured home and allegedly defective exterior siding were not part of an "integrated product" and that homeowners could therefore sue siding manufacturer for damage caused to the home), and Elite Prof'ls, Inc. v. Carrier Corp., 827 P.2d 1195, 1202 (Kan. App. 1992) (holding that a trucking company could recover in tort for meat that spoiled when a refrigeration unit purchased from defendant malfunctioned; in the court's view, the meat constituted "harm to property other than the refrigeration unit itself"), with Travelers Indem. Co. v. Dammann & Co., Inc., 594 F.3d 238 (3d Cir. 2010) (holding that a manufacturer of vanilla extract must rely on contract remedies against a supplier of vanilla beans when the beans were discovered to contain mercury after they had been incorporated into the manufacturer's extract). In the latter case, the court noted that the "product itself"/"other property" distinction of *Saratoga Fishing* is being replaced in many jurisdictions by a more fine-grained test rooted in the parties' expectations: "The majority of jurisdictions employ some variation of a test under which tort remedies are unavailable for property damage experienced by the owner where the damage was a foreseeable result of a defect at the time the parties contractually determined their respective exposure to risk, regardless whether the damage was to the 'goods' themselves or to 'other property.'" 594 F.3d at 250. For discussion of these issues, see Comment *e* to §19 of the Restatement (Third).

On the issue of tort recovery for economic loss in the products liability context, see Gary T. Schwartz, Economic Loss in American Tort Law: The Examples of *J'Aire* and of Products Liability, 23 San Diego L. Rev. 37 (1986); and Ralph C. Anzivino, The Disappointed Expectations Test and the Economic Loss Doctrine, 92 Marq. L. Rev. 749 (2009).

Law and Policy: Policy Objectives Supporting Strict Liability in Tort for Defective Products

A number of policy objectives have been advanced by courts and commentators in support of imposing strict liability in tort on commercial sellers of defective products. Among these objectives are: (1) compensating injured plaintiffs more adequately; (2) spreading losses among those who consume products; (3) forcing sellers to make good on implied representations of safety; (4) redressing the disappointment of consumer expectations; (5) deterring the marketing of defective products; (6) easing the evidentiary burden on plaintiffs to prove the sellers' negligence; and (7) controlling wasteful accident costs. Is there any way to tie these objectives together into an overarching philosophy? Consider the following excerpt.

James A. Henderson, Jr., Coping with the Time Dimension in Products Liability

69 Cal. L. Rev. 919, 931-39 (1981)

In general, strict liability is thought to be preferable to negligence because it better enhances social utility by reducing the costs associated with accidents and because it promotes fairness. Strict liability is believed to increase utility by satisfying four major objectives: encouraging investment in product safety, discouraging consumption of hazardous products, reducing transaction costs, and promoting loss spreading. . . .

Strict liability promotes investment in product safety, the so-called "risk control" objective, by imposing liability rules that encourage manufacturers to find ways to reduce or eliminate avoidable product risks. Although in theory this same objective is satisfied by holding manufacturers liable only for their negligence, those who advocate strict liability suggest that manufacturers escape a significant portion of negligence-based liability. An action sounding in negligence presents the plaintiff with difficult issues of proof, such as what a manufacturer with expertise in the field should have known. Manufacturers also may be able to destroy adverse test results and frustrate plaintiffs' attempts to demonstrate that the defendant knew of the hazards. Knowing that the average plaintiff has difficulty in establishing negligence, manufacturers may be willing to bet on escaping liability, or at least large judgments, and thus may limit their efforts to reduce product risks. A regime of strict liability, which does not consider the manufacturer's knowledge, eliminates the practical difficulties involved in litigating a negligence claim. Manufacturers will be less likely to escape liability and will have a greater incentive to invest in efforts to reduce product risks.

Strict liability has also been justified on the ground that it reduces the consumption of risky products by increasing their cost and so placing them at a disadvantage in the market. This second objective, frequently referred to as "market deterrence," rests on the assumption that consumers tend to underassess the risks associated with various products. Unless consumers are reminded of these risks by price increments reflecting manufacturers' liability insurance costs, including the costs of insuring against accidents not worth trying to prevent, they will overconsume relatively risky products. Lower consumption of these products will result in fewer accidents, thereby reducing the costs of product liability insurance. Unlike the risk control objective, market deterrence is not achieved to the same extent, even in theory, by imposing liability only for negligence: a relatively hazardous product will escape liability if its benefits are sufficient to justify its risks and a reasonable person would not have made it safer at the time of its distribution. In that event, the product will reflect the relevant avoidance costs, but will not reflect the costs of insuring against those accidents that are not worth trying to prevent.

The third objective traditionally thought to be promoted by strict liability is the reduction of transaction costs, which include the costs of operating the accident reparation system. Strict liability reduces these costs by simplifying the proof necessary to establish liability. Since the plaintiff need not put forward evidence of the defendant's negligence, often a difficult, costly, and time consuming process, the costs of trials under a strict liability rule should be lower than they would be under a negligence rule.

The final utility objective concerns reducing dislocation costs that occur when a single individual or business must bear the full accident loss. The costs of repairing the damage or replacing what has been lost, whether borne by an unsuccessful plaintiff or by a liable defendant, may financially destroy the loss bearer. The additional social costs represented by the uncompensated victim who becomes a public charge, or by the manufacturer who goes into bankruptcy, must also be counted as costs of accidents. These dislocation costs can be reduced by spreading accident losses among a large number of persons by means of insurance. In general, manufacturers are believed to be better able to obtain insurance than are consumers, and are assumed to be able to pass on most, if not all, of the insurance costs by raising the prices of products. Under a negligence approach, manufacturers who are not negligent escape liability; even very large accident costs caused by dangerous products will not be shifted to defendants who have acted reasonably. Under strict liability, more of such costs are shifted to manufacturers and their insurers, thus decreasing dislocation costs to the extent of the increased liability.

In addition to the first four objectives aiming at the promotion of social utility, strict products liability traditionally has been supported on the ground that it responds to shared notions of fairness. This writer confesses to a certain degree of skepticism regarding the relevance of fairness, as a consideration separate from utility, to the question of whether producers should be held strictly liable. When a producer is negligent in designing, manufacturing, or marketing a product, it is easy to appreciate the relevance of fairness principles to the question of liability. But the allocation of accident losses to producers irrespective of fault seems to be primarily a means of reducing social waste rather than a means of achieving fairness. Yet, the fact that courts and commentators persist in rationalizing strict products liability in terms of fairness strongly suggests that fairness should be examined. Thus, rather than circumventing fairness in this analysis, or attempting once and for all to settle the question of its relevance to strict products liability, an effort will be made to identify those fairness rationales that seem to support strict liability.

Of the many fairness rationales relied upon by courts and commentators, three offer possible justifications for strict products liability. All three rationales rely to some extent on intuition for their support, and all present analytical difficulties. In order to understand these rationales, it will be useful to consider how they support the traditional imposition of strict liability for harm caused by manufacturing defects.

First, strict liability may be justified on fairness grounds because the product that contains a hidden manufacturing defect that causes harm disappoints the consumer's or user's reasonable expectations with regard to safety. The producer may not have been negligent, and the plaintiff may have understood as a general proposition that mistakes can happen. However, when the plaintiff has paid value for the product, he has a right to expect that it will not fail dangerously in its intended use. Moreover, producers typically try to communicate impressions of infallibility that create consumer confidence in the product. Intuitively it seems appropriate to allow the plaintiff in such a case to claim compensation based on the unfair disappointment of his reasonable expectations.

Second, strict liability for manufacturing defects may be justified because in distributing its products, some of which contain hidden manufacturing defects, the producer may be said to be deliberately taking the physical well-being of those who are injured by the product. The producer is like an actor who shoots into a crowd. The producer, like the shooter, does not know who will be injured; but as surely as the shooter knows that someone will be shot, the producer knows that someone will be injured. Both the shooter and the producer can also estimate the number of victims. The shooter loads his gun with a certain number of bullets, and the producer accepts a certain defect rate when setting the level of quality control for its products. Having set a defect rate, the producer can predict the number of accidents, and thus, the number of accident victims. Choosing to limit quality control means accepting a certain number of accidents; so in a sense, the eventual victims of this choice are harmed deliberately. Of course, the shooter is presumably not privileged, and thus commits a battery when he shoots into the crowd. In contrast, the producer is here assumed to have made the economically reasonable decision in choosing to limit quality control. Consequently, the producer can be said to be privileged in the sense that it will not be found liable under a system of negligence even though its conduct caused harm to others. However, there is precedent for holding an actor liable to others for harm deliberately inflicted even when the actor is privileged to act. The best that can be said for the manufacturer is that it has behaved in an economically rational manner; but that does not alter the fact that its deliberate decision has condemned users and consumers to suffer harm. On this view, the manufacturer should in fairness be required to compensate the injured victims.

Finally, strict liability for manufacturing defects may be justified on fairness grounds because it causes the financial burden of accidents to be borne by those who use, and therefore benefit directly from, the product. From this perspective, the producer is a conduit through which accident costs are shifted from injured persons who do not directly benefit from the product to those persons who do. When a defective product distributed by a nonnegligent producer causes an accident in which a nonuser or nonconsumer bystander is injured, the producer who is held strictly liable shifts the costs to those who purchase and use or consume the product. The bystander-plaintiff's claim is supported by the fairness principle that "those who benefit should pay." Of course, the principle applies only crudely. Some nonusers and nonconsumers benefit indirectly from the use and consumption of the products that cause them injury. Also, spreading the costs pro rata on a per-product rather than on a per-use basis causes some users and consumers to bear more, and some less, than their fair share of the burden. Moreover, recovery on the basis of strict liability is not restricted to bystanders; users and consumers also recover for harm caused by manufacturing defects. However, within these narrow limitations strict liability for manufacturing defects seem to be supported by the "benefits/burdens" fairness principle.

All three fairness rationales represent responses to situations in which accident costs are imposed on certain persons without their express or tacit consent. The "benefits/burdens" rationale, with its concern for bystanders who in no way consent to being victims, is most clearly concerned with consent. The other rationales reflect similar perspectives. The "consumer expectations" rationale relies on the assumption that producers, through advertising, entice purchasers into a misplaced sense of security so that the consent seemingly given by purchasers to their exposure to product-related risks is more properly viewed as involuntary. Finally, the "deliberate taking" rationale, although it purports to focus on the deliberateness of the manufacturer's quality control decisions, relies on the idea of nonconsensual "taking."

Given that strict products liability is firmly established in all American jurisdictions, it is useful to consider what one might call the *boundaries* of the subject. For example, what qualifies as a "product"? The Restatement (Third) defines this term as follows:

§19. Definition of "Product"

For purposes of this Restatement:

(a) A product is tangible personal property distributed commercially for use or consumption. Other items, such as real property and electricity, are products when the context of their distribution and use is sufficiently analogous to the distribution and use of tangible personal property that is appropriate to apply the rules stated in this Restatement.

(b) Services, even when provided commercially, are not products. . . .

Issues regarding what is a product arise frequently. For example, in Blaha v. Stuard, 640 N.W.2d 85 (S.D. 2002), the court held that a dog, which defendants had sold to plaintiffs (it subsequently attacked plaintiffs' daughter), was not a product because, according to the court, living creatures have no fixed nature. In Engelhardt v. Rogers Group, Inc., 132 F. Supp. 2d 757 (E.D. Ark. 2001), a highway that had been resurfaced by defendant was held not to be a product after a driver on the highway was killed as a result of another vehicle hydroplaning. The court ruled that a highway was neither a "tangible object" nor a "good" as defined by Arkansas statutes, and thus could not be a product. One fascinating area of litigation concerns books, movies, and games alleged to contain "defective" ideas. Courts typically refuse to extend products liability law to such media content. See, e.g., Winter v. G. P. Putnam's Sons, 938 F.2d 1033 (9th Cir. 1991) (plaintiffs relied on advice of mushroom encyclopedia to harvest and consume mushrooms that severely poisoned them; publisher of encyclopedia could not be held liable under products liability law); Sanders v. Acclaim Entm't, 188 F. Supp. 2d 1264 (D. Colo. 2002) (Columbine shooting victims' families failed to state a strict liability claim against game software makers who allegedly inspired school shooting because intangible thoughts and ideas are not products). For an analysis of how courts determine whether something is a product, see Charles E. Cantu, A Continuing Whimsical Search for the True Meaning of the Term "Product" in Products Liability Litigation, 35 St. Mary's L.J. 341 (2004).

So far, all of the cases we have examined have involved commercial sellers of new products who are in the business of selling the product causing the injury. To a large extent, although not completely, §402A reaches only such sellers. To what extent should, and has, strict liability in tort been applied in other contexts? In reacting to the following discussion of this question, it is important to emphasize that the issue is not one of liability or no liability. Even if strict liability in tort does not apply, the defendant may still be exposed to liability in negligence or breach of implied warranty. But you should also appreciate that to the extent that it is more difficult for the plaintiff to recover under one of those other bases, the issue as a practical matter may be one of liability or no liability.

Courts disagree on the question of whether to impose liability on commercial sellers of used products. In Crandell v. Larkin & Jones Appliance Co., 334 N.W.2d 31 (S.D. 1983), the seller of a used clothes dryer was held strictly liable for harm caused by a fire that started when a thermostat failed. The defendant had sold the dryer as a "Quality Reconditioned Unit." See also Gaumer v. Rossville Truck and Tractor Co., Inc., 202 P.3d 81, 86 (Kan. App. 2009) ("No exception for sellers of used products has ever been recognized by our Supreme Court."). In a somewhat narrower opinion than *Crandell,* the New Jersey Supreme Court held that strict liability applies to defective repairs or new component parts replaced by a dealer who sells used products. Realmuto v. Straub Motors, 322 A.2d 440, 444 (N.J. 1974). Accord Gaumer v. Rossville Truck & Tractor Co., 257 P.3d 292 (Kan. 2011) (after comprehensive survey of authority pro and con, court concludes that Kansas Product Liability Act imposes strict liability on used product sellers); Peterson v. Lou Bachrodt Chevrolet Co., 329 N.E.2d 785 (Ill. 1975).

Other courts believe that strict liability is not appropriate in used products cases in which the seller does not introduce the defect into the product. See, e.g., La Rosa v. Superior Court, 176 Cal. Rptr. 224 (Ct. App. 1981); Cataldo v. Lazy Days R.V. Ctr., Inc., 920 So. 2d 174 (Fla. Dist. Ct. App. 2006); Allenberg v. Bentley Hedges Travel Serv., 22 P.3d 223 (Okla. 2001); Tillman v. Vance Equip. Co., 596 P.2d 1299 (Or. 1979). See generally James A. Henderson, Jr., Extending the Boundaries of Strict Products Liability: Implications of the Theory of the Second Best, 128 U. Pa. L. Rev. 1036, 1081-85 (1980).

Section 8 of the Restatement (Third) deals with a commercial seller's liability for defective used products. The two primary subsections impose liability when a defect (a) results from the seller's failure to exercise reasonable care; or (b) is a manufacturing defect and the seller's marketing of the product would cause a reasonable person in the position of the buyer to expect the used product to present no greater risk of defect than if the product were new. Section 8 defines a used product as a product that, prior to the time of sale or other distribution, is commercially sold or otherwise distributed to a buyer not in the commercial chain of distribution and used for some period of time.

Another important boundary area concerns who are sellers or distributors. What about defendants who supply products in the course of performing what are essentially services? Providers of pure services are not considered product sellers or providers, and thus do not fall within the ambit of strict products liability. However, providers of services remain liable for negligence, as would be expected. The issue becomes more difficult in what could be called "hybrid" situations where actors provide both products and services in a single transaction. In Newmark v. Gimbel's Inc., 258 A.2d 697 (N.J. 1969), the Supreme Court of New Jersey held that a beauty parlor patron who was injured by defective permanent wave solution could hold the beauty parlor strictly liable in tort. The court distinguished an earlier decision refusing to impose strict liability on a dentist on the ground that "the essence of the relationship [of the dentist] with his patient was the furnishing of professional skill and services," whereas the beautician was engaged "in a commercial enterprise." Id. at 702. The decision in *Newmark* highlights an interesting aspect of products liability law: the apparent ease with which the strict liability doctrine may be rendered inapplicable by characterizing what the defendant has supplied as "service" rather than "goods." Doctrinally, the distinction has support. Both the Uniform Commercial Code (§2-102) and §402A of the Restatement (Second) purport to apply only to transactions characterizable as sales of goods or products. Many of the early cases raising the "goods vs. services" issue were brought by plaintiffs injured by contaminated food served in restaurants. Cf. Cushing v. Rodman, discussed at p. 520, above.

The Restatement (Third) contains the following important boundary provision:

> §20. Definition of "One Who Sells or Otherwise Distributes"
>
> For purposes of this restatement:
>
> (a) One sells a product when, in a commercial context, one transfers ownership thereto either for use or consumption or for resale leading to ultimate use or consumption. Commercial product sellers include, but are not limited to, manufacturers, wholesalers, and retailers.
>
> (b) One otherwise distributes a product when, in a commercial transaction other than a sale, one provides the product to another either for use or consumption or as a preliminary step leading to ultimate use or consumption. Commercial nonsale product distributors include, but are not limited to, lessors, bailors, and those who provide products to others as a means of promoting either the use or consumption of such products or some other commercial activity.
>
> (c) One also sells or otherwise distributes a product when, in a commercial transaction, one provides a combination of products and services and either the transaction taken as a whole, or the product component thereof, satisfies the criteria in Subsection (a) or (b).

In Cintrone v. Hertz Truck Leasing & Rental Service, 212 A.2d 769 (N.J. 1965), the Supreme Court of New Jersey faced the question whether strict liability applied to a commercial lessor of trucks. The plaintiff was injured when the brakes on a truck rented from defendant by the plaintiff's employer failed, causing an accident. The defendant had rented a fleet of trucks to the employer, along with a promise to maintain them in good working order. At the time of the accident the truck was over two years old. Reversing the trial court's dismissal of the plaintiff's strict liability count, the New Jersey high court held that a commercial vehicle lessor impliedly warrants that its vehicles are in safe working order regardless of the actual age of the vehicle. The court concluded (212 A.2d at 778):

> When the implied warranty or representation of fitness arises, for how long should it be considered viable? Since the exposure of the user and the public to harm is great if the rented vehicle fails during ordinary use on a highway, the answer must be that it continues for the agreed rental period. The public interests involved are justly served only by treating an obligation of that nature as an incident of the business enterprise. The operator of the rental business must be regarded as possessing expertise with respect to the service life and fitness of his vehicles for use. That expertise ought to put him in a better position than the bailee to detect or to anticipate flaws or defects or fatigue in his vehicles. Moreover, as between bailor for hire and bailee the liability for flaws or defects not discoverable by ordinary care in inspecting or testing ought to rest with the bailor just as it rests with a manufacturer who buys components containing latent defects from another maker, and installs them in the completed product, or just as it rests with the retailer at the point of sale to the consumer. And, with respect to failure of a rented vehicle from fatigue, since control

of the length of the lease is in the lessor, such risk is one which in the interest of the consuming public as well as of the members of the public traveling the highways, ought to be imposed on the rental business.

The Restatement (Third) treats commercial lessors in a manner consistent with *Cintrone*. See Comment *c* to §20. See also Svege v. Mercedes-Benz Credit Corp., 329 F. Supp. 2d 272 (D. Conn. 2004). In contrast to commercial lessors, finance lessors are far less likely to be actively involved in the production of the good subject to lease or in a position to place pressure on producers to act reasonably For this reason, courts rarely subject them to products liability. See, e.g., Arriaga v. CitiCapital Commercial Corp., 85 Cal. Rptr. 3d 143 (Ct. App. 2008) (concluding that finance lessor was not subject to strict products liability). Similar reasoning led the Supreme Court of Texas in New Texas Auto Auction Services, L.P. v. Gomez De Hernandez, 249 S.W.3d 400 (2008), to conclude that an auctioneer who sold a vehicle at auction was nevertheless not a "seller" for purposes of products liability.

Problem 32

Your firm represents the El Papagayo Verde restaurant, defendant in a suit brought by a restaurant patron. The complaint contains counts in both negligence and strict liability. The senior partner handling the case asked for your assistance. At the time of the accident eight months ago, the plaintiff, Tom Walters, and his wife, Mary Jean, had just ordered dinner at the restaurant. Mr. Walters was tasting the wine they had chosen to celebrate their anniversary when the glass shattered in his hand, causing deep cuts and possible permanent injury. The plaintiff seeks to recover against El Papagayo Verde on the basis of negligence and strict liability. Pedro Nejarte, the waiter who served the wine, and Mrs. Walters insist that Mr. Walters was drinking normally and did not mishandle the glass. El Papagayo Verde opened nine months before the accident. When it began its operation, all glasses used by the restaurant were new. El Papagayo Verde continually replaces glasses that break, so it is unclear exactly how long the particular glass in this case had been in service. The turnover rate among the kitchen staff at El Papagayo Verde is quite high. Consequently, the plaintiff has been unable to gather direct evidence supporting the conclusion that El Papagayo Verde's employees were negligent in their handling of glasses in general or this particular glass.

The partner in charge of this case wants you to prepare a memorandum assessing the strengths of both the negligence and strict liability counts. He also wants you to anticipate, and meet, the plaintiff's likely arguments in support of his claims.

2. The Plaintiff's Prima Facie Case: Causation

The actual cause and proximate cause requirements developed in Chapters 2 and 4 apply in products liability cases regardless of whether the theory relied on is negligence, warranty, or strict liability in tort, and regardless of the type of defect involved. Section 2-715 of the Uniform Commercial Code establishes that "consequential damages resulting from the seller's breach include . . . injury to person or property *proximately resulting* from any breach of warranty" (emphasis added); §402A of the Restatement (Second) of Torts establishes seller's liability "for physical harm . . . *caused to* the ultimate user and consumer, or to his property" (emphasis added); and §1 of the Restatement (Third) refers to the seller being "subject to liability for harm . . . *caused by* the defect" (emphasis added). These provisions have been interpreted so as to impose actual cause and proximate cause requirements similar to the requirements under negligence principles. Thus, the plaintiff must show that the product caused the injury, was distributed by the defendant, and, but for the defect, the accident either would not have happened or would not have been so harmful to the plaintiff. The plaintiff must also show that the resulting injury to the plaintiff was within the range of foreseeable risks created by the defect. Moreover, courts will occasionally recognize the conduct of third persons as "efficient intervening causes" sufficient to relieve the defendant seller of liability to the plaintiff.

a. Actual Causation (Cause-in-Fact)

A recurring issue involves whether asbestos plaintiffs have sufficiently proven that their exposures to defendants' products caused their subsequent injuries. In Weakley v. Burnham Corp., 871 A.2d 1167 (D.C. Ct. App. 2005), the plaintiff claimed that his exposure to asbestos dust while servicing asbestos-containing boilers manufactured by defendants caused his debilitating asbestosis. His inability to identify exactly whose boilers he had worked on over a 15-year period caused the trial court to enter summary judgment against him. Reversing and remanding for trial, the court of appeals held that proof merely that the plaintiff had worked at a job site where, at some point in time, defendants' products had been used would not suffice. At a minimum, the plaintiff must prove that he and the defendants' products had been "in the same place at the same time." (871 A.2d at 1175). The court concluded:

> The "same place at the same time" standard, . . . provides the key to Weakley's appeal. Weakley has stated under oath that he "frequently" worked on boilers manufactured by each of the appellees, and that he has thus been present at the same place and at the same time, and "regularly" exposed to, the asbestos that he attributes to the appellees. It is true that as to two of the defendants . . . Weakley has not been able to identify the time or place of any contact with those defendants' products. Nevertheless, he has asserted that he has "frequently" been in the immediate presence of, and has worked on, these defendants' boilers. . . . We do not read the "same time and same place" minimum standard as requiring the plaintiff to recall and specify a *particular* time and a *particular* place. . . .
>
> Weakley must, of course, also establish that his exposure to each defendant's product was a "substantial factor" contributing to his having contracted asbestosis. For summary judgment purposes, however, this element is satisfied by Dr. Casolaro's expert testimony. This witness' analysis may not be without its difficulties, and his diagnosis could perhaps come under adversarial fire, but such issues are for the trier of fact, and are not suitable for resolution by summary judgment.

The issue to which Casolaro, the plaintiff's expert, testified in *Weakley* was whether the plaintiff's exposure to a particular defendant's boiler was sufficiently substantial to support a jury finding of actual causation. In Lohrmann v. Pittsburgh Corning Corp., 782 F.2d 1156 (4th Cir. 1986), the court of appeals established a test requiring the plaintiff to prove with specificity the frequency and regularity of exposure to, and the proximity with, defendant's products. *Lohrmann* reflects the view that, for a plaintiff who has had countless exposures to many other asbestos-containing products over a period of time, a brief exposure to a particular defendant's product should not suffice to support a claim against that defendant.

Lohrmann is widely accepted by American courts, although a few jurisdictions continue to follow a "one fiber" rule according to which any exposure to asbestos is considered a substantial factor. For decisions following the stricter approach of *Lohrmann* see Betz v. Pneumo Abex, LLC, 44 A.3d 27 (Pa. 2012); Holcomb v. Georgia Pacific, LLC, 289 P.3d 188 (Nev. 2012); Borg-Warner Corp. v. Flores, 232 S.W.3d 765 (Tex. 2007); Monsanto Co. v. Hall, 912 So. 2d 134 (Miss. 2005). For discussion, see David Bernstein, Getting to Causation in Toxic Tort Cases, 74 Brook. L. Rev. 51 (2009); Jane Stapleton, The Two Explosive Proof-of-Causation Doctrines Central to Asbestos Claims, 74 Brook. L. Rev. 1011 (2009). The most conceptually difficult actual causation cases have been those in which the plaintiff is harmed by a defective product that is both unidentified by trademark or insignia and in no way unique to the defendant. In the classic example of such a defendant identification case, the plaintiff is harmed by a defective unit of a type of product manufactured and distributed by many companies, under circumstances where the plaintiff cannot prove which company actually produced and distributed the defective, harm-causing product unit. Most cases of this sort are design and warning, rather than manufacturing defect, cases.

The most famous examples in the past two decades have involved personal injuries allegedly resulting from plaintiffs' prenatal exposure to diethylstilbestrol (DES). The harmful products in those cases were allegedly defective by reason of their design and marketing; they did not contain manufacturing defects. Some courts have responded in ways that allow injured plaintiffs to overcome otherwise fatal gaps in their proofs of causation by joining as defendants all, or most, of the companies manufacturing and distributing DES during the time periods relevant to their cases. The best known of these decisions, following in the footsteps of Summers v. Tice, p. 132, above, is Sindell v. Abbott Labs., 607 P.2d 924 (Cal.), *cert. denied,* 449 U.S. 912 (1980), discussed at pp. 141-142, above. In that case, each defendant was held liable in proportion to its share of the DES market. *Sindell* dropped like a bombshell on the American legal scene. It became the focal point of much controversy as to whether private tort litigation was capable of dealing with mass tort. Courts and commentators have lined up on both sides of the issue, with controversy continuing to this day. Although the predominant reaction of courts to market share and other "group liability" theories has been negative, important exceptions continue to appear, as noted in Chapter 2. In retrospect, *Sindell* and its progeny may represent an example of courts attempting to work their way to a solution to a difficult problem of proving causation, only to flounder on the practical difficulties of unmanageability. The question remains open whether judicial floundering is worse than no governmental response at all.

b. Proximate (Legal) Causation

Union Pump Co. v. Allbritton

898 S.W.2d 773 (Tex. 1995)

OWEN, JUSTICE.

The issue in this case is whether the condition, act, or omission of which a personal injury plaintiff complains was, as a matter of law, too remote to constitute legal causation. Plaintiff brought suit alleging negligence, gross negligence, and strict liability, and the trial court granted summary judgment for the defendant. The court of appeals reversed and remanded, holding that the plaintiff raised issues of fact concerning proximate and producing cause. 888 S.W.2d 833. Because we conclude that there was no legal causation as a matter of law, we reverse the judgment of the court of appeals and render judgment that plaintiff take nothing.

On the night of September 4, 1989, a fire occurred at Texaco Chemical Company's facility in Port Arthur, Texas. A pump manufactured by Union Pump Company caught fire and ignited the surrounding area. This particular pump had caught on fire twice before. Sue Allbritton, a trainee employee of Texaco Chemical, had just finished her shift and was about to leave the plant when the fire erupted. She and her supervisor Felipe Subia, Jr., were directed to and did assist in abating the fire.

Approximately two hours later, the fire was extinguished. However, there appeared to be a problem with a nitrogen purge valve, and Subia was instructed to block in the valve. Viewing the facts in a light most favorable to Allbritton, there was some evidence that an emergency situation existed at that point in time. Allbritton asked if she could accompany Subia and was allowed to do so. To get to the nitrogen purge valve, Allbritton followed Subia over an aboveground pipe rack, which was approximately two and one-half feet high, rather than going around it. It is undisputed that this was not the safer route, but it was the shorter one. Upon reaching the valve, Subia and Allbritton were notified that it was not necessary to block it off. Instead of returning by the route around the pipe rack, Subia chose to walk across it, and Allbritton followed. Allbritton was injured when she hopped or slipped off the pipe rack. There is evidence that the pipe rack was wet because of the fire and that Allbritton and Subia were still wearing fireman's hip boots and other firefighting gear when the injury occurred. Subia admitted that he chose to walk over the pipe rack rather than taking a safer alternative route because he had a "bad habit" of doing so.

Allbritton sued Union Pump, alleging negligence, gross negligence, and strict liability theories of recovery, and accordingly, that the defective pump was a proximate or producing cause of her injuries. But for the pump fire, she asserts, she would never have walked over the pipe rack, which was wet with water or firefighting foam.

Following discovery, Union Pump moved for summary judgment. To be entitled to summary judgment, the movant has the burden of establishing that there is no genuine issue of material fact and that it is entitled to judgment as a matter of law. A defendant who moves for summary judgment must conclusively disprove one of the elements of each of the plaintiff's causes of action. Lear Siegler, Inc. v. Perez, 819 S.W.2d 470, 471 (Tex. 1991). All doubts must be resolved against Union Pump and all evidence must be viewed in the light most favorable to Allbritton. Id. The question before this Court is whether Union Pump established as a matter of law that neither its conduct nor its product was a legal cause of Allbritton's injuries. Stated another way, was Union Pump correct in contending that there was no causative link between the defective pump and Allbritton's injuries as a matter of law?

Negligence requires a showing of proximate cause, while producing cause is the test in strict liability. Proximate and producing cause differ in that foreseeability is an element of proximate cause, but not of producing cause. Id. Proximate cause consists of both cause in fact and foreseeability. Cause in fact means that the defendant's act or omission was a substantial factor in bringing about the injury which would not otherwise have occurred. A producing cause is "an efficient, exciting, or contributing cause, which in a natural sequence, produced injuries or damages complained of, if any." Common to both proximate and producing cause is causation in fact, including the requirement that the defendant's conduct or product be a substantial factor in bringing about the plaintiff's injuries.

Lear Siegler, 819 S.W.2d at 472 n.1 (quoting Restatement (Second) of Torts §431 cmt. *e* (1965)).

At some point in the causal chain, the defendant's conduct or product may be too remotely connected with the plaintiff's injury to constitute legal causation. As this Court noted in City of Gladewater v. Pike, 727 S.W.2d 514, 518 (Tex. 1987), defining the limits of legal causation "eventually mandates weighing of policy considerations." See also Springall v. Fredericksburg Hospital and Clinic, 225 S.W.2d 232, 235 (Tex. Civ. App.—San Antonio 1949, no writ), in which the court of appeals observed:

> [T]he law does not hold one legally responsible for the remote results of his wrongful acts and therefore a line must be drawn between immediate and remote causes. The doctrine of "proximate cause" is employed to determine and fix this line and "is the result of an effort by the courts to avoid, as far as possible the metaphysical and philosophical niceties in the age-old discussion of causation, and to lay down a rule of general application which will, as nearly as may be done by a general rule, apply a practical test, the test of common experience, to human conduct when determining legal rights and legal liability."

Id. at 235 (quoting City of Dallas v. Maxwell, 248 S.W. 667, 670 (Tex. Comm'n App. 1923, holding approved)).

Drawing the line between where legal causation may exist and where, as a matter of law, it cannot, has generated a considerable body of law.[1] Our Court has considered where the limits of legal causation should lie in the factually analogous case of Lear Siegler, Inc. v. Perez, [819 S.W.2d 470 (Tex. 1991), discussed in Chapter 4, pp. 308-309]. The threshold issue was whether causation was negated as a matter of law in an action where negligence and product liability theories were asserted. . . . [W]e found a comment to the Restatement (Second) of Torts, section 431, instructive on the issue of legal causation:

> In order to be a legal cause of another's harm, it is not enough that the harm would not have occurred had the actor not been negligent. . . . The negligence must also be a substantial factor in bringing about the plaintiff's harm. The word "substantial" is used to denote the fact that the defendant's conduct has such an effect in producing the harm as to lead reasonable men to regard it as a cause, using that word in the popular sense, in which there always lurks the idea of responsibility, rather than in the so-called "philosophic sense," which includes every one of the great number of events without which any happening would not have occurred.

Lear Siegler, 819 S.W.2d at 472 (quoting Restatement (Second) of Torts §431 cmt. *a* (1965)).

As this Court explained in *Lear Siegler,* the connection between the defendant and the plaintiff's injuries simply may be too attenuated to constitute legal cause. 819 S.W.2d at 472. Legal cause is not established if the defendant's conduct or product does no more than furnish the condition that makes the plaintiff's injury possible. Id. This principle applies with equal force to proximate cause and producing cause. Id. at 472 n.1.

1. In the seminal decision in Palsgraf v. Long Island Railroad Co., 248 N.Y. 339, 162 N.E. 99 (1928), for example, a railway guard knocked explosives from under the arm of a passenger who was hurrying to board a train. The resulting explosion caused scales some distance away to fall on the plaintiff. The majority in *Palsgraf* held that as a matter of law, the defendant owned no duty to the plaintiff because "[t]he risk reasonably to be perceived defines the duty to be obeyed; . . . it is risk to another or to others within the range of apprehension." Id. 162 N.E. at 100. In his dissent in *Palsgraf,* Judge Andrews opined that the decision should turn not on duty but on proximate cause. In analyzing proximate cause, he recognized: "What we do mean by the word 'proximate' is that, because of convenience, of public policy, of a rough sense of justice, the law arbitrarily declines to trace a series of events beyond a certain point." Id. at 103 (Andrews, J., dissenting).

This Court similarly considered the parameters of legal causation in Bell v. Campbell, 434 S.W.2d 117, 122 (Tex. 1968). In *Bell*, two cars collided, and a trailer attached to one of them disengaged and overturned into the opposite lane. A number of people gathered, and three of them were attempting to move the trailer when they were struck by another vehicle. Id. at 119. This Court held that the parties to the first accident were not a proximate cause of the plaintiffs' injuries, reasoning:

> All acts and omissions charged against respondents had run their course and were complete. Their negligence did not actively contribute in any way to the injuries involved in this suit. It simply created a condition which attracted [the plaintiffs] to the scene, where they were injured by a third party.

Id. at 122.

In *Bell*, this Court examined at some length decisions dealing with intervening causes and decisions dealing with concurring causes. The principles underlying the various legal theories of causation overlap in many respects, but they are not coextensive. While in *Bell*, this Court held "the injuries involved in this suit were not proximately caused by any negligence of [defendants] but by an independent and intervening agency," id., we also held "[a]ll forces involved in or generated by the first collision had come to rest, and no one was in any real or apparent danger therefrom[,]" id. at 120, and accordingly, that the "[defendants'] negligence was not a concurring cause of [the plaintiffs'] injuries." Id. at 122. This reasoning applies with equal force to Allbritton's claims.

Even if the pump fire were in some sense a "philosophic" or "but for" cause of Allbritton's injuries, the forces generated by the fire had come to rest when she fell off the pipe rack. The fire had been extinguished, and Allbritton was walking away from the scene. Viewing the evidence in the light most favorable to Allbritton, the pump fire did no more than create the condition that made Allbritton's injuries possible. We conclude that the circumstances surrounding her injuries are too remotely connected with Union Pump's conduct or pump to constitute a legal cause of her injuries. See *Lear Siegler*, 819 S.W.2d at 472.

Accordingly, we reverse the judgment of the court of appeals and render judgment that plaintiff take nothing.

Union Pump Co. v. Allbritton generated both a concurring and a dissenting opinion. The concurrence chides the majority for "unnecessarily perpetrating confusion" by "conflat[ing] foreseeability and other policy issues with cause in fact." According to the concurrence, the causation analysis should include two steps. First, one must ask whether the defendant's actions, or the product's defect, was the cause-in-fact of the plaintiff's injury. This "but for" prong is devoid of any policy considerations; the task is simply to determine whether the plaintiff's injury was "philosophically" caused by defendant's negligence. Once this hurdle has been passed, "the court should consider . . . whether the policies or principles at the heart of [the] cause of action dictate a further limitation on liability." While acknowledging that the pump defect was a but-for cause-in-fact of the plaintiff's injury, indeed was a substantial cause of her injury, the concurrence concludes that policy considerations prevent the defect from being a legal cause (898 S.W.2d at 784):

> In this case, the injury to Allbritton was not foreseeable. [Her] injuries were all the result of a needlessly dangerous shortcut taken after the crisis had subsided. Holding Union Pump

> liable for Allbritton's failure to use proper care in exiting the area of the fire after the crisis ended is akin to holding it liable for an auto accident she suffered on the way home, even though the accident probably would not have occurred had she left after her normal shift. Foreseeability allows us to cut off Union Pump's liability at some point; I would do so at the point the crisis had abated or at the point Allbritton and Subia departed from their usual, safe path.

The dissent declares that the defendant is not entitled to summary judgment (898 S.W.2d at 786):

> The record reflects that at the time Sue Allbritton's injury occurred, the forces generated by the fire in question had not come to rest. Rather, the emergency situation was continuing. The whole area of the fire was covered in water and foam; in at least some places, the water was almost knee-deep. Allbritton was still wearing hip boots and other gear, as required to fight the fire. . . .

In Ford Motor Co. v. Ledesma, 242 S.W.3d 32 (Tex. 2007), the court returned to these issues after a products liability defendant challenged the adequacy of jury instructions that had used the same causation language as *Union Pump*:

> To say that a producing cause is "an efficient, exciting, or contributing cause that, in a natural sequence, produces the incident in question" is incomplete and, more importantly, provides little concrete guidance to the jury. Juries must ponder the meaning of "efficient" and "exciting" in this context. These adjectives are foreign to modern English language as a means to describe a cause, and offer little practical help to a jury striving to make the often difficult causation determination in a products case.
>
> Defining producing cause as being a substantial factor in bringing about an injury, and without which the injury would not have occurred, is easily understood and conveys the essential components of producing cause that (1) the cause must be a substantial cause of the event in issue and (2) it must be a but-for cause, namely one without which the event would not have occurred. This is the definition that should be given in the jury charge.

Would this formulation have affected the outcome in *Union Pump*?

Note: Postscript on Causation and Daubert

Expert testimony is crucial in proving causation in many product liability cases, especially in cases involving prescription drugs and toxic products. As discussed in Chapter 2, pp. 125-127, above, the somewhat controversial opinion by the United States Supreme Court in Daubert v. Merrell Dow Pharmaceuticals, Inc., made a significant change in the admissibility of expert testimony by abandoning the traditional requirement that expert opinion be generally accepted in the scientific community and by giving courts more discretion in deciding the issue of admissibility. If the trial judge holds the plaintiff's only evidence of causation inadmissible, the claim will almost certainly be defeated before reaching the jury. Therefore, with admissibility of expert testimony being practically dispositive, one can easily imagine how hotly contested this issue becomes.

Recent decisions demonstrate the importance of experts and *Daubert*. In Rink v. Cheminova, Inc., 400 F.3d 1286 (11th Cir. 2005), plaintiffs brought a class action to recover against a pesticide manufacturer for injuries allegedly caused by a defective pesticide used to combat a medfly infestation in Florida. The plaintiffs' expert relied on an inferential methodology in giving his opinion that the pesticide had become dangerously defective (and thereby capable of causing plaintiffs' injuries) because of unusually high temperatures in the facility in which it was stored. Not only did the expert give his opinion that the defective pesticide caused plaintiffs' injuries, but also the plaintiffs' treating physicians testified to the same effect based on their previous experiences diagnosing similar occurrences. The district court excluded the expert's testimony and entered summary judgment for the manufacturer because the treating physicians' testimony did not suffice, standing alone. The court of appeals affirmed, concluding that the expert's testimony "required the kind of scientifically unsupported 'leap of faith' which is condemned by *Daubert*" (400 F.3d at 1292). See also Carlson v. Bioremedi Therapeutic Sys., Inc., 822 F.3d 194 (5th Cir. 2016) (district court abused its discretion by admitting testimony of defendants' expert and sole testifying witness without *Daubert* scrutiny); Kilpatrick v. Breg, Inc., 613 F.3d 1329 (11th Cir. 2010) (expert testimony that pain pump caused injury properly excluded based on unreliable use of differential diagnosis methodology); Watson v. Ford Motor Co., 699 S.E.2d 169 (S.C. 2010) (trial court erred in admitting expert testimony that electromagnetic interference caused vehicle cruise control system to malfunction; expert's general expertise on electricity and wiring insufficient to inform judgment regarding the specific cause of the accident and the feasibility of an alternative design).

One notable decision resisting the trend toward exceedingly stringent gatekeeping of experts is Milward v. Acuity Specialty Products Group, Inc., 639 F.3d 11 (1st Cir. 2011). In that case, plaintiff worker and his spouse sought to demonstrate that his rare form of leukemia was caused by routine workplace exposure to benzene-containing products manufactured by defendant. The trial court ruled plaintiffs' general causation expert inadmissible under *Daubert*. The First Circuit panel reversed, holding that the trial court abused its discretion by refusing to consider the expert's "'weight of the evidence' methodology in which he considered five lines of evidence drawn from the peer-reviewed scientific literature on leukemia and benzene." Id. at 16. Instead, the trial court had examined the lines of evidence separately, deeming each unreliable individually without ever considering their cumulative impact. For contrasting academic views of the *Milward* opinion decision, compare David Bernstein, The Misbegotten Judicial Resistance to the Daubert Revolution, 89 Notre Dame L. Rev. 27, 62-67 (2013), and Aaron D. Twerski and Lior Sapir, Sufficiency of the Evidence Does Not Meet *Daubert* Standards: A Critique of the Green-Sanders Proposal, 23 Widener L.J. 641, 660 (2014) (both critiquing "weight of the evidence" methodology), with Michael D. Green, Pessimism About *Milward,* 3 Wake. Forest J.L. & Pol'y 41 (2013) (offering a spirited defense).

It should be noted that even if the trial judge admits expert testimony, the judge may still decide, upon hearing all of the evidence, that the plaintiff has not met the burden to reach the jury. In Meister v. Medical Engineering Corp., 267 F.3d 1123 (D.C. Cir. 2001), the plaintiff alleged that breast implants manufactured by the defendant caused her to suffer from scleroderma, a serious skin disease. The trial judge allowed the testimony of the plaintiff's two experts on the relationship between silicone and scleroderma. After the defendant introduced significant evidence to contradict the plaintiff's experts, the jury found for the plaintiff. The trial judge, however, granted the defendants' renewed motion for judgment as a matter of law and entered judgment for the defendants, which was upheld on appeal. Despite the testimony of the plaintiff's experts, the evidence, according to both the trial and appellate courts, was insufficient to support a finding for the plaintiff.

The difficulties that plaintiffs encounter with *Daubert* and its judicial followers have prompted sharp academic responses. See, e.g., Julie A. Seaman, A Tale of Two *Dauberts*,

47 Ga. L. Rev. 889 (2013); Margaret A. Berger & Aaron D. Twerski, Uncertainty and Informed Choice: Unmasking *Daubert*, 104 Mich. L. Rev. 257 (2005).

3. Affirmative Defenses Based on Plaintiff's Conduct

To the extent that the plaintiff relies on traditional negligence principles in a products liability case, presumably the plaintiff will be barred from recovery, or recovery will be reduced, if the trier of fact finds the plaintiff to have been contributorily negligent. When the plaintiff relies on the theories of implied warranty or strict liability in tort, however, the way to recovery may be made easier in this regard. The Restatement (Second) position is stated in the following comment to §402A:

> *n. Contributory negligence.* Since the liability with which this Section deals is not based upon negligence of the seller, but is strict liability, the rule applied to strict liability cases applies. Contributory negligence of the plaintiff is not a defense when such negligence consists merely in a failure to discover the defect in the product, or to guard against the possibility of its existence. On the other hand the form of contributory negligence which consists in voluntarily and unreasonably proceeding to encounter a known danger, and commonly passes under the name of assumption of risk, is a defense under this Section as in other cases of strict liability. If the user or consumer discovers the defect and is aware of the danger, and nevertheless proceeds unreasonably to make use of the product and is injured by it, he is barred from recovery.

In Haglund v. Phillip Morris, Inc., 847 N.E.2d 315 (Mass. 2006), a widow brought a wrongful death action against a cigarette manufacturer based on allegations that the cigarettes could have been designed to be non-addictive, thereby allowing her husband to quit smoking. The defendant argued in defense that the plaintiff's decision to begin and continue smoking, with knowledge of the risks, was an "unreasonable use," and thus barred recovery. The trial court denied the plaintiff's motion to preclude the defense and, after the plaintiff stipulated that her husband knew the risks and acted unreasonably, denied the plaintiff's claim as a matter of law. The Supreme Court of Massachusetts affirmed the denial of plaintiff's motion to preclude, but reversed the dismissal of the action, concluding (847 N.E.2d at 319-20):

> [The unreasonable use] defense presumes that the product at issue is, in normal circumstances, reasonably safe and capable of being reasonably safely used, and therefore that the consumer's unreasonable use of the product he knows to be defective and dangerous is appropriately penalized. Here, however, both Phillip Morris and the plaintiff agree that cigarette smoking is inherently dangerous and that there is no such thing as a safe cigarette. Because no cigarette can be safely used for its ordinary purpose, smoking, there can be no nonunreasonable use of cigarettes. Thus the [unreasonable use] defense, which serves to deter unreasonable use of products in a dangerous and defective state, will, in the usual course, be inapplicable.
>
> However, we also agree with Phillip Morris that, in certain conceivable scenarios, an individual consumer's behavior may be so overwhelmingly unreasonable in light of the consumer's knowledge about, for example, a specific medical condition from which he suffers, that the unreasonable use defense may be invoked. The jury determine unreasonable use from the specific factual context of each case, and we are loath to foreclose assertion of the defense as a matter of law in every cigarette-related product liability action.

> Because the plaintiff's motion for summary judgment . . . was brought early in the litigation, we reverse the judgment of dismissal to afford the parties the opportunity to develop more fully the evidence supporting their claims and defenses. . . .

The Restatement (Third) ducks these issues by referring to the plaintiff's conduct failing to conform "to generally applicable rules establishing appropriate standards of care" and to "generally applicable rules apportioning responsibility." See §17.

Murray v. Fairbanks Morse

610 F.2d 149 (3d Cir. 1979)

ROSENN, CIR. J. This appeal raises several issues, including novel and important questions as to whether a comparative negligence statute may be applied and, if so, to what extent, in an action for personal injuries brought under twin theories of strict products liability and common law principles of negligence. The jury returned a verdict in favor of the plaintiff, Norwilton Murray, in the sum of two million dollars against the manufacturer, Beloit Power Systems, Inc. (Beloit). The jury, in response to special interrogatories, found that plaintiff's negligence was a proximate cause of his injuries and that he was at fault to the extent of five percent. The trial judge reduced the verdict accordingly and judgment was thereupon entered for the plaintiff. Beloit's motion for a new trial was denied and it appealed. . . .

I

At the time of the accident, Norwilton Murray, a thirty-four year old experienced instrument fitter, was employed by Litwin Corporation, an installer of equipment. On July 21, 1974, Murray and a co-worker were installing an electrical control panel at the Hess Oil Refinery in the Virgin Islands. The panel was built by Beloit to Litwin's specifications and Litwin's engineer approved it at Beloit's factory before it was shipped. Litwin intended to install the panel on a platform over an open space approximately ten feet above the concrete floor of the refinery. There was evidence, however, that Beloit had not been so informed. At Litwin's request the unit had been purposely left open at the bottom so that conduits from below could be attached to it. The control panel was removed from its shipping crate and a cherry-picker hoisted it by its metal lifting eyes onto the platform. In order to protect the integrity of the delicate instrumentation inside the panel, Beloit had attached two iron cross-members to the open bottom of the unit to stabilize it during shipping. Murray's task was to align the holes in the base of the control panel with predrilled holes in the platform and secure the unit with mounting bolts. Because the holes were not perfectly aligned when the cherry-picker deposited the unit on the foundation, Murray chose to use a crow-bar to rock the approximately one and a half ton unit into alignment.

The accident occurred when Murray put his weight on one of the iron cross-members by leaning over the open space at the bottom of the unit to bolt it to the platform. The cross-member gave way and Murray fell approximately ten feet to the concrete floor incurring severe injuries to his spine. It was determined at trial that the cross-member gave way because it had been only temporarily or "tack-welded" to the unit, instead of being secured by a permanent or "butt-weld." . . .

Murray brought a products liability action against Beloit alleging alternative theories of strict liability under Restatement (Second) of Torts §402A and common law negligence. He contended that the control panel was defective because the cross-member had been only tack-welded to the unit. Beloit defended with expert evidence to prove that Murray's method of installation was highly dangerous and Beloit argued that Murray assumed the risk of injury posed by his manner of installation. The district court, holding that the Virgin Islands comparative negligence statute, 5 V.I.C. §1451 (1978) was applicable to a strict products liability action, instructed the jury that if they found Beloit liable and Murray negligent, to reduce Murray's award by the percentage attributable to his fault.

The jury returned a verdict finding Beloit liable under both the strict products liability and the negligence counts. The jury also found Murray's negligence in installing the unit to constitute five percent fault for the injuries. The jury awarded Murray $2,000,000 in damages. This sum, when reduced by the five percent fault attributable to Murray and the reduction to present value of his future earnings, amounted to $1,747,000. Although noting that the verdict was very high, the district court denied defendant's motion for a new trial.

[The court's discussion of preliminary issues is omitted.]

III

We now turn to the claims of both parties that damages were improperly apportioned. Murray has cross-appealed and we shall first consider whether his award should have been reduced by the five percent fault attributed to his negligence in causing his injuries. We must determine whether the district court was correct in applying the Virgin Islands comparative negligence statute, 5 V.I.C. §1451 in a strict products liability action. . . .

In the present case, Beloit requested a jury instruction that Murray's voluntary assumption of risk would constitute a complete bar to recovery. Murray, on the other hand, requested an instruction that ordinary contributory negligence was not a defense to a section 402A action. The district court declined to issue either instruction and instead, applying the Virgin Islands comparative negligence statute, instructed the jury that they could reduce any award for Murray by whatever fault they ascribed to his negligence in causing the accident. Judge Young later explained his position:

> The Court is of the opinion that neither of the positions advanced by the parties should govern the law of strict products liability in the Virgin Islands, but that both plaintiff's want of ordinary due care in his use of the product and plaintiff's unreasonable exposure to a known and appreciable risk of injury should work to diminish plaintiff's recovery in a §402A type action in proportion to the amount of causative culpable conduct attributable to plaintiff. The mere failure of plaintiff to discover or guard against the existence of a defect where plaintiff had no reason to suspect the same would not constitute a defense in a §402A type action.

Murray v. Beloit Power Systems, Inc., 450 F. Supp. 1145, 1147 (D.V.I. 1978) (footnote omitted). . . .

IV

We are faced with an initial problem not fully considered by the district court. As indicated above, comparative negligence has been adopted by statute in the Virgin Islands, 5 V.I.C.

§1451. The statute provides that contributory negligence is replaced by comparative negligence "[i]n any action based upon *negligence* to recover for injury to person or property. . . ." 5 V.I.C. §1451(a) (emphasis supplied). . . .

In applying the Virgin Islands comparative negligence statute to this suit, the district court expressly adopted the "position and policy considerations advanced by the Wisconsin Supreme Court in Powers v. Hunt-Wesson Foods, Inc., 64 Wis. 2d 532, 219 N.W.2d 393 (1974), and Dippel v. Sciano, 37 Wis. 2d 443, 155 N.W.2d 55 (1967)." 450 F. Supp. at 1147. The *Dippel* case was the first decision to apply a comparative negligence statute to a strict products liability action. . . . The Wisconsin approach is to view the strict products liability action as "akin to negligence per se" and therefore within the purview of the comparative negligence statute. 155 N.W.2d at 64. By adopting the Wisconsin approach, the district court justified the application of the Virgin Islands comparative negligence statute, arguably limited to negligence actions, to strict products liability.

We disagree with the district court's adoption of Wisconsin's gloss on section 402A actions as negligence per se. The Restatement makes it quite clear that strict liability is imposed on the defendant even if he has exercised "all possible care in the preparation and sale of his products." Restatement (Second) of Torts §402A(2)(a). The focus of the strict products liability action is on the condition of the product and not on the conduct of the defendant. . . . The advantage of strict products liability theory is that the plaintiff need only prove the existence of a product defect and not that negligence caused it. The problem is that products liability cases are often tried on alternative theories of negligence and strict liability and the temptation to view strict liability as a species of presumptive negligence is inviting. We decline any such invitation because we believe that a satisfactory union of strict liability and comparative negligence principles cannot be conceptually achieved by converting an action predicated upon a product defect into a hybrid action adulterated by proof of personal misconduct. . . .

V

We agree with the district court that the use of comparative principles in section 402A actions can achieve a more equitable allocation of the loss from product related injuries. We are mindful, however, of the current conceptual confusion among the courts, and the difficulties confronting us in comparing plaintiff's personal conduct with the strict liability of the defendant for his product defect. . . .

The elimination of the need to prove defendant's negligence has led some to view strict products liability as a "no-fault" doctrine to which the application of comparative negligence principles is simply not conceptually feasible. According to Dean Wade, however, fault is still present in strict products liability cases despite the focus on the product defect:

> In the case of products liability, the fault inheres primarily in the nature of the product. The product is "bad" because it is not duly safe; it is determined to be defective and (in most jurisdictions) unreasonably dangerous. . . . [S]imply maintaining the bad condition or placing the bad product on the market is enough for liability. . . . One does not have to stigmatize conduct as negligent in order to characterize it as fault.

Wade, [Products Liability and Plaintiff's Fault, 29 Mercer L. Rev. 373, 377 (1978)] (footnotes omitted). Dean Aaron Twerski adds perspective on the relationship between defect and fault: "In this imperfect world it is not an outrageous inference that a bad defect most probably stems from serious fault — even if the fault need not nor cannot be established." Twerski, From Defect to Cause to Comparative Fault — Rethinking Some Product Liability Concepts, 60 Marq. L. Rev. 297, 331 (1977).

The substitution of the term fault for defect, however, would not appear to aid the trier of fact in apportioning damages between the defect and the conduct of the plaintiff. The key conceptual distinction between strict liability theory and negligence is that the plaintiff need not prove faulty *conduct* on the part of the defendant in order to recover. The jury is not asked to determine if the defendant deviated from a standard of care in producing his product. There is no proven faulty conduct of the defendant to compare with the faulty conduct of the plaintiff in order to apportion the responsibility for an accident. Although we may term a defective product "faulty," it is qualitatively different from the plaintiff's conduct that contributes to his injury. A comparison of the two is therefore inappropriate. The characterization of both plaintiff's negligent conduct and the defect as faulty may provide a semantic bridge between negligence and strict liability theories, but it provides neither a conceptual nor pragmatic basis for apportioning the loss for a particular injury.

We believe that if the loss for a particular injury is to be apportioned between the product defect and the plaintiff's misconduct, the only conceptual basis for comparison is the causative contribution of each to the particular loss or injury. In apportioning damages we are really asking how much of the injury was caused by the defect in the product versus how much was caused by the plaintiff's own actions. We agree with the Ninth Circuit when it noted that comparative causation "is a conceptually more precise term than 'comparative fault' since fault alone without causation does not subject one to liability." Pan-Alaska Fisheries, Inc. v. Marine Construction & Design Co., 565 F.2d 1129, 1139 (9th Cir. 1977). The appropriate label for the quality of the act is insignificant. . . . Thus, the underlying task in each case is to analyze and compare the causal conduct of each party regardless of its label. Although fault, in the sense of the defendant's defective product or the plaintiff's failure to meet a standard of care, must exist before a comparison takes place,[12] the comparison itself must focus on the role each played in bringing about the particular injury. . . .

The relevant causation inquiry in a strict products liability suit should be whether the product defect "caused-in-fact" some or all of the injury and whether the plaintiff's faulty conduct "caused-in-fact" all or some of the injury. If the answer to both these questions is affirmative, the issue of proximate cause becomes relevant. Were there any intervening causes or unforeseeable consequences which would absolve the defendant of liability for the defect or the plaintiff for his conduct? It is conceivable that in any given accident, both the product defect and the plaintiff's conduct may be substantial factors in bringing about the injury. Under a comparative causation approach, once the jury has determined that the product defect caused the injury, the defendant is strictly liable for the harm caused by his defective product. The jury, however, would be instructed to reduce the award of damages "in proportion to the plaintiff's contribution to his own loss or injury." *Pan-Alaska Fisheries,* supra, 565 F.2d at 1139.

The use of causation as the conceptual bridge between the plaintiff's conduct and the defendant's product in no way jeopardizes the conceptual integrity of the strict products liability action. The focus is still on the product defect. Semantically, apportioning damages in strict products liability cases may be termed a system of "comparative

12. We believe the initial determination of fault is necessary to avoid situations in which conduct that is reasonable on the part of the plaintiff might contribute causally to an injury and the plaintiff would accordingly bear part of the loss. Only when conduct fails to meet a societal standard of reasonable care should the casual link between conduct and injury be examined.

fault" but the real division occurs along lines of causation.[13] However, "because the term 'comparative fault' appears to be commonly accepted and used," id., we shall use that label to represent a system of apportioning damages in strict products liability cases. . . .

VI

Once a conceptually viable way of apportioning damages in section 402A actions is established, the key inquiry is whether such a system is consistent with the policy goals of strict product liability. As we have indicated already, a central goal of the strict liability action is to relieve the plaintiff of proof problems associated with existing negligence and warranty theories. A system of comparative fault which proceeds to apportion damages on the basis of causation in no way disturbs the plaintiff's burden of proof. The plaintiff still need only prove the existence of a defect causally linked to the injury. The defendant's burden is to prove plaintiff's contributory fault. . . .

The recognition of contributory fault as an absolute bar to recovery would improperly shift the total loss to the plaintiff. Under a system of comparative fault, however, there are good reasons for allowing some form of contributory fault to be considered in reducing damages. When plaintiff's conduct is faulty, i.e., he exposes himself to an unreasonable risk of harm which causes part of his injuries, the manufacturer should not be required to pay that portion of the loss attributable to the plaintiff's fault. Under a comparative system, the future cost of the defendant's product will accurately represent the danger it has caused and not the danger caused by plaintiff's own fault.[14]

[The court left unresolved the question of whether to apply comparative fault to assumption of the risk and product misuse.]

VII

The foregoing analysis leads us to conclude that a system of comparative fault may effectively operate in strict products liability cases and will result in a more equitable apportionment of the loss for product related injuries while furthering the valid policy goals behind the strict products liability action. We accordingly hold that a system of pure comparative fault should be applied to Restatement §402A actions in the Virgin Islands.

13. Indeed, this appears to be the thrust of the new Proposed Uniform Comparative Fault Act. Under this proposed model act, strict liability is included definitionally within the scope of the term "fault." Uniform Comparative Fault Act §1(b). This is accomplished by attributing fault to the defectiveness of the product. See Wade, supra, 29 Mercer L. Rev. at 377. However, the Uniform Act recognizes that "[l]egal requirements of causal relation apply both to fault as the basis for liability and to contributory fault." Uniform Comparative Fault Act §1(b). In determining the percentages of fault attributed to each part, the Uniform Act states that "the trier of fact shall consider both the nature of the conduct and the damages claimed." Id. §2(b).

14. There is a legitimate concern, however, that if contributory negligence, in the sense of failing to discover the product defect, is recognized as a category of plaintiff's fault, almost every case of products liability will be open to loss apportionment through protracted litigation. Defendants will always argue that the plaintiff negligently failed to find the defect. Such a defense might intrude on another goal of strict products liability, that of discouraging the introduction of obviously defective products into the stream of commerce. If the plaintiff can be held responsible for not discovering the defect, there is an incentive to make defects obvious and not eliminate them from products. But when the plaintiff is contributorily at fault, in the sense of exposing himself to an unreasonable risk of harm in the use of the product, such conduct is to be considered plaintiff's legal fault, thereby triggering the comparative causation analysis. This view is consistent with the position adopted by Judge Young in his memorandum opinion in the instant case. 450 F. Supp. at 1147.

Under this system, fault is ascribed to the defendant once his product is found to be defective. If fault on the part of the plaintiff is also present, the trier of fact shall reduce the damage award in proportion to the plaintiff's causal contribution to his own injury. Under our holding, the plaintiff shall not be barred from recovery even if his fault is determined to be greater than that of the defendant.

The task before us now is to determine what effect our holding has on the apportionment of the loss for Murray's injuries. . . .

Our review of the record reveals that Beloit introduced expert testimony to prove that Murray's method of installation was highly dangerous. Beloit's expert testified that Murray could have taken safety measures to avoid or minimize the risk of a fall. . . .

Balanced against this evidence was testimony from Murray's supervisor and co-worker that the method used to install the unit was commonly employed without difficulty. Murray's supervisor testified that over an eighteen-year period he had installed approximately 400 units in this fashion. . . .

We cannot say as a matter of law that the jury's assessment of five percent fault to Murray under the strict liability count was against the weight of the evidence. . . .

Because we perceive no error in the district court's judgment under either the strict products liability or negligence counts, the judgment of the district court is affirmed. . . .

The problem addressed in *Murray* is often referred to as the "apples and oranges" problem: Can the "apples" of strict liability be compared to the "oranges" of plaintiff negligence? The court thought that the two theories of liability are so different that "conceptually" the comparison could not be made. The court did think it came up with a solution to the problem: comparative causation. Another solution is that contained in §8 of the Restatement (Third) of Torts: Apportionment of Liability (2000):

> §8. Factors for Assigning Shares of Responsibility
>
> Factors for assigning percentages of responsibility to each person whose legal responsibility has been established include
>
> (a) the nature of the person's risk-creating conduct, including any awareness of indifference with respect to the risks created by the conduct and any intent with respect to the harm created by the conduct; and
>
> (b) the strength of the causal connection between the person's risk-creating conduct and the harm.

Comment *a* to this section is skeptical whether any comparison based on culpability can be made: "'Assigning shares of culpability' could be misleading if it were not made clear that 'culpability' refers to 'legal culpability,' which may include strict liability." While the Restatement admits that it is not possible to make a precise comparison between conduct that is negligent and conduct that carries strict liability, it relies on the phrase "assigning shares of responsibility," which it believes is "a less confusing phrase because it suggests that the fact finder, after considering the relevant factors, *assigns* shares of responsibility rather than *compares* incommensurate quantities." Even so, the drafters use the phrase "comparative responsibility" (the title to Topic I of this Restatement is "Basic Rules of Comparative Responsibility") because of its widespread acceptance by courts.

Quite apart from whether courts will make fault comparisons in these cases, recovery will in any event be barred if causation is not established. Thus, in Control Techniques, Inc. v. Johnson, 762 N.E.2d 104 (Ind. 2002), the plaintiff brought suit against the manufacturer and installer of a circuit breaker after he was badly burned while testing it. At trial, the jury awarded the plaintiff $2 million, and assigned 80 percent of the fault to the company that installed the breaker, 15 percent to the plaintiff, and 5 percent to the manufacturer. In affirming the verdict against the manufacturer, the Indiana Supreme Court considered the relationship between Indiana's Comparative Fault Act and proximate cause (762 N.E.2d at 109):

> Under the Comparative Fault Act, liability is to be apportioned among persons whose fault caused or contributed to causing the loss in proportion to their percentages of "fault" as found by the jury. As a result, the jury is first required to decide whether an actor's negligence was a proximate cause of the plaintiff's injury. To say there is a "superseding cause" foreclosing one actor's liability is to say that the superseding event was not reasonably foreseeable to that actor. This is simply another way of saying, in comparative fault terms, that the original actor did not cause the harm and receives zero share of any liability.

Thus, when a break in proximate causation occurs, even a highly culpable defendant is off the hook completely.

An interesting aspect of comparative fault/causation analysis in products cases involves the question of its applicability when the product defect consists of a failure of a product design to save the plaintiff from injury if and when the user negligently causes an accident while using the product. Cf. Restatement (Third) of Torts: Products Liability §16 cmt. *f* and Reporters' Note (1998) (documenting split of authority on this issue). Thus, in Alami v. Volkswagen of Am., Inc., 766 N.E.2d 574 (N.Y. 2002), the plaintiff brought an action for the enhanced injuries caused to her husband when the floorboard in his Volkswagen Jetta improperly buckled upon impacting a steel utility pole, despite the fact that her husband's drunkenness caused him to drive off the road and into the pole. The trial court and intermediate appellate court granted summary judgment for the defendant. The New York high court reversed and remanded for trial. The court reasoned that if the defendant breached its duty to protect the driver in the event of a crash, the initial cause of the accident should neither preclude nor diminish liability. The court concluded that "[p]laintiff . . . asks only that Volkswagen honor its well-recognized duty to produce a product that does not unreasonably enhance or aggravate a user's injuries." 766 N.E.2d at 577. In Jahn v. Hyundai Motor Co., 773 N.W.2d 550 (Iowa 2009), the court thoroughly reviewed the case law on this issue and determined that the *Alami* approach is a minority view. In support of applying comparative fault principles, the court noted that "it would be unfair to impose costs of substandard plaintiff conduct on manufacturers, who would presumably pass on some or all of those costs to users and consumers, including those who use and consume products safely and wisely." Id. at 554-55. See also Wolf v. Toyota Motor Co., 2013 WL6596833 at *9 (Del. Sup. Ct. 2013) (also surveying jurisdictions like *Jahn* and determining that "[t]he majority rule approach is the better reasoned approach: manufacturer defendants in a 'crashworthiness' claim may file a third-party complaint against original tortfeasor to allow for proper allocation of fault and to present a more complete account of the accident to the jury").

Scholarly treatment of the subject of comparative fault and its applicability to products litigation has been extensive. See, e.g., Richard W. Wright, The Logic and Fairness of Joint and Several Liability, 23 Memphis St. U. L. Rev. 45 (1992); Mary J. Davis, Individual and Institutional Responsibility: A Vision for Comparative Fault in Products Liability, 39 Vill. L.

Rev. 281 (1994); Scott Giesler, Comment, The Uncertain Future of Assumption of Risk in California, 28 Loy. L.A. L. Rev. 1495 (1995); Mark M. Hager, What's (Not!) in a Restatement? ALI Issue-Dodging on Liability Apportionment, 33 Conn. L. Rev. 77 (2000); David G. Owen, Products Liability: User Misconduct Defenses, 52 S.C. L. Rev. 1 (2000).

B. Liability for Defective Product Designs

Cases involving allegedly defective product designs play a significant role in products liability litigation. Until the late 1960s and early 1970s, when something of an explosion in product design litigation occurred, claims based on defective design succeeded only in two limited categories of cases. The first of these might be called *flawed design* cases. If the plaintiff could show that the design caused the product to fail to perform its intended function—if the design was self-defeating in a dangerous way so as to cause injury—courts would treat the design defect the same as if it were a manufacturing defect. Indeed, given the functional similarities between manufacturing defects and these types of inadvertent design errors, it is often difficult to tell from reading the earlier decisions whether the defect was a manufacturing defect or a bad design. Thus, in the California decision in Greenman v. Yuba Power Products, Inc., p. 528, above, the defect that caused the plaintiff's injuries was a loose set screw on a home power lathe which allowed a piece of wood to fly out of the machine and strike the plaintiff. It is not clear from the opinion whether the wrong screw had been mistakenly installed in the particular machine used by the plaintiff, in which case the particular power tool had a manufacturing defect, or whether the screw was the one called for in the tool's specifications, in which case the power tool had a defective design. Either way, the tool was unreasonably dangerous because of the self-defeating characteristic of the inadequate set screw, and the court had no trouble in concluding that it could be found to be defective.

The Restatement (Third) recognizes the functional interchangeability of manufacturing defect and defective design in the context of product malfunction. Thus, Comment *b* to §3, the "res ipsa" section that allows an inference of defect from the fact that the product failed to perform its manifestly intended function (see p. 535, above), contains the following observations:

> Although the rules in this Section . . . most often apply to manufacturing defects, occasionally a product design causes the product to malfunction in a manner identical to that which would ordinarily be caused by a manufacturing defect. Thus, an aircraft may inadvertently be designed in such a way that, in new condition and while flying within its intended performance parameters, the wings suddenly and unexpectedly fall off, causing harm. In theory, of course, the plaintiff in such a case would be able to show how other units in the same production line were designed, leading to a showing of a reasonable alternative design under §2(b). As a practical matter, however, when the incident involving the aircraft is one that ordinarily occurs as a result of product defect, and evidence in the particular case establishes that the harm was not solely the result of causes other than product defect existing at time of sale, it should not be necessary for the plaintiff to incur the cost of proving whether the failure resulted from a manufacturing defect or from a defect in the design of the product. Section 3 allows the trier of fact to draw the inference that the product was defective whether due to a manufacturing defect or a design defect. Under those circumstances, the plaintiff need not specify the type of defect responsible for the product malfunction.

In earlier cases, when the product designs were not self-defeating in the just-described way, plaintiffs had a more difficult time convincing courts to condemn them as defective. Thus, if the power lathe in the *Greenman* case had functioned exactly as the designer had intended, and if the plaintiff had been injured when he caught his fingers in the drive belt connecting the motor to the spindle, it is not clear that a court 40 or 50 years ago would have imposed liability on the manufacturer. The plaintiff could have argued that the belt should have been shielded in some manner. But earlier courts might have been disposed to blame the accident on the carelessness of the plaintiff-user in failing to cope with an obvious risk, rather than on any shortcomings in the lathe's design. Indeed, in a leading case close in its facts to the power lathe hypothetical, the New York Court of Appeals established the general rule that there would be no liability for injuries caused by an obvious risk created by a product's design. See Campo v. Scofield, 95 N.E.2d 802 (N.Y. 1950). This rule, which came to be known as the *patent danger rule,* effectively insulated manufacturers from most of the risks presented by their conscious design choices, such as the decision in the hypothetical not to put a guard on the drive belt of the power lathe.

The second basic category of cases in which courts have traditionally imposed liability for defective designs are *express warranty cases,* where the seller had expressly warranted that the product would perform safely and not cause injuries of the sort suffered by the plaintiff. Thus, in the hypothetical case involving the power lathe, the injured plaintiff would have had a better chance of recovery if the manufacturer had promised that "your hand cannot get caught in the belt."

One of the best known express warranty decisions from this earlier era is Baxter v. Ford Motor Co., 12 P.2d 409 (Wash. 1932), in which the defendant car manufacturer advertised that the windshields in its new cars would not shatter "under the hardest impact." The plaintiff was injured when a rock struck his windshield and shattered the glass, blinding him in one eye. The court permitted recovery on the basis of express warranty, even though the plaintiff was not in privity with the defendant manufacturer. Express warranty is today available to an injured plaintiff whenever the injury-causing feature of the design fails to measure up to promises of safety made by the defendant. See, e.g., Forbes v. General Motors Corp., 935 So. 2d 869 (Miss. 2006), in which the plaintiff sustained serious injuries when the front end of her car struck another vehicle. Although the collision was severe enough to damage her car, the air bag did not deploy. The trial court directed a verdict for the defendant. The Supreme Court of Mississippi reversed and remanded, holding that a jury could find that the manufacturer breached an express warranty in the owner's manual that stated that if a front-end collision was "hard enough," the air bag would deploy.

The general rule governing express warranties is set out in the Uniform Commercial Code as follows:

§2-313. Express Warranties by Affirmation, Promise, Description, Sample

(1) Express warranties by the seller are created as follows:

(a) Any affirmation of fact or promise made by the seller to the buyer which relates to the goods and becomes part of the basis of the bargain creates an express warranty that the goods shall conform to the affirmation or promise.

(b) Any description of the goods which is made part of the basis of the bargain creates an express warranty that the goods shall conform to the description.

> (c) Any sample or model which is made part of the basis of the bargain creates an express warranty that the whole of the goods shall conform to the sample or model.
>
> (2) It is not necessary to the creation of an express warranty that the seller use formal words such as "warrant" or "guarantee" or that he have a specific intention to make a warranty, but an affirmation merely of the value of the goods or a statement purporting to be merely the seller's opinion or commendation of the goods does not create a warranty.

It will be observed that §2-313 does not require that the plaintiff rely on the express warranty, but only that the warranty "become part of the basis of the bargain." This has been interpreted to require that the warranties be made in reasonable proximity, in time and space, to the sale. Consistent with the holding in *Baxter,* there is no requirement that the plaintiff be in privity of contract with the defendant.

McCormack v. Hankscraft Co.

278 Minn. 322, 154 N.W.2d 488 (1967)

ROGOSHESKE, JUSTICE. Plaintiff appeals from the judgment entered upon an order of the district court granting judgment n.o.v. and a conditional new trial in favor of defendant, Hankscraft Company, Inc. . . .

Viewing, as we must, the evidence and all permissible inferences most favorably to the sustaining of the verdict, the jury reasonably could have found the following facts.

In October 1957, Andrea's father, Donald McCormack, purchased from a retail drugstore an electric Hankscraft steam vaporizer manufactured by defendant. It was purchased pursuant to the advice of a doctor to be used as a humidifier for Andrea, then 8 months old, who had just returned from being hospitalized for croup and pneumonia. After unpacking the vaporizer, Andrea's parents read the instruction booklet accompanying the unit from "cover to cover." Then, following defendant's printed instructions, they put the vaporizer to use in the treatment of Andrea. Thereafter, from time to time as the need arose, it was used for the young children of the family in the prescribed manner, including the use of it unattended throughout the night, without any problem. . . .

In the spring of 1960, the children had colds and Mrs. McCormack desired to use the vaporizer but found it "wasn't working." She went to the same self-service drugstore and purchased another Hankscraft vaporizer similar to the first unit. She personally selected it without the aid or recommendation of any clerk because it was a Hankscraft, knowing defendant to be a manufacturer of a number of products for children and relying upon defendant's prior representations contained in the booklet accompanying the first vaporizer that its vaporizers were "safe" and "practically foolproof," as well as advertisements representing them to be "tip-proof." This second vaporizer, purchased in a sealed carton, was known as Model 202A, and its general appearance as to size and shape and its method of operation were identical with the first unit. It was accompanied by an instruction booklet substantially identical to that furnished with the first vaporizer, which Mrs. McCormack again completely read.

This second vaporizer had been used about a half dozen times without incident when, on November 20, 1960, it was again set up for use in a small bedroom in the northwest corner of the house, occupied by Andrea, then 3 years and 9 months old, and her baby sister, Alison, 1 year and 10 months old. Andrea slept in a regular single bed and Alison in a crib. To the east of the doorway of this bedroom is an adjoining bathroom, which Andrea frequently used during the night. The doors of the bedrooms and bathroom were habitually left open and a light was usually burning in the bathroom. Andrea's bed was located in what might be described as the southwest corner of the room with the headboard against the doorway wall. The crib was in the northeast corner. A chifforobe stood next to the crib against the north wall. Andrea's mother set up the vaporizer at about 8 p.m. on a seat-step-type metal kitchen stool about 2 1/2 feet high. She placed the stool in front of and against the chifforobe. The electric cord was extended behind the chifforobe and plugged into an outlet located there. The stool was about 4 feet from the foot of Andrea's bed. When steam started coming from the hole in the top of the unit, Mrs. McCormack left the room. After visiting a neighbor until about 11 p.m., she did some ironing, and at about 1:30 a.m., she returned to the room to replenish the water supply in the vaporizer. Using some type of "mitt," she lifted the cap and poured water from a milk bottle into the jar. She then went to bed.

At about 2:30 a.m., Mrs. McCormack heard a terrible scream and got out of bed. She found Andrea lying on the floor of her bedroom, screaming. The metal stool was upright, but the vaporizer was on the floor and the water had come out of the jar. The vaporizer had separated into its three component parts — a glass jar, a metal pan, and a plastic top-heating unit. The electric cord was still plugged into the electric outlet. In some manner, Andrea, while intending to go to the bathroom, had tipped over the vaporizer and caused the water in the jar to spill upon her body.

Andrea was rushed to the hospital for treatment. More than 30 percent of her body had severe burns; she was suffering from shock; and her condition was critical for some time. She had third-degree burns on her chest, shoulders, and back. Skingraft surgery was performed on her twice. She was hospitalized for 74 1/2 days. Ten days later she was admitted to the Kenny Institute for treatment. She remained there 102 days and thereafter was taken to the Mayo Clinic, where she had further surgery in August 1961. At the time of the trial, Andrea had heavy scar tissue on her chest, stomach, legs, arms, and neck; a deformed jaw; restricted movement of her head; an irregular posture; and the prospect of 6 to 12 more surgical procedures during her lifetime. Her condition is largely permanent.

The "automatic-electric" vaporizer in question is of normal design and consists of three component parts — an aluminum pan which serves as a base, a 1-gallon glass jar or water reservoir which is inserted into the pan, and a black plastic cap to which is fastened a black plastic heating-chamber tube.

The glass jar, 6 5/8 inches square and 8 inches high, is a so-called "standard gallon pickle jar" not specially manufactured as a component part. The top opening is 4 1/2 inches in diameter and its outer neck has a male-type glass thread. To fill the jar to a designated fill mark requires .73 gallon of water.

The aluminum pan, which is made to fit the bottom of the jar, is 4 inches high. It has two plastic lifting and carrying handles. Four projections, 3/4 inch in diameter and 1/8 inch in height, are regularly spaced on the bottom of the pan and serve as feet for the unit.

The plastic cap and heating chamber assembly has a dome-like appearance in its upper portion, which is 5 inches in diameter and 2 3/4 inches high. Enclosed in a plastic tube which attaches to the upper portion are two narrow, 8-inch-long steel electrodes which extend from the underside of the cap and are fastened to terminals which connect to an electric plug-in type cord. This cord, about 6 feet long, is attached to the terminals through a hole in the cap. Opposite the electric cord is a round steam hole 3/16 inch in diameter. Directly below this there is moulded into the top a "medicament hollow." The heating chamber tube enclosing the electrodes is about 7 5/8 inches long. It consists of a lower section 5 1/8 inches long, which tapers upward from 1 1/2 inches to 1 7/8 inches in diameter, and an upper section 2 1/2 inches long and 3 inches in diameter. The upper section has a flange 3 3/4 inches in diameter through which three screws are used to fasten both sections to the cap. A hole 1/8 inch in diameter is in the bottom of the lower section through which water in the jar reaches the electrodes. Eight holes 1/4 inch in diameter are in the bottom of the upper section. They are intended to relieve any steam pressure that might build up inside the lower tube or the jar should the steam hole become obstructed and also to guard against "any chance of water spitting out the steam hole." The cap and heating chamber assembly, by its own weight, rests loosely upon the glass jar with the black tube extending down into the jar. There are no threads inside the plastic cap or any other means provided to fasten the cap to the threaded neck of the jar. This design and construction were intended by defendant to serve as a safety measure to avoid any buildup of steam in the glass jar, but it also has the result of allowing the water in the jar to gush out instantaneously when the vaporizer is tipped over. This unit can be tipped over easily by a child through the exertion of about 2 pounds of force.

To operate the vaporizer in accordance with the instructions contained in defendant's booklet, the "entire plastic cover" is removed, the glass jar is filled to the filling market with tap water containing minerals, and the cord is plugged into an electric outlet, whereupon "(t)he vaporizer will produce a gentle cloud of steam within a few minutes." The heating unit is designed so that it automatically turns off whenever the water in the jar decreases to a certain level. As the booklet pictorially illustrates, the water from the jar enters the lower section of the heating chamber through the small hole at the bottom. Here it is heated until it boils and is vaporized into steam, which passes out of the unit through the hole in the cap.

Tests made of the unit established that after about 4 minutes of operation the water in the heating chamber reaches 212 degrees Fahrenheit and steam emanates from the steam port. Although the water in the jar outside the heating chamber does not reach the boiling point, the upper portion of this water does reach 211 degrees within 35 minutes of operation and the middle portion reaches 211 degrees within 3 hours. The temperature of the outside of the jar ranges from 172 degrees after about 1 hour to 182 degrees after 5 hours. Thus, during most of the 6- to 8-hour period in which the unit is designed to operate without refilling, the water in the reservoir is scalding hot, since water of 145-degree temperature will burn and 180-degree water will cause third-degree burns on a child 5 years old.

By touch, a user can determine that the water in the jar outside the heating unit, as well as the jar and the plastic cap, becomes hot during the operation of the vaporizer. However, there is no movement of the water in the jar and no means by which a user could discern by sight or touch that this reserve water in the jar became and remained scalding hot. Plaintiff's parents, relying upon their understanding of what defendant represented in its instruction booklet, were reasonably led to believe up to the time of plaintiff's injury that, since steam was generated only in the heating unit, the temperature of the water in the jar during the entire operation of the vaporizer remained the same as when put in. At all of the times when replenishing the water in either the first or second vaporizer, plaintiff's mother followed the routine of removing the entire plastic cover by using some "glove" or "mitt" as a precaution against the steam. She would leave the cord plugged in, add water to the jar, replace the cover, wait until steam appeared, and then leave the unit unattended in the room. As her testimony implied, she at no time discovered by touching or handling the unit when it was in use that the temperature of any part of the water in the jar became hot.

The instruction booklet furnished by defendant did not disclose the scalding temperatures reached by the water in the jar, nor was any warning given as to the dangers that could result from an accidental upset of the unit. While plaintiff's mother realized that the unit could be tipped over by a sufficient external force, she justifiably relied upon defendant's representations that it was "safe," "practically foolproof," and "tip-proof." She understood this to mean that the unit "was safe to use around (her) children" and that she "didn't have to worry" about dangers when it was left unattended in a child's room since this was the primary purpose for which it was sold.

In its booklet and advertising, defendant in fact made the representations relied upon by plaintiff's mother. In addition to the simple operating instructions and a pictorial "cutaway" indicating how the steam is generated by the electrodes in the heating chamber, the booklet stated:

"WHY THE HANKSCRAFT VAPORIZER IS SUPERIOR TO OTHERS IN DESIGN.

"Your vaporizer will run all night on one filling of water, directing a steady, gentle flow of medicated steam exactly where it is needed. No attention is necessary.

"It's safe, too, and practically foolproof. Since the water itself makes the electric contact, the vaporizer shuts off automatically when the water is gone. The electric unit cannot burn out."

The booklet also had a picture of a vaporizer sending steam over a baby's crib, alongside which was printed:

"For most effective use, the vaporizer should be placed at least four feet away from the person receiving treatment, and should not be placed above the patient's level." . . .

Plaintiff called two expert witnesses, whose qualifications in the field of product design were unquestioned. Both testified that the design of the vaporizer was defective principally in that it failed to provide a means for securing the plastic cover to the jar in a manner which would prevent the water in the jar from instantaneously discharging when the unit was tipped over. In the opinion of both, the unit could be tipped over with little force and this defective design created a risk of bodily harm to a child if the unit were left operating and unattended in the room. This defect could have been eradicated by the adoption of any one of several practical and inexpensive alternative designs which utilized simple and well known techniques to secure the top to the jar. Any of these alternative designs could have been employed by defendant prior to its production of the second vaporizer by the application of sound product-design principles current at that time. Among these alternative designs was that of making threads on the inside of the plastic top so it could screw onto the jar and the putting of two or three small holes in the top, which would take care of any danger that steam would build up inside the jar. Both witnesses stated that such a change in design was essential to make the unit safe for its intended use because the presence of near-boiling water in the jar was not discernible by sight or touch and not warning of the risk of harm was contained in defendant's instruction booklet. . . .

Plaintiff urges that defendant was negligent both in its failure to give any warning of the dangers inherent in the use of the vaporizer and in its adoption of an unsafe design. Plaintiff claims among other things that defendant, in undertaking to instruct as to the use of its vaporizer, violated its duty to use due care when it failed to inform that the water in the jar got scalding hot with temperatures up to 211 degrees Fahrenheit and to warn of the dangers of serious injury if the unit were upset during operation. Defendant concedes it gave no such warning but vigorously argues that a warning was not necessary since the fact that the water in the jar becomes and remains hot should be obvious to any user.

In support of its position, defendant claims that anyone touching the jar or plastic top after the vaporizer had been working for some time would realize they are hot and conclude the water in the jar is also hot, and that because the instructions indicate that steam is produced in the plastic heating chamber, a reader would necessarily conclude the water in the jar is hot since the heating unit obviously comes into direct contact with such water.

Plaintiff, on the other hand, contends that a warning is necessary because the average user would not realize that this water becomes hot, much less that it becomes scalding hot. Plaintiff relies upon the undisputed evidence that there is no boiling activity of the reserve water in the jar and that there is no way short of actual temperature measurements to discern by sight or touch that this water reaches the dangerous temperature of 211 degrees. Further, plaintiff relies upon the evidence that the instructions furnished by defendant served to allay any suspicions a user might otherwise have as to the near-boiling temperature of the water or any apprehension of danger by indicating that the vaporizer was safe to use unattended in a child's room throughout the night. Moreover, both of plaintiff's parents testified that neither had in fact become aware of the temperature of the water nor realized the danger that, if the unit were upset while in use, the water could scald and inflict third-degree burns on a child.

We have little difficulty in reaching the conclusion that the evidence justified the jury in finding that defendant failed to exercise reasonable care to inform users, including plaintiff's parents, of the scalding temperatures of the water and to warn of the dangers reasonably foreseeable in the use of the vaporizer. Surely the evidence does not as a matter of law compel a conclusion that the true nature and gravity of the dangers which could result from the scalding water in the jar were sufficiently obvious to most potential users as to preclude the jury from finding that due care required an appropriate warning. Under the court's instruction, the jury could, and quite likely did, conclude that defendant knew or should have reasonably foreseen that the primary use of its vaporizer involved the danger that a child might be severely burned by the rapid discharge of near-boiling water upon an intentional or accidental upset, and that a substantial number of users would not become aware of the scalding temperature of the water nor realize the potential dangers of using the vaporizer unattended in a child's room unless adequate information and an appropriate warning were given so that parents would take extraordinary precautions. These findings, together with defendant's utter failure to warn, and the finding that the dangers inherent in the vaporizer's use were not obvious and were outside the realm of common knowledge of potential users (especially in view of defendant's representations of safety) are, we hold, supported by the evidence and alone justified the jury's verdict of liability.

We similarly conclude and hold that the evidence is also sufficient to support the jury's verdict of liability on the ground that defendant was negligent in adopting an unsafe design. It is well established that a manufacturer, despite lack of privity of contract, has a duty to use reasonable care in designing its product so that those it should expect will use it are protected from unreasonable risk of harm while the product is being used for its intended use. A breach of such duty renders the manufacturer liable. Clearly, such a duty was owed to plaintiff for defendant admitted that the primary, intended use of the vaporizer was for the treatment of children's colds and croup.

The proof is sufficient to support plaintiff's claim of defective design in that, among other defects, defendant failed to exercise reasonable care in securing the plastic cover to the jar to guard against the reasonably foreseeable danger that a child would tip the unit over when it was in use and be seriously burned by coming in contact with the scalding water that would instantaneously gush out of the jar.

[In a footnote the court concludes that the plaintiff's proof on the tippability issue failed in that there was no showing that the design modifications suggested by the plaintiff's experts would have prevented the vaporizer from tipping in this case.]

To urge that a vaporizer is not a dangerous instrumentality is not persuasive to a reviewing court when the evidence reasonably permits a finding that a simple, practical, inexpensive, alternative design which fastened the top to the jar would have substantially reduced or eliminated the danger which caused plaintiff's injuries. Defendant's experts testified that the design adopted was to guard against an explosion because of a buildup of steam in the heating unit and jar, but the jury could have accepted the testimony of plaintiff's experts which indicated the use of defendant's design was not necessary to accomplish this purpose. Moreover, the fact that at the time the second vaporizer was purchased many other brands of vaporizers on the market were designed in basically this same manner, while certainly relevant, did not necessarily bar the jury from concluding that the exercise of due care required the adoption of a different design.

We also find no merit in defendant's contention that it was not negligent because any defect caused by its failure to secure the heating unit to the jar was obvious. Clearly the jury could have justifiably found that users, particularly children such as plaintiff who was a mere child of 3 years of age, are incapable of meaningfully comprehending the true nature and gravity of the risk to them that results from a product's design and of effectively acting so as to avoid the danger. The jury could have concluded that protection of this class of persons required that defendant in the exercise of due care should have adopted one of the safe alternative designs. While the evidence with respect to this issue required a resolution of the conflicts in the testimony of expert witnesses, the jury was free to adopt the opinions of plaintiff's witnesses and to reach a verdict of liability on this ground of negligence also.

We also conclude that the evidence was sufficient to support a finding of liability upon a breach of an express warranty.

We are persuaded that whether the previously quoted language of the booklet, particularly in combination with the picture of a vaporizer sending steam over a body's crib, amounted to an express warranty that it was "safe" for a user to let this vaporizer run all night in a child's room without attention was a jury question. No particular words are required to constitute an express warranty, and the representations made must be interpreted as an ordinary person would understand their meaning, with any doubts resolved in favor of the user. Since parents instinctively exercise great care to protect their children from harm, the jury could justifiably conclude that defendant's representations were factual (naturally tending to induce a buyer to purchase) and not mere "puffing" or "sales talk." . . .

Reversed with directions to enter judgment upon the verdict.

In Uloth v. City Tank Corp., 384 N.E.2d 1188 (Mass. 1978), the court considered the interactive capabilities of warnings and designs to reduce risk. Plaintiff's foot was amputated when he caught it in a pincer between the blade and compaction chamber of a garbage truck on which he was working. Plaintiff claimed that he jumped on the back step of the garbage truck as it was moving from one stop to the next. In the process he lost his balance and his left foot went toward the loading sill of the garbage compaction chamber. When the blade meets the loading sill it creates a shear point, with the blade and sill acting like scissors. The descending panel caught the plaintiff's foot and dragged it into the trash hopper, severing it from his leg.

The defendant argued that the simple and obvious scissor-like quality of the machine was itself a totally adequate warning of the dangers of the garbage truck. Plaintiff argued that a design alternative such as a stop-bar, an interrupted cycle, or a "dead-man control" would have reduced the danger of a shear point accident. Affirming judgment for plaintiff, the Massachusetts high court rejected the defendant's warning argument:

> An adequate warning may reduce the likelihood of injury to the user of a product in some cases. We decline, however, to adopt any rule which permits a manufacturer or designer to discharge its total responsibility to workers by simply warning of the dangers of a product. Whether or not adequate warnings are given is a factor to be considered on the issue of negligence, but warnings cannot absolve the manufacturer or designer of all responsibility for the safety of the product. . . .
>
> [A] warning is not effective in eliminating injuries due to instinctual reactions, momentary inadvertence, or forgetfulness on the part of a worker. One of the primary purposes of safety devices is to guard against such foreseeable situations.
>
> Balanced against the somewhat limited effectiveness of warnings is the designer's ability to anticipate and protect against possible injuries. If a slight change in design would prevent serious, perhaps fatal, injury, the designer may not avoid liability by simply warning of the possible injury. [384 N.E.2d at 1192.]

The new Restatement agrees with the court's conclusions in *Uloth* (§2, Comment *l*):

> *l. Relationship between design and instruction or warning.* Reasonable designs and instructions or warnings both play important roles in the production and distribution of reasonably safe products. In general, when a safer design can reasonably be implemented and risks can reasonably be designed out of a product, adoption of the safer design is required over a warning that leaves a significant residuum of such risks. For example, instructions and warnings may be ineffective because users of the product may not be adequately reached, may be likely to be inattentive, or may be insufficiently motivated to follow the instructions or heed the warnings. However, when an alternative design to avoid risks cannot reasonably be implemented, adequate instructions and warnings will normally be sufficient to render the product reasonably safe. . . . Warnings are not, however, a substitute for the provision of a reasonably safe design.

Troja v. Black & Decker Manufacturing Co.

62 Md. App. 101, 488 A.2d 516 (1985)

GILBERT, C.J. This appeal involves a personal injury action grounded in strict liability.

On January 10, 1979, Michael Troja accidentally amputated his thumb while he was operating a radial arm saw manufactured by Black and Decker Manufacturing Company, Inc. . . .

At the close of Troja's case before Judge Raymond G. Thieme and a jury, the judge granted Black and Decker's motion for a directed verdict on the defective design portion of Troja's strict liability count. Judge Thieme ruled that Troja had failed to produce any legally sufficient evidence of the economic feasibility of a proposed alternative radial arm saw design, or of the existence of the technology necessary to produce such a product in 1976, the year the particular saw was manufactured. . . .

Troja argues that the trial court: 1) abused its discretion in precluding an expert witness from stating an opinion in regard to the economic and technological feasibility of a proposed safeguard for the radial arm saw; 2) erred in directing a verdict on the issue of design defect based on the court's findings that Troja failed to produce legally sufficient evidence to warrant submission of that issue to the jury. . . .

The alleged villain in this litigation is a twelve inch radial arm saw, DeWalt Model No. 780, manufactured by Black and Decker in 1976. Troja had borrowed the saw from Robert Krohn, who had hired Troja to build a bar. Troja and Krohn removed the saw from its metal base and stand in order that it could be carried from Krohn's basement to the work site in the bar. The guide fence and metal base were left behind. Bereft of its base, the saw was placed directly on the floor. Troja rigged a makeshift guide fence by securing an aluminum level to the saw with two "C" clamps. At the time of his injury, Troja was using the saw to make a cross-cut. He had dispensed with his makeshift fence and guided the wood into the saw blade with his bare hand.

A "DeWalt Instruction & Maintenance Manual" accompanied the 1976 DeWalt Model No. 780. The manual contained instructions, illustrated with photographs, on the subjects of assembly, operation, and maintenance of the saw. The manual included instructions for performing various types of cuts. The proper procedure for executing a cross-cut was explained and illustrated.

The Design Defect

Troja contends that because the saw was designed so that the guide fence was easily removable, the absence of a safety feature that would prevent the saw from running when the fence was not in place rendered it unreasonably dangerous.

Maryland, in Phipps v. General Motors Corp., 278 Md. 337, 363 A.2d 955 (1976), embraced the theory of strict liability in tort actions. There the Court expressly adopted the elements contained in the Restatement (Second) of Torts, §402A (1965). . . .

Section 402A requires a court, in a design defect case, to weigh "the utility of risk inherent in the design against the magnitude of the risk." Phipps v. General Motors Corp., 278 Md. at 345, 363 A.2d at 959. The court, *Phipps* tells us, ought to implement a balancing process to decide whether the product in question was unreasonably dangerous.

One helpful guide to the balancing process was recommended in Wade, On the Nature of Strict Tort Liability for Products, 44 Miss. L.J. 825, 837-838 (1973). Wade suggests seven factors that should be weighed in determining whether a given product is "reasonably safe." Those factors are:

(1) The usefulness and desirability of the product — its utility to the user and to the public as a whole.
(2) The safety aspects of the product — the likelihood that it will cause injury, and the probable seriousness of the injury.
(3) The availability of a substitute product which would meet the same need and not be as unsafe.
(4) The manufacturer's ability to eliminate the unsafe character of the product without impairing its usefulness or making it too expensive to maintain its utility.
(5) The user's ability to avoid danger by the exercise of care in the use of the product.
(6) The user's anticipated awareness of the dangers inherent in the product and their avoidability, because of general public knowledge of the obvious condition of the product, or of the existence of suitable warnings or instructions.
(7) The feasibility, on the part of the manufacturer, of spreading the loss by setting the price of the product or carrying liability insurance.

In some instances the risk is "inherently unreasonable," and no balancing test is necessary. An example of an inherently unreasonable risk is where, as in *Phipps,* the gas pedal of a new automobile suddenly and without warning sticks, causing the vehicle to accelerate.

The failure of the manufacturer, in the case sub judice, to incorporate a safety system such as the one proposed by Troja is not an inherently unreasonable risk. Therefore, in order to create a jury issue on the liability of Black and Decker because of a defective design, Troja was required to produce evidence from which the jury could determine the former's unreasonableness in manufacturing a saw, in 1976, without a safety system. In Singleton v. International Harvester Co., 685 F.2d 112 (4th Cir. 1981), the Fourth Circuit held that in order to carry a case to the jury, the evidence should show: the technological feasibility of manufacturing a product with the suggested safety device at the time the suspect product was manufactured; the availability of the materials required; the cost of production of the suggested device; price to the consumer, including that of the suggested device; and the chances of consumer acceptance of a model incorporating such features. The design alternative proposed in *Singleton* was a roll-over protective structure for a tractor which had upended or toppled, trapping the operator beneath it. Because Singleton's experts failed to provide the foundation information required, the court affirmed the trial court's directed verdict on the issue of defective design.

Troja contends that Judge Thieme erred when he refused to allow an expert in the field of "machine guarding safety systems" to testify that a radial saw design, incorporating a safety device described as an "interlock system," could have been developed in 1976. Gerald Rennell, who was offered by Troja as an expert, testified that he had taken courses in machine guarding and industrial safety. He said that he had been employed as a "safety engineer" and a "loss-control inspector." Although Rennell suggested that Black and Decker could have incorporated a "safety interlock feature," which would have prevented the saw from running when the guide fence was not in place, he acknowledged that he had no experience in radial arm saw design. Rennell was unable to furnish a design demonstrating the actual placement of such a system, or to explain how it could be integrated in the saw without interfering with the functions for which the fence would normally not be employed. The expert's bald statement that a safety interlock device could be implemented without great cost to the manufacturer was not supported by any data regarding the cost of the materials necessary to include such a feature. Moreover, Rennell did not conduct any tests to determine the feature's actual utility. Despite the trial court's pointed comments that it would exclude Rennell's testimony as to the feasibility of incorporating the proposed safety device, unless the expert established a foundation, Troja opted not to question his witness with respect to those areas. Inasmuch as there was an absence of a proper foundation for the expert's statement relative to a safety interlock device, the trial court excluded all testimony regarding the economic/technological feasibility in 1976 of producing a saw with the proposed safety system. We agree with Judge Thieme. The record simply does not support Troja's assertion that the trial court incorrectly excluded Rennell's testimony. . . .

When we view the evidence and all the inferences which may reasonably be drawn therefrom in a light most favorable to Troja, we are left with the inescapable conclusion that there simply was no legally sufficient evidence of design defect for the jury to consider. . . . The trial court properly granted the manufacturer's motion for a directed verdict on the issue of design defect. . . .

Judgment affirmed.

What if a product manufacturer offers safety enhancements as an additional purchase option to consumers rather than as part of the basic product? Ideally, optional safety devices can be seen as market-based responses to risk-management problems, giving consumers the ability to make personally tailored decisions about how much to invest in product safety. Courts have struggled with the question of whether to, in essence, delegate responsibility to market actors by refusing to hold product manufacturers liable when they fail to include optional safety devices as part of standard product equipment. One of the authors of this book has argued that courts should apply a no-duty rule when sellers offer optional safety features but consumers choose not to use them. See James A. Henderson, Jr. & Aaron D. Twerski, Optional Safety Devices: Delegating Product Design Responsibility to the Market, 45 Ariz. St. L.J. 1399 (2013). In the article, Professors Henderson and Twerski suggest that a product should not be considered defectively designed "based on the omission of a safety device when the product seller offers the device as an option at the time of sale and a reasonable seller would expect those who purchase for use and consumption to make reasonable decisions regarding whether or not to include the safety device in the design." *Id.* at 1424. For a case adopting this approach, see Parks v. Ariens Co., 2015 WL 3960901 (N.D. Iowa 2015). For further discussion of the potential for "private" market-derived solutions to product risk-benefit decision making, see Richard C. Ausness, "Danger Is My Business": The Right to Manufacture Unsafe Products, 67 Ark. L. Rev. 827 (2014); James A. Henderson, Jr., The Constitutive Dimensions of Tort: Promoting Private Solutions to Risk-Management Problems, 40 Fla. St. U. L. Rev. 221 (2013).

Many courts have articulated their design liability tests in risk-utility terms. See, e.g., Wilson v. Piper Aircraft Corp., 577 P.2d 1322 (Or. 1978); Turner v. General Motors Corp., 584 S.W.2d 844 (Tex. 1979); Morningstar v. Black & Decker Mfg. Co., 253 S.E.2d 666 (W. Va. 1979). Some have also mandated that the jury be instructed as to risk-utility factors. The New York Court of Appeals in Voss v. Black & Decker Mfg. Co., 450 N.E.2d 204 (N.Y. 1983), was explicit on this matter. After reiterating Wade's seven factors, set out in *Troja,* the court concluded: "Pertinent factors in the individual case, when evaluated as to whether or not they are applicable, should form the basis for charging the jury as to how it should evaluate the evidence in order to decide whether a product is not reasonably safe." Id. at 403. Other courts have held that risk-utility factors are only for the court in deciding whether plaintiff has established a prima facie case and are not to be given to the jury. See, e.g., Turner v. General Motors Corp., above.

Many state legislatures and courts require that in order to succeed in a case alleging defective design, a plaintiff must establish the availability of a reasonable alternative design. The Louisiana statute (La. Rev. Stat. Ann. §9:2800.56 (West 2010)) is illustrative. It provides:

> A product is unreasonably dangerous in design if, at the time the product left its manufacturer's control:
>
> (1) There existed an alternative design for the product that was capable of preventing the claimant's damage; and
>
> (2) The likelihood that the product's design would cause the claimant's damage and the gravity of that damage outweighed the burden on the manufacturer of adopting such alternative design and the adverse effect, if any, of such alternative design on the utility of the product. An adequate warning about a product shall be considered in evaluating the likelihood of damage when the manufacturer has used reasonable care to provide the adequate warning to users and handlers of the product.

Similar statutes have been enacted in Mississippi, Ohio, New Jersey, and Texas. Judicial support for the need to establish a reasonable alternative design is substantial, although a few courts continue to prefer a more open-ended risk-utility test, in which the availability of a reasonable alternative design is merely one factor among several. See, e.g., Vautour v. Body Masters Sports Indus., Inc., 784 A.2d 1178 (N.H. 2001); Bustos v. Hyundai Motor Co., 243 P.3d 440, 452 (N.M. Ct. App. 2010).

Not only has the risk-utility approach been adopted by courts and legislatures, but it also has the support of the overwhelming majority of commentators. See, e.g., Sheila L. Birnbaum, Unmasking the Test for Defect: From Negligence [to Warranty] to Strict Liability to Negligence, 33 Vand. L. Rev. 593 (1980); Richard A. Epstein, Products Liability: The Search for the Middle Ground, 56 N.C. L. Rev. 643 (1978); James A. Henderson, Jr., Renewed Judicial Controversy over Defective Product Design: Toward the Preservation of an Emerging Consensus, 63 Minn. L. Rev. 773 (1979); Aaron D. Twerski, A Moderate and Restrained Federal Product Liability Bill: Targeting the Crisis Areas for Resolution, 18 U. Mich. J.L. Ref. 575 (1985).

The Restatement (Third) adopts the design standard applied in *McCormack* and *Troja*, above:

> §2. Categories Of Product Defect
>
> A product is defective when, at the time of sale or distribution, it contains a manufacturing defect, is defective in design, or is defective because of inadequate instructions or warnings. A product: . . .
>
> (b) is defective in design when the foreseeable risks of harm posed by the product could have been reduced or avoided by the adoption of a reasonable alternative design by the seller or other distributor, or a predecessor in the commercial chain of distribution, and the omission of the alternative design renders the product not reasonably safe; . . .
>
> COMMENT
>
> *d.* Design defects: general considerations. . . . The requirement in Subsection (b) that plaintiff show a reasonable alternative design applies in most instances even though the plaintiff alleges that the category of product sold by the defendant is so dangerous that it should not have been marketed at all. See Comment e. Common and widely distributed products such as alcoholic beverages, firearms and above-ground swimming pools may be found to be defective only upon proof of the requisite conditions in Subsections (a), (b), or (c). If such products are defectively manufactured or sold without reasonable warnings as to their danger when such warnings are appropriate, or if reasonable alternative designs could have been adopted, then liability under §§1 and 2 may attach. Absent proof of defect under those Sections, however, courts have not imposed liability for categories of products that are generally available and widely used and consumed, even if they pose substantial risks of harm. Instead, courts generally have concluded that legislatures and administrative agencies can, more appropriately than courts, consider the desirability of commercial distribution of some categories of widely used and consumed, but nevertheless dangerous, products.
>
> ILLUSTRATION:
>
> 4. XYZ Co. manufactures above-ground swimming pools that are four feet deep. Warnings are embossed on the outside of the pools in large letters stating "DANGER—DO NOT DIVE." In disregard of the warnings, Mary, age 21, dove head first into an XYZ pool and suffered serious injury. Expert testimony establishes that when Mary's outstretched hands hit the pool's slippery vinyl bottom her hands slid apart, causing her to strike her head against the bottom of the pool. For the purposes of this Illustration it is assumed that the

warnings were adequate and that the only issue is whether the above-ground pool was defectively designed because the bottom was too slippery. All the expert witnesses agree that the vinyl pool liner that XYZ utilized was the best and safest liner available and that no alternative, less slippery liner was feasible. Mary has failed to establish defective design under Subsection (b).

COMMENT

e. Design defects: possibility of manifestly unreasonable design. Several courts have suggested that the designs of some products are so manifestly unreasonable, in that they have low social utility and high degree of danger, that liability should attach even absent proof of a reasonable alternative design. In large part the problem is one of how the range of relevant alternative designs is described. For example, a toy gun that shoots hard rubber pellets with sufficient velocity to cause injury to children could be found to be defectively designed within the rule of Subsection (b). Toy guns unlikely to cause injury would constitute reasonable alternatives to the dangerous toy. Thus, toy guns that project ping pong balls, soft gelatin pellets, or water might be found to be reasonable alternative designs to a toy gun that shoots hard pellets. However, if the realism of the hard-pellet gun, and thus its capacity to cause injury, is sufficiently important to those who purchase and use such products to justify the court's limiting consideration to toy guns that achieve realism by shooting hard pellets, then no reasonable alternative will, by hypothesis, be available. In that instance, the design feature that defines which alternatives are relevant — the realism of the hard-pellet gun and thus its capacity to injure — is precisely the feature on which the user places value and of which the plaintiff complains. If a court were to adopt this characterization of the product, and deem the capacity to cause injury an egregiously unacceptable quality in a toy for use by children, it could conclude that liability should attach without proof of a reasonable alternative design. The court would declare the product design to be defective and not reasonably safe because the extremely high degree of danger posed by its use or consumption so substantially outweighs its negligible social utility that no rational, reasonable person, fully aware of the relevant facts, would choose to use, or to allow children to use, the product.

COMMENT

f. Design defects: factors relevant in determining whether the omission of a reasonable alternative renders a product not reasonably safe. Subsection (b) states that a product is defective in design if the omission of a reasonable alternative design renders the product not reasonably safe. A broad range of factors may be considered in determining whether an alternative design is reasonable and whether its omission renders a product not reasonably safe. The factors include, among others, the magnitude and probability of the foreseeable risks of harm, the instructions and warnings accompanying the product, and the nature and strength of consumer expectations regarding the product. The relative advantages and disadvantages of the product as designed and as it alternatively could have been designed may also be considered. Thus, the likely effects of the alternative design on production costs; the effects of the alternative design on product longevity, maintenance, repair, and esthetics; and the range of consumer choice among products are factors that may be taken into account. Plaintiff is not necessarily required to introduce proof on all of these factors; their relevance, and the relevance of other factors, will vary from case to case. Depending on the mix of these factors, a number of variations in the design of a given product may meet the test in Subsection (b). On the other hand, it is not a factor under Subsection (b) that the imposition of liability would have a negative effect on corporate earnings or would reduce employment in a given industry.

When evaluating the reasonableness of a design alternative, the overall safety of the product must be considered. It is not sufficient that the alternative design would have reduced or prevented the harm suffered by the plaintiff if it would also have introduced into the product other dangers of equal or greater magnitude. . . .

> In many cases, the plaintiff must rely on expert testimony. Subsection (b) does not, however, require the plaintiff to produce a prototype in order to make out a prima facie case. Thus, qualified expert testimony on the issue suffices, even though the expert has produced no prototype, if it reasonably supports the conclusion that a reasonable alternative design could have been practically adopted at the time of sale. . . .

Parish v. Jumpking, Inc.

719 N.W.2d 540 (Iowa 2006)

LARSON, JUSTICE.

James Parish was severely injured while using a trampoline manufactured by the defendant, Jumpking, Inc. Parish sued Jumpking on theories of defective design of the trampoline, and negligence in failing to warn of the danger in using it. The defendant moved for summary judgment, which was granted, and the plaintiff appealed. We affirm.

I. Facts and Prior Proceedings

In June of 1999, Delbert Parish (the plaintiff's brother) and Shelley Tatro purchased a Jumpking fourteen-foot trampoline for use in their backyard. They set up the trampoline, and Delbert tried it out by attempting a somersault. He nearly fell off the trampoline, prompting Delbert and Shelley to purchase a "fun ring"—a netlike enclosure with one entry point onto the trampoline. While the plaintiff was visiting his brother on September 11, 1999, he attempted to do a back somersault on the trampoline, but he landed on his head and was rendered a quadriplegic. In August 2001 Parish filed suit, on his own behalf and on behalf of his minor son, against Jumpking, as designer and manufacturer of the trampoline and its enclosure.

II. The Issues

The district court entered summary judgment against the plaintiff on all claims, and he argues on appeal that this was error because there were genuine issues of material fact on his design-defect claim, and on the adequacy of Jumpking's warnings. He also contends that the "open and obvious" defense is not applicable to a design-defect case, and in any event, there was an issue of material fact as to its application here. . . .

IV. The Defective Design Claim

In *Wright v. Brooke Group Ltd.*, 652 N.W.2d 159 (Iowa 2002), we adopted sections 1 and 2 of the Restatement (Third) of Torts: Products Liability [hereinafter Restatement]. Section 2 of the Restatement recognizes three types of product defect:

> A product is defective when, at the time of sale or distribution, it contains a manufacturing defect, is defective in design, or is defective because of inadequate instructions or warnings. A product:
>
> . . . .

> (b) is defective in design when the foreseeable risks of harm posed by the product could have been reduced or avoided by the adoption of a reasonable alternative design by the seller or other distributor, or a predecessor in the commercial chain of distribution, and the omission of the alternative design renders the product not reasonably safe[.]

The plaintiff's first argument is that the district court erred in granting summary judgment on his design-defect claim under section 2(b). Under a design-defect claim, a plaintiff is essentially arguing that, even though the product meets the manufacturer's design specifications, the specifications themselves create unreasonable risks. To succeed under section 2(b), a plaintiff must ordinarily show the existence of a reasonable alternative design, *Wright,* 652 N.W.2d at 169, and that this design would, at a reasonable cost, have reduced the foreseeabilty of harm posed by the product. Restatement §2 cmt. *d.*

The Restatement recognizes exceptions to the requirement of a reasonable alternative design, but the plaintiff relies on only one: that the design was "manifestly unreasonable" under Restatement §2(b) cmt. *e.* Under that comment,

> the designs of some products are so manifestly unreasonable, in that they have low social utility and high degree of danger, that liability should attach even absent proof of a reasonable alternative design.

The plaintiff concedes that he has not offered an alternative design; rather, he argues a trampoline is so inherently dangerous that a reasonable design alternative is not available. He contends there is no safe way to use a trampoline in a backyard, and it must be used only by properly trained and qualified participants under supervision.

The Restatement provides this illustration of a manifestly unreasonable product under comment *e:*

> ABC Co. manufactures novelty items. One item, an exploding cigar, is made to explode with a loud bang and the emission of smoke. Robert purchased the exploding cigar and presented it to his boss, Jack, at a birthday party arranged for him at the office. Jack lit the cigar. When it exploded, the heat from the explosion lit Jack's beard on fire causing serious burns to his face. If a court were to recognize the rule identified in this Comment, the finder of fact might find ABC liable for the defective design of the exploding cigar even if no reasonable alternative design was available that would provide similar prank characteristics. The utility of the exploding cigar is so low and the risk of injury is so high as to warrant a conclusion that the cigar is defective and should not have been marketed at all.

Restatement §2(b) cmt. *e,* illus. 5.

Application of the "manifestly unreasonable" exception presents an issue of first impression in Iowa. However, the wording of section 2(b) and virtually all commentary on it suggest that this exception should be sparingly applied. In fact, such exceptions to the requirement of a reasonable alternative design were "grudgingly accepted by the Reporters," Keith C. Miller, *Myth Surrenders to Reality: Design Defect Litigation in Iowa,* 51 Drake L. Rev. 549, 564 (2003), suggesting that the drafters did not intend for there to be any exceptions to this requirement. One of the reporters to the Restatement agrees:

> [B]ear in mind that our comment *e* talks about extremely dangerous products with very low social utility. It substitutes for the qualitative problem, in the general design area, a kind of quantitative solution. We admit that there may be times, and I think they'd be rare, probably

> non-existent, when a product might come to court, to you, that was so bad, so very outloud bad, so very antisocial, that it would tug against the very grain of the way you were raised.

James A. Henderson, Jr., *The Habush Amendment: Section 2(b) comment e,* 8–Fall Kan. J.L. & Pub. Pol'y 86, 86 (1998).

Suits involving common and widely distributed products are more likely than others to require the showing of a reasonable alternative. According to the Restatement,

> Common and widely distributed products such as alcoholic beverages, firearms, and above-ground swimming pools may be found to be defective only upon proof of [a reasonable alternative design]. If such products are . . . sold without reasonable warnings as to their danger . . . then liability under §§1 and 2 may attach. Absent proof of defect under those Sections, however, courts have not imposed liability for categories of products that are generally available and widely consumed, even if they pose substantial risks of harm.

Restatement §2(b) cmt. *d.*

While comment *e* recognizes the possibility that egregiously dangerous products might be held defective for that reason alone, the Restatement has noted that "a clear majority of courts that have faced the issue have refused so to hold." Restatement §2, American Case Law and Commentary on Issues Related to Design-Based Liability, at 87. In this commentary, the Restatement discussed several cases imposing liability under comment *e* but observed that "[e]ach of these judicial attempts at imposing such liability have either been overturned or sharply curtailed by legislation." *Id.* at 89.

Under our summary judgment rules,

> [w]hen a motion for summary judgment is made and supported as provided in this rule, an adverse party may not rest upon the mere allegations or denials in the pleadings, but the response, by affidavits or as otherwise provided in this rule, *must set forth specific facts showing that there is a genuine issue for trial. If the adverse party does not so respond, summary judgment, if appropriate, shall be entered.*

Iowa R. Civ. P. 1.981(5) (emphasis added). As previously noted, a genuine issue of fact is presented if a reasonable fact finder could return a verdict or decision for the nonmoving party based upon those facts. *Junkins,* 421 N.W.2d at 132. By adopting section 2 of the Restatement in *Wright,* we also adopted comment *e.* In the present case, the issue is whether a reasonable fact finder could conclude the trampoline was manifestly unreasonable in its design within the meaning of comment *e* as interpreted by the commentary surrounding it and the cases applying it.

> In cases involving common and widely distributed products, courts generally have concluded that legislatures and administrative agencies can, more appropriately than courts, consider the desirability of commercial distribution of some categories of widely used and consumed, but nevertheless dangerous, products.

Restatement §2(b) cmt. *d.*

It is undisputed that trampolines are common and widely distributed products. In fact, the evidence showed approximately fourteen million people use them. Even data produced by the plaintiff in his resistance to summary judgment showed that in 2002 only 2.1% of trampolines were associated with injuries, and only one-half of one percent of jumpers were injured. The Consumer Product Safety Commission, based on 1997 and 1998 injury data, concluded trampolines ranked twelfth among recreational use products in terms of injuries. They rated below such common activities as basketball, bicycle riding, football, soccer, and skating.

The benefits of trampolining include use in cardiovascular workouts and other medical treatments, including "bouncing" therapy for children with cystic fibrosis. Trampolining obviously provides valuable exercise and entertainment.

We conclude that the plaintiff has failed to generate a genuine issue of fact sufficient to except this product from the alternative-design requirement of section 2(b), and the plaintiff's design-defect claim under that section must therefore be rejected.

V. The Warnings

The plaintiff also claims the trampoline did not incorporate adequate warnings and that a genuine issue of fact was generated on that issue.

Under the Restatement, a product

> is defective because of inadequate instructions or warnings when the foreseeable risks of harm posed by the product could have been reduced or avoided by the provision of reasonable instructions or warnings by the seller or other distributor, or a predecessor in the commercial chain of distribution, and the omission of the instructions or warnings renders the product not reasonably safe.

Restatement §2(c).

The trampoline in this case, and its surrounding fun ring, together provide numerous warnings. Three warnings are placed permanently on the pad of the trampoline and advise the user:

> WARNING
>
> Do not land on head or neck.
> Paralysis or death can result, even if you land in the middle of the trampoline mat (bed).
> To reduce the chance of landing on your head or neck, do not do somersaults (flips).
> Only one person at a time on trampoline.
> Multiple jumpers increase the chances of loss of control, collision, and falling off.
> This can result in broken head, neck, back, or leg.
> This trampoline is not recommended for children under 6 years of age.

These warnings also include nationally recognized warning symbols cautioning against those activities. During manufacture, Jumpking also places one warning on each of the eight legs of the trampoline, and the design is such that the only way to assemble the trampoline is to have these warnings facing out so they are visible to the user. Jumpking further manufactures two printed (nonpictorial) warnings that are sewn onto the trampoline bed itself. It also provides a warning placard for the owner to affix to the trampoline that contains both the pictorial warning and the language regarding safe use of the trampoline, and it provides an owner's manual that contains the warnings as found on the trampoline as well as additional warnings regarding supervision and education. It is undisputed that these warnings exceed the warnings required by the American Society for Testing and Material (ASTM).

Warnings are also provided with the fun ring. Jumpking provides eight warning stickers to be placed on the legs of the fun ring during assembly, and Shelley Tatro recalls installing them as directed. Jumpking provided extra warnings on the fun ring because it was aware that the fun ring may partially cover warnings on the legs of the trampoline. It also provides a warning placard with the fun ring to be placed at the door of the fun ring containing the pictorial warnings and additional language required by the ASTM. The fun ring comes with a separate owner's manual that provides additional warnings.

The Restatement recognizes that users must pay some attention for their own safety:

> Society does not benefit from products that are excessively safe — for example, automobiles designed with maximum speeds of 20 miles per hour — any more than it benefits from products that are too risky. Society benefits most when the right, or optimal, amount of product safety is achieved. *From a fairness perspective, requiring individual users and consumers to bear appropriate responsibility for proper product use prevents careless users and consumers from being subsidized by more careful users and consumers, when the former are paid damages out of funds to which the latter are forced to contribute through higher product prices.*

Restatement §2 cmt. *a* (emphasis added).

In this case, it is undisputed that the three warnings affixed to the pad of the trampoline and the placards that came with both the trampoline and the fun ring warned against the specific conduct in which the plaintiff was engaged at the time of his injury, i.e., attempting somersaults or flips. We conclude that a reasonable fact finder could not conclude that the defendant's warnings were inadequate, and we affirm the district court's summary judgment on that claim.

Because we find summary judgment was properly ordered on the grounds discussed, we do not address the plaintiff's "open and obvious" argument.

AFFIRMED.

In Higgins v. Intex Recreation Corp., 99 P.3d 421 (Wash. Ct. App. 2004), a jury apportioned 35 percent liability to the manufacturer of the Extreme Sno-Tube II, a vinyl inflatable snow tube. Plaintiff was struck and severely injured by an out-of-control adult who was riding the Sno-Tube after plaintiff attempted to stop the adult from unknowingly hitting a young child in his path. Plaintiff argued at trial that the Sno-Tube was defectively designed because it permitted riders to travel at great speeds and to inadvertently turn backward, thereby increasing the chances of an accident. Intex argued "that if the Sno-Tube did not go fast and rotate it would not be a Sno-Tube." Id. at 424. The court upheld the jury verdict, noting that "[t]here is evidence . . . from which a jury could conclude that the placement of ribs or ridges on the bottom of the Sno-Tube . . . would keep the rider facing downhill. The rider could then see obstacles and direct the tube." Id. at 425. Would that design still be a Sno-Tube? How would you formulate a test for determining when a redesigned product no longer fits within the category represented by the defendant's product? Cf. Restatement (Third) of Torts: Products Liability §2 cmts. *d-f* (1998); Evans v. Lorrilard, 990 N.E.2d 997 (Mass. 2013) ("The essential question is not whether the safer alternative design [of a lower tar and nicotine cigarette] is an 'ordinary cigarette' but whether adoption of the safer alternative design would result in undue interference with the cost or performance of the product, thereby making the alternative unreasonable.").

Notwithstanding the difficulty of defining a product's specific "category," courts have been quick to reject the concept of product category liability. See, e.g., S.F. v. Archer Daniels Midland Co., 594 Fed. Appx. 11 (2d. Cir. 2014) (affirming dismissal of suit against manufacturer of high fructose corn syrup for allegedly causing diabetes because, under New York law, "a design-defect claim will not stand if the only alternative is an outright ban"); Fabiano v. Philip Morris Inc., 29 Misc. 3d 395, 909 N.Y.S.2d 314, 320 (Sup. Ct. N.Y. County 2010) (observing "the vast majority of courts have been markedly unreceptive to the call that they displace markets, legislatures, and governmental agencies by decreeing whole categories of products to be outlaws"). One may still on occasion find a court considering product category liability, see, e.g., McCarthy v. Olin Corp., 119 F.3d 148, 173-174 (2d Cir. 1997) (Calabresi, J., dissenting) (suggesting that hollow-point bullets might appropriately be subjected to product category liability), Ruiz-Guzman v. Amvac Chem. Corp., 7 P.3d 795 (Wash. 2000) (entertaining the possibility that a pesticide may fail risk-utility balancing even absent proof of a RAD), but such occasions are rare. Would military-style assault weapons, which have been used by civilians in a number of mass shootings in the United States in recent years, constitute a good candidate for a rare application of product category liability?

Problem 33

A partner in your law firm has asked you to prepare a memorandum analyzing the potential merits of a products liability case that has been brought against your client, Ford Motor Company. The plaintiff in the case, Trey Washington, suffered severe injuries when the 2006 Hyundai Accent he was driving was struck from behind by a 2002 Ford Excursion sport utility vehicle (SUV) manufactured by your client. The accident occurred on a two-lane rural highway. Mr. Washington was driving within the 45 mph speed limit when he noticed several deer stopped on the highway ahead. Mr. Washington brought his vehicle to a controlled stop. Due to the angle of the setting sun, the driver of the SUV behind him did not notice the deer or the brake lights from Mr. Washington's car until it was too late to avoid a collision. The SUV struck Mr. Washington's car with so much force that he suffered severe spinal injuries, notwithstanding proper deployment of the air bag system in his vehicle. The driver of the SUV was unharmed.

The file contains a memorandum prepared by an automotive design expert retained by your firm, which begins by describing in general terms the safety risks posed by SUVs to drivers and passengers of other vehicles. Both the National Highway Traffic and Safety Administration (NHTSA) and the Insurance Institute for Highway Safety (IIHS) have conducted large-scale studies demonstrating that occupants of passenger vehicles are significantly more likely to suffer fatal or serious injuries when struck by an SUV than by another passenger vehicle. The expert explains that SUVs were originally designed as specialty vehicles for off-road use and for heavy towing and hauling. For this reason, the vehicles were built using frame, weight, and suspension features characteristic of trucks rather than ordinary passenger vehicles.

Some of these design features created safety risks to the occupants of the SUVs themselves, the best known of which is the propensity for SUVs to roll over. Others implicated the safety of occupants of other vehicles that might be struck by an SUV. For instance, the frame height of many SUVS is such that, in an accident with a passenger vehicle, the

SUV's bumper overrides the bumper of the other vehicle, resulting in crashes with much greater force and injury potential to the occupants of the other vehicle. Although the NHTSA requires passenger vehicles to be built within a prescribed height range to ensure that vehicle bumpers meet during crashes, SUVs are classified as trucks and are therefore exempt from the requirement.

The most deadly override incidents involve side crashes, in which the SUV may crash directly through the door and into the cabin of the other vehicle. For front and rear crashes, in contrast, portions of the body of the passenger vehicle typically are designed to crush during impact, absorbing crash force and lowering the risk of injury. Beginning in the early 2000s, SUV manufacturers began making design adjustments to reduce the risk of override. For some models, bumper and vehicle height were reduced, although this also had the effect of reducing the SUV's off-road capabilities and the SUV driver's sense of "command" over the road. Many SUV manufacturers instead maintained the height of the vehicles but added an additional, lower-mounted safety bar intended to engage the bumpers of other vehicles and reduce risk to their occupants. In fact, your client pioneered this design feature in the late 1990s, and it was included in the 2002 Ford Excursion that struck Mr. Washington.

Beyond reducing the risk of override, however, there is only so much that can be done to reduce the disproportionate risk posed by SUVs to occupants of other vehicles. To facilitate off-road driving, cargo hauling, and towing, SUVs must generally be built on a truck frame, which is considerably stiffer than the frame of a passenger vehicle. In a collision with a passenger vehicle, the SUV frame will transfer crash energy to the other vehicle, which, unlike the SUV, is designed to crush during impact. These design differences, along with the sheer difference in mass between the two vehicles, mean that the other vehicle will bear the brunt of the force created by the impact. In essence, the other vehicle becomes the crush zone for the SUV since the SUV is designed for bulk and rigidity. The resulting disparity in crash risk can be dramatic: The IIHS found that when extremely large SUVs such as the Ford Excursion or the Chevy Suburban collide with average-size passenger vehicles, the driver of the other vehicle is 48 times more likely to die than the SUV driver.

The engineer's report does note that many small and midsize SUVs are designed to be lighter and lower-riding than conventional SUVs. Often, these models are built on an automobile, rather than a truck, frame and chassis. These design changes reduce the risk of damage to other vehicles and injury to their occupants. However, they also reduce the SUV's off-road, hauling, and towing capabilities, as well as provide a markedly different driver experience due to the smaller stature of the vehicle. Although the vast majority of SUVs are never actually driven off-road or used to haul or tow extreme loads, marketing studies suggest that consumers significantly value the psychological experience of driving an outsized, powerful vehicle. The engineer's report quotes one industry marketing executive as saying, "You don't ask how often people actually use these capabilities because it doesn't really matter to them — they get to feel like Superman wherever they are." The report concludes by noting the engineer's opinion that, although the injuries suffered by Mr. Washington could have been reduced or avoided if the Ford Excursion were built on an automobile frame, the design change would have resulted in an altogether different category of vehicle.

The main issue that the partner would like you to address in your memorandum is whether there is any substantial chance that Mr. Washington will reach the jury with a claim that the Ford Excursion design is defective. He recognizes that the file is far from complete, and that further factual inquiry will be necessary if your firm proceeds with the case. What he wants at this stage is for you to identify the legal issues likely to be involved and to assess the client's chances of success with respect to each, making reasonable factual assumptions wherever necessary. He would also like you to identify the major avenues for further investigation. Assume that Troja v. Black & Decker and Parish v. Jumpking, Inc., above, are the latest decisions by your state's higher court on the subject of defective design.

Note: Design Defect and Daubert

One of the subthemes in this casebook has been the admissibility of expert testimony in proving certain aspects of the plaintiff's case. As discussed earlier in this chapter, issues involving the admissibility of evidence often arise involving causation, especially general causation in cases involving toxic substances. When plaintiffs rely on experts, judges must rule on the admissibility of the testimony, in many courts requiring application of the principles set forth in the Daubert v. Merrell Dow decision by the Supreme Court, p. 125, above. These principles are also relevant to the question of proof of design defect. Thus, to prove a reasonable alternative design, plaintiffs may call upon experts to provide the technical background that judges, lawyers, and juries lack.

In Lauzon v. Senco Products, Inc., 270 F.3d 681 (8th Cir. 2001), the plaintiff shot himself in the thumb with a nailing gun that he was using to roof a garage. The plaintiff relied on an engineer to prove that the design of the gun, a rapid-firing nailer that fired nails when the operator simultaneously held the trigger and bounced the contact point of the gun along the surface of the work, was defective. An alternative design that, according to the expert, fired only upon a release and re-depression of the trigger, was safer, and already existed. Interestingly, the manufacturer marketed the gun for the very purpose of its rapid-fire quality. However, the expert pointed out that the rapid-firing quality of the design made the gun prone to "double-fire," whereby the gun shot one nail and, upon recoil, sometimes unexpectedly fired a second. The trial court, citing *Daubert*, excluded the expert's testimony. The court of appeals reversed, noting that while *Daubert* controls, several factors weigh toward admitting the evidence. The more dispositive factors appeared to be (1) although "general acceptance" is no longer automatically dispositive after *Daubert*, in this case it substantially favored the testimony of the expert, and (2) the expert's theories were highly testable.

At this point, you might reconsider the Maryland appellate court's decision in *Troja*, above. Although decided before *Daubert*, was the issue in *Troja* essentially the same — that courts should be wary of expert testimony that appears to have been "cooked up" solely for purposes of the litigation before them?

Heaton v. Ford Motor Co.

248 Or. 467, 435 P.2d 806 (1967)

GOODWIN, J. The plaintiff appeals a judgment entered after an involuntary nonsuit in a products-liability case involving a wheel on a Ford 4-wheel-drive pickup truck. The principal question is whether the plaintiff produced sufficient evidence to support his allegation that the wheel was dangerously defective.

Plaintiff purchased the truck new in July 1963 to use for hunting and other cross-country purposes as well as for driving upon paved highways. He drove the truck some 7,000 miles without noticing anything unusual about its performance. Prior to the day of the accident the truck had rarely been off the pavement, and plaintiff swore that it had never been subjected to unusual stress of any kind.

On the day of the accident, however, the truck, while moving on a "black-top" highway at normal speed, hit a rock which plaintiff described as about five or six inches in diameter. The truck continued uneventfully for about 35 miles, when it left the road and tipped over.

After the accident, the rim of the wheel was found to be separated from the "spider." Witnesses described the "spider" as the interior portion of the wheel which is attached to the vehicle by the lug nuts. The twelve rivets connecting the rim to the spider appeared to have been sheared off. The spider, according to one witness, showed signs of having been dragged along the ground. There was also a large dent in the rim and a five-inch cut in the inner tube at a spot within the tire that was adjacent to the dent in the rim. Only three of the rivets which had held the rim on the spider were found after the accident. . . .

In the type of case in which there is no evidence, direct or circumstantial, available to prove exactly what sort of manufacturing flaw existed, or exactly how the design was deficient, the plaintiff may nonetheless be able to establish his right to recover, by proving that the product did not perform in keeping with the reasonable expectations of the user. When it is shown that a product failed to meet the reasonable expectations of the user the inference is that there was some sort of defect, a precise definition of which is unnecessary. If the product failed under conditions concerning which an average consumer of that product could have fairly definite expectations, then the jury would have a basis for making an informed judgment upon the existence of a defect. The case at bar, however, is not such a case. . . .

The court's function is to decide whether the evidence furnishes a sufficient basis for the jury to make an informed decision. If the record permits, the jury determines whether the product performed as an ordinary consumer would have expected. In the case at bar the record furnishes no basis for a jury to do anything but speculate.

Where the performance failure occurs under conditions with which the average person has experience, the facts of the accident alone may constitute a sufficient basis for the jury to decide whether the expectations of an ordinary consumer of the product were met. High-speed collisions with large rocks are not so common, however, that the average person would know from personal experience what to expect under the circumstances. Nor does anything in the record cast any light upon this issue. The jury would therefore be unequipped, either by general background or by facts supplied in the record, to decide whether this wheel failed to perform as safely as an ordinary consumer would have expected. To allow the jury to decide purely on its own intuition how strong a truck wheel should be would convert the concept of strict liability into the absolute liability of an insurer.

The argument has been made that the question of the ordinary consumer's expectations should be treated for jury purposes in the same way that the question of reasonable conduct in a negligence case is treated. But in deciding in a negligence case what is reasonable conduct, the jury is deciding in a context of "right and wrong" how someone *should* have behaved. In making this decision they are presumed to know the relevant factors. If not, such information is provided, as in a medical malpractice case where there is expert testimony as to the proper standards.

In the defective-product area, courts have already decided how strong products *should* be: They should be strong enough to perform as the ordinary consumer expects. In deciding what the reasonable consumer expects, the jury is not permitted to decide how strong products should be, nor even what consumers should expect, for this would in effect be the same thing. The jury is supposed to determine the basically factual question of what reasonable consumers do expect from the product. Where the jury has no experiential basis for knowing this, the record must supply such a basis. In the absence of either common experience or evidence, any verdict would, in effect, be the jury's opinion of how strong the product *should* be. Such an opinion by the jury would be formed without the benefit of data concerning the cost or feasibility of designing and building stronger products. Without reference to relevant factual data, the jury has no special qualifications for deciding what is reasonable. . . .

While the matter was never presented to the trial court, and thus requires no extended discussion in this appeal, the plaintiff has referred in this court to certain advertising published by the defendant, to reinforce the plaintiff's claim that a consumer would have expected the wheel in question to be engineered and manufactured in such a manner as to withstand the kind of force applied to it in this case. The plaintiff does not contend that the advertising constituted misrepresentation under Restatement (Second) of Torts §402B, but rather that the advertising in general tends to create expectations of strength and durability under Section 402A. A general impression of durability, however, does not help a customer to form an expectation about the breaking point of a wheel. A "rugged" Ford truck could be expected to negotiate rough terrain, including five-or-six-inch rocks, at appropriate off-the-road speeds, but it does not follow that a user could expect the same thing at highway speeds. If such expectations do exist, the record should contain evidence to support the inference that they do.

Affirmed.

O'CONNELL, J. (dissenting).

. . . It is plaintiff's position that the theory of strict liability should be deemed applicable whenever a person is injured as a result of exposing himself to a hazard in reasonable reliance upon the capabilities of a product as represented by the seller. The gist of plaintiff's argument is summed up as follows:

> . . . It is not unreasonable to suggest that the driver of a vehicle promoted as "solid," "rugged" and "built like a truck" will subject that vehicle and its passengers to hazards to which he would not subject a vehicle otherwise promoted. With specific reference to this case, it is not unreasonable to surmise that a driver of a vehicle so promoted who runs over a rock on the highway will not even consciously consider the possibility of stopping to check for damage because he takes it for granted that such an impact will not harm a vehicle which he has been conditioned to think of as "solid," "rugged," and "like a truck."

Plaintiff, then, is asking us to "take judicial notice of facts which form part of the common knowledge of people who possess average intelligence. . . ."

Apparently the majority opinion would hold that there was a failure of proof, irrespective of whether the question of strict liability is for the court or jury in a case of this kind. I disagree. If we had been presented with the same facts with the modification that plaintiff had struck a rock one inch in diameter rather than a five-inch rock, I am sure that the majority would have held that at least a jury question was made out. The beginning point of our reasoning would be that a manufacturer of automobiles must construct wheels of sufficient durability to withstand the impact of one-inch rocks, because one-inch rocks are not an uncommon obstacle on highways. A buyer could reasonably expect to have the wheel withstand such an impact and it would not be unreasonable for him to proceed on his journey after the impact. However, the buyer could not reasonably expect a wheel to remain safe after striking a rock two feet in diameter at seventy miles an hour. Somewhere along the continuum between one inch and two feet it will be necessary to draw a line.

The line is drawn by deciding whether a manufacturer should be required to construct a wheel of such durability as to withstand the impact of a rock of the size in question. Whether the manufacturer has that duty in a particular case should depend, it seems to me, upon whether the manufacturer could reasonably foresee the likelihood that the hazard would be encountered by those using the product, and this would, of course, depend to some extent upon the representations made by the manufacturer with respect to the durability of the product.

The manufacturer's conduct must be measured against a standard of reasonableness, a standard similar to that employed in determining whether a defendant is negligent. Here, however, we do not measure defendant's conduct in terms of fault but simply upon the basis of its foreseeability. A jury is just as well equipped to judge the reasonableness of defendant's conduct on this score as it is when the inquiry is made as to defendant's negligence. The members of the jury draw upon their experiences and observations and set up some kind of a standard as a measure against which to appraise the defendant's conduct in the particular case. They would be justified in concluding that the wheel in this case was unreasonably dangerous according to the test stated in Restatement (Second) of Torts §402A, p. 352 (1965), requiring a finding that "[t]he article sold must be dangerous to an extent beyond that which would be contemplated by the ordinary consumer who purchases it, with the ordinary knowledge common to the community as to its characteristics."

The majority apparently would require some evidence of what this community standard is. How is this to be done? Certainly this is not the type of question which calls for the testimony of an expert witness. Are we to call lay witnesses to testify what "would be contemplated by the ordinary customer"? If that is required in the present case, it would be equally necessary in an ordinary negligence case to inform the jury of the community standard on such questions as the reasonableness of conduct in driving a car with respect to speed, lookout and control.

But we submit these questions of the reasonableness of defendant's conduct to the jury and, subject to the right of the court to decide as a matter of law that the standard was or was not met, we are willing to trust the jury's judgment as to the community standard and to appraise the defendant's conduct in light of it.

I believe that the question of defendant's liability is kept from the jury in the present case not because there is a lack of evidence upon which to sustain a verdict for plaintiff, but because the majority of the court, finding the imposition of strict liability a severe burden upon the seller, attempts to limit that burden by distorting the concept of the jury's function.

SLOAN, J., joins in this dissent.

The test for defective design adopted by the Oregon high court in *Heaton* has come to be known as the "consumer expectations" test. Although the strong majority of jurisdictions apply a risk-utility test, the consumer expectations test garners the support of some courts. See, e.g., Braswell v. Cincinnati Inc., 731 F.3d 1081, 1089 (10th Cir. 2013) (Given the lack of "any indication that the Oklahoma Supreme Court is inclined to adopt the risk-utility test, we will continue to apply the consumer expectations test to design defect cases."); Aubin v. Union Carbide Corp., 177 So. 3d 489, 494 (Fla. 2015) ("[W]e conclude that the definition of design defect . . . which utilizes the consumer expectations test, instead of utilizing the risk utility test and requiring proof of a reasonable alternative design, best vindicates the purposes underlying the doctrine of strict liability."). One question under the consumer expectations test is whether the court is concerned with the expectations of a reasonable person or with the actual expectations of the plaintiff. The Supreme Court of California has made it clear that "the jury considers the expectations of a hypothetical reasonable consumer, rather than those of the particular plaintiff in the case." Campbell v. General Motors Corp., 649 P.2d 224, 233 n.6 (Cal. 1982).

A well-known decision that combines a consumer expectations test for design defect with a risk-utility standard is Barker v. Lull Engineering Co., 573 P.2d 443 (Cal. 1978). The plaintiff in that case was a young, relatively inexperienced worker whose supervisor asked him to operate a high-lift loader on a sloping work site. The regular operator, learning of the location at which the loader would be operated that day and realizing the dangers presented by the rough, sloping terrain, had called in sick. The loader was a large machine capable of lifting heavy loads on forks similar to those on a forklift.

On the day of the accident in which he received injuries, the plaintiff first leveled the loader by means of a lever on the floor between his legs. As he was lifting a load of lumber to the second story of a building under construction, the loader appeared to begin to tip. Heeding the warnings from several co-workers, the plaintiff jumped from the loader and started to run. The loader tipped over, causing the load to fall on the plaintiff. The plaintiff's expert testified that the loader's relatively narrow wheel base made it unstable and likely to tip. Outriggers could have been incorporated in the design that would have made it more stable, preventing the accident. Also, the loader should have been equipped with a roll bar and a seat belt. In addition, the expert testified the lever used to level the machine should have been protected from accidental bumping, and the transmission should have had a "park" position.

Defendant's experts contradicted all of plaintiff's arguments. The court instructed the jury "that strict liability for a defect in design of a product is based on a finding that the product was unreasonably dangerous for its intended use." The jury returned its verdict for the defendant manufacturer. On appeal, the Supreme Court of California reversed and remanded (573 P.2d at 457-58):

> If a jury in determining liability for a defect in design is instructed only that it should decide whether or not there is "a defective design," it may reach to the extreme conclusion that the plaintiff, having suffered injury, should without further showing, recover; on the other hand, it may go to the opposite extreme and conclude that because the product matches the intended design the plaintiff, under no conceivable circumstances, could recover. The submitted definition eschews both extremes and attempts a balanced approach.
>
> We hold that a trial judge may properly instruct the jury that a product is defective in design (1) if the plaintiff demonstrates that the product failed to perform as safely as an ordinary consumer would expect when used in an intended or reasonably foreseeable manner, or (2) if the plaintiff proves that the product's design proximately caused his injury and the defendant fails to prove . . . that on balance the benefits of the challenged design outweigh the risk of danger inherent in such design.

The *Barker* decision has come to be understood as adopting a two-pronged test for defective design: the first prong is consumer expectations, and the second prong is risk-utility. Several other courts utilize the *Barker* two-pronged test for design-based liability, albeit with some nontrivial variations among them. See, e.g., In re Methyl Tertiary Butyl Ether (MTBE) Prods. Liab. Litig., 2015 WL 3763645 (S.D.N.Y. 2015) (applying Puerto Rico law); Tincher v. Omega Flex, Inc., 104 A.3d 328 (Pa. 2014); Knitz v. Minster Mach. Co., 432 N.E.2d 814 (Ohio), *cert. denied,* 459 U.S. 857 (1982); Gen. Motors Corp. v. Farnsworth, 965 P.2d 1209 (Alaska 1998); Acoba v. Gen. Tire, Inc., 986 P.2d 288 (Haw. 1999); Jackson v. Gen. Motors Corp., 60 S.W.3d 800 (Tenn. 2001); Mikolajczyk v. Ford

Motor Co., 901 N.E.2d 329 (Ill. 2008). However, it appears that only California and Alaska have coupled the two-pronged liability test with a shift to defendant of the burden of proof on the risk-utility issue.

Soule v. General Motors Corp.

8 Cal. 4th 548, 882 P.2d 298, 34 Cal. Rptr. 2d 607 (1994)

BAXTER, J.

Plaintiff's ankles were badly injured when her General Motors (GM) car collided with another vehicle. She sued GM, asserting that defects in her automobile allowed its left front wheel to break free, collapse rearward, and smash the floorboard into her feet. GM denied any defect and claimed that the force of the collision itself was the sole cause of the injuries. Expert witnesses debated the issues at length. Plaintiff prevailed at trial, and the Court of Appeal affirmed the judgment.

We granted review to resolve . . . [whether] a product's design [may] be found defective on grounds that the product's performance fell below the safety expectations of the ordinary consumer . . . if the question of how safely the product should have performed cannot be answered by the common experience of its users. . . .

Facts

On the early afternoon of January 16, 1984, plaintiff was driving her 1982 Camaro in the southbound center lane of Bolsa Chica Road, an arterial street in Westminster. There was a slight drizzle, the roadway was damp, and apparently plaintiff was not wearing her seat belt. A 1972 Datsun, approaching northbound, suddenly skidded into the path of plaintiff's car. The Datsun's left rear quarter struck plaintiff's Camaro in an area near the left front wheel. Estimates of the vehicles' combined closing speeds on impact vary from 30 to 70 miles per hour.

The collision bent the Camaro's frame adjacent to the wheel and tore loose the bracket that attached the wheel assembly (specifically, the lower control arm) to the frame. As a result, the wheel collapsed rearward and inward. The wheel hit the underside of the "toe pan" — the slanted floorboard area beneath the pedals — causing the toe pan to crumple, or "deform," upward into the passenger compartment.

Plaintiff received a fractured rib and relatively minor scalp and knee injuries. Her most severe injuries were fractures of both ankles, and the more serious of these was the compound compression fracture of her left ankle. This injury never healed properly. In order to relieve plaintiff's pain, an orthopedic surgeon fused the joint. As a permanent result, plaintiff cannot flex her left ankle. She walks with considerable difficulty, and her condition is expected to deteriorate.

After the accident, the Camaro was acquired by a salvage dealer, Noah Hipolito. Soon thereafter, plaintiff's son, Jeffrey Bishop, and her original attorney, Richard Hawkins, each inspected and photographed the car and its damaged floorboard area. The failed bracket assembly was retrieved. However, Hipolito later discarded the damaged toe pan, repaired the Camaro, and resold it. Thus, except for the bracket assembly, no part of the vehicle was retained as evidence.

Plaintiff sued GM for her ankle injuries, asserting a theory of strict tort liability for a defective product. She claimed the severe trauma to her ankles was not a natural consequence of the accident, but occurred when the collapse of the Camaro's wheel caused the toe pan to crush violently upward against her feet. Plaintiff attributed the wheel collapse to a manufacturing defect, the substandard quality of the weld attaching the lower control arm bracket to the frame. She also claimed that the placement of the bracket, and the configuration of the frame, were defective designs because they did not limit the wheel's rearward travel in the event the bracket should fail.

The available physical and circumstantial evidence left room for debate about the exact angle and force of the impact and the extent to which the toe pan had actually deformed. The issues of defect and causation were addressed through numerous experts produced by both sides in such areas as biomechanics, metallurgy, orthopedics, design engineering, and crash-test simulation.

Plaintiff submitted the results of crash tests, and also asserted the similarity of another real-world collision involving a 1987 Camaro driven by Dana Carr. According to plaintiff's experts, these examples indicated that Camaro accidents of similar direction and force do not generally produce wheel bracket assembly failure, extensive toe pan deformation, or severe ankle injuries such as those plaintiff had experienced. These experts opined that without the deformation of the toe pan in plaintiff's car, her accident could not have produced enough force to fracture her ankles.

A metallurgist testifying on plaintiff's behalf examined the failed bracket from her car. He concluded that its weld was particularly weak because of excess "porosity" caused by improper welding techniques. Plaintiff's experts also emphasized the alternative frame and bracket design used by the Ford Mustang of comparable model years. They asserted that the Mustang's design, unlike the Camaro's, provided protection against unlimited rearward travel of the wheel should a bracket assembly give way.

GM's metallurgist disputed the claims of excessive weakness or porosity in the bracket weld. Expert witnesses for GM also countered the assertions of defective design. GM asserted that the Camaro's bracket was overdesigned to withstand forces in excess of all expected uses. According to expert testimony adduced by GM, the Mustang's alternative frame and bracket configuration did not fit the Camaro's overall design goals and was not distinctly safer for all collision stresses to which the vehicle might be subjected. Indeed, one witness noted, at least one more recent Ford product had adopted the Camaro's design. . . .

The court instructed the jury that a manufacturer is liable for "enhanced" injuries caused by a manufacturing or design defect in its product while the product is being used in a foreseeable way. Over GM's objection, the court gave the standard design defect instruction without modification. . . . This instruction advised that a product is defective in design "if it fails to perform as safely as an ordinary consumer would expect when used in an intended *or* reasonably foreseeable manner or if there is a risk of danger inherent in the design which outweighs the benefit of the design." (Italics added.)

The jury was also told that in order to establish liability for a design defect under the "ordinary consumer expectations" standard, plaintiff must show (1) the manufacturer's product failed to perform as safely as an ordinary consumer would expect, (2) the defect existed when the product left the manufacturer's possession, (3) the defect was a "legal cause" of plaintiff's "enhanced injury," and (4) the product was used in a reasonably foreseeable manner. . . .

In a series of special findings, the jury determined that the Camaro contained a defect (of unspecified nature) which was a "legal cause" of plaintiff's "enhanced injury." . . . Plaintiff received an award of $1.65 million.

GM appealed. Among other things, it argued that the trial court erred by instructing on ordinary consumer expectations in a complex design-defect case, and by failing to give GM's special instruction on causation.

Following one line of authority, the Court of Appeal concluded that a jury may rely on expert assistance to determine what level of safe performance an ordinary consumer would expect under particular circumstances. Hence, the Court of Appeal ruled, there was no error in use of the ordinary consumer expectations standard for design defect in this case. . . .

Discussion

1. Test for design defect

[The courts' treatment of California law, including the decision in Barker v. Lull Engineering, above, is omitted.]

In *Barker,* we offered two alternative ways to prove a design defect, each appropriate to its own circumstances. The purposes, behaviors, and dangers of certain products are commonly understood by those who ordinarily use them. By the same token, the ordinary users or consumers of a product may have reasonable, widely accepted minimum expectations about the circumstances under which it should perform safely. Consumers govern their own conduct by these expectations, and products on the market should conform to them.

In some cases, therefore, "ordinary knowledge . . . as to . . . [the product's] characteristics" (Rest. 2d Torts, supra, §402A, com. *i,* p. 352) may permit an inference that the product did not perform as safely as it should. *If* the facts permit such a conclusion, and *if* the failure resulted from the product's design, a finding of defect is warranted without any further proof. The manufacturer may not defend a claim that a product's design failed to perform as safely as its ordinary consumers would expect by presenting expert evidence of the design's relative risks and benefits.[3]

However, as we noted in *Barker,* a complex product, even when it is being used as intended, may often cause injury in a way that does not engage its ordinary consumers' reasonable minimum assumptions about safe performance. For example, the ordinary consumer of an automobile simply has "no idea" how it should perform in all foreseeable situations, or how safe it should be made against all foreseeable hazards. (*Barker,* supra.)

An injured person is not foreclosed from proving a defect in the product's design simply because he cannot show that the reasonable minimum safety expectations of its ordinary consumers were violated. Under *Barker*'s alternative test, a product is still defective if its design embodies "excessive preventable danger" . . . that is, unless "the benefits of the . . . design outweigh the risk of danger inherent in such design" (id.). But this determination involves technical issues of feasibility, cost, practicality, risk, and benefit (id., at p. 431, 143 Cal. Rptr. 225, 573 P.2d 443) which are "impossible" to avoid. . . . In such cases, the jury *must* consider the manufacturer's evidence of competing design considerations . . . and the issue of design defect cannot fairly be resolved by standardless reference to the "expectations" of an "ordinary consumer."

3. For example, the ordinary consumers of modern automobiles may and do expect that such vehicles will be designed so as not to explode while idling at stoplights, experience sudden steering or brake failure as they leave the dealership, or roll over and catch fire in two-mile-per-hour collisions. If the plaintiff in a product liability action proved that a vehicle's design produced such a result, the jury could find forthwith that the car failed to perform as safely as its ordinary consumers would expect, and was therefore defective.

As we have seen, the consumer expectations test is reserved for cases in which the *everyday experience* of the product's users permits a conclusion that the product's design violated *minimum* safety assumptions, and is thus defective *regardless of expert opinion about the merits of the design.* It follows that where the minimum safety of a product is within the common knowledge of lay jurors, expert witnesses may not be used to demonstrate what an ordinary consumer would or should expect. Use of expert testimony for that purpose would invade the jury's function (see Evid. Code, §801, subd. (a)), and would invite circumvention of the rule that the risks and benefits of a challenged design must be carefully balanced whenever the issue of design defects goes beyond the common experience of the product's users.[4]

By the same token, the jury may not be left free to find a violation of ordinary consumer expectations whenever it chooses. Unless the facts actually permit an inference that the product's performance did not meet the minimum safety expectations of its ordinary users, the jury must engage in the balancing of risks and benefits required by the second prong of *Barker.*

Accordingly, as *Barker* indicated, instructions are misleading and incorrect if they allow a jury to avoid this risk-benefit analysis in a case where it is required. Instructions based on the ordinary consumer expectations prong of *Barker* are not appropriate where, as a matter of law, the evidence would not support a jury verdict on that theory. Whenever that is so, the jury must be instructed solely on the alternative risk-benefit theory of design defect announced in *Barker.*[5]

GM suggests that the consumer expectations test is improper whenever "crashworthiness," a complex product, or technical questions of causation are at issue. Because the variety of potential product injuries is infinite, the line cannot be drawn as clearly as GM proposes. But the fundamental distinction is not impossible to define. The crucial question in each individual case is whether the circumstances of the product's failure permit an inference that the product's design performed below the legitimate, commonly accepted minimum safety assumptions of its ordinary consumers.[6]

GM argues at length that the consumer expectations test is an "unworkable, amorphic, fleeting standard" which should be entirely abolished as a basis for design defect. In GM's view, the test is deficient and unfair in several respects. First, it defies definition. Second, it focuses not on the objective condition of products, but on the subjective, unstable, and often unreasonable opinions of consumers. Third, it ignores the reality that ordinary consumers know little about how safe the complex products they use can or should be made. Fourth, it invites the jury to isolate the particular consumer, component, accident, and injury before it instead of considering whether the whole product fairly accommodates the

4. Plaintiff insists that manufacturers should be forced to design their products to meet the "objective" safety demands of a "hypothetical" reasonable consumer who is fully informed about what he or she should expect. Hence, plaintiff reasons, the jury may receive expert advice on "reasonable" safety expectations for the product. However, this function is better served by the risk-benefit prong of *Barker.* There, juries receive expert advice, apply clear guidelines, and decide accordingly whether the product's design is an acceptable compromise of competing considerations. . . .

5. Plaintiff urges that any limitation on use of the consumer expectations test contravenes *Greenman*'s purpose to aid hapless consumers. But we have consistently held that manufacturers are not insurers of their products, they are liable to tort only when "defects" in their products cause injury. (E.g., Daly v. General Motors Corp. (1978) 20 Cal. 3d 725, 733, 144 Cal. Rptr. 380, 575 P.2d 1162; *Cronin,* supra, 8 Cal. 3d 121, 133.) *Barker* properly articulated that a product's design is "defective" only if it violates the "ordinary" consumer's safety expectations, or if the manufacturer cannot show the design's benefits outweigh its risks. . . .

6. Contrary to GM's suggestion, ordinary consumer expectations are not irrelevant simply because expert testimony is required to prove that the product failed as marketed, or that a condition of the product as marketed was a "substantial," and therefore "legal," cause of injury. We simply hold that the consumer expectations test is appropriate only when the jury, fully apprised of the circumstances of the accident or injury, may conclude that the product's design failed to perform as safely as its ordinary consumers would expect.

competing expectations of all consumers in all situations (see Daly v. General Motors Corp., supra). Fifth, it eliminates the careful balancing of risks and benefits which is essential to any design issue. . . .

We fully understand the dangers of improper use of the consumer expectations test. However, we cannot accept GM's insinuation that ordinary consumers lack any legitimate expectations about the minimum safety of the products they use. In particular circumstances, a product's design may perform so unsafely that the defect is apparent to the common reason, experience, and understanding of its ordinary consumers. In such cases, a lay jury is competent to make that determination. . . .

Applying our conclusions to the facts of this case, however, we agree that the instant jury should not have been instructed on ordinary consumer expectations. Plaintiff's theory of design defect was one of technical and mechanical detail. It sought to examine the precise behavior of several obscure components of her car under the complex circumstances of a particular accident. The collision's exact speed, angle, and point of impact were disputed. It seems settled, however, that plaintiff's Camaro received a substantial oblique blow near the left front wheel, and that the adjacent frame members and bracket assembly absorbed considerable inertial force.

An ordinary consumer of automobiles cannot reasonably expect that a car's frame, suspension, or interior will be designed to remain intact in any and all accidents. Nor would ordinary experience and understanding inform such a consumer how safely an automobile's design should perform under the esoteric circumstances of the collision at issue here. Indeed, both parties assumed that quite complicated design considerations were at issue, and that expert testimony was necessary to illuminate these matters. Therefore, injection of ordinary consumer expectations into the design defect equation was improper.

We are equally persuaded, however, that the error was harmless, because it is not reasonably probable defendant would have obtained a more favorable result in its absence. . . .

Here there were no instructions which specifically remedied the erroneous placement of the consumer expectations alternative before the jury. Moreover, plaintiff's counsel briefly reminded the jury that the instructions allowed it to find a design defect under either the consumer expectations or risk-benefit tests. However, the consumer expectations theory was never emphasized at any point. As previously noted, the case was tried on the assumption that the alleged design defect was a matter of technical debate. Virtually all the evidence and argument on design defect focused on expert evaluation of the strengths, shortcomings, risks, and benefits of the challenged design, as compared with a competitor's approach. . . .

Under these circumstances, we find it highly unlikely that a reasonable jury took that path. We see no reasonable probability that the jury disregarded the voluminous evidence on the risks and benefits of the Camaro's design, and instead rested its verdict on its independent assessment of what an ordinary consumer would expect. Accordingly, we conclude, the error in presenting that theory to the jury provides no basis for disturbing the trial judgment.[8]

[Discussion of other issues omitted.]

8. In a separate argument, raised for the first time in GM's brief on the merits, both GM and the Council urge us to reconsider *Barker*'s holding — embodied in the standard instruction received by this jury — that under the risk-benefit test, the manufacturer has the burden of proving that the utility of the challenged design outweighs its dangers. (*Barker,* supra. . . .) We explained in *Barker* that placement of the risk-benefit burden on the manufacturer is appropriate because the considerations which influenced the design of its product are "peculiarly within . . . [its] knowledge." (Id. . . .) Furthermore, we observed the "fundamental policies" of *Greenman* dictate that a manufacturer who seeks to escape design defect liability on risk-benefit grounds "should bear the burden of persuading the trier of fact that its product should not be judged defective. . . ." (Id. . . .)

Conclusion

The trial court erred when it instructed on the consumer expectations test for design defect. . . . However, [the] error [did not cause] actual prejudice. Accordingly, the judgment of the Court of Appeal, upholding the trial court judgment in favor of plaintiff, is affirmed.

KENNARD, GEORGE, WERDEGAR BOREN, JJ., concur.

[Concurring opinions omitted.]

In Morson v. San Diego Superior Court, 109 Cal. Rptr. 2d 343 (2001), a California intermediate appellate court refused to apply the consumer expectations prong of the test for defective design to a claim that latex rubber gloves had caused allergic reactions in health care workers. The court held that the consumer expectations test was applicable only when the product failure was so straightforward as to negate the need for expert testimony. The plaintiffs' design claims against the glove manufacturer could only be brought under the risk-utility prong of the *Barker/Soule* standard, and required competent expert testimony regarding the feasibility of alternative designs to reduce the risks to allergic users. See also Tillman v. C.R. Bard, Inc., 2015 WL 1456657, at *25 (M.D. Fla. 2015) ("Because this case pertains to a complex medical device, accessible to the consumer only through a physician, the Court finds that the consumer-expectation test is not applicable here."). Although many of the two-prong test jurisdictions do tend to demarcate the tests' applicability based on this simple/complex product failure divide, others, such as the Izzarelli v. R.J. Reynolds Tobacco Co. case set out below, pp. 594-595, believe that the simple/complex distinction cleaves too bluntly.

One jurisdiction that went farthest toward carving out an independent role for consumer expectations in the design defect context was Wisconsin. See Green v. Smith & Nephew AHP, Inc., 629 N.W.2d 727 (Wis. 2001), in which the court held that the consumer expectations test applied to design claims based on the same facts as in *Morson*. The Wisconsin high court in *Green* held that the consumer expectations test applied to all claims of defective design whether or not they pertained to a complex product. In 2011, however, the state of Wisconsin passed legislation abandoning the consumer expectations test in favor of the Products Liability Restatement model. Act of Jan. 27, 2011, sec. 31, §895.047(1)(a) Wis. Sess. Laws 1, 6-7 (codified at Wis. Stat. §895.047(1)(a)).

The Restatement (Third) adopts a risk-utility standard for design defect claims (see §2(b), p. 536, above), and rejects consumer expectations as a general, stand-alone test for defective design (§2, comment *g*):

> *g. Consumer expectations: general considerations.* Under Subsection (b), consumer expectations do not constitute an independent standard for judging the defectiveness of product designs. Courts frequently rely, in part, on consumer expectations when discussing liability based on other theories of liability. Some courts, for example, use the term

---

GM argues that *Barker* unfairly requires the manufacturer to "prove a negative"—i.e., the absence of a safer alternative design. The Council suggests our "peculiar knowledge" rationale is unrealistic under liberal modern discovery rules. We are not persuaded. *Barker* allows the evaluation of competing designs, but it does not require proof that the challenged design is the safest possible alternative. The manufacturer need only show that given the inherent complexities of design, the benefits of its chosen design outweigh the dangers. Moreover, modern discovery practice neither redresses the inherent technical imbalance between manufacturer and consumer nor dictates that the injured consumer should bear the primary burden of evaluating a design developed and chosen by the manufacturer. GM and the Council fail to convince us that *Barker* was incorrectly decided in this respect.

> "reasonable consumer expectations" as an equivalent of "proof of a reasonable, safer design alternative," since reasonable consumers have a right to expect product designs that conform to the reasonableness standard in Subsection (b). Other courts, allowing an inference of defect to be drawn when the incident is of a kind that ordinarily would occur as a result of product defect, observe that products that fail when put to their manifestly intended use disappoint reasonable consumer expectations. See §3. [p. 535, above.] However, consumer expectations do not play a determinative role in determining defectiveness. Consumer expectations, standing alone, do not take into account whether the proposed alternative design could be implemented at reasonable cost, or whether an alternative design would provide greater overall safety. Nevertheless, consumer expectations about product performance and the dangers attendant to product use affect how risks are perceived and relate to foreseeability and frequency of the risks of harm, both of which are relevant under Subsection (b). See Comment *f.* Such expectations are often influenced by how products are portrayed and marketed and can have a significant impact on consumer behavior. Thus, although consumer expectations do not constitute an independent standard for judging the defectiveness of product designs, they may substantially influence or even be ultimately determinative on risk-utility balancing in judging whether the omission of a proposed alternative design renders the product not reasonably safe.

Part of the reason for rejecting the consumer expectations test as an independent marker of design defect was the Restatement (Third) Reporters' view that courts in actual practice almost always rest a finding of defectiveness on evidence of a reasonable alternative design, irrespective of whether their doctrine is phrased in terms of consumer expectations. See Aaron D. Twerski & James H. Henderson, Jr., Manufacturers' Liability for Defective Product Designs: The Triumph of Risk-Utility, 74 Brook. L. Rev. 1061 (2008). Even defenders of the view that a consumer expectations test might be desirable have agreed with the Reporters' assessment. See Douglas A. Kysar, The Expectations of Consumers, 103 Colum. L. Rev. 1700, 1706 (2003) (reviewing consumer expectations — based decisions and concluding that, "as predicted by the Reporters, the decisions tend to fit quite comfortably within the doctrinal framework established by the Third Restatement, despite the courts' proclamations to the contrary").

A good example is the case of Mikolajczyk v. Ford Motor Co., cited above for adopting the *Barker* two-pronged test for design defect. Although the *Mikolajczyk* court stated that it was retaining consumer expectations as a stand-alone test, it also indicated that once either party introduced evidence relevant to a risk-utility test, then consumer expectations become but one factor under the risk-utility test. 901 N.E. 2d at 352. In Show v. Ford Motor Co., 659 F.3d 584 (7th Cir. 2011), plaintiffs injured in a rollover accident argued that their 1993 Ford Explorer was defectively designed due to instability. Writing for a unanimous panel, Judge Easterbrook affirmed the trial judge's grant of summary judgment to defendant manufacturer:

> Plaintiffs' argument that jurors should be able to rely on their own expectations as consumers reflects a belief that "expectations" are all that matters. Yet because under *Mikolajczyk* the consumer-expectations approach is just a means of getting at some issues that bear on the question whether a product is unreasonably dangerous, it is impossible to dispense with expert knowledge. . . .
>
> Counsel for the plaintiffs repeat the mantra that cars "just don't roll over in low-speed collisions" unless defectively designed. How do they know that? The record doesn't tell us even why this car rolled over, let alone what cars usually do in particular kinds of collisions — or what design changes could reduce the rollover rate, by how much. . . .
>
> Because consumer expectations are just one factor in the inquiry whether a product is unreasonably dangerous, a jury unassisted by expert testimony would have to rely on speculation. This record does not show whether 1993 Explorers are unduly (or

> unexpectedly) dangerous, because it lacks evidence about many issues, such as: (a) under what circumstances they roll over; (b) under what circumstances consumers expect them to do so; (c) whether it would be possible to reduce the rollover rate; and (d) whether a different and safer design would have averted this particular accident. All of these are subjects on which plaintiffs bear the burden of proof. [Id. at 587-588]

Another jurisdiction that combines a limited role for consumer expectations with risk-utility analysis is Connecticut. In Potter v. Chicago Pneumatic Tool Co., 694 A.2d 1319 (Conn. 1997), the court held that juries may be able to infer a defect in design without expert testimony under certain circumstances, but not for cases "involving complex product designs in which an ordinary consumer may not be able to form expectations of safety." Id. at 1333. In such cases, the court held that Connecticut law requires application of a "modified consumer expectation test" that focuses on "various factors that balance the utility of the product's design with the magnitude of its risks." Id.

The *Potter* case left many questions unanswered, including the often determinative one of whether consumer expectations of a product's hazards can be used defensively by product manufacturers to, in essence, preclude plaintiff's demonstration of a reasonable alternative design. The following decision brings considerable clarity.

Izzarelli v. R.J. Reynolds Tobacco Co.

136 A.3d 1232 (Conn. 2016)

McDonald, J.

We have been asked by the United States Court of Appeals for the Second Circuit to consider whether the "[g]ood tobacco" exception to strict products liability contained in comment (i) to §402A of the Restatement (Second) of Torts [("The article sold must be dangerous to an extent beyond that which would be contemplated by the ordinary consumer. . . . Good tobacco is not unreasonably dangerous merely because the effects of smoking may be harmful; but tobacco containing something like marijuana may be unreasonably dangerous.")] precludes an action in this state against a cigarette manufacturer for including additives and manipulating the nicotine in its cigarettes in a manner that ultimately increases the user's risk of cancer. . . .

This case requires us to revisit our seminal strict product liability precedent, Potter v. Chicago Pneumatic Tool Co., 241 Conn. 199, 694 A.2d 1319 (1997), and to clarify the proper purview of the two strict liability tests recognized in that case: the ordinary consumer expectation test and the modified consumer expectation test. We conclude that the modified consumer expectation test is our primary strict product liability test, and the sole test applicable to the present case. Because the obvious danger exceptions to strict liability in comment (i) to §402A of the Restatement (Second), including "[g]ood tobacco," are not dispositive under the multifactor modified consumer expectation test, we answer the certified question in the negative. . . .

I

. . . In 1997, in *Potter*, this court considered the viability of our ordinary consumer expectation test for design defect cases. The defendants in that case had requested that the court abandon that test for such cases in favor of the risk-utility test in the second tentative draft of the Restatement (Third) of Torts. The court declined to adopt the test in the draft Restatement (Third). The court viewed an absolute requirement of proof of a feasible alternative design to impose an undue burden on plaintiffs and to preclude claims that should be valid even in the absence of such proof.

Although the court in *Potter* maintained its allegiance to §402A, it acknowledged criticisms of the ordinary consumer expectation test and decided that some change in our law was necessary because that test also could preclude relief for valid claims. In particular, the court pointed to the problem of complex products for which a consumer might not have informed safety expectations. The court was concerned, however, with shifting the focus to the conduct of the manufacturer and in turn abandoning strict liability. Accordingly, the court decided to adopt a test that would incorporate risk-utility factors into the ordinary consumer framework. Under the "modified" consumer expectation test, the jury would weigh the product's risks and utility and then inquire, in light of those factors, whether a "reasonable consumer would consider the product design unreasonably dangerous." Id., at 221, 694 A.2d 1319. The court's sample jury instruction incorporated the definition of unreasonably dangerous from comment (i) to §402A of the Restatement (Second) and then provided a nonexclusive list of factors that could be used to determine what an ordinary consumer would expect. "The availability of a feasible alternative design is a factor that a plaintiff may, rather than must, prove in order to establish that a product's risks outweigh its utility." Id., at 221, 694 A.2d 1319.

The court in *Potter* emphasized that . . . the ordinary consumer expectation test would be appropriate when the incident causing injury is so bizarre or unusual that the jury would not need expert testimony to conclude that the product failed to meet the consumer's expectations. . . .

Potter was decided at a point in time when Connecticut design defect jurisprudence was not well developed. Indeed, as the present case illustrates, because actions under our liability act often have been brought in federal court, this court has had limited opportunities to do so. Subsequent case law and commentary has indicated that *Potter* was not clear as to when resort to each test would be appropriate and under what circumstances both tests properly could be submitted to a jury. . . . The present case is a paradigmatic example of the confusion left in *Potter*'s wake. The defendant contends that, under *Potter*, only the ordinary consumer expectation test applies to the present case because the modified test is limited to complex designs for which consumers lack safety expectations. The plaintiff contends that, under *Potter*, the modified consumer expectation test is the default test with the ordinary test limited to res ipsa type cases, in which the consumer's minimum expectations of the product have not been met. We have not been presented with an opportunity since *Potter* to address squarely our design defect standards. We therefore take this opportunity to revisit *Potter* and dispel the ambiguity created by it, with the advantage of hindsight informed by almost two decades of subsequent developments in product liability law.

II

. . . For the reasons set forth subsequently, we reach the following conclusions regarding the standards for a strict product liability action based on defective design generally and in the present case. Under *Potter*, the modified consumer expectation test is our primary test. The ordinary consumer expectation test is reserved for cases in which the product failed to meet the ordinary consumer's minimum safety expectations, such as res ipsa type cases. A jury could not reasonably conclude that cigarettes that cause cancer fail to meet the consumer's minimum safety expectations. Therefore, the plaintiff was required to proceed under the modified consumer expectation test. Comment (i) to §402A of the Restatement (Second) does not present a per se bar to recovery under the modified consumer expectation test. Accordingly, the answer to the certified question is "no."

To begin, we acknowledge that there is language in *Potter*, as well as in subsequent Connecticut case law, that could support each of the following interpretations of our strict liability standards for design defects: (1) the ordinary consumer expectation test is the primary test, with the modified consumer expectation test reserved exclusively for complex product designs for which an ordinary consumer could not form safety expectations (simple/complex divide); (2) the modified consumer expectation test is the default test, with the ordinary consumer expectation test reserved for products that fail to meet minimum safety expectations; and (3) a plaintiff may elect to proceed under either test or both tests, such that, even if the claim fails under the ordinary consumer expectation test, the plaintiff may prevail under the modified consumer expectation test with the assistance of expert testimony.

We are not persuaded that *Potter* intended to draw a simple/complex divide. The court in *Potter* pointed to the problem in proving consumers' safety expectations for complex products because that concern was implicated in the case before the court and was the most obvious misfit for the ordinary consumer expectation test. *Potter* involved pneumatic hand tools alleged to be defective because they exposed users to excessive vibration, which in turn caused permanent vascular and neurological damage to the users' hands. The plaintiffs relied on expert testimony from various engineers and industry standards to prove their case. Id., at 204-206, 694 A.2d 1319. Notably, although concerns about proof for complex products was foremost in the court's mind when adopting the modified test, the court stated no limitations on the circumstances in which that test could be applied. Instead, all of the limitations discussed were in reference to the application of the ordinary consumer expectation test.

Moreover, a simple/complex divide would not be ideal because the line between these categories is not always clear. Indeed, one could readily categorize the defendant's Salem cigarettes as a complex product because of the hundreds of ingredients incorporated into Salem cigarettes, as well as the myriad physical, chemical and biochemical variables that were considered in designing that product. Alternatively, one could view the defendant's cigarettes as a simple product if characterized as nothing more than a nicotine delivery system that carries a known risk of causing cancer.

We observe that other jurisdictions that apply both a consumer expectation test and a risk-utility test have rejected the simple/complex divide. See, e.g., Mikolajczyk v. Ford Motor Co., 231 Ill.2d 516, 528-41, 327 Ill. Dec. 1, 901 N.E.2d 329 (2008) (rejecting argument that risk-utility test is only test to be applied if product is complex and if injury occurred in circumstances unfamiliar to average consumer and that consumer expectation test is reserved for cases involving simple products or everyday circumstances).

Although some of the shortcomings of the ordinary consumer expectation test have been best illustrated in relation to complex designs, the concerns with this test have never been limited to such designs. See, e.g., J. Beasley, Products Liability and the Unreasonably Dangerous Requirement (1981) p. 88 (asserting that consumer expectation test has "little logical application to new products, where no expectation of safety may have developed, or to obscure products with a limited market, where the number of consumers is not conducive to a clear consensus," and also noting opposite problem, that "if an entire industry rejects a safe design and uses an unsafe one, the unsafe one may have become expected"); see also S. Birnbaum, "Unmasking the Test for Design Defect: From Negligence [to Warranty] to Strict Liability to Negligence," 33 Vanderbilt L. Rev. 593, 613-15 (1980) (discussing generally applicable concerns with ordinary consumer expectation test). One significant concern has been that the ordinary consumer expectation test, which deems unreasonable only those dangers that would not be anticipated by an ordinary consumer, could preclude recovery whenever a product's dangers were open and obvious.

The court in *Potter* had no occasion to address this concern. Nonetheless, it is evident that limiting the modified test to complex products for which the consumer could not form safety expectations would be antithetical to the public policies informing our product liability law. A consequence of such a limitation would be to immunize manufacturers even when they readily could have reduced or eliminated the product's danger. It could also immunize manufacturers for design decisions that increase the risk of known dangers, as in the present case. Our legislature's express rejection of comparative or contributory negligence as a bar to recovery in a strict liability action would be in tension with a sweeping immunity based solely on the consumer's knowledge. Moreover, *Potter* expanded our product liability tests to remove impediments to recovery.

More fundamentally, providing such immunity would remove an important incentive to improving product safety. For this reason, there has been a clear and overwhelming trend in other jurisdictions to allow consumers to pursue defective product design claims despite open and obvious dangers, usually under a multifactor risk-utility test.

Making the modified consumer expectation test our default test for design defect claims, and reserving the ordinary consumer expectation test for those products that fail to meet legitimate, commonly accepted minimum safety expectations, provides a safety incentive that is consonant with our state's public policies. Moreover, such a framework is the only one that can be reconciled with this court's direction in *Potter* that the jury could be instructed on both tests if supported by the evidence. Allowing the jury to consider both tests is only logical if the standard, and not merely the nature of proof, differs under each test. If the two tests were merely alternative methods of proving the same standard — the product failed to meet the ordinary consumer's expectations — then a jury's verdict that this standard was not met under one test could not logically be reconciled with a verdict that this standard was met under the other test. Either the product met the ordinary consumer's expectations, or it did not. If, however, one test sets the floor for recovery — a product that meets minimum safety expectations — then a verdict for the defendant on that test logically could be reconciled with a plaintiff's verdict on a test that sets a higher standard. In other words, a product might meet the consumer's minimum safety expectations because the product's dangers are known or obvious but nonetheless be defective because it could have been designed to be less dangerous without unreasonably compromising cost or utility (e.g., a table saw lacking a safety guard).

Accordingly, we hold that, under our product liability law, the ordinary consumer expectation test is reserved for those limited cases in which a product fails to meet a consumer's legitimate, commonly accepted minimum safety expectations. Expert testimony on product design is not needed to prove the product's defect, nor is the utility of the product's design an excuse for the undisclosed defect. All other cases should be determined under the modified consumer expectation test.

With this clarification of our law, it is evident that the plaintiff in the present case properly could proceed only under the modified consumer expectation test. A cigarette that exposes the user to carcinogens and the attendant risk of cancer cannot be said to fail to meet an ordinary consumer's legitimate, commonly accepted minimum safety expectations. To establish the defect, the plaintiff's case required expert testimony on cigarette design and manufacture, as well as the feasibility of an alternative design. . . .

Finally, we turn to the question of whether comment (i) to §402A of the Restatement (Second) is a per se bar to the plaintiff's recovery under the modified consumer expectation test. We conclude that it is not.

Comment (i) to §402A serves a limited role under the modified consumer expectation test. Although the modified test asks the jury to weigh various factors through the ultimate lens of the consumer's expectations, as a functional and practical matter that weighing process supplants the definition in comment (i) of unreasonably dangerous. In other words, the factors that the court in *Potter* identified essentially provide the jury with information that a fully informed consumer would know before deciding whether to purchase the product. When the consumer has specific product expectations that differ from those factors, those too may be factored into the weighing process. It could be that, in a given case, the consumer's expectations of the product would be the determinative factor.

To allow the ordinary consumer's awareness of the product's potential danger to preclude recovery as a matter of law, however, would make Connecticut an outlier and defeat our intention in relegating the ordinary consumer expectation test to a more limited role. Indeed, irrespective of the incorporation of the definition of unreasonably dangerous from comment (i) to §402A into the modified test, it would be contrary to the public policy of this state to incorporate the exceptions in comment (i) insofar as they would immunize a manufacturer from liability for manipulating the inherently dangerous properties of its product to pose a greater risk of danger to the consumer.

We answer the certified question "no."

In this opinion Eveleigh, Robinson and Vertefeuille, Js., concurred.

[The concurring opinion of Zarella, J., joined by Espinosa, J., which argued for explicit adoption of the Restatement (Third) of Torts, Products Liability design defect standard, is omitted. In response to the concurrence, the majority opinion stated:

> The concurring justices would go further and take this occasion to adopt the test in the Restatement (Third) of Torts. We decline to consider that issue in the present case principally because neither party sought to have the jury charged under the Restatement (Third) test, which would have required the jury to make a finding that was not required under either of our current tests, namely, that there was a feasible, safer alternative. Although the plaintiff did present evidence on that matter, the jury was free to conclude that Salem cigarettes are unreasonably dangerous even if it did not credit that evidence. Therefore, we conclude that it is appropriate and sufficient in the present case to clarify the circumstances under which the existing tests apply rather than adopt a new legal standard.

[Id. at n. 11]

Problem 34

The facts from Problem 33, p. 580, above, are incorporated by reference. The partner in charge of that case would like to know if there is any substantial chance of reaching the jury with a design claim on the assumption that your jurisdiction applies a consumer expectations standard in judging defective design.

C. Liability for Failure to Instruct or Warn

As reflected in some of the decisions set forth in the preceding section on defective designs, whenever a commercial seller markets a product, the seller must provide needed instructions regarding proper use and must warn of hidden risks. If adequate instructions and warnings are not provided to purchasers and users, the seller may be liable for supplying a defective product even if the product in question is free from manufacturing defects and even if the product design is not, judged on its own merits, unreasonably dangerous. In many cases the plaintiff will rely on traditional negligence principles, alleging that the defendant's duty of care has been breached. Failure to provide adequate instructions or warning can also support a conclusion that the product, as marketed, is defective, and thus the seller is strictly liable in tort. The following comment to §402A of the Restatement (Second) explains how failure-to-warn supports strict liability:

> *j. Directions or warning*. In order to prevent the product from being unreasonably dangerous, the seller may be required to give directions or warning, on the container, as to its use. The seller may reasonably assume that those with common allergies, as for example to eggs or strawberries, will be aware of them, and he is not required to warn against them. Where, however, the product contains an ingredient to which a substantial number of the population are allergic, and the ingredient is one whose danger is not generally known, or if known is one which the consumer would reasonably not expect to find in the product, the seller is required to give warning against it, if he has knowledge, or by the application of reason, developed human skill and foresight should have knowledge, of the presence of the ingredient and the danger. Likewise in the case of poisonous drugs, or those unduly dangerous for other reasons, warnings as to use may be required.
>
> But a seller is not required to warn with respect to products, or ingredients in them, which are only dangerous, or potentially so, when consumed in excessive quantity, or over a long period of time, when the danger, or potentiality of danger, is generally known and recognized. Again the dangers of alcoholic beverages are an example, as are also those of foods containing such substances as saturated fats, which may over a period of time have a deleterious effect upon the human heart.
>
> Where warning is given, the seller may reasonably assume that it will be read and heeded; and a product bearing such a warning, which is safe for use if it is followed, is not in defective condition, nor is it unreasonably dangerous.

One question raised by the preceding comment, with its requirement that the seller know of the risks or be in the position that he should have known, is whether the approach in §402A is different in substance from traditional negligence principles.

Sheckells v. AGV Corp.

987 F.2d 1532 (11th Cir. 1993)

Birch, Circuit Judge.

Plaintiff Charles Sheckells ("Sheckells"), the natural father and guardian of John Sheckells, an incapacitated adult, appeals from the grant of summary judgment in favor of AGV, a defendant in the underlying product liability action. The grant of summary judgment in favor of AGV is Affirmed in Part and Reversed in Part.

I. Background

John Sheckells was injured when he lost control of his motorcycle after striking debris in the road. At the time of the accident, he was wearing a helmet manufactured by AGV. On behalf of his son, Sheckells filed suit against AGV alleging that the helmet was defectively designed and manufactured and that the defendants failed to warn that the helmet would not afford any significant protection from certain reasonably foreseeable impacts. On appeal, Sheckells has abandoned his theory of defective design and appeals the judgment only upon the failure to warn theory.

When purchased, the helmet contained a warning label affixed to the inside of the helmet, stating in substance that "some reasonably foreseeable impacts may exceed this helmet's capability to protect against severe injury or death." In addition, the helmet was packaged with a consumer notice that informs the purchaser that "[y]our helmet is the single most important piece of safety equipment you own and should be treated as such." The notice further states that "NO HELMET, including your AGV helmet, can protect the wearer against all foreseeable impacts" and that "NO WARRANTY OR REPRESENTATION IS MADE AS TO THIS PRODUCT'S ABILITY TO PROTECT THE USER FROM ANY INJURY OR DEATH. THE USER ASSUMES ALL RISKS."

In opposition to summary judgment, Sheckells offered the deposition testimony of Dr. Joseph L. Burton, the Chief Medical Examiner for the City of Atlanta. With regard to the failure to warn claim, Dr. Burton testified that Department of Transportation and Snell Memorial Foundation impact tests are conducted at speeds of only 15 to 20 miles an hour and that no motorcycle helmet marketed today provides any assurance of protecting the wearer from facial or brain injury at speeds of 30 or 45 miles an hour. Further, he opined that the average purchaser of a helmet would not know these facts.

The district court entered summary judgment in favor of AGV on the failure to warn theory on the ground that it was open and obvious that the AGV helmet would not protect an operator traveling at 30 to 45 miles an hour. Sheckells appeals the grant of summary judgment.

II. Discussion . . .

In this diversity action, AGV's duty to warn of hazards posed by the use of its products is determined by Georgia law. . . . Under Georgia law, a manufacturer is subject to liability for failure to warn if it "(a) knows or has reason to know that the chattel is or is likely to be dangerous for the use for which it is supplied, and (b) has no reason to believe that those for whose use the chattel is supplied will realize its dangerous condition and (c) fails to exercise reasonable care to inform them of its dangerous condition or of the facts which make it likely to be dangerous." Greenway v. Peabody Intl. Corp., 163 Ga. App. 698, 703, 294 S.E.2d 541, 545-546 (1982) (quoting Restatement (Second) of Torts §388). Georgia law imposes no duty on a manufacturer to warn of a danger associated with the use of its product if that danger is open or obvious.

> [T]here is no duty resting upon the manufacturer or seller to warn of a product-connected danger which is obvious, or of which the person who claims to be entitled to warning knows, should know, or should, in using the product, discover.

294 S.E.2d at 546 (quoting Annotation, Products Liability — Duty to Warn, 76 A.L.R.2d 9, 28-29 (1961)).

At his deposition, Dr. Burton testified that, although no motorcycle helmet on the market today would provide any assurance of protecting an operator from facial or brain injury at a speed of 30 to 45 miles an hour, "the average buyer of a helmet would not know that." Dr. Burton also testified that representations made by vendors of motorcycles and helmets may lull a purchaser into a false sense of security regarding the amount of protection provided by a helmet. Dr. Burton concluded that, in order to dispel this impression, some warning should accompany the helmet to educate the user that the helmet provides no significant protection at speeds exceeding 30 to 45 miles an hour. Thus, Dr. Burton's deposition, viewed in the light most favorable to the plaintiff, suggests that the failure of a motorcycle helmet to protect the wearer at speeds over 30 to 45 miles an hour is not an open or obvious danger.

AGV presented no evidence tending to show that it is open or obvious that its helmet would not protect the wearer at speeds of 30 to 45 miles an hour. That the parties' experts agree that no helmet currently marketed could protect a wearer traveling at speeds of 45 miles an hour does not mean that this fact is patent to a purchaser. Presumably, these experts are "expert" for the reason that they possess knowledge not generally shared with the public. As noted by the Greenway court, the focus of the open or obvious danger rule is upon "those for whose use the chattel is supplied." 294 S.E.2d at 545-546.

The district court relied on several Georgia cases for the proposition that "it is a matter of common knowledge that operating a motorcycle carries with it certain inherent dangers." While recognizing the inherent hazard of operating a motorcycle, these cases do not establish as a matter of Georgia law that safety precautions, such as a helmet, openly and obviously provide insignificant protection at speeds of 30 to 45 miles an hour. Further, those cases where the Georgia courts have concluded that a peril associated with a product is open or obvious suggest that summary judgment was inappropriate based on the factual record before the district court. The Georgia courts have determined that, under certain circumstances, operating a product without the safety features included by the manufacturer is an open or obvious hazard. See, e.g., Weatherby v. Honda Motor Co., 195 Ga. App. 169, 393 S.E.2d 64, 67 (1990) (danger in operating motorcycle with uncapped fuel tank is open and obvious). Additionally, the Georgia cases reveal that the observable absence of a safety feature is likely to be considered an open and obvious danger. In each of these cases, however, the absence of the safety feature in question was apparent to the purchaser by a simple visual inspection. By contrast, it is not obvious from an observation of the AGV helmet that this product provides only minimal protection against collision when the motorcycle is operated at speeds of 30 to 45 miles an hour. Conceivably, a purchaser might expect more from "the single most important piece of safety equipment" that he or she owns. Further, Dr. Burton's testimony suggests that the limited degree of protection afforded by wearing a helmet is not common knowledge. The evidence presented by the plaintiff was sufficient to raise an issue of fact regarding the open or obvious nature of this hazard. Thus, in granting summary judgment for AGV with respect to the failure to warn claim, the district court erred by resolving a material and genuinely disputed issue of fact against the plaintiff.

AGV further contends that summary judgment was appropriate based on either of two issues not reached by the district court. First, AGV argues that John Sheckells did not read the allegedly inadequate warnings, and, thus, the failure to warn was not a proximate cause of his injuries. AGV relies on John Sheckells's deposition testimony that he did not remember reading the warning label affixed to the helmet or the literature that was packaged with the helmet. John Sheckells did not testify that he did not read the warnings, only that he did not remember doing so. Based on the factual record before the district court, it is possible that this failure to remember was due to his memory loss, suffered as a result of the accident. Additionally, Charles Sheckells testified at his deposition that he discussed the consumer warnings with his son at the time the helmet was purchased. Therefore, there is a genuine dispute of material fact as to proximate cause, and summary judgment is inappropriate.

AGV also maintains that summary judgment was proper since the warnings included with the helmet were adequate as a matter of law. The district court did not reach this issue. The consumer information packaged with the helmet explains that no helmet "can protect the wearer against all foreseeable impacts." While this warning informs the purchaser that certain foreseeable impacts exceed the helmet's capacity to protect the wearer, it falls short of informing the purchaser that the helmet will not provide any significant degree of protection at speeds of 30 to 45 miles an hour. Dr. Burton's testimony, viewed in the light most favorable to Sheckells, establishes a lack of consumer awareness of the degree of protection provided by a helmet at median and high speeds. AGV has not, at this stage of the litigation, proffered sufficient facts to show that this warning was sufficient as a matter of law.

The consumer information sheet also informs the purchaser that no warranty or representation is made as to the helmet's ability to protect the user from any injury or death and that the user assumes all risks. AGV contends that this statement, couched in language typically used in disclaimers of legal responsibility, also serves as a warning to purchasers. Whether this language was sufficient to warn the user that the helmet, which was described in the consumer information as "the single most important piece of safety equipment you own," would provide no significant protection at speeds of over 30 to 45 miles an hour is, at this stage of the proceeding, a disputed issue of fact.

III. Conclusion

The grant of summary judgment in favor of AGV is affirmed with regard to the claim of defective design or manufacture. In granting summary judgment on the failure to warn theory, however, the district court erred by resolving a disputed and material issue of fact regarding the open or obvious nature of the limited protection provided by AGV's helmet. Summary judgment on the failure to warn claim is therefore reversed.

In Westry v. Bell Helmets, Inc., 487 N.W.2d 781 (Mich. Ct. App. 1992), on substantially the same facts as in *Sheckells*, the court of appeals affirmed a summary judgment for defendant manufacturer on the ground that the risks of serious injury from high-speed motorcycle crashes were open and obvious.

When reasonable persons can differ as to the obviousness of the danger, the issue is for the trier of fact. See Restatement (Third) of Torts: Products Liability §2, cmt. *j* (1998). One area in which courts have differed on the issue of whether risks are obvious involves trampolines. Cf. Parish v. Jumpking, p. 575, supra, which focused on the design aspects of trampoline liability. Consistent with that case, appellate courts have been hard on plaintiffs who bring failure-to-warn claims against trampoline manufacturers. Thus, in Sollami v. Eaton, 747 N.E.2d 375 (Ill. App. Ct. 2001), the intermediate appellate court reversed the trial court's ruling for defendant and held that the risks presented by a trampoline were not open and obvious to teenage users as a matter of law. The court of appeals held that extensive warnings provided in the instruction manual indicated the defendant manufacturer's superior knowledge regarding using the trampoline without adult supervision, and imposed a duty to warn of those risks other than in a manual that teenagers were not likely to read. The Illinois Supreme Court reversed the intermediate appellate court and affirmed the trial court's ruling that the risks of harm from a trampoline are obvious to teenage users as a matter of law. See Sollami v. Eaton, 772 N.E.2d 215 (Ill. 2002).

Another group of cases in which the obviousness of the risks has been the subject of controversy involves alcoholic beverages. The general rule is that the risks of excessive drinking are obvious and therefore need not be warned against. See, e.g., Cook v. MillerCoors, LLC, 872 F. Supp. 2d 1346 (M.D. Fla. 2012) (holding that the risks of consuming excessive amounts of an alcoholic beverage are reasonably obvious even though the beverage in question was also marketed as an energy drink); Maguire v. Pabst Brewing Co., 387 N.W.2d 565 (Iowa 1986) (no duty to warn of the dangers of drinking too much beer prior to driving automobile). But there have been exceptions. In Hon v. Stroh Brewery Co., 835 F.2d 510 (3d Cir. 1987), plaintiff's decedent died from pancreatitis at the age of 26. Medical experts supported plaintiff's claim that relatively moderate consumption of beer distributed by defendant — two or three cans per night on an average of four nights a week for a period of six years — caused his fatal disease. The district court granted summary judgment for defendant, relying on the general rule that the risks of drinking alcohol are widely known. The court of appeals reversed, concluding (835 F.2d at 514):

> [The medical] affidavits provide evidence tending to show that beer in the quantity and manner [decedent] consumed it can have fatal consequences. Nothing in the record suggests that [decedent] was aware of this fact, however. Moreover [one medical] affidavit tends to show that the general public is unaware that consumption at this level and in this manner can have any serious adverse effects. There is no evidence in the record that the public appreciates any hazard that may be associated with this kind of consumption.

Query: On the reasonable assumption that the risks of such moderate beer consumption are extremely remote — that the defendant would have discharged its duty if it had warned that the risk was "one in a million" — could a reasonable jury find that the warning would have caused a beer-loving young man in his twenties to give up beer for the rest of his life? Or should that consideration matter? For an argument that strict liability may be, at least in theory, warranted on the facts of *Hon*, see James A. Henderson, Jr., Echoes of Enterprise Liability in Product Design and Marketing Litigation, 87 Cornell L. Rev. 958, 989-90 (2002) (these "remote risk" cases are functionally similar to manufacturing defect cases, and manufacturers should be strictly liable to the occasional victims, whether or not the manufacturers warn against the risks).

The Restatement (Third) adopts the following standard for defects based on failure to instruct or warn:

> §2. Categories of Product Defect
>
> A product is defective when, at the time of sale or distribution, it contains a manufacturing defect, is defective in design, or is defective because of inadequate instructions or warnings. A product: . . .

(c) is defective because of inadequate instructions or warnings when the foreseeable risks of harm posed by the product could have been reduced or avoided by the provision of reasonable instructions or warnings by the seller or other distributor, or a predecessor in the commercial chain of distribution, and the omission of the instructions or warnings renders the product not reasonably safe.

COMMENT

j. Warnings: obvious and generally known risks. In general, a product seller is not subject to liability for failing to warn or instruct regarding risks and risk-avoidance measures that should be obvious to, or generally known by, foreseeable product users. When a risk is obvious or generally known, the prospective addressee of a warning will or should already know of its existence. Warning of an obvious or generally-known risk in most instances will not provide an effective additional measure of safety. Furthermore, warnings that deal with obvious or generally-known risks may be ignored by users and consumers and may diminish the significance of warnings about non-obvious, not-generally-known risks. Thus, requiring warnings of obvious or generally-known risks could reduce the efficacy of warnings generally. When reasonable minds may differ as to whether the risk was obvious or generally known, the issue is to be decided by the trier of fact. The obviousness of risk may bear on the issue of design defect rather than failure to warn. See Comments d and g.

One context in which the adequacy of a warning takes on additional layers of complexity is when the product's foreseeable user or bystander victim does not read at all or does not read English. Should manufacturers have a duty to provide warnings in pictorial or non-English language format? In Farias v. Mr. Heater, Inc., 684 F.3d 1231 (2012), plaintiff, a Florida resident who spoke only Spanish, purchased defendant's propane gas heater from a major hardware retailer and used it inside of her home contrary to warnings provided in English and through pictures. After failing to close a gas valve on the heater, plaintiff's home caught fire and was severely damaged. The court held that Florida law does not require Spanish-language warnings absent a showing that defendant specifically targeted "Spanish-speaking customers through the use of Hispanic media." Id. at 1236. In Campos v. Firestone Tire & Rubber Co., 485 A.2d 305 (N.J. 1984), plaintiff was born and raised in Portugal, and did not read English. He was injured while installing a new truck tire on a three-piece rim assembly manufactured by defendant. An adequate warning in English was supplied and prominently posted at the workplace. Plaintiff's expert argued that defendant should have produced a graphic or symbolic warning regarding the risks of inserting one's hand in the assembly during tire inflation — a sign containing a picture of a hand inside the assembly, with a red diagonal line through it, similar to international road signs. The high court concluded that a jury could find that defendant breached its duty to warn, and remanded the case for a new trial. See also Torres-Rios v. LPS Labs., Inc., 152 F.3d 11 (1st Cir. 1998) (symbolic warning adequate even though product was sold in Puerto Rico where the dominant language is Spanish). For an argument that in certain situations manufacturers should bear a duty in the United States to provide warnings in Spanish, see Keith Sealing, Peligro!: Failure to Warn of a Product's Inherent Risk in Spanish Should Constitute a Product Defect, 11 Temp. Pol. & Civ. Rts. L. Rev. 153, 154 (2001).

What if a defendant's product will foreseeably be used with another product — not manufactured or sold by defendant — and that *other* product carries a risk of injury? Confronted by just this issue through the case of In re New York City Asbestos Litigation,

2016 WL 3495191 (N.Y. June 28, 2016), the Court of Appeals of New York held that manufacturers of the non-injurious product may nevertheless have a duty to warn under certain circumstances:

> In deciding whether a manufacturer has a duty to warn certain users of its product about the hazards of using that product with another company's product, we must consider whether the manufacturer is in a superior position to know of and warn against those hazards, for in all failure-to-warn cases, this is a major determinant of the existence of the duty to warn. Furthermore, where one manufacturer's product is a durable item designed for continuous use with the other manufacturer's fungible product, which by contrast deteriorates relatively quickly and is designed to be replaced, the manufacturer of the durable product typically is in the best position to guarantee that those who use the two products together will receive a warning; the end user is more likely to interact with the durable product over an extended period of time, and hence he or she is more likely to inspect warnings on that item or in associated documentation, than to review warnings supplied by the maker of the "wear item". Accordingly, because a manufacturer who learns that its product is used in conjunction with another company's product has the knowledge and ability to warn of the dangers of the joint use of the products, especially if the other company's product is a "wear item," the manufacturer's superior position to warn is a factor — though by no means dispositive — supporting the recognition of a duty to warn under certain circumstances.
>
> Recognition of a manufacturer's duty to warn against the certain perils of using its product with another company's product will likely have a balanced and manageable economic impact. The manufacturer incurs a relatively modest cost from complying with the duty because the cost of issuing a warning about combined uses of its product and another product under certain circumstances is not significantly more burdensome than the manufacturer's pre-existing duty to warn of the dangers of using the manufacturer's product separately — a well-established cost that is itself relatively low.
>
> Nor is the cost of liability and litigation likely to become unreasonable. Prior judicial recognition of a manufacturer's duty to warn of the perils of reasonably foreseeable uses of its product has not imposed extreme or unreasonable financial liability on manufacturers, and there is no evidence before us that judicial approval of a duty to warn about the hazards of the combined use of two manufacturers' products, if sensibly confined, would saddle manufacturers with an untenable financial burden, especially given that they can obtain insurance coverage for this type of liability. . . .
>
> [T]he manufacturer of a product has a duty to warn of the danger arising from the known and reasonably foreseeable use of its product in combination with a third-party product which, as a matter of design, mechanics or economic necessity, is necessary to enable the manufacturer's product to function as intended.

The product at issue in the case was a valve manufactured for use in high-pressure, high-temperature steam pipes which the defendant manufacturer knew would require asbestos-based sealing components. Thus, the opinion may represent another of the exceptional tort doctrines brought about specifically in response to the massive public health crisis of asbestos. Nevertheless, the court took pains to stress that its "decision here adds but a note to a familiar anthem in failure-to-warn jurisprudence." Id. at *13. Do you agree? For discussion, see James A. Henderson, Jr., Sellers Of Safe Products Should Not Be Required To Rescue Users From Risks Presented By Other, More Dangerous Products, 37 Sw. U. L. Rev. 595 (2008).

Note: The Causation Conundrum in Warning Defect Cases

Upon reading many of these failure-to-warn decisions, one may ask, "What good would a warning have done?" In some cases, it seems doubtful that a warning would have affected the plaintiff's behavior even if it had been given. On the other hand, the plaintiff might have made different choices if given full information. In response to the obvious difficulties of answering such a question, a number of courts have held that when a product is sold without a warning, a rebuttable presumption arises that the consumer would have read any warning provided by the manufacturer and acted so as to minimize the risks. In Jacobs v. Technical Chem. Co., 480 S.W.2d 602 (Tex. 1972), the Texas high court affirmed an alternative holding of the trial court giving the plaintiff a new trial on what, without a presumption, would have been very weak evidence of causation. See also Reyes v. Wyeth Labs., 498 F.2d 1264 (5th Cir.), *cert. denied*, 419 U.S. 1096 (1974); Nissen Trampoline Co. v. Terre Haute First Nat'l Bank, 332 N.E.2d 820 (Ind. Ct. App. 1975), *rev'd on other grounds*, 358 N.E.2d 974 (Ind. 1977); Cunningham v. Charles Pfizer & Co., 532 P.2d 1377 (Okla. 1974).

The trend in favor of applying a "heeding presumption" in causation cases is substantial. See, e.g., Tenbarge v. Ames Taping Tool Sys. Inc., 190 F.3d 862 (8th Cir. 1999) (applying Missouri law) (manufacturer of dry wall taping gun, who provided no warning of repetitive stress injury, was subject to a rebuttable presumption that had a warning been given it would have been heeded); Pavlik v. Lane Ltd./Tobacco Exporters Int'l, 135 F.3d 876, 883 (3d Cir. 1998) (predicting that Pennsylvania would adopt a heeding presumption in failure-to-warn cases); Maya v. Johnson & Johnson, 97 A.3d 1203 (Pa. Super. Ct. 2014) (deciding that the trial court erred in failing to instruct the jury on the heeding presumption in a case involving Children's Motrin). On the other hand, the court in Rivera v. Philip Morris, Inc., 209 P.3d 271 (Nev. 2009), rejected the heeding presumption. The court first referenced the distinction between §402A cmt. *j* of the Second Restatement (which implies that manufacturers can escape design defect liability through the provision of adequate warnings) and §2 cmt. *l* of the Third Restatement (which does not grant adequate warnings such wide exculpatory effect). Siding firmly with the Third Restatement on this matter, the *Rivera* court reasoned that the heeding presumption undermines the goal of preferring design solutions over warnings: "[I]t is better public policy not to encourage a reliance on warnings because this will help ensure that manufacturers continue to strive to make safe products." Id. at 277. Do you agree with the court's analysis?

How much evidence should serve to rebut the presumption that, if a warning had been given, the plaintiff would have heeded it? In Colgrove v. Cameron Machine Co., 172 F. Supp. 2d 611 (W.D. Pa. 2001), the plaintiff accidentally stepped on a foot-switch made without a safety guard. The switch activated a paper-winding machine that caught and crushed the plaintiff's arm. The plaintiff claimed the manufacturer of the foot-switch should have warned of the possibility of accidental tripping. The manufacturer argued, inter alia, that a warning would not have prevented the accident. The court, in denying defendant's motion for judgment as a matter of law, explained how the heeding presumption applied in this case (172 F. Supp. 2d at 617):

> To recover . . . Colgrove must establish that the alleged defect was the proximate cause of his injuries. As the Third Circuit put it in Pavlik, "To reach a jury on a failure to warn theory of liability, the evidence must be such as to support a reasonable inference, rather than a guess, that the existence of an adequate warning might have prevented the injury." However, Colgrove is aided in making his case by a rebuttable presumption that a warning, if given, would have been heeded. . . . To rebut this presumption, [defendant] would need

> to show that [plaintiff's company] was informed of the danger of the unguarded foot-switch, and chose to disregard that information.

The court went on to explain that although awareness of a danger on the part of the plaintiff, when he continues in his behavior, is usually enough to rebut the presumption, in this case the plaintiff alleged that it was failure to warn the plaintiff's employer that caused the injury. Thus, proof of the plaintiff's awareness of the unguarded switch being dangerous did not rebut the heeding presumption.

In Bachtel v. TASER Int'l, Inc., 747 F.3d 965 (8th Cir. 2014), a police officer's use of a taser led to the death of a detainee. The deceased's mother sued the taser manufacturer, bringing warning and design defect claims. Because police officers typically receive instructions on the use of such products from superior officers rather than from the manufacturer's packaging information, and because the particular officer who fatally used the taser had not read the manufacturer's warnings, the court found no causation as a matter of law for plaintiff's failure-to-warn claim. The court also suggested that to sustain the heeding presumption, plaintiff should have presented expert testimony as to "the effect of a warning on a police officer in the field." Id. at 970. Does imposing this expert evidentiary requirement effectively remove the heeding presumption in this case?

Perhaps surprisingly, a demonstration that in actuality plaintiff failed to read a warning does not automatically prove that defendant's communication of the warning was sufficient. In Bryant v. BGHA, Inc., 9 F. Supp. 3d 1374 (M.D. Ga. 2014), plaintiff sued under a failure-to-warn theory after falling while descending a hunting stand without securing the provided ratchet straps. Paper instructions packaged along with the hunting stand stated in bold, capitalized text that "vital ratchet straps are included and necessary for the . . . [hunting stand]. Do not attempt to use these ladderstands without all vital ratchet straps secured." Id. at 1381. The court ruled that plaintiff's admission that he did not read the warnings provided with the stand precluded recovery on the theory that the defendant failed "to provide adequate warning of the product's potential risk." Id. at 1395. However, the court held that the plaintiff could still seek to challenge "the adequacy of the efforts of the manufacturer or seller to communicate the dangers of the product to the buyer or user." In fact, plaintiff's failure to read the warning could provide important "circumstantial evidence" that defendant failed to communicate its warnings adequately, which raised a question of fact for the jury. Id. *Bryant* seems to show that defeating the heeding presumption does not necessarily bar plaintiff's failure-to-warn claim, but can raise and even contribute to a different theory of recovery under failure-to-warn.

For discussion regarding the challenges posed by causation analysis in the failure-to-warn context, see Aaron D. Twerski & Neil B. Cohen, Resolving the Dilemma of Nonjusticiable Causation in Failure-to-Warn Litigation, 84 S. Cal. L. Rev. 125 (2010).

Problem 35

Your firm represents the Bambi Peanut Butter Company (BPB) in an action recently brought against it. Karen and Peter Jones have brought the action to recover as guardians for their two-year-old daughter, Pamela, and on their own behalf. The complaint alleges that nine months ago, when Pamela was 16 months old, Karen Jones fed her a peanut butter sandwich made with Bambi Peanut Butter. The complaint alleges that the child choked on the peanut butter when the sticky, viscous substance lodged in the back of her mouth and in her throat, cutting off her breathing capacity. By the time Karen could clear the baby's throat, Pamela had suffered irreversible brain damage. The complaint does not allege that the peanut butter was different from ordinary peanut butter. Instead, it alleges that BPB failed to supply a warning to Karen Jones that babies under two years of age cannot manage eating peanut butter and should not be fed it, given the risk of possible fatal choking. No warning accompanied the Bambi Peanut Butter, and the complaint alleges that Karen Jones did not know of the dangers. Had she been warned, the complaint asserts, she never would have fed the peanut butter sandwich to Pamela.

The Joneses seek to recover as guardians for their daughter and also for Karen's mental upset and emotional distress at witnessing the tragedy and Peter's, at learning of it shortly after it occurred. How will you defend this case on behalf of BPB?

Moore v. Ford Motor Co.

332 S.W.3d 749 (Mo. 2011) (en banc)

STITH, Judge.

I. Factual and Procedural Background

In April 2005, [Jeanne and Monty Moore] purchased a 2002 Ford Explorer. On November 1, 2005, the day of the collision, Ms. Moore was 6 feet tall and weighed approximately 300 pounds. She was stopped to make a left turn in the Explorer when she was hit from behind by another vehicle. At impact, the driver's seat collapsed backward and Ms. Moore's head and shoulders hit the back seat, fracturing her T9 vertebra. The injury rendered Ms. Moore a paraplegic.

Ms. Moore and her husband sued Ford under theories of negligent failure to warn, strict liability failure to warn, negligent design and strict liability design defect. The Moores' counsel explained their failure to warn claims during his opening statement as follows:

> The third reason we've sued Ford arises from simple common sense. *Nowhere in the owner's manual or on the on-product labels did Ford tell people who might use the Explorer that it intended the front seats to collapse in a rear impact.* That's information we contend in this trial that people are entitled to know before they sit in those front seats. Just as important, I think, that's information we contend in this case that people are entitled to know before they put their children or loved ones behind these seats. None of that information was given to consumers by Ford. *If Jeanne and Monty would have been warned by Ford or instructed by Ford that the seats in the 2002 Explorer were intended to collapse in a rear impact, they may never have bought their car and we wouldn't be here* (emphasis added).

At trial, Ms. Moore testified that she paid attention to weight warnings when she purchased products because of her size and because her husband and son were both tall and heavy. Ms. Moore testified that she routinely read warnings, instructions and manuals if they involved something in which she was interested. Ms. Moore further testified that, after she purchased the vehicle but prior to the wreck, she looked through the owner's manual for information about other matters and, in doing so, saw no listing of maximum weight limits for the front seats. Ms. Moore also testified that she saw no warnings that the seats of the Explorer might collapse backward in a rear-end impact. In her words, she "figured that, you know, if you had that you would go forward." Ms. Moore further testified, without objection, that she would not have bought the Explorer had she known that the seats were not designed for people of her size. . . .

At the close of the Moores' case, Ford moved for a directed verdict on all counts. In opposing this motion, the Moores further articulated why they had made a case on their failure to warn claims:

> The subject Explorer is devoid of *any warning whatsoever* telling its customers like Jeanne that *the seat in the Explorer is dangerously susceptible to breaking and collapsing in a mild to moderate impact when holding an occupant of Mrs. Moore's size and weight, or that this condition leads to a loss of restraint that can allow an occupant to strike the rear seat causing spinal cord injuries and paralysis.* (emphasis added).

The trial court granted the motion for directed verdict on the Moores' failure to warn claims. . . . After opinion by the court of appeals, this Court accepted transfer. . . .

III. The Trial Court Erred in Directing a Verdict on the Failure to Warn Claims

A. Failure to Warn of Higher Risk when Seats Used by Overweight Persons.

The Moores contend that they made a submissible case of strict liability for failure to warn in that the Explorer lacked any warnings that the front seats could collapse in rear impacts and were not tested or designed to perform with occupants of Ms. Moore's size.

The elements of a cause of action for strict liability failure to warn are: (1) the defendant sold the product in question in the course of its business; (2) the product was unreasonably dangerous at the time of sale when used as reasonably anticipated without knowledge of its characteristics; (3) the defendant did not give adequate warning of the danger; (4) the product was used in a reasonably anticipated manner; and (5) the plaintiff was damaged as a direct result of the product being sold without an adequate warning. . . .

There is no dispute that the Moores presented substantial evidence with respect to the first and fourth elements in that (1) Ford stipulated that it designed, manufactured and sold the Explorer involved in this case, and (4) there is no dispute that by driving the car, Ms. Moore was using the Explorer in a reasonably anticipated manner at the time of the accident. There also is no dispute that no warnings were given as to whether the seats were designed for a person of Ms. Moore's size or that they were designed to collapse backward in rear-impact collisions. Ford strongly disputes, however, that the Moores adduced sufficient evidence that the Explorer was unreasonably dangerous when used as reasonably anticipated without knowledge of its characteristics.

. . . [M]any products that otherwise might be dangerous can be used safely if adequate instructions for use are given and if warnings of dangers are adequate. Failure to warn claims are concerned with how a lack of warning about a product, and the user's resultant lack of knowledge about the product's dangers or safe use, may give rise to an unreasonable danger to the consumer. In such a case, it would not be inconsistent for a jury to find that a product's design is not unreasonably dangerous in itself but that, without an accompanying warning imparting knowledge of the product's dangerous characteristics or safe use, the otherwise non-defective product is unreasonably dangerous. . . .

Viewing the evidence in the light most favorable to the Moores and drawing all inferences in their favor, they adduced sufficient evidence for the jury to find that the Explorer was unreasonably dangerous without a warning imparting knowledge of its characteristics despite the finding that the design of the seats themselves was not defective. Louis D'Aulerio, one of the Moores' experts, testified that pull testing he conducted showed that the point of failure for a 2002 Explorer seat is 16,870 inch pounds. Mr. D'Aulerio then calculated the forces that were generated on Ms. Moore's seat in the wreck given the change in velocity, sustained "g-forces" and her weight. Mr. D'Aulerio testified that although the change in velocity for the collision was as low as 12.8 miles per hour, due to Ms. Moore's weight and other calculations, the Explorer seat endured forces of 15,800 to 19,000 inch pounds. Mr. D'Aulerio testified that this calculation showed that, in rear-end collisions at mild to moderate speeds — 12.8 to 17.2 miles per hour change in velocity — given Ms. Moore's weight, the forces in the crash exceeded the seat's capability. The jury was entitled to consider whether the Explorer seat was rendered unreasonably dangerous when not accompanied with a warning of its greater potential to collapse under the circumstances of a low to moderate rear-end collision while carrying a person of Ms. Moore's weight.

Ford argues that the type of danger presented by its seats is not amenable to a simple warning because the seat is safe for use by people of Ms. Moore's weight in normal driving conditions and in most accidents, other designs present other dangers, and the risk of danger varies with the type and speed of accident. Ford argues that because the Moores never state precisely what an appropriate warning would have said, such a warning could not realistically be made; the Moores, therefore, failed to make their case of failure to warn. This Court disagrees.

Ford does not cite any Missouri law placing the burden on the plaintiff to propose the wording of an adequate warning to make a submissible case.[2] While both Ford and the dissenting opinion note that Indiana apparently does place this burden on plaintiff, Indiana appears to be unique in this regard. . . . Indeed, Washington specifically provides that the plaintiff in a failure to warn case need not "prove the exact wording of an adequate warning." Ayers v. Johnson & Johnson Baby Products Co., 59 Wash. App. 287, 797 P.2d 527, 531 (1990). The other cases cited by the dissent do not concern whether a plaintiff must propose specific alternative language for a warning, much less require plaintiff to do so, but rather discuss generally the types of issues that may be relevant in a failure to warn case, including the feasibility of giving a warning about the danger at issue. . . .

The broad principles the dissent cites concerning relevance and feasibility do not address Ford's real difficulty here, which seems to be in how to phrase its warning. But Ford has not cited any authority that the difficulty of phrasing an adequate warning excuses the failure to give any warning. While the warning alleged to be needed here may take some thought to construct, in the absence of a showing that giving a warning simply would not be technically feasible, any remaining difficulty Ford might have in formulating the precise wording to use in the warning does not negate its need to warn but rather emphasizes the need to do so carefully.[6]

2. Of course, prudence and good lawyering may dictate that a plaintiff do so. In their response to Ford's motion for directed verdict, the Moores did explain the basic structure of what they believed to be an adequate warning. The Moores argued that Ford should have told "its customers . . . that the seat in the Explorer is dangerously susceptible to breaking and collapsing in a mild to moderate impact when holding an occupant of Ms. Moore's size and weight, or that this condition leads to a loss of restraint that can allow an occupant to strike the rear seat causing spinal cord injuries and paralysis."

6. Moreover, this Court's holding will not lead to a requirement that Ford must provide detailed warnings about how each part of the car will behave for persons of all different weights, sizes and shapes. The Court holds only that

VII. Conclusion

For the reasons set out above, the directed verdict for Ford on the Moores' . . . failure to warn claims is reversed. In all other respects, the judgment is affirmed. The cause is remanded.

TEITELMAN, WOLFF and BRECKENRIDGE, JJ., concur. PRICE, C.J., dissents in separate opinion filed. FISCHER, J., concurs in opinion of PRICE, C.J. RUSSELL, J., not participating.

WILLIAM RAY PRICE, JR., Chief Justice[, dissenting].

In this case a six foot tall, three hundred pound woman, Ms. Moore, was driving a 2002 Ford Explorer. The Ford was struck from behind by another vehicle, causing Ms. Moore's seat to collapse backward, despite the seat being one of the more secure in the industry. The collapse resulted in the fracture of Ms. Moore's T9 vertebra. . . .

Notwithstanding the failure of the plaintiffs to offer any evidence of a feasible, adequate warning that would have avoided the injury, the majority reverses the trial court's directed verdict ruling. I respectfully dissent and would affirm the trial courts ruling with respect to the failure to warn claims. . . .

To make a submissible failure to warn case in Indiana, a plaintiff must offer some evidence of the content or placement of a warning that would have prevented the danger posed by the product in question. Nissen Trampoline Co. v. Terre Haute First Nat'l Bank, 265 Ind. 457, 358 N.E.2d 974, 978 (1976); Morgen v. Ford Motor Co., 797 N.E.2d 1146, 1152 (Ind. 2003). Such evidence is "indispensable to a rational conclusion that the product was defective and unreasonably dangerous to the user without warnings, and to a rational conclusion that such unreasonably dangerous condition was the proximate cause of the accident and injury." Nissen Trampoline, 358 N.E.2d at 978. Failure to offer evidence of this nature imposes upon courts the onerous duty of hypothesizing warnings that would alter a plaintiff's behavior or, as is the case here, they may choose to ignore the inquiry altogether. Id.

Other jurisdictions also require plaintiffs to offer evidence as to what specific warnings would have been sufficient to avoid injury in order to establish a prima facie case for failure to warn. . . . To require anything less invites not only a roving jury instruction, but the danger of subjecting a manufacturer to liability for failing to do the impossible. . . .

Despite the fact that the seat in question was one of the safest in the industry, the Moores argue that when people of a particular size are traveling at a particular speed the seat may fail. Thus, a hypothetical warning, as to the likelihood that the seats might collapse, must be in the form of a sliding-scale, varying among a myriad of factors, including weight of occupants, height of occupants and the velocity of impact. Tellingly, the Moores failed to offer any evidence as to the wording of this problematic warning, its feasibility or where it might have been placed. . . .

Because the Moores failed to offer any evidence as to what a feasible, adequate warning might say or where it might be placed, they did not make a submissible case. . . .

---

where, as here, the evidence shows that Ford knew its design meant that its seats were more likely to collapse backward in rear-end collisions when used by persons of more than normal weight, subjecting them to the risk of serious injuries such as those sustained by Ms. Moore, a jury could find that it had a duty to warn the consumer of that increased risk so the consumer could make an informed choice whether to use the seats despite that danger. Only if a comparable showing were made that other features rendered the product unreasonably dangerous in the absence of an adequate warning would a failure to warn claim be submissible as to other features of a vehicle, as that is the standard for recovery under Missouri law.

Plaintiffs in *Moore* attacked defendant's warning as inadequate without attempting to offer a reasonable alternative warning (RAW). In contrast, plaintiffs in Nilson v. Hershey Entm't & Resorts Co., 649 F. Supp. 2d 378 (M.D. Pa. 2009), offered a RAW through expert testimony. Plaintiffs were parents of a boy who at age eleven lost hearing in his left ear shortly after riding a roller coaster at defendant's amusement park. Plaintiffs alleged that the park's warnings on the roller coaster—essentially that the ride involved "speed changes and unexpected forces"—did not adequately advise riders of the potential dangers involved. Plaintiffs' expert proposed an alternative warning that would more specifically alert riders that the physical stresses they would experience would be severe: "WARNING!!! THIS IS A HIGH SPEED RIDE WITH RAPID JOLTS IN SHARP TURNS AND HARD DIPS. DO NOT RIDE UNLESS YOU ARE PREPARED FOR THE MOST SEVERE LEVEL OF PHYSICAL IMPACT AND THRILL." Id. at 388. The trial court, in ruling against plaintiffs as a matter of law, did not see "any informative significant difference in Plaintiffs' expert's suggested alternative warning and the warning actually on the [roller coaster]." Id. Why didn't the expert propose a straightforward warning that riding defendant's roller coaster could lead to hearing loss?

One of the authors has argued that the proposal of a RAW should be seen as a necessary element of plaintiff's prima facie case, akin to the RAD requirement for design defect cases. See Aaron D. Twerski & James A. Henderson, Jr., Fixing Failure to Warn, 90 Ind. L.J. 237, 254 (2015) ("[A]llowing the plaintiff to allege failure to warn without specifically setting forth the relevant details—the medium and, if written, the text, placement, color, and size of the proposed warning—condones a cause of action without any standard and allows a jury to intuit causation without being required to test its finding against what a real-world warning would have said. . . ."). If "prudence and good lawyering may dictate that a plaintiff [submit a RAW]," as the *Moore* court indicated in footnote 2, above, why do plaintiffs' lawyers object to a formal requirement of the RAW as a doctrinal matter? If you think a plaintiff must supply a RAW to maintain a successful failure-to-warn claim, is the plaintiff required to supply expert testimony supporting the RAW's adequacy? For a subsequent interpretation of the rule in Indiana addressing this question, see Cook v. Ford Motor Co., 913 N.E.2d 311, 327 n.9 (Ind. Ct. App. 2009), which explained that "[a]lthough evidence of an alternate adequate warning may be required, an expert is not necessarily the sole source of such evidence."

Note: The Special Context of Prescription Drugs and Medical Devices

Harmful side effects caused by prescription drugs and other medical products give rise to an interesting subset of failure-to-warn cases. The general rule is that drug companies owe patients duties to use reasonable care in testing their products and in warning prescribing and treating physicians regarding harmful side effects. Under this "learned intermediary rule," if timely and adequate warnings are given to doctors, drug companies will not be liable for injuries caused by the drugs. See, e.g., Cochran v. Brooke, 409 P.2d 904 (Or. 1966). The general rule is that pharmacies must only pass on warnings supplied to them by manufacturers. In narrow circumstances, such as where a pharmacy has information that a patient will have a harmful reaction to a drug, the court may impose upon a pharmacy an independent duty to warn. See, e.g., Happel v. Wal-Mart Stores, Inc., 766 N.E.2d 1118 (Ill. 2002).

Most courts follow the learned intermediary rule whereby manufacturers are not required to give warnings directly to patients. See Tyree v. Boston Scientific Corp., 56

F. Supp. 3d 826, 828 (S.D. W.Va. 2014) (reviewing jurisdictions and concluding that "the total number of states employing some iteration of the learned intermediary doctrine [is] forty-eight (including D.C.)"). But some state courts have recognized a duty owed by drug manufacturers to warn patients directly in certain contexts. Thus, in MacDonald v. Ortho Pharmacy Corp., 475 N.E.2d 65 (Mass.), *cert. denied,* 794 U.S. 920 (1985), the Supreme Judicial Court of Massachusetts reversed a JNOV and ordered judgment on a jury verdict for plaintiff on a claim that the drug manufacturer had failed adequately to warn a young mother directly of the risks of stroke from taking an oral contraceptive. The court concluded (475 N.E.2d at 69-70):

> The rule in jurisdictions that have addressed the question of the extent of a manufacturer's duty to warn in cases involving prescription drugs is that the prescribing physician acts as a "learned intermediary" between the manufacturer and the patient, and "the duty of the ethical drug manufacturer is to warn the doctor, rather than the patient, [although] the manufacturer is directly liable to the patient for a breach of such duty." Oral contraceptives, however, bear peculiar characteristics which warrant the imposition of a common law duty on the manufacturer to warn users directly of associated risks. Whereas a patient's involvement in decision-making concerning use of a prescription drug necessary to treat a malady is typically minimal or nonexistent, the healthy, young consumer of oral contraceptives is usually actively involved in the decision to use "the pill," as opposed to other available birth control products, and the prescribing physician is relegated to a relatively passive role. . . .
>
> [Moreover,] the birth control pill is specifically subject to extensive Federal regulation. The FDA has promulgated regulations designed to ensure that the choice of "the pill" as a contraceptive method is informed by comprehensible warnings of potential side effects. These regulations, and subsequent amendments, have their basis in the FDA commissioner's finding, after hearings, that "[b]ecause oral contraceptives are ordinarily taken electively by healthy women who have available to them alternative methods of treatment, and because of the relatively high incidence of serious illnesses associated with their use, . . . users of these drugs should, without exception, be furnished with written information telling them of the drug's benefits and risks." . . .
>
> The oral contraceptive thus stands apart from other prescription drugs in light of the heightened participation of patients in decisions relating to use of "the pill"; the substantial risks affiliated with the product's use; the feasibility of direct warnings by the manufacturer to the user; the limited participation of the physician (annual prescriptions); and the possibility that oral communications between physicians and consumers may be insufficient or too scanty standing alone fully to apprise consumers of the product's dangers at the time the initial selection of a contraceptive method is made as well as at subsequent points when alternative methods may be considered. We conclude that the manufacturer of oral contraceptives is not justified in relying on warnings to the medical profession to satisfy its common law duty to warn, and that the manufacturer's obligation encompasses a duty to warn the ultimate user. Thus, the manufacturer's duty is to provide to the consumer written warnings conveying reasonable notice of the nature, gravity, and likelihood of known or knowable side effects, and advising the consumer to seek fuller explanation from the prescribing physician or other doctor of any such information of concern to the consumer.

More recently, a few courts have noted the explosion in direct-to-consumer advertising and other changes in the market for health care services as reasons supporting abandonment of the learned intermediary doctrine for suits against prescription drug and device manufacturers. See, e.g., Perez v. Wyeth Labs. Inc., 734 A.2d 1245 (N.J. 1999); State ex rel. Johnson & Johnson Corp. v. Karl, 647 S.E.2d 899 (W. Va. 2007).

Should manufacturers have a duty to warn hospitals who procure prescription drugs and medical devices, in addition to the doctors who dispense them to patients? In Taylor v. Intuitive Surgical, Inc., 355 P.3d 309 (Wash. Ct. App. 2015), the court found that a manufacturer's duty runs only to the physician, not the hospital, thereby affirming a jury verdict finding the device manufacturer not liable. A dissenting judge argued that "[w]hile a physician is a gatekeeper between the manufacturer and the unwarned patient, a physician is not a gatekeeper between the manufacturer and the unwarned *hospital* because the physician does not use independent judgment to determine which medical products a hospital should receive and what information a hospital needs to know about those products." Id. at 318. Instead, the dissent claimed that "the hospital exercises independent judgment to determine which medical products it should purchase and receives information about those products directly from the manufacturer." Id. Does it make a difference to your view of this case that the product at issue in *Taylor* was an advanced robotic surgery device known as the da Vinci System, and that the manufacturer recommends that purchasing hospitals establish training and credentialing protocols for surgeons prior to letting them use the device? Id. at 311.

The Restatement (Third) contains the following section dealing with prescription drugs and medical devices:

§6. Liability of Seller or Other Distributor for Harm Caused by Defective Prescription Drugs and Medical Devices

(a) A manufacturer of a prescription drug or medical device who sells or otherwise distributes a defective drug or medical device is subject to liability for harm to persons caused by the defect. A prescription drug or medical device is one that may be legally sold or otherwise distributed only pursuant to a health care provider's prescription.

(b) For purposes of liability under Subsection (a), a prescription drug or medical device is defective if at the time of sale or other distribution the drug or medical device:

(1) contains a manufacturing defect as defined in §2(a); or

(2) is not reasonably safe due to defective design as defined in Subsection (c); or

(3) is not reasonably safe due to inadequate instructions or warnings as defined in Subsection (d).

(c) A prescription drug or medical device is not reasonably safe due to defective design if the foreseeable risks of harm posed by the drug or medical device are sufficiently great in relation to its foreseeable therapeutic benefits that reasonable health care providers, knowing of such foreseeable risks and therapeutic benefits, would not prescribe the drug or medical device for any class of patients.

(d) A prescription drug or medical device is not reasonably safe because of inadequate instructions or warnings if reasonable instructions or warnings regarding foreseeable risks of harm are not provided to:

(1) prescribing and other health care providers who are in a position to reduce the risks of harm in accordance with the instructions or warnings; or

(2) the patient when the manufacturer knows or has reason to know that health care providers will not be in a position to reduce the risks of harm in accordance with the instructions or warnings.

(e) A retail seller or other distributor of a prescription drug or medical device is subject to liability for harm caused by the drug or device if:

(1) at the time of sale or other distribution the drug or medical device contains a manufacturing defect as defined in §2(a); or

(2) at or before the time of sale or other distribution of the drug or medical device the retail seller or other distributor fails to exercise reasonable care and such failure causes harm to persons.

Clearly, the Restatement (Third) endorses the learned intermediary rule in §6(d)(1), subject to limited exceptions in (d)(2) and to a caveat in Comment *e* that the Restatement (Third) "leaves to developing case law whether exceptions to the learned intermediary rule" should be adopted in direct-to-consumer advertising or other situations. Subsection (e) adopts the rules described earlier regarding the liability of retail sellers, including pharmacies. By far the most controversial aspect of §6 has been its treatment of design-based liability in subsection (c). Professor Henderson explains how subsection (c) came to be drafted in James A. Henderson, Jr., Prescription Drug Design Liability Under the Proposed Restatement (Third) of Torts: A Reporter's Perspective, 48 Rutgers L. Rev. 471 (1996). For a criticism of subsection (c), see George W. Conk, Is There a Design Defect in the Restatement (Third) of Torts: Products Liability?, 109 Yale L.J. 1087 (2000). Professor Henderson and his co-reporter reply in James A. Henderson, Jr. & Aaron D. Twerski, Drug Designs Are Different, 111 Yale L.J. 151 (2001). Conk replies, yet again, in George W. Conk, The True Test: Alternative Safer Designs for Drugs and Medical Devices in a Patent-Constrained Market, 49 UCLA L. Rev. 737 (2002). An overview of the Restatement (Third)'s treatment of medical technologies can be found in Lars Noah, This Is Your Products Liability Restatement on Drugs, 74 Brook. L. Rev. 839 (2009).

For discussion of failure-to-warn and the increased marketing of prescription drugs, see Richard C. Ausness, "There's Danger Here, Cherie!" Liability for the Promotion and Marketing of Drugs and Medical Devices for Off-Label Uses, 73 Brook. L. Rev. 1253 (2008); Richard C. Ausness, Will More Aggressive Marketing Practices Lead to Greater Tort Liability for Prescription Drug Manufacturers?, 37 Wake Forest L. Rev. 97 (2002).

The courts in the failure-to-warn cases considered thus far have all spoken as if the basis of liability were negligence. Indeed, it is difficult to see how strict liability for failure to warn could have been applied in those cases — "failure," after all, implies some sort of shortcoming on the part of the defendant. One court, however, has purported to apply genuine strict liability for failure to warn. In Beshada v. Johns-Manville Products Corp., 447 A.2d 539 (N.J. 1982), the plaintiffs were workers and survivors of deceased workers who claimed to have contracted various lung ailments, including lung cancer, from exposure to defendants' asbestos products. The defendants asserted that at the time of the exposure they did not know and could not have known that their products caused such ailments. The trial court refused plaintiffs' motion to strike that defense and the plaintiffs appealed. The Supreme Court of New Jersey reversed and ordered the defense stricken.

In a subsequent decision, the New Jersey Supreme Court addressed the question of whether the holding in *Beshada* applied in prescription drug cases, and held that it did not. See Feldman v. Lederle Labs., 479 A.2d 374 (N.J. 1984). In Gogol v. Johns-Manville Sales Corp., 595 F. Supp. 971 (D.N.J. 1984), the district court concluded that "the import of *Feldman* . . . is that one rule applies to asbestos products, and a different rule applies to non-asbestos products." Id. at 974. The court recognized that the defendant's equal protection arguments were not without merit, but declined to upset the New Jersey rule on that ground.

A clear majority of U.S. jurisdictions reject the *Beshada* approach. See, e.g., Anderson v. Owens-Corning Fiberglas Corp., 810 P.2d 549 (Cal. 1991); Restatement (Third) of Torts: Products Liability §2, cmt. *a* (1998) ("Most courts agree that, for the liability system to be fair and efficient, the balancing of risks and benefits in judging product design and marketing must be done in light of the knowledge of risks and risk-avoidance techniques reasonably available at the time of distribution."). However, a minority of states appear willing to hold manufacturers responsible for risks that were unknowable at the time of distribution. Thus, in Sternhagen v. Dow Co., 935 P.2d 1139, 1142-46 (Mont. 1997), the Montana Supreme Court rejected a "state of the art" defense to failure-to-warn causes of action as contrary to strict products liability. Instead, the court applied an "imputation of knowledge doctrine" whereby the manufacturer is deemed to have knowledge of a "product's undiscovered or undiscoverable dangers" as "more consistent with existing Montana laws." Such a doctrine "reinforces [the courts'] commitment to provide maximum protection for consumers, while still assuring an appropriate limitation to a manufacturer's liability." In Malcolm v. Evenflo Co., Inc., 217 P.3d 514 (Mont. 2009), the high court cited *Sternhagen* in support of a decision to exclude evidence that a product had complied with applicable safety regulations, reasoning that such evidence would, like a "state of the art" defense, inappropriately inject negligence principles into strict liability law.

Most commentators have argued against imputing time-of-trial knowledge to a product seller. See generally James A. Henderson, Jr., Coping with the Time Dimension in Products Liability, 69 Cal. L. Rev. 919 (1981); Alan Schwartz, Products Liability, Corporate Structure, and Bankruptcy: Toxic Substances and the Remote Risk Relationship, 14 J. Legal Stud. 689 (1985); Ellen Wertheimer, Unknowable Dangers and the Death of Strict Products Liability: The Empire Strikes Back, 60 U. Cin. L. Rev. 1183 (1992). The last-cited article surveys the cases and finds that an overwhelming majority of courts refuse to impute time-of-trial knowledge to a manufacturer. For an article defending the view that tort law should provide strong incentives to discover hidden risks during research and innovation phases of product development, see Mary Lyndon, Tort Law and Technology, 12 Yale J. on Reg. 137 (1995).

D. Statutory Reform of Products Liability

1. Reform in State Legislatures

Legislative activity at the state level, although widespread, has for the most part occurred piecemeal. Only a few states have passed comprehensive products liability legislation. See, e.g., Idaho Code §§6-1401 et seq. (1990); Ind. Code §§34-20 et seq. (1998); Ky. Rev. Stat. Ann. §§411.300 et seq. (Banks-Baldwin 1991); Wash. Rev. Code. Ann. §§7.72.010 et seq. (West 1991); Tex. Civ. Prac. & Rem. Code Ann. §§82.001 et seq. (1993). Illinois, which had already enacted comprehensive tort reform legislation, enacted additional reforms in 1995. These substantial reforms were struck down in their entirety on a variety of state constitutional grounds. See Best v. Taylor Mach. Works, 689 N.E.2d 1057 (Ill. 1997). Other state courts have been more receptive to legislative reforms. See, e.g., Arbino v. Johnson & Johnson, 880 N.E.2d 420 (Ohio 2007) (noneconomic damages cap not unconstitutional); Garhart *ex rel.* Tinsman v. Columbia/Healthone, L.L.C., 95 P.3d 571 (Colo. 2004) (rejecting constitutional challenges to medical malpractice damages cap); Rhyne v. K-Mart Corp., 594 S.E.2d 1 (N.C. 2004) (rejecting challenges to cap on punitive damages award); Gourley *ex rel.* Gourley v. Nebraska Methodist Health System, Inc., 663 N.W.2d 43 (Neb. 2003) (medical malpractice damages cap upheld). In Illinois, the state legislature responded to *Best* by enacting new tort reform legislation targeting medical malpractice litigation. Certain procedural portions of the legislation were implicitly rejected by the state high court in O'Casek v. Children's Home and Aid Soc. of Illinois, 892 N.E.2d 994 (Ill. 2008). Then, in Lebron v. Gottlieb Memorial Hosp., 930 N.E.2d 895 (Ill. 2010), the court squarely declared the damages cap portion of the legislation to be unconstitutional.

As of 2016, legislatures in nearly every state have enacted laws addressing a variety of subjects to deal with "the tort crisis," real or imagined. Most of the legislation seeks to provide some measure of protection to manufacturers who claim to be hard-hit by the far-reaching decisions of courts. The American Tort Reform Association, a lobbying group, maintains a comprehensive online database of tort reform measures that have been adopted in each state, along with a tally of which measures have been upheld or rejected on constitutional grounds. See http://www.atra.org/legislation/states (last visited August 2, 2016).

Some of this statutory reform has been directed specifically at products liability, such as in Mississippi where the state legislature passed a statute that allows passive middlemen to escape liability in products cases. See Miss. Code Ann. §11-1-63(h) (2004) ("It is the intent of this section to immunize innocent sellers who are not actively negligent, but instead are mere conduits of a product."). Significantly more legislation has been aimed not at products liability litigation in particular but rather at tort cases in general. For example, Mississippi, Georgia, and Illinois have implemented procedural reforms aimed at limiting access to their courts to out-of-state plaintiffs. These measures are aimed at curtailing "forum shopping" by plaintiff's lawyers. South Carolina, along with several other states that have implemented similar reforms (see supra at p. 138), has abolished joint and several liability against all defendants who are 50 percent or less responsible. The same legislation bars recovery when plaintiffs are 51 percent or more responsible. Such reforms will, of course, impact products liability cases, mostly in ways that are believed to benefit defendants. For more information on recent reform activity in state legislatures, see James A. Henderson Jr., Asbestos Litigation Madness: Have the States Turned a Corner?, 20 Mealey's Litig. Rep.: Asbestos 5-8 (Jan. 10, 2006); 3 Prod. Liab. Rep. (CCH) ¶¶90,000 et seq. (compendium of state statutes, arranged alphabetically and updated periodically).

Cases like *Best* have sparked much controversy over the role of courts in tort and products liability reform. For an argument that these courts have wrongfully interfered with their respective legislatures, see Victor E. Schwartz & Leah Lorber, Judicial Nullification of Civil Justice Reform Violates the Fundamental Federal Constitutional Principle of Separation of Powers: How to Restore the Right Balance, 32 Rutgers L.J. 907 (2001).

One additional point for consideration is the potential role of the federal Constitution in legislative efforts to reform tort liability. As has been noted, state constitutions may impinge on efforts at reform, causing legislation to be set aside on a number of grounds. To date, however, little if any such legislation has been overturned on the basis of the federal Constitution. An article by John C. P. Goldberg, The Constitutional Status of Tort Law: Due Process and the Right to a Law for the Redress of Wrongs, 115 Yale L.J. 524 (2005), argues that the United States Constitution presents obstacles to legislative reform of the tort system. Goldberg explains that the common law and the framers of the federal Constitution regarded civil suits noninstrumentally, primarily as a means for actors to redress private injuries. Given this history, Goldberg argues that rights of redress in tort should be viewed as protected by the requirements of due process. On this view, these fundamental civil rights should be protected by a more stringent standard than the rational basis test traditionally applied by courts in evaluating legislation curtailing or limiting the right to sue in tort. For a more general defense of products liability law, also informed by the civil redress perspective, see John C.P. Goldberg & Benjamin C. Zipursky, The Easy

Case for Products Liability Law: A Response to Professors Polinsky and Shavell, 123 Harv. L. Rev. 1919 (2010).

2. Reform in the United States Congress

With 50 state legislatures going their own ways, and with 50 state court systems all possessing their own, individualized doctrinal biases, the quest for a uniform solution to the products liability crisis, not surprisingly, has turned to Congress. From 1979 onward, bills have been introduced each year (in either the House or the Senate) to "federalize" and thus (hopefully) to render uniform much of present-day products liability law. Some of these proposals have been quite modest and directed toward a limited number of issues; others have attempted to regulate many, but not all, aspects of products litigation.

In 1996, proponents of federal legislative reform came close to success. Both houses of Congress passed the Common Sense Product Liability Legal Reform Act of 1996. In April 1996, President Clinton vetoed the legislation. He expressed his dislike for provisions of the bill dealing with curtailment of joint and several liability and those capping punitive damage awards. Reformers returned again in 1998, introducing the Product Liability and Reform Act of 1998. The bill, among other things, capped punitive damages for small businesses at the greater of $250,000 or twice compensatory damages. The bill had good prospects for passage on the merits (and probably would have been signed by the President) but failed to receive enough votes to invoke cloture (an end to debate), foreclosing passage. The failure occurred after the Majority Leader, Trent Lott, hand-wrote his own amendment into the margin of the bill at the last minute, effectively immunizing a large employer in his home state from products liability lawsuits. This angered Democrats, who had been admonished not to add amendments of their own and who claimed to have been left in the dark regarding Lott's amendment. While Lott denied hiding anything, his last-minute amendment appears to have provided opponents with enough political ammunition to kill the bill. See Legislation: Product Liability Measure Dies Again After Senate Bid to Invoke Cloture Fails, Prod. Liab. Daily d2 (BNA) (July 10, 1998).

While Congress has not, as of the fall of 2016, promulgated comprehensive products liability reform, it has taken a piecemeal approach similar to that used by some state legislatures. See, e.g., 21 U.S.C. §§1601-1606 (Biomaterials Access Assurance Act) and 49 U.S.C. §40101 (Federal Aviation Administration Authorization Act of 1994). Faced with the potential for a national crisis when analysts predicted massive computer shutdowns at the change of the millennium, the federal and state legislatures passed "Y2K" tort reforms, intended to prevent products liability litigation from crippling the technology industry. See Y2K Act, Pub. L. No. 106-37 (1999). A similar congressional response to the September 11, 2001 terrorist attack, intended to protect the airline industry from crushing tort liability, is described in Chapter 9, supra. More generally, for an argument that the federal government needs to continue toward a federalized tort reform and a proposal for one such program, see Victor E. Schwartz & Mark A. Behrens, A Proposal for Federal Products Liability Reform in the New Millennium, 4 Tex. Rev. L. & Pol'y 261 (2000). For reflections on the tort reform movement in general, see Michael P. Allen, A Survey and Some Commentary on Federal "Tort Reform," 39 Akron L. Rev. 909 (2006); F. Patrick Hubbard, The Nature and Impact of the "Tort Reform" Movement, 35 Hofstra L. Rev. 437 (2006); Julie Davies, Reforming the Tort Reform Agenda, 25 Wash. U. J.L. & Pol'y 119 (2007); Joanna M. Shepherd, Tort Reforms' Winners and Losers: The Competing Effects of Care and Activity Levels, 55 UCLA L. Rev. 905 (2008).

Congress has enacted one procedural reform that exerts a considerable impact on products liability litigation. The Class Action Fairness Act of 2005 (CAFA) grants federal district courts original jurisdiction over class actions where the amount in controversy exceeds five million dollars, subject to certain other requirements, and provides for removal of such class actions from state courts to federal courts. The Act also provides for broader judicial review of class action settlements. See Class Action Fairness Act of 2005, Pub. L. No. 109-2, 119 Stat. 4. The Act has resulted in a greater percentage of class actions being heard in the federal courts, where corporate defendants believe they are treated more fairly than in state courts. For a collection of views on CAFA, see Symposium, Fairness to Whom? Perspectives on the Class Action Fairness Act of 2005, 156(6) U. Pa. L. Rev. (2008). One empirical study from that symposium concludes that, with the exception of Republican-appointed male judges, the federal judiciary has tended to interpret CAFA in narrow ways, resulting in less incursion onto state jurisdiction than anticipated. Kevin M. Clermont & Theodore Eisenberg, CAFA Judicata: A Tale of Waste and Politics, 156 U. Pa. L. Rev. 1553 (2008).

For a time, Congress considered legislation aimed at solving problems arising from asbestos litigation. Asbestos-related injuries have produced an enormous amount of tort litigation over recent decades, threatening entire industries with financial destruction. The Fairness in Asbestos Injury Resolution Act (FAIR), first introduced in 2003, would have removed asbestos claims from the courts altogether and created a no-fault compensation system run by an Office of Asbestos Disease Compensation to be created within the U.S. Department of Labor. Under the 2005 version of FAIR, the compensation system would process and evaluate asbestos claims according to levels of injury, and award compensation based on predetermined schedules. The funds required, which would have been in the hundreds of billions of dollars, were to be provided by federal assessments on the businesses and insurers that would otherwise face tort liability for asbestos-related injuries. The FAIR bill failed to attract wide support from either victims or businesses and was never passed by Congress.

Chapter 8

Damages

Section A of this chapter takes up the rules by which the injury to the plaintiff is translated into a dollar amount. In working through this section, it is important to keep in mind the practical interrelationship between the damages covered here and the liability issues covered in the preceding chapters. These issues are not resolved in isolation from each other; particularly in the settlement process, the parties' assessments of liability and damages are combined so that the amount that the plaintiff receives, if any, depends as much on the extent of the injury as it does on the clarity of the defendant's liability. Even in cases that go to trial, it is commonly assumed that juries, and perhaps even judges, fuse the issues in reaching compromise verdicts. Thus, while it is necessary for pedagogical reasons to focus here on the rules of damages largely to the exclusion of liability considerations, this is not an accurate reflection of the actual manner in which the torts process unfolds.

Section B covers punitive damages, a long-standing means of awarding "exemplary" damages against especially egregious tortfeasors, but one that has come under increasing political and constitutional attack.

A. Compensatory Damages

The basic tort measure of compensatory damages is the amount of money necessary to restore the plaintiff to the preinjury condition. Often, a complete restoration cannot physically be accomplished, and in such cases damages include the monetary value of the difference between the plaintiff's preinjury and postinjury conditions. However useful "making the plaintiff whole" may be as a heuristic for assessing damages, it is important to remember that tort law empowers wronged individuals to seek a remedy against their *particular* wrongdoers. Thus, even when complete restoration of the plaintiff's preinjury condition is not possible or when full compensation is not an appropriate measure of damages for other reasons, tort law still seeks to offer the plaintiff "satisfaction" in the form of the right to extract recovery from his specific antagonist. This feature usefully distinguishes tort law from other systems, such as insurance or publicly funded compensation schemes, that are in the business of annulling or compensating for losses but that do not directly address the social rupture that has occurred between the plaintiff and the defendant. Indeed, it might be most accurate to say that tort law is aimed at providing "fair" rather than "full" compensation for wrongs, because "many [plaintiffs] appropriately obtain a remedy in the form of less-than-full compensation or more-than-full compensation." John C. P. Goldberg, Two Conceptions of Tort Damages: Fair v. Full Compensation, 55 DePaul L. Rev. 435, 437 (2006). In this section, we consider the rules of compensatory damages in cases of personal injury, wrongful death, and property damage.[1]

1. Compensatory damages in tort cases are not limited to the damages taken up in this section. Other categories of damages are taken up in the chapters dealing with the substantive bases of liability to which they are appropriate. See, e.g., Chapter 12, Defamation, and Chapter 14, Commercial Torts.

1. Personal Injury

a. Medical Expenses

The subject of medical expenses presents relatively few difficulties because these expenses tend to be the most concrete and objectively demonstrable items advanced by the plaintiff. In order to be compensable, the expense must be reasonably related to the defendant's wrongful conduct. The most common such items are doctors' bills, X-rays, hospital bills, and the like. Mental health treatment is an allowable item of medical expense. See Musa v. Jefferson County Bank, 620 N.W.2d 797 (Wis. 2001). Recovery has also been permitted for an assortment of expenses related to the plaintiff's physical condition or to medical treatment. For example, in Reilly v. U.S., 665 F. Supp. 976 (D.R.I. 1987), the plaintiffs, parents of an infant daughter permanently disabled as a result of physician negligence, recovered the cost of architectural modifications of their home, a specially modified van, and the costs of operating the vehicle. And in Moore v. Kroger Co., 800 F. Supp. 429 (N.D. Miss. 1992), *aff'd*, 18 F.3d 936 (5th Cir. Miss. 1994), a mother acting as conservator of her comatose son recovered the cost of her travel to and from the treatment center where he resided.

Not only must the expenses have been reasonably necessitated by the invasion of the plaintiff's person, but also they must be reasonable in amount. The plaintiff who goes for treatment to three medical specialists when a reasonable person would have gone to one will probably not recover for the expense of the extra two. Nor will the plaintiff recover fully for bills from even a single doctor that are later found to be excessively high.

Related to the question of whether the plaintiff has spent too much on medical treatment is the question of whether the plaintiff has spent too little. Under the "avoidable consequences rule," the plaintiff generally cannot recover for consequences of the defendant's wrong that the plaintiff could have avoided by taking reasonable harm-reducing measures. See 3 Jacob A. Stein, Stein on Personal Injury Damages §18:1 (3d ed. 1997). Thus, in personal injury cases, to recover fully the plaintiff ordinarily must take reasonable steps to mitigate the injuries, including, according to one court, losing weight if that is medically advised to reduce the extent of the plaintiff's injuries. See Aisole v. Dean, 574 So. 2d 1248 (La. 1991). If the plaintiff has unreasonably refused medical care, the damages will be based on what would have happened had the reasonable care been followed, including, according to one court, the cost of reasonable medical expenses not in fact incurred. See Sette v. Dakis, 48 A.2d 271 (Conn. 1946). Of course, the important question here is whether the plaintiff's failure or refusal to submit to a proposed treatment is reasonable. Should the plaintiff's tort recovery be reduced because of a refusal to undergo an operation that involves some risk of death? Risk of paralysis? Do not all operations involve some degree of risk?

What if the refusal of the plaintiff to seek what otherwise would be reasonable medical care is based on religious beliefs? In Williams v. Bright, 230 A.D.2d 548, 658 N.Y.S.2d 910, appeal dismissed, 90 N.Y.2d 935, 686 N.E.2d 1368 (1997), an injured plaintiff refused treatment that almost certainly would have restored her to her pre-injury condition on the ground that, because she was a devout Jehovah's Witness, her religion barred her from undertaking the surgery. The trial court instructed the jury that, although plaintiffs ordinarily are required to act reasonably to mitigate their damages, in the instant case the jurors must consider the plaintiff's religion in evaluating the reasonableness of her conduct:

> You have to accept as a given that the dictates of her religion forbid blood transfusions.
>
> And so you have to determine . . . whether she . . . *acted reasonably as a Jehovah's Witness* in refusing surgery which would involve blood transfusions.
>
> Was it reasonable for her, not what you would do or your friends or family, was it reasonable for her given her beliefs, without questioning the validity or the propriety of her beliefs? [230 A.D.2d at 551]

An intermediate appeals court rejected the trial judge's instruction, arguing that it effectively required the jury — and by extension the court and the state — to endorse plaintiff's religion and its tenets. Instead, the court proscribed the following addition to the standard jury instruction on mitigation of damages:

> In considering whether the plaintiff acted as a reasonably prudent person, you may consider the plaintiff's testimony that she is a believer in the Jehovah's Witness faith, and that as an adherent of that faith, she cannot accept any medical treatment which requires a blood transfusion. I charge you that such belief is a factor for you to consider, together with all the other evidence you have heard, in determining whether the plaintiff acted reasonably in caring for her injuries, keeping in mind, however, that the overriding test is whether the plaintiff acted as a reasonably prudent person, under all the circumstances confronting her. [230 A.D.2d at 556-557]

Two earlier cases, like *Williams,* held that the jury could take the plaintiff's belief in faith healing into account in determining the reasonableness of the refusal to accept traditional medical care. See Lange v. Hoyt, 159 A. 575 (1932), and Christiansen v. Hollings, 112 P.2d 723 (Cal. Ct. App. 1941), both of which involved Christian Scientists as plaintiffs. Other courts, however, have refused to recognize religious beliefs as providing a valid reason for refusing medical treatment. See, e.g., Munn v. Algee, 924 F.2d 568 (5th Cir.), *cert. denied,* 502 U.S. 900 (1991), involving a member of the Jehovah's Witnesses, who had refused to undergo a medically necessary blood transfusion citing religious beliefs. The court of appeals was concerned that the "case-by-case" approach of *Lange* and *Christiansen* would require the jury to assess the reasonableness of the religious basis of the plaintiff's refusal to accept medical treatment. The court felt that such an assessment might violate the Establishment Clause of the First Amendment to the United States Constitution; however, because of the procedural posture of the case, the court did not have to resolve that issue. The "reasonable believer" approach of *Williams, Lange,* and *Christiansen* is advanced in Note, Reason, Religion, and Avoidable Consequences, 67 N.Y.U. L. Rev. 1111 (1992). See also Note, Medical Care, Freedom of Religion, and Mitigation of Damages, 87 Yale L.J. 1466 (1978), which argues that the avoidable consequences rule violates the First Amendment rights of those whose religious beliefs prevent them from seeking medical care. See also Guido Calabresi, Ideals, Beliefs, Attitudes and the Law (1985). Chapter 3 of that book, entitled "The Beliefs of a Reasonable Person," is particularly relevant to this issue.

In addition to reasonably incurred medical expenses, future medical expenses are also recoverable, but they must be proved by a reasonable probability (see Marchetti v. Ramirez, 688 A.2d 1325 (Conn. 1997)), and will commonly be reduced to present value (see Thorpe v. Bailey, 386 A.2d 668 (Del. 1978)). Some states have enacted tort reform statutes that require reduction of future expenses to present value. See, e.g., Mich. Comp. Laws Ann. §600.630(1)(c) (West 1995).

Can the plaintiff recover "medical monitoring" expenses, not for the future treatment of any injury, but to determine whether the plaintiff incurs injury in the future? The United States Supreme Court, in a case arising under the Federal Employers' Liability Act,[2] ruled that there can be no such recovery in the absence of a present injury. See Metro-North Commuter R.R. Co. v. Buckley, 521 U.S. 424 (1997). Similarly, the court in June v. Union Carbide Corp., 577 F.3d 1234 (10th Cir. 2009) interpreted the Price-Anderson Act of 1957, which governs civil liability claims arising out of nuclear incidents, to require actual physical manifestation of bodily injury before plaintiffs may seek to recover medical expenses.

Some state courts have been more receptive to medical monitoring claims. For instance, the court in Donovan v. Philip Morris USA, Inc., 914 N.E.2d 891 (Mass. 2009), ruled that an existing physical injury is not necessary, relying on the following reasoning:

> Our tort law developed in the late Nineteenth and early Twentieth centuries, when the vast majority of tortious injuries were caused by blunt trauma and mechanical forces. We must adapt to the growing recognition that exposure to toxic substances and radiation may cause substantial injury which should be compensable even if the full effects are not immediately apparent. When competent medical testimony establishes that medical monitoring is necessary to detect the potential onset of a serious illness or disease due to physiological changes indicating a substantial increase in risk of harm from exposure to a known hazardous substance, the element of injury and damage will have been satisfied and the cost of that monitoring is recoverable in tort. No particular level or quantification of increase in risk of harm is necessary, so long as it is substantial and so long as there has been at least a corresponding subcellular change. This should address any concern over false claims, yet permit a genuinely injured person to recover legitimate expenses without having to overcome insurmountable problems of proof in this difficult and complex area. . . . The expense of medical monitoring is thus a form of future medical expense and should be treated as such.
>
> In conclusion, each plaintiff must prove the following: (1) The defendant's negligence (2) caused (3) the plaintiff to become exposed to a hazardous substance that produced, at least, subcellular changes that substantially increased the risk of serious disease, illness, or injury (4) for which an effective medical test for reliable early detection exists, (5) and early detection, combined with prompt and effective treatment, will significantly decrease the risk of death or the severity of the disease, illness or injury, and (6) such diagnostic medical examinations are reasonably (and periodically) necessary, conformably with the standard of care, and (7) the present value of the reasonable cost of such tests and care, as of the date of the filing of the complaint.

See also Bower v. Westinghouse Elec. Corp., 522 S.E.2d 424 (W. Va. 1999) (adopting a similar set of criteria for medical monitoring claims); Meyer v. Fluor Corp., 220 S.W.3d 712 (Mo. 2007) (same); and Sadler v. PacifiCare of Nevada, 340 P. 3d 1264 (Nev. 2014) (declining to identify specific criteria for medical monitoring claims, but holding that a plaintiff may satisfy the injury requirement for such claims if he or she is reasonably required to undergo medical monitoring beyond what would have been recommended if

2. The Federal Employers' Liability Act (45 U.S.C.A. §§51-60) provides for compensation to railroad employees injured as the result of work-related activities. Liability of the employer-railroad is based on negligence. Assumption of the risk and contributory negligence are not defenses, but the contributory negligence of the employee serves to reduce recovery, except in cases in which the railroad's negligence constitutes a violation of a statute enacted for the safety of employees.

the plaintiff had not been exposed to the defendant's negligent act). In contrast, state courts rejecting the medical monitoring cause of action include Caronia v. Philip Morris USA, 5 N.E.3d 11 (N.Y. 2013), Lowe v. Philip Morris USA, Inc., 183 P.3d 181 (Or. 2008), Sinclair v. Merck & Co., Inc., 948 A.2d 587 (N.J. 2008), and Paz v. Brush Engineered Materials, Inc., 949 So. 2d 1 (Miss. 2007). For a thorough review of how courts have addressed medical monitoring claims, see Victor E. Schwartz & Cary Silverman, The Rise of 'Empty Suit' Litigation. Where Should Tort Law Draw the Line?, 80 Brook. L. Rev. 599 (2015).

Even more basic than the question of whether the plaintiff's expenses are "reasonable" is the question of whether the plaintiff has undergone an "expense." Where the plaintiff is fully compensated by medical insurance, for example, is there an expense for which recovery from the defendant will be allowed? The general rule in this country regarding the effect of plaintiff's obtaining benefits from sources other than the defendant is stated in Gelsomino v. Mendonca, 723 A.2d 300, 301 (R.I. 1999), as follows:

> The collateral source doctrine mandates that evidence of payments made to an injured party from sources independent of a tort-feasor are inadmissible and shall not diminish the tort-feasor's liability to the plaintiff. "The rationale of this rule is that the injured person is entitled to be made whole, since it is no concern of the tort-feasor that someone else completely unconnected with the tort-feasor has aided his victim," and the "wrongdoer, responsible for injuring the plaintiff, should not receive [this] windfall." [Internal citations omitted.]

The plaintiff in this case was a teacher injured when the defendant police officer negligently drove his cruiser into a portable classroom while pursuing another vehicle. The trial court erred in allowing the jury to consider evidence of payments to the teacher from a disability pension. The defendant officer was entitled to no reduction in damages due to the pension. Defendant city, which employed both the officer and the teacher, was entitled to a reduction only for those portions of the pension that it could prove it had paid into the teacher's account. Would the Rhode Island court have reached the same result if it had applied the rule of the following case?

Coyne v. Campbell

11 N.Y.2d 372, 183 N.E.2d 891 (1962)

Froessel, J. On July 5, 1957, plaintiff sustained a whiplash injury when his automobile was struck in the rear by a motor vehicle driven by defendant. Inasmuch as plaintiff is a practicing physician and surgeon, he received medical treatment, physiotherapy and care from his professional colleagues and his nurse, and incurred no out-of-pocket expenses therefor. Nevertheless, in his bill of particulars, he stated that his special damages for medical and nursing care and treatment amounted to $2,235. The trial court ruled that the value of these services was not a proper item of special damages, and that no recovery could be had therefor since they had been rendered gratuitously. He thus excluded evidence as to their value. The sole question here presented is the correctness of this ruling.

In the leading case of Drinkwater v. Dinsmore (80 N.Y. 390) we unanimously reversed a plaintiff's judgment entered upon a jury verdict, because defendant was precluded from showing that plaintiff had been paid his wages by his employer during the period of his incapacitation. We held such evidence admissible on the theory that plaintiff was entitled to recover only his pecuniary losses, of which wages gratuitously paid were not an item. With respect to medical expenses, we stated (p. 393) that "the plaintiff must show what he paid the doctor, and can recover only so much as he paid or was bound to pay." Although decided more than 80 years ago, the *Drinkwater* case has continuously been and still is recognized as the prevailing law of this State.

As recently as 1957, the Legislature declined to enact a proposed amendment to the Civil Practice Act, the avowed purpose of which (1957 Report of N.Y. Law Rev. Comm., p. 223) was "to abrogate the rule of Drinkwater v. Dinsmore, 80 N.Y. 390 (1880) and to conform New York law to the rule followed in most states that payments from collateral sources do not reduce the amount recoverable in a personal injury action." . . . The Legislature and not the judiciary is the proper body to decide such a policy question involving the accommodation of various interests. We should not now seek to assume their powers and overrule their decision not to change the well-settled law of this State. No matter what may be the rule in other jurisdictions, *Drinkwater* is still the law in this State.

We find no merit in plaintiff's contention that the medical and nursing services for which damages are sought were supported by consideration. Plaintiff testified that he did not have to pay for the physiotherapy, and his counsel confirmed the fact that "these various items were not payable by the doctor nor were they actual obligations of his, and that he will not have to pay them."

Plaintiff's colleagues rendered the necessary medical services gratuitously as a professional courtesy. It may well be that as a result of having accepted their generosity plaintiff is under a moral obligation to act for them in a similar manner, should his services ever be required; such need may never arise, however, and in any event such a moral obligation is not an injury for which tort damages, which "must be compensatory only" may be awarded. A moral obligation, without more, will not support a claim for legal damages. . . .

We are also told that the physiotherapy treatments which plaintiff received from his nurse consumed approximately two hours per week, and that they were given during the usual office hours for which she received her regular salary. Plaintiff does not claim that he was required to or in fact did pay any additional compensation to his nurse for her performance of these duties, and, therefore, this has not resulted in compensable damage to plaintiff.

Finally, we reject as unwarranted plaintiff's suggestion that our decision in Healy v. Rennert (9 N.Y.2d 202, 206) casts doubt on the continued validity of the *Drinkwater* rule in a case such as the instant one. In *Healy,* we held that it was error to permit defendants to establish on cross-examination that plaintiff was a member of a health insurance plan and that he was receiving increased disability pension benefits. In that case, however, the plaintiff had given value for the benefits he received; he paid a premium for the health insurance, and had worked for 18 years, in order to be eligible for the disability retirement benefits. We were not confronted with — and did not attempt to pass upon — a situation where the injured plaintiff received wholly gratuitous services for which he had given no consideration in return and which he was under no legal obligation to repay. In short, insurance, pension, vacation and other benefits which were contracted and paid for are not relevant here. Gratuitous services rendered by relatives, neighbors and friends are not compensable.

. . . It would hardly be fair in a negligence action, where damages are compensatory and not punitive, to change the *Drinkwater* rule of long standing in the face of the Legislature's refusal to do so, and to punish a defendant by requiring him to pay plaintiff for a friend's generosity. If we were to allow a plaintiff the reasonable value of the services of the physician who treated him gratuitously, logic would dictate that the plaintiff would then be entitled to the reasonable value of such services, despite the fact that the physician charged him but a fraction of such value. Such a rule would involve odd consequences, and in the end simply require a defendant to pay a plaintiff the value of a gift.

The judgment appealed from should be affirmed.

CHIEF JUDGE DESMOND (concurring). The reason why this plaintiff cannot include in his damages anything for physicians' bills or nursing expense is that he had paid nothing for those services. . . .

Settled and consistent precedents provide the answer to the question posed by this appeal. Neither justice nor morality require a different answer. Diminution of damages because medical services were furnished gratuitously results in a windfall of sorts to a defendant but allowance of such items although not paid for would unjustly enrich a plaintiff.

I vote to affirm.

FULD, J. (dissenting). It is elementary that damages in personal injury actions are awarded in order to compensate the plaintiff, but, under an established exception, the collateral source doctrine — which we recognized in Healy v. Rennert (9 N.Y.2d 202) — a wrongdoer will not be allowed to deduct benefits which the plaintiff may have received from another source. To put the matter broadly, the defendant should not be given credit for an amount of money, or its equivalent in services, received by the plaintiff from other sources. "The rationale of the collateral source doctrine in tort actions," it has been said, "is that a tort-feasor should not be allowed to escape the pecuniary consequences of his wrongful act merely because his victim has received benefit from a third party" (Note, 26 Fordham L. Rev. 372, 381).

In the *Healy* case, this court held that, if one is negligently injured by another, the damages recoverable from the latter are diminished neither (1) by the fact that the injured party has been indemnified for his loss by insurance effected by him nor (2) by the fact that his medical expenses were paid by HIP or some other health insurance plan (p. 206). In the case before us, the plaintiff suffered injuries and required medical and nursing care. He had no health insurance, but he received the necessary medical care and services from fellow doctors without being required to pay them in cash. In addition, he received physiotherapy treatments from the nurse employed by him in his office and to whom he, of course, paid a salary.

I fail to see any real difference between the situation in Healy v. Rennert and the case now before us. In neither case was the injured person burdened with any charges for the medical services rendered and, accordingly, when the defendant is required to pay as "damages" for those services or their value, such damages are no less "compensatory" in the one case than in the other. Nor do I understand why a distinction should be made depending upon whether the medical services were rendered gratuitously or for a consideration.[1] What difference should it make, either to the plaintiff or to the defendant, whether an injured plaintiff has his medical bills taken care of by an insurer or by a wealthy uncle or by a fellow doctor? Certainly, neither the uncle, who acted out of affection, nor the doctor, impelled by so-called professional courtesy, intended to benefit the tort-feasor.

1. I shall assume that in this case the doctors' services were given gratuitously, though a strong argument could be made to the contrary, that is, that they were supported by consideration in that the plaintiff came under a duty to reciprocate and render medical services to his colleagues. Be that as it may, though, I see no basis for labeling the physiotherapy treatments given by the plaintiff's salaried nurse gratuitous. They were given during the nurse's normal working day for which she received wages from the plaintiff. Had she not been required to give such treatments, she would undoubtedly have been free to perform other work for the plaintiff.

The crucial question in cases such as this is whether the tort-feasor would, in fairness and justice, be given credit for the amounts, or their equivalent in services, which the plaintiff has received from some collateral source. The collateral source doctrine is not, and should not be, limited to cases where the plaintiff had previously paid consideration (in the form of insurance premiums, for instance) for the benefit of services which he receives or where there has been a payment of cash or out-of-pocket expenses. The rationale underlying the rule is that a wrongdoer, responsible for injuring the plaintiff, should not receive a windfall. Were it not for the fortuitous circumstance that the plaintiff was a doctor, he would have been billed for the medical services and the defendant would have had to pay for them. The medical services were supplied to help the plaintiff, not to relieve the defendant from any part of his liability or to benefit him. It should not matter, in reason, logic or justice, whether the benefit received was in return for a consideration or given gratuitously, or whether it represented money paid out or its equivalent in services.

The rule reflected by the decision in Drinkwater v. Dinsmore (80 N.Y. 390) is court made and, accordingly, since I believe . . . that it is not only "completely opposite to the majority rule," but also "unfair, illogical and unduly complex," I cannot vote for its perpetuation. Indeed, as I have already indicated, an even stronger case for its repudiation is made out by our recent decision in Healy v. Rennert (9 N.Y.2d 202, supra).

I would reverse the judgment appealed from and direct a new trial.

JUDGES DYE, VAN VOORHIS, BURKE, and FOSTER concur with JUDGE FROESSEL; CHIEF JUDGE DESMOND concurs in a separate opinion; JUDGE FULD dissents in an opinion.

Judgment affirmed.

It may, of course, be difficult to determine whether the service is really gratuitous. For example, one court permitted recovery of expenses already paid for by Medicare (Berg v. United States, 806 F.2d 978 (10th Cir. 1986), *cert. denied,* 482 U.S. 913 (1987)), but not for expenses paid for by a different governmental program, the Civilian Health and Medical Program of the Uniformed Services (Mays v. United States, 806 F.2d 976 (10th Cir. 1986)). The court stated that the important distinction between the two sources is that the former is supported by a special social security tax paid for by its beneficiaries, while the latter is paid for out of general governmental revenue.

On one view, everyone pays for publically funded medical care programs through taxes. Perhaps for this reason, most courts have applied the collateral source rule to gratuitously rendered governmental services, such as free medical care rendered by a veterans' hospital (see Ulrich v. Veterans' Admin. Hosp., 853 F.2d 1078 (2d Cir. 1988)); state-operated mental health facilities (see Werner v. Lane, 393 A.2d 1329 (Me. 1978)); and special services for students with handicaps furnished by a public school (see Williston v. Ard, 611 So. 2d 274 (Ala. 1992)).

But what about services rendered gratuitously due to a personal relationship with the plaintiff? In Hill v. U.S., 81 F.3d 118 (10th Cir.), *cert. denied*, 519 U.S. 810 (1996), the court held that plaintiff parents could recover the value of round-the-clock care they gave their disabled daughter after a district court found the care to be the same in quality as that provided by a licensed practical nurse.

Several states have, by statute, substantially abrogated the collateral source rule in tort cases. These statutes sometimes provide an offset to the reduction by some amount, reflecting the fact that the collateral source benefits may have been paid for by the plaintiff, or someone else acting on the plaintiff's behalf. See, e.g., N.Y. Civ. Prac. L. & R. 4545(a), which provides that the collateral source reduction is to be offset by the amount of premiums paid by the plaintiff for the benefits for the two-year period immediately preceding the accrual of the cause of action, and by the projected future cost to the plaintiff of maintaining the benefits.

The constitutionality of a number of statutes abrogating the collateral source rule has been challenged under both state constitutions and the United States Constitution, with varying results. Upholding a statute that permits the introduction of evidence of collateral source payments in personal injury cases is Heinz v. Chicago Road Investment Co., 549 N.W.2d 47 (Mich. Ct. App. 1996), *rev. denied,* 567 N.W.2d 250 (Mich. 1997). A similar statute was held unconstitutional on state equal protection and due process grounds in American Legion Post Number 57 v. Leahey, 681 So. 2d 1337 (Ala. 1996). However, the Alabama Supreme Court overturned its decision in *Leahey,* thus reviving the statute that permits the introduction of evidence of collateral source payments, in Marsh v. Green, 782 So. 2d 223 (Ala. 2000).

Another way of avoiding double recovery, which is the main concern of statutes abrogating the collateral source rule, is to permit the collateral source to be subrogated to the rights of the plaintiff against the defendant. *Subrogation* is a device that puts the collateral source "in the shoes of the plaintiff," so that the collateral source can recover from the defendant to the extent of the obligation to the plaintiff. The right of the collateral source to subrogation will ordinarily arise only out of contract. For example, if a medical expense insurer has paid the plaintiff for the latter's bills, the insurer will be able to recover the amount of such payment from the tortfeasor only if the insurance contract authorizes it.

If no subrogation agreement exists, the insurer who has paid medical expenses usually has no right to subrogation. See, e.g., Perriera v. Redigar, 778 A.2d 429 (N.J. 2001). Courts following this view generally perceive medical insurance more as a form of investment by the insured that simply imposes on the insurer a duty to pay, rather than as a form of indemnification protecting the insured from medical expense losses. Courts have been willing, however, to examine the insurance policy to determine if it is one of indemnification rather than investment. If the policy appears to be written more in the language of the former, courts may allow subrogation even in the absence of an express clause. See, e.g., Cunningham v. Metropolitan Life Ins. Co., 360 N.W.2d 33 (Wis. 1985). The Florida statute abrogating the collateral source rule, Fla. Stat. §768.76, provides that the defendant is not entitled to a reduction to the extent that the collateral source is entitled to subrogation.

An emerging issue related to the collateral source rule concerns how to value the disparity between the amount that hospitals and doctors bill a patient and the lower negotiated amount that health maintenance organizations and other insurance providers actually end up paying. Plaintiffs argue that the savings negotiated on their behalf are a benefit received from a third party that should be excluded from evidence on the same general rationale that supports the collateral source rule. See White v. Jubitz Corp., 219 P.3d 566, 583 (Or. 2009) ("[T]he plaintiff in a personal injury action is entitled to claim and recover from a tortfeasor the reasonable value of the medical services charged without limitation to the sums for which plaintiff is legally liable, that plaintiff has paid for those services, or that a third party has paid on plaintiff's behalf."). Defendants, on the other hand, argue that health care providers routinely bill excessive amounts that they have no expectation of actually recovering; thus, allowing plaintiffs to recover the full stated amount of medical bills would result in a windfall. See Haygood v. De Escabedo, 356 S.W.3d 390 (Tex. 2012) ("To impose liability for medical expenses that a health care provider is not entitled to charge does not prevent a windfall to a tortfeasor; it creates one for a claimant. . . ."); Jacques v. Manton, 928 N.E.2d 434, 438 (Ohio 2010) ("[P]ermitting introduction of evidence of [write-offs] allows the fact-finder to determine the actual amount of medical expenses incurred as a result of the defendant's conduct. This result supports the traditional goal of compensatory damages — making the plaintiff whole."). The following case provides an extensive analysis.

Howell v. Hamilton Meats & Provisions, Inc.

52 Cal. 4th 541, 257 P.3d 1130, 139 Cal. Rptr.3d 325 (2011)

WERDEGAR, J. When a tortiously injured person receives medical care for his or her injuries, the provider of that care often accepts as full payment, pursuant to a preexisting contract with the injured person's health insurer, an amount less than that stated in the provider's bill. In that circumstance, may the injured person recover from the tortfeasor, as economic damages for past medical expenses, the undiscounted sum stated in the provider's bill but never paid by or on behalf of the injured person? We hold no such recovery is allowed, for the simple reason that the injured plaintiff did not suffer any economic loss in that amount. . . . The collateral source rule, which precludes deduction of compensation the plaintiff has received from sources independent of the tortfeasor from damages the plaintiff "would otherwise collect from the tortfeasor" (*Helfend v. Southern Cal. Rapid Transit Dist.* (1970) 2 Cal. 3d 1, 6, 84 Cal. Rptr. 173, 465 P.2d 61 (*Helfend*)), ensures that plaintiff here may recover in damages the amounts her insurer paid for her medical care. The rule, however, has no bearing on amounts that were included in a provider's bill but for which the plaintiff never incurred liability because the provider, by prior agreement, accepted a lesser amount as full payment. . . .

Factual And Procedural Background

Plaintiff Rebecca Howell was seriously injured in an automobile accident negligently caused by a driver for defendant Hamilton Meats & Provisions, Inc. (Hamilton). At trial, Hamilton conceded liability and the necessity of the medical treatment plaintiff had received, contesting only the amounts of plaintiff's economic and noneconomic damages. . . .

Plaintiff's surgeon and her husband each testified that the total amount billed for her medical care up to the time of trial was $189,978.63, and the jury returned a verdict awarding that same amount as damages for plaintiff's past medical expenses.

Hamilton then made a "post-trial motion to reduce past medical specials pursuant to [Hanif v. Housing Authority (1988) 200 Cal. App.3d 635, 246 Cal. Rptr. 192 (*Hanif*)]," seeking a reduction of $130,286.90, the amount assertedly "written off" by plaintiff's medical care providers, Scripps Memorial Hospital Encinitas (Scripps) and CORE Orthopaedic Medical Center (CORE). . . .

In opposition, plaintiff argued reduction of the medical damages would violate the collateral source rule. She supported her opposition with copies of the patient agreements she had signed with Scripps, in which she agreed to pay Scripps's "usual and customary charges" for the medical care she was to receive, and with CORE, in which she agreed to pay any part of the physician's fee her insurance did not pay.

The trial court granted Hamilton's motion, reducing the past medical damages award "to reflect the amount the medical providers accepted as payment in full." Accordingly, the court reduced the judgment by $130,286.90.

The Court of Appeal reversed the reduction order, holding it violated the collateral source rule. . . .

We granted Hamilton's petition for review.

Discussion

. . . When, as here, the costs of medical treatment are paid in whole or in part by a third party unconnected to the defendant, the collateral source rule is implicated. The collateral source rule states that "if an injured party receives some compensation for his injuries from a source wholly independent of the tortfeasor, such payment should not be deducted from the damages which the plaintiff would otherwise collect from the tortfeasor." (*Helfend, supra,* 2 Cal. 3d at p. 6, 84 Cal. Rptr. 173, 465 P.2d 61). . . .

The California history of the substantive question at issue — whether recovery of medical damages is limited to the amounts providers actually are paid or extends to the amounts of their undiscounted bills — begins with *Hanif, supra,* 200 Cal. App. 3d 635, 246 Cal. Rptr. 192.

The injured plaintiff in *Hanif* was a Medi–Cal recipient, and the amounts Medi–Cal paid for his medical care were, according to his evidence, substantially lower than the "reasonable value" of the treatment (apparently the same as the hospital bill, as the opinion notes the hospital had "'written off'" the difference). (*Hanif, supra,* 200 Cal. App. 3d at p. 639, 246 Cal. Rptr. 192.) Although there was no evidence the plaintiff was liable for the difference, the court in a bench trial awarded the plaintiff the larger, "reasonable value" amount. (*Ibid.*) The appellate court held the trial court had overcompensated the plaintiff for his past medical expenses; recovery should have been limited to the amount Medi–Cal had actually paid on his behalf. (*Id.* at pp. 639, 643-644, 246 Cal. Rptr. 192.) . . .

Hanif's rationale was straightforward. While California courts have referred to the "reasonable value" of medical care in delineating the measure of recoverable damages for medical expenses, in this context "'[r]easonable value' is a term of limitation, not of aggrandizement." (*Hanif, supra,* 200 Cal. App. 3d at p. 641, 246 Cal. Rptr. 192.) The "detriment" the plaintiff suffered (Civ. Code, §3281), his pecuniary "loss" (*id.,* §3282), was only what Medi–Cal had paid on his behalf; to award more was to place him in a better financial position than before the tort was committed. (*Hanif,* at pp. 640-641, 246 Cal. Rptr. 192.) A tort plaintiff's recovery for medical expenses, the *Hanif* court opined, is limited to the amount "paid or incurred for past medical care and services, whether by the plaintiff or by an independent source. . . ." (*Id.* at p. 641, 246 Cal. Rptr. 192.) . . .

A. *Hanif* and the Measure of Damages for Past Medical Expenses

We agree with the *Hanif* court that a plaintiff may recover as economic damages *no more* than the reasonable value of the medical services received and is not entitled to recover the reasonable value if his or her actual loss was less. (*Hanif, supra,* 200 Cal. App. 3d at p. 641, 246 Cal. Rptr. 192.) California decisions have focused on "reasonable value" in the context of *limiting* recovery to reasonable expenditures, not expanding recovery beyond the plaintiff's actual loss or liability. To be recoverable, a medical expense must be both incurred *and* reasonable.

The rule that a plaintiff's expenses, to be recoverable, must be both incurred *and* reasonable accords, as well, with our damages statutes. "Damages must, in all cases, be reasonable. . . ." (Civ. Code, §3359.) But if the plaintiff negotiates a discount and thereby receives services for less than might reasonably be charged, the plaintiff has not suffered a pecuniary loss or other detriment in the greater amount and therefore cannot recover damages for that amount. (*Id.,* §§3281, 3282.) The same rule applies when a collateral source, such as the plaintiff's health insurer, has obtained a discount for its payments on the plaintiff's behalf. . . .

B. *Hanif* and Private Health Insurance

Plaintiff contends *Hanif*'s limitation on recovery, even if correct as to Medi–Cal recipients, does not logically apply to plaintiffs, like her, with private medical insurance. The appellate court below agreed, reasoning that "Howell, who was privately insured, incurred personal liability for her medical providers' usual and customary charges," whereas the plaintiff in *Hanif* "incurred no personal liability for the medical charges billed to Medi–Cal." Observing that *Hanif* stated the measure of recovery for medical expenses was the amounts actually "paid or incurred" (*Hanif, supra,* 200 Cal. App. 3d at p. 641, 246 Cal. Rptr. 192), plaintiff argues she *incurred* liability for the full amount of Scripps's and CORE's bills when she signed patient agreements with those providers and accepted their services.

We find the distinction unpersuasive. Evidence presented at the posttrial hearing showed Scripps and CORE accepted the discounted amounts as full payment pursuant to preexisting agreements with PacifiCare, plaintiff's managed care plan. Since those agreements were in place when plaintiff sought medical care from the providers and signed the patient agreements, her prospective liability was limited to the amounts PacifiCare had agreed to pay the providers for the services they were to render. Plaintiff cannot meaningfully be said ever to have incurred the full charges. . . .

Hanif noted one exception to its rule, viz., for medical services that are gratuitously provided or discounted, an exception included in the Restatement section on which the court relied (Rest. 2d Torts, §911, com. h, pp. 476-477). The question arises whether this exception, if accepted, limits *Hanif*'s logic in a manner important to the present issue. That is, if a plaintiff, as the Restatement provides, may recover the reasonable value of donated medical services — services for which neither the plaintiff nor the plaintiff's insurer paid — should a plaintiff also be permitted to recover other amounts that were not paid but were reasonably billed by the provider, including the negotiated rate differential? If the amount of a gratuitous discount would be considered a collateral source payment, should the amount of a negotiated discount be treated in the same way?

The Restatement reflects the widely held view that the collateral source rule applies to gratuitous payments and services. . . . California law is less clear on the point. . . .

Assuming California follows the Restatement's view that a plaintiff may recover the value of donated services under the collateral source rule, this exception to *Hanif*'s limitation on recovery does not, we believe, militate against applying *Hanif*'s rule — that only amounts paid or incurred are recoverable — to medical expenses paid by the plaintiff's insurer. Medical providers that agree to accept discounted payments by managed care organizations or other health insurers as full payment for a patient's care do so not as a gift to the patient or insurer, but for commercial reasons and as a result of negotiations. As plaintiff herself explains, hospitals and medical groups obtain commercial benefits from their agreements with health insurance organizations; the agreements guarantee the providers prompt payment of the agreed rates and often have financial incentives for plan members to choose the providers' services. . . . That plaintiffs are not permitted to recover undiscounted amounts from those who have injured them creates no danger these negotiations and agreements will disappear; the medical provider has no financial reason to care whether the tortfeasor is charged with or the plaintiff recovers the negotiated rate differential. . . .

C. Windfall to the Tortfeasor

Nor does the tortfeasor obtain a "windfall" merely because the injured person's health insurer has negotiated a favorable rate of payment with the person's medical provider. When an injured plaintiff has received collateral compensation or benefits as a gift, allowing a deduction from damages in that amount would result in a windfall for the tortfeasor and underpayment for the injury. Because the tortfeasor would not pay the full cost of his or her negligence or wrongdoing, the deduction would distort the deterrent function of tort law. . . . Analogously, if it were established a medical provider's full bill generally represents the value of the services provided, and the discounted price negotiated with the insurer is an artificially low fraction of that true value, one could make a parallel argument that relieving the defendant of paying the full bill would result in underdeterrence. The complexities of contemporary pricing and reimbursement patterns for medical providers, however, do not support such a generalization. . . .

We do not suggest hospital bills always exceed the reasonable value of the services provided. [P]rices for a given service can vary tremendously, sometimes by a factor of five or more, from hospital to hospital in California. With so much variation, making any broad generalization about the relationship between the value or cost of medical services and the amounts providers bill for them — other than that the relationship is not always a close one — would be perilous. . . .

[I]t is not possible to say generally that providers' full bills represent the real value of their services, nor that the discounted payments they accept from private insurers are mere arbitrary reductions. Accordingly, a tortfeasor who pays only the discounted amount as damages does not generally receive a windfall and is not generally underdeterred from engaging in risky conduct.

D. The Negotiated Rate Differential as Insurance Benefit

If the negotiated rate differential is not a gratuitous payment by the provider to the injured plaintiff (recoverable, at least in the Restatement's view, under the collateral source rule), nor an arbitrary reduction (arguably recoverable to prevent a defense windfall and underdeterrence), is it, as plaintiff contends and the Court of Appeal held, recoverable as a benefit provided to the insured plaintiff under her policy? Plaintiff contends the negotiated rate differential represents the monetary value of the administrative and marketing advantages a provider obtains through its agreement with the insurer. Having incurred liability for the full price of her medical care, plaintiff maintains, she then received the benefit of having her insurer extinguish that obligation through a combination of cash payments and noncash consideration in the amount of the negotiated rate differential. Both parts of this consideration being benefits accruing to her under her policy, for which she paid premiums, both parts should assertedly be recoverable under the collateral source rule.

We disagree. As previously discussed, plaintiff did not incur liability for her providers' full bills, because at the time the charges were incurred the providers had already agreed on a different price schedule for PacifiCare's . . . members. Having never incurred the full bill, plaintiff could not recover it in damages for economic loss. For this reason alone, the collateral source rule would be inapplicable. . . .

The negotiated rate differential lies outside the operation of the collateral source rule also because it is not primarily a benefit to the plaintiff and, to the extent it does benefit the plaintiff, it is not provided as "compensation for [the plaintiff's] injuries." (*Helfend, supra,* 2 Cal. 3d at p. 6, 84 Cal. Rptr. 173, 465 P.2d 61). . . . [E]ven when the overall savings a health insurance organization negotiates for itself can be said to benefit an insured indirectly — through lower premiums or copayments, for example — it would be rare that these indirect benefits would coincidentally equal the negotiated rate differential for the medical services rendered the plaintiff.

Finally, while the providers presumably did obtain some commercial advantages by virtue of their agreements with PacifiCare, plaintiff's insurer, the *global* value of those advantages cannot be equated to the amount of the negotiated rate differential for plaintiff's *individual* care. . . . For a given medical service to a given plaintiff, therefore, the amount of the negotiated rate differential may be higher or lower than the average discount over the range of services offered. The negotiated rate differential in a particular case thus does not necessarily reflect the commercial advantages the provider obtained in exchange for accepting a discounted payment *in that case.*

We conclude the negotiated rate differential is not a collateral payment or benefit subject to the collateral source rule. We emphasize, however, that the rule applies with full force here and in similar cases. Plaintiff here recovers the amounts paid on her behalf by her health insurer as well as her own out-of-pocket expenses. . . . Plaintiff thus receives the benefits of the health insurance for which she paid premiums: her medical expenses have been paid per the policy, and those payments are not deducted from her tort recovery. . . .

We Concur: Cantil–Sakauye, C.J., Kennard, Baxter, Chin, And Corrigan, JJ.

Dissenting Opinion by Klein, J.

I respectfully dissent. I agree Rebecca Howell (Howell), who was insured by PacifiCare under a preferred provider organization (PPO) health insurance policy, is not entitled to recover the gross amount of her potentially inflated medical bills. However, I disagree with the majority insofar as it concludes Howell's recovery of medical damages must be capped at the discounted amount her medical providers agreed to accept as payment in full from her insurer. Rather, Howell should be entitled to recover the *reasonable value* or market value of such services, as determined by expert testimony at trial, just as would be the case if the injured person had not purchased insurance or if the medical services had been donated.

The majority . . . creates a significant exception to this state's long-standing collateral source rule. The majority draws a bright line and limits Howell's recovery of medical damages to "no more than the medical providers accepted in full payment for their services." Thus, Howell is left in a worse position than an uninsured individual or one who was a donee of medical services, persons who are entitled to recover the full reasonable value of their medical care. Neither law nor policy supports such an anomalous outcome.

The majority holds the "negotiated rate differential" (the *difference* between the original billed amount of $189,978.63 and the lesser amount accepted by the providers as payment in full) lies outside the operation of the collateral source rule because the plaintiff did not suffer any economic loss in the amount of the negotiated rate differential and therefore said sum is not recoverable by plaintiff.

The majority fails to recognize the difference between the *reasonable value* of Howell's care (hypothetically, $75,000) and the *lesser sum* Howell's preferred providers agreed to accept as *payment in full* ($59,691.73), did constitute a payment by others, namely, the medical providers, toward the cost of treating Howell. Howell's medical providers, as participants in PacifiCare's PPO network, *wrote off* a portion of her bills, pursuant to their agreements with PacifiCare. By acquiring the PPO policy, Howell purchased not only indemnity coverage but also access to the negotiated discounts between her health insurer and her medical providers. Therefore, any difference between the *reasonable value* of Howell's treatment, and the *lesser amount* the providers agreed to accept as *payment in full,* was a benefit Howell is entitled to retain under the collateral source rule. There is little justification for allowing a defendant tortfeasor to avoid liability for the reasonable value of a plaintiff's medical expenses, where such value exceeds the negotiated payment. . . .

Under the reasonable value approach, in the event the reasonable value of a plaintiff's treatment *exceeds* the amount the medical providers have agreed to accept as payment in full from plaintiff's insurer, such difference would be allocated to the plaintiff, rather than to the defendant tortfeasor. This approach preserves the long-standing collateral source rule, and at the same time, prevents a plaintiff from recovering excessive damages based on potentially inflated medical bills.

. . . [I]t should be recognized that where an insured plaintiff prevails and obtains an award of economic damages for past medical expenses from a third party, the insured generally is contractually required to reimburse the health insurer to the extent the insured recovers on her judgment against the tortfeasor. In addition to having to reimburse the health insurer, the plaintiff will have incurred attorney fees to prosecute the claim for economic damages.

Thus, because the plaintiff's award of economic damages for past medical expenses is likely to be largely transferred from the defendant (or from the defendant's insurer) to the plaintiff's insurer and to the plaintiff's attorney, the award is not likely to yield a windfall to the plaintiff.

In addition, it should be recognized the collateral source rule serves to protect the "person who has invested years of insurance premiums to assure [her] medical care." (*Helfend, supra,* 2 Cal.3d at pp. 9-10, 84 Cal. Rptr. 173, 465 P.2d 61.) However, the award of compensatory damages does not expressly include reimbursement to the plaintiff for those premiums. It is only through the application of the collateral source rule that the plaintiff is rewarded for maintaining his or her own health insurance for personal injuries.

For all these reasons, any perceived windfall to the plaintiff as a consequence of the collateral source rule represents a relatively minor portion of plaintiff's overall recovery of economic damages. Further, as between the injured person and the tortfeasor, the equities dictate such benefit should be allocated to the injured party, not to the negligent tortfeasor. Indeed, it is difficult to understand just what policy considerations justify denying the thrifty or prudent plaintiff who has purchased private health insurance the full benefit of his or her own foresight, and instead, transferring that benefit to the tortfeasor. . . .

Problem 36

You have received the following memorandum from a partner in your firm:

> My client is Sandra Fuller, the daughter of an old friend. Sandra, who was 23 at the time, was injured in an automobile accident about a year ago. The liability issues are fairly routine, but there is a problem with respect to damages that I need your help on. Sandra's back was severely injured. Her doctor has prescribed conservative treatment, but the pain has persisted. The doctor told her that there are medicines that would substantially reduce the pain, but she has refused to take them. As a teenager, Sandra became involved with cocaine. About three years ago, she realized that she was addicted, and at the recommendation of a friend, joined the "Martinists," a religious group that opposes the use of all drugs, including those for purely medicinal purposes. The Martinists were very effective in dealing with Sandra's addiction. She was able to kick the cocaine habit, and is a dedicated believer in the Martinists.
>
> Three months ago, Sandra's father met a Dr. Wolverton at a party. Dr. Wolverton has studied pain for many years, and has been experimenting with ultra-sound and electrical shock treatments for the relief of pain. His methods are very controversial and have not been accepted by the medical profession. Dr. Wolverton told Sandra's father that he would treat Sandra for her back pain at no cost. While Sandra would have been willing to pay for the treatment, she agreed to volunteer since it offered a drug-free treatment for pain. She has been undergoing treatment by Dr. Wolverton for two months, and reports that the treatments have helped but have not eliminated the pain. Dr. Wolverton has told me that with time the pain will be completely eliminated, but he has refused to say just how long it will take. I have talked with an orthopedic surgeon at the medical school, and he is very doubtful as to the efficacy of the Wolverton treatments. He is confident that the accepted drug therapy would be more effective, relatively inexpensive, and nonaddictive.
>
> I have a meeting next week with Catherine Riggs, who represents the insurance company of Lawrence Melby, the driver of the other car. I want to work up an initial demand, and I would like your help determining how these facts will affect Sandra's claim for pain and suffering and medical expenses.

b. Lost Earnings and Impairment of Earning Capacity

(1) The Basic Measure of Recovery

From a strictly economic point of view, impairment of ability to earn may be the most justifiable element of general compensatory damages. The loss or impairment of a person's capacity to earn a living, unless compensated, may result in a life of subsistence and dependence on others. In a typical case involving serious bodily injury, the plaintiff is incapacitated for a period, during which some or all of the earnings the plaintiff would have received are lost; later, the condition improves to the point that the plaintiff is able to return to work, albeit with difficulty, and to achieve something less than the former earnings level. The plaintiff in such a case will be seeking to recover for both the earnings actually lost up to the time of the trial or settlement and the diminution in the capacity to earn in the future. In this type of case, the dividing line between lost earnings and impairment of earning capacity is drawn in time: out-of-pocket losses up to the time of trial or settlement constitute the former; anticipated losses in the future constitute the latter. Thus, for example, if the plaintiff had been earning $3,000 a month prior to the accident (that is, with a demonstrated earning capacity of $3,000 a month) and thereafter experiences a three-month total disability during which no earnings are received, followed by a return to work at a diminished earnings rate of $2,250 a month (that is, a permanent 25 percent disability), and the trial takes place 18 months after the accident, the plaintiff will be seeking to recover $20,250 in lost earnings ($9,000 for three months total disability and $11,250 for 15 months partial disability) and a lump sum for impairment of earning capacity equal to the anticipated loss of $750 a month for the rest of the plaintiff's life.

Of course, not all cases are so simple, as the following decisions make clear.

Ruzzi v. Butler Petroleum Co.

527 Pa. 1, 588 A.2d 1 (1991)

PAPADAKOS, JUSTICE.

[Plaintiff Ruzzi was servicing the sign at a gas station owned by defendant Zinsser and supplied with fuel by defendant Butler Petroleum, when used fuel tanks near the sign exploded. At trial, the jury found against Butler Petroleum and defendant Shockey, the tanks' vendor, on the issue of liability. Plaintiff called an expert witness, Jarrell, who testified as to lost earning capacity. Shockey appealed various aspects of Jarrell's testimony to the Superior Court, which affirmed on those issues. Only the portion of the Pennsylvania Supreme Court opinion relating to Shockey's appeal of Jerrell's testimony on future earnings is included here.

After examining the expert witness's credentials, the court found he was qualified to testify, that expert testimony on earning capacity was appropriate, and that Jarrell's testimony was neither speculative nor lacking in foundation.] . . .

Shockey also claims that Jarrell's testimony was contrary to the evidence. The basis of this claim is that at the time of trial Ruzzi was employed by AMG Sign Company at a less physically demanding job, but at the same salary he made before the injury. The error in this claim is that it ignores the difference between actual loss of earnings and loss of earning capacity. This court discussed the difference between these concepts as follows:

> The defendants contend that there was no evidence of impairment of earning power and that the fact that Bochar's wages were higher after the accident than before proves no deterioration of earning ability. A tortfeasor is not entitled to a reduction in his financial responsibility because, through fortuitous circumstances or unusual application on the part of the injured person, the wages of the injured person following the accident are as high or even higher than they were prior to the accident. Parity of wages may show lack of impairment of earning power if it confirms other physical data that the injured person has completely recovered from his injuries. Standing alone, however, parity of wages is inconclusive. The office worker, who loses a leg has obviously had his earning ability impaired even though he can still sit at a desk and punch a comptometer as vigorously as before. It is not the status of the immediate present which determines capacity for remunerative employment. Where permanent injury is involved, the whole span of life must be considered. Has the economic horizon of the disabled person been shortened because of the injuries sustained as the result of the tortfeasor's negligence? That is the test.

Bochar v. J.B. Martin Motors, Inc., 374 Pa. 240, 244, 97 A.2d 813, 815 (1953). (Footnotes omitted.)

Shockey's claim is without merit, for the fact of Ruzzi's current employment at the same salary as before the injury does not, as this court explained in *Bochar,* negate his claim for a diminished earning capacity. Earning capacity has to do with the injured person's economic horizons, not his actual earnings, and the fact that Ruzzi was fortunate enough to earn as much as he had formerly earned, but at a new and less physically demanding job, does not establish that a loss of earning capacity, on these facts, is contrary to the evidence.

Finally, Shockey contends that the expert testimony was inadmissible because it went beyond the scope of Jarrell's pretrial report. In particular, Shockey claims that although the pretrial report addresses future wage loss, it does not address diminished earning capacity, and thus, does not place Shockey on notice that the expert would testify as to diminished earning capacity. We disagree with Shockey's characterization of Jarrell's pre-trial report furnished to Shockey pursuant to pertinent discovery rules.

As stated earlier in *Bochar v. J.B. Martin Motors, Inc.,* lost earning capacity involves the question, "Has the economic horizon of the disabled person been shortened because of the injuries sustained as a result of the tortfeasor's negligence?"

Jarrell's report states that, based on his understanding of Dr. Flit's testimony, Ruzzi was permanently injured and would never again be able to perform work of the type he had performed before the accident. Instead, he would be limited to light duty work where he could frequently change positions and not lift over twenty pounds. Jarrell also stated, in the last paragraph of his report:

> It [future earnings loss] is based on AMG Sign Company's continuing willingness to provide Mr. Ruzzi with employment on an "as able to work, as light duty work is available" basis. Should that willingness cease or should AMG Sign Company go out of business, Mr. Ruzzi would have to re-enter the open labor market where he would face the well known difficulties of the unemployed handicapped. Their unemployment rate is typically twice that of the non-handicapped, and their average earnings are 54%-82% of those of the non-handicapped (Employer Attitudes Towards Hiring Persons With Disabilities, Human Resources Center publication, 1978).

At trial, Jarrell testified that "countless studies done on the earnings of an impaired handicap [sic] versus the earnings of a nonimpaired, nonhandicapped" person indicate that the handicapped person suffers a loss of 17% earning capacity.

Since lost earning capacity is the limitation of economic horizons, and since Jarrell's report describes not only the nature of Ruzzi's injuries, but also, in Jarrell's opinion, what would happen to Ruzzi were he forced to compete on an open job market, including a prediction that he would be able to earn no more than 82% of his former salary (an 18% loss of earning capacity), the testimony was within the scope of the report and it was not error to admit Jarrell's expert testimony.

The order of Superior Court is affirmed.

The task of placing a dollar value on diminution of earning capacity can involve a good deal of guesswork. The variables that determine, at least theoretically, the size of the award for diminished earning capacity are: (1) the plaintiff's basic earning capacity; (2) the percentage by which the plaintiff's earning capacity has been diminished — which is often difficult to assess with any certainty, and rough fractions such as 25 or 50 percent, supported by expert medical testimony, are typically employed; (3) the expected duration of the disability; and, if permanent (4) the life expectancy of the plaintiff — obviously, the longer the plaintiff is likely to live, the greater will be the cumulative loss of earnings potential. On this last point, life expectancy tables are usually employed, such as Table 8-1, which is taken from the Internal Revenue Regulations (26 C.F.R. §1.401(a)(9)-9).

In states that do not establish the controlling life expectancy table by statute,[3] this matter may become the subject of disagreement between the parties. Life expectancy tables vary considerably depending on when they were constructed and the type of data that was used. There are even "work life expectancy" tables, prepared by the Bureau of Labor Statistics and others, upon which defense lawyers often base their calculations of diminished earning capacity. See, e.g., Ciecka et al., A Markov Process Model of Work-Life Expectancies Based on Labor Market Activity in 1997-98, 9 J. Legal Econ. 33 (1999). Courts sometimes accept this idea of the plaintiff's "expected working life," and use it instead of the more ordinarily employed "life expectancy." See, e.g., Williams v. United States, 435 F.2d 804 (1st Cir. 1970), a case arising under the Federal Employers' Liability Act,[4] in which the court assumed the plaintiff would have worked until age 60. Observe that in every instance it is the individual plaintiff's actual life expectancy immediately preceding the accident that is the measure of recovery. Except where by statute the trier of fact must rely exclusively on the standard life expectancy tables, the defendant may attempt to prove that the individual plaintiff had a shorter than average life expectancy. See, e.g., Oxford v. Hamilton, 763 S.W.2d 83 (Ark. 1989) (evidence of plaintiff's heavy drinking permissible to assist jury in determining life expectancy).

Where the injuries caused by the defendant's conduct have the effect of shortening the plaintiff's expected life, the plaintiff will recover for the total impairment in his earning capacity for the number of years by which his life expectancy has been shortened. Plaintiffs on occasion have sought compensation for a shortening of life expectancy separate from other economic and noneconomic elements of damages, but American courts have traditionally rejected such claims. The reason usually given for denying recovery is stated by the court in Downie v. U.S. Lines Co., 359 F.2d 344, 347 (3d Cir. 1966), *cert. denied,* 385 U.S. 897 (1966):

> We believe that the rule [that the shortening of one's life expectancy is a compensable element of damages] is not feasible because of the incalculable variables which may enter into any attempt to place value on life; absent some workable criteria, a damage award would be base speculation.

However, compensatory damages for shortened life expectancy have long been allowed in British courts (see, e.g., Flint v. Lovell, 1 K.B. 354 (1935)). Several American jurisdictions are now allowing recovery for shortened life expectancy, or what one court termed the "noneconomic value of being alive," as an element separate from lost income, pain and suffering. See, e.g., U.S. v. Anderson, 669 A.2d 73 (Del. 1995); Alexander v. Scheid, 726 N.E.2d 272 (Ind. 2000); Durham v. Marberry, 156 S.W.3d 242 (Ark. 2004).

In attaching a dollar value to the plaintiff's earning capacity, it is necessary in cases involving self-employed persons to separate out from the plaintiff's income any return from business investments. See Wesson v. F. M. Heritage Co., 386 A.2d 217 (Conn. 1978).

3. For an example of a statutory life expectancy table, see N.C. Gen. Stat. §8-46.
4. See footnote 2, above.

TABLE 8-1
Ordinary Life Annuities — One Life — Expected Return Multiples
[i.e., Life Expectancies]

Ages		*Multiples [Life Expectancies]*	*Ages*		*Multiples [Life Expectancies]*	*Ages*		*Multiples [Life Expectancies]*
Male	*Female*		*Male*	*Female*		*Male*	*Female*	
6	11	65.0	41	46	33.0	76	81	9.1
7	12	64.1	42	47	32.1	77	82	8.7
8	13	63.2	43	48	31.2	78	83	8.3
9	14	62.3	44	49	30.4	79	84	7.8
10	15	61.4	45	50	29.6	80	85	7.5
11	16	60.4	46	51	28.7	81	86	7.1
12	17	59.5	47	52	27.9	82	87	6.7
13	18	58.6	48	53	27.1	83	88	6.3
14	19	57.7	49	54	26.3	84	89	6.0
15	20	56.7	50	55	25.5	85	90	5.7
16	21	55.8	51	56	24.7	86	91	5.4
17	22	54.9	52	57	24.0	87	92	5.1
18	23	53.9	53	58	23.2	88	93	4.8
19	24	53.0	54	59	22.4	89	94	4.5
20	25	52.1	55	60	21.7	90	95	4.2
21	26	51.1	56	61	21.0	91	96	4.0
22	27	50.2	57	62	20.3	92	97	3.7
23	28	49.3	58	63	19.6	93	98	3.5
24	29	48.3	59	64	18.9	94	99	3.3
25	30	47.4	60	65	18.2	95	100	3.1
26	31	46.5	61	66	17.5	96	101	2.9
27	32	45.6	62	67	16.9	97	102	2.7
28	33	44.6	63	68	16.2	98	103	2.5
29	34	43.7	64	69	15.6	99	104	2.3
30	35	42.8	65	70	15.0	100	105	2.1
31	36	41.9	66	71	14.4	101	106	1.9
32	37	41.0	67	72	13.8	102	107	1.7
33	38	40.0	68	73	13.2	103	108	1.5
34	39	39.1	69	74	12.6	104	109	1.3
35	40	38.2	70	75	12.1	105	110	1.2
						106	111	1.0
36	41	37.3	71	76	11.6	107	112	.8
37	42	36.5	72	77	11.0	108	113	.7
38	43	35.6	73	78	10.5	109	114	.6
39	44	34.7	74	79	10.1	110	115	.5
40	45	33.8	75	80	9.6	111	116	0

One of the most difficult elements in the impairment of earning capacity formula is the first one suggested above — the assessment of the plaintiff's basic capacity to earn. Many courts have relied on actuarial tables that calculate workers' expected lifetime earnings based on race, among other demographic variables, an approach that may inadvertently incorporate the effects of historical prejudice and injustice into a plaintiff's damages award. This practice has come under attack by scholars, see Martha Chamallas & Jennifer B. Wriggins, The Measure of Injury (2010), and judges, see McMillan v. City of New York, 253 F.R.D. 247 (E.D.N.Y. 2008) (Weinstein, J.) (holding that the use of race-based actuarial tables is unconstitutional); G.M.M. v. Kimpson, 116 F. Supp. 3d 126 (E.D.N.Y. 2015) (holding in the context of a lead paint case that the defense could not introduce statistical evidence that the three-year-old plaintiff, because he was Hispanic, was less likely to obtain post-secondary degrees in order to reduce damages) (Weinstein, J.). An additional source of difficulty is the fact that the plaintiff's earning capacity probably would not have remained constant. The plaintiff will often be able to establish that, but for the injuries, further training and experience would have led to an increased earning capacity (Henry v. National Union Fire Ins. Co., 542 So. 2d 102 (La. Ct. App. 1989)), but the defendant will almost always be able to argue that the earning capacity would have declined toward the end of plaintiff's life (see, e.g., Aretz v. United States, 456 F. Supp. 397 (S.D. Ga. 1978)).[5] For an interesting case study that traces the projected earning capacity of a plaintiff year by year, see Sigmund A. Horvitz & Ronald D. Krist, Measuring the Loss of Earning Capacity, 36 Tex. B.J. 411 (1973).

In addition to uncertainty regarding future earnings, plaintiffs also may face uncertainty regarding the onset and severity of their physical injuries. In Mauro v. Raymark Industries, 561 A.2d 257 (N.J. 1989), plaintiff presented evidence that he had suffered workplace exposure to asbestos fibers which caused thickening of his chest walls and that, in the opinion of a state-provided doctor, "there is some evidence that this exposure may increase the risk of development of lung cancer." Id. at 258. Because plaintiff's experts were unable to opine that it was more likely than not plaintiff would contract cancer, the trial judge refused to permit the jury to award damages for plaintiff's enhanced risk of contracting cancer. The judge did, however, permit the jury to consider compensation for medical monitoring expenses and pain and suffering related to plaintiff's fear of contracting cancer. On appeal, the New Jersey Supreme Court first noted that its case law relaxes statue-of-limitations and single-controversy requirements to allow plaintiffs in toxic tort cases to bring subsequent claims for personal injury in the event that they do develop a disease such as lung cancer in the future. The court then concluded:

> [O]ur case law affords toxic-tort plaintiffs the right to receive full compensation for any provable diminution of bodily health, accommodating all damage claims attributable to present injury and deferring compensation only for disease not yet incurred and not reasonably probable to occur. Recognition of present claims for medical surveillance and emotional distress realistically addresses significant aspects of the present injuries sustained by toxic-tort plaintiffs, and serves as an added deterrent to polluters and others responsible for the wrongful use of toxic chemicals. In our view, these developments in New Jersey law affecting toxic-tort plaintiffs argue persuasively against modification of the reasonable-probability standard in such cases. We therefore will not disturb the trial court's refusal to submit to the jury plaintiff's damage claim based on his enhanced risk of cancer. . . . [Id. at 267]

5. There is a lengthy subsequent history to this case, none of which changes the point for which it is cited in the text. The last opinion in the history is Aretz v. United States, 660 F.2d 531 (5th Cir. 1981).

Justice Handler dissented, arguing that the majority's adherence to traditional legal rules regarding causation and damages was "ritualistic," id. at 269. He continued:

> In my view, the majority's solution of allowing the plaintiff to sue defendant later if he develops cancer is unfair and unjust and does not comport with broader notions of sound public policy. In light of current knowledge and experience, there is no valid reason why plaintiff's enhanced risk of cancer should not be considered an element of a present injury caused by the defendant and to be compensated now. Due to this injury, plaintiff may have to alter his lifestyle to avoid cancer-causing agents that may be present in foods or the environment and atmosphere to prevent the likelihood of developing cancer. Plaintiff may also be prevented from obtaining certain jobs — such as in chemical factories — because his enhanced risk of cancer make him more vulnerable to other workplace injuries. In addition, his health and life insurance premiums will be greater because the insurance companies will charge plaintiff for his enhanced risk of developing cancer. [Id. at 271]

Many courts that have addressed the issue have agreed with the majority in *Mauro* and have permitted recovery for future harm only if the plaintiff has evidence that such harm is probable. See, e.g., Pollock v. Johns-Manville Sales Corp., 686 F. Supp. 489 (D.N.J. 1988). However, some courts allow plaintiffs to recover damages for harm that has a smaller probability of occurring, so long as plaintiffs present adequate evidence to establish the probability of future harm. See, e.g., Cincinnati Ins. Co. v. Samples, 192 S.W.3d 311 (Ky. 2006) (evidence of 15-20 percent chance of future harm sufficient for jury to award damages).

While Justice Handler would have permitted the plaintiff in *Mauro* to get to the jury although the chance of future harm was, according to the evidence, less than 51 percent, he did not state how the evidence should affect the jury's decision. Perhaps implicit in his opinion is the thought that the jury would reduce, but not eliminate, the plaintiff's recovery based on the evidence relating to the chance of future harm. That thought was made explicit by a concurring judge in Jordan v. Bero, 210 S.E.2d 618, 641 (W. Va. 1974):

> Accordingly the jury would be instructed that from all the evidence they should determine what the overall probability is that the plaintiff will suffer future damages, and that from all of the evidence they should determine the amount of monetary damages to which the plaintiff would be entitled if the disabilities which doctors reasonably believe are possible actually come to pass. The jury would then be instructed to multiply the amount of future damages reasonably to be expected times the probability of those damages actually occurring and arrive at a figure which will compensate the plaintiff for the possibility of future injuries. It would appear that in a major damage suit the jury could be aided by expert testimony with regard to probability analysis to make the problem comprehensible to the average layman.

In Patriello v. Kalman, 576 A.2d 474 (Conn. 1990), the Supreme Court of Connecticut overruled an earlier case, Healy v. White, 378 A.2d 540 (Conn. 1977), that, like *Mauro,* had held that the plaintiff could recover for future harm only if the probability of the harm exceeded 50 percent. The plaintiff's evidence in *Patriello* was that there was an 8 to 16 percent chance of future injury. The court ruled that the plaintiff who suffers a "present injury which has resulted in an increased risk of future harm is entitled to compensation to the extent that the future harm is likely to occur." 576 A.2d at 484. The court made it clear that the plaintiff could recover only for a reduced amount based on the probability of future harm, not for the full extent of the harm should it occur. The court did not specifically address the issue of what the plaintiff's recovery should be if the chance of future harm exceeds 50 percent, but dictum indicates that the plaintiff in such a case might recover in full. Can you think of any arguments for reducing recovery in all cases in which the chance of future harm is less than 100 percent?

Because allowing damages for future harm carries the risk of punishing defendants for an injury that never materializes, an increasing number of courts are basing those damages on the percentage probability that the harm will occur. See, e.g., Alexander v. Scheid, 726 N.E.2d 272 (Ind. 2000); Dillon v. Evanston Hosp., 771 N.E.2d 357 (Ill. 2002). Arguments for allocating damages between the plaintiff and defendant based on the chances of future injury are made in Joseph H. King, Causation, Valuation and Chance in Personal Injury Torts Involving Preexisting Conditions and Future Consequences, 90 Yale L.J. 1353 (1981); Andrew R. Klein, A Model for Enhanced Risk Recovery in Tort, 56 Wash. & Lee L. Rev. 1173 (1999).

Grayson v. Irvmar Realty Corp.

7 A.D.2d 436, 184 N.Y.S.2d 33 (1959)

BREITEL, J. The principal issue raised in this personal injury negligence case is whether the court, in permitting the jury to award substantial damages to plaintiff for impairment or frustration of her inchoate operatic career, committed error. In addition, defendant contends that the damages awarded are, in any event, excessive. Some question is also raised as to liability, but it does not merit discussion.

Plaintiff, a young woman who is engaged seriously in the study of music looking to the development of an operatic career, sustained a fractured leg and an alleged impairment of her hearing as a result of a fall on the sidewalk in front of defendant's premises. The act of negligence charged was the failure to light properly a construction sidewalk bridge. . . . The jury awarded damages in the amount of $50,000.

There is no dispute that one tortiously injured may recover damages based upon the impairment of future earning capacity. There is also no dispute that the assessment of damages may be based upon future probabilities and is not confined to actual earnings prior to the accident. The unusual issue tendered in this case is whether there may be a similar assessment where the probability of future earnings is not based upon any prior actual engagement in the vocational earning of income. In that respect it is not unlike the situation in death actions where the pecuniary benefit to survivors must be determined with respect to children or very young people whose income potentiality has not yet been developed. The situation, on the other hand, is a little different, again, from that of young persons training for occupations, especially professions, where the probability of completion of training is high, and the resultant earning of at least a modal income is equally highly probable. The reason for this last difference is that in the case of persons of rare and special talents many are called but few are chosen. For those who are not chosen, the probabilities of exploiting their talents financially are minimal or totally negative. In this class would fall the musical artist, the professional athlete, and the actor.

It should be clear that one possessed of rare and special talents is entitled to recover damages for tortious injury to the development of those talents. This, too, may have a pecuniary value which is assessable, albeit without the degree of precision one would require in a commercial case. On this view, the court properly submitted to the jury the question of assessing the damages to plaintiff's operatic career, inchoate though it may have been. But, in the light of the proper distinctions, the jury's award of $50,000 was grossly excessive.

At the time of the accident plaintiff was twenty-one and had been graduated from high school. Since some undisclosed age as a child, she had studied music and singing. This included five years of instrumental instruction. In the later years she had a professional teacher of voice and studied under an opera coach. When she left school she participated successively in operatic workshops. As part of her operatic studies it was necessary to learn the various foreign languages closely associated with classic opera. While engaged in her studies she made a large number of appearances, all without income, on the radio, in benefit performances, and in workshop-productions of opera. Her voice teacher and opera coach testified that she had a superior voice and, as a consequence, had a bright future, in their opinion, in the opera. There was testimony that plaintiff was preparing for a European debut.

Plaintiff sustained her injuries when she fell, catching her foot in a hole. Her leg was then fractured. At the same time her head struck the surface, as a result of which she claims she sustained an impairment of hearing. The alleged hearing impairment has largely cleared up, leaving, however, a sequela of an impairment of pitch. Although she has continued to study singing and made a number of appearances of the same character as she had made before the accident, it is claimed that the impairment of pitch has limited her performance and that this is likely to be permanent. This claim was supported by her voice teacher and by medical testimony. However, there was highly credible proof from an eminent physician selected from the court-designated medical panel, offered by defendant, to the effect that any impairment of hearing she had was due to a diseased condition which existed before the accident. The jury might well have, but did not, accept this testimony, despite still other proof that plaintiff had had ear trouble prior to the accident.

As already noted, it is undisputed that a person tortiously injured is entitled to recover for impairment of future earning capacity, without limitation to the actual earnings which preceded the accident. In death actions, and in the cases of injuries, involving very young people whose vocational potentialities have not yet been developed, the courts have allowed assessment of damages based on future, and not presently realized, earning capacity. . . .

In the case of young people engaged in the study for occupations or professions requiring a great deal of preliminary or formal training the courts have also permitted the assessment of damages based on future earning potential after the training period would have been completed. And even in the case of singers, and presumably, therefore, in the case of other musical artists, some courts in other jurisdictions have had occasion to permit juries to assess damages based on future earning potential although at the time of the accident the would-be artist's career is inchoate.

On this analysis the jury in this case was very properly permitted to assess the damages with respect to plaintiff's inchoate operatic career. But the award it made was highly excessive.

It is at this point that the distinction must be made between persons who largely exploit native talents and those who exploit intensive training. It is notable that those who exploit rare and special talents may achieve exceedingly high financial rewards, but that the probability of selection for the great rewards is relatively low. On the other hand, those who, provided they have the intelligence and opportunities, train for the more skilled occupations and professions, not so heavily dependent upon unusual native gifts, will more likely achieve their objectives.

The would-be operatic singer, or the would-be violin virtuoso, or the would-be actor, are not assured of achieving their objectives merely because they have some gifts and complete the customary periods of training. Their future is a highly speculative one, namely, whether they will ever receive recognition or the financial perquisites that result from such recognition. Nevertheless, the opportunities exist and those opportunities have an economic value which can be assessed, although, obviously, without any precision. But a jury may not assume that a young student of the opera who has certain gifts will earn the income of an operatic singer, even in the median group.

In determining, therefore, the amount to be recovered, the jury may consider the gifts attributed to plaintiff; the training she has received; the training she is likely to receive; the opportunities and the recognition she already has had; the opportunities she is likely to have in the future; the fact that even though the opportunities may be many, that the full realization of those opportunities is limited to the very few; the fact that there are many other risks and contingencies, other than accidents, which may divert a would-be vocal artist from her career; and, finally, that it is assessing directly not so much future earning capacity as the opportunities for a practical chance at such future earning capacity.

The foregoing factors to be considered must reflect substantial development in the would-be artist's career. Every gleam in a doting parent's eye and every self-delusion as to one's potentialities must be skeptically eradicated. The jury is not to assess within the limits of wishful thinking but is to assess the genuine potentialities, although not yet realized, as evidenced by objective circumstances. Thus viewed, plaintiff here was undoubtedly serious about her operatic career; but, except from her teachers, she had not achieved any spectacular or extraordinary recognition for her talents. It is not the dilettante interest that has a pecuniary value, but the genuine opportunity to engage in a serious artistic career. In this context no effort has been made to consider the possible issues, sometimes tendered, as to the compensability for artistic pursuits indulged in solely for self-enjoyment, but impaired as a result of tortious injury.

Based on the preceding discussion and the proof in this case, and allowing for the injury sustained by plaintiff to her leg, any verdict in excess of $20,000 is excessive.[6] . . .

Judgment reversed, on the law and on the facts, and a new trial granted, unless plaintiff stipulates to accept a judgment in the reduced amount of $20,000, in which event the judgment is modified in that respect and, as so modified, affirmed, with costs to defendant-appellant. Settle order on notice.

All concur except VALENTE and MCNALLY, J.J., who concur in part and dissent in part. . . .

In *Grayson,* there was little doubt that the plaintiff's injury was permanent, but she had no well-defined existing occupation that could function as the basic measure of the value of impaired capacity to earn. The two groups of persons most likely to present problems of this sort are homemakers and the young. The problems with respect to homemakers are

6. If the trial judge, or the court on appeal, determines that the damages as set by the jury clearly exceed or are clearly less than is warranted by the evidence, a remittitur or additur can be ordered. Theoretically, in the case of remittitur, if the plaintiff refuses to accept the lower amount of damages determined by the court to be the most the jury on the evidence could award, a new trial will be awarded. In the case of additur, the choice is put to the defendant—agree to the increased award the court has determined as the least amount supported by the evidence or face a new trial. Remittitur and additur cannot be ordered simply because the judge disagrees with the amount of the jury award; the standard is usually stated to be whether the jury award "shocks the conscience" of the court. [Eds.]

likely to occur less frequently as more of them join the labor force outside the home. If a plaintiff is injured during what is clearly a temporary withdrawal from the labor market during, for example, the early years of childrearing, the plaintiff may have a career that would furnish the basis of a claim for impaired earning capacity. More troublesome are cases involving plaintiffs who have never worked, or have worked only sporadically, outside the home. A number of approaches have been used or suggested. Some courts permit a homemaker to recover for impaired earning capacity based upon existing, though unused, capacity. In this approach it is irrelevant that the homemaker was not engaged in any particular commercial employment outside the home at the time of injury. See, e.g., Brandao v. Wal-Mart Stores, Inc., 803 So. 2d 1039 (La. Ct. App. 2001), which held that a trial court did not abuse its discretion by allowing a jury to award damages for loss of past and future earning capacity to a full-time homemaker and parent.

Perhaps the most common approach to putting a market value on the services that a typical homemaker performs for the family is to reach a figure that represents their total replacement cost. See, e.g., DeLong v. Erie County, 455 N.Y.S.2d 887 (N.Y. App. Div. 1982), *aff'd,* 457 N.E.2d 717 (N.Y. 1983), in which there was expert testimony that the replacement cost of services performed by a 28-year-old housewife with three children was $527,659. Occasionally, courts seem to permit a subjective assessment of the impaired value by the jury, much in the same way it is permitted to attach a value to other intangible elements of damages, such as pain and suffering. See, e.g., Florida Greyhound Lines Inc. v. Jones, 60 So. 2d 396 (Fla. 1952).

The commentators, particularly those with a law and economics orientation, seem to prefer the method of assessing damages that refers to "opportunity costs"—the income that the homemaker could have earned in the market. See Richard Posner, Economic Analysis of Law 193 (6th ed. 2003).

Cases involving permanent injury to young persons are even more difficult. With the very young, there is likely to be very little proof that the plaintiff could or would have entered any particular occupation. In such cases, a good bit of speculation is allowed. See, e.g., Estevez v. United States, 72 F. Supp. 2d 205 (S.D.N.Y. 1999), in which the plaintiff was two years old.

Some of the factors upon which courts have based their determinations of a child's future earning capacity are the minimum wage (see McNeil v. United States, 519 F. Supp. 283 (D.S.C. 1981)) and intelligence and skill tests administered by a school prior to the child's injury (see Martin v. United States, 471 F. Supp. 6 (D. Ariz. 1979)).

Of more immediate concern to law students is the question of the point in a student's educational development at which a claim for impaired ability to become a lawyer might be recognized. In one case, Kenton v. Hyatt Hotels Corp., 693 S.W.2d 83 (Mo. 1985), the plaintiff was a law student when she was injured, and she was permitted to recover impaired earning capacity damages based on what she would have earned as a lawyer. On the other hand, the plaintiff in Waldorf v. Shuta, 896 F.2d 723 (3d Cir. 1990), was not able to recover such damages. In this case, the plaintiff's aspirations of a legal profession amounted to little more than a "gleam in the eye"; the plaintiff was a high school dropout, although he had gotten a high school equivalency diploma while in the military. He had worked as a paralegal; he had been denied admission to a four-year college, but had completed one year of a two-year program, in which he had taken courses in tennis, acting, and photography. The court stated that, while the plaintiff wanted to become a lawyer, no evidence supported the conclusion that he was likely to fulfill that ambition.

(2) Adjustments in Reaching the Final Recovery Figure

Thus far, the tacit assumption has been that once the difficult assessments of earning capacity and percentage of disability are made, the plaintiff's recovery for future impairment of earning capacity is calculated by multiplying those two elements together and then multiplying their product by the plaintiff's expected period of disability. Thus, in the earlier example of the plaintiff with a $1,000 a month earning capacity and a 25 percent permanent disability, if we posit a life expectancy of 30 years it might be assumed that his recovery for future impairment would be $90,000 (that is, $1,000 a month × .25 × 360 months). However, in most jurisdictions the plaintiff would, on the foregoing assumptions, receive something less than the full $90,000, a reduction that takes into account the fact that the recovery will be received immediately, in a lump sum, rather than in increments over the years. Because the money can be put into the bank and earn interest, the amount received is in most states adjusted downward. What the plaintiff will receive is the present value of the right to receive $250 a month for 30 years — that is, the sum of money which, invested at a given rate of interest, will permit the plaintiff to withdraw $250 a month for 30 years, with the fund to be exhausted upon the final withdrawal.

Courts in this country refer to the process of calculating this lump sum as reducing the recovery to present value. Actually, this phrase is misleading insofar as it suggests that a gross sum is first reached (e.g., the $90,000 figure in the preceding hypothetical example) and then reduced to a lower figure to reflect the earning power of the lump sum. Instead, the present value of the right to receive a certain income for a certain period is calculated in the first instance, from standard charts prepared for the purpose. These charts, such as Table 8-2, show the present value of the right to receive one dollar for *x* number of years at *y* rate of interest.

The manner in which this chart is used to calculate the plaintiff's recovery for impairment of earning capacity is best illustrated with an example. Assume that a court were to determine that a fair and conservative rate of interest that a plaintiff might be expected to earn on his recovery is 6 percent. What is the present value at 6 percent compounded annually of the right to receive $3,000 a year for 30 years? Locating year "30" on the chart and running it over to the "6%" column, we find the present value of the right to receive one dollar a year at 6 percent for 30 years is 13.765. The right to receive $3,000 a year at the same rate is 3,000 times as great, or $41,295, a figure slightly less than one-half of the $90,000 figure calculated earlier. The reason why a $41,295 lump sum recovery will allow the plaintiff to receive $3,000 a year for 30 years is reflected in the fact that, at 6 percent, $2,477.70 will be generated in interest in the first year.[7] Thus, of the first $3,000 presumably withdrawn by the plaintiff at the end of the first year, only $522.30 will actually come from the principal, that is, from the lump sum paid by the defendant. Over the 30 years of annual payouts, the amount of interest in each payment will go down and the amount of principal will go up.

The extent to which damages for impaired future capacity should or should not be reduced to present value has been the subject of some debate. For example, in Beaulieu v. Elliot, 434 P.2d 665 (Alaska 1967), the court declined to follow the majority rule that damages should be reduced to present value. The court reasoned that the interest earned on a lump sum merely offsets inflation, leaving the plaintiff more or less whole.

7. The plaintiff may withdraw the money more often than once a year, in smaller increments — e.g., at the rate of $250 a month. We are here assuming an annual withdrawal of $3,000 in order to keep the calculations simple and to make relevant the discount chart which is based on interest compounded annually rather than monthly.

TABLE 8-2
Present Value of One Dollar Per Annum
(Payable at the end of each year for the number of years indicated)

Yr.	*3%*	*4%*	*5%*	*6%*
1	.971	.962	.952	.943
2	1.914	1.886	1.859	1.833
3	2.829	2.775	2.723	2.673
4	3.717	3.630	3.546	3.465
5	4.580	4.452	4.330	4.212
6	5.417	5.242	5.076	4.917
7	6.230	6.002	5.786	5.582
8	7.020	6.733	6.463	6.210
9	7.786	7.435	7.108	6.802
10	8.530	8.111	7.722	7.360
11	9.253	8.761	8.306	7.887
12	9.954	9.385	8.863	8.384
13	10.635	9.986	9.394	8.853
14	11.296	10.563	9.899	9.295
15	11.938	11.118	10.380	9.712
16	12.561	11.652	10.838	10.106
17	13.166	12.166	11.274	10.477
18	13.754	12.659	11.690	10.828
19	14.324	13.134	12.085	11.158
20	14.878	13.590	12.462	11.470
21	15.415	14.029	12.821	11.764
22	15.937	14.451	13.163	12.042
23	16.444	14.857	13.489	12.303
24	16.936	15.247	13.799	12.550
25	17.413	15.622	14.094	12.783
26	17.877	15.983	14.375	13.003
27	18.327	16.330	14.643	13.211
28	18.764	16.663	14.898	13.406
29	19.189	16.984	15.141	13.591
30	19.600	17.292	15.373	13.765
31	20.000	17.589	15.593	13.929
32	20.389	17.874	15.803	14.084
33	20.766	18.148	16.003	14.230
34	21.132	18.411	16.193	14.368
35	21.487	18.665	16.374	14.498

Under this theory, which a few states adopt, the court assumes that inflation and interest will completely offset each other, such that no discounting is necessary. A clear majority of courts addressing the matter have rejected the total offset method used by the court in *Beaulieu*. In fact, the Alaska state legislature reversed the *Beaulieu* rule in 1986 in order to bring Alaska courts in line with other states in reducing future damages to their present value. See Alaska Statute 09.17.040; Sherbahn v. Kerkove, 987 P.2d 195 (Alaska 1999). Some courts increase the amount of recovery based upon a predicted inflation rate. See, e.g., *In re* Eastern and Southern Dists. Asbestos Litig., 772 F. Supp. 1380 (E.D.N.Y. & S.D.N.Y. 1991), *aff'd in part and rev'd in part (on other grounds) sub* nom, *In re* Brooklyn Navy Yard Asbestos Litig., 971 F.2d 831 (2d Cir. 1992). More courts have adopted an inflation-adjusted rate for discounting to present value and use a rate lower than the then current low-risk rate of return on investments. The leading case is Feldman v. Allegheny Airlines, Inc., 524 F.2d 384 (2d Cir. 1975), in which the predicted annual inflation rate of 2.87 percent was subtracted from the current savings bank interest rate of 4.14 percent and rounded off to an adjusted discount rate of 1.5 percent. Most courts, even those rejecting the total offset method, now make some adjustment for the effects of inflation in reducing the plaintiff's recovery to present value. See generally Dan B. Dobbs, Dobbs Law of Remedies: Damages-Equity-Restitution, §8.5 (West 1993); Stein on Personal Injury Damages, 3d §15:5.

Yet another possible adjustment in the plaintiff's recovery for impaired earning capacity stems from the fact that certain damages are not subject to taxation under §104(a)(2) of the Internal Revenue Code, which excludes as taxable income the damages "received (whether by suit or agreement and whether as lump sums or as periodic payments) on account of personal physical injuries or physical sickness." (Prior to 1996, the exclusion of tort awards from income taxes was not limited to those damages stemming from physical injury. All personal awards, physical or not, escaped federal income tax.) Notwithstanding the non-taxability of awards for impaired earning capacity, at one time most courts refused to adjust downward the award to reflect a hypothetical after-tax income. The leading case was McWeeney v. New York, N.H. & H.R.R., 282 F.2d 34 (2d Cir.), *cert. denied,* 364 U.S. 870 (1960). However, in a wrongful death action arising under the Federal Employers' Liability Act, the Supreme Court of the United States ruled that courts should instruct juries on reducing damages for lost earning capacity to an after-tax amount. See Norfolk & Western Ry. v. Liepelt, 444 U.S. 490 (1980). In Fanetti v. Helenic Lines, Ltd., 678 F.2d 424 (2d Cir. 1982), *cert. denied,* 463 U.S. 1206 (1983), the Second Circuit ruled that *Liepelt* applies to all actions for future earnings that are brought under federal law.

Some states have adopted *Liepelt* (see, e.g., Ruff v. Weintraub, 519 A.2d 1384 (N.J. 1987)), but a far greater number have rejected a reduction of damages to an after-tax amount (see, e.g., Blake v. Clein, 903 So. 2d 710 (Miss. 2005)). It is worth noting that while the Supreme Court in *Liepelt* found a worker's after-tax income to be the appropriate basis upon which to project future lost earnings, the court, in dicta, also indicated that the lump sum damage award should be increased by the amount of income tax that would have to be paid on the earnings of the award. This suggestion was accepted by the Ninth Circuit in DeLucca v. United States, 670 F.2d 843 (9th Cir. 1982).

In general, see J. Martin Burke & Michael K. Friel, Tax Treatment of Employment-Related Personal Injury Awards: The Need for Limits, 50 Mont. L. Rev. 13 (1989); Joseph M. Dodge, Taxes and Torts, 77 Cornell L. Rev. 143 (1992).

Problem 37

A partner in your firm has asked you to help her in connection with a case she is handling for Henry Milo. Milo, who is now 37 years old, owned and operated a plumbing business until two years ago. About three years ago, he was involved in an automobile accident that resulted in the loss of his left arm. The partner has sued Andrew Trumball, who was driving the automobile in which Milo was a passenger. The legal issues involved in the case are fairly routine, except with respect to Milo's damages for impaired earning capacity.

At the time of the accident, Milo's gross income from his plumbing business was $90,000 a year. Without his left arm, Milo could no longer function as a plumber, and about a year after the accident he sold the business to an employee. He now is in a Baptist seminary where he is studying to become a minister. In current dollars, Milo can expect to make about $40,000 a year when he graduates later this year. If he does well, he can expect to get a church of his own three or four years after graduating, with a salary in current dollars of about $45,000. His future income will be hard to predict — it will depend on the size and location of his church. Ministers in urban churches earn more than those in small town and rural churches. Milo is at the top of his class, and he could pretty much choose among available churches. His current intention is to find a rural, relatively poor church where he feels he could accomplish more than in a larger, wealthier situation.

For several years before the accident, Milo had been thinking of getting out of the plumbing business and following his father's footsteps into the clergy. In fact, he had applied to several seminaries in the month before the accident. Milo is quite philosophical about the loss of his arm and has come to view it as a message from God directing him to leave his business and join the ministry.

The partner would like a memorandum indicating how you would present the impairment of earning capacity element most favorably to the client.

c. Pain, Suffering, and Other Intangible Elements

From a purely monetary point of view, recovery for noneconomic loss has become the preeminent element of recovery in personal injury cases. It has been estimated that in products liability and medical malpractice cases, recovery for intangible harm accounts, for nearly 50 percent of the total recovery. See The American Law Institute, Reporters' Study — Enterprise Responsibility for Personal Injury 201 (1991). For children, the elderly, non-working spouses, and other plaintiffs without paid employment, noneconomic damages can make up an even greater share. In Walters v. Hitchcock, 237 Kan. 31, 697 P.2d 847 (1985), for instance, plaintiff was a stay-at-home mother with four minor children. A negligently performed thyroid surgery left her with permanent esophageal damage and a crude reconstructed throat that was fashioned from part of her colon. After summarizing the pain, disfigurement, and embarrassment caused by plaintiff's condition, the court upheld a jury verdict of $2,000,000, only $59,000 of which represented actual damages.

Pain and suffering is the most difficult element of recovery to measure. One device permitted in some states as a guide to juries is the *per diem argument,* under which the plaintiff's attorney suggests to the jury a dollar value for the plaintiff's pain for whatever time segment the attorney chooses. For example, the attorney might suggest that one hundred dollars would be reasonable compensation for one hour's intense physical pain. Ten hours a day would be one thousand dollars; one year would be $365,000; 20 years would be $7,300,000. In Debus v. Grand Union Stores, 621 A.2d 1288 (Vt. 1993), the court explored the rationales for and against the *per diem* method of calculating damages:

> The principal reason advanced against per diem arguments is that a jury's verdict must be based on the evidence before it, and a per diem figure, which is not in evidence, allows the jury to calculate damages based solely on the argument of counsel. Further, courts have reasoned that a per diem argument unfairly assumes that pain is constant, uniform, and

> continuous, and that the pain will prevail for the rest of plaintiff's life. Therefore, it creates an "illusion of certainty. . . ."
>
> On the other hand, jurisdictions that have allowed per diem arguments counter that sufficient safeguards exist in the adversarial system to overcome the objections to its use. They point out that a plaintiff's hypothesis on damages, even if presented on a per diem basis, must be reasonable or suffer serious and possibly fatal attack by opposing counsel; further, the notion that pain is constant and uniform may be easily rebutted by reference to the evidence or the jury's own experience. . . .

Courts are divided as to whether damages for pain and suffering should be discounted to present value. Yes, according to Wright v. Maersk Line, 84 Fed. App. 123 (2d Cir. 2003). No, according to Brant v. Brockhold, 532 N.W.2d 801 (Iowa 1995).

In Compensation and Revenge, 40 San Diego L. Rev. 1387 (2003), Emily Sherwin argues that the "practice of awarding lump sums for future pain and suffering without discounting to present value confirms that these awards are not seriously understood to conform to actual loss." Id. at 1393. Instead, Professor Sherwin believes that pain and suffering awards serve underlying normative goals that have "a close affinity to revenge." Id. at 1389.

As Professor Sherwin's argument suggests, pain and suffering is a broad concept that may include a number of more or less separate factors, the most common of which is the physical pain associated with the injury. To recover for this, the injured person must have been conscious. See Estate of Swarthout v. Beard, 190 N.W.2d 373 (Mich. Ct. App. 1971), *rev'd on other grounds sub nom.* Smith v. City of Detroit, 202 N.W.2d 300 (Mich. 1972); Blunt v. Zinni, 302 N.Y.S.2d 504 (App. Div. 1969). But the plaintiff need not be aware of what is happening. See Walsh v. Staten Island Obstetrics & Gynecology Assocs., P.C., 598 N.Y.S.2d 17 (N.Y. App. Div. 1993), in which the court ruled that a child in a vegetative state for his "short, eight-year life," but who responded to painful and pleasurable stimuli, can recover for pain and suffering. In some cases, a relatively brief period of consciousness before death has been held sufficient to support a verdict for physical pain and suffering. In Wiggins v. Lane & Co., 298 F. Supp. 194 (E.D. La. 1969), the plaintiff's decedent was knocked with great force from a pile-driving rig on which he was working and fell 50 feet to the deck below. Medical experts testified that he probably died when he hit the deck, but offered no opinions as to whether he was conscious during the fall. On this evidence, the jury was permitted to find that the decedent suffered pain from the time he was struck until he died, and the trial judge refused to set aside an award of $10,000 for that period.

Courts also allow recovery for mental suffering stemming from humiliation, shame, embarrassment, and loss of sleep caused by tortious conduct. Recovery for mental suffering associated with bodily disfigurement is also includible as an element of pain and suffering. In Ocampo v. Paper Converting Mach. Co., 2005 U.S. Dist. LEXIS 17107 (D. Ill. 2005), for example, the plaintiff suffered permanent disfigurement after she was "scalped" when her hair was caught in a machine she was working with. As a result, she became "depressed" and claimed to "feel scarred on the inside as well." The court upheld a total award of $5,612,000, of which $2.3 million represented damages for disfigurement. For an argument that psychological evidence suggests that individuals adapt far better to disabling injuries than might be expected, and that noneconomic damages should perhaps be lowered accordingly, see Samuel R. Bagenstos & Margo Schlanger, Hedonic Damages, Hedonic Adaptation, and Disability, 60 Vand. L. Rev. 745 (2007).

McDougald v. Garber

73 N.Y.2d 246, 536 N.E.2d 372 (1989)

WACHTLER, CHIEF JUDGE. This appeal raises fundamental questions about the nature and role of nonpecuniary damages in personal injury litigation. By nonpecuniary damages, we mean those damages awarded to compensate an injured person for the physical and emotional consequences of the injury, such as pain and suffering and the loss of the ability to engage in certain activities. Pecuniary damages, on the other hand, compensate the victim for the economic consequences of the injury, such as medical expenses, lost earnings and the cost of custodial care.

The specific questions raised here deal with assessment of nonpecuniary damages and are (1) whether some degree of cognitive awareness is a prerequisite to recovery for loss of enjoyment of life and (2) whether a jury should be instructed to consider and award damages for loss of enjoyment of life separately from damages for pain and suffering. We answer the first question in the affirmative and the second question in the negative.

I

On September 7, 1978, plaintiff Emma McDougald, then 31 years old, underwent a Caesarean section and tubal ligation at New York Infirmary. Defendant Garber performed the surgery; defendants Armengol and Kulkarni provided anesthesia. During the surgery, Mrs. McDougald suffered oxygen deprivation which resulted in severe brain damage and left her in a permanent comatose condition. This action was brought by Mrs. McDougald and her husband, suing derivatively, alleging that the injuries were caused by the defendants' acts of malpractice.

A jury found all defendants liable and awarded Emma McDougald a total of $9,650,102 in damages, including $1,000,000 for conscious pain and suffering and a separate award of $3,500,000 for loss of the pleasures and pursuits of life. The balance of the damages awarded to her were for pecuniary damages — lost earnings and the cost of custodial and nursing care. Her husband was awarded $1,500,000 on his derivative claim for the loss of his wife's services. On defendants' posttrial motions, the Trial Judge reduced the total award to Emma McDougald to $4,796,728 by striking the entire award for future nursing care ($2,353,374) and by reducing the separate awards for conscious pain and suffering and loss of the pleasures and pursuits of life to a single award of $2,000,000 (McDougald v. Garber, 132 Misc. 2d 457, 504 N.Y.S.2d 383). Her husband's award was left intact. On cross appeals, the Appellate Division affirmed (135 A.D.2d 80, 524 N.Y.S.2d 192) and later granted defendants leave to appeal to this court.

II

. . . At trial, defendants sought to show that Mrs. McDougald's injuries were so severe that she was incapable of either experiencing pain or appreciating her condition. Plaintiffs, on the other hand, introduced proof that Mrs. McDougald responded to certain stimuli to a sufficient extent to indicate that she was aware of her circumstances. Thus, the extent of Mrs. McDougald's cognitive abilities, if any, was sharply disputed.

The parties and the trial court agreed that Mrs. McDougald could not recover for pain and suffering unless she were conscious of the pain. Defendants maintained that such consciousness was also required to support an award for loss of enjoyment of life. The court, however, accepted plaintiffs' view that loss of enjoyment of life was compensable without regard to whether the plaintiff was aware of the loss. Accordingly, because the level of Mrs. McDougald's cognitive abilities was in dispute, the court instructed the jury to consider loss of enjoyment of life as an element of nonpecuniary damages separate from pain and suffering. . . .

We conclude that the court erred, both in instructing the jury that Mrs. McDougald's awareness was irrelevant to their consideration of damages for loss of enjoyment of life and in directing the jury to consider that aspect of damages separately from pain and suffering.

III

We begin with the familiar proposition that an award of damages to a person injured by the negligence of another is to compensate the victim, not to punish the wrongdoer. The goal is to restore the injured party, to the extent possible, to the position that would have been occupied had the wrong not occurred. To be sure, placing the burden of compensation on the negligent party also serves as a deterrent, but purely punitive damages — that is, those which have no compensatory purpose — are prohibited unless the harmful conduct is intentional, malicious, outrageous, or otherwise aggravated beyond mere negligence.

Damages for nonpecuniary losses are, of course, among those that can be awarded as compensation to the victim. This aspect of damages, however, stands on less certain ground than does an award for pecuniary damages. An economic loss can be compensated in kind by an economic gain; but recovery for noneconomic losses such as pain and suffering and loss of enjoyment of life rests on "the legal fiction that money damages can compensate for a victim's injury" (Howard v. Lecher, 42 N.Y.2d 109, 111, 397 N.Y.S.2d 363, 366 N.E.2d 64). We accept this fiction, knowing that although money will neither ease the pain nor restore the victim's abilities, this device is as close as the law can come in its effort to right the wrong. We have no hope of evaluating what has been lost, but a monetary award may provide a measure of solace for the condition created.

Our willingness to indulge this fiction comes to an end, however, when it ceases to serve the compensatory goals of tort recovery. When that limit is met, further indulgence can only result in assessing damages that are punitive. The question posed by this case, then, is whether an award of damages for loss of enjoyment of life to a person whose injuries preclude any awareness of the loss serves a compensatory purpose. We conclude that it does not.

Simply put, an award of money damages in such circumstances has no meaning or utility to the injured person. An award for the loss of enjoyment of life "cannot provide [such a victim] with any consolation or ease any burden resting on him. . . . He cannot spend it upon necessities or pleasures. He cannot experience the pleasure of giving it away" (Flannery v. United States, 4th Cir., 718 F.2d 108, 111, *cert. denied,* 467 U.S. 1226, 104 S. Ct. 2679, 81 L. Ed. 2d 874).

We recognize that, as the trial court noted, requiring some cognitive awareness as a prerequisite to recovery for loss of enjoyment of life will result in some cases "in the paradoxical situation that the greater the degree of brain injury inflicted by a negligent defendant, the smaller the award the plaintiff can recover in general damages"

(McDougald v. Garber, 132 Misc. 2d 457, 460, 504 N.Y.S.2d 383, supra). The force of this argument, however — the temptation to achieve a balance between injury and damages — has nothing to do with meaningful compensation for the victim. Instead, the temptation is rooted in a desire to punish the defendant in proportion to the harm inflicted. However relevant such retributive symmetry may be in the criminal law, it has no place in the law of civil damages, at least in the absence of culpability beyond mere negligence.

Accordingly, we conclude that cognitive awareness is a prerequisite to recovery for loss of enjoyment of life. We do not go so far, however, as to require the fact finder to sort out varying degrees of cognition and determine at what level a particular deprivation can be fully appreciated. With respect to pain and suffering, the trial court charged simply that there must be "some level of awareness" in order for plaintiff to recover. We think that this is an appropriate standard for all aspects of nonpecuniary loss. No doubt the standard ignores analytically relevant levels of cognition, but we resist the desire for analytical purity in favor of simplicity. A more complex instruction might give the appearance of greater precision but, given the limits of our understanding of the human mind, it would in reality lead only to greater speculation. We turn next to the question whether loss of enjoyment of life should be considered a category of damages separate from pain and suffering.

IV

There is no dispute here that the fact finder may, in assessing nonpecuniary damages, consider the effect of the injuries on the plaintiff's capacity to lead a normal life. Traditionally, in this State and elsewhere, this aspect of suffering has not been treated as a separate category of damages; instead, the plaintiff's inability to enjoy life to its fullest has been considered one type of suffering to be factored into a general award for nonpecuniary damages, commonly known as pain and suffering.

Recently, however, there has been an attempt to segregate the suffering associated with physical pain from the mental anguish that stems from the inability to engage in certain activities, and to have juries provide a separate award for each.

Some courts have resisted the effort, primarily on the ground that duplicative and therefore excessive awards would result. Other courts have allowed separate awards, noting that the types of suffering involved are analytically distinguishable. Still other courts have questioned the propriety of the practice but held that, in the particular case, separate awards did not constitute reversible error. . . .

We do not dispute that distinctions can be found or created between the concepts of pain and suffering and loss of enjoyment of life. If the term "suffering" is limited to the emotional response to the sensation of pain, then the emotional response caused by the limitation of life's activities may be considered qualitatively different. But suffering need not be so limited — it can easily encompass the frustration and anguish caused by the inability to participate in activities that once brought pleasure. Traditionally, by treating loss of enjoyment of life as a permissible factor in assessing pain and suffering, courts have given the term this broad meaning.

If we are to depart from this traditional approach and approve a separate award for loss of enjoyment of life, it must be on the basis that such an approach will yield a more accurate evaluation of the compensation due to the plaintiff. We have no doubt that, in general, the total award for nonpecuniary damages would increase if we adopted the rule. That separate awards are advocated by plaintiffs and resisted by defendants is sufficient evidence that larger awards are at stake here. But a larger award does not by itself indicate that the goal of compensation has been better served.

The advocates of separate awards contend that because pain and suffering and loss of enjoyment of life can be distinguished, they must be treated separately if the plaintiff is to be compensated fully for each distinct injury suffered. We disagree. Such an analytical approach may have its place when the subject is pecuniary damages, which can be calculated with some precision. But the estimation of nonpecuniary damages is not amenable to such analytical precision and may, in fact, suffer from its application. Translating human suffering into dollars and cents involves no mathematical formula; it rests, as we have said, on a legal fiction. The figure that emerges is unavoidably distorted by the translation. Application of this murky process to the component parts of nonpecuniary injuries (however analytically distinguishable they may be) cannot make it more accurate. If anything, the distortion will be amplified by repetition.

Thus, we are not persuaded that any salutary purpose would be served by having the jury make separate awards for pain and suffering and loss of enjoyment of life. We are confident, furthermore, that the trial advocate's art is a sufficient guarantee that none of the plaintiff's losses will be ignored by the jury.

The errors in the instructions given to the jury require a new trial on the issue of nonpecuniary damages to be awarded to plaintiff Emma McDougald. Defendants' remaining contentions are either without merit, beyond the scope of our review or are rendered academic by our disposition of the case.

Accordingly, the order of the Appellate Division, insofar as appealed from, should be modified, with costs to defendants, by granting a new trial on the issue of nonpecuniary damages of plaintiff Emma McDougald, and as so modified, affirmed.

TITONE, JUDGE (dissenting).

The majority's holding represents a compromise position that neither comports with the fundamental principles of tort compensation nor furnishes a satisfactory, logically consistent framework for compensating nonpecuniary loss. Because I conclude that loss of enjoyment of life is an objective damage item, conceptually distinct from conscious pain and suffering, I can find no fault with the trial court's instruction authorizing separate awards and permitting an award for "loss of enjoyment of life" even in the absence of any awareness of that loss on the part of the injured plaintiff. Accordingly, I dissent. . . .

The capacity to enjoy life — by watching one's children grow, participating in recreational activities, and drinking in the many other pleasures that life has to offer — is unquestionably an attribute of an ordinary healthy individual. The loss of that capacity as a result of another's negligent act is at least as serious an impairment as the permanent destruction of a physical function, which has always been treated as a compensable item under traditional tort principles. Indeed, I can imagine no physical loss that is more central to the quality of a tort victim's continuing life than the destruction of the capacity to enjoy that life to the fullest.

Unquestionably, recovery of a damage item such as "pain and suffering" requires a showing of some degree of cognitive capacity. Such a requirement exists for the simple reason that pain and suffering are wholly subjective concepts and cannot exist separate and apart from the human consciousness that experiences them. In contrast, the destruction of an individual's capacity to enjoy life as a result of a crippling injury is an objective fact that does not differ in principle from the permanent loss of an eye or limb. As in the case of a lost limb, an essential characteristic of a healthy human life has been wrongfully taken, and, consequently, the injured party is entitled to a monetary award as a substitute. . . .

The majority has rejected separate recovery, in part because it apparently perceives some overlap between the two damage categories and in part because it believes that the goal of enhancing the precision of jury awards for nonpecuniary loss would not be advanced.

However, the overlap the majority perceives exists only if one assumes, as the majority evidently has, that the "loss of enjoyment" category of damages is designed to compensate only for "*the emotional response* caused by the limitation of life's activities" and "*the frustration and anguish caused by* the inability to participate in activities that once brought pleasure" (emphasis added), both of which are highly *subjective* concepts.

In fact, . . . while the victim's "emotional response" and "frustration and anguish" are elements of the award for pain and suffering, the "limitation of life's activities" and the "inability to participate in activities" that the majority identifies are recoverable under the "loss of enjoyment of life" rubric. Thus, there is no real overlap, and no real basis for concern about potentially duplicative awards where, as here, there is a properly instructed jury.

Finally, given the clear distinction between the two categories of nonpecuniary damages, I cannot help but assume that permitting separate awards for conscious pain and suffering and loss of enjoyment of life would contribute to accuracy and precision in thought in the jury's deliberations on the issue of damages. . . . In light of the concrete benefit to be gained by compelling the jury to differentiate between the specific objective and subjective elements of the plaintiff's nonpecuniary loss, I find unpersuasive the majority's reliance on vague concerns about potential distortion owing to the inherently difficult task of computing the value of intangible loss. My belief in the jury system, and in the collective wisdom of the deliberating jury, leads me to conclude that we may safely leave that task in the jurors' hands.

For all of these reasons, I approve of the approach that the trial court adopted in its charge to the jury. Accordingly, I would affirm the order below affirming the judgment.

A number of courts have recently sided with Judge Titone's dissent and have held that damages for loss of enjoyment of life (now often referred to as hedonic damages) is an item of recovery separate from that for pain and suffering. See, e.g., Bennett v. Lembo, 761 A.2d 494 (N.H. 2000); Boan v. Blackwell, 541 S.E.2d 242 (S.C. 2001). In general, see Comment, Joyless Life and Lifeless Joy: The Recovery of Hedonic Damages by Plaintiffs in a Persistent Vegetative State, 50 San Diego L. Rev. 721 (2013); and Comment, Nonpecuniary Damages for Comatose Tort Victims, 61 Geo. L.J. 1547 (1973).

Legislatures in recent years have been critical of recovery for intangible harm, and as a part of the explosion in legislative tort reform, a number of states have enacted statutes limiting recovery for that element of harm. See, e.g., Alaska Stat. §09.17.010 (noneconomic damages limited to the greater of $400,000 or the plaintiff's life expectancy times $8,000 per year, except that cases of "severe permanent physical impairment or severe disfigurement" have a limit of the greater of $1 million or the plaintiff's life expectancy times $25,000 per year); Colo. Rev. Stat. §13-21-102.5 (noneconomic damages limited to $500,000, but may not exceed $250,000 unless "the court finds justification by clear and convincing evidence," and with an annual inflation adjustment beginning in 1998). A great number of state reforms and federal reform proposals have fixated on $250,000 as the appropriate cap amount, apparently drawing that number from California's pioneering noneconomic damages cap passed in 1975, despite the enormous erosion of purchasing power represented by that amount due to inflation over the intervening decades. See Amanda K. Edwards, Medical Malpractice Non-Economic Damages Caps, 43 Harvard J. on Legis. 213 (2006). A few states have gone further to provide statutory caps on damages in certain kinds of actions, preventing any recovery above the caps regardless of whether the damages stem from economic or noneconomic losses. See, e.g., Colo. Rev.

Stat. §13-64-302 (limiting damages in tort cases against health care providers or health care professionals to $1,000,000).

The effects of damage caps are not entirely clear. A recent empirical study suggests that caps on noneconomic losses may not, on the whole, have a strong effect on reducing awards. The author of the study hypothesizes that this is the result of, among other things, a "crossover effect," in which noneconomic damages in excess of the cap spill over into the category of economic damages, which generally remain unlimited. See Catherine M. Sharkey, Unintended Consequences of Medical Malpractice Damage Caps, 80 N.Y.U. L. Rev. 391 (2005). Evidence also suggests that noneconomic damages caps have a disproportionate impact on female plaintiffs given that, "while overall men tend to recover greater total damages, juries consistently award women more in noneconomic loss damages than men, and that the noneconomic portion of women's total damage awards is significantly greater than the percentage of men's total recoveries attributable to noneconomic damages." Lucinda M. Finley, The Hidden Victims of Tort Reform: Women, Children, and the Elderly, 53 Emory L.J. 1263, 1266 (2004).

Statutory damage caps have been the subject of constitutional attack, with varying results explainable in part by differences in the state constitutions. Upholding the statutes are Kirkland v. Blaine County Med. Ctr., 4 P.3d 1115 (Idaho 2000), and Estate of Verba v. Ghaphery, 543 S.E.2d 347 (W. Va.), *aff'd,* 552 S.E.2d 406 (W. Va. 2000). Ruling that the damage cap statutes are unconstitutional are State ex rel. Ohio Academy of Trial Lawyers v. Sheward, 715 N.E.2d 1062 (Ohio 1999) (comprehensive tort reform statute violated separation of powers doctrine); Lakin v. Senco Products, Inc., 987 P.2d 463 (Or. 1999) (damage cap violates state constitutional right to jury trial); and Best v. Union Pacific R.R. Co., 689 N.E.2d 1057 (Ill. 1997) (violates state constitutional prohibition of special legislation). For a powerful argument that, as a matter of federal constitutional law, "all American citizens have a right to a body of law for the redress of private wrongs that generates meaningful and judicially enforceable limits on tort reform legislation," see John C. P. Goldberg, The Constitutional Status of Tort Law: Due Process and the Right to a Law for the Redress of Wrongs, 115 Yale L.J. 524 (2005). Although the author refrains from arguing that this due process right would entitle individuals to any specific tort rule, principle, or form of relief, his argument does appear to support the legitimacy of courts' striking down those legislative reforms they deem to have gone "too far."

Another concern expressed by critics of the existing process is that it involves "horizontal" unfairness—plaintiffs with substantially similar injuries recover significantly different amounts. This results from the fact that the jury in each case hears only the evidence in that case, and does not have a basis for comparing that case with other similar cases. One way to achieve greater equality between similar cases would be to provide juries with information about the awards for intangible harm in those similar cases. See, e.g., II. The American Law Institute, Reporters' Study—Enterprise Responsibility for Personal Injury 223-29 (1991). For a more detailed proposal, see Randall R. Bovbjerg, Frank A. Sloan & James F. Blumstein, Valuing Life and Limb in Tort: Scheduling "Pain and Suffering," 83 Nw. U. L. Rev. 908 (1989).

Problem 38

A partner in the firm with which you are an associate has asked for your assistance on the Sidney Rothman case. Rothman is seeking to recover against Tompkins Department

Stores, Inc., in whose store Mr. Rothman recently fell and suffered what his doctor has diagnosed as a herniated disc in his lower back. The lawyer for Reliance Insurance Company, which carries the liability insurance covering Tompkins Department Stores, Inc., has an appointment to see the partner next week to discuss settlement of the case. The partner wants you to analyze the file so that you can make a recommendation as to the range within which the case should be settled.

In responding to this assignment, you are to consider the case that follows (Jones v. Harris, p. 666, below) to be the most recent reported case from your state dealing with the subject of recovery for low back injuries. In addition, there exist rules of thumb which are routinely referred to (though by no means followed unswervingly) in settlement negotiations. Generally, in what are usually referred to as the smaller cases, insurance companies recognize a range of from three to five times out-of-pocket loss, including work time lost (this amount is usually referred to as the "specials"), depending upon such factors as the severity and duration of pain and the like.[8] Where the plaintiff is represented by a lawyer, insurance companies may on occasion go as high as ten times specials in these smaller cases. For cases of a more serious or unusual nature, the rule of thumb multiples just described tend to give way to more individualized consideration of the unique factors of the particular case. One of the senior partners in your firm, who has had a great deal of trial experience in personal injury cases, recently explained his views of what a lawyer might expect a jury to return in a herniated disc case. Without a myelogram or subsequent laminectomy confirmation, the range of probable recovery is approximately \$20,000 to \$75,000. With myelographic confirmation but no surgery, the range is \$75,000 to \$200,000. Where surgery has been performed, the range jumps to \$200,000 to \$500,000 or more. The partner explained that these are at best only general categories with respect to which he gears his expectations in low back cases. The first category, for example, includes what he calls the "doubtful diagnosis" cases. Even without a myelogram, if the diagnosis is firm, the case may be treated almost as favorably as other cases with myelographic confirmation. Moreover, the categories reflect a range of cases as to the certainty of liability, from rather doubtful liability to clear liability. "Clear liability always adds to the value of a case — even if only a sprained finger is involved," he suggests. The partner referred you to a few supreme court cases somewhat in point; the most recent is Jones v. Harris (p. 666, below). A couple of the cases were decided some time ago and thus are of more limited usefulness. One case, decided on appeal in 1983, upheld a judgment of \$50,000 for a 46-year-old woman who had a 15 percent permanent disability as a result of a neck injury and a 5 percent permanent disability in her lower back. There was no evidence of future loss of income, and no myelographic confirmation, but she did testify that she could no longer ride horses, build corrals, or dance as she had before the accident. Another case, decided on appeal in 1995, involved a 66-year-old retired male with a herniated disc, which was confirmed by a myelogram. His annual earnings before the accident ranged from \$25,000 to \$30,000. His disability appears to have been substantial. The judgment for damages of \$120,000 for loss of future earnings, and \$50,000 for pain and suffering was upheld. "In the final analysis," the partner added, "while generalizations are helpful, each case has its own twists, and in working up any case, particularly the bigger ones, it is important to focus on the particular facts of that case."

The following documents are from the file on the Sidney Rothman case.

8. It is not proper, however, for the trial judge to use this approach in calculating damages. In Hayhurst v. LaFlamme, 441 A.2d 544 (R.I. 1982), the court reversed the trial judge's method of calculating damages for pain and suffering by multiplying lost wages and medical expenses by five.

Client's Statement

Name: Sidney L. Rothman *Date:* March 17

My name is Sidney L. Rothman. I am 42 years old, married, with three children, ages 11, 13 and 15. I am employed as a civil engineer with Grayson & Sons.

On November 20 last year, I had driven downtown to do some shopping for my wife's birthday. At about 3:00 in the afternoon, I entered Tompkins Department Store to look for a wrist watch. I went first to the sporting goods department on the sixth floor to look at tennis racquets. I had taken the elevator. I decided not to buy one and took the elevator down to the second floor to the jewelry department. I bought a watch and had it wrapped. Straight ahead from the counter where I bought the watch is a stairway leading to the main floor. I started down the stairs toward the main floor. I would guess that it was around 3:45 or 4:00 by then. I don't know how many steps there are in that staircase or how high the staircase is. It is covered with carpeting. I was about a third of the way down the stairs when a clerk approached me coming up the stairs with a pile of boxes. He turned to say hello to someone to my left, and walked right into me, causing me to lose my balance. I could feel that I was falling and I tried to keep my balance by pushing against the wall. I was too far from the railing on the right side to grab it. I must have spun around, because I landed very heavily in a sitting position on the bottom step. There wasn't anyone ahead of me on the stairs so I had a clear fall to the bottom. I didn't have any packages or anything else in my hands. I was looking straight ahead, as I always do when I go down stairs. I don't remember anything else about the fall because it all happened so fast.

I experienced immediate and terrible pain in my right lower back and I was unable to rise from the position in which I had fallen. Several persons who identified themselves as store personnel, whose names I do not know, helped me walk to a rest area nearby in the store, from which I was taken shortly after in an ambulance to the Great Oaks Hospital. The ambulance was from Shafer's Ambulance Service.

I spent seven nights in the hospital, undergoing various tests and treatments. My doctor, Dr. William M. Peters, decided against an operation at this time. I was discharged on November 27, and spent approximately one week in bed at home, during which time my wife cared for me.

I returned to work on December 18, but as yet I have been unable to return to my normal activities, which include field trips of various sorts to construction jobs being performed by our company. At the present time I am on a salary with Grayson & Sons, making over $120,000 a year before taxes. Since I came with the firm, I have advanced steadily and am presently in charge of our heavy construction department.

The pain in my back has diminished some since the fall in the department store, but I have been unable to engage in many of the activities which I was accustomed to before the accident, such as tennis and doing jobs around the house. Since my discharge from the hospital I have worn a brace on my back, and I have seen my doctor a number of times. However, the pain and the accompanying incapacity continue. I have had recurrent attacks of pain in my lower back throughout most of my adult life, but it has never lasted more than two or three days and it has never incapacitated me in any appreciable way.

I have read this statement, and it is true to the best of my knowledge and belief.

/s/ David J. Richards */s/Sidney L. Rothman*

William M. Peters, M.D.
240 West Plain Street

March 23

Richards & Berger, Attorneys
4000 Main Street

Dear Sirs:

Mr. Sidney Rothman has been a patient of mine for over 11 years. I was called to see him at the Great Oaks Hospital on the afternoon of November 20, last year. The patient reported having fallen earlier that day, injuring his lower back. He complained of severe pain in the lumbo-sacral area with accompanying pain in the posterior right calf, indicating some sciatic nerve root involvement in the right thigh and leg. Examination of the patient on November 20, including employment of the Nafzigger test and the straight leg raising test indicated the strong possibility of a herniated disc being present at the L5-S1 levels. X-ray examination the following day revealed a narrowing of the lumbar 4-5 sacral interspace, suggesting that the herniation was located at the level of the fifth lumbar disc space. No earlier X-rays of the lumbar area are available for purposes of comparison. Based upon my examination of the patient and the X-rays, it is my opinion that the patient is suffering from a herniated disc at the L5 level. During the patient's stay in the hospital, I called Dr. Hall Gordon, an orthopedic surgeon with a great deal of experience in these matters. His diagnosis was consistent with mine.

In cases of this sort I advise my patients to employ conservative treatment for an indefinite period of time before resorting to surgery. Therefore, I recommended several weeks bed rest and extended diathermy treatments of the area affected. In addition, a Williams-type back brace has been employed in an effort to achieve stabilization of the patient's lower spine in order to promote a resolution of the nerve root involvement. However, in some cases of this type, despite physiotherapy to the patient's spine, low back pain persists. If the pain persists in Mr. Rothman's case, I will recommend that he undergo a CAT scan, and if that shows a problem, it will probably be necessary for him to undergo a myelographic examination. Eventually, surgical stabilization and removal of the herniated disc may be required. Surgery of this sort is expensive and involves some risks of paralysis to the patient, and I therefore prefer to give conservative treatment every chance in cases of this sort.

As for the cause of the herniation in this case, it was probably produced by the patient's fall on November 20. There is no indication of any other possible cause. The patient has a history of some back pain in the past, but it is doubtful it would have been caused by a herniated disc in light of the active nature of his life during this period. The X-rays reveal no arthritis or any other congenital defects or traumatically produced conditions other than the herniation in question which could in any way be contributing to Mr. Rothman's present incapacity.

Sincerely,

William M Peters

William M. Peters, M.D.

Randolph Copich, M.D.
Sanford Medical Building

March 27

Richards & Berger, Attorneys at Law
4000 Main Street

Dear Sirs:

At the request of the Reliance Insurance Company, I have examined Sidney L. Rothman for the purpose of evaluating the condition of his lower back in connection with a fall he is said to have had on a stairway in Tompkins Department Store. The results of my examination are as follows:

First, it is by no means certain that the patient, Mr. Rothman, has experienced any injury to his back beyond the spraining of certain ligaments in the lumbar region. I have examined the X-rays taken later on November 22, last year, and I have had additional X-rays taken at my clinic, and in both instances it is impossible to detect a fracture of any of the vertebrae or a herniation of any of the intervertebral discs. There is at most a slight narrowing of the lumbar 4-5 sacral interspace, but that is perfectly consistent with the natural condition of the patient's spine. Without a CAT scan and myelographical examination of the area in question, which I am told the attending physician, Dr. Peters, is opposed to, it is impossible to conclude that the patient is suffering from a herniated disc.

Second, it is not at all clear that any traumatically produced injury to the patient's lower back originated with his fall on November 20. My interview of the patient indicates that he has suffered some intermittent lower back pain for more than twenty years. It appears that he played football both in high school and in college, and it is very possible that some injury to his lower back occurred during that period. It is possible (and, in light of the patient's history of low back pain, probable) that he exposed the lumbar region to severe shock and trauma resulting in a chronic instability of the vertebrae at the L5-S1 level. The fall on November 20 may have merely aggravated what could properly be described as a preexisting condition of instability.

In any event, it is my opinion that the patient has a marked tendency to exaggerate the pain he claims to be suffering in this case, and that the physical indications do not support his subjective descriptions of pain.

Sincerely,

Randolph Copich

Randolph Copich, M.D.

Grayson & Sons
Civil Engineers

March 24

Richards & Berger, Attorneys
4000 Main Street

Dear Sirs:

Mr. Sidney Rothman has been part of our organization here at G. & S. for 9 years. He is a most competent engineer and, at least until his recent accident, was one of our most valuable supervisors. His salary for this year will, with bonuses, exceed $160,000. He missed approximately 4 weeks of work due to the accident, but we paid him without deduction for the time he lost. We have assured him that he need not worry over his position with our firm, but frankly his present physical condition does cause some concern in our minds over his future usefulness to us. As you probably know, civil engineering of the sort we are engaged in is an active, "get up and go" occupation requiring a lot of physical activity. Jobs must be checked at construction sites, and so on. Sid Rothman was probably headed for a position of major responsibility in our construction operations. It is possible that in another five years or so he might have been part of our executive management picture, at a salary in excess of $200,000 a year. If he does not manage eventually to pull himself together physically, however, it is difficult to predict the role he may be playing in the future growth and development of our company.

Sincerely,

Parker G. Grayson

Parker G. Grayson, President

October 15

Richards & Berger, Attorneys at Law
4000 Main Street

Dear Mr. Richards:

As you requested when I visited your office, I am writing this letter to keep you up to date on my physical condition at the present time. I don't know if this hurts our case or not, but I have followed Dr. Peters' orders and have avoided all strenuous physical exercise and the like, and it seems to be paying off. At my last visit to Dr. Peters' office earlier this week, we discussed my progress and more or less concluded that an operation won't be necessary after all. As he explained, it is my decision. The way things are going, it looks like this thing will resolve itself with just taking it easy. I have had to give up tennis, and I haven't gotten back to a full schedule at work, but I honestly think that in time I will be able to return to these activities.

I have finally collected all the bills for my medical expenses, which I am enclosing. As you can see, they total $20,685.24. Of that amount, $16,126.28 was covered by my medical insurance, and I am enclosing the statements from Blue Cross.

If I can be of any further help in preparing our case, just let me know.

Best regards,

Sidney L. Rothman

Sidney L. Rothman

William M. Peters, M.D.
240 West Plain Street

October 16

Richards & Berger, Attorneys
4000 Main Street

Dear Mr. Richards:

Pursuant to your request by letter dated October 11, I am writing to bring you up to date on the progress of Sidney Rothman. Briefly stated, he appears to be responding quite favorably to the conservative treatments that I have prescribed, and it does not appear that, barring some unforeseeable mishap or reinjury to his lower back, an operation will be necessary. He is still somewhat restricted in his physical activities, and may never be able fully to return to his former routine of heavy physical exercise without suffering a recurrence of pain. He is a remarkably fit individual, however, and I personally believe, at his present rate of recovery, that he will have achieved what might be called a "return to normal activity" within six months to a year. Whether he will ever play tennis again is somewhat in doubt, but he should be able to return to full activities in connection with his job.

In your letter, you asked what the medical costs of an operation on Mr. Rothman's back would be, if it were to come to that. It is impossible to be precise, but I can assure you that it would be expensive. My conservative estimate is that it would be approximately $125,000. It is possible that it could be a bit less, and may even be more, depending on what would be determined to be needed at the time of the surgery, and how much medical costs will have gone up. As I have indicated, I believe that surgery will not be necessary, but of course it can't be ruled out completely.

Sincerely,

William M Peters

William M. Peters, M.D.

Contingent Fee Agreement

Date March 17

The Client, Sidney L. Rothman
(Name and Address)

Retains the Attorney Richards & Berger, 4000 Main St.
(Name and Address)

To represent him in the following matter:

The Client hereby agrees to pay the Attorney from any recovery in the above matter in accordance with the following schedule:

1. Settlement before suit is instituted	25%
2. Settlement after suit is instituted but before trial	33 1/3%
3. Recovery or settlement after commencing trial but before entry of case in appellate court	40%
4. Recovery or settlement after entry of case in appellate court	50%

These percentages shall apply to the full amount of recovery or settlement without deduction for expenses and disbursements. The Client shall be liable to the Attorney regardless of the outcome of the case for such expenses and disbursements.

Sidney L. Rothman
(Signature of Client)

David J. Richards
(Signature of Attorney)

Bailey, Back Injuries

Basic Personal Injury Anatomy 159, 161-63, 165-67, 171 (Collins and Wood eds., 1965)

I. Anatomy of Back

A. Spinal Column

1. [§5.1] Components

The spinal column is a flexible assemblage of individual segments of bone called vertebrae. There are normally seven cervical (neck) vertebrae, twelve dorsal or thoracic (chest) vertebrae, and five lumbar (low back) vertebrae. Each section moves with the structures above and below. The sacrum is composed of five vertebrae that fused during the early stage of embryonic life to form a solid body mass. . . .

Each vertebra is described by a number: C-2, L-1, D-12, etc. . . .

B. Vertebrae

1. [§5.3] Vertebral Body . . .

The bodies of the vertebrae are connected by the intervertebral disc structures made up of a tough ring of annulus fibrosus and a semigelatinous nucleus pulposus. On its upper (superior) and lower (inferior) surfaces, each vertebral body is covered with a thin plate of hyaline cartilage.

C. Intervertebral Disc

1. [§5.5] Location . . .

The discs or fibrocartilages are interposed between the surfaces of the vertebral bodies from the second cervical vertebra to the sacrum, and they form strong bonds between the adjacent vertebra. . . .

2. Components

a. [§5.6] Annulus Fibrosus

Each intervertebral disc has two constituents, the annulus fibrosus and the nucleus pulposus. The annulus fibrosus is composed of laminae (layers) of fibrous tissue. . . .

b. [§5.7] Nucleus Pulposus

The nucleus pulposus has a pulpy or mucoid character, is yellowish in color, and has a consistency somewhat like gristle. . . . The nucleus is somewhat plastic in nature, and because of this it tends to obey the law of fluids when there is movement of the vertebral column — it is neither compressible nor expansible. . . .

3. [§5.8] Function

The elasticity of the disc under pressure indicates that it functions as a shock absorber for the vertebrae. . . .

It should be evident that the amount of force to which the annulus fibrosus is subjected with various activities of the spine is tremendous. Its anatomy suggests great strength. Not only must it resist the pressures exerted on it by the nucleus pulposus, but it must act also as a retainer, during extreme bending, because it binds the vertebral bodies together. . . .

II. Mechanics of Rupture

A. [§5.15] Location

About 95 percent of all ruptures of the lumbar intervertebral disc occur between the fourth and fifth lumbar, or fifth lumbar and first sacral, vertebrae. The remaining 5 percent occur between the third and fourth or second and third lumbar vertebrae. Rupture of the annulus fibrosus fibers allows displacement or herniation of the nucleus pulposus.

Jones v. Harris

896 So. 2d 237 (La. Ct. App. 2005)

Patricia Rivet Murray, J.

This is a personal injury action arising out of a motor vehicle accident. From a judgment in favor of the plaintiffs, Jacquelyn Jones, and her husband, Jack Jones, the Defendants . . . appeal. The central issues Defendants raise on this appeal are whether the accident caused Mrs. Jones' back injury, the necessity of surgical treatment of that injury, the extent of that injury, and the alleged excessiveness of the damages awarded for that injury. For the reasons that follow, we affirm.

Factual and Procedural Background

On June 30, 1998, Mrs. Jones was driving on Canal Street . . . when the rental vehicle she was driving was rear ended by a Jeep driven by Ms. Harris. . . . At the time of the accident, Ms. Harris was in the course and scope of her employment with the State.

On February 3, 1999, Mrs. Jones filed suit against Ms. Harris and her insurer, Allstate. Mr. Jones joined in the suit to assert a loss of consortium claim. On November 16, 1999, the Joneses filed an amended petition adding the State as a defendant. The trial court granted the Joneses' motion for summary judgment on liability. Defendants did not contest that decision.

In February 2004, a three-day jury trial was held on the issues of causation and damages. The jury rendered a verdict in Mrs. Jones' favor, assessing her damages as follows:

Past Medical Expenses	$154,326
Future Medical Expenses	80,000
Loss of Past Wages	80,206
Loss of Future Wages/ Earning Capacity Including Loss of Fringe Benefits	348,864
General Damages [Pain and Suffering]	500,000
Total Damages	$1,163,396

The jury also awarded $40,000 in loss of consortium damages to Mr. Jones. The trial court rendered judgment in accord with the jury's verdict. . . . The trial court denied the State's motions for judgment notwithstanding the verdict and new trial. This appeal followed.

Discussion

On appeal, Defendants challenge four of the jury's awards; to-wit: (1) general damages [pain and suffering]; (2) loss of past wages; (3) loss of future wages/earnings capacity, including fringe benefits; and (4) loss of consortium. We separately address each award.

General Damages [Pain and Suffering]

The jury awarded Mrs. Jones $500,000 in general damages. Defendants argue that this award is clearly excessive. La. C.C. art.1999 . . . provides that "[w]hen damages are insusceptible of precise measurement, much discretion shall be left to the court for the reasonable assessment of these damages. . . ."

Because "[r]easonable persons frequently disagree about the measure of general damages in a particular case," a general damage award may be disturbed on appeal only when "the award is, in either direction, beyond that which a reasonable trier of fact could assess for the effects of the particular injury to the particular plaintiff under the particular circumstances." [Youn v. Maritime Overseas Corp.], 623 So. 2d at 1261. The jurisprudential theme that has emerged is that "the discretion vested in the trier of fact is 'great,' and even vast, so that an appellate court should rarely disturb an award of general damages." Id.

Although Defendants invite us to resort to a consideration of awards for generically similar injuries and contend that the award in this case is disproportionate to such prior awards, the jurisprudence is settled that "resort to prior awards is only appropriate after an appellate court has concluded that an 'abuse of discretion' has occurred." Cone v. National Emergency Services, Inc., 747 So. 2d 1085, 1089. Because we find no abuse of discretion, a comparison of prior awards is not appropriate. Instead, we focus our analysis of the effects of this particular injury on this particular plaintiff under the particular circumstances of this case.

Our review of the record shows that upon the impact of the accident, Mrs. Jones testified that she was thrown forward and the seatbelt jerked her back and locked her into the seat. That night she experienced stiffness in her neck and lower back for which she took Motrin. During the next nine days she continued taking over-the-counter medication for the escalating pain in her left leg and lower back. On referral by a long time friend (who also is her attorney), she sought treatment with Dr. L.S. Kewalramani.

On July 9, 1998, Dr. Kewalramani first saw Mrs. Jones. On the first visit, Mrs. Jones complained of pain in the lower back, the left buttock, the left shoulder, and the neck region. . . . During the nine-day period between the date of the accident and the date she first saw Dr. Kewalramani, she reported that she took Motrin, but her pain continued and gradually increased in severity.

Dr. Kewalramani testified that his initial examination of Mrs. Jones revealed mild spasms in her neck and back and localized tenderness at the L5-S1 level. On the first visit, Dr. Kewalramani advised Mrs. Jones to get x-rays of the cervical spine, lumbar spine, and hip joints. He also prescribed a theragesic cream and other medication.

On her next visit, Dr. Kewalramani gave her a home physical therapy program to follow. He also interpreted the x-rays of her lumbar spine. . . . He . . . testified that the x-rays confirmed his initial impression regarding the L5-S1 level being the problem area.

For the next several months, Dr. Kewalramani continued to treat Mrs. Jones conservatively. On each visit, she showed signs of improvement. At the January 14, 1999 visit, Dr. Kewalramani discharged her with the recommendation that she continue with the home physical therapy program. He gave her a prescription for a small amount of medication and instructed her to call his office if she experienced any exacerbation of pain.

Ten months later, on November 12, 1999, Mrs. Jones returned to Dr. Kewalramani complaining of progressively increasing lumbar pain and discomfort radiating along the left lower extremity. According to Dr. Kewalramani's report, Mrs. Jones told him that she was hoping the pain would improve with time, that her husband was calling her crippled, that she was concerned because she was experiencing radiating pain down her right leg, and that she could not live without the medication. Dr. Kewalramani testified that she denied having any new injury or trauma. Based on her complaints, Dr. Kewalramani ordered [several tests.] Based on the [test] results coupled with the fact that he had treated her conservatively for a lengthy period over which she had progressed and then regressed, Dr. Kewalramani recommended that Mrs. Jones get a second opinion from a neurosurgeon of her choice. She selected Dr. Kenneth Vogel.

Dr. Vogel recommended to Mrs. Jones that she undergo a micro-surgical diskectomy. . . . On April 4, 2001, Mrs. Jones underwent a microsurgical laminectomy, L5-S1, left; lumbar medial branch neurotomy, L4-5 and L5-S1, left and a lumbar epidural block. In his operating report, Dr. Vogel stated that he was able to see through the microscope that the disc herniation at L5-S1 had actually occurred. . . .

[Over the next three years, Mrs. Jones continued to receive various treatments from Dr. Kewalramani and underwent further operative procedures with Dr. Vogel.]

At the State's request, Dr. Walter Abbott saw Mrs. Jones on January 21, 2004. Dr. Abbott testified by deposition that Mrs. Jones' medical condition on that date was low back pain and some degree of referred pain into the left and right side. . . . Based on his review of the MRIs and other tests and her prior diagnosis, Dr. Abbott testified that it was his opinion that surgery was not necessary. In his report, Dr. Abbott opined that the initial MRI showed Mrs. Jones' back injury to be a "minimal problem" and did not show a disc herniation but rather a degenerative disc at L5-S1. Dr. Abbott testified that there was a definite change in her condition for the worse after surgery and that "surgery is not without trauma." As to causation, he attributed her back pain not to the accident, but to the surgeries. As to her future prognosis, he testified that he did not believe there would be much improvement and that she is "probably pretty much stuck with what she has," which he defined as "fatal back syndrome," a "failed effort to treat a very minor problem."

. . . Credibility determinations, including evaluating expert witness testimony, are for the trier of fact. Such credibility determinations are factual findings governed by the well-settled manifest error standard of review. . . . Given that both Dr. Vogel and Dr. Kewalrami, Mrs. Jones' treating physicians, related Mrs. Jones' back injury to the accident, we cannot say the jury was manifestly erroneous in resolving this conflicting expert testimony in Mrs. Jones' favor.

Returning to the issue of whether the general damage award was excessive, we note that general damages may be established in three ways: (i) the circumstances of the case, (ii) expert medical testimony, and (iii) the tort victim's testimony. In this case, Mrs. Jones' evidence on this issue consisted primarily of her own testimony and that of her two treating physicians. The circumstances of the rear-end collision were undisputed and were not especially significant. . . .

Mrs. Jones testified that she presently still has pain. She testified that she presently is aggravated because she lost her job after the first surgery. She explained that she was under the impression that she would be able to return to her job as an insurance underwriter at Lafayette Insurance after the first surgery. Although she continued working until immediately before her first surgery (March 31, 2001 was her last day of work), she lost her job when she was unable to return to work for over twelve weeks following the first surgery. She explained that Lafayette Insurance has a policy that if an employee is not back to work in twelve weeks, it has the right to replace that employee. Mrs. Jones testified that she felt the application of the policy to her was unfair as she had worked for the company for twenty-five years. She further testified that she called Lafayette Insurance after the first surgery, but was told that no job was available.

Mrs. Jones still further testified that she did not believe she could work because she has a problem getting up out of bed in the morning. She testified that she has to get up before her husband leaves for work so that he is there to assist her. She described her daily activities as including doing her home physical therapy program. She stressed her inability to sit or lay down for a lengthy period. She testified that she has two back braces and that she sleeps in one of them and sometimes wakes up at 4:00 a.m. with pain. She testified that they had to install both a handicapped toilet and a shower in their house for her. As to the need for the latter, she noted that on one occasion she was stuck in the tub for forty-five minutes.

Mrs. Jones characterized herself as an active person before the accident. She listed the activities she previously enjoyed doing as including shooting pool, going out dancing, and bowling. Since the accident she testified she is no longer able to do these activities. Another activity that she identified as impaired due to the accident is her ability to engage in activities with her grandchildren, such as lifting them.

Considering the particular effects of the particular injuries on this particular plaintiff coupled with the great discretion accorded the jury's decision on damages, we cannot say that the jury's award of $500,000 to Mrs. Jones for her pain and suffering was an abuse of discretion.

Loss of Past Wages

An analysis of an award for past wages of a salaried employee is generally a straightforward mathematical calculation. Such is the case here. . . .

Loss of Future Wages/Earning Capacity, Including Loss of Fringe Benefits

. . . In determining a proper future lost wage award, factors to be considered are: "the plaintiff's physical condition before the injury, the plaintiff's past work history and work consistency, the amount the plaintiff probably would have earned absent the injury complained of, and the probability that the plaintiff would have continued to earn wages over the remainder of his working life." *Myers,* 638 So. 2d at 379. Applying those factors here, Mrs. Jones' physical condition before the injury was good. She had a stable, consistent work history; for twenty-five years she worked for the same employer, Lafayette Insurance. At the time of the accident, her yearly income was roughly $29,000. Mrs. Jones testified that she planned to continue working at her job until she was sixty-five years old so that she could get collect full company benefits. Given these facts, we cannot say the jury abused its discretion in awarding $348,864 for loss of future wages.

Loss of Consortium

. . . When asked about the activities he and his wife enjoyed before the accident, Mr. Jones replied that they enjoyed going for walks. Specifically, he testified that they would go for walks downtown and at the Riverwalk. He testified that since the accident his wife has "slowly backed away from walking." He further replied that before the accident his wife would help with cooking and barbecuing for the family, but since the accident she is unable to do so.

Lastly, when asked whether their intimacy has been affected by the accident, Mr. Jones replied that it has been affected, that it has gotten "really bad," and that he has learned to live with it. Given these facts, we cannot say the jury abused its discretion in awarding Mr. Jones $40,000 for loss of consortium. See Runnels v. Esteves, 550 So. 2d 1225 (La. App. 4 Cir. 1989) (affirming $45,000 award for loss of consortium).

Decree

For the foregoing reasons, the judgment of the trial court is affirmed.

AFFIRMED.

Mechanisms for Resolving Disputes: Settlement

One of the main purposes of the materials in this section is to introduce the student to the settlement process as an indispensable mechanism for resolving disputes in our system. For every torts dispute that is resolved by means of the formal adjudicative process, many more are resolved by means of settlement. The expense and delay incident to adjudication contribute to the pressures on both parties to settle, especially in cases involving relatively small claims. The inherent unpredictability of adjudication also exerts pressure to settle, even in the minority of cases where the damages may be very large. Contrary to what one might have otherwise assumed, it is the uncertainty, and not the certainty, of a given case that exerts the greater pressure upon the parties to settle prior to final judicial determination. Whenever the plaintiff and defendant in a torts dispute enter into settlement negotiations, they assume the roles of seller and buyer in a contractual setting. If a mutually agreeable settlement figure is reached, the plaintiff sells to the defendant the right to bring legal action and receives from the defendant a liquidated, lump sum payment in money. The promise not to sue that the plaintiff makes it legally binding to the same extent as any other promise given for adequate consideration, and may be raised by the defendant as an absolute bar to any later action by the plaintiff based upon the claim in question. It follows that in order for a settlement to take place, both sides to a dispute must believe that they stand to gain from the contemplated contractual exchange. Both parties must believe, in other words, that they have something to lose by proceeding further with the formal torts process. It is the uncertainty inherent in most cases that helps to provide the setting necessary for both parties to see some substantial benefit in resorting to the settlement process. See Stewart J. Schwab & Michael Heise, Splitting Logs: An Empirical Perspective on Employment Discrimination Settlements, 96 Cornell L. Rev. 931, 937-38 (2011) (describing "ambiguity aversion" as one common cognitive tendency favoring settlement over trial).

One method to encourage the settlement of disputes without trial in cases brought in federal court is embodied in Rule 68 of the Federal Rules of Civil Procedure. Under this rule, if one party makes an offer of settlement that is rejected by the other, the rejecting party must pay the costs incurred after the offer is made if the outcome to that party is not more favorable than the offer. For a discussion of the application and limitations of the rule, see Jay N. Varon, Promoting Settlements and Limiting Litigation Costs by Means of Offer of Judgment: Some Suggestions for Using and Revising Rule 68, 33 Am. U. L. Rev. 813 (1984); Ian H. Fisher, Federal Rule 68, A Defendant's Subtle Weapon: Its Use and Pitfalls, 14 DePaul Bus. L.J. 89 (2001).

The preceding paragraphs may imply that settlement occurs, if at all, before trial and judgment. In the vast majority of settled cases, that is the point in the process when settlement does occur. But a case may be settled after judgment is entered at the trial, and even after the case has been appealed. In fact, one study of Rand Corporation's Institute for Civil Justice indicates that 20 percent of plaintiffs end up recovering less than their judgments at the trials, and that settlements account for 62 percent of that number. See L.A. Times, July 7, 1987, at 3, col. 1.

The plaintiff's lawyer conducts a great many, perhaps the substantial majority of, settlement negotiations with representatives of insurance companies. Were it not for the insurance money it would not be worth the lawyer's time and the plaintiff's expense to advance the claim in many cases. In any event, it is worthwhile to reflect a moment upon the manner in which insurance companies approach the settlement process. In a word, they approach it with a singular absence of sentimentality. They are not charitable organizations; they are privately owned business institutions designed and operated to maximize profits. Short of fraudulent or otherwise illegal conduct, the company managers are encouraged in our free enterprise system to settle cases brought against those they insure for as little as possible.

The mechanics of how this objective is accomplished are straightforward enough. The representative of the insurance company assigned to handle a claim seeks to determine what is commonly referred to as the company's exposure to liability — that is, the amount (up to applicable policy limits) representing the maximum which the company reasonably might be called upon by a jury to pay upon a finding of liability, adjusted by a factor representing the realistic probability of such a finding. From this base figure a reserve is created on the books of the company which statistical experience dictates should cover the company's exposure to liability. The reserve is an amount out of the general assets of the company that has been set aside for application, when and if needed, to the case until it is finally resolved. It appears as a liability on the company's books. If the plaintiff ultimately obtains a judgment in excess of this reserve, then of course the company must pay it up to (and sometimes exceeding) policy limits. But the reserve represents the company expert's opinion of what the plaintiff is likely to receive, adjusted by the probability of receiving it. It is never revealed to the plaintiff and represents from the company's point of view a ceiling on what they will be willing to settle for. Actually, the goal of the claims manager will be to settle for a figure substantially below the reserve in a particular case, thereby creating at least the impression that the manager has saved his company money. It should come as no surprise that in order to provide enough room to maneuver comfortably below the reserve figure, the first figure the claims manager advances will often appear depressingly low to the plaintiff.

From the point of view of the plaintiff's attorney, an evaluation process is followed which is very similar to that just described, except that no reserve is created and the figures arrived at are, therefore, not formalized to the same extent. The plaintiff's lawyer is in a more flexible position relative to the bargaining process. The client may and probably will place pressure upon his attorney to obtain a generous settlement. But the client is rarely in a position to judge what is "generous," relatively speaking, and may in the end look largely to the attorney for assurances that the settlement obtained is a fair one. In any event, it is clear that the plaintiff will start off asking for more than the insurer is likely to pay to leave adequate room for the give and take of bargaining. The plaintiff's lawyer ordinarily will not ask what he or she believes to be a preposterous figure. Not only must the lawyer appear to be minimally desirous of settling the case in order for the insurance company to take the offer seriously and begin to make serious counteroffers; but also the lawyer faces the difficult task of explaining to even the timid client why "we asked for 10,000 but settled for 10."

And so the settlement process is formally launched with a demand by the plaintiff who usually (but by no means always) goes first, and a responding counteroffer by the defendant. Usually, these figures are separated by some distance, but they should not be too far apart or the settlement process breaks down. Essentially, it is like the bartering that accompanies the purchase and sale of any item of questionable or arguable value.

The literature on the settlement process is rich and varied. For helpful overviews, see Roger Fisher, William Ury & Bruce Patton, Getting to Yes: Negotiating Agreement Without Giving In (2d ed. 1991); Robert H. Mnookin, Scott R. Peppet & Andrew S. Tulumello, Beyond Winning: Negotiating to Create Value in Deals and Disputes (2000); Donald G. Gifford, A Context-Based Theory of Strategy Selection in Legal Negotiations, 46 Ohio St. L.J. 41 (1985). Many articles appear in lawyers' professional journals and are written from the perspective of either the plaintiff's or defendant's lawyer. The negotiation process has now become the subject of more neutral academic study and many law schools have courses in negotiation. See Robert M. Bastress & Joseph D. Harbaugh, Interviewing, Counseling, and Negotiating — Skills for Effective Representation (1990).

The Lawyer's Professional Responsibility: Problems of the Plaintiff's Lawyer in the Settlement Process

As the preceding note indicates, a substantial body of literature addresses the techniques that are available to lawyers to maximize their clients' positions in the settlement process. In contrast, commentators pay relatively little attention to the professional problems that may arise during the settlement negotiations. To the extent they do, most discussion focuses on the thorny issue of whether, and to what extent, lawyers may fudge, bluff, or otherwise dissemble during negotiations, notwithstanding the general requirements of truthfulness in statements to others found in Model Rule of Professional Conduct 4.1 (2016), on the theory that somehow ethical obligations are suspended or applied different within the negotiation context. For a fascinating overview of these issues along with empirical evidence regarding attorney attitudes and behavior, see Art Hinshaw & Jess K. Alberts, Doing the Right Thing: An Empirical Study of Attorney Negotiation Ethics, 16 Harv. Negot. L. Rev. 95 (2011).

Many other ethical problems arise because in making the decision to settle or not, the lawyer may find that his or her own personal interests are at odds with those of the client. One example of this potential conflict stems from the fact that most successful, experienced plaintiffs' lawyers make a good portion of their livelihood from settling, not trying, cases. As younger lawyers, they established reputations as fierce and effective trial adversaries. Later, with their reputations accepted, defendants and insurance companies are more willing to settle with them at more acceptable figures. Of course, if what has just been described is accepted at least as a possibility, then it is equally possible that a younger, less well-established attorney may have a personal interest in taking a relatively higher percentage of cases to formal adjudication — how else is he or she to establish the reputation upon which to base the more profitable practice of settling almost all cases?

Another potential source of ethical problems is the contingent fee contract, an example of which is set out above. Under such a contract, the lawyer's compensation does not depend directly on how much effort has been expended to achieve a particular recovery, but rather on the phase the case is at when recovery is achieved. Thus, a lawyer may in a particular case be able to shift from one phase to another by, for example, filing suit or commencing trial, without a substantial increase in work. And with larger cases such a shift may result in a significant increase in compensation even if there is no increase in recovery. Pressures of a different sort operate with smaller cases. In such cases, the higher fee percentage applicable to a later phase will often not provide sufficient additional dollars to make the extra effort of moving to that phase worthwhile to the lawyer. The very human temptation exists, then, to accept many more cases than would otherwise be feasible and then to resolve every doubt in favor of settlement. The lawyer may thus come to have a vested interest in settling all but the most glaring examples of inadequate compensation. The torts practice pursued in this direction takes on the features of a volume wholesaler. Some of the stresses and strains resulting from the contingent fee system are discussed in Frederick B. MacKinnon, Contingent Fees for Legal Services: A Study of Professional Economics and Responsibilities (1964).

Some states have adopted rules relating to contingent fees which set limits on the amount of the fee without regard to the phase at which the case is disposed of. In New Jersey, for instance, contingent fees are controlled by the following rule:

> (c) In any matter where a client's claim for damages is based upon the alleged tortious conduct of another . . . , an attorney shall not contract for, charge, or collect a contingent fee in excess of the following limits:
>
> (1) 33⅓% on the first $750,000 recovered;
>
> (2) 30% on the next $750,000 recovered;
>
> (3) 25% on the next $750,000 recovered;
>
> (4) 20% on the next $750,000 recovered; and
>
> (5) on all amounts recovered in excess of the above by application for reasonable fee in accordance with the provisions of paragraph (f) hereof; and
>
> (6) where the amount recovered is for the benefit of a client who was a minor or mentally incapacitated when the contingent fee arrangement was made, the foregoing limits shall apply, except that the fee on any amount recovered by settlement . . . shall not exceed 25%. . . .
>
> (f) If at the conclusion of a matter an attorney considers the fee permitted by paragraph (c) to be inadequate, an application on written notice to the client may be made to the Assignment Judge . . . for the hearing and determining of a reasonable fee in light of all the circumstances.

Rule 1:21-7, New Jersey Court Rules Ann. The constitutionality of an earlier version of this rule was upheld in American Trial Lawyers Assn. v. New Jersey Supreme Court, 330 A.2d 350 (N.J. 1974). A few moments of reflection will suggest that this system generates its own set of professional stresses. Since the lawyer's percentage share of the recovery may decrease as the recovery increases, the extra effort needed to produce a higher recovery for the client may not be worth it from the lawyer's point of view. This fee system can also exacerbate the problem mentioned below that arises when a lawyer is handling more than one case with the same insurer. Because the lawyer will get a larger portion of the lower settlement, it will be possible for multicase settlements to be so structured as to increase the lawyer's fee while decreasing the overall recovery.

The lawyer's personal financial condition may also influence the decision whether or not to settle. Settling claims rather than trying them, or settling them earlier than they should be, may be the answer to a lawyer's immediate need for funds. This would be particularly true in urban areas, where delay before trial can be measured in years. Another situation in which the temptation is presented to place the client's interests in a secondary position arises when a lawyer who has several different clients with separate claims against the same defendant, or against the same insurance company, meets with the opposing party to settle the several claims together. It is obvious that such a practice puts the plaintiff's lawyer in the position of potentially divided loyalty with respect to the several clients. If the lawyer strikes what he or she believes to be a "hard bargain" with respect to claim number one, this may put the lawyer at a disadvantage when the negotiating parties immediately turn their attention to claim number two. One particularly bad practice is settlement in the aggregate, whereby a single figure for all the claims the lawyer has with the company is agreed upon, with the lawyer dividing this figure among the clients as he or she sees best.

It is difficult to determine how often lawyers engage in these practices. In one study of settlement practices, the author concluded that such conduct did not appear to be a major problem.[9] Part of the difficulty in judging the performance of lawyers in this respect is that it is almost impossible to determine if hidden, but improper, motives lead to unwise settlements. And apart from aggregate settlements, which, in the absence of informed consent by each client, are clear violations of the rules of ethics (Model Rules of Professional Conduct 1.8(g) (2016)), no objective standard is available by which most settlements can be characterized as good or bad. Each case tends to have enough unique aspects so that the range of acceptability is wide enough to make firm, critical judgments difficult. This is not to suggest that lawyers frequently engage in these practices; but the pressures do exist. As with so many problems of professional responsibility, the most effective control is the lawyer's awareness of these personal pressures and a willingness to put the client's interests first. See Terry Thomason, Are Attorneys Paid What They Are Worth? Contingent Fees and the Settlement Process, 20 J. Legal Stud. 187 (1991), in which the author, using economic analysis, answers in the negative the question posed by the title. See also Ted Schneyer, Legal-Process Constraints on the Regulation of Lawyers' Contingent Fee Contracts, 47 DePaul L. Rev. 371 (1998), in which the author argues that courts and disciplinary agencies cannot meaningfully regulate contingent fee amounts through occasional ex post facto reviews under a reasonableness standard because of the lack of an appropriate baseline standard.

Other problems of professional responsibility occur in the context of settlement negotiations, not because the interests of the lawyer and client conflict, but because of the lawyer's desire to do the best she can for the client. One particularly stressful situation, even for the

9. See H. Laurence Ross, Settled Out of Court: The Social Process of Insurance Claims Adjustment 83 (1980).

conscientious lawyer, arises in cases involving relatively serious injury. In such cases, clients may have an immediate need for funds to meet their living expenses. A prompt settlement may satisfy this need, but the amount obtained will probably be lower than could have been had if the client were financially able to wait out the negotiation process for a longer time. The lawyer's own interest may be on the side of postponing settlement in order to reach a higher figure, because under the contingent fee contract he receives more compensation from higher settlements. Under these circumstances, the temptation is great for the lawyer to advance living expenses to the hard-pressed client to remove the pressure for an early but unwise settlement. The rules of ethics prohibit this (see Model Rules of Professional Conduct 1.8(e) (2016)), but not all jurisdictions have followed the rule and academics have criticized it severely for its impacts on indigent clients and access to justice. See, e.g., Philip G. Schrag, The Unethical Ethics Rule: Nine Ways To Fix Model Rule Of Professional Conduct 1.8(E), 28 Geo. J. Legal Ethics 39 (2015); Louis S. Rulli, Roadblocks To Access To Justice: Reforming Ethical Rules To Meet The Special Needs Of Low-Income Clients, 17 U. Pa. J.L. & Soc. Change 347 (2014).

2. Wrongful Death

One of the peculiarities of the common law was the effect of the plaintiff's death upon the right to recover damages in a tort action. No cause of action existed for the death itself, and any cause of action to recover for physical injuries tortiously caused by the defendant's conduct abated — terminated — with the plaintiff's death. See Wex S. Malone, The Genesis of Wrongful Death, 17 Stan. L. Rev. 1043 (1965); T. A. Smedley, Wrongful Death — Bases of the Common Law Rules, 13 Vand. L. Rev. 605 (1960). Thus, if the plaintiff were killed outright by the defendant, no civil action would lie, and if the plaintiff died — even of old age — before obtaining a judgment against the defendant, any cause of action would die. Similarly, if the defendant were to die before judgment, the cause of action would abate.

This state of the law has been changed in England and in every state in the United States. Today, by statute, the death of the plaintiff before judgment has far less devastating effects upon existing or potential rights of recovery against the tortious defendant. Two basic types of statutes accomplish this result. In all jurisdictions, survival statutes prevent abatement of existing causes of action due to the death of either party, and in many jurisdictions, wrongful death statutes create causes of action that allow recovery when tortious conduct of the defendant causes someone's death. Many states have separate statutes of both types. In those jurisdictions which do not have a separate wrongful death statute, the courts have construed the general survival statute to create rights of recovery based upon tortiously caused deaths.

The measures of recovery under these two types of statute differ, reflecting the differences in the underlying statutory objectives. Under survival statutes, the basic measure of recovery is what the plaintiff's decedent would have been able to recover had he or she survived; under wrongful death statutes, the basic measure of recovery is the harm caused to the decedent's family by the defendant's conduct. There are two major approaches to measuring the plaintiff's recovery under wrongful death statutes. One type of wrongful death statute is patterned after the earliest English statute, Lord Campbell's Act, 1846, 9 & 10 Vict., ch. 93, and measures recovery by the loss (including, in many states, grief and mental anguish) suffered by the surviving family members and next of kin of the decedent. This is the most widely adopted measure of recovery for wrongful death in the United

States. The other type of statute, in effect in a minority of states, measures recovery by the pecuniary loss suffered by the decedent's estate.

Apart from the preceding broad generalizations, the wrongful death statutes vary considerably from state to state with respect to most of the important provisions. Therefore, the point of departure in any wrongful death case is the controlling statute. For an emotionally and analytically powerful treatment of the subject of wrongful death damages, see Andrew J. McClurg, Dead Sorrow: A Story About Loss and a New Theory of Wrongful Death Damages, 85 B.U. L. Rev. 1 (2005), in which the author grapples with the accidental death of his own fiancé and proposes a series of reforms to better acknowledge the intrinsic value of lost life and the grief it causes.

3. Injury to Personal Property

Compared to the rules involved in measuring damages for personal injury and death, the rules in cases of injury to personal property are simple and straightforward. The basic measure is the difference between the market value of the property before the injury and its market value after. If for practical purposes the item has been totally destroyed, the market value after the injury will be the salvage value, if any. Furthermore, in some jurisdictions a plaintiff's total recovery may be limited to an amount not exceeding the preaccident value of the property (see, e.g., Magnolia Petroleum Co. v. Harrell, 66 F. Supp. 559 (W.D. Okla. 1946). See generally 3 Dan B. Dobbs, Remedies 835-922 (2d ed. 1993).

For an interesting argument that damages should not be available for negligent injury to property, see Richard Abel, Should Tort Law Protect Property Against Accidental Loss?, 23 San Diego L. Rev. 79 (1986).

B. Punitive Damages

The torts process imposes punitive damages in order to punish especially opprobrious behavior. One prominent instrumental argument is that punitive damages are necessary in order to deter antisocial conduct that is unlikely to be detected by victims. When stealthy wrongdoers are apprehended, add-on damages beyond compensatories seem appropriate in order to make up for the times that similar wrongdoing escapes detection. See A. Mitchell Polinsky & Steven Shavell, Punitive Damages: An Economic Analysis, 111 Harv. L. Rev. 869 (1998) (laying out the basic argument for a punitive damages formula that explicitly incorporates a defendant's likelihood of escaping liability). Others contend that punitive damages are best understood as a form of private retribution whereby nongovernmental plaintiffs are empowered to impose punishment on their wrongdoers. See Anthony Sebok, Punitive Damages: From Myth to Theory, 92 Iowa L. Rev. 957 (2007); Benjamin C. Zipursky, A Theory of Punitive Damages, 84 Tex. L. Rev. 105 (2005). Still others have suggested that punitive damages may "fill the gap" between the compensatory damages meant to capture the harms that particularly egregious conduct inflicts upon individual plaintiffs, and the harms inflicted upon society at large. See Catherine M. Sharkey, The BP Oil Spill Settlements, Classwide Punitive Damages, and Societal Deterrence, 64 DePaul L. Rev. 681 (2014). Regardless of the underlying rationale, courts disagree regarding the types of conduct that should expose defendants to punitive damages and apply a range of legal standards such as a "conscious disregard for the consequences" (Ford Motor Co. v.

Stubblefeld, 319 S.E.2d 470 (Ga. 1984)); an "evil mind," which may entail evil acts, spiteful motive, or outrageous conduct creating a substantial risk of tremendous harm (Volz v. Coleman Co., Inc., 748 P.2d 1191 (Ariz. 1987)); and a "wanton disregard for safety" (Axen v. American Home Products Corp., 974 P.2d 224 (Or. Ct. App. 1999)). Judges in Maryland, at one time, typically gave juries the following instruction on punitive damages:

> Implied malice, which the plaintiffs have to prove in order to recover punitive damages in this case, requires a finding by you of a wanton disposition, grossly irresponsible to the rights of others, extreme recklessness and utter disregard for the rights of others. . . .

In Owens-Illinois, Inc. v. Zenobia, 601 A.2d 633 (Md. 1992), involving an award of punitive damages against an asbestos manufacturer for failure to warn of the dangerousness of its product, Maryland's high court amended the traditional instruction, supra, by requiring that actual, rather than merely implied, malice be proven. Actual malice refers to conduct characterized by evil motive or intent to injure or deceive. Id. at 650. Maryland's high court also required that the higher standard of actual malice be proven by clear and convincing evidence, rather than merely a preponderance of the evidence. A dissenting opinion in *Zenobia* argued that setting a higher threshold for punitive damages eligibility should be accomplished solely by changing the burden of proof and not by adjusting the standard from implied to actual malice. Id. at 662-63. The dissent argued that situations involving implied malice, i.e., examples of outrageously reckless conduct, may be as deserving of punishment as intentionally inflicted injuries under a totality-of-the-circumstances approach.

Of course, the risk of overdeterrence looms larger in connection with punitive than with compensatory damages. Sending a signal of sufficient strength to punish and deter egregiously antisocial behavior without discouraging risky but socially beneficial activities presents a considerable challenge. Heightened burdens of proof accompanied by stingier legal standards for awarding punitive damages reflect judicial concern that a more generous standard may result in debilitating financial costs to potentially undeserving defendants. However, the empirical evidence in support of this concern is mixed. See Theodore Eisenberg, Jeffrey J. Rachlinski & Martin T. Wells, Reconciling Experimental Incoherence with Real World Coherence in Punitive Damages, 54 Stan. L. Rev. 1239 (2002) (reviewing available empirical evidence on punitive damages awards and concluding that "researchers have not identified either a crazy pattern of awards or a substantial series of actual punitive damage awards that constitute a shocking pattern of incoherence or unfairness"). See also Theodore Eisenberg et al., Juries, Judges, and Punitive Damages: Empirical Analysis Using the Civil Justice Survey of State Courts 1992, 1996, and 2001 Data, 3 J. Empirical Legal Stud. 263 (2006).

One issue that arises frequently in connection with punitive damages is the possibility that multiple punitive awards will be granted sequentially, to different plaintiffs, based on the same conduct that happens to cause harm to a number of victims. This may result, in the aggregate, in unfair and inefficiently excessive punishment. The possibility of multiple punishments will be considered below in connection with the unconstitutionality of allegedly excessive punitive damages awards. One scholar has suggested that a national registry of punitive awards be established, by which previous awards for the same conduct would be taken into account in setting appropriate punitive damages awards in the future. See Jim Gash, Solving the Multiple Punishments Problem: A Call for a National Punitive Damages Registry, 99 Nw. Univ. L. Rev. 1613 (2004-05).

Considerable state legislation aims at controlling the amount of punitive damage awards, evidencing a mistrust in the ability or willingness of courts to control jury discretion in this respect. A fairly common method is the establishing of a maximum that can be awarded. See, e.g., Code of Va. §§8.01-38.1 (total punitive damages cannot exceed $350,000 in "any action"); Tex. Civ. Prac. & Rem. Code §41.008 (punitive award cannot exceed the greater of (1) twice the amount of economic damages, plus noneconomic damages (capped at $750,000), and (2) $200,000).

The constitutionality of punitive damages has been the subject of considerable litigation. In Browning-Ferris Indus. of Vt., Inc. v. Kelko Disposal, Inc., 492 U.S. 257 (1989), the Supreme Court ruled that the "excessive fines" clause in the Eighth Amendment to the United States Constitution does not bar punitive damages. In Pacific Mutual Ins. Co. v. Haslip, 499 U.S. 1 (1991), the Court considered, and rejected, a due process attack on the punitive damages regime of Alabama. In upholding the Alabama law, the Court said (499 U.S. at 18):

> One must concede that unlimited jury discretion — or unlimited judicial discretion for that matter — in the fixing of punitive damages may invite extreme results that jar one's constitutional sensibilities. We need not, and indeed we cannot, draw a mathematical bright line between the constitutionally acceptable and the constitutionally unacceptable that would fit every case. We can say, however, that general concerns of reasonableness and adequate guidance from the court when the case is tried to a jury properly enter into the constitutional calculus. With these concerns in mind, we review the constitutionality of the punitive damages awarded in this case. . . .
>
> [B]efore its ruling in the present case, the Supreme Court of Alabama had elaborated and refined the . . . criteria for determining whether a punitive award is reasonably related to the goals of deterrence and retribution. It was announced that the following could be taken into consideration in determining whether the award was excessive or inadequate: (a) whether there is a reasonable relationship between the punitive damages award and the harm likely to result from the defendant's conduct as well as the harm that actually has occurred; (b) the degree of reprehensibility of the defendant's conduct, the duration of that conduct, the defendant's awareness, any concealment, and the existence and frequency of similar past conduct; (c) the profitability to the defendant of the wrongful conduct and the desirability of removing that profit and of having the defendant also sustain a loss; (d) the "financial position" of the defendant; (e) all the costs of litigation; (f) the imposition of criminal sanctions on the defendant for its conduct, these to be taken in mitigation; and (g) the existence of other civil awards against the defendant for the same conduct, these also to be taken in mitigation.
>
> The application of these standards, we conclude, imposes a sufficiently definite and meaningful constraint on the discretion of Alabama fact finders in awarding punitive damages. The Alabama Supreme Court's post-verdict review ensures that punitive damages awards are not grossly out of proportion to the severity of the offense and have some understandable relationship to compensatory damages. While punitive damages in Alabama may embrace such factors as the heinousness of the civil wrong, its effect upon the victim, the likelihood of its recurrence, and the extent of defendant's wrongful gain, the fact finder must be guided by more than the defendant's net worth. Alabama plaintiffs do not enjoy a windfall because they have the good fortune to have a defendant with a deep pocket.

Although the Alabama punitive damages law withstood United States Supreme Court scrutiny in *Haslip,* it was found wanting in BMW of N. Am., Inc. v. Gore, 517 U.S. 559 (1996). The Alabama Supreme Court had approved a $2 million punitive damage award to the plaintiff (the court reduced a jury award of $4 million to $2 million), although the actual damage to the plaintiff was $4,000. In holding that this award was unconstitutional, the U.S. Supreme Court said (517 U.S. at 574-75):

> Elementary notions of fairness enshrined in our constitutional jurisprudence dictate that a person receive fair notice not only of the conduct that will subject him to punishment but also of the severity of the penalty that a State may impose. Three guideposts, each of which indicates that BMW did not receive adequate notice of the magnitude of the sanction that Alabama might impose . . . lead us to the conclusion that the $2 million award against BMW is grossly excessive: the degree of reprehensibility of the [defendant's conduct]; the disparity between the harm or potential harm suffered by [the plaintiff] and his punitive damages award; and the difference between this remedy and the civil penalties authorized or imposed in comparable cases.

On remand, the Supreme Court of Alabama ordered a remittitur of the award to $50,000. BMW of N. Am., Inc. v. Gore, 701 So. 2d 507 (Ala. 1997).

State Farm Mutual Automobile Insurance Co. v. Campbell

123 S. Ct. 1513 (2003)

JUSTICE KENNEDY delivered the opinion of the Court.

We address once again the measure of punishment, by means of punitive damages, a State may impose upon a defendant in a civil case. The question is whether, in the circumstances we shall recount, an award of $145 million in punitive damages, where full compensatory damages are $1 million, is excessive and in violation of the Due Process Clause of the Fourteenth Amendment to the Constitution of the United States.

I

In 1981, Curtis Campbell (Campbell) was driving with his wife, Inez Preece Campbell, in Cache County, Utah. He decided to pass six vans traveling ahead of them on a two-lane highway. Todd Ospital was driving a small car approaching from the opposite direction. To avoid a head-on collision with Campbell, who by then was driving on the wrong side of the highway and toward oncoming traffic, Ospital swerved onto the shoulder, lost control of his automobile, and collided with a vehicle driven by Robert G. Slusher. Ospital was killed, and Slusher was rendered permanently disabled. The Campbells escaped unscathed. . . .

In the ensuing wrongful death and tort action, Campbell insisted he was not at fault. Early investigations did support differing conclusions as to who caused the accident, but "consensus was reached early on by the investigators and witnesses that Mr. Campbell's unsafe pass had indeed caused the crash." . . . Campbell's insurance company, petitioner State Farm Mutual Automobile Insurance Company (State Farm), nonetheless decided to contest liability and declined offers by Slusher and Ospital's estate (Ospital) to settle the claims for the policy limit of $50,000 ($25,000 per claimant). State Farm also ignored the advice of one of its own investigators and took the case to trial, assuring the Campbells that "their assets were safe, that they had no liability for the accident, that [State Farm] would represent their interests, and that they did not need to procure separate counsel." . . . To the contrary, a jury determined that Campbell was 100 percent at fault, and a judgment was returned for $185,849, far more than the amount offered in settlement.

At first State Farm refused to cover the $135,849 in excess liability. Its counsel made this clear to the Campbells: "'You may want to put for sale signs on your property to get things moving.'" . . . Nor was State Farm willing to post a supersedeas bond to allow Campbell to appeal the judgment against him. Campbell obtained his own counsel to appeal the verdict. During the pendency of the appeal, in late 1984, Slusher, Ospital, and the Campbells reached an agreement whereby Slusher and Ospital agreed not to seek satisfaction of their claims against the Campbells. In exchange the Campbells agreed to pursue a bad faith action against State Farm and to be represented by Slusher's and Ospital's attorneys. The Campbells also agreed that Slusher and Ospital would have a right to play a part in all major decisions concerning the bad faith action. No settlement could be concluded without Slusher's and Ospital's approval, and Slusher and Ospital would receive 90 percent of any verdict against State Farm.

In 1989, the Utah Supreme Court denied Campbell's appeal in the wrongful death and tort actions. . . . State Farm then paid the entire judgment, including the amounts in excess of the policy limits. The Campbells nonetheless filed a complaint against State Farm alleging bad faith, fraud, and intentional infliction of emotional distress. The trial court initially granted State Farm's motion for summary judgment because State Farm had paid the excess verdict, but that ruling was reversed on appeal. . . . On remand State Farm moved *in limine* to exclude evidence of alleged conduct that occurred in unrelated cases outside of Utah, but the trial court denied the motion. At State Farm's request the trial court bifurcated the trial into two phases conducted before different juries. In the first phase the jury determined that State Farm's decision not to settle was unreasonable because there was a substantial likelihood of an excess verdict.

Before the second phase of the action against State Farm we decided *BMW of North America, Inc. v. Gore,* 517 U.S. 559, L. Ed. 2d 809 (1996), and refused to sustain a $2 million punitive damages award which accompanied a verdict of only $4,000 in compensatory damages. Based on that decision, State Farm again moved for the exclusion of evidence of dissimilar out-of-state conduct. . . . The trial court denied State Farm's motion. . . .

The second phase addressed State Farm's liability for fraud and intentional infliction of emotional distress, as well as compensatory and punitive damages. The Utah Supreme Court aptly characterized this phase of the trial:

> State Farm argued during phase II that its decision to take the case to trial was an "honest mistake" that did not warrant punitive damages. In contrast, the Campbells introduced evidence that State Farm's decision to take the case to trial was a result of a national scheme to meet corporate fiscal goals by capping payouts on claims company wide. This scheme was referred to as State Farm's "Performance, Planning and Review," or PP&R, policy. To prove the existence of this scheme, the trial court allowed the Campbells to introduce extensive expert testimony regarding fraudulent practices by State Farm in its nation-wide operations. Although State Farm moved prior to phase II of the trial for the exclusion of such evidence and continued to object to it at trial, the trial court ruled that such evidence was admissible to determine whether State Farm's conduct in the Campbell case was indeed intentional and sufficiently egregious to warrant punitive damages. . . .

Evidence pertaining to the PP&R policy concerned State Farm's business practices for over 20 years in numerous States. Most of these practices bore no relation to third-party automobile insurance claims, the type of claim underlying the Campbells' complaint against the company. The jury awarded the Campbells $2.6 million in compensatory damages and $145 million in punitive damages, which the trial court reduced to $1 million and $25 million respectively. Both parties appealed.

The Utah Supreme Court sought to apply the three guideposts we identified in *Gore, supra,* . . . and it reinstated the $145 million punitive damages award. Relying in large part on the extensive evidence concerning the PP&R policy, the court concluded State Farm's conduct was reprehensible. The court also relied upon State Farm's "massive wealth" and on testimony indicating that "State Farm's actions, because of their clandestine nature, will be punished at most in one out of every 50,000 cases as a matter of statistical probability," . . . and concluded that the ratio between punitive and compensatory damages was not unwarranted. Finally, the court noted that the punitive damages award was not excessive when compared to various civil and criminal penalties State Farm could have faced, including $10,000 for each act of fraud, the suspension of its license to conduct business in Utah, the disgorgement of profits, and imprisonment. . . . We granted certiorari. . . .

II

We recognized in *Cooper Industries, Inc. v. Leatherman Tool Group, Inc.,* 532 U.S. 424, . . . that in our judicial system compensatory and punitive damages, although usually awarded at the same time by the same decisionmaker, serve different purposes. . . . Compensatory damages "are intended to redress the concrete loss that the plaintiff has suffered by reason of the defendant's wrongful conduct." . . . (citing Restatement (Second) of Torts §903, pp. 453-454 (1979)). By contrast, punitive damages serve a broader function; they are aimed at deterrence and retribution. *Cooper Industries, supra.* . . .

While States possess discretion over the imposition of punitive damages, it is well established that there are procedural and substantive constitutional limitations on these awards. . . . The reason is that "elementary notions of fairness enshrined in our constitutional jurisprudence dictate that a person receive fair notice not only of the conduct that will subject him to punishment, but also of the severity of the penalty that a State may impose." . . . To the extent an award is grossly excessive, it furthers no legitimate purpose and constitutes an arbitrary deprivation of property. . . .

Although these awards serve the same purposes as criminal penalties, defendants subjected to punitive damages in civil cases have not been accorded the protections applicable in a criminal proceeding. This increases our concerns over the imprecise manner in which punitive damages systems are administered. We have admonished that "punitive damages pose an acute danger of arbitrary deprivation of property. Jury instructions typically leave the jury with wide discretion in choosing amounts, and the presentation of evidence of a defendant's net worth creates the potential that juries will use their verdicts to express biases against big businesses, particularly those without strong local presences." . . .

In light of these concerns, in *Gore supra,* . . . we instructed courts reviewing punitive damages to consider three guideposts: (1) the degree of reprehensibility of the defendant's misconduct; (2) the disparity between the actual or potential harm suffered by the plaintiff and the punitive damages award; and (3) the difference between the punitive damages awarded by the jury and the civil penalties authorized or imposed in comparable cases. . . . We reiterated the importance of these three guideposts in *Cooper Industries* and mandated appellate courts to conduct *de novo* review of a trial court's application of them to the jury's award. . . . Exacting appellate review ensures that an award of punitive damages is based upon an "'application of law, rather than a decisionmaker's caprice.'" . . .

III

Under the principles outlined in *BMW of North America, Inc. v. Gore*, this case is neither close nor difficult. It was error to reinstate the jury's $145 million punitive damages award. We address each guidepost of *Gore* in some detail.

A

"The most important indicium of the reasonableness of a punitive damages award is the degree of reprehensibility of the defendant's conduct." . . . We have instructed courts to determine the reprehensibility of a defendant by considering whether: the harm caused was physical as opposed to economic; the tortious conduct evinced an indifference to or a reckless disregard of the health or safety of others; the target of the conduct had financial vulnerability; the conduct involved repeated actions or was an isolated incident; and the harm was the result of intentional malice, trickery, or deceit, or mere accident. . . . The existence of any one of these factors weighing in favor of a plaintiff may not be sufficient to sustain a punitive damages award; and the absence of all of them renders any award suspect. It should be presumed a plaintiff has been made whole for his injuries by compensatory damages, so punitive damages should only be awarded if the defendant's culpability, after having paid compensatory damages, is so reprehensible as to warrant the imposition of further sanctions to achieve punishment or deterrence. . . .

Applying these factors in the instant case, we must acknowledge that State Farm's handling of the claims against the Campbells merits no praise. The trial court found that State Farm's employees altered the company's records to make Campbell appear less culpable. State Farm disregarded the overwhelming likelihood of liability and the near-certain probability that, by taking the case to trial, a judgment in excess of the policy limits would be awarded. State Farm amplified the harm by at first assuring the Campbells their assets would be safe from any verdict and by later telling them, postjudgment, to put a for-sale sign on their house. While we do not suggest there was error in awarding punitive damages based upon State Farm's conduct toward the Campbells, a more modest punishment for this reprehensible conduct could have satisfied the State's legitimate objectives, and the Utah courts should have gone no further.

This case, instead, was used as a platform to expose, and punish, the perceived deficiencies of State Farm's operations throughout the country. The Utah Supreme Court's opinion makes explicit that State Farm was being condemned for its nationwide policies rather than for the conduct directed toward the Campbells. 65 P.3d at 1143 ("The Campbells introduced evidence that State Farm's decision to take the case to trial was a result of a national scheme to meet corporate fiscal goals by capping payouts on claims company wide."). This was, as well, an explicit rationale of the trial court's decision in approving the award, though reduced from $145 million to $25 million. . . . ("[T]he

Campbells demonstrated, through the testimony of State Farm employees who had worked outside of Utah, and through expert testimony, that this pattern of claims adjustment under the PP&R program was not a local anomaly, but was a consistent, nationwide feature of State Farm's business operations, orchestrated from the highest levels of corporate management.").

The Campbells contend that State Farm has only itself to blame for the reliance upon dissimilar and out-of-state conduct evidence. The record does not support this contention. From their opening statements onward the Campbells framed this case as a chance to rebuke State Farm for its nationwide activities. . . . ("You're going to hear evidence that even the insurance commission in Utah and around the country are unwilling or inept at protecting people against abuses."); . . . ("[T]his is a very important case. . . . It transcends the Campbell file. It involves a nationwide practice. And you, here, are going to be evaluating and assessing, and hopefully requiring State Farm to stand accountable for what it's doing across the country, which is the purpose of punitive damages."). This was a position maintained throughout the litigation. In opposing State Farm's motion to exclude such evidence under *Gore*, the Campbells' counsel convinced the trial court that there was no limitation on the scope of evidence that could be considered under our precedents. . . .

A State cannot punish a defendant for conduct that may have been lawful where it occurred. . . . Nor, as a general rule, does a State have a legitimate concern in imposing punitive damages to punish a defendant for unlawful acts committed outside of the State's jurisdiction. Any proper adjudication of conduct that occurred outside Utah to other persons would require their inclusion, and, to those parties, the Utah courts, in the usual case, would need to apply the laws of their relevant jurisdiction. *Phillips Petroleum Co. v. Shutts,* 472 U.S. 797. . . .

Here, the Campbells do not dispute that much of the out-of-state conduct was lawful where it occurred. They argue, however, that such evidence was not the primary basis for the punitive damages award and was relevant to the extent it demonstrated, in a general sense, State Farm's motive against its insured. Brief for Respondents 46-47 ("Even if the practices described by State Farm were not malum in se or malum prohibitum, they became relevant to punitive damages to the extent they were used as tools to implement State Farm's wrongful PP&R policy."). This argument misses the mark. Lawful out-of-state conduct may be probative when it demonstrates the deliberateness and culpability of the defendant's action in the State where it is tortious, but that conduct must have a nexus to the specific harm suffered by the plaintiff. A jury must be instructed, furthermore, that it may not use evidence of out-of-state conduct to punish a defendant for action that was lawful in the jurisdiction where it occurred. . . .

For a more fundamental reason, however, the Utah courts erred in relying upon this and other evidence: The courts awarded punitive damages to punish and deter conduct that bore no relation to the Campbells' harm. A defendant's dissimilar acts, independent from the acts upon which liability was premised, may not serve as the basis for punitive damages. A defendant should be punished for the conduct that harmed the plaintiff, not for being an unsavory individual or business. Due process does not permit courts, in the calculation of punitive damages, to adjudicate the merits of other parties' hypothetical claims against a defendant under the guise of the reprehensibility analysis, but we have no doubt the Utah Supreme Court did that here. . . . Punishment on these bases creates the possibility of multiple punitive damages awards for the same conduct; for in the usual case nonparties are not bound by the judgment some other plaintiff obtains. . . .

The Campbells have identified scant evidence of repeated misconduct of the sort that injured them. Nor does our review of the Utah courts' decisions convince us that State Farm was only punished for its actions toward the Campbells. Although evidence of other acts need not be identical to have relevance in the calculation of punitive damages, the Utah court erred here because evidence pertaining to claims that had nothing to do with a third-party lawsuit was introduced at length. Other evidence concerning reprehensibility was even more tangential. For example, the Utah Supreme Court criticized State Farm's investigation into the personal life of one of its employees and, in a broader approach, the manner in which State Farm's policies corrupted its employees. . . . The Campbells attempt to justify the courts' reliance upon this unrelated testimony on the theory that each dollar of profit made by underpaying a third-party claimant is the same as a dollar made by underpaying a first-party one. . . . For the reasons already stated, this argument is unconvincing. The reprehensibility guidepost does not permit courts to expand the scope of the case so that a defendant may be punished for any malfeasance, which in this case extended for a 20-year period. In this case, because the Campbells have shown no conduct by State Farm similar to that which harmed them, the conduct that harmed them is the only conduct relevant to the reprehensibility analysis.

B

Turning to the second *Gore* guidepost, we have been reluctant to identify concrete constitutional limits on the ratio between harm, or potential harm, to the plaintiff and the punitive damages award. *Gore, supra*, at 582, 116 S. Ct. 1589 ("[W]e have consistently rejected the notion that the constitutional line is marked by a simple mathematical formula, even one that compares actual *and potential* damages to the punitive award."); . . . We decline again to impose a bright-line ratio which a punitive damages award cannot exceed. Our jurisprudence and the principles it has now established demonstrate, however, that, in practice, few awards exceeding a single-digit ratio between punitive and compensatory damages, to a significant degree, will satisfy due process. In *Haslip*, in upholding a punitive damages award, we concluded that an award of more than four times the amount of compensatory damages might be close to the line of constitutional impropriety. 499 U.S., at 23-24. . . . We cited that 4-to-1 ratio again in *Gore*. 517 U.S., at 581. . . . The Court further referenced a long legislative history, dating back over 700 years and going forward to today, providing for sanctions of double, treble, or quadruple damages to deter and punish. . . . While these ratios are not binding, they are instructive. They demonstrate what should be obvious: Single-digit multipliers are more likely to comport with due process, while still achieving the State's goals of deterrence and retribution, than awards with ratios in range of 500 to 1, . . . or, in this case, of 145 to 1.

Nonetheless, because there are no rigid benchmarks that a punitive damages award may not surpass, ratios greater than those we have previously upheld may comport with due process where "a particularly egregious act has resulted in only a small amount of economic damages." . . . The converse is also true, however. When compensatory damages are substantial, then a lesser ratio, perhaps only equal to compensatory damages, can reach the outermost limit of the due process guarantee. The precise award in any case, of course, must be based upon the facts and circumstances of the defendant's conduct and the harm to the plaintiff.

In sum, courts must ensure that the measure of punishment is both reasonable and proportionate to the amount of harm to the plaintiff and to the general damages recovered. In the context of this case, we have no doubt that there is a presumption against an award that has a 145-to-1 ratio. The compensatory award in this case was substantial; the

Campbells were awarded $1 million for a year and a half of emotional distress. This was complete compensation. The harm arose from a transaction in the economic realm, not from some physical assault or trauma; there were no physical injuries; and State Farm paid the excess verdict before the complaint was filed, so the Campbells suffered only minor economic injuries for the 18-month period in which State Farm refused to resolve the claim against them. The compensatory damages for the injury suffered here, moreover, likely were based on a component which was duplicated in the punitive award. Much of the distress was caused by the outrage and humiliation the Campbells suffered at the actions of their insurer; and it is a major role of punitive damages to condemn such conduct. Compensatory damages, however, already contain this punitive element. . . .

The Utah Supreme Court sought to justify the massive award by pointing to State Farm's purported failure to report a prior $100 million punitive damages award in Texas to its corporate headquarters; the fact that State Farm's policies have affected numerous Utah consumers; the fact that State Farm will only be punished in one out of every 50,000 cases as a matter of statistical probability; and State Farm's enormous wealth. . . . Since the Supreme Court of Utah discussed the Texas award when applying the ratio guidepost, we discuss it here. The Texas award, however, should have been analyzed in the context of the reprehensibility guidepost only. The failure of the company to report the Texas award is out-of-state conduct that, if the conduct were similar, might have had some bearing on the degree of reprehensibility, subject to the limitations we have described. Here, it was dissimilar, and of such marginal relevance that it should have been accorded little or no weight. The award was rendered in a first-party lawsuit; no judgment was entered in the case; and it was later settled for a fraction of the verdict. With respect to the Utah Supreme Court's second justification, the Campbells' inability to direct us to testimony demonstrating harm to the people of Utah (other than those directly involved in this case) indicates that the adverse effect on the State's general population was in fact minor.

The remaining premises for the Utah Supreme Court's decision bear no relation to the award's reasonableness or proportionality to the harm. They are, rather, arguments that seek to defend a departure from well-established constraints on punitive damages. While States enjoy considerable discretion in deducing when punitive damages are warranted, each award must comport with the principles set forth in *Gore*. Here the argument that State Farm will be punished in only the rare case, coupled with reference to its assets (which, of course, are what other insured parties in Utah and other States must rely upon for payment of claims) had little to do with the actual harm sustained by the Campbells. The wealth of a defendant cannot justify an otherwise unconstitutional punitive damages award. . . . ("[Wealth] provides an open-ended basis for inflating awards when the defendant is wealthy. . . . That does not make its use unlawful or inappropriate; it simply means that this factor cannot make up for the failure of other factors, such as 'reprehensibility,' to constrain significantly an award that purports to punish a defendant's conduct"). The principles set forth in *Gore* must be implemented with care, to ensure both reasonableness and proportionality.

C

The third guidepost in *Gore* is the disparity between the punitive damages award and the "civil penalties authorized or imposed in comparable cases." . . . We note that, in the past, we have also looked to criminal penalties that could be imposed. . . . The existence of a criminal penalty does have bearing on the seriousness with which a State views the wrongful action. When used to determine the dollar amount of the award, however, the criminal penalty has less utility. Great care must be taken to avoid use of the civil process to assess criminal penalties that can be imposed only after the heightened protections of a criminal trial have been observed, including, of course, its higher standards of proof. Punitive damages are not a substitute for the criminal process, and the remote possibility of a criminal sanction does not automatically sustain a punitive damages award.

Here, we need not dwell long on this guidepost. The most relevant civil sanction under Utah state law for the wrong done to the Campbells appears to be a $10,000 fine for an act of fraud . . . an amount dwarfed by the $145 million punitive damages award. The Supreme Court of Utah speculated about the loss of State Farm's business license, the disgorgement of profits, and possible imprisonment, but here again its references were to the broad fraudulent scheme drawn from evidence of out-of-state and dissimilar conduct. This analysis was insufficient to justify the award.

IV

An application of the *Gore* guideposts to the facts of this case, especially in light of the substantial compensatory damages awarded (a portion of which contained a punitive element), likely would justify a punitive damages award at or near the amount of compensatory damages. The punitive award of $145 million, therefore, was neither reasonable nor proportionate to the wrong committed, and it was an irrational and arbitrary deprivation of the property of the defendant. The proper calculation of punitive damages under the principles we have discussed should be resolved, in the first instance, by the Utah courts.

The judgment of the Utah Supreme Court is reversed, and the case is remanded for proceedings not inconsistent with this opinion.

It is so ordered.

[The dissenting opinions by Justices Scalia and Thomas are omitted.]

[Justice Ginsburg (dissenting) reviews the evidence of State Farm's conduct and finds it to be outrageous.]

The Court dismisses the evidence describing and documenting State Farm's PP&R policy and practices as essentially irrelevant, bearing "no relation to the Campbells' harm." . . . It is hardly apparent why that should be so. What is infirm about the Campbells' theory that their experience with State Farm exemplifies and reflects an overarching underpayment scheme, one that caused "repeated misconduct of the sort that injured them," . . . ? The Court's silence on that score is revealing: Once one recognizes that the Campbells did show "conduct by State Farm similar to that which harmed them," . . . it becomes impossible to shrink the reprehensibility analysis to this sole case, or to maintain, at odds with the determination of the trial court . . . that "the adverse effect on the State's general population was in fact minor," *ante*, at 1525.

Evidence of out-of-state conduct, the Court acknowledges, may be "probative [even if the conduct is lawful in the state where it occurred] when it demonstrates the deliberateness and culpability of the defendant's action in the State where it is tortious. . . ." "Other acts" evidence concerning practices both in and out of State was introduced in this case to show just such "deliberateness" and "culpability." The evidence was admissible, the trial court ruled: (1) to document State Farm's "reprehensible" PP&R program; and (2) to "rebut [State Farm's] assertion that [its] actions toward the Campbellswere inadvertent errors or mistakes in judgment." . . . Viewed in this light, there surely was "a nexus" . . . between much of the "other acts" evidence and "the specific harm suffered by [the Campbells]." . . .

When the Court first ventured to override state-court punitive damages awards, it did so moderately. The Court recalled that "in our federal system, States necessarily have considerable flexibility in determining the level of punitive damages that they will allow in different classes of cases and in any particular case." *Gore,* 517 U.S., at 568. . . . Today's decision exhibits no such respect and restraint. No longer content to accord state-court judgments "a strong presumption of validity," . . . the Court announces that "few awards exceeding a single-digit ratio between punitive and compensatory damages, to a significant degree, will satisfy due process." . . . Moreover, the Court adds, when compensatory damages are substantial, doubling those damages "can reach the outermost limit of the due process guarantee." . . . In a legislative scheme or a state high court's design to cap punitive damages, the handiwork in setting single-digit and 1-to-1 benchmarks could hardly be questioned; in a judicial decree imposed on the States by this Court under the banner of substantive due process, the numerical controls today's decision installs seem to me boldly out of order. . . .

I remain of the view that this Court has no warrant to reform state law governing awards of punitive damages. . . . Even if I were prepared to accept the flexible guides prescribed in *Gore*, I would not join the Court's swift conversion of those guides into instructions that begin to resemble marching orders. For the reasons stated, I would leave the judgment of the Utah Supreme Court undisturbed. . . .

In Williams v. Philip Morris, Inc., 127 P.3d 1165 (Or. 2006), the Oregon high court reviewed a punitive damages award of $79.5 million that had been assessed against the defendant tobacco manufacturer in light of its decades-long fraudulent publicity campaign. Despite the fact that compensatory damages in the case were set at $500,000 and despite an earlier order from the United States Supreme Court to reconsider the punitives award in light of the *State Farm* decision, the Oregon high court affirmed the award given the defendant's "carefully calculated program spanning decades," one that involved "trickery and deceit" and one that, in a criminal context, would constitute second-degree manslaughter. 127 P.3d 1165, 1177-78. Subsequently, the United States Supreme Court again vacated the Oregon court's judgment, reasoning that the award might have unconstitutionally punished the defendant for behavior that harmed nonparties, "i.e., injury that it inflicts upon those who are, essentially, strangers to the litigation." Philip Morris USA v. Williams, 549 U.S. 346, 353 (2007). Following yet another remand, the Oregon Supreme Court determined that its prior decision could be affirmed on independent state procedural grounds, effectively ending the proceedings without addressing the constitutional question. Williams v. Philip Morris Inc., 344 Or. 45, 176 P.3d 1255 (Or. 2008). For discussion of the litigation, see Catherine M. Sharkey, Federal Incursions and State Defiance: Punitive Damages in the Wake of Philip Morris v. Williams, 46 Willamette L. Rev. 449 (2010); and Anthony Sebok, After Philip Morris v. Williams: What Is Left of the "Single-Digit" Ratio?, 2 Charleston L. Rev. 287 (2008).

As the Philip Morris v. Williams odyssey makes clear, state and lower federal courts have struggled with the implications of the *State Farm* decision. One recurring issue involves suits challenging environmental harm and other difficult-to-monetize injuries. Although the Supreme Court in *State Farm* indicated that such contexts "may" justify departure from the single-digit ratio limit, lower courts have yet to work out when and how such departures should proceed. See Alexandra B. Klass, Punitive Damages and Valuing Harm, 92 Minn. L. Rev. 83 (2007). *State Farm* also implies that "a few" double-digit (or higher) awards involving reprehensible defendant conduct in the context of low compensatory damages might be constitutional.

In Simon v. San Paolo Holding Co., 113 P.3d 63 (Cal. 2005), a case involving intentionally fraudulent promises in negotiations for the sale of property, the court set a maximum punitive award that exceeded a single-digit multiplier, but only just barely: The court set the maximum punitive award at $50,000, or ten times the compensatory award. Id. at 81. In Seltzer v. Morton, 154 P.3d 561 (Mont. 2007), the court determined that the low level of compensatory damages awarded in the case, combined with the egregiousness of the defendant's behavior, justified looking to other factors, including the defendant's net worth. Rather than evaluate whether exceeding a single-digit ratio is appropriate in a given case, courts also may focus on the relevant compensatory award that forms the basis of comparison. For instance, in Action Marine, Inc. v. Cont'l Carbon Inc., 481 F.3d 1302 (11th Cir. 2007), the court held that under applicable state law, an attorney fee award to prevailing plaintiffs is compensatory in nature, and thus can be included as part of the actual damages award to justify a higher level of punitive damages. For its own part, the United States Supreme Court continues to indicate a preference for very low ratios. In Exxon Shipping Co. v. Baker, 554 U.S. 471 (2008), the Court ruled that under federal maritime law, punitive damages are limited to a 1:1 ratio with compensatory damages. Although not a constitutional holding, the case may signal where the Court would move should it again take up the issue of due process constraints on punitive damages.

For scholarly reactions to the punitive damages controversy focusing on manageability, see Sara D. Guardino & Richard A. Daynard, Punishing Tobacco Industry Misconduct: The Case for Exceeding a Single Digit Ratio Between Punitive and Compensatory Damages, 67 U. Pitt. L. Rev. 1 (2005) (concluding that a powerful financial sanction is needed to deter lethal misbehavior when the defendant makes billions of dollars addicting consumers to its deadly product); Andrew C.W. Lund, The Road from Nowhere? Punitive Damages Ratios After *BMW v. Gore* and *State Farm Mutual Automobile Insurance Co. v. Campbell*, 20 Touro L. Rev. 943 (2005) (concluding that the Supreme Court's shift of emphasis to ratio guideposts was necessary in order to communicate with lower courts); and Michael P. Allen, The Supreme Court, Punitive Damages and State Sovereignty, 13 Geo. Mason L. Rev. 1 (2004) (arguing against mathematical formulas to reduce punitive damages and recommending an emphasis on competent jury instructions). For contributions from a law and economics vantage point, see Steve P. Calandrillo, Penalizing Punitive Damages: Why the Supreme Court Needs a Lesson in Law and Economics, 78 Geo. Wash. L. Rev. 774 (2010) (arguing that "the Supreme Court's arbitrary due process litmus test of ten times compensatory damages as a ceiling on punitive damages makes zero sense from an economic analysis point of view"), and W. Kip Viscusi, The Challenge of Punitive Damages Mathematics, 30 J. Legal Stud. 315 (2001) (arguing that the economic framework would not work in practice, despite its theoretical appeal).

For empirical research on punitive damages, see Neil Vidmar & Mirya Holman, The Frequency, Predictability, and Proportionality of Jury Awards of Punitive Damages in State Courts in 2005: A New Audit, 43 Suffolk U. L. Rev. 855 (2010) (reviewing extensive new empirical evidence regarding the practice of punitive damages awards); Theodore Eisenberg & Martin T. Wells, The Significant Association Between Punitive and Compensatory Damages in Blockbuster Cases: A Methodological Primer, 3 J. Empirical Legal Stud. 175 (2006) (noting the strong, statistically significant relationship between compensatory and punitive awards); Theodore Eisenberg, Neil LaFountain, Brian Ostrom, David Rottman & Martin T. Wells, Juries, Judges, and Punitive Damages: An Empirical Study, 87 Cornell L. Rev. 743 (2002) (concluding that compensatory damages are the most powerful predictor of punitive awards and that damage awards generally do not meaningfully differ between bench and jury trials).

Chapter 9

The Role of Insurance in the Torts Process

From an instrumental perspective, tort law may be seen to serve two primary functions: deterrence, whereby threats of liability pressure potential injurers to invest optimally in care; and loss distribution, whereby victims' losses are spread through various forms of injurers' insurance. In the middle portion of the last century, American tort theorists relied on loss distribution rationales to argue in support of expanding theories of strict liability, holding commercial actors increasingly liable for the harms their activities caused. The theory was that such actors would spread victims' losses, or the costs of insurance covering injurers' liability for those losses, in their price structures. In the last decades of the twentieth century, torts scholars largely gave up on the loss distribution rationale and emphasized deterrence as the primary instrumental objective of tort.[1] Systems of social insurance other than tort had expanded rapidly in the second half of the century, performing the loss distribution function more efficiently, at lower transaction costs, than the tort system.[2] The apparent administrative advantages of non-tort systems of compensation appeared to be so strong that scholars began arguing for wholesale abandonment of tort law, as discussed in Chapter 10. Yet the fact remains that the tort system does compensate many accident victims, totaling upwards of a hundred billion dollars a year in compensation benefits, thus continuing to serve a significant loss distribution function. And the billions of dollars in compensation payments each year by liability insurance providers occur against the backdrop of the tort system and its principles of civil responsibility. Thus, relating the torts system to the institution of insurance remains an essential undertaking.

The purpose of this chapter is to both introduce the fundamental concepts of insurance, including its social (e.g., social security), private first-party (e.g., victim's loss insurance), and private third-party (e.g., injurer's liability insurance) forms, and sketch how they interact with tort. Social and first-party insurance exists, of course, wholly independently of the tort system. Life and health insurance — and property insurance against natural calamities — typically compensate for losses having nothing to do with human wrongdoing. But when tortious conduct causes losses, problems arise concerning how various forms of first-party insurance payouts should interact with the monetary benefits that may come to the injured victim in the form of tort damages. You have already encountered the *collateral source rule* in this book, where benefits derived from these forms of social and private first-party insurance are ignored in the calculation of tort recoveries. And you may know that some jurisdictions have abolished this traditional rule in recent years. This chapter revisits these issues on a somewhat grander scale, letting you see

1. Scholars also began to revive noninstrumental theories, such as corrective justice and civil recourse theories. See the law and policy note on p. 36 supra.

2. See generally Kenneth S. Abraham, Twenty-first Century Insurance and Loss Distribution in Tort Law, in Exploring Tort Law 81-84 (M. Stuart Madden ed., 2005). The conventional account of the development of tort theory, as described in the text, has undergone a significant historical revision. As John Witt has demonstrated, cooperative insurance societies during the nineteenth century represented an important privately organized precursor to the kind of loss distribution function that twentieth-century scholars envisioned for tort law. See John Fabian Witt, Toward a New History of American Accident Law: Classical Tort Law and the Cooperative First Party Insurance Movement, 114 Harv. L. Rev. 690 (2001).

the "bigger picture." Third-party insurance — liability insurance that potential injurers purchase or otherwise put in place to cover tort liabilities they may incur from their activities — is, of course, necessarily related to the tort system. This chapter explores both the theoretical aspects of the insurance-tort relationship and two issues of practical concern: first, the extent to which liability insurers can be reached directly by claimants and thus become the "real" defendants; and second, the obligations of insurers to their insureds to settle liability claims in good faith.

A. The History and Functions of Insurance Generally

Kenneth S. Abraham, Insurance Law and Regulation: Cases and Materials

3-7 (6th ed. 2015)

A. The Nature and Functions of Insurance . . .

How Insurance Works

In the simplest sense, the function of insurance is to protect the policyholder in the event of a future loss. A more sophisticated description, however, recognizes three separate insurance functions. The first is *risk-transfer* from comparatively risk-averse to less risk-averse or risk-neutral parties. A risk-neutral party is indifferent as between a small risk of suffering a large loss and greater risk of suffering a small loss, when each risk has the same *expected value* — the probability of a loss multiplied by its magnitude if it occurs. In contrast, a risk-averse party would prefer the large risk of suffering a small loss to a smaller risk of suffering the large loss. . . .

Individuals (and most business entities) are generally risk-averse with respect to low-probability, high-magnitude losses, such as the prospect of a home burning down. Economists explain this as a function of the diminishing marginal utility of wealth. This concept reflects the intuition that events substantially diminishing a person's wealth will generally have a *disproportionately* large impact on that person's well-being relative to smaller losses of wealth. . . .

The second function of insurance is *risk-pooling*, or diversification. Insurance companies are not intrinsically risk-neutral. Rather, by insuring a large number of insureds posing homogeneous and independent risks, an insurer can transform these risks into a highly predictable set of obligations. This is an application of the law of large numbers. To illustrate, if one flips a coin 10 times, the likelihood that the flips will produce 3, 4, 5, 6, or 7 flips of heads (i.e. conform to the expected distribution of heads and tails) is about 90%. But if one flipped a coin 100 times, the likelihood that between 30 and 70 of these flips would be heads would be much greater than 90%, or even 99%. In other words, as one increases the number of coin flips, the distribution of heads and tails becomes more and more likely to reflect the expected distribution of 50% heads and 50% tails. Insurance operates in the same way: the pooling of individual risks largely eliminates uncertainty, as reflected by the fact that each year a relatively predictable and stable number of individuals get into car accidents, experience house fires, and are sued for negligence. Insurance is thus a vehicle by which risk-averse parties combine to share and thereby reduce their collective risk. The insurance company's profits constitute payment for providing this service to its policyholders and for bearing the residual risk that losses will vary beyond the range predicted.

The third function of insurance is *risk-allocation*. Insurers not only accept the transfer of risks and then pool them. In charging for the coverage they provide, insurers attempt to set a price that is proportional to the degree of risk posed by each insured. Insurers thereby allocate risk to groups of insureds posing similar or identical degrees of risk. Different methods of risk classification measure risks in different ways. But by classifying risks and then pricing coverage in accordance with their classifications, insurers can create incentives for insureds to appropriately limit the degree of risk they post. For instance by charging more for health insurance to those who smoke cigarettes, insurers may encourage smokers to quit.

Any given insurance arrangement accomplishes these three functions in varying degrees. For example, a particular insurance policy will transfer some but by no means all the risks faced by the insured. In addition, because an insurer's effort at risk diversification through pooling is always imperfect, insurers inevitably face a greater or lesser degree of risk themselves. Finally, obtaining the information necessary to classify risks and price accordingly is not cost-free; consequently, risk-allocation normally can proceed only to the point at which further refinement is not worthwhile. . . .

The Social Functions of Insurance

Insurance not only performs the direct economic functions of risk transfer, risk pooling, and risk allocation. Because over time insurance has come to occupy so important a place in our way of life, insurance also plays a number of social roles. Arguably in both positive and negative ways, insurance constrains and in a sense helps constitute social life. For example, insurance affects our norms. When health insurance covers contraception or mental health needs, these services gradually come to be seen as appropriate forms of medical treatment. And when homeowners insurance premiums are reduced because a home contains smoke detectors, it becomes irresponsible not to have them installed. Insurance sometimes is also a surrogate regulator or instrument of governance. In most states it is unlawful to drive a car without liability insurance. Drivers who cannot obtain liability insurance at tolerable cost because of their accident records are effectively prohibited from driving, though admittedly they still may drive in violation of law and at considerable financial risk to themselves and their potential victims. Similarly, physicians who cannot obtain malpractice insurance may be denied hospital admitting privileges and marginalized in their medical practices. Finally, insurance is a kind of equalizer. It takes money from the lucky and gives it to the unlucky. In so doing it smooths out some of the differences among people that would otherwise result from bad luck. I may still suffer if I become ill and can no longer work, but if I have disability insurance my income will be maintained.

These sorts of insights have been developed by a group of "insurance and society" scholars whose work has shed new light on the way that insurance operates in practice. See, e.g., Richard V. Erickson et al., Insurance as Governance (2003); Tom Baker & Jonathan Simon (eds.), Embracing Risk (2002). One of the long-term legal implications of these insights is that insurance can often operate as a substitute for government regulation of safety. See Omri Ben-Shahar & Kyle D. Logue, Outsourcing Regulation: How Insurance Reduces Moral Hazard, 111 Mich. L. Rev. 197 (2012). Another, even broader, implication may be that insurance does not fit comfortably within the public-private dichotomy. Private insurers are not agents of government, and therefore are not subject to the standards that restrict the scope of government's discretion. Insurers, for example, are not and probably should not be required to accord their applicants and policyholders with full-blown due process and equal protection. But given the social role and importance of insurance, we may need standards for regulating the behavior of private insurers that recognize their unique public role. See Kenneth S. Abraham, Four Conceptions of Insurance, 161 U. Pa. L. Rev 653 (2013).

B. *The Problems of Adverse Selection and Moral Hazard*

If the insurance market functioned perfectly, law would have a much less important role to play in regulating insurance than it does in practice. Among other things, consumers of insurance would know exactly what they wanted and what was offered to them, insurers would know what to charge for each form of coverage, and the purchase of insurance by one party would have no impact on anyone else. The ideal of the perfectly functioning market, however, is never achieved in practice.

Insurance markets are especially susceptible to two well-known market failures: adverse selection and moral hazard. Both of these market failures arise from policyholders having better information than insurers regarding their risk levels. Of course, quite often the tables are turned, and insurers possess better information than policyholders about relevant information, such as the content of insurance policies. For now though, we focus on adverse selection and moral hazard, which are fundamental to understanding insurance products and market practices in addition to the law that governs them.

Adverse Selection. Other things being equal, a party facing a high risk of loss is more likely to seek insurance than a party facing a low risk. If potential policyholders know better than insurers whether they pose comparatively high or low risk prior to acquiring insurance, then adverse selection may occur: when insurers charge each party the same price for coverage, then high-risk parties elect to be insured in greater proportion than low-risk parties, and insurers are forced to raise the price of coverage. As a result of the increased price, some of the comparatively low-risk parties that had previously been insured decline to purchase coverage or purchase less of it, the average degree of risk posed by the insurer's policyholders rises, and the insurer is forced to raise prices again, thus restarting the cycle of adverse selection. . . .

Eventually the insurer's risk pool either unravels completely, or an equilibrium is reached in which some low-risk parties purchase less coverage than they would otherwise desire and others purchase none. In either case, low-risk parties buy less coverage and high-risk parties buy more coverage than they would if insurers could distinguish the risk posed by different policyholders. For classic economic expositions of the problem, see Michael D. Rothschild & Joseph E. Stiglitz, Equilibrium in Competitive Insurance Markets: An Essay on the Economics of Imperfect Information, 90 Q. J. Econ. 629 (1976); George Akerloff, The Market for "Lemons": Quality Uncertainty and the Market Mechanism, 84 Q. J. Econ. 488 (1970).

Moral Hazard. The term moral hazard originated in insurance law as a description of the risk that an insured or insurance beneficiary would deliberately destroy the subject matter that was insured in order to obtain payment of an insurance benefit. For example, in 18th century England it was possible to purchase insurance on the lives of strangers. This was a form of gambling rather than true insurance. As in ordinary gambling, when the insured death occurred, the policyholder would not merely avoid a loss, but would actually obtain a gain. Moreover, because of this prospect it was the policyholder's interest for the party whose life was insured to die sooner rather than later. The policyholder therefore had an incentive to cause the insured death to occur. Because of this moral hazard, eventually . . . the practice of insuring without an "insurable interest" in the insured subject matter — an interest engendered by love and affection or an economic relationship — was prohibited. The term moral hazard now often refers more generally to the tendency of any insured party to exercise less care to avoid an insured loss than would be exercised if the loss were not insured.

Like adverse selection, moral hazard is fundamentally an information asymmetry problem: if insurers could costlessly monitor the ongoing behavior of their insureds, insurance would not be plagued by moral hazard. Because premiums could be charged in proportion to the level of care actually exercised by the insured, there would be no incentive for insured parties to exercise less care than those who were uninsured. But of course insurers cannot costlessly monitor the levels of care their insureds exercise. Consequently, because of this imperfect information, moral hazard is a common threat to the functioning of insurance.

Combating Threats to the Insurance Function. Insurers attempt to combat adverse selection and moral hazard with a variety of devices. They engage in "underwriting," the process of screening and evaluating applications to determine the degree of risk posed by prospective insureds; they classify insureds based on the degree of risk posed and set premium levels accordingly; they experience-rate, or charge premiums for coverage renewals based in part on the insured's loss experience during the previous policy period; they include deductible, coinsurance, and dollar limits of coverage in policies so that all losses are not fully insured; they do not let people buy insurance on the lives of strangers, or on property in which the prospective policyholder has no interest; and they fashion the terms of coverage so that unusual risks are not insured by standard policies and so that the results of inordinately dangerous behavior are not insured. . . .

Although the threat posed by adverse selection should not be underestimated, neither should it be exaggerated. See Peter Siegelman, Adverse Selection in Insurance Markets: An Exaggerated Threat, 113 Yale L.J. 1223 (2004); Tom Baker, Containing the Promise of Insurance: Adverse Selection and Risk Classification, 9 Conn. Ins. L.J. 371 (2003); George L. Priest, The Current Insurance Crisis and Modern Tort Law, 96 Yale L.J. 1521 (1987). In certain respects insurers know more about applicants than the applicants know themselves. Insurers maintain data about the characteristics that affect risk levels, for example, that individuals do not possess. Applicants may think that they pose higher or lower risks than they actually pose, or may have no intuition about the issue. In these situations adverse selection is likely to be weak or nonexistent. In addition, it is risk-aversion that prompts the demand for insurance in the first place. Risk-averse insureds have a tendency to become and to remain insured even if they are charged somewhat more for coverage than perfect actuarial calculations would dictate. The result is an often-tolerable level of cross-subsidization from low-risk individuals to high-risk individuals within any given risk pool. In this sense every risk classification involves some redistribution of risk, up to the point where the factors that prevent adverse selection begin to dissolve.

B. *Viewing the Tort System from a Loss Distribution Perspective*

Kenneth S. Abraham, Twenty-first Century Insurance and Loss Distribution in Tort Law

In Exploring Tort Law 85-91, 102, 106-10 (M. Stuart Madden ed., 2005) (footnotes omitted)

II. The Tort System in an Insurance Perspective

A. Generally

. . . [T]ort is just one component of a larger system of compensation for personal injury and illness. Viewing tort not in isolation from this larger system, but as a part of it, helps to reveal tort's comparatively modest scope. The sheer amount of money spent each year to compensate the victims of injury and illness tell[s] a story that words alone do not adequately capture.

B. The Tort System

The total direct cost of the tort system is roughly $233 billion per year. This is a more than one-hundred-fold increase since 1950, when tort costs were about $2 billion. The increase in tort costs during this period has outstripped economic growth by a factor of three. Not all of this sum, however, is paid on account of losses associated with personal injury and illness. Some portion of the total is paid in connection with claims for property damage, for pure economic loss, and for losses associated with dignitary torts such as defamation and invasion of privacy. For the sake of simplicity I will assume conservatively that 75 percent of the $233 billion annual cost of tort is the result of claims for personal injury and illness. Consequently, the proper figure to keep in mind for purposes of comparison with other sources is a direct tort cost of $175 billion.

The percentage of this sum that is paid to personal injury and illness victims cannot be pinpointed exactly. One . . . estimate is that only 46 percent of all expenditures, which based on the above calculation amounts to about $80 billion per year, is paid to victims. There is also somewhat less recent data on particular sub-fields within tort. Only a bit more than half of all money expended on automobile liability goes to victims. In contrast, products liability and medical malpractice pay a considerably smaller portion of their expenditures to victims — perhaps as little as one-third.

Only half or even less of what we spend on tort is paid to victims, of course, because the system spends a great deal for the individualized fact-finding regarding negligence, causation, and damages that are so characteristic of tort. The theory of corrective justice requires monetary awards that are carefully tailored to the evidence of each particular plaintiff's past and probable future losses, both economic and emotional. And the search for optimal deterrence dovetails with this individualized tailoring of awards. To achieve deterrence the system must strive to threaten and to impose liability on defendants for all, but no more than all, of the costs that their negligence causes. Making this determination can be costly. In this respect the two approaches that compete for the dominance of tort theory converge, both requiring that a considerable portion of the tort dollar be spent on the cost of administration rather than on compensation itself.

C. Workers' Compensation

Workers' compensation pays benefits for injuries "arising out of or in the course of employment." Benefits paid by this nonfault system of compensation for job-related injuries are lower than those paid by tort, $46 billion as compared to tort's $80 billion. Because workers' compensation is essentially a system of absolute liability on the part of the employer, however, fact-finding as to liability is usually unnecessary. As a consequence, the cost of administration related to that issue is generally low. Therefore, workers' compensation pays a much higher percentage of the total dollars it expends in benefits than does tort — over 82 percent.

D. Health Insurance

By far the largest non-tort source of compensation for personal injury and illness is health insurance. Health care costs in the United States exceed $1.1 trillion per year. Third-party payments made for direct health care costs (as distinguished from medical research, etc.) total about $846 billion per year, of which payments by public sources such as Medicare, Medicaid, and other, smaller programs account for $423 billion, and private insurance for roughly the same amount. Together these sources pay about 79 percent of all personal health care expenditures, leaving individuals to pay $194 billion per year themselves. A significant portion of these personal expenditures is incurred by persons with no health insurance or inadequate insurance: about 15 percent of the population has no health insurance at all.

E. Life Insurance

Life insurance is also a significant method of loss distribution. The average insured household is covered by nearly $200,000 of life insurance. Fixing the proper of amount of life insurance benefits to figure into the calculus requires some estimation, however, because life insurance represents both insurance and savings. Each year over $44 billion is paid to the beneficiaries of life insurance policyholders as death benefits. But an additional $31 billion is paid as living benefits, in the form of cash surrender or investment return. An indeterminate portion of this sum is undoubtedly used by recipients to cover injury and illness costs.

Life insurance has sometimes been considered to be payment to assuage grief. But it is more accurate and useful to conceive of life insurance as compensation for loss of earning power or human capital. A household that purchases insurance on the life of its principal income earner is not buying protection against grief; rather, it is insuring against the possibility that it will be deprived of support by the premature death of the insured. Life insurance is therefore best understood mainly as a method of compensating for income lost because of death resulting from illness or injury. On this view, although $200,000 may seem like a significant amount of insurance, it is in fact inadequate protection against lost income for virtually all families — at current interest rates this sum would yield an annual income of less than $10,000.

F. Disability Insurance

The majority of payments for disability — income lost because of the inability to work — are made by the Social Security Disability program. This program pays about $55 billion per year for total, long-term disability. But the average monthly benefit is only $814 to each disabled beneficiary and $238 to children of disabled beneficiaries. Statistics on benefits paid by privately purchased long-term disability insurance are difficult to obtain, because these payouts are comparatively small — they may be on the order of $10 billion per year. Roughly 25 percent of private sector employees have long term disability insurance — although the discrepancy in the percentage of individuals in different wage groups who are covered is striking. Whereas 47 percent of white-collar employees are covered, only 13 percent of blue collar employees are. In addition, benefits paid for short-term disability, in the form of paid sick leave, are available to about one-half of the work force. Based on the data available, my very rough estimate is that the magnitude of these payments is $23 billion per year. Thus, payouts from all these forms of disability coverage total about $88 billion annually.

Putting these figures together, as reflected in Table 9-1, yields a rough idea of the quantitative importance of tort liability within our broader system of compensation for illness and injury. In very rough terms, that broader system costs about $1.7 trillion annually, of which $175 billion, or about 10 percent, is for personal injury and illness tort costs. Looking at percentages of benefits paid rather than percentages of costs, $1.1 trillion in benefits is paid each year, of which about $80 billion, or just over 7 percent, is paid to the relevant subset of tort victims.

Thus, . . . tort plays a small role in our system of public and private loss distribution. Moreover, tort is also a comparatively inefficient compensation mechanism, in that it pays a much smaller percentage of its expenditures to victims than [do] the other approaches. And because the other approaches compensate on a broader basis, they are superior not only at loss distribution but also at risk distribution. On the other hand, payments made by the overall system are far from sufficient to compensate all the victims of illness and injury

TABLE 9-1
Annual Personal Injury and Illness Compensation Costs (in $ Billions)

	Expenditures [including Administrative Costs]	*Benefits Paid [to Victims]*
Tort	175	80
Workers Compensation	56	46
Health Insurance	1100	846
Health Care Out-of-Pocket	194	–
Life Insurance	48	44
Disability Insurance	96	88
Total	1669	1104

for all their losses. Although there is therefore at least a potential []role to be played by tort in filling the gaps in our overall loss distribution system, the question is whether expanding tort or the features of our broader system of compensation is the better method of addressing this problem.

[The author observes that, although the tort system is remarkably less efficient as a loss-distribution mechanism than the other systems of social and first-party market insurance, tort serves the deterrence objective better than do the other systems. The answer to the question he identifies in the last quoted paragraph — whether to expand tort or to expand reliance on first-party insurance — is answered largely by means of the collateral source rule. Refusing to deduct nontort insurance benefits from tort recoveries and then subrogating the insurers to the victim's rights to tort recovery — the traditional rule in this country — is thought to maximize the deterrence potential of tort. Abolishing the traditional rule — deducting nontort benefits from tort recoveries — would make first-party insurance the primary source of victims' benefits while reducing the deterrence effects of tort. After considering possible variations on the collateral-source theme, the author proposes a bold new departure from tradition.]

IV. Toward a New Treatment of Collateral Sources

[I]t is time to take a step back and look at the big picture. We have seen that the central challenge for tort law's treatment of collateral sources is how to preserve deterrence while at the same time taking advantage of the much greater efficiency of first-party and social insurance as methods of compensation. Offsets sacrifice deterrence in order to accord these forms of insurance loss-distributional priority. Nonoffsets preserve deterrence, but at the cost of some combination of possible overcompensation, significant administrative expense, and making tort — an inefficient loss distributor — the primary source of compensation. We are thus faced with a choice between unsatisfactory alternatives.

Two principles can help lead away from this dilemma. The first principle, already noted, is that first-party and social insurance are superior to tort as methods of affording compensation, because the compensable event under these systems is simple and easily applied. The result is that a much higher proportion of the money invested in loss distribution finds its way into the pockets of victims under first-party and social insurance than in tort. The second principle is that, from a loss-distributional standpoint, out-of-pocket expenses should have a higher compensation priority than intangible loss. It may be arguable that awarding pain and suffering damages serves corrective justice; and in my view awards of at least some damages for pain and suffering are necessary to promote optimal deterrence. But although pain and suffering is a real social cost, the loss that pain and suffering damages reflect cannot be "distributed" by awarding victims monetary compensation. The victims of pain and suffering do not need their losses distributed; they need their pain and suffering relieved. Paying damages for pain and suffering does not relieve pain and suffering. It is instead an economic substitute for relief, as well as a means of attempting to ensure that the plaintiff's counsel fees can be paid without depriving her of compensation for out-of-pocket loss.

Combining these two principles with the desirability of preserving deterrence suggests an alternative approach. We should permit potential tort victims to invest their available insurance dollars more heavily in first-party insurance, protecting them against the risk of suffering out-of-pocket loss, rather than on tort "insurance." But we should continue to threaten defendants with liability for the full social cost of harm they cause, including intangible loss.

A number of scholars have proposed full-subrogation approaches that would allow this ideal to be approached. In one way or another they propose authorizing plaintiffs to sell their tort causes of action in return for additional protection against out-of-pocket loss. What these approaches amount to, using the kind of terminology I employed in Part II, is "nonoffsets with total collateral recovery." The plaintiff would continue to have formal tort rights, but her first-party insurance contract would provide that her total tort recovery — not merely the benefits already paid or payable by the insurer — would be returned to her insurer as subrogation reimbursement. The plaintiff would then be a plaintiff in name only, since the real party in interest would be her first-party insurer.

This general approach would preserve the deterrence that is a central feature of the nonoffset approaches but would enable potential tort claimants to transform their right to recover pain and suffering damages into less expensive, or more broadly protective, first-party insurance. Of course, the details of this approach need to be worked out. . . . It ought to be provided as an option for policyholders to accept or reject, and even then only after significant efforts have been made to ensure that the policyholder has given informed consent to the arrangement. That way, the state would not decide the proper mix of tort rights and insurance for all individuals; that decision would be made individually rather than collectively, as is now done.

Because the vast majority of private first-party insurance is employment-related group health insurance, a method of returning premiums saved or providing additional coverage to the individual policyholders electing the option would have to be developed as well. A method of designating the insurer that would hold the the newly-enhanced right of subrogation reimbursement would also be required. It is easy enough to picture a bifurcation, however, under which health insurers, for example, received the right to payment of all damages for out-of-pocket expenses and conscious pain and suffering, whereas the right to recover damages for wrongful death was transferred to life insurers, with corresponding reductions in premiums or increases in the amounts of coverage provided by these sources.

The victims of torts might also have to be provided with an incentive to participate actively in the insurer's conduct of tort suits, since victims would effectively become mere witnesses without any economic stake in the outcome. Some sharing of pain and suffering damages by the victim and the insurer above a specified level might prove to be an optimal method of obtaining this participation. Because certain insurance companies might come to specialize in this form of recovery, and as a secondary market involving tort lawyers representing these insurers probably would develop, competition among insurers would likely generate a variety of options. Finally, the subrogation reimbursement rights of other collateral sources would have to be preserved, so that (for example) disability insurers were reimbursed by health insurers out of the tort recoveries that health insurers obtained. . . .

This approach might well help to fill part of the gap in the fabric of protection against out-of-pocket loss that still remains and so troubles both the tort and social welfare systems. As noted earlier, there are still substantial gaps in the fabric of protection provided by first-party insurance. Fifteen percent or more of the population has no health insurance; nearly one-fifth of the cost of out-patient medical care is uninsured; few income-earners have private or public disability insurance that provides more than slightly above subsistence level wage-loss protection, many having only social security protection against long-term, total disability; and most families have insufficient life insurance to protect them against the income loss they would suffer upon the death of the principal wage-earner in the family.

Tort has not filled these gaps, nor has political action on the health and disability insurance fronts for several decades now. Perhaps by creating a market for potential tort claims, revision of the collateral source rule can do what we have thus far failed to do — contribute to the provision of sufficient health-care and income-loss protection for everyone in the United States. If the uninsured cannot now afford to pay for health and disability insurance with currently available funds, some of them may be willing to pay part of the necessary premium for such coverage by transferring their right to recover for personal injury in tort to these insurers, in return for insurance coverage that they can afford. We would then have achieved greater loss distribution, not by expanding the scope of tort liability, but by modifying the relationship between tort recoveries and collateral sources and creating a means by which tort rights can be transformed into superior forms of insurance. I do not want to argue that this change alone would be sufficient to provide health or disability insurance to all the uninsured. But it might make a start.

At the same time, the effects on the market for legal services might be salutary. At present, the contingent-fee system is necessary at least in part because plaintiffs have no other way to manage the huge payment that would otherwise be due their attorneys. Once the purchasers of the services of plaintiffs' personal injury attorneys are more often also first-party insurers, they may be able to take advantage of the greater clout that the reform would put in their hands. A more competitive and perhaps very different market for the services of personal injury attorneys might be the result.

Conclusion

The world of insurance has changed enormously since the collateral source rule was first developed. At that time the payment of insurance benefits to tort plaintiffs by collateral sources was a rarity. Now this is routine. Similarly, the reasons for the exemption of life insurance from standard subrogation rules and practices no longer apply. But gaps in the fabric of first-party and social insurance protection still exist. By looking at tort and this fabric of protection as one system, we can see that neither the collateral source rule as we know it nor legislative reversals of the rule optimize the deterrence and insurance functions of this system. To achieve this goal, individuals should be given the right to transfer full subrogation rights to first-party insurers, in return for lower premiums or expanded insurance.

Jane Stapleton, Tort, Insurance and Ideology

58 Modern L. Rev. 820, 820-821, 825-826, 833-37, 843-845 (1995)
(footnotes omitted)

When misfortune befalls an individual, our social and legal arrangements may provide a variety of responses other than to let the losses associated with it lie where they fell. For example, the misfortune may have been the subject of private insurance taken out by the victim and at a level the victim chose. The risk of the misfortune may have been socialised by being covered by, say, a scheme of social insurance or social welfare. A third response is restoration of the victim, that is provision to the victim of a financial measure which attempts as far as money is able to return the victim to the position he was in before the misfortune occurred. Clearly, tort qualifies as a form of the third response because the measure of damages in tort is restorative of the victim; but is it also a form of the first two responses and, if so, what are the ramifications of this?

. . . My aim in this article is to emphasise that whether one thinks the existing catchment of tort (or existing forms of social insurance and social welfare) should be reduced, leaving individuals merely with the support they can afford from first party insurance or hope to receive from charity, is profoundly a matter of ideology. The reason this requires emphasis is that confusing tort with the other forms of support for misfortune can lead, and has recently led in the United States, to the presentation of these choices as apolitical and their resolution in favour of retrenchment of tort as merely the working through of inexorable logic.

In this article I will deal with tort's relationship with insurance. Concentrating first on the common but vague claim that tort is somehow 'about insurance,' I will argue that neither actual insurance nor insurability are or should be relevant to the reach and shape of tort liability. I then hope to explain why continued confusion on this point can lead to the conflation of tort with the insurance model of response to misfortune. Once this 'tort as insurance' construction of liability is embraced, the normative agenda for the future of tort inexorably points to retrenchment: an agenda, it can then be claimed, which arises from the mere logic of what tort is about and not from any ulterior ideological motive. Exploding the ideological subtext of the 'tort as insurance' fallacy then frees us not only to formulate coherently the central question of the future of tort (this is the question of which of life's misfortunes justify the full restorative response tort extracts from the defendant), but also to admit the ideological nature of the analysis required for resolution of this question. . . .

[Before addressing the normative merits of viewing tort law through the lens of insurance, Professor Stapleton first argues that the "tort-as-insurance" argument fails to provide a convincing descriptive account of the tort system:]

The traditional view is that so long as tort (and indeed civil liability in general) is viewed and structured as a system of individual responsibility, we cannot convincingly draw a moral distinction between defendants merely on the basis of their capacity to share or offload that responsibility onto others in an insurance pool. Since in tort it is always individuals who are the initial overt target of a suit, we cannot convincingly ignore the symbolic structure of individual responsibility this entails. In other words, it would seem morally incoherent for the liability insurance factor to have any independent force, for it would mean that there would be cases, for example, in which the fact that tipped the balance in favour of the defendant being held liable would simply be that he had or could have had liability insurance cover, while an equally culpable but uninsured or uninsurable actor would escape. It is not self-evident why the latter party taking an uninsured or uninsurable risk should be so favoured and his victim denied the law's protection on this account. Even if the normative insurance argument only operates at the broad level of the insurability of a generic activity, this would still imply that the fact that an individual is required to pay personally should be a reason not to impose upon him a rule of individual responsibility. Stated in this general way (rather than in limited terms of, say, indeterminacy of liability), the insurance argument seems absurd. . . .

[W]hat about the normative issue of whether we should see tort as insurance? In the United States, this idea has recently gained currency from the writings of influential scholars (whom I will loosely call the "Yale Lawyers" [Eds: Yale Law professors George Priest and Alan Schwartz are among leading proponents of the "tort-as-insurance" argument identified by the author]). They attempt to legitimise the tort-as-insurance argument in two ways. First, they allege that this was how, in the postwar period, eminent scholars and judges saw tort (that it was a way of providing insurance to victims) and that this was the basis on which new liabilities were built. Here it is worth noting that the insurance construction of tort may seem particularly seductive where liability has been imposed for outcomes which reasonable care would not have prevented (i.e., strict liabilities) because, by definition, the defendant does not have the option of responding by taking preventative measures. The fallacy that US product manufacturers have been exposed to such strict liability since the early 1960s fuelled the descriptive claims of the 'tort-as-insurance' scholars. For them there can be no economic justification for strict liability on the basis of deterrence, so the only economic explanation for a strict liability would be to provide insurance and this would then justify only an insurance measure of damages for such liabilities. Secondly, the Yale lawyers also make an independent normative argument based on autonomy in favour of seeing tort-as-insurance. Before we look at these claims, it should be noted that if such a benchmark of insurance can be legitimated in one of these ways, it then would provide the means by which the scope of tort could be attacked, for judged by that benchmark tort provides excessive coverage. Moreover, that attack and the reform agenda of retrenchment it suggests can appear to be apolitical and merely something we all agree.

[Professor Stapleton argues that judges and torts scholars who supported the expansion of liability in the twentieth century were not exclusively, or even primarily, motivated by a torts-as-insurance vision.]

The Yale lawyers also try to legitimise the tort-as-insurance construction of tort law on the basis of an independent normative argument. The actual starting point for this is the underplayed assumption, extraordinary to British eyes, that the plaintiff and the defendant were or could have been linked by bargaining relationship(s). Making this assumption, it is then said that the result of imposing tort liability on the defendant will be that in future those in the position of the defendant will pass their new liability insurance costs down the chain in the price the defendant charges for the relevant good or service, so that in the end those in the position of the plaintiff will be called on to pay for the new tort protection themselves. Step 2 is to assume that, since this could be portrayed as potential plaintiffs having in effect to pay for the protection tort has given them, this apparent insurance effect of tort should in fact be recognised as the intended goal of tort. That is, by imposing liability on such defendants, courts should be seen as ensuring customers are provided with insurance against the risk of (tortious) injury by the defendant. Step 3 then notes that whichever way a victim receives protection, be it by first party insurance or by a tort entitlement, in the end he will have to pay for that protection himself and that therefore, in wealth terms, obtaining protection by tort does not enhance the wealth of the victim. The fourth step in the argument points out that to provide protection in this way acts regressively against the poor since, although the burden of the liability premiums is passed on equally to all potential victims, rich and poor alike, once injured a rich victim can usually extract higher damages from the pool of liability insurance of which the defendant is a member than a poor person whose lost wages are lower. What is more, it is said, the poor person may well not 'want' cover for certain losses (because he does not have the resources to pay for them), so 'forcing' him to pay for this via the tort system is said to trample on the autonomy of the poor. Relying on this regressive characteristic of obtaining protection by tort and its alleged invasion of autonomy, the exponents of the 'tort-as-insurance' construction argue for the radical retrenchment of tort. In other words, the counter-intuitive, indeed the astonishing conclusion which is made, is that, particularly in the interests of the class of poor plaintiffs, plaintiffs should receive less protection from tort. . . .

There are two analytical problems with this 'tort-as-insurance' line of analysis. First, it relies on an assumption that all plaintiffs and defendants are or could be linked by a chain of consensual bargaining. Yet this is wholly at odds with how tort law is conventionally understood, namely as that set of obligations which can arise between two parties even if they are strangers to one another. Landmark tort cases in both the United States and United Kingdom testify to this. It may well be that, in some contexts, we should develop principles to limit tort liability where there is the chance of appropriate channels of bargaining linking the plaintiff and defendant. But we cannot assume that between plaintiff and defendant there is always the potential for appropriate bargaining and then use this assumption, first to construe all tort liability as intended merely as a form of insurance, and then to justify evaluation of the comparative 'efficiency' of tort as an avenue of providing insurance to the victim relative to first party insurance.

Secondly, the fundamental logical flaw in the tort-as-insurance construction of tort law is the same as the one identified in the comparative insurability approach sometimes argued for in the United Kingdom and the Commonwealth. By assuming that the victim needs insurance, we are assuming that he cannot as of right require the defendant to protect his relevant interests. It impliedly rejects the possibility that sometimes there are reasons why the law may want to grant him that right and the accompanying entitlement to a restorative measure of damages: for example, because it wants to deter certain conduct of defendants or because it regards the injury as a wrong which 'justice' requires to be 'corrected', or an 'outcome' for which the defendant should be held responsible. . . .

I have a further and more basic complaint about the tort-as-insurance construction: that, while it masquerades as an apolitical analysis of what we all agree tort is about, it is in fact profoundly political. It stresses concerns about autonomy and dependency while ignoring concerns about deterrence and corrective justice. The tort-as-insurance argument also generates a reform strategy which is radically redistributional whereby business is enriched and injured individuals are stripped of protection, yet neither of these consequences is squarely acknowledged. . . .

[Stapleton notes that "for victims the grant of tort protection can significantly affect the wealth of their class." This is because potential victims of product defects are, under a strict liability system, "relieved of any perceived need to protect themselves from the risk of manufacturer carelessness by paying for first party insurance cover for that risk." Stapleton further claims that, under the tort reform strategy "suggested by the tort-as-insurance construction of tort law," victims of product defects would "henceforth have to pay for the protection which hitherto they had not had to buy but were entitled to as of right" while manufacturers would no longer feel "a real economic pressure because they were unable simply to pass on all liability costs onto their customers would now go scot-free. Any deterrence incentives generated in the past by the now-abandoned liability (even if only spread over an imperfectly differentiated risk pool) would be lost. Moreover, because they would be relieved of any economic pressures that liability had imposed upon them, it would tend to make them wealthier and their activities more profitable."]

Commentators and judges should think twice before making off-hand comments that insurance should be relevant to the scope of tort liability, that judges should take into account 'the realities of insurance' or that they should address the comparative insurability of parties. Such statements are dangerous. They are not only indeterminate criteria but can mislead us into suppressing any corrective justice or deterrence goals we may have for tort liability and this then opens the door for the more radical argument that tort is a surrogate for first party insurance. This latter tort-as-insurance criterion then inexorably points to the need for the retrenchment of tort entitlements. But, far from being a construction of tort law with which we all agree, it is one with little judicial support and one which is based on ideological assumptions about the weight to be given to concerns about autonomy and dependency. Of course, resort to ideological assumptions here is inescapable because whether we should deploy tort, with its full restorative measure, to help the victim of a specific misfortune is not a matter of legal logic but a debatable political question. It is true that one factor in that debate is a concern to preserve autonomy and not force individuals to pay for protection for which they do not want to pay. Another concern is not positively to encourage a dependency culture by allowing victims to free-ride on this particular system of support for misfortune. Both of these are valid and healthy restraining influences on the growth of tort (as well as systems of socialised risk). But they are not trump cards. Against them must be weighed other concerns. These include the moral view that sometimes individuals are entitled (without payment) not to be physically damaged by the careless act of the defendant. Another is the interest in deterring certain conduct by requiring injurers to pay the full social costs of the injuries they cause. Where we resolve this balancing of concerns in favour of pro-liability factors so that a tort entitlement is recognised, that entitlement is clearly not designed as a mimic of insurance: first, because there is no need for insurance since these factors support an entitlement; secondly, because the measure of damages is restorative. . . .

The scope of tort liability is a political question and concerns about autonomy and dependency are valid factors to be weighed in that balance. If the pool of tort liability is now thought to be overflowing, there is nothing wrong in identifying all such countervailing factors more carefully than in the past. But this should be done openly, acknowledging that the weight given to each factor is a matter of personal political judgment. It should also be acknowledged that for many people the degree to which they find dependency, free-riding or inroads into autonomy objectionable is heavily coloured by the weight they give other pro-liability values and concerns for which the core of tort law has long stood. For example, though in my view any distaste for the dependency culture should be brought to bear with greater stringency on commercial plaintiffs complaining about economic disappointment in their risktaking, I personally do not think it should be of much weight in cases of personal injuries caused by the defendant's affirmative act. Those who argue for the retrenchment of tort from the tort-as-insurance perspective should acknowledge their political emphasis on dependency and autonomy concerns and be required to justify the enrichment of injurers which such retrenchment would generate. What the tort-as-insurance idea teaches those who choose to defend the core of tort entitlements (and programmes of socialised risk) is that it is crucial to prevent certain ideas such as insurability, autonomy and dependency being asserted as apolitical trumps in the debate about how society should respond to misfortunes. We must separate out pro-liability concerns and countervailing factors more carefully, subject them openly to our own political weightings and not be afraid of acknowledging where and why our preferred boundaries of the pool of tort entitlements lie.

After reading the scholarly excerpts from Professors Abraham and Stapleton, what are your thoughts about the effort to analyze tort law and tort reform measures through the lens of insurance? Does the torts-as-insurance construction ignore fundamental features and functions of the tort system, as Professor Stapleton argues? Do the insurance-minded reformers continue to have an important practical point, whether or not Professor Stapleton is accurate in her critique?

C. The Effects of Liability Insurance on the Torts Process

The basic mechanics of liability insurance are relatively simple. The insurance company and the insured enter into a contract, embodied in the policy, whereby in exchange for the premium paid by the insured the company agrees to defend any claim against the insured covered by the policy and to pay to the claimant any amount, subject to deductibles and up to the limits stated in the policy,[3] that the insured injurer becomes legally obligated to pay to the victim. In addition to having the duty to defend, the insurer also has the right to defend, and thus takes over the effective management of the claim. In most cases where coverage is clear and the policy limits are more than sufficient to pay any judgment, the insured assumes a decidedly secondary role and is more like a witness than a party. Typically, the insured does not participate actively in the settlement negotiations, and any unauthorized settlement agreed to by the insured is not binding on the insurer. Indeed, the decision to settle or defend the claim is more often than not made by the insurer with little or no consultation with the insured. (Technically the insured must concur in the settlement, but when the insurer pays all of it, insureds almost never object.) And if the claim does go to trial, in nearly every instance the lawyer for the defense will be selected and paid by the insurer. Thus, from the perspective of everyone involved with the claim, the real defender of the claim is the insurer.

The role that liability insurance money plays in the nitty-gritty of the torts process is discussed in Tom Baker, Blood Money, New Money and the Moral Economy of Tort Law in Action, 35 Law & Soc. Rev. 275 (2001). "Blood money" refers to money from individuals' own pockets, as contrasted with "insurance money." The loss of blood money is potentially devastating for many defendants, and the threat of such a loss looms over many professions — particularly those in the medical field. However, defendants rarely have to pay out such blood money. Professor Baker concludes this is due to a norm within the plaintiffs' bar which views suing for blood money as a punitive measure meted out only in egregious circumstances. Other scholars believe that blood money is rarely sought because it is "unprofitable for plaintiffs' attorneys to pursue defendants' personal assets" due to the delays and risks inherent in such pursuits. See Charles Silver, David A. Hyman, Bernard S. Black & Myungho Paik, Policy Limits, Payouts, and Blood Money: Medical Malpractice Settlements in the Shadow of Insurance, 5 U.C. Irvine L. Rev. 559 (2015). Either way, given the reality that liability insurers defend claims and pay the judgments and settlements, it is not surprising that plaintiffs would try to make insurers up-front parties to litigation.

1. The Insurance Company as the Real Party in Interest

Shingleton v. Bussey

223 So. 2d 713 (Fla. 1969)

[The plaintiff was injured by the defendant in an automobile collision. Although the plaintiff brought suit against both the defendant and the defendant's insurance company, the trial court dismissed the claim against the insurance company. The plaintiff's appeal

3. Liability insurance is available with different limits of liability. With automobile insurance, the limits are usually stated as a certain amount for each person injured, and generally a higher amount for each accident. The obligation to defend is typically without a monetary limit, and may thus exceed in value the insurer's obligation to pay claims.

raised the question whether injured victims of motor vehicle accidents may sue directly as third-party beneficiaries of the liability insurance coverage held by their tortfeasor.]

ERVIN, C.J. . . . In the present case, the policy of insurance contains provisions to the effect that no action shall lie against the insurer until the amount of the obligation of the insured shall have been finally determined by judgment and that the policy shall not give any right to join the insurer in any action to determine the liability of an insured. We are aware that a majority of those jurisdictions which have had occasion to adjudicate the efficacy of such clauses are aligned in sustaining them as a bar to direct action against and joinder of an insurer in an action to determine the liability of an insured. See Appleman, 8 Insurance Law and Practice, §§4851-66. However, we are convinced that the time has arrived when the legal reasons advanced in favor of joinder and direct action against an insurer outweigh and preponderate over the traditional notions asserted to justify precluding an injured third party from enjoying such rights. Compare Georgia Southern & Florida Ry. Co. v. Seven-Up Bottling Co. (Fla.), 175 So. 2d 39. . . . It can hardly be disputed that motor vehicle liability insurance is a subject necessarily lending itself to regulation imposed by the State in the exercise of its police power. It is a subject affected with a public interest and its regulation in a multiple of ways for the protection of the general public has become of more and more importance in the passage of years and changing times. This being the case, it is not unreasonable to restrict or limit the effect of express contractual provisions where the same collide with those considerations which affect the interests of the public generally. Where, for example, they collide with principles of due process and equal protection, and the right to a full and adequate remedy of law guaranteed all citizens.

The provisions prohibiting joinder and direct action in the case sub judice do not merely attempt to defer the liability of the insurer, but in addition seek to defer, subject to the same condition, the right of an injured third party beneficiary to maintain a cause of action against the insurer. In the modern world which is fraught with public safety hazards, it is unrealistic that mass liability insurance coverage designed to afford protective benefits for the general public should contain such condition precedent as a barrier to the right of identified members of the protected class to pursue a speedy, realistic and adequate recovery action. This hardly comports with Section 4, Declaration of Rights, State Constitution, F.S.A., that the courts shall be open so that persons injured shall have remedy by due course of law without denial or delay.

Admittedly, a contract of insurance can be entered into which imposes certain reasonable conditions or limitations on the responsibility of the insurer to pay out the proceeds or benefits contemplated by the contract. But such conditions cannot unreasonably burden or curtail the otherwise actionable right of a third party beneficiary to sue jointly the parties charged with liability, viz., the tort-feasor and the insurer of the tort-feasor. The insurer is, of course, not a joint tort-feasor. The unfettered right of a plaintiff to sue defendants jointly is so universal and essential to due process that it can rarely be curtailed or restricted by private contract between potential defendants. An insurer is free not to enter into a liability policy with an insured, but if it does so it cannot unreasonably circumscribe its potential liability under the contract by stipulating therein restraints upon the right of the third party beneficiary to sue directly an insurer contingently or secondarily liable and to join the insurer as a defendant in the action to determine the liability of the insured.

Such a view is particularly warranted where as in the present case the injured party plaintiff is a nonconsenting party to the contract and derives standing as a third party beneficiary entitled to sue in a direct joint action to recover the benefits of the policy by virtue of operation of law.

The insured may agree to conditions vis-à-vis the insurer to waive his own constitutional rights and curtail or postpone his remedies under the policy, but it is a contradiction of public policy to contract for liability coverage for members of the public and simultaneously deny a beneficiary thereunder the ordinary rights of a litigant to sue for such coverage through the restraint of a "no joinder" clause. It is an anomaly in the law and discriminatory for the parties to a contract to attempt to deny nonconsenting members of the public a full, complete, adequate remedy at law which is constitutionally guaranteed all citizens.

The insured and the insurer cannot constitutionally contract away or postpone the speedy and adequate remedy the law affords a third party, nor impose unusual limitations upon the latter's right to jointly sue adverse parties. Balanced, therefore, against the public policy of this state favoring the elimination of multiplicity of suits and unreasonable impediments to the remedial process of adjudication of adversary rights conferred by the operation of substantive principles of law, we think the "no joinder" restriction in the subject policy goes much too far and therefore should be construed as securing for the insurer only the right to assert the nonliability and not the nonjoinder of the insured with the insurer as a condition precedent to the liability of the insurer.

In reaching the foregoing conclusion, we are cognizant that the primary reason advanced in those jurisdictions which have sustained "no joinder clauses" in the area of liability insurance is that such a clause serves to prevent prejudice to the insurer through the prophylactic effect of isolating from the jury's consideration any knowledge that coverage for the insured exists. Such a result is deemed desirable because of the notion that a jury is prone to find negligence or to augment damages, if it thinks that an affluent institution such as an insurance company will bear the loss. See Appleman, 8 Insurance Law and Practice, §4861. While we will not go so far as to assert that the above proposition has been all but obliterated by the more recent indications to the effect that the injection of insurance does not operate to increase the size of jury verdicts, we do think the stage has now been reached where juries are more mature. Accordingly, a candid admission at trial of the existence of insurance coverage, the policy limits of same, and an otherwise aboveboard revelation of the interest of an insurer in the outcome of the recovery action against insured should be more beneficial to insurers in terms of diminishing their overall policy judgment payments to litigating beneficiaries than the questionable "ostrich head in the sand" approach which may often mislead juries to think insurance coverage is greater than it is. . . .

The District Court in its decision has ably spelled out the interests of an insurer in actively participating in the litigation brought against its insured. In addition to the reasons assigned by the District Court for such participation, there are certain facets to the question of joinder which we believe emphatically support the objective of a single law suit as a measure for affording complete adjudication of the tripartite interests whether they be concurrent or conflicting.

It is not altogether improbable that situations may arise where an injured third party has a very real interest in promptly aligning the insurer with the insured in a recovery action in order to timely adjudicate all questions concerning the coverage supplied the insured by the insurer. . . . Delays of the insured in filing proof of claim, claims of excess or other insurance, claims of misrepresentation, failure to seek early arbitration, and a variety of other defenses growing out of policy provisions can be asserted vis-à-vis the liability of the insurer against the insured which may operate, and often do, to defeat recovery by the injured third party beneficiary. . . .

A feasible approach to remedy the potential dangers inherent in the above described situations appears to be afforded by the joinder of the insurer. If joinder is allowed initially, all the cards are on the table and all interrelated claims and defenses can be heard and adjudicated reciprocally among all parties and the plaintiff will have the same initial right as insurer now avails itself against plaintiff to protect his rights against the insurer. In this manner the interests of all the parties and the concomitant right to expeditiously litigate the same in concert are preserved.

If it should clearly appear in pretrial procedures that joinder of the insurer interposes issues between insured and insurer in particular case situations likely to unduly complicate trial of the questions pertaining to the liability of the insured to the injured third party and commensurate damages to be awarded, it would be a simple process under our liberal civil rules for the trial judge on timely motion to sever such complicating issues between insurer and insured for separate trial or adjudication. But such separation for adjudication of issues between insurer and insured would not remove from the case the identity of all parties joined nor their claims and defenses and their right to participate and protect their respective interests.

For the foregoing reasons, we affirm the judgment of the District Court of Appeal, 1st District, on the merits. We recede from all prior decisions in conflict herewith.

By and large, courts have not followed *Shingleton* in creating a third party direct action against an insurer, apart from what is permitted by statute or by a policy itself. See White v. Goodville Mut. Cas. Co., 596 P.2d 1229 (Kan. 1979); Allen v. Pomroy, 277 A.2d 727 (Me. 1971); but see Watson v. Aetna Cas. & Sur. Co., 675 N.Y.S.2d 367 (App. Div. 1998) (creating more limited right for claimant to bring action against insurer for damages when it has already obtained judgment against insured on the issue of liability). However, many state statutes do permit direct actions by third parties against liability insurers. In general, these actions may only be brought after a claimant has a judgment against the insured. See, e.g., Ala. Code §27-23-2; N.Y. Ins. Law §3420. A minority of state statutes establish the right of a claimant to bring a direct action against a liability insurer at the outset of the case in a limited set of circumstances. See, e.g., La. Rev. Stat. Ann. §22:1269; (direct action allowed when insured has, *inter alia*, committed offense against insured's children or spouse); Ga. Code Ann. §40-2-140 (direct action allowed when insured is motor carrier); Wis. Stat. Ann. §632.24 (direct action allowed when claimant alleges negligence by insured).

While few state legislatures have created expansive rights of direct action against insurers, many more have established, with respect to automobile accidents, compulsory liability insurance and financial responsibility statutes. Compulsory liability insurance statutes require that minimum liability insurance be purchased in order to register an automobile. See, e.g., Ind. Code §9-25-4. Financial responsibility laws require drivers involved in accidents to provide proof of the ability to pay for subsequent damages or face suspension of their driver's license. The typical form of compliance is proof of insurance, see, e.g., N.H. Rev. Stat. Ann. §264.21.

2. Conflicts of Interest in the Defense and Settlement of Tort Claims

What was said earlier about the active role of the liability insurer and the passive role of the insured in defending claims and paying judgments against the insured is accurate only when there is no conflict of interest between the insurer and the insured. There are two common scenarios in which such a conflict may arise: denial of coverage and refusal to settle.

The insurer may deny coverage for a variety of reasons. The insurer may assert, for example, that the insured did not give the insurer the timely notice of the claim that is required by all liability insurance policies. Also, since liability policies do not cover harm that the insured intentionally causes, the insurer may argue that on the facts of the claim the insured intentionally injured the claimant. The conflict between the insurer's interests and those of the insured is clear in cases like these.

When the insurer disputes coverage, it has several options. It can notify the insured that it denies coverage and will not participate in the defense of the underlying claim. The coverage issue could then be addressed either before or after the underlying claim is resolved. The process for the earlier resolution of the coverage issue is an action for a declaratory judgment. The process for a later resolution could be a suit against the insurer by the claimant on the judgment against the insured. But even if the insured prevails against the claimant, it could still be determined that the insurer should have defended the claim — an issue to be resolved by a suit for defense costs brought by the insured against the insurer. The insurer can also agree to defend the claim under a "reservation of rights" or a "non-waiver agreement," both of which permit the insurer to defend the claim while preserving the insurer's right to dispute coverage later.

Refusals to settle typically stem from claims in excess of the policy limits. Liability policies commonly place two sorts of dollar limits on the insurer's obligation to pay the claim: a per occurrence limit and a per claim limit. If the policy, for example, limits the insurer's liability to $100,000 for any one claim, and the claim is for $500,000, what is best for the insured may be very different from what is best for the insurer. The insured would want the case settled for anything up to $100,000 to protect the insured completely from personal liability. The insurer, on the other hand, may prefer to litigate such a claim, even if it seems valid, hoping to avoid any liability at all. There would be no problem, of course, if the insurer's decision to litigate ends up in a verdict for less than the policy limits. But what if the decision backfires — the insurer refuses to settle and the verdict is for more than the policy limits? The decision below is one court's attempt to articulate the nature of the duty to settle.

Crisci v. Security Insurance Co.

66 Cal. 2d 425, 426 P.2d 173, 58 Cal. Rptr. 13 (1967)

Peters, J. In an action against The Security Insurance Company of New Haven, Connecticut, the trial court awarded Rosina Crisci $91,000 (plus interest) because she suffered a judgment in a personal injury action after Security, her insurer, refused to settle the claim. Mrs. Crisci was also awarded $25,000 for mental suffering. Security has appealed.

June DiMare and her husband were tenants in an apartment building owned by Rosina Crisci. Mrs. DiMare was descending the apartment's outside wooden staircase when a tread gave way. She fell through the resulting opening up to her waist and was left hanging 15 feet above the ground. Mrs. DiMare suffered physical injuries and developed a very severe psychosis. In a suit brought against Mrs. Crisci the DiMares alleged that the step broke because Mrs. Crisci was negligent in inspecting and maintaining the stairs. They contended that Mrs. DiMare's mental condition was caused by the accident, and they asked for $400,000 as compensation for physical and mental injuries and medical expenses.

Mrs. Crisci had $10,000 of insurance coverage under a general liability policy issued by Security. The policy obligated Security to defend the suit against Mrs. Crisci and authorized the company to make any settlement it deemed expedient. Security hired an experienced lawyer, Mr. Healy, to handle the case. Both he and defendant's claims manager believed that unless evidence was discovered showing that Mrs. DiMare had a prior mental illness, a jury would probably find that the accident precipitated Mrs. DiMare's psychosis. And both men believed that if the jury felt that the fall triggered the psychosis, a verdict of not less than $100,000 would be returned.

An extensive search turned up no evidence that Mrs. DiMare had any prior mental abnormality. As a teenager Mrs. DiMare had been in a Washington mental hospital, but only to have an abortion. Both Mrs. DiMare and Mrs. Crisci found psychiatrists who would testify that the accident caused Mrs. DiMare's illness, and the insurance company knew of this testimony. Among those who felt the psychosis was not related to the accident were the doctors at the state mental hospital where Mrs. DiMare had been committed following the accident. All the psychiatrists agreed, however, that a psychosis could be triggered by a sudden fear of falling to one's death.

The exact chronology of settlement offers is not established by the record. However, by the time the DiMares' attorney reduced his settlement demands to $10,000, Security had doctors prepared to support its position and was only willing to pay $3,000 for Mrs. DiMare's physical injuries. Security was unwilling to pay one cent for the possibility of a plaintiff's verdict on the mental illness issue. This conclusion was based on the assumption that the jury would believe all of the defendant's psychiatric evidence and none of the plaintiff's. Security also rejected a $9,000 settlement demand at a time when Mrs. Crisci offered to pay $2,500 of the settlement.

A jury awarded Mrs. DiMare $100,000 and her husband $1,000. After an appeal, the insurance company paid $10,000 of this amount, the amount of its policy. The DiMares then sought to collect the balance from Mrs. Crisci. A settlement was arranged by which the DiMares received $22,000, a 40 percent interest in Mrs. Crisci's claim to a particular piece of property, and an assignment of Mrs. Crisci's cause of action against Security. Mrs. Crisci, an immigrant widow of 70, became indigent. She worked as a babysitter, and her grandchildren paid her rent. The change in her financial condition was accompanied by a decline in physical health, hysteria, and suicide attempts. Mrs. Crisci then brought this action.

The liability of an insurer in excess of its policy limits for failure to accept a settlement offer within those limits was considered by this court in Comunale v. Traders & General Ins. Co., 50 Cal. 2d 654 [328 P.2d 198 (1958)]. It was there reasoned that in every contract, including policies of insurance, there is an implied covenant of good faith and fair dealing that . . . requires the insurer to settle in an appropriate case although the express terms of the policy do not impose the duty; that in determining whether to settle the insurer must give the interests of the insured at least as much consideration as it gives to its own interests; and that when "there is great risk of a recovery beyond the policy limits so that the most reasonable manner of disposing of the claim is a settlement which can be made within those limits, a consideration in good faith of the insured's interest required the insurer to settle the claim." (50 Cal. 2d at p. 659.)

In determining whether an insurer has given consideration to the interests of the insured, the test is whether a prudent insurer without policy limits would have accepted the settlement offer.

Several cases, in considering the liability of the insurer, contain language to the effect that bad faith is the equivalent of dishonesty, fraud, and concealment. Obviously a showing that the insurer has been guilty of actual dishonesty, fraud, or concealment is relevant to the determination whether it has given consideration to the insured's interest in considering a settlement offer within the policy limits. The language used in the cases, however, should not be understood as meaning that in the absence of evidence establishing actual dishonesty, fraud, or concealment no recovery may be had for a judgment in excess of the policy limits. Comunale v. Traders & General Ins. Co., supra, 50 Cal. 2d 654, 658-659, makes it clear that liability based on an implied covenant exists whenever the insurer refuses to settle in an appropriate case and that liability may exist when the insurer unwarrantedly refuses an offered settlement where the most reasonable manner of disposing of the claim is by accepting the settlement. Liability is imposed not for a bad faith breach of the contract but for failure to meet the duty to accept reasonable settlements, a duty included within the implied covenant of good faith and fair dealing. Moreover . . . recovery may be based on unwarranted rejection of a reasonable settlement offer and . . . the absence of evidence, circumstantial or direct, showing actual dishonesty, fraud, or concealment is not fatal to the cause of action.

Amicus curiae argues that, whenever an insurer receives an offer to settle within the policy limits and rejects it, the insurer should be liable in every case for the amount of any final judgment whether or not within the policy limits. As we have seen, the duty of the insurer to consider the insured's interest in settlement offers within the policy limits arises from an implied covenant in the contract, and ordinarily contract duties are strictly enforced and not subject to a standard of reasonableness. Obviously, it will always be in the insured's interest to settle within the policy limits when there is any danger, however slight, of a judgment in excess of those limits. Accordingly the rejection of a settlement within the limits where there is any danger of a judgment in excess of the limits can be justified, if at all, only on the basis of interests of the insurer, and, in light of the common knowledge that settlement is one of the usual methods by which an insured receives protection under a liability policy, it may not be unreasonable for an insured who purchases a policy with limits to believe that a sum of money equal to the limits is available and will be used so as to avoid liability on his part with regard to any covered accident. In view of such expectation an insurer should not be permitted to further its own interests by rejecting opportunities to settle within the policy limits unless it is also willing to absorb losses which may result from its failure to settle.

The proposed rule is a simple one to apply and avoids the burdens of a determination whether a settlement offer within the policy limits was reasonable. The proposed rule would also eliminate the danger that an insurer, faced with a settlement offer at or near the policy limits, will reject it and gamble with the insured's money to further its own interests. Moreover, it is not entirely clear that the proposed rule would place a burden on insurers substantially greater than that which is present under existing law. The size of the judgment recovered in the personal injury action when it exceeds the policy limits, although not conclusive, furnishes an inference that the value of the claim is the equivalent of the amount of the judgment and that acceptance of an offer within those limits was the most reasonable method of dealing with the claim.

Finally, and most importantly, there is more than a small amount of elementary justice in a rule that would require that, in this situation where the insurer's and insured's interests necessarily conflict, the insurer, which may reap the benefits of its determination not to settle, should also suffer the detriments of its decision. . . .

[T]he evidence is clearly sufficient to support the determination that Security breached its duty to consider the interests of Mrs. Crisci in proposed settlements. Both Security's attorney and its claims manager agreed that if Mrs. DiMare won an award for her psychosis, that award would be at least $100,000. Security attempts to justify its rejection of a settlement by contending that it believed Mrs. DiMare had no chance of winning on the mental suffering issue. That belief in the circumstances present could be found to be unreasonable. Security was putting blind faith in the power of its psychiatrists to convince the jury when it knew that the accident could have caused the psychosis, that its agents had told it that without evidence of prior mental defects a jury was likely to believe the fall precipitated the psychosis, and that Mrs. DiMare had reputable psychiatrists on her side. Further, the company had been told by a psychiatrist that in a group of 24 psychiatrists, 12 could be found to support each side.

The trial court found that defendant "knew that there was a considerable risk of substantial recovery beyond said policy limits" and that "the defendant did not give as much consideration to the financial interests of its said insured as it gave to its own interests." That is all that was required.

The judgment is affirmed.

TRAYNOR, C.J., MCCOMB, J., TOBRINER, J., MOSK, J., and BURKE, J. concurred.

The court in *Crisci* set the boundaries of the insurer's duty broadly, in a manner generous to the insured. While many states have adopted similar views of the duty to settle, see, e.g., Contreras v. U.S. Sec. Ins. Co., 927 So. 2d 16, 21 (Fla. Dist. Ct. App. 2006); Short v. Dairyland Ins. Co., 334 N.W.2d 384, 387-88 (Minn. 1983), none have adopted the *Crisci* court's suggestion that insurers could be held strictly liable for unsuccessful settlements. Indeed, some courts have adopted a far more narrow vision of the duty to settle: that, in the absence of bad faith conduct, an insurer cannot be liable for unsuccessful settlements. See, e.g., Pavia v. State Farm Mut. Auto. Ins. Co., 626 N.E.2d 24, 27-28 (N.Y. 1993). These differing approaches are important, and can determine the success of an insured's claim against an insurer. In the end, however, courts generally acknowledge that insurers owe the insured some duty to settle in the face of reasonably prudent settlement offers within policy limits. See Leo P. Martinez, The Restatement of the Law of Liability Insurance and the Duty to Settle, 68 Rutgers U.L. Rev. 155 (2015).

Courts are split on whether the duty to settle applies in situations where claimants do *not* make offers to settle within the policy limits. See Maine Bonding & Cas. Co. v Centennial Ins. Co. 298 Or. 514 (1985) (affirming judgment against insurer for bad-faith failure to initiate settlement negotiations). But see, e.g., Chandler v. Am. Fire & Cas. Co., 879 N.E.2d 396, 400 (Ill. App. Ct. 2007) (holding that the duty to settle does not arise until a third party demands settlement within policy limits); see also Annotation, 51 A.L.R.5th 701 (1997) (listing cases). In addition, some courts have imposed liability on insurance companies even when those insurers have settled *within* policy limits. See, e.g., Roehl Transp., Inc. v. Liberty Mut. Ins. Co., 784 N.W.2d 542 (Wis. 2010) (holding the defendant insurer liable because it failed to make good faith settlement efforts that could have reduced the insured's deductible liability). Moreover, in cases involving multiple insurers of the same insured, courts have held insurers liable for excess judgment when the claimant's offer to settle exceeded the policy limits of any individual insurer but fell within the aggregate policy limits of the multiple insurers. See, e.g., Howard v. Am. Nat'l Fire Ins. Co., 115 Cal. Rptr. 3d 42, 65-66 (Ct. App. 2010).

Once it is determined that the insurer has breached the duty to settle, most jurisdictions hold that the insurer is liable to the insured for an excess judgment even if the insured has not actually satisfied the judgment, and even if the insured is financially unable to do so. See Michael F. Aylward, Understanding Bad Faith, in 1 New Appleman Insurance Law Practice Guide: Coverage Analysis and Prelitigation Procedures §6.08[3], at 6-27 (Jeffrey E. Thomas, Leo P. Martinez, Marc S. Mayerson & Douglas R. Richmond eds., 2015) §6.08[3]. The court in Frankenmuth Mutual Insurance Co. v. Keeley, 461 N.W.2d 666 (Mich. 1990), took a middle-of-the-road approach. The court ruled that the insured can get a current judgment against the insurer for the amount of the excess judgment, but that the insurer would have to make payments on that judgment only as the insured acquired new assets subject to attachment.

Punitive damages may also be awarded against the insurer, but courts generally require some sort of aggravated behavior beyond "simple" bad faith or negligence. See, e.g., Sloan v. State Farm Mut. Auto. Ins. Co., 85 P.3d 230, 232 (N.M. 2004) (requiring reckless disregard, dishonest judgment, or otherwise malicious, willful, or wanton conduct); see generally Steven S. Ashley, Bad Faith Actions — Liability and Damages §8.06 (2d ed. 1997).

In an attempt to avoid the risk of liability in excess of policy limits, some insureds have attempted to settle with the injured party without the insurer. However, attempts to make the settlement binding on the insurer have reached mixed results, even if the insurer acted in bad faith in rejecting the settlement offer. See, e.g., Hamilton v. Maryland Cas. Co., 41 P.3d 128, 136 (Cal. 2002) (insured, who settled the claim with the injured party after the insurer rejected a settlement offer within the policy limits, could not sustain a bad faith action for damages against the insurer, because "[a] defending insurer cannot be bound by a settlement made without its participation and without any actual commitment on its insured's part to pay the judgment, even where the settlement has been found to be in good faith"). But see United Servs. Auto. Ass'n v. Morris, 741 P.2d 246 (Ariz. 1987) (a settlement reached by the insured and the claimant is binding on the insurer if the insured can prove that she acted reasonably and prudently in settling the claim).

In general, see Michael F. Aylward, Other People's Money: Insurer Liability for Failing to Settle Within Policy Limits, 54 Fed'n Def. & Corp. Couns. Q. 267 (2004); Symposium, Bad Faith in Contracts and Insurance, 72 Tex. L. Rev. 1203 (1994). For a helpful treatment of the duty of an insurance company to settle, see generally Kent D. Syverud, The Duty to Settle, 76 Va. L. Rev. 1113 (1990).

Problem 39

A partner of the firm in which you are an associate has given you the file dealing with the claim of Matilda Jones against Diedre Gertzweiler. Your firm represents Eagle Insurance Company, Gertzweiler's insurer. Jones and Gertzweiler are neighbors, and both are in their mid-50s. A little over a year ago, Jones dropped in at Gertzweiler's home for a morning cup of coffee. After finishing her coffee, Jones started to walk to the kitchen counter. On the way, she tripped on the corner of a rug, fell, and hit her head on the edge of the counter. She suffered serious and permanent head injuries. You have concluded that while liability is doubtful, the injuries, apart from any doubts about liability, would support recovery of somewhere near $150,000. The file indicated that the limits on Gertzweiler's policy were $200,000 per person and $500,000 per accident.

Taking into account both the doubtful liability and the seriousness of the injuries, you concluded that Eagle should make an initial offer of settlement of $25,000, and in no event go higher than $40,000. On the basis of your evaluation, an offer of $25,000 was submitted to Jones's lawyer. At a conference with the partner last week, she told you that Jones's lawyer has responded with a demand of $50,000. This turns out to be the limit of Gertzweiler's liability coverage — someone at Eagle had made a mistake in reporting the higher limits to your firm. The partner has also told you that the highest court of your jurisdiction has just handed down an opinion that follows *Crisci.* The partner asked you whether you would now abandon your resistance point of $40,000 and recommend that the offer of $50,000 be accepted. The partner is concerned that if Eagle rejects the $50,000 offer, and Jones wins at the trial, the company will be exposed to a claim for bad faith refusal to settle and may end up paying an amount well in excess of the $50,000 policy limit. If your assessment of damages is accurate, the company's liability could amount to as much as $150,000, apart from the possibility of recovery by the insured of punitive damages or damages for mental upset. The partner wonders if it would be wise for the company to avoid that exposure at the cost of $10,000, the difference between your initial resistance point and the policy limits.

What advice will you give to the partner with respect to whether Eagle Insurance should settle for the policy limits, or stay with your initial resistance point of $40,000?

The Lawyer's Professional Responsibility: Conflicts of Interest in Liability Insurance Cases

Under the typical liability insurance policy, the insurer has both the right and the duty to defend a claim against its insured. If the insurer is unable to settle the claim through its own claims process, it will usually name an attorney to handle the case. In such a situation, the lawyer designated to defend the insured has a client-lawyer relationship with the insured, and owes the same duties to the insured that the insurer does. See, e.g., State Farm Fire & Cas. Ins. Co. v. Mabry, 497 S.E.2d 844 (Va. 1998). See also Restatement (Third) of the Law Governing Lawyers §134 (2000). While the lawyer is selected by the insurer, and for that reason must look after its interests, the insurer's interests may conflict with those of the insured. When that occurs, the lawyer must act carefully to avoid representing persons with conflicting interests.

The rules of professional responsibility permit a lawyer to represent clients with differing interests in the same matter so long as the lawyer "reasonably believes that the lawyer will be able to provide competent and diligent representation to each affected client," and both have consented, after consultation, to the dual representation. Model Rules of Professional Conduct, Rule 1.7 (2016).

One of the more frequently recurring conflict of interest situations is that involved in *Crisci*, in which the claim exceeds the policy limits. See generally, Ellen S. Pryor & Charles Silver, Defense Lawyers' Professional Responsibilities: Part I — Excess Exposure Cases, 78 Tex. L. Rev. 599 (2000). The common procedure in such cases is for the company, or its attorney, to write the insured an "excess claim" letter inviting the insured to secure her own attorney to protect her interests. In the majority of cases, where the insured does not secure independent representation, the excess claim letter does not relieve the attorney retained by the company from his or her duties to the insured. The attorney is under a continuing duty to represent the interests of the insured, and must advise of any offers of settlement from the claimant, and may later have to withdraw from representing the insured if the conflict becomes irreconcilable. See Hamilton v. State Farm Mut. Auto. Ins. Co., 511 P.2d 1020 (Wash. Ct. App. 1973).

The possible existence of a policy defense can also be the source of a conflict of interest when an attorney is retained by the insurer to represent the insured. For example, a conflict can arise when, without notifying the insured, such an attorney gathers evidence on which to base a coverage defense for the insurer that the insured had failed to provide timely notice of the accident. *See* Employers Cas. Co. v. Tilley, 496 S.W.2d 552 (Tex. 1973). One of the more troublesome of the policy defense cases involves a claim that the insured intentionally injured the claimant, a claim not normally covered by liability insurance. While the insurer and the insured both would prefer the insured to prevail no matter what theory is relied on at the trial, the insurer may be able to avoid liability by supporting the intentional harm claim. The insured, if he is to lose at all, would naturally prefer a judgment based on negligence or recklessness, which would make the insurer ultimately liable. In Burd v. Sussex Mut. Ins. Co., 56 N.J. 383, 267 A.2d 7 (1970), the court held in such a case that it was proper for the attorney to withdraw from representing the insured, compelling the insured to select his own attorney to defend the claim. The coverage question would then be litigated in a later case, and if it were determined that the claim was covered by the policy, the insurer would be liable not only for the judgment against the insured, but also for the latter's attorneys' fees and expenses. A different resolution was suggested in Employers' Fire Ins. Co. v. Beals, 240 A.2d 397 (R.I. 1968) — the appointment of two attorneys by the insurer, one to represent the insurer and the other, the insured.

Chapter 10

Compensation Systems as Alternatives to the System of Tort Liability Based on Fault

Criticisms of the traditional tort system as a way of allocating accidental personal injury losses have been with us for decades, as have alternative mechanisms aimed at providing compensation to victims through streamlined, aggregative procedures. For a description of aggregate claims settlement practices that the authors describe as "tort law by other means," see Samuel Issacharoff & John Fabian Witt, The Inevitability of Aggregate Settlement, 57 Vand. L. Rev. 1571 (2004). Frequently voiced criticisms of the tort system include: (a) that it is inefficient — too little money ends up as compensation for injury and too much is siphoned off by the process of handling claims; (b) that it undercompensates the seriously injured and overcompensates the slightly injured; and (c) that compensation, if it is paid at all, is not paid promptly, at the time when it would do the most good. These criticisms are thought to take on added weight in the context of mass torts, where concerns of conflict of interest and inadequate representation also loom large. See generally David Marcus, Some Realism About Mass Torts, 75 U. Chi. L. Rev. 1949 (2008); Richard A. Nagareda, Mass Torts in a World of Settlement (2007).

The validity of these criticisms is hotly disputed, but proposals have emerged, some already adopted and others still on the drawing board, that are designed to provide compensation that is quicker, fairer, and more efficient. These alternative systems have the following characteristics in common:

1. The key to compensation is no longer fault; rather, it is an activity-connected event, which makes causation the central issue for recovery;
2. Explicit use is made of insurance — indeed, the claim for compensation is made against an insurer rather than one who has caused the harm; and
3. Compensation for intangible harm is largely not available, and compensation for economic loss may be less than actual loss.

Two contexts in which these compensation systems have been adopted involve workplace and automobile accidents. Non-fault compensation systems also have been proposed for medical and product-related injuries, but have not been implemented on a large scale, in part because of the difficulty in deciding what events would trigger compensation. An adverse medical outcome, for example, may result from the existing condition of the patient or from some shortcoming of the medical professional. If medical compensation will not be available to all who suffer heart attacks, there must be some method of sorting out those who should be compensated from those who should not. It is difficult, although it may not be impossible, to draw a line between the compensable and the noncompensable that does not in some way relate to the "fault" of the medical professional.

Any attempt to establish a non-fault compensation system for product-related injuries would also run into problems. For example, if the injured person had been driving while intoxicated and had run off the road into a utility pole, which product manufacturer should be responsible for the driver's injuries and pay the compensation? The manufacturer of the alcoholic beverage? Of the automobile? Of the utility pole? All three?

This chapter will focus on two compensation systems that have been widely implemented — workers' compensation and no-fault automobile insurance. The third section in the chapter will explore expansions of no-fault to medical and vaccine-related injuries; the growing use of public and private non-fault compensation mechanisms in the United States following large-scale disasters such as the events of September 11, 2001, or the British Petroleum oil spill of 2010; and the New Zealand social accident insurance scheme, which has almost totally replaced the tort system by allocating accidental injury losses through a variety of non-fault compensation systems. The final section offers selections from one recent scholarly effort to take stock of alternative compensation schemes and their relationship to the torts system.

A. Workers' Compensation

One of the significant impacts of the Industrial Revolution in this country in the latter half of the nineteenth century was the rapid increase in industrial accidents and employee injuries. Unsafe working conditions combined with expansion of the industrial work force to produce a steady stream, and then a flood, of disabling accidents. Many injured employees who were no longer able to earn wages became charges on the public. And for every worker injured or killed on the job there were likely to be dependent family members who would also have to look to public assistance for economic survival. The problem was compounded by the difficulties the disabled worker encountered in recovering compensation from the employer in the form of tort damages. In the first place, fault had to be shown on the part of someone as the proximate cause of his injuries. Even if negligence could be proved, if the person at fault happened to be a co-worker, as was very often the case, the employer was immunized from liability by the fellow servant rule, which barred recovery from a common master for the negligence of a fellow servant.[1] And even where the employer was shown to be directly at fault, or where some exception to the fellow servant rule was available, the doctrines of assumption of the risk and contributory negligence often barred recovery. See, e.g., Lamson v. American Ax & Tool Co., 58 N.E. 585 (Mass. 1900) (Holmes, C.J.) (dismissing personal injury action by employee who complained of unsafe working conditions because "[h]e stayed, and took the risk" and he "did so none the less that the fear of losing his place was one of his motives"). Injured employees might, in appropriate cases, succeed in actions against third persons. However, because the great majority of industrial accidents did not involve strangers to the employment relationship, the availability of tort actions against third persons remained almost totally theoretical. Studies of the economic impact of industrial accidents prior to workers' compensation reveal a system under which most workers injured on the job received little or no compensation through the tort system. See Arthur Larson & Lex K. Larson, Larson's Workers' Compensation Law §2.05 (2001).

Common law judges came under significant strain during the late nineteenth and early twentieth centuries, as shocking rates of injury and death among industrial workers were difficult to square with prevailing tort doctrines and the free labor ideology that supported

1. The landmark case is Priestley v. Fowler, [1837] 3 M. & W. 1, 150 Reprint 1030. The leading American case is Farwell v. Boston & Worcester R., 4 Metc. (Mass.) 49 (1842).

them. An ideal of freely bargaining, self-possessed workers helped to justify tort defenses such as assumption of risk and the fellow servant rule. Yet, as the American workplace changed dramatically in character, those same doctrines seemed to become primarily a shield for capital owners rather than an enabler of autonomy for labor. Although judges did experiment with new principles and practices for redressing the industrial carnage that came before them, they ultimately lost out to the systems of workers' compensation that proliferated throughout state legislatures. Early in the last century, legislative and public concern over the mounting problem of disabled, uncompensated workers led to the enactment of workers' compensation statutes in several states. By 1920 all but eight states had such statutes. The last state to fall in line was Mississippi, in 1949. These workers' compensation schemes largely displaced the common law of tort, workers' cooperative movements, and other institutional responses to the accident crisis. As the legal historian John Witt has argued, part of tort law's adaptive disadvantage was its inability to assimilate new social scientific ways of apprehending the industrial landscape. While classical tort doctrines seemed capable of rationalizing away any individual case of workplace suffering, aggregated accident data presented instead a policy problem of historically unprecedented magnitude. "[I]n the face of such statistical regularities, classical tort law's attempt to assign fault and responsibility through individualized inquiry into each work-accident case seemed beside the point." John Fabian Witt, The Accidental Republic 144 (2004).

Workers' compensation serves a number of purposes. In exchange for relinquishing the right to sue employers in tort for their work-related injuries, workers are provided with certainty and predictability of compensation. The compensation system is designed to prevent the destitution of the injured worker, regardless of fault. The predictability of workers' compensation also benefits employers, allowing them to better insure against injuries and pass the cost of that insurance along in the price of the goods and services the employers distribute commercially. In addition, the workers' compensation system also gives the injured worker an incentive to return to work by providing a somewhat lower payoff than what the worker would be earning at work. Workers' compensation is also meant to decrease social costs, both by allowing the parties to avoid protracted litigation and by decreasing the cost to the government of administrating the fault-based tort liability system.

Workers' compensation statutes vary considerably from state to state, although there are core features that almost all statutes share. All provide compensation for what might loosely be called work-related injuries without regard to either employee or employer fault, although fault is not entirely irrelevant under some statutes. All statutes provide somewhat limited compensation for impaired capacity to earn; most provide unlimited compensation for medical expenses. None compensate for intangible harm as such, although some observers believe that claims adjusters find other ways to provide some compensation for significant emotional or other intangible harms. In exchange for this package of non-fault benefits, employees give up the right to recover against employers in tort; workers' compensation is said to be the exclusive remedy for work-related injuries. Most workers' compensation laws operate, at least initially, through an administrative rather than through a judicial process.

Not all workers and employers are covered. Some statutes exempt employers of, for example, three or fewer employees. The Massachusetts act, outlined below, does not cover professional athletes who are compensated for work-related injuries, and real estate brokers who work only on commission. Also excluded are "casual" employees — those who are not employed in the employer's business. Some statutes also exempt agricultural employees.

The Massachusetts act (Mass. Gen. Laws Ann. ch. 152) is fairly representative. A covered employer must buy workers' compensation insurance, or qualify as a self-insurer. Most employers choose to buy workers' compensation insurance. An injured employee must notify the employer, who in turn will notify the insurer. After investigation and medical examinations, most claims are settled informally between the employee and the insurer. As workers' compensation was originally conceived, the hope was that an injured employee would not need to be represented by an attorney. While many claims are disposed of directly by the employee and the insurer, lawyers are an important part of the process. Indeed, many lawyers specialize in workers' compensation claims.

If settlement is not reached at this preliminary stage, the employee must file a request for a hearing before the Industrial Accident Board. The Board functions something like a court, although its orders are not self-executing. The party that loses before the Board can appeal the decision to the Superior Court. In reviewing the Board's decision, the court is limited to deciding whether the Board's decision is supported by the evidence or affected by an erroneous interpretation of the law; the Board's findings of fact are given the same status as those made by the jury in a civil case.

The sections of the Massachusetts act setting the amount of compensation are complicated, and what follows is a somewhat simplified statement of what an injured employee can recover. Medical expenses, including appropriate vocational training for workers who cannot resume their prior occupations, are recoverable in full. But compensation for impaired earning capacity — usually called "work loss" — is limited. If the employee is totally incapacitated, the employee is entitled to 60 percent of the employee's preinjury weekly wage, for a period not exceeding 156 weeks. If the injury is permanent and total, additional compensation kicks in after the expiration of the compensation for total incapacity, and is two-thirds of the employee's weekly wage. Compensation for partial incapacity is pegged at 60 percent of the difference between the worker's preinjury wage and what the worker can earn after the injury. The act also calls for reasonable burial costs, not exceeding eight times the average weekly wage in the state, and for death benefits to dependents, in the event that the injury results in death.

In addition to compensation for incapacity and burial expenses, the act provides for lump-sum payment for certain specific injuries. For example, if the injury results in the amputation of a leg, the worker is entitled to the statewide average weekly wage multiplied by 39; if both legs are amputated, the multiplier is 96. For the loss of hearing in both ears, the multiplier is 77. The act provides additional compensation for dependents of the injured worker.

In calculating the total compensation to which the worker is entitled, the act adopts the collateral source rule: Workers' compensation recovery is not reduced by any amount the worker receives from some other source. And finally, under appropriate circumstances, a worker may opt to receive a "lump sum" — roughly, the present value of whatever future payments the worker would otherwise be entitled to.

While it is accurate to characterize workers' compensation as non-fault, under the Massachusetts act, fault can still be relevant. If the injury is caused by the "serious and wilful misconduct" of the injured employee, the employee is not entitled to compensation, although if the injury causes death, the employee's dependents' rights to compensation are not affected. An injured employee is entitled to double compensation if the injury is caused by "serious and wilful misconduct" of the employer.

Not all injured employees are entitled to workers' compensation — to be compensable, the injury must have the requisite connection to the employment. In Massachusetts, as in most other states, the injury must "arise out of and in the course" of the employment. Some courts appear to treat this language as establishing a single requirement — that of "work connection." See, e.g., Thornton v. Chamberlain Mfg. Corp., 300 A.2d 146 (N.J. 1973), in which the court ordered compensation paid to a claimant who was attacked and injured by a former co-employee who was motivated by an on-the-job dispute, although the attack took place off the employment premises and nine days after the claimant left the employment. Most courts, however, treat the "arising out of and in the course of" language as imposing two separate requirements, each of which must be met to establish compensability. See, e.g., Gilbert v. USF Holland, Inc., 637 N.W.2d 194 (Iowa 2001) ("in the course of" satisfied, but not "arising out of"); Clodgo v. Rentavision, Inc., 701 A.2d 1044 (Vt. 1997) ("arising out of" satisfied, but not "in the course of").

Anderson v. Save-A-Lot, Ltd.

989 S.W.2d 277 (Tenn. 1999)

DROWOTA, J.

In this workers' compensation case, we consider for the first time whether an employee who has been sexually harassed by a supervisor in the course of employment may recover workers' compensation benefits from the employer. . . .

I. Facts & Procedural History

Since this case is presented to us on summary judgment, we summarize the evidence in the light most favorable to the plaintiff, the non-moving party. The record demonstrates that the plaintiff, Bernice Anderson ("Anderson"), was employed by defendant Save-A-Lot Foods as a co-assistant manager of a grocery store in Memphis. Anderson testified in a deposition that she was repeatedly sexually harassed on a daily basis by her immediate supervisor, Kenneth Bush ("Bush"), during the course of her employment. . . .

When Anderson first started working in the . . . store, Bush approached her, stating that he "knew how I got my job and what I had been doing with the other managers, [and] that he wanted the same thing." Anderson testified that Bush routinely followed her around the store, making lewd gestures and remarks to her. For instance, it is alleged that Bush repeatedly made graphic sexual comments about her body, requested that Anderson engage in sexual relations with him and accused her of having sex with co-workers. Bush would often grab Anderson's hand or bump up against her when he made these remarks. Anderson also alleged encounters in which Bush would "literally run up to me and get as close as he could to me and stare me up and down and then bust out laughing." In addition, on numerous occasions Bush, in the presence of Anderson, made inappropriate remarks about the body parts of the cashiers in the store.

. . . Ultimately, after Anderson reported the incidents to other management employees, an investigation was conducted, and Anderson was transferred to another store. Anderson alleges that as a result of Bush's harassing conduct, she suffers from post-traumatic stress disorder and depression and, consequently, has incurred medical expenses and has been unable to work. A psychiatrist who examined Anderson gave her a sixty (60%) percent permanent psychiatric impairment rating.

Anderson filed this Complaint for Workers' Compensation, seeking reimbursement for her medical expenses and lost earnings. In addition, Anderson filed a complaint in federal court alleging violations of the Tennessee Human Rights Act and Title VII of the Civil

Rights Act of 1964. After considering the deposition testimony proffered by the plaintiff, the trial court in the present case granted summary judgment to the defendants. It is unclear from the record whether the trial court found that a plaintiff may not recover workers' compensation benefits for sexual harassment injuries as a matter of law, or whether the trial court found that Anderson failed to demonstrate in this particular instance that she suffered an injury that arose out of her employment. [T]he Special Workers' Compensation Appeals Panel reversed the decision of the trial court. Concluding that Anderson's injury arose out of and in the course of her employment, the Panel found that Anderson would not have suffered an injury "but for" her employment.

II. Analysis . . .

Tennessee's Workers' Compensation Law applies to covered employees who suffer from "personal injury or death by accident arising out of and in the course of employment without regard to fault as a cause of the injury or death." Under this two-pronged test, a plaintiff must prove by a preponderance of the evidence that: (1) the injury arose out of her employment; and (2) the injury occurred during the course of her employment.

There is no dispute in this case that the alleged injury occurred in the course of Anderson's employment with Save-A-Lot. Viewing the "time, place and circumstances" surrounding the alleged harassment, it is clear that such incidents occurred while Anderson was on the premises of Save-A-Lot, performing duties on behalf of her employer. The crucial inquiry in this case concerns whether the alleged injury arose out of Anderson's employment. For years this Court has avoided applying "artificial labels" by advocating a steadfast test to determine when an injury arises out of employment. This struggle that has confronted our courts was discussed in Bell v. Kelso Oil Co., 597 S.W.2d 731 (Tenn. 1980):

> This Court and others over the years have attempted, with little success, to wring more certainty and specificity from the terse words "arising out of and in the course of employment." This has resulted in various judicial "tests" and "doctrines," such as, the "positional doctrine," the "peculiar hazard doctrine," the "foreseeability" test, the "street-risk doctrine," and others.
>
> It is difficult, perhaps impossible, to compose a formula which will clearly define the line between accidents and injuries which arise out of and in the course of employment to those which do not; hence, in determining whether an accident arose out of and in the course of the employment, each case must be decided with respect to its own attendant circumstances and not by resort to some formula.
>
> In this endeavor, the relation of the employment to the injury is the essential point of inquiry. . . .
>
> Generally, an injury arises out of and in the course of the employment if it has a rational causal connection to the work and occurs while the employee is engaged in the duties of his employment; and, any reasonable doubt as to whether an injury "arose out of the employment" is to be resolved in favor of the employee. [. . .]
>
> We have said that an injury arises out of the employment "when there is apparent to the rational mind, upon consideration of all the circumstances, a causal connection between the conditions under which the work [was] required to be performed and the resulting injury."

Bell, 597 S.W.2d at 733-34.

The defendants contend that claims for sexual harassment are properly brought pursuant to federal and state civil rights statutes, as well as tort suits, and do not fall within the ambit of Tennessee's Workers' Compensation Law. The defendants assert that Anderson's alleged injury was not due to a risk inherent to her employment or a risk that is a normal component of the employment relationship. Because Save-A-Lot did not have policies facilitating or condoning the alleged harassment and because the alleged incidents were not motivated by a desire to further the business of the employer, the defendants argue that the injury did not arise from Anderson's employment but, instead, was personal to Kenneth Bush. Thus, they contend that, as a matter of law, summary judgment was properly granted to the defendants.

It is well-settled that an employee may recover workers' compensation benefits for emotional injuries, such as stress, arising out of employment so long as the mental disorder can be traced to an "identifiable, stressful, work-related event producing a sudden mental stimulus such as fright, shock or excessive unexpected anxiety."

[The court then analyzed earlier Tennessee cases and cases from other jurisdictions.]

III. Conclusion

After carefully considering the rationale of these decisions and the facts of this case, we conclude that Anderson has failed to demonstrate that her alleged injury arose out of her employment. . . . On one hand, it is logical to construe Bush's purported activity as seeking to further a personal perverse sexual desire. It is equally logical to interpret Bush's conduct as being motivated by a demented animosity against Anderson in which he seeks to control and humiliate her. Under any interpretation, we find that it would be unreasonable to characterize Bush's motivation as anything other than "purely personal in nature" and not related to furthering the business of the employer. Anderson has not made any allegation suggesting that Bush was provoked to act in the best interest of Save-A-Lot, nor does the record support such an inference.

Furthermore, there is no indication that the nature of Save-A-Lot's business was such that the risk of harassment was a "reasonably considered hazar[d]" so that it was a normal component of Anderson's employment relationship. There is no allegation that Save-A-Lot requires or encourages employees to engage in any practice or dress in any manner that may invite sexual advances. Moreover, there is no suggestion of an established policy or systematic behavior by the employer in which sexual harassment is condoned. In fact, Anderson testified that to her knowledge Bush was the only Save-A-Lot employee who engaged in inappropriate harassing conduct.

The record strongly indicates that the alleged harassment had absolutely no "connect[ion] with what [Anderson] had to do in fulfilling her responsibilities of employment" with Save-A-Lot. It is clear under Tennessee law that the fact that Anderson was exposed to Bush during the course of her employment is not dispositive. The record simply does not demonstrate that sexual harassment was an inherent risk to which Anderson was exposed when she accepted employment with Save-A-Lot. To the contrary, the alleged harassment was an unanticipated risk that was not a condition of Anderson's employment. Accordingly, we find that Anderson's alleged injury is not compensable under the Tennessee Workers' Compensation Law.

Our holding is supported by public policy justifications. The Tennessee Workers' Compensation Law was enacted to "provide compensation for loss of earning power or capacity sustained by workmen through injuries in industry." We question whether the drafters ever contemplated that the statute would cover injuries suffered as a result of sexual harassment.

In fact, the Tennessee Human Rights Act ("THRA") was enacted to provide a remedy for the type of injuries that the plaintiff alleges. The remedies provision of the THRA, as well as its federal counterpart, Title VII of the Civil Rights Act of 1964, is designed to fully compensate victims of sexual harassment in the workplace. Moreover, it is conceivable that a contrary ruling would thwart the intent of the framers of the THRA to provide sexual harassment victims with a full recovery, since employer defendants would argue that THRA suits brought by employee plaintiffs are barred by the Tennessee workers' compensation exclusivity of remedies provision.

The judgment of the trial court granting summary judgment to the defendants is hereby affirmed. Costs of this appeal are taxed to the plaintiff.

The result in *Anderson* has both negative and positive implications for the claimant. On the down side, the claimant is unable to recover from workers' compensation. But on the up side, since workers' compensation does not cover the sexual harassment claim, the victim is free to pursue tort claims against the employer. Another case following the *Anderson* court's approach is Horodyskyj v. Karanian, 32 P.3d 470 (Colo. 2001), in which the employer attempted to assert the affirmative defense that it was immune from suit due to the fact that the alleged sexual harassment arose out of plaintiff's employment and was thus covered by workers' compensation. However, the court held that on the facts of the case, the sexual harassment complained of did not arise out of the plaintiff's employment, and allowed the tort claims to proceed. A lower court in Colorado subsequently distinguished *Horodyskyj* when an employee sought workers' compensation for mental distress allegedly suffered due to retaliatory harassment he experienced at work after testifying on behalf of a fellow employee in her federal sexual harassment suit. The court reasoned that "[a]lthough claimant's decision to testify in the lawsuit was personal, there is no evidence in the record to suggest that the harassment he experienced as a consequence grew out of any personal relationship or personal dispute." Public Service of Colorado v. Industrial Claim Appeals Office of State, 68 P.3d 583, 586 (Colo. App. 2003).

Courts examine the requirement of "arising out of/in the course of" in many contexts. One commonly recurring context involves injuries suffered while the employee is going to or coming from work. As a general rule, injuries arising in this context are not compensable. See La Croix v. Omaha Public Schools, 582 N.W.2d 283, 285 (Neb. 1998). Exceptions to the "going and coming" rule are numerous, however. See, e.g., Labadie v. Norwalk Rehab. Servs., 875 A.2d 485 (Conn. 2005), in which the employee was a nurse who was on her way from home to visit a patient, her first assignment of the day. The court held that the employee was entitled to compensation under a "service to the employer" exception to the general rule. See also Duke *ex rel.* Duke v. Parker Hannifin Corp., 925 So. 2d 893 (Miss. Ct. App. 2005), in which the court lists seven separate exceptions to the "going and coming" rule. For instance, an employee injured on a coffee break may recover under workers' compensation even if she has left her place of work and is injured while walking to a convenience store. Misek v. CNG Financial, 660 N.W.2d 495 (Neb. 2003).

The situation where an employee is attacked by some outside person also presents an "arising out of/in the course of" issue. If the attack stems in some way from the employment, courts ordinarily will find a sufficient connection for compensation. In Zoucha v. Touch of Class Lounge, 690 N.W.2d 610 (Neb. 2005), the court allowed compensation to an employee leaving work who was assaulted and robbed in the parking lot by a patron of the establishment in which she worked. In contrast, consider Panpat v. Owens-Brockway Glass Container, Inc., 49 P.3d 773 (Or. 2002), in which the decedent was shot and killed at her workplace by a co-employee with whom the decedent had a romantic relationship. The court stated that because the relationship was purely personal, the required work connection was missing, the injury was not covered by workers' compensation, and suit against the employer in negligence could proceed.

Courts also face cases where the injuries do not occur while the person is on the job, but are otherwise related to employment. The court in Shuler v. Gregory Elec., 622 S.E.2d 569 (S.C. Ct. App. 2005), held that the spouse and children of an employee who was killed in a car accident when returning home from physical therapy for a work-connected injury were entitled to workers' compensation death benefits because the death would not have occurred but for the mandated physical therapy. Conversely, some injuries that clearly occur while the person is on the job will nevertheless not be considered to "arise out of" the employment if "there was no condition of his employment, no risk of his employment activities, and no hazard in his workplace that was related to his injury." Lakeside Casino v. Blue, 743 N.W.2d 169, 178 (Iowa 2007). Applying these principles, the Iowa Supreme Court determined that a worker injured climbing stairs at the workplace did have the requisite relationship between employment and injury, while workers injured walking across a level floor, straightening up from signing a document, or turning to flush a toilet did not. See id. at 177-78.

Another issue related to the "arising out of/in the course of" requirement is whether the exclusive remedy provision of the compensation statute applies. If the injury does not arise out of and in the course of the employment, personal injury remedies may be available against the employer. In fact, even if the employment connection is satisfied, the exclusivity provision may not necessarily bar tort recovery. Many statutes, for instance, do not bar tort suits against the employer if the employer intentionally causes the injury. See, e.g., Mich. Comp. Laws Ann. §418.131. Often these intentional injury exceptions are judicially created, apparently out of discomfort with the limited damages awarded under workers' compensation schemes in the face of what appears to be egregious employer behavior. In Johnson v. BP Chemicals, Inc., 707 N.E.2d 1107 (Ohio 1999), for instance, the court ruled that the intent requirement is satisfied if it is established that the employer knew with substantial certainty that the injury to the employee would result from the unsafe working conditions.[2] The court also held that an attempt by the Ohio legislature to limit the exception to the exclusivity provision to "an act committed by an employer in which the employer deliberately and intentionally injures, causes an occupational disease of, or causes the death of an employee" (Ohio RC 2745.01(D)(1)) violated the state constitution.

Several years earlier, the Supreme Court of Ohio defined "injury" within the workers' compensation exclusivity provision not to include a "nonphysical injury with purely psychological consequences." Kerans v. Porter Paint Co., 575 N.E.2d 428, 431 (Ohio 1991). In this case, the plaintiff sought to recover compensation from her employer for harms she suffered as a victim of sexual harassment by her supervisor, also an employee of the defendant. The plaintiff faced something of a dilemma because, on the one hand, the workers' compensation recovery scheme offered little compensation for psychiatric and emotional harms such as those suffered by victims of sexual harassment. On the other hand, if the plaintiff sought to escape the exclusivity of workers' compensation through the

2. Recall Garratt v. Dailey, Ch. 1, above, in this regard. Compare Helf v. Chevron U.S.A., Inc., 203 P.3d 962 (Utah 2009) (holding that in Utah the intentional tort exception to workers' compensation exclusivity requires not merely substantial certainty, which implies probabilistic knowledge, but that the employer actually "knew or expected that injury would occur to a particular employee performing a specific task").

intentional tort exception, then she would be less likely to recover against her employer, given that respondeat superior liability is more difficult to establish for intentional torts than for negligence. The majority seemed to recognize her dilemma, and therefore offered a way out of the workers' compensation scheme not through the intentional tort exception, but by characterizing her harm as one that fell wholly without the coverage of the statutory regime. In that manner, her most plausible claims against the defendant — ones based on inadequate supervision and other negligent acts by the defendant company itself — could proceed. Three dissenting justices objected to the "creation of a new tort against an employer which has no foundation in common law." Id. at 436. Moreover, the dissenters felt that the majority's construction of the workers' compensation statute raised serious separation of powers concerns:

> Traditionally, we have been reluctant to adopt exceptions to the exclusive-remedy rule and this position has come from an unwillingness to tamper with the terms of a legislative bargain provided in exchange for the relinquishment of some prior vested rights. Either an expansive interpretation of the intentional tort exception or the development of new negligent tort actions would thwart the basic purpose of the statutory and constitutional scheme by eroding the exclusivity of the remedy provided by the Workers' Compensation Act.

Id. at 438-39.

The dissenters were vindicated in Kaminski v. Metal & Wire Prods. Co., 927 N.E.2d 1066 (Ohio 2010), a case examining another legislative attempt to limit the reach of the intentional tort exception in Ohio. The relevant statute provided that an employee could pursue direct tort actions when "the employer committed the tortious act with the intent to injure another or with the belief that the injury was substantially certain to occur." The phrase "substantially certain," however, was defined by the statute as acting "with deliberate intent to cause an employee to suffer an injury, a disease, a condition, or death." Id. at 1079 (quoting R.C. 2745.01). Thus, what appeared to be two avenues of intentional tort recovery actually converged into one. Notwithstanding the obvious legislative intent to overrule *Johnson,* which had defined substantially certain knowledge in the more conventional way and deemed that avenue of tort recovery constitutionally required, the court in *Kaminski* upheld the new employer intentional tort statute. Two years later, the court stood by its narrow interpretation of "substantially certain," insisting that the statute's peculiar definition could not be a mere "scrivener's error." Houdek v. Thyssenkrupp Materials N.A., 983 N.E.2d 1253, 1258 (Ohio 2012). See also Franklin Corp. v. Tedford, 18 So. 3d 215, 221 (Miss. 2009) (requiring "actual intent to injure the employee" in order to circumvent workers' compensation).

Problem 40

A partner in your law firm has asked you to look at a case for her. The client is John Tomassi, a 32-year-old assistant manager at the local Burkhart's department store, part of a nationwide chain. He has worked for Burkhart's for seven years. Recently he suffered severe personal injuries while on the job. Preliminary investigation into the facts of the matter has revealed the following:

Three months ago, John was working a late shift, as he had done numerous times in the past. One of his duties was to help close up at 10:00 P.M. The local Burkhart's store consists of two buildings located about 50 feet apart. As part of closing the store, John collects the receipts from the cash registers in the smaller building and takes them in a lock-box to the larger building across the parking lot so that all of the receipts can be put in the safe and taken to the bank the following morning. On the night in question, John was walking across the parking lot with the day's receipts when an unknown assailant attacked him from behind. The parking lot is poorly lit, and John was unable to see his attacker prior to the assault. The assailant struck John in the back of the head with a piece of pipe, grabbed the lock-box, and ran. The assailant has not been identified. John suffered a fractured skull, which caused a mild brain injury. He spent several weeks in the hospital and continues to suffer from persistent, incapacitating headaches and dizziness.

The neighborhood in which the store is located has deteriorated in recent years, with rising incidents of gang activity and theft. Over the past nine months, several stores in the vicinity have reported break-ins, and a year ago a local gang burglarized and vandalized the store that John helps to manage. In response, the Burkhart management at the corporate headquarters formulated a policy whereby, in such "high-risk" areas, the receipts from the previous day's sales were to be left in a safe in the smaller building overnight and carried to the large building the next morning. The policy also directed that a security guard would accompany whoever was responsible for carrying the receipts in the morning. This policy was finalized by the corporate office and sent to the local branch of the store over five months before John's injury. However, despite John's complaints that he was worried for his safety while carrying that much money alone at night, the head manager of the local store did not implement the new policy, saying the cost of providing a security guard was currently too high and that it was easier to keep things as they were until the store was doing better financially. At the end of one discussion about the issue, which occurred three weeks before the attack on John, the head manager told John: "You know, if you feel unsafe, you should maybe carry a can of Mace or something. Beyond that, I can't help you." After discussing the incident with local law enforcement agents, you have learned that if the change in corporate policy had been implemented, the attack very probably would not have occurred.

John has come to your firm inquiring about his rights and asking about his chances for tort recovery. The partner wants your opinion as to whether these facts favor the possibility of reaching the jury in a tort action against Burkhart's under the intentional tort exception to the workers' compensation exclusivity provision. If successful, a tort action would pay much more generously than workers' compensation benefits. The partner directs you to apply the two-prong analysis used in the following case to identify the strengths and weaknesses of John's situation. She wants your opinion regarding the likelihood of John's success in tort specifically.

Laidlow v. Hariton Machinery Co., Inc.

790 A.2d 884 (N.J. 2002)

LONG, J.

The Workers' Compensation system has been described as an historic "trade-off" whereby employees relinquish their right to pursue common-law remedies in exchange for prompt and automatic entitlement to benefits for work-related injuries. Millison v. E.I. du Pont de Nemours & Co., 101 N.J. 161, 174, 501 A.2d 505 (1985). That characterization is only broadly accurate. In fact, not every worker injured on the job receives compensation benefits and not all conduct by an employer is immune from common-law suit.

The Legislature has declared that certain types of conduct by the employer and the employee will render the Workers' Compensation bargain a nullity. Thus, for example, a worker whose death or injury is "intentionally" self-inflicted or results from a "willful" failure to make use of a safety device, furnished and required by the employer, will be ineligible for benefits. Likewise, an employer who causes the death or injury of an employee by committing an "intentional wrong" will not be insulated from common-law suit. N.J.S.A. 34:15-8; *Millison*, supra, 101 N.J. at 169.

The described limitations involve intentional wrongful conduct committed either by the worker or the employer. Underlying those limitations is the idea that such conduct neither constitutes "a natural risk of" nor "arises out of" the employment, the very notions at the heart of the Workers' Compensation bargain in the first instance.

The focus of this appeal is conduct by an employer that is alleged to constitute an intentional wrong under N.J.S.A. 34:15-8. We are called on to revisit our holding in *Millison*; resolve conflicting interpretations of it; and apply that decision to a case in which an injured employee claims that his employer has removed a safety device from a dangerous machine, knowing that the removal was substantially certain to result in injury to its workers and, in addition, deliberately and systematically deceived safety inspectors into believing that the machine was properly guarded. We hold that, in those circumstances, the employee's allegations, if proven, meet both the conduct and context prongs of *Millison*, thus entitling the employee to pursue his common-law remedies.

I

Rudolph Laidlow (Laidlow) suffered a serious and debilitating injury when his hand became caught in a rolling mill he was operating at his place of employment, AMI-DDC, Inc. (AMI). Laidlow sustained a crush and degloving injury resulting in partial amputations of the index, middle, ring and small fingers of his dominant left hand. Laidlow sued AMI on an intentional tort theory. He also named his supervisor, Richard Portman (Portman), in the suit for discovery purposes. AMI answered, denying the allegations of the complaint, and moved for summary judgment on the basis of the Workers' Compensation bar.

Under Rule 4:46-2, a movant will be granted summary judgment if the court finds, after reviewing the full motion record in the light most favorable to the adverse party, that there is no genuine issue of material fact. It is with that standard in mind that we view the facts presented on AMI's motion.

AMI is in the business of manufacturing electrical products. Laidlow has been employed by AMI since August 7, 1978. On December 11, 1992, Laidlow was performing his job as a "set up man," which required him to work with a rolling mill that changed the dimension of heated metal bars when they were inserted into the mill. Laidlow manually inserted the bars into a "channel" that guided them into the mill, and often had to apply pressure to the bars with his hand in order to feed them into the rollers. On the day of the accident, Laidlow's glove became caught by the unguarded nip point as he was pushing a bar of silver into the channel. His gloved hand was pulled toward the mill's rollers. An eyewitness, Laidlow's co-worker Steven Smozanek, described the incident as follows: "The rollers are approximately 18 inches in diameter, and as he was feeding the bar into the roller, it pulled his hand against the roller, not into the roller, and as it pulled the hand against the roller, it just ripped the glove and the skin right off his hand."

On a prior occasion, Laidlow's glove had also become hooked on a bar, but he was able to slip his hand out of the glove before it was pulled into the machine. Smozanek described a similar incident when he was working on the mill and his gloved hand had snagged on a bar, but he too was able to pull his hand out of the glove just in time to escape injury. Those close calls were reported to AMI.

After the rolling mill was purchased by AMI in 1978, the company arranged to have a safety guard installed. However, the safety guard was "never" engaged; from 1979 to the date of Laidlow's accident in 1992, the guard always was "tied up." According to Laidlow, the guard was placed in its proper position only when Occupational Safety and Health Administration (OSHA) inspectors came to the plant. On those occasions, Portman, Laidlow's supervisor, would instruct employees to release the wire that was holding up the safety guard. As soon as the OSHA inspectors left, the safety guard would again be disabled.

Laidlow operated the mill without the safety guard in place for approximately twelve to thirteen years. During that period, except for the "near misses" referred to earlier, there were apparently no accidents with the mill until Laidlow was seriously injured during the incident at issue here.

Laidlow spoke to Portman regarding the safety guard three times during the period immediately preceding his accident. Approximately two weeks prior to the accident, Laidlow asked Portman to restore the guard. Several weeks before that, he spoke to Portman because a new operator was going to work on the mill and Laidlow thought the guard should be restored to its operative position. Additionally, one week before the incident, Laidlow again expressed concern that a new, inexperienced operator would be working on the mill, and told Portman that it was dangerous not to use the guard. According to Laidlow, the guard was never restored. Portman responded to his requests by stating that "it was okay" and "not a problem," and by "walk[ing] away." Laidlow never refused to operate the mill without the safety guard in place nor spoke with any other superior in the company about the safety guard.

AMI concedes that the guard was removed for "speed and convenience." In addition, Gerald Barnes, a professional engineer retained by Laidlow, certified that AMI "knew there was a virtual certainty of injury to Mr. Laidlow or a fellow work[er] arising from the operation of the mill without a guard."

On those facts, the trial court concluded that Laidlow failed to demonstrate an "intentional wrong" under N.J.S.A. 34:15-8 and that Workers' Compensation was his exclusive remedy. Accordingly, the trial court granted AMI's motion for summary judgment, along with a similar motion filed by Portman.

The Appellate Division affirmed the dismissals, concluding that there was no evidence of an intentional wrong by AMI to warrant an exception from the Workers' Compensation bar. The panel relied on the lack of any accident over a twelve-year period and determined that OSHA violations alone, in the absence of proof of deliberate intent to injure, would not satisfy the intentional wrong standard. The court dismissed the suit against Portman because Laidlow failed to demonstrate any need to pursue discovery.

Judge Lintner dissented, contending that the record, fairly read, presented a jury issue regarding intentional wrong; that the lack of injuries over the twelve-year period was not dispositive of the issue of substantial certainty of injury; that, coupled with the guard's removal, AMI's deceptive practices with regard to OSHA provided conclusive evidence of "context" under *Millison*; and that Laidlow should have been allowed to obtain discovery from Portman because Portman was in a unique position to provide evidence of what the employer knew.

The appeal is before us as of right under Rule 2:2-1(a)(2) based on the dissenting opinion below. We granted Amicus status to the Trial Lawyers of America (ATLA-NJ) and New Jersey Manufacturer's Insurance Company (NJM).

II

In essence, Laidlow's argument is that the combination of the employer's disabling of the safety guard and deception of OSHA presents a triable issue on whether such conduct meets the definition of an "intentional wrong." AMI counters that under *Millison*, an intentional wrong requires a "deliberate intention to injure" and that Laidlow concedes that no one at AMI harbored such an intention. AMI also maintains that *Millison* specifically declared that the removal of a safety device fails to meet the intentional wrong standard. To the extent that recent Appellate Division decisions suggest the contrary, AMI argues that those cases should be disapproved. Furthermore, AMI argues that even if removal of a safety guard could qualify in some circumstances as an intentional wrong, the absence of any prior injury on its machine and Laidlow's successful experience in operating the machine without an accident for over twelve years obviates that possibility in this case.

NJM supports AMI's position that, under *Millison*, the standard for an intentional wrong requires proof of an employer's subjective intent to injure and that the deliberate removal or alteration of a safety guard does not constitute a "deliberate intent to injure." NJM also claims that the OSHA violations are legally irrelevant under *Millison*.

The heart of ATLA-NJ's position is that AMI and NJM totally mischaracterize *Millison*. ATLA contends that *Millison* specifically rejected the notion that an intentional wrong requires a deliberate intent to injure on the part of the employer; that *Millison* never declared that removal of a safety device failed to meet the standard for an intentional wrong; that the Appellate Division's reliance on the lack of prior accidents on the mill machine allows for "one free injury" contrary to our public policy; and that there is a jury question regarding whether the employer's actions constituted an intentional wrong.

III

Our decision in *Millison* is obviously at the root of this case and a review of our holding there is essential. In *Millison*, we were faced with the question of "what categories of employer conduct will be sufficiently flagrant so as to constitute an 'intentional wrong,' thereby entitling a plaintiff to avoid the 'exclusivity' bar of N.J.S.A. 34:15-8?" *Millison*, supra, 101 N.J. at 176, 501 A.2d 505. That statute reads:

> Such agreement shall be a surrender by the parties thereto of their rights to any other method, form or amount of compensation or determination thereof than as provided in this article and an acceptance of all the provisions of this article, and shall bind the employee and for compensation for the employee's death shall bind the employee's personal representatives, surviving spouse and next of kin, as well as the employer, and those conducting the employer's business during bankruptcy or insolvency.
>
> If an injury or death is compensable under this article, a person shall not be liable to anyone at common law or otherwise on account of such injury or death for any act or omission occurring while such person was in the same employ as the person injured or killed, except for intentional wrong. N.J.S.A. 34:15-8.

That is the so-called exclusive remedy provision of the Workers' Compensation Act, often referred to as the Workers' Compensation bar. *Millison* confronted that provision in the context of an occupational disease caused by exposure to asbestos during employment.

The appeal in *Millison* challenged a trial court's grant of summary judgment to an employer based on N.J.S.A. 34:15-8 in connection with plaintiffs' claim that the employer knowingly exposed them to an occupational disease. That court simultaneously denied summary judgment to the company doctors with respect to whom plaintiffs alleged the fraudulent concealment of their asbestos-related diseases. The Appellate Division affirmed the grant of summary judgment to the employer and reversed the denial of summary judgment to the physicians because there was no evidence that they "deliberately intended" to injure the workers.

We granted plaintiffs' petition for certification. Before us, plaintiffs argued that "their charges that defendants knowingly and deliberately exposed employees to a hazardous work environment and fraudulently concealed existing occupational diseases are sufficient to fall within the Act's limited 'intentional wrong' exception and to take their injuries outside the intended scope of the Compensation Act." *Millison*, supra, 101 N.J. at 170.

In addressing that contention, we recounted the history of the intentional wrong exception that had led the Appellate Division to its conclusion that only an employer's deliberate intent to injure was sufficient to vault the exclusivity bar. We also identified the precedents underlying the Appellate Division's ruling. [Description of earlier rulings requiring "deliberate intention" omitted.]

We recognized that those cases traced their rationale to Professor Larson's narrow and limited approach to intentional wrong and quoted extensively from his treatise. Specifically, we cited the following section:

> Even if the alleged conduct goes beyond aggravated negligence, and includes such elements as knowingly permitting a hazardous work condition to exist, knowingly ordering claimant to perform an extremely dangerous job, willfully failing to furnish a safe place to work, or even willfully and unlawfully violating a safety statute, this still falls shorts of the kind of actual intention to injure that robs the injury of accidental character. . . .
>
> If these decisions seem rather strict, one must remind oneself that what is being tested here is not the degree of gravity or depravity of the employer's conduct, but rather the narrow issue of intentional versus accidental quality of the precise event producing injury. The intentional removal of a safety device or toleration of a dangerous condition may or may not set the stage for an accidental injury later. But in any normal use of the words, it cannot be said, if such an injury does happen, that this was deliberate infliction of harm comparable to an intentional left jab to the chin. 2A A. Larson, The Law of Workmen's Compensation s 68.13 at 13-22 to 13-27 (1983) (footnotes omitted).

What is critical, and what often has been misunderstood, is that we cited Professor Larson and the cases relying on his approach for informational, not precedential, purposes. *Millison*, in fact, specifically rejected Professor Larson's thesis that in order to obtain redress outside the Workers' Compensation Act an employee must prove that the employer subjectively desired to harm him. In place of Larson's theory, we adopted Dean Prosser's broader approach to the concept of intentional wrong.

Under Prosser's approach, an intentional wrong is not limited to actions taken with a subjective desire to harm, but also includes instances where an employer knows that the consequences of those acts are substantially certain to result in such harm. See W. Prosser and W. Keeton, The Law of Torts 569 (5th ed.1984).

In abandoning Larson's purely subjective approach in favor of substantial certainty, we stated: "In adopting a 'substantial certainty' standard, we acknowledge that every undertaking, particularly certain business judgments, involve some risk, but that willful employer misconduct was not meant to go undeterred." Id. at 178.

Put another way, we recognized that Larson's "deliberate intent to injure" standard would sweep under its protection employer conduct that the Legislature never intended to insulate. By adopting Prosser's "substantial certainty" standard, we delineated another method by which a plaintiff could prove an intentional wrong. . . . Although noting in *Millison* that we were not repudiating earlier decisions [requiring deliberate intention,] we recognized that those decisions had been modified to the extent that an intentional wrong can be shown not only by proving a subjective desire to injure, but also by a showing, based on all the facts and circumstances of the case, that the employer knew an injury was substantially certain to result. In addition to adopting Prosser's "substantial certainty" test relative to conduct, in *Millison* we added a crucial second prong to the test:

> Courts must examine not only the conduct of the employer, but also the context in which that conduct takes place: may the resulting injury or disease, and the circumstances in which it is inflicted on the worker, fairly be viewed as a fact of life of industrial employment, or is it rather plainly beyond anything the legislature could have contemplated as entitling the employee to recover only under the Compensation Act? Id. at 179, 501 A.2d 505.

By the addition of the context prong, *Millison* required courts to assess not only whether the employer acted with knowledge that injury was substantially certain to occur, but also whether the injury and the circumstances surrounding it were part and parcel of everyday industrial life or plainly outside the legislative grant of immunity. In other words, under *Millison*, if only the conduct prong is satisfied, the employer's action will not constitute an intentional wrong within the meaning of N.J.S.A. 34:15-8. That standard will be met only if both prongs of *Millison* are proved.

Applying the newly adopted standard to the facts in *Millison*, we concluded, with respect to the defendant employer, that:

> count one of plaintiffs' complaints seeking damages beyond those available through workers' compensation for their initial work-related occupational diseases must fall. Although defendants' conduct in knowingly exposing plaintiffs to asbestos clearly amounts to deliberately taking risks with employees' health, as we have observed heretofore the mere knowledge and appreciation of a risk — even the strong probability of a risk — will come up short of the "substantial certainty" needed to find an intentional wrong resulting in avoidance of the exclusive-remedy bar of the compensation statute. In the face of the legislature's awareness of occupational diseases as a fact of industrial employment, we are constrained to conclude that plaintiffs-employees' initial resulting occupational diseases must be considered the type of hazard of employment that the legislature anticipated would be compensable under the terms of the Compensation Act and not actionable in an additional civil suit. Ibid.

Regarding the defendant physicians' conduct, however, we reached a different conclusion:

> Plaintiffs have, however, pleaded a valid cause of action for aggravation of their initial occupational diseases under the second count of their complaints. Count two alleges that in

> order to prevent employees from leaving the workforce, defendants fraudulently concealed from plaintiffs the fact that they were suffering from asbestos-related diseases, thereby delaying their treatment and aggravating their existing illnesses. . . .
>
> These allegations go well beyond failing to warn of potentially-dangerous conditions or intentionally exposing workers to the risks of disease. There is a difference between, on the one hand, tolerating in the workplace conditions that will result in a certain number of injuries or illnesses, and, on the other, actively misleading the employees who have already fallen victim to those risks of the workplace. An employer's fraudulent concealment of diseases already developed is not one of the risks an employee should have to assume. Such intentionally-deceitful action goes beyond the bargain struck by the Compensation Act. . . . The legislature, in passing the Compensation Act, could not have intended to insulate such conduct from tort liability. . . .

Recapping, a number of principles relevant to the present inquiry can be distilled from *Millison*. First, although we recognized the need for a chary interpretation of the intentional wrong exception to the Workers' Compensation bar so that the exception would not "swallow up" the rule, we clearly rejected Larson's narrow and limited approach that required subjective intention to injure. Second, in rejecting that approach, we also declined to adopt Larson's conclusion concerning the effect of removal of a safety device. At the very least, that issue remained open after *Millison*.

Third, we adopted Prosser's substantial certainty test for intentional wrong, a test encompassing acts that the employer knows are substantially certain to produce injury even though, strictly speaking, the employer does not will that result. Fourth, although we did not repudiate [early case law] outright, our adoption of the "substantial certainty" standard as a complement to the "subjective desire" standard governing conduct plainly modified that line of cases. Fifth, under *Millison*, in order for an employer's act to lose the cloak of immunity of N.J.S.A. 34:15-8, two conditions must be satisfied: (1) the employer must know that his actions are substantially certain to result in injury or death to the employee, and (2) the resulting injury and the circumstances of its infliction on the worker must be (a) more than a fact of life of industrial employment and (b) plainly beyond anything the Legislature intended the Workers' Compensation Act to immunize. . . .

V

We turn now to the case at bar. . . . [W]e are satisfied that under our well-established standards for summary judgment . . . summary judgment should have been denied to AMI and the case sent to a jury on the issue of substantial certainty.

The evidence with inferences in favor of Laidlow is powerful. The rolling mill is a dangerous machine because it requires an employee to manually feed material into a nip point. . . . Apparently recognizing that principle, after its purchase AMI provided a safety guard for the rolling mill. Yet, for 13 years, from 1979 to 1992 when Laidlow was injured, the guard was inactivated by AMI nearly 100% of the time the machine was in use. During that period, Laidlow and a fellow employee had experienced close calls with the nip point of the unguarded mill. Those were potentially serious accidents in which the employees' gloves were ripped off by the machine and their fingers saved only by the cloth in the gloves. Those close calls were reported to AMI to no avail. They were persuasive evidence that AMI knew not only that injury was substantially certain to occur, but also that when it did occur it would be very serious, as Laidlow's injury turned out to be. Within the month prior to his accident, Laidlow asked his supervisor three times to restore the guard because the unguarded machine was dangerous and because new and inexperienced employees would be operating it. Nothing was ever done. . . .

AMI argues that the absence of prior accidents obviates a possible finding of "substantial certainty" by a jury. We disagree. To be sure, reports of prior accidents like prior "close-calls" are evidence of an employer's knowledge that death or injury are substantially certain to result, but they are not the only such evidence. Likewise, the absence of a prior accident does not mean that the employer did not appreciate that its conduct was substantially certain to cause death or injury. In short, we disagree with AMI and the Appellate Division that the absence of a prior accident on the rolling mill ended any inquiry regarding intentional wrong. That is simply a fact, like the close-calls, that may be considered in the substantial certainty analysis.

Turning to the facts in this record, we are satisfied that a reasonable jury could conclude, in light of all surrounding circumstances, including the prior close-calls, the seriousness of any potential injury that could occur, Laidlow's complaints about the absent guard, and the guilty knowledge of AMI as revealed by its deliberate and systematic deception of OSHA, that AMI knew that it was substantially certain that the removal of the safety guard would result eventually in injury to one of its employees. Thus, a jury question was presented on that issue.

A finding that the substantial certainty prong was satisfied does not end our inquiry. Laidlow's allegations, if proved, also must satisfy the context prong of *Millison* to preclude AMI from summary judgment. We have concluded that if Laidlow's allegations are proved, however, the context prong of *Millison* would be met. Indeed, if an employee is injured when an employer deliberately removes a safety device from a dangerous machine to enhance profit or production, with substantial certainty that it will result in death or injury to a worker, and also deliberately and systematically deceives OSHA into believing that the machine is guarded, we are convinced that the Legislature would never consider such actions or injury to constitute simple facts of industrial life. On the contrary, such conduct violates the social contract so thoroughly that we are confident that the Legislature would never expect it to fall within the Worker's Compensation bar.

Our holding is not to be understood as establishing a per se rule that an employer's conduct equates with an "intentional wrong" within the meaning of N.J.S.A. 34:15-8 whenever that employer removes a guard or similar safety device from equipment or machinery, or commits some other OSHA violation. Rather, our disposition in such a case will be grounded in the totality of the facts contained in the record and the satisfaction of the standards established in *Millison* and explicated here.

VI

. . . Obviously, the proofs at trial may not track the employee's allegations. Thus, the employer may, even after a jury returns a verdict in the employee's favor regarding substantial certainty, apply to the trial court for reconsideration of the context issue based on the difference between the facts actually established at trial and what plaintiff alleged would be proved. With that possibility in mind, where the evidence is in conflict regarding the allegations relied on by the trial court for its preliminary context evaluation, the court should secure from the jury a resolution of those conflicts by way of a carefully crafted jury verdict form.

VII

The judgment of the Appellate Division is reversed. The matter is remanded for trial after plaintiff is afforded a reasonable opportunity to complete discovery concerning Portman.

Laidlow and several other cases discussed above are examples of a phenomenon that arises in many alternative compensation schemes—what Professor Nora Freeman Engstrom has labeled "exit." As time passes, injured employees find new ways to avoid the exclusivity of workers' compensation remedies in order to seek recovery in the tort system. See Nora Freeman Engstrom, Exit, Adversarialism, and the Stubborn Persistence of Tort, 6 J. Tort L. 75, 83-84 (2013). In *Laidlow*, for instance, the employee achieved exit through an expansive interpretation of the "intentional wrong" doctrine. But note that injured employees are not the only ones who try to avoid workers' compensation. In *Anderson*, it was the employer who escaped workers' compensation through the "arising out of" requirement. Altogether, the many doctrines of workers' compensation law allow a surprisingly high rate of workplace injuries to wind up in the tort system.

Despite its imperfections, workers' compensation has been part of the American industrial landscape for over a century. One recent reform, spearheaded in Oklahoma, attempted to change the shape of workers' compensation. Under a 2013 Oklahoma law, companies were permitted to opt out of the state's workers' compensation scheme and write their own employee injury compensation plans. Okla. Stat. Ann. tit. 85A, §202 (2013). Proponents of the opt-out system argued that it reduces costs for businesses and increases employee satisfaction. Investigative reports, however, were critical of the opt-out statute, finding that the reform favors employers over employees by limiting the types of injuries covered, reducing benefits, and narrowing the timeframe to bring a claim. Michael Grabell & Howard Berkes, Inside Corporate America's Campaign to Ditch Workers' Comp, ProPublica, Oct. 13, 2015, https://www.propublica.org/article/inside-corporate-americas-plan-to-ditch-workers-comp. In late 2016, the Oklahoma Supreme Court struck down the opt-out provision as a constitutionally impermissible "special law" that subjected certain classes of workers to disparate treatment. Vasquez v. Dillard's, Inc., 2016 WL 4804078 (Okla. 2016).

B. Compensation for Victims of Automobile Accidents

Much of the criticism directed at the torts system of allocating losses from personal injuries has focused on those stemming from automobile accidents. In general, the system stands accused of overcompensating the slightly injured, undercompensating the seriously injured, delaying the payment of claims, absorbing high costs in processing claims, encouraging dishonesty in the making and paying of claims, and causing high, to the point of being unaffordable, liability insurance premiums. The most comprehensive empirical study of automobile accidents was conducted by the United States Department of Transportation, which culminated in a multivolume report released in 1970.

The most influential work kindling an interest in removing automobile accident losses from the torts system is that of then Professor, now Judge, Robert Keeton and Professor

Jeffrey O'Connell. In their book, Basic Protection for the Traffic Victim: A Blueprint for Reforming Automobile Insurance (1965), they presented a detailed proposal that would replace much of the traditional negligence insurance system of compensation for personal injuries caused by automobile accidents. The key features of the Basic Protection Plan are:

(1) Compulsory insurance providing for compensation for economic loss of up to $10,000, without regard to fault, for injuries "arising out of the ownership, maintenance, or use of a motor vehicle." Economic loss consists of income actually lost, expenses reasonably incurred by the injured person for services he would have performed for himself but for the injury, and reasonable medical and rehabilitation expenses.
(2) Reduction of the amount of compensation due by any amount received from a collateral source, such as medical insurance and sick leave plans (but not life insurance or "gratuities"), and by an amount representing the income tax that would be paid were the compensation taxable.
(3) Exemption from liability in tort for the first $5,000 of damages for pain and suffering and for the first $10,000 of other tort damages.
(4) Periodic payments of benefits on a monthly basis, with lump-sum payment only when a court rules that it "is in the best interests of the claimant."

Massachusetts was the first state to enact a no-fault automobile insurance statute. In 1967, a bill patterned after the Keeton-O'Connell Basic Protection Plan was passed by the House of Representatives, but was defeated in the Senate. This setback for no-fault was only temporary, and the Massachusetts legislature enacted the Personal Injury Protection Act (Mass. Gen. Laws ch. 90, §§34A, 34M, and 34N, and ch. 231, §6D), which became effective in 1971.

No-fault statutes were subsequently adopted by a number of states and they come in almost endless variations. In some states no-fault insurance is compulsory, and in others it is only elective — insurance companies must offer the coverage, but it need not be purchased. The statutes also vary in the amount of no-fault benefits that are payable. No-fault compensation is limited to out-of-pocket expenses, usually medical and related expenses and lost wages. Some statutes have an aggregate limit for both; others specify separate limits.

"True" no-fault requires some sort of tort exemption applicable to the operator causing the injury. All such statutes exempt the operator from tort liability for out-of-pocket no-fault benefits that are paid and, to some extent, from liability for pain and suffering. The most important variations among "true" no-fault statutes relate to the amount of no-fault benefits available, and to the extent to which recovery for intangible harm may still be had.

The Massachusetts and Michigan statutes tend toward the extremes with respect to both. In Massachusetts, there is an overall limit of $8,000 in benefits for economic loss, and a limit of $2,000 for medical expenses. See Mass. Gen. Laws Ann. ch. 90, §34A. Under the Michigan statute, there is no dollar limit to reasonable medical expenses. Recovery for work loss is limited to the three years after the accident, with a limit of $5,189 for a 30-day period, adjusted for inflation beginning October 1, 2013. See Mich. Comp. Laws Ann. ch. 500, §3107.

Massachusetts allows tort recovery for pain and suffering if medical expenses exceed $2,000, or if the injury is serious, such as death or loss of a body member. See Mass. Gen. Laws. Ann. ch. 231, §6(D). Michigan permits tort recovery for "noneconomic loss" only if the injury results in "death, serious impairment of body function, or permanent serious disfigurement." See Mich. Comp. Laws Ann. ch. 500, §3135. Interpreting the precise meaning of this eligibility threshold has proven difficult for the Michigan courts and legislature. See David Perlow, It's Time for a Tune Up: Torquing Michigan's "Faulty" Automobile-Insurance System, 24 T.M. Cooley L. Rev. 281 (2007).

As with workers' compensation (see *Anderson,* p. 721, above) no-fault automobile insurance involves coverage problems. No-fault statutes generally require that, to be compensable, the injury must arise out of the ownership, operation, maintenance, or use of the insured automobile, paralleling the "arising out of/in the course of" language common to most workers' compensation laws. Also paralleling workers' compensation, the no-fault coverage language has generated considerable litigation.

McKenzie v. Auto Club Insurance Association

458 Mich. 214, 580 N.W.2d 424 (1998)

TAYLOR, JUSTICE.

This case presents the issue whether plaintiff is entitled to personal injury protection (PIP) benefits under the no-fault act, M.C.L. §500.3101 et seq.; M.S.A. §24.13101 et seq., for injuries sustained when he was nonfatally asphyxiated while sleeping in a camper/trailer attached to his pickup truck. We conclude that plaintiff's injury is not covered by the no-fault act because it did not arise out of the use of a motor vehicle "as a motor vehicle" as required by M.C.L. §500.3105(1); M.S.A. §24.13105(1). Whether an injury arises out of the use of a motor vehicle "as a motor vehicle" turns on whether the injury is closely related to the transportational function of automobiles. We accordingly reverse the judgment of the Court of Appeals and remand for entry of summary disposition in favor of defendant.

I

The basic facts are undisputed. While on a hunting trip, plaintiff and Hughie McKenzie slept in a camper/trailer attached to the back of plaintiff's pickup truck. The camper/trailer was equipped with a propane-fueled, forced-air heater. Ostensibly, because of either poor ventilation or improper exhaust in the unit itself, carbon monoxide fumes from the heater leaked into the camper/trailer and overcame the two men. Fortunately, they were found the following day and recovered after being hospitalized.

Plaintiff filed the present suit for PIP benefits under his no-fault insurance contract with defendant. Defendant moved for summary disposition, contending that there was no coverage because the camper/trailer was not being used "as a motor vehicle" at the time the injury occurred as required by §3105. The trial court granted summary disposition for plaintiff. . . .

II

This case turns on whether plaintiff's injury, incurred while sleeping in a parked camper/trailer, arose out of the use of a motor vehicle "as a motor vehicle" as contemplated by

§3105. We are able to arrive at this ultimate question because all agree that this injury was occasioned while a person was occupying the vehicle as required by M.C.L. §500.3106(1)(c); M.S.A. §24.13106(1)(c).

It is well to begin our analysis with the basic axioms of statutory construction: The rules of statutory construction are well established. First and foremost, we must give effect to the Legislature's intent. If the language of a statute is clear and unambiguous, the plain meaning of the statute reflects the legislative intent and judicial construction is not permitted. Further, we are to give statutory language its ordinary and generally accepted meaning. [Citation omitted.]

The "use of a motor vehicle 'as a motor vehicle'" limitation on no-fault coverage[4] had its origins in the Uniform Motor Vehicle Accident Reparations Act. . . .

As a matter of English syntax, the phrase "use of a motor vehicle 'as a motor vehicle'" would appear to invite contrasts with situations in which a motor vehicle is not used "as a motor vehicle." This is simply to say that the modifier "as a motor vehicle" assumes the existence of other possible uses and requires distinguishing use "as a motor vehicle" from any other uses. White it is easily understood from all our experiences that most often a vehicle is used "as a motor vehicle," i.e., to get from one place to another, it is also clear from the phrase used that the Legislature wanted to except those other occasions, rare as they may be, when a motor vehicle is used for other purposes, e.g., as a housing facility of sorts, as an advertising display (such as at a car dealership), as a foundation for construction equipment, as a mobile public library, or perhaps even when a car is on display in a museum. On those occasions, the use of the motor vehicle would not be "as a motor vehicle," but as a housing facility, advertising display, construction equipment base, public library, or museum display, as it were. It seems then that when we are applying the statute, the phrase "as a motor vehicle" invites us to determine if the vehicle is being used for transportational purposes.

Accordingly, we are convinced that the clear meaning of this part of the no-fault act is that the Legislature intended coverage of injuries resulting from the use of motor vehicles when closely related to their transportational function and only when engaged in that function.[7]

Moreover, requiring that an injury be closely associated with the transportational function of a vehicle before coverage is triggered has support in much of our prior case law. We acknowledge that the expressed rationale of these cases was not articulated in terms of transportational function, and, indeed, some cannot be reconciled with this approach, but many are consistent with a focus on transportational function to determine whether the injuries at issue in those cases arose out of the use of a motor vehicle "as a motor vehicle."

4. M.C.L. §500.3105(1); M.S.A. §24.13105(1) provides: "Under personal protection insurance an insurer is liable to pay benefits for accidental bodily injury arising out of the ownership, operation, maintenance or use of a motor vehicle as a motor vehicle, subject to the provisions of this chapter."

7. The dissent accuses us of judicial activism. It is always gratifying to hear members of the judiciary concern themselves with judicial restraint and proper deference to the Legislature. We fully agree with these principles. But the dissent's concern is misplaced here. We have acted in accord with venerable norms of statutory construction by focusing on the language and syntax of the statute and then painstakingly endeavoring to be faithful to it even on pain of having to overrule some of our previous opinions. This repudiation of earlier efforts never comes easily to any judicial body and that is the case here. We have then not taken on a legislative role. Rather, it is paradoxically the dissent that attempts to rewrite the statute by effectively omitting portions of it. It is the dissent's position that an injury arising out of any intended use of a motor vehicle triggers coverage. This would accord no meaning to the phrase "as a motor vehicle." This a court cannot do, as we must read a statute to give meaning to every portion. That is what we have done and what separates us from the dissent.

In Turner v. Auto Club Ins. Ass'n, 448 Mich. 22, 528 N.W.2d 681 (1995), a truck involved in a multiple vehicle accident smashed into a building and started a fire when the truck's gas tank exploded. This Court held that the damage to the building arose out of the use of the truck "as a motor vehicle." Id. at 32, 528 N.W.2d 681. This holding was not surprising in that it indicated that no-fault insurance generally covers damage directly resulting from an accident involving moving motor vehicles. This, of course, is consistent with the approach that focuses on transportational function because moving motor vehicles are quite obviously engaged in a transportational function.

In Putkamer v. Transamerica Ins. Corp. of America, 454 Mich. 626, 636-637, 563 N.W.2d 683 (1997), this Court held that injuries incurred while entering a vehicle with the intent to travel arose out of the use of a motor vehicle as a motor vehicle. Because entering a vehicle in order to travel in it is closely related to the transportational function, *Putkamer* also comports with this approach.

In Winter v. Automobile Club of Michigan, 433 Mich. 446, 446 N.W.2d 132 (1989), this Court denied no-fault insurance coverage when it held that an injury resulting when a cement slab fell from a crane attached to a parked tow truck did not arise out of the use of a motor vehicle "as a motor vehicle." The *Winter* Court's holding turned on the fact that the truck was parked and none of the exceptions set forth in §3106 applied. Accordingly, it was unnecessary to explicitly consider whether the injury arose out of the use of a motor vehicle "as a motor vehicle," as opposed to some other use. However, this holding is nonetheless consistent with the approach posited here because the injury arose out of the use of a motor vehicle as a foundation for construction equipment and was not closely associated with the transportational function. . . .

The dissent relies heavily on Bialochowski v. Cross Concrete Pumping Co., 428 Mich. 219, 407 N.W.2d 355 (1987), which is also inconsistent with the approach posited here. In *Bialochowski,* this Court concluded that an injury incurred while a cement truck was unloading its product arose out of the use of a motor vehicle as a motor vehicle. The Court stated at 228, 407 N.W.2d 355:

> Motor vehicles are designed and used for many different purposes. The truck involved in this case is a cement truck capable of pouring cement at elevated levels. Certainly one of the intended uses of this motor vehicle (a motor vehicle under the no-fault act) is to pump cement. The accident occurred while this vehicle was being used for its intended purpose. We hold that the phrase "use of a motor vehicle as a motor vehicle" includes this use.

We find this holding utterly antithetical to the language of §3105. As discussed above, §3105's requirement that injuries arise out of the use of a motor vehicle "as a motor vehicle" clearly distinguishes use "as a motor vehicle" from other possible uses. *Bialochowski* eviscerates this distinction by holding that the use of the vehicle at issue to pump cement constitutes use "as a motor vehicle." Obviously, motor vehicles are designed and used for various purposes as the *Bialochowski* Court noted. In fact, only in the context of various possible uses would a limitation to use "as a motor vehicle" be necessary. Where the Legislature explicitly limited coverage under §3105 to injuries arising out of a particular use of motor vehicles — use "as a motor vehicle" — a decision finding coverage for injuries arising out of any other use, e.g., to pump cement, is contrary to the language of the statute. Accordingly, we are convinced that *Bialochowski* was wrongly decided.

Entirely apart from this direct criticism of *Bialochowski,* we do not think it constitutes adequate support for the dissent's proposed rule that any intended use of a multipurpose vehicle constitutes use "as a motor vehicle."

First, this Court's subsequent decision in *Winter,* supra at 455, 446 N.W.2d 132, explicitly limited *Bialochowski:* Insofar as it related to the "as a motor vehicle" language, *Bialochowski* decided a narrow issue: whether a dual-purpose vehicle is not necessarily in use as a motor vehicle when it is being used for a nonlocomotive purpose. *Bialochowski* held that coverage is not necessarily precluded solely because there was no "vehicular movement" at the time of the injury.

This all means that the *Winter* Court read *Bialochowski* to only establish that vehicular movement was not necessary to constitute use of a motor vehicle "as a motor vehicle." Here, the dissent's reading of *Bialochowski* as meaning that any intended use of a multipurpose vehicle is use "as a motor vehicle" effectively overrules the *Winter* Court's limitation of *Bialochowski.* . . .

What we have, then, is the dissent resuscitating a broad reading of *Bialochowski* without even doffing its cap to the later and thus controlling limitation thereof by *Winter.* Moreover, the dissent fails to explicitly consider and give meaning to the language of the statute or to apply cases . . . that appropriately made such an analysis. This is a peculiar, and unfortunate, exercise of our judicial tasks.

In summary, we think that the language of the statute ought to control and that *Bialochowski* is inadequate support for the rule advocated by the dissent.

Accordingly, we hold that whether an injury arises out of the use of a motor vehicle "as a motor vehicle" under §3105 turns on whether the injury is closely related to the transportational function of motor vehicles.

If we apply this test here, it is clear that the requisite nexus between the injury and the transportational function of the motor vehicle is lacking. At the time the injury occurred, the parked camper/trailer was being used as sleeping accommodations. This use is too far removed from the transportational function to constitute use of the camper/trailer "as a motor vehicle" at the time of the injury. Thus, we conclude that no coverage is triggered under the no-fault act in this instance. . . .

For these reasons, we reverse the judgment of the Court of Appeals and remand for entry of an order granting defendant's motion for summary disposition.

BRICKLEY, BOYLE, and WEAVER, JJ., concur with TAYLOR, J.

MICHAEL F. CAVANAGH, JUSTICE (dissenting).

This case calls on us to determine whether the plaintiff is entitled to personal protection insurance benefits under the no-fault act for injuries resulting from a nonfatal asphyxiation that occurred while he was sleeping in a camper/trailer attached to his pickup truck. Because I find that, under the tests enunciated in our past decisions, plaintiff meets the requirements of the act and is entitled to benefits, I dissent from the majority's holding. It appears that the majority's effort today adds a transportational use limitation to the statute where the Legislature has inserted no such term. Accordingly, I would affirm the judgment of the Court of Appeals, finding the plaintiff entitled to summary disposition in his favor on his claim for no-fault benefits.

. . . We are, therefore, presented only with the need to determine whether the motor vehicle here was used as a motor vehicle, as required by subsection 3105(1) as a precursor to coverage. . . .

An analysis of our past decisions reveals that there are two distinct steps required to determine if a motor vehicle at the time of injury, was being used as a motor vehicle. The first step arises initially from Bialochowski v. Cross Concrete Pumping Co., 428 Mich. 219, 407 N.W.2d 355 (1987).

In *Bialochowski,* we addressed a situation where a pump attached to a parked concrete truck exploded, injuring the plaintiff. Focusing on the remedial nature of the no-fault act, and the balancing undertaken by the Legislature in enacting the statute, we found that it was clear that use "as a motor vehicle" "is not limited to normal vehicular movement on a highway." In that case, we also determined that when a multipurpose vehicle was used for one of its intended purposes it was used "as a motor vehicle." This establishes the parameters of the first step in my analysis. . . .

For at least 15 years, the published appellate decisions of this state have pointed clearly toward the resolution I would reach in this case. Besides comporting with my analysis, this trend points toward another consideration. Because no-fault benefits have clearly applied to situations involving camper/trailers, such as the one before us, I am confident that . . . insurers have been on notice that they were liable for coverage in these instances. Accordingly, insurers have been at least capable of determining their rates for insuring such vehicles in light of such liability. To the extent that insurers could have, and in fact may have, charged for insuring such a risk, policy considerations do not support the windfall that acceptance of the defendant's arguments would entail.

In view of the clear requirements of *Bialochowski,* and in light of the policy considerations discussed above, our task should not be difficult. I would find the camper/trailer to have been used for one of its intended purposes, sheltering sleeping campers. Hence, under *Bialochowski,* I would find that the camper/trailer was used "as a motor vehicle."

II

My analysis, however, is not yet complete. Our past decisions indicate that, in addition to a determination under subsection 3105(1) of usage of a motor vehicle "as a motor vehicle," I must also determine whether there was a sufficient causal connection between this usage as a motor vehicle and the plaintiff's injury. Thornton v. Allstate Ins. Co., 425 Mich. 643, 391 N.W.2d 320 (1986).

While *Thornton* is often cited as having discussed the use of a motor vehicle "as a motor vehicle," as it has been by the parties here, a close analysis of our decision reveals that we clearly decided that case on the basis of causation. As we have previously noted, "[i]n *Thornton* there was no question but that the taxi was being used 'as a motor vehicle.' However, this Court found a lack of causal connection between that use and the plaintiff's injury." Rather than involving a subsection 3105(1) question, this second step of my inquiry concerns causation. Where causation is lacking, coverage will not be found, despite usage of a motor vehicle "as a motor vehicle." The important distinction here, which must be emphasized given the confusion evidenced by some of the arguments presented, is that our decision in *Thornton* was one of causation, not one concerning the presence or use of a motor vehicle "as a motor vehicle."

Thornton concerned the availability of no-fault benefits when a taxi driver was shot during an armed robbery of his cab. We found benefits to be unavailable, owing to a strained relationship with the driver's use of the motor vehicle as a motor vehicle. As we noted, "the relation of the gunshot wound to the functional use of a motor vehicle as a motor vehicle was at most merely 'but for,' incidental, and fortuitous."

In *Thornton,* we found that the robber's bullet was too far removed from the use of a motor vehicle to allow recovery of no-fault benefits. Indeed, the fact that Mr. Thornton was operating a vehicle at that time had little to do with his injury. While we agreed that there might be an incidental or fortuitous connection (i.e., operating a taxicab might make one somewhat more likely to be the victim of an armed robbery), the vehicle was merely the locale of his injury. What injured Mr. Thornton had no connection to his vehicle. Rather, a gunman chose to shoot him, and the fact that Mr. Thornton happened to be driving his vehicle at the time was an insufficient basis for allowing benefits.[10]

Conversely, the plaintiff here was not injured by some outside force or actor. Rather, it was the malfunction of the vehicle itself. The vehicle was not merely the locale of the injury, but rather was an integral part of it. Therefore, the causal connection was not the "tenuous" one of *Thornton,* but rather one of an integral nature, and, hence, coverage should obtain.

III

The majority, of course, seems to believe that *Bialochowski* "eviscerates" the distinction of §3105 regarding use as a motor vehicle, and, furthermore, that apparently Winter v. Automobile Club of Michigan, 433 Mich. 446, 446 N.W.2d 132 (1989), should be read to eviscerate *Bialochowski.* While it is fairly clear that *Winter,* authored by a dissenter in *Bialochowski,* went to great lengths to attack *Bialochowski,* the actual holding of the case was very narrow. To the extent that the majority reads *Winter*'s rather expansive dicta to apply to a case where the actual *Winter* issue is conceded, I cannot agree.

As to the "evisceration" of the distinction of §3105, this section, of course, speaks of use of a motor vehicle "as a motor vehicle." While this provision has certainly led to a fair amount of controversy, I cannot accept this as a rationale to undertake what the majority purports to do: replace "as a motor vehicle" with "for a transportational function." As my brethren in the majority have frequently pointed out in other contexts, and as we should all agree, where the Legislature has used language that is less than clear, we may be called on to interpret it, but we have no call, or right, to merely replace the Legislature's language with language of our own choosing. I turn to our past decisions to apply a consistent approach to an interpretation of this difficult section. While I tend to agree that the Legislature needs to clarify this section, rather than awaiting such a change in the statute, it appears the majority simply elects to make it.[11]

IV

A review of our past decisions indicates that an analysis under subsection 3105(1) to determine whether an insurer is liable for coverage on the basis of the use of a motor vehicle "as a motor vehicle" involves two discrete steps. First, we must determine whether the vehicle was being used for its intended purpose or, in the case of a multipurpose vehicle,

10. Note, again, that there was no question that the vehicle in *Thornton* was being used "as a motor vehicle." If Mr. Thornton's paralysis resulted not from a bullet but from a crash or from injuring his neck upon striking a pothole, there is no doubt that there would have been coverage.

11. In fact, the majority fails to admit the state of the law that it is today upsetting. At best, the Court might say that today it finally corrects a long-neglected area of law. At worst, the Court simply engages in result-oriented judicial activism and encourages litigants to steadfastly insist on litigation to enforce matters of settled law, and to continually resist settlement of claims and pursue review before this Court, regardless of the failure of past attempts, in the hope that a majority of the Court will simply favor their view this time. As one of my colleagues has noted, judicial activism can occur toward any particular result, and the Court's decision today, I fear, encourages litigants to seek out such activism and find hope in the prospect of it occurring in their favor. I decline to join such action.

for one of its intended purposes. Second, we must determine whether this usage had a sufficient causal relationship to the injury to support an award of benefits. For the reasons stated above, I find the answers to both questions in this case to be affirmative.

This case is clearly answered under our existing case law, and I would decline to undertake a realignment of our precedent to find otherwise. I would affirm the result of the Court of Appeals, finding the plaintiff entitled to summary disposition on his claim for no-fault benefits.

MALLETT, C.J., and MARILYN J. KELLY, J., concur with MICHAEL F. CAVANAGH, J.

The sufficiency of the connection between the injury and the insured automobile is presented in many contexts. The one discussed in the dissent in *McKenzie* involves intentionally inflicted harm. See, e.g., Klemmetsen v. Am. Family Mut. Ins. Co., 2006 U.S. Dist. LEXIS 32047 (Colo. 2006) (no coverage for injuries to driver violently assaulted while attempting to get into his car); Kennedy v. Auto Club of Michigan, 544 N.W.2d 750 (Mich. Ct. App.), *app. denied,* 557 N.W.2d 312 (Mich. 1996) (no coverage for injuries to passenger injured by projectile thrown through window of insured automobile). On the other hand, the court in Blish v. Atlanta Cas. Co., 736 So. 2d 1151 (Fla. 1999), held that there was coverage when the driver was attacked and robbed while changing a tire; and the court in White v. American Cas. Ins. Co., 756 N.E.2d 1208 (Mass. App. Ct. 2001), held that coverage existed for a driver who sounded his car horn, causing a dog to bolt out of the house toward the car and bite the driver.

After an initial flush of success, no-fault automobile insurance has fallen on hard times. No state has enacted a no-fault statute since 1975, and several no-fault statutes have been repealed. Criticisms of no-fault have centered on its costs, particularly in states with generous benefits, such as Michigan, and on the loss of the right of many victims of automobile accidents to recover in full for intangible harm. A study by the Rand Institute, for instance, concluded that states with no-fault automobile insurance have had greater increases in premiums and claim costs than states without no-fault. See James M. Anderson, Paul Heaton & Stephen J. Carroll, The U.S. Experience with No-Fault Automobile Insurance: A Retrospective (2010). See also DiProspero v. Penn, 874 A.2d 1039 (N.J. 2005) (describing difficulties with New Jersey's no-fault scheme). One common scapegoat for no-fault's recent struggles is the plaintiffs bar. Professor Jeffrey O'Connell, one of the early advocates of no-fault insurance, lamented, "The trial lawyers water it down, shoot it in the kneecap, and then protest that it doesn't work well." Karl Stark, No-Fault Insurance Idea Draws Renewed Interest, Phila. Inquirer, Feb. 2, 2003, at E1. An alternative explanation for high costs is that auto-insurers lobbied for and obtained primary payer status, rather than secondary status as the original Keeton-O'Connell plan had envisioned. This arrangement displaced medical insurers as the primary payers and arguably created perverse incentives in the provision of medical care. See Nora Freeman Engstrom, An Alternative Explanation for No-Fault's "Demise," 61 DePaul L. Rev. 303, 338-341 (2012).

Confronted with various criticisms of early no-fault schemes, Professor O'Connell proposed a system that would merge no-fault and tort. This "choice system" allows drivers to choose between something like traditional no-fault insurance and something like traditional recovery in tort. Legislation based on this idea has been introduced in several sessions of Congress, beginning in 1997. See generally Jeffrey O'Connell, Peter Kinzler & Hunter Bates, A Federal Bill, with Commentary, to Allow Choice in Auto Insurance,

7 Conn. Ins. L.J. 511 (2001). Although New Jersey and Pennsylvania use variants of the choice system, efforts to adopt a federal choice bill like the one proposed by Professor O'Connell died off by the early 2000s. For a comprehensive consideration of no-fault automobile insurance in general, see Gary T. Schwartz, Auto No-Fault and First Party Insurance: Advantages and Problems, 73 S. Cal. L. Rev. 611 (2000).

C. No-Fault: Beyond Work- and Automobile-Related Accident Losses

As should be clear from the materials in the chapter so far, the tort system of allocating personal injury losses has come under considerable attack. Those who have sought to change the system have proceeded along two very different lines. One line has been to work within the system and to seek changes in the substantive rules and procedures by which tort law allocates losses. The most dramatic of the recent changes have come largely through legislation and involve such items as caps on damages, and the abrogation of joint and several liability and of the collateral source rule. These changes, and others, are discussed at various points throughout this casebook.

The second line of attack, documented in the preceding sections of this chapter, seeks to replace the torts system in part with one not based on fault. Workers' compensation is such a system. A more limited inroad into the torts system is no-fault automobile insurance. This section explores the second line of attack through additional — and, in some cases, far more ambitious — examples.

1. No-Fault Compensation for Medical and Vaccine-Related Injuries

Suggestions for expanding the no-fault concept beyond work- and automobile-related accidents abound.[3] One set of proposals would replace medical malpractice claims with a no-fault system. One effort at bringing no-fault principles to bear in medical malpractice cases that legislatures implemented is birth-related neurological injuries. A no-fault system for such injuries was enacted into law in Virginia in 1987. See Va. Code Ann. §§38.2-5000 to 38.2-5021. The following description is taken from Note, Innovative No-Fault Reform for an Endangered Specialty, 74 Va. L. Rev. 1487, 1489-94 (1988) (footnotes have been omitted):

> The Injured Infant Act was created for the purpose of
>
> > seeking to assure the lifetime care of infants with birth-related neurological injuries, fostering an environment that will increase the availability of medical malpractice insurance at a reasonable cost for physicians and hospitals providing obstetrical

3. One of the earliest proposals is contained in the report ABA Commission on Medical Professional Liability, Designated Compensable Event System: A Feasibility Study (1979). Other suggestions appear in Paul Weiler, Medical Malpractice on Trial 132-58 (1991); II Reporters' Study, Enterprise Liability for Personal Injury 514-15 (American Law Institute 1991); Jeffrey O'Connell, Abandoning Tort Liability: Elective No-Fault Insurance for Many Kinds of Injuries, 60 Minn. L. Rev. 501 (1976). One professor has even proposed expanding no-fault to legal malpractice. See Melissa Mortazavi, A No-Fault Remedy for Legal Malpractice?, 44 Hofstra L. Rev. 471 (2015).

> services, and promoting the availability of obstetrical care to indigent and low-income patients.

The Act creates a program similar to workers' compensation in that those who recover under its terms give up whatever right they may have had to bring a tort action against the health care providers attending the delivery. The definition of eligible infants is narrow— the drafters of the Act estimate that it will apply to only about forty births in the state per year. The Act applies only to live births in which there is

> injury to the brain or spinal cord of an infant caused by the deprivation of oxygen or mechanical injury occurring in the course of labor, delivery or resuscitation in the immediate post-delivery period in a hospital which renders the infant permanently nonambulatory, aphasic [having a defect or loss in the power of expression], incontinent, and in need of assistance in all phases of daily living.

In addition, the birth must have occurred on or after January 1, 1988 at a hospital participating in the program, and a participating physician must have provided obstetric services. Specifically excluded from coverage under the Act are claims involving "disability or death caused by genetic or congenital abnormalities." Claims filed more than ten years after the birth of the injured child are barred.

The Act creates the Virginia Birth-Related Neurological Injury Compensation Program (Program), which is governed by a Board of Directors (Board), each member of which is appointed by the Governor for a three-year term. The Board administers the Birth-Related Neurological Injury Compensation Fund (Fund). Participation in the Program is not mandatory for either physicians or hospitals. Obstetricians who want to participate in the Program pay $5,000 into the Fund each year, while all other physicians licensed in the state, including those who do not practice obstetrics, are assessed $250 per year. Participating hospitals pay a sum equal to $50 multiplied by the number of deliveries made during the prior year, with a cap of $150,000 per hospital per year. If these assets are inadequate to maintain the Fund on an actuarially sound basis, a premium tax of up to one-quarter of one percent of net direct premiums written in the state will be assessed on all liability insurance carriers in the state. All of these payments will go directly into the Fund, which is designed to be self-sufficient—none of the money for the Program is to come from the state's general revenues.

Claims filed pursuant to the Act are heard and determined by the Industrial Commission of Virginia (Commission), which also handles the state's workers' compensation claims. A panel of three physicians chosen pursuant to a plan developed by the deans of the state's medical schools review each claim and make a recommendation to the Commission "as to whether the injury alleged is a birth-related neurological injury" coming within the statutory scheme. This provision establishes an automatic source of independent, expert medical opinion in lieu of that which a malpractice plaintiff would produce for trial. The Commission is required to hold a hearing on any claim within 120 days of its filing, assuring swifter compensation for those newborns covered by the Act than is currently available through the tort system. The only parties to the hearing are the claimant and the Program. Although compensation is awarded under the Act without regard to fault, each claim is automatically referred to the state licensing agencies of the physicians and hospital involved for investigation of any possible substandard care. All factual findings of the Commission are conclusive and binding.

Upon a determination by the Industrial Commission that an infant comes within the terms of the Act, the Commission will award a remedy limited to net economic loss less any amount received from collateral sources. The award is paid out as it accrues, rather than in a lump sum as a civil remedy typically would be. In addition to reasonable medical expenses, the award compensates for reasonable expenses, including attorney's fees, and loss of earnings from the age of eighteen.

> In addition to its goal of making liability insurance for obstetricians more available and affordable by removing from the tort system the claims of catastrophically injured newborns, the Act also attempts to facilitate access to medical care for indigents. This problem has become especially acute for the indigent, because physicians are increasingly reluctant to handle these often "high-risk" deliveries. To address this problem, the Injured Infant Act requires obstetricians and hospitals who wish to obtain the advantages of the Act's coverage to agree to work with local health departments in developing "a program to provide obstetrical care to patients eligible for Medical Assistance Services and to patients who are indigent, and upon approval of such program by the Commissioner of Health, to participate in its implementation."

Florida has a similar statute. See Fla. Stat. ch. 766.301-316. For a critique of the Florida statute, see Sandy Martin, Comment, NICA — Florida Birth-Related Neurological Injury Compensation Act: Four Reasons Why This Malpractice Reform Must Be Eliminated, 26 Nova L. Rev. 609-45 (2002). For more general commentary on the pros and cons of no-fault compensation schemes for medical injury, see Randall R. Bovbjerg & Frank A. Sloan, No-Fault for Medical Injury: Theory and Evidence, 67 U. Cin. L. Rev. 53 (1998), and David M. Studdert & Troyen A. Brennan, Toward a Workable Model of "No Fault" Compensation for Medical Injury in the United States, 27 Am. J.L. & Med. 225 (2001).

The federal government also has instituted no-fault compensation schemes in the medical arena. For instance, in 2006 Congress passed the Public Readiness and Emergency Preparedness Act, P.L. No. 109-148, empowering the Secretary of the Health and Human Services (HHS) Department to declare a public health emergency and extend tort immunity to manufacturers of vaccines and other pandemic and epidemic products. The premise of the act is that, in order to rapidly develop and deploy countermeasures to bioterrorism or other public health dangers, manufacturers, physicians, and other involved actors need protection from potentially crushing financial risks such as tort liability. The only exception to legal immunity during a declared emergency is for "willful misconduct" that plaintiffs prove through "clear and convincing evidence." The act orders the HHS Secretary to promulgate regulations "that further restrict the scope of actions or omissions . . . that may qualify as 'willful misconduct.'" The Secretary is further instructed to award compensation to individuals harmed by the administration of a public health countermeasure, although such compensation is contingent on the establishment of funding by later congressional acts. Finally, the act provides that no federal or state court shall have jurisdiction to review the decisions made by the Secretary under the act. In late 2008 the Secretary declared a public health emergency with respect to smallpox countermeasures, ordering liability protection both retroactively to January 2008 and prospectively until December 31, 2015. See Declaration Under the Public Readiness and Emergency Preparedness Act, 73 Fed. Reg. 61,869 (Oct. 17, 2008). For a history of the use of liability protections to confront public health crises, see Karen Shichman Crawford & Jeffrey Axelrad, Legislative Modification to Tort Liability: The Unintended Consequence of Public Health and Bioterrorism Threats, 45 Creighton L. Rev. 337 (2012).

Public health measures such as provision of vaccines provide a compelling case for alternative compensation mechanisms. From the individual's perspective, vaccinations seem to offer little chance of gain and the potential for significant loss. After all, if everyone else gets vaccinated, then the risk of infection to the individual is low while the risk of side effects may be high. Of course, if everyone else follows this same logic, then no one will become vaccinated and the risk of infection will become quite high. For this reason, the benefits of a vaccinated populace are a form of public good, and governments are often forced to mandate vaccinations, at least until the disease is thought to be fully eradicated. Thus, those individuals who suffer side effects — often unavoidable — from the vaccination have a strong argument for compensation, as they have borne a concentrated and often involuntary loss in order to benefit the public health generally. On the other hand, if vaccine manufacturers are saddled with the full costs of compensation, they may have inadequate incentives to develop and market their products.

To address concerns over medical injury to children from vaccines and the financial threat to vaccine manufacturers from tort liability, the United States adopted the National Childhood Vaccine Injury Act of 1986 (hereinafter "Vaccine Act"). Among the Vaccine Act's goals is "providing a streamlined system for compensation in rare instances where an injury results from vaccination." Whitney S. Waldenberg & Sarah E. Wallace, When Science Is Silent: Examining Compensation of Vaccine-Related Injuries When Scientific Evidence of Causation is Inconclusive, 42 Wake Forest L. Rev. 303, 305 (2007). To operationalize the Vaccine Act, the National Vaccine Injury Compensation Program ("Vaccine Fund") was established through an industry-wide tax, and it offers compensation to eligible claimants on a no-fault basis. More than $3 billion has been paid out from the program since 1988. See U.S. Dept. of Health and Human Services, National Vaccine Injury Compensation Program, available at http://www.hrsa.gov/vaccinecompensation/data/index.html.

Persons eligible to file a claim include injured patients and parents or legal guardians bringing a claim on behalf of their children. To establish eligibility the claimant must typically show that the vaccine is among those listed in a table maintained by the Secretary of the HHS, the Vaccine Injury Table, and that the vaccine was administered in the United States. The Vaccine Injury Table serves to ease the burden of proving causation by establishing general causal presumptions for certain vaccine-injury pairings. Specifically, the table establishes categories of vaccines, representative complications arising from those vaccines, and a time interval in which the complication must be observed. For claimants whose injuries fit these criteria, causation is presumed. If the injury does not meet the criteria, the claimant can proceed "off-Table" by attempting to show actual causation through competent medical evidence. See Brandon L. Boxler, Note, What to Do with *Daubert:* How to Bring Standards of Reliable Scientific Evidence to the National Vaccine Injury Compensation Program, 52 Wm. & Mary L. Rev. 1319, 1336-37 (2011).

The Vaccine Act allows a person injured by one of the enumerated vaccines to sue the Department of Health and Human Services. Once a suit is brought, a special master is assigned to the petitioner's case. 42 U.S.C. §300aa-11(a)(1). Beyond the submission of a required affidavit and medical records, 42 U.S.C. §300aa-11(c)(2), the claim consideration process is relatively simple. Notably absent from the proceedings are discovery, cross-examination, pleadings, and a formal trial. See Victor E. Schwartz & Liberty Mahshigian, National Childhood Vaccine Injury Act of 1986: An Ad Hoc Remedy or a Window for the Future?, 48 Ohio St. L.J. 387, 391 (1987). The special master may order discovery or production of evidence in certain cases, and the master alone will perform these functions. In most cases, the only issues relevant to the proceedings are "whether the petitioner suffered a compensable injury" and "the extent of compensable damages." Id. Decisions of the special master are also appealable to the U.S. Court of Federal Claims, the court of appeals of the Federal Circuit, and ultimately the U.S. Supreme Court. 42 U.S.C §300aa-12(f). One repeatedly appealed issue involves the failure of special masters to find adequate evidence of a causal link between certain childhood vaccines and autism. See, e.g., Cedillo v. Secretary of Health & Human Servs., 617 F.3d 1328 (Fed. Cir. 2010). This vaccine-injury linkage has been alleged by numerous advocacy groups but has not been accepted for inclusion in the Vaccine Injury Table and remains a highly controversial issue. See Boxler, supra.

For successful claimants, compensation is awarded for both "actual unreimbursable expenses" and "reasonable projected unreimbursable expenses." 42 U.S.C. §300aa-15(a)(1)(A). These past and reasonably projected future expenses include "diagnosis and medical or other remedial care determined to be reasonably necessary," as well as "rehabilitation, developmental evaluation, special education, vocational training and placement, case management services, counseling, emotional or behavioral therapy, residential and custodial care and service expenses, special equipment, related travel expenses, and facilities determined to be reasonably necessary." 42 U.S.C. §300aa-15(a)(1)(A)(iii). However, because only "unreimbursable" expenses are covered, the collateral source rule does not apply under the program. In the event of a death, an automatic award of $250,000 is made. Additionally, pain and suffering up to $250,000 in damages may be awarded. Reasonable costs, including attorneys' fees, are also eligible for recovery. 42 U.S.C. §300aa-15(a). Interestingly, if a claim for compensation is denied, the claimant may still receive attorney's fees if the special master or court feels that the action was brought in good faith and there was a reasonable basis for the injury claim. 42 U.S.C. §300aa-15(e)(1).

Of importance is the requirement that all claims for compensation arising out of a vaccine injury must first go through the Vaccine Act process. However, those dissatisfied with the compensation they receive under the Vaccine Act may pursue recovery in a traditional tort forum. The dissatisfied individual must expressly reject the compensation and then file suit in state or federal court. Although success may result in a larger damages award, including avoidance of the $250,000 cap on pain and suffering damages, this approach entails risks and additional costs. For instance, in pursuing this route the claimant loses the benefit of relaxation of the standards of proof for causality that the Vaccine Act grants. The claimant must also contend with the Vaccine Act's preemption provision, which bars state tort law liability for any "vaccine-related injury or death [that] resulted from side effects that were unavoidable even though the vaccine was properly prepared and was accompanied by proper directions and warnings." 42 U.S.C. §300aa-22(b)(1). The Supreme Court has interpreted this somewhat cryptic provision to bar all product liability claims that proceed on a design defect theory, leaving only manufacturing and warning defect causes of action available to plaintiffs in state court. See Bruesewitz v. Wyeth LLC, 131 S. Ct. 1068 (2011).

Professor Nora Freeman Engstrom has written critically of the Vaccine Fund claims process, asserting that it suffers from many of the flaws that mark the tort system it was supposed to displace. See A Dose of Reality for Specialized Courts: Lesson from the VICIP, 163 U. Pa. L. Rev. 1631, 1698 (2015). Despite the Vaccine Fund's success in promoting research and stabilizing prices, Engstrom argues, Vaccine Fund adjudication has slipped into a litigation-like adversarialism that lasts an average of five-and-a-half years — much longer than the average adjudication in tort. Id. at 1685, 1712.

2. Dealing with Disaster: Public and Private Compensation Funds as Alternatives to Tort Litigation

The Exxon Valdez oil spill of 1989 resulted in extensive damage to Prince William Sound, Alaska, along with significant financial, emotional, and cultural consequences for local fisherman, Native Alaskan tribes, and others who depended on the affected ecosystem. Ensuing litigation resulted in a $5 billion punitive damages verdict against Exxon, which was handed down in 1994. At the time the jury announced its verdict, the lead plaintiffs' attorney, Brian O'Neill, hugged his three-year-old son, whereupon one of Exxon's lawyers said to him, "He'll be in college before you get any of that money." Richard Lempert, Low Probability/High Consequence Events: Dilemmas of Damage Compensation, 58 DePaul L. Rev. 357, 368-69 (2009). The Exxon attorney's prediction proved remarkably accurate: After numerous appeals and delays, including a precedent-setting trip to the U.S. Supreme Court, Exxon finally consented in 2009 to the entry of judgment against it for punitive damages in the amount of $507.5 million. See Exxon Valdez v. Exxon Mobil, 568 F.3d 1077 (9th Cir. 2009).

The protracted and costly Exxon Valdez litigation experience has loomed large in the minds of potential claimants and policymakers in the wake of subsequent disasters, such as Hurricane Katrina in 2005 and the British Petroleum oil spill of 2010. While some scholars continue to support the role of tort liability in preventing and redressing mass-scale harms, see, e.g., Daniel A. Farber, Tort Law in the Era of Climate Change, Katrina, and 9/11: Exploring Liability for Extraordinary Risks, 43 Val. U. L. Rev. 1075 (2009), others have looked to the September 11th Victim Compensation Fund as a promising alternative model.

Less than two weeks after the terrorist attacks of September 11, 2001, Congress passed the Air Transportation Safety and System Stabilization Act (ATSSSA), which, among other things, established a pool of public money to compensate eligible victims of the 9/11 attacks. The major impetus for the 9/11 Fund was to mitigate the financial hardship that might otherwise have crippled the airline industry if it were subjected to tort liability for the attacks, but it also served to provide victims of the attacks with remedies for their injuries. In general, the 9/11 Fund presented qualified claimants with the option of electing a no-fault remedy for physical harm or death stemming from the immediate aftermath of the attacks, while preserving a limited right to sue in tort for those choosing not to participate in the 9/11 Fund. But these options were "either/or" alternatives: Anyone filing a claim with the 9/11 Fund automatically waived all rights against domestic tort defendants. The legislation that created the 9/11 Fund called for a Special Master to promulgate regulations and administer the fund. Because Congress intended prompt recovery, claimants were required to file their claims within two years after these regulations were established.

After a claimant filed with the fund, a claims evaluator reviewed the claim for eligibility, the extent of the harm, and the amount of compensation due. Eligibility turned on showing causation, which required that the injury be the direct result of one of the air crashes constituting the September 11 attacks. If a claim was determined eligible, either the claims evaluator calculated a "presumed award" based on predetermined criteria or the claimant proceeded directly to a hearing on compensation. If a presumed award was calculated, the claimant could either accept the award or request a hearing and present evidence of individualized circumstances meriting recovery beyond the presumed award. Compensation was based on several factors, including the "extent of the harm to the claimant" (including both economic and noneconomic losses), the specific facts underlying the claim, and the particular circumstances of the claimant, such as the victim's income and the number of surviving dependents. The 9/11 Fund did not adopt the collateral source rule, so recovery from certain alternative sources, such as life insurance, was ultimately deducted from the award. Negligence was not considered under the 9/11 Fund and punitive damages were not available. The Special Master was required to make a determination within 120 days after a claim was filed. The Special Master's determination was final, and appeal was not available from this decision.

Alternatively, for those who chose to bring suit under traditional tort theories, the ATSSSA also maintained limited recovery in tort.[4] The act mandated that those who elected not to participate in the 9/11 Fund could recover only up to "the limits of liability coverage maintained by the air carrier," about $1.5 billion per plane. In addition, the act mandated that the substantive law governing the claim was that of the state in which the crash occurred and that the U.S. District Court for the Southern District of New York had original and exclusive jurisdiction over claims arising out of the events of September 11.

Some critics of the 9/11 Fund consider it too narrow in scope, in view of its being limited to injuries stemming from the September 11 attacks. Why, they ask, were victims of the September 11 tragedy compensated, but not victims of other terrorist attacks, such as those who died in the 1995 bombing in Oklahoma City, or even victims of natural disasters (a particularly salient query in the wake of Hurricane Katrina in 2005)? Similar complaints were made that the 9/11 Fund did not compensate persons whose injuries manifested well after the "immediate aftermath" of the events, such as those injured by inhalation of toxic particles released by the crash.[5] Additionally, the 9/11 Fund was criticized for not doing enough to compensate high-income victims of the disaster: The income tables the fund incorporated in calculating compensation were capped at $231,000 a year, which was less than the annual income of a number of those who died in the attacks. On the other hand, some criticized the 9/11 Fund for making any distinction in the amount of compensation provided based on income level. These critics argued, in part, that the 9/11 Fund should have been viewed as a form of charity or a symbolic honoring of those injured or killed, and thus income-based distinctions in the awards were inappropriate and perhaps insulting. For an article addressing these criticisms, among others, and the effectiveness of the 9/11 Fund in general, see Robert M. Ackerman, The September 11th Victim Compensation Fund: An Effective Administrative Response to National Tragedy, 10 Harv. Negot. L. Rev. 135 (2005).

Despite these criticisms, participation in the 9/11 Fund was high. According to Ackerman, "the overwhelming majority (99%) of potential death claimants filed somewhere; 97% filed with the fund, while only 2% chose to file [tort claims]." The 9/11 Fund awarded a total of approximately $7.049 billion to 5,560 claimants. Awards for death claims ranged from $250,000 to $7.1 million, and awards for personal injury ranged from $500 to $8.6 million. Administrative costs of managing the fund amounted to only 1.2 percent of the total awards, a startling contrast to tort litigation. On the whole, especially given the hasty

4. The tort claims have thus far largely progressed as might be expected. One major decision, *In re* September 11 Litig., 280 F. Supp. 2d 279 (S.D.N.Y. 2003), held that the defendant airlines, airport security companies, airport operators, airplane manufacturer, and operators and owners of the World Trade Center each owed a duty to the plaintiffs in that the plaintiffs had stated a legally sufficient claim against each defendant, and denied the defendants' motions to dismiss. Not surprisingly, settlements have followed steadily in the wake of this ruling. See, e.g., *In re* September 11 Property Damage Litig., 650 F.3d 145 (2d Cir. 2011) (property damage claimants); *In re* World Trade Ctr. Disaster Site Litig., 871 F. Supp. 2d 263 (S.D.N.Y 2012) (emergency personnel and others involved in rescue and cleanup operations). For an overview written by the judge and special masters of this litigation, see Alvin K Hellerstein, James A. Henderson Jr. & Aaron D. Twerski, Managerial Judging: The 9/11 Responders' Tort Litigation, 98 Cornell L. Rev. 127 (2012).

5. In December 2010 Congress passed the James Zadroga 9/11 Health and Compensation Act, which reopened the 9/11 Fund and provided $2.8 billion in compensation for those with health problems, primarily respiratory difficulties, caused by the attacks. Torts attorney and expert Sheila Birnbaum was named to act as Special Master of the reopened fund. See Anemona Hartocollis, Eligibility Area for 9/11 Compensation Is Expanded, N.Y. Times, June 22, 2011, at A17. Congress reauthorized the Zadroga Act in December 2015, allowing individuals to receive compensation from the 9/11 Fund for another five years. See James Zadroga 9/11 Victim Compensation Fund Reauthorization Act, Pub. L. No. 114-113, 129 Stat. 3000 (2015).

enactment, Ackerman argues that in light of what could be reasonably expected of the 9/11 Fund, it was a relative success. It managed to provide economic redress promptly and lessened the hardship facing the injured and the families of those who died in the attacks, while providing sufficient financial protection to the airlines to allow them to continue operating.

Citing the 9/11 Fund favorably, John Witt has written that many twenty-first-century threats to the environment, human health, and safety simply exceed the grasp of the tort system:

> Diverse new risks, including nuclear disasters, global warming, genetically modified organisms, and any number of complex systems whose compromise might lead to catastrophic results, present challenges on a scale that seems to defy even the most innovative accident-law institutions on the contemporary scene. Because we lack aggregatable experience with such catastrophes, these new catastrophic risks move beyond the actuarial model that emerged in the work-accident experience. Statistical models of risk like those that animated developments in the law of accidents a century ago simply cannot be assembled in the absence of the requisite time-series data. In this regard, the federal compensation fund set up in the wake of the September 11, 2001 attack on the World Trade Center may be a harbinger of the kinds of departures from traditional practice that we may be compelled to adopt in a world of mass risks and postmodern technologies.

Witt, supra, at 208-09 (footnote omitted). Yet critics argue that traditional adjudication serves purposes that cannot be replicated by alternative compensation mechanisms, including the articulation of collectively expressed norms of responsibility and allocations of fault. One striking finding in this respect is that nearly 40 percent of a sample of 9/11 Fund claimants reported that they would be willing to spend some of their recovery to pursue a declaratory judgment action determining fault and responsibility for the harms that they or their loved ones suffered. Gillian K. Hadfield, Framing the Choice Between Cash and the Courthouse: Experiences with the 9/11 Victim Compensation Fund, 42 Law & Soc'y Rev. 645, 670 tbl. 7 (2008).

Debate lingers as to whether and how similar compensation funds should be created to deal with future large-scale tragedies, or even as a response to continuing problems such as violent crime. For example, Julie Goldscheid suggests that the 9/11 Fund may provide a model for the reform of existing state compensation programs for the victims of violent crime to make those programs more "victim friendly" and potentially broader in scope. See Julie Goldscheid, Crime Victim Compensation in a Post-9/11 World, 79 Tul. L. Rev. 167 (2004). Additionally, the Minnesota state legislature looked to the 9/11 Fund when it devised a compensation mechanism for victims of an interstate bridge collapse in Minneapolis that killed 13 and injured numerous others. See Mike Steenson & Joseph Michael Sayler, The Legacy of the 9/11 Fund and the Minnesota I-35W Bridge-Collapse Fund: Creating a Template for Compensating Victims of Future Mass-Tort Catastrophes, 35 Wm. Mitchell L. Rev. 524, 526 (2009). In contrast, Kenneth Feinberg — the Special Master of the 9/11 Fund — argued that the fund should not be used as a model for other endeavors to compensate the victims of catastrophic events, including terrorist acts. See Kenneth R. Feinberg, The Unprecedented Effort to Compensate the Victims of 9/11, at 178 (2005), reviewed in Robert L. Rabin, September 11 Through the Prism of Victim Compensation: What Is Life Worth?, 106 Colum. L. Rev. 464 (2006).

Notwithstanding his reservations, Feinberg again found himself at the center of a massive compensation effort following the British Petroleum (BP) oil spill disaster of 2010. On

April 20 of that year, an explosion occurred on the Deepwater Horizon oil rig in the Gulf of Mexico, eventually leading to the largest marine oil spill in history.[6] The Deepwater Horizon was an impressive piece of technology, capable of staying within 5 feet of a well head in the open seas using thrusters and GPS technology. Before attempting to establish the Maconda Prospect site in the Gulf, the Deepwater Horizon had successfully drilled a 35,000-feet-deep well below 4,000 feet of water. Nevertheless, 36 hours after the explosion on April 20, in which 11 workers were killed and flames were visible from 35 miles away, the rig sank.

Addressing the nation on June 15, 2010, President Barack Obama said:

> Already, this oil spill is the worst environmental disaster America has ever faced. And unlike an earthquake or a hurricane, it's not a single event that does its damage in a matter of minutes or days. The millions of gallons of oil that have spilled into the Gulf of Mexico are more like an epidemic, one that we will be fighting for months and even years.

President Barack Obama, "Remarks by the President to the Nation on the BP Oil Spill" (June 15, 2010), http://www.whitehouse.gov/the-press-office/remarks-president-nation-bp-oil-spill. The next day President Obama announced that BP would establish a $20 billion escrow fund and claims processing mechanism, known as the Gulf Coast Claims Facility (GCCF). Facing potential liability under the Oil Pollution Act of 1990 (OPA) and other laws, potentially including state tort law, BP had already established a makeshift settlement procedure, but the GCCF replaced it with a third-party-administered fund overseen by Feinberg and his firm, Feinberg Rozen, LLP. See Gulf Coast Claims Facility, Frequently Asked Questions, available at http://www.gulfcoastclaimsfacility.com/faq.

Perhaps understandably, the GCCF has proven more controversial than the 9/11 Fund. Unlike the potential liability that faced airlines after the September 11 disaster, liability under existing statutory and common law duties for BP and its corporate partners was much clearer in the case of the Deepwater Horizon disaster, rendering the GCCF a possibly less attractive alternative compared with the 9/11 Fund. See Chapter 4, Section B.4 (discussing recovery for economic loss). And unlike the congressional act that funded, structured, and specified oversight of the post-9/11 compensation process, the GCCF is a purely private mechanism. Despite its seeming endorsement by President Obama, the GCCF was created entirely by BP in cooperation with Feinberg and his firm, which is being paid directly by BP to process claims and limit the company's exposure to lawsuits. This design has not escaped scrutiny. Addressing allegations that Feinberg and his firm had allowed professional conflicts of interest to affect their efforts to persuade claimants to eschew litigation and participate in the GCCF, a federal district judge issued something of a "Miranda warning" for private claims settlement facilities, ordering Feinberg and his associates to:

> (1) Refrain from contacting directly any claimant that they know or reasonably should know is represented by counsel, whether or not said claimant has filed a lawsuit or formal claim. (2) Refrain from referring to the GCCF, Ken Feinberg, or Feinberg Rozen, LLP (or their representatives), as "neutral" or completely "independent" from BP. . . . (3) Begin any communication with a putative class member with the statement that the individual has a right to consult with an attorney of his/her own choosing prior to accepting any settlement

6. For a comprehensive report on the causes, consequences, and implications of the British Petroleum disaster, including references for much of the information contained in this brief overview, see National Commission on the BP Deepwater Horizon Oil Spill and Offshore Drilling, Deep Water: The Gulf Oil Disaster and the Future of Offshore Drilling (2011).

> or signing a release of legal rights. (4) Refrain from giving or purporting to give legal advice to unrepresented claimants, including advising that claimants should not hire a lawyer. (5) Fully disclose to claimants their options under OPA if they do not accept a final payment. . . . (6) Advise claimants that the "pro bono" attorneys and "community representatives" retained to assist GCCF claimants are being compensated directly or indirectly by BP.

Order and Reasons, In re Oil Spill by the Oil Rig "Deepwater Horizon" in the Gulf of Mexico, on April 20, 2010, MDL No. 2179, 2011 WL 323866 (E.D. La. Feb. 2, 2011). Professor Linda S. Mullenix an early skeptic of the GCCF, wrote:

> Not all fund approaches to resolving mass claims are the same, and not all funds are fungible. Nonetheless, "funds" are now invoked with almost talismanic approval, as a preferred means for providing compensation to disaster victims outside the litigation system. Moreover, the Gulf Coast Claims Facility provides a stellar example of the unseemly pressure exerted on disaster victims to quickly seek relief through a fund mechanism, rather than retaining counsel and filing a lawsuit. With the advent of the GCCF, commentators ought to ask probing questions concerning who benefits from these mechanisms and whether the GCCF model in particular serves the interests of justice and for whom.
>
> The greatest justifications for fund resolution of mass claims are grounded in values of efficiency and economy. The theory underlying fund resolution of claims is that by avoiding the litigation system, claimants receive quick, easy payment of claims and eliminate the risks, transaction costs, and delays inherent in litigation. These themes have pervaded Feinberg's repeated appeals to claimants to settle with both the September 11th Victim Compensation Fund and the Gulf Coast Claims Facility.
>
> However, one may legitimately question whether efficiency and economy ought to be the bellwether metrics of a successful compensation program. In contrast, other commentators have suggested that compensation programs ought to be evaluated by the core substantive values of democratic governance, which include the values of participation, accountability, transparency, rationality, personal autonomy, equality, due process, and other social capital values necessary to promote civil society.

Prometheus Unbound: The Gulf Coast Claims Facility as a Means for Resolving Mass Torts Claims — A Fund Too Far, 71 La. L. Rev. 819, 913-14 (2011) (footnotes omitted). Indeed, the GCCF has had a mixed record. The upside is that the GCCF has distributed billions of dollars to persons hurt by the oil spill. The downside is that Gulf Coast residents have voiced concerns about inadequate transparency, accountability, and consistency in the distribution of funds. See Joan Flocks & James Davies, The Deepwater Horizon Disaster Compensation Process as Corrective Justice: Views from the Ground Up, 84 Miss. L.J. 1, 22-30 (2014).

Unsatisfied with the GCCF, many Gulf Coast residents joined class action lawsuits against BP. In 2012, Judge Carl Barbier approved a settlement creating an uncapped fund that would provide for six types of damages, including economic loss and real property damage. See In re Oil Spill by Oil Rig Deepwater Horizon in Gulf of Mexico, on Apr. 20, 2010, 910 F. Supp. 2d 891, 903 (E.D. La. 2012), aff'd sub nom. In re Deepwater Horizon, 739 F.3d 790 (5th Cir. 2014). Professors Samuel Issacharoff and D. Theodore Rave have argued that this class settlement provides better payouts to claimants than the GCCF, despite the high transaction costs of litigation. See The BP Oil Spill Settlement and the Paradox of Public Litigation, 74 La. L. Rev. 397 (2014). According to one estimate, cleanup costs, civil liability, and criminal fines associated with the oil spill will add up to over $50 billion in losses for BP and its codefendants. Catherine M. Sharkey, The BP Oil Spill Settlements, Classwide Punitive Damages, and Societal Deterrence, 64 DePaul L. Rev. 681, 704 (2015). For comparative insight, see the thorough review of Japan's legal and compensatory response to its Fukushima nuclear meltdown disaster, in Eric A. Feldman, Fukushima: Catastrophe, Compensation, and Justice in Japan, 62 DePaul L. Rev. 335 (2013).

3. More Sweeping Compensation Systems: The New Zealand Experience

As of yet, proposals in this country to replace the entire tort system with a system in which fault plays no part have not reached the legislative halls. Some sentiment has been voiced in support of such sweeping change. See, e.g., American Bar Association, Report of the Action Committee to Improve the Tort Liability System 6 (1987):

> There are . . . members of the Commission who hold the view that meaningful improvement in the system of compensating injury victims can better be achieved by adopting a social insurance or no-fault recovery scheme that assures compensation of basic economic loss to every accident victim and promotes incentives to greater safety either through contributions to the funding of the reparation scheme, utilization of criminal and administrative sanctions, or a combination of these strategies.

See also Stephen D. Sugarman, Compensation for Accidental Personal Injury: What Nations Might Learn from Each Other, 38 Pepp. L. Rev. 597 (2011); Kenneth S. Abraham & Lance Liebman, Private Insurance, Social Insurance, and Tort Reform: Toward a New Vision of Compensation for Illness and Injury, 93 Colum. L. Rev. 75 (1993); Stephen D. Sugarman, Doing Away with Personal Injury Law (1989).

Dramatic changes in the system of allocating personal injury losses have been in effect in New Zealand since the early 1970s. As a response to a number of perceived problems of the tort system, especially the failure to provide adequate compensation to accident victims, New Zealand enacted the Accident Compensation Act of 1972. The Act built upon the country's existing workers' compensation scheme and created a government-administered no-fault compensation system to provide benefits for all those suffering "injury by accident." An essential element of the act was that no showing of fault was required for recovery under the plan. In exchange for the many benefits provided under the act, accident victims were barred from exercising common law rights to sue in tort for damages for death or personal injury. However, in the rare situation where a particular injury was not covered by the act (possibly by virtue of a restrictive interpretation of "injury by accident"), the victim was not precluded from seeking recovery through a tort action for damages. The New Zealand courts have also held that suits for exemplary damages against tortfeasors are not precluded by the act. See, e.g., Auckland City Council v. Blundell [1986] 1 N.Z. L.R. 732.

The original act was based on an underlying philosophy of collective responsibility and was designed to establish a program of social insurance. Thus, although the plan at first provided benefits only for accident victims, it was hoped that the plan would eventually cover victims of disease and illness as well. However, a shift in the governing party of New Zealand resulted in a changed perception of the purpose of the plan as well as reforms to the benefits provided. The new government no longer viewed the no-fault system as a social insurance scheme, but rather maintained the plan as a system of accident insurance. The change in philosophy was reflected in a new title for the act, the Accident Rehabilitation and Compensation Insurance Act 1992 (ARCIA). See Richard S. Miller, An Analysis and Critique of the 1992 Changes to New Zealand's Accident Compensation Scheme, 52 Md. L. Rev. 1070 (1993). Further shifting political winds were reflected in the title of a later overhaul of ARCIA — the Injury Prevention, Rehabilitation and Compensation Act 2001 — which itself was recently renamed the Accident Compensation Act 2001, bringing at least the name of the scheme full circle to its 1972 origins. With the exception of a brief period of experimentation with privatization in the late 1990s, the New Zealand scheme has been administered throughout its history by a government agency, currently known as the Accident Compensation Corporation (ACC).

The ACC provides benefits for personal injuries, including physical and mental harms, that arise due to accident, medical treatment, gradual work-related processes, and sexual abuse or assault. Most accident victims are covered, including visitors injured in New Zealand and New Zealand residents injured abroad. However, not every benefit extends to all accident victims. The most important distinction is that, with insignificant exceptions, only wage earners are entitled to earnings-related compensation; loss of earning capacity of injured non-earners, such as those working at home, remains largely uncompensated. Wage earners receive 80 percent of lost earnings after an initial one-week period of nonpayment. If the accident is work-related, the employer must ordinarily pay for the first week. After the first week, the ACC pays for all earners' injuries, whether sustained on or off the job, subject to certain caps on weekly earnings amounts. The plan provides earnings replacement for as long as the victim is unable to work, or until retirement age, with a wage inflation adjustment.

The ACC is generous in its coverage of medical treatment and hospital care, and offers wider options for care than New Zealand's socialized medical system offers to victims of illness that is not accident-related. The plan also pays for ambulance expenses, nursing care expenses, dental expenses, and expenses for artificial limbs. These benefits accrue to any victim injured in an accident. In addition to providing medical expenses, the ACC is charged with the responsibility of promoting the rehabilitation of accident victims. To this end, resources are provided to assist victims in assessing their needs and options. Financial assistance for purchase or modification of motor vehicles, modification of a residence, child care, and equipment are also provided when necessary to further the independence of the injured.

The original act provided lump-sum payments for permanent loss or impairment of bodily functions, loss of capacity for enjoying life, disfigurement, and pain and suffering. These payments for noneconomic losses were provided in lieu of the potentially large awards granted under common law tort actions. Often such payments constituted the principal compensation to disabled non–wage earners. For a period of time, ARCIA eliminated compensation for these noneconomic losses, moving the system away from its origin as a substitute for the tort action, and leaving non–wage earners with little real means of compensation. In place of payments for noneconomic loss, the 1992 act created an "independence allowance" for persons with total disability, which was supposed to enable the injured to meet the additional, miscellaneous costs of disability. Subsequent legislation has restored the lump-sum payment system for permanent injuries that occur after April 1, 2002. A similar cycle of initially broad coverage, contraction, and then re-expansion occurred with respect to the ACC's coverage of medical accidents. The current act provides coverage for expenses arising from a "treatment injury," a concept that is intended to be broader than medical negligence but not so broad as to include the natural progression of disease or illness. See Peter H. Schuck, Tort Reform, Kiwi-Style, 27 Yale L. & Pol'y Rev. 187, 191-96 (2008). Finally, the ACC pays for several additional benefits, including compensation for funeral expenses, constant personal attention for a victim when such care is necessary, substitute household services previously provided by the victim, and earnings-related compensation to the surviving dependent family members of an earner who dies as a result of an accident.

The ACC is funded by a combination of direct levies and general government revenues. Covered expenses are paid for from different accounts depending on the type of injury. Broadly speaking, levies on employers, set according to firm size and industry accident history, fund compensation for work-related accidents; levies on the earnings of workers fund non-work-related accidents of earners; general tax revenues fund compensation for accidents of non-earners; levies on motor vehicle owners in the form of license fees and fuel taxes fund compensation for motor vehicle accidents; and the earners and non-earners funds are used in combination to cover medical treatment injuries.

The ACC faced a major test in early 2011, as the second extreme earthquake in just six months hit Christchurch, the largest city on New Zealand's South Island. Fatalities totaled 181, making it the second deadliest natural disaster in New Zealand history, while property damage estimates made it easily the country's costliest disaster. Within weeks, the ACC received as many as 7,133 earthquake-related injury claims, including those of numerous elderly victims who required hip replacements and other orthopedic surgeries. See Martin Johnston, Elderly Face Slow Recovery After Quake, N.Z. Herald, April 8, 2011, at A005. Not long after the quake the head of the ACC was quoted as saying, "There is no question that this is the largest claim in the 37-year history of our unique ACC scheme." John Hartevelt, ACC Takes Another Big Hit on Top of Pike River Claims, Dominion Post, March 3, 2011, at 5. Acknowledging that the ACC would face significant budgetary strain from the disaster, the Minister continued: "Yes it is a hit, but this is why I have no difficulty in saying to New Zealanders, this is why you pay your ACC levies — so those that are traumatised, those that are injured, those that are bereaved in circumstances like the Christchurch earthquake have the security that ACC will be there for them and their families. An earthquake is the ultimate accident — nobody is to blame." Id.

For a discussion of political roadblocks that could potentially prevent adoption of a no-fault system similar to New Zealand's in the United States, see Matthew Hitzhusen, Crisis and Reform: Is New Zealand's No-Fault Compensation System a Reasonable Alternative to the Medical Malpractice Crisis in the United States?, 22 Ariz. J. Int'l & Comp. Law 649 (2005). For a critical analysis of the New Zealand plan, see James A. Henderson, Jr., The New Zealand Accident Compensation Reform, 48 U. Chi. L. Rev. 781 (1981).

D. "Exit" and "Adversarialism" in Alternative Compensation Systems

This chapter has examined several systems outside of tort law that provide compensation for accidental personal injury losses. The potential benefits of these systems include lower administrative costs, greater predictability, quicker payments, and less chilling of desirable activity (e.g. vaccination and vaccine development). As the preceding sections show, however, these programs sometimes do not function as smoothly as their architects expect. Professor Nora Freeman Engstrom, whose work has been cited throughout this chapter, has identified two phenomena that plague many alternative compensation systems: "exit" and "adversarialism."

Nora Freeman Engstrom, Exit, Adversarialism, and the Stubborn Persistence of Tort

6 J. Tort. L. 75 (2013) (footnotes omitted)

1. Introduction

The tort system is much maligned — for the unpredictability of its judgments, the stinginess (or, some say, profligacy) of its awards, and the slow pace, exorbitant cost, and adversarial nature of its operation. But what to do? Reformers have debated that question for over a century.

Suggestions, not surprisingly, abound — so many, in fact, they can be mapped on a continuum. On the one end, we may situate modest reform ideas such as the "discouragement" reforms so popular and prevalent in recent decades. Premised on the notion that there is "too much" tort litigation, these reforms — such as caps on contingency fees, limits on punitive or noneconomic damages, and modifications to joint and several liability and the collateral source rule — are aimed at dampening plaintiffs' desire and capacity to sue, thus reducing litigation's volume and intensity. In so doing, these reforms offer not a fundamental reorientation of the tort liability system, but more accurately, "less of the same." Next, moving somewhere toward the continuum's midpoint, we might situate somewhat more fundamental reforms, such as increased reliance on contract or a push toward enterprise liability, particularly in the medical malpractice realm. Then, on the far end of the continuum, we would locate undeniably ambitious no-fault ideas.

Unlike those favoring discouragement mechanisms, those favoring no-fault or "replacement" regimes do not necessarily believe there is "too much" litigation. Rather, they believe that the litigation we do have, for at least particular kinds of claims, is misdirected, taking too long, costing too much, and compensating too few. As such, reformers seek to shuttle various categories of claims away from the tort system and into (typically) free-standing, newly minted administrative tribunals. There, it is assumed, with the fault obstacle gone, procedures simplified, and damages curtailed (and often paid not on an individualized basis, but pursuant to strict schedules), compensation can be more easily, cheaply, quickly, amicably, consistently, and predictably delivered.

The no-fault idea is surely attractive, and nearly a half-century after Professor Jeffrey O'Connell's publication of *Basic Protection for the Traffic Victim* — which, with the stroke of a pen, kicked off the modern no-fault movement — the idea's allure endures. Indeed, in recent years, tailored no-fault plans have been proposed dozens of times, for everything from airline accidents, to those who contract HIV after transfusion with tainted blood, to those hurt in schoolyard play, to those injured in athletic competition, to victims of medical malpractice, to those harmed following contact with (variously) prescription drugs, medical devices, contraceptives, asbestos, lead paint, cigarettes, and firearms. It seems, in fact, that someone takes to the airwaves to suggest that a no-fault scheme be created whenever a truly vexing mass tort comes along.

Still, the no-fault idea has not been everywhere accepted. Indeed, for nearly as long as they've been championed, no-fault plans have been subject to harsh, sometimes scathing, criticism. Some of these critics seize on the notion that no-fault mechanisms run counter to

Americans' individualized conception of justice or, relatedly, permit "guilty" tortfeasors to dodge responsibility for their misdeeds. Others question the wisdom or humanity of eliminating or significantly curtailing compensation for pain and suffering, especially for those victims whose economic loss might be comparatively insubstantial. Still others raise constitutional objections, charging that no-fault mechanisms run afoul of state right-to-trial and open-court provisions or violate bedrock Seventh and Fourteenth Amendment guarantees. Applying law and economics principles, others contend that no-fault plans sacrifice tort's deterrent function, resulting in more accidents, more injuries, and higher social costs. Finally, still others complain that existing no-fault reforms, focusing as they do on particular litigation "hot-spots," do not go nearly far enough. Thus, rather than our existing, piecemeal mechanisms — which carve various categories of claims out of the civil justice system while leaving the remainder intact — these commentators champion far more encompassing, often government-funded, reform.

Much ink has been spilled adjudicating these important, and fundamental, disputes. My aim here is in some ways more modest. Tabling the question of whether existing or imagined no-fault mechanisms are constitutional, as well as the broader question of whether they are (or would be) on balance beneficial, sensible, or equitable, in the pages that follow, I take our current replacement regimes on their own terms.

I note that, at enactment, these reforms set out to divert certain claims from the tort system, and they also sought to deliver payment to qualifying claimants simply, expeditiously, and predictably, without adversarial processes or significant attorney involvement. Against that ambition, I then evaluate four of the boldest experiments with no-fault compensation in the United States. . . . This investigation reveals that all four of our most ambitious no-fault experiments have, in certain respects, failed. Seepage from no-fault regimes and into the tort system has been a persistent problem, substantially diluting no-fault's ostensible advantages. And, even when compensation has been provided within our existing regimes, that compensation has only infrequently been delivered as amicably, as expeditiously, or as easily as reformers anticipated.

Furthermore, interrogating these struggles, I find that there is a heretofore unidentified commonality between the problems plaguing America's no-fault mechanisms. I call these the problems of exit and adversarialism. Across substantive areas, that is, no-fault mechanisms have become plagued by the problem of exit, as claimants seeking full compensation make end-runs around no-fault, either to evade the regime entirely or to supplement no-fault's comparatively meager benefits with more generous payments, available only within traditional tort. Or, they have become bogged down by adversarialism, marked by longer times to decision and increased combativeness, attorney involvement, and utilization of formal adjudicatory procedures. Some regimes, including auto no-fault and the [Vaccine Fund], display just one of these afflictions. Others, like workers' compensation and neurological birth injury funds, display traces of both.

Interestingly — and suggesting a fertile ground for future inquiry — these problems do not seem to appear in the reforms' early years. With time, across substantive areas, however, the problems do show up. And, with broad implications for our design and deployment of future no-fault mechanisms, these problems ultimately impair no-fault's effectiveness.

This insight complicates conventional wisdom, which posits that moving from a tort-based system to a no-fault system will markedly streamline procedures, promote predictability, speed payments, limit court congestion, quell combativeness, and reduce the need for attorney involvement. And, more fundamentally, it suggests that tort law exerts a more powerful gravitational pull than scholars and policymakers have previously recognized.

The urge to return to the tort system is strong. It is difficult to resist. And even when claims are effectively cordoned off and handled within a self-contained no-fault regime, over time, those regimes tend to acquire an adversarial cast that make them resemble, to a surprising extent, none other than their tort law ancestor.

[In the body of the article, Engstrom examines the phenomena of exit and adversarialism in workers' compensation, automobile no-fault, the Vaccine Fund, and the Florida and Virginia birth injury funds. — Eds.]

. . . In the past, when forecasting a proposed scheme's costs and benefits, it might have been reasonable to assume that boundaries demarcating where tort ends and no-fault begins could be easily drawn and efficiently policed — and also that adversarial processes would invariably and radically subside, as cases were cordoned off and relocated to freestanding administrative tribunals. This essay challenges those assumptions. Second, and more broadly, this essay seeks to follow (however modestly) in Jeffrey O'Connell's proud footsteps. Professor O'Connell has taught us patiently, persistently, and by vivid example, that only by endeavoring really to understand a regime's frailties can we begin the arduous work of effecting its repair. Following in O'Connell's legacy, I suggest, only by truly understanding what ails our existing systems of no-fault compensation — and learning the sometimes bitter lessons that come from those experiences — can we possibly begin the difficult work of designing better, more equitable, and more durable reforms.

Chapter 11

Dignitary Wrongs and Intentional Infliction of Mental Upset

In this chapter, we consider four intentional torts having at their core the protection of interests in peace of mind and basic human dignity. We have already considered one such tort in Chapter 1 — offensive battery. We begin this chapter by briefly revisiting that subject. Two of the other intentional torts taken up here — assault and false imprisonment — have their roots in the early common law[1] and are well-established legal wrongs. The fourth, intentional infliction of mental upset, is a more recent development and functions as a means of reaching antisocial conduct that does not fall squarely within the definitions of the other dignitary torts.

A. Offensive Battery

Chapter 1 addresses the tort of battery. While some cases in that chapter involve some type of bodily harm, it is important to recognize that courts do not necessarily require a plaintiff to prove actual bodily harm to succeed with a battery claim. For example, in Fisher v. Carrousel Motor Hotel, p. 321, the manager of a restaurant grabbed plaintiff's plate from his hand and shouted that plaintiff, a "Negro," would not be served in the club. The court allowed plaintiff to recover, finding that offensive and insulting physical contact was sufficient for a battery claim, even though no bodily harm resulted.

However, the law does not permit recovery by extremely sensitive persons who become offended at the slightest contact. Rather, the contact must offend a "reasonable sense of personal dignity." Brzoska v. Olson, 668 A. 2d 1355, 1361 (Del. 1995). In *Brzoska*, plaintiffs brought an action against a dentist who treated them without disclosing that he was infected with the AIDS virus. Testing revealed that plaintiffs had not become infected with the virus, but they sought recovery for their mental upset over having been contacted physically by the defendant while he was carrying the virus and thus potentially able to transmit the infection. The Supreme Court of Delaware affirmed the lower court's entry of summary judgment for the defendant, concluding:

> In sum, we find that, without actual exposure to HIV, the risk of its transmission is so minute that any fear of contracting AIDS is *per se* unreasonable. We therefore hold, *as a matter of law,* that the incidental touching of a patient by an HIV-infected dentist while performing ordinary, consented-to dental procedures is insufficient to sustain a battery claim in the absence of a channel for HIV infection. In other words, such contact is "offensive" only if it results in actual exposure to the HIV virus. . . .

1. Indeed, one of the earliest recorded opinions in tort law involves assault. I de S v. W de S, [1348] Y.B. Lib. Ass. fo. 99, placitum 60. In this classic torts case, the defendant had banged on the door of a tavern with a hatchet, and swung the hatchet in the direction of the tavern keeper's wife after she informed him that the tavern was closed. For this assault, the defendant was held liable for damages of half a mark.

> [N]othing in this record suggests any bleeding from Dr. Owens or that any wound or lesions ever came into contact with a break in the skin or mucous membrane of any of the plaintiffs. Plaintiffs have failed to demonstrate any evidence of actual exposure to potential HIV transmission beyond mere unsupported supposition.

Id. at 1364-65.

Claims alleging offensive battery arise frequently in sexual harassment cases. For example, In Doe v. Lake Oswego Sch. Dist., 353 Or. 321 (2013), the Supreme Court of Oregon held that reaching under a child's clothing and fondling him in front of a class of students constitutes offensive battery, and reversed the district court's grant of summary judgment for defendant. Even though plaintiffs, elementary school children at the time of battery, filed the claim many years after the fondling had occurred and conceded that they did not appreciate the touching was offensive at the time, the court allowed the offensive battery claim to proceed.

Though less common than sexual abuse cases, infringement of religious liberties also can lead to offensive battery claims. In Kumar v. Gate Gourmet, Inc., 325 P.3d 193 (Wash. 2014), plaintiff airport employees brought a class action against their employer, challenging the employer's meal policy, which barred employees from bringing their own food to work (for security reasons), leaving only employer-provided food for the employees to eat. Plaintiffs alleged that defendant, through practices such as misrepresenting pork meatballs as being made from turkey, "deceived them into eating food in violation of their religious beliefs, knowing that this would cause an offensive contact." Id. at 205. The court held that plaintiffs had adequately stated a claim for offensive battery.

Note: A Postscript on Intent—Must the Defendant Intend to Offend?

In *Vosburg,* which appears at the beginning of Chapter 1, the jury specifically found that defendant, Putney, did not intend to harm plaintiff, even though Putney conceded that he intended to kick plaintiff lightly on the shin. One view of the decision under modern law (Wisconsin was still developing its law of battery in the 1890s, when the case was decided) is that the contact with plaintiff's shin was offensive, given the surrounding circumstances (school room called to order, etc.), and therefore defendant committed a battery even though he did not intend to cause harm. But this view of the case raises the question of whether the defendant must at least intend to offend the plaintiff by the intended contact. Would it be sufficient that the defendant intended the contact and that a reasonable person would have been offended? To test this question of law, suppose that the jury in *Vosburg* had answered two further questions as follows:

Q: Did the defendant intend to offend the plaintiff when he (the defendant) kicked him?
A: No.
Q: Did the plaintiff take offense at being kicked, prior to suffering harm?
A: No.

If these questions and answers had been part of the trial record in *Vosburg,* how do you suppose the Supreme Court of Wisconsin would have reacted to plaintiff's battery claim? How should a court respond under current law? Cf. White v. Muniz, 999 P.2d 814 (Colo. 2000) (observing a range of views and approaches among jurisdictions and concluding that "the law of Colorado requires the jury to conclude that defendant both intended the contact and intended it to be harmful or offensive"). Contrary to *White*, most courts that have addressed the issue hold that the only intent required is the intent to cause the contact. See *Brzoska*, supra, at 1360 ("The intent necessary for battery is the intent to make contact with the person, not the intent to cause harm."). A draft of the American Law Institute's forthcoming work on intentional torts labels this difference of approach the "single intent v. dual intent" issue and sides with the single-intent rule. Restatement (Third) of Torts: Intentional Torts to Persons §102 cmt. b (Am. Law Inst., Tentative Draft No. 1, April 8, 2015).

A related question is whether the doctrine of transferred intent should be available to plaintiffs who allege offensive, as opposed to physically harmful, battery. In Hendrix v. Burns, 43 A.3d 415 (Md. Ct. Spec. App. 2012), the court surveyed case law and commentary and held that the doctrine should be applicable in any case alleging an intent to cause harmful or offensive contact. In that case, plaintiff sought to apply the doctrine to defendant who had been engaged in an ongoing "road rage" incident with a third party but accidentally struck plaintiff's car. Because the incident involved harmful physical contact, the court's holding with respect to merely offensive contact should likely be considered dictum. But see Restatement (Third) of Torts: Intentional Torts to Persons §111 (Am. Law Inst., Tentative Draft No. 1, April 8, 2015) (stating that the doctrine of transferred intent should be available for harmful or offensive battery, assault, and false imprisonment).

B. Assault

Restatement (Second) of Torts

§21. Assault

(1) An actor is subject to liability to another for assault if

(a) he acts intending to cause a harmful or offensive contact with the person of the other or a third person, or an imminent apprehension of such a contact, and

(b) the other is thereby put in such imminent apprehension.

(2) An action which is not done with the intention stated in Subsection (1, a) does not make the actor liable to the other for an apprehension caused thereby although the act involves an unreasonable risk of causing it and, therefore, would be negligent or reckless if the risk threatened bodily harm.

§29. Apprehension of imminent and future contact

(1) To make the actor liable for an assault he must put the other in apprehension of an imminent contact.

(2) An act intended by the actor as a step toward the infliction of a future contact, which is so recognized by the other, does not make the actor liable for an assault under the rule stated in §21.

Read v. Coker

[1853] 13 C.B. 850, 138 Eng. Rep. 1437

The cause was tried before Talfourd, J., at the first sitting in London in Easter Term last. The facts which appeared in evidence were as follows: — The plaintiff was a paper-stainer, carrying on business in the City Road, upon premises which he rented of one Molineux, at a rent of 8s. per week. In January 1852, the rent being sixteen weeks in arrear, the landlord employed one Holliwell to distrain for it. Holliwell accordingly seized certain presses, lathes, and other trade fixtures, and, at the plaintiff's request, advanced him 16£ upon the security of the goods, for the purpose of paying off the rent. The plaintiff, being unable to redeem his goods, on the 23rd of February applied to the defendant for assistance. The goods were thereupon sold to the defendant by Holliwell, on the part of Read, for 25£. 11s.6d.; and it was agreed between the plaintiff and the defendant, that the business should be carried on for their mutual benefit, the defendant paying the rent of the premises and other outgoings, and allowing the plaintiff a certain sum weekly.

The defendant becoming dissatisfied with the speculation, dismissed the plaintiff on the 22nd of March. On the 24th, the plaintiff came to the premises, and refusing to leave when ordered by the defendant, the latter collected together some of his workmen, who mustered round the plaintiff, tucking up their sleeves and aprons, and threatened to break his neck if he did not go out; and, fearing that the men would strike him if he did not do so, the plaintiff went out. This was the assault complained of in the first count. Upon this evidence, the learned judge left it to the jury to say, whether there was an intention on the part of the defendant to assault the plaintiff, and whether the plaintiff was apprehensive of personal violence if he did not retire. The jury found for the plaintiff on this count, damages one farthing. . . .

Byles, Serjt., on a former day in this term, in pursuance of leave reserved to him at the trial, moved for a rule nisi to enter the verdict for the defendant . . . or for a new trial on the ground of misdirection, and that the verdict was not warranted by the evidence. That which was proved . . . clearly did not amount to an assault. . . . To constitute an assault, there must be something more than a threat of violence. An assault is thus defined in Buller's Nisi Prius, p. 15, — "An assault is an attempt or offer, by force or violence, to do a corporal hurt to another, as, by pointing a pitchfork at him, when standing within reach; presenting a gun at him [within shooting distance]; drawing a sword, and waving it in a menacing manner, &c. But no words can amount to an assault, though perhaps they may in some cases serve to explain a doubtful action, as, if a man were to lay his hand upon his sword, and say, 'If it were not assize time, he would not take such language'; the words would prevent the action from being construed to be an assault, because they shew he had no intent to do him any corporal hurt at that time: Tuberville v. Savage, 1 Mod. 3." . . . [Jervis, C.J. If a man comes into a room, and lays his cane on the table, and says to another, "If you don't go out, I will knock you on the head," would not that be an assault?] Clearly not: it is a mere threat, unaccompanied by any gesture or action towards carrying it into effect. The direction of the learned judge as to this point was erroneous. He should have told the jury, that, to constitute an assault, there must be an attempt, coupled with a present ability to do personal violence to the party; instead of leaving it to them, as he did, to say what the plaintiff thought, and not what they (the jury) thought was the defendant's intention. There must be some act done denoting a present ability and an intention to assault.

[A rule nisi was granted.]

Jervis, C.J. I am of opinion that this rule . . . must be discharged. If anything short of actual striking will in law constitute an assault, the facts here clearly shewed that the defendant was guilty of an assault. There was a threat of violence exhibiting an intention to assault, and a present ability to carry the threat into execution. . . .

Maule, Cresswell, and Talfourd, JJ., concurring. Rule discharged. . . .

Beach v. Hancock

27 N.H. 223 (1853)

Trespass, for an assault.

Upon the general issue it appeared that the plaintiff and defendant, being engaged in an angry altercation, the defendant stepped into his office, which was at hand, and brought out a gun, which he aimed at the plaintiff in an excited and threatening manner, the plaintiff being three or four rods distant. The evidence tended to show that the defendant snapped the gun twice at the plaintiff, and that the plaintiff did not know whether the gun was loaded or not, and that, in fact, the gun was not loaded.

The court ruled that the pointing of a gun, in an angry and threatening manner, at a person three or four rods distant, who was ignorant whether the gun was loaded or not, was an assault, though it should appear that the gun was not loaded, and that it made no difference whether the gun was snapped or not.

The court, among other things, instructed the jury that, in assessing the damages, it was their right and duty to consider the effect which the finding of light or trivial damages in actions for breaches of the peace, would have to encourage a disregard of the laws and disturbances of the public peace.

The defendant excepted to these rulings and instructions.

The jury, having found a verdict for the plaintiff, the defendant moved for a new trial by reason of said exceptions.

Gilcrest, C.J. . . . One of the most important objects to be attained by the enactment of laws and the institutions of civilized society is, each of us shall feel secure against unlawful assaults. Without such security society loses most of its value. Peace and order and domestic happiness, inexpressively more precious than mere forms of government, cannot be enjoyed without the sense of perfect security. We have a right to live in society without being put in fear of personal harm. But it must be a reasonable fear of which we complain. And it surely is not unreasonable for a person to entertain a fear of personal injury, when a pistol is pointed at him in a threatening manner, when, for aught he knows, it may be loaded, and may occasion his immediate death. The business of the world could not be carried on with comfort, if such things could be done with impunity.

We think the defendant guilty of an assault, and we perceive no reason for taking any exception to the remarks of the court. Finding trivial damages for breaches of the peace, damages incommensurate with the injury sustained, would certainly lead the ill-disposed to consider an assault as a thing that might be committed with impunity. But, at all events, it was proper for the jury to consider whether such a result would or would not be produced.

Judgment on the verdict.

Modern cases generally reject the "present ability" requirement of Read v. Coker, and ask instead whether a reasonable person would have felt danger or threat of physical harm. In Bouton v. Allstate Insurance Co., 491 So. 2d 56 (La. Ct. App. 1986), the plaintiff claimed that a 13-year-old boy committed an assault upon him by going to the front door of plaintiff's house on Halloween night dressed in military fatigues and carrying a plastic model submachine gun. The plaintiff shot and killed the boy, believing him to be an armed assailant. After plaintiff's acquittal on second degree murder charges, plaintiff brought this action against the boy's insurers, alleging that the boy's assault caused plaintiff to be tried criminally, incur legal expenses, lose his job, and suffer a damaged reputation. The court rejected this claim as a matter of law, stating that a reasonable person under these circumstances would not have been apprehensive of imminent harmful bodily contact.

Of course, in many cases an ability to cause harm *will* be present when an assault occurs. In Hughes v. Metro. Gov't of Nashville & Davisonson County, 340 S.W.3d 352 (Tenn. 2011), plaintiff suffered injuries after a municipal public works employee drove a front-end loader toward plaintiff and forced him to jump awkwardly over a guardrail. Plaintiff hoped to characterize the employee's actions as mere negligence in order to stay within defendant's waiver of sovereign immunity for torts committed by city employees. Citing extensive evidence that the employee intended to frighten plaintiff and, indeed, had a history of attempting to scare coworkers and otherwise engage in "horseplay" involving heavy equipment, the court held that the actions constituted an intentional tort of assault, not negligence, and hence was not included in the waiver.

C. False Imprisonment

Restatement (Second) of Torts

§35. False Imprisonment

(1) An actor is subject to liability to another for false imprisonment if

(a) he acts intending to confine the other or a third person within boundaries fixed by the actor, and

(b) his act directly or indirectly results in such a confinement of the other, and

(c) the other is conscious of the confinement or is harmed by it.

(2) An act which is not done with the intention stated in Subsection (1, a) does not make the actor liable to the other for a merely transitory or otherwise harmless confinement, although the act involves an unreasonable risk of imposing it and therefore would be negligent or reckless if the risk threatened bodily harm.

Whittaker v. Sanford

110 Me. 77, 85 A. 399 (1912)

Savage, J. Action for false imprisonment. The plaintiff recovered a verdict for $1100. The case comes up on defendant's exceptions and motion for a new trial.

[The plaintiff had been a member of a religious sect which had colonies in Maine and in Jaffa, Syria, and of which the defendant was the leader. Some months prior to the alleged imprisonment, the plaintiff, while in Jaffa, announced her intention to leave the sect. The defendant, with the help of the plaintiff's husband, persuaded the plaintiff to return to the United States aboard the sect's palatial yacht, the Kingdom. The defendant promised the plaintiff that she and her children would be free to leave the ship any time they were in port. After their arrival in Maine, the plaintiff asked to be put ashore with her children and baggage, and the defendant refused. (The plaintiff eventually gained her release on a writ of habeas corpus.) There was evidence that the plaintiff had been ashore a number of times, had been on numerous outings and had been treated as a guest during her stay aboard the yacht. According to the uncontradicted evidence, at no time did anyone physically restrain the plaintiff except for the defendant's refusal, once the plaintiff announced her decision to quit the yacht, to let the plaintiff use a small boat to take herself, her children, and her belongings ashore. Throughout the entire episode, the plaintiff's husband was with her and repeatedly tried to persuade her to change her mind and remain with the sect.]

. . . The court instructed the jury that the plaintiff to recover must show that the restraint was physical, and not merely a moral influence, that it must have been actual physical restraint, in the sense that one intentionally locked into a room would be physically restrained, but not necessarily involving physical force upon the person; that it was not necessary that the defendant, or any person by his direction, should lay his hand upon the plaintiff, that if the plaintiff was restrained so that she could not leave the yacht Kingdom by the intentional refusal to furnish transportation as agreed, she not having it in her power to escape otherwise, it would be a physical restraint and unlawful imprisonment. We think the instructions were apt and sufficient. If one should, without right, turn the key in a door, and thereby prevent a person in the room from leaving, it would be the simplest form of unlawful imprisonment. The restraint is physical. The four walls and the locked door are physical impediments to escape. How is it different when one who is in control of a vessel at anchor, within practical rowing distance from the shore, who has agreed that a guest on board shall be free to leave, there being no means to leave except by rowboats, wrongfully refuses the guest the use of a boat? The boat is the key. By refusing the boat he turns the key. The guest is as effectually locked up as if there were walls along the sides of the vessel. The restraint is physical. The impassable sea is the physical barrier. . . .

But the damages awarded seem to us manifestly excessive. The plaintiff, if imprisoned, was by no means in close confinement. She was afforded all the liberties of the yacht. She was taken on shore by her husband to do shopping and transact business at a bank. She visited neighboring islands with her husband and children, on one of which they enjoyed a family picnic. The case lacks the elements of humiliation and disgrace that frequently attend false imprisonment. She was respectfully treated as a guest in every way, except that she was restrained from quitting the yacht for good and all.

The certificate will be,

Exceptions overruled. If the plaintiff remits all of the verdict in excess of $500, within 30 days after the certificate is received by the clerk, motion overruled; otherwise, motion sustained.

The "moral influence" aspects of the *Whittaker* decision arise today in the context of struggles of parents to free their children from the control and influence of religious sects. If the children are unemancipated minors, presumably their parents may legally establish and restore their rights to custody. But because the children in these cases are often grown adults, parents must allege that their children are being held tortiously against their wills. Consistent with the holding in *Whittaker,* false imprisonment is not found when the only restraints on the children are moral; allegations that the children have been brainwashed, and must be returned to their parents for "deprogramming," will not suffice even when the parents' right to custody in such circumstances are established by special statutes. Thus, in Katz v. Superior Court, 141 Cal. Rptr. 234 (Ct. App. 1977), the court granted the petition of the adult children to prohibit the enforcement of court orders appointing their parents as temporary guardians for the purpose of permitting the children to be deprogrammed from the ideas and attitudes allegedly instilled in them by the Rev. Sun Myung Moon's Unification Church. Courts have also declined to punish certain religious practices that otherwise would be tortious in a secular context. For instance, in Pleasant Glade Assembly of God v. Schubert, 264 S.W.3d 1 (Tex. 2008), the defendant church was entitled to free exercise protection from liability under the First Amendment for former church member's emotional distress and false imprisonment claims resulting from the defendants' "laying hands" on the plaintiff when she allegedly underwent demonic possession.

While courts are reluctant to support efforts by parents to gain custody of their adult children, they are also reluctant to interfere with those efforts by imposing tort liability upon persons who attempt to persuade members to leave religious sects. Thus, in Weiss v. Patrick, 453 F. Supp. 717 (D.R.I. 1978), *aff'd*, 588 F.2d 818 (1st Cir. 1978), *cert. denied*, 442 U.S. 929 (1979), the court ruled in favor of defendants against plaintiff, a member of the Unification Church, who brought an action alleging that defendants had conspired to violate her civil rights and claiming damages for assault, battery, and false imprisonment. Defendants had been hired by plaintiff's mother to persuade plaintiff to leave the church. Although plaintiff testified that she had been kidnapped and held forcibly against her will, the district court found that plaintiff had merely been exposed to lawful efforts to convince her to change her way of life.

Given the substantial physical area in which plaintiff was free to move in *Whittaker*, defendant might have argued that no imprisonment occurred at all. In Shen v. Leo A. Daly Co., 222 F.3d 472 (8th Cir. 2000), plaintiff was an agent of defendant, stationed in Taiwan. Plaintiff alleged that, after defendant terminated the agency under circumstances for which defendant was responsible, he was falsely imprisoned in Taiwan. Plaintiff also included a contract claim premised on defendant's alleged breach of the covenant of good faith and fair dealing. The court ruled that defendant was entitled to judgment as a matter of law on the false imprisonment count, stating (Id. at 477):

> [Plaintiff's] confinement . . . was to a whole country. He was free to move about Taiwan, and was not restrained in any way in his daily activities. Although it is difficult to define exactly how close the level of restraint must be, in this case the country of Taiwan is clearly too great an area within which to be falsely imprisoned.

Rougeau v. Firestone Tire & Rubber Co.

274 So. 2d 454 (La. Ct. App. 1973)

Savoy, J. Deryl D. Rougeau instituted this tort suit against his ex-employer, Firestone Tire and Rubber Company, seeking damages for . . . false imprisonment . . . alleged to have occurred during the investigations by agents of defendant concerning missing property at defendant's Lake Charles plant. The trial judge denied recovery to plaintiff, and we affirm the judgment of the trial judge.

Plaintiff was employed as a guard-fireman at defendant's plant in Lake Charles. Two lawnmowers belonging to the defendant were allegedly stolen during plaintiff's working shift. Local management enlisted the aid of E. E. Drummond, Corporate Security Manager of Firestone Tire and Rubber Company, to investigate the thefts. . . .

. . . The facts revealed that Drummond and two employees of defendant and plaintiff went to his home to search for the missing property. Plaintiff, on advice of his attorney, refused to allow the search. Drummond, the employees of defendant, and plaintiff returned to the plant. Plaintiff was asked to wait in the guardhouse. Two guards were instructed to keep plaintiff in the guardhouse. However, both guards stated they did not consider plaintiff to be a prisoner. Plaintiff was allowed to leave when he fell ill. The total amount of time which plaintiff spent in the guardhouse did not exceed thirty minutes.

We agree with the trial judge that plaintiff was not falsely imprisoned. At no time was he totally restrained. Additionally, plaintiff never revealed to anyone that he did not want to stay in the guardhouse, thus showing his implied consent to stay.

In Faniel v. Chesapeake & Potomac Telephone Co., 404 A.2d 147 (D.C. 1979), an employee who was suspected by her employer of stealing telephone equipment brought an action for false imprisonment based on allegations that she had been forced against her will to accompany her employer's security personnel to her home to locate and recover the equipment. The trial court entered judgment for defendant employer notwithstanding a jury verdict for plaintiff. On evidence similar to that in the *Rougeau* case, the court of appeals affirmed, holding that there was no evidence that plaintiff employee, who agreed to accompany the security officers to her home, had yielded to threats, either express or implied, or to physical force. In response to plaintiff's argument that she had not agreed to a detour during the trip to her home, the court of appeals pointed out that plaintiff had not objected or asked to leave the car, and thus had failed to negate her prior consent to take the trip.

Another issue that might have been addressed by the court in *Rougeau* is whether plaintiff must have been aware of the confinement in order to recover. Section 35 of the Restatement (Second), above, requires that plaintiff must either be aware of the confinement or be harmed by it. This limitation has been attacked by some commentators as overly restrictive. See, e.g., 1 Fowler V. Harper, Fleming James, Jr. & Oscar S. Gray, The Law of Torts §3.6 (3d ed. 1996).

Coblyn v. Kennedy's, Inc.

359 Mass. 319, 268 N.E.2d 860 (1971)

Spiegel, J. This is an action of tort for false imprisonment. At the close of the evidence the defendants filed a motion for directed verdicts which was denied. The jury returned verdicts for the plaintiff in the sum of $12,500. The case is here on the defendants' exceptions to the denial of their motion and to the refusal of the trial judge to give certain requested instructions to the jury.

We state the pertinent evidence most favorable to the plaintiff. On March 5, 1965, the plaintiff went to Kennedy's, Inc. (Kennedy's), a store in Boston. He was seventy years of age and about five feet four inches in height. He was wearing a woolen shirt, which was "open at the neck," a topcoat and a hat. "[A]round his neck" he wore an ascot which he had "purchased . . . previously at Filenes." He proceeded to the second floor of Kennedy's to purchase a sport coat. He removed his hat, topcoat and ascot, putting the ascot in his pocket. After purchasing a sport coat and leaving it for alterations, he put on his hat and coat and walked downstairs. Just prior to exiting through the outside door of the store, he stopped, took the ascot out of his pocket, put it around his neck, and knotted it. The knot was visible "above the lapels of his shirt." The only stop that the plaintiff made on the first floor was immediately in front of the exit in order to put on his ascot.

Just as the plaintiff stepped out of the door, the defendant Goss, an employee, "loomed up" in front of him with his hand up and said: "Stop. Where did you get that scarf?" The plaintiff responded, "[W]hy?" Goss firmly grasped the plaintiff's arm and said: "[Y]ou better go back and see the manager." Another employee was standing next to him. Eight or ten other people were standing around and were staring at the plaintiff. The plaintiff then said, "Yes, I'll go back in the store" and proceeded to do so. As he and Goss went upstairs to the second floor, the plaintiff paused twice because of chest and back pains. After reaching the second floor, the salesman from whom he had purchased the coat recognized him and asked what the trouble was. The plaintiff then asked: "[W]hy 'these two gentlemen stop me?'" The salesman confirmed that the plaintiff had purchased a sport coat and that the ascot belonged to him.

The salesman became alarmed by the plaintiff's appearance and the store nurse was called. She brought the plaintiff to the nurse's room and gave him a soda mint tablet. As a direct result of the emotional upset caused by the incident, the plaintiff was hospitalized and treated for a "myocardial infarct."

Initially, the defendants contend that as a matter of law the plaintiff was not falsely imprisoned. They argue that no unlawful restraint was imposed by either force or threat upon the plaintiff's freedom of movement. However, "[t]he law is well settled that '[a]ny genuine restraint is sufficient to constitute an imprisonment . . . ' and '[a]ny demonstration of physical power which, to all appearances, can be avoided only by submission, operates as effectually to constitute an imprisonment, if submitted to, as if any amount of force had been exercised. If a man is restrained of his personal liberty by fear of a personal difficulty, that amounts to a false imprisonment' within the legal meaning of such term." Jacques v. Childs Dining Hall Co., 244 Mass. 438, 438-439, 138 N.E. 843.

We think it is clear that there was sufficient evidence of unlawful restraint to submit this question to the jury. Just as the plaintiff had stepped out of the door of the store, the defendant Goss stopped him, firmly grasped his arm and told him that he had "better go back and see the manager." There was another employee at his side. The plaintiff was an elderly man and there were other people standing around staring at him. Considering the plaintiff's age and his heart condition, it is hardly to be expected that with one employee in front of him firmly grasping his arm and another at his side the plaintiff could do other than comply with Goss's "request" that he go back and see the manager. . . .

The defendants next contend that the detention of the plaintiff was sanctioned by G.L. c. 231, §94B, inserted by St. 1958, c. 337. This statute provides as follows: "In an action for false arrest or false imprisonment brought by any person by reason of having been detained for questioning on or in the immediate vicinity of the premises of a merchant, if such person was detained in a reasonable manner and for not more than a reasonable length of time by a person authorized to make arrests or by the merchant or his agent or servant authorized for such purpose and if there were reasonable grounds to believe that the person so detained was committing or attempting to commit larceny of goods for sale on such premises, it shall be a defence to such action. If such goods had not been purchased and were concealed on or amongst the belongings of a person so detained it shall be presumed that there were reasonable grounds for such belief."

The defendants argue in accordance with the conditions imposed in the statute that the plaintiff was detained in a reasonable manner for a reasonable length of time and that Goss had reasonable grounds for believing that the plaintiff was attempting to commit larceny of goods held for sale.

It is conceded that the detention was for a reasonable length of time. We need not decide whether the detention was effected in a reasonable manner for we are of opinion that there were no reasonable grounds for believing that the plaintiff was committing larceny and, therefore, he should not have been detained at all. However, we observe that Goss's failure to identify himself as an employee of Kennedy's and to disclose the reasons for his inquiry and actions, coupled with the physical restraint in a public place imposed upon the plaintiff, an elderly man, who had exhibited no aggressive intention to depart, could be said to constitute an unreasonable method by which to effect detention.

The pivotal question before us as in most cases of this character is whether the evidence shows that there were reasonable grounds for the detention. At common law in an action for false imprisonment, the defense of probable cause, as measured by the prudent and cautious man standard, was available to a merchant. In enacting G.L. c. 231, §94B, the Legislature inserted the words, "reasonable grounds." Historically, the words "reasonable grounds" and "probable cause" have been given the same meaning by the courts. . . .

The defendants assert that the judge improperly instructed the jury in stating that "grounds are reasonable when there is a basis which would appear to the reasonably prudent, cautious, intelligent person." In their brief, they argue that the "prudent and cautious man rule" is an objective standard and requires a more rigorous and restrictive standard of conduct than is contemplated by G.L. c. 231 §94B. The defendants' requests for instructions, in effect, state that the proper test is a subjective one, viz., whether the defendant Goss had an honest and strong suspicion that the plaintiff was committing or attempting to commit larceny. . . .

If we adopt the subjective test as suggested by the defendants, the individual's right to liberty and freedom of movement would become subject to the "honest . . . suspicion" of a shopkeeper based on his own "inarticulate hunches" without regard to any discernible facts. In effect, the result would be to afford the merchant even greater authority than that given to a police officer. In view of the well established meaning of the words "reasonable grounds" we believe that the Legislature intended to give these words their traditional meaning. This seems to us a valid conclusion since the Legislature has permitted an individual to be detained for a "reasonable length of time." . . .

Applying the standard of reasonable grounds as measured by the reasonably prudent man test to the evidence in the instant case, we are of opinion that the evidence warranted the conclusion that Goss was not reasonably justified in believing that the plaintiff was engaged in shoplifting. There was no error in denying the motion for directed verdicts and in the refusal to give the requested instructions.

Exceptions overruled.

A more recent case with similar facts is McCann v. Wal-Mart Stores, Inc., 210 F. 3d 51 (1st Cir. 2000). As the McCanns were leaving the store, two Wal-Mart employees stepped out in front of the McCanns' shopping cart, blocking their path to the exit. The employees told the mother that her children were not allowed in the store because they had been caught stealing on a prior occasion. In fact, the employees were mistaken. Despite Debra McCann's protestations, one of the employees told the McCanns that the police had been called, and the McCanns "had to go with her." The mother did not resist the employees' direction because "she believed that she had to go with [them] and that the police were coming." Id. at 53. Wal-Mart asserted that under Maine law, the jury had to find "actual, physical restraint," but the court retorted that a literal application of "actual, physical restraint would put Maine law broadly at odds with not only the Restatement but with a practically uniform body of common law in other states that accepts the mere threat of physical force, or a claim of lawful authority to restrain, as enough to satisfy the confinement requirement for false imprisonment." Id. at 54.

The court's opinion in *Coblyn* implies that the decisions of shop owners to detain potential shoplifters should be subject to the same level of scrutiny as that applied to police officers. False imprisonment claims are sometimes brought against law enforcement officials under state tort law, in addition to constitutional challenges. See, e.g., Bennett v. Ohio Dep't of Rehabilitation & Correction, 573 N.E.2d 633 (Ohio 1991) (even if an initial confinement was lawful, defendant Department of Corrections could be found liable for the tort of false imprisonment if it intentionally continued to confine an inmate despite knowledge that the privilege initially justifying that confinement no longer existed). In Hollins v. City of New York, 2014 WL 836950 (S.D.N.Y. 2014), the court held that a valid false imprisonment claim had been stated based on allegations that police handcuffed plaintiff, a 12-year old child residing in an apartment being searched by police, for three to four hours, including a substantial period of time after the search had been completed.

Notwithstanding the similarities, might there be good reason for courts to afford retailers greater latitude than police and corrections officers? Note that an erroneous detention imposes costs not only on the falsely accused patron, but also on the business itself in terms of an immediate and probably permanent loss of the customer's good will. Thus, a merchant might have a natural incentive to avoid overzealous efforts to detect shoplifting. Some courts do appear more deferential than the *Coblyn* court to the decisions of shop owners concerning the need to detain potential shoplifters. For example, in Wal-Mart Stores, Inc. v. Resendez, 962 S.W.2d 539 (Tex. 1998), the plaintiff Resendez was eating peanuts from a bag marked with a Wal-Mart price sticker while she shopped at the defendant's store. A store security guard followed Resendez and watched her place the empty bag under a rose bush, purchase some items, and leave. Having determined that Resendez did not pay for the bag of peanuts, the security guard escorted her back into the store, where she was detained for fifteen minutes until a police officer arrived and arrested her. Resendez objected that, although she no longer had the receipt, she had purchased the peanuts the day before at another Wal-Mart store. After her misdemeanor peanut-theft conviction was overturned, Resendez brought an action against Wal-Mart for false imprisonment. On appeal from a jury verdict for Resendez, the supreme court reversed the judgment, holding that (962 S.W.2d at 540) "[i]n a false imprisonment case, if the alleged detention was performed with the authority of law, then no false imprisonment occurred. . . . The 'shopkeeper's privilege' expressly grants an employee the authority of law to detain a customer to investigate the ownership of property in a reasonable manner and for a reasonable period of time if the employee has a reasonable belief that the customer has stolen or is attempting to steal store merchandise." Statutes in a number of other states provide immunity for retail businesses' reasonable detention of shoplifters. See, e.g., N.Y. Gen. Bus. §218 (McKinney 2011); Mich, Comp. Laws Ann. §600.2917 (West 2011); Okla. Stat. Ann. tit. 22, §1344 (West 2011); La. Code Crim. Proc. Ann. art. 215 (2010).

Sindle v. New York City Transit Authority

33 N.Y.2d 293, 307 N.E.2d 245 (1973)

NY Court of Appeals (highest)

JASEN, J. At about noon on June 20, 1967, the plaintiff, then 14 years of age, boarded a school bus owned by the defendant, New York City Transit Authority, and driven by its employee, the defendant Mooney. It was the last day of the term . . . and the 65 to 70 students on board the bus were in a boisterous and exuberant mood. Some of this spirit expressed itself in vandalism, a number of students breaking dome lights, windows, ceiling panels and advertising poster frames. There is no evidence that the plaintiff partook in this destruction.

The bus made several stops at appointed stations. On at least one occasion, the driver admonished the students about excessive noise and damage to the bus. When he reached the Annadale station, the driver discharged several more passengers, went to the rear of the bus, inspected the damage and advised the students that he was taking them to the St. George police station.

The driver closed the doors of the bus and proceeded, bypassing several normal stops. As the bus slowed to turn onto Woodrow Road, several students jumped without apparent injury from a side window at the rear of the bus. Several more followed, again without apparent harm, when the bus turned onto Arden Avenue.

At the corner of Arden Avenue and Arthur Kill Road, departing from its normal route, the bus turned right in the general direction of the St. George police station. The plaintiff, intending to jump from the bus, had positioned himself in a window on the right-rear side. Grasping the bottom of the window sill with his hands, the plaintiff extended his legs (to mid-thigh), head and shoulders out of the window. As the bus turned right, the right rear wheels hit the curb and the plaintiff either jumped or fell to the street. The right rear wheels then rolled over the midsection of his body, causing serious personal injuries.

The plaintiff, joined with his father, then commenced an action to recover damages for negligence and false imprisonment. At the outset of the trial, the negligence cause was waived and plaintiffs proceeded on the theory of false imprisonment. At the close of the plaintiffs' case, the court denied defendants' motion to amend their answers to plead the defense of justification. The court also excluded all evidence bearing on the justification issue.

We believe that it was an abuse of discretion for the trial court to deny the motion to amend and to exclude the evidence of justification. It was the defendants' burden to prove justification — a defense that a plaintiff in an action for false imprisonment should be prepared to meet — and the plaintiffs could not have been prejudiced by the granting of the motion to amend. The trial court's rulings precluded the defendants from introducing any evidence in this regard and were manifestly unfair. Accordingly, the order of the Appellate Division must be reversed and a new trial granted.

In view of our determination, it would be well to outline some of the considerations relevant to the issue of justification. In this regard, we note that, generally, restraint or detention, reasonable under the circumstances and in time and manner, imposed for the purpose of preventing another from inflicting personal injuries or interfering with or damaging real or personal property in one's lawful possession or custody is not unlawful. . . . Also, a parent, guardian or teacher entrusted with the care or supervision of a child may use physical force reasonably necessary to maintain discipline or promote the welfare of the child.

Similarly, a school bus driver, entrusted with the care of his student-passengers and the custody of public property, has the duty to take reasonable measures for the safety and protection of both — the passengers and the property. In this regard, the reasonableness of his actions — as bearing on the defense of justification — is to be determined from a consideration of all the circumstances. At a minimum, this would seem to import a consideration of the need to protect the persons and property in his charge, the duty to aid the investigation and apprehension of those inflicting damage, the manner and place of the occurrence, and the feasibility and practicality of other alternative courses of action.

With regard to the proper measure of damages, an ancillary but nevertheless important question of law is presented — namely, whether a plaintiff's negligence in attempting to extricate himself from an unlawful confinement should diminish his damages for bodily injuries sustained as a result of the false imprisonment. In this regard, plaintiff has been awarded damages of $500 for mental anguish and $75,000 for bodily injuries. The plaintiff father has been awarded damages of $750 for loss of services and $5,797 for medical expenses.

Where the damages follow as a consequence of the plaintiff's detention without justification an award may include those for bodily injuries. And although confinement reasonably perceived to be unlawful may invite escape, the person falsely imprisoned is not relieved of the duty of reasonable care for his own safety in extricating himself from the unlawful detention. In this regard, it has been held that alighting from a moving vehicle, absent some compelling reason, is negligence per se. Therefore, upon retrial, if the trier of fact finds that plaintiff was falsely imprisoned but that he acted unreasonably for his own safety by placing himself in a perilous position in the window of the bus preparatory to an attempt to alight, recovery for the bodily injuries subsequently sustained would be barred.

For the reasons stated, the order of the Appellate Division should be reversed and the case remitted for a new trial.

FULD, C.J., and BURKE, BREITEL, GABRIELLI, JONES, and WACHTLER, JJ., concur.

Order reversed, without costs, and a new trial granted.

D. *Intentional Infliction of Mental Upset*

William L. Prosser, Insult and Outrage

44 Cal. L. Rev. 40, 40-43 (1956)

By the middle of this century, it appears to be quite generally recognized that the nameless wrong which, for lack of anything better, usually is called the intentional infliction of mental suffering, or mental anguish or mental disturbance, or emotional distress, has such distinct and definite features of its own that it is entitled to be regarded as a separate tort.

[I]t is no longer disputed that in a proper case the action for such a tort will lie, without resort to any assault, defamation, or other traditional basis of liability. . . .

Certain assumptions may be made at the outset. The . . . tort . . . encountered from the beginning the same objections which have been raised against any liability for mental disturbance negligently inflicted: the unsatisfactory character of the injury, "too subtle and speculative to be capable of admeasurement by any standard known to the law," and so evanescent, intangible, peculiar and variable with the individual as to be beyond prediction or anticipation; and the "wide door" which might be opened, not only to fictitious claims, but to litigation in the field of trivialities and mere bad manners. The leading case which broke through the shackles in 1897 was Wilkinson v. Downton in England, in which a practical joker amused himself by telling a woman that her husband had been smashed up in an accident and was lying at The Elms at Leytonstone with both legs broken, and that she was to go at once in a cab with two pillows to fetch him home. The shock to her nervous system produced serious and permanent physical consequences, which at one time threatened her reason, and entailed weeks of suffering and incapacity. The court no doubt regretted that the defendant could not, like that other false informer Titus Oates, be whipped from Aldgate to Newgate and from Newgate to Tyburn; and as in many another hard case, the enormity of the outrage overthrew the settled rule of law.

As other outrageous cases began to accumulate, the courts continued to struggle to find some familiar and traditional basis of liability; and wherever it was possible without too obvious pretense, the recovery was rested upon a technical assault, battery, false imprisonment, trespass to land, nuisance, or invasion of the right of privacy. The independent cause of action served as a peg upon which to hang the mental damages; and there are many such cases which on their facts fall fairly within the scope of the "new tort." Gradually too many cases appeared in which no such traditional ground could be discovered; and somewhere around 1930 it began to be generally recognized that the intentional infliction of mental disturbance, at least by extreme and outrageous conduct, could be a cause of action in itself. . . .

It may . . . be assumed that "mental anguish" requires no definition. By whatever name it passes, from nervous shock to emotional upset, it is familiar enough as an element of compensable damages in cases of personal injury, where the admitted difficulty of measuring its financial equivalent never has been regarded as an insuperable obstacle. . . . It includes all highly unpleasant mental reactions, such as fright, horror, grief, shame, humiliation, anger, embarrassment, chagrin, disappointment, worry and nausea. It must of course be proved; and since it is easily feigned and difficult to deny, the courts have tended quite naturally to insist upon some guarantee of genuineness, either in the form of physical consequences which can be attested objectively, or in the nature of the defendant's conduct and the circumstances of the case.

Calvert Magruder, Mental and Emotional Disturbances in the Law of Torts

49 Harv. L. Rev. 1033, 1035 (1936)

[I]t is true . . . that the common law has been reluctant to recognize the interest in one's peace of mind as deserving of general and independent legal protection, even as against intentional invasions. Conceivably a principle might have been developed that mental distress purposely caused is actionable unless justified, thus casting upon the defendant the burden of establishing some privilege by way of rebutting the prima facie liability. That this was not done is hardly to be ascribed to any inherent difficulty in assessing damages. . . . Rather it was due to policy considerations of a different sort. Adoption of the suggested principle would open up a wide vista of litigation in the field of bad manners, where relatively minor annoyances had better be dealt with by instruments of social control other than the law. Quite apart from the question how far peace of mind is a good thing in itself, it would be quixotic indeed for the law to attempt a general securing of it. Against a large part of the frictions and irritations and clashing of temperaments incident to participation in a community life, a certain toughening of the mental hide is a better protection than the law could ever be. Furthermore, in an ad hoc manner, and perhaps not very scientifically, the courts have in large measure afforded legal redress for mental or emotional distress in the more outrageous cases, without formulating too broad a general principle.

Prosser's attempt to outline this "new tort" and his effort to limit its scope to avoid the problems suggested by Magruder are embodied in §46 and accompanying commentary of the Restatement (Second) of Torts:

§46. Outrageous Conduct Causing Severe Emotional Distress

(1) One who by extreme and outrageous conduct intentionally or recklessly causes severe emotional distress to another is subject to liability for such emotional distress, and if bodily harm to the other results from it, for such bodily harm.

(2) Where such conduct is directed at a third person, the actor is subject to liability if he intentionally or recklessly causes severe emotional distress

(a) to a member of such person's immediate family who is present at the time, whether or not such distress results in bodily harm, or

(b) to any other person who is present at the time, if such distress results in bodily harm. . . .

COMMENT:

d. Extreme and outrageous conduct. The cases thus far decided have found liability only where the defendant's conduct has been extreme and outrageous. It has not been enough that the defendant has acted with an intent which is tortious or even criminal, or that he has intended to inflict emotional distress, or even that his conduct has been characterized by "malice," or a degree of aggravation which would entitle the plaintiff to punitive damages for another tort. Liability has been found only where the conduct has been so outrageous in character, and so extreme in degree, as to go beyond all possible bounds of decency, and to be regarded as atrocious, and utterly intolerable in a civilized community. Generally, the case is one in which the recitation of the facts to an average member of the community would arouse his resentment against the actor, and lead him to exclaim, "Outrageous!"

The liability clearly does not extend to mere insults, indignities, threats, annoyances, petty oppressions, or other trivialities. The rough edges of our society are still in need of a good deal of filing down, and in the meantime plaintiffs must necessarily be expected and required to be hardened to a certain amount of rough language, and to occasional acts that are definitely inconsiderate and unkind. There is no occasion for the law to intervene in every case where some one's feelings are hurt. There must still be freedom to express an unflattering opinion, and some safety valve must be left through which irascible tempers may blow off relatively harmless steam. See Magruder, Mental and Emotional Disturbance in the Law of Torts, [49] Harvard Law Review 1033, 1053 (1936). It is only where there is a special relation between the parties, as stated in §48,[2] that there may be recovery for insults not amounting to extreme outrage.

Note that §45 of the Restatement (Third) of Torts: Liability for Physical and Emotional Harm (2010) is virtually identical to §46 of the Restatement (Second). Where the Third Restatement differs is the addition of the doctrine of transferred intent; the emotional harm directed at one person but resulting in emotional harm of another is nevertheless treated as an intentional tort. See id. at cmt. i. For instance, in Kinsler v. Int'l House of Pancakes, Inc., 799 N.Y.S.2d 863 (N.Y. 2005), the court sustained plaintiff's infant daughter's claim under

2. §48. Special Liability of Public Utility for Insults by Servants.

A common carrier or other public utility is subject to liability to patrons utilizing its facilities for gross insults which reasonably offend them, inflicted by the utility's servants while otherwise acting within the scope of their employment. [Eds.]

the "transferred intent" doctrine for damages arising from an asthma attack and emotional distress the daughter suffered as a result of alleged defamatory accusations made against her mother. For a contrary view see Bourne v. Mapother & Mapother, P.S.C., 998 F. Supp. 2d 495 (S.D. W. Va. 2014) (holding that "the doctrine of transferred intent is not appropriate in the IIED context given the personal nature of the tort").

State Rubbish Collectors Association v. Siliznoff

38 Cal. 2d 330, 240 P.2d 282 (1952)

TRAYNOR, J. On February 1, 1948, Peter Kobzeff signed a contract with the Acme Brewing Company to collect rubbish from the latter's brewery. Kobzeff had been in the rubbish business for several years and was able to secure the contract because Acme was dissatisfied with the service then being provided by another collector, one Abramoff. Although Kobzeff signed the contract, it was understood that the work should be done by John Siliznoff, Kobzeff's son-in-law, whom Kobzeff wished to assist in establishing a rubbish collection business.

Both Kobzeff and Abramoff were members of the plaintiff State Rubbish Collectors Association, but Siliznoff was not. The by-laws of the Association provided that one member should not take an account from another member without paying for it. Usual prices ranged from five to ten times the monthly rate paid by the customer, and disputes were referred to the board of directors for settlement. After Abramoff lost the Acme account he complained to the association, and Kobzeff was called upon to settle the matter. Kobzeff and Siliznoff took the position that the Acme account belonged to Siliznoff, and that he was under no obligation to pay for it. After attending several meetings of plaintiff's board of directors Siliznoff finally agreed, however, to pay Abramoff $1,850 for the Acme account and join the association. The agreement provided that he should pay $500 in 30 days and $75 per month thereafter until the whole sum agreed upon was paid. Payments were to be made through the association, and Siliznoff executed a series of promissory notes totaling $1,850. None of these notes was paid, and in 1949 plaintiff association brought this action to collect the notes then payable. Defendant cross-complained and asked that the notes be cancelled because of duress and want of consideration. In addition he sought general and exemplary damages because of assaults made by plaintiff and its agents to compel him to join the association and pay Abramoff for the Acme account. The jury returned a verdict against plaintiff and for defendant on the complaint and for defendant on his cross-complaint. It awarded him $1,250 general and special damages and $7,500 exemplary damages. The trial court denied a motion for a new trial on the condition that defendant consent to a reduction of the exemplary damages to $4,000. Defendant filed the required consent, and plaintiff has appealed from the judgment.

Plaintiff's primary contention is that the evidence is insufficient to support the judgment. Defendant testified that shortly after he secured the Acme account, the president of the association and its inspector, John Andikian, called on him and Kobzeff. They suggested that either a settlement be made with Abramoff or that the job be dropped, and requested Kobzeff and defendant to attend a meeting of the association. At this meeting defendant was told that the association "ran all the rubbish from that office, all the rubbish hauling," and that if he did not pay for the job they would take it away from him. "'We would take it away, even if we had to haul for nothing.' . . . [O]ne of them mentioned that I had better pay up, or else." Thereafter, on the day when defendant finally agreed to pay for the account, Andikian visited defendant at the Rainier Brewing Company, where he was collecting rubbish. Andikian told defendant that "'We will give you up till tonight to get down to the board meeting and make some kind of arrangements or agreements about the Acme Brewery, or otherwise we are going to beat you up.' . . . He says he either would hire somebody or do it himself. And I says, 'Well, what would they do to me?' He says, well, they would physically beat me up first, cut up the truck tires or burn the truck, or otherwise put me out of business completely. He said if I didn't appear at that meeting and make some kind of an agreement that they would do that, but he says up to then they would let me alone, but if I walked out of that meeting that night they would beat me up for sure." Defendant attended the meeting and protested that he owed nothing for the Acme account and in any event could not pay the amount demanded. He was again told by the president of the association that "that table right there [the board of directors] ran all the rubbish collecting in Los Angeles and if there was any routes to be gotten that they would get them and distribute them among their members. . . ." After two hours of further discussion defendant agreed to join the association and pay for the Acme account. He promised to return the next day and sign the necessary papers. He testified that the only reason "they let me go home, is that I promised that I would sign the notes the very next morning." The president "made me promise on my honor and everything else, and I was scared, and I knew I had to come back, so I believe he knew I was scared and that I would come back. That's the only reason they let me go home." Defendant also testified that because of the fright he suffered during his dispute with the association he became ill and vomited several times and had to remain away from work for a period of several days.

Plaintiff contends that the evidence does not establish an assault against defendant because the threats made all related to action that might take place in the future; that neither Andikian nor members of the board of directors threatened immediate physical harm to defendant. We have concluded, however, that a cause of action is established when it is shown that one, in the absence of any privilege, intentionally subjects another to the mental suffering incident to serious threats to his physical well-being, whether or not the threats are made under such circumstances as to constitute a technical assault.

In the past it has frequently been stated that the interest in emotional and mental tranquillity is not one that the law will protect from invasion in its own right. As late as 1934 the Restatement of Torts took the position that "The interest in mental and emotional tranquillity and, therefore, in freedom from mental and emotional disturbance is not, as a thing in itself, regarded as of sufficient importance to require others to refrain from conduct intended or recognizably likely to cause such a disturbance." (Restatement, Torts, §46, Comment *c*.) The Restatement explained the rule allowing recovery for the mere apprehension of bodily harm in traditional assault cases as an historical anomaly (§24, Comment *c*), and the rule allowing recovery for insulting conduct by an employee of a common carrier as justified by the necessity of securing for the public comfortable as well as safe service. (§48, Comment *c*.)

The Restatement recognized, however, that in many cases mental distress could be so intense that it could reasonably be foreseen that illness or other bodily harm might result. If the defendant intentionally subjected the plaintiff to such distress and bodily harm resulted, the defendant would be liable for negligently causing the plaintiff bodily harm. (Restatement, Torts, §§306, 312.) Under this theory the cause of action was not founded on a right to be free from intentional interference with mental tranquillity, but on the right to be free from negligent interference with physical well-being. A defendant who intentionally subjected another to mental distress without intending to cause bodily harm would nevertheless be liable for resulting bodily harm if he should have foreseen that the mental distress might cause such harm.

The California cases have been in accord with the Restatement in allowing recovery where physical injury resulted from intentionally subjecting the plaintiff to serious mental distress.

The view has been forcefully advocated that the law should protect emotional and mental tranquillity as such against serious and intentional invasions and there is a growing body of case law supporting this position. . . .

There are persuasive arguments and analogies that support the recognition of a right to be free from serious, intentional, and unprivileged invasions of mental and emotional tranquillity. If a cause of action is otherwise established, it is settled that damages may be given for mental suffering naturally ensuing from the acts complained of, and in the case of many torts, such as assault, battery, false imprisonment, and defamation, mental suffering will frequently constitute the principal element of damages. In cases where mental suffering constitutes a major element of damages it is anomalous to deny recovery because the defendant's intentional misconduct fell short of producing some physical injury.

It may be contended that to allow recovery in the absence of physical injury will open the door to unfounded claims and a flood of litigation, and that the requirement that there be physical injury is necessary to insure that serious mental suffering actually occurred. The jury is ordinarily in a better position, however, to determine whether outrageous conduct results in mental distress than whether that distress in turn results in physical injury. From their own experience jurors are aware of the extent and character of the disagreeable emotions that may result from the defendant's conduct, but a difficult medical question is presented when it must be determined if emotional distress resulted in physical injury. Greater proof that mental suffering occurred is found in the defendant's conduct designed to bring it about than in physical injury that may or may not have resulted therefrom.

That administrative difficulties do not justify the denial of relief for serious invasions of mental and emotional tranquillity is demonstrated by the cases recognizing the right of privacy. Recognition of that right protects mental tranquillity from invasion by unwarranted and undesired publicity. As in the case of the protection of mental tranquillity from other forms of invasion, difficult problems in determining the kind and extent of invasions that are sufficiently serious to be actionable are presented. Also the public interest in the free dissemination of news must be considered. Nevertheless courts have concluded that the problems presented are not so insuperable that they warrant the denial of relief altogether.

In the present case plaintiff caused defendant to suffer extreme fright. By intentionally producing such fright it endeavored to compel him either to give up the Acme account or pay for it, and it had no right or privilege to adopt such coercive methods in competing for business. In these circumstances liability is clear. . . .

Plaintiff contends finally that the damages were excessive. The question of excessiveness is addressed primarily to the discretion of the trial court, and an award that stands approved by that court will not be disturbed on appeal unless it appears that the jury was influenced by passion or prejudice. With respect to the general damages the trial court concluded that the jury was not so influenced, and on the record before us we cannot say that it was. The excessiveness, if any, of the award of exemplary damages was cured by the trial court's reduction of those damages to $4,000.

The judgment is affirmed. GIBSON, C.J., SHENK, EDMONDS, CARTER, SCHAUER, and SPENCE, JJ., concurred.

The judicial fear of a "runaway tort" is not triggered by cases like *Siliznoff.* Serious threats of grievous physical harm are plainly not part of the everyday friction of life, and the likelihood that such threats will produce severe emotional distress in their recipient is open to little doubt. Similarly, several other limited categories of cases have typically provoked untroubled applications of the tort of intentional infliction of mental upset. One area involves debt collection practices that, while not as physically threatening as those involved in *Siliznoff,* nonetheless pass beyond the realm of acceptable business practice. For example, in Ford Motor Credit Co. v. Sheehan, 373 So. 2d 956 (Fla. Dist. Ct. App.), *cert. dismissed,* 379 So. 2d 204 (Fla. 1979), judgment for plaintiff was affirmed based on proof that defendant, in order to locate the debtor, falsely represented that the debtor's children had been involved in a serious automobile accident. In Boyle v. Wenk, 392 N.E.2d 1053 (Mass. 1979), the Supreme Judicial Court of Massachusetts held that it was for the jury to determine whether defendant creditor's conduct in telephoning plaintiff, whom defendant knew had just returned from the hospital, resulting in serious emotional and physical harm to plaintiff, was merely "rude and clumsy" or was "extreme and outrageous." Id. at 1058. And in Moorhead v. J. C. Penney Co., 555 S.W.2d 713 (Tenn. 1977), the Supreme Court of Tennessee reversed the trial court's dismissal of a complaint that alleged repeated and threatening demands for the repayment of a nonexistent debt over an extended period. The fact that the defendant apologized when the accounting error was finally corrected did not bar recovery for its prior conduct.

Another established foothold for intentional infliction of mental upset claims involves the mishandling of corpses and related funeral and burial services. In Meyer v. Nottger, 241 N.W.2d 911 (Iowa 1976), for example, the high court of Iowa reversed a trial court dismissal and held that plaintiff's complaint had stated a claim for intentional infliction of severe mental upset. Plaintiff alleged that defendant lied to plaintiff in order to induce plaintiff to hire defendant, made a false statement to plaintiff that the deceased's body was emitting an objectionable odor that required a more expensive casket sealer, and prevented plaintiff and his family from viewing the body through various deceptive means. Similarly, the court in Gray Brown-Service Mortuary, Inc. v. Lloyd, 729 So. 2d 280 (Ala. 1999), upheld the claim of the plaintiff widower for mental upset where it was found that the defendant mausoleum had dealt with an unbearable odor problem in its facility by applying a caustic chemical onto the remains of the plaintiff's deceased wife, binding her casket with duct tape, and then later tossing the remains in the woods.

Both *Meyer* and *Gray Brown-Service Mortuary, Inc.* are at a considerable remove from cases like *Siliznoff.* The defendant mortuaries, for example, were hardly attempting to distress the bereaved plaintiffs; instead, they were hoping that their shady practices would go entirely unnoticed by the mourners. Indeed, in this regard, it is open to debate whether defendants' actions satisfied even the "reckless" requirement of §46 of the Restatement (Second) of Torts. See, e.g., Heitzman v. Thompson, 705 N.W.2d 426 (Neb. 2005), in which the court described a defendant mortician's conduct in failing to obtain consent to embalm a body and transporting the body without a required state license "unprofessional or careless — but not outrageous." Id. at 433. The willingness of many courts nonetheless to recognize intentional infliction claims in these contexts probably reflects several considerations, including, most obviously, the peculiar vulnerability to mental upset of family members in facing death and burial of a loved one.

Another possible argument explaining the judicial leniency toward plaintiffs in such cases follows from deterrence theory. In general, the law's ability to discourage unacceptable behavior is a combined function of the wrongdoer's likelihood of being caught, the ease with which liability is imposed on the apprehended, and the magnitude of the punishment thus imposed. In certain classes of cases, including shady behavior of funeral homes, the chances of detecting wrongful behavior are seriously impaired. Furthermore, the grief and vulnerability of bereaved family members undermines their ability to police the conduct of funeral home personnel. Thus, most wrongful behavior goes undetected. And even when it is discovered, potential plaintiffs are often too distraught to pursue legal remedies. In such cases, the law, in an effort to send a deterrent signal of sufficient strength, may lower the barriers to imposing liability and amplify the damages that are consequently imposed.

Somewhat similar concerns are presented by cases involving mental upset caused by the conduct of hospitals and other health care providers, although courts may be less willing to interpret the intent requirement leniently in this context as they appear to be in the case of mausoleums and funeral homes. In Burges v. Perdue, 721 P.2d 239 (Kan. 1986), plaintiff agreed to a partial autopsy of her son's body, but specifically refused to consent to an examination of his brain. The doctor who obtained the consent failed to inform the county coroner of its limited nature, and the decedent's brain was removed and sent to the Kansas Neurological Institute for examination. Upon discovering the error, another doctor called plaintiff, told her that the Institute had her son's "brain in a jar," and asked her what she would like to have done with it. The court found that the behavior of the latter doctor was not outrageous, because the doctor who called plaintiff had done so out of concern and a desire to resolve any impropriety. Similarly, in Childers v. Geile, 367 S.W.3d 576 (Ky. 2012), summary judgment was awarded to defendant obstetrician on an intentional infliction of emotional distress claim arising from defendant's incorrect diagnosis that plaintiff had miscarried her fetus, followed by defendant's prescription of a contraction-inducing medicine that resulted in the premature birth and death of the fetus. Despite the tragic circumstances, the court held that no reasonable fact finder could conclude that defendant acted with intent or reckless disregard of plaintiff's right to be spared from outrageous conduct causing emotional distress.

Several courts have found that insurance companies may be held liable for emotional distress after canceling the policies of their insureds. In Liberty Mutual Insurance Co. v. Steadman, 968 So. 2d 592 (Fla. Dist. Ct. App. 2007), the court held that a health insurer who delayed authorizing approval for a lung transplant for nine months in the hope that the patient would die before it had to pay for the surgery is liable for emotional distress. The court found that, as a matter of law, the insurer's conduct was outrageous. Similarly, in Hailey v. California Physicians Service, 69 Cal. Rptr. 3d 789 (Ct. App. 2007), an insurer who delayed cancellation of a health insurance policy (on grounds of misrepresentation by the insured) until after the insured incurred over $450,000 in medical bills following an automobile accident was held liable for intentional infliction of emotional distress. The court denied summary judgment to the insurer, finding that the facts raised the specter that the insurers' final decision to rescind "may not have come about because of omissions in the application, but because of the substantial medical bills resulting from [the] automobile accident." Id. at 808.

Most potential intentional infliction of emotional distress claims arise in less unusual circumstances, forcing courts to pay more careful attention to the appropriate boundaries of liability. As we have seen throughout these materials, a central method by which courts define the parameters of liability is through their decisions to enter judgment on the pleadings, to direct verdicts, or to allow cases to go to the jury. These gatekeeper decisions reflect the efforts of courts in the present context to draw meaningful lines between outrageousness and mere obnoxiousness. In Moncada v. West Coast Quartz Corp., 221 Cal. App. 4th 768 (App. 6th Dist. 2013), for instance, the court was faced with a claim that defendants repeatedly promised plaintiffs that if they continued to work for a company until it was sold, plaintiffs would be paid a significant bonus from the sale proceeds. Plaintiffs relied on this promise to their detriment by remaining employed at the company, and forgoing other employment and personal opportunities. The court held that the alleged conduct was not extreme or outrageous, but rather part of the "callous" workings of the market:

> Here, the allegations . . . consist of defendants misleading plaintiffs into believing they would be compensated in an amount that would allow them to retire if they continued to work for West Coast until the company was sold. While the allegations of defendants' conduct[,] if true, demonstrate a callous disregard for plaintiffs' professional and personal well-being, the alleged conduct as stated is not extreme or outrageous to support a cause of action for intentional infliction of emotional distress. [Id. at 780-781]

Gatekeeper decisions by the court become especially significant in the context of claims premised on racially or ethnically derogatory conduct. In Taylor v. Metzger 152 N.J. 490 (1998), the Supreme Court of New Jersey reversed the trial court's grant of summary judgment for the defendant, holding that a single derogatory racial comment directed against an employee by her supervisor gave rise to a tort action for intentional infliction of emotional distress. Plaintiff Carrie Taylor, a Black woman, worked as a sheriff's officer in the office of defendant Henry Metzger. Taylor claimed that Metzger, the county sheriff, called her a "jungle bunny" in the presence of another supervisor. Taylor believed the remark to be a "demeaning and derogatory racial slur" that caused her to become a "nervous wreck" and immediately begin crying. Id. at 495. Although Taylor did not lose any income and her basic job duties remained unchanged following the incident, she lost her position as floor supervisor and "felt she suffered a loss of dignity and self-respect." Id. at 497. Taylor began consulting a psychiatrist, Dr. Ira L. Fox, periodically for the next year. He diagnosed her condition as "post-traumatic stress disorder," concluding that the disorder was "directly related [to] and caused by the incident to her person when she was reportedly called a jungle bunny by Mr. Metzger." Id. In reversing the trial court's dismissal of the claim, the New Jersey high court explained that while "a single racial slur spoken by a stranger on the street does not amount to extreme and outrageous conduct . . . a jury could reasonably conclude that the power dynamics of the workplace contribute to the extremity and the outrageousness." Id. at 511. Thus, "the fact that defendant uttered only one slur toward plaintiff does not, as a matter of law, preclude his conduct from being extreme and outrageous." Id. Furthermore, the court noted that under the average person standard, properly adapted to reflect the characteristics of Taylor, "a jury could reasonably find that [Metzger's] conduct would have a devastating effect on the average African American. . . ." Id. at 689. Therefore, the court determined that Taylor presented sufficient evidence to withstand summary judgment on her intentional inflicting of emotional distress claim.

The tailored standard adopted by the *Taylor* court finds support in a wealth of social science research concerning the effects of perceived discriminatory speech and conduct on performance and well-being. A large body of research shows that perceived experiences with discrimination adversely affects one's health, including through psychological and physiological stress responses and through changes in behavior. See E.A. Pascoe & L. S. Richman, Perceived Discrimination and Health: A Meta-analytic Review, 135 Psych. Bull. 531 (2009). For instance, experiencing discrimination is associated with greater prevalence of hypertension. See Mario Sims, et al., Perceived Discrimination and Hypertension Among African Americans in the Jackson Heart Study, 102 Am. J. Pub. Health S258 (2012). Likewise, studies have found consistent associations between exposure to discrimination and a wide range of Diagnostic and Statistical Manual of Mental Disorders (DSM) diagnosed mental disorders. See T.T. Lewis, C.D. Cogburn & D.R. Williams, Self-Reported Experiences of Discrimination and Health: Scientific Advances, Ongoing Controversies, and Emerging Issues, 11 Ann. Rev. Clin. Psych. 407 (2015). A growing body of literature examines hormonal and neural effects of racial discrimination and identifies potential neurobiological pathways by which discrimination affects mental health, generally finding the experience of discrimination to be similar to that of experiencing chronic social stress. Maximus Bergera & Zoltán Sarnyaiab, "More than Skin Deep": Stress Neurobiology and Mental Health Consequences of Racial Discrimination, 18 Stress: Intl. J. on the Biology of Stress 1 (2015).

After experiencing derogatory treatment, targets of prejudice often come to anticipate future mistreatment. This increase in vigilance can mobilize the stress response, which has physiological as well as psychological consequences. See Pamela J. Sawyer et al., Discrimination and the Stress Response: Psychological and Physiological Consequences of Anticipating Prejudice in Interethnic Interaction, 102 Am. J. Public Health 1020 (2012) (demonstrating this effect among Latina study participants who interacted with a White partner known to hold prejudiced views). Anticipatory stress directly interferes with cognitive processing, leading to impaired performance on a variety of tasks. Indeed, a substantial literature developed over the past two decades demonstrates that members of minority groups may perform worse on tests and other tasks when a stereotype about their racial or ethnic group has been made salient. See Hannah-Hanh D. Nguyen & Ann Marie Ryan, Does Stereotype Threat Affect Test Performance of Minorities and Women? A Meta-Analysis of Experimental Evidence, 93 J. Applied Psych. 1314 (2008). "Stereotype threat" effects of this sort have been shown in at least one study to occur simply due to the presence of an examiner or evaluator of a different race than the non-dominant minority group member. See A.D. Thames, A. D., et al., Effects of Stereotype Threat, Perceived Discrimination, and Examiner Race on Neuropsychological Performance: Simple as Black and White?, 19 J. Intl. Neuropsych. Soc. 583 (2013). Likewise, some recent research suggests that subtle forms of bias and discrimination (e.g., "microaggressions") may impair the cognitive functioning of Black and Latino individuals even worse than blatant discrimination of the sort present in *Taylor*. The cognitive burden of managing reactions to subtle or ambiguous discrimination appears to take an especially heavy toll on members of stigmatized groups. See Mary C. Murphy, et al., Cognitive Costs of Contemporary Prejudice, Group Processes & Intergroup Relations (2013); J. Salvatore & J.N. Shelton, Cognitive Costs of Exposure to Racial Prejudice, 18 Psych. Sci. 810 (2007). In short, discriminatory behavior in the workplace may contribute to adverse performance and a sense of frustration and isolation for minority individuals. Both physiologically and psychologically, discriminatory behavior seems capable of giving rise to severe consequences, despite the childhood promise that "words will never hurt me."

Notwithstanding the weight of social science evidence such as this, courts often hold as matter of law that the use of racial slurs or other discriminatory conduct does not create a claim for intentional infliction of mental upset. In Irving v. J. L. Marsh, Inc., 360 N.E.2d 983 (Ill. App. Ct. 1977), for instance, the plaintiff sought a refund for returned merchandise. The defendant's employee wrote the n-word on the refund slip he gave the plaintiff: "arrogant [] refused exchange/says he doesn't like product." The court found that the employee's conduct was insufficient to support a valid cause of action. Similarly, in Lopez v. Target Corp., 676 F.3d 1230 (11th Cir. Fla. 2012), a Latino customer was refused service by a cashier who said pointedly, "I'm closed to YOU!" The court held that the cashier's alleged conduct, although reprehensible, was not outrageous enough to maintain an intentional infliction of emotional distress action under Florida law, which requires a truly extreme level of outrageousness in cases of verbal abuse. See also Harris v. Sutton Motor Sales & RV Consignments Corp., 406 F. App'x 181, 183 (9th Cir. 2010) (co-workers' use of racial epithet, "although unquestionably offensive," did not amount to an "extraordinary transgression of the bounds of socially tolerable conduct," which is required to sustain a claim of intentional infliction of emotional distress); Johnson v. Fambrough, 706 So. 2d 739, 741 (Ala. Civ. App. 1997) (court of appeals affirmed trial court's grant of defendant employer's motion for summary judgment, concluding that "the [plaintiff] employee failed to provide any substantial evidence that the employer's use of the 'n' word caused her, in any way, to suffer emotional distress."); Lay v. Roux Labs., Inc., 379 So. 2d 451 (Fla. Dist. Ct. App. 1980) (affirming dismissal of a complaint for intentional infliction of emotional distress based on the use of a racial epithet toward plaintiff by defendant's parking supervisor during an argument over a parking space).

The court in *Taylor* credits plaintiff's claim that the average member of her racial group is likely to be sensitive to racial slurs. Cf. Roth v. Wiese, 716 N.W.2d 419 (Neb. 2006) (construing "outrageousness" of harassing phone calls by defendant uncle in light of his sexual abuse of plaintiff niece some 30 years earlier). However, in Wiggs v. Courshon, 355 F. Supp. 206 (S.D. Fla. 1973), the court seemed to take an opposite tack. Although the court refused to grant the defendant's motion for a new trial after a jury returned a verdict in favor of the plaintiffs, who had been called a racial epithet and subjected to obscene insults by defendant's waitress in a dispute over a dinner order, the court nonetheless concluded that the damages were excessive and therefore ordered a remittitur. The court observed:

> As to the amount of the verdicts, not only were the judicial eyebrows raised at the size of these verdicts, but the judicial conscience was profoundly shocked. . . . The court condemns the uncivil outburst and rude remarks made by defendant's waitress, but does such an inexcusable insult justify the award of $25,000 under these circumstances? Plainly not. We all have ethnic and racial backgrounds and the court notes that there is at least one and usually several epithets ascribed to any ethnic group members, the use of which offends some members of the group. Despite that, it is certain a line would quickly form by members of any ethnic group to receive $25,000 as balm for an ethnic or racial epithet. The indefensibility of the size of the verdict is plainer still when we place it in context of an epithet delivered in a dispute over the ingredients of a dinner entree when that remark caused neither out-of-pocket expenses to the members of the ethnic group nor any apparent mental or emotional injury.

In its order of remittitur, the court set appropriate damages for the plaintiffs collectively at $2,500. But does the court's analysis make sense in terms of the test set out in §46 of the Restatement (Second) of Torts? Can the plaintiff be outraged, but just a little?

In addition to racial hostility, courts also frequently face claims premised on emotionally distressing speech and conduct of a sexual nature. In Samms v. Eccles, 358 P.2d 344 (Utah 1961), plaintiff Marcia Samms sought to recover damages from David Eccles for severe emotional distress she suffered as a result of Eccles's continuing indecent proposals directed at her. Samms alleged that Eccles "repeatedly and persistently called her by phone at various hours including late at night, soliciting her to have illicit sexual relations with him," and on one occasion he visited her residence and indecently exposed himself. Id. at 345. Samms charged that as a result of Eccles' proposals, she "suffered great anxiety and fear for her personal safety and severe emotional distress." Id. The trial court dismissed the claim on the ground that Samms failed to show any basis upon which relief could be granted. Holding that the trial court erred in dismissing the action, the Supreme Court of Utah explained that an action for severe emotional distress is recognized absent bodily impact or physical injury "where the defendant intentionally engaged in some conduct toward the plaintiff, (a) with the purpose of inflicting emotional distress or, (b) where any reasonable person would have known that such would result and his actions are of such a nature as to be considered outrageous and intolerable in that they offend against the generally accepted standards of decency and morality." Id. at 347. Thus the court concluded that, while "under usual circumstances the solicitation to sexual intercourse would not be actionable," aggravated situations like Samms's are "clearly distinguishable" and "the facts were sufficiently disclosed that the case she proposes to prove could be found to fall within the requirements [for severe emotional distress]." Id.

In Brandon v. County of Richardson, 261 Neb. 636 (2001), the Supreme Court of Nebraska addressed a situation of hostility and abuse motivated by plaintiff's gender identification. On December 31, 1993, Teena Brandon, Lisa Lambert, and Phillip Devine were found murdered in Lambert's home in Richardson County. John L. Lotter and Thomas M. Nissen were convicted of the murders. Following the death of her daughter, Brandon's mother, JoAnn Brandon, brought an action against Richardson County and Sheriff Laux for negligence, wrongful death, and intentional infliction of emotional distress in connection with Brandon's murder and the events leading up to her death. Lotter and Nissan beat and raped Brandon violently at a party, allegedly in part because Brandon had been identifying as a male. When Brandon reported the sexual assault to the authorities, Sheriff Laux subjected her to tape-recorded questioning of an extremely graphic nature. Evidence also showed that Sheriff Laux was aware of Lotter and Nissen's criminal past and the fact that the two had made threats on Brandon's life following the rape. The district court, sitting without a jury, found the county negligent in failing to protect Brandon, but denied recovery on intentional infliction of emotional distress on the ground that Laux's conduct did not reach the level of extreme or outrageous.

Reversing on appeal, the Supreme Court of Nebraska explained that "the relationship between the parties and the susceptibility of the plaintiff to emotional distress are important factors to consider" and thus "conduct which might otherwise be considered merely rude or abusive may be deemed outrageous when the defendant knows that the plaintiff is particularly susceptible to emotional distress." Id. at 657. Determining as a matter of law that Laux's conduct was extreme and outrageous, the Nebraska high court noted such factors as Brandon's particularly vulnerable emotional state, Laux's abuse of a position of power, Laux's crude and dehumanizing language, and the intimidating tone utilized by the Laux throughout his questioning.

Ford v. Revlon, Inc.

153 Ariz. 38, 734 P.2d 580 (1987)

Facts

Leta Fay Ford worked for the purchasing department of Revlon, Inc. (Revlon) in Phoenix, Arizona. She began her employment in 1973 as a secretary. She worked her way up to junior buyer and buyer positions over the ten years of her employment at Revlon. In October 1979, Revlon hired Karl Braun as the new manager for the purchasing department, which made him Ford's supervisor.

On 3 April 1980, Braun invited Ford to a dinner ostensibly to discuss business away from the office. Ford agreed and met Braun at a Phoenix restaurant. The business discussion, however, turned to more personal topics. At the end of the dinner, Ford started to leave. Braun told her that she was not going anywhere and to sit down because he planned to spend the night with her. When Ford rejected his advances, Braun told her, "you will regret this." Ford testified at trial that after this incident her working relationship with Braun was strained and uncomfortable. Ford did not report the dinner incident nor the adverse working atmosphere to Revlon management.

On 3 May 1980, Revlon held its annual service awards picnic. Braun followed Ford for most of the day. At one point, [Braun actually assaulted Ford, submitted her to unwanted touching of a sexual nature, and made repeated vulgar statements regarding what he planned to do to her].

Later in May of 1980, Ford began a series of meetings with various members of Revlon management to report her complaints. Ford first spoke with the Phoenix Revlon comptroller, Robert Lettieri, who had authority to recommend hiring, firing, discipline, and promotions. Ford told him about the incidents with Braun and that she was afraid of Braun and wanted help. Lettieri said that he would speak to someone in personnel about her complaint and that she also should talk to personnel.

In early June of 1980, Ford spoke to Cecelia Domin, the personnel manager for the clerical and technical group in the Phoenix plant. In the Revlon management hierarchy, Domin reported directly to the director of personnel and worked with the plant manager of executives. When meeting with Domin, Ford was very emotional, her hands were shaking, and she was crying. Ford told Domin about the incidents and said that she was afraid of Braun. On 23 June 1980, Ford spoke to Robert Kosciusko, the personnel manager for executives. Ford also told him about the incidents, that she was afraid of Braun, and that the strain was making her sick.

In August of 1980, Ford met again with Domin and additionally with Martin Burstein, the director of personnel at the Phoenix plant. Again Ford complained about the incidents and told them that she was afraid of Braun. Burstein told Ford that he would talk to a Revlon vice president and that he would get back to her. Also in August, Ford spoke to John Maloney, a manager in receiving and stores. Maloney suggested that Ford contact Marie Kane at Revlon headquarters in New Jersey. Kane, a manager of human resources, was a "trouble shooter" and a veteran of the Phoenix personnel department.

In November of 1980, Ford telephoned Kane in New Jersey to report her concerns about Braun and her frustrations about the work situation. At this time, it had been six months since Ford first complained of Braun's conduct and no action had been taken. Kane then reported the details of her conversation with Ford to her boss, David Coe, the vice president of industrial relations and operations. Kane also informed Coe that Ford was becoming ill because of the problem. Coe's response was that the matter was not their concern at the corporate level and that the matter should be sent back to the local level and handled in Phoenix. Coe instructed Kane to telephone Burstein so that he could solve the problem. Kane did speak to Burstein, who promised to take care of the problem immediately.

When, as of December 1980, no action had been taken on Ford's complaint, Ford telephoned Kane again and informed her that Braun was continuing his harassment by calling her into his office and telling her that he wanted to destroy her, that she made him nervous, and that so long as she worked for him she was never going to go anywhere. He also called her into his office and did not allow her to sit down and would stare at her and not speak to her. According to Ford, Kane responded that it was a lot to absorb and that she would have to talk to someone else about it and that she would get back to Ford. After a few days had elapsed and Kane had not telephoned Ford, Ford again called Kane, who was out, and left a message. It was January 1981 before Kane returned Ford's call. Kane told Ford that the situation was too hot for her to handle and that she did not want to be involved. Kane suggested that Ford put the matter in the back of her mind and try to forget the situation. Around this time, Ford also contacted Gene Tucker, a corporate Equal Employment Opportunity (EEO) specialist, and asked him for help. Tucker said that he would have to talk to Harry Petrie, the vice president of industrial relations and personnel in New York. Tucker did not get back to Ford.

During the time of the harassment, Ford developed high blood pressure, a nervous tic in her left eye, chest pains, rapid breathing, and other symptoms of emotional stress. Ford felt weak, dizzy, and generally fatigued. Ford consulted a physician about her condition.

On 23 February 1981, Ford submitted a written request for a transfer out of the purchasing department. On 24 February 1981, Braun placed Ford on a 60-day probation because of her allegedly poor work performance. On 25 February 1981, a meeting finally was held in personnel at Ford's demand so she could have something done about her situation with Braun. Ford was able to have Tucker arrange a meeting with them and with Domin and Burstein. Ford again gave the details of her complaint against Braun and her fear of him. Ford also submitted a handwritten complaint which read in part:

> I want to officially register a charge of sexual harassment and discrimination against K. Braun.
>
> I am asking for protection from Karl Braun. I have a right to be protected.
>
> I am collapsing emotionally and physically and I can't go on.

At this meeting on 25 February 1981, Braun was called in and confronted. After the meeting, Burstein and Domin told Ford that Braun would be closely monitored. Burstein also testified that he investigated Ford's allegation, which he said took him about three weeks.

Not until three months later, on 8 May 1981, however, did Burstein submit a report on Ford's complaint to vice president Coe; the report confirmed Ford's charge of sexual assault and recommended that Braun be censured. On 28 May 1981, a full year and one month after Braun's initial act of harassment, Braun was issued a letter of censure from Revlon.

In October of 1981, Ford attempted suicide.

On 5 October 1981, Revlon terminated Braun. Braun testified at trial that the reason given him for his termination was that he did not fit into the Revlon organization, partially because of the way he handled the "Ford situation."

In April of 1982, Ford sued both Braun and Revlon for assault and battery, and for intentional infliction of emotional distress.

The jury found Braun liable for assault and battery but not liable for intentional infliction of emotional distress. The jury found Revlon liable for intentional infliction of emotional distress but not liable for assault and battery. Damages awarded to Ford by the jury were assessed against Braun in the amount of $100 compensatory damages and $1,000 punitive damages, and assessed against Revlon in the amount of $10,000 compensatory damages and $100,000 punitive damages. Only Revlon appealed. Therefore, the only issue on appeal was whether Revlon was liable for intentional infliction of emotional distress. The court of appeals in a memorandum decision reversed the judgment of the trial court, holding that since Braun (as agent) was found not guilty of intentional infliction of emotional distress, then Revlon (as principal) could not be found guilty. We granted review because we disagreed with this limitation on the liability of Revlon.

Independent Tort Liability of the Employer

The court of appeals held that Revlon could not be liable for intentional infliction of emotional distress if Braun was not liable. The court of appeals stated:

> Even though the jury found Braun did assault Ford on May 3, 1980, it found that the assault and his subsequent acts, whatever they were found to be, were insufficient to hold him liable for intentional or reckless infliction of emotional distress. Revlon's liability is inextricably tied to the acts of Braun. Since Braun's acts did not constitute intentional or reckless infliction of emotional distress, then the inaction of Revlon on Ford's complaint certainly could not reach that level.

We disagree. Admittedly, when the master's liability is based solely on the negligence of his servant, a judgment in favor of the servant is a judgment in favor of the master. DeGraff v. Smith, 62 Ariz. 261, 157 P.2d 342 (1945). When the negligence of the master is independent of the negligence of the servant, the result may be different. As noted by the court of appeals:

> We recognize that where there is independent negligence on the part of the master, the master may be liable, apart from his derivative liability for his servant's wrongful acts. In such a case, a judgment in favor of the servant will not ordinarily bar a recovery against the master. However, the master must have "'been guilty of acts on which *independently of the acts of the servant,* liability may be predicated.'" (Emphasis supplied.)

We believe that the analysis should be the same in intentional tort cases. In a case factually similar to this one, the U.S. Court of Appeals for the Fourth Circuit recognized that a corporation could be liable for intentional infliction of emotional distress because its supervisor was aware of the sexual harassment of an employee by a manager and failed to stop it even though the *underlying* harassment might not rise to the level of either assault and battery or intentional infliction of emotional distress. Davis v. United States Steel Corp., 779 F.2d 209, 211 (4th Cir. 1985). The Fourth Circuit held that although the acts and behavior of the manager were despicable, they did not rise to the level of providing a basis for recovery by the complainant against the corporation for assault and battery or intentional infliction of emotional distress. The court went on to say, however, that "the situation is otherwise with respect to [the employer] and [its] failure to take any action." Id. at 212. We believe that Revlon's failure to investigate Ford's complaint was independent of Braun's abusive treatment of Ford.

Is Revlon Liable for Intentional Infliction of Emotional Distress?

Elements of the tort of intentional infliction of emotional distress have been set out by this court, relying upon the language of the Restatement of Torts.

The three required elements are: *first,* the conduct by the defendant must be "extreme" and "outrageous"; *second,* the defendant must either intend to cause emotional distress or recklessly disregard the near certainty that such distress will result from his conduct; and *third,* severe emotional distress must indeed occur as a result of defendant's conduct.

We believe that the conduct of Revlon met these requirements. First, Revlon's conduct can be classified as extreme or outrageous. Ford made numerous Revlon managers aware of Braun's activities at company functions. Ford did everything that could be done, both within the announced policies of Revlon and without, to bring this matter to Revlon's attention. Revlon ignored her and the situation she faced, dragging the matter out for months and leaving Ford without redress. Here is sufficient evidence that Revlon acted outrageously.

Second, even if Revlon did not intend to cause emotional distress, Revlon's reckless disregard of Braun's conduct made it nearly certain that such emotional distress would in fact occur. Revlon knew that Braun had subjected Ford to physical assaults, vulgar remarks, that Ford continued to feel threatened by Braun, and that Ford was emotionally distraught, all of which led to a manifestation of physical problems. Despite Ford's complaints, Braun was not confronted for nine months, and then only upon *Ford's* demand for a group meeting. Another three months elapsed before Braun was censured. Revlon not only had actual knowledge of the situation but it also failed to conduct promptly any investigation of Ford's complaint.

Third, it is obvious that emotional distress did occur. Ample evidence, both medical and otherwise, was presented describing Ford's emotional distress. Ford testified about her emotional distress and her development of physical complications caused by her stressful work environment. The evidence convinced the jury, which found that emotional distress had occurred.

We also note that Revlon had set forth a specific policy and several guidelines for the handling of sexual harassment claims and other employee complaints, yet Revlon recklessly disregarded these policies and guidelines. Ford was entitled to rely on the policy statements made by Revlon.

Once an employer proclaims a policy, the employer may not treat the policy as illusory. We hold that Revlon's failure to take appropriate action in response to Ford's complaint of sexual harassment by Braun constituted the tort of intentional infliction of emotional distress.

Arizona Workers' Compensation Law

Revlon contends that this matter is controlled by Arizona Workers' Compensation laws and not by tort law. We disagree. Ford's severe emotional distress injury was found by the jury to be not unexpected and was essentially nonphysical in nature. As the trial court stated:

> Evidence established that this tort was committed through defendant's action and inaction to plaintiff's complaints made over a period in excess of eight months. Such action and inaction and the resulting emotional injury to the plaintiff were therefore not "unexpected," accidental, or physical in nature so as to limit plaintiff's recovery to the workmen's compensation claim under A.R.S. §§23-1021(B) and 1043.01(B).

Ford v. Revlon, Inc., No. C-457854, slip op. at 15 (Super. Ct. Maricopa County, June 15, 1984). A.R.S. §23-1021(B) provides, in relevant part, that

> Every employee covered by insurance in the state compensation fund who is injured *by accident* arising out of and in the course of employment . . . shall be paid such compensation (emphasis added). . . .

A.R.S. §23-1043.01(B) sets forth the limiting standard for compensation under the statute for physiological injury. This section states: "A mental injury . . . shall not be considered a personal injury by accident . . . and is not compensable . . . unless . . . unexpected, unusual or extraordinary stress . . . or some physical injury . . . was a substantial contributing cause."

The acts by Braun and Revlon were not "accidents." Indeed, the jury found both parties liable for the intentional offenses in which they engaged: Braun for assault and battery and Revlon for emotional distress. An injured employee may enforce common-law liability against his or her employer if not encompassed by statute.

The decision of the court of appeals is vacated. The judgment of the trial court is reinstated.

GORDON, C.J., and JACK D. H. HAYS, RETIRED J., concur.

[The concurring opinion of FELDMAN, VICE CHIEF JUSTICE, is omitted.]

Sexual harassment often combines elements of assault, battery, and intentional infliction of mental upset. In addition to the challenge of getting a court to recognize intentional infliction of mental upset as independent of assault or battery, a plaintiff must also avoid the pitfalls of workers' compensation and respondeat superior limitations. Workers' compensation statutes were enacted to spread the costs of injuries resulting from workplace hazards and are intended to be an employee's exclusive remedy against his or her employer. (See p. 718, above.) Courts have split on whether sexual harassment should be considered compensable under the statutes. As *Ford* demonstrates, some jurisdictions allow recovery outside of workers' compensation for sexual harassment in the workplace. See also Gerber v. Vincent's Men's Hairstyling, Inc., 57 So. 3d 935, 938 (Fla. Dist. Ct. App. 2011) (employee's sexual harassment was not barred by the exclusive remedy provision of Florida's Workers' Compensation Statute; sexual harassment is not a "risk inherent in the work environment," and the exclusive remedy provision "does not apply [w]hen an employer commits an intentional tort"); Kerans v. Porter Paint Co., 575 N.E.2d 428 (Ohio 1991); Byrd v. Richardson-Greenshields Sec., Inc., 552 So. 2d 1099 (Fla. 1989). Other courts hold that sexual harassment claims fit within the plain language of the statutes and, absent legislative determination otherwise, workers' compensation remedies — which typically focus on accidental physical injuries and therefore offer little in the way of compensation for emotional and dignitary harms such as sexual harassment — preclude tort recovery. See, e.g., Green v. Wyman-Gordon Co., 664 N.E.2d 808 (Mass. 1996); Konstantopoulos v. Westvaco Corp., 690 A.2d 936 (Del. 1996).

Paralleling state law rules allowing tort recovery for sexual harassment, Congress enacted the Civil Rights Act of 1964 with a provision that provides a cause of action against an employer who discriminates on the basis of sex. See 42 U.S.C. §2000e et seq. Successful plaintiffs under Title VII may obtain "such affirmative action as may be appropriate," which often includes reinstatement, back pay, retroactive seniority benefits, and sometimes even punitive damages. See Note, Damages for Sexual Harassment under Title VII and State Tort Law, 10 Cap. U. L. Rev. 657, 662-66 (1981). Thus, plaintiffs typically join Title VII claims with state law tort actions in attempting to obtain full recovery for injuries suffered from sexual harassment. Unfortunately for plaintiffs, some courts consider the tort claims to be part of the Title VII claims and deny separate recovery on both. See, e.g., Otto v. Heckler, 781 F.2d 754 (9th Cir. 1986). Other courts hold that intentional infliction of emotional distress claims are precluded when the gravamen of plaintiff's complaint is a different common law or statutory remedy. Thus, where plaintiff's emotional distress claim is based on the same allegations as those supporting a sexual harassment claim, the former claim is held invalid. Bookman v. AIDS Arms, Inc., 2014 WL 4968189 (N.D. Tex. 2014). Likewise, state civil rights laws may preempt common law offensive battery claims in the context of sexual harassment against an employer. See Waffle House, Inc. v. Williams, 313 S.W.3d 796 (Tex. 2010) (barring common law tort claim against defendant employer for allowing employee to sexually harass plaintiff co-worker).

In addition to struggling with the issue of damages under Title VII, courts have continued to confront the question of what sort of employer conduct will constitute a cause of action for sexual harassment. Courts easily determine that denial of a tangible employment benefit is actionable. Thus in Barnes v. Costle, 561 F.2d 983 (D.C. 1977), the plaintiff could recover when her job was terminated after she refused her supervisor's sexual demands. (Some states provide broad protection to employees discharged for socially unacceptable reasons. Later decisions have expanded the criteria regarding whether harassment affected the "terms, conditions, or privileges of employment" under Title VII. The Supreme Court has held that harassment creating a "hostile workplace" is actionable under the statute. See Meritor Savings Bank v. Vinson, 477 U.S. 57 (1986), in which a supervisor's demands for the plaintiff to participate in sexual activity were held to have created an "intimidating, hostile or offensive" environment, regardless of whether such demands were linked to the offering or denial of economic job benefits. In a subsequent decision, Harris v. Forklift Systems, Inc., 510 U.S. 17 (1993), the Supreme Court clarified the *Vinson* test by holding that a plaintiff asserting a hostile workplace claim need not establish that the conduct in issue caused a tangible psychological injury. Instead, the plaintiff need show only that the conduct created an environment that a reasonable person would find hostile or abusive. The Court observed:

> Whether an environment is "hostile" or "abusive" can be determined only by looking at all the circumstances. These include the frequency of the discriminatory conduct; its severity; whether it is physically threatening or humiliating, or a mere offensive utterance; and whether it unreasonably interferes with an employee's work performance. The effect on the employee's psychological well-being is, of course, relevant to determining whether

> the plaintiff actually found the environment abusive. But while psychological harm, like any other relevant factor, may be taken into account, no single factor is required.

510 U.S. at 23. See generally Susan Estrich, Sex at Work, 43 Stan. L. Rev. 813 (1991); Kathryn Abrams, The New Jurisprudence of Sexual Harassment, 83 Cornell L. Rev. 1169 (1998); Vicki Schultz, Reconceptualizing Sexual Harassment, 107 Yale L.J. 1683 (1998).

As awareness of sexual harassment has expanded, courts have recognized that harmful behavior can occur through all manner of gender and sexuality configurations. In Oncale v. Sundowner Offshore Services, Inc., 523 U.S. 75 (1998), the Supreme Court reversed a grant of summary judgment for the defendant male employees, who had subjected the plaintiff, a male co-worker, to sex-related, humiliating actions, physical assaults, and the threat of rape aboard the oil platform where they worked. Remanding the case for trial, the Supreme Court noted that there was "no justification in the statutory language or our precedents for a categorical rule excluding same-sex harassment claims from the coverage of Title VII." 523 U.S. at 79. In Caravantes v. 53rd St. Partners, LLC, 2012 WL 3631276 (S.D.N.Y. 2012), plaintiffs were held to have failed to prove by a preponderance of the evidence that a sexual game played among male employees at a restaurant was anything more than "horseplay." However, one plaintiff successfully demonstrated that a sexual relationship urged upon him by a male supervisor went beyond game parameters, forcing him to compromise his sexual autonomy in order to get through the work day and causing him severe distress. In Lewis v. City of Benicia, 224 Cal. App. 4th 1519 (App. 1st Dist. 2014), summary judgment for defendant supervisor was reversed, because an inference that the supervisor engaged in a pervasive pattern of same-gender harassment against plaintiff was supported by a course of alleged conduct that included numerous gifts and frequent lunch purchases, along with some sexual jokes and displays of pornographic computer images, over a period of several months.

Problem 41

Sonia Sanchez has come to your firm seeking advice on whether to pursue a civil action against her ex-boyfriend, Allan Warner. According to Sonia, she began dating Allan casually the summer after her freshman year of college. During that time, Sonia and Allan shared several sexual encounters, the first such encounters of Sonia's life. Before one of their dates near the end of the summer, Allan arranged with two of his friends to set up a hidden video camera in the bedroom where Allan intended to have sexual intercourse with Sonia. The resulting videotape begins with the three boys making crude comments and jokes about Sonia and then proceeds to capture Sonia and Allan's sexual encounter from later that night. Allan played the tape for several of his friends shortly after the encounter, and rumors of the tape's existence and contents circulated widely in Allan's and Sonia's respective social circles. Sonia claims that she suffered severe humiliation and emotional upset from the videotape and the gossip surrounding it. She has withdrawn from classes and stopped dating or being sexually active. She also has sought counseling for her emotional upset. Sonia wants to obtain compensation for her tangible and intangible harms. She also hopes to attract publicity to the boys' wrongdoing, so that "no one thinks they can get away with treating people this way."

Based on her story, does Sonia have a claim for intentional infliction of emotional distress? If not, what elements are likely to be found wanting? Are there other risks of going forward with the claim that Sonia should consider?

Like most states, your state has not adopted a freestanding tort of negligent infliction of emotional distress, but instead recognizes certain limited exceptions to the general rule of nonrecovery for negligently inflicted emotional harm, such as bystander, special relationship, or direct victim exceptions (see Chapter 4). Would any of these exceptions permit Sonia to recover against Allan and his friends in negligence? Assume in the alternative that both Sonia and your firm want to take Sonia's case as an opportunity to advocate for the recognition of a freestanding negligent infliction of emotional distress tort. What arguments for and against the tort do you imagine will be available?

To what extent does the First Amendment protect the defendant from an intentional infliction of mental upset claim brought by a plaintiff as a result of something the defendant said? The answer is unclear. For years most courts avoided the issue, either by finding that the plaintiff's injury was caused by conduct as well as speech on the part of the defendant, or by concluding that the defendant's speech was not sufficiently outrageous to satisfy the substantive requirements of the tort. But in Hustler Magazine v. Falwell, 485 U.S. 46 (1988), the Supreme Court held that a public figure, televangelist Jerry Falwell, could not recover for intentional infliction of mental upset arising from the publication of a vicious "ad parody," absent a showing that the ad contained a false statement of fact and that the defendant, in publishing the ad, acted with actual malice. Thus, the decision appeared to subject claims for the intentional infliction of mental upset to constitutional constraints similar to those applying to the tort of defamation, which are discussed in detail in Chapter 12. The scope of the constitutional privilege remains unclear, however. The *Falwell* decision focused on the status of the plaintiff as a public figure, as well as the value of the ideas expressed in the ad parody. See also Jones v. City of Philadelphia, 893 A.2d 837 (Pa. 2006) (upholding dismissal of intentional infliction of mental distress claim by a public official whose remarks at a city meeting were described by defendants as anti-Semitic). To what extent does the following case clarify the scope of First Amendment protection for outrageous speech?

Snyder v. Phelps

131 S. Ct. 1207, 179 L. Ed. 2d 172 (2011)

Chief Justice Roberts delivered the opinion of the Court.

A jury held members of the Westboro Baptist Church liable for millions of dollars in damages for picketing near a soldier's funeral service. The picket signs reflected the church's view that the United States is overly tolerant of sin and that God kills American soldiers as punishment. The question presented is whether the First Amendment shields the church members from tort liability for their speech in this case.

I

A

Fred Phelps founded the Westboro Baptist Church in Topeka, Kansas, in 1955. The church's congregation believes that God hates and punishes the United States for its tolerance of homosexuality, particularly in America's military. The church frequently communicates its views by picketing, often at military funerals. In the more than 20 years that the members of Westboro Baptist have publicized their message, they have picketed nearly 600 funerals. Marine Lance Corporal Matthew Snyder was killed in Iraq in the line of duty. Lance Corporal Snyder's father selected the Catholic church in the Snyders' hometown of Westminster, Maryland, as the site for his son's funeral. Local newspapers provided notice of the time and location of the service.

Phelps became aware of Matthew Snyder's funeral and decided to travel to Maryland with six other Westboro Baptist parishioners (two of his daughters and four of his grandchildren) to picket. On the day of the memorial service, the Westboro congregation members picketed on public land adjacent to public streets near the Maryland State House, the United States Naval Academy, and Matthew Snyder's funeral. The Westboro picketers carried signs that were largely the same at all three locations. They stated, for instance: "God Hates the USA/Thank God for 9/11," "America is Doomed," "Don't Pray for the USA," "Thank God for IEDs," "Thank God for Dead Soldiers," "Pope in Hell," "Priests Rape Boys," "God Hates Fags," "You're Going to Hell," and "God Hates You."

The church had notified the authorities in advance of its intent to picket at the time of the funeral, and the picketers complied with police instructions in staging their demonstration. The picketing took place within a 10- by 25-foot plot of public land adjacent to a public street, behind a temporary fence. That plot was approximately 1,000 feet from the church where the funeral was held. Several buildings separated the picket site from the church. The Westboro picketers displayed their signs for about 30 minutes before the funeral began and sang hymns and recited Bible verses. None of the picketers entered church property or went to the cemetery. They did not yell or use profanity, and there was no violence associated with the picketing.

The funeral procession passed within 200 to 300 feet of the picket site. Although Snyder testified that he could see the tops of the picket signs as he drove to the funeral, he did not see what was written on the signs until later that night, while watching a news broadcast covering the event.

B

Snyder filed suit against Phelps, Phelps's daughters, and the Westboro Baptist Church (collectively Westboro or the church) in the United States District Court for the District of Maryland under that court's diversity jurisdiction. Snyder alleged five state tort law claims [including] intentional infliction of emotional distress. . . . Westboro moved for summary judgment, contending, in part, that the church's speech was insulated from liability by the First Amendment.

At trial, Snyder described the severity of his emotional injuries. He testified that he is unable to separate the thought of his dead son from his thoughts of Westboro's picketing, and that he often becomes tearful, angry, and physically ill when he thinks about it. Expert witnesses testified that Snyder's emotional anguish had resulted in severe depression and had exacerbated pre-existing health conditions.

A jury found for Snyder on the intentional infliction of emotional distress and held Westboro liable for $2.9 million in compensatory damages and $8 million in punitive damages. Westboro filed several post-trial motions, including a motion contending that the jury verdict was grossly excessive and a motion seeking judgment as a matter of law on all claims on First Amendment grounds. The District Court remitted the punitive damages award to $2.1 million, but left the jury verdict otherwise intact.

In the Court of Appeals, Westboro's primary argument was that the church was entitled to judgment as a matter of law because the First Amendment fully protected Westboro's speech. The Court of Appeals agreed. The court reviewed the picket signs and concluded that Westboro's statements were entitled to First Amendment protection because those statements were on matters of public concern, were not provably false, and were expressed solely through hyperbolic rhetoric.

We granted certiorari.

II

To succeed on a claim for intentional infliction of emotional distress in Maryland, a plaintiff must demonstrate that the defendant intentionally or recklessly engaged in extreme and outrageous conduct that caused the plaintiff to suffer severe emotional distress. The Free Speech Clause of the First Amendment—"Congress shall make no law . . . abridging the freedom of speech"—can serve as a defense in state tort suits, including suits for intentional infliction of emotional distress.

Whether the First Amendment prohibits holding Westboro liable for its speech in this case turns largely on whether that speech is of public or private concern, as determined by all the circumstances of the case. "[S]peech on 'matters of public concern' . . . is 'at the heart of the First Amendment's protection.'" The First Amendment reflects "a profound national commitment to the principle that debate on public issues should be uninhibited, robust, and wide-open." Accordingly, "speech on public issues occupies the highest rung of the hierarchy of First Amendment values, and is entitled to special protection." "'[N]ot all speech is of equal First Amendment importance,'" however, and where matters of purely private significance are at issue, First Amendment protections are often less rigorous. That is because restricting speech on purely private matters does not implicate the same constitutional concerns as limiting speech on matters of public interest: "[T]here is no threat to the free and robust debate of public issues; there is no potential interference with a meaningful dialogue of ideas"; and the "threat of liability" does not pose the risk of "a reaction of self-censorship" on matters of public import.

Speech deals with matters of public concern when it can "be fairly considered as relating to any matter of political, social, or other concern to the community," or when it "is a subject of legitimate news interest; that is, a subject of general interest and of value and concern to the public." The arguably "inappropriate or controversial character of a statement is irrelevant to the question whether it deals with a matter of public concern." . . . Deciding whether speech is of public or private concern requires us to examine the "'content, form, and context'" of that speech, "'as revealed by the whole record.'" As in other First Amendment cases, the court is obligated "to 'make an independent examination of the whole record' in order to make sure that 'the judgment does not constitute a forbidden intrusion on the field of free expression.'" In considering content, form, and context, no factor is dispositive, and it is necessary to evaluate all the circumstances of the speech, including what was said, where it was said, and how it was said.

The "content" of Westboro's signs plainly relates to broad issues of interest to society at large, rather than matters of "purely private concern." While [Westboro's] messages may fall short of refined social or political commentary, the issues they highlight—the political and moral conduct of the United States and its citizens, the fate of our Nation, homosexuality in the military, and scandals involving the Catholic clergy — are matters of public import. The signs certainly convey Westboro's position on those issues, in a manner designed . . . to reach as broad a public audience as possible. And even if a few of the signs — such as "You're Going to Hell" and "God Hates You" — were viewed as containing messages related to Matthew Snyder or the Snyders specifically, that would not change the fact that the overall thrust and dominant theme of Westboro's demonstration spoke to broader public issues.

Apart from the content of Westboro's signs, Snyder contends that the "context" of the speech — its connection with his son's funeral — makes the speech a matter of private rather than public concern. The fact that Westboro spoke in connection with a funeral, however, cannot by itself transform the nature of Westboro's speech. Westboro's signs, displayed on public land next to a public street, reflect the fact that the church finds much to condemn in modern society. Its speech is "fairly characterized as constituting speech on a matter of public concern," and the funeral setting does not alter that conclusion.

Snyder argues that the church members in fact mounted a personal attack on Snyder and his family, and then attempted to "immunize their conduct by claiming that they were actually protesting the United States' tolerance of homosexuality or the supposed evils of the Catholic Church." We are not concerned in this case that Westboro's speech on public matters was in any way contrived to insulate speech on a private matter from liability. Westboro had been actively engaged in speaking on the subjects addressed in its picketing long before it became aware of Matthew Snyder, and there can be no serious claim that Westboro's picketing did not represent its "honestly believed" views on public issues. There was no pre-existing relationship or conflict between Westboro and Snyder that might suggest Westboro's speech on public matters was intended to mask an attack on Snyder over a private matter.

Snyder goes on to argue that Westboro's speech should be afforded less than full First Amendment protection "not only because of the words" but also because the church members exploited the funeral "as a platform to bring their message to a broader audience." There is no doubt that Westboro chose to stage its picketing at the Naval Academy, the Maryland State House, and Matthew Snyder's funeral to increase publicity for its views and because of the relation between those sites and its views — in the case of the military funeral, because Westboro believes that God is killing American soldiers as punishment for the Nation's sinful policies.

Westboro's choice to convey its views in conjunction with Matthew Snyder's funeral made the expression of those views particularly hurtful to many, especially to Matthew's father. The record makes clear that the applicable legal term — "emotional distress" — fails to capture fully the anguish Westboro's choice added to Mr. Snyder's already incalculable grief. But Westboro conducted its picketing peacefully on matters of public concern at a public place adjacent to a public street. Such space occupies a "special position in terms of First Amendment protection." "[W]e have repeatedly referred to public streets as the archetype of a traditional public forum," noting that "'[t]ime out of mind' public streets and sidewalks have been used for public assembly and debate."

That said, "[e]ven protected speech is not equally permissible in all places and at all times." Westboro's choice of where and when to conduct its picketing is not beyond the Government's regulatory reach — it is "subject to reasonable time, place, or manner restrictions" that are consistent with the standards announced in this Court's precedents. . . .

We have identified a few limited situations where the location of targeted picketing can be regulated under provisions that the Court has determined to be content neutral. In *Frisby,* for example, we upheld a ban on such picketing "before or about" a particular residence, 487 U.S., at 477. In Madsen v. Women's Health Center, Inc., we approved an injunction requiring a buffer zone between protesters and an abortion clinic entrance. 512 U.S. 753, 768 (1994). The facts here are obviously quite different, both with respect to the activity being regulated and the means of restricting those activities.

Simply put, the church members had the right to be where they were. Westboro alerted local authorities to its funeral protest and fully complied with police guidance on where the picketing could be staged. The picketing was conducted under police supervision some 1,000 feet from the church, out of the sight of those at the church. The protest was not unruly; there was no shouting, profanity, or violence.

The record confirms that any distress occasioned by Westboro's picketing turned on the content and viewpoint of the message conveyed, rather than any interference with the funeral itself. A group of parishioners standing at the very spot where Westboro stood, holding signs that said "God Bless America" and "God Loves You," would not have been subjected to liability. It was what Westboro said that exposed it to tort damages.

Given that Westboro's speech was at a public place on a matter of public concern, that speech is entitled to "special protection" under the First Amendment. Such speech cannot be restricted simply because it is upsetting or arouses contempt. . . .

The jury here was instructed that it could hold Westboro liable for intentional infliction of emotional distress based on a finding that Westboro's picketing was "outrageous." "Outrageousness," however, is a highly malleable standard with "an inherent subjectiveness about it which would allow a jury to impose liability on the basis of the jurors' tastes or views, or perhaps on the basis of their dislike of a particular expression." In a case such as this, a jury is "unlikely to be neutral with respect to the content of [the] speech," posing "a real danger of becoming an instrument for the suppression of . . . 'vehement, caustic, and sometimes unpleasan[t]'" expression. Such a risk is unacceptable; "in public debate [we] must tolerate insulting, and even outrageous, speech in order to provide adequate 'breathing space' to the freedoms protected by the First Amendment." What Westboro said, in the whole context of how and where it chose to say it, is entitled to "special protection" under the First Amendment, and that protection cannot be overcome by a jury finding that the picketing was outrageous.

For all these reasons, the jury verdict imposing tort liability on Westboro for intentional infliction of emotional distress must be set aside. . . .

IV

Our holding today is narrow. We are required in First Amendment cases to carefully review the record, and the reach of our opinion here is limited by the particular facts before us. As we have noted, "the sensitivity and significance of the interests presented in clashes between First amendment and [state law] rights counsel relying on limited principles that sweep no more broadly than the appropriate context of the instant case. Westboro believes that America is morally flawed; many Americans might feel the same about Westboro. Westboro's funeral picketing is certainly hurtful and its contribution to public discourse may be negligible. But Westboro addressed matters of public import on public property, in a peaceful manner, in full compliance with the guidance of local officials.

The speech was indeed planned to coincide with Matthew Snyder's funeral, but did not itself disrupt that funeral, and Westboro's choice to conduct its picketing at that time and place did not alter the nature of its speech.

Speech is powerful. It can stir people to action, move them to tears of both joy and sorrow, and — as it did here — inflict great pain. On the facts before us, we cannot react to that pain by punishing the speaker. As a Nation we have chosen a different course — to protect even hurtful speech on public issues to ensure that we do not stifle public debate. That choice requires that we shield Westboro from tort liability for its picketing in this case.

The judgment of the United States Court of Appeals for the Fourth Circuit is affirmed.

It is so ordered.

[The concurring opinion of BREYER, J., is omitted.]

ALITO, J., dissenting.

Our profound national commitment to free and open debate is not a license for the vicious verbal assault that occurred in this case. . . . The Court now holds that the First Amendment protected respondents' right to brutalize Mr. Snyder. I cannot agree.

I

Respondents and other members of their church have strong opinions on certain moral, religious, and political issues, and the First Amendment ensures that they have almost limitless opportunities to express their views. . . .

It does not follow, however, that they may intentionally inflict severe emotional injury on private persons at a time of intense emotional sensitivity by launching vicious verbal attacks that make no contribution to public debate. To protect against such injury, "most if not all jurisdictions" permit recovery in tort for the intentional infliction of emotional distress (or IIED). . . .

Although the elements of the IIED tort are difficult to meet, respondents long ago abandoned any effort to show that those tough standards were not satisfied here. Instead, they maintained that the First Amendment gave them a license to engage in such conduct. They are wrong. . . .

IV

The Court concludes that respondents' speech was protected by the First Amendment for essentially three reasons, but none is sound.

First — and most important — the Court finds that "the overall thrust and dominant theme of [their] demonstration spoke to" broad public issues. As I have attempted to show, this portrayal is quite inaccurate; respondents' attack on Matthew was of central importance. But in any event, I fail to see why actionable speech should be immunized simply because it is interspersed with speech that is protected. The First Amendment allows recovery for defamatory statements that are interspersed with nondefamatory statements on matters of public concern, and there is no good reason why respondents' attack on Matthew Snyder and his family should be treated differently.

Second, the Court suggests that respondents' personal attack on Matthew Snyder is entitled to First Amendment protection because it was not motivated by a private grudge, but I see no basis for the strange distinction that the Court appears to draw. Respondents' motivation — "to increase publicity for its views" — did not transform their statements attacking the character of a private figure into statements that made a contribution to debate on matters of public concern. Nor did their publicity-seeking motivation soften the sting of their attack. And as far as culpability is concerned, one might well think that wounding statements uttered in the heat of a private feud are less, not more, blameworthy than similar statements made as part of a cold and calculated strategy to slash a stranger as a means of attracting public attention.

Third, the Court finds it significant that respondents' protest occurred on a public street, but this fact alone should not be enough to preclude IIED liability. To be sure, statements made on a public street may be less likely to satisfy the elements of the IIED tort than statements made on private property, but there is no reason why a public street in close proximity to the scene of a funeral should be regarded as a free-fire zone in which otherwise actionable verbal attacks are shielded from liability. If the First Amendment permits the States to protect their residents from the harm inflicted by such attacks — and the Court does not hold otherwise — then the location of the tort should not be dispositive. A physical assault may occur without trespassing; it is no defense that the perpetrator had "the right to be where [he was]." And the same should be true with respect to unprotected speech. Neither classic "fighting words" nor defamatory statements are immunized when they occur in a public place, and there is no good reason to treat a verbal assault based on the conduct or character of a private figure like Matthew Snyder any differently. . . .

Because I cannot agree either with the holding of this Court . . . I would reverse the decision below and remand for further proceedings. . . .

VI

Respondents' outrageous conduct caused petitioner great injury, and the Court now compounds that injury by depriving petitioner of a judgment that acknowledges the wrong he suffered.

In order to have a society in which public issues can be openly and vigorously debated, it is not necessary to allow the brutalization of innocent victims like petitioner. I therefore respectfully dissent.

Did the *Snyder* majority understate the degree to which IIED claims are carefully cabined under state common law to provide private law remedies for only the most outrageous and widely reviled behavior? Consider the following reaction from a leading proponent of the "civil recourse" school of tort theory:

> Those who complain that the concept of outrageousness is too vague and subjective to withstand First Amendment scrutiny are ignoring the structure of the common law of torts, in general, and operating without an adequate understanding of the tort of IIED, in particular. Tort law, unlike criminal law or regulation, is not a series of general prohibitions or restrictions promulgated and then enforced by the state. It is a system for empowering private parties to use the courts to redress wrongful injuries done to them by others. This does not mean due process disappears and vagueness does not matter, but it does mean that the rule-of-law norms that the Due Process Clause is understood to entail, particularly within our federalist system, cannot be evaluated in quite the way that one would evaluate a criminal statute. What is critical — apart from jurisdictional concerns — is that the

> plaintiff's claim be anchored as an injury to him; that the law's treatment of his conduct as a wrongful injuring of the plaintiff be adequately rooted in precedent and social understanding regarding the wrongs and rights of community members; that the precedent and social understanding reflect a legitimate conceptualization of correlative rights and duties; and that the individual upon whom liability is imposed can, in some sense, be expected to be aware that the community regards the kind of injuring he did to the plaintiff as a wrongful injuring. Looked at from this point of view, the tort of intentional infliction of emotional distress through outrageous conduct is almost tailor-made to respect community members' rights to be free of tort liability for emotional harm in all but the rarest case. The conduct of the Phelpses in Westminster, Maryland, fell squarely within the domain in which a private right of action for imposition of severe emotional distress is actionable.

Benjamin C. Zipursky, *Snyder v. Phelps*, Outrageousness, and the Open Texture of Tort Law, 60 DePaul L. Rev. 473, 477-478 (2011).

Chapter 12

Defamation

Defamation is one of the most complex torts. The sources of the complexity lie in the historical origins of the law,[1] and in the difficulties of reconciling the important but often conflicting interests in the protection of reputation and freedom of speech. Although common law courts had already developed certain privileges and defenses to insulate the free expression of ideas and opinions from liability, these doctrines were no longer purely discretionary following the Supreme Court's partial "constitutionalization" of defamation law in New York Times Co. v. Sullivan, discussed in Section B, below. Later cases have expanded the reach of the First Amendment into the law of defamation, and how much remains of the traditional law is somewhat in doubt. Section A of this chapter contains a general description of the traditional law of defamation as it has developed apart from the constitutional cases. In Section B, we set out the principal lines of constitutional development. Section C concludes the chapter by describing a proposal for a uniform act that seeks to bring about a clearer and more appropriate balance between the interests in reputation and in speech. As you read these materials, note carefully the ways in which the common law of defamation did, and did not, anticipate the concerns of the Supreme Court.

A. The Traditional Law

The law of defamation protects the interest in reputation. The basic elements of an action for defamation are:

(1) *A defamatory statement.* Not all insults are actionable; the general rule is that to be defamatory, a statement must hold the plaintiff up to "hatred, ridicule, or contempt."
(2) *Publication.* The basis of the plaintiff's cause of action is the harm suffered from the reaction of others and not hurt feelings. The defamatory statement must, therefore, be published — that is, communicated to a third person.
(3) *Harm.* In some circumstances, the plaintiff must prove actual harm from the publication of the defamatory statement in order to recover. In other instances, there is no need for such proof. The requirements with respect to proof of harm are reflected in the categories of damages that may be recovered. There are two categories of compensatory damages — special and general — that are uniquely defined in the context of defamation law. See Section 2.a, below. In addition, punitive damages may be recovered.

1. The history of the law of defamation defies brief restatement. In general, see R. C. Donnelly, History of Defamation, 1949 Wis. L. Rev. 99; Van Vechten Veeder, The History and Theory of the Law of Defamation, 3 Colum. L. Rev. 546 (1903), and 4 Colum. L. Rev. 33 (1904). Closely related is the criminal law of libel, which also has become overlaid with constitutional dimensions. See Garrison v. Louisiana, 379 U.S. 64 (1964).

If the plaintiff is successful in establishing a prima facie case, the defendant may be able to avoid liability by setting up either of two defenses:

(1) *Privilege.* The privilege to publish a defamatory statement may be either absolute or qualified. An absolute privilege is available in situations in which the interest in free expression totally outweighs interests in reputation and affords the speaker the utmost level of protection from liability. A qualified privilege rests on a more limited interest of permitting free expression between the publisher and the audience and generally insulates the speaker from liability unless he or she acts with actual malice.
(2) *Truth.* Truth is not part of the plaintiff's prima facie case in a suit for defamation, but rather must be established by the defendant.

1. What Constitutes Defamation

a. The General Standard

Since the interest that the law of defamation seeks to protect is the integrity of the plaintiff's reputation, the defamatory communication must do more than hurt the plaintiff's feelings. It must be of a nature to cause others to react adversely to the plaintiff. As a result, defamation is traditionally defined as a statement that holds one up to hatred, ridicule, or contempt. In New York, for instance, a defamatory expression has been defined as one that "tends to expose a person to hatred, contempt or aversion, or to induce an evil or unsavoury opinion of him in the minds of a substantial number in the community." Nichols v. Item Publishers, Inc., 132 N.E.2d 860, 861-62 (N.Y. 1956). A somewhat broader definition is supplied by §559 of the Restatement (Second) of Torts:

> A communication is defamatory if it tends so to harm the reputation of another as to lower him in the estimation of the community or to deter third persons from associating or dealing with him.

Even this definition is too limited for some courts. For example, in the classic English case Youssoupoff v. Metro-Goldwyn-Mayer Pictures, Ltd., 50 T.L.R. 581 (C.A. 1934), the plaintiff, a Russian princess, claimed that the defendant's motion picture defamed her by portraying her as a woman who had been raped by the notorious Russian monk Rasputin. Although the film did not suggest that the plaintiff was guilty of any misbehavior, the appellate court affirmed a lower court decision for the plaintiff. The court approved the trial judge's definition, which included statements causing persons "to be shunned or avoided," and added its own gloss by characterizing as defamatory "a false statement about a man to his discredit. . . ." To the defendant's assertion that the motion picture was not defamatory, the court responded (50 T.L.R. at 584):

> [T]his is the argument as I understand it: "To say of a woman that she is raped does not impute unchastity." From that we get to this, which was solemnly put forward, that to say of a woman of good character that she has been ravished by a man of the worst possible character is not defamatory. That argument was solemnly presented to the jury, and I only wish the jury could have expressed, and that we could know, what they thought of it, because it seems to me to be one of the most legal arguments that were ever addressed to, I will not say a business body, but a sensible body.

The medium of the defamatory communication does not have to be the written or spoken word; actions, gestures, pictures, and other visual representations may also be defamatory. In Schultz v. Frankfort Marine Accident & Plate Glass Ins. Co., 139 N.W. 386 (Wis. 1913), the court held that detectives who were "rough shadowing" — a form of surveillance designed to publicly harass and humiliate its object — the plaintiff had defamed him. And in Burton v. Crowell Publishing Co., 82 F.2d 154 (2d Cir. 1936), a photograph in an advertisement was held to be defamatory. The plaintiff in this case, a well-known equestrian, had posed for a picture showing him holding a saddle from which hung a large girth. The girth appeared to be attached to the plaintiff rather than the saddle. Characterizing the picture as "grotesque, monstrous, and obscene," the court commented on the unique way in which a picture can defame:

> If the advertisement is a libel, it is such in spite of the fact that it asserts nothing whatever about the plaintiff, even by the remotest implications. . . . [I]t is patently an optical illusion, and carries its correction on its face as much as though it were a verbal utterance which expressly declared that it was false. It would be hard for words so guarded to carry any sting, but the same is not true of caricatures, and this is an example; for notwithstanding all we have just said, it exposed the plaintiff to overwhelming ridicule. [82 F.2d at 155.]

Defamation litigation often results when the content of the publication focuses on sex. Accusations that the plaintiff is an adulterer are clearly defamatory. See, e.g., Barreca v. Nickolas, 683 N.W.2d 111, 116 (Iowa 2004) (noting that adultery accusations have conventionally been treated as slander per se); City of Fairbanks v. Rice, 20 P.3d 1097 (Alaska 2000) (same). Accusations of sex or other sexual behavior while working can also qualify as defamatory, as in Young v. Gannett Satellite Info. Network, Inc., 734 F.3d 544, 548 (6th Cir. 2013) (newspaper improperly alleged that a police officer "had sex with a woman while on the job"). Other statements like those in *Youssoupoff* and *Burton* may raise eyebrows but do not so directly accuse the plaintiff of sexual misbehavior. See, e.g., Vigil v. Rice, 397 P.2d 719 (N.M. 1964) (doctor's false report to school authorities that a 13-year-old student was pregnant was ruled defamatory); Sauerhoff v. Hearst Corp., 538 F.2d 588 (4th Cir. 1976) (a married plaintiff was defamed when the defendant referred to a woman who was not the plaintiff's wife as his "girl friend"); Clark v. American Broadcasting Cos., 684 F.2d 1208 (6th Cir. 1982), *cert. denied,* 460 U.S. 1040 (1983) (a television documentary on street prostitution showing plaintiff walking toward the camera was capable of creating the impression that plaintiff was a prostitute); and Robinson v. Radio One, Inc., 695 F. Supp. 2d 425 (N.D. Tex. 2010) (defendant's broadcast, which referred to the plaintiff as a "gay security guard" may constitute defamation as applied even if it is no longer treated as defamation per se given that state's criminal sodomy statute was declared unconstitutional).

The business world also furnishes its share of defamation cases. Statements that the plaintiff is a bad credit risk or that he cheats his customers are defamatory. Merchants who criticize a competitor's goods in a way that impugns the latter's integrity may also be liable for defamation. See, e.g., Rosenberg v. J. C. Penney Co., 86 P.2d 696 (Cal. Ct. App. 1939) (defendant's comment that gym shorts sold by plaintiff were "poorly made seconds or prison-made merchandise" was defamatory in light of plaintiff's known claim to sell only first-grade goods). The First Circuit, and a number of other courts, have followed the Second Restatement, and ruled that a "false statement concerning the quality of goods . . . is not actionable as defamation per se unless 'made under circumstances and in a manner that implies that the manufacturer or vendor is dishonest, fraudulent or incompetent'." Ira Green, Inc. v. Military Sales & Serv. Co., 775 F.3d 12, 22-23 (1st Cir. 2014). A merchant may suffer harm to reputation in more particular ways, such as in Braun v. Armour & Co., 173 N.E. 845 (N.Y. 1930), which held that an advertisement listing a kosher meat market as a seller of Armour's Star Bacon was defamatory. And in Metabolife Intern., Inc. v. Wornick, 264 F.3d 832 (9th Cir. 2001), the plaintiff challenged several statements contained in a journalistic report regarding its herbal diet product, including claims that "every expert" asked by the defendants believed the product is "not safe," that the product has not been tested for safety, that the product contains the same main ingredient as methamphetamine, and that "You can die from taking this product." On the other hand, in Seaton v. TripAdvisor LLC, 728 F.3d 592, 599 (6th Cir. 2013), an aggrieved hotel owner unsuccessfully filed a claim against TripAdvisor for his hotel's inclusion on its "2011 Dirtiest Hotels" list. The court reasoned that TripAdvisor's list constituted nonactionable opinion and "rhetorical hyperbole." Finally, as in Burton v. Teleflex Inc., 707 F.3d 417 (3d Cir. 2013), some statements by corporations cannot be taken as defamatory under any circumstances, such as stating that a former employee "left the company to pursue other opportunities."

By and large, parodies and satires have been held not to be defamatory on the ground that reasonable people would not take such publications to be statements of actual facts. See, e.g., Hustler Magazine v. Falwell, 485 U.S. 46 (1988), involving a parody of a liquor advertisement in which the plaintiff, a well-known religious leader, was portrayed as having a sexual dalliance with his mother in an outhouse. The jury found that the parody was not defamatory because no reasonable person would believe the parody to be true. In New Times, Inc. v. Isaacks, 146 S.W.3d 144 (Tex. 2004), the court granted summary judgment to a defendant newspaper that had lampooned a local judge after the judge ordered a 13-year-old boy to juvenile detention because he wrote a Halloween story that was found to contain "terroristic threats." The newspaper published a satirical article depicting the same judge as jailing a six-year-old girl "for writing a book report about 'cannibalism, fanaticism, and disorderly conduct' based on Maurice Sendak's classic children's book *Where the Wild Things Are*." Id. at 148. In the court's view, no reasonable reader could conclude that the article described actual facts when viewed in its entirety. A court ruled similarly in Corsi Farah v. Esquire Magazine, 736 F.3d 528 (D.C. Cir. 2013), when faced with a defamation claim brought by the author and publisher of a book questioning Barack Obama's eligibility to serve as President. In an online blog post, defendant reported that thousands of copies of the book had been pulled from the shelves and purchasers had been offered their money back. The court held that a reasonable reader would not understand the article at issue as providing real news, given *Esquire*'s "history of publishing satirical stories, with recent topics ranging from Osama Bin Laden's television-watching habits to 'Sex Tips from Donald Rumsfeld'." Id. at 537.

Like the tolerance for satire and parody, it is also not unreasonable for the law to expect people to have a certain toughness of hide with respect to vulgarisms. Common epithets such as "bastard" and "son of a bitch," because they are almost never taken in a literal sense, are only mildly offensive except to the most sensitive. Given the proper circumstances, however, even these epithets may be defamatory. See, e.g., Capps v. Watts, 246 S.E.2d 606 (S.C. 1978), in which the words "paranoid sonofabitch" were actionable where they could be found to impute qualities to the plaintiff which were incompatible with the exercise of his office as an administrator of a state association for the blind. And in Spence v. Flynt, 816 P.2d 771 (Wyo. 1991), *cert. denied,* 503 U.S. 984 (1992), the court held that summary judgment was not appropriate in a case involving a vulgar diatribe against a lawyer for representing Andrea Dworkin, a prominent anti-pornography activist and feminist theorist, in a suit against *Hustler* magazine. But opprobrious terms describing one's personal outlook are not generally actionable. The court in Raible v. Newsweek, Inc., 341 F. Supp. 804 (W.D. Pa. 1972), found the characterization "bigot" not defamatory, stating that descriptions of a person's political, religious, economic, or sociological philosophies are not defamatory. A federal appeals court has called terms such as "fascist" and "fellow traveler" amorphous expressions of opinion that cannot defame. Buckley v. Littell, 539 F.2d 882 (2d Cir. 1976), *cert. denied,* 429 U.S. 1062 (1977).

Whether or not the charge that one is a Communist or a Communist sympathizer is defamatory has been an on-again, off-again proposition in American law. For cases from the 1920s through the early 1950s, which show how courts' attitudes have adapted with the changing political relationship between the United States and the Soviet Union, see Annotation, 33 A.L.R.2d 1196 (1954). For a more thorough overview of "allegedly objectionable political or social beliefs or principles as defamation," see Annotation, 62 A.L.R.4th 314 (1988). The statement does not have to be taken as defamatory by the general public to be actionable. It suffices if the statement is perceived to be defamatory by a smaller community, such as the one in which the plaintiff works. See Sharratt v. Housing Innovations, Inc., 310 N.E.2d 343 (Mass. 1974). Occasionally, courts have been asked to make moral judgments about the values that lead the audience to react adversely to the statement; and some have argued that a plaintiff's reputation must suffer in the eyes of "right-thinking" people for a statement to be defamatory. In general, American courts have rejected this formulation, preferring the view that a statement is defamatory if so perceived by a significant segment of the community even if that segment's views seem unsavory or dishonorable. As Justice Holmes stated in Peck v. Tribune Co., 214 U.S. 185, 190 (1909): "No conduct is hated by all. That it will be known by a large number, and will lead an appreciable fraction of that number to regard the plaintiff with contempt, is enough to do her practical harm." And in Grant v. Reader's Digest Ass'n Inc., 151 F.2d 733 (2d Cir. 1945), *cert. denied,* 326 U.S. 797 (1946), the court stated, with respect to an accusation that the plaintiff was a legislative representative of the Communist party (151 F.2d 734-35):

> A man may value his reputation even among those who do not embrace the prevailing moral standards; and it would seem that the jury should be allowed to appraise how far he should be indemnified for the disesteem of such persons. . . . We do not believe, therefore, that we need say whether "right-thinking" people would harbor similar feelings toward a lawyer, because he had been an agent for the Communist Party, or was a sympathizer with its aims and means. It is enough if there be some, as there certainly are, who would feel so, even though they would be "wrong-thinking" people if they did.

Not all courts, however, ignore the values of the audience. In Connelly v. McKay, 28 N.Y.S.2d 327 (Sup. Ct. 1941), the defendant had falsely accused the plaintiff, who ran a gas station and guest house catering to truck drivers, of informing the Interstate Commerce Commission of truckers who violated Commission regulations. There is little question that many truck drivers would regard such a person hostilely, but the court held that the statement was not defamatory, relying in part on language that appears in §559 cmt. *e* of the Restatement of Torts, which provides:

> The fact that a communication tends to prejudice another in the eyes of even a substantial group is not enough if the group is one whose standards are so anti-social that it is not proper for the courts to recognize them.

See also Albright v. Morton, 321 F. Supp. 2d 130 (D. Mass. 2004), in which the district court rejected as "offensive" plaintiff's argument that a statement claiming that the plaintiff was homosexual should be considered libelous per se, and Robinson v. Radio One, Inc., 695 F. Supp. 2d 425 (N.D. Tex. 2010), above. For a discussion on homosexuality and defamation, see Haven Ward, "I'm Not Gay, M'kay?" Should Falsely Calling Someone a Homosexual Be Defamatory?, 44 Ga. L. Rev. 739 (2010).

Some persons, such as those with a history of criminal activity, have been held to be "libel-proof" with respect to certain sorts of statements. A plaintiff is libel-proof if she already has a sufficiently bad reputation with respect to a certain trait, so that a defamatory statement about that trait cannot harm her, even if it is false and made with malice. See, e.g., Jackson v. Longcope, 476 N.E.2d 617 (Mass. 1985); Ray v. Time, Inc., 452 F. Supp. 618 (W.D. Tenn. 1976), *aff'd,* 582 F.2d 1280 (6th Cir. 1978). In the latter case, the plaintiff was the person convicted of killing Martin Luther King. In Guccione v. Hustler Magazine, Inc., 800 F.2d 298 (2d Cir. 1986), *cert. denied,* 479 U.S. 1091 (1987), the plaintiff, the publisher of *Penthouse* magazine, was held to be libel-proof with respect to an accusation that he had committed adultery. Further, in Kevorkian v. American Medical Ass'n, 602 N.W.2d 233 (Mich. Ct. App. 1999), *appeal denied,* 613 N.W.2d 720, *reconsideration denied,* 620 N.W.2d 849 (Mich. 2000), *cert. denied,* 532 U.S. 995 (2001), the court held that statements about a physician who illegally assisted suicide, such as that he "serves merely as a reckless instrument of death," engages in "criminal practices," and is "a killer," were not defamatory. The court said that with respect to "assisted suicides," the plaintiff was libel-proof.

The Supreme Court of New Hampshire, in Thomas v. Telegraph Publishing Co., 929 A.2d 993, 1005 (2007), similarly adopted an "issue-specific" version of the libel-proof doctrine, holding that when "the plaintiff engaged in criminal or antisocial behavior in the past . . . widely reported to the public," the evidence may support the conclusion, "as a matter of law, that the plaintiff's reputation could not have suffered from the publication of the false and libelous statement" concerning the previously reported issue. The court cautioned, however, that the doctrine should be applied only "with caution and sparingly," which the court backed up by reversing a trial court ruling that plaintiff was libel-proof in light of inadequate publicity of plaintiff's 20 prior criminal convictions. Id. In Stern v. Cosby, 645 F. Supp. 2d 258 (S.D.N.Y. 2010), the court also refused to rule that a deceased celebrity's lawyer and friend was libel-proof merely because he had appeared in an unflattering light in tabloid newspaper articles and a reality television program featuring the celebrity. The libel-proof concept was rejected in Liberty Lobby, Inc. v. Anderson, 746 F.2d 1563 (D.C. Cir. 1984), *vacated on other grounds,* 477 U.S. 242 (1986), in which the court expressed doubt about its ability to determine whether the plaintiff's reputation had already been so badly damaged that it could not be further harmed by a new libel. In fact, some courts decline to rule on whether a person is libel-proof. See, e.g., Armistead v. Minor, 815 So. 2d 1189 (Miss. 2002) (court held that a determination of libel-proof status is always a jury question). However, some courts — in particular, the Second Circuit and New York district courts — still consider whether someone is libel-proof, even in the absence of criminal convictions. See, e.g., Frydman v. Verschleiser, No. 14-CV-05903 (JGK), 2016 WL 1128203, at *13 (S.D.N.Y. Mar. 22, 2016); and Guccione v. Hustler Magazine, Inc., 800 F.2d 298 (2d Cir. 1986). In general, see Joseph H. King, Jr.,

The Misbegotten Libel-Proof Doctrine and the "Gordian Knot" Syndrome, 29 Hofstra L. Rev. 343 (2000).

b. Interpretation of the Statement

The general rule is that if the statement about the plaintiff is capable of several meanings, one of which is not defamatory, the plaintiff must establish that the audience would take the statement in its defamatory sense. For example, in Washington Post Co. v. Chaloner, 250 U.S. 290 (1919), the defendant published a story that the plaintiff "shot and killed John Gillard, while the latter was abusing his wife, who had taken refuge at Merry Mills, Chaloner's home." Applying District of Columbia law, the trial judge had ruled as a matter of law that the story implied that the plaintiff had committed murder. In reversing, the Supreme Court stated (250 U.S. at 293-94):

> Counsel for [plaintiff] admit (and properly so) that, upon the authorities, a published item saying "C shot and killed G," without more, would not be libelous per se — it does not set forth the commission of a crime in unambiguous words. And we are unable to conclude that, as matter of law, addition of the words "while the latter was abusing his wife, who had taken refuge at Merry Mills, Chaloner's home" would convert such a statement into a definite charge of murder. On the contrary they might at least suggest to reasonable minds that the homicide was without malice.

Illinois follows a stronger *innocent construction rule,* under which the plaintiff cannot recover if the statement is reasonably capable of a nondefamatory meaning or of referring to someone other than plaintiff. See Bryson v. News Am. Publications, 672 N.E.2d 1207 (Ill. 1996). Thus, in Global Relief Foundation, Inc. v. New York Times Co., 2003 WL 403135 (N.D. Ill. 2003), *aff'd* 390 F.3d 973 (7th Cir. 2004), the court dismissed a libel suit against a news organization that had claimed the federal government was investigating plaintiff, an Islamic charity, for having ties to terrorists. As one of the grounds for dismissal, the court noted that an article that failed to specifically reference the plaintiff by name could have been construed by readers as referring to a different charity. In Muzikowski v. Paramount Pictures Corp., 322 F.3d 918 (7th Cir. 2003), on the other hand, the court held that merely labeling a movie "fictitious" did not afford defendant the protection of the innocent construction rule. Rather, plaintiff still could demonstrate that the movie was based on his life and that statements in the movie could not reasonably be construed as applying to anyone else.

In establishing the defamatory meaning of a statement, the plaintiff is not limited to its words (although, as will be seen, if resort to extrinsic facts is necessary, that statement may not be actionable without proof of special damages). Extrinsic facts necessary to make the statement defamatory are called the *inducement,* and the defamatory meaning based on such facts is called the *innuendo.* In Cassidy v. Daily Mirror Newspapers, Ltd., [1929] 2 K.B. 331, the defendant had published a story that one Cassidy had announced his engagement to "Miss X." The plaintiff was Mrs. Cassidy, and she proved that she lived with Cassidy as his wife (the inducement). The story would then have the meaning that she was an immoral woman in that she lived with Cassidy as his wife but without marrying him (the innuendo). In Rubin v. U.S. News & World Report, Inc., 271 F.3d 1305, 1306-08 (11th Cir. 2001), the defendant published a news article alleging that much of the global gold trade was illegitimate and stating that the plaintiff "concedes . . . [that] there's a dual economic system in the jewelry industry" and that "there's on the books and there's off the books." The court of appeals affirmed dismissal of the complaint, concluding that no libel by implication had occurred because "a reader would only see [plaintiff] as a knowledgeable gold refiner who has cooperated to be interviewed as a source of information on the industry." Id. In contrast, the Fourth Circuit refused to dismiss a suit against the *New York Times* and one of its columnists for articles published about the anthrax mailing that occurred in the fall of 2001. *See* Hatfill v. New York Times Co., 416 F.3d 320 (4th Cir. 2005). Despite a statement in the challenged column that the plaintiff, a scientist, was assumed to be "an innocent man caught in a nightmare," the appeals court held that "the unmistakable theme" of the article was that the scientist should be investigated more closely by the government. Id. at 333.

Chau v. Lewis

771 F.3d 118 (2d Cir. 2014)

Wesley, Circuit Judge:

Plaintiffs–Appellants Wing F. Chau and Harding Advisory LLC appeal from a March 29, 2013 judgment of the United States District Court for the Southern District of New York (Daniels, J) dismissing their claims of libel against Defendants–Appellees author Michael Lewis, his source, Steven Eisman, and Lewis's publisher, W.W. Norton, for twenty-six allegedly defamatory statements in Lewis's book *The Big Short*. The district court granted Defendants' motion for summary judgment and dismissed each of Plaintiffs' claims. We Affirm the district court's grant of summary judgment.

Background

The United States' housing market collapse in 2008-2009 and the ensuing global financial crisis are widely considered the worst financial disasters since the Great Depression; their causes have been hotly debated. One of the many books that explore the genesis of the financial decline is *The Big Short: Inside the Doomsday Machine*, written by Defendant Michael Lewis and published in 2010 by Defendant W.W. Norton. A work of non-fiction, *The Big Short* looks at a "small group of iconoclasts who 'shorted,' or bet against, the subprime mortgage bond market at a time when most investors thought real estate prices would continue to rise (i.e., were 'long')." One of the so-called "iconoclasts" described in *The Big Short* is Defendant Steve Eisman, who managed a hedge fund and served as one of Lewis's sources for the book. . . .

Thankfully, we do not have to weigh in on the root of America's fiscal crisis. The task before us is much more focused: to determine whether one chapter of *The Big Short*— Chapter 6, titled *Spider-Man at the Venetian* — contains statements that are defamatory to Plaintiffs Wing Chau and his business Harding Advisory.

Chapter 6 comprises twenty-four pages of the 270-page, ten-chapter book, and one-third of that chapter focuses on a dinner conversation that took place in January 2007 at the Wynn Las Vegas Hotel during the 2007 American Securitization Forum. The dinner was notable in its design to introduce people who shorted the market to the people who went long. Eisman was in attendance and was seated next to Chau.

Chau, an "investment professional," is the founder and owner of Harding Advisory LLC. . . . At the time of the January 2007 dinner, Harding was a top-ranked manager of Collateralized Debt Obligations[2] (commonly known as "CDOs") and was on its way to issuing more asset-backed CDOs by volume than any other CDO manager.

Spider-Man at the Venetian recounts Eisman's interaction and discussions with Chau at that dinner and paints CDO managers in general, and Plaintiffs in particular, in a negative light. In response to this chapter's representations, Chau sued Lewis for writing, Norton for publishing, and Eisman for communicating to Lewis twenty-six allegedly defamatory statements. . . .

[The court reproduces in detail the statements, which portray Wing Chau variously as: "the sucker"; "a fool"; "the engine of doom;" a huckster selling to investors instruments that were "the equivalent of three levels of dog shit lower than the original bonds" underlying CDOs, while further encouraging "tens of thousands of actual human being to be handed money they could never afford to repay"; a self-serving opportunist who sold out his own position in CDOs while continuing to market them to others; a "double agent — a character who seemed to represent the interests of investors when he better represented the interests of Wall Street bond trading desks"; a "moron" or a "crook" who did not "give a fuck about the investors in this thing"; and a "front man" for "Wall Street firms" who "would rather have $50 billion in crappy CDOs than none at all, as he was paid mainly on volume."]

Discussion

. . . In New York, a plaintiff must establish five elements to recover in libel: (1) a written defamatory factual statement concerning the plaintiff; (2) publication to a third party; (3) fault; (4) falsity of the defamatory statement; and (5) special damages or per se actionability. On closer inspection, the first element of these five is actually composed of multiple parts: there must be (A) a writing, it must be (B) defamatory, it must be (C) factual — that is, not opinion — and it must be (D) about the plaintiff, not just a general statement. . . .

A. Statements that Simply Are Not Defamatory in Meaning

Not all (or even most) maligning remarks can be considered defamatory. A statement is defamatory if it exposes an individual "to public hatred, shame, obloquy, contumely, odium, contempt, ridicule, aversion, ostracism, degradation or disgrace, or . . . induce[s] an evil opinion of one in the minds of right-thinking persons, and . . . deprive[s] one of their confidence and friendly intercourse in society." Kimmerle v. N.Y. Evening Journal, Inc., 262 N.Y. 99, 102, 186 N.E. 217 (1933). A statement, therefore, can meet all of the other elements of defamation — be factual, published, false, and about the plaintiff — but still not be actionable if it fails to rise to the necessary level of derogation. . . .

[A number of the challenged statements] are not reasonably susceptible to a defamatory connotation and are therefore non-actionable. [One statement], for example, purports to quote Chau stating "I've sold everything out." It is unclear how such a quote, true or not, could produce hatred, shame, or contempt of Chau or his business. Perhaps it would give

2. Though largely irrelevant for purposes of this discussion, a CDO is a type of structured asset-backed security that evolved to encompass the mortgage and mortgage-backed securities market. Their ready availability and decline in quality is largely credited with fueling the subprime mortgage crisis.

Harding's investors more confidence if their money managers also had an equity stake in the investments, but that they did not does not make the statement defamatory. [Another statement], which describes Chau as "almost giddily" telling Eisman that he had "passed all the risk," is also non-defamatory: passing risk is the business of a money manager, and we cannot characterize this as defamatory. Moreover, Lewis's (or Eisman's) characterization of Chau as "almost gidd[]y" is a subjective assessment and an opinion. This same logic applies to . . . Chau's statement that he would "rather have $50 billion in crappy CDOs than none at all, as he was paid mainly on volume"[, which] merely conveys a fundamental truth: $10 worth of a lousy security is worth more than none at all. Similarly, being paid on volume is a statement that is generally applicable to brokers, dealers, and firms. It is unclear how an ordinary reader would interpret this, in context, as defamatory. . . .

B. Opinion

As mentioned above, only factual statements are actionable as defamation or libel. This is because, in part, New York law protects derogatory statements which may be categorized as "opinion" as opposed to "fact.". . . .

In the instant case, the district court correctly held that [a number of the challenged statements] are non-actionable opinions. In [several statements], the use of phrasing such as, "I had no idea . . ." and "I didn't know . . ." are particular customs or signals to readers that something is opinion, not fact. Likewise, the epithets . . . — "sucker," "fool," "front-man," "industrial waste," "pilot[]" of the "ship of doom," and "crooks or morons" — are hyperbole and therefore not actionable opinion. While someone may not appreciate being called a fool, it is an expression of one's view of another, and moreover might not reflect reality: history has shown many "fools" to have indeed been visionaries. Time may prove the insult misguided, but the insult is not itself a fact — but rather, is one's perception of facts — at the time it is uttered.

C. Not of and Concerning Plaintiff

In New York, a plaintiff cannot sustain a libel claim if the allegedly defamatory statement is not "of and concerning plaintiff" but rather only speaks about a group of which the plaintiff is a member. As many of the statements concern "CDO managers" generally, the district court correctly held that they are not "of and concerning" Chau. This includes [statements that] respectively describe the "CDO manager's job;" the "typical CDO manager;" "[t]he last thing you wanted [from] a CDO manager;" and the "double agent" created by the bond market. Though Chau is described in the book as a CDO manager, these statements are solely about the group.

D. Substantial Truth

Falsity of a statement is needed to make out a claim of libel. But in defamation law, as in life, determinations of fact and fiction are not zero-sum. In New York, a statement need not be completely true, but can be substantially true, as when the overall "gist or substance of the challenged statement" is true. Printers II, Inc. v. Prof'ls Publ'g, Inc., 784 F.2d 141, 146-47 (2d Cir.1986).

Statements . . . which describe Plaintiffs' goal to "maximize dollars in [their] care;" their "love [of] guys who short [their] market" and Chau's "main fear . . . that the U.S. economy would strengthen" thus minimizing the number of people betting against the subprime mortgage market . . . are all completely or substantially true. . . . Chau's entire business operated by having people to bet against. Bets are simply gambles that the result of an event — here, mortgage defaults that would devalue CDOs — will favor their side of the wager. While some may cringe at the thought of investing money as a gamble, such bets are the nature of much of the financial market and are especially the case with CDOs. . . .

Conclusion

Chapter 6 of *The Big Short* portrays Chau as starting out from a series of simple finance-related jobs to becoming the founder and principal of a financial firm managing CDOs, which provided him with what many Americans hope for — great wealth. The market events of 2008 and 2009 may undoubtedly influence one's perception as to whether going long on CDOs meant Chau was a fool, or Chau was a rube, or his motivations were avarice; but hindsight cannot give such opinions a defamatory meaning. Lewis's various implications that Chau was wrong about the mortgage market are not actionable.

The law of defamation in New York is predicated on the free exchange of ideas and viewpoints. That marketplace can wound one's pride — for words can offend or insult — but simple slights are not the stuff of defamation. . . . It is understandable that Chau was displeased by a book that laid a good share of the blame for the financial crisis at the feet of Wall Street banks — and the advisors they chose to manage the CDOs — that collapsed so spectacularly. Before the crash, Chau was a top manager of asset-backed CDOs. By the time the book was published, every CDO managed by Chau was either in default, liquidated, or downgraded to junk status, and his investors incurred substantial losses that would damage any money manager's reputation. Our dissenting brother exploits Chau's fate as context for his view that the Defendants' writing did not have an "innocent meaning[ ]"; our view is that a non-defamatory reflection on this disastrous chapter of our nation's financial history would not necessarily have an "innocent meaning" for those depicted.

We have considered all of Plaintiffs' contentions on this appeal and have found them to be without merit. For the reasons above, the judgment of the district court is AFFIRMED as to all statements.

WINTER, Circuit Judge, dissenting:

A trier of fact could easily find the following.

Appellant is the only CDO manager mentioned by name in the relevant chapter of the book and is depicted as the poster child for the CDO managers described [as having caused or contributed to the economic crisis]. Appellant is portrayed as lining his own pockets and foisting doomed-to-fail portfolios upon investors. Although he was paid to monitor the amount of risk in the fund's portfolio, he worried only about volume because he was paid by volume. And, knowing that the default rate of residential mortgages was sufficient to wipe out the fund's holdings, appellant sold all his interests in the fund, passing all the risk to the fund's investors, who believed he was monitoring that risk. The portrayal of the appellant is particularly graphic because it purports to show his state of mind and his actions out of his own mouth.

The book states that appellant managed a fund controlling "roughly $15 billion, invested in nothing but CDOs backed by the triple-B tranche of a mortgage bond," described as "dog shit." The book states that appellant had little training or background in CDO management because he had "spent most of his career working sleepy jobs at sleepy life insurance companies." While appellant was paid to manage these investments to reduce risk, "he actually didn't spend a lot of time worrying about what was in CDOs." Indeed, the book portrays appellant as not caring about how much risk was borne by the fund's investors. Appellant is said to have stated that "he would rather have $50 billion in crappy CDOs than none at all, as he was paid mainly on volume." . . .

The book's author admits that he does not use a fact checker, and much of what the book says about the appellant is known even now (before a trial) as false. For example, appellant's fund did not manage "nothing but CDOs backed by the triple-B tranche of a mortgage bond." In fact, 38% of the assets were more highly rated. For another example, appellant spent only two of his 12-year career at life insurance companies, sleepy or not, and had substantial experience in CDO management. He did not make $26 million annually; his income was one-tenth of that.

These falsehoods provide the scenic background for the portrayal of the appellant as engaging in conduct that a trier of fact could find amounted to fraud in order to line appellant's own pockets. This portrayal can be described as non-defamatory only by declining to view it as a whole; by taking some of the statements and quotations entirely out of the context in which they were made; by finding that some statements have only a single and non-defamatory meaning when the book clearly intended a different and defamatory meaning, one adopted by readers, or so a trier could find; and by labeling some statements as opinion without regard to the facts that they imply. . . .

My colleagues find [the challenged statements] non-defamatory because, they say, passing risk is the business of money managers; but the book alleges far more than informed risk passing. It describes the appellant as not doing the monitoring of risk he was paid to do, privately caring only about volume rather than reducing risk because he was paid by volume, and, as he learned of the growing number of defaults in amounts that wiped out the fund's portfolio, selling his interests in the fund to pass all risk on to buyers who were deceived into believing that the risk was being vetted. This description could easily serve as the opening statement in a civil or criminal fraud trial. . . .

I, therefore, respectfully dissent.

A further problem of interpretation involves a defamatory statement that makes no direct reference to the plaintiff. Proof that such a statement was taken by the audience to refer to the plaintiff is called the *colloquium.* In Stanton v. Metro Corp., 438 F.3d 119 (1st Cir. 2005), the court of appeals reversed a district court's conclusion that a photograph accompanying a magazine article was not defamatory as matter of law. The defendant had published a photograph of the plaintiff along with four other young people as part of an article entitled "The Mating Habits of the Suburban High School Teenager." The article advanced the claim that "teenagers in the greater Boston area have become more sexually promiscuous over the span of the last decade." Id. at 123. A small-print disclaimer at the beginning of the article read, "The individuals pictured are unrelated to the people or events described in this story." Id. at 122. Nevertheless, the court of appeals ruled that readers could reasonably draw the inference that plaintiff was sexually promiscuous, given the small size and placement of the disclaimer and the content of the publication as a whole.

In responding to the defendant's claim that the presence of an express disclaimer rendered any defamatory reading of the article necessarily incorrect, the court stated that "determining whether an allegedly defamatory statement can reasonably bear that construction as matter of law should not be confused with a search for its meaning in the objective sense." Id. at 127. So long as a "considerable and respectable segment of the community," id. at 128, would draw the inference, even if incorrectly, defamation may lie, and the decision is for the trier of fact.

A difficult problem is also presented when the defendant has made a defamatory statement about a group of which the plaintiff is a member. If the group is sufficiently small that the plaintiff is identifiable as the one defamed, then the action will be sustained. For instance, an allegedly defamed lawyer was ruled to be identifiable in a press release issued by a state court judge that had referred to a particular litigant's "stable of lawyers" and accused them of "a vitriolic campaign of judge-shopping" and "spurious and unethical legal actions and false allegations." Although not expressly named in the release, plaintiff was ruled identifiable because only six lawyers constituted the "stable." Yoder v. Workman, 224 F. Supp. 2d 1077 (S.D. W. Va. 2002). A larger group was involved in Fawcett Publications, Inc. v. Morris, 377 P.2d 42 (Okla. 1962), *cert. denied,* 376 U.S. 513 (1964). In this case, the plaintiff was permitted to recover based upon the statement that the football team of which he was a member used amphetamines, although there were 60 to 70 others on the team at the time. In Neiman-Marcus v. Lait, 13 F.R.D. 311 (S.D.N.Y. 1952), the defendants, in a book titled *U.S.A. Confidential,* asserted that the saleswomen in a large department store were call girls. There were 382 saleswomen in all, and the action was brought by 30 of them. In dismissing their complaint, the court said (13 F.R.D. at 316):

> [W]here the group or class disparaged is a large one, absent circumstances pointing to a particular plaintiff as the person defamed, no individual member of the group or class has a cause of action. . . .
>
> Giving the plaintiff saleswomen the benefit of all legitimate favorable inferences, the defendants' alleged libel cannot reasonably be said to concern more than the saleswomen as a class. There is no language referring to some ascertained or ascertainable person. Nor is the class so small that it follows that defamation of the class infects the individual of the class. This Court so holds as a matter of law since it is of the opinion that no reasonable man would take the writers seriously and conclude from the publication a reference to any individual saleswoman.

In search of a bright line rule, the court in Barger v. Playboy Enterprises, Inc., 564 F. Supp. 1151 (N.D. Cal. 1983), *aff'd,* 732 F.2d 163 (9th Cir.), *cert. denied,* 469 U.S. 853 (1984), stated that if the group is larger than 25, its members cannot recover based upon defamatory statements about the group. In this case, the article depicted the sexual activities of the "brides" and "mommas" of the members of the Hell's Angels motorcycle gang. In general, see Note, A Communitarian Defense of Group Libel Laws, 101 Harv. L. Rev. 682 (1988); Note, Group Defamation: Five Guiding Factors, 64 Tex. L. Rev. 591 (1985).

2. Remedies

a. Damages

The rules governing damages for defamation follow the classic division between compensatory and punitive damages. While the awarding of punitive damages proceeds along conventional lines, the awarding of compensatory damages does not. There are two categories of compensatory damages — special and general damages, both of which are defined in a way unique to the law of defamation. Furthermore, for some types of defamation, the plaintiff will not be able to recover unless there is proof of special damages. Thus, the rules of damages for defamation have importance not only in determining how much the plaintiff may recover, but also in determining whether he or she can recover at all.

(1) Special Damages

It is generally held that special damages are limited to pecuniary losses directly caused by the reaction of others to the defamatory statement. See Terwilliger v. Wands, 17 N.Y. 54 (1858), which, in spite of its age, is still a leading case on the point. Typical sources of special damages include loss of credit, or of a job, or of customers. Such damages do not arise because the plaintiff has been harmed emotionally, or even physically, but because others, motivated by the defamatory statement, have refused to do business with the plaintiff or the plaintiff has otherwise suffered identifiable economic harm.

(2) General Damages

If the plaintiff has shown special damages, or if the case is one in which there may be recovery without having to prove them, the plaintiff is entitled to recover general damages. General damages include the mental anguish and associated economic losses that are not included under special damages. In addition, general damages are presumed to flow from certain kinds of defamation, and little in the way of proof has to be presented to support an award. See Michael K. Steenson, Presumed Damages in Defamation Law, 40 Wm. Mitchell L. Rev. 1492 (2014). The extent of indefiniteness of proof permitted is illustrated by Judge Wyzanski's charge to the jury in Curley v. Curtis Publishing Co., 48 F. Supp. 29, 34, 35, 36 (D. Mass. 1942):

> In a libel suit, the appropriate measure of damages is the loss of reputation suffered by the plaintiff, the physical pain which he has suffered, and the mental anguish which he has suffered. . . .
>
> You are entitled to take into account the standing of the plaintiff in the community and group in which he moves. You are entitled to take into account the extent of the publication of which complaint is made. All those are proper elements. . . .
>
> As to damages — damages are an element about which a Judge has no better knowledge than a jury. You are practical men. You know what the consequences practically are of articles which are defamatory and not true or privileged, and articles which are defamatory and are malicious.
>
> [Y]our experience is sufficient to decide the matter, and twelve of you are much better estimators than I alone would be.

Because by their nature general damages cannot be established with precision, a court can exert little control over a jury's verdict. Unless the award shocks the judicial conscience or is the obvious result of passion or prejudice, reviewing courts are reluctant to overturn verdicts for such damages, whether the plaintiff complains that the award was inadequate or the defendant that it was excessive. See, e.g., Eulo v. Deval Aerodynamics, Inc., 47 F.R.D. 35 (E.D. Pa. 1969), *aff'd in part and rev'd in part,* 430 F.2d 325 (3d Cir. 1970), *cert. denied,* 401 U.S. 974 (1971) (jury is the "supreme arbiter" of damage awards in defamation cases, and the court would not overturn the jury's verdict of 6 cents on a $300,000 claim); Kansas Elec. Supply Co. v. Dun & Bradstreet, Inc., 448 F.2d 647 (10th Cir. 1971), *cert. denied,* 405 U.S. 1026 (1972) (the court was "extremely reluctant" to set aside the verdict of $100,000 even though no special damages were proven); and Time, Inc. v. Firestone, 424 U.S. 448 (1976) (the court had "no warrant" for reexamining a $100,000 award for plaintiff's "anxiety and concern" over an inaccurate report of the grounds for her divorce).

(3) Punitive Damages

If the plaintiff proves that the defendant published the defamatory statement with malice, the plaintiff may be entitled to punitive damages. The malice that must be proved has been called actual malice, express malice, or malice in fact, and it has been defined variously as bad faith, ill will, hatred, intent to injure, vindictiveness, and wanton or reckless indifference to the plaintiff's rights. Wrongful motive may be almost impossible to prove directly, and courts accept evidence of other matters as indicia of malice, such as the defendant's knowledge of the falsity of the statement or the failure to try to verify the truth of the statement, failure to publish a retraction, excessive publication of the statement, or the presence of an overall scheme of harassment. One explanation of punitive damages is contained in Reynolds v. Pegler, 123 F. Supp. 36 (S.D.N.Y. 1954). The plaintiff won a jury verdict of one dollar for compensatory damages and a total of $175,000 in punitive damages from three defendants. In denying the defendants' motion to set aside the verdict for punitive damages as excessive, the court stated (123 F. Supp. at 37-38):

> In effect, the defendants urge that the giving of punitive damages is dependent upon, and must bear relationship to, the allowance of actual damages. But the applicable law is to the contrary and is too firmly rooted to admit of argument. . . .
>
> To adopt the contrary view now urged by the defendants would mean that a defamer gains a measure of immunity no matter how venomous or malicious his attack simply because of the excellent reputation of the defamed; it would mean that the defamer, motivated by actual malice, becomes the beneficiary of that unassailable reputation and so escapes punishment. It would require punitive damages to be determined in inverse ratio to the reputation of the one defamed.

Query whether the court's analysis is in tension with the Supreme Court's more recent economic due process jurisprudence which encourages defendants to challenge the constitutionality of punitive damages awards based in part on their numerical relationship to plaintiffs' actual damages. See Chapter 8, Section B, above.

b. Retraction

Under the traditional common law rule, a demand by the plaintiff that the defendant retract the defamatory statement was not a prerequisite to recovery. But if the defendant published a retraction, this would be taken into account in calculating damages. Although some courts have held that a retraction may affect only punitive damages, most take it into account with respect to compensatory damages as well, reasoning that the harm caused by a false assertion may also be alleviated at least partially by a genuine retraction. In general, see Laurence H. Eldredge, The Law of Defamation 543-63 (1978).

A number of states have enacted retraction statutes applicable to news media. Some states, like California under Cal. Civ. Code §48a (West 2010), limit the plaintiff to actual damages unless a demanded retraction has not been published. Others, like Wisconsin under Wis. Stat. Ann. §895.05 (West 2011), make a demand for retraction a prerequisite for bringing the action. The constitutionality of retraction statutes has been attacked, with mixed results. The California statute was upheld in Werner v. Southern California Associated Newspapers, 216 P.2d 825 (Cal. 1950). The Montana statute, which requires a demand for retraction as a condition of bringing suit, was held unconstitutional in Madison v. Yunker, 589 P.2d 126 (Mont. 1978), under a state constitutional provision requiring that "a speedy remedy [be] afforded for every injury." A provision of the Arizona constitution that the "right of action to recover damages for injuries shall never be abrogated, and the amount recovered shall not be subject to any statutory limitation," was held to override that state's retraction statute in Boswell v. Phoenix Newspapers, 730 P.2d 186 (Ariz. 1986), *cert. denied,* 481 U.S. 1029 (1987).

c. Injunctions

Because First Amendment case law so disfavors prior restraints on the freedoms of speech and the press, injunctions against the publication of defamatory statements are generally not available. See Kramer v. Thompson, 947 F.2d 666 (3d Cir. 1991), *cert. denied,* 504 U.S. 940 (1992); 1 Rodney A. Smolla, Law of Defamation §9.88 (2001). In one unusual case, Lothschuetz v. Carpenter, 898 F.2d 1200 (6th Cir. 1990), the appeals court enjoined the further publication of a statement that had been judicially determined to be defamatory. But other courts have suggested that injunctive relief would not be available even as against the precise republication of a statement that had already been adjudicated libelous. See, e.g., Metropolitan Opera Ass'n, Inc. v. Local 100, Hotel Emps. & Rest. Emps. Int'l Union, 239 F.3d 172, 178 (2d Cir. 2001).

3. The Libel/Slander Distinction

As was stated at the beginning of the subsection on damages, for some types of defamation the plaintiff must prove special damages to recover at all. The principal distinction is between *slander* (oral defamation) and *libel* (written defamation). Subject to important exceptions, there can be no recovery for slander absent proof of special damages, whereas no such proof is necessary to recover for libel. Whatever the historical justifications for this distinction, it has come under strong fire. One critic is A. P. Herbert, who penned a series of fictional and humorous English cases and published them as The Uncommon Law (1935). In Chicken v. Ham, Mr. Herbert, writing as the Lord Chancellor, observed (p. 73):

> A layman, with the narrow outlook of a layman on these affairs, might rashly suppose that it is equally injurious to say at a public meeting, 'Mr. Chicken is a toad,' and to write upon a postcard, 'Mr. Chicken is a toad.' But the unselfish labours of generations of British jurists have discovered between the two some profound and curious distinctions. For example, in order to succeed in an action for slander the injured party must prove that he has suffered some actual and special damage, whereas the victim of a written defamation need not; so that we have this curious result, that in practice it is safer to insult a man at a public meeting than to insult him on a postcard, and that which is written in the corner of a letter is in law

> more deadly than that which is shouted from the house-tops. My Lords, it is not for us to boggle at the wisdom of our ancestors, and this is only one of a great body of juridical refinements handed down to us by them, without which few of our profession would be able to keep body and soul together.

In routine cases, the distinction between libel and slander, whether sensible or not, is easy enough to apply.[2] But modern electronic communication has added new dimensions. Motion pictures were absorbed into the law of libel without much difficulty. A film is printed, even if what the audience sees is a projection of the film. Radio and television, however, do not lend themselves so easily to classification. Videotaped and filmed programs on television would seem closely analogous to motion pictures, and some courts have held accompanying defamation to be libel. Live broadcasts are more difficult. They are oral and transitory, but have wide circulation, similar to newspapers and magazines. Predictably, different courts have reacted differently, some holding them to be slander, others libel. Some courts have introduced an additional refinement: If the words are off-the-cuff, the defamation is slander; if read from a script the defamation is libel. Section 568A of the Restatement (Second) of Torts, on the other hand, characterizes all broadcast defamation as libel, whether read from a script or not. Some states have dealt with the problem by statute.

a. Slander

There can be no recovery for slander absent proof of special damage, unless what the defendant has said falls into a category of slander per se. The theory behind making some statements actionable per se is that some charges are so serious that harm to the plaintiff's reputation resulting in economic loss is almost certain to follow. The four traditional categories of slander per se are:

(1) Statements that the plaintiff has committed a crime. In general, not any crime will do. American courts usually take the position that the crime must be serious, one involving moral turpitude. Section 571 of the Restatement (Second) of Torts provides that the crime must be punishable by imprisonment in a state or federal institution or be regarded by the public as involving moral turpitude. Comment *g* defines *moral turpitude* as "shameful wickedness, so extreme a departure from ordinary standards of honesty, good morals, justice or ethics as to be shocking to the moral sense of the community." The illustrative offenses included in the comment range from those commonly considered grievous, such as treason, murder, arson, rape, criminal assault, and kidnapping, to those which are less abhorrent, such as bootlegging or filing fraudulent tax returns.

(2) Statements that the plaintiff has a loathsome disease. There are not many diseases that would lead people to regard the plaintiff with sufficient revulsion to justify the presumption of economic loss. In 1863, the Supreme Judicial Court of Massachusetts, in "George, The Count Joannes" v. Burt, 88 Mass. (6 Allen) 236, 239 (1863), stated that there were only three: "An action for oral slander, in charging the plaintiff with disease, has been confined to the imputation of such loathsome and infectious maladies as would make him an object of disgust and aversion, and banish him from human society. We believe the only examples which adjudged cases furnish are the plague, leprosy, and venereal disorders."

Like the claim that plaintiff has a particular sexual orientation, the accusation of diseased status raises questions about whether the touchstone for reputational harm should be the

2. The summary in this paragraph is based on Rodney A. Smolla, Law of Defamation §1.14 (2001).

actual perceptions of the community or the perceptions we would like to believe represent our community and its values. For instance, during the 1990s, commentators wondered whether "AIDS [has] replaced leprosy as a 'loathsome disease' . . . or are we now too enlightened to attach a social stigma to any disease?" Robert M. Ackerman, Bringing Coherence to Defamation Law Through Uniform Legislation: The Search for an Elegant Solution, 72 N.C. L. Rev. 291, 296 n.13 (1994). In McCune v. Neitzel, 457 N.W.2d 803 (Neb. 1990), the trial judge ruled that a statement that the plaintiff had AIDS was slander per se. The defendant did not appeal from the ruling. See also Karen M. Markin, Still Crazy After All These Years: The Enduring Defamatory Power of Mental Disorder, 29 L. & Psychol. Rev. 155 (2005), in which the author argues that the continuing social and cultural stigmatization of mental illness leads courts to find claims that an individual suffers from mental illness to be defamatory.

(3) Statements damaging to one's business, trade, or profession. The presumption that the plaintiff has suffered economic loss as a direct result of the defamation has its strongest logical justification in this category. A person's reputation is important to business, and loss of business is likely to follow when that reputation is disparaged. Thus, accusations that the plaintiff is a bad credit risk, or is dishonest, or mismanages business affairs are actionable without proof of special damages. For example, in Demers v. Meuret, 512 P.2d 1348 (Or. 1973), a statement that the plaintiff, an airport manager, was "a demented old man" who "might come out and chop up our airplanes with an axe" was held to be slander per se. See also Dugan v. Mittal Steel USA Inc., 929 N.E.2d 184 (Ind. 2010) (a supervisor's accusations of fraud or theft by plaintiff former employee to co-workers constituted defamation per se). The defamatory statement must relate to the plaintiff's qualifications to conduct his business, or to the way he conducts it. Thus, in Liberman v. Gelstein, 605 N.E.2d 344 (N.Y. 1992), statements by a tenant that his landlord "threw a punch at me," "called my daughter a slut," and "threatened to kill me" were held not to be slander per se because the statements were unrelated to the plaintiff as a landlord. See also Rufeh v. Schwartz, 858 N.Y.S.2d 194 (App. Div. 2008) (holding that a prospective home seller's statement to a school superintendant that the plaintiff buyer's children were unfit to attend was too broad to constitute slander per se to the plaintiff's business, trade, or profession).

(4) Statements that a woman is unchaste. This category of slander per se was late in developing, having been created by statute in Victorian England in 1891 following a period of intense social scrutiny of female sexual behavior. Many states have followed the English lead, sometimes by statute, other times by judicial decision. Men are not protected by this rule, raising questions about its continued viability in the wake of numerous Supreme Court cases striking down sex- or gender-based classifications on equal protection grounds. Oddly, no recent cases seem to have directly addressed the question. But see Sauerhoff v. Hearst Corp., 388 F. Supp. 117 (D. Md. 1974) (upholding female-specific slander per se doctrine in the face of male plaintiff's constitutional challenge). Comment *c* to §574 of the Restatement (Second) of Torts suggests that the distinction between males and females may be unconstitutional, but does not speculate whether, if it is unconstitutional, the rule will be extended to males, or the category abandoned altogether.

b. Libel

The rule that proof of special damages is not needed to support recovery in libel is modified in some states by the libel per quod-libel per se distinction. In states distinguishing between the two kinds of libel, only libel per se is actionable without proof of special damages. To constitute libel per se, the statement must be defamatory on its face. See, e.g., Monroe-Trice v. UNUM, 2002 WL 483312 (S.D.N.Y. 2002) (statements in disability insurance doctor's report that referred to plaintiff's interaction with prostitutes constituted libel per se; thus, plaintiff need not prove special damages). If there is need to look outside the statement for facts which will make it defamatory, it is libel per quod, and the plaintiff must show special damage to recover.

There is some disagreement among commentators as to whether the majority of American jurisdictions observe the "libel per se"/"libel per quod" distinction or follow the English rule that special damages do not have to be proven in libel actions. Commentators also disagree about which view is the better rule of law. The original torts Restatement makes no note of the diverging course set by some American courts and points instead to the justifications for the English rule. See Restatement of Torts, §569, cmt. *b.* The Restatement (Second) calls the "libel per se"/"libel per quod" distinction a minority view and observes that the rule's principal justification has been preempted by recent constitutional decisions. See Restatement (Second) of Torts §569, cmt. *b.* For the view that most states allow recovery in a libel action without proof of special damage and that this is the preferable position, see Lawrence H. Eldredge, The Spurious Rule of Libel per Quod, 79 Harv. L. Rev. 733 (1966). For the view that most states observe the "libel per se"/ "libel per quod" distinction and that it is the better mode of analysis, see William L. Prosser, More Libel per Quod, 79 Harv. L. Rev. 1629 (1966). The two positions are discussed in Francis D. Murnaghan, From Figment to Fiction to Philosophy—The Requirement of Proof of Damages in Libel Actions, 22 Cath. U. L. Rev. 1 (1972), in which the author concludes that there should be no recovery for general, unproven damages in any case.

4. Publication

To satisfy the requirement of publication, the plaintiff must show that the defamatory statement has been communicated by the defendant to a third person. The person who publishes the statement is liable even if it is a mere report of something heard from someone else. This is so even if the source of the story is carefully identified. Conversely, a person is generally not liable for another voluntary and unauthorized repetition of defamatory matter unless the republication was the natural and probable consequence of the original communication. For example, in Oberman v. Dun & Bradstreet, Inc., 586 F.2d 1173 (7th Cir. 1978), a credit reporting agency was held not liable for defamatory material in a confidential report issued to a bank when a realty company obtained the report through a bank director who was a salesman for the realty company. The court ruled that it was not foreseeable that a confidential report would fall into the hands of a third party in this way.

A number of cases have arisen in which the defendant has written a letter to the plaintiff containing defamatory material, and the plaintiff has shown the letter to another. In general, the courts have concluded that the publication in this circumstance is made by the plaintiff rather than the defendant. But there are occasions in which the defendant will be responsible for the publication, despite the plaintiff's involvement. In Hedgpeth v. Coleman, 111 S.E. 517 (N.C. 1922), the defendant sent a letter to the plaintiff, a 14-year-old boy, accusing him of theft. The plaintiff showed the letter to his brother, who in turn showed it to their father. The court held the defendant responsible for the communication of the letter to the plaintiff's brother and father.

One "self-publication" context arising with increasing frequency involves a discharged employee's disclosure to a prospective employer of the grounds for the discharge. Holding that the former employer may be a publisher of the employee's statement of the grounds for the discharge are Churchey v. Adolph Coors Co., 759 P.2d 1336 (Colo. 1988), and Lewis v. Equitable Life Assurance Society, 389 N.W.2d 876 (Minn. 1986). In so ruling, the court in *Churchey* stated (759 P.2d at 1345):

> When the originator of the statement reasonably can foresee that the defamed person will be compelled to repeat a defamatory statement to a third party, there is a strong causal link between the originator's actions and the harm caused to the defamed person; this causal connection makes the imposition of liability reasonable. If publication could be based on the defamed person's freely-made decision to repeat a defamatory remark, however, the defendant would be held liable for damages which the plaintiff reasonably could have avoided. . . . Imposing liability for self-publication which is "likely" but not compelled would unnecessarily deter such communication.

Subsequently, the Colorado and Minnesota legislatures enacted statutes barring actions based on self-publication in this context. See Minn. Stat. §181.933 (d) (2016); Colo. Rev. Stat. §13-25-125.5 (2016). More recent judicial opinions seem to have joined this tide against the tort of compelled self-defamation. See Cweklinsky v. Mobil Chemical Co., 837 A.2d 759 (Conn. 2004), in which the court reviewed existing case law and concluded, "public policy concerns favor the rejection of the doctrine of compelled self-publication defamation." Courts have taken different positions with respect to intrabusiness communications. Some courts have held that there is no publication when the communication takes place between persons within a business unit who are legitimately concerned with the matter being communicated. See, e.g., Mims v. Metropolitan Life Ins. Co., 200 F.2d 800 (5th Cir. 1952), *cert. denied,* 345 U.S. 940 (1953); Rowe v. Isbell, 599 So. 2d 35 (Ala. 1992). Other courts have held that there is a publication under these circumstances, and handle the matter as one involving a qualified privilege. See, e.g., Bals v. Verduzco, 600 N.E.2d 1353 (Ind. 1992). What if the communication is by the defendant to the plaintiff's agent? The court in Reece v. Finch, 562 So. 2d 195 (Ala. 1990), held that there was no publication.

One who "disseminates" as opposed to "publishes" a defamatory statement may escape liability. *Disseminators* are those who distribute the material, but who have no effective control over its content, such as newspaper distributors, libraries, and telephone companies. According to §581 of the Restatement (Second) of Torts, one who "delivers or transmits defamatory matter published by a third person is subject to liability if, but only if, he knows or has reason to know of its defamatory character." This section also states that television and radio broadcasters are considered publishers, rather than disseminators.

A more recent issue is how to characterize Internet service providers. Although this question was initially heavily contested in the courts, Congress settled the issue in 1996 when it enacted the Communications Decency Act (CDA). Section 230 of the act expressly provides that "no provider or user of an interactive computer service shall be treated as the publisher or speaker of any information provided by another information content provider." 47 U.S.C. §230(c)(1). Zeran v. America Online, Inc., 129 F.3d 327 (4th Cir. 1997), *cert. denied,* 324 U.S. 937 (1998), was the first reported case to interpret the act. The case arose when the provider failed to remove certain joke advertisements, posted anonymously, that named plaintiff as the vendor of T-shirts bearing offensive and tasteless slogans regarding the bombing of the Oklahoma City federal building. While the act clearly immunized publishers, the plaintiff argued that AOL was a distributor, and that distributor liability remained intact under the statute. The court disagreed: "Assuming arguendo that Zeran has satisfied the [knowledge] requirements for imposition of distributor liability, this theory of liability is merely a subset, or a species, of publisher liability, and is therefore also foreclosed by §230." 129 F.3d at 332. See also Noah v. AOL Time Warner, Inc., 261 F. Supp. 2d 532 (E.D. Va. 2003) (applying *Zeran*).

Blumenthal v. Drudge, 992 F. Supp. 44 (D.D.C. 1998), illustrates the broad immunity granted by the CDA. The case involved a defamation suit against AOL and Internet gossip columnist Matt Drudge brought by a White House aide. The court held AOL immune from suit under the CDA where, unlike *Zeran,* the statements in question were not posted by an anonymous individual. Indeed, AOL had contracted with and compensated the gossip columnist; had retained certain editorial rights, including the right to require changes in content and to remove it; and had affirmatively promoted the columnist as a new source of unverified instant gossip. See also Nemet Chevrolet, Ltd. v. Consumeraffairs.com, Inc., 591 F.3d 250 (4th Cir. 2009) (defendant interactive website provider was not liable for defamatory posts about plaintiff automobile dealership). In Batzel v. Smith, 333 F.3d 1018 (9th Cir. 2003), the appeals court afforded immunity to the moderator of a listserv and website operator who posted an allegedly defamatory e-mail authored by a third party, even though the third party told defendant that he would not have forwarded the message had he known it would be posted. On the other hand, as one recent court reminded, "No case of which this court is aware has immunized a defendant from allegations that *it* created tortious content." Anthony v. Yahoo Inc., 421 F. Supp. 2d 1257, 1262-63 (N.D. Cal. 2006) (refusing to dismiss claim that defendant Yahoo Inc. includes fake, expired, and otherwise misleading personal ads in its online dating service). Although §230 of the CDA immunizes online publishers of third-party content, there may still be valid contract claims for detrimental reliance in failing to remove defamatory content. In Barnes v. Yahoo!, Inc., 570 F.3d 1096 (9th Cir. 2009), the plaintiff sought to cancel fraudulently created indecent profiles, which included nude photographs of the plaintiff, posted by her ex-boyfriend. Yahoo! took approximately two months to remove the profiles, even though Barnes contacted Yahoo! several times and followed official Yahoo! protocol in making her requests. Barnes sued Yahoo! for failing to remove the content after being notified, thus "treat[ing] Yahoo not as a publisher, but rather as one who undertook to perform a service and did it negligently." Id. at 1102. The district court granted Yahoo!'s motion to dismiss under §230 of the CDA, and the Ninth Circuit agreed that a claim for negligent undertaking was still protected under the act. Id. at 1105-06. Nevertheless, the Ninth Circuit remanded the case under a promissory estoppel theory for failing to remove the profile. Id. at 1108-09. How, if at all, are the effects on a potential victim from breach of a promise not to publish different from a decision to publish, which is immunized by the CDA? The court also notes that §230 of the CDA was intended to immunize any defendant who otherwise could be treated as a publisher for purposes of liability. The plaintiff's promissory estoppel theory seems to treat Yahoo! as a publisher, because only a publisher could meaningfully make, and break, a promise to remove the offending material. This case may signal a certain amount of judicial discontent with the breadth of the CDA, particularly given the prevalence of online harassment.

Another complex problem in the law of defamation that is exacerbated in the online context involves multiple publications in newspapers and magazines. Traditionally, each successive republication of a defamatory statement constitutes a separate tort. With the onset of mass communications, most states continued to apply the same rule to multiple but simultaneous publications, a development that had significant implications for statute of limitations purposes and that exposed media defendants to potentially endless litigation. The modern trend is instead toward a "single publication" rule, under which a statement is considered to be a new publication, giving rise to an additional cause of action, only if it constitutes a new "edition" of the original statement. In Firth v. State, 775 N.E.2d 463 (N.Y. 2002), the New York Court of Appeals applied the single publication rule to an allegedly defamatory report posted on an Internet site, rejecting the plaintiff's argument that each "hit" or viewing of the online report constituted a new publication. The court also held that adding an unrelated report to the same site did not constitute a new edition for purposes of the single publication rule, because viewing such modifications as new editions "would either discourage the placement of information on the Internet or slow the exchange of such information, reducing the Internet's advantages." Id. at 467. See also Clark v. Viacom Int'l Inc., 617 F. App'x 495, 503 (6th Cir. 2015) (observing that "[a]fter *Firth*, no other court in the country has failed to extend the single publication rule to the online domain"). Obviously, when publication occurs in more than one state, very difficult conflict of law problems are presented. See Luther L. McDougal III, Robert L. Felix & Ralph U. Whitten, American Conflicts Law 454-55 (5th ed. 2001).

For a sampling of the extensive commentary generated by the topic of defamation law and the Internet, see Bryant Storm, The Man Behind the Mask: Defamed Without a Remedy, 33 N. Ill. U. L. Rev. 393 (2013); Jeff Kosseff, Defending Section 230: The Value of Intermediary Immunity, 15 J. Tech. L. & Pol'y 123 (2010); Jae Hong Lee, Batzel v. Smith & Barrett v. Rosenthal: Defamation Liability For Third-Party Content on the Internet, 19 Berkeley Tech. L.J. 469 (2004); Michael Hadley, The Gertz Doctrine and Internet Defamation, 84 Va. L. Rev. 477 (1998); David R. Sheridan, Zeran v. AOL and the Effect of Section 230 of the Communications Decency Act upon Liability for Defamation on the Internet, 61 Alb. L. Rev. 147 (1997).

5. The Basis of Liability

The traditional basis of liability in defamation can be put briefly: Aside from the malice necessary to defeat a conditional privilege, liability, with two exceptions, is strict, and the state of the defendant's mind is irrelevant.[3] The plight of the defendant in Cassidy v. Daily Mirror Newspapers, Ltd., [1929] 2 K.B. 331, p. 781, above, illustrates this. Cassidy, who was also known as Corrigan, was well known in racing circles as a bon vivant and womanizer. At one racing meet, he posed for a photographer with a woman whom he identified as his betrothed. He gave the photographer permission to announce the engagement. The photographer sent the photograph to the defendant's newspaper, which published it with the caption "Mr. M. Corrigan, the race horse owner, and [Miss X] whose engagement has been announced. . . ." The court affirmed a judgment entered on a jury verdict for the plaintiff, Cassidy's wife, notwithstanding that defendant did not know the fact which made the publication libelous, stating (2 K.B. at 341-42):

> It is said that this decision would seriously interfere with the reasonable conduct of newspapers. I do not agree. If publishers of newspapers, who have no more rights than private persons, publish statements which may be defamatory of other people, without inquiry as to their truth, in order to make their paper attractive, they must take the consequences, if on subsequent inquiry, their statements are found to be untrue or capable of defamatory and

3. Reflecting the strict liability core of the libel action, the law in this area has been stated by one court as follows: "The question . . . is not who was aimed at, but who was hit." Laudati v. Stea, 117 Atl. 422, 424 (R.I. 1922).

> unjustifiable inferences. . . . To publish statements and inquire into their truth afterwards, may seem attractive and up to date. Only to publish after inquiry may be slow, but at any rate it would lead to accuracy and reliability.

In reaching its decision, the court relied on the classic strict liability case, E. Hulton & Co. v. Jones, [1910] A.C. 20. There the defendant printed a story in its newspaper written by a Paris correspondent, which in part ran:

> 'Whist! there is Artemus Jones with a woman who is not his wife, who must be, you know — the other thing!' whispers a fair neighbor of mine excitedly to her bosom friend's ear. Really, is it not surprising how certain of our fellow-countrymen behave when they come abroad? Who would suppose by his goings on, that he is a churchwarden at Peckham?

The plaintiff was Thomas Artemus Jones, not of Peckham but from North Wales; nor was he a churchwarden. But he did produce witnesses who testified that they read the article and thought it referred to the plaintiff. Both the trial court and the House of Lords on appeal accepted the defendant's assertion that he had never heard of the plaintiff and had used "Artemus Jones" as a fictitious name. Nonetheless, judgment for the plaintiff on the jury verdict was affirmed. Lord Loreburn's opinion states, in part (id. at 23-24):

> A person charged with libel cannot defend himself by shewing that he intended in his own breast not to defame, or that he intended not to defame the plaintiff, if in fact he did both. He has none the less imputed something disgraceful and has none the less injured the plaintiff. A man in good faith may publish a libel believing it to be true, and it may be found by the jury that he acted in good faith believing it to be true, and reasonably believing it to be true, but that in fact the statement was false. Under those circumstances he has no defence to the action, however excellent his intention.

One exception to strict liability relates to publication. The defendant is not liable absent intent to publish or negligence in publishing. For example, if the defendant accuses the plaintiff of something that is defamatory with the intent that no one other than the plaintiff hear it, the defendant is not liable if it is overheard without negligence on the defendant's part. Thus, in Harbridge v. Greyhound Lines, Inc., 294 F. Supp. 1059 (E.D. Pa. 1969), it was held that the defendant was not liable for an allegedly defamatory statement to the plaintiff's wife in a telephone conversation with the plaintiff, when the wife, unknown to the defendant, was listening in on the plaintiff's telephone.

6. Defenses

The law of defamation has developed a highly technical and labyrinthine set of defenses with which the defendant can meet the plaintiff's equally technical and labyrinthine prima facie case. These defenses include that the publication of the defamatory statement was privileged and that the statement is true.

a. Privilege

The privilege to publish a defamatory statement may be either absolute or qualified. Both are complete defenses, but the latter may be lost under some circumstances, while the former cannot be lost at all. The defendant with an absolute privilege can, without liability, publish a statement known to be false and do it with the most evil of intentions. As might be expected, this complete immunity from liability will not be lightly granted and is generally limited to situations in which the communication is with the consent of the plaintiff, or is by a government official in the performance of governmental duties, or is between husband and wife, or is a broadcast required under various state and federal "equal time" statutes.

The defendant is free to publish a defamatory statement about the plaintiff if the latter has consented to it. In Cassidy v. Daily Mirror Newspapers, Ltd., p. 822 above, for instance, Cassidy himself could not recover since he was the source of the story and solicited its publication. One recurring problem is the letter of recommendation. The plaintiff who asks the defendant for such a letter does not necessarily consent to the inclusion of defamatory material. But if the plaintiff knows or has reason to believe that the defendant will include such material, it is arguable that there is consent. Such a situation might arise when the defendant, a former employer perhaps, has derogatory information that the plaintiff should expect the defendant to include in any reference letter. Richardson v. Gunby, 127 P. 533 (Kan. 1912), illustrates how fine the line can get. The plaintiff requested one Neal to ask the defendant for information concerning a cement company, where the plaintiff was the secretary, and its officers. Defendant responded with a letter stating, "no one locally has any faith in the integrity or ability of its officers. Its secretary is regarded as one of the most tricky men in this community and a good man to leave strictly alone, and all of his projects." In a suit for libel based on this letter, the defendant argued that the plaintiff could not recover because he solicited the letter for the purpose of creating a cause of action, and thus consented to its publication. The court stated that this was correct as far as it went, but added the following qualification (127 P. at 536):

> If, however, the plaintiff instigated or set on foot the inquiry for the purpose of ascertaining whether the defendant . . . was disseminating evil reports concerning the cement company or its officers, in order that such influences might be counteracted, or for any other proper purpose, and not for the purpose of predicating an action for damages in his own behalf, he was not estopped from maintaining an action.

Consent to defamatory statements may also be based on contract, as in Joftes v. Kaufman, 324 F. Supp. 660 (D.D.C. 1971). In this case, the court ruled that the plaintiff consented to the publications of allegedly defamatory letters explaining reasons for the plaintiff's discharge from his employment, the letters having been sent pursuant to a contractual grievance procedure initiated by the plaintiff.

The most important absolute privilege is extended to parties involved in the conduct of government affairs, whether they exercise a judicial, legislative, or executive function. This privilege rests on the notion that free expression and full disclosure of information is so essential to the proper functioning of governmental processes that it outweighs any private interest in reputation. Thus, it is usually held that the official participants in a judicial proceeding—judge, jury, attorneys, litigating parties, and witnesses—may make defamatory statements with impunity before and during a judicial proceeding as long as the statements relate to some part of the proceeding. See, e.g., Bochetto v. Gibson, 860 A.2d 67, 71 (Pa. 2004) (defendant is entitled to absolute immunity for "communications which are issued in the regular course of judicial proceedings and which are pertinent and material to the redress or relief sought"). Thus, in Harris v. Riggenbach, 633 N.W.2d 193 (S.D. 2001), an attorney's affidavit submitted in litigation was absolutely privileged, even though the plaintiff asserted that the attorney acted in bad faith in submitting the affidavit. See also Simms v. Seaman, 129 Conn. App 651 (2011) (defendant attorney was held immune from liability for his misstatement of material fact during postjudgment proceedings that resulted in defamation to the plaintiff).

The privilege attending communications made in the course of judicial proceedings is generally extended to those made in administrative proceedings of a judicial or quasi-judicial nature, such as medical board investigations and teacher decertification proceedings. One court, Carradine v. State, 511 N.W.2d 733 (Minn. 1994), has extended the privilege to statements made by police officers, whether spoken during an arrest or written in an arrest report. See also Lutz v. Nelson, 788 N.W.2d 58 (Minn. 2010) (the court extended privilege against defamation suits to members of a watershed board conducting an investigation); Hagberg v. California Fed. Bank FSB, 81 P.3d 244 (Cal. 2004) (construing state statutory privilege to immunize statements made when citizen contacts law enforcement personnel to report suspected criminal activity); Oritz v. Delaware River Port Auth., No. 09-6062, 2010 WL 1994911 (E.D. Pa. May 17, 2010) (citizens' statements made to initiate an internal investigation were held to be both issued as a matter of regular course of the proceedings and material to the proceedings and thus enjoyed an "absolute privilege," shielding the citizens from a defamation claim). The privilege also extends to "fair and accurate" republications. In Sahara Gaming Corp. v. Culinary Workers Union Local 226, 984 P.2d 164 (Nev. 1999), the court held that the republication of the allegations of a complaint were privileged, even if the republication was made with the intent to cause damage to the plaintiff. The privilege may also apply to somewhat peripheral documents. Thus, in Butler v. Hearst-Argyle Television, Inc., 49 S.W.3d 116 (Ark. 2001), the court extended the privilege to an affidavit filed in connection with a motion to recuse a prosecutor involved in the underlying case. However, most courts require that the reproduced document must in some way directly connect with a proceeding. See, e.g., Lindeman v. Lesnick, 604 S.E.2d 55 (2004) (refusing to apply absolute privilege to statements made in a memorandum concerning a workers' compensation claim when no claim had been filed with the workers' compensation commission).

The privilege is also available to members of state and national legislatures while they are functioning as such. It has been embodied in Article I, Section 6 of the Constitution of the United States: ". . . and for any Speech or Debate in either House, [the Senators and Representatives of Congress] shall not be questioned in any other Place." Section 590 of the Restatement (Second) states that "[a] member of the Congress of the United States or of a State or local legislative body is absolutely privileged to publish defamatory matter concerning another in the performance of his legislative functions." The privilege is not limited to floor debates on proposed legislation, but extends to all legislative branch activity. Thus, in Whalen v. Hanley, 63 P.3d 254 (Alaska 2003), the court afforded legislative immunity to state representatives who had questioned the activity of executive branch officials during committee meetings. The absolute privilege has also been extended to witnesses in legislative proceedings, so long as the testimony relates to the legislative proceedings. See Riddle v. Perry, 40 P.3d 1128 (Utah 2002); Restatement (Second) of Torts §590A.

For executive and administrative officers of state and federal governments, courts traditionally drew no distinction between public officials and private individuals. In Barr v. Matteo, 360 U.S. 564 (1959), however, the Supreme Court held that an absolute privilege should attach so long as the challenged statements or actions were taken "within the outer perimeter of [the official's] line of duty." In Westfall v. Erwin, 484 U.S. 292, 297-98 (1988), the Supreme Court substantially narrowed this official immunity defense, holding that federal employees could not assert immunity from liability for common law torts unless the conduct at issue was discretionary in nature. Congress responded by passing the Westfall Act, H.R. Rep. No. 700, 100th Cong., 2d Sess. 3-4 (1988), reprinted in 1988 U.S.C.C.A.N. 5945, 5946-47, which amended the Federal Tort Claims Act to provide immunity to all federal employees for common law torts committed within the scope of their employment, instead providing that the exclusive remedy for such torts is through an action against the United States.

Although Barr v. Matteo stated that the privilege attaches to federal officials no matter how minor their governmental role, many states limit their own common law tort immunity to top officials. Additionally, most states extend qualified immunity only to state officials; thus, "a public official is shielded from liability only when discretionary acts within the scope of the official's authority are done in good faith and are not malicious or corrupt." Aspen Exploration Corp. v. Sheffield, 739 P.2d 150 (Alaska 1987). The *Aspen Exploration* court decided to adopt a middle course between these two approaches, extending absolute immunity to some, but not all, state officials, based on the following factors (id. at 159-60):

(1) The nature and importance of the function that the officer performed to the administration of government (i.e., the importance to the public that this function be performed; that it be performed correctly; that it be performed according to the best judgment of the officer unimpaired by extraneous matters);
(2) The likelihood that the officer will be subjected to frequent accusations of wrongful motives and how easily the officer can defend against these allegations; and
(3) The availability to the injured party of other remedies or other forms of relief (i.e. whether the injured party can obtain some other kind of judicial review of the correctness or validity of the officer's action).

Most of the cases dealing with communications between husband and wife have concluded that there is no publication. These cases have rested on the ancient fiction that the husband and wife are one, and that one cannot publish to oneself. A more likely explanation, however, is that courts believe that the marital relationship should be a private one, unencumbered by potential interference from the state in the form of ex post scrutiny of spousal communications. For a discussion of the history of the husband and wife privilege in defamation law, see Laurence H. Eldredge, The Law of Defamation 416-417 (1978). For influential accounts of the dichotomy between public and private spheres and how it has manifested itself generally in American law and culture, see Catharine A. MacKinnon, Toward a Feminist Theory of the State (1989); Alan Freeman & Elizabeth Mensch, The Public-Private Distinction in American Law and Life, 36 Buff. L. Rev. 237 (1987); Frances Olsen, The Family and the Market: A Study of Ideology and Legal Reform, 96 Harv. L. Rev. 1497 (1983); Symposium, The Public/Private Distinction, 130 U. Pa. L. Rev. 1289 (1982).

Under the Federal Communications Act of 1934 (47 U.S.C.A. §315), a radio or television broadcaster who permits a candidate for public office to use its station for campaign purposes must afford equal broadcasting opportunity to other candidates for the same office. This statute also prohibits the broadcaster from censoring the material so broadcast. The Supreme Court ruled in Farmers' Educational & Coop. Union v. WDAY, Inc., 360 U.S. 525 (1959), that the broadcaster is absolutely immune from liability for defamatory statements made during equal time broadcasts.

Beyond those occasions calling for an absolute immunity from liability, there are many situations in which it is appropriate to afford a more limited protection to the publication of defamatory matter. For instance, the qualified privilege of the defendant to publish defamatory statements for self-protection is somewhat analogous to the privileges of self-defense and defense of property. It is proper for the defendant to protect against the plaintiff's statement by calling the plaintiff a liar, but only if that statement serves to explain the plaintiff's motives. Thus, if the plaintiff accused the defendant of embezzlement, it would be proper for the defendant to state the plaintiff is the embezzler and is trying to cover up his own crime. It would be improper for the defendant to add that the plaintiff is a horse thief who for that reason cannot be believed. As to the nature of the privilege of reply, see generally Annotation, 41 A.L.R.3d 1083 (1972).

Marking out the limits of qualified privileges based on the interests of the audience in hearing a communication has been particularly troublesome. Generally, the privilege is not available to the idle gossip or the self-appointed watchdog of the community's morals. Thus, In Watt v. Longsdon, [1930] 1 K.B. 103 (Ct. App.), a letter from a friend of the plaintiff and his wife to the wife detailing the plaintiff's extramarital activities was not privileged. Factors that are likely to be important in finding a qualified privilege are whether the defendant is a relative or personal adviser to the person to whom he communicates the information, and whether the defendant has been asked for the information. But the cases do not fall into any clear pattern. The Restatement (Second) of Torts is a satisfactory statement of the privilege:

§595. Protection of Interest of Recipient or a Third Person

(1) An occasion makes a publication conditionally privileged if the circumstances induce a correct or reasonable belief that

(a) there is information that affects a sufficiently important interest of the recipient or a third person, and

(b) the recipient is one to whom the publisher is under a legal duty to publish the defamatory matter or is a person to whom its publication is otherwise within the generally accepted standards of decent conduct.

(2) In determining whether a publication is within generally accepted standards of decent conduct it is an important factor that

(a) the publication is made in response to a request rather than volunteered by the publisher or

(b) a family or other relationship exists between the parties.

Cases in which this privilege has been found to exist are Lester v. Powers, 596 A.2d 65 (Me. 1991) (communication from alumna of college to college in connection with tenure review process of alumna's former teacher), and McClure v. American Family Mutual Ins. Co., 223 F.3d 845 (8th Cir. 2000) (communications about insurer's agents to other agents, clients, and the public). In addition, numerous examples exist of situations in which the publisher and the audience share a common interest. Thus, in Gohari v. Darvish, 767 A.2d 321 (Md. 2001), the court held that a communication from a franchisee to his franchisor about a former employee of the franchisee was privileged. The former employee had applied for a franchise from the franchisor, and the communication was in response to an inquiry by the franchisor.

A somewhat narrower privilege applies to public statements about matters of public concern. The general rule is that fair comment on such matters as current political issues and endeavors in the arts, sciences, and sports are privileged insofar as the comment is one of opinion. See Leddy v. Narragansett Television, L.P., 843 A.2d 481, 488 (R.I. 2004) (defendant television station's "implied opinion that plaintiff was 'ripping off the system' by accepting a tax-free disability pension while collecting a salary for working at a full-time job constituted fair comment on a matter of public interest, based on the disclosed and nondefamatory fact that plaintiff was collecting a municipal disability pension while working as a fire investigator for the state"). Although the privilege does not extend to misstatements of fact, it has not always been easy to distinguish between opinion and fact for the purpose of this rule. For example, in Piscatelli v. Smith, 12 A.3d 164 (Md. Ct. Spec. App. 2011), *cert. granted*, 20 A.3d 115 (Md.), a newspaper article suggesting plaintiff's involvement in a double murder was held to be an expression of opinion; and in Myers v. Boston Magazine Co., 403 N.E.2d 376 (Mass. 1980), a statement that the plaintiff is "the only sportscaster in town enrolled in a course in remedial speaking" was at most an opinion that his reading style needed improvement. On the other hand, in Eikhoff v. Gilbert, 83 N.W. 110 (Mich. 1900), a statement that a candidate for the state legislature had "championed measures opposed to the moral interests of the community" was held to be an assertion of fact. A minority of states have extended the fair comment privilege to include statements of fact, at least under some circumstances. See Coleman v. MacLennan, 98 Pac. 281 (Kan. 1908); Dairy Stores, Inc. v. Sentinel Publishing Co., 516 A.2d 220 (N.J. 1986).

In recent years, nearly half of the states have enacted "anti-SLAPP" (Strategic Lawsuits Against Public Participation) statutes. See Public Participation Project, http://www.anti-slapp.org/your-states-free-speech-protection/ (last visited October 28, 2016). These statutes are designed to permit citizens to petition governmental bodies on issues of public concern without fear that they might be sued in retaliation by interested parties. A typical example of a SLAPP would be a suit brought by a large land developer against environmental or neighborhood associations opposed to the developer's plans, where the developer's goal is not necessarily to prevail as a legal matter, but rather to deter opposition by making it expensive and discomforting. The term SLAPP was coined by two University of Denver professors, and arose out of their ten-year interdisciplinary study of politically motivated litigation. See Penelope Canan & George W. Pring, Studying Strategic Lawsuits Against Public Participation: Mixing Quantitative and Qualitative Approaches, 22 L. & Soc'y Rev. 385 (1988). Although scholars have debated the actual incidence and severity of SLAPPs, see Note, The Legal Literature on SLAPPs: A Look Behind the Smoke Nine Years After Professors Pring and Canan First Yelled "Fire!," 9 U. Fla. J.L. & Pub. Pol'y 85 (1997), the impression remains widely shared that public involvement in politically contested matters may be chilled by the threat of frivolous defamation or other tort suits brought by well-heeled plaintiffs.

The qualified privilege to publish defamatory matter may be lost if the defendant abuses it. Courts generally assert that the privilege will be defeated only if the defendant is guilty of actual malice — ill will toward the plaintiff or reckless indifference to the plaintiff's rights. But it is clear that the courts have used this term much more loosely. According to §§599-605 of the Restatement of Torts, the privilege is abused if the defendant does not believe in the truth of the defamatory matter, or even if believing it, does not have reasonable grounds for the belief. The privilege may also be forfeited if in publishing the defamatory matter, the defendant does not act for a proper purpose, that is, to protect the interest for which the privilege is granted in the first place. An abuse of privilege by publication with an improper purpose was involved in MacLean v. Scripps, 17 N.W. 815 (Mich. 1883), in which a jury found that a newspaper published defamatory matter in order to create a sensation and for the sole purpose of increasing circulation.

The privilege may also be lost through excessive publication. Ordinarily, the purposes for which the privilege exists can be satisfied by limited publication. The employee who suspects a fellow employee of tapping the till need not call a press conference to alert the employer, nor announce it in front of other employees. Under certain circumstances, however, broad publication may be reasonable. For example, in Merlo v. United Way of America, 43 F.3d 96 (4th Cir. 1994), United Way discharged its chief financial officer and called a press conference to publicize a report critical of his financial practices during his tenure. The court held that publication through the national media was a reasonable means of communicating the pertinent facts to millions of donors.

b. Truth

For civil libel claims, truth has historically been a complete defense. The effect of making truth a defense is that the plaintiff comes into court with a spotless reputation. Given the difficulties the defendant may encounter in proving truth, this can be a tremendous advantage for the plaintiff.

One problem facing the defendant is the particularity with which the truth of the statement must be shown. The truth may differ in some respects from the statement, and the question is one of how great a difference will be tolerated. The defendant cannot prove the truth of a statement that the plaintiff stole a horse on January 15 by showing that it was a cow stolen on September 28, even if it does prove that the plaintiff is a thief. On the other hand, proof that the plaintiff stole the horse on January 16 ought to be close enough. At one time the courts tended to be sticklers for detail, and in one case, Sharpe v. Stephenson, 34 N.C. 348 (1851), the court stated that the defendant could not show the truth of a statement that the plaintiff had criminal intercourse with a certain person at a particular time and place with proof of criminal intercourse with that person but at a different time and place. However, hostility to truth as a defense has moderated over the years. In Fort Worth Press Co. v. Davis, 96 S.W.2d 416 (Tex. Civ. App. 1936), the court stated that "substantial," not literal, truth is enough, and held that a statement that the plaintiff mayor had squandered $80,000 of public funds was true enough, although the actual amount was $17,500. And in Guccione v. Hustler Magazine, Inc., 800 F.2d 298 (2d Cir. 1986), *cert. denied,* 479 U.S. 1091 (1987), the court ruled that a statement that the plaintiff was an adulterer was true, although the plaintiff's actual adultery had ended with his divorce three years before the story was printed. The court stated that the "test is whether the statement, as it was published, had a different effect on the mind of the reader than the actual literal truth." 800 F.2d at 301-02. Additionally, "[m]inor inaccuracies do not amount to falsity," as ruled in Masson v. New Yorker Magazine, Inc., 501 U.S. 496 (1991), and it is "irrelevant whether trained lawyers or judges might with the luxury of time have chosen more precise words." The Supreme Court followed this rule in Air Wisconsin Airlines Corp. v. Hoeper, 134 S. Ct. 852, 856 (2014), where statements concerning a potentially armed and unstable pilot were deemed not to be "materially false."

A different judicial attitude toward the "substantial truth" notion is illustrated by Kentucky Kingdom Amusement Company v. Belo Kentucky, Inc., 179 S.W.3d 785 (Ky. 2005). In this case, a television news station broadcast allegedly defamatory reports regarding an incident in which several roller coaster passengers at an amusement park were injured. The challenged statements included a claim that "State inspectors . . . think the ride is too dangerous"; that the ride had "malfunctioned"; and that the plaintiff "removed a key component of the ride." Id. at 788. The plaintiff argued that these statements were defamatory because, although a state inspector had issued a stop operation order on the ride, he had not expressly stated that it was "too dangerous"; the accident had occurred because of operator error, not "malfunction" in a mechanical sense; and the part removed by the plaintiff was a dispatch brake motor that was not a "key component," despite one witness testifying that it would have prevented the accident.

The court upheld a substantial jury award, rejecting the defendant's argument that the broadcast reports were "substantially true" when evaluated in full context. The court stated (id. at 791-92):

> The doctrine of "substantially true" is a convenient and necessary phrase invented by lawyers and judges to apply in very narrow and limited circumstances and related only to incidental information and not to essential conduct. . . . That is not the case here. Truth is a relatively easy concept to ascertain. It is generally defined as accuracy or correctness. Here, the broadcasts were fundamentally inaccurate as [they] related to the comments "too dangerous," "ride malfunctioned," and "removed a key component."

In contrast to this fairly deterministic and literalist approach, a vigorous dissent argued that the challenged statements "are unmistakably substantially true when viewed in their full context" and that immunizing such statements from liability when they concern public figures or matters of public concern is essential to avoid "self-censorship by the media in its conduct of its most essential role." Id. at 800-01.

Some courts have extended the truth defense to include an "own words" defense to defamation. This doctrine posits that an accurate quote of a statement made by the plaintiff is not defamatory because "a plaintiff cannot be defamed by the use of his own words." Smith v. School Dist. of Philadelphia, 112 F. Supp. 2d 417, 429 (E.D. Pa. 2000) (plaintiff did not state a claim when he alleged that he was defamed when two school officials "leaked" to the principal his letter that expressed belief that some teachers at the school discriminated against African-American students). See also Van Buskirk v. CNN, 284 F.3d 977 (9th Cir. 2002) (a televised news broadcast that paraphrased plaintiff's statements about the United States military's actions in Laos was not defamatory because the plaintiff admitted that he made the statements to reporters).

7. Judge, Jury, and Burden of Proof

The Restatement (Second) of Torts in §613 sets out the commonly accepted rules for allocating the burden of proof between the plaintiff and the defendant. The plaintiff has the burden of proof as to most issues of fact that may arise in a defamation case. Thus, for example, the plaintiff must prove, as a part of his prima facie case, that the statement is defamatory and that the audience understood its defamatory meaning, and, if required, that he suffered special damages. The defendant has the burden of proving that the publication was privileged. However, the plaintiff has the burden of proving that a qualified privilege was abused by the defendant.

The rules relating to the allocation of functions between judge and jury are contained in §§614-619 of the Restatement (Second). Under these rules, the judge determines whether the statement could be taken as defamatory by the audience and whether the publication was privileged. The jury determines whether the statement was understood by the audience as defamatory, whether it is true, and whether a qualified privilege was abused.

Problem 42

You have just finished an interview with Gary Carlson, a professor in the chemistry department of Colchester College, a small, private liberal arts college. He wants to know if he can sue the *National Inquisitor* for defamation. The *National Inquisitor* is a weekly "supermarket" publication that carries a variety of sensationalistic stories. Like other publications of the type, it has the reputation for playing loosely with the truth. The article is titled "Drugs on Campus." The portion relating to Carlson is:

> In our investigation into drug use at American colleges and universities, we visited Colchester College. Given its bucolic location, you might think that drugs would not be a problem. That's what we thought, but we were wrong. The use of cocaine and marijuana is pervasive, not only by students but by the faculty and administration as well. For example, we heard of a party at which marijuana was freely available, and you can imagine the orgy when everyone got good and high. We asked Professor Gary Carlson, a self-styled expert on marijuana, about it, but he would not talk to our reporters. We did find out that Professor Carlson is a member of NORML (National Organization for the Repeal of Marijuana Laws), so his reluctance to speak on the record is understandable.

On the page on which this paragraph appeared was a photograph of Carlson and some students taken at his home. The photograph depicted an informal scene, in which most of the people, including Carlson, were smoking. The caption under the photograph said: "Drugs at College — Prof. Entertains Students at Home."

The story related to you by Carlson is that he has conducted several carefully controlled experiments designed to determine the effects of marijuana in general and on AIDS victims in particular. He has used both students and non-students in the experiments, with the advance approval of the college administration and of the appropriate federal and state agencies. Carlson admits that he smoked marijuana a few times out of curiosity as a graduate student 15 years ago, but not since then. Carlson does not know how the *National Inquisitor* came into possession of the photograph. He occasionally conducted experiments in his home, and he thinks that the photograph was taken by someone present at one of them, who then gave the photograph to a *National Inquisitor* reporter. The cigarette Carlson was smoking was not marijuana but an ordinary cigarette. He does not belong to NORML, although he has communicated with officials in the organization from time to time as a source of information.

Carlson is not particularly concerned with the effect the article might have on his own career. The university and the scientific communities are aware that his involvement with marijuana is limited to scientific studies and are unlikely to take the article seriously. The wags among his acquaintances have had a field day at his expense, however. Carlson's primary concern is with the impact on the college. Already some alumni and parents have sent letters expressing concern about the moral climate at Colchester. Since Carlson has tenure, he is not afraid that his position is in any danger, but a decline in the funds raised could have an adverse effect on the chemistry department as well as the college as a whole.

Based on your knowledge of the law of defamation gained from the text preceding this problem, prepare a memorandum for the file indicating:

1. A preliminary analysis of the law that you expect would control the claim;
2. Any additional facts you will need to make an evaluation of Carlson's potential claim, where you are likely to be able to get the facts, and any problems you may encounter in the investigation; and

3. Your opinion as to whether in any event Carlson should carry the matter to suit. The following observations from Clarence Morris and C. Robert Morris, Jr., Morris on Torts 376-78 (2d ed. 1980), may help you in this regard:

> A dishonored client who wants a lawyer to file a libel suit may be actuated by several different motives. The client may want compensation for financial losses caused by the slur. Usually the victim is outraged and would like to make the harasser squirm. Sometimes the complainant wants to grab a chance to receive a great deal of money. Perhaps the most decent goal of a person dishonored is an urgent need for exculpation and vindication. These motives seldom occur singly, and a defamed client often hopes to reach more than one objective.
>
> Counsel representing a smeared client whose major motive is the rehabilitation of reputation must proceed with circumspection. When vindication is the client's principal need, the wisest course may involve sacrificing other objectives in order to get a prompt, prominent, and full retraction. An out-and-out apology will often neutralize dishonor more effectively than successful litigation ending in a substantial judgment. An early and large money settlement without complete retraction is often unthinkable to one who urgently needs to clear his or her name; even though the dishonored person widely publicizes the settlement, the rancorous vilifier may, in replay, circulate the imputation that the victim seemed willing to sell honor for a price. Sometimes, especially when the defamation results in heavy financial losses, the astute counsel for a claimant may be able to persuade the libeler both to retract and to pay for all or part of the harm done. . . . The risk of incurring both liability and legal expenses in such a case may bring the libeler around not only to publishing a retraction but also to paying for all or some of the claimant's financial loss. Retraction, however, does not always protect one defamed from suffering extraordinarily large damages, recoverable only through litigation.
>
> When a disparaged person brings and loses a defamation suit, further resort to litigation will probably reestablish or reenforce the plaintiff's disrepute. The technical reasons for losing a libel suit are many and are rarely understood by the public. An honorable person who has been defamed can lose a case on a number of grounds that have nothing to do with the plaintiff's deserved reputation. The victim can be defeated by the libeler's constitutional privileges of freedom of expression, the libeler's common law privilege, the plaintiff's inability to prove the right kind of fault or to establish the right kind of damages, and so on. The besmirched plaintiff's acquaintances, once the libel suit is lost, are likely to believe that the defamation was true; a plaintiff's ironclad proof of falsity is overshadowed when the court awesomely dismisses the case. Most claimants who genuinely desire a rehabilitated reputation should be advised not to sue when risk of failure is substantial.
>
> A claimant who desires to litigate must be prepared, once started, to fight all the way to the end. The plaintiff must stand ready to appeal if the case is lost at the trial, since subsidence may imply an admission that the disparagement was true.
>
> Counsel should view with special caution a proposal to bring suit on a subtle or somewhat trivial defamation. Like any witness, a disparaged plaintiff who takes the stand is subject to impeachment by cross-examination intended to show acts of misconduct evincing bad moral character; conviction of a crime involving moral turpitude, if such has been the case; or bad reputation for truth and veracity. Even one who can prove all elements of a postrevolution libel case may not be well served when his or her past has been less than perfect. The litigant's opponent may offer proof calculated to show that the claimant's "actual damages" could have resulted from widespread knowledge of misdeeds having no relation to the defendant's disparagement. Only plaintiffs with good records are likely to come out of a libel suit with better reputations than they had going in. Oscar Wilde unwisely sued on a libel that was proven true. The civil suit's sequel was an indictment, and Wilde was convicted. His two years' experience in prison is reflected in his woeful Ballad of Reading Gaol.
>
> Defamation plaintiffs who collect substantial judgments have not necessarily acted in their best interests. Slurs are often less damaging than the derided person[al] fancies.

> Defamations, like most communications, seldom are fully apprehended; many people who hear or read aspersions neither clearly identify the person affronted nor remember the scorn for long. Those well acquainted with the victim will generally not believe false accusations. Litigation, at its various stages and over a substantial period of time, republicizes the defamation. Fragments of trials and appeals are reported as they happen. Many who know that legal proceedings are in progress never follow their entire course; others who read about a final judgment often forget who won. When a defendant vigorously contests a suit for publishing a defamation, some people will sententiously say that so much smoke without some fire is unlikely.
>
> The well-known victim of prominent and persistent vilification may have little to lose, other than legal costs, by bringing a libel suit. Some litigation victories are newsworthy and easily understood; they are especially exculpatory and reparative when judgment awards the plaintiff substantial damages. There are, then, only a modicum of cases in which counsel should recommend filing a defamation suit and prosecuting it vigorously to its conclusion.

B. The Constitutional Issues

1. New York Times Co. v. Sullivan and Its Progeny: Protecting Defamatory Statements Relating to Public Officials

In 1964, the Supreme Court of the United States ruled that defamatory statements relating to public officials are entitled to protection under the First Amendment to the Constitution of the United States. New York Times Co. v. Sullivan, 376 U.S. 254 (1964). In this case, the plaintiff, an elected Commissioner of Public Affairs of Montgomery, Alabama, sued the New York Times Co. and four individual defendants for an allegedly libelous statement made in a newspaper advertisement published in the *Times*. The statement accused city police of violating the civil rights of black students and of harassing Dr. Martin Luther King for his civil rights activities. Although the plaintiff was not named in the advertisement, he claimed that it referred to him because he supervised the Montgomery police department. He was successful in the Alabama courts, receiving a $500,000 judgment. The Supreme Court reversed, holding that a public official may not recover damages for defamation relating to his official conduct unless he proves that the defendant published the statement with actual malice. The Court defined actual malice as either knowledge of the falsity of the statement or "reckless disregard" of whether or not the statement is false. The Court also ruled that the plaintiff must establish malice with "convincing clarity," and that the Court will independently review the evidence to determine for itself that the plaintiff has discharged this heavy burden.[4] The Court based its decision in part on the commitment a democratic nation must have to uninhibited debate about important public issues. According to the Court, the common law defense of truth is an inadequate safeguard to prevent citizens from self-censoring their criticism of the government (376 U.S. at 279):

> Under such a rule, would-be critics of official conduct may be deterred from voicing their criticism, even though it is believed to be true and even though it is in fact true, because of doubt whether it can be proved in court or fear of the expense of having to do

4. In Bose v. Consumers Union of United States, Inc., 466 U.S. 485 (1984), the Court reaffirmed its statement in *New York Times* that appellate courts must determine, after an independent review of the record, that the plaintiff has established malice with clear and convincing proof. In so doing, it rejected the "clearly erroneous" standard of appellate review of facts set out in Federal Rule 52(a). In Anderson v. Liberty Lobby, 477 U.S. 242 (1986), the Court ruled that the "clear and convincing" burden of proof applicable to the malice issue applies to the trial judge in deciding motions for summary judgment as well as to the jury.

> so. . . . The rule thus dampens the vigor and limits the variety of public debate. It is inconsistent with the First and Fourteenth Amendments.

In addition, the Court said that private individuals and other critics of government officials should have the "fair equivalent" of the immunity enjoyed by public officials under Barr v. Matteo, discussed at p. 825, above.

The impact, both practical and symbolic, of the *New York Times* case is difficult to overstate. See generally Symposium: The Press and the Constitution 50 Years After *New York Times v. Sullivan*, 48 Ga. L. Rev. 691 (2014). Under *New York Times,* the two most important issues that would have to be dealt with in later cases concern the facts the plaintiff must prove to establish actual malice and the determination of who is a public official.

a. Actual Malice

As stated above, *actual malice* for constitutional purposes refers to the defendant's attitude, not toward the plaintiff, but rather toward the falsity of the statement; the plaintiff can recover only by establishing that the defendant knew the statement was false, or published it with reckless disregard of its falsity. As to the latter requirement, the Court in St. Amant v. Thompson, 390 U.S. 727, 730-31 (1968), observed:

> "Reckless disregard," it is true, cannot be fully encompassed in one infallible definition. Inevitably its outer limits will be marked out through case-by-case adjudication, as is true with so many legal standards for judging concrete cases, whether the standard is provided by the Constitution, statutes, or case law. . . . [R]eckless conduct is not measured by whether a reasonably prudent man would have published, or would have investigated before publishing. There must be sufficient evidence to permit the conclusion that the defendant in fact entertained serious doubts as to the truth of his publication. Publishing with such doubts shows reckless disregard for truth or falsity and demonstrates actual malice.

Ventura v. Kyle

8 F. Supp. 3d 1115 (D. Minn. 2014)

Richard H. Kyle, District Judge. This defamation action arises from a passage in decedent Chris Kyle's autobiography describing an altercation with Plaintiff Jessie Ventura during a Navy SEAL's wake. In his book, Kyle wrote that Ventura made offensive comments about the SEALs and their service in the Iraq war, so Kyle "laid him out." Ventura claims Kyle fabricated the encounter to gain publicity. He commenced this action against Kyle asserting claims for defamation, appropriation, and unjust enrichment. While this action was pending, Kyle was tragically killed, and his wife, Taya Kyle, acting as executrix of his estate, now moves for summary judgment on Ventura's claims. For the reasons that follow, her Motion will be denied.

Background

Jesse Ventura is a well-known former wrestler, actor, and Governor of Minnesota, who served as a member of the Navy Special Forces Underwater Demolition/SEAL Teams during the Vietnam War. Chris Kyle was a Navy SEAL sniper and author of an autobiography entitled *American Sniper, the Autobiography of the Most Lethal Sniper in U.S.*

Military History. The book, which was released January 3, 2012, reached number one on the New York Times' Bestseller list by January 29, 2012, and in June 2012, Warner Brothers purchased the rights to a film adaptation.

In *American Sniper*, Kyle wrote a subchapter captioned "Punching Out Scruff Face" about an alleged altercation with Ventura. According to Kyle, the encounter took place at McP's, a bar in Coronado, California, on October 12, 2006, during a wake for Kyle's comrade, Mike Monsoor, who was killed in the line of duty. The subchapter reads as follows:

> AFTER THE FUNERAL WE WENT TO A LOCAL BAR FOR THE WAKE proper. As always, there were a bunch of different things going on at our favorite nightspot, including a small party for some older SEAL's and UDT members who were celebrating the anniversary of their graduation. Among them was a celebrity I'll call Scruff Face.
>
> Scruff served in the military; most people seem to believe he was a SEAL. As far as I know, he was in the service during the Vietnam conflict but not actually in the war. I was sitting there with Ryan and told him that Scruff was holding court with some of his buddies.
>
> "I'd really like to meet him," Ryan said.
>
> "Sure." I got up and went over to Scruff and introduced myself.
>
> "Mr. Scruff Face, I have a young SEAL over here who's just come back from Iraq. He's been injured but he'd really like to meet you."
>
> Well, Scruff kind of blew us off. Still, Ryan really wanted to meet him, so I brought him over. Scruff acted like he couldn't be bothered.
>
> *All right.*
>
> We went back over to our side of the bar and had a few more drinks. In the meantime, Scruff started running his mouth about the war and everything and anything he could connect to it. President Bush was an asshole. We were only over there because Bush wanted to show up his father. We were doing the wrong thing, killing men and women and children and murdering.
>
> And on and on. Scruff said he hates America and that's why he moved to Baja California. 9/11 was a conspiracy.
>
> And on and on some more.
>
> The guys were getting upset. Finally, I went over and tried to get him to cool it.
>
> "We're all here in mourning," I told him. "Can you just cool it? Keep it down."
>
> "You deserve to lose a few," he told me. Then he bowed up as if to belt me.
>
> I was uncharacteristically level-headed at that moment.
>
> "Look," I told him, "why don't we just step away from each other and go on our way?" Scruff bowed up again. This time he swung.
>
> Being level-headed and calm can last only so long. I laid him out.
>
> Tables flew. Stuff happened. Scruff Face ended up on the floor.
>
> I left.
>
> Quickly.
>
> I have no way of knowing for sure, but rumor has it he showed up at the BUD/S graduation with a black eye.

Although he does not name Ventura in print, Kyle has confirmed in television, radio, and print interviews that "Scruff Face" is Ventura. In early January 2012, Kyle appeared on the Opie & Anthony Show, a talk-radio program, and the O'Reilly Factor, a talk show, retelling the above-quoted story about Ventura and repeating Ventura's alleged statement, "You deserve to lose a few guys." The story also appeared on FOX News.

Kyle maintained that "the events that happened in [the] book are true" and that "the essence of what was said is accurate." He testified in his deposition that he was standing on the sidewalk outside the bar with four or five people around and Ventura was talking loudly about how he disagreed with President Bush, the Iraq War, and the SEALs' tactics. Ventura told him they "deserved to lose a few" and took on an aggressive posture. At this point, he thought Ventura might hit him, so he punched Ventura in the face, knocking him to the ground, and then turned and ran down the street toward Danny's (another SEAL bar nearby where Kyle and others continued to drink after McP's that night).

Kyle could identify only one witness who had heard Ventura say, "You deserved to lose a few," and saw him punch Ventura: Jeremiah Dinnell. Dinnell testified that he saw Kyle and Ventura arguing on the patio, heard Ventura say that "with what [they] were doing overseas [they] deserve to lose a few guys," and then saw Kyle punch him in the face, underneath the eye. Dinnell could not recall if or how Ventura fell after the punch or whether there was any blood. Dinnell did not see where Kyle went afterward but he, Dinnell, took off toward Danny's. Laura deShazo also stated she saw an unidentified male hit Ventura at McP's that night and several witnesses testified to seeing Ventura getting up from the ground and Kyle leaving. Still others who were at McP's did not witness any altercation but testified to hearing about it from Kyle or other SEALs later that night at Danny's or at breakfast the following morning. Although Dinnell was the only one who allegedly heard Ventura say the SEALs "deserved to lose a few," several of Kyle's witnesses testified to hearing Ventura express disagreement with President Bush, the Iraq War, and the SEALs' tactics.

Ventura denies both the statements attributed to him and that Kyle ever laid a hand on him. According to Ventura, he spent the weekend attending events for the BUD/S Class 258 graduation and the bicentennial reunion of his BUD/S class, Class 58. Although Ventura could not remember specific dates, his rental-car records reflect that he arrived in San Diego at approximately 7:30 p.m. on October 12, 2006. Ventura recalls going to McP's with his friends who were also there for the reunion, the DeWitts and Mike Gotchey. Although he could not recall which night he was at McP's — either the night before or after the graduation ceremony — he was certain that when he was at McP's, the DeWitts were there with him and that a group of younger SEALs were there for a wake. He recalls spending the evening engaged in conversation with his friends on the patio of McP's and meeting several people who approached their table to talk to him. He denies having any verbal or physical confrontation with Kyle or anyone else that night.

The DeWitts and Gotchey averred that they went to McP's with Ventura after the BUD/S graduation ceremony, but Ventura maintains this was an error, as later discovered evidence including photographs, the program of events for their BUD/S class reunion, and the date of Monsoor's wake, all indicated that they were at McP's on October 12, the night before the ceremony. Gotchey and the DeWitts averred they were with Ventura the entire evening and that the events described in *American Sniper* never happened. They recall several of the younger SEALs and others approached Ventura to meet him, but do not recall whether Kyle was one of them. They state Ventura did not exchange hostile words with anyone, was not involved in any physical altercation, and never stated the SEALs were murdering innocent people or deserved to lose a few. Ventura has also produced the declaration of Robert Leonard, who was at McP's that night until 11 p.m. and does not recall any arguments or physical fights, nor does he recall hearing Ventura make any offensive comments.

The following day at the BUD/S graduation ceremony, no witness observed any indication that Ventura had been punched in the face, such as bruising, swelling, or abrasions, including Wayne Robertson, who stood next to Ventura for photos and interacted with him throughout the day. And none of Ventura's witnesses heard mention of a fight at McP's. Ventura has submitted photographs of himself taken at McP's and at the graduation ceremony the next day, in which no injuries are visible. As Ventura was on blood-thinning medication at the time, he maintains that a punch in the face from a "220-pound trained killer" would have resulted in noticeable bruising and/or bleeding.

Ventura commenced the instant action against Kyle in February 2012, asserting claims of defamation, appropriation, and unjust enrichment. Kyle moved for partial summary judgment in the fall of 2012, which Motion was denied. In February 2013, Kyle was killed by a fellow veteran, against whom criminal charges are currently pending in Texas. His wife, Taya Kyle, was appointed executrix of his estate and substituted as the Defendant in this action in July 2013. Discovery has since been completed, and Taya Kyle now moves for summary judgment on Ventura's claims. . . .

Analysis

I. Defamation

Where the plaintiff is a public figure, which the parties agree Ventura is, a defamation claim requires: (1) a false and defamatory statement about the plaintiff; (2) an unprivileged publication of that statement to a third party; (3) a tendency to harm the plaintiff's reputation in the community; and (4) the defendant acted with "actual malice." The burden is on the plaintiff to prove each of these elements. Here, Defendant disputes whether Kyle's statements were false and whether he acted with actual malice.

i. Material Falsity

To succeed on a defamation claim, a plaintiff must prove the defendant's statement was materially false. Masson v. New Yorker Magazine, Inc., 501 U.S. 496, 517, 111 S. Ct. 2419, 115 L.Ed.2d 447 (1991). . . . Defendant asserts Kyle's statements were substantially true and Ventura cannot prove otherwise. While Defendant has presented testimony supporting the truth of Kyle's statements, Ventura has also presented testimony and corroborating evidence contravening it.

Ventura has submitted sworn statements of several people present at McP's with him (Mike Gotchey, Bill DeWitt, Charlene DeWitt, and Robert Leonard) who deny hearing him make the statements Kyle attributed to him in American Sniper and deny seeing Kyle punch him. . . .

Accordingly, the Court considers these affidavits as evidence in Ventura's favor, along with the affidavits of Leonard and Robertson, and Ventura's own testimony. But the evidence in the case does not come down to just eyewitness statements on both sides; Ventura has also submitted corroborating photographs of himself at the graduation ceremony the following day in which no injuries are visible, despite Kyle's allegation that he punched Ventura (not a small man himself) in the face with such force that he knocked him to the ground. Altogether, Ventura has proffered sufficient evidence upon which a jury could conclude that Kyle's statements were materially false.

ii. Actual Malice

Assuming for the sake of argument that Kyle's statements were false, Defendant asserts Ventura cannot prove Kyle acted with actual malice. . . . Defendant argues that Ventura has not presented sufficient evidence of actual malice because his evidence only relates to the truth of Kyle's statements and not Kyle's state of mind specifically.

Defendant's assertion that actual malice cannot be inferred from a false statement is only true if the statement relates to an ambiguous event. Under such circumstances, a defendant could unknowingly misinterpret the event, leading to a statement that is false but made without actual malice. But Kyle's story does not recount an ambiguous event. While it is possible Kyle could have misinterpreted Ventura's comments to him and innocently published a false account of them, this reasoning does not apply to Kyle's account of "punching out" Ventura. If Ventura proves that statement was false — that is, if a jury does not believe Kyle punched Ventura — it follows that Kyle fabricated it. And if a jury concludes Kyle fabricated part of the story, it could reasonably conclude he fabricated the rest of his story about Ventura.

In conclusion, Ventura has presented sufficient evidence to create a genuine issue of fact as to whether Kyle knowingly (or recklessly) published false statements about him. Accordingly, his defamation claim will be left for a jury to resolve. . . .

Conclusion

Based on the foregoing, and all the files, records, and proceedings herein, IT IS ORDERED that Defendant's Motion for Summary Judgment is DENIED.

Generally, the determination of whether actual malice has been proved with convincing clarity does not rest on any one factor, but results from an accumulation of evidence that is held to amount to reckless disregard of the truth. Cases in which plaintiffs have succeeded in establishing malice include Smith v. Anonymous Joint Enter., 793 N.W.2d 533 (Mich. 2010), in which the Supreme Court of Michigan concluded that plaintiff presented clear and convincing evidence at trial to support the jury's finding that defendants John Stanek and Donald Barrows defamed plaintiff by mass-mailing copies of a personnel report containing false information about her; Carson v. Allied News Co., 482 F. Supp. 406 (N.D. Ill. 1979), in which the defendant had distorted and altered facts contained in his source material and had fabricated entire conversations; and Goldwater v. Ginzburg, 414 F.2d 324 (2d Cir. 1969), *cert. denied,* 396 U.S. 1049 (1970), involving purported psychiatric evaluations of a presidential candidate. But the burden of proving actual malice through clear and convincing evidence is so heavy that few plaintiffs are able to meet it.

For example, in Dickey v. CBS Inc., 583 F.2d 1221 (3d Cir. 1978), the trial court held that, although the defendant was unconcerned whether the defamatory material it had broadcast was true or not, it was nonetheless not liable because it had not in fact entertained serious doubts about the truth of the charges. The appellate court affirmed the decision because it believed that CBS's reliance on the author of the statement, a veteran congressman who knew the plaintiff and who refused to retract the charges, was justified. In Heishman, Inc. v. Fox Television Stations, Inc., 217 F. Supp. 2d 690 (E.D. Va. 2002), a car dealership sued a television station after a four-second shot of a license plate showing the car dealer's name was included in a report on the fraudulent practice of selling flood-damaged cars. Five separate reviewers within the television station had failed to notice the dealer's name in the footage, a collective failure that plaintiff argued rose to the level of recklessness. The court rejected plaintiff's argument because it believed the argument "wrongly equates efforts to exercise due care with recklessness merely because the efforts do not succeed [and], if accepted, would discourage efforts to exercise due care through the use of multiple reviewers." Id. at 695. For other examples of cases in which plaintiff fails to establish actual malice, see, e.g., Levesque v. Doocy, 560 F.3d 82 (1st Cir. 2009); CACI Premier Tech., Inc. v. Rhodes, 536 F.3d 280 (4th Cir. 2008); Schatz v. Republican State Leadership Comm., 777 F. Supp. 2d 181 (D. Me. Apr. 7, 2011); Kipper v. NYP Holdings Co., 912 N.E.2d 26 (N.Y. 2009). For a thorough analysis of how the actual malice standard is and should be applied in light of the institutional context of contemporary media organizations, see Randall P. Bezanson & Gilbert Cranberg, Institutional Reckless Disregard for Truth in Public Defamation Actions Against the Press, 90 Iowa L. Rev. 887 (2005).

While the failure to investigate or discover the truth will not necessarily constitute malice, the purposeful avoidance of the truth may well be enough. See Harte-Hanks Communications, Inc. v. Connaughton, 491 U.S. 657 (1989). In Suzuki Motor Corp. v. Consumers Union of U.S., Inc., 292 F.3d 1192 (9th Cir. 2002), the court of appeals reversed summary judgment on behalf of Consumers Union (CU), a nonprofit consumer product testing organization, in a case arising out of reports by CU that the Suzuki Samurai automobile had a dangerously high rollover tendency. The court ruled that CU reasonably could be found to have had a high awareness of the probable falsity of its report in light of evidence that the organization altered its test design and had a financial motivation to report dramatic findings. The court also held that "in the face of obvious reasons to doubt the accuracy of its Samurai story, [defendant] did not act reasonably in dispelling those doubts, thereby raising the inference that [defendant] knew of the story's falsity." Id. at 1203. Rehearing en banc was subsequently denied, 330 F.3d 1110 (9th Cir.), *cert. denied,* 540 U.S. 983 (2003), over a strenuous dissent by Judge Kozinski that was joined by ten Ninth Circuit judges. After thoroughly evaluating CU's testing methodology and claims, the dissenting opinion concluded, at 1123:

> I have read CU's review of the Samurai and Suzuki's criticism of its methodology. After all that, I can only say I would long hesitate before letting anyone I care about drive or ride in one of these vehicles. If Suzuki wanted me to disregard CU's conclusions, it should have taken the money it spent on this lawsuit and hired an independent agency to run tests showing that CU's criticisms are unfounded. It could also have tried to improve its product to moot criticism in the future. But, until today, I had thought the one option not available to a company in Suzuki's position was to use its vast financial resources to drag its critics through the gauntlet of our immensely expensive litigation machine. I continue to hope I'm right, or this will be a sad day indeed for consumer organizations and those who rely on them for information vital to their health and safety.

b. Public Officials, Public Figures, and Matters of Public Concern

Like actual malice, the question of who is a public official for the purposes of the *New York Times* rule has also been the subject of considerable litigation. In Rosenblatt v. Baer, 383 U.S. 75, 85-86 (1966), the Court stated that the public official designation applies to government employees "who have, or appear to the public to have, substantial responsibility for or control over the conduct of governmental affairs," and to governmental positions important enough that "the public has an independent interest in the qualifications and performance of the person who holds it beyond the general public interest in the qualifications and performance of all government employees."

A wide assortment of public employees, no matter where they fall in the hierarchy of officialdom, have been held to be public officials, including city police officers, court clerks, fire department captains, and school teachers. See, e.g., Lane v. MPG Newspaper, 781 N.E.2d 800 (Mass. 2003), in which the court held that even a low-ranking elected town official must meet the actual malice standard. But in LeDoux v. Northwest Publishing, Inc., 521 N.W.2d 59 (Minn. Ct. App. 1994), the court held that a city maintenance supervisor was not a public official, nor was a high school principal in Ellerbee v. Mills, 422 S.E.2d 539 (Ga. 1992). See also Anaya v. CBS Broad., Inc., 626 F. Supp. 2d 1158 (D.N.M. 2008) (procurement assistant at the Los Alamos National Laboratory is not a public official). The category of public officials has also been interpreted to include many persons not normally thought of as public employees. See Monitor Patriot Co. v. Roy, 401 U.S. 265 (1971) (candidate for public office); Klahr v. Winterble, 418 P.2d 404 (Ariz. Ct. App. 1966) (member of student senate at state university); Turley v. W.T.A.X., Inc., 236 N.E.2d 778 (Ill. App. Ct. 1968) (architect involved in construction of a public building and in a position to influence the expenditure of public funds); Doctors Convalescent Center, Inc. v. East Shore Newspapers, Inc., 244 N.E.2d 373 (Ill. App. Ct. 1968) (nursing home licensed by state and which housed patients who were wards of the state). In Jenoff v. Hearst Corp., 453 F. Supp. 541 (D. Md. 1978), *aff'd,* 644 F.2d 1004 (4th Cir. 1981), the court refused to rule that the plaintiff, a volunteer undercover police informant, was a public official, pointing out that the nature of his activities precluded such a designation. According to the court in Bufalino v. Associated Press, 692 F.2d 266 (2d Cir. 1982), *cert. denied,* 462 U.S. 1111 (1983), the status of the plaintiff may have as much to do with how the allegedly defamatory story refers to him as with his actual status. The plaintiff in that case was the town attorney, but the court refused to characterize him as a public official because the story about him only referred to him as an attorney; the story did not identify him as a public official, nor did the defendant establish that the plaintiff's name was recognized in the town as a public official.

In Curtis Publishing Co. v. Butts, 388 U.S. 130 (1967), the Supreme Court held that the *New York Times* rule should be extended to "public figures," not just public officials. In this consolidated case, Butts was a college athletic director and former football coach accused in a magazine article of furnishing his team's plays to the coach of a rival team. Walker was a retired army general who took part in the events surrounding the use of federal troops to integrate a southern university. In an opinion announcing the judgment of the Court but joined by only three justices, Justice Harlan explained that both Butts and Walker were public figures, Butts by virtue of his position, and Walker because he had voluntarily injected himself into a public controversy. Furthermore, both plaintiffs had access to the media so that they could refute false accusations, and both were of continuing interest to the public. However, Justice Harlan asserted in his opinion that a recovery by either plaintiff could not be viewed as a vindication of government policy, as was the case in *New York Times,* and he therefore advanced a standard of liability that was less rigorous than the actual malice standard imposed on *New York Times* plaintiffs but more demanding than the common law. He suggested a rule by which a public figure could recover for defamation if it could be proved that the defendant's conduct has been "highly unreasonable" so that it constituted "an extreme departure from the standards of investigation and reporting ordinarily adhered to by responsible publishers." 388 U.S. at 155.

The majority, however, did not support Justice Harlan's intermediate standard, preferring instead Chief Justice Warren's opinion adopting the *New York Times* standard for cases involving public figure plaintiffs. Warren reasoned that the increasing concentration of power in private sectors of society means that many who are not public officials "are nevertheless, intimately involved in the resolution of important public questions or, by reason of their fame, shape events in areas of concern to society at large." 388 U.S. at 164. For that reason, and because they have access to the media to offer countering statements and accounts, Warren concluded that the *New York Times* standard should also be applied to public figure plaintiffs.

After the *Butts* case was decided, a further category of matters of public interest or concern emerged in lower court cases. If the challenged statements were determined to be related to a matter of legitimate public concern, the plaintiff had to meet the *New York Times* standard even if the plaintiff was not deemed to be a public figure. This public concern concept gained acceptance by a plurality of the Supreme Court in Rosenbloom v. Metromedia, Inc., 403 U.S. 29 (1971), in which the Court held that the plaintiff, a magazine distributor, could not recover for statements asserting that he sold obscene literature. Justice Brennan concluded in his plurality opinion that the *New York Times* privilege should apply to defamatory statements relating to private persons if the statements relate to matters of general or public interest. He emphasized society's interest in being informed about certain issues, and reasoned that this interest does not diminish merely because a private individual, however involuntarily, is involved.

Gertz v. Robert Welch, Inc.

418 U.S. 323, 94 S. Ct. 2997, 41 L. Ed. 2d 789 (1974)

MR. JUSTICE POWELL delivered the opinion of the Court.

This Court has struggled for nearly a decade to define the proper accommodation between the law of defamation and the freedoms of speech and press protected by the First Amendment. With this decision we return to that effort. We granted certiorari to reconsider the extent of a publisher's constitutional privilege against liability for defamation of a private citizen.

I

In 1968 a Chicago policeman named Nuccio shot and killed a youth named Nelson. The state authorities prosecuted Nuccio for the homicide and ultimately obtained a conviction for murder in the second degree. The Nelson family retained petitioner Elmer Gertz, a reputable attorney, to represent them in civil litigation against Nuccio.

[Respondent published an article in his magazine accusing the petitioner of being part of a Communist conspiracy against the police. The article also stated that petitioner belonged to two Marxist organizations. Petitioner brought this action for libel against the respondent in federal district court, and after the evidence was completed, the trial judge directed a verdict for petitioner on the liability issues, since it was undisputed that the article contained false statements which constituted libel per se. After a verdict for the petitioner of $50,000, the trial judge granted the respondent's motion for judgment notwithstanding the verdict on the ground that the article was about a matter of public interest and thus entitled to the protection of the *New York Times* rule, and that actual malice had not been convincingly demonstrated. The court of appeals affirmed.] . . .

III

We begin with the common ground. Under the First Amendment there is no such thing as a false idea. However pernicious an opinion may seem, we depend for its correction not on the conscience of judges and juries but on the competition of other ideas. But there is no constitutional value in false statements of fact. Neither the intentional lie nor the careless error materially advances society's interest in "uninhibited, robust, and wide-open" debate on public issues. New York Times Co. v. Sullivan, 376 U.S., at 270. They belong to that category of utterances which "are no essential part of any exposition of ideas, and are of such slight social value as a step to truth that any benefit that may be derived from them is clearly outweighed by the social interest in order and morality." Chaplinsky v. New Hampshire, 315 U.S. 568, 572 (1942).

Although the erroneous statement of fact is not worthy of constitutional protection, it is nevertheless inevitable in free debate. . . . Our decisions recognize that a rule of strict liability that compels a publisher or broadcaster to guarantee the accuracy of his factual assertions may lead to intolerable self-censorship. Allowing the media to avoid liability only by proving the truth of all injurious statements does not accord adequate protection to First Amendment liberties. . . . The First Amendment requires that we protect some falsehood in order to protect speech that matters.

The need to avoid self-censorship by the news media is, however, not the only societal value at issue. If it were, this Court would have embraced long ago the view that publishers and broadcasters enjoy an unconditional and indefeasible immunity from liability for defamation. Such a rule would indeed obviate the fear that the prospect of civil liability for injurious falsehood might dissuade a timorous press from the effective exercise of First Amendment freedoms. Yet absolute protection for the communications media requires a total sacrifice of the competing value served by the law of defamation.

The legitimate state interest underlying the law of libel is the compensation of individuals for the harm inflicted on them by defamatory falsehoods. We would not lightly require the State to abandon this purpose, for, as Mr. Justice Stewart has reminded us, the individual's right to the protection of his own good name "reflects no more than our basic concept of the essential dignity and worth of every human being—a concept at the root of any decent system of ordered liberty. The protection of private personality, like the protection of life itself, is left primarily to the individual states under the Ninth and Tenth Amendments. But this does not mean that the right is entitled to any less recognition by this Court as a basic of our constitutional system." Rosenblatt v. Baer, 383 U.S. 75, 92-93 (1963) (opinion of Stewart, J.). . . .

[W]e have no difficulty in distinguishing among defamation plaintiffs. The first remedy of any victim of defamation is self-help—using available opportunities to contradict the lie or correct the error and thereby to minimize its adverse impact on reputation. Public officials and public figures usually enjoy significantly greater access to the channels of effective communication and hence have a more realistic opportunity to counteract false statements than private individuals normally enjoy. Private individuals are therefore more vulnerable to injury, and the state interest in protecting them is correspondingly greater.

More important than the likelihood that private individuals will lack effective opportunities for rebuttal, there is a compelling normative consideration underlying the distinction between public and private defamation plaintiffs. An individual who decides to seek governmental office must accept certain necessary consequences of that involvement in public affairs. He runs the risk of closer public scrutiny than might otherwise be the case. And society's interest in the officers of government is not strictly limited to the formal discharge of official duties. As the Court pointed out in Garrison v. Louisiana, 379 U.S. 64, 77 (1964), the public's interest extends to "anything that might touch on an official's fitness for office. . . . Few personal attributes are more germane to fitness for office than dishonesty, malfeasance, or improper motivation, even though these characteristics may also affect the official's private character."

Those classed as public figures stand in a similar position. Hypothetically, it may be possible for someone to become a public figure through no purposeful action of his own, but the instances of truly involuntary public figures must be exceedingly rare. For the most part those who attain this status have assumed roles of especial prominence in the affairs of society. Some occupy positions of such persuasive power and influence that they are deemed public figures for all purposes. More commonly, those classed as public figures have thrust themselves to the forefront of particular public controversies in order to influence the resolution of the issues involved. In either event, they invite attention and comment.

Even if the foregoing generalities do not obtain in every instance, the communications media are entitled to act on the assumption that public officials and public figures have voluntarily exposed themselves to increased risk of injury from defamatory falsehoods concerning them. No such assumption is justified with respect to a private individual. He has not accepted public office nor assumed an "influential role in ordering society." Curtis Publishing Co. v. Butts, . . . 388 U.S., at 164 (opinion of Warren, C.J.). He has relinquished no part of his interest in the protection of his own good name, and consequently he has a more compelling call on the courts for redress of injury inflicted by defamatory falsehood. Thus, private individuals are not only more vulnerable to injury than public officials and public figures; they are also more deserving of recovery.

For these reasons we conclude that the States should retain substantial latitude in their efforts to enforce a legal remedy for defamatory falsehood injurious to the reputation of a private individual. . . .

We hold that, so long as they do not impose liability without fault, the States may define for themselves the appropriate standard of liability for a publisher or broadcaster of defamatory falsehood injurious to a private individual. This approach provides a more equitable boundary between the competing concerns involved here. It recognizes the strength of the legitimate state interest in compensating private individuals for wrongful injury to reputation, yet shields the press and broadcast media from the rigors of strict liability for defamation. At least this conclusion obtains where, as here, the substance of the defamatory statement "makes substantial danger to reputation apparent." This phrase places in perspective the conclusion we announce today. Our inquiry would involve considerations somewhat different from those discussed above if a State purported to condition civil liability on a factual misstatement whose content did not warn a reasonably prudent editor or broadcaster of its defamatory potential. Such a case is not now before us, and we intimate no view as to its proper resolution.

IV

Our accommodation of the competing values at stake in defamation suits by private individuals allows the States to impose liability on the publisher or broadcaster of defamatory falsehoods on a less demanding showing than that required by *The New York Times.* This conclusion is not based on a belief that the considerations which prompted the adoption of the *The New York Times* privilege for defamation of public officials and its extension to public figures are wholly inapplicable to the context of private individuals. Rather, we endorse this approach in recognition of the strong and legitimate state interest in compensating private individuals for injury to reputation. But this countervailing state interest extends no further than compensation for actual injury. For the reasons stated below, we hold that the States may not permit recovery of presumed or punitive damages, at least when liability is not based on a showing of knowledge of falsity or reckless disregard for the truth.

The common law of defamation is an oddity of tort law, for it allows recovery of purportedly compensatory damages without evidence of actual loss. Under the traditional rules pertaining to actions for libel, the existence of injury is presumed from the fact of publication. Juries may award substantial sums as compensation for supposed damage to reputation without any proof that such harm actually occurred. The largely uncontrolled discretion of juries to award damages where there is no loss unnecessarily compounds the potential of any system of liability for defamatory falsehood to inhibit the vigorous exercise of First Amendment freedoms. Additionally, the doctrine of presumed damages invites juries to punish unpopular opinion rather than to compensate individuals for injury sustained by the publication of a false fact. More to the point, the States have no substantial interest in securing for plaintiffs such as this petitioner gratuitous awards of money damages far in excess of any actual injury.

We would not, of course, invalidate state law simply because we doubt its wisdom, but here we are attempting to reconcile state law with a competing interest grounded in the constitutional command of the First Amendment. It is therefore appropriate to require that state remedies for defamatory falsehood reach no farther than is necessary to protect the legitimate interest involved. It is necessary to restrict defamation plaintiffs who do not prove knowledge of falsity or reckless disregard for the truth to compensation for actual injury. We need not define "actual injury," as trial courts have wide experience in framing appropriate jury instructions in tort action. Suffice it to say that actual injury is not limited to out-of-pocket loss. Indeed, the more customary types of actual harm inflicted by defamatory falsehood include impairment of reputation and standing in the community, personal humiliation, and mental anguish and suffering. Of course, juries must be limited by appropriate instructions, and all awards must be supported by competent evidence concerning the injury, although there need be no evidence which assigns an actual dollar value to the injury.

We also find no justification for allowing awards of punitive damages against publishers and broadcasters held liable under state-defined standards of liability for defamation. In most jurisdictions jury discretion over the amounts awarded is limited only by the gentle rule that they not be excessive. Consequently, juries assess punitive damages in wholly unpredictable amounts bearing no necessary relation to the actual harm caused. And they remain free to use their discretion selectively to punish expressions of unpopular views. Like the doctrine of presumed damages, jury discretion to award punitive damages unnecessarily exacerbates the danger of media self-censorship, but, unlike the former rule, punitive damages are wholly irrelevant to the state interest that justifies a negligence standard for private defamation actions. They are not compensation for injury. Instead, they are private fines levied by civil juries to punish reprehensible conduct and to deter its future occurrence. In short, the private defamation plaintiff who establishes liability under a less demanding standard than that stated by *New York Times* may recover only such damages as are sufficient to compensate him for actual injury.

V

Notwithstanding our refusal to extend the *New York Times* privilege to defamation of private individuals, respondent contends that we should affirm the judgment below on the ground that petitioner is either a public official or a public figure. There is little basis for the former assertion. . . .

Respondent's characterization of petitioner as a public figure raises a different question. That designation may rest on either of two alternative bases. In some instances an individual may achieve such pervasive fame or notoriety that he becomes a public figure for all purposes and in all contexts. More commonly, an individual voluntarily injects himself or is drawn into a particular public controversy and thereby becomes a public figure for a limited range of issues. In either case such persons assume special prominence in the resolution of public questions.

Petitioner has long been active in community and professional affairs. He has served as an officer of local civil groups and of various professional organizations, and he has published several books and articles on legal subjects. Although petitioner was consequently well-known in some circles, he had achieved no general fame or notoriety in the community. None of the prospective jurors called at the trial had ever heard of petitioner prior to this litigation, and respondent offered no proof that this response was atypical of the local population. We would not lightly assume that a citizen's participation in community and professional affairs rendered him a public figure for all purposes. Absent clear evidence of general fame or notoriety in the community, and pervasive involvement in the affairs of society, an individual should not be deemed a public personality for all aspects of his life. It is preferable to reduce the public figure question to a more meaningful context by looking to the nature and extent of an individual's participation in the particular controversy giving rise to the defamation.

In this context it is plain that petitioner was not a public figure. He played a minimal role at the coroner's inquest, and his participation related solely to his representation of a private client. He took no part in the criminal prosecution of officer Nuccio. Moreover, he never discussed either the criminal or civil litigation with the press and was never quoted as having done so. He plainly did not thrust himself into the vortex of this public issue, nor did he engage the public's attention in an attempt to influence its outcome. We are persuaded that the trial court did not err in refusing to characterize petitioner as a public figure for the purpose of this litigation.

We therefore conclude that the *New York Times* standard is inapplicable to this case and that the trial court erred in entering judgment for respondent. Because the jury was allowed to impose liability without fault and was permitted to presume damages without proof of injury, a new trial is necessary. We reverse and remand for further proceedings in accord with this opinion.

It is so ordered.

[The concurring opinion of JUSTICE BLACKMUN, and the dissenting opinions of CHIEF JUSTICE BURGER and JUSTICES DOUGLAS, BRENNAN, and WHITE are omitted.]

At the retrial, the jury determined that the defendant was guilty of actual malice, and the trial judge entered judgment for the plaintiff on the verdict for $100,000 in compensatory damages and for $300,000 in punitive damages. The judgment was affirmed on appeal in Gertz v. Robert Welch, Inc., 680 F.2d 527 (7th Cir. 1982), *cert. denied,* 459 U.S. 1226 (1983).

The first post-*Gertz* case to reach the Supreme Court was Time, Inc. v. Firestone, 424 U.S. 448 (1976). The case arose out of a report of the plaintiff's divorce published in the defendant's magazine. The plaintiff and her husband had sued each other for divorce in Florida, the husband claiming extreme cruelty and adultery. The husband's petition was granted, but there was no specification of the grounds in the decree, beyond a statement that neither party "has shown the least susceptibility to domestication." The defendant reported that the plaintiff's husband was granted a divorce on grounds of extreme cruelty and adultery. After the defendant refused to print a retraction, the plaintiff brought this action. The Florida Supreme Court affirmed a judgment of $100,000 for the plaintiff, from which the defendant appealed. Writing for the majority, Justice Rehnquist rejected Time's contention that Mrs. Firestone was a public figure. In the Court's view the plaintiff had not assumed a role of special prominence in the affairs of society, since her prominence was limited to the Palm Beach social circle; she had not thrust herself into any public controversy in an attempt to influence its resolution; her involvement in the litigation was involuntary, since the legal system compelled parties seeking a divorce to dissolve their marriage judicially. The Court also emphasized that a public controversy was not to be equated with all controversies of interest to the public, warning that to do so would be to reinstate *Rosenbloom.* Justice Marshall in dissent argued that the majority had reinstated *Rosenbloom,* despite its protestations to the contrary, with its discussion of whether the plaintiff's divorce action was a matter of "public controversy." In Justice Marshall's view, the plaintiff was a public figure for the purposes of the divorce litigation. She had greater access to the media than do private persons generally, as evidenced by the fact that press coverage of her activities was frequent enough to warrant her subscribing to a press-clipping service; she had voluntarily assumed a position of social prominence and thus could be fairly held to have assumed the risk of defamatory statements; finally, she had held several press conferences during the course of her long divorce trial, which had attracted national media coverage.

As one court has stated, trying to draw the line between public figures and private individuals is "much like trying to nail a jellyfish to the wall." Rosanova v. Playboy Enterprises, Inc., 411 F. Supp. 440, 443 (S.D. Ga. 1976). A five-factor test for determining whether the plaintiff is a limited-purpose public figure has evolved:

> (1) the plaintiff had access to channels of effective communication; (2) the plaintiff voluntarily assumed a role of special prominence in a public controversy; (3) the plaintiff

> sought to influence the resolution or outcome of the controversy; (4) the controversy existed prior to the publication of the defamatory statements; and (5) the plaintiff retained public figure status at the time of the alleged defamation. [Wells v. Liddy, 186 F.3d 505, 534 (4th Cir. 1999), *cert. denied,* 528 U.S. 1118 (2000).]

The cases tend to be context-specific, so generalizations are difficult to make. Holding plaintiffs to be public figures, either all-purpose or limited, are: Makaeff v. Trump Univ., LLC, 715 F.3d 254 (9th Cir. 2013) (holding that Trump University was a limited public figure for purposes of controversy regarding its allegedly fraudulent practices because "large scale, aggressive advertising can inject a person or entity into a public controversy that arises from the subject of that advertising"); Steaks Unlimited, Inc. v. Deaner, 623 F.2d 264 (3d Cir. 1980) (extensive advertising and promotion by steak retailer rendered it public figure); Nichols v. Moore, 396 F. Supp. 2d 783 (E.D. Mich. 2005) (brother and suspected accomplice of Oklahoma City bomber Terry Nichols); Atlanta Journal-Constitution v. Jewell, 555 S.E.2d 175 (Ga. Ct. App. 2001), *cert. denied sub nom.* Jewell v. Cox Enters., Inc., 123 S. Ct. 75 (2002) (security guard who gave several television interviews after bombing in Atlanta's Olympic Park); Reuber v. Food Chem. News, Inc., 925 F.2d 703 (4th Cir.), *cert. denied,* 501 U.S. 1212 (1991) (whistleblowing scientist for National Cancer Institute); Rebozo v. Washington Post Co., 637 F.2d 375 (5th Cir.), *cert. denied,* 454 U.S. 964 (1981) (well-known friend of a former president); Carson v. Allied News Co., 529 F.2d 206 (7th Cir. 1976) (wife of late night talk show host); James v. Gannett Co., 353 N.E.2d 834 (N.Y. 1976) (professional belly dancer).

Holding plaintiffs not to be public figures are Armstrong v. Shirvell, 596 F. App'x 433 (6th Cir. 2015) (student council president of a large university); Lassonde v. Stanton, 956 A.2d 332 (N.H. 2008) (plaintiff helped construct a home for a disabled man in conjunction with a reality television program); Mathis v. Daly, 695 S.E.2d 807 (N.C. Ct. App. 2010) (former CEO of the Haywood County Council on Aging); Klentzman v. Brady, 312 S.W.3d 886 (Tex. App. 2009) (son of the chief deputy sheriff for Fort Bend County); Wayment v. Clear Channel Broadcasting, Inc., 116 P.3d 271, 281 (Utah 2005) (prominent local television reporter where defendant "provided no evidence that [the reporter] wielded any particular social or political influence"); Krauss v. Globe Int'l Inc., 674 N.Y.S.2d 662 (App. Div. 1998) (ex-husband of TV personality); Warford v. Lexington Herald-Leader Co., 789 S.W.2d 758 (Ky. 1990), *cert. denied,* 498 U.S. 1047 (1991) (assistant college basketball coach); Dodrill v. Arkansas Democrat Co., 590 S.W.2d 840 (Ark. 1979), *cert. denied,* 444 U.S. 1076 (1980) (attorney suspended from practice). One court has even held that a plaintiff may be a public figure with respect to some, but not all defendants in the same lawsuit, even when plaintiff's claims are premised on identical published statements. See Chafoulias v. Peterson, 668 N.W.2d 642 (Minn. 2003).

The Court in *Gertz* stated that "it might be possible for someone to become a public figure through no purposeful action of his own, but the instances of truly involuntary public figures must be exceedingly rare."[5] 418 U.S. at 345. The Court's assertion has proved to be

5. Along the lines of the *Gertz* quotation, the Supreme Court held that the media cannot convert the plaintiff from a private figure to a public figure by simply making the plaintiff the subject of a story. In Hutchinson v. Proxmire, 443 U.S. 111 (1979), the Court ruled that a researcher applying for public financing was not a public figure. That the plaintiff's response to a statement criticizing his research project was carried by some newspapers did not mean that he had the kind of access to the media discussed in *Gertz.* The Court stated that the plaintiff's access to the media must predate the alleged defamatory statement, and must be of a "regular and continuing" nature. To the same effect is Wolston v. Reader's Digest Association, 443 U.S. 157 (1979).

correct — very few reported decisions have concluded that the plaintiff was an "involuntary public figure." In holding that the plaintiff, a secretary caught up in the Watergate break-in, was not an involuntary public figure, the court of appeals in Wells v. Liddy, cited above, set out two characteristics of one who would be such a public figure: (1) that the person was a "central figure in a significant public controversy" and (2) that "the [person] has taken some action, or failed to act when action was required, in circumstances in which a reasonable person would understand that publicity would likely inhere." 186 F.3d at 539-40. The court characterized the second requirement as being in the nature of an "assumption of the risk."

The Supreme Court in *Gertz* specifically left it to the states to determine whether a malice or negligence standard should be applied in cases of private individuals as plaintiffs. Most courts considering the issue have opted for negligence. See, e.g., Rouch v. Enquirer & News of Battle Creek, 487 N.W.2d 205 (Mich. 1992); Capuano v. Outlet Co., 579 A.2d 469 (R.I. 1990). The Indiana Supreme Court adopted the malice standard in Journal-Gazette Co., Inc. v. Bandido's, Inc., 712 N.E.2d 446 (Ind.), *cert. denied,* 528 U.S. 1005 (1999). An intermediate mental state standard was adopted by the court in Huggins v. Moore, 726 N.E.2d 456, 460 (N.Y. 1999). Reaffirming an earlier case, the court stated that a media defendant is liable only if it "acted in a grossly irresponsible manner without due consideration for the standards of information gathering and dissemination ordinarily followed by responsible parties."

Gertz did not involve purely private defamation — a private individual suing a non-media defendant. Some courts have altered the common law basis of liability in favor of negligence in these cases. See, e.g., Jacron Sales Corp. v. Sindorf, 350 A.2d 688 (Md. 1976). Other courts have continued to apply strict liability. See, e.g., Harley-Davidson Motorsports, Inc. v. Markley, 568 P.2d 1359 (Or. 1977). Some light may have been shed on this issue by the various opinions in Dun & Bradstreet, Inc. v. Greenmoss Builders, Inc., 472 U.S. 749 (1985), which principally held that proof of New York Times malice is not required to support an award of presumed or punitive damages if the story does not involve a matter of public concern. In addition, five justices, one who concurred in and four who dissented from the result in that case, specifically addressed whether Gertz should be limited to media defendants and agreed at least on that point that it should not. In Snead v. Redland Aggregates, Ltd., 998 F.2d 1325 (5th Cir. 1993), *cert. dismissed,* 511 U.S. 1050 (1994), the court stated that the Dun & Bradstreet plurality opinion supported common law standards for purely private cases and held that the Constitution imposes no minimum standard of fault in such libel cases. This issue is discussed in Rodney A. Smolla, Dun & Bradstreet, Hepps, and Liberty Lobby: A New Analytic Primer on the Future Course of Defamation, 75 Geo. L.J. 1519 (1987). Another issue discussed by Professor Smolla in this article is whether public officials and figures have any "private" lives to which the malice standard would not apply. Professor Smolla suggests that courts might be receptive to distinguishing between public officials for that purpose, according those well up in the "policymaking hierarchy" little in the way of private lives, with increasing privacy available as cases move down the ladder of the hierarchy. See also James C. Mitchell, The Accidental Purist: Reclaiming the Gertz All Purpose Public Figure Doctrine in the Age of "Celebrity Journalism," 22 Loy. L.A. Ent. L. Rev. 559 (2002), who argues that the actual malice burden should fall only on defamatory statements that are sufficiently connected to the celebrities' influence in public affairs, and not on extremely personal matters.

2. Milkovich v. Lorain Journal Co. and Its Progeny: Distinguishing "Fact" from "Opinion"

Milkovich v. Lorain Journal Co.

497 U.S. 1, 110 S. Ct. 2695, 111 L. Ed. 2d 1 (1990)

CHIEF JUSTICE REHNQUIST delivered the opinion of the Court. Respondent J. Theodore Diadiun authored an article in an Ohio newspaper implying that petitioner Michael Milkovich, a local high school wrestling coach, lied under oath in a judicial proceeding about an incident involving petitioner and his team which occurred at a wrestling match. Petitioner sued Diadiun and the newspaper for libel, and the Ohio Court of Appeals affirmed a lower court entry of summary judgment against petitioner. This judgment was based in part on the grounds that the article constituted an "opinion" protected from the reach of state defamation law by the First Amendment to the United States Constitution. We hold that the First Amendment does not prohibit the application of Ohio's libel laws to the alleged defamations contained in the article.

[The article that was the basis of the suit appeared in a newspaper owned by respondent Lorain Journal, and] bore the heading "Maple beat the law with the 'big lie,'" beneath which appeared Diadiun's photograph and the words "TD Says." The carryover page headline announced ". . . Diadiun says Maple told a lie." The column contained the following passages:

> . . . A lesson was learned (or relearned) yesterday by the student body of Maple Heights High School, and by anyone who attended the Maple-Mentor wrestling meet of last Feb. 8.
>
> A lesson which, sadly, in view of the events of the past year, is well they learned early.
>
> It is simply this: If you get in a jam, lie your way out.
>
> If you're successful enough, and powerful enough, and can sound sincere enough, you stand an excellent chance of making the lie stand up, regardless of what really happened.
>
> The teachers responsible were mainly Maple wrestling coach, Mike Milkovich, and former superintendent of schools, H. Donald Scott.
>
> Anyone who attended the meet, whether he be from Maple Heights, Mentor, or impartial observer, knows in his heart that Milkovich and Scott lied at the hearing after each having given his solemn oath to tell the truth.
>
> But they got away with it.
>
> Is that the kind of lesson we want our young people learning from their high school administrators and coaches?
>
> I think not.

Petitioner commenced a defamation action against respondents . . . alleging that the headline of Diadiun's article and the 9 passages quoted above "accused plaintiff of committing the crime of perjury, an indictable offense in the State of Ohio, and damaged plaintiff directly in his lifetime occupation of coach and teacher, and constituted libel per se."

[The Court's detailing of the proceedings below is omitted. The result of those proceedings is that summary judgment in favor of the respondents was affirmed on the ground that "the article in question was constitutionally protected opinion." Certiorari was granted "to consider the important questions raised by the Ohio courts' recognition of a constitutionally-required 'opinion' exception to the application of its defamation laws."] We now reverse.

Since the latter half of the 16th century, the common law has afforded a cause of action for damage to a person's reputation by the publication of false and defamatory statements.

In Shakespeare's Othello, Iago says to Othello:

> Good name in man and woman, dear my lord,
> Is the immediate jewel of their souls.
> Who steals my purse steals trash;
> 'Tis something, nothing;
> 'Twas mine, 'tis his, and has been slave to thousands;
> But he that filches from me my good name
> Robs me of that which not enriches him,
> And makes me poor indeed.

Act III, scene 3.

Defamation law developed not only as a means of allowing an individual to vindicate his good name, but also for the purpose of obtaining redress for harm caused by such statements. As the common law developed in this country, apart from the issue of damages, one usually needed only allege an unprivileged publication of false and defamatory matter to state a cause of action for defamation. The common law generally did not place any additional restrictions on the type of statement that could be actionable. Indeed, defamatory communications were deemed actionable regardless of whether they were deemed to be statements of fact or opinion. See, e.g., Restatement of Torts, §§565-567. As noted in the 1977 Restatement (Second) of Torts §566, Comment *a:*

> Under the law of defamation, an expression of opinion could be defamatory if the expression was sufficiently derogatory of another as to cause harm to his reputation, so as to lower him in the estimation of the community or to deter third persons from associating or dealing with him. . . . The expression of opinion was also actionable in a suit for defamation, despite the normal requirement that the communication be false as well as defamatory. . . . This position was maintained even though the truth or falsity of an opinion — as distinguished from a statement of fact — is not a matter that can be objectively determined and truth is a complete defense to a suit for defamation.

However, due to concerns that unduly burdensome defamation laws could stifle valuable public debate, the privilege of "fair comment" was incorporated into the common law as an affirmative defense to an action for defamation. "The principle of 'fair comment' afford[ed] legal immunity for the honest expression of opinion on matters of legitimate public interest when based upon a true or privileged statement of fact." 1 F. Harper & F. James, Law of Torts §5.28, p. 456 (1956) (footnote omitted). As this statement implies, comment was generally privileged when it concerned a matter of public concern, was upon true or privileged facts, represented the actual opinion of the speaker, and was not made solely for the purpose of causing harm. See Restatement of Torts, supra, §606. "According to the majority rule, the privilege of fair comment applied only to an expression of opinion and not to a false statement of fact, whether it was expressly stated or implied from an expression of opinion." Restatement (Second) of Torts, supra, §566, Comment *a.* Thus under the common law, the privilege of "fair comment" was the device employed to strike the appropriate balance between the need for vigorous public discourse and the need to redress injury to citizens wrought by invidious or irresponsible speech.

[The Court's discussion of the earlier Supreme Court cases imposing constitutional restraints on the common law of defamation is omitted.]

Respondents would have us recognize, in addition to the established safeguards discussed above, still another First Amendment-based protection for defamatory statements which are categorized as "opinion" as opposed to "fact." For this proposition they rely principally on the following dictum from our opinion in *Gertz* [v. Robert Welch, Inc., 418 U.S. 323, 94 S. Ct. 2997, 41 L. Ed. 2d 789 (1974)]:

> Under the First Amendment there is no such thing as a false idea. However pernicious an opinion may seem, we depend for its correction not on the conscience of judges and juries but on the competition of other ideas. But there is no constitutional value in false statements of fact.

418 U.S., at 339-340, 94 S. Ct., at 3007 (footnote omitted).

Read in context, . . . the fair meaning of the passage is to equate the word "opinion" in the second sentence with the word "idea" in the first sentence. Under this view, the language was merely a reiteration of Justice Holmes' classic "marketplace of ideas" concept. See Abrams v. United States, 250 U.S. 616, 630, 40 S. Ct. 17, 22, 63 L. Ed. 1173 (1919) (Holmes, J., dissenting) ("[T]he ultimate good desired is better reached by free trade in ideas . . . the best test of truth is the power of the thought to get itself accepted in the competition of the market.").

Thus we do not think this passage from *Gertz* was intended to create a wholesale defamation exemption for anything that might be labeled "opinion." . . . Not only would such an interpretation be contrary to the tenor and context of the passage, but it would also ignore the fact that expressions of "opinion" may often imply an assertion of objective fact.

If a speaker says, "In my opinion John Jones is a liar," he implies a knowledge of facts which lead to the conclusion that Jones told an untruth. Even if the speaker states the facts upon which he bases his opinion, if those facts are either incorrect or incomplete, or if his assessment of them is erroneous, the statement may still imply a false assertion of fact. Simply couching such statements in terms of opinion does not dispel these implications; and the statement, "In my opinion Jones is a liar," can cause as much damage to reputation as the statement, "Jones is a liar." . . .

Apart from their reliance on the *Gertz* dictum, respondents do not really contend that a statement such as, "In my opinion John Jones is a liar," should be protected by a separate privilege for "opinion" under the First Amendment. But they do contend that in every defamation case the First Amendment mandates an inquiry into whether a statement is "opinion" or "fact," and that only the latter statements may be actionable. They propose that a number of factors developed by the lower courts (in what we hold was a mistaken reliance on the *Gertz* dictum) be considered in deciding which is which. But we think the "breathing space" which "freedoms of expression require in order to survive," is adequately secured by existing constitutional doctrine without the creation of an artificial dichotomy between "opinion" and fact.

Foremost . . . a statement on matters of public concern must be provable as false before there can be liability under state defamation law, at least in situations, like the present, where a media defendant is involved. Thus, unlike the statement, "In my opinion Mayor Jones is a liar," the statement, "In my opinion Mayor Jones shows his abysmal ignorance by accepting the teachings of Marx and Lenin," would not be actionable. . . . [A] statement of opinion relating to matters of public concern which does not contain a provably false factual connotation will receive full constitutional protection.[6]

Next, [protection is provided] for statements that cannot "reasonably [be] interpreted as stating actual facts" about an individual. . . . This provides assurance that public debate will not suffer for lack of "imaginative expression" or the "rhetorical hyperbole" which has traditionally added much to the discourse of our Nation.

The *New York Times–Butts* and *Gertz* culpability requirements further ensure that debate on public issues remains "uninhibited, robust, and wide-open," New York Times [Co. v. Sullivan], 376 U.S., at 270, 84 S. Ct., at 720 [(1964)]. Thus, where a statement of "opinion" on a matter of public concern reasonably implies false and defamatory facts regarding public figures or officials, those individuals must show that such statements were made with knowledge of their false implications or with reckless disregard of their truth. Similarly, where such a statement involves a private figure on a matter of public concern, a plaintiff must show that the false connotations were made with some level of fault as required by *Gertz.*

We are not persuaded that, in addition to these protections, an additional separate constitutional privilege for "opinion" is required to ensure the freedom of expression guaranteed by the First Amendment. The dispositive question in the present case then becomes whether or not a reasonable factfinder could conclude that the statements in the Diadiun column imply an assertion that petitioner Milkovich perjured himself in a judicial proceeding. We think this question must be answered in the affirmative. . . . This is not the sort of loose, figurative or hyperbolic language which would negate the impression that the writer was seriously maintaining petitioner committed the crime of perjury. Nor does the general tenor of the article negate this impression.

We also think the connotation that petitioner committed perjury is sufficiently factual to be susceptible of being proved true or false. A determination of whether petitioner lied in this instance can be made on a core of objective evidence by comparing, *inter alia,* petitioner's testimony [in two proceedings below].

The numerous decisions discussed above establishing First Amendment protection for defendants in defamation actions surely demonstrate the Court's recognition of the Amendment's vital guarantee of free and uninhibited discussion of public issues. But there is also another side to the equation; we have regularly acknowledged the "important social values which underlie the law of defamation," and recognize that "[s]ociety has a pervasive and strong interest in preventing and redressing attacks upon reputation." Rosenblatt v. Baer, 383 U.S. 75, 86, 86 S. Ct. 669, 676, 15 L. Ed. 2d 597 (1966). Justice Stewart in that case put it with his customary clarity:

> The right of a man to the protection of his own reputation from unjustified invasion and wrongful hurt reflects no more than our basic concept of the essential dignity and worth of every human being—a concept at the root of any decent system of ordered liberty.
>
> The destruction that defamatory falsehood can bring is, to be sure, often beyond the capacity of the law to redeem. Yet, imperfect though it is, an action for damages is the only hope for vindication or redress the law gives to a man whose reputation has been falsely dishonored.

Id., at 92-93, 86 S. Ct., at 679-680 (Stewart, J., concurring).

6. Does the Chief Justice move too quickly here? What if Mayor Jones does not, in fact, accept the teachings of Marx and Lenin? [Eds.]

We believe our decision in the present case holds the balance true. The judgment [below] is reversed and the case remanded for further proceedings not inconsistent with this opinion.

Reversed.

[The dissenting opinion of Justice Brennan is omitted.]

Milkovich has been seen as changing the law that made "opinion" immune to defamation litigation; that is, if the statement were defined as opinion, there could be no recovery in defamation based on it. See David A. Anderson, Is Libel Law Worth Reforming?, 140 U. Pa. L. Rev. 487, 507 (1991). Several cases illustrate the impact that *Milkovich* has had on the courts. First, in Unelko Corp. v. Rooney, 912 F.2d 1049 (9th Cir. 1990), *cert. denied,* 499 U.S. 961 (1991), the defendant stated in a nationally televised program that he had tried a product made by the plaintiff and that "[i]t didn't work." In a decision rendered before *Milkovich,* the trial judge entered summary judgment in favor of the defendant on the ground that the statement was one of opinion, not of fact. The court of appeals disagreed with this assessment of the case, stating that "a factfinder could conclude that Rooney's statement that [the product] 'didn't work' implied an assertion of objective fact." 912 F.2d at 1055. In Yetman v. English, 811 P.2d 323 (Ariz. 1991), the defendant said of the plaintiff at a political meeting, "What kind of a communist do we have up here that thinks it's improper to protect your interests?" The court held that in the context, whether the statement was an assertion of fact or was "political invective or hyperbole" and thus protected opinion was an issue of fact for the jury. Finally, in Flamm v. American Ass'n of University Women, 201 F.3d 144 (2d Cir. 2000), the court ruled that a statement in a directory of lawyers that the plaintiff was an "ambulance chaser" interested in taking only "slam dunk cases" implied a statement of fact that the plaintiff engaged in improper solicitation of cases.

Other courts, however, have given defendants more leeway in using very derogatory expressions to describe plaintiffs and their activities. Thus, in Hickey v. Capital Cities/ABC, Inc., 792 F. Supp. 1195 (D. Or. 1992), the court entered summary judgment for defendant, which had broadcast a characterization of plaintiff's laboratory animal supply operation as "a black market in stolen pets," "a low, repulsive crime," and "a rotten trade." And in Sullivan v. Conway, 157 F.3d 1092 (7th Cir. 1998), the court ruled that an assertion that the plaintiff "was a very poor lawyer" was a nonactionable statement of opinion. Similarly, in Phantom Touring, Inc. v. Affiliated Publications, 953 F.2d 724 (1st Cir.), *cert. denied,* 504 U.S. 974 (1992), the defendant newspaper carried a story suggesting that the plaintiff was misleading the public in the marketing of a production of "Phantom of the Opera" by failing to call clear attention to the fact that the plaintiff's production was not the more popular Andrew Lloyd Webber version. In affirming the dismissal of the complaint, the court ruled that expressions such as "rip-off," "fraud," and "a snake-oil job" could not reasonably be found to be anything other than expressions of opinion. Finally, in Horsley v. Rivera, 292 F.3d 695 (11th Cir. 2002), an anti-abortion activist published on his website names of doctors who perform abortions, crossing out names of those who have been killed. The court ruled that he could not recover against a nationally televised talk-show host who called the activist "an accomplice to murder" because the talk-show host spoke figuratively and no reasonable viewer would believe that he was literally accusing the plaintiff of a felony. See also Horsley v. Feldt, 304 F.3d 1125 (11th Cir. 2002) (same plaintiff could not recover against abortion rights activists who had stated that plaintiff has "the blood of these doctors on [his] hands"); Schatz v. Republican State Leadership Comm., 669 F.3d 50, 52 (1st Cir. 2012) (allowing that in a political race contestants can, with impunity, "badmouth their opponents, hammering them with unfair and one-sided attacks"); Mink v. Knox, 613 F.3d 995, 1006 (10th Cir. 2010) (altered photographs of a professor, wearing dark sunglasses and a Hitler-like mustache, are protected because "fantasy, parody, rhetorical hyperbole, or imaginative expression" cannot be reasonably interpreted as stating actual facts); Gardner v. Martino, 563 F.3d 981, 989 (9th Cir. 2009) (talk show host's statement that "Polaris sucks" is a nonactionable "obvious exaggeration"); ZL Techs., Inc. v. Gartner, 709 F. Supp. 2d 789 (N.D. Cal. 2010) (defendant's report, placing plaintiff in an unfavorable position in its "Magic Quadrant," a proprietary map that divides vendors into four quadrants in declining order of desirability, constitutes nonactionable opinion).

Milkovich does not, of course, preclude a state from according more protection to speech under state law than does the U.S. Supreme Court under the Constitution. In Immuno AG. v. J. Moor-Jankowski, 567 N.E.2d 1270 (N.Y.), *cert. denied,* 500 U.S. 954 (1991), the Court of Appeals of New York did extend broader protection to speech than *Milkovich.* The plaintiff sued the defendant, the editor of a scientific journal, for publishing a letter critical of the plaintiff's plans for hepatitis research on chimpanzees in West Africa. The court read *Milkovich* as establishing a rule that "except for special situations of loose, figurative, hyperbolic language, statements that contain or imply assertions of provably false fact will likely be actionable." 567 N.E.2d at 1275. On this test, the court believed it could be found that the letter did contain statements of fact. The court ruled, however, that under New York law, the "full context" of the statement should be taken into account, and that the letter as a whole

> would not have been viewed by the average reader of the Journal as conveying actual facts about plaintiff [and] it would be plain to the reasonable reader of this scientific publication that [the letter writer] was voicing no more than a highly partisan point of view.

567 N.E.2d at 1281. One important factor to the court was that the defamation appeared in a letter to the editor.

> The public forum function of letters to the editor is closely related in spirit to the "marketplace of ideas" and oversight and informational values that compelled recognition of the privileges of fair comment, fair report and the immunity accorded expression of opinion. These values are best effectuated by according defendant some latitude to publish a letter to the editor on a matter of legitimate public concern — the letter's author, affiliation, bias and premises fully disclosed, rebuttal openly invited — free of defamation litigation. A publication that provides a forum for such statements on controversial matters is not acting in a fashion "at odds with the premises of democratic government and with the orderly manner in which economic, social, or political change is to be effected" (Garrison v. Louisiana, 379 U.S. 64, 75, [85 S. Ct. 209, 216, 13 L. Ed. 2d 125 (1964)]), but to the contrary is fostering those very values.

567 N.E.2d at 1281-82. See also Wampler v. Higgins, 752 N.E.2d 962 (Ohio 2001). The protection that is, and should be, extended to letters published by the media is discussed in Marc A. Franklin, Libel and Letters to the Editor: Toward an Open Forum, 57 U. Colo. L. Rev. 651 (1986).

Professor Thomas criticizes the categorization of statements as fact or opinion in Jeffrey E. Thomas, A Pragmatic Approach to Meaning in Defamation Law, 34 Wake Forest L.

Rev. 333 (1999). He argues that the courts should evaluate the meaning that the average reader or listener would attribute to the statement, and not whether the statement could be characterized as fact or opinion. He thinks the result in *Milkovich* was right, but that some later lower courts have unduly remained focused on the categorical approach to allegedly defamatory statements, overlooking the fact that a pragmatic approach focused on linguistic factors might provide a more sensible and workable alternative.

Problem 43

In what way would your analysis of Problem 42, p. 831 above, be altered as a result of the constitutional developments discussed in this section?

C. Assessment and Criticism of Current Defamation Law

1. The Realities of Defamation Litigation

Obviously, the Supreme Court in *New York Times* and later cases hoped that the more stringent malice standard would discourage the bringing of defamation suits. See also Philadelphia Newspapers, Inc. v. Hepps, 475 U.S. 767 (1986), which held, contrary to the traditional common law rule, that the burden is on the plaintiff to prove the falsity of the statement. Whether the Court has succeeded in its goal is difficult to determine, given the numerous variables that confound any attempt to identify the impact of the Court's jurisprudence on defamation litigation, including especially the explosion of new forms of media and communications technologies over the past three decades. What does seem clear, however, is that media defendants have been afforded substantial legal protection. See, e.g., Riley v. Harr, 292 F.3d 282 (1st Cir. 2002), which deployed a variety of constitutional and common law doctrines to find non-actionable several challenged statements from the nonfiction book *A Civil Action*, which plaintiff had argued depicted him in a defamatory light. Indeed, after analyzing the results of litigation tracking undertaken by the Libel Defense Resource Center, Professor David A. Logan, in Libel Law in the Trenches: Reflections on Current Data on Libel Litigation, 87 Va. L. Rev. 503, 520 (2001), concluded:

> One could say that the *New York Times* . . . constitutional regime has provided the media with something approaching an absolute privilege to defame; a reasonable publisher should worry about having to pay substantial libel damages as much as she worries about being struck by lightning.

On the other hand, it does not appear that money is a central motivation for pursuing defamation claims and, thus, plaintiffs may continue to bring defamation suits, despite their low likelihood of success. Professor Lidsky, for instance, has observed a rise in libel suits by corporate defendants against individual participants in Internet discussion forums, where the goals of the litigation "are not even arguably about recovering money damages," but rather are to silence critics and manage public perceptions. Lyrissa Barnett Lidsky, Silencing John Doe: Defamation & Discourse in Cyberspace, 49 Duke L.J. 855, 859 (2000). According to an empirical study that observed defamation plaintiffs more generally, only 20 percent admitted that they had compensation as their primary goal. Rather, plaintiffs appear to be more concerned with revenge and correcting the record. See Randall P. Bezanson, Libel Law and the Realities of Libel Litigation: Setting the Record Straight, 71 Iowa L. Rev. 226 (1985). It is just as well that money does not figure prominently in the decision to sue, for another study determined that defamation plaintiffs were successful in only 20 percent of the reported cases. Excluding two very large awards, recoveries averaged only $20,000, out of which the plaintiffs had to pay their costs and legal fees. Settlements averaged only $7,000, before costs and fees. Randall P. Bezanson, The Libel Suit in Retrospect: What Plaintiffs Want and What Plaintiffs Get, 74 Cal. L. Rev. 789 (1986).

2. Possible Legislative Reform

Recent years have seen growing dissatisfaction with the way in which the law of defamation, including the constitutional rules, strikes the balance between the interest in reputation and the interest in free speech. See David Kohler, Forty Years After *New York Times v. Sullivan*: The Good, the Bad, and the Ugly, 83 Or. L. Rev. 1203 (2004). As one critic of the defamation scene observed:

> The present law of libel is a failure. It denies most defamation victims any remedy, and at the same time chills speech by encouraging high litigation costs and occasional large judgments.

David A. Anderson, Is Libel Law Worth Reforming?, 140 U. Pa. L. Rev. 487, 550 (1991). See also Shannon M. Heim, The Role of Extra-judicial Bodies in Vindicating Reputational Harm, 15 CommLaw Conspectus 401, 403 (2007) (proposing "the use of state news councils as an alternative to traditional libel litigation for a more effective vindication of reputational injury").

Another critic of the current law of defamation is Professor Randall P. Bezanson, who argued for change in The Libel Tort Today, 45 Wash. & Lee L. Rev. 535, 556 (1988):

> At least in the mass communication, or media, setting, the libel tort today represents a very different set of interests from those reflected in the common law tort. The interests are essentially regulatory and punitive. The libel tort today represents a civil penalty for general publication in an irresponsible manner of an injurious falsehood about a person or entity. A finding of falsity is based on the content of the challenged statement and the subjective intent of the publisher, not on its meaning as understood in the real dynamics of actual communication. Injury is premised upon the logical consequences of the false fact and attendant emotional stress, not on community-based perceptions of reputation and harm. Irresponsibility is based on judicially-created standards of journalistic process and editorial judgment, not on concepts of privilege that reflect social value and abjure judgments of fault.
>
> Whatever may be said against or in favor of such a tort, it is a far cry from the common law concepts of reputation, compensation, publication, and privilege. For those whose interest is in protecting reputation, today's libel tort fails in almost all respects to do so. It underprotects the community-based interest in reputation, and overprotects the reputationally-unrelated interests in truth, responsible journalism, and freedom from emotional harm. For those whose interest is in protecting the press from unnecessary inhibition and government control of the standards of journalism, today's libel tort is anathema, for

> the chief consequence of libel today is inhibition of the press from violating judicially-crafted standards of journalism. Finally, for those who placed faith in the privileges created by New York Times Co. v. Sullivan and its progeny, today's libel tort must be discouraging, if not utterly devastating, for it falls substantially short of safeguarding press freedom and fails to safeguard individual reputation as well.
>
> Whether in our instinct for reform we should return to the imperfectly realized common law interests or formulate new approaches that depart from both our present and our past, we need to build change on an understanding of where we are today and how we got there. For my part, today's libel tort is profoundly and fundamentally disquieting in a society that attempts to strike a balance between reputation and freedom of expression. Change in the libel system is therefore an imperative. But this should be neither a shocking nor an unsettling conclusion, for change is the one common thread that extends throughout the libel tort's long and arduous history.

Objections of this sort are not new. But as yet, legislatures have not attempted broad intervention into defamation law, as they have with respect to personal injury law — no doubt because constitutional law substantially circumscribes the permitted scope of legislative action. Nonetheless, a movement has emerged for legislative reformation of the law of defamation — a reformation that is much more sweeping than the recent legislative reforms of tort law.[7] The movement began with the Libel Reform Project of the Annenberg Washington Program. Under the direction of Professor Rodney A. Smolla, the project developed its comprehensive "Proposal for the Reform of Libel Law" in 1988. The basic thrust of the proposal is to provide an alternative to damage actions in which the truth or falsity of the statement would be determinative. See Rodney A. Smolla & Michael J. Gaertner, The Annenberg Libel Reform Proposal: The Case for Enactment, 31 Wm. & Mary L. Rev. 25 (1989). That facet of the proposal has emerged in a series of drafts of a Uniform Defamation Act prepared by the National Conference of Commissioners on Uniform State Laws, the latest of which is dated March 23, 1993, although there are significant differences between the two proposals. The act would permit a defendant to submit an "offer of termination" to the plaintiff. To be effective, the offer would have to stipulate that the defendant does not assert the truth of the statement, and offer to publish a correction. If accepted by the plaintiff, the action would be dismissed; if rejected, the plaintiff's recovery, if any, would be limited to economic damages. The act would also permit the plaintiff to bring an action for "vindication," rather than for damages. The central issue would be the falsity of the statement; the fault of the defendant would not be relevant, nor would the defendant be able to rely on a conditional privilege. For an extensive discussion of the history of the Uniform Act, see Robert M. Ackerman, Bringing Coherence to Defamation Law Through Uniform Legislation: The Search for an Elegant Solution, 72 N.C. L. Rev. 291 (1994). The proposed act met with substantial opposition from a variety of quarters, and the Reporter has recommended that it be withdrawn from further consideration by the Commissioners. Part of the Uniform Defamation Act has survived for further consideration by the Commissioners, however, and was approved by them in the form of the Uniform Correction or Clarification of Defamation Act.

7. Reform proposals of a more theoretical bent also have appeared. For an argument that the "actual malice" rule should be abandoned in favor of a legislatively established rule that would permit public figures to recover the amount that the media profited from the defamatory statement, see Kristian D. Whitten, The Economics of Actual Malice: A Proposal for Legislative Change to the Rule of New York Times v. Sullivan, 32 Cumb. L. Rev. 519 (2002).

The ABA's House of Delegates endorsed the act in 1994 by a vote of 176 to 130 and, as of 2016, it had been adopted in three states, North Dakota, Texas, and Washington. The act requires a potential plaintiff to make a timely and adequate request for a correction or clarification from the defendant. If the defendant makes a sufficient correction, as defined by the act, the person may only recover provable economic loss as mitigated by the correction.

Chapter 13

Invasion of Privacy

The right to recover for invasion of privacy had its genesis in a law review article: Samuel D. Warren & Louis D. Brandeis, The Right to Privacy, 4 Harv. L. Rev. 193 (1890). The article was prompted by what Warren viewed as outrageous reporting by the Boston newspapers of his and his wife's social activities, including the printing of guest lists from the Warrens' dinner parties. After this article appeared, courts, and occasionally legislatures, built on the ideas of Warren and Brandeis and almost all states now recognize, in some form, the right to recover for invasion of privacy. Most courts have followed the analysis advanced by Prosser in an article from which the following excerpts are taken:

William L. Prosser, Privacy

48 Cal. L. Rev. 383, 390-403, 405-06 (1960)

[In this article, Prosser undertakes a comprehensive survey of right to privacy cases, and concludes that not one tort but rather a set of four torts, each protecting a different interest, has emerged.]

I. Intrusion

[Prosser first discusses the early cases falling into this category, which involved physical intrusions into such places as the plaintiff's home or hotel room.]

The principle was, however, soon carried beyond such physical intrusion. It was extended to eavesdropping upon private conversations by means of wire tapping and microphones; and there are three decisions, . . . which have applied the same principle to peering into the windows of a home. . . . The tort has been found in the case of unauthorized prying into the plaintiff's bank account. . . .

It is clear, however, that there must be something in the nature of prying or intrusion, and mere noises which disturb a church congregation, or bad manners, harsh names and insulting gestures in public, have been held not to be enough. It is also clear that the intrusion must be something which would be offensive or objectionable to a reasonable man, and that there is no tort when the landlord stops by on Sunday morning to ask for the rent.

It is clear also that the thing into which there is prying or intrusion must be, and be entitled to be, private. . . . On the public street, or in any other public place, the plaintiff has no right to be alone, and it is no invasion of his privacy to do no more than follow him about. Neither is it such an invasion to take his photograph in such a place, since this amounts to nothing more than making a record, not differing essentially from a full written description, of a public sight which any one present would be free to see. . . .

It appears obvious that the interest protected by this branch of the tort is primarily a mental one. It has been useful chiefly to fill in the gaps left by trespass, nuisance, the intentional infliction of mental distress, and whatever remedies there may be for the invasion of constitutional rights.

II. Public Disclosure of Private Facts

. . . First, the disclosure of the private facts must be a public disclosure, and not a private one. There must be, in other words, publicity. It is an invasion of the right to publish in a newspaper that the plaintiff does not pay his debts, or to post a notice to that effect in a window on the public street or cry it aloud in the highway; but, . . . it has been agreed that it is no invasion to communicate that fact to the plaintiff's employer, or to any other individual, or even to a small group, unless there is some breach of contract, trust or confidential relation which will afford an independent basis for relief. . . .

Second, the facts disclosed to the public must be private facts, and not public ones. Certainly no one can complain when publicity is given to information about him which he himself leaves open to the public eye, such as the appearance of the house in which he lives, or the business in which he is engaged. . . .

. . . The decisions indicate that anything visible in a public place may be recorded and given circulation by means of a photograph, to the same extent as by a written description, since this amounts to nothing more than giving publicity to what is already public and what any one present would be free to see. . . .

Third, the matter made public must be one which would be offensive and objectionable to a reasonable man of ordinary sensibilities. All of us, to some extent, lead lives exposed to the public gaze or to public inquiry, and complete privacy does not exist in this world except for the eremite in the desert. Any one who is not a hermit must expect the more or less casual observation of his neighbors and the passing public as to what he is and does, and some reporting of his daily activities. The ordinary reasonable man does not take offense at mention in a newspaper of the fact that he has returned from a visit, or gone camping in the woods, or that he has given a party as his house for his friends; and very probably Mr. Warren would never have had any action for the reports of his daughter's wedding. The law of privacy is not intended for the protection of any shrinking soul who is abnormally sensitive about such publicity. It is quite a different matter when the details of sexual relations are spread before the public gaze, or there is highly personal portrayal of his intimate private characteristics or conduct. . . .

III. False Light in the Public Eye

. . . One form in which [this tort] occasionally appears . . . is that of publicity falsely attributing to the plaintiff some opinion or utterance. A good illustration of this might be the fictitious testimonial used in advertising. . . . More typical are spurious books and articles, or ideas expressed in them, which purport to emanate from the plaintiff. In the same category are the unauthorized use of his name as a candidate for office, or to advertise for witnesses of an accident, or the entry of an actor, without his consent, in a popularity contest of an embarrassing kind.

Another form in which this branch of the tort frequently has made its appearance is the use of the plaintiff's picture to illustrate a book or an article with which he has no reasonable connection. . . .

Still another form in which the tort occurs is the inclusion of the plaintiff's name, photograph and fingerprints in a public a "rogues' gallery" of convicted criminals, when he has not in fact been convicted of any crime. . . .

The false light need not necessarily be a defamatory one, although it very often is, and a defamation action will also lie. It seems clear, however, that it must be something that would be objectionable to the ordinary reasonable man under the circumstances, and that, as in the case of disclosure, the hypersensitive individual will not be protected. . . .

The false light cases obviously differ from those of intrusion, or disclosure of private facts. The interest protected is clearly that of reputation, with the same overtones of mental distress as in defamation. There is a resemblance to disclosure; but the two differ in that one involves truth and the other lies, one private or secret facts and the other invention. Both require publicity. There has been a good deal of overlapping of defamation in the false light cases, and apparently either action, or both, will very often lie. The privacy cases do go considerably beyond the narrow limits of defamation, and no doubt have succeeded in affording a needed remedy in a good many instances not covered by the other tort.

It is here, however, that one disposed to alarm might express the greatest concern over where privacy may be going. The question may well be raised, and apparently still is unanswered, whether this branch of the tort is not capable of swallowing up and engulfing the whole law of public defamation; and whether there is any false libel printed, for example, in a newspaper, which cannot be redressed upon the alternative ground. If that turns out to be the case, it may well be asked, what of the numerous restrictions and limitations which have hedged defamation about for many years, in the interest of freedom of the press and the discouragement of trivial and extortionate claims? Are they of so little consequence that they may be circumvented in so casual and cavalier a fashion?

IV. Appropriation

. . . [T]here are a great many decisions in which the plaintiff has recovered when his name or picture, or other likeness, has been used without his consent to advertise the defendant's product, or to accompany an article sold, to add luster to the name of a corporation, or for other business purposes. . . .

It is the plaintiff's name as a symbol of his identity that is involved here, and not his name as a mere name. There is, as a good many thousand John Smiths can bear witness, no such thing as an exclusive right to the use of any name. . . . It is when he makes use of the name to pirate the plaintiff's identity for some advantage of his own, as by impersonation to obtain credit or secret information, or by posing as the plaintiff's wife, or providing a father for a child on a birth certificate, that he becomes liable. It is in this sense that "appropriation" must be understood.

On this basis, the question before the courts has been first of all whether there has been appropriation of an aspect of the plaintiff's identity. It is not enough that a name which is the same as his is used in a novel, a comic strip, or the title of a corporation, unless the context or the circumstances, or the addition of some other element, indicate that the name is that of the plaintiff. . . .

Once the plaintiff is identified, there is the further question whether the defendant has appropriated the name or likeness for his own advantage. . . . [I]t has been held that the mere incidental mention of the plaintiff's name in a book or a motion picture or even in a commentary upon news which is part of an advertisement, is not an invasion of his privacy; nor is the publication of a photograph or a newsreel in which he incidentally appears.

It seems sufficiently evident that appropriation is quite a different matter from intrusion, disclosure of private facts, or a false light in the public eye. The interest protected is not so much a mental as a proprietary one, in the exclusive use of the plaintiff's name and likeness as an aspect of his identity. It seems quite pointless to dispute over whether such a right is to be classified as "property." If it is not, it is at least, once it is protected by the law, a right of value upon which the plaintiff can capitalize by selling licenses. . . .

Courts overwhelmingly have adopted Prosser's "four tort" approach to privacy law. One exception is New York — in Robertson v. Rochester Folding Box Co., 64 N.E. 442 (N.Y. 1902), the court of appeals held that there is no common law right of privacy in New York. See also Messenger v. Gruner & Jahr Printing and Publishing, 727 N.E.2d 549 (N.Y. 2000).[1] Not surprisingly, the Restatement of Torts (Second) has incorporated Prosser's approach into §§652A-652E dealing with invasions of privacy. (Prosser was the reporter for the Restatement (Second) of Torts when these sections were drafted and approved.) Given the judicial approval of Prosser's approach, this chapter also incorporates that organization. However, the "four tort" approach should not be seen as a tidy and uncontestable construction of privacy doctrine. Instead, as Judge Biggs of the U.S. Court of Appeals for the Third Circuit memorably remarked, the state of privacy law is very much "that of a haystack in a hurricane." Ettore v. Philco Television Broadcasting Co., 229 F.2d 481, 485 (3d Cir. 1956). For a critical analysis of Prosser's approach, see Neil M. Richards & Daniel J. Solove, Prosser's Privacy Law: A Mixed Legacy, 98 Cal. L. Rev. 1887 (2010). And for an effort to update Prosser's taxonomy of privacy interests in light of both "the breathtaking rise of the Information Age" and the various areas of law that concern privacy in addition to tort, see Daniel J. Solove, A Taxonomy of Privacy, 154 U. Pa. L. Rev. 477 (2006).

Nor should judicial acceptance of Prosser's rubric be taken to mean that there is agreement as to the values that underlie the privacy torts. A number of commentators have disagreed with Prosser on that issue. For example, Professor Edward J. Blaustein, in his article, Privacy as an Aspect of Human Dignity: An Answer to Dean Prosser, 39 N.Y.U. L. Rev. 962 (1964), argues in favor of a single tort, having as its purpose the protection of personal dignity. A different view is advanced in Robert C. Post, The Social Foundations of Privacy: Community and Self in the Common Law Tort, 77 Cal. L. Rev. 957 (1989); the author argues that the purpose of privacy law should be to protect "rules of civility." Professor Randall P. Benzanson, in *The Right to Privacy* Revisited: Privacy, News, and Social Change, 1890-1990, 80 Cal. L. Rev. 1133 (1992), asserts that privacy law should protect persons' control of information. More recent authors have eschewed the attempt to identify a single or dominant purpose of privacy law, and instead have identified several diverse interests and values that are typically subsumed under the broad heading of privacy. See Jonathan Kahn, Privacy as a Legal Principle of Identity Maintenance, 33 Seton Hall. L. Rev. 371 (2003); Daniel J. Solove, Conceptualizing Privacy, 90 Cal. L. Rev. 1087 (2002); Robert C. Post, Three Concepts of Privacy, 89 Geo. L.J. 2087 (2001). Finally, Professor Eugene Volokh argues that — whatever the force and underlying values of privacy law — a slew of *other* tort law duties perversely incentivize parties to compromise privacy interests

1. One year after the *Robertson* case, New York adopted a statute that prohibited the use of an individual's name or likeness for advertising or trade purposes without the person's consent. *See* Act of Apr. 6, 1903, ch. 132, §§1-2, 1903 N.Y. Laws 308.

in order to satisfy their obligations of reasonable monitoring, investigation, and disclosure. See Eugene Volokh, Tort Law vs. Privacy, 114 Colum. L. Rev. 879 (2014).

The following overview of Prosser's four torts should enable you to draw at least some tentative conclusions on the meaning and significance of privacy as a legal construct.

A. *Intrusion*

Hamberger v. Eastman

106 N.H. 107, 206 A.2d 239 (1964)

The plaintiffs, husband and wife, brought companion suits for invasion of their privacy against the defendant who owned and rented a dwelling house to the plaintiffs. . . .

The declaration in the suit by the husband reads as follows:

"In a plea of the case, for that the defendant is the owner of a certain dwelling house . . . which was, and still is, occupied by the plaintiff and his family as a dwelling house on a weekly rental basis; that said dwelling house is located adjacent to and abutting other land of the defendant whereon the defendant maintains his place of residence, together with his place of business.

"That, sometime during the period from October, 1961, to October 15, 1962, the defendant, wholly without the knowledge and consent of the plaintiff, did willfully and maliciously invade the privacy and sanctity of the plaintiff's bedroom, which he shared with his wife in their dwelling house, by installing and concealing a listening and recording device in said bedroom; that this listening and recording device, which was concealed in an area adjacent to the bed occupied by the plaintiff and his wife was attached and connected to the defendant's place of residence by means of wires capable of transmitting and recording any sounds and voices originating in said bedroom.

"That, on or about October 15, 1962, plaintiff discovered the listening and recording device which defendant had willfully and maliciously concealed in his bedroom, and the plaintiff, ever since that time and as a direct result of the actions of the defendant, has been greatly distressed, humiliated, and embarrassed and has sustained and is now sustaining, intense and severe mental suffering and distress, and has been rendered extremely nervous and upset, seriously impairing both his mental and physical condition, and that the plaintiff has sought, and still is under, the care of a physician; that large sums have been, and will be in the future, expended for medical care and attention; that because of his impaired mental and physical condition, the plaintiff has been and still is unable to properly perform his normal and ordinary duties as a father and as a husband, and has been unable to properly perform his duties at his place of employment, and has been otherwise greatly injured."

The declaration in the suit by the wife is identical, with appropriate substitutes of the personal pronoun, and omission of the allegation of inability to perform duties at her place of employment.

In both actions the defendant moved to dismiss on the ground that on the facts alleged, no cause of action is stated. The Court . . . reserved and transferred the cases to the Supreme Court without ruling.

Kenison, C.J. The question presented is whether the right of privacy is recognized in this state. There is no controlling statute and no previous decision in this jurisdiction which decides the question. Inasmuch as invasion of the right of privacy is not a single tort but consists of four distinct torts, it is probably more concrete and accurate to state the issue in the present case to be whether this state recognizes that intrusion upon one's physical and mental solitude or seclusion is a tort. . . .

We have not searched for cases where the bedroom of husband and wife has been "bugged" but it should not be necessary — by way of understatement — to observe that this is the type of intrusion that would be offensive to any person of ordinary sensibilities. What married "people do in the privacy of their bedrooms is their own business so long as they are not hurting anyone else." Ernst and Loth, For Better or Worse 79 (1952). The Restatement, Torts, §867 provides that "a person who unreasonably and seriously interferes with another's interest in not having his affairs known to others . . . is liable to the other." As is pointed out in Comment *d* "liability exists only if the defendant's conduct was such that he should have realized that it would be offensive to persons of ordinary sensibilities. It is only where the intrusion has gone beyond the limits of decency that liability accrues. These limits are exceeded where intimate details of the life of one who has never manifested a desire to have publicity are exposed to the public. . . ."

The defendant contends that the right of privacy should not be recognized on the facts of the present case as they appear in the pleadings because there are no allegations that anyone listened or overheard any sounds or voices originating from the plaintiffs' bedroom. The tort of intrusion on the plaintiffs' solitude or seclusion does not require publicity and communication to third persons although this would affect the amount of damages. . . . The defendant also contends that the right of privacy is not violated unless something has been published, written or printed and that oral publicity is not sufficient. Recent cases make it clear that this is not a requirement.

If the peeping Tom, the big ear and electronic eavesdropper (whether ingenious or ingenuous) have a place in the hierarchy of social values, it ought not to be at the expense of a married couple minding their own business in the seclusion of their bedroom who have never asked for or by their conduct deserved a potential projection of their private conversations and actions to their landlord or to others. Whether actual or potential such "publicity with respect to private matters of purely personal concern is an injury to personality. It impairs the mental peace and comfort of the individual and may produce suffering more acute than that produced by a mere bodily injury." III Pound, Jurisprudence 58 (1959). The use of parabolic microphones and sonic wave devices designed to pick up conversations in a room without entering it and at a considerable distance away makes the problem far from fanciful.

It is unnecessary to determine the extent to which the right of privacy is protected as a constitutional matter without the benefit of statute. For the purposes of the present case it is sufficient to hold that the invasion of the plaintiffs' solitude or seclusion, as alleged in the pleadings, was a violation of their right of privacy and constituted a tort for which the plaintiffs may recover damages to the extent that they can prove them. "Certainly, no right deserves greater protection, for, as Emerson has well said, 'solitude, the safeguard of mediocrity, is to genius the stern friend.'" Ezer, Intrusion on Solitude: Herein of Civil Rights and Civil Wrongs, 21 Law in Transition 63, 75 (1961).

The motion to dismiss should be denied.

Remanded.

All concurred.

Many intrusion cases are like *Hamberger* in that they involve physical invasions of the plaintiff's property. See, e.g., Engman v. Southwestern Bell Tel. Co., 591 S.W.2d 78 (Mo. Ct. App. 1979), and Gonzales v. Southwestern Bell Tel. Co., 555 S.W.2d 219 (Tex. Civ. App. 1977). In both of these cases telephone company employees entered the homes of the plaintiffs to remove telephones after service had been terminated. In *Gonzales*, the fact that the plaintiffs were not at home at the time of the entry did not defeat their claim. And in *Engman*, the court ruled that the telephone company tariff, pursuant to which the defendant retained title to telephones and was authorized to enter customers' premises to remove them, did not insulate the defendant from liability. In connection with the latter case, consider Florida Publishing Co. v. Fletcher, 340 So. 2d 914 (Fla. 1976), *cert. denied*, 431 U.S. 930 (1977), in which the court ruled that a newspaper reporter covering a story about a fire at the plaintiff's home had consent by "custom and usage" to enter the home with a fire marshal and a police officer investigating the fire.

Intrusion overlaps considerably with trespass actions, and often plaintiffs will allege both. The presence or absence of an invasion or trespass may often turn on consent. Consent, in certain circumstances, may be obtained through fraud or subterfuge without exposing the intruder to liability. In Desnick v. American Broadcasting Cos., Inc., 44 F.3d 1345 (7th Cir. 1995), for example, investigative journalists for Prime Time Live sent "testers," claiming to be patients, into plaintiff's eye care centers to see if the centers were recommending unnecessary cataract surgery. The Seventh Circuit held no action for trespass or invasion of privacy would lie. Chief Judge Posner stated (44 F.3d at 1351):

> [S]ome cases . . . deem consent effective even though it was procured by fraud. There must be *something* to this surprising result. Without it a restaurant critic could not conceal his identity when he ordered a meal, or a browser pretend to be interested in merchandise that he could not afford to buy. Dinner guests would be trespassers if they were false friends who never would have been invited had the host known their true character, and a consumer who in an effort to bargain down an automobile dealer falsely claimed to be able to buy the same car elsewhere at a lower price would be a trespasser in the dealer's showroom. Some of these might be classified as privileged trespasses, designed to promote competition. Others might be thought justified by some kind of implied consent — the restaurant critic for example might point by way of analogy to the use of the "fair use" defense by book reviewers charged with copyright infringement and argue that the restaurant industry as a whole would be injured if restaurants could exclude critics. But most such efforts at rationalization would be little better than evasions. The fact is that consent to an entry is often given legal effect even though the entrant has intentions that if known to the owner of the property would cause him for perfectly understandable and generally ethical or at least lawful reasons to revoke his consent.

Several courts have resisted the *Desnick* opinion's apparently broad acceptance of consent obtained through misrepresentation. In Pitt Sales, Inc. v. King World Productions, Inc., 383 F. Supp. 2d 1354 (S.D. Fla. 2005), for instance, the court emphasized that "the issue before it is not whether a misrepresentation vitiates consent, but whether the acts of the party accused of the trespass do not exceed, or are not in conflict with, the purposes for which such consent was given." Id. at 1367. In that case, a producer for *Inside Edition* posed as a door-to-door sales representative for a magazine sales company in order to secretly record the company's activities. The court held that a factual question existed regarding whether the defendants' acts exceeded or conflicted with the nominal basis of the plaintiff's consent. Id. In so ruling, the court relied heavily on Food Lion v. Capital Cities/ABC, Inc., 194 F.3d 505 (4th Cir. 1999), a prominent case in which two American

Broadcasting Company (ABC) reporters using false resumes secured employment with the plaintiff for the undisclosed purpose of investigating the plaintiff's food handling practices. The Fourth Circuit upheld an award based on trespass, reasoning that "[a]lthough Food Lion consented to [the reporter's] entry to do her job, she exceeded the consent when she videotaped in non-public areas of the store and worked against her second employer, Food Lion, in doing so." Id. at 519.

As *Desnick*, *Pitt Sales*, and *Food Lion* illustrate, a recurring factual context for intrusion claims involves the use of aggressive investigatory techniques by journalists. One of the most prominent such cases was Nader v. General Motors Corp., 255 N.E.2d 765 (N.Y. 1970), arising out of a book by the plaintiff, Ralph Nader, *Unsafe at Any Speed*, which criticized the defendant's automobiles. Based on a research paper written by Nader while he was a law student, *Unsafe at Any Speed* is credited by many with launching the modern consumer rights and auto safety movements. According to Nader, General Motors was less supportive of his efforts than were consumers. Specifically, the plaintiff alleged that the defendant:

> (1) conducted a series of interviews with acquaintances of the plaintiff, "questioning them about, and casting aspersions upon (his) political, social . . . racial and religious views . . . ; his integrity; his sexual proclivities and inclinations; and his personal habits"; (2) kept him under surveillance in public places for an unreasonable length of time; (3) caused him to be accosted by girls for the purpose of entrapping him into illicit relationships; (4) made threatening, harassing and obnoxious telephone calls to him; (5) tapped his telephone and eavesdropped, by means of mechanical and electronic equipment, on his private conversations with others; and (6) conducted a "continuing" and harassing investigation of him. [255 N.E.2d at 767.]

In response to these allegations, the court ruled that under District of Columbia law the telephone tapping and eavesdropping would constitute invasions of privacy, as would the surveillance if it were "overzealous." Id. at 772. The other allegations would not support an action for invasion of privacy, according to the court, but might support recovery for intentional infliction of emotional harm. Id. at 770. The case was settled before trial for $425,000, most of which Nader used to start a consumer advocacy organization, the Center for Study of Responsive Law. The president of General Motors at the time, James Roche, appeared before a United States Senate subcomittee in 1966 and apologized to Nader. That same year, Congress passed two expansive statutes that formed the basis of modern highway safety regulation. See Highway Safety Act of 1966, Pub. L. No. 89-564, 80 Stat. 731 (codified at 23 U.S.C. §§401-404 (2000)); National Traffic and Motor Vehicle Safety Act of 1966, Pub. L. No. 89-563, 80 Stat. 718 (codified at 49 U.S.C. §§30101-30170 (2000)). For an interesting account of the Nader-General Motors controversy by the plaintiff's attorney, see Stuart M. Speiser, Lawsuit 1-118 (1980). For a recent case involving similar investigatory practices, see Meyer v. Kalanick, 2016 WL 3981369 at *1 (S.D.N.Y. 2016) ("It is a sad day when, in response to the filing of a commercial lawsuit, a corporate defendant feels compelled to hire unlicensed private investigators to conduct secret personal background investigations of both the plaintiff and his counsel. It is sadder yet when these investigators flagrantly lie to friends and acquaintances of the plaintiff and his counsel in an (ultimately unsuccessful) attempt to obtain derogatory information about them.").

In David A. Logan, Masked Media: Judges, Juries, and the Law of Surreptitious Newsgathering, 83 Iowa L. Rev. 161, 163-64 (1997), the author analyzes the issues in cases like

Desnick, *Pitt Sales*, *Food Lion*, and *Nader* and concludes that there should be room for tort litigation, despite the public interests served by aggressive newsgathering tactics:

> This Article . . . proposes an inelegant solution to the vexing problems presented by surreptitious newsgathering. If a reporter violates "generally applicable" state tort law (e.g., commits fraud and trespass), she should be subject to liability and an award of compensatory and, in extreme circumstances, punitive damages. The damages available, however, should be sharply cabined to avoid creating excessive disincentives to engage in investigative reporting. Recognizing that the "primary purpose (of tort law) is to make a fair adjustment of the conflicting claims of the litigating parties," these limits should arise primarily from state law, with judges using familiar common-law principles.

Reflecting the spirit of Professor Logan's proposal, the *Food Lion* plaintiff sought only nominal damages of one dollar for its trespass claim. See 194 F.3d at 516-17.

Shulman v. Group W Productions, Inc.

18 Cal. 4th 200, 955 P.2d 469, 74 Cal. Rptr. 2d 843 (1998)

WERDEGAR, JUSTICE. . . .

In the present case, we address the balance between privacy and press freedom in the commonplace context of an automobile accident. Plaintiffs, two members of a family whose activities and position did not otherwise make them public figures, were injured when their car went off the highway, overturning and trapping them inside. A medical transport and rescue helicopter crew came to plaintiffs' assistance, accompanied on this occasion by a video camera operator employed by a television producer. The cameraman filmed plaintiffs' extrication from the car, the flight nurse and medic's efforts to give them medical care during the extrication, and their transport to the hospital in the helicopter. The flight nurse wore a small microphone that picked up her conversations with other rescue workers and with one of the plaintiffs. This videotape and sound track were edited into a segment that was broadcast, months later, on a documentary television show, *On Scene: Emergency Response.* Plaintiffs, who consented neither to the filming and recording nor to the broadcasting, allege the television producers thereby intruded into a realm of personal privacy and gave unwanted publicity to private events of their lives.

The trial court granted summary judgment for the producers on the ground that the events depicted in the broadcast were newsworthy and the producers' activities were therefore protected under the First Amendment to the United States Constitution. The Court of Appeal reversed, finding . . . legal error on the trial court's part as to both plaintiffs' intrusion claims. Agreeing with some, but not all, of the Court of Appeal's analysis, we conclude summary judgment was [improper] as to their cause of action for intrusion. . . .

Discussion

Influenced by Dean Prosser's analysis of the tort actions for invasion of privacy (Prosser, Privacy (1960), 48 Cal. L. Rev. 381) and the exposition of a similar analysis in the Restatement Second of Torts sections 652A-652E, California courts have recognized . . . the privacy cause of action pleaded by plaintiffs here: . . . intrusion into private places, conversations or other matters. . . .

II. Intrusion

Of the four privacy torts identified by Prosser, the tort of intrusion into private places, conversations or matter is perhaps the one that best captures the common understanding of an "invasion of privacy." . . .

As stated in [Miller v. National Broadcasting Co., 232 Cal. Rptr. 668 (1986) (*Miller*)] and the Restatement, . . . the action for intrusion has two elements: (1) intrusion into a private place, conversation or matter, (2) in a manner highly offensive to a reasonable person. We consider the elements in that order.

We ask first whether defendants "intentionally intrude[d], physically or otherwise, upon the solitude or seclusion of another," that is, into a place or conversation private to [plaintiffs]. . . . To prove actionable intrusion, the plaintiff must show the defendant penetrated some zone of physical or sensory privacy surrounding, or obtained unwanted access to data about, the plaintiff. The tort is proven only if the plaintiff had an objectively reasonable expectation of seclusion or solitude in the place, conversation or data source.

Cameraman Cooke's mere presence at the accident scene and filming of the events occurring there cannot be deemed either a physical or sensory intrusion on plaintiffs' seclusion. Plaintiffs had no right of ownership or possession of the property where the rescue took place, nor any actual control of the premises. Nor could they have had a reasonable expectation that members of the media would be excluded or prevented from photographing the scene; for journalists to attend and record the scenes of accidents and rescues is in no way unusual or unexpected.

Two aspects of defendants' conduct, however, raise triable issues of intrusion on seclusion. First, a triable issue exists as to whether both plaintiffs had an objectively reasonable expectation of privacy in the interior of the rescue helicopter, which served as an ambulance. Although the attendance of reporters and photographers at the scene of an accident is to be expected, we are aware of no law or custom permitting the press to ride in ambulances or enter hospital rooms during treatment without the patient's consent. Other than the two patients and Cooke, only three people were present in the helicopter, all Mercy Air staff. As the Court of Appeal observed, "[i]t is neither the custom nor the habit of our society that any member of the public at large or its media representatives may hitch a ride in an ambulance and ogle as paramedics care for an injured stranger."

Second, Ruth [one of the plaintiffs] was entitled to a degree of privacy in her conversations with Carnahan [the flight nurse] and other medical rescuers at the accident scene, and in Carnahan's conversations conveying medical information regarding Ruth to the hospital base. Cooke, perhaps, did not intrude into that zone of privacy merely by being present at a place where he could hear such conversations with unaided ears. But by placing a microphone on Carnahan's person, amplifying and recording what she said and heard, defendants may have listened in on conversations the parties could reasonably have expected to be private. . . .

Whether Ruth expected her conversations with Nurse Carnahan or the other rescuers to remain private and whether any such expectation was reasonable are, on the state of the record before us, questions for the jury. We note, however, that several existing legal protections for communications could support the conclusion that Ruth possessed a reasonable expectation of privacy in her conversations with Nurse Carnahan and the other rescuers. A patient's conversation with a provider of medical care in the course of treatment including emergency treatment, carries a traditional and legally well-established expectation of privacy. . . .

Ruth's claim require[s] her . . . only to prove that she had an objectively reasonable expectation of privacy in her conversations. Whether the circumstances of Ruth's extrication and helicopter rescue would reasonably have indicated to defendants, or to their agent, Cooke, that Ruth would desire and expect her communications to Carnahan and the other rescuers to be confined to them alone, and therefore not to be electronically transmitted and recorded, is a triable issue of fact in this case. . . .

We turn to the second element of the intrusion tort, offensiveness of the intrusion. . . . The *Miller* court explained that determining offensiveness requires consideration of all the circumstances of the intrusion, including its degree and setting and the intruder's "motives and objectives." The *Miller* court concluded that reasonable people could regard the camera crew's conduct in filming a man's emergency medical treatment in his home, without seeking or obtaining his or his wife's consent, as showing "a cavalier disregard for ordinary citizens' rights of privacy" and, hence, as highly offensive.

We agree with the *Miller* court that all the circumstances of an intrusion, including the motives or justification of the intruder, are pertinent to the offensiveness element. Motivation or justification becomes particularly important when the intrusion is by a member of the print or broadcast press in the pursuit of news material. Although, as will be discussed more fully later, the First Amendment does not immunize the press from liability for torts or crimes committed in an effort to gather news, the constitutional protection of the press does reflect the strong societal interest in effective and complete reporting of events, an interest that may — as a matter of tort law — justify an intrusion that would otherwise be considered offensive.

In deciding, therefore, whether a reporter's alleged intrusion into private matters (i.e., physical space, conversation or data) is "offensive" and hence actionable as an invasion of privacy, courts must consider the extent to which the intrusion was, under the circumstances, justified by the legitimate motive of gathering the news. Information collecting techniques that may be highly offensive when done for socially unprotected reasons — for purposes of harassment, blackmail or prurient curiosity, for example — may not be offensive to a reasonable person when employed by journalists in pursuit of a socially or politically important story. . . .

The mere fact the intruder was in pursuit of a "story" does not, however, generally justify an otherwise offensive intrusion; offensiveness depends as well on the particular method of investigation used. At one extreme, "'routine . . . reporting techniques,'" such as asking questions of people with information . . . could rarely, if ever, be deemed an actionable intrusion. At the other extreme, violation of well-established legal areas of physical or sensory privacy — trespass into a home or tapping a personal telephone line, for example — could rarely, if ever, be justified by a reporter's need to get the story. Such acts would be deemed highly offensive even if the information sought was of weighty public concern; they would also be outside any protection the Constitution provides to newsgathering.

Between these extremes lie difficult cases, many involving the use of photographic and electronic recording equipment. Equipment such as hidden cameras and miniature cordless and directional microphones are powerful investigative tools for newsgathering, but may also be used in ways that severely threaten personal privacy. California tort law provides no bright line on this question; each case must be taken on its facts.

On this summary judgment record, we believe a jury could find defendants' recording of Ruth's communications to Carnahan and other rescuers, and filming in the air ambulance, to be "'highly offensive to a reasonable person.'" With regard to the depth of the intrusion, a reasonable jury could find highly offensive the placement of a microphone on a medical rescuer in order to intercept what would otherwise be private conversations with an injured patient. In that setting, as defendants could and should have foreseen, the patient would not know her words were being recorded and would not have occasion to ask about, and object or consent to, recording. Defendants, it could reasonably be said, took calculated advantage of the patient's "vulnerability and confusion." Arguably, the last thing an injured accident victim should have to worry about while being pried from her wrecked car is that a television producer may be recording everything she says to medical personnel for the possible edification and entertainment of casual television viewers.

For much the same reason, a jury could reasonably regard entering and riding in an ambulance — whether on the ground or in the air — with two seriously injured patients to be an egregious intrusion on a place of expected seclusion. Again, the patients, at least in this case, were hardly in a position to keep careful watch on who was riding with them, or to inquire as to everyone's business and consent or object to their presence. A jury could reasonably believe that fundamental respect for human dignity requires the patients' anxious journey be taken only with those whose care is solely for them and out of sight of the prying eyes (or cameras) of others.

Nor can we say as a matter of law that defendants' motive — to gather usable material for a potentially newsworthy story — necessarily privileged their intrusive conduct as a matter of common law tort liability. A reasonable jury could conclude the producers' desire to get footage that would convey the "feel" of the event — the real sights and sounds of a difficult rescue — did not justify either placing a microphone on Nurse Carnahan or filming inside the rescue helicopter. Although defendants' purposes could scarcely be regarded as evil or malicious (in the colloquial sense), their behavior could, even in light of their motives, be thought to show a highly offensive lack of sensitivity and respect for plaintiffs' privacy. A reasonable jury could find that defendants, in placing a microphone on an emergency treatment nurse and recording her conversation with a distressed, disoriented and severely injured patient, without the patient's knowledge or consent, acted with highly offensive disrespect for the patient's personal privacy comparable to, if not quite as extreme as, the disrespect and insensitivity demonstrated in *Miller.*

Turning to the question of constitutional protection for newsgathering, one finds the decisional law reflects a general rule of *nonprotection:* the press in its newsgathering activities enjoys no immunity or exemption from generally applicable laws. "It is clear that the First Amendment does not invalidate every incidental burdening of the press that may result from the enforcement of civil and criminal laws of general applicability. Under prior cases, otherwise valid laws serving substantial public interests may be enforced against the press as against others, despite the possible burden that may be imposed." [Quoting Branzborg v. Hayes, 408 U.S. 665, 682-683 (1972).] . . .

[D]efendants enjoyed no constitutional privilege, merely by virtue of their status as members of the news media, to eavesdrop . . . or otherwise to intrude tortiously on private places, conversations or information. . . .

As should be apparent from the above discussion, the constitutional protection accorded newsgathering, if any, is far narrower than the protection surrounding the publication of truthful material; consequently, the fact that a reporter may be seeking "newsworthy" material does not in itself privilege the investigatory activity. The reason for the difference is simple: the intrusion tort, unlike that for publication of private facts, does not subject the press to liability for the contents of its publications. Newsworthiness, as we stated earlier, is a complete bar to liability for publication of private facts and is evaluated with a high degree of deference to editorial judgment. The same deference is not due, however, when the issue is not the media's right to publish or broadcast what they choose, but their right to intrude into secluded areas or conversations in pursuit of publishable material. At most, the Constitution may preclude tort liability that would "place an impermissible burden on newsgatherers."

Defendants urge a rule more protective of press investigative activity. Specifically, they seek a holding that "when intrusion claims are brought in the context of newsgathering conduct, that conduct be deemed protected so long as (1) the information being gathered is about a matter of legitimate concern to the public and (2) the underlying conduct is lawful (i.e., was undertaken without fraud, trespass, etc.)." Neither tort law nor constitutional precedent and policy supports such a broad privilege.

As to constitutional policy, we repeat that the threat of infringement on the liberties of the press from intrusion liability is minor compared with the threat from liability for publication of private facts. . . . [B]ut no constitutional precedent or principle of which we are aware gives a reporter general license to intrude in an objectively offensive manner into private places, conversations or matters merely because the reporter thinks he or she may thereby find something that will warrant publication or broadcast.

Conclusion . . .

[T]he state may not intrude into the proper sphere of the news media to dictate what they should publish and broadcast, but neither may the media play tyrant to the people by unlawfully spying on them in the name of newsgathering. Summary judgment for the defense was . . . improper as to the cause of action for invasion of privacy by intrusion. . . .

CHIN, JUSTICE, . . . dissenting. . . .

I dissent . . . from the plurality's holding that plaintiffs' "intrusion" cause of action should be remanded for trial. . . .

Ruth's expectations notwithstanding, I do not believe that a reasonable trier of fact could find that defendants' conduct in this case was "highly offensive to a reasonable person," the test adopted by the plurality. Plaintiffs do not allege that defendants, though present at the accident rescue scene and in the helicopter, interfered with either the rescue or medical efforts, elicited embarrassing or offensive information from plaintiffs, or even tried to interrogate or interview them. Defendants' news team evidently merely recorded newsworthy events "of legitimate public concern" as they transpired. Defendants' apparent motive in undertaking the supposed privacy invasion was a reasonable and nonmalicious one: to obtain an accurate depiction of the rescue efforts from start to finish. The event was newsworthy, and the ultimate broadcast was both dramatic and educational, rather than tawdry or embarrassing.

No illegal trespass on private property occurred, and any technical illegality arising from defendants' recording Ruth's conversations with medical personnel was not so "highly offensive" as to justify liability. Recording the innocuous, inoffensive conversations that occurred between Ruth and the nurse assisting her and filming the seemingly routine, though certainly newsworthy, helicopter ride may have technically invaded plaintiffs' private "space," but in my view no "highly offensive" invasion of their privacy occurred.

We should bear in mind we are not dealing here with a true "interception" — e.g., a surreptitious wiretap by a third party — of words spoken in a truly private place — e.g., in a psychiatrist's examining room, an attorney's office, or a priest's confessional. Rather, here the broadcast showed Ruth speaking in settings where others could hear her, and the fact that she did not realize she was being recorded does not ipso facto transform defendants' newsgathering procedures into *highly* offensive conduct within the meaning of the law of intrusion.

In short, to turn a jury loose on the defendants in this case is itself "highly offensive" to me. I would reverse the judgment of the Court of Appeal with directions to affirm the summary judgment for defendants on all causes of action.

As *Shulman* makes clear, the intrusion tort is not limited to physical invasions of the plaintiff's property that constitute trespass. Whether the defendant has unlawfully intruded into the plaintiff's "space" has arisen in a variety of contexts:

Eavesdropping. *Hamberger*, above, is one of many cases involving the surreptitious use of listening devices. See, e.g., Billings v. Atkinson, 489 S.W.2d 858 (Tex. 1973) (telephone wiretapping held to be an invasion of privacy); Dietemann v. Time, Inc., 449 F.2d 245 (9th Cir. 1971) (use of hidden camera and microphone by which conversation with plaintiff in his den relayed to tape recorder in automobile parked nearby held to be an invasion). In Fischer v. Hooper, 732 A.2d 396 (N.H. 1999), the court ruled that whether the defendant's post-divorce recording of his wife's telephone conversations with their daughter "exceeded the bounds of decency" was a jury issue.

Videotaping. In Lewis v. LeGrow, 670 N.W.2d 675 (Mich. Ct. App. 2003), three ex-girlfriends brought statutory and common law invasion of privacy claims against a boyfriend who had secretly videotaped their sexual encounters with him. The court held that a jury could reasonably conclude that this conduct constituted an unreasonable intrusion upon the seclusion of the plaintiffs, even if they did consent to having sexual relations with defendant. See id. at 689. But see Bowens v. Ary, Inc., 794 N.W.2d 842, *reconsideration denied*, 796 N.W.2d 475 (Mich. 2011) (no reasonable juror could conclude that plaintiffs had a reasonable expectation of privacy in the recorded conversation that took place backstage prior to a high-profile concert); Spilfogel v. Fox Broadcasting Co., No. 10-12507, 2011 WL 2623578 (11th Cir. July 5, 2011) (plaintiff's erratic behavior on a public street was not private, and defendant network did not violate her privacy by airing the incident on the show *COPS*); Hougum v. Valley Mem'l Homes, 574 N.W.2d 812, 818 (N.D. 1998) (department store security officer's "relatively brief visual intrusion" of plaintiff masturbating in restroom held not actionable).

Does a defendant need to actually view intimate occurrences in order for plaintiff to successfully state a claim? "No" according to Koeppel v. Speirs, 808 N.W.2d 177 (Iowa 2011), in which an employer installed a hidden video camera in a workplace bathroom, purportedly to investigate whether one of two female employees was engaged in misconduct. The employer defended on the ground that the camera was never functional and thus neither employee was ever viewed or recorded. The Iowa Supreme Court noted a split of authority on the question of whether intrusion can occur without actual perception: "The point of disagreement among courts across the nation essentially boils down to whether the harm sought to be remedied by the tort is caused by accessing information from the plaintiff in a private place or by placing mechanisms in a private place that are capable of doing so at the hand of the defendant." Id. at 184. The court concluded that so long as a fact finder determines the hidden video equipment could have been functional at some point so as to invade plaintiff's privacy, then the cause of action can proceed even without evidence that defendant actually viewed intimate occurrences.

Sound Enhancement. In Marich v. MGM/UA Telecommunications, Inc., 7 Cal. Rptr. 3d 60 (2003), parents of a deceased child sued the producers and distributors of a television show entitled, *LAPD: Life on the Beat*. The defendants broadcast a sound-enhanced recording of the telephone call in which the parents first learned of their son's death from Los Angeles police officers. The court rejected plaintiffs' argument that the act of enhancing the sound constituted a separate intrusion, stating that "[w]hat a defendant does with a surreptitious recording after obtaining it may affect the measure of damages . . . but it is not a new 'obtaining'" sufficient to support an independent tort. 113 Cal. App. 4th at 432, 7 Cal. Rptr. 3d at 72-73.

Unwanted (and Repetitious) Telephone Calls. Can the systematic attempt to reach someone by phone against their wishes give rise to an intrusion action? Efforts by creditors and their collection agencies to contact debtors often become the subject of such intrusion claims, with varying results. Compare, e.g., Jacksonville State Bank v. Barnwell, 481 So. 2d 863 (Ala. 1985) (borrower had valid invasion of privacy claim against bank for a "series of harassing telephone calls"), with Beneficial Finance Co. v. Lamos, 179 N.W.2d 573 (Iowa 1970) (repeated telephone calls by a creditor to plaintiff, relating to debt, at latter's place of business not an invasion of privacy). See generally Franklyn S. Haiman, Speech v. Privacy: Is There a Right Not to Be Spoken To?, 67 Nw. L. Rev. 153 (1972).

Excessive Surveillance. In Clayton v. Richards, 47 S.W.3d 149 (Tex. 2001), the court held that whether a private investigator, who set up video surveillance equipment in a couples' bedroom, committed an invasion of privacy on the husband was an issue for the jury, even though the investigator had set up the equipment at the wife's direction. In remanding the case for trial, the court of appeals noted that actual physical presence was not necessary to commit the tort, and even if the private investigator only offered technical assistance in the use of such equipment, the jury could still find him liable for invasion of privacy. See also Galella v. Onassis, 353 F. Supp. 196 (S.D.N.Y. 1971), *aff'd in part, rev'd in part*, 487 F.2d 986 (2d Cir. 1973) (photographer's conduct in recording daily lives of widow and children of assassinated president was an invasion of privacy); but see Villanova v. Innovative Investigations, Inc., A-0654-10T2, 2011 WL 2638134 (N.J. Super. Ct. App. Div. July 7, 2011) (placement of GPS tracking unit in plaintiff's vehicle did not amount to an invasion of privacy). However, when surveillance is undertaken with a legitimate purpose, courts have held that the person whose conduct is alleged to be an invasion of privacy acted under a qualified privilege. See, e.g., I.C.U. Investigations, Inc. v. Jones, 780 So. 2d 685 (Ala. 2000) (filming of plaintiff urinating in his front yard not an intrusion when the purpose was to investigate the legitimacy of plaintiff's workers' compensation claim, and the means used were not offensive or objectionable).

Sexual Harassment. See, e.g., Busby v. Trustwal Sys. Corp., 551 So. 2d 322 (Ala. 1989) (summary judgment motion by defendant denied where plaintiffs alleged that repeated offensive questions, comments, and physical contacts by supervisor in the workplace constituted an invasion of privacy). For a suggestion that "privacy torts can supplement sexual harassment law, but they cannot supplant it" in light of the systemic focus and the norm-altering goals of the antidiscrimination movement, see Robert C. Post, Three Concepts of Privacy, 89 Geo. L.J. 208 (2001).

The Future of Privacy. In a prominent book at the turn of the millennium, Jeffrey Rosen sought to identify a "phenomenon that affects all Americans: namely, the erosion of privacy at home, at work, and in cyberspace, so that intimate personal information . . . is increasingly vulnerable to being wrenched out of context and exposed to the world." Jeffrey Rosen, The Unwanted Gaze: The Destruction of Privacy in America 3 (2000). Rosen's diagnosis seems even more accurate today following the advent of ubiquitous internet access, social media, and video capture possibilities via smartphones. Such technologies have had a dramatic impact on national debates regarding police conduct and the intersection of law enforcement and race. See, e.g., Jocelyn Simonson, Copwatching, 104 Cal. L. Rev. 391 (2016); Justin Marceau & Alan K. Chen, Free Speech and Democracy in the Video Age, 116 Colum. L. Rev. 991 (2016). They also will undoubtedly impact tort law and consumer protection. Significant emerging areas of debate include: (a) whether individuals should have a "right to be forgotten," i.e., a legal entitlement to force internet search engines and content providers to remove objectionable personal information from the internet, see Miquel Peguera, The Shaky Ground of the Right to Be Delisted, 18 Vand. J. Ent. & Tech. L. 507 (2016); (b) whether privacy law should create a "right to quantitative privacy" to address the rise of "Big Data" analytic techniques that can, for instance, enable retailers to determine which of their female customers are pregnant before those customers have even told their friends, see Kate Crawford & Jason Schultz, Big Data and Due Process: Toward a Framework to Redress Predictive Privacy Harms, 55 B.C. L. Rev. 93 (2014); and (c) what role litigation should play in the deterrence and compensation of harms caused by data breaches involving consumer credit cards and other personal information, see Sasha Romanosky, David A. Hoffman & Alessandro Acquisti, Empirical Analysis of Data Breach Litigation, 11 J. Empirical Legal Stud. 74 (2014).

B. Public Disclosure of Private Facts

Diaz v. Oakland Tribune, Inc.

139 Cal. App. 3d 118, 188 Cal. Rptr. 762 (1983)

Barry-Deal, A.J. Plaintiff Toni Ann Diaz (Diaz) sued the Oakland Tribune, Inc., owners and publishers of the Oakland Tribune (The Tribune), and Sidney Jones (Jones), one of its columnists, for invasion of privacy. Diaz claimed that the publication of highly embarrassing private facts in Jones' March 26, 1978, newspaper column was unwarranted and malicious and caused her to suffer severe emotional distress. The jury awarded Diaz $250,000 in compensatory damages and $525,000 in punitive damages ($25,000 against Jones and $500,000 against the Tribune). Judgment was entered on February 14, 1980. Defendants' motion for a new trial based on insufficiency of the evidence, errors of law, and excessive damages was denied. This timely appeal followed. As discussed below, we reverse the judgment because of instructional errors.

The facts are for the most part undisputed. Diaz is a transsexual. She was born in Puerto Rico in 1942 as Antonio Diaz, a male. She moved to California from New York in 1964. Suffice it to say that for most of her life Diaz suffered from a gender identification problem and the anxiety and depression that accompanied it. She testified that since she was young she had had the feeling of being a woman. . . . In 1975 gender corrective surgery was performed by the Stanford staff.

According to Diaz the surgery was a success. By all outward appearances she looked and behaved as a woman and was accepted by the public as a woman. According to her therapist, Dr. Sable, her physical and psychological identities were now in harmony.

Diaz scrupulously kept the surgery a secret from all but her immediate family and closest friends. She never sought to publicize the surgery. She changed her name to Toni Ann Diaz and made the necessary changes in her high school records, her social security records, and on her driver's license. She tried unsuccessfully to change her Puerto Rican birth certificate. She did not change the gender designation on her draft card, however, asserting that it would be a useless gesture, since she had previously been turned down for induction.

Following the surgery she no longer suffered from the psychological difficulties that had plagued her previously. In 1975 she enrolled in the College of Alameda (the College), a two-year college. . . .

In spring 1977, she was elected student body president for the 1977-1978 academic year, the first woman to hold that office. Her election and an unsuccessful attempt to unseat her were reported in the College newspaper, the Reporter, in the May 17, June 1, and June 14, 1977, editions. At no time during the election did Diaz reveal any information about her sex-change operation.

In 1977 Diaz was also selected to be the student body representative to the Peralta Community College Board of Trustees (the Board). Diaz's selection as student body representative, together with her photograph, appeared in the June 1977 issue of the Peralta Colleges Bulletin.

Near the middle of her term as student body president, Diaz became embroiled in a controversy in which she charged the College administrators with misuse of student funds. The March 15, 1978, issue of the Tribune quoted Diaz's charge that her signature had improperly been "rubber stamped" on checks drawn from the associated students' accounts.

On March 24, 1978, an article in the Alameda Times-Star, a daily newspaper, mentioned Diaz in connection with the charge of misuse of student body funds.

Shortly after the controversy arose, Jones was informed by several confidential sources that Diaz was a man. Jones considered the matter newsworthy if he could verify the information. Jones testified that he inspected the Tribune's own files and spoke with an unidentified number of persons at the College to confirm this information. It was not until Richard Paoli, the city editor of the Tribune, checked Oakland city police records that the information that Diaz was born a man was verified. The evidence reveals that in 1970 or 1971, prior to the surgery, Diaz was arrested in Oakland for soliciting an undercover police officer, a misdemeanor.

On March 26, 1978, the following item appeared in Jones' newspaper column: "More Education Stuff: The students at the College of Alameda will be surprised to learn their student body president, Toni Diaz, is no lady, but is in fact a man whose real name is Antonio."

"Now I realize, that in these times, such a matter is no big deal, but I suspect his female classmates in P.E. 97 may wish to make other showering arrangements."

Upon reading the article, Diaz became very depressed and was forced to reveal her status, which she had worked hard to conceal. Diaz testified that as a result of the article she suffered from insomnia, nightmares, and memory lapses. She also delayed her enrollment in Mills College, scheduled for that fall.

In her complaint Diaz did not charge that any of the information was untrue, only that defendants invaded her privacy by the unwarranted publicity of intimate facts. Defendants defended on the ground that the matter was newsworthy and hence was constitutionally protected.

At trial the jury returned a special verdict and found that (1) defendants did publicly disclose a fact concerning Diaz; (2) the fact was private and not public; (3) the fact was *not* newsworthy; (4) the fact was highly offensive to a reasonable person of ordinary sensibilities; (5) defendants disclosed the fact with knowledge that it was highly offensive or with reckless disregard of whether it was highly offensive; and (6) the disclosure proximately caused injury or damage to Diaz.

In this appeal defendants challenge the jury's finding on issues Nos. (2) and (3) above. Defendants also urge instructional error and attack the awards of compensatory and punitive damages. Before we address these issues, it is useful briefly to discuss the competing rights involved herein: the right to privacy and the right to free speech and press.

Background

The concept of a common-law right to privacy was first developed in a landmark article by Warren and Brandeis, The Right to Privacy (1890) 4 Harv. L. Rev. 193, and has been adopted in virtually every state. The specific privacy right with which we are concerned is the right to be free from public disclosure of private embarrassing facts, in short, "the right to be let alone." (Melvin v. Reid (1931) 112 Cal. App. 285, 289, 297 P. 91.) . . .

The public disclosure cause of action is distinct from a suit for libel or "false light," since the plaintiff herein does not challenge the accuracy of the information published, but asserts that the publicity is so intimate and unwarranted as to outrage the community's notion of decency. . . .

Of course, the right to privacy is not absolute and must be balanced against the often competing constitutional right of the press to publish newsworthy matters. . . . The First Amendment protection from tort liability is necessary if the press is to carry out its constitutional obligation to keep the public informed so that they may make intelligent decisions on matters important to a self-governing people. (See Cox Broadcasting Corp. v. Cohn, . . . 420 U.S. at pp. 491-493, 95 S. Ct. at pp. 1044-1045.)

However, the newsworthy privilege is not without limitation. Where the publicity is so offensive as to constitute a "morbid and sensational prying into private lives for its own sake, . . ." it serves no legitimate public interest and is not deserving of protection. (See Virgil v. Time, Inc., . . . 527 F.2d at p. 1129; Rest. 2d Torts, §652D, Com. *h.*)

As discerned from the decisions of our courts, the public disclosure tort contains the following elements: (1) public disclosure (2) of a private fact (3) which would be offensive and objectionable to the reasonable person and (4) which is not of legitimate public concern. . . .

Instructional Error

At the outset defendants urge that the trial court misinstructed the jury (1) on the right to privacy and (2) that defendants had the burden of proving newsworthiness. We agree and find that either of these errors was prejudicial and requires reversal.

1. The Right to Privacy

Plaintiff Diaz proffered a jury instruction properly defining the right to privacy.[12] However, the trial court, sua sponte, added the following language: "It prevents business

12. The complete instruction reads as follows: "The California Constitution provides that all persons have an inalienable right of privacy. It is the right to live one's life in seclusion, without being subjected to unwarranted or undesirable publicity. In short, it's the right to be left alone."

or government interests from misusing information gathered for one purpose in order to serve other purposes, or to embarrass us. *This right should be abridged only when there is a compelling public need.*" (Emphasis added.)

The language contained in the last sentence was taken from White v. Davis (1975) 13 Cal. 3d 757, 120 Cal. Rptr. 94, 533 P.2d 222. The trial court misplaced its reliance on that case. In *White*, supra, plaintiff challenged covert police surveillance of University of California at Los Angeles students in their classrooms. There, the court required the *government* to demonstrate a "'compelling public need'" for the intrusion. (Id., at p. 775, 120 Cal. Rptr. 94, 533 P.2d 222.) That case did not attempt to balance the competing rights of free speech and press against the right to privacy. Rather, it recognized the heavy burden on the government to justify interference with First Amendment freedoms. (Id., at pp. 767-773, 120 Cal. Rptr. 94, 553 P.2d 222.)

Unlike the government's activity in *White*, defendants' publication of the article is a preferred right which is not encumbered by the presumption of illegality. Defendants enjoy the right to publish information in which the public has a *legitimate interest.* (See Briscoe v. Reader's Digest Association, Inc., . . . 4 Cal. 3d at p. 541, 93 Cal. Rptr. 866, 483 P.2d 34; Virgil v. Time, Inc., supra, 527 F.2d at pp. 1128-1129; Rest. 2d Torts, supra, §652D, Com. *d.*) To require that the article meet the higher "'compelling public need'" standard would severely abridge this constitutionally recognized right of free speech and press.

After examining the entire record, we cannot say that this error was harmless. The instruction misstated the law concerning defendants' right to publish newsworthy matters and necessarily lessened plaintiff's burden of proof. Since plaintiff's verdict may have rested on this erroneous theory, the judgment must be reversed. . . .

2. The Burden of Proving Newsworthiness

[The court ruled that the burden to prove that the story lacked newsworthiness is on the plaintiff; its discussion of this point is omitted.]

The Public Disclosure Tort

1. Private Facts

Defendants next argue that the evidence establishes as a matter of law that the fact of Diaz's original gender was a matter of public record, and therefore its publicity was not actionable.[16] In support of their contention defendants rely on Cox Broadcasting Corp. v. Cohn, supra, 420 U.S. 469, 95 S. Ct. 1029, 43 L. Ed. 2d 328. That reliance is misplaced.

Generally speaking, matter which is already in the public domain is not private, and its publication is protected. . . .

In *Cox Broadcasting Corp.*, the Supreme Court ruled that Cohn, the father of a deceased rape victim, could not maintain a disclosure action against media defendants who identified Cohn's daughter as the victim during the television coverage of the murder trial. (Cox Broadcasting Corp. v. Cohn, supra, 420 U.S. at pp. 496-497, 95 S. Ct. at 1046-1047.) Central to the court's conclusion was the fact that the reporter obtained the victim's

16. Defendants do not challenge the jury's findings that (1) the matter was publicized and (2) the fact was highly offensive to a reasonable person. There is ample evidence in the record to support these findings.

name from the indictment, which had been shown to him in open court. (Id., at p. 496, 95 S. Ct. at 1046.)

In a very narrow holding, the court ruled that a state may not impose sanctions on the accurate publication of the name of a rape victim obtained from judicial records which are maintained in connection with a public prosecution and which themselves are open to public inspection. (Id., at p. 491, 95 S. Ct. at 1044.) Importantly, the court expressly refused to address the broader question of whether the truthful publication of facts obtained from public records can ever be subjected to civil or criminal liability. (Ibid.)

Because of its narrow holding, *Cox Broadcasting Corp.* gives us little guidance.

Here there is no evidence to suggest that the fact of Diaz's gender-corrective surgery was part of the public record. To the contrary, the evidence reveals that Diaz took affirmative steps to conceal this fact by changing her driver's license, social security, and high school records, and by lawfully changing her name. The police records, upon which Jones relied, contained information concerning one Antonio Diaz. No mention was made of Diaz's new name or gender. In order to draw the connection, Jones relied upon unidentified confidential sources. Under these circumstances, we conclude that Diaz's sexual identity was a private matter.

We also do not consider Diaz's *Puerto Rican* birth certificate to be a public record in this instance. In any event, defendants did not rely on that document and cannot be heard to argue that the information contained therein is public.

Moreover, matter which was once of public record may be protected as private facts where disclosure of that information would not be newsworthy. (See Briscoe v. Reader's Digest Association, Inc., supra, 4 Cal. 3d at pp. 537-538, 93 Cal. Rptr. 866, 483 P.2d 34 [publication of identity of ex-offender for past crime was held to be improper]; Melvin v. Reid, supra, 112 Cal. App. at pp. 290-291, 297 P. 91 [disclosure of plaintiff's past life as a prostitute, seven years after she reformed, was actionable].)

2. Newsworthiness

As discussed above, whether the fact of Diaz's sexual identity was newsworthy is measured along a sliding scale of competing interests: the individual's right to keep private facts from the public's gaze versus the public's right to know. . . . In an effort to reconcile these competing interests, our courts have settled on a three-part test for determining whether matter published is newsworthy: "'[1] the social value of the facts published, [2] the depth of the article's intrusion into ostensibly private affairs, and [3] the extent to which the party voluntarily acceded to a position of public notoriety.'" (Briscoe v. Reader's Digest Association, Inc., supra, 4 Cal. 3d at p. 541, 93 Cal. Rptr. 866, 483 P.2d 34.)

Defendants argue that in light of Diaz's position as the first female student body president of the College, her "questionable gender" was a newsworthy item. As a subsidiary contention, they assert that the issue of newsworthiness should not have been submitted to the jury. We address the latter contention first.

a. Newsworthiness as a Jury Question

Whether a publication is or is not newsworthy depends upon contemporary community mores and standards of decency. . . . This is largely a question of fact, which a jury is uniquely well-suited to decide. . . .

Defendants argue that the right to publish would suffer at the hands of a jury which, unlike the trial judge, would be more likely to use a general verdict in order to punish unpopular speech and persons. In Virgil v. Time, Inc., supra, 527 F.2d 1122, the Court of Appeals for the Ninth Circuit in a California case recognized this danger. However, that court concluded that any risk of prejudice may be checked by close judicial scrutiny at the stages of litigation such as summary judgment, directed verdict, and judgment notwithstanding the verdict. (Id., at p. 1130.) Our trial court judges are entirely capable of correcting such jury overreaching. . . .

b. Newsworthiness as a Matter of Law

Next, defendants urge that, as the first female student body president of the College, Diaz was a public figure, and the fact of her sexual identity was a newsworthy item as a matter of law. We disagree.

It is well settled that persons who voluntarily seek public office or willingly become involved in public affairs waive their right to privacy on matters connected with their public conduct. . . . The reason behind this rule is that the public should be afforded every opportunity of learning about any facet which may affect that person's fitness for office. . . .

However, the extent to which Diaz voluntarily acceded to a position of public notoriety and the degree to which she opened her private life are questions of fact. . . . As student body president, Diaz was a public figure for some purposes. However, applying the three-part test enunciated in *Briscoe*, we cannot state that the fact of her gender was newsworthy per se.

Nor does the fact that she was the first woman student body president, in itself, warrant that her entire private life be open to public inspection. The public arena entered by Diaz is concededly small. Public figures more celebrated than she are entitled to keep some information of their domestic activities and sexual relations private. . . .

Nor is there merit to defendant's claim that the changing roles of women in society make this story newsworthy. This assertion rings hollow. The tenor of the article was by no means an attempt to enlighten the public on a contemporary social issue. Rather, as Jones himself admitted, the article was directed to the students at the College about their newly elected president. Moreover, Jones' attempt at humor at Diaz's expense removes all pretense that the article was meant to educate the reading public. The social utility of the information must be viewed in context, and not based upon some arguably meritorious and unintended purpose.

Therefore, we conclude that the jury was the proper body to answer the question whether the article was newsworthy or whether it extended beyond the bounds of decency.

Insufficient Evidence of Malice

Defendants next urge that the award of punitive damages was improper, since there was insufficient evidence to support a finding of malice on the part of either defendant. The evidence demonstrated that Jones published the article without first contacting Diaz, although he knew that the information contained therein would have a "devastating" impact on her. He testified that he attempted to obtain Diaz's telephone number from his unidentified sources but was unsuccessful. He admitted that he never telephoned the College in order to contact Diaz. Jones also stated that his comment about Diaz's classmates in "P.E. 97" making other shower arrangements was a joke, an attempt to be "flip."

In order to justify the imposition of punitive damages, "the defendant '". . . must act with the intent to vex, injure, or annoy, or with a conscious disregard of the plaintiff's rights."'" (Taylor v. Superior Court (1979) 24 Cal. 3d 890, 895, 157 Cal. Rptr. 693, 598 P.2d 854, emphasis omitted). . . .

Viewing the article as a whole, as well as Jones' conduct in preparing the article, we cannot say as a matter of law that there was insufficient evidence to support a finding of malice.

Here Jones knew that Diaz would certainly suffer severe emotional distress from the publicity alone. Nevertheless, he added to the indignity by making Diaz the brunt of a joke. The defendants' knowledge of the extent and severity of plaintiff's injuries is relevant to a finding of malice. . . . The jury could reasonably have inferred from these facts that Jones acted with the intent to outrage or humiliate Diaz or that he published the article with a conscious disregard of her rights.

The fact that Jones verified the story with unidentified sources does not negate the finding of malice. The jury could well have concluded that Jones' effort to discuss the article with Diaz was de minimis when compared to the magnitude of the expected harm. This is especially true since Jones was under no deadline to publish this article. Under these circumstances, the jury could have reasonably concluded that Jones' conduct evidenced a callous and conscious disregard for Diaz's privacy interests. . . . Accordingly, the jury acted well within its discretion in awarding punitive damages.

The Oakland Tribune, Inc., was also liable for punitive damages since the newspaper publishing company reviewed and approved Jones' article for publication. . . .

We are mindful of the dangerous, inhibiting effect on speech and press a large punitive damage award can have. . . . If upon retrial the plaintiff recovers a judgment, we caution the trial court to scrutinize strictly any award of punitive damages to ensure that it is not used to silence unpopular persons or speech and that it does not exceed the proper level necessary to punish and deter similar behavior. . . .

Excessive Compensatory Damage Award

Finally, defendants urge that the compensatory damage award was excessive. The jury awarded Diaz $250,000, largely for emotional and psychological injury caused by the article. Diaz's special damages for psychotherapy approximated $800.

The evidence adduced at trial established that following the publication of the article Diaz became very depressed and withdrawn. She suffered from insomnia and experienced nightmares. She had frequent memory lapses and experienced difficulty in her social relationships. As a result, in September 1978 she began psychotherapy treatments with Allen Sable, Ph.D.

The actual injury involved herein is not limited to out-of-pocket loss. It generally includes "impairment of reputation and standing in the community, personal humiliation, and mental anguish and suffering." (See Gertz v. Robert Welch, Inc., . . . 418 U.S. at p. 350, 94 S. Ct. at p. 3012.) The harm Diaz alleged to have suffered is not easily quantifiable, and the amount of damages must necessarily be left to the sound discretion of the jury. . . .

As a rule all presumptions are in favor of the judgment. . . . A reviewing court must not interfere with the verdict unless it can be said that it was the result of "passion or prejudice" on the part of the jury. . . .

Here the jury fixed the damages after hearing the evidence and being properly instructed. The evidence of Diaz's emotional distress and suffering was uncontradicted. That Diaz was able to earn high marks in her classes after the incident does not necessarily minimize or negate the emotional trauma she suffered and will continue to suffer.

Also, the trial judge denied a motion for a new trial based on this same issue. While that determination is not binding upon this court, it is entitled to great weight. . . .

The jury and the trial judge were in the best position to evaluate the scope and severity of Diaz's injuries. They heard the testimony and observed the witnesses. Although the amount of the award is high, it cannot be said that it is so grossly disproportionate, considering the past and future pain and humiliation, as to be excessive as a matter of law.

The judgment is reversed.

SCOTT, ACTING P.J., concurs. [The concurring opinion of FEINBERG, J., is omitted.]

For a thorough review of how claims involving privacy interests of lesbian, gay, bisexual, and transgender plaintiffs have fared in court, see Anita L. Allen, Privacy Torts: Unreliable Remedies for LGBT Plaintiffs, 98 Cal. L. Rev. 1711 (2010). Note that the court in *Diaz* did not indicate a clear distinction between public figures and private persons for the purposes of the public disclosure tort, as does the post–*New York Times* law of defamation. Nor does §652D of the Restatement (Second) of Torts, which sets out the doctrinal elements of a valid public disclosure claim. This section bases liability on whether the matter "would be highly offensive to a reasonable person" and "is not of a legitimate concern to the public." The comments refer to "the customs of the time and place," and to "the customs and conventions of the community." It is, Comment *h* states, a "matter of the community mores." Even a motion picture actress, this comment asserts, is entitled to keep some aspects of her life to herself.

Public disclosure of the plaintiff's sex life is not always actionable. In Sipple v. Chronicle Publishing Co., 201 Cal. Rptr. 665 (Ct. App. 1984), the court upheld summary judgment in a case in which the defendants published the fact that the plaintiff, an ex-Marine, was homosexual. The plaintiff had grabbed the arm of a person about to shoot the then President Ford. In reporting the story, the defendants disclosed the fact that the plaintiff was a "prominent member of the San Francisco gay community," questioned whether President Ford failed to praise the plaintiff's heroism because of prejudice, and quoted politician Harvey Milk as expressing hope that "maybe this [event] will help break the stereotype." Id. at 666. The plaintiff brought suit because members of his family were unaware of his sexuality and abandoned him after the stories were reported. The court ruled that plaintiff's sexuality was a public, rather than a private, fact because he was well known in homosexual political and social circles. The court also ruled that in any event, the plaintiff's homosexuality was newsworthy. As to this, in California the newsworthiness of a story may be as much influenced by the style in which the information is presented as by its substance:

> Moreover, and perhaps even more to the point, the record shows that the publications were not motivated by a morbid and sensational prying into appellant's private life but rather were prompted by legitimate political considerations, i.e., to dispel the false public opinion

> that gays were timid, weak and unheroic figures and to raise the equally important political question whether the President of the United States entertained a discriminatory attitude or bias against a minority group such as homosexuals. [201 Cal. Rptr. at 670.]

Some courts do, however, give considerable weight to whether the plaintiff is a public figure when analyzing the public disclosure tort. One of the leading cases is Sidis v. F-R Pub. Corp., 113 F.2d 806 (2d Cir.), *cert. denied*, 311 U.S. 711 (1940). The plaintiff as a child was a mathematical genius; he had lectured to distinguished mathematicians at the age of 11, and graduated from Harvard when he was 16. He dropped from public view for several years, until an article published by the defendant in The New Yorker, entitled "Where Are They Now," detailed the idiosyncratic habits and characteristics of the plaintiff and brought him back to the public gaze. In affirming the trial judge's dismissal of the action, the court said (113 F.2d at 809):

> William James Sidis was once a public figure. As a child prodigy, he excited both admiration and curiosity. Of him great deeds were expected. In 1910, he was a person about whom the newspapers might display a legitimate intellectual interest in the sense meant by Warren and Brandeis, as distinguished from a trivial and unseemly curiosity. But the precise motives of the press we regard as unimportant. And even if Sidis had loathed public attention at that time, we think his uncommon achievements and personality would have made the attention permissible. Since then Sidis has cloaked himself in obscurity, but his subsequent history, containing as it did the answer to the question of whether or not he had fulfilled his early promise, was still a matter of public concern. The article in The New Yorker sketched the life of an unusual personality, and it possessed considerable popular news interest.
>
> We express no comment on whether or not the news worthiness of the matter printed will always constitute a complete defense. Revelations may be so intimate and so unwarranted in view of the victim's position as to outrage the community's notions of decency. But when focused upon public characters, truthful comments upon dress, speech, habits, and the ordinary aspects of personality will usually not transgress this line. Regrettably or not, the misfortunes and frailties of neighbors and "public figures" are subjects of considerable interest and discussion to the rest of the population. And when such are the mores of the community, it would be unwise for a court to bar their expression in the newspapers, books, and magazines of the day.

The court in *Sidis* seemed to take the position that "once a public figure, always a public figure" — a position with which some other courts have agreed. See, e.g., Montesano v. Donrey Media Group, 668 P.2d 1081 (Nev. 1983), *cert. denied*, 466 U.S. 959 (1984). The State of California at one point took a different view. In Briscoe v. Reader's Digest Ass'n, Inc., 483 P.2d 34 (Cal. 1971), for example, the complaint alleged that the defendant named the plaintiff in a magazine article on truck hijacking in connection with an 11-year-old incident in which the plaintiff hijacked a truck and had a gun battle with the police. The complaint also alleged that, following the incident, the plaintiff became rehabilitated and led a respectable life, and that the article caused his daughter and his friends to scorn and abandon him. In ruling that the complaint stated a cause of action, the court observed (483 P.2d at 44):

> We do not hold today that plaintiff must prevail in his action. It is for the trier of fact to determine (1) whether plaintiff has become a rehabilitated member of society, (2) whether identifying him as a former criminal would be highly offensive and injurious to the

> reasonable man, (3) whether defendant published this information with a reckless disregard for its offensiveness, and (4) whether any independent justification for printing plaintiff's identity existed. We hold today only that, as pleaded, plaintiff has stated a valid cause of action, sustaining the demurrer to plaintiff's complaint was improper, and that the ensuing judgment must therefore be reversed.

The *Briscoe* decision was overruled in Gates v. Discovery Communications, Inc., 101 P.3d 552, (Cal. 2004). The court concluded that subsequent U.S. Supreme Court first amendment cases "have fatally undermined *Briscoe*'s holding that a media defendant may be held liable in tort for recklessly publishing true but not newsworthy facts concerning a rehabilitated former criminal, insofar as that holding applies to facts obtained from public official court records." Id. at 559-60.

Even persons who are not public figures can get caught up in events that are, or could be found to be by the jury, matters of legitimate public interest. For example, in Shulman v. Group W Productions, Inc., 955 P.2d 469 (Cal. 1998), set out on p. 867, the plaintiffs also filed a "public disclosure of private facts" suit. The court ruled that, although the plaintiffs' intrusion suit survived a motion for summary judgment, the public disclosure claim did not. The court stated that the broadcast of the interview with the accident victim was a matter "of legitimate public interest" as a matter of law. Consider also Doe v. Berkeley Publishers, 496 S.E.2d 636 (S.C.), *cert. denied*, 525 U.S. 963 (1998), in which the defendant reported that the plaintiff had been sexually assaulted while the latter was in prison. Although the trial court had directed a verdict for the defendant, the intermediate appeals court held that a jury question existed regarding whether publication of the plaintiff's name in particular was a matter of public significance. In a three paragraph opinion, the Supreme Court of South Carolina concluded that "[t]he Court of Appeals erred in separating the plaintiff's identity from the event. Under state law, if a person, whether willingly or not, becomes an actor in an event of public or general interest, then the publication of his connection with such an occurrence is not an invasion of his right to privacy." Id. at 637 (citation omitted).

The public disclosure tort requires disclosure to the public, but just what the "public" is has been the subject of much litigation. In Shattuck-Owen v. Snowbird Corp., 16 P.3d 555 (Utah 2000), the court held that the showing of a surveillance video tape, made in connection with an investigation of a sexual assault of an employee, to other employees was not a disclosure to the public. In Robert C. Ozer, P.C. v. Borquez, 940 P.2d 371 (Colo. 1997), the court stated that the disclosure must be made "to a large number of persons or the general public." The court did not indicate, however, how large a "large number" has to be to constitute a public disclosure; the facts and circumstances of each case must be taken into consideration in determining whether the disclosure was sufficiently public so as to support a claim for invasion of privacy.

One deeply challenging context involving the constitutionality of public disclosure actions concerns the publication of the names of victims of crimes, particularly rape, child molestation, and other sexual assaults, such as the prison sexual assault at issue in Doe v. Berkeley Publishers, supra. The United States Supreme Court addressed these issues in Cox Broadcasting v. Cohn, 420 U.S. 469 (1975), concluding that a Georgia privacy statute was unconstitutional as applied to a reporter who published the name of a 17-year-old rape-murder victim, after the reporter learned the name from a publicly available indictment in the case. Partially in response to this holding, some states passed statutes requiring that sex crime victims' names be withheld from public records, while still seeking to criminally and civilly punish those who publish the victims' names if they are obtained in some other fashion. The next case concerned just such a regime.

The Florida Star v. B.J.F.

491 U.S. 524, 109 S. Ct. 2603, 105 L. Ed. 2d 443 (1989)

Justice Marshall delivered the opinion of the Court.

Florida Stat. §794.03 (1987) makes it unlawful to "print, publish, or broadcast . . . in any instrument of mass communication" the name of the victim of a sexual offense.[3] Pursuant to this statute, appellant *The Florida Star* was found civilly liable for publishing the name of a rape victim which it had obtained from a publicly released police report. The issue presented here is whether this result comports with the First Amendment. We hold that it does not.

[The plaintiff reported to the county sheriff's department that she had been raped and robbed by an unknown person. The report of the department contained the name of the plaintiff, and was put in the press room, where it was seen by a reporter for the defendant's newspaper. The reporter prepared a story for the "Police Reports" section of the newspaper, which included the name of the plaintiff. The story was published as written, although the naming of a rape victim was contrary to the policy of the paper. The plaintiff sued the sheriff's department and the defendant, alleging a violation of §794.03. The plaintiff settled with the department before trial for $2,500.

At the trial, the plaintiff testified as to the emotional harm she suffered as a result of the article, stemming in part from phone calls to her mother from a man who said that he would rape her again. The trial judge denied the defendant's motion for a directed verdict, and the jury returned a verdict against the defendant for $75,000 in compensatory and $25,000 in punitive damages. The trial judge offset the amount paid by the sheriff's department against the compensatory award. The judgment for the plaintiff on the jury verdict was affirmed by the Florida District Court of Appeal, and the Florida Supreme Court denied review.]

II

The tension between the right which the First Amendment accords to a free press, on the one hand, and the protections which various statutes and common-law doctrines accord to personal privacy against the publication of truthful information, on the other, is a subject we have addressed several times in recent years. Our decisions in cases involving government attempts to sanction the accurate dissemination of information as invasive of privacy, have not, however, exhaustively considered this conflict. On the contrary, although our decisions have without exception upheld the press' right to publish, we have emphasized each time that we were resolving this conflict only as it arose in a discrete factual context.

3. The statute provides in its entirety:

> Unlawful to publish or broadcast information identifying sexual offense victim.—No person shall print, publish, or broadcast, or cause or allow to be printed, published, or broadcast, in any instrument of mass communication the name, address, or other identifying fact or information of the victim of any sexual offense within this chapter. An offense under this section shall constitute a misdemeanor of the second degree, punishable as provided in §775.082, §775.083, or §775.084.

Fla. Stat. §794.03 (1987).

The parties to this case frame their contentions in light of a trilogy of cases which have presented, in different contexts, the conflict between truthful reporting and state-protected privacy interests. In Cox Broadcasting Corp. v. Cohn, 420 U.S. 469, 95 S. Ct. 1029, 43 L. Ed. 2d 328 (1975), we found unconstitutional a civil damages award entered against a television station for broadcasting the name of a rape-murder victim which the station had obtained from courthouse records. In Oklahoma Publishing Co. v. Oklahoma County District Court, 430 U.S. 308, 97 S. Ct. 1045, 51 L. Ed. 2d 355 (1977), we found unconstitutional a state court's pretrial order enjoining the media from publishing the name or photograph of an 11-year-old boy in connection with a juvenile proceeding involving that child which reporters had attended. Finally, in Smith v. Daily Mail Publishing Co., 443 U.S. 97, 99 S. Ct. 2667, 61 L. Ed. 2d 399 (1979), we found unconstitutional the indictment of two newspapers for violating a state statute forbidding newspapers to publish, without written approval of the juvenile court, the name of any youth charged as a juvenile offender. The papers had learned about a shooting by monitoring a police band radio frequency and had obtained the name of the alleged juvenile assailant from witnesses, the police, and a local prosecutor.

Appellant takes the position that this case is indistinguishable from *Cox Broadcasting*. Alternatively, it urges that our decisions in the above trilogy, and in other cases in which we have held that the right of the press to publish truth overcame asserted interests other than personal privacy, can be distilled to yield a broader First Amendment principle that the press may never be punished, civilly or criminally, for publishing the truth. Appellee counters that the privacy trilogy is inapposite, because in each case the private information already appeared on a "public record," and because the privacy interests at stake were far less profound than in the present case. In the alternative, appellee urges that *Cox Broadcasting* be overruled and replaced with a categorical rule that publication of the name of a rape victim never enjoys constitutional protection.

We conclude that imposing damages on appellant for publishing B.J.F.'s name violates the First Amendment, although not for either of the reasons appellant urges. Despite the strong resemblance this case bears to *Cox Broadcasting*, that case cannot fairly be read as controlling here. The name of the rape victim in that case was obtained from courthouse records that were open to public inspection, a fact which Justice White's opinion for the Court repeatedly noted. . . . Significantly, one of the reasons we gave in *Cox Broadcasting* for invalidating the challenged damages award was the important role the press plays in subjecting trials to public scrutiny and thereby helping guarantee their fairness. That role is not directly compromised where, as here, the information in question comes from a police report prepared and disseminated at a time at which not only had no adversarial criminal proceedings begun, but no suspect had been identified.

Nor need we accept appellant's invitation to hold broadly that truthful publication may never be punished consistent with the First Amendment. Our cases have carefully eschewed reaching this ultimate question, mindful that the future may bring scenarios which prudence counsels our not resolving anticipatorily. See, e.g., Near v. Minnesota ex rel. Olson, 283 U.S. 697, 716, 51 S. Ct. 625, 75 L. Ed. 1357 (1931) (hypothesizing "publication of the sailing dates of transports or the number and location of troops"); see also Garrison v. Louisiana, 379 U.S. 64, 72, n.8, 74, 85 S. Ct. 209, 215, n.8, 216, 13 L. Ed. 2d 125 (1964) (endorsing absolute defense of truth "where discussion of public affairs is concerned," but leaving unsettled the constitutional implications of truthfulness "in the discrete area of purely private libels"). . . . We continue to believe that the sensitivity and significance of the interests presented in clashes between First Amendment and privacy rights counsel relying on limited principles that sweep no more broadly than the appropriate context of the instant case.

In our view, this case is appropriately analyzed with reference to such a limited First Amendment principle. It is the one, in fact, which we articulated in *Daily Mail* in our synthesis of prior cases involving attempts to punish truthful publication: "[I]f a newspaper lawfully obtains truthful information about a matter of public significance then state officials may not constitutionally punish publication of the information, absent a need to further a state interest of the highest order." 443 U.S., at 103, 99 S. Ct., at 2671. . . .

. . . Appellee argues that a rule punishing publication furthers three closely related interests: the privacy of victims of sexual offenses; the physical safety of such victims, who may be targeted for retaliation if their names become known to their assailants; and the goal of encouraging victims of such crimes to report these offenses without fear of exposure.

At a time in which we are daily reminded of the tragic reality of rape, it is undeniable that these are highly significant interests, a fact underscored by the Florida Legislature's explicit attempt to protect these interests by enacting a criminal statute prohibiting much dissemination of victim identities. We accordingly do not rule out the possibility that, in a proper case, imposing civil sanctions for publication of the name of a rape victim might be so overwhelmingly necessary to advance these interests as to satisfy the *Daily Mail* standard. For three independent reasons, however, imposing liability for publication under the circumstances of this case is too precipitous a means of advancing these interests to convince us that there is a "need" within the meaning of the *Daily Mail* formulation for Florida to take this extreme step. . . .

First is the manner in which appellant obtained the identifying information in question. As we have noted, where the government itself provides information to the media, it is most appropriate to assume that the government had, but failed to utilize, far more limited means of guarding against dissemination than the extreme step of punishing truthful speech. That assumption is richly borne out in this case. B.J.F.'s identity would never have come to light were it not for the erroneous, if inadvertent, inclusion by the Department of her full name in an incident report made available in a pressroom open to the public. . . .

That appellant gained access to the information in question through a government news release makes it especially likely that, if liability were to be imposed, self-censorship would result. Reliance on a news release is a paradigmatically "routine newspaper reporting techniqu[e]." *Daily Mail*, 443 U.S., at 103, 99 S. Ct., at 2671. The government's issuance of such a release, without qualification, can only convey to recipients that the government considered dissemination lawful, and indeed expected the recipients to disseminate the information further. Had appellant merely reproduced the news release prepared and released by the Department, imposing civil damages would surely violate the First Amendment. The fact that appellant converted the police report into a news story by adding the linguistic connecting tissue necessary to transform the report's facts into full sentences cannot change this result.

A second problem with Florida's imposition of liability for publication is the broad sweep of the negligence per se standard applied under the civil cause of action implied from §794.03. Unlike claims based on the common law tort of invasion of privacy, see Restatement (Second) of Torts §652D (1977), civil actions based on §794.03 require no case-by-case findings that the disclosure of a fact about a person's private life was one that a reasonable person would find highly offensive. On the contrary, under the per se theory of negligence adopted by the courts below, liability follows automatically from publication. This is so regardless of whether the identity of the victim is already known throughout the community; whether the victim has voluntarily called public attention to the offense; or whether the identity of the victim has otherwise become a reasonable subject of public concern — because, perhaps, questions have arisen whether the victim fabricated an assault by a particular person. Nor is there a scienter requirement of any kind under §794.03, engendering the perverse result that truthful publications challenged pursuant to this cause of action are less protected by the First Amendment than even the least protected defamatory falsehoods: those involving purely private figures, where liability is evaluated under a standard, usually applied by a jury, of ordinary negligence. . . .

Third, and finally, the facial underinclusiveness of §794.03 raises serious doubts about whether Florida is, in fact, serving, with this statute, the significant interests which appellee invokes in support of affirmance. Section 794.03 prohibits the publication of identifying information only if this information appears in an "instrument of mass communication," a term the statute does not define. Section 794.03 does not prohibit the spread by other means of the identities of victims of sexual offenses. An individual who maliciously spreads word of the identity of a rape victim is thus not covered, despite the fact that the communication of such information to persons who live near, or work with, the victim may have consequences as devastating as the exposure of her name to large numbers of strangers. . . .

When a State attempts the extraordinary measure of punishing truthful publication in the name of privacy, it must demonstrate its commitment to advancing this interest by applying its prohibition evenhandedly, to the small-time disseminator as well as the media giant. Where important First Amendment interests are at stake, the mass scope of disclosure is not an acceptable surrogate for injury. A ban on disclosures effected by "instrument[s] of mass communication" simply cannot be defended on the ground that partial prohibitions may effect partial relief. . . .

III

Our holding today is limited. We do not hold that truthful publication is automatically constitutionally protected, or that there is no zone of personal privacy within which the State may protect the individual from intrusion by the press, or even that a State may never punish publication of the name of a victim of a sexual offense. We hold only that where a newspaper publishes truthful information which it has lawfully obtained, punishment may lawfully be imposed, if at all, only when narrowly tailored to a state interest of the highest order, and that no such interest is satisfactorily served by imposing liability under §794.03 to appellant under the facts of this case. The decision below is therefore

Reversed.

[The concurring opinion of JUSTICE SCALIA is omitted.]

JUSTICE WHITE, with whom THE CHIEF JUSTICE and JUSTICE O'CONNOR join, dissenting.

"Short of homicide, [rape] is the 'ultimate violation of self.'" Coker v. Georgia, 433 U.S. 584, 597, 97 S. Ct. 2861, 2869, 53 L. Ed. 2d 982 (1977) (opinion of White, J.). For B.J.F., however, the violation she suffered at a rapist's knife-point marked only the beginning of her ordeal. A week later, while her assailant was still at large, an account of this assault — identifying by name B.J.F. as the victim — was published by The Florida Star. As a result, B.J.F. received harassing phone calls, required mental health counseling, was forced to move from her home, and was even threatened with being raped again.

Yet today, the Court holds that a jury award of $75,000 to compensate B.J.F. for the harm she suffered due to the Star's negligence is at odds with the First Amendment. I do not accept this result.

The Court reaches its conclusion based on an analysis of three of our precedents and a concern with three particular aspects of the judgment against appellant. I consider each of these points in turn, and then consider some of the larger issues implicated by today's decision.

I

The Court finds its result compelled, or at least supported in varying degrees, by three of our prior cases: Cox Broadcasting Corp. v. Cohn, 420 U.S. 469, 95 S. Ct. 1029, 43 L. Ed. 2d 328 (1975); Oklahoma Publishing Co. v. Oklahoma County District Court, 430 U.S. 308, 97 S. Ct. 1045, 51 L. Ed. 2d 355 (1977); and Smith v. Daily Mail Publishing Co., 443 U.S. 97, 99 S. Ct. 2667, 61 L. Ed. 2d 399 (1979). I disagree. None of these cases requires the harsh outcome reached today.

Cox Broadcasting reversed a damages award entered against a television station, which had obtained a rape victim's name from public records maintained in connection with the judicial proceedings brought against her assailants. While there are similarities, critical aspects of that case make it wholly distinguishable from this one. First, in *Cox Broadcasting*, the victim's name had been disclosed in the hearing where her assailants pleaded guilty; and, as we recognized, judicial records have always been considered public information in this country. . . . In fact, even the earliest notion of privacy rights exempted the information contained in judicial records from its protections. See Warren & Brandeis, The Right to Privacy, 4 Harv. L. Rev. 193, 216-217 (1890). Second, unlike the incident report at issue here, which was meant by state law to be withheld from public release, the judicial proceedings at issue in *Cox Broadcasting* were open as a matter of state law. Thus, in *Cox Broadcasting*, the state-law scheme made public disclosure of the victim's name almost inevitable; here, Florida law forbids such disclosure. See Fla. Stat. §794.03 (1987).

These facts — that the disclosure came in judicial proceedings, which were open to the public — were critical to our analysis in *Cox Broadcasting*. The distinction between that case and this one is made obvious by the penultimate paragraph of *Cox Broadcasting*:

> We are reluctant to embark on a course that would make public records generally available to the media but would forbid their publication if offensive. . . . [T]he First and Fourteenth Amendments will not allow exposing the press to liability for truthfully publishing information released to the public in official court records. If there are privacy interests to be protected in judicial proceedings, the States must respond by means which avoid public documentation or other exposure of private information. . . . Once true information is disclosed in public court documents open to public inspection, the press cannot be sanctioned for publishing it.

Cox Broadcasting, supra, at 496, 95 S. Ct., at 1047 (emphasis added).

Cox Broadcasting stands for the proposition that the State cannot make the press its first line of defense in withholding private information from the public — it cannot ask the press to secrete private facts that the State makes no effort to safeguard in the first place. In this case, however, the State has undertaken "means which avoid [but obviously, not altogether prevent] public documentation or other exposure of private information." No doubt this is why the Court frankly admits that "*Cox Broadcasting* . . . cannot fairly be read as controlling here." . . .

II

We are left, then, to wonder whether the three "independent reasons" the Court cites for reversing the judgment for B.J.F. support its result.

The first of these reasons relied on by the Court is the fact "appellant gained access to [B.J.F.'s name] through a government news release." "The government's issuance of such a release, without qualification, can only convey to recipients that the government considered dissemination lawful," the Court suggests. So described, this case begins to look like the situation in *Oklahoma Publishing*, where a judge invited reporters into his courtroom, but then tried to forbid them from reporting on the proceedings they observed. But this case is profoundly different. Here, the "release" of information provided by the government was not, as the Court says, "without qualification." As the Star's own reporter conceded at trial, the crime incident report that inadvertently included B.J.F.'s name was posted in a room that contained signs making it clear that the names of rape victims were not matters of public record, and were not to be published. The Star's reporter indicated that she understood that she "[was not] allowed to take down that information" (i.e., B.J.F.'s name) and that she "[was] not supposed to take the information from the police department." Thus, by her own admission the posting of the incident report did not convey to the Star's reporter the idea that "the government considered dissemination lawful"; the Court's suggestion to the contrary is inapt.

Instead, Florida has done precisely what we suggested, in *Cox Broadcasting*, that States wishing to protect the privacy rights of rape victims might do: "respond [to the challenge] by means which *avoid* public documentation or other exposure of private information." 420 U.S., at 496, 95 S. Ct., at 1047 (emphasis added). By amending its public records statute to exempt rape victims' names from disclosure, Fla. Stat. §119.07(3)(h) (1983), and forbidding its officials from releasing such information, Fla. Stat. §794.03 (1983), the State has taken virtually every step imaginable to prevent what happened here. This case presents a far cry, then, from *Cox Broadcasting* or *Oklahoma Publishing*, where the State asked the news media not to publish information it had made generally available to the public: here, the State is not asking the media to do the State's job in the first instance.

Unfortunately, as this case illustrates, mistakes happen: Even when States take measures to "avoid" disclosure, sometimes rape victims' names are found out. As I see it, it is not too much to ask the press, in instances such as this, to respect simple standards of decency and refrain from publishing a victims' name, address, and/or phone number.[6]

6. The Court's concern for a free press is appropriate, but such concerns should be balanced against rival interests in a civilized and humane society. An absolutist view of the former leads to insensitivity as to the latter.

This was evidenced at trial, when the Florida Star's lawyer explained why the paper was not to blame for any anguish caused B.J.F. by a phone call she received, the day after the Star's story was published, from a man threatening to rape B.J.F. again. Noting that the phone call was received at B.J.F.'s home by her mother (who was babysitting B.J.F.'s children while B.J.F. was in the hospital), who relayed the threat to B.J.F., the Star's counsel suggested:

> [I]n reference to the [threatening] phone call, it is sort of blunted by the fact that [B.J.F.] didn't receive the phone call. Her mother did. And if there is any pain and suffering in connection with the phone call, it has to lay in her mother's hands. I mean, my God, she called [B.J.F.] up at the hospital to tell her [of the threat] — you know, I think that is tragic, but I don't think that is something you can blame the Florida Star for.

2 Record 154-155.

While I would not want to live in a society where freedom of the press was unduly limited, I also find regrettable an interpretation of the First Amendment that fosters such a degree of irresponsibility on the part of the news media.

Second, the Court complains that appellant was judged here under too strict a liability standard. The Court contends that a newspaper might be found liable under the Florida court's negligence per se theory without regard to a newspaper's scienter or degree of fault. Ante, at 2612. The short answer to this complaint is that whatever merit the Court's argument might have, it is wholly inapposite here, where the jury found that appellant acted with "reckless indifference towards the rights of others," 2 Record 170, a standard far higher than the *Gertz* standard [Gertz v. Robert Welch, Inc., 418 U.S. 323, 94 S. Ct. 2997, 41 L. Ed. 2d 789 (1974)] the Court urges as a constitutional minimum today. Ante, at 2612. B.J.F. proved the Star's negligence at trial — and, actually, far more than simple negligence; the Court's concerns about damages resting on a strict liability or mere causation basis are irrelevant to the validity of the judgment for appellee.

But even taking the Court's concerns in the abstract, they miss the mark. Permitting liability under a negligence per se theory does not mean that defendants will be held liable without a showing of negligence, but rather, that the standard of care has been set by the legislature, instead of the courts. The Court says that negligence per se permits a plaintiff to hold a defendant liable without a showing that the disclosure was "of a fact about a person's private life . . . that a reasonable person would find highly offensive." Ibid. But the point here is that the legislature — reflecting popular sentiment — has determined that disclosure of the fact that a person was raped is categorically a revelation that reasonable people find offensive. And as for the Court's suggestion that the Florida courts' theory permits liability without regard for whether the victim's identity is already known, or whether she herself has made it known — these are facts that would surely enter into the calculation of damages in such a case. In any event, none of these mitigating factors was present here; whatever the force of these arguments generally, they do not justify the Court's ruling against B.J.F. in this case.

Third, the Court faults the Florida criminal statute for being underinclusive: §794.03 covers disclosure of rape victims' names in "'instrument[s] of mass communication,'" but not other means of distribution, the Court observes. Ante, at 2612-2613. But our cases which have struck down laws that limit or burden the press due to their underinclusiveness have involved situations where a legislature has singled out one segment of the news media or press for adverse treatment, see, e.g., *Daily Mail* (restricting newspapers and not radio or television), or singled out the press for adverse treatment when compared to other similarly situated enterprises, see, e.g., Minneapolis Star & Tribune Co. v. Minnesota Commr. of Revenue, 460 U.S. 575, 578, 103 S. Ct. 1365, 1368, 75 L. Ed. 2d 295 (1983). Here, the Florida law evenhandedly covers all "instrument[s] of mass communication" no matter their form, media, content, nature, or purpose. It excludes neighborhood gossips because presumably the Florida Legislature has determined that neighborhood gossips do not pose the danger and intrusion to rape victims that "instrument[s] of mass communication" do. Simply put: Florida wanted to prevent the widespread distribution of rape victims' names, and therefore enacted a statute tailored almost as precisely as possible to achieving that end. . . .

Consequently, neither the State's "dissemination" of B.J.F.'s name, nor the standard of liability imposed here, nor the underinclusiveness of Florida tort law requires setting aside the verdict for B.J.F. . . .

III . . .

Of course, the right to privacy is not absolute. Even the article widely relied upon in cases vindicating privacy rights, Warren & Brandeis, The Right to Privacy, 4 Harv. L. Rev. 193

(1890), recognized that this right inevitably conflicts with the public's right to know about matters of general concern — and that sometimes, the latter must trump the former. Resolving this conflict is a difficult matter, and I fault the Court not for attempting to strike an appropriate balance between the two, but rather, fault it for according too little weight to B.J.F.'s side of [the] equation, and too much on the other.

I would strike the balance rather differently. Writing for the Ninth Circuit, Judge Merrill put this view eloquently:

> Does the spirit of the Bill of Rights require that individuals be free to pry into the unnewsworthy private affairs of their fellowmen? In our view it does not. In our view, fairly defined areas of privacy must have the protection of law if the quality of life is to continue to be reasonably acceptable. The public's right to know is, then, subject to reasonable limitations so far as concerns the private facts of its individual members.

Virgil v. Time, Inc., 527 F.2d 1122, 1128 (1975), *cert. denied*, 425 U.S. 998, 96 S. Ct. 2215, 48 L. Ed. 2d 823 (1976). . . .

I do not suggest that the Court's decision today is a radical departure from a previously charted course. The Court's ruling has been foreshadowed.

In Time, Inc. v. Hill, 385 U.S. 374, 383-384, n.7, 87 S. Ct. 534, 539-540, n.7, 17 L. Ed. 2d 456 (1967), we observed that — after a brief period early in this century where Brandeis' view was ascendant — the trend in "modern" jurisprudence has been to eclipse an individual's right to maintain private any truthful information that the press wished to publish. More recently, in *Cox Broadcasting*, 420 U.S. at 491, 95 S. Ct., at 1044, we acknowledged the possibility that the First Amendment may prevent a State from ever subjecting the publication of truthful but private information to civil liability. Today, we hit the bottom of the slippery slope.

I would find a place to draw the line higher on the hillside: a spot high enough to protect B.J.F.'s desire for privacy and peace-of-mind in the wake of a horrible personal tragedy. There is no public interest in publishing the names, addresses, and phone numbers of persons who are the victims of crime — and no public interest in immunizing the press from liability in the rare cases where a State's efforts to protect a victim's privacy have failed.

Consequently, I respectfully dissent.

In Cape Publications, Inc. v. Hitchner, 549 So. 2d 1374 (Fla.), *appeal denied*, 493 U.S. 929 (1989), the court held that the publication of a story involving child abuse, which included the names of the persons involved, was newsworthy and could not be made the basis of an invasion of privacy action, notwithstanding a Florida statute that prohibited the disclosure of child abuse proceedings. The prosecutor in the case had shown the file to the reporter. For in-depth discussion of potential tensions between journalism market pressures, First Amendment values, and invasion of privacy actions, see Richard T. Karcher, Tort Law and Journalism Ethics, 40 Loy. U. Chi. L.J. 781 (2009).

In State v. Globe Communications Corp., 648 So. 2d 110 (Fla. 1994), the defendant, a supermarket tabloid, was criminally prosecuted for violating a Florida statute which provided:

> No person shall print, publish, or broadcast, or cause or allow to be printed, published, or broadcast, in any instrument of mass communication the name, address, or other

> identifying fact or information of the victim of any sexual offense within this chapter. An offense under this section shall constitute a misdemeanor of the second degree. . . .

The defendant had identified a woman allegedly raped by a member of a well-known political family, and published her name in two issues of its paper. The court held that the statute violated the free speech provisions of both the United States and Florida Constitutions. Id. at 114.

In Doe 2 v. Associated Press, 331 F.3d 417 (4th Cir. 2003), the court of appeals held that a news organization could not be held liable to a sexual abuse victim for publishing the victim's name after learning it during the perpetrator's sentencing hearing. The sentencing judge in the criminal proceeding had ordered all reporters present not to disclose any sexual assault victims' name in press accounts of the hearing. Because no reporter had objected to the secrecy order, plaintiff was led to believe that his anonymity would be protected despite testifying in open court against his assailant. The Fourth Circuit rejected plaintiff's intrusion and invasion of privacy claims, stating that "[p]laintiff may have successfully alleged poor judgment on the part of the [defendant], but he has not made out a case of tortious conduct under South Carolina law." Id. at 422.

At least one court has responded to constitutional challenges brought against the public disclosure tort by simply refusing to recognize it as an independently viable action. In Hall v. Post, 372 S.E.2d 711 (N.C. 1988), the court asserted that with respect to facts that are "newsworthy," the free speech clause of the First Amendment generates constitutional problems with the application of tort liability. If, on the other hand, the disclosed facts are private, then the court believed that the tort overlaps with intentional infliction of emotional harm. Thus, the court concluded (372 S.E.2d at 717):

> [A]ny possible benefits which might accrue to plaintiffs are entirely insufficient to justify adoption of the constitutionally suspect private facts invasion of privacy tort which punishes defendants for the typically American act of broadly proclaiming the truth by speech or writing.

Note, though, that re-styling the tort claim as one for intentional infliction of emotional harm does not avoid the difficult First Amendment issues alluded to by the court. See Hustler Magazine, Inc. v. Falwell, 485 U.S. 46 (1988) (applying "actual malice" standard to intentional infliction of emotional distress claims against public figures).

C. False Light

Godbehere v. Phoenix Newspapers, Inc.

162 Ariz. 335, 783 P.2d 781 (1989)

Feldman, Vice Chief Justice.

Richard G. Godbehere, a former Maricopa County Sheriff, and several deputies and civilian employees of the sheriff's office (plaintiffs) brought this action against Phoenix Newspapers, Inc., the publisher of The Arizona Republic and Phoenix Gazette, and fourteen editors and reporters of the two newspapers (publishers), for libel and false light invasion of privacy. The trial court granted publishers' motion to dismiss for failure to state a claim as to the invasion of privacy claims, but refused to dismiss the other counts of the complaint. Plaintiffs appealed and the court of appeals affirmed. We granted review to determine whether Arizona should recognize a cause of action for false light invasion of privacy, and if so, what the proper standard should be. . . .

Facts

In the spring and summer of 1985, publishers printed over fifty articles, editorials, and columns (the publications) about plaintiffs' various law enforcement activities. The publications stated that the plaintiffs engaged in illegal activities, staged narcotics arrests to generate publicity, illegally arrested citizens, misused public funds and resources, committed police brutality, and generally were incompetent at law enforcement. Plaintiffs alleged in their eighteen-count complaint that the publications were false, damaged their reputations, harmed them in their profession, and caused them emotional distress. Publishers moved to dismiss all eighteen counts of the complaint for failure to state a claim, and the court dismissed the false light invasion of privacy claims. . . .

On appeal, plaintiffs argued that Arizona should follow the Restatement (Second) of Torts §652E (1977) (hereafter Restatement), which provides in part:

> One who gives publicity to a matter concerning another that places the other before the public in a false light is subject to liability to the other for invasion of his privacy, if
>
> (a) the false light in which the other was placed would be highly offensive to a reasonable person, and
>
> (b) the actor had knowledge of or acted in reckless disregard as to the falsity of the publicized matter and the false light in which the other would be placed.

Discussion . . .

B. Privacy in Arizona

Arizona first recognized an action for invasion of privacy in Reed v. Real Detective Publishing Co., 63 Ariz. 294, 162 P.2d 133 (1945). Reed involved the unauthorized publication of the plaintiff's photograph. Subsequently, our court of appeals recognized the Restatement's four-part classification of the tort.

Although most jurisdictions that recognize a cause of action for invasion of privacy have adopted the Restatement standard of "highly offensive to a reasonable person" or a similar standard, Arizona courts of appeals' decisions have imposed a stricter standard. Rather than following the Restatement, these decisions have held that where the damage alleged is emotional, the plaintiff must prove the elements of the tort of intentional infliction of emotional distress in addition to proving invasion of privacy. To recover for invasion of privacy, a plaintiff must show that the defendant's conduct was "extreme and outrageous." No other state requires a plaintiff to prove that the defendant committed "outrage" in a false light action.

Publishers urge this court to adopt the court of appeals' view. They argue that there is no need for an independent tort of false light invasion of privacy because the action overlaps two other recognized torts: defamation and intentional infliction of emotional distress. These, publishers contend, cover the field and permit recovery in meritorious cases, thus making the false light action an unnecessary burden on the media's first amendment rights. To consider this argument, we must examine the distinctions between the false light action and the torts of intentional infliction of emotional distress and defamation.

C. False Light Invasion of Privacy and Intentional Infliction of Emotional Distress

Arizona has turned to Restatement §46 to define intentional infliction of emotional distress, also known as the tort of outrage. This section provides:

> (1) one who by extreme and outrageous conduct intentionally or recklessly causes severe emotional distress to another is subject to liability for such emotional distress, and if bodily harm to the other results from it, for such bodily harm.

The element of "extreme and outrageous conduct" requires that plaintiff prove defendant's conduct exceeded "all bounds usually tolerated by decent society . . . and [caused] mental distress of a very serious kind." . . .

Publishers emphasize that actions for both intentional infliction of emotional distress and invasion of privacy provide compensation for emotional distress or damage to sensibility. Thus, the injury from both torts is similar. Although this may be true, the fact that two different actions address the same injury is no reason to refuse to recognize torts that protect against different wrongful conduct. For example, three victims may suffer broken legs in the following ways: (1) a defendant negligently drives a car into the first victim's car; (2) a defendant's defective product injures the second victim; and (3) a defendant, without justification, attacks the third. Each victim would have a different tort claim: negligence, strict liability, and battery. The fact that each victim suffers the same type of injury does not preclude recognizing separate tort actions. Each tort theory developed separately to deter and provide redress against a different type of wrongful conduct.

Thus, the fact that outrage and invasion of privacy both provide redress for emotional injury does not persuade us that the actions are "merged" or that plaintiffs should be required to prove the former in an action for the latter. The outrage tort protects against conduct so extreme that it would induce "an average member of the community . . . to exclaim, 'outrageous!'" Restatement §46 Comment *d.* False light invasion of privacy, however, protects against the conduct of knowingly or recklessly publishing false information or innuendo that a "reasonable person" would find "highly offensive." Although false publication may constitute outrageous conduct and vice versa, it is also true that the same wrongful conduct will not always satisfy the elements of both tort actions. Because each action protects against a different type of tortious conduct, each has its place, and the common injury should not abrogate the action.

Nor do we believe that recognizing the false light action without requiring plaintiffs to prove outrage will circumvent the "stringent standards" of the emotional distress tort. The standards for proving false light invasion of privacy are quite "stringent" by themselves. For example, the plaintiff in a false light case must prove that the defendant published with knowledge of the falsity or reckless disregard for the truth. This standard is as stringent as the intentional infliction of emotional distress requirement that the plaintiff prove the defendant "intentionally or recklessly caused" the emotional distress. . . .

We conclude, therefore, that the two torts exist to redress different types of wrongful conduct. Situations exist where a jury could find the defendant's publication of false information or innuendo was not outrageous but did satisfy the false light elements. Thus, we believe the tort action for false light invasion of privacy provides protection against a narrow class of wrongful conduct that falls short of "outrage," but nevertheless should be deterred.

D. Invasion of Privacy and Defamation

A second argument advanced by publishers is that little distinction exists between a tort action for false light invasion of privacy and one for defamation. Thus, because defamation actions are available, they argue, Arizona need not recognize false light invasion of privacy. Again, we disagree.

Although both defamation and false light invasion of privacy involve publication, the nature of the interests protected by each action differs substantially. A defamation action compensates damage to reputation or good name caused by the publication of false information. To be defamatory, a publication must be false and must bring the defamed person into disrepute, contempt, or ridicule, or must impeach plaintiff's honesty, integrity, virtue, or reputation.

Privacy, on the other hand, does not protect reputation but protects mental and emotional interests. Under this theory, a plaintiff may recover even in the absence of reputational damage, as long as the publicity is unreasonably offensive and attributes false characteristics. However, to qualify as a false light invasion of privacy, the publication must involve "a major misrepresentation of [the plaintiff's] character, history, activities or beliefs," not merely minor or unimportant inaccuracies. Restatement §652E Comment *c*.

Another distinction between defamation and false light invasion of privacy is the role played by truth. To be defamatory, a publication must be false, and truth is a defense. A false light cause of action may arise when something untrue has been published about an individual, or when the publication of true information creates a false implication about the individual. In the latter type of case, the false innuendo created by the highly offensive presentation of a true fact constitutes the injury.[2]

Thus, although defamation and false light often overlap, they serve very different objectives. The two tort actions deter different conduct and redress different wrongs. A plaintiff may bring a false light invasion of privacy action even though the publication is not defamatory, and even though the actual facts stated are true. . . .

2. A good example of a false light cause of action based on implication is Douglass v. Hustler Magazine, Inc., 769 F.2d 1128 (7th Cir. 1985), *cert. denied*, 475 U.S. 1094, 106 S. Ct. 1489, 89 L. Ed. 2d 892 (1986). In *Douglass*, the plaintiff posed nude, consenting to the publication of her photographs in Playboy magazine. Her photographer subsequently left the employ of Playboy for Hustler magazine, a publication of much lower standing in the journalistic community. He sold her photographs to Hustler, which published them. The plaintiff sued for the nonconsensual use of the photographs. Plaintiff had no cause of action for defamation, because essentially, there was nothing untrue about the photographs. She posed for them and, as published, they did not misrepresent her. She also had no claim for outrage. She voluntarily posed for the photographs and consented to their publication in Playboy. Publication was not "outrageous," as it may have been if she were photographed without her knowledge and the photos published without her initial consent. However, the court upheld her recovery for false light invasion of privacy. The jury may have focused on the differences between Playboy and Hustler and concluded that to be published in Hustler, as if she had posed for that publication, falsely placed her in a different light than the Playboy publication. 769 F.2d at 1138.

F. Free Speech Considerations

As in defamation, a public official in a false light action must always show that the defendant published with knowledge of the false innuendo or with reckless disregard of the truth. Any doubt about the application of the actual malice element of the false light tort to public figures has been eliminated. In Hustler Magazine, Inc. v. Falwell, 485 U.S. 46, 108 S. Ct. 876, 99 L. Ed. 2d 41 (1988), the Supreme Court held that a public figure plaintiff must prove Times v. Sullivan actual malice in order to recover for intentional infliction of emotional distress. Although *Hustler* was an intentional infliction case, the language used by the Court is so broad that it applies to any tort action relating to free speech, particularly "in the area of public debate about public figures." See *Hustler*, 485 U.S. at 53, 108 S. Ct. at 881.[6] Additional protection for free speech comes from the principle that protection for privacy interests generally applies only to private matters. . . .

G. Is False Light Available in This Case?

Finally, publishers contended that even if we recognize false light actions, the action does not lie in this case. They argue that not only do the publications discuss matters of public interest, but plaintiffs have no right of privacy with respect to the manner in which they perform their official duties. We agree. . . .

A number of jurisdictions take the position that because false light is a form of invasion of privacy, it must relate only to the private affairs of the plaintiff and cannot involve matters of public interest. It is difficult to conceive of an area of greater public interest than law enforcement. Certainly the public has a legitimate interest in the manner in which law enforcement officers perform their duties. Therefore, we hold that there can be no false light invasion of privacy action for matters involving official acts or duties of public officers.

Consequently, we adopt the following legal standard: A plaintiff cannot sue for false light invasion of privacy if he or she is a public official and the publication relates to performance of his or her public life or duties. We do not go so far as to say, however, that a public official has no privacy rights at all and may never bring an action for invasion of privacy. Certainly, if the publication presents the public official's private life in a false light, he or she can sue under the false light tort, although actual malice must be shown.

The Supreme Court has held that "the public official designation applies at the very least to those among the hierarchy of government employees who have, or appear to the public to have, substantial responsibility for or control over the conduct of governmental affairs." Rosenblatt v. Baer, 383 U.S. 75, 85, 86 S. Ct. 669, 676, 15 L. Ed. 2d 597 (1966). Police and other law enforcement personnel are almost always classified as public officials. The publications at issue concern the discharge of their public duties and do not relate to private affairs. Therefore, plaintiffs have no claim for false light invasion of privacy.

6. To this point, we have spoken of false light as requiring that the plaintiff show actual malice. Restatement §652E seems to state that requirement, but the Caveat to that section states that the Institute "takes no position" on whether, under some circumstances, a nonpublic figure may recover for false light invasion of privacy where he does not show actual malice but does show negligent publication. *See also* Restatement §652E comment on clause (b). Because this case does not present the issue, we also take no position on the validity of a false light action for negligent publication. Suffice it to say that in this case, where we deal with publications concerning public officers performing public duties, the First Amendment controls.

We affirm the trial court's dismissal of the false light claim. Because we disagree with the court of appeals' reasoning, we vacate that opinion and remand to the trial court for further proceedings consistent with this opinion.

Notwithstanding decisions like *Godbehere*, some commentators have argued the false light tort completely overlaps other torts, and for that reason should not be recognized as a distinct category of invasion of privacy. This point was first made in Harry Kalven, Jr., Privacy in Tort Law — Were Warren and Brandeis Wrong?, 31 Law & Contemp. Probs. 327 (1966). More recently, the anti–false light cudgel was taken up by Professor J. Clark Kelso in his article False Light Privacy: A Requiem, 32 Santa Clara L. Rev. 783 (1993). Professor Kelso characterized the tort as "Prosser's Folly" and asserted that

> [n]one of the cases Prosser cited in support of false light privacy came close to recognizing such a tort. False light existed only in Prosser's mind.

Id. at 788. Professor Kelso surveyed over 600 cases, and concluded that in none of them was false light essential to the outcome. The "core" of the false light case, he stated, "lies elsewhere, in defamation, in misappropriation, or in intentional infliction of emotional distress." Id. at 785.

Numerous states have agreed with Professor Kelso. The Supreme Court of Minnesota, in Lake v. Wal-Mart Stores, Inc., 582 N.W.2d 231 (1998), rejected the false light tort, but did state that it would recognize the other three right to privacy categories. Similarly, the Supreme Court of Florida also rejected false light but recognized defamation by false implication in Jews for Jesus, Inc. v. Rapp, 997 So. 2d 1098 (2008). The Supreme Court of Colorado also declined to recognize the false light privacy category in Denver Publishing Company v. Bueno, 54 P.3d 893 (2002). The court felt that the limited areas in which the false light tort plays an independent doctrinal role were especially problematic from the perspective of free speech concerns:

> Because tort law is intended both to recompense wrongful conduct and to prevent it, it is important that it be clear in its identification of that wrongful conduct. The tort of false light fails that test. The sole area in which it differs from defamation is an area fraught with ambiguity and subjectivity. Recognizing "highly offensive" information, even framed within the context of what a reasonable person would find highly offensive, necessarily involves a subjective component. The publication of highly offensive material is more difficult to avoid than the publication of defamatory information that damages a person's reputation in the community. In order to prevent liability under a false light tort, the media would need to anticipate whether statements are "highly offensive" to a reasonable person of ordinary sensibilities even though their publication does no harm to the individual's reputation. To the contrary, defamatory statements are more easily recognizable by an author or publisher because such statements are those that would damage someone's reputation in the community. In other words, defamation is measured by its results; whereas false light invasion of privacy is measured by perception. It is even possible that what would be highly offensive in one location would not be in another, or what would have been highly offensive in 1962 would not be highly offensive in 2002. In other words, the standard is difficult to quantify, and shifts based upon the subjective perceptions of a community. [54 P.3d at 903-04]

Nonetheless, a majority of courts continue to recognize false light as an independent tort. See id. at 897 (observing that as of 2002, "thirty state courts acknowledge false light as a viable claim in their jurisdictions"). Still other courts seem to view false light invasion of privacy as equivalent to defamation, while nonetheless treating the two categories as viable, independent torts. See, for instance, Solano v. Playgirl, Inc., 292 F.3d 1078 (9th Cir. 2002), which reversed summary judgment against plaintiff, a popular television actor, who had claimed false light invasion of privacy based on defendant's use of his photograph on its magazine cover in a manner that suggested plaintiff appeared nude inside the magazine. While permitting plaintiff's false light claim to proceed to the jury, the court also acknowledged that "[a]n action for invasion of privacy by placing the plaintiff in a false light in the public eye is in substance equivalent to a libel claim." Id. at 1083 n.2. The law is surveyed and the minority view rejecting the false light tort is criticized in Note, Let There Be False Light: Resisting the Growing Trend Against an Important Tort, 84 Minn. L. Rev. 713 (2000). See also James B. Lake, Restraining False Light: Constitutional and Common Law Limits on a "Troublesome Tort," 61 Fed. Comm. L.J. 625 (2009).

D. Appropriation

Prosser's fourth category of tortious privacy invasion concerns the nonconsensual commercial use of some element of plaintiff's name or likeness. A frequent context for such claims is the unauthorized use of plaintiff's image in defendant's commercial advertisement, as in one of the first privacy cases in this country. See Pavesich v. New England Life Ins. Co., 50 S.E. 68 (Ga. 1905). For a more recent example, see Coton v. Televised Visual X-Ography, Inc., 740 F. Supp. 2d 1299 (M.D. Fla. 2010) (unauthorized use of plaintiff's self-portrait on the cover of a pornographic movie entitled the plaintiff to compensatory damages for harm to her reputation in addition to copyright infringement). Plaintiff's image or likeness need not be exact. For example, the court in Faulkner v. Hasbro, Inc., 2016 WL 3965200 (D.N.J. 2016), held that plaintiff Harris Faulkner, a professional television journalist, had successfully stated a claim against defendant toy manufacturer for introducing a "Harris Faulkner Hamster Doll" into its "Littlest Pet Shop" toy line. The court reasoned that plaintiff was "entitled to adduce evidence that as a child plays inside this fictionalized, highly interactive world, s/he may see or put into the girl hamster doll named Harris Faulkner the identity, persona, and characteristics of the real Harris Faulkner." Id. at *2. Nor is wrongful appropriation limited to the use of plaintiff's name or likeness. For instance, in Carson v. Here's Johnny Portable Toilets, Inc., 698 F.2d 831 (6th Cir. 1983), the court held that defendant's use of the phrase "Here's Johnny," which was a signature phrase used to introduce plaintiff's nightly talk show, constituted tortious appropriation.

The commercial appropriation tort is related to, but distinct from, a "right of publicity" tort that originated in Haelan Laboratories, Inc. v. Topps Chewing Gum, Inc., 202 F.2d 866 (2d Cir. 1953), and that has since been adopted by approximately half of the states either by common law or by statute. See, e.g., Toney v. L'Oreal USA, Inc., 406 F.3d 905 (7th Cir. 2004) (construing Illinois Right of Publicity Act). As the Nevada Supreme Court has stated:

> The distinction between these two torts is the interest each seeks to protect. The appropriation tort seeks to protect an individual's personal interest in privacy; the personal injury is measured in terms of the mental anguish that results from the

> appropriation of an ordinary individual's identity. The right to publicity seeks to protect the *property* interest that a celebrity has in his or her name; the injury is not to personal privacy, it is the economic loss a celebrity suffers when someone else interferes with the property interest that he or she has in his or her name. We consider it critical in deciding this case that recognition be given to the difference between the *personal*, injured-feelings quality involved in the appropriation privacy tort and the *property*, commercial value quality involved in the right of publicity tort.

People for the Ethical Treatment of Animals v. Bobby Berosini, Ltd., 895 P.2d 1269, 1283 (Nev. 1995). Despite the distinct lineages of the two torts and the separate interests that they seek to protect, courts and litigants often use the terms interchangeably, and facts supporting a claim for one tort will frequently also support a claim for the other. For an engaging historical analysis, see Samantha Barbas, From Privacy to Publicity: The Tort of Appropriation in the Age of Mass Consumption, 61 Buff. L. Rev. 1119, 1125 (2013) (arguing that "[t]he right of publicity eclipsed the right of privacy when modern consumer culture came to see loss of profit as the more serious and probable consequence of the unauthorized commercial exploitation of a person's image, rather than harm to one's dignity or emotions").

A key factor involved in both the appropriation and the right of publicity torts is the use by defendant of plaintiff's name or likeness for trade or business purposes. Comment *d* to §652C, which sets out the commercial appropriation tort, states:

> No one has the right to object merely because his name or appearance is brought before the public, since neither is in any way a private matter and both are open to public observation. It is only when the publicity is given for the purpose of appropriating to the defendant's benefit the commercial or other values associated with the name or the likeness that the right of privacy is invaded.

In Toffoloni v. LFP Publishing Group, 572 F.3d 1201 (11th Cir. 2009), *Hustler* magazine published nude photographs of the plaintiff that had been taken 20 years prior to her death. The plaintiff, along with her son, had been murdered by her professional wrestler husband, Christopher Benoit. The defendant asserted that there was substantial public interest in the story of the life, career, and tragic death of Benoit (who committed suicide after killing his wife and son), and in the parallel story of the plaintiff, her modest beginnings and youthful interest in modeling, and her violent death. Applying Georgia law, the federal court of appeals held that the publication of the nude photographs was not incidental to the article, which was concededly of public interest. Rather, the article was incidental to the photographs. The story was only of tangential relevance to the magazine's desire to publish the photographs for commercial gain. "[S]omeone's notorious death [does not] constitute[] a carte blanche for the publication of any and all images of that person during his or her life . . . regardless of whether those images are of any relevance to the incident currently of public concern." Id. at 1210.

In Raymen v. United Senior Association, Inc., 2005 WL 607916 (D.D.C. 2005), the court held that anticipated charitable contributions could be considered sufficient to satisfy the commercial purpose aspect of the appropriation tort. In a mail campaign opposing same-sex marriage, defendant had used a photograph of plaintiffs, two men, kissing as they awaited their opportunity to wed following a newly established right to same-sex marriage in Multnomah County, Oregon. The court concluded that the defendant's use of the photograph was for its own financial gain, given that the defendant sought financial contributions to further its political activities.

A similar argument regarding "indirect" financial interests has repeatedly failed with respect to the entertainment industry. For instance, in Tyne v. Time Warner Entertainment Company, 901 So. 2d 802 (Fla. 2005), the Supreme Court of Florida held that the term "commercial purpose" within Florida's commercial misappropriation statute did not apply to motion pictures, which do not directly promote a product or service, despite the obvious and significant business motivations of the Hollywood film industry. Thus, survivors of individuals killed in a fishing vessel during a North Atlantic storm could not proceed under the statute against producers of a film that depicted the tragic events. See also Almeida v. Amazon.com, Inc., 456 F.3d 1316 (11th Cir. 2006) (defendant retailer entitled to summary judgment on misappropriation claim because, in selling "Anjos Proibidos" book that included an underage photograph of plaintiff on its cover, defendant did not directly promote a product or service). Why would the "indirect" financial interests argument be deemed adequate in the context of money-raising efforts by political interest groups but not profiteering by the film industry?

Another key question under the commercial appropriation tort concerns how the interest of states in protecting the commercial value of personality should be balanced against the interests in promoting artistic expression and in permitting free and open discussion on matters of legitimate public concern. In Nichols v. Moore, 334 F. Supp. 2d 944 (E.D. Mich. 2004), a federal district court dismissed a right of publicity claim brought by Terry Nichols against filmmaker Michael Moore. Nichols had been investigated but not charged in connection with the Oklahoma City bombing, for which Nichols's brother and Timothy McVeigh were convicted. Moore's documentary film *Bowling for Columbine* addressed Nichols's role in the bombing as part of a broader treatment of violence in American society. The court dismissed Nichols's publicity claim on First Amendment grounds, reasoning "courts have been consistently unwilling to recognize the right of publicity cause of action where the plaintiff's name or picture was used in connection with a matter of public interest, be it news or entertainment." Id. at 956. Compare *Nichols* with Jordan v. Jewel Food Stores, Inc., 743 F.3d 509 (7th Cir. 2014), in which a grocery store chain unsuccessfully argued that its logo-emblazoned advertisements congratulating Michael Jordan on his induction into the Basketball Hall of Fame were noncommercial speech and therefore insulated from liability. For an attempt to integrate the right of publicity with First Amendment and copyright law, see Thomas F. Cotter & Irina Y. Dmitrieva, Integrating the Right of Publicity with First Amendment and Copyright Preemption Analysis, 33 Colum. J.L. & Arts 165 (2010).

In re NCAA Student-Athlete Name & Likeness Licensing Litigation

724 F.3d 1268 (9th Cir. 2013)

Bybee, Circuit Judge:

. . . In this case, we must balance the right of publicity of a former college football player against the asserted First Amendment right of a video game developer to use his likeness in its expressive works.

The district court concluded that the game developer, Electronic Arts ("EA"), had no First Amendment defense against the right-of-publicity claims of the football player, Samuel Keller. We affirm. . . .

I

Samuel Keller was the starting quarterback for Arizona State University in 2005 before he transferred to the University of Nebraska, where he played during the 2007 season. EA is the producer of the *NCAA Football* series of video games, which allow users to control avatars representing college football players as those avatars participate in simulated games. In *NCAA Football*, EA seeks to replicate each school's entire team as accurately as possible. Every real football player on each team included in the game has a corresponding avatar in the game with the player's actual jersey number and virtually identical height, weight, build, skin tone, hair color, and home state. EA attempts to match any unique, highly identifiable playing behaviors by sending detailed questionnaires to team equipment managers. Additionally, EA creates realistic virtual versions of actual stadiums; populates them with the virtual athletes, coaches, cheerleaders, and fans realistically rendered by EA's graphic artists; and incorporates realistic sounds such as the crunch of the players' pads and the roar of the crowd.

EA's game differs from reality in that EA omits the players' names on their jerseys and assigns each player a home town that is different from the actual player's home town. However, users of the video game may upload rosters of names obtained from third parties so that the names do appear on the jerseys. In such cases, EA allows images from the game containing athletes' real names to be posted on its website by users. Users can further alter reality by entering "Dynasty" mode, where the user assumes a head coach's responsibilities for a college program for up to thirty seasons, including recruiting players from a randomly generated pool of high school athletes, or "Campus Legend" mode, where the user controls a virtual player from high school through college, making choices relating to practices, academics, and social life.

In the 2005 edition of the game, the virtual starting quarterback for Arizona State wears number 9, as did Keller, and has the same height, weight, skin tone, hair color, hair style, handedness, home state, play style (pocket passer), visor preference, facial features, and school year as Keller. In the 2008 edition, the virtual quarterback for Nebraska has these same characteristics, though the jersey number does not match, presumably because Keller changed his number right before the season started.

Objecting to this use of his likeness, Keller filed a putative class-action complaint in the Northern District of California asserting, as relevant on appeal, that EA violated his right of publicity under California Civil Code §3344 and California common law. EA moved to strike the complaint as a strategic lawsuit against public participation ("SLAPP") under California's anti-SLAPP statute, Cal. Civ. Proc. Code §425.16, and the district court denied the motion. We have jurisdiction over EA's appeal pursuant to 28 U.S.C. §1291. See Batzel v. Smith, 333 F.3d 1018, 1024–26 (9th Cir.2003).

II

California's anti-SLAPP statute is designed to discourage suits that "masquerade as ordinary lawsuits but are brought to deter common citizens from exercising their political or legal rights or to punish them for doing so." Batzel, 333 F.3d at 1024 (internal quotation marks omitted). The statute provides:

> A cause of action against a person arising from any act of that person in furtherance of the person's right of petition or free speech under the United States Constitution or the

> California Constitution in connection with a public issue shall be subject to a special motion to strike, unless the court determines that the plaintiff has established that there is a probability that the plaintiff will prevail on the claim.

Cal. Civ. Proc. Code §425.16(b)(1). We have determined that the anti-SLAPP statute is available in federal court. . . .

EA did not contest before the district court and does not contest here that Keller has stated a right-of-publicity claim under California common and statutory law. Instead, EA raises . . . affirmative defenses derived from the First Amendment[, the most important of which invokes California's "transformative use" defense to right-of-publicity claims.]

A

The California Supreme Court formulated the transformative use defense in Comedy III Productions, Inc. v. Gary Saderup, Inc., 25 Cal. 4th 387, 106 Cal. Rptr. 2d 126, 21 P.3d 797 (2001). The defense is "a balancing test between the First Amendment and the right of publicity based on whether the work in question adds significant creative elements so as to be transformed into something more than a mere celebrity likeness or imitation." Id. 106 Cal. Rptr. 2d 126, 21 P.3d at 799. The California Supreme Court explained that "when a work contains significant transformative elements, it is not only especially worthy of First Amendment protection, but it is also less likely to interfere with the economic interest protected by the right of publicity." Id. 106 Cal. Rptr. 2d 126, 21 P.3d at 808. . . .

Comedy III gives us at least five factors to consider in determining whether a work is sufficiently transformative to obtain First Amendment protection. See J. Thomas McCarthy, The Rights of Publicity and Privacy §8:72 (2d ed. 2012). First, if "the celebrity likeness is one of the 'raw materials' from which an original work is synthesized," it is more likely to be transformative than if "the depiction or imitation of the celebrity is the very sum and substance of the work in question." Comedy III, 106 Cal. Rptr. 2d 126, 21 P.3d at 809. Second, the work is protected if it is "primarily the defendant's own expression"—as long as that expression is "something other than the likeness of the celebrity." Id. This factor requires an examination of whether a likely purchaser's primary motivation is to buy a reproduction of the celebrity, or to buy the expressive work of that artist. McCarthy, supra, §8:72. Third, to avoid making judgments concerning "the quality of the artistic contribution," a court should conduct an inquiry "more quantitative than qualitative" and ask "whether the literal and imitative or the creative elements predominate in the work." Comedy III, 106 Cal. Rptr. 2d 126, 21 P.3d at 809. Fourth, the California Supreme Court indicated that "a subsidiary inquiry" would be useful in close cases: whether "the marketability and economic value of the challenged work derive primarily from the fame of the celebrity depicted." Id. 106 Cal. Rptr. 2d 126, 21 P.3d at 810. Lastly, the court indicated that "when an artist's skill and talent is manifestly subordinated to the overall goal of creating a conventional portrait of a celebrity so as to commercially exploit his or her fame," the work is not transformative. Id. . . .

[I]n No Doubt v. Activision Publishing, Inc., the California Court of Appeal addressed Activision's *Band Hero* video game. 192 Cal. App. 4th 1018, 122 Cal. Rptr. 3d 397, 400 (2011), petition for review denied, 2011 Cal. LEXIS 6100 (Cal. June 8, 2011) (No. B223996). In *Band Hero*, users simulate performing in a rock band in time with popular songs. Id. at 401. Users choose from a number of avatars, some of which represent actual rock stars, including the members of the rock band No Doubt. Id. at 401. Activision licensed No Doubt's likeness, but allegedly exceeded the scope of the license by permitting users to manipulate the No Doubt avatars to play any song in the game, solo or with members of other bands, and even to alter the avatars' voices. Id. at 402. The court held that No Doubt's right of publicity prevailed despite Activision's First Amendment defense because the game was not "transformative" under the *Comedy III* test. It reasoned that the video game characters were "literal recreations of the band members," doing "the same activity by which the band achieved and maintains its fame." Id. at 411. According to the court, the fact "that the avatars appear in the context of a videogame that contains many other creative elements[ ] does not transform the avatars into anything other than exact depictions of No Doubt's members doing exactly what they do as celebrities." Id. The court concluded that "the expressive elements of the game remain manifestly subordinated to the overall goal of creating a conventional portrait of No Doubt so as to commercially exploit its fame." Id. (internal quotation marks omitted). . . .

[W]e conclude that EA's use of Keller's likeness does not contain significant transformative elements such that EA is entitled to the defense as a matter of law. The facts of *No Doubt* are very similar to those here. EA is alleged to have replicated Keller's physical characteristics in *NCAA Football*, just as the members of No Doubt are realistically portrayed in *Band Hero*. Here, as in *Band Hero*, users manipulate the characters in the performance of the same activity for which they are known in real life — playing football in this case, and performing in a rock band in *Band Hero*. The context in which the activity occurs is also similarly realistic — real venues in *Band Hero* and realistic depictions of actual football stadiums in *NCAA Football*. As the district court found, Keller is represented as "what he was: the starting quarterback for Arizona State" and Nebraska, and "the game's setting is identical to where the public found [Keller] during his collegiate career: on the football field." Keller v. Elec. Arts, Inc., No. C 09–1967 CW, 2010 WL 530108, at *5 (N.D. Cal. Feb. 8, 2010).

. . . Given that *NCAA Football* realistically portrays college football players in the context of college football games, the district court was correct in concluding that EA cannot prevail as a matter of law based on the transformative use defense at the anti-SLAPP stage. . . .

AFFIRMED.

THOMAS, Circuit Judge, dissenting:

Because the creative and transformative elements of Electronic Arts' *NCAA Football* video game series predominate over the commercial use of the athletes' likenesses, the First Amendment protects EA from liability. Therefore, I respectfully dissent.

I

. . . Although [the five considerations identified in *Comedy III*] are often distilled as analytical factors, Justice Mosk was careful in *Comedy III* not to label them as such. Indeed, the focus of *Comedy III* is a more holistic examination of whether the transformative and creative elements of a particular work predominate over commercially based literal or imitative depictions. The distinction is critical, because excessive deconstruction of *Comedy III* can lead to misapplication of the test. And it is at this juncture that I must respectfully part ways with my colleagues in the majority. . . .

A

The first step in conducting a balancing is to examine the creative work at issue. At its essence, EA's *NCAA Football* is a work of interactive historical fiction. Although the game changes from year to year, its most popular features predominately involve role-playing by the gamer. For example, a player can create a virtual image of himself as a potential college football player. The virtual player decides which position he would like to play, then participates in a series of "tryouts" or competes in an entire high school season to gauge his skill. Based on his performance, the virtual player is ranked and available to play at select colleges. The player chooses among the colleges, then assumes the role of a college football player. He also selects a major, the amount of time he wishes to spend on social activities, and practice—all of which may affect the virtual player's performance. He then plays his position on the college team. In some versions of the game, in another mode, the virtual player can engage in a competition for the Heisman Trophy. In another popular mode, the gamer becomes a virtual coach. The coach scouts, recruits, and develops entirely fictional players for his team. The coach can then promote the team's evolution over decades of seasons.

The college teams that are supplied in the game do replicate the actual college teams for that season, including virtual athletes who bear the statistical and physical dimensions of the actual college athletes. But, unlike their professional football counterparts in the *Madden NFL* series, the NCAA football players in these games are not identified.

The gamers can also change their abilities, appearances, and physical characteristics at will. Keller's impressive physical likeness can be morphed by the gamer into an overweight and slow virtual athlete, with anemic passing ability. And the gamer can create new virtual players out of whole cloth. Players can change teams. The gamer could pit Sam Keller against himself, or a stronger or weaker version of himself, on a different team. Or the gamer could play the game endlessly without ever encountering Keller's avatar. In the simulated games, the gamer controls not only the conduct of the game, but the weather, crowd noise, mascots, and other environmental factors. Of course, one may play the game leaving the players unaltered, pitting team against team. But, in this context as well, the work is one of historic fiction. The gamer controls the teams, players, and games.

Applying the *Comedy III* considerations to *NCAA Football* in proper holistic context, the considerations favor First Amendment protection. The athletic likenesses are but one of the raw materials from which the broader game is constructed. The work, considered as a whole, is primarily one of EA's own expression. The creative and transformative elements predominate over the commercial use of likenesses. The marketability and economic value of the game comes from the creative elements within, not from the pure commercial exploitation of a celebrity image. The game is not a conventional portrait of a celebrity, but a work consisting of many creative and transformative elements. . . .

B

Although one could leave the analysis with an examination of the transformative and creative aspects of the game, a true balancing requires an inquiry as to the other side of the scales: the publicity right at stake. Here, as well, the *NCAA Football* video game series can be distinguished from the traditional right of publicity cases, both from a quantitative and a qualitative perspective.

As a quantitative matter, *NCAA Football* is different from other right of publicity cases in the sheer number of virtual actors involved. Most right of publicity cases involve either one celebrity, or a finite and defined group of celebrities. . . .

In contrast, *NCAA Football* includes not just Sam Keller, but thousands of virtual actors. This consideration is of particular significance when we examine, as instructed by *Comedy III*, whether the source of the product marketability comes from creative elements or from pure exploitation of a celebrity image. There is not, at this stage of the litigation, any evidence as to the personal marketing power of Sam Keller, as distinguished from the appeal of the creative aspects of the product. Regardless, the sheer number of athletes involved inevitably diminish the significance of the publicity right at issue. . . . Put another way, if an anonymous virtual player is tackled in an imaginary video game and no one notices, is there any right of publicity infringed at all?

The sheer quantity of the virtual players in the game underscores the inappropriateness of analyzing the right of publicity through the lens of one likeness only. Only when the creative work is considered in complete context can a proper analysis be conducted.

As a qualitative matter, the essence of *NCAA Football* is founded on publicly available data, which is not protected by any individual publicity rights. It is true that EA solicits and receives information directly from colleges and universities. But the information is hardly proprietary. Personal vital statistics for players are found in college programs and media guides. Likewise, playing statistics are easily available. In this respect, the information used by EA is indistinguishable from the information used in fantasy athletic leagues, for which the First Amendment provides protection, or much beloved statistical board games, such as Strat-O-Matic. An athlete's right of publicity simply does not encompass publicly available statistical data.

Further, the structure of the game is not founded on exploitation of an individual's publicity rights. The players are unidentified and anonymous. It is true that third-party software is available to quickly identify the players, but that is not part of the EA package. And the fact that the players can be identified by the knowledgeable user by their position, team, and statistics is somewhat beside the point. The issue is whether the marketability of the product is driven by an individual celebrity, or by the game itself. Player anonymity, while certainly not a complete defense, bears on the question of how we balance the right of publicity against the First Amendment. This feature of the game places it in stark contrast with *No Doubt*, where the whole point of the enterprise was the successful commercial exploitation of the specifically identified, world-famous musicians.

Finally, as a qualitative matter, the publicity rights of college athletes are remarkably restricted. This consideration is critical because the "right to exploit commercially one's celebrity is primarily an economic right." Gionfriddo v. Major League Baseball, 94 Cal. App. 4th 400, 114 Cal. Rptr. 2d 307, 318 (2001). NCAA rules prohibit athletes from benefitting economically from any success on the field. NCAA Bylaw 12.5 specifically prohibits commercial licensing of an NCAA athlete's name or picture. NCAA, 2012-13 NCAA Division I Manual §12.5.2.1 (2012). Before being allowed to compete each year, all Division I NCAA athletes must sign a contract stating that they understand the prohibition on licensing and affirming that they have not violated any amateurism rules. In short, even if an athlete wished to license his image to EA, the athlete could not do so without destroying amateur status. Thus, an individual college athlete's right of publicity is extraordinarily circumscribed and, in practical reality, nonexistent.[5]

5. The issue of whether this structure is fair to the student athlete is beyond the scope of this appeal, but forms a significant backdrop to the discussion. The NCAA received revenues of $871.6 million in fiscal year 2011-12, with 81% of the money coming from television and marketing fees. However, few college athletes will ever receive any professional compensation. The NCAA reports that in 2011, there were 67,887 college football players. Of those, 15,086 were senior players, and only 255 athletes were drafted for a professional team. Thus, only 1.7% of seniors received any subsequent professional economic compensation for their athletic endeavors. NCAA, Estimated Probability of Competing in Athletics Beyond the High School Interscholastic

In sum, even apart from consideration of transformative elements, examination of the right of publicity in question also resolves the balance in favor of the First Amendment. The quantity of players involved dilutes the commercial impact of any particular player and the scope of the publicity right is significantly reduced by the fact that: (1) a player cannot own the individual, publicly available statistics on which the game is based; (2) the players are not identified in the game; and (3) NCAA college athletes do not have the right to license their names and likenesses, even if they chose to do so.

II

Given the proper application of the transformative use test, Keller is unlikely to prevail. The balance of interests falls squarely on the side of the First Amendment. The stakes are not small. The logical consequence of the majority view is that all realistic depictions of actual persons, no matter how incidental, are protected by a state law right of publicity regardless of the creative context. This logic jeopardizes the creative use of historic figures in motion pictures, books, and sound recordings. Absent the use of actual footage, the motion picture *Forrest Gump* might as well be just a box of chocolates. Without its historical characters, *Midnight in Paris* would be reduced to a pedestrian domestic squabble. The majority's holding that creative use of realistic images and personas does not satisfy the transformative use test cannot be reconciled with the many cases affording such works First Amendment protection. I respectfully disagree with this potentially dangerous and out-of-context interpretation of the transformative use test.

For these reasons, I respectfully dissent.

For a similar holding and dissenting opinion in a parallel suit arising under New Jersey law, see Hart v. Electronic Arts, Inc., 717 F.3d 141 (3d Cir. 2013). One context in which the "transformative use" test has been inconsistently deployed is in the collection and promotion of amateur nude video footage. In Lane v. M.R.A. Holdings, LLC, 242 F. Supp. 2d 1205 (M.D. Fla. 2002), a 17-year-old girl who had exposed her breasts to a stranger with a camera sued for misappropriation when the video footage was included in a commercially marketed "Girls Gone Wild" video. The court rejected her claim, arguing that "it is irrefutable that the *Girls Gone Wild* video is an expressive work created solely for entertainment purposes." Id. at 1213. In Bosely v. Wildwett.com, 310 F. Supp. 2d 914 (N.D. Ohio 2004), on the other hand, the court took a less charitable view of the artistic merits of amateur nude video collections. Plaintiff, a regionally prominent television news anchor, sued to restrain the commercial use of videotaped images of her participation in a wet t-shirt contest at a Florida nightclub. The court granted a preliminary injunction, reasoning that the defendant's product contained images that "are mere copies of [plaintiff's] performance and are not protected material." Id. at 928. See also Bullard v. MRA Holding,

---

Level (2011), available at http://www.ncaa. org/wps/wcm/connect/public/ncaa/pdfs/2011/2011+probability+of+going+pro.

And participation in college football can come at a terrible cost. The NCAA reports that, during a recent five-year period, college football players suffered 41,000 injuries, including 23 non-fatal catastrophic injuries and 11 fatalities from indirect catastrophic injuries. NCAA, Football Injuries: Data From the 2004/05 to 2008/09 Seasons, available at http://www.ncaa. org/wps/wcm/connect/public/ncaa/health+and+safety/sports+injuries/resources/football+ injuries.

LLC, 890 F. Supp. 2d 1323 (N.D. Ga. 2012) (certifying question to Georgia Supreme Court whether defendants' use of plaintiff's semi-nude image, captured after plaintiff exposed herself while on spring break at the age of fourteen, on cover of video box and in nationwide television advertisements, constituted misappropriation of likeness for commercial use under Georgia law).

While the law may protect the plaintiff against appropriation of small segments of the plaintiff's identity, there may be less protection if what is appropriated is the plaintiff's whole life. In Spahn v. Julien Messner, Inc., 221 N.E.2d 543 (N.Y. 1966), the plaintiff, a very successful major league pitcher, sued the defendant for the latter's unauthorized biography of the plaintiff. The court held that truth is a complete defense in cases involving reports about newsworthy events and people. But, the court ruled, if the biography is "fictionalized," the plaintiff may be able to recover. This latter aspect of appropriation law of *Spahn* was found constitutionally wanting in Time, Inc. v. Hill, 385 U.S. 374 (1967). The plaintiffs were a family that had been held hostage in their homes for several hours by three escaped prisoners. An article in *Life*, a magazine published by the defendant, was based on that incident, and on a later novel and play called *The Desperate Hours*, depicting a similar incident, although there were many factual differences between the actual events and the later novel and play. The plaintiffs' claim alleged that the magazine article intended to, and did, create the impression that the novel and play accurately portrayed what happened to the plaintiffs. A judgment for the plaintiffs was affirmed by the Court of Appeals of New York, but was reversed by the Supreme Court, which ruled that to recover based on the falsity of the article, the plaintiffs had to establish *New York Times* malice — that is, that the defendant either knew that the article was false, or acted in reckless disregard of its truth or falsity.[2]

2. There is some confusion as to whether *Hill* is an appropriation or false light case. The plaintiff's cause of action was based on a New York statute providing for a recovery by "[a]ny person whose name, portrait or picture is used within this state for advertising purposes or for the purposes of trade without the written consent" of that person. But the Supreme Court in a later case characterized the action as one involving false light. If *Hill* really is a false light case, however, it adds nothing to the law, at least as that law is set out in the Restatement (Second); proof that the defendant knew or acted in reckless disregard of the falsity is a part of the plaintiff's case under §652E. As a historical aside, the attorney for the plaintiffs in the Supreme Court was Richard M. Nixon.

Chapter 14

Commercial Torts: Misrepresentation and Interference with Business Relations

A. Misrepresentation

This section considers the tort liability of one who misleads and thereby harms another by means of false representations in the course of business dealings. We are all familiar with the classic example of the con artist defrauding an unsuspecting victim, and it is hardly surprising that the law should provide a remedy in those relatively rare instances in which the con artist is brought into court. The vast majority of misrepresentation cases, however, are not so clear. Considerable leeway exists within which persons in a bargaining relationship may deal sharply with one another and may take advantage of each other's ignorance or lack of experience. One of the tasks in the cases that follow will be to trace the fine line that separates hard, effective bargaining from actionable misrepresentation. This task is made more difficult by the unreliability of morality as a guide. As we shall see, courts sometimes impose liability even when the misrepresentation was totally innocent, and they sometimes deny recovery even when it can be shown that the defendant willfully misled the plaintiff.

The following formulation appears in Pace v. Parrish, 247 P.2d 273, 274-75 (Utah 1952), and will suffice as a starting point for analysis of this subject:

> This being an action in deceit based on fraudulent misrepresentations, the burden was upon plaintiffs to prove all of the essential elements thereof. These are: (1) That a representation was made; (2) concerning a presently existing material fact; (3) which was false; (4) which the representor either (a) knew to be false, or (b) made recklessly, knowing that he had insufficient knowledge upon which to base such representation; (5) for the purpose of inducing the other party to act upon it; (6) that the other party, acting reasonably and in ignorance of its falsity; (7) did in fact rely upon it; (8) and was thereby induced to act; (9) to his injury and damage.

The rules that govern liability for fraudulent misrepresentation are set forth in §§525-549 of the Restatement (Second) of Torts and generally reflect the elements set forth above. (The Restatement divides its coverage of misrepresentation into two chapters: Chapter 22, which includes the above-mentioned sections and covers business transactions, and Chapter 23, which covers nonbusiness transactions.) The Restatement also contains rules establishing liability for concealment and nondisclosure (§§550 and 551), negligent misrepresentation (§§552, 552A, and 552B), and innocent misrepresentation (§552C). The American Law Institute has begun to revise its earlier treatments of the subject of misrepresentation as part of its Restatement (Third) of Torts: Liability for Economic Harm project.

Before addressing the substantive elements of the tort, it is useful to consider briefly the subject of damages as it relates to recovery for misrepresentation. The first and most basic principle is that the plaintiff must have suffered actual harm in order to recover on a theory of misrepresentation. See, e.g., Casey v. Welch, 50 So. 2d 124 (Fla. 1951); Dilworth v. Lauritzen, 424 P.2d 136 (Utah 1967). See generally Glenn A. McCleary, Damage as Requisite to Rescission for Misrepresentation, 36 Mich. L. Rev. 1, 227 (1937). As for the measure of the plaintiff's recovery in a misrepresentation case, there are two basic rules: the "out-of-pocket" rule, and the "benefit-of-the-bargain" rule. The former sounds classically in tort, and measures the recovery by the difference in value between what the plaintiff gave up in the business transaction and what was received. The latter, which rings of contract, measures the recovery by the difference in value between what the plaintiff actually received and what would have been received had the defendant's representations been true. The out-of-pocket rule looks backward, and seeks to restore the plaintiff to the position held before the transaction; the benefit-of-the-bargain rule looks forward, and seeks to place the plaintiff in the same position that would have been held after the transaction had the defendant's representations not been false. The Restatement does not provide for recovery for emotional harm damages in misrepresentation actions, even when the misrepresentation is intentional. Most courts follow the Restatement in this regard, and disallow such damages. See, e.g., Brogan v. Mitchell, 692 N.E.2d 276 (Ill. 1998). Some courts have allowed damages for emotional harm in fraud cases. See, e.g., Kilduff v. Adams, Inc., 593 A.2d 478 (Conn. 1991); Hoffman v. Stamper, 867 A.2d 276 (Md. 2005). In general, see Andrew L. Merritt, Damages for Emotional Distress in Fraud Litigation: Dignitary Torts in a Commercial Society, 42 Vand. L. Rev. 1 (1989); Annotation, 11 A.L.R.5th 88 (1993).

The basic difference between the out-of-pocket and benefit-of-the-bargain measures of recovery may best be understood by means of a concrete example. Suppose that *A* sells a house to *B* and fraudulently misrepresents the condition of the property. Assume that the actual value of the house is $20,000; that the sale price is $30,000; and that the value of the house if the representations had been true would be $35,000. Under the out-of-pocket rule, if successful in a misrepresentation action, *B* would receive $10,000—the difference between what was paid and what was actually received. Under the benefit-of-the-bargain approach, *B* would recover $15,000—the difference between what was actually received and what would have been received had *A*'s representations been true. The former measure of recovery is similar to rescission in equity, a remedy traditionally available as an adjunct to a contract action. However, rescission involves the returning by the plaintiff of the property to the defendant and the refunding by the defendant of the total purchase price. The out-of-pocket rule in misrepresentation cases does not involve giving up the property (which the plaintiff may wish to retain), but instead involves the payment by the defendant of an amount of money which, together with the plaintiff's retention of the property, will make the plaintiff whole.

To some extent, the applicable damages rule will depend upon the type of case presented. Given the decidedly contract flavor of the benefit-of-the-bargain rule, it is not surprising that in most instances plaintiffs in misrepresentation actions will be limited to damages measured by the out-of-pocket rule. (There are cases, of course, in which the out-of-pocket rule will actually give the plaintiff a higher recovery—do you see how?) However, the provisions of the Restatement (Second) of Torts provide a fairly flexible approach. Section 549 of the Restatement (Second) of Torts extends the benefit-of-the-bargain rule to all cases of fraudulent misrepresentation, providing the plaintiff can prove damages "with reasonable certainty." Sections 552 and 552B, imposing liability upon a defendant who negligently supplies false information in the course of defendant's business, profession, or employment, or in a transaction in which the defendant has a pecuniary interest, speak in terms of compensating the plaintiff for both out-of-pocket and consequential pecuniary losses. And §552C, permitting recovery in some cases involving innocent misrepresentation, limits the measure of damages to out-of-pocket losses. For further discussion of the out-of-pocket rule versus the benefit-of-the-bargain rule for cases involving fraudulent misrepresentation, see Jill Wieber Lens, Honest Confusion: The Purpose of Compensatory Damages in Tort and Fraudulent Misrepresentation, 59 U. Kan. L. Rev. 231 (2011).

In addition, the overlap of the tort and contract theories that is apparent in misrepresentation cases raises the question of whether courts trying such cases should allow punitive damages. Traditionally, contract law does not impose punitive damages and thus such damages would be unavailable for a misrepresentation claim brought in contract. However, such damages are potentially available in tort. See, e.g., Schipporeit v. Khan, 775 N.W.2d 503 (S.D. 2009) (discussing the "independent tort doctrine"). Some have argued that traditional contract damages tend to leave plaintiffs undercompensated and defendants underdeterred because the breach of contract may not be discovered and sued upon. Allowing misrepresentation as an independent tort, with the possibility of punitive damages, works to offset these effects, particularly in egregious contract cases, such as when a breaching party attempts to misrepresent or conceal the breach. See Catherine Paskoff Chang, Note, Two Wrongs Can Make Two Rights: Why Courts Should Allow Tortious Recovery for Intentional Concealment of Contract Breach, 39 Colum. J.L. & Soc. Probs. 47 (2005). On the other hand, some scholars and judges have resisted the expansion of tort liability and the possibility of punitive damages. In All-Tech Telecom, Inc. v. Amway Corp., 174 F.3d 862, 865 (7th Cir. 1999), for example, Judge Posner argues that plaintiffs should not be permitted to escalate their contract disputes to charges of tortious misrepresentation when they could have protected themselves adequately and more efficiently by insisting that important oral representations be embodied in written contracts. Posner argues that there is no need to provide tort remedies for misrepresentation, as contract law adequately addresses the issue and tort remedies interfere with how contract law has balanced the policy issues relating to cases of misrepresentation. As you work through the cases in this section, you should be alert to the importance of the damages issue, and you should consider whether the plaintiffs might have sought alternative remedies to those apparently considered by the courts.

1. The Nature of the Defendant's Representation

Adams v. Gillig

199 N.Y. 314, 92 N.E. 670 (1910)

On and prior to June 2, 1908, the plaintiff was the owner in fee simple of a lot of land one hundred feet front and about one hundred and sixty feet in depth, situated on the east side of Elmwood avenue in the city of Buffalo, and also of two other lots of land fronting on Highland avenue in said city, and which run back to and adjoin the first-mentioned lot. The lots fronting on Highland avenue had houses on them, and the lot fronting on Elmwood avenue was vacant. The immediate neighborhood of said lots, so far as the same have been built upon, is devoted exclusively to residences.

The defendant sought to purchase a portion of the plaintiff's lot fronting on Elmwood avenue and stated that he desired to purchase the same for residence purposes. The negotiations were carried on with the plaintiff's agents, and the defendant stated to the representative of the plaintiff's agents and also to the agents themselves that he intended to build dwellings upon the lot if purchased. The plaintiff's agents communicated to her the statement of the defendant and his offers, and she asked her agents if they were sure the sale would not affect the value of the remaining vacant lot, and she was told by her agents that the defendant would build either single or double houses upon the lot so to be purchased.

The representations of the defendant that he intended to build dwellings on the lot to be purchased by him were false and fraudulent and made with the intent to deceive the plaintiff. The plaintiff relied upon the representations of the defendant that he intended to build dwellings upon the lot when purchased, and believing such statements to be true, executed and delivered to him a deed of sixty-five feet front and one hundred and sixty feet in depth in consideration of $5,525.

During all the time that the defendant was negotiating for the purchase of the lot in question he intended to build a public automobile garage thereon, which fact was unknown to the plaintiff and which the defendant fraudulently concealed from her. . . .

The plaintiff was deceived by said misrepresentations of the defendant and the construction of the proposed garage will greatly damage the remaining property belonging to the plaintiff. It will decrease the value of the remaining vacant lot on Elmwood avenue about one-half, and the value of her lots, with houses fronting on Highland avenue, about one-fourth. The referee found in favor of the plaintiff and directed a reconveyance of the property. From the judgment entered upon the report of the referee an appeal was taken to the Appellate Division of the Supreme Court where it was affirmed by a divided court.

CHASE, J. Any contract induced by fraud as to a matter material to the party defrauded is voidable. There are many rules as to what constitutes an inducement by fraud, and also affecting the general statement that any contract will be set aside for fraud, that have been established as necessary to protect the rights of all the parties to a contract, which need not be stated in this discussion, except so far as they affect the particular transaction under consideration.

It may be assumed that promises of future action that are a part of the contract between the parties, to be binding upon them, must be stated in the contract. An oral restrictive covenant, or any oral promise to do or refrain from doing something affecting the property about which a written contract is made and executed between the parties, will not be enforced, not because the parties should not fulfill their promises and their legal and moral obligations, but because the covenants and agreements being promissory and contractual in their nature and a part of, or collateral to a principal contract, the entire agreement between the parties must be deemed to have been merged in the writing. The value of a writing would be very seriously impaired if the rule mentioned in regard to including the entire agreement in such writing is not enforced.

A strict enforcement of such rule tends to greater security and safety in business transactions and leaves less opportunity for dishonesty and false swearing, induced, perhaps, by a change of purpose or a failure to obtain the result that was anticipated when the transaction was originally consummated and reduced to writing. Such rule makes it necessary for the parties to a written contract to include everything therein pertaining to the subject-matter of the principal contract, and if by mistake or otherwise an oral agreement, a part of the transaction, is omitted from the writing, it can only be made effective and enforceable by a reformation of the writing, so that the same shall include therein the entire agreement between the parties. . . .

It is not claimed on this appeal that the defendant made promises which became a part of the contract, or that the deed could be reformed by including therein restrictive covenants. The rule in regard to including the entire agreement between the parties in the writing does not take away or detract from the general rule by which a contract can always be set aside for fraud affecting the transaction as to a material fact that is not promissory in its nature. Any statement of an existing fact material to the person to whom it is made that is false and known by the person making it to be false and which is made to induce the execution of a contract, and which does induce the contract, constitutes a fraud that will sustain an action to avoid the contract if the person making it is injured thereby.

We have in this case findings by the trial court sustained by the record, which show that the defendant purposely, intentionally and falsely stated to the plaintiff that he desired to purchase a portion of her vacant lot for the purpose of building a dwelling or dwellings thereon. He must have known that if he thereby induced her to convey to him such portion of the lot and his intention to build a garage thereon was carried out it would injure her to an extent in excess of the full consideration to be paid by him to her for such lot.

The plaintiff relied upon the defendant's honesty and good faith in the purchase, and was apparently willing to take her chances of a subsequent change in his intention, or of his selling the lot to another whose intentions and purposes might be entirely different.

The simple question in this case is, therefore, whether the alleged intention of the defendant to build a dwelling or dwellings upon the lot which he sought to purchase is such a statement of an existing material fact as authorizes the court to cancel the deed because of the fraud.

. . . The intent of a person is sometimes difficult to prove, but it is nevertheless a fact and a material and existing fact that must be ascertained in many cases, and when ascertained determines the rights of the parties to controversies. The intent of Gillig was a material existing fact in this case, and the plaintiff's reliance upon such fact induced her to enter into a contract that she would not otherwise have entered into. The effect of such false statement by the defendant of his intention cannot be cast aside as immaterial simply because it was possible for him in good faith to have changed his mind or to have sold the property to another who might have a different purpose relating thereto. As the defendant's intention was subject to change in good faith at any time it was of uncertain value. It was, however, of some value. It was of sufficient value so that the plaintiff was willing to stand upon it and make the conveyance in reliance upon it.

The use of property in a particular manner changes from time to time and restrictive covenants of great value at one time may become a source of serious embarrassment at a later date. The fact that restrictive covenants cannot ordinarily be drawn to bend to changed conditions has made many purchasers disinclined to accept conveyances with such covenants. A restrictive covenant in a deed may be of sufficient importance to justify a refusal by a contractee to accept a conveyance subject to such conditions. A person in selling property may be quite willing to execute and deliver a deed thereof without putting restrictive covenants therein and in reliance upon the good faith of express, unqualified assurances of the present intention of the prospective purchaser. In such case the intention is material and the statement of such intention is the statement of an existing fact.

Unless the court affirms this judgment, it must acknowledge that although a defendant deliberately and intentionally, by false statements, obtained from a plaintiff his property to his great damage it is wholly incapable of righting the wrong, notwithstanding the fact that by so doing it does in no way interfere with the rules that have grown up after years of experience to protect written contracts from collateral promises and conditions not inserted in the contract.

We are of the opinion that the false statements made by the defendant of his intention should, under the circumstances of this case, be deemed to be a statement of a material, existing fact of which the court will lay hold for the purpose of defeating the wrong that would otherwise be consummated thereby. . . .

We do not concede the accuracy of the statement made before us on behalf of the defendant to the effect that false statements similar to the one made by the defendant to induce the execution of the deed by the plaintiff are common in business transactions, but if true, and controversies arise over the retention of the fruits of such frauds, and the fraudulent inducement is conceded or proven beyond reasonable controversy, the transactions will not have the approval and sanction of the courts.

The judgment should be affirmed, with costs.

Cullen, C.J., Gray, Vann, Werner, Willard, Bartlett and Hiscock, JJ., concur.

Judgment affirmed.

Vulcan Metals Co. v. Simmons Manufacturing Co.

248 F. 853 (C.C.A.N.Y. 1918)

[This is an appeal from two cases which were tried together in the district court. The first case was a deceit action brought by Vulcan Metals Co. (Vulcan) against Simmons Manufacturing Co. (Simmons) based upon misrepresentations allegedly made by Simmons to Vulcan in the course of the sale by Simmons to Vulcan of tools, dies and equipment, including patents, for the manufacture of vacuum cleaners. The second case was an action by Simmons against Vulcan on three notes given by Vulcan as part of the purchase price. In the second case, Vulcan raised the misrepresentations by way of defense and counterclaim. The evidence introduced during the trial in the district court is described as follows in the syllabus to the court's opinion:

"[The misrepresentations upon which Vulcan relies] were of two classes — those touching the efficiency of the vacuum cleaner; and, second, that no attempt had been made to market the machines by the Simmons Manufacturing Company.

"The first of these classes is substantially the same as those contained in a booklet issued by the Simmons Manufacturing Company for the general sale of the vacuum cleaners. . . . The booklet is in general the ordinary compilation, puffing the excellence and powers of the vacuum cleaner, and asserting its superiority over all others of a similar sort. . . .

"The second class of misrepresentations was that the Simmons Manufacturing Company had not sold the machine, or made any attempt to sell it; that they had not shown it to any one; that it had never been on the market, and that no one outside of the company officials and the men in the factory knew anything about it. . . .

"There was evidence that the machines, when exploited by the Vulcan Metals Company, Incorporated, proved to be ineffective and of little or no value, and that their manufacture was discontinued by that company not very long after they had undertaken it. There was also evidence that several of the Western agents of the Simmons Manufacturing Company had had the machines in stock and had attempted to market some of them; that they had been unsuccessful in these efforts, owing for the most part to the fact that the water pressures, where they had been sold, had not been sufficient to establish the necessary vacuum. . . ."

The district court directed a verdict in favor of Simmons in both actions, and from judgments entered thereon Vulcan appealed.]

L. HAND, J. (after stating the facts as above). The first question is of the misrepresentations touching the quality and powers of the patented machine. These were general commendations, or, in so far as they included any specific facts, were not disproved; e.g., that the cleaner would produce 18 inches of vacuum with 25 pounds water pressure. They raise, therefore, the question of law how far general "puffing" or "dealers' talk" can be the basis of an action for deceit.

The conceded exception in such cases has generally rested upon the distinction between "opinion" and "fact"; but that distinction has not escaped the criticism it deserves. An opinion is a fact, and it may be a very relevant fact; the expression of an opinion is the assertion of a belief, and any rule which condones the expression of a consciously false opinion condones a consciously false statement of fact. When the parties are so situated that the buyer may reasonably rely upon the expression of the seller's opinion, it is no excuse to give a false one. And so it makes much difference whether the parties stand "on an equality." For example, we should treat very differently the expressed opinion of a chemist to a layman about the properties of a composition from the same opinion between chemist and chemist, when the buyer had full opportunity to examine. The reason of the rule lies, we think, in this: There are some kinds of talk which no sensible man takes seriously, and if he does he suffers from his credulity. If we were all scrupulously honest, it would not be so; but, as it is, neither party usually believes what the seller says about his own opinions, and each knows it. Such statements, like the claims of campaign managers before election, are rather designed to allay the suspicion which would attend their absence than to be understood as having any relation to objective truth. It is quite true that they induce a compliant temper in the buyer, but it is by a much more subtle process than through the acceptance of his claims for his wares.

In the case at bar, since the buyer was allowed full opportunity to examine the cleaner and to test it out, we put the parties upon an equality. It seems to us that general statements as to what the cleaner would do, even though consciously false, were not of a kind to be taken literally by the buyer. As between manufacturer and customer, it may not be so; but this was the case of taking over a business, after ample chance to investigate. Such a buyer, who the seller rightly expects will undertake an independent and adequate inquiry into the actual merits of what he gets, has no right to treat as material in his determination statements like these. . . .

As respects the representation that the cleaners had never been put upon the market or offered for sale, the rule does not apply; nor can we agree that such representations could not have been material to Freeman's decision to accept the contract. The actual test of experience in their sale might well be of critical consequence in his decision to buy the business, and the jury would certainly have the right to accept his statement that his reliance upon these representations was determinative of his final decision. We believe that the facts as disclosed by the depositions of the Western witnesses were sufficient to carry to the jury the question whether those statements were false. It is quite true, as the District Judge said, that the number of sales was small, perhaps not 60 in all; but they were scattered in various parts of the Mountain and Pacific States, and the jury might conclude that they were enough to contradict the detailed statements of Simmons that the machines had been kept off the market altogether. . . .

The next question is as to whether any such misrepresentations were conclusively cured by the recital in the contract of purchase as follows: "The party of the first part [the

Simmons Company] has been engaged in the manufacture of a certain type of vacuum cleaning machines, and the parties of the first and second part [the National Suction Cleaner Company] have been engaged in the sale thereof."

We all agree that an adequate retraction of the false statement before Freeman executed the contract would be a defense. Whether this be regarded as terminating the consequences of the original wrong, or as a correction of it, is of little importance. Further, we agree that, even if Freeman had in fact never learned of the retraction, it would serve, if given under such circumstances as justified the utterer in supposing that he would. For example, a letter actually delivered into his hands containing nothing but a retraction would be a defense, though it abundantly appeared that he had never read it. His loss might still be the consequence, and the reasonable consequence, but for the letter, of the original fraud; but the writer would have gone as far as necessary to correct that fraud, and we should not be disposed to hold it as an insurer that its correction should be effective. . . . I . . . do not think that [the recital in this contract] was certain to catch the eye of the reader, and that therefore neither was the defendant's duty of retraction inevitably discharged, nor, what is nearly the same thing, did the defendant show beyond question that Freeman actually saw it. As a retraction the recital was a defense, and the defendant had the burden of proof. As notice to Freeman actually conveyed, it may have been only evidence upon the causal sequence between the wrong and the injury; but we attach no great significance to that distinction. The fact that he signed the contract appears to us to be some evidence upon which the jury might say that he could not have seen the recital. That depends upon how much importance they think he attached to the original representation, and that depends in turn upon what they thought of his story. If they did believe that the representation was of critical consequence in his decision, they might infer that he did not see it, or he would not have gone on without some explanation. The very silence of the testimony upon the question might be taken to infer that he had not noticed it, even at the trial, just as it might also be taken to indicate that he had fabricated the whole story, and hoped the recital would escape the notice of the defendant. In any event, the interpretation of the whole transaction appears to us not to be so clear that reasonable people might not come to opposite conclusions upon it, and that involves a submission to the jury. It is perhaps of some importance that no allusion to the recital appears in the record.

It results from the foregoing that the judgment in the action for deceit must be reversed. In the action upon the notes the judgment upon the notes will be affirmed, because the Vulcan Metals Company, Incorporated, did not make any offer to return the machines, tools, and patents, which were not shown to be without any value, and consequently it was in no position to rescind. The judgment in that action dismissing the counterclaim must, however, be reversed, since the counterclaim involved the same facts as the complaint in the action for deceit. . . .

Judgment in the action of deceit reversed, and new trial ordered. Judgment in the action on the notes affirmed so far as it gives judgment on the notes, and reversed so far as it dismisses the counterclaim, and new trial upon the counterclaim ordered.

[Upon rehearing, the court dismissed Vulcan's counterclaim on the notes.]

Swinton v. Whitinsville Savings Bank

311 Mass. 677, 42 N.E.2d 808 (1942)

[A demurrer to the declaration was sustained by the trial court. The plaintiff appealed.]

QUA, J. The declaration alleges that on or about September 12, 1938, the defendant sold the plaintiff a house in Newton to be occupied by the plaintiff and his family as a dwelling; that at the time of the sale the house "was infested with termites, an insect that is most dangerous and destructive to buildings"; that the defendant knew the house was so infested; that the plaintiff could not readily observe this condition upon inspection; that, "knowing the internal destruction that these insects were creating in said house," the defendant falsely and fraudulently concealed from the plaintiff its true condition; that the plaintiff at the time of his purchase had no knowledge of the termites, exercised due care thereafter, and learned of them about August 30, 1940; and that, because of the destruction that was being done and the dangerous condition that was being created by the termites, the plaintiff was put to great expense for repairs and for the installation of termite control in order to prevent the loss and destruction of said house.

There is no allegation of any false statement or representation, or of the uttering of a half truth which may be tantamount to a falsehood. There is no intimation that the defendant by any means prevented the plaintiff from acquiring information as to the condition of the house. There is nothing to show any fiduciary relation between the parties, or that the plaintiff stood in a position of confidence toward or dependence upon the defendant. So far as appears the parties made a business deal at arm's length. The charge is concealment and nothing more; and it is concealment in the simple sense of mere failure to reveal, with nothing to show any peculiar duty to speak. The characterization of the concealment as false and fraudulent of course adds nothing in the absence of further allegations of fact.

If this defendant is liable on this declaration every seller is liable who fails to disclose any nonapparent defect known to him in the subject of the sale which materially reduces its value and which the buyer fails to discover. Similarly it would seem that every buyer would be liable who fails to disclose any nonapparent virtue known to him in the subject of the purchase which materially enhances its value and of which the seller is ignorant. The law has not yet, we believe, reached the point of imposing upon the frailties of human nature a standard so idealistic as this. That the particular case here stated by the plaintiff possesses a certain appeal to the moral sense is scarcely to be denied. Probably the reason is to be found in the facts that the infestation of buildings by termites has not been common in Massachusetts and constitutes a concealed risk against which buyers are off their guard. But the law cannot provide special rules for termites and can hardly attempt to determine liability according to the varying probabilities of the existence and discovery of different possible defects in the subjects of trade. The rule of nonliability for bare nondisclosure has been stated and followed by this court. . . . It is adopted in the American Law Institute's Restatement of Torts, §551. See Williston on Contracts (Rev. ed.) §§1497, 1498, 1499.

The order sustaining the demurrer is affirmed, and judgment is to be entered for the defendant.

So ordered.

The court in Obde v. Schlemeyer, 353 P.2d 672 (Wash. 1960), held that a selling home owner does have an affirmative duty to disclose the presence of termites to the buyer. Such a duty of disclosure, the court said, exists whenever "justice, equity, and fair dealing" require it.

While the rule of nonliability laid out in *Swinton* is still good law, see e.g., Ingaharro v. Blanchette, 440 A.2d 445 (N.H. 1982) (holding that no duty exists to disclose the inadequacy of the water supply in a residential property sale), the trend has been to extend the duty to disclose. The duty is not limited in its application to termites, but is often extended to include many things such as disclosure of structural defects, past murders on the property, the proximity of toxic waste dumps, even ghosts and poltergeists that supposedly haunt the property. Reed v. King, 193 Cal. Rptr. 130 (Ct. App. 1983) (murders on property); Stambovsky v. Ackley, 572 N.Y.S.2d 672 (App. Div. 1991) (hauntings). See also Andrea M. Guttridge, Redefining Residential Real Estate Disclosure: Why Energy Consumption Should Be Disclosed Prior to the Sale of Residential Real Property, 37 Rutgers L. Rec. 164 (2010) (arguing that a home's high energy consumption constitutes a material defect that should require disclosure).

The cases in this subsection presume an intent on the defendant's part to deceive the plaintiff and present the question of what sort of conduct by the defendant will amount to a misrepresentation of fact sufficient to form the basis for tort liability. Although these cases do not raise the point, it should be fairly obvious that the defendant need not actually use words or employ language in order to misrepresent material facts. Thus, in Salzman v. Maldaver, 24 N.W.2d 161 (Mich. 1946), the court refused to dismiss a complaint that alleged that the defendant, who sold a number of stacks of damaged aluminum metal sheets to the plaintiff, had deliberately misled the plaintiff by placing an undamaged sheet on the top of each stack of damaged sheets, under circumstances where it was impractical for the plaintiff to move the stacks in order to check their condition for himself. Similarly, in Jones v. West Side Buick Auto Co., 93 S.W.2d 1083 (Mo. Ct. App. 1936), the turning back of the odometer of a used car by the defendant-seller was held sufficient to constitute a misrepresentation of the number of miles the car had previously been driven. (In 1972, Congress enacted the Motor Vehicle Information and Cost Savings Act, 15 U.S.C. §1901 et seq., rendering it illegal to change the odometer with the intent to alter the number of miles shown. Violations are punishable by substantial fines. The court of appeals in Edgar v. Fred Jones Lincoln-Mercury of Oklahoma City, Inc., 524 F.2d 162 (10th Cir. 1975), held that the federal act did not preempt the common law of the states imposing liability for fraudulent misrepresentation.)

The classic formulation of the rule that a misstatement of present intention may be sufficient to constitute an actionable misrepresentation of fact is that of Lord Bowen in Edgington v. Fitzmaurice, L.R. 29 Ch. Div. 459, 483 (1882): "[T]he state of a man's mind is as much a fact as the state of his digestion."

As the *Swinton, Obde*, and *Ingaharro* cases, above, suggest, the subject of fraudulent nondisclosure has received a considerable amount of judicial attention. Other cases that have held that nondisclosures are not actionable include Harshman II Dev. Co., L.L.C. v. Meijer Stores Ltd. P'ship, 938 N.E.2d 53 (Ohio Ct. App. 2010) (seller of commercial real estate parcel failed to disclose to buyer that the property contained jurisdictional wetlands); Stevenson v. Baum, 75 Cal. Rptr. 2d 904 (Ct. App. 1998) (vendor of a mobile home park failed to disclose to the buyer the existence of an oil company's pipeline easement); and Cooper & Co., Inc. v. Bryant, 440 So. 2d 1016 (Ala. 1983) (real estate broker hired by seller did not disclose to buyer crack in foundation of house). Section 551 of the first Restatement of Torts, to which the court in *Swinton* makes reference, has been revised. The original §551 had placed a duty upon actors to disclose in three basic situations: where a fiduciary or other similar relation of trust and confidence exists between the parties; where subsequently acquired information is recognized by the actor to make untrue or misleading a previous representation; and where the actor subsequently ascertains that a misrepresentation not originally made for the purpose of being acted upon is about to be acted upon by the other party to the business transaction. The second of these situations is illustrated in a decision by the Supreme Court of Ohio that suggests the relative liberality with which courts today are likely to impose duties to disclose. In Miles v. McSwegin, 388 N.E.2d 1367 (Ohio 1979), a judgment for the plaintiffs was affirmed when the defendant real estate broker, who had described the property purchased by the plaintiffs as "a good sound house," subsequently learned that the house was infested with termites. See also Bursey v. Clement, 387 A.2d 346 (N.H. 1978).

Section 551 of the Restatement (Second) describes two additional circumstances under which a duty to disclose will arise: where, with respect to "facts basic to the transaction," the actor knows or believes that disclosure of additional matters is necessary to prevent a partial statement of the facts from being misleading; and where the actor knows that the other party is about to enter into the transaction under a mistake as to such facts and that the other party, "because of the relationship between them, the customs of the trade or other objective circumstances, would reasonably expect a disclosure of those facts." Accord Restatement (Third) of Torts Liability for Economic Harms §13 (Am. Law Inst., Tentative Draft No. 1, 2012). These additional provisions greatly enlarge the circumstances under which a duty to disclose will be imposed. It remains to be seen whether it makes sense any longer to speak, as the court in *Swinton* spoke, of "the rule of nonliability for bare nondisclosure." A number of cases indicate a judicial willingness to expand nondisclosure liability, particularly in the context of real estate transactions. In Reed v. King, 193 Cal. Rptr. 130 (Ct. App. 1983), the court ruled that a claim by a buyer against the seller of a house and his real estate broker was improperly dismissed; the complaint alleged that the defendants had not disclosed that the house was the site of a multiple murder, which substantially lowered the market value of the house. In Easton v. Strassburger, 199 Cal. Rptr. 383 (Ct. App. 1984), the court ruled that the seller's real estate broker was liable not only for failing to disclose to the buyer defects in the land of which he actually knew—here the susceptibility to earth slides of the land on which the house was built—but also for failing to act reasonably to discover such defects.

A recent effort to hold the line on the expansion of disclosure obligations occurred in Milliken v. Jacono, 60 A.3d 133 (Pa. Super. Ct. 2012), in which the court decided that the seller's failure to disclose that the house was the site of a murder/suicide did not constitute negligent misrepresentation. The court argued that the holding in *Reed*, supra, creates a slippery slope, requiring sellers not only to disclose objective defects but also subjective defects.

2. Scienter, Negligence, and Strict Liability

Derry v. Peek

14 App. Cas. 337 (House of Lords, 1889)

[This action was brought by Sir Henry William Peek against the chairman of the Plymouth, Devonport and District Tramways Company, William Derry, and four company directors for having fraudulently misrepresented to him that the company was authorized in moving its carriages to use steam power instead of horses, thereby inducing him to purchase shares in the company. By a special act of Parliament (45 & 46 Vict. c. clix), the company had been authorized to build certain tramways.]

By sect. 35 the carriages used on the tramways might be moved by animal power and, with the consent of the Board of Trade, by steam or any mechanical power for fixed periods and subject to the regulations of the Board.

By sect. 34 of the Tramways Act 1870 (33 & 34 Vict. c. 78), which section was incorporated in the special Act, "all carriages used on any tramway shall be moved by the power prescribed by the special Act, and where no such power is prescribed, by animal power only."

In February 1883 the appellants as directors of the company issued a prospectus containing the following paragraph: —

"One great feature of this undertaking, to which considerable importance should be attached, is, that by the special Act of Parliament obtained, the company has the right to use steam or mechanical motive power, instead of horses, and it is fully expected that by means of this a considerable saving will result in the working expenses of the line as compared with other tramways worked by horses."

Soon after the issue of the prospectus the respondent, relying, as he alleged, upon the representations in this paragraph and believing that the company had an absolute right to use steam and other mechanical power, applied for and obtained shares in the company.

The company proceeded to make tramways, but the Board of Trade refused to consent to the use of steam or mechanical power except on certain portions of the tramways.

[As a result of the decision of the Board of Trade,] the company was wound up, and the [plaintiff] in 1885 brought an action of deceit against the [defendants] claiming damages for the fraudulent misrepresentations of the defendants whereby the plaintiff was induced to take shares in the company.

[At the trial, the plaintiff and defendants testified that they were aware that the consent of the Board of Trade was necessary for the company to use steam power, but that they either assumed that consent had been given or would be given in due course.

The trial judge dismissed the plaintiff's action, concluding that the defendants believed that the company had the authority described in the prospectus, that their belief in this regard was not unreasonable, and that their conduct was not so reckless or careless that they should be held liable in deceit. The decision of the trial judge was reversed by the Court of Appeal (COTTON L.J., SIR J. HANNEN, and LOPES L.J.), who held that although the defendants honestly believed their statement to the plaintiff was true they made it without any reasonable ground for believing it to be true, and therefore should be liable to make good to the plaintiff the loss suffered by him in purchasing the shares. The defendants appealed from the decision of the Court of Appeal to the House of Lords, where the decision of the intermediate court was unanimously set aside and the decision of the trial judge restored.]

LORD HERSCHELL: —

My Lords, in the statement of claim in this action the respondent, who is the plaintiff, alleges that the appellants made in a prospectus issued by them certain statements which were untrue, that they well knew that the facts were not as stated in the prospectus, and made the representations fraudulently, and with the view to induce the plaintiff to take shares in the company.

"This action is one which is commonly called an action of deceit, a mere common law action." This is the description of it given by Cotton L.J. in delivering judgment. I think it important that it should be borne in mind that such an action differs essentially from one brought to obtain rescission of a contract on the ground of misrepresentation of a material fact. The principles which govern the two actions differ widely. Where rescission is claimed it is only necessary to prove that there was misrepresentation; then, however honestly it may have been made, however free from blame the person who made it, the contract, having been obtained by misrepresentation, cannot stand. In an action of deceit, on the contrary, it is not enough to establish misrepresentation alone; it is conceded on all hands that something more must be proved to cast liability upon the defendant, though it has been a matter of controversy what additional elements are requisite. I lay stress upon this because observations made by learned judges in actions for rescission have been cited and much relied upon at the bar by counsel for the respondent. Care must obviously be observed in applying the language used in relation to such actions to an action of deceit. Even if the scope of the language used extends beyond the particular action which was being dealt with, it must be remembered that the learned judges were not engaged in determining what is necessary to support an action of deceit, or in discriminating with nicety the elements which enter into it.

[An extended treatment of the authorities is omitted.]

Having now drawn attention, I believe, to all the cases having a material bearing upon the question under consideration, I proceed to state briefly the conclusions to which I have been led. I think the authorities establish the following propositions: First, in order to sustain an action of deceit, there must be proof of fraud, and nothing short of that will suffice. Secondly, fraud is proved when it is shewn that a false representation has been made (1) knowingly, or (2) without belief in its truth, or (3) recklessly, careless whether it be true or false. Although I have treated the second and third as distinct cases, I think the third is but an instance of the second, for one who makes a statement under such circumstances can have no real belief in the truth of what he states. To prevent a false statement [from] being fraudulent, there must, I think, always be an honest belief in its truth. And this probably covers the whole ground, for one who knowingly alleges that which is false, has obviously no such honest belief. Thirdly, if fraud be proved, the motive of the person guilty of it is immaterial. It matters not that there was no intention to cheat or injure the person to whom the statement was made. . . .

In my opinion making a false statement through want of care falls far short of, and is a very different thing from, fraud, and the same may be said of a false representation honestly believed though on insufficient grounds. . . . [T]he whole current of authorities, with which I have so long detained your Lordships, shews to my mind conclusively that fraud is essential to found an action of deceit, and that it cannot be maintained where the acts proved cannot properly be so termed. . . . But for the reasons I have given I am unable to hold that anything less than fraud will render directors or any other persons liable to an action of deceit.

At the same time I desire to say distinctly that when a false statement has been made the questions whether there were reasonable grounds for believing it, and what were the means of knowledge in the possession of the person making it, are most weighty matters for consideration. The ground upon which an alleged belief was founded is a most important test of its reality. I can conceive many cases where the fact that an alleged belief was destitute of all reasonable foundation would suffice of itself to convince the Court that it was not really entertained, and that the representation was a fraudulent one. So, too, although means of knowledge are . . . a very different thing from knowledge, if I thought that a person making a false statement had shut his eyes to the facts or purposely abstained from inquiring into them, I should hold that honest belief was absent, and that he was just as fraudulent as if he had knowingly stated that which was false. . . .

I quite admit that the statements of witnesses as to their belief are by no means to be accepted blindfold. The probabilities must be considered. Whenever it is necessary to arrive at a conclusion as to the state of mind of another person, and to determine whether his belief under given circumstances was such as he alleges, we can only do so by applying the standard of conduct which our own experience of the ways of men has enabled us to form; by asking ourselves whether a reasonable man would be likely under the circumstances so to believe. I have applied this test, with the result that I have a strong conviction that a reasonable man situated as the defendants were, with their knowledge and means of knowledge, might well believe what they state they did believe, and consider that the representation made was substantially true. . . .

I think the judgment of the Court of Appeal should be reversed. [Lord Halsbury, L.C., Lord Watson, Lord Bramwell and Lord Fitzgerald delivered concurring opinions.]

Order of the Court of Appeal reversed; order of [the trial judge] restored.

International Products Co. v. Erie Railroad

244 N.Y. 331, 155 N.E. 662 (1927)

Andrews, J.

[Plaintiff expected a valuable shipment of goods to arrive via steam ship, after which plaintiff arranged for the goods to be stored at defendant railroad company's warehouse docks. The goods in question were covered by insurance during shipment and the coverage would be extended if plaintiff informed the insurance provider of the precise location of the goods after unloading. In response to plaintiff's query specifying this reason for needing to know the goods' location, defendant's agent informed plaintiff that the goods had arrived and were stored at dock F. Plaintiff in turn informed its insurer. In fact, the goods did not arrive in New York for several days after this representation was made. After arrival, half of the goods were stored at dock D, rather than dock F. When dock D was later destroyed by fire with all of its contents, plaintiff was unable to obtain insurance due to the erroneous location information provided by plaintiff to its insurance carrier in reliance on defendant's representation.]

Confining ourselves to the issues before us we eliminate any theory of fraud or deceit. Had they been present other questions would arise. We come to the vexed question of liability for negligent language. In England the rule is fixed. "Generally speaking there is no such thing as liability for negligence in word as distinguished from act." (Pollock on Torts [12th ed.], p. 565; Fish v. Kelby, 17 C.B. [N.S.] 194.) Dicta to the contrary may be found in earlier cases. But since Peek v. Derry (L.R. 14 A.C. 337), although what was said was not necessary to the decision, the law is clearly to the effect "that no cause of action is maintainable for a mere statement, although untrue, and although acted upon to the damage of the person to whom the statement is made unless the statement be false to the knowledge of the person making it" (Dickson v. Reuters Telegram Co., Ltd., L.R. 1877, 3 C.P. Div. 1), or as said elsewhere "we have to take it as settled that there is no general duty to use any care whatever in making statements in the way of business or otherwise, on which other persons are likely to act." (9 Law Quarterly Review, 292.) And the same principle has been applied in equity although it had been supposed that here, at least, there was often a remedy for negligent misrepresentation.

These cases have not been without criticism. The denial, under all circumstances, of relief because of the negligently spoken or written word, is, it is said, a refusal to enforce what conscience, fair dealing and the usages of business require. The tendency of the American courts has been towards a more liberal conclusion. The searcher of a title employed by one, who delivers his abstract to another to induce action on the faith of it, must exercise care. So must a physician who assures a wife that she may safely treat the infected wound of her husband or hired by another, examines a patient and states the result of his diagnosis. So of a telegraph company, stating that a telegram was delivered when in fact it was not. And the liability of such a company to the receiver for the erroneous transcription of a telegram has also sometimes been placed on this ground.

In New York we are already committed to the American as distinguished from the English rule. In some cases a negligent statement may be the basis for a recovery of damages. . . .

Obviously, however, the rule we have adopted has its limits. Not every casual response, not every idle word, however damaging the result, gives rise to a cause of action. Chancellor Kent might not be held responsible for an error in one of his "Battery opinions." As he himself said, they cost nothing and bind no one. Liability in such cases arises only where there is a duty, if one speaks at all, to give the correct information. And that involves many considerations. There must be knowledge or its equivalent that the information is desired for a serious purpose; that he to whom it is given intends to rely and act upon it; that if false or erroneous he will because of it be injured in person or property. Finally the relationship of the parties, arising out of contract or otherwise, must be such that in morals and good conscience the one has the right to rely upon the other for information, and the other giving the information owes a duty to give it with care. An inquiry made of a stranger is one thing; of a person with whom the inquirer has entered or is about to enter into a contract concerning the goods which are or are to be its subject is another. Even here the inquiry must be made as the basis of independent action. We do not touch the doctrine of caveat emptor. But in a proper case we hold that words negligently spoken may justify the recovery of the proximate damages caused by faith in their accuracy.

When such a relationship as we have referred to exists may not be precisely defined. All that may be stated is the general rule. In view of the complexity of modern business each case must be decided on the peculiar facts presented. The same thing is true, however, in the usual action for personal injuries. There whether negligence exists depends upon the relations of the parties, the thing done or neglected, its natural consequences, and many other considerations. No hard and fast line may be drawn.

Here, as we view the facts, the duty to speak with care if it spoke at all, rested on the defendant. We have it about to become the bailee of the plaintiff's goods; the inquiry made by him with whom it was dealing for the purpose as it knew of obtaining insurance; the realization that the information it gave was to be relied upon and that if false the insurance obtained would be worthless. We have an inquiry such as might be expected in the usual course of business made of one who alone knew the truth. We have a negligent answer, untrue in fact, actual reliance upon it, and resulting proximate loss. True the answer was not given to serve the purposes of the defendant itself. This we regard as immaterial.

If there was negligence justifying a recovery we cannot hold the plaintiff guilty of contributory negligence as a matter of law. Whether or not it should have discovered the error by an inspection of the bill of lading when it received it was a question of fact.

We have confined our decision to the precise issues before us. We do not consider what might be the result under other conditions or whether a recovery might not be had upon other grounds. If the testimony is to be interpreted as the defendant claims it should be; if the statement as to the dock was a mere expression of present intention, still it might be claimed that under the circumstances due care required notice if such intention was subsequently changed. Or under either interpretation it might be said some principle of estoppel might be applied. Or if we are to take the wider view of contracts sometimes proposed, then that a recovery on this theory is permissible. All this we pass by. Such questions we will consider when they are required by the decision we must reach. Until then we express no opinion.

The judgment [for the plaintiff on a directed verdict for the plaintiff] appealed from should be affirmed, with costs.

CARDOZO, C.J., POUND, CRANE and LEHMAN, J.J., concur; KELLOGG, J., absent.

Judgment affirmed.

The holding of the New York court in the *International Products Co.* case is recognized in most American jurisdictions and is reflected in §552 of the Restatement (Second) of Torts. Liability will be imposed on those who, in the course of their businesses or professions, or in other transactions in which they have pecuniary interests, negligently supply false information for the guidance of others in their business transactions. See also Restatement (Third) of Torts Liability for Economic Harms §5 (Am. Law Inst., Tentative Draft No. 1, 2012). As mentioned earlier at the beginning of this section, §552B limits the damages for negligent misrepresentation to those necessary to compensate the plaintiff for the pecuniary harm thereby caused, including the traditional out-of-pocket measure and other consequential pecuniary losses. The plaintiff may not, however, recover the benefit of the bargain. See Johnson v. Healy, 405 A.2d 54, 58 (1978) (declining to award full repair cost measure of damages that significantly exceeded reliance measure because "policy dictates limitation to diminution of value to avoid unreasonable economic waste"). As subsequent materials will reveal, these rules governing negligent misrepresentation are most frequently applied to persons, such as accountants, who are in the business or profession of supplying information to be used in making business decisions. But the rule has been held inapplicable in a case in which the plaintiff alleged that he relied on information in the *Wall Street Journal* about bonds in which he invested. The information turned out to be false, and the plaintiff's action for negligent misrepresentation was dismissed. See Gutter v. Dow Jones, Inc., 490 N.E.2d 898 (Ohio 1986).

Tort liability for innocent misrepresentation is recognized in the Restatement (Second) of Torts:

§552C. MISREPRESENTATION IN SALE, RENTAL OR EXCHANGE TRANSACTION

(1) One who, in a sale, rental or exchange transaction with another, makes a misrepresentation of a material fact for the purpose of inducing the other to act or to refrain from acting in reliance upon it, is subject to liability to the other for pecuniary loss caused to him by his justifiable reliance upon the misrepresentation, even though it is not made fraudulently or negligently.

(2) Damages recoverable under the rule stated in this section are limited to the difference between the value of what the other has parted with and the value of what he has received in the transaction.

CAVEAT

The Institute expresses no opinion as to whether there may be other types of business transactions, in addition to those of sale, rental and exchange, in which strict liability may be imposed for innocent misrepresentation under the conditions stated in this Section.

Although the court in the *Johnson* case mingles principles of tort and warranty law, there may be some utility in keeping them separate in determining liability for innocent misrepresentation. Indeed, it may be important to keep both tort and warranty principles separate from equitable principles of restitution. The following comment to §552C attempts to explain why these distinctions may be necessary.

> *b. Relationship to action for restitution or breach of warranty.* The remedy provided in this Section is very similar to that afforded under the law of restitution. It differs, however, in a material respect. The plaintiff is permitted to retain what he has received and recover damages, rather than rescind and seek restitution, in which case he must return what he received. The tort action for damages may have a definite advantage to the plaintiff in cases in which he is unable to restore what he received in its original condition; when he has made improvements or for other reasons finds it desirable to keep what he has received rather than return it; when he is barred from rescission by delay or has so far committed himself that he has lost the remedy by an election; or when for some other reason, such as the defendant's change of position, restitution is not available to him. It may even in many cases be a better solution from the point of view of the defendant himself, since it permits the transaction to stand, rather than be upset at a later date.
>
> In view of the many similarities of the rule set forth in this Section to the restitutionary remedy, it is difficult to say with certainty whether this rule should be regarded as one of strict liability in the law of torts, eliminating the requirement of intent or negligence in making the representation, or one of the law of restitution, eliminating the requirement of rescinding and restoring the status quo. Under either classification the rule of this Section retains its usefulness.
>
> It should be added that in cases involving the sale of goods, and probably in other transactions, a somewhat similar remedy has been available in the action for breach of warranty. The latter action, despite its historic relationship to tort, has been subject to important contract defenses, notably among them the parol evidence rule. This is made explicit by the Uniform Commercial Code. (See U.C.C. §2-202.) Further, in cases involving the sale of goods, most of the innocent misrepresentations made actionable by this Section would also be actionable under the Code on the theory of breach of warranty. But it does not necessarily follow that actions for damages founded upon innocent misrepresentation are preempted by the Code. The measure of damages provided by this Section differs from the traditional measure of damages for breach of warranty (now embodied in the Code). Under this Section, damages are solely restitutionary in character. In contrast, the measure of damages for breach of warranty includes compensation for benefit of the bargain and for consequential losses. This difference argues for viewing the tort action under this Section as unburdened by contract (or Code) defenses. However, this issue has gone virtually unnoticed in the jurisdictions that give damages in tort for innocent misrepresentation. In a case in which, as a practical matter, the amount recoverable under this Section is substantially the same as the amount recoverable for breach of warranty, the argument against recognition of defenses traditional to the warranty action loses much of its force.

3. Reliance and Contributory Negligence

Pelkey v. Norton

149 Me. 247, 99 A.2d 918 (1953)

TIRREL, J. This is an action "on the case" for deceit.

The plaintiff, who is a dealer in automobiles and trucks in the town of Topsham, alleged that he and the defendant entered into an agreement for the purchase and sale of a 1951

Packard automobile, by the terms of which the plaintiff sold the defendant a 1951 Packard automobile for a total sales price of $3,007.84, and in payment thereof, the defendant paid to the plaintiff the sum of $1,807.84 in cash and sold or, as the term is commonly used, "traded in" a truck towards the purchase price of the Packard automobile, for which the plaintiff "allowed" the defendant a credit on the purchase of $1,200, making payment in full.

The truck which the defendant sold or traded in was a 1947 Chevrolet truck. The plaintiff contends that at the time of their negotiation for the sale of the Packard automobile, the truck owned by the defendant was represented to be a 1949 Chevrolet truck by the defendant; whereas in truth and fact the truck was a 1947 model, and was known by the defendant to be a 1947 model, but was falsely represented by the defendant to induce the plaintiff to allow a greater amount as its trade-in value.

The undisputed testimony of witnesses for the plaintiff indicates the facts to be, — the plaintiff is an automobile dealer and had been for several years. On the date alleged in the declaration the defendant went to the place of business of the plaintiff and conversation was had between the parties concerning the sale by the plaintiff to the defendant of a 1951 Packard sedan. The selling price of the Packard, including extras, handling charges, and taxes, including the State sales tax, was $3,007.84. The defendant was the owner of a Chevrolet dump truck which he wished to "trade in" as part payment for the Packard sedan. It was, of course, essential for the plaintiff to know the year of manufacture of the truck in order to make the proper allowance as its "trade-in" value. The defendant informed the plaintiff it was a 1949 truck, saying: "I ought to know, I bought it new." The year of manufacture may be determined by securing serial and motor numbers imprinted on the frame and motor and by then referring to a certain book showing the year of manufacture. Included in the serial number is a key letter. The plaintiff by himself or his agents obtained certain numbers and a serial letter from the impression on the car. A mistake was apparently made in reading the letter Q as O. No serial letter O was revealed in the Dealers Book. The letter Q, if read correctly, would have informed the plaintiff that the Chevrolet truck was a 1947 model. The 1947 and 1949 models were of the same general appearance. The plaintiff then asked the defendant to show him the original bill of sale but was informed by defendant that it was at his son's house in North Yarmouth. The difference in the trade-in price between a 1949 model and a 1947 model was approximately $700. The plaintiff allowed the trade-in price of a 1949 model. Applications for registration of this same truck signed by the defendant and introduced by plaintiff as exhibits show the year model as a 1947. The plaintiff sold this truck to a third person as a 1949 model who later informed the plaintiff of the error in the date of the model and brought suit for damages against this plaintiff.

Upon completion of the plaintiff's evidence the defendant rested, and moved for a directed verdict for the defendant, which was granted, to which the plaintiff seasonably filed his exceptions. After the motion for a directed verdict was granted for the defendant, and before judgment was rendered, the plaintiff filed a motion for a directed verdict for the plaintiff, which motion was denied, and to which denial the plaintiff also took exceptions.

The plaintiff now prosecutes in this court on his exceptions to the granting of the motion for a directed verdict for the defendant and the denial of the motion for a directed verdict for the plaintiff.

The presiding Justice, in a short summation to the jury, before directing the verdict for the defendant, gave his reasons based on the case of Benjamin H. Coffin v. Winfred S. Dodge, 146 Me. 3, explaining to the jury that among the elements of deceit is one that a plaintiff in such a case must prove "that the plaintiff did not know the representation to be false, and by the exercise of reasonable care could not have ascertained its falsity."

In Coffin v. Dodge, supra, we said on pages 5 and 6: "In the case of Crossman v. Bacon & Robinson, 119 Me. 105, 109, the elements in deceit are stated to be '(1) a material representation which is (2) false and (3) known to be false, or made recklessly as an assertion of fact without knowledge of its truth or falsity and (4) made with the intention that it shall be acted upon and (5) acted upon with damage. In addition to these elements it must also be proved that the plaintiff (6) relied upon the representations (7) was induced to act upon them and (8) did not know them to be false, and by the exercise of reasonable care could not have ascertained their falsity. Every one of these elements must be proved affirmatively to sustain an action of deceit.'"

There is a well recognized exception to or limitation upon so much of the foregoing clause numbered (8) as requires proof that the plaintiff by the exercise of reasonable care could not have ascertained the falsity of the representation. . . .

The limitation on the foregoing clause numbered (8) is that one cannot escape liability for *intentional misrepresentation* on the ground that the plaintiff negligently relied thereon. In Bixler v. Wright, 116 Me. 133, 139 we said: "The law dislikes negligence. It seeks properly to make the enforcement of men's rights depend in very considerable degree upon whether they have been negligent in conserving and protecting their rights. But the law abhors fraud. And when it comes to an issue whether fraud shall prevail or negligence, it would seem that a court of justice is quite as much bound to stamp out fraud as it is to foster reasonable care." . . .

Many decisions hold that one guilty of actual fraud may not excuse his own wrongful acts by claiming that the person defrauded was guilty of contributory negligence.

In Eastern Trust & Banking Company v. Andrew W. Cunningham, 103 Me. 455, 465, 466, the court said:

> But the defendant contends further that if the plaintiff did not know, it ought to have known, and would have known but for its own negligence. We think this defense cannot avail. There are cases which hold that where one carelessly relies upon a pretence of inherent absurdity and incredibility, upon mere idle talk, or upon a device so shadowy as not to be capable of imposing upon anyone, he must bear his misfortune, if injured. He must not shut his eyes to what is palpably before him. But that doctrine, if sound, is not applicable here. We think the well settled rule to be applied here is that if one intentionally misrepresents to another facts particularly within his own knowledge, with an intent that the other shall act upon them, and he does so act, he cannot afterwards excuse himself by saying "You were foolish to believe me." It does not lie in his mouth to say that the one trusting him was negligent. In this case the fact whether or not there were funds in the Gardiner bank to meet the checks was peculiarly within the knowledge of the defendant. The rule is stated in Pollock on Torts, §252, as follows: — "It is now settled law that one who chooses to make positive assertions without warrant shall not excuse himself by saying that the other party need not have relied upon them. He must show that his representation was not in fact relied upon. In short, nothing will excuse a culpable misrepresentation short of proof that it was not relied upon, either because the other party knew the truth, or because he *relied wholly* on his own investigations, or because the alleged fact did not influence his actions at all." (Emphasis ours.) . . .

The present case is clearly distinguishable from Coffin v. Dodge, supra. The facts bring it within the limitation on the general rules laid down therein. In this record there is testimony which, if believed by the jury, would justify a finding that the defendant was guilty of an actual, intentional, false and fraudulent misrepresentation to the plaintiff. If so, negligence on the part of the plaintiff in reliance thereon was no defense to his action of deceit. There was sufficient evidence in this record to justify a finding by the jury of the existence of every essential element of actionable fraud.

On this record it was error to direct a verdict for the defendant and the plaintiff's exception thereto must be sustained. . . .

Exception to direction of verdict for the defendant sustained.

Pelkey follows the generally accepted rule that the plaintiff must rely upon the defendant's misrepresentation and the reliance must be justifiable under the circumstances. See John C. P. Goldberg, Anthony J. Sebok & Benjamin C. Zipursky, The Place of Reliance in Fraud, 48 Ariz. L. Rev. 1001 (2006). Thus, the plaintiff's actual knowledge of the facts will bar recovery. See, e.g., Williams v. Bisson, 46 A.2d 708 (Me. 1946), wherein the plaintiff knew the true facts regarding erroneous recitals in a deed. And in *Ex parte* Leo, 480 So. 2d 572 (Ala. 1985), the plaintiff indicated by his conduct that he did not rely on representations as to the square footage of the house he bought from the defendant; the plaintiff had access to the house and had made some measurements himself.

The difficult cases are those in which the plaintiff actually relies, but under circumstances where the defendant may argue that the plaintiff's reliance was unreasonable. See, e.g., Johnson v. Waterfront Servs. Co., 909 N.E.2d 342, 350 (Ill. App. Ct. 2009) ("The question of justifiable reliance takes into account both what the plaintiff knew and what he could have learned through the exercise of ordinary prudence. In other words, a plaintiff may not close his eyes and then claim that he has been deceived by others.") (internal citations omitted). Where the defendant has been guilty of actual fraud, a majority of courts have sided with Pelkey v. Norton in turning a deaf ear to the argument that the plaintiff should have discovered the truth. See Restatement (Second) of Torts §545A; Roda v. Berko, 81 N.E.2d 912 (Ill. 1948). A classic statement of this position appears in Chamberlin v. Fuller, 9 A. 832, 836 (Vt. 1887): "No rogue should enjoy his ill-gotten plunder for the simple reason that his victim is by chance a fool." Section 540 of the Restatement (Second) makes clear that the recipient of a fraudulent misrepresentation of fact is justified in relying on its truth even if its falsity would have been revealed by an investigation.

On the other hand, when the misrepresentation is merely negligent and not fraudulent, contributory negligence will in most jurisdictions bar the plaintiff's recovery (see §552A, Restatement (Second) of Torts) or reduce it if comparative fault rules apply (see Gilchrist Timber Co. v. ITT Rayonier Co., 696 So. 2d 334 (Fla. 1997)). In Estate of Braswell v. People's Credit Union, 602 A.2d 510 (R.I. 1992), the court ruled that contributory negligence will not bar recovery for pecuniary loss stemming from negligent misrepresentations in consumer transactions. In some states, contributory negligence will not bar a restitution claim based on negligent misrepresentation. See Wilson v. Came, 366 A.2d 474 (N.H. 1976). And when the defendant is held strictly liable under §552C, above, the plaintiff is only required to show justifiable reliance on the innocent misrepresentation. Does it seem strange to you that innocent misrepresenters are treated more harshly than negligent misrepresenters with regard to the effects of the plaintiff's contributory negligence?

Corva v. United Services Automobile Association

108 A.D. 2d 631, 485 N.Y.S.2d 264 (1985)

Before SANDLER, J.P., and CARRO, BLOOM and KASSAL, JJ.

MEMORANDUM DECISION. . . .

Plaintiff was a passenger in an automobile on March 29, 1979 when it was involved in an accident with a motor vehicle owned by Donald Sabia. Plaintiff retained the firm of Mangiatordi & Corpina (M & C) to represent her. Sabia was insured by United Services Automobile Association (USAA). Upon notification of the accident USAA employed Dahle Lassonde & Co., Inc., (Dahle) and Jack L. Hall to protect its interests. Negotiations ensued between M & C and Dahle and Hall as a result of which the matter was settled for $15,000, allegedly because Dahle and Hall represented to M & C that that was the limit of Sabia's coverage. The complaint alleges that Sabia carried insurance with USAA in excess of $15,000 and seeks compensatory and punitive damages. Dahle and Hall and USAA interposed separate defenses. Each set forth a cross-complaint against M & C asserting that M & C violated its duty of care to Corva by not independently verifying the policy limits in the policy of insurance issued by USAA and that therefore, in the event of a recovery by Corva against the cross-claimants, or any of them, those found liable to Corva will be entitled to indemnity or contribution from M & C.

M & C moved to dismiss the third and fourth party complaints. Special Term granted the motion. We reverse and reinstate these complaints. . . . Paragraph 15 of the complaint alleges:

> . . . That the aforesaid representations were made with the knowledge that they were false, or there should have been knowledge that they were false; or were made with wanton, gross and reckless disregard as to whether they were true or false, with a pretense of knowledge when in fact there was no knowledge, without taking the necessary and proper steps to ascertain the truth of the said representations which were ascertainable and available all with knowledge that the plaintiff was relying and would act upon said representations.

To the extent to which the cross-complaints seek contribution from M & C on the theory that M & C's violation of its duty of care to Corva contributed to the loss sustained, the cross-complaints would appear to be legally sufficient. It is of course well established that New York law permits an apportionment of damages among culpable parties "regardless of the degree or nature of the concurring fault" and that contribution is permitted even in favor of an intentional wrongdoer if the parties are subject to liability to plaintiff for damages for the same injury.

In dismissing the cross-complaints, Special Term . . . concluded that plaintiff could succeed in its main action only on showing that M & C had justifiably relied upon the misrepresentation alleged and that such a finding would be inconsistent with a determination that M & C had violated its duty of care to its client by not independently verifying the policy limits. The flaw in this analysis lies in the erroneous assumption that the standard for determining justifiable reliance in an action for fraud and misrepresentation is identical with the standard of reasonable care in a negligence or malpractice action. The standards are in fact quite different.

In discussing the requirement of justifiable reliance in a misrepresentation case, a leading authority observed:

> The plaintiff's conduct must not be so utterly unreasonable, in light of the information open to him, that the law may properly say that his loss is his own responsibility. . . . If he is a

> person of normal intelligence, experience and education, he may not put faith in representations which any such normal person would recognize at once as preposterous, as, for example, that glasses, once fitted, will alter shape and adapt themselves to the eye, or which are shown by facts within his observation to be so patently and obviously false that he must have closed his eyes to avoid discovery of the truth. . . . Prosser, Law of Torts (4th ed.) pp. 715, 716.

The standard of reasonable care in negligence or malpractice actions is obviously quite different, and it is clearly theoretically possible that M & C could have justifiably relied on the alleged misrepresentations for purposes of the plaintiff's action and still have been at fault in failing independently to inquire into the policy limits.

In the foregoing observations we of course intimate no opinion as to the merits of the cross-complaints. There is obviously something unappealing in the notion that someone who has deceived another should be entitled to contribution for the damage caused by the deception because the deceived person had imprudently relied on the truthfulness of the representation. All we decide here is that the cross-complaints may not be dismissed as a matter of law.

All concur.

If the plaintiff's unreasonable conduct relates not to reliance on the misrepresentation but to the failure to avoid or reduce the loss after the transaction is completed, then the plaintiff's fault may affect recovery in the usual way under contributory or comparative negligence principles. See ESCA Corp. v. KPMG Peat Marwick, 959 P.2d 651 (Wash. 1998). But this is not the same situation as the one raised by *Corva*, is it?

Misrepresentations ordinarily induce plaintiffs to act in reliance on them. What if a misrepresentation allegedly causes a plaintiff to refrain from acting? In Small v. Fritz Companies, Inc. 65 P.3d 1255 (Cal. 2003), the defendant company released a financial report that had been either negligently or fraudulently prepared based on improper accounting, misrepresenting the company's financial situation as better than it actually was. When the report's falsity was discovered, the company's stock plummeted and the plaintiffs, who had allegedly retained their stock based on the report, lost money. The California high court recognized a cause of action for stockholders induced to refrain from selling their stock by negligent or fraudulent misrepresentations made in financial reports distributed to a wide spectrum of people. The court disagreed with the defendant's primarily policy-based arguments that this would unreasonably expand liability and held that where a plaintiff can prove actual reliance, the defendant is liable.

4. Liability to Third Persons

Ultramares Corp. v. Touche

255 N.Y. 170, 174 N.E. 441 (1931)

Cardozo, C.J. The action is in tort for damages suffered through the misrepresentations of accountants, the first cause of action being for misrepresentations that were merely negligent and the second for misrepresentations charged to have been fraudulent.

In January, 1924, the defendants, a firm of public accountants, were employed by Fred Stern and Co., Inc., to prepare and certify a balance sheet exhibiting the condition of its business as of December 31, 1923. They had been employed at the end of each of three years preceding to render a like service. Fred Stern & Co., Inc., which was in substance Stern himself, was engaged in the importation and sale of rubber. To finance its operations, it required extensive credit and borrowed large sums of money from banks and other lenders. All this was known to the defendants. The defendants knew also that in the usual course of business the balance sheet when certified would be exhibited by the Stern company to banks, creditors, stockholders, purchasers or sellers, according to the needs of the occasion, as the basis of financial dealings. Accordingly, when the balance sheet was made up, the defendants supplied the Stern company with thirty-two copies certified with serial numbers as counterpart originals. Nothing was said as to the persons to whom these counterparts would be shown or the extent or number of the transactions in which they would be used. In particular there was no mention of the plaintiff, a corporation doing business chiefly as a factor, which till then had never made advances to the Stern company, though it had sold merchandise in small amounts. The range of the transactions in which a certificate of audit might be expected to play a part was as indefinite and wide as the possibilities of the business that was mirrored in the summary.

By February 26, 1924, the audit was finished and the balance sheet made up. It stated assets in the sum of $2,550,671.88 and liabilities other than capital and surplus in the sum of $1,479,956.62, thus showing a net worth of $1,070,715.26. Attached to the balance sheet was a certificate as follows:

Touche, Niven & Co.
Public Accountants
Eighty Maiden Lane
New York

February 26, 1924.

Certificate of Auditors

We have examined the accounts of Fred Stern & Co., Inc., for the year ending December 31, 1923, and hereby certify that the annexed balance sheet is in accordance therewith and with the information and explanations given us. We further certify that, subject to provision for federal taxes on income, the said statement, in our opinion, presents a true and correct view of the financial condition of Fred Stern & Co., Inc., as at December 31, 1923.

TOUCHE, NIVEN & CO.
Public Accountants

Capital and surplus were intact if the balance sheet was accurate. In reality both had been wiped out, and the corporation was insolvent. The books had been falsified by those in charge of the business so as to set forth accounts receivable and other assets which turned out to be fictitious. The plaintiff maintains that the certificate of audit was erroneous in both its branches. The first branch, the asserted correspondence between the accounts and the balance sheet, is one purporting to be made as of the knowledge of the auditors. The second branch, which certifies to a belief that the condition reflected in the balance sheet presents a true and correct picture of the resources of the business, is stated as a matter of opinion. In the view of the plaintiff, both branches of the certificate are either fraudulent or negligent. As to one class of assets, the item of accounts receivable, if not also as to others, there was no real correspondence, we are told, between balance sheet and books, or so the triers of the facts might find. If correspondence, however, be assumed, a closer examination of supporting invoices and records, or a fuller inquiry directed to the persons appearing on the books as creditors or debtors, would have exhibited the truth.

[The plaintiff corporation loaned money to Stern & Co. in reliance upon the audit certified by the defendant, and suffered losses when Stern & Co. went into bankruptcy.]

This action, brought against the accountants in November, 1926, to recover the loss suffered by the plaintiff in reliance upon the audit, was in its inception one for negligence. On the trial there was added a second cause of action asserting fraud also. The trial judge dismissed the second cause of action without submitting it to the jury. As to the first cause of action, he reserved his decision on the defendants' motion to dismiss, and took the jury's verdict. They were told that the defendants might be held liable if with knowledge that the results of the audit would be communicated to creditors they did the work negligently, and that negligence was the omission to use reasonable and ordinary care. The verdict was in favor of the plaintiff for $187,576.32. On the coming in of the verdict, the judge granted the reserved motion. The Appellate Division affirmed the dismissal of the cause of action for fraud, but reversed the dismissal of the cause of action for negligence, and reinstated the verdict. The case is here on cross-appeals.

The two causes of action will be considered in succession, first the one for negligence and second that for fraud.

(1) We think the evidence supports a finding that the audit was negligently made, though in so saying we put aside for the moment the question whether negligence, even if it existed, was a wrong to the plaintiff. [The court's description of the defendant's negligence is omitted.]

If the defendants owed a duty to the plaintiff to act with the same care that would have been due under a contract of employment, a jury was at liberty to find a verdict of negligence upon a showing of a scrutiny so imperfect and perfunctory. . . .

We are brought to the question of duty, its origin and measure.

The defendants owed to their employer a duty imposed by law to make their certificate without fraud, and a duty growing out of contract to make it with the care and caution proper to their calling. Fraud includes the pretense of knowledge when knowledge there is none. To creditors and investors to whom the employer exhibited the certificate, the defendants owed a like duty to make it without fraud, since there was notice in the circumstances of its making that the employer did not intend to keep it to himself. A different question develops when we ask whether they owed a duty to these to make it without negligence. If liability for negligence exists, a thoughtless slip or blunder, the failure to detect a theft or forgery beneath the cover of deceptive entries, may expose accountants to a liability in an indeterminate amount for an indeterminate time to an indeterminate class. The hazards of a business conducted on these terms are so extreme as to enkindle doubt whether a flaw may not exist in the implication of a duty that exposes to these consequences. We put aside for the moment any statement in the certificate which involves the representation of a fact as true to the knowledge of the auditors. If such a statement was made, whether believed to be true or not, the defendants are liable for deceit in the event that it was false. The plaintiff does not need the invention of novel doctrine to help it out in such conditions. The case was submitted to the jury and the verdict was returned upon the theory that even in the absence of a misstatement of a fact there is a liability also for erroneous opinion. The expression of an opinion is to be subject to a warranty implied by law. What, then, is the warranty, as yet unformulated, to be? Is it merely that the opinion is honestly conceived and that the preliminary inquiry has been honestly pursued, that a halt has not been made without a genuine belief that the search has been reasonably adequate to bring disclosure of the truth? Or does it go farther and involve the assumption of a liability for any blunder or inattention that could fairly be spoken of as negligence if the controversy were one between accountant and employer for breach of a contract to render services for pay?

The assault upon the citadel of privity is proceeding in these days apace. How far the inroads shall extend is now a favorite subject of juridical discussion. . . . In the field of the law of torts a manufacturer who is negligent in the manufacture of a chattel in circumstances pointing to an unreasonable risk of serious bodily harm to those using it thereafter may be liable for negligence though privity is lacking between manufacturer and user (MacPherson v. Buick Motor Co., 217 N.Y. 382). A force or instrument of harm having been launched with potentialities of danger manifest to the eye of prudence, the one who launches it is under a duty to keep it within bounds. Even so, the question is still open whether the potentialities of danger that will charge with liability are confined to harm to the person, or include injury to property. In either view, however, what is released or set in motion is a physical force. We are now asked to say that a like liability attaches to the circulation of a thought or a release of the explosive power resident in words. . . .

In Glanzer v. Shepard [233 N.Y. 236, 135 N.E. 275 (1922)] the seller of beans requested the defendants, public weighers, to make return of the weight and furnish the buyer with a copy. This the defendants did. Their return, which was made out in duplicate, one copy to the seller and the other to the buyer, recites that it was made by order of the former for the use of the latter. The buyer paid the seller on the faith of the certificate which turned out to be erroneous. We held that the weighers were liable at the suit of the buyer for the moneys overpaid. Here was something more than the rendition of a service in the expectation that the one who ordered the certificate would use it thereafter in the operations of his business as occasion might require. Here was a case where the transmission of the certificate to another was not merely one possibility among many, but the "end and aim of the transaction," as certain and immediate and deliberately willed as if a husband were to order a gown to be delivered to his wife, or a telegraph company, contracting with the sender of a message, were to telegraph it wrongly to the damage of the person expected to receive it. The bond was so close as to approach that of privity, if not completely one with it. Not so in the case at hand. No one would be likely to urge that there was a contractual relation, or even one approaching it, at the root of any duty that was owing from the defendants now before us to the indeterminate class of persons who, presently or in the future, might deal with the Stern company in reliance on the audit. In a word, the service rendered by the defendant in Glanzer v. Shepard was primarily for the information of a third person, in effect, if not in name, a party to the contract, and only incidentally for that of the formal promisee. In the case at hand, the service was primarily for the benefit of the Stern company, a convenient instrumentality for use in the development of the business, and only incidentally or collaterally for the use of those to whom Stern and his associates might exhibit it thereafter. Foresight of these possibilities may charge with liability for fraud. The conclusion does not follow that it will charge with liability for negligence.

[The opinion next discusses International Products Co. v. Erie R.R., above, and distinguishes it on the ground that there existed in that case a "determinate relation, that of bailor and bailee, with peculiar opportunity for knowledge on the part of the bailee as to the subject-matter of the statement and with a continuing duty to correct it if erroneous."]

From the foregoing analysis the conclusion is, we think, inevitable that nothing in our previous decisions commits us to a holding of liability for negligence in the circumstances of the case at hand, and that such liability, if recognized, will be an extension of the principle of those decisions to different conditions, even if more or less analogous. The question then is whether such an extension shall be made.

The extension, if made, will so expand the field of liability for negligent speech as to make it nearly, if not quite, coterminous with that of liability for fraud. Again and again, in decisions of this court, the bounds of this latter liability have been set up, with futility the fate of every endeavor to dislodge them. Scienter has been declared to be an indispensable element except where the representation has been put forward as true of one's own knowledge, or in circumstances where the expression of opinion was a dishonorable pretense. Even an opinion, especially an opinion by an expert, may be found to be fraudulent if the grounds supporting it are so flimsy as to lead to the conclusion that there was no genuine belief back of it. Further than that this court has never gone. Directors of corporations have been acquitted of liability for deceit though they have been lax in investigation and negligent in speech. This has not meant, to be sure, that negligence may not be evidence from which a trier of the facts may draw an inference of fraud (Derry v. Peek, [L. R.] 14 A.C. 337, 369, 375, 376), but merely that if that inference is rejected, or, in the light of all the circumstances, is found to be unreasonable, negligence alone is not a substitute for fraud. Many also are the cases that have distinguished between the willful or reckless representation essential to the maintenance at law of an action for deceit, and the misrepresentation, negligent or innocent, that will lay a sufficient basis for rescission in equity. If this action is well conceived, all these principles and distinctions, so nicely wrought and formulated, have been a waste of time and effort. They have even been a snare, entrapping litigants and lawyers into an abandonment of the true remedy lying ready to the call. The suitors thrown out of court because they proved negligence, and nothing else, in an action for deceit, might have ridden to triumphant victory if they had proved the self-same facts, but had given the wrong another label, and all this in a State where forms of action have been abolished. So to hold is near to saying that we have been paltering with justice. A word of caution or suggestion would have set the erring suitor right. Many pages of opinion were written by judges the most eminent, yet the word was never spoken. We may not speak it now. A change so revolutionary, if expedient, must be wrought by legislation. . . .

Our holding does not emancipate accountants from the consequences of fraud. It does not relieve them if their audit has been so negligent as to justify a finding that they had no genuine belief in its adequacy, for this again is fraud. It does no more than say that if less than this is proved, if there has been neither reckless misstatement nor insincere profession of an opinion, but only honest blunder, the ensuing liability for negligence is one that is bounded by the contract, and is to be enforced between the parties by whom the contract has been made. We doubt whether the average business man receiving a certificate without paying for it and receiving it merely as one among a multitude of possible investors, would look for anything more.

(2) The second cause of action is yet to be considered.

The defendants certified as a fact, true to their own knowledge, that the balance sheet was in accordance with the books of account. If their statement was false, they are not to be exonerated because they believed it to be true. We think the triers of the facts might hold it to be false. . . .

In this connection we are to bear in mind the principle already stated in the course of this opinion that negligence or blindness, even when not equivalent to fraud, is none the less evidence to sustain an inference of fraud. At least this is so if the negligence is gross. . . .

We conclude, to sum up the situation, that in certifying to the correspondence between balance sheet and accounts the defendants made a statement as true to their own knowledge, when they had, as a jury might find, no knowledge on the subject. If that is so, they may also be found to have acted without information leading to a sincere or genuine belief when they certified to an opinion that the balance sheet faithfully reflected the condition of the business. . . .

Upon the defendants' appeal as to the first cause of action, the judgment of the Appellate Division should be reversed, and that of the Trial Term affirmed, with costs in the Appellate Division and in this court.

Upon the plaintiff's appeal as to the second cause of action, the judgment of the Appellate Division and that of the Trial Term should be reversed, and a new trial granted, with costs to abide the event.

POUND, CRANE, LEHMAN, KELLOGG, O'BRIEN and HUBBS, JJ., concur.

Judgment accordingly.

In Credit Alliance Corp. v. Arthur Andersen & Co., 483 N.E.2d 110 (N.Y. 1985), the Court of Appeals of New York held that to be liable to third persons in negligence, "(1) the accountants must have been aware that the financial reports were to be used for a particular purpose or purposes; (2) in the furtherance of which a known party or parties was intended to rely; and (3) there must have been some conduct on the part of the accountants linking them to that party or parties, which evinces the accountants' understanding of that party or parties' reliance." 483 N.E.2d at 118. The Court of Appeals has made it clear that the accountant's knowledge that the third person will rely on the accountant's work is not enough to impose liability. See Iselin v. Landau, 522 N.E.2d 21 (N.Y. 1988). Knowledge plus face-to-face meetings of the plaintiff with the accountant satisfied the third requirement of *Credit Alliance* in Walpert, Sullivan & Blumenthal, P.A. v. Katz, 762 A.2d 582 (Md. 2000).

A somewhat more restrictive rule than that expressed in *Ultramares* and *Credit Alliance* was adopted by the court in Shelden v. Bernett, 754 P.2d 256 (Alaska 1988). The court held that in giving tax advice, an accountant is liable for negligent misrepresentation only to those the accountant specifically intends to rely on the advice, and then only if the accountant makes that intent known. For further discussion of the liability of accountants for negligent misrepresentations, see Jay M. Feinman, Liability of Accountants for Negligent Auditing: Doctrine, Policy, and Ideology, 31 Fla. St. U. L. Rev. 17 (2003). For an argument that negligent misrepresentation is best conceptualized as a contractual claim akin to promissory estoppel and other reliance-based contract law doctrines, see Mark P. Gergen, Negligent Misrepresentation as Contract, 101 Cal. L. Rev. 953 (2013).

To some extent, the subject of the liability of accountants and others for negligent misrepresentations has been supplemented by federal statutes and regulations governing the sale of securities in this country. Actions may be brought under several sections of the Securities Act of 1933 (15 U.S.C. §77) and the Securities Exchange Act of 1934 (15 U.S.C. §78) by investors financially harmed by misleading or fraudulent representations or nondisclosures accompanying the sale of securities. See, e.g., Stoneridge Inv. Partners, LLC v. Scientific-Atlanta, 552 U.S. 148 (2008); see generally Louis Loss, Joel Seligman & Troy Paredes, Fundamentals of Securities Regulation ch. 11 (5th ed. 2003). Additionally, Section 933 of the Dodd–Frank Wall Street Reform and Consumer Protection Act (15 U.S.C. §78o–7(m)) extended investors' private rights of action against accountants and securities analysts under the Securities Exchange Act to include credit rating agencies.

Although most of the cases have involved accountants and auditors, courts have extended third-party liability to other occupations. See, e.g., First State Sav. Bank v. Albright & Assocs. of Ocala, Inc., 561 So. 2d 1326 (Fla. Dist. Ct. App.), *rev. denied*, 576 So. 2d 284 (Fla. 1990) (land appraiser); Ossining Union Free Sch. Dist. v. Anderson LaRocca Anderson, 539 N.E.2d 91 (N.Y. 1989) (engineers and architects); John Martin Co., Inc. v. Morse/Diesel, Inc., 819 S.W.2d 428 (Tenn. 1991) (subcontractor). See also Seth E. Lipner & Lisa A. Catalano, The Tort of Giving Negligent Investment Advice, 39 U. Memphis L. Rev. 663 (2009). The following case arose out of the subprime mortgage collapse which helped fuel the financial crisis of 2008. In it, the largest U.S. state pension fund challenged the role of investment rating companies in helping to sustain investor demand for mortgage-backed securities notwithstanding signs of risk and volatility in the housing market.

California Public Employees' Retirement System v. Moody's Investors Service, Inc.

226 Cal. App. 4th 643, 172 Cal. Rptr. 3d 238 (Ct. App. 2014), rev. denied, 2014 Cal. LEXIS 9404 (Cal. Aug. 25, 2014)

JENKINS, J.

This is an appeal from an order denying the special motion to strike of defendants Moody's Investors Service, Inc., Moody's Corporation and The McGraw-Hill Companies, Inc. (collectively, Rating Agencies or defendants) against plaintiff California's Public Employees' Retirement System (CalPERS). . . . The trial court reached this decision after finding that . . . dismissal at this stage would be improper because CalPERS successfully demonstrated a probability of prevailing on the merits of its sole claim of negligent misrepresentation. According to the Rating Agencies, the trial court's finding of a probability of prevailing on the merits is erroneous. . . . For reasons set forth below, we affirm the trial court's order in its entirety. . . .

Factual and Procedural Background

On July 9, 2009, CalPERS, the largest state public pension fund in the United States, filed a complaint against the Rating Agencies asserting causes of action for negligent misrepresentation and negligent interference with prospective economic advantage. The complaint challenged the veracity of the Rating Agencies' assignment of highly favorable credit ratings to three structured investment vehicles (SIVs) that ultimately collapsed, causing billions of dollars in losses to CalPERS and other investors. According to the complaint, in 2006 and early 2007, CalPERS, through its agents, invested approximately $1.3 billion of its assets in medium-term notes and commercial paper issued by these SIVs after the Rating Agencies assigned the debt their highest "AAA" or equivalent ratings. When the SIVs subsequently entered bankruptcy or receivership in 2007 or 2008, CalPERS lost "hundreds of millions, and perhaps more than $1 billion."

As a general matter, these ratings represent an agency's assessment of the likelihood that a SIV noteholder will be paid the expected amount of principal and interest through the note's maturity date. Before assigning a particular rating, the Rating Agency conducts detailed research and risk analysis with respect to the SIV notes. Once a rating is given, it is published in the SIV's offering materials made available to potential investors. . . .

CalPERS contends: "High credit ratings were critical to the SIVs' existence." Without the high ratings indicating stable financial returns, the SIVs would not have attracted buyers, like CalPERS, with institutional policies restricting note purchases to investment grade products. In other words, CalPERS alleges, had the Rating Agencies not given their highest ratings to Cheyne, Stanfield and Sigma [three SIVs], it would not have purchased their debt issues and suffered the significant investment losses when, in 2007 and 2008, the SIVs suffered a series of downgrades and were eventually forced to wind down.

Discussion

The Rating Agencies contend CalPERS failed to make a prima facie case of negligent misrepresentation for four reasons. . . . Specifically, the Rating Agencies contend CalPERS failed to produce substantial evidence with respect to each of the following essential elements of its claim: (1) a misrepresented past or existing material fact with respect to the SIV ratings; (2) the absence of a reasonable basis for believing the SIV ratings were true when published; (3) a legal duty owed by the Rating Agencies to CalPERS with respect to the SIV ratings; and (4) actual and justifiable reliance by CalPERS on the SIV ratings. . . .

1. Are ratings actionable statements?

At first glance, resolving whether ratings are actionable misrepresentations for purposes of this tort seems quite straightforward given the oft-stated rule that a speaker's opinion about a future event is not a statement about a past or existing material fact. "It is hornbook law that an actionable misrepresentation must be made about past or existing facts; statements regarding future events are merely deemed opinions." (San Francisco Design Center Associates v. Portman Companies (1995) 41 Cal. App. 4th 29, 43-44 [50 Cal. Rptr. 2d 716]. . . . Here, for example, the complaint describes the SIV ratings as "'address[ing] the *likelihood* that investors will receive payments as promised' and 'address[ing] the *expected* loss posed to investors in relation to timely payment of interest (if applicable) and timely payment of principal at par on the final legal maturity date,'" allegations that appear to place the ratings within this nonactionable realm of opinion or prediction. (Italics added.)

However, as CalPERS is quick to note: "Under certain circumstances, expressions of professional opinion are treated as representations of fact. When a statement, although in the form of an opinion, is 'not a casual expression of belief' but 'a deliberate affirmation of the matters stated,' it may be regarded as a positive assertion of fact. (Gagne v. Bertran (1954) 43 Cal. 2d 481, 489 [275 P.2d 15].) Moreover, when a party possesses or holds itself out as possessing superior knowledge or special information or expertise regarding the subject matter and a plaintiff is so situated that it may reasonably rely on such supposed knowledge, information, or expertise, the defendant's representation may be treated as one of material fact. (Gagne v. Bertran, supra, 43 Cal. 2d at p. 489 [275 P.2d 15]; Cohen v. S & S Construction Company (1983) 151 Cal. App. 3d 941, 946, [201 Cal. Rptr. 173]. . . .

Relying on this exception to the general rule, CalPERS argues the ratings in this case are not merely "casual statements of belief," but rather "deliberate assertions based on analysis of non-public, confidential information, and assigned after the Rating Agencies participated in structuring the SIV's." As such, CalPERS reasons, the ratings should be deemed actionable expressions of professional opinion rather than nonactionable predictions regarding future events. [To support its reasoning, CalPERS provided, and the court reviewed, declarations from several former credit rating agency employees.]

We agree with CalPERS this evidence reflects . . . not only that the Rating Agencies employed superior knowledge and special information and expertise to assign ratings to the SIVs, they employed their special knowledge, information and expertise to participate in, and exert control over, the very construction of the SIVs. As such, we agree with CalPERS a prima facie case has been made that the ratings are actionable as "professional opinions" or "deliberate affirmations of fact" regarding the nature and quality of the SIV product. . . .

2. Was there a reasonable basis for believing the ratings were accurate?

Next, with respect to whether the Rating Agencies had the requisite reasonable basis for believing in the integrity of the ratings at the time of their publication, the complaint describes the following circumstances. . . .

[The court restates the complaint's description of the Rating Agencies use of flawed methodologies and unreasonable assumptions in their evaluations of the SIVs. CalPER's also presented evidence that the SIVs paid fees to the Rating Agencies according to the percentage of the SIV's securities sold. Pursuant to their financial incentive, the Agencies then issued high ratings to these SIVs.]

This evidence presented . . . suffices to prove a prima facie case the Rating Agencies lacked a reasonable basis for believing the accuracy or truthfulness of their ratings.

3. Did the Rating Agencies intend to influence CalPERS?

We now turn to the issue of whether the Rating Agencies, when issuing the ratings, intended to influence CalPERS in its decision to invest in the SIV market, such that they assumed a legal duty to CalPERS with respect to these ratings. Where, as here, a negligent misrepresentation claim is brought against the provider of a professional opinion based on special knowledge, information or expertise regarding a company's value, the California Supreme Court requires the following:

> "The representation must have been made with the intent to induce plaintiff, or a particular class of persons to which plaintiff belongs, to act in reliance upon the representation in a specific transaction, or a specific type of transaction, that defendant intended to influence. Defendant is deemed to have intended to influence [its client's] transaction with plaintiff whenever defendant knows with substantial certainty that plaintiff, or the particular class of persons to which plaintiff belongs, will rely on the representation in the course of the transaction. [However,] [i]f others become aware of the representation and act upon it, there is no liability even though defendant should reasonably have foreseen such a possibility." [Bily v. Arthur Young & Co. (1992) 3 Cal. 4th 370, 390, 407-408, 11 Cal. Rptr. 2d 51, 834 P.2d 745 (*Bily*)]. . . .

This evidence, in our view, supports a reasonable inference that the Rating Agencies supplied their ratings with knowledge of the existence of a well defined type of transaction which the ratings were intended to influence. . . . Quite simply, this is not a case where it is alleged the defendant "merely knew" of the possibility its professional opinions were being shared with third parties. This is a case where CalPERS alleges the Rating Agencies, first, helped create the underlying products and, second, assigned and published ratings on those products that were then prominently featured in marketing materials given to investors interested in purchasing them. (Cf. [Nutmeg Securities, Ltd. v. McGladrey & Pullen (2001) 92 Cal. App. 4th 1435, 1444, 112 Cal. Rptr. 2d 657] ["where an 'outside' or 'independent' accountant prepares as well as audits a corporation's financial records it is liable for negligent misrepresentation to those third parties who reasonably and foreseeably relied on the financial records, the audit, or both"].)

Accordingly, we decline to hold, at this stage of the litigation, that, as a matter of law, the Rating Agencies owed no duty to CalPERS with respect to the ratings under California law. (Bily, supra, 3 Cal. 4th at p. 408, 11 Cal. Rptr. 2d 51, 834 P.2d 745.)

4. Did CalPERS actually and justifiably rely on the SIV ratings?

We now address the fourth element of the negligent misrepresentation tort — to wit, whether CalPERS actually and justifiably relied on the ratings when purchasing the SIVs. . . .

A. Actual Reliance.

To make a prima facie showing of actual reliance, CalPERS offered declarations from several witnesses. . . . [The witnesses stated that CalPER's investment guidelines limited the purchase of SIVs to those with high credit ratings, testimony that the Rating Agencies challenged as inadmissible and inconclusive.]

. . . However, whatever the merits of the Rating Agencies' arguments, CalPERS's evidence of actual reliance is, at a minimum, sufficient to make a prima facie case that it would not have invested in the SIVs if the representations reflected in the ratings had not been made.

B. Justifiable Reliance.

"Besides actual reliance, a plaintiff must also show 'justifiable' reliance, i.e., circumstances were such to make it reasonable for the plaintiff to accept the defendant's statements without an independent inquiry or investigation. The reasonableness of the plaintiff's reliance is judged by reference to the plaintiff's knowledge and experience. Except in the rare case where the undisputed facts leave no room for a reasonable difference of opinion, the question of whether a plaintiff's reliance is reasonable is a question of fact." OCM Principal Opportunities Fund, L.P. v. CIBC World Markets Corp. (2007) 157 Cal. App. 4th 835, 864-865, 68 Cal. Rptr. 3d 828.

In disputing that CalPERS has made a prima facie showing of justifiable reliance, the Rating Agencies rely on the comprehensive disclaimers of liability accompanying their ratings. . . .

While the language in these disclaimers may indeed be comprehensive, as CalPERS points out, it does not speak to the allegations at hand: mainly, that the Rating Agencies promulgated ratings despite lacking a reasonable basis to believe in the ratings' accuracy. We agree. Indeed, the law is clear that, generally speaking, "'[a] plaintiff will be denied recovery only if his conduct is manifestly unreasonable in the light of his own intelligence or information. It must appear that he put faith in representations that were 'preposterous' or 'shown by facts within his observation to be so patently and obviously false that he must have closed his eyes to avoid discovery of the truth.' Even in case of a mere negligent misrepresentation, a plaintiff is not barred unless his conduct, in the light of his own information and intelligence, is preposterous and irrational. The effectiveness of disclaimers is assessed in light of these principles." (OCM Principal, supra, 157 Cal. App. 4th at p. 865, 68 Cal. Rptr. 3d 828.) In this case, the presence of certain disclaimers does not necessarily render CalPERS's investment decisions preposterous or irrational.

The Rating Agencies also make much of CalPERS's high level of market sophistication in arguing their reliance was unjustified. However, CalPERS's sophistication, on our record, does not preclude a finding of justifiable reliance. CalPERS has presented evidence that the SIV market existed in a "shroud of secrecy" and very few persons, even within the Rating Agencies themselves, were privy to the SIVs' composition. As such, it is hardly surprising the relevant investor class may have significantly relied on the ratings.

Accordingly, for the reasons stated, we affirm the trial court's finding that a prima facie case of reliance exists on this record.

Disposition

The trial court's order . . . is affirmed in full. The parties shall bear their own costs on appeal.

McGuiness, P.J., and Siggins, J., concurred.

Is the result in *CalPERS* supported by the Third Restatement's scienter provision which states that "[a] misrepresentation is fraudulent if the maker of it . . . knows that he does not have the confidence in the accuracy of his representation that he states or implies"? Restatement (Third) of Torts Liability for Economic Harms §13 (Am. Law Inst., Tentative Draft No. 1, 2012). Or perhaps the new Restatement's provision on liability for misrepresentation of opinion, which permits liability not only for cases in which "the parties are in a fiduciary or confidential relationship," but also when "the defendant claims to have expertise or other knowledge not accessible to the plaintiff, and offers the opinion to provide a basis for reliance by the plaintiff"? Restatement (Third) of Torts Liability for Economic Harms §14 (Am. Law Inst., Tentative Draft No. 1, 2012).

Of considerable interest to the legal profession is the extent to which lawyers may be liable for misrepresentation to persons other than their clients. Two federal district court cases took opposite positions as to whether New York law under *Credit Alliance* would impose third-person liability on lawyers. The court in Crossland Savings FSB v. Rockwood Insurance Co., 692 F. Supp. 1510 (S.D.N.Y. 1988), held that *Credit Alliance* applies only to accountants, and so refused to impose liability for negligent misrepresentation against an attorney in favor of one with whom the attorney was not in a contractual relationship. A different judge in the same federal district held in Vereins-Und Westbank, AG v. Carter, 691 F. Supp. 704 (S.D.N.Y. 1988), that *Credit Alliance* does apply to attorneys. Which of the two federal district judges is correct as to the liability of lawyers in New York may be unresolved, but it is clear that the Court of Appeals of New York will apply *Credit Alliance* to others besides accountants. See *Ossining Union Free School District*, cited above.

The failure of large numbers of federally insured savings and loan associations (S&Ls) in the 1980s and 1990s resulted in a search for sources of compensation for the consequent losses that has focused on lawyers. One law firm agreed to a fine of $41 million for its misconduct in connection with the failure of one S&L. In general, see Donald C. Langevoort, Where Were the Lawyers? A Behavioral Inquiry into Lawyers' Responsibility for Clients' Fraud, 46 Vand. L. Rev. 75 (1993); Symposium, 66 S. Cal. L. Rev. 985 (1993). The liability of lawyers to third persons for negligent misrepresentations in securities matters is discussed in Stuart Cohn, Securities Counseling for New and Developing Companies, ch. 20.11 (1993).

As a general rule, a defendant's liability for intentional misrepresentation extends only to those victims the defendant intended to, or had reason to foresee would, rely on the misrepresentation. See Restatement (Second) of Torts §531; Bily v. Arthur Young & Co., cited above. Liability for innocent misrepresentation is limited under §552C to sale, rental, and exchange transactions, and applies only when the defendant made a representation "of material fact for the purpose of inducing the other to act or to refrain from acting in reliance on it," and the other justifiably relied on the representation.

B. *Interference with Business Relations*

1. Intentional Interference with Contractual Relations

Wilkinson v. Powe

300 Mich. 275, 1 N.W.2d 539 (1942)

Bushnell, J. Plaintiff Jay D. Wilkinson brought this action against defendants Powe and Stinson, individually and doing business as Shamrock Creamery, charging them with wrongfully procuring a breach of plaintiff's contract with certain farmers to haul their milk.

In 1932 plaintiff and his father, David Wilkinson, began to haul milk for farmers to the Oakland Creamery and built up their first milk route. Later, they ceased to deliver milk to the Oakland Creamery and began to deliver to the Shamrock Creamery. The Wilkinsons developed a second milk route in 1934 or 1935. A written agreement covering the year 1937 was entered into between the Wilkinsons and the farmers on their milk routes in December of 1936. The Wilkinsons agreed to haul milk to Pontiac creameries and the farmers agreed to pay them 25 cents per hundred. Prior to 1937, the arrangement between the Wilkinsons and the farmers was not evidenced by a written contract. The principal and heavier route was 97 miles and the other 94 miles. In April of 1937, David H. Wilkinson assigned all of his interest in the milk routes to plaintiff Jay D. Wilkinson.

Shortly after the execution of the written agreement, defendant Powe told the Wilkinsons that he wanted to take over the larger route and offered in exchange for the route the trade-in value of plaintiff's old truck, and told plaintiff he would give him a job in the creamery. Plaintiff then informed Powe of the existence of the written contract and refused to give up the route. About three months later Powe informed plaintiff that he would be required to replace the open stake racks on his trucks with insulated bodies because of a municipal ordinance. After plaintiff made this change in his trucks, he was unable to get his trucks into the creamery and the milk had to be handled by hand. This led to friction between the parties.

On May 29, 1937, defendant Powe sent a letter to the farmers doing business with plaintiff, worded as follows:

> For reasons which are vital to our business, we the Shamrock Creamery, have decided that on and after June 1st, we will purchase no milk except that which is picked up by our own trucks at the farm.
>
> Nothing on your part has occasioned or made necessary this change, and we are hopeful that you will continue to sell us your milk. Pursuant to the change made, our trucks will call at your place Tuesday afternoon, June 1st, to pick up your milk, if you desire to continue business with us.
>
> Trusting that our business relationship may continue and be of mutual benefit, I am,
>
> Yours very truly
> (Signed) *T. M. Powe*,
> Shamrock Creamery

The particular season of the year in which the letter was written was described by a witness as being the "lush" season for milk when the available supply is about double that of other months of the year. This letter resulted in a meeting of some of the farmers to consider the situation. As a result of the request made by some of these farmers at the meeting, defendants sent out a notice dated June 1, 1937, reading:

> We have agreed to let Jay D. Wilkinson's trucks continue to haul the milk they have been hauling to our milk plant for the first 10 days of June, 1937. Disregard the notices you received today May 31st until June 11th.

On June 10th, Powe wrote a letter to Wilkinson in which he said:

> We have caused to be served on all farmers affected by the same a duplicate of the attached letter. Due to a verbal agreement made in consideration of the wish of some of those affected the date stated was extended to June 11, 1937.
>
> Since we understand that you have a contract of some nature with many of the farmers in question we are inclosing a copy of said letter, so that you may govern yourself accordingly.

Wilkinson was unable to find another suitable market for milk after June 10th and was soon forced to abandon his routes. Defendants have since hauled the milk of practically all the farmers formerly under contract with plaintiff.

Plaintiff alleged in his declaration that defendants' object was to prevent him from protecting the farmers on his routes from false, fraudulent, and dishonest practices in the testing, weighing and price paid for milk. This was denied by defendants. They claimed their reason for deciding to haul the milk was that plaintiff failed to deliver the milk on time or in a proper condition, and that the action was taken to protect themselves and their customers by insuring a steady supply of good cream and wholesome milk. The testimony is in conflict on this point; but since the jury found for plaintiff, it must be assumed that they resolved this question against the defendants.

Plaintiff claimed damages in the sum of $5,000, and testified that each of his routes had a value of $2,000. The jury returned a verdict in the sum of $4,000. On a former trial by jury, a verdict of $5,000 was rendered and judgment entered thereon. Subsequently a new trial was granted. On this, the second trial, decision on a motion for directed verdict having been reserved, the trial judge entered a judgment for no cause of action. . . .

The crux of the [trial] court's opinion is expressed as follows:

> A factual situation justifying the submission of the issue to a jury for the assessment of the damages is not present. The jury verdict must be predicated upon a circumstance which does not take into consideration the defendants' right to discontinue its source of supply at any time. To find for the plaintiff is a sympathetic attempt to give legal security to one, who, in a precarious position, acted unwisely. . . . Without their acceptance (defendants) of the product the routes had no value. Lawful action, not unlawful action, then eliminated any value the routes may have had.

If the trial court is to be sustained, the judgment must stand on one of two grounds; first, that, in procuring the breach of contract, defendants were exercising what is often designated as a "superior" or "absolute" right, i.e., to refuse to accept further delivery of milk from plaintiff and, therefore, no justification was necessary; or second, that the injury, if any, was the result of defendants' refusal to accept deliveries of milk from plaintiff, and the breach of contract by the farmers was not the proximate cause of plaintiff's injury. [The court approves the principle laid down in Lumley v. Gye, below.] . . .

If the defendants in the instant case had merely refused to accept further delivery of milk by plaintiff, they would have been clearly within their legal rights, although this would have resulted in a breach of contract between plaintiff and the farmers. But defendants did more. Their letters of May 29th and June 1st show active solicitation of a breach of the contract and their refusal to accept delivery of milk was merely another step in bringing about the breach.

Almost analogous facts, so far as the principle is concerned, are found in Knickerbocker Ice Co. v. Gardiner Dairy Co., 107 Md. 556 (69 Atl. 405, 16 L.R.A. [N. S.] 746). In the *Gardiner* case, plaintiff Gardiner Company was engaged in the dairy business and required a large quantity of ice during the spring and summer months. In order to meet its requirements, it entered into a contract with the Sumwalt Company to deliver not exceeding 20 tons of ice a day until the completion of plaintiff's plant, then in the course of construction, at a price of $5 per ton, delivered. Sumwalt at the time was purchasing ice in large quantities from the defendant, Knickerbocker Ice Company, and when defendant learned of the contract between Gardiner and Sumwalt, it notified Sumwalt that it would refuse to deliver any ice whatever to it unless it refrained from delivering ice to Gardiner. Being compelled by the exigencies of its business to secure ice from Knickerbocker, and alarmed by the threat, Sumwalt breached its contract with Gardiner and advised it that this was done because of the action of Knickerbocker. Gardiner was thereby compelled to purchase ice directly from Knickerbocker at a price considerably greater and on less advantageous terms. The court discussed Lumley v. Gye, below, and other authorities, and held that (p. 567):

> If the Knickerbocker company had simply refused to furnish the Sumwalt company with ice, the Gardiner company would not, for that reason alone, have a remedy against the Knickerbocker company. Such action would not necessarily be unlawful or wrongful, but, if the Knickerbocker company refused to furnish the Sumwalt company if it furnished the

> Gardiner company, although it knew it was under contract to do so, in order to get the business of the Gardiner company for itself on its own terms, then it was unlawful thus to interfere with the contract between the Sumwalt company and the Gardiner company. So, without further pursuing that branch of the case, we are of the opinion that the demurrer was properly overruled, as the declaration stated an actionable wrong, even if there had been no express allegation of malice.

The editor states in the annotations of 16 L.R.A. (N.S.) at page 747, that: "Although the doctrine is denied by some courts, the weight of authority at the present time sustains Knickerbocker Ice Co. v. Gardiner Dairy Co."

Substituting defendant for Knickerbocker, the farmers for Sumwalt, and plaintiff for Gardiner, there is a parallel in principle. Instead of refusing to sell, as in the *Gardiner* case, defendants in the instant case refused to purchase from the farmers unless they broke their contract with plaintiff and thereby brought about the breach.

Defendants' refusal to accept further deliveries of milk by plaintiff was wrongful in the light of the evidence in the instant case because it was done to accomplish an unlawful purpose, i.e., to bring about a breach of contract. It therefore follows that the problem of proximate cause disappears from consideration in the case. Defendants cannot be heard to say that they should not be held liable for the injury caused plaintiff by their unlawful acts merely because they could have caused the same injury by a lawful act.

The right to perform a contract and to reap the profits resulting therefrom, and the right to compel performance by the other party, is generally regarded as a property right. The direct consequence of defendants' acts was to destroy plaintiff's routes, and plaintiff is entitled to recover their value.

That a few of the farmers on the routes had not signed the contracts is beside the point. Plaintiff certainly had an understanding with them, and there is no testimony to show that they would not have continued to employ plaintiff to haul their milk if defendants had not interfered.

The damages allowed by the jury are supported by the testimony. The order for entry of judgment notwithstanding the verdict is vacated and the cause remanded for entry of judgment upon the verdict. Costs to appellant.

Chandler, C.J., and Boyles, North, Starr, Wiest, Butzel, and Sharpe, JJ., concurred.

The most famous decision imposing tort liability upon one who intentionally induces another to breach a contract with a third party is Lumley v. Gye, 2 El. & Bl. 216, 118 Eng. Rep. 749 (Q.B. 1853). The plaintiff had a contract with the singer Johanna Wagner (Richard Wagner's niece) whereby the latter was to perform exclusively for the former during the term of the contract. The defendant, knowing of the contract, "enticed and procured Wagner to refuse to perform" for the plaintiff. The court held that the plaintiff could recover damages for defendant's wrongful interference with the contract.[1] Although at first the doctrine established in Lumley v. Gye was approached somewhat hesitantly by both English and American courts (see William Schofield, The Principle of Lumley v. Gye and Its Application, 2 Harv. L. Rev. 19 (1888)), it is now fully accepted both in England (see, e.g., Thompson v. Deakin, [1952] ch. 646) and in this country (see, e.g., Wilkinson v. Powe, above, and Restatement (Second) of Torts §§766-774A). A broad range of

1. In the equally famous companion case, Lumley v. Wagner, 1 De G.M. & G. 604, 42 Eng. Rep. 687 (1852), the court enjoined Wagner from breaking her agreement not to perform for anyone other than the plaintiff.

contractual relations are protected, including agreements which are unenforceable (see, e.g., F.D. Hill & Co. v. Wallerich, 407 P.2d 956 (Wash. 1965)), or terminable (see, e.g., Hammonds v. Aetna Casualty & Surety Co., 237 F. Supp. 96 (N.D. Ohio 1965)). These elements of unenforceability and terminability may affect the measure of damages to which the plaintiff is entitled, but they do not bar recovery against one who has intentionally interfered with the relationship.

In order to recover in these cases, the plaintiff must show that the defendant's interference with contractual relations was intentional — it is not enough that the defendant acted negligently. See §766(C), Restatement (Second) of Torts. However, even intentional interference will not always, or perhaps even usually, result in liability. Courts require more than mere intentional interference with a contract; rather, the interference must additionally be improper. See, e.g., Safeway Ins. Co. v. Guerrero, 106 P.3d 1020 (Ariz. 2005). Section 766 of the Restatement (Second) adopts the rule that the interference must be improper as well as intentional. According to the comments, both the purpose and the means used are relevant to the issue of whether the actor acted improperly. In addition, §767 lists seven factors to be taken into account in evaluating the defendant's conduct:

(a) the nature of the actor's conduct,
(b) the actor's motive,
(c) the interests of the other with which the actor's conduct interferes,
(d) the interests sought to be advanced by the actor,
(e) the social interests in protecting the freedom of action of the actor and the contractual interests of the other,
(f) the proximity or remoteness of the actor's conduct to the interference and
(g) the relations between the parties.

Where the contract interfered with is found to be against public policy, however, the plaintiff will not be allowed to recover. See Restatement (Second) of Torts §774. Even legitimate contracts may be interfered with without liability, so long as such interference furthers some public interest. Thus in Brimelow v. Casson, [1924] 1 ch. 302, the defendants, representatives of an actors' union, were accused of having interfered with the contractual relationship between the plaintiff, who managed a burlesque troupe known as Wu Tut Tut Revue, and the operators of the various theaters in which the troupe appeared. Evidence showed that the performers in the plaintiff's chorus line were grossly underpaid and as a result had been forced to take up prostitution. The defendants had persuaded the theater owners to refuse to honor their contracts with the plaintiff unless he paid the chorus members higher wages, and as a consequence the troupe's tour through southern England was interrupted. Referring to what the judge on appeal called "the good sense of this tribunal," the plaintiff's complaint was dismissed.

The fact patterns to which these rules have been applied are varied. In Australian Gold, Inc. v. Hatfield, 436 F.3d 1228 (10th Cir. 2006), the plaintiffs sold certain tanning products to various distributors. The contract between the plaintiffs and the distributors prohibited the distributors from reselling the products to anyone who would then sell them over the Internet. One of the distributors sold the products to the defendants, who were using fictitious company names to resell the products on the Internet. The defendants were aware of the contractual restrictions on the resale of the products that prohibited the distributor from selling to them, and were using the fictitious company names to try to evade detection of their wrongful purchasing of the products from the distributor. The plaintiffs sued the defendants for, among other things, interfering with the plaintiffs' contractual arrangement with the distributor. The appeals court upheld a verdict for the plaintiffs for tortious interference with contract.

Courts have also addressed claims of intentional interference with contracts in cases involving solicitation of a party's clients by the party's former employees. In Adler, Barish, Daniels, Levin & Creskoff v. Epstein, 393 A.2d 1175 (Pa. 1978), *cert. denied*, 442 U.S. 907 (1979), the Supreme Court of Pennsylvania upheld an injunction in favor of a law firm against former salaried associates prohibiting them from contacting the law firm's clients in order to induce them to transfer their legal work to the new firm formed by the former associates. The court in Koeppel v. Schroder, 505 N.Y.S.2d 666 (App. Div. 1986), reached a different result, asserting that a client has an absolute right to terminate an existing relationship with an attorney without cause; former partners of a law firm were thus free to use legal and proper means to solicit clients of that firm. To support recovery in such cases, the court stated that there must be a wrongful interference, such as that involving fraud. The court in Fred Siegel Co., L.P.A. v. Arter & Hadden, 707 N.E.2d 853, *reconsideration denied*, 709 N.E.2d 1216 (Ohio 1999), ruled that a violation of the ethical rules relating to solicitation would not in itself be a sufficient basis for characterizing the solicitation of former clients as improper. But the court also concluded that the use of client lists, which are protected as trade secrets, could constitute improper means. In general, see Vincent R. Johnson, Solicitation of Law Firm Clients by Departing Partners and Associates: Tort, Fiduciary, and Disciplinary Liability, 50 U. Pitt. L. Rev. 1 (1988).

Also of interest to the legal profession is Cross v. American Country Insurance Co., 875 F.2d 625 (7th Cir. 1989), which held that a liability insurer wrongfully interfered with an attorney's contingent fee contract by settling directly with the attorney's injured client. The insurer was aware that the attorney represented and had a contract with the injured person.

In a widely publicized case, a Texas jury returned a verdict in favor of Pennzoil based on Texaco's conduct in enticing Getty Oil Co. to back out of a merger agreement with Pennzoil. The appellate court affirmed the verdict for the plaintiff of $7.53 billion in compensatory damages, but reduced the $3 billion punitive damage award to $1 billion in Texaco, Inc. v. Pennzoil Co., 729 S.W.2d 768 (Tex. App. 1987), *cert. dismissed*, 485 U.S. 994 (1988). At the time, Texas law required Texaco to post a bond in the amount of the verdict to appeal the decision. Texaco's unsuccessful challenge to that law is reported at Pennzoil Co. v. Texaco, Inc., 481 U.S. 1 (1987). For a discussion of the *Pennzoil* case from a variety of perspectives, see Symposium, 9 Rev. of Litig. 1 (1990).

Although at-will contracts — those which either party may terminate at any time for any reason — would seem to be among the "prospective contracts" discussed in the next section, some courts have held that interference with such contracts can give rise to a claim for tortious interference with contract. See, e.g., Wesco Autobody Supply, Inc. v. Ernest, 243 P.3d 1069, 1083 (Idaho 2010) ("Liability may arise for tortious interference with a contract even where the contract is terminable at will because, until it has been terminated by one party, the contract is valid and subsisting and a defendant may not improperly interfere with it."); Huff v. Swartz, 606 N.W.2d 461 (Neb. 2000).

As is typical of many areas in which concepts of tort and contract intersect, the damages issue has produced some confusion and controversy in these cases. By and large, a tort, rather than a contract, measure of damages has been accepted. See Restatement (Second) of Torts §774A. Thus, instead of just basing damages on the position the plaintiff would have occupied had the defendant not interfered, courts have allowed successful plaintiffs to recover for all harm proximately resulting from the defendant's conduct. In an appropriate case the plaintiff will be allowed to recover for mental upset and suffering. Section

774A calls for recovery if the harm is "reasonably to be expected to result from the interference." The Oregon Supreme Court in Mooney v. Johnson Cattle Co., Inc., 634 P.2d 1333 (Or. 1981), surveyed the law and adopted a modification of the Restatement rule. (In rejecting the Restatement formulation, the court observed in a footnote that even the Reporters conceded that existing case law did not support recovery.) The court ruled that to recover, the emotional distress "must be a common and predictable result of disrupting the *type* of relationship or transaction rather than a result 'reasonably to be expected' in the particular situation." 634 P.2d at 1338. This rule seems close to the Restatement (Second) of Contracts provision with respect to recovery for emotional harm. Section 353 calls for such recovery in breach of contract cases if the harm is a "particularly likely result" of the breach. Two judges dissented in *Mooney*, arguing that recovery for emotional harm for intentional interference with contract should be treated like any other intentional infliction of such harm, and should be controlled by §46, Restatement (Second) of Torts, discussed in Section D of Chapter 11, above. Punitive damages also may be awarded in appropriate cases. See Duff v. Engelberg, 47 Cal. Rptr. 114 (Cal. Ct. App. 1965); Leigh Furniture & Carpet Co. v. Isom, 657 P.2d 293 (Utah 1982); Annotation, 44 A.L.R.4th 1078 (1986).

In general, see Nili Cohen-Grabelsky, Interference with Contractual Relations and Equitable Doctrines, 45 Mod. L. Rev. 241 (1982); and Fred S. McChesney, Tortious Interference with Contract Versus "Efficient" Breach: Theory and Empirical Evidence, 28 J. Legal Stud. 131 (1999).

In the cases considered so far, the plaintiffs alleged that the defendants deterred third parties from performing their contracts with the plaintiffs. Courts have considered extending the tort in two other contexts:

1. When the plaintiff claims that the defendant has made it more costly for the plaintiff to perform a contract with a third party. In Shafir v. Steele, 727 N.E.2d 1140 (Mass. 2000), the court held that such a claim is maintainable. The court relied on the Restatement (Second) of Torts §766A, which provides for recovery in this type of case.

2. When the plaintiff alleges that the defendant has tortiously interfered with the defendant's own contract. According to Applied Equipment Corp. v. Litton Saudi Arabia Ltd., 869 P.2d 454 (Cal. 1994), a party cannot interfere with its own contract. The court stated that to recognize such a cause of action would be to obliterate the "vital and established distinctions between contract and tort theories of liability by effectively allowing the recovery of tort damages for an ordinary breach of contract." 869 P.2d at 457.

2. Intentional Interference with Prospective Contracts

Tuttle v. Buck

107 Minn. 145, 119 N.W. 946 (1909)

This appeal was from an order overruling a general demurrer to a complaint in which the plaintiff alleged:

That for more than ten years last past he has been and still is a barber by trade, and engaged in business as such in the village of Howard Lake, Minnesota, where he resides, owning and operating a shop for the purpose of his said trade. That until the injury hereinafter complained of his said business was prosperous, and plaintiff was enabled thereby to comfortably maintain himself and family out of the income and profits thereof, and also to save a considerable sum per annum, to wit, about $800. That the defendant, during the period of about twelve months last past, has wrongfully, unlawfully, and maliciously endeavored to destroy plaintiff's said business, and compel plaintiff to abandon the same. That to that end he has persistently and systematically sought, by false and malicious reports and accusations of and concerning the plaintiff, by personally soliciting and urging plaintiff's patrons no longer to employ plaintiff, by threats of his personal displeasure, and by various other unlawful means and devices, to induce, and has thereby induced, many of said patrons to withhold from plaintiff the employment by them formerly given. That defendant is possessed of large means, and is engaged in the business of a banker in said village of Howard Lake, at Dassel, Minnesota, and at divers other places, and is nowise interested in the occupation of a barber; yet in the pursuance of the wicked, malicious, and unlawful purpose aforesaid, and for the sole and only purpose of injuring the trade of the plaintiff, and of accomplishing his purpose and threats of ruining the plaintiff's said business and driving him out of said village, the defendant fitted up and furnished a barber shop in said village for conducting the trade of barbering. That failing to induce any barber to occupy said shop on his own account, though offered at nominal rental, said defendant, with the wrongful and malicious purpose aforesaid, and not otherwise, has during the time herein stated hired two barbers in succession for a stated salary, paid by him, to occupy said shop, and to serve so many of plaintiff's patrons as said defendant has been or may be able by the means aforesaid to direct from plaintiff's shop. That at the present time a barber so employed and paid by the defendant is occupying and nominally conducting the shop thus fitted and furnished by the defendant, without paying any rent therfor, and under an agreement with defendant whereby the income of said shop is required to be paid to defendant, and is so paid in partial return for his wages. That all of said things were and are done by defendant with the sole design of injuring the plaintiff, and of destroying his said business, and not for the purpose of serving any legitimate interest of his own. That by reason of the great wealth and prominence of the defendant, and the personal and financial influence consequent thereon, he has by the means aforesaid, and through other unlawful means and devices by him employed, materially injured the business of the plaintiff, has largely reduced the income and profits thereof, and intends and threatens to destroy the same altogether, to plaintiff's damage in the sum of $10,000.

ELLIOTT, J. (after stating the facts as above).

It has been said that the law deals only with externals, and that a lawful act cannot be made the foundation of an action because it was done with an evil motive. In Allen v. Flood, [1898] A.C. 1, 151, Lord Watson said that, except with regard to crimes, the law does not take into account motives as constituting an element of civil wrong. . . . In Jenkins v. Fowler, 24 Pa. 308, Mr. Justice Black said that "malicious motives make a bad act worse, but they cannot make that wrong which, in its own essence, is lawful." . . .

Such generalizations are of little value in determining concrete cases. They may state the truth, but not the whole truth. Each word and phrase used therein may require definition and limitation. Thus, before we can apply Judge Black's language to a particular case, we must determine what act is "in its own essence lawful." . . . It is not at all correct to say that the motive with which an act is done is always immaterial, providing the act itself is not unlawful. Numerous illustrations of the contrary will be found in the civil as well as the criminal law.

We do not intend to enter upon an elaborate discussion of the subject, or become entangled in the subtleties connected with the words "malice" and "malicious." We are not able to accept without limitations the doctrine above referred to, but at this time content ourselves with a brief reference to some general principles.

It must be remembered that the common law is the result of growth, and that its development has been determined by the social needs of the community which it governs. It is the resultant of conflicting social forces, and those forces which are for the time dominant leave their impress upon the law. It is of judicial origin, and seeks to establish doctrines and rules for the determination, protection, and enforcement of legal rights. Manifestly it must change as society changes and new rights are recognized. To be an efficient instrument, and not a mere abstraction, it must gradually adapt itself to changed conditions. Necessarily its form and substance have been greatly affected by prevalent economic theories.

For generations there has been a practical agreement upon the proposition that competition in trade and business is desirable, and this idea has found expression in the decisions of the courts as well as in statutes. But it has led to grievous and manifold wrongs to individuals, and many courts have manifested an earnest desire to protect the individual from the evils which result from unrestrained business competition. The problem has been to so adjust matters as to preserve the principle of competition and yet guard against its abuse to the unnecessary injury to the individual. So the principle that a man may use his own property according to his own needs and desires, while true in the abstract, is subject to many limitations in the concrete. Men cannot always, in civilized society, be allowed to use their own property as their interests or desires may dictate without reference to the fact that they have neighbors whose rights are as sacred as their own. The existence and well-being of society require that each and every person shall conduct himself consistently with the fact that he is a social and reasonable person. The purpose for which a man is using his own property may thus sometimes determine his rights. . . .

Many of the restrictions which should be recognized and enforced result from a tacit recognition of principles which are not often stated in the decisions in express terms. Sir Frederick Pollock notes that not many years ago it was difficult to find any definite authority for stating as a general proposition of English law that it is wrong to do a wilful wrong to one's neighbor without lawful justification or excuse. But neither is there any express authority for the general proposition that men must perform their contracts. Both principles in this generality of form and conception, are modern and there was a time when neither was true. After developing the idea that law begins, not with authentic general principles, but with the enumeration of particular remedies, the learned writer continues: "If there exists, then, a positive duty to avoid harm, much more must there exist the negative duty of not doing wilful harm, subject, as all general duties must be subject, to the necessary exceptions. The three main heads of duty with which the law of torts is concerned, namely, to abstain from wilful injury, to respect the property of others, and to use due diligence to avoid causing harm to others, are all alike of a comprehensive nature." Pollock, Torts (8th ed.), p. 21. He then quotes with approval the statement of Lord Bowen that "at common law there was a cause of action whenever one person did damage to another, wilfully and intentionally, without just cause or excuse." . . .

It is freely conceded that there are many decisions contrary to this view; but, when carried to the extent contended for by the appellant, we think they are unsafe, unsound, and illy adapted to modern conditions. To divert to one's self the customers of a business rival by the offer of goods at lower prices is in general a legitimate mode of serving one's own interest, and justifiable as fair competition. But when a man starts an opposition place of business, not for the sake of profit to himself, but regardless of loss to himself, and for the sole purpose of driving his competitor out of business, and with the intention of himself retiring upon the accomplishment of his malevolent purpose, he is guilty of a wanton wrong and an actionable tort. In such a case he would not be exercising his legal right, or doing an act which can be judged separately from the motive which actuated him. To call such conduct competition is a perversion of terms. It is simply the application of force without legal justification, which in its moral quality may be no better than highway robbery.

Nevertheless, in the opinion of the writer this complaint is insufficient. It is not claimed that it states a cause of action for slander. No question of conspiracy or combination is involved. Stripped of the adjectives and the statement that what was done was for the sole purpose of injuring the plaintiff, and not for the purpose of serving a legitimate purpose of the defendant, the complaint states facts which in themselves amount only to an ordinary everyday business transaction. There is no allegation that the defendant was intentionally running the business at a financial loss to himself, or that after driving the plaintiff out of business the defendant closed up or intended to close up his shop. From all that appears from the complaint he may have opened the barber shop, energetically sought business from his acquaintances and the customers of the plaintiff, and as a result of his enterprise and command of capital obtained it, with the result that the plaintiff, from want of capital, acquaintance, or enterprise, was unable to stand the competition and was thus driven out of business. The facts thus alleged do not, in my opinion, in themselves, without reference to the way in which they are characterized by the pleader, tend to show a malicious and wanton wrong to the plaintiff.

A majority of the justices, however, are of the opinion that, on the principle declared in the foregoing opinion, the complaint states a cause of action, and the order is therefore affirmed.

Affirmed.

JAGGARD, J., dissents.

The court in Katz v. Kapper, 44 P.2d 1060 (Cal. Ct. App. 1935), was considerably less sympathetic to the plaintiff than was the court in *Tuttle*. In *Katz*, the plaintiff and the defendants were rivals in the wholesale fish business in Los Angeles. The complaint alleged that the defendants, with the "sole intention" of putting the plaintiff out of business, threatened customers of the plaintiff that if they continued to buy fish from the plaintiff, the defendants would open a retail store and sell fish at prices so low that the customers would be driven out of business. The complaint further alleged that the defendants did open a retail store and sold at lower than wholesale prices, resulting in many customers shifting their purchases from the plaintiff to the defendants. In affirming the order sustaining the defendants' demurrer to the complaint, the court stated (44 P.2d at 1062):

> The defendants are not charged with making any effort to deprive plaintiff of his trade except by transferring the same to themselves. This is essentially business competition. The defendants did or threatened to do nothing other than to gain a business advantage proportionate to the losses sustained by plaintiff, and by the accomplishment of that end their purposes would have been satisfied. It cannot be said that the methods used by the defendants were unlawful. They threatened plaintiff's customers with the ruination of their businesses if they continued to trade with plaintiff, but a threat is not unlawful if it is to do a lawful thing. . . .
>
> The fact that the methods used [by defendants] were ruthless, or unfair, in a moral sense, does not stamp them as illegal. It has never been regarded as the duty or province of the courts to regulate practices in the business world beyond the point of applying legal or equitable remedies in cases involving acts of oppression or deceit which are unlawful. . . . The demurrer to the complaint was properly sustained.

Wal-Mart Stores, Inc. v. Sturges

44 Tex. Sup. Ct. J. 486, 52 S.W.3d 711 (Tex. 2001)

Justice Hecht delivered the opinion of the Court.

Texas, like most states, has long recognized a tort cause of action for interference with a prospective contractual or business relation even though the core concept of liability— what conduct is prohibited—has never been clearly defined. Texas courts have variously stated that a defendant may be liable for conduct that is "wrongful," "malicious," "improper," of "no useful purpose," "below the behavior of fair men similarly situated," or done "with the purpose of harming the plaintiff," but not for conduct that is "competitive," "privileged," or "justified," even if intended to harm the plaintiff. Repetition of these abstractions in the case law has not imbued them with content or made them more useful, and tensions among them, which exist not only in Texas law but American law generally, have for decades been the subject of considerable critical commentary.

This case affords us the opportunity to bring a measure of clarity to this body of law. From the history of the tort in Texas and elsewhere, and from the scholarly efforts to analyze its boundaries, we conclude that to establish liability for interference with a prospective contractual or business relation the plaintiff must prove that it was harmed by the defendant's conduct that was either independently tortious or unlawful. By "independently tortious" we mean conduct that would violate some other recognized tort duty. We must explain this at greater length, but by way of example, a defendant who threatened a customer with bodily harm if he did business with the plaintiff would be liable for interference because his conduct toward the customer—assault—was independently tortious, while a defendant who competed legally for the customer's business would not be liable for interference. Thus defined, an action for interference with a prospective contractual or business relation provides a remedy for injurious conduct that other tort actions might not reach (in the example above, the plaintiff could not sue for assault), but only for conduct that is already recognized to be wrongful under the common law or by statute.

Because the defendant's conduct in this case was not independently tortious or unlawful . . . we reverse the court of appeals' judgment and render judgment for the defendant.

I

[The plaintiffs had contracted to purchase a vacant lot—"Tract 2"—next to a Wal-Mart store. The plaintiffs then entered into negotiations to lease the lot to Fleming Foods, a Texas grocery chain. Wal-Mart management decided that it would like to acquire Tract 2 for the purpose of expanding its existing store. Wal-Mart informed Fleming by telephone of its desire to acquire Tract 2, and failing that it would close its existing store and relocate elsewhere. Fleming then ended its negotiations with the plaintiffs—it did not want to build a store on Tract 2 if Wal-Mart relocated.]

The plaintiffs sued Wal-Mart for tortiously interfering with their prospective lease with Fleming. . . . The plaintiffs' actual damages claim . . . was . . . the profits the plaintiffs would have made on the Fleming lease. The jury found Wal-Mart liable. . . . [T]he district court submitted to the jury two questions with accompanying instructions as follows:

> Did Wal-Mart wrongfully interfere with Plaintiffs' prospective contractual agreement to lease the property to Fleming?

> Wrongful interference occurred if (a) there was a reasonable probability that Plaintiffs would have entered into the contractual relation, and (b) Wal-Mart intentionally prevented the contractual relation from occurring with the purpose of harming Plaintiffs.
>
> Was Wal-Mart's intentional interference with Plaintiffs' prospective lease agreement with Fleming justified?
>
> An interference is "justified" if a party possesses an interest in the subject matter equal or superior to that of the other party, or if it results from the good faith exercise of a party's rights, or the good faith exercise of a party's mistaken belief of its rights.

The jury answered "yes" to the first question and "no" to the second. Wal-Mart offered no objection to this part of the jury charge that is relevant to our consideration of the case. The jury assessed $1 million actual damages [and] assessed $500,000 punitive damages. . . . [T]he trial court rendered judgment on the interference claim, awarding actual and punitive damages. . . .

. . . The court of appeals affirmed the award of actual damages but remanded for a retrial of punitive damages. . . .

We granted Wal-Mart's petition for review.

II

Wal-Mart argues that there is no evidence to support the jury's verdict that it wrongfully interfered with the plaintiffs' prospective lease with Fleming or that it was not justified in acting as it did. Our analysis of these arguments is complicated because it must be made in light of the jury charge that the district court gave without objection, even though, as we conclude, the charge's statement of the law was not entirely correct. We will focus on Wal-Mart's argument that there is no evidence of wrongful interference: that is, in the language of the jury charge, no evidence that Wal-Mart acted "with the purpose of harming Plaintiffs." To resolve this issue, we must understand what kind of conduct is legally harmful and constitutes tortious interference. Whenever two competitors vie for the same business advantage, as Wal-Mart and Sturges did over the acquisition of Tract 2, one's success over the other can almost always be said to harm the other. Wal-Mart's evidentiary challenge here raises the question of what harm must be proved to constitute tortious interference. To answer this question, we look to the historical development of the interference torts in other jurisdictions and in Texas and survey every Texas case involving a claim of intentional interference with prospective relations. We then analyze the evidence in this case.

[The court's comprehensive discussion of the law in general, and of Texas law in particular, is omitted.]

We therefore hold that to recover for tortious interference with a prospective business relation a plaintiff must prove that the defendant's conduct was independently tortious or wrongful. By independently tortious we do not mean that the plaintiff must be able to prove an independent tort. Rather, we mean only that the plaintiff must prove that the defendant's conduct would be actionable under a recognized tort. Thus, for example, a plaintiff may recover for tortious interference from a defendant who makes fraudulent statements about the plaintiff to a third person without proving that the third person was actually defrauded. If, on the other hand, the defendant's statements are not intended to deceive, . . . then they are not actionable. Likewise, a plaintiff may recover for tortious interference from a defendant who threatens a person with physical harm if he does business with the plaintiff. The plaintiff need prove only that the defendant's conduct toward the prospective customer would constitute assault. Also, a plaintiff could recover for tortious interference by showing an illegal boycott, although a plaintiff could not recover against a defendant whose persuasion of others not to deal with the plaintiff was lawful. Conduct that is merely "sharp" or unfair is not actionable and cannot be the basis for an action for tortious interference with prospective relations, and we disapprove of cases that suggest the contrary. These examples are not exhaustive, but they illustrate what conduct can constitute tortious interference with prospective relations.

The concepts of justification and privilege are subsumed in the plaintiff's proof, except insofar as they may be defenses to the wrongfulness of the alleged conduct. For example, a statement made against the plaintiff, though defamatory, may be protected by a complete or qualified privilege. Justification and privilege are defenses in a claim for tortious interference with prospective relations only to the extent that they are defenses to the independent tortiousness of the defendant's conduct. Otherwise, the plaintiff need not prove that the defendant's conduct was not justified or privileged, nor can a defendant assert such defenses.

In reaching this conclusion we treat tortious interference with prospective business relations differently than tortious interference with contract. It makes sense to require a defendant who induces a breach of contract to show some justification or privilege for depriving another of benefits to which the agreement entitled him. But when two parties are competing for interests to which neither is entitled, then neither can be said to be more justified or privileged in his pursuit. If the conduct of each is lawful, neither should be heard to complain that mere unfairness is actionable. Justification and privilege are not useful concepts in assessing interference with prospective relations, as they are in assessing interference with an existing contract.

III

With this understanding of what conduct is prohibited by the tort of interference with prospective contractual or business relations and what conduct is not prohibited, we return to the evidence of this case. As we have already noted, we must assess Wal-Mart's argument that no evidence supports a finding of wrongful interference with the plaintiffs' prospective agreement with Fleming Foods in light of the jury charge to which Wal-Mart did not object, even though the charge does not correctly state the law. We must therefore consider whether the plaintiffs offered any evidence from which the jury could find, as the trial court instructed them, that Wal-Mart acted "with the purpose of harming Plaintiffs." As we have shown, however, harm that results only from lawful competition is not compensable by the interference tort. We must look to see whether there is evidence of harm from some independently tortious or unlawful activity by Wal-Mart.

The plaintiffs tell us that their interference claim is based on the telephone conversation between Hudson, Wal-Mart's realtor, and Callaway, Fleming's manager of store development. Specifically, the plaintiffs complain of Hudson's "ultimatum" to Callaway that if Wal-Mart were not able to acquire Tract 2 for expansion, it would relocate its store. The plaintiffs contend that Hudson's statement was false and therefore fraudulent. To be fraudulent a statement must be material and false, the speaker must have known it was false or acted recklessly without regard to its falsity, the speaker must have intended that the statement be acted on, and hearer must have relied on it. The plaintiffs do not dispute that Wal-Mart had undertaken to identify stores which could not be expanded and to relocate them, that it attempted to acquire Tract 2 as an alternative to relocating the Nederland store, and that as Hudson told Callaway, if Wal-Mart could not acquire Tract 2 it would relocate. The only evidence the plaintiffs cite in support of their contention is that at the time Hudson called Callaway Wal-Mart had not begun efforts to relocate; that as a general matter Wal-Mart preferred to expand rather than relocate; and that there was room on Tract 1 for some expansion of the store. The fact that Wal-Mart had not begun to relocate its store when Hudson talked with Callaway is no evidence that his statement was false. The plaintiffs point to no evidence that Wal-Mart's general preference for expansion over relocation, or the possibilities for some expansion on Tract 1 [which was adjacent to the Wal-Mart store, and on which Wal-Mart had a lease for the development of the store], would have made it decide not to relocate. Indeed, if Tract 1 had been adequate for Wal-Mart's intended expansion, it would not have needed to acquire Tract 2.

Thus, no evidence supports the plaintiffs' contention that Hudson's statement to Callaway was fraudulent or that Hudson intended to deceive Callaway, and the plaintiffs do not contend that Wal-Mart's conduct was otherwise illegal or tortious. The record contains no evidence to indicate that Wal-Mart intended the plaintiffs any harm other than what they would necessarily suffer by Wal-Mart's successful acquisition of Tract 2, which they were both pursuing, by entirely lawful means. We therefore conclude that there is no evidence to support a judgment for the plaintiffs on their interference claim. . . .

For the reasons we have explained, we reverse the judgment of the court of appeals and render judgment that the plaintiffs take nothing.

[The concurring opinion of JUSTICE O'NEILL is omitted.]

In general, courts have been less willing to protect interests in prospective business relations than they have been to protect interests in existing contracts. See, e.g., Carvel Corp. v. Noonan, 818 N.E.2d 1100 (N.Y. 2004); Guard-Life Corp. v. S. Parker Hardware Mfg. Corp., 406 N.E.2d 445 (N.Y. 1980). However, the structure of the Restatement (Second) of Torts with respect to the former is similar to that with respect to the latter. Section 766B establishes the basic tort, and provides that one who "intentionally and improperly interferes with another's prospective contractual relation is subject to liability" for the pecuniary loss sustained. Section 767, listing the factors relevant to whether the actor acted improperly, applies to §766B as well as to §766, which deals with existing contracts. In addition, there is a separate §768 applicable only to §766B, which permits interference in a competition context. According to this section, the interference is not improper if "wrongful means" are not used, the interference does not result in an unlawful restraint of trade, and its purpose is in part to advance the actor's interest in competition. The Supreme Court of Utah in Leigh Furniture & Carpet Co. v. Isom, 657 P.2d 293 (Utah 1982), concluded that the Restatement approach is too complex, and established the following as elements of the plaintiff's claim (657 P.2d at 304):

> (1) that the defendant intentionally interfered with plaintiff's existing or potential economic relations,
> (2) for an improper purpose or by improper means,
> (3) causing injury to the plaintiff.

It is not clear how this differs from the Restatement. The court also stated that it would recognize privilege as a defense, although it did not indicate what sort of privilege it had in mind, other than by referring to an earlier case involving a first amendment claim of privilege to engage in a boycott. See Searle v. Johnson, 646 P.2d 682 (Utah 1982). However, in Eldridge v. Johndrow, 345 P.3d 553 (Utah 2015), Utah eliminated improper-purpose liability for tortious interference, meaning that the plaintiff must demonstrate the use of improper means. The court argued that improper-purpose liability created evidentiary problems and provided businesses with inadequate notice of their rights and duties. This holding follows the trend of eliminating or cabining the role of purpose and placing greater weight on wrongful conduct. 345 P.3d at 564.

Nostrame v. Santiago

213 N.J. 109 (2013)

Justice Hoens delivered the opinion of the Court.

This appeal arises from a dispute between two attorneys over their successive representation of a client. Plaintiff Frank J. Nostrame, Esq., alleges that defendant Mazie Slater Katz & Freeman, LLC (Mazie Slater), along with another unidentified person, wrongfully induced his client, defendant Natividad Santiago, to discharge him and to be substituted in his place as her counsel. Plaintiff asserts that defendant Mazie Slater thereby engaged in tortious interference with his contractual relationship with his client, making the law firm liable to him in tort. Plaintiff further argues that because his retainer agreement with Santiago was for a contingent fee, defendant's tortious behavior caused him to sustain a substantial loss that he should be entitled to recover from the law firm.

Defendant Mazie Slater contends that because the client always retained the right to be represented by counsel of her choosing, the law firm was free to discuss her case with her and to undertake her representation in plaintiff's place. Mazie Slater further asserts that plaintiff was fully compensated for his representation because he was reimbursed for the expenses he incurred and was paid a fee, based on quantum meruit, for the services he performed prior to his discharge. . . .

I.

This dispute arises in the context of a motion to dismiss plaintiff's complaint for failure to state a claim upon which relief may be granted. As a result, we derive the facts from plaintiff's complaint and the exchange of correspondence between counsel in connection with the motion to dismiss, and we recite them in the light most favorable to plaintiff.

In October 2006, defendant Natividad Santiago underwent cataract surgery that resulted in a significant injury to her eye. On January 18, 2007, she met with plaintiff to consult with him about the possibility of pursuing a medical malpractice claim that would compensate her for her injuries. Santiago signed a contingent fee agreement in which she retained plaintiff to represent her and she signed authorizations to permit him to obtain copies of her medical records. Plaintiff secured the needed records, engaged in research, and consulted with one or more medical experts. He filed a complaint on Santiago's behalf on May 23, 2007. During this time, Santiago moved to Florida to live with her daughter, Betsy, and plaintiff asserts that he communicated with both of them by telephone to monitor Santiago's medical condition and to keep her apprised of his efforts on her behalf. According to plaintiff, Santiago scheduled an appointment to discuss her case with him on June 1, 2007, and when she failed to appear, he called and spoke with her daughter who could not explain her absence.

That same day, however, plaintiff received a letter from Santiago, dated May 31, 2007, discharging him as her counsel. The letter further instructed plaintiff to turn over Santiago's file to Mazie Slater and requested that plaintiff not contact her because her decision was final. Plaintiff asserts that the letter, which Santiago signed, was drafted by Mazie Slater.

In spite of the direction that he not contact Santiago, plaintiff called and wrote to her, trying to determine why he had been discharged. In a letter, dated June 6, 2007, plaintiff defended his handling of the litigation in response to what he described as Santiago's complaint that he "had done nothing to further [her] case." Santiago forwarded the letter to her new attorney at the Mazie Slater firm, Adam Slater, who directed plaintiff in writing to cease all further contact with Santiago and who demanded that he turn over his file. . . .

Thereafter, Mazie Slater settled Santiago's malpractice suit and filed its motion to discharge plaintiff's lien. Adam Slater certified that a $1,200,000 settlement had been reached which, after payment of expenses, resulted in $358,396.31 in attorneys' fees. The law firm asserted that plaintiff was not entitled to any portion of that fee because he had filed the complaint prematurely and had done little to advance the litigation prior to being discharged. Plaintiff countered with a certification of services describing the work he had performed and asserted that he was entitled to be compensated at an hourly rate equivalent to the one that Slater had used in an earlier filing with the court. At about the same time, plaintiff filed his complaint in this matter, seeking an additional award of damages in the nature of a contingent fee based on his claim that Mazie Slater had tortiously interfered with his contract with defendant Natividad Santiago by inducing her to discharge him.

[The trial court denied defendants' motion to dismiss plaintiff's complaint. The Appellate Division granted defendants' motion for leave to appeal and reversed the order of the trial court and dismissed plaintiff's complaint with prejudice. The New Jersey Supreme Court granted plaintiff's petition for review.]

III.

This appeal requires us to first address whether, and under what circumstances, a discharged attorney might be able to sustain a cause of action sounding in tortious interference against a successor attorney. Our resolution of this question rests on a consideration of fundamental principles governing the attorney-client relationship and traditional concepts of tort and contract.

As we have held, "[a] client is always entitled to be represented by counsel of his own choosing[,]" and an attorney "'may do nothing which restricts the right of the client to repose confidence in any counsel of his choice.'" [citation omitted]. Indeed, the client is free to discharge the attorney at any time, without being subject to suit for breach of contract, because the agreement between an attorney and client is a contract that is terminable at will. . . .

The recognized family of business torts includes both claims for tortious interference with a contract, see Restatement (Second) of Torts §766, and claims for tortious interference with a prospective contractual relationship, see id. §766B. Although plaintiff characterized his claim as sounding in tortious interference with a contract, because the contract between an attorney and client is terminable at will, another attorney's interference with it must technically be analyzed in accordance with the principles governing the latter variety of tort. See id. §766 comment g (explaining that "interest in a contract terminable at will is primarily an interest in future relations between the parties, and . . . is closely analogous to interference with prospective contractual relations").

We need not delve deeply into the differences between the two torts nor need we recite all of the proof elements that are ordinarily required to sustain a cause of action based on either tort because the dispute before us is narrowly circumscribed. Relevant to this appeal, both of these torts have as their focus the means by which one has interfered with the contractual relationship, whether that contractual relationship is existing or prospective. In either circumstance, liability rests upon whether the interfering act is intentional and improper. See, e.g., id. §§766, 766B. . . .

There can be no doubt that inducing another to end a contractual relationship through acts that amount to fraud or defamation would be wrongful. But even in the context of ordinary business competitors, our understanding of wrongfulness has been broadened beyond these traditional categories. Our Appellate Division, for example, has recognized that deceit and misrepresentation can constitute wrongful means. See Shebar v. Sanyo Bus. Sys. Corp., 218 N.J. Super. 111, 118, 526 A.2d 1144 (App. Div.1987) (holding that using deceit to prevent employee from accepting alternate employment while planning to terminate him would be actionable), aff'd, 111 N.J. 276, 544 A.2d 377 (1988). Similarly, our courts have concluded that "violence, fraud, intimidation, misrepresentation, criminal or civil threats, and/or violations of the law" are among the kinds of conduct that would be considered to be "wrongful means." E Z Sockets, Inc. v. Brighton–Best Socket Screw Mfg. Inc., 307 N.J. Super. 546, 559, 704 A.2d 1364 (Ch. Div.1996), aff'd, 307 N.J. Super. 438, 704 A.2d 1309 (App. Div.1997). On the other hand, lesser sorts of behavior have been found to fall short of constituting wrongful means in the ordinary business context. See Ideal Dairy Farms, Inc. v. Farmland Dairy Farms, Inc., 282 N.J. Super. 140, 205-06, 659 A.2d 904 (App. Div.) (holding that "vigorous" solicitation of competitor company's customers was not wrongful), certif. denied, 141 N.J. 99, 660 A.2d 1197 (1995); C.R. Bard, Inc. v. Wordtronics Corp., 235 N.J. Super. 168, 174, 561 A.2d 694 (Law Div.1989) (holding that "sneaky" or "underhanded" acts are not "wrongful means").

The behaviors that have been identified as wrongful means would support a cause of action in general and there is nothing that insulates attorneys from being liable if they use such means in pursuing clients. In the unique context of attorneys, however, there are other acts that could also be considered to be wrongful means. Attorneys are not competitors for business in the ordinary sense of that term or as that term is used in the Restatement. On the contrary, their behavior is governed by our [Rules of Professional Conduct (RPCs)], some of which bear directly on the behavior in which they may and may not engage when seeking to attract clients.

Attorneys may not "make false or misleading communications about the lawyer, the lawyers' services, or any matter in which the lawyer has or seeks a professional involvement." RPC 7.1(a). They may not "create an unjustified expectation about results[,]" RPC 7.1(a)(2), or, except in defined circumstances, compare their services with those of other lawyers, RPC 7.1(a)(3). In advertising their services, attorneys face additional limitations and prohibitions that serve the goal of keeping their communications "predominantly informational." See RPC 7.2.

Attorneys are also bound by ethical strictures in their personal contacts with prospective clients. See RPC 7.3. Communications with prospective clients are generally permitted, see RPC 7.3(a), and plaintiff's argument that they are barred by RPC 4.2 fails to recognize that

RPC 4.2 prohibits communication when the attorney and the client stand in essentially adversarial positions. Although that prohibition is irrelevant to this dispute, in the context of an attorney's communications with prospective clients in general there are many limitations imposed on the content and timing of such contacts. See, e.g., RPC 7.3(b)(1) (prohibiting contact with persons whose physical, mental or emotional state interferes with exercise of judgment); RPC 7.3(b)(3) (prohibiting communications that involve "coercion, duress or harassment"); RPC 7.3(b)(4) (governing timing of contact with victims of mass disasters). Attorneys, moreover, are limited in their communications relating to their fields of practice, designations and certifications, RPC 7.4, and even in their behavior relating to their firm name and letterhead, RPC 7.5.

Unlike the relatively confined circumstances in which, at least under the Restatement, ordinary business competitors would be found to have engaged in improper or wrongful means, our supervisory authority over attorneys, as expressed in the RPCs, creates a further series of limitations that bear upon whether an attorney who approaches a client already represented might be found to have utilized improper or wrongful means. It is not simply that they are prohibited from making statements about another attorney that are defamatory or that amount to fraud. Rather, they may not make misrepresentations, may not use tactics to pressure or harass, may not, except in defined circumstances, make comparisons, may not disparage other attorneys, and may not offer promises about results. Just as Mazie Slater argues that permitting plaintiff's claim to proceed would interfere with Santiago's right to repose confidence in their firm as her attorneys, so, too, must they abide by their ethical obligations lest they do likewise to Santiago's relationship with plaintiff.

Competition among attorneys for clients is a part of the practice of law. Striking the balance between competition that abides within the bounds set forth by the ethical strictures of the RPCs and that which does not requires careful consideration. In the end, a lawyer who improperly or wrongfully interferes with the attorney-client relationship of another will have more to fear than a lawsuit by his predecessor; he or she will likely be in violation of our ethical rules as well.

IV.

With these principles as our guide, we consider the questions presented by this appeal. First, the complaint's assertions that the client failed to appear for a meeting, discharged her attorney, asked that her file be transferred, and directed that the former lawyer not contact her, fall well short of identifying the sort of wrongful means that would give rise to a cognizable claim for tortious interference. Those, however, were the only facts known to plaintiff when he filed his complaint.

Second, even applying the generous standard used in addressing a motion to dismiss for failure to state a claim upon which relief can be granted, this pleading fails. . . . [P]laintiff's complaint asserted merely that he had a contingent fee agreement with a client, that she arranged for a meeting, that she did not appear, and that she thereafter discharged him, asking him to send her file to the lawyers she had retained in his place and directing that he not contact her further. Although plaintiff urges us to glean from that series of events that Mazie Slater induced the client to discharge him, perhaps aided by another unknown person, plaintiff's complaint did not assert, and he cannot point to any fact that suggests, that the means employed were improper or wrongful.

Third, although we are well aware of our admonition . . . that dismissals . . . should ordinarily be without prejudice and that plaintiffs generally should be permitted to file an amended complaint to cure the defects in their pleading, we find no warrant for such relief here. . . . [P]laintiff conceded that he had no further facts to plead, instead filing the complaint in the hope that he could use the tools of discovery to uncover evidence of wrongdoing. In that context, dismissal with prejudice was entirely appropriate lest his former client and her newly-chosen attorney be subjected to a mere fishing expedition, a remedy that would raise the specter of chilling any client's exercise of the free choice to select counsel that we have accorded them. . . .

[B]ecause we recognize that the paramount right to be protected is the right of the client to choose counsel freely, and because we do not intend to countenance litigation between successive counsel that is unsupported by facts known at the time of filing, we direct that any complaint filed in the future based on such a cause of action plead the facts and circumstances that constitute the allegedly wrongful means with specificity and particularity. Because plaintiff's complaint is based on nothing more than his unsupported suspicion that his client would not have discharged him absent some wrongful or improper means, it fails to state a claim upon which relief can be granted.

V.

The judgment of the Appellate Division is affirmed as modified.

Chief Justice Rabner, Justices Lavecchia and Albin, and Judges Rodriguez and Cuff (both temporarily assigned) join in Justice Hoens's Opinion. Justice Patterson did not participate.

For affirmance as modification — Chief Justice Rabner and Justices Lavecchia, Albin, Hoens, Rodriguez (t/a) and Cuff (t/a) — 6.

Opposed — None.

Examples can be cited in which attorney defendants have crossed the line from proper competition to improper conduct, however "improper" is defined. See, e.g., Reeves v. Hanlon, 95 P.3d 513 (Cal. 2004) (upholding judgment against defendant lawyers who, when resigning from plaintiff law firm, improperly induced other at-will employees to quit and work for the defendants' new firm and destroyed or misappropriated information important to the plaintiffs). For more on the special problems that claims for tortious interference with contract present when both parties are attorneys, particularly regarding how recognition of such claims restricts the ability of clients to choose which lawyers should represent them, see Alex B. Long, The Business of Law and Tortious Interference, 36 St. Mary's L.J. 925 (2005).

While most of the intentional interference with a contractual relationship cases involve claims by plaintiffs against their competitors, not all fall into that category. In McGuire v. Tarmac Environmental Co., 293 F.3d 437 (8th Cir. 2002), the plaintiff alleged that the defendants deprived him of the brokerage fee that was due him on a real property sale contract between the defendants. The plaintiff introduced the purchaser and seller of the property, negotiated over the terms, and arranged meetings between them. The purchaser of the property resented the fact that the plaintiff would earn a commission of $250,000 for his role in the transaction. The defendants decided to cut him off from the matter by having the seller first transfer the property to a sister corporation that was not previously involved in the sale, and then have the sister corporation sell the property to the buyer. The court of appeals stated that two questions are significant in determining whether there was intentional interference with contract: "(1) did [defendants] actively and affirmatively take steps to induce the breach; and if so, (2) would the contracts have been performed absent [the] interference?" The court determined that there was sufficient evidence for the jury to have answered yes to these questions, and affirmed the jury's award of both compensatory and punitive damages.

Not all courts require that there be an existing contract to find intentional interference.

Baker v. Dennis Brown Realty, Inc.

121 N.H. 640, 433 A.2d 1271 (1981)

BROCK, J. This case is an action in tort for the intentional interference with a prospective contractual relationship brought by a prospective purchaser of certain real estate against the seller's real estate agent. The Concord District Court . . . found for the plaintiff and entered a judgment of $3,525.29. On the defendant's appeal, we affirm in part.

In June 1978, the plaintiff, Sharon Baker, was seeking to purchase a home in Concord and enlisted the services of Keeler Family Realty. An agent of that firm, Jody Keeler, examined the listings in the Multiple Listing Service and found a home that he thought could be of interest to the plaintiff. Because the defendant, Dennis Brown Realty, Inc., held an exclusive listing authorization from the home's owner, Sarah Landry, the plaintiff's real estate agent contacted the defendant firm to arrange for the plaintiff to be shown the home.

On June 22, 1978, the home was shown to the plaintiff by her own agent and an agent of the defendant firm, Faye Olson. In the event that the plaintiff was to purchase the home, the two real estate agencies involved would share equally in the sales commission under a co-brokerage agreement.

Upon seeing the property, the plaintiff immediately decided that she wished to buy it and offered $26,900, the *full* asking price. The two agents immediately drafted an unconditional purchase and sale agreement, which the plaintiff signed.

At about the same time another agent from the defendant firm, Douglas Bush, arrived on the premises. He informed the plaintiff and her agent that only the full asking price would be acceptable to the seller and asked to see the purchase and sale agreement. After reviewing the document, Mr. Bush insisted that two conditions be added to the agreement; bank financing and the sale of the plaintiff's home. Due to the plaintiff's particular situation, both she and her own agent advised Mr. Bush that these conditions were not necessary because she already had obtained bank financing for up to $33,000. Mr. Bush insisted, however, and she finally acquiesced to his demands.

By this time Faye Olson, the other agent of the defendant firm, had already cancelled other appointments that she had made to show the home. Twenty minutes later, however, Mr. Bush showed the home to his own clients, the Piars. He informed the Piars that there was an outstanding offer for the full asking price, and the Piars then offered $300 more. Mr. Bush then prepared a purchase and sale agreement for the Piars (buyers) to sign. Although he inserted a condition in the offer relating to bank financing, he did not insert a condition for the sale of the Piars home; a term he had insisted be placed in the plaintiff's offer. The Piars' offer and the plaintiff's offer were then communicated to the seller without anyone from the defendant firm notifying the plaintiff that a higher offer had been made for the home. Mr. Bush did not tell the seller about the possibility of obtaining a higher offer from the plaintiff and the seller accepted the Piars' offer. Because the Piars had dealt exclusively with the defendant firm the entire sales commission went to the defendant, and Mr. Bush received 35 per cent of that commission. Even if the plaintiff had made a higher offer and eventually purchased the home, the defendant firm and Mr. Bush would have received a substantially smaller commission due to the co-brokerage agreement.

The plaintiff was ultimately able to purchase a similar property in the same neighborhood, but at a price $3,100 greater than the amount that she had offered to purchase the Landry home. . . .

The defendant first argues that an offer to purchase real estate creates no legally protected interest or right if the offer is in fact not accepted. . . . However, the present action is not on the contract but rather is one in tort for the *intentional* interference with a prospective contractual relationship, . . . an action that has been recognized in this State for some time. . . . See also Hanger One, Inc. v. Davis Associates, Inc., 121 N.H. [586], —, 431 A.2d 792, 794 (1981). "One who, without a privilege to do so, induces or otherwise purposely causes a third person not to . . . enter into or continue a business relation with another is liable to the other for the harm caused thereby." . . .

The trial court, in ruling upon the parties' requests for findings of fact, found facts which clearly support its determination that the defendant's agent "purposely caused" the seller "not to enter into a business relation" with the plaintiff.

Once it has been established that the defendant induced or otherwise caused the seller not to enter into a contract with the plaintiff, a determination must be made as to whether the defendant's action was privileged. "An action for interference with contractual relations cannot succeed . . . where the defendant's actions were justified [or privileged] under the circumstances." Bricker v. Crane, 118 N.H. at 252, 387 A.2d at 323. As the seller's real estate agent, the defendant might have some degree of privilege in situations such as are involved here but certainly not an absolute one that would blanket him in complete immunity. Moreover, the burden is on the defendant to show that his actions were privileged. . . . Here, the trial court, after considering the evidence presented, ruled that the defendants' actions were not privileged. Because there is no transcript of the testimony below, we are in no position to say either that the trial court abused its discretion or that there was insufficient evidence to support its ruling.

Only one issue remains in this case and that is the question whether the damages awarded were speculative.

[The court then ruled that the correct measure of damages is the difference between the price of the home that the plaintiff actually purchased and plaintiff's offer on the home involved in this case.]

. . . It is the defendant's position that this award too is speculative because, had the defendant informed the plaintiff of the second offer on the home, a bidding contest or "auction" would have resulted, and it is impossible to determine where it would have stopped. No doubt there is some truth to this argument, and we cannot say with certainty what the result would have been had the defendant not isolated the plaintiff out of contention for the home. Nevertheless, "'the difficulty of determining the sum which will recompense a person' wronged by another is no reason for not allowing the injured party damages." . . .

Judgment for the plaintiff in the sum of $3,100.

BATCHELDER, J., did not sit; the others concurred.

Cases in which liability has been imposed for interference with prospective relationships have largely been limited to those involving contracts. Other types of expectancies have not received the same degree of legal protection from interference. Thus, in Trautwein v. Harbourt, 123 A.2d 30 (N.J. Super. App. Div.), *cert. denied*, 125 A.2d 233 (N.J. 1956), a plaintiff who complained that he had been willfully and maliciously excluded from a fraternal organization was denied relief as a matter of law. But cf. Deon v. Kirby Lumber Co., 111 So. 55 (La. 1926), in which the court held that the plaintiff's allegation that the defendant had acted maliciously to deprive the plaintiff and his family of the society of their friends and neighbors stated a cause of action under Louisiana law. The only expectancies other than those related to prospective contracts to which the Restatement (Second) of Torts extends legal protection are the interests of a prospective donee in an inheritance or gift. See §774B of the Restatement (Second) of Torts.

Liability for interference with both existing and prospective contracts is discussed in Harvey S. Perlman, Interference with Contract and Other Economic Expectancies: A Clash of Tort and Contract Doctrine, 49 U. Chi. L. Rev. 61 (1982), and William J. Woodward, Contractarians, Community, and the Tort of Interference with Contract, 80 Minn. L. Rev. 1103 (1996).

Chapter 15

Global Dimensions of Tort Law

The conceptual heart of Anglo-American tort law remains very much fixed on the paradigmatic tort of *A* wrongfully injuring *B*. In this simple fact setting, two private individuals residing within the same political community engage in a brief, blunt, and relatively contained encounter. Adjudication of the dispute is simplified because the identity of the parties and the cause and extent of the harm are believed to be clearly identifiable. The encounter typically is thought to pose no spillover effects on other individuals, especially not individuals who reside outside of the state or territory whose courts eventually will adjudicate the dispute. From this perspective, the role of tort law appears relatively circumscribed, existing primarily to deter or provide compensation for the occasional wrongful harms that occur in an otherwise self-regulating sphere of private relations and interactions between individuals in liberal society. To the extent that something more dramatic or broad-sweeping is needed in the way of legal intervention, citizens are expected to direct their concerns to the political branches.

As we have seen throughout this casebook, however, changes in social and economic relations, as well as advances in scientific knowledge and understanding, have strained the classical conception of tort law. For instance, the development of sophisticated epidemiological and toxicological methods of causal inference have led to situations in which courts can know with great certainty that a substance causes harm at an aggregate, population-wide level, but still be quite uncertain whether any particular plaintiff's harm was caused by the substance at issue. Similarly, in *Sindell* and other market share liability cases, pp. 139-144, above, courts faced a situation in which the plaintiffs' harm was known to have been caused by the specific product that all relevant defendants manufactured and sold in a virtually identical form, but in which the plaintiffs still could not identify which *particular* defendant or defendants sold the product to their mothers during pregnancy.

The standard conception also is strained in cases involving indirect harms, such as those that give rise to bystander liability, special instances of recovery for purely economic loss, or liability that extends despite the intervening conduct of other, more culpable actors. In these cases, courts move somewhat beyond the classical framework of legal relations existing solely between two "transacting" individuals, *A* and *B*. Instead, courts find that *A*'s conduct sometimes gives rise to liability to a third person, *C*, even when *A*'s connection to *C* is attenuated or absent altogether. Thus, in *Tarasoff*, p. 279, above, the court found a limited duty owed by psychotherapists to foreseeable victims with whom the psychotherapists had no direct relationship whatsoever. Similarly, in *Herrera*, p. 326, above, the court relied on sociological evidence regarding the correlation between car theft and automobile accidents to impose a legal duty of care on a car dealer whose negligence led to the theft of a vehicle, which in turn led to a harmful accident with a plaintiff who otherwise had no connection to the defendant car dealer. In each of these instances, the courts move beyond a classic *A*-wrongfully-injures-*B* dyadic framework to recognize more complex and interrelated webs of causation and responsibility.

This chapter strains the conceptual heart of tort law even further by asking how far its doctrinal and procedural framework can be "scaled up" to higher geographic and political levels of generality without entertaining insurmountable difficulties. Section A begins by addressing the controversial question of whether and when domestic courts should hear ordinary tort suits brought by foreign plaintiffs premised on conduct or harm that occurs outside the United States. Section B then turns to the Alien Tort Statute, 28 U.S.C. §1350, a statute that grants federal courts limited jurisdiction to hear civil liability claims brought by foreign plaintiffs for a "tort . . . committed in violation of the law of nations or a treaty of the United States." As the reader can see, both Sections A and B remain focused on the adjudication of claims brought by or against private parties; however, the parties involved are more geographically removed than the typical plaintiffs seen in domestic tort suits.

Section C then turns to the context of torts between states or other governmental bodies within a single federal system. By examining early United States Supreme Court cases involving claims of nuisance and other tortious harm between states, the section demonstrates the existence and use of tort principles to adjudicate certain kinds of harms that today are more conventionally addressed by legislation and regulation. Although much of this federal common law of torts has been preempted by modern environmental, health, and safety legislation, the principles remain significant because they establish a background set of rights and responsibilities that states negotiate against as new kinds of harm develop or are recognized, and as states advocate changes to existing forms of legislation and regulation. The early cases also are important because they provide a basis in Section D for understanding the application of tort rules and principles between nations. As will be seen, much of the development of international tort law has been driven by an analogy to the historical invocation of tort principles between states and other subnational governmental bodies. Both Sections C and D therefore invite the reader to ponder what shape tort law has taken — or may yet take — when it is applied between public actors such as cities, states, or nations, as opposed to private actors such as individuals and firms.

Notwithstanding the cases and materials presented in this chapter, it should be emphasized that the role of tort law at present is relatively minor in the overall effort to "regulate" global systems such as international product markets or shared environmental spaces such as the atmosphere or the oceans. Still, if the growth of environmental, health, and safety regulation *within* nations provides any indication of how regulation will develop *between* nations, then there may indeed be an intermediate phase in which tort law is asked to play a prominent role at the global level. If that is the case, then judges, policymakers, and scholars will need to consider carefully what institutions and procedures are used to implement tort law on this broader scale. An organizing theme of this book has been that tort law cannot be fully understood — its potentials and pitfalls properly appreciated — unless one devotes careful attention to process. The materials in this chapter provide perhaps the clearest demonstration of this theme, for in the "scaling up" of tort law's concepts to higher levels of geographic and political abstraction, courts and other adjudicatory bodies invite a range of practical and procedural — not just moral and political — challenges.

A. *The Extraterritorial Reach of Domestic Law*

The U.S. Supreme Court has held that, before a state or federal court may exercise personal jurisdiction over a defendant, the defendant must receive notice, there must be constitutionally sufficient "minimum contacts" between the defendant and the forum in order to satisfy the due process clause, and there must be a statutory grant of authority to the court to exercise jurisdiction. See Asahi Metal Indus. Co. v. Superior Court of California, Solano

County, 480 U.S. 102 (1987); International Shoe Co. v. Washington, 326 U.S. 310 (1945). In the case of a lawsuit seeking recovery in tort against a corporation based on activities that occur abroad, the personal jurisdiction requirements are easily met by bringing suit against the defendant in its state of incorporation or in its state of domicile, which typically is held to be the location of its corporate headquarters. See World-Wide Volkswagen v. Woodson, 444 U.S. 286, 291 (1980); Milliken v. Meyer, 311 U.S. 457, 462 (1940). In such cases, "[a] court may assert general jurisdiction over foreign (sister-state or foreign-country) corporations to hear any and all claims against them when their affiliations with the State are so 'continuous and systematic' as to render them essentially at home in the forum State." Daimler AG v. Bauman, 134 S. Ct. 746, 754 (2014) (quotation and citation omitted). See also Lea Brilmayer, Jennifer Haverkamp & Buck Logan, A General Look at General Jurisdiction, 66 Tex. L. Rev. 721, 728-35 (1988) (noting that domicile, residence, principal place of business, and place of incorporation have traditionally enjoyed special constitutional status as bases for personal jurisdiction).

When general jurisdiction cannot be asserted, plaintiff must demonstrate specific jurisdiction, which in the tort context typically is done through a showing of purposeful availment of the jurisdiction by defendant sufficient to establish that "defendant's activities manifest an intention to submit to the power of a sovereign." J. McIntyre Mach., Ltd. v. Nicastro, 564 U.S. 874, 882 (2011). In a products liability suit, for instance, plaintiff must show that defendant deliberately targeted the jurisdiction in some manner that goes beyond merely placing its goods in the stream of commerce: "The defendant's transmission of goods permits the exercise of jurisdiction only where the defendant can be said to have targeted the forum; as a general rule, it is not enough that the defendant might have predicted that its goods will reach the forum State." Id. at 882 (criticizing the "stream of commerce" metaphor that appeared in *Asahi*).

As the remainder of this section demonstrates, the satisfaction of personal jurisdiction requirements alone does not guarantee that the plaintiff's case will be heard in her forum of choice. In addition to due process limitations, courts have developed a cluster of related doctrines that are designed to allow a court to decline jurisdiction in circumstances where the court finds that adjudication more properly should occur in a different forum. The most important of these doctrines — forum non conveniens — is addressed in the following state law case, while others are addressed in Section B, below, in connection with the federal Alien Tort Statute.

Dow Chemical Co. v. Castro Alfaro

786 S.W.2d 674 (Tex. 1990)

[Plaintiff Domingo Castro Alfaro, a Costa Rican resident and employee of the Standard Fruit Company, and several other Costa Rican employees and their spouses, brought suit against Dow Chemical Company and Shell Oil Company. The plaintiffs alleged that they suffered personal injuries as a result of their exposure to dibromochloropropane (DBCP), a pesticide manufactured by Dow and Shell and used by Standard Fruit, although banned in the United States. The plaintiffs alleged that they suffered various serious medical problems as a result of the exposure, including sterility. A Texas district court dismissed the plaintiffs' complaint, citing the doctrine of forum non conveniens, which affords courts discretion to decline to hear cases in certain circumstances, such as when the plaintiff's selection of forum would work an undue hardship on the defendant or when exercise of jurisdiction would threaten comity between sovereign governments.

In a brief majority opinion, the Texas Supreme Court concluded that, by enacting §71.031 of the Texas Civil Practice and Remedies Code,[1] the state legislature abolished forum non conveniens. Several concurring and dissenting opinions then engage in a much more broad-sweeping and heated exchange regarding the role of tort law in an era of economic globalization. Excerpts from these opinions follow.]

DOGGETT, JUSTICE, concurring.

Because its analysis and reasoning are correct I join in the majority opinion without reservation. I write separately, however, to respond to the dissenters who mask their inability to agree among themselves with competing rhetoric. In their zeal to implement their own preferred social policy that Texas corporations not be held responsible at home for harm caused abroad, these dissenters refuse to be restrained by either express statutory language or the compelling precedent, previously approved by this very court, holding that forum non conveniens does not apply in Texas. To accomplish the desired social engineering, they must invoke yet another legal fiction with a fancy name to shield alleged wrongdoers, the so-called doctrine of forum non conveniens. The refusal of a Texas corporation to confront a Texas judge and jury is to be labeled "inconvenient" when what is really involved is not convenience but connivance to avoid corporate accountability.

The dissenters are insistent that a jury of Texans be denied the opportunity to evaluate the conduct of a Texas corporation concerning decisions it made in Texas because the only ones allegedly hurt are foreigners. Fortunately Texans are not so provincial and narrow-minded as these dissenters presume. Our citizenry recognizes that a wrong does not fade away because its immediate consequences are first felt far away rather than close to home. Never have we been required to forfeit our membership in the human race in order to maintain our proud heritage as citizens of Texas.

The dissenters argue that it is inconvenient and unfair for farmworkers allegedly suffering permanent physical and mental injuries, including irreversible sterility, to seek redress by suing a multinational corporation in a court three blocks away from its world headquarters and another corporation, which operates in Texas this country's largest chemical plant. Because the "doctrine" they advocate has nothing to do with fairness and convenience and everything to do with immunizing multinational corporations from accountability for their alleged torts causing injury abroad, I write separately.

I. The Facts

. . . Shell Oil Company is a multinational corporation with its world headquarters in Houston, Texas. Dow Chemical Company, though headquartered in Midland, Michigan, conducts extensive operations from its Dow Chemical USA building located in Houston. Dow operates this country's largest chemical manufacturing plant within 60 miles of

1. At the time of the *Dow Chemical Company* litigation, §71.031 provided, in relevant part:

> (a) An action for damages for the death or personal injury of a citizen of this state, of the United States, or of a foreign country may be enforced in the courts of this state, although the wrongful act, neglect, or default causing the death or injury takes place in a foreign state or country, if:
>
> (1) a law of the foreign state or country or of this state gives a right to maintain an action for damages for the death or injury;
>
> (2) the action is begun in this state within the time provided by the laws of this state for beginning the action; and
>
> (3) in the case of a citizen of a foreign country, the country has equal treaty rights with the United States on behalf of its citizens. . . . [Eds.]

Houston in Freeport, Texas. The district court where this lawsuit was filed is three blocks away from Shell's world headquarters, One Shell Plaza in downtown Houston.

Shell has stipulated that all of its more than 100,000 documents relating to DBCP are located or will be produced in Houston. Shell's medical and scientific witnesses are in Houston. The majority of Dow's documents and witnesses are located in Michigan, which is far closer to Houston (both in terms of geography and communications linkages) than to Costa Rica. The respondents have agreed to be available in Houston for independent medical examinations, for depositions and for trial. Most of the respondents' treating doctors and co-workers have agreed to testify in Houston. Conversely, Shell and Dow have purportedly refused to make their witnesses available in Costa Rica.

The banana plantation workers allegedly injured by DBCP were employed by an American company on American-owned land and grew Dole bananas for export solely to American tables. The chemical allegedly rendering the workers sterile was researched, formulated, tested, manufactured, labeled and shipped by an American company in the United States to another American company. The decision to manufacture DBCP for distribution and use in the third world was made by these two American companies in their corporate offices in the United States. Yet now Shell and Dow argue that the one part of this equation that should not be American is the legal consequences of their actions.

II. Forum Non Conveniens — A Common Law Doctrine Out of Control

As a reading of Tex. Civ. Prac. & Rem. Code Ann. §71.031 (Vernon 1986) makes clear, the doctrine of forum non conveniens has been statutorily abolished in Texas. The decision in Allen v. Bass, 47 S.W.2d 426 (Tex. Civ. App.–El Paso 1932, writ ref'd), approved by this court, clearly holds that, upon a showing of personal jurisdiction over a defendant, article 4678, now section 71.031 of the Texas Civil Practice & Remedies Code, "opens the courts of this state to citizens of a neighboring state and gives them an absolute right to maintain a transitory action of the present nature and to try their cases in the courts of this state." Id. at 427.

Displeased that *Allen* stands in the way of immunizing multinational corporations from suits seeking redress for their torts causing injury abroad, the dissenters doggedly attempt to circumvent this precedent. Unsuccessful with arguments based upon Texas law, they criticize the court for not justifying its result on public policy grounds.

A. Using the "Doctrine" to Kill the Litigation Altogether

... A forum non conveniens dismissal is often, in reality, a complete victory for the defendant. As noted in Irish Nat'l Ins. Co. v. Aer Lingus Teoranta, 739 F.2d 90, 91 (2d Cir. 1984),

> [i]n some instances, . . . invocation of the doctrine will send the case to a jurisdiction which has imposed such severe monetary limitations on recovery as to eliminate the likelihood that the case will be tried. When it is obvious that this will occur, discussion of convenience of witnesses takes on a Kafkaesque quality — everyone knows that no witnesses ever will be called to testify.

In using the term forum non conveniens, "the courts have taken refuge in a euphemistic vocabulary, one that glosses over the harsh fact that such dismissal is outcome-determination in a high percentage of the forum non conveniens cases. . . ." Robertson,

Forum Non Conveniens in America and England: "A Rather Fantastic Fiction," 103 L.Q. Rev. 398, 409 (1987). Empirical data available demonstrate that less than four percent of cases dismissed under the doctrine of forum non conveniens ever reach trial in a foreign court.[5] A forum non conveniens dismissal usually will end the litigation altogether, effectively excusing any liability of the defendant. The plaintiffs leave the courtroom without having had their case resolved on the merits.[6]

B. The Gulf Oil Factors — Balanced Toward the Defendant

Courts today usually apply forum non conveniens by use of the factors set forth at length in Gulf Oil Corp. v. Gilbert, 330 U.S. 501, 508-09, 67 S. Ct. 839, 843-44, 91 L. Ed. 1055 (1947). Briefly summarized, those factors are (i) the private interests of the litigants (ease and cost of access to documents and witnesses); and (ii) the public interest factors (the interest of the forum state, the burden on the courts, and notions of judicial comity). In the forty-three years in which the courts have grappled with the Gulf Oil factors, it has become increasingly apparent that their application fails to promote fairness and convenience. Instead, these factors have been used by defendants to achieve objectives violative of public policy.

1. *The Obsolete Private Interest Factors*

. . . In his dissent, Justice Gonzalez correctly crystallizes the private interest factors as "those considerations that make the trial of a case relatively easy, expeditious, and inexpensive for the parties." 786 S.W.2d 695. Advances in transportation and communications technology have rendered the private factors largely irrelevant:

> A forum is not necessarily inconvenient because of its distance from pertinent parties or places if it is readily accessible in a few hours of air travel. It will often be quicker and less expensive to transfer a witness or a document than to transfer a lawsuit. Jet travel and satellite communications have significantly altered the meaning of "non conveniens."

5. Professor David Robertson of the University of Texas School of Law attempted to discover the subsequent history of each reported transnational case dismissed under forum non conveniens from Gulf Oil v. Gilbert, 330 U.S. 501, 67 S. Ct. 839, 91 L. Ed. 1055 (1947) to the end of 1984. Data was received on 55 personal injury cases and 30 commercial cases. Of the 55 personal injury cases, only one was actually tried in a foreign court. Only two of the 30 commercial cases reached trial. See Robertson, supra, at 419.

6. Such a result in the name of "convenience" would undoubtedly follow a dismissal under forum non conveniens in the case at bar. The plaintiffs, who earn approximately one dollar per hour working at the banana plantation, clearly cannot compete financially with Shell and Dow in carrying on the litigation. More importantly, the cost of just one trip to Houston to review the documents produced by Shell would exceed the estimated maximum possible recovery in Costa Rica. In an unchallenged affidavit, a senior Costa Rican labor judge stated that the maximum possible recovery in Costa Rica would approximate 100,000 colones, just over $1,080 at current exchange rates. Assuming such a recovery were possible, no lawyer, in Costa Rica or elsewhere, could afford to take such a case — against two giant corporations vigilantly defending themselves in litigation. Further, Costa Rica permits neither jury trials nor depositions of nonparty witnesses. Attempting to depose a Dow representative concerning the company's knowledge of DBCP hazards will prove to be an impossible task as Dow is not required to produce that person in Costa Rica. It is not unlikely that Shell and Dow seek a forum non conveniens dismissal not in pursuit of fairness and convenience, but rather as a shield against the litigation itself. If successful, Shell and Dow, like many American multinational corporations before them, would have secured a largely impenetrable shield against meaningful lawsuits for their alleged torts causing injury abroad.

Calavo Growers of California v. Belgium, 632 F.2d 963, 969 (2d Cir. 1980) (Newman J., concurring). See also McGee v. International Life Ins. Co., 355 U.S. 220, 223, 78 S. Ct. 199, 201, 2 L. Ed. 2d 223 (1957) ("[M]odern transportation and communication have made it much less burdensome for a party sued to defend himself in a State where he engages in economic activity."). . . . In sum, the private factors are no longer a predominant consideration — fairness and convenience to the parties have been thrust out of the forum non conveniens equation. As the "doctrine" is now applied, the term "forum non conveniens" has clearly become a misnomer.

2. *The Public Interest Factors*

The three public interest factors asserted by Justice Gonzalez may be summarized as (1) whether the interests of the jurisdiction are sufficient to justify entertaining the lawsuit; (2) the potential for docket backlog; and (3) judicial comity.

a. The Interest of Texas

The dissenting members of the court falsely attempt to paint a picture of Texas becoming an "irresistable forum for all mass disaster lawsuits," Gonzalez dissent, 786 S.W.2d 690, and for "personal injury cases from around the world," Hecht dissent, 786 S.W.2d 707. They suggest that our citizens will be forced to hear cases in which "[t]he interest of Texas in these disputes is likely to be . . . slight," Cook dissent, 786 S.W.2d 697. Although these suppositions undoubtedly will serve to stir public debate, they have little basis in fact.

The dissenting justices each know that for a Texas jury to hear a case, Texas must obtain in personam jurisdiction over the defendants in question. See Gulf Oil, 330 U.S. at 504, 67 S. Ct. at 841 ("[T]he doctrine of forum non conveniens can never apply if there is an absence of jurisdiction or mistake of venue."). . . . Due process mandates that these requirements be satisfied before a Texas court may assert jurisdiction over a defendant. The personal jurisdiction-due process analysis will ensure that Texas has a sufficient interest in each case entertained in our state's courts.

Specifically, Texas has a substantial interest in the case at bar. As stated previously, this suit has been filed against Shell, a corporation with its world headquarters in Texas, doing extensive business in Texas and manufacturing chemicals in Texas. The suit arose out of alleged acts occurring in Texas and alleged decisions made in Texas. The suit also has been filed against Dow, a corporation with its headquarters in Michigan, but apparently having substantial contacts with Texas. Dow operates the country's largest chemical plant in Texas, manufacturing chemicals within sixty miles of the largest population center in Texas, where millions of Texans reside. Shell and Dow cannot now seek to avoid the Texas civil justice system and a jury of Texans.

b. Docket Backlog

The next justification offered by the dissenters for invoking the legal fiction of "inconvenience" is that judges will be overworked. Not only will foreigners take our jobs, as we are told in the popular press; now they will have our courts. The xenophobic suggestion that foreigners will take over our courts "forcing our residents to wait in the corridors of our courthouses while foreign causes of action are tried," Gonzalez dissent, 786 S.W.2d at 690, is both misleading and false.

It is the height of deception to suggest that docket backlogs in our state's urban centers are caused by so-called "foreign litigation." This assertion is unsubstantiated empirically both in Texas and in other jurisdictions rejecting forum non conveniens. Ten states, including Texas, have not recognized the doctrine. Within these states, there is no evidence that the docket congestion predicted by the dissenters has actually occurred. The best evidence, of course, comes from Texas itself. Although foreign citizens have enjoyed the statutory right to sue defendants living or doing business here since the 1913 enactment of the predecessor to Section 71.031 of the Texas Civil Practice and Remedies Code, reaffirmed in the 1932 decision in *Allen*, Texas has not been flooded by foreign causes of action. . . .

c. Judicial Comity

Comity — deference shown to the interests of the foreign forum — is a consideration best achieved by rejecting forum non conveniens. Comity is not achieved when the United States allows its multinational corporations to adhere to a double standard when operating abroad and subsequently refuses to hold them accountable for those actions. As S. Jacob Scherr, Senior Project Attorney for the Natural Resources Defense Counsel, has noted

> There is a sense of outrage on the part of many poor countries where citizens are the most vulnerable to exports of hazardous drugs, pesticides and food products. At the 1977 meeting of the UNEP Governing Council, Dr. J.C. Kiano, the Kenyan minister for water development, warned that developing nations will no longer tolerate being used as dumping grounds for products that had not been adequately tested "and that their peoples should not be used as guinea pigs for determining the safety of chemicals."

Comment, U.S. Exports Banned For Domestic Use, But Exported to Third World Countries, 6 Int'l Tr. L.J. 95, 98 (1980-81) [hereinafter "U.S. Exports Banned"].

Comity is best achieved by "avoiding the possibility of 'incurring the wrath and distrust of the Third World as it increasingly recognizes that it is being used as the industrial world's garbage can.'" Note, Hazardous Exports from a Human Rights Perspective, 14 Sw. U. L. Rev. 81, 101 (1983) [hereinafter "Hazardous Exports"] (quoting Hon. Michael D. Barnes (Representative in Congress representing Maryland)).[10] . . .

III. Public Policy & the Tort Liability of Multinational Corporations in United States Courts

The abolition of forum non conveniens will further important public policy considerations by providing a check on the conduct of multinational corporations (MNCs). See Economic Approach, 22 Geo. Wash. J. Int'l L. & Econ. at 241. The misconduct of even a few multinational corporations can affect untold millions around the world. For example, after the United States imposed a domestic ban on the sale of cancer-producing TRIS-treated children's sleepwear, American companies exported approximately 2.4 million pieces to Africa, Asia and South America. A similar pattern occurred when a ban was proposed for baby pacifiers that had been linked to choking deaths in infants. Hazardous

10. A senior vice-president of a United States multinational corporation acknowledged that "[t]he realization at corporate headquarters that liability for any [industrial] disaster would be decided in the U.S. courts, more than pressure from Third World governments, has forced companies to tighten safety procedures, upgrade plants, supervise maintenance more closely and educate workers and communities." Wall St. J., Nov. 26, 1985, at 22, col. 4 (quoting Harold Corbett, senior vice-president for environmental affairs at Monsanto Co.).

Exports, supra, 14 Sw. U. L. Rev. at 82. These examples of indifference by some corporations towards children abroad are not unusual.[13]

The allegations against Shell and Dow, if proven true, would not be unique, since production of many chemicals banned for domestic use has thereafter continued for foreign marketing. Professor Thomas McGarity, a respected authority in the field of environmental law, explained:

> During the mid-1970s, the United States Environmental Protection Agency (EPA) began to restrict the use of some pesticides because of their environmental effects, and the Occupational Safety and Health Administration (OSHA) established workplace exposure standards for toxic and hazardous substances in the manufacture of pesticides. . . . [I]t is clear that many pesticides that have been severely restricted in the United States are used without restriction in many Third World countries, with resulting harm to fieldworkers and the global environment.

McGarity, Bhopal and the Export of Hazardous Technologies, 20 Tex. Int'l L.J. 333, 334 (1985) (citations omitted). By 1976, "29 percent, or 161 million pounds, of all the pesticides exported by the United States were either unregistered or banned for domestic use." McWilliams, Tom Sawyer's Apology: A Reevaluation of United States Pesticide Export Policy, 8 Hastings Int'l & Comp. L. Rev. 61, 61 & n. 4 (1984). It is estimated that these pesticides poison 750,000 people in developing countries each year, of which 22,500 die. Id. at 62. Some estimates place the death toll from the "improper marketing of pesticides at 400,000 lives a year." Id. at 62 n. 7.

Some United States multinational corporations will undoubtedly continue to endanger human life and the environment with such activities until the economic consequences of these actions are such that it becomes unprofitable to operate in this manner. At present, the tort laws of many third world countries are not yet developed. . . . When a court dismisses a case against a United States multinational corporation, it often removes the most effective restraint on corporate misconduct. See an Economic Approach, supra, 22 Geo. Wash. J. Int'l L. & Econ. at 241.

The doctrine of forum non conveniens is obsolete in a world in which markets are global and in which ecologists have documented the delicate balance of all life on this planet. The parochial perspective embodied in the doctrine of forum non conveniens enables corporations to evade legal control merely because they are transnational. This perspective ignores the reality that actions of our corporations affecting those abroad will also affect Texans. Although DBCP is banned from use within the United States, it and other similarly banned chemicals have been consumed by Texans eating foods imported from Costa Rica and elsewhere. See D. Weir & M. Schapiro, Circle of Poison 28-30, 77, 82-83 (1981).[15] In the absence of meaningful tort liability in the United States for their actions, some

13. A subsidiary of Sterling Drug Company advertised Winstrol, a synthetic male hormone severely restricted in the United States since it is associated with a number of side effects that the F.D.A. has called "virtually irreversible," in a Brazilian medical journal, picturing a healthy boy and recommending the drug to combat poor appetite, fatigue and weight loss. U.S. Exports Banned, supra, 6 Int'l Tr. L.J. at 96. The same company is said to have marketed Dipyrone, a painkiller causing a fatal blood disease and characterized by the American Medical Association as for use only as "a last resort," as "Novaldin" in the Dominican Republic. "Novaldin" was advertised in the Dominican Republic with pictures of a child smiling about its agreeable taste. Id. at 97. "In 1975, thirteen children in Brazil died after coming into contact with a toxic pesticide whose use had been severely restricted in this country." Hazardous Exports, supra, 14 Sw. U. L. Rev. at 82.

15. Less than one per cent of the imported fruits and vegetables are inspected for pesticides. General Accounting Office, Pesticides: Better Sampling and Enforcement Needed on Imported Food GAO/RCED-86-219 (Sept. 26, 1986), at 3. The GAO found that of the 7.3 billion pounds of bananas imported into the F.D.A.'s Dallas District (covering Texas) from countries other than Mexico in 1984, not a single sample was checked for illegal pesticide residues such as DBCP. Id. at 53. Even when its meager inspection program discovers illegal pesticides, the F.D.A.

multinational corporations will continue to operate without adequate regard for the human and environmental costs of their actions. This result cannot be allowed to repeat itself for decades to come.

As a matter of law and of public policy, the doctrine of forum non conveniens should be abolished. Accordingly, I concur.

PHILLIPS, CHIEF JUSTICE, dissenting.

I respectfully dissent. For the reasons stated in Justice Hecht's dissenting opinion, I would hold that the doctrine of forum non conveniens is not foreclosed by Tex. Civ. Prac. & Rem. Code §71.031. . . . Unlike my fellow dissenters, however, I lack the prescience to foretell whether dire consequences will follow. As the existence or not of forum non conveniens has long been an open question in Texas, our courts have traditionally attracted a number of actions originating in foreign jurisdictions. Today's decision will probably accelerate that trend, but to what extent, and with what effect, I do not know. . . .

GONZALEZ, JUSTICE, dissenting.

Under the guise of statutory construction, the court today abolishes the doctrine of forum non conveniens in suits brought pursuant to section 71.031 of the Civil Practice and Remedies Code. This decision makes us one of the few states in the Union without such a procedural tool, and if the legislature fails to reinstate this doctrine, Texas will become an irresistible forum for all mass disaster lawsuits. See generally, Note, Foreign Plaintiffs and Forum Non Conveniens: Going Beyond Reyno, 64 Tex. L. Rev. 193 (1985). "Bhopal"-type litigation, with little or no connection to Texas will add to our already crowded dockets, forcing our residents to wait in the corridors of our courthouses while foreign causes of action are tried.[2] . . .

[Justice Gonzalez discusses the history of the forum non conveniens doctrine, concluding that the legislature did not intend to abolish the doctrine when it adopted the predecessor statute to section 71.031. In his view, the original intent of the jurisdictional statute was to ensure that Texas citizens have a right to pursue claims in Texas state courts, even when their injury occurs in a foreign nation. It was not, therefore "intended to give citizens of foreign countries an absolute right to maintain suits in Texas or to strip our courts of their equitable common law power to, on occasion and under certain circumstances, dismiss disputes that have only a tenuous connection to Texas."]

In conclusion, I have no intent, much less "zeal" to implement social policy as Justice Doggett charges. That is not our role. It is clear that if anybody is trying to advance a particular social policy, it is Justice Doggett. I admire his altruism, and I too sympathize with the plight of the plaintiffs. However, the powers of this court are well-defined, and the sweeping implementations of social welfare policy Justice Doggett seeks to achieve by abolishing the doctrine of forum non conveniens are the exclusive domain of the legislature.

For all of the above reasons, I dissent.

COOK, JUSTICE, dissenting.

---

rarely sanctions the shipper or producer. Id. at 4. The GAO found only eight instances over a six year period where any punitive action whatsoever was taken. Id. "United States consumers have suffered as pesticide-treated crops are imported to the United States, thus completing a circle of poison." McGarity, supra, 20 Tex.Int'l L.J. at 334. . . .

2. For example, in July 1988, there was an oil rig disaster in Scotland. A Texas lawyer went to Scotland, held a press conference, and wrote letters to victims or their families. He advised them that they had a good chance of trying their cases in Texas where awards would be much higher than elsewhere. Houston Post, July 18, 1988, at 13A, col. 1; The Times (London), July 18, 1988, at 20A, col. 1; Texas Lawyer, Sept. 26, 1988 at 3.

Like turn-of-the-century wildcatters, the plaintiffs in this case searched all across the nation for a place to make their claims. Through three courts they moved, filing their lawsuits on one coast and then on the other. By each of those courts the plaintiffs were rejected, and so they continued their search for a more willing forum. Their efforts are finally rewarded. Today they hit pay dirt in Texas.

No reason exists, in law or in policy, to support their presence in this state. The legislature adopted within the statute the phrase "may be enforced" to permit plaintiffs to sue in Texas, irrespective of where they live or where the cause of action arose. The legislature did not adopt this statute, however, to remove from our courts all discretion to dismiss. To use the statute to sweep away, completely and finally, a common law doctrine painstakingly developed over the years is to infuse the statute with a power not contained in the words. Properly read, the statute is asymmetrical. Although it confers upon the plaintiffs an absolute right to bring claims in our courts, it does not impose upon our courts an absolute responsibility to entertain those claims.

Even if the statute supported the court's interpretation, however, I would remain unwilling to join in the opinion. The decision places too great a burden on defendants who are citizens of our state because, by abolishing forum non conveniens, the decision exposes our citizens to the claims of any plaintiff, no matter how distant from Texas is that plaintiff's home or cause of action. The interest of Texas in these disputes is likely to be as slight as the relationship of the plaintiffs to Texas. The interest of other nations, on the other hand, is likely to be substantial. For these reasons, I fear the decision allows assertions of jurisdiction by Texas courts that are so unfair and unreasonable as to violate the due process clause of the federal constitution. . . .

HECHT, JUSTICE, dissenting.

Today the Court decrees that citizens of a foreign nation, Costa Rica, who claim to have been injured in their own country have an absolute right to sue for money damages in Texas courts. This same invitation extends to the citizens of every nation which would allow a Texas resident to sue in its courts in the most unlikely event he should ever want to. Citizens of foreign nations injured in Texas may certainly sue here; in some cases, they may sue in Texas even though they were injured elsewhere. But for this Court to give aliens injured outside Texas an absolute right to sue in this state inflicts a blow upon the people of Texas, its employers and taxpayers, that is contrary to sound policy. . . .

The plain language of [section 71.031] is permissive: the actions described "may be enforced in the courts of this state." The statute thus prohibits dismissal of an action within its ambit solely because plaintiffs reside or the action arose outside Texas. The Legislature has plainly opened the door to such actions; but the Court tears the door off its hinges. Not only does the statute allow foreign actions, the Court says, it mandates them. The Court would be correct if the statute stated that the actions it describes "shall be enforced in the courts of this state." But it does not say so. The statute does not create an absolute right to bring a personal injury action in Texas no matter how little it has to do with this state, how inconvenient it is to the parties, and how burdensome it is to the courts and the people of Texas who must pay for them. The statute certainly does not explicitly revoke the rule of forum non conveniens.

. . . The dearth of authority for the Court's unprecedented holding is disturbing. Far more disconcerting, however, is the Court's silence as to why the rule of forum non conveniens should be abolished in personal injury and death cases, either by the Legislature or by the Court. If the Legislature did abolish the rule of forum non conveniens by statute in 1913, what does the Court think the Legislature expected to accomplish for the people of this state? The benefit to the plaintiffs in suing in Texas should be obvious: more money, as counsel was candid enough to admit in oral argument.[10] This advantage to suing in American courts has not escaped international notice. England's Lord Denning, for example, has observed, "As a moth is drawn to the light, so is a litigant drawn to the United States. If he can only get his case into their courts, he stands to win a fortune." Smith Kline & French Laboratories Ltd. v. Bloch, (1983) 2 All E.R. 72, 74, in Note, Foreign Plaintiffs and Forum Non Conveniens: Going Beyond "Reyno," 64 Tex. L. Rev. 193, 197-8, n. 28 (1985).

But what purpose beneficial to the people of Texas is served by clogging the already burdened dockets of the state's courts with cases which arose around the world and which have nothing to do with this state except that the defendant can be served with citation here? Why, most of all, should Texas be the only state in the country, perhaps the only jurisdiction on earth, possibly the only one in history, to offer to try personal injury cases from around the world? Do Texas taxpayers want to pay extra for judges and clerks and courthouses and personnel to handle foreign litigation? If they do not mind the expense, do they not care that these foreign cases will delay their own cases being heard? As the courthouse for the world, will Texas entice employers to move here, or people to do business here, or even anyone to visit? What advantage for Texas does the Court see, or what advantage does it think the Legislature envisioned, that no other jurisdiction has ever seen, in abolishing the rule of forum non conveniens for personal injury and death cases? Who gains? A few lawyers, obviously. But who else? If the Court has good answers to these questions, why does it not say so in its opinion? If there are no good answers, then what the Court does today is very pernicious for the state.[11]

. . . The trial court in the present case did not provide this essential basis for its decision to dismiss this case. I cannot determine from the record before us whether the trial court was correct in dismissing this case on the grounds of forum non conveniens. Consequently, I would reverse the trial court's dismissal of the case and remand to that court for further consideration in light of this opinion. I would, however, reverse the judgment of the court of appeals to the extent that it precludes the possibility of dismissal after proper application of the rule of forum non conveniens. I would hold, not that the rule of forum non conveniens should be applied in this case, but only that it can be applied in a proper case. I would intimate no decision on whether this would be shown to be a proper case after further proceedings in the trial court.

10. It is equally plain to me that defendants want to be sued in Costa Rica rather than Texas because they expect that their exposure will be less there than here. However, it also seems plain to me that the Legislature would want to protect the citizens of this state, its constituents, from greater exposure to liability than they would face in the country in which the alleged wrong was committed. This would be incentive for the Legislature not to abolish the rule of forum non conveniens.

11. Justice Doggett's concurring opinion undertakes to answer these questions that the Court ignores. It suggests that there are essentially two policy reasons to abolish the rule of forum non conveniens: to assure that injured plaintiffs can recover fully, and to assure that American corporations will be fully punished for their misdeeds abroad. Neither reason is sufficient. If the defendants in this case were Costa Rican corporations which plaintiffs could sue only in Costa Rica, plaintiffs would be limited to whatever recovery they could obtain in Costa Rican courts. The concurring opinion has not explained why Costa Rican plaintiffs who claim to have been injured by American corporations are unjustly treated if they are required to sue in their own country where they could only sue if they had been injured by Costa Rican corporations. In other words, why are Costa Ricans injured by an American defendant entitled to any greater recovery than Costa Ricans injured by a Costa Rican defendant, or a Libyan defendant, or an Iranian defendant? Moreover, the concurring opinion does not explain why the American justice system should undertake to punish American corporations more severely for their actions in a foreign country than that country does. If the alleged conduct of the defendants in this case is so egregious, why has Costa Rica not chosen to afford its own citizens the recovery they seek in Texas? One wonders how receptive Costa Rican courts would be to the pleas of American plaintiffs against Costa Rican citizens for recovery of all the damages that might be available in Texas, or anywhere else for that matter.

The plaintiffs in this case are certainly entitled to justice. But so are the people of Texas. And it may well be that justice for both groups requires that these plaintiffs pursue their remedies fully in Costa Rica, their home. I therefore dissent.

In *Dow Chemical Company*, the court held that the specific jurisdictional grant of §71.031 for non-resident tort suits precluded forum non conveniens dismissal, whether under the traditional common law approach or under the codified standard of §71.051 of the Texas civil procedure code. Shortly after *Dow Chemical Company*, the Texas legislature amended its rules of civil procedure to provide that the doctrine of forum non conveniens does apply in any wrongful death or personal injury action brought by a non-resident, despite the terms of §71.031. The statute also expressly states that a "court may not stay or dismiss a plaintiff's claim under [the forum non conveniens provision] if the plaintiff is a legal resident of this state." Tex. Civ. Prac. & Rem. Code Ann. §71.051(e) (2015). As the Texas Supreme Court has noted, this latter provision has a broad and somewhat remarkable significance: "The formula is simple: plaintiff + legal residence = right to a Texas forum." In re Ford Motor Co., 442 S.W.3d 265, 270 (Tex. 2014). In *In re Ford Motor Co.*, the Court interpreted this sweeping provision to require Ford Motor Company to defend Texas wrongful death claims involving two Mexican residents and a car accident that took place in Mexico, because the survivor of the crash, a Mexican citizen, sued the estate of a Mexican decedent in Texas state court. After the case, the Texas legislature amended the statute again to clarify that the legal residency exception to forum non conveniens applies only to plaintiffs who are legal residents of Texas or derivative claimants of legal residents of Texas, and to redefine "plaintiff" to exclude representatives, administrators, guardians and next friends unless they are a derivative claimant of a Texas resident. Cf. In re Bridgestone Americas Tire Operations, LLC, 459 S.W.3d 565 (Tex. 2015) (decided before the new amendments passed but holding that Texas resident serving as "next friend" of his sister and brother-in-law's children, who had survived an automobile accident in Mexico that killed their parents, could not take advantage of the Texas resident exception to the forum non conveniens statute).

As indicated in *Dow Chemical Company*, although the principles of forum non conveniens are not constitutionally required, the Supreme Court's pronouncements on the subject have been influential in the state courts. In Piper Aircraft Co. v. Reyno, 454 U.S. 235 (1981), the Supreme Court examined the doctrine in a case arising out of an airplane crash that took place in Scotland. The court of appeals held that courts could not dismiss cases based on forum non conveniens when the substantive law of the alternative forum (e.g., Scotland) is less favorable to the plaintiff than her chosen forum (e.g., the U.S. District Court in Pennsylvania). In reversing, the Supreme Court held that an unfavorable difference in substantive law is merely one factor to consider among many when applying forum non conveniens. The Court specifically noted that the doctrine "is designed in part to help courts avoid conducting complex exercises in comparative law." Moreover, the Court argued that the court of appeals ruling would cause American courts to become fora of choice for international plaintiffs and, thus, "[t]he flow of litigation into the United States would increase and further congest already crowded courts." Still, the Court did note that the obvious inadequacy of the alternative forum is an important factor weighing in favor of plaintiff's chosen forum. Thus, for instance, dismissal "would not be appropriate where the alternative forum does not permit litigation of the subject matter of the dispute." 454 U.S. at 252.

An important application of the forum non conveniens doctrine occurred following a disastrous chemical leak at a pesticide plant owned and operated by Union Carbide India in Bhopal, India. On the morning of December 3, 1984, approximately 40 tons of methyl isocyanate escaped from the plant, leading to several thousand deaths, forced evacuation of 250,000, and continuing serious health problems for an additional 100,000, including blurred vision, lung diseases, intestinal bleeding, and various neurological and psychological disorders. Union Carbide India was more than 50 percent owned by Union Carbide Corporation, a New York company. Before the disaster, the parent company had sent a team of investigators to Bhopal to inspect the plant. Their report found a number of hazardous conditions and made major safety recommendations that were never implemented. Among other problems, a portion of the safety equipment at the plant had been broken for months prior to the accident. Although an alarm was eventually sounded by the plant an hour after the gas escape, local residents had not received information or training to understand the alarm's significance. See David Hunter, James Salzman & Durwood Zaelke, International Environmental Law and Policy 1466-67 (2d ed. 2002).

Dozens of lawsuits were filed against the Union Carbide companies in the United States and hundreds more in India. The U.S. actions were consolidated and assigned to the U.S. District Court for the Southern District of New York by the Judicial Panel on Multidistrict Litigation. See *In re* Union Carbide Corporation Gas Plant Disaster at Bhopal, India in December, 1984, 601 F. Supp. 1035 (Jud. Pan. Mult. Lit. 1985). Union Carbide sought dismissal of the U.S. actions based on the doctrine of forum non conveniens. Strikingly, the Indian government opposed dismissal on the explicit ground that it did not believe its court system could provide adequate and speedy compensation to the thousands of victims. See Sheila L. Birnbaum & Douglas W. Dunham, Foreign Plaintiffs and Forum Non Conveniens, 16 Brooklyn J. Int'l L. 241, 257 (1990). Nevertheless, the federal district judge granted Union Carbide's dismissal motion:

> It is difficult to imagine how a greater tragedy could occur to a peacetime population than the deadly gas leak in Bhopal on the night of December 2-3, 1984. The survivors of the dead victims, the injured and others who suffered, or may in the future suffer due to the disaster, are entitled to compensation. This Court is firmly convinced that the Indian legal system is in a far better position than the American courts to determine the cause of the tragic event and thereby fix liability. Further, the Indian courts have greater access to all the information needed to arrive at the amount of the compensation to be awarded the victims.
>
> . . . Plaintiffs, including the Union of India, have argued that the courts of India are not up to the task of conducting the Bhopal litigation. They assert that the Indian judiciary has yet to reach full maturity due to the restraints placed upon it by British colonial rulers who shaped the Indian legal system to meet their own ends. Plaintiffs allege that the Indian justice system has not yet cast off the burden of colonialism to meet the emerging needs of a democratic people.
>
> The Court thus finds itself faced with a paradox. In the Court's view, to retain the litigation in this forum, as plaintiffs request, would be yet another example of imperialism, another situation in which an established sovereign inflicted its rules, its standards and values on a developing nation. This Court declines to play such a role. The Union of India is a world power in 1986, and its courts have the proven capacity to mete out fair and equal justice. To deprive the Indian judiciary of this opportunity to stand tall before the world and to pass judgment on behalf of its own people would be to revive a history of subservience and subjugation from which India has emerged. India and its people can and must vindicate their claims before the independent and legitimate judiciary created there since the Independence of 1947.

> . . . Therefore, the consolidated case is dismissed on the grounds of forum non conveniens under the following conditions:
>
> 1. Union Carbide shall consent to submit to the jurisdiction of the courts of India, and shall continue to waive defenses based upon the statute of limitations;
> 2. Union Carbide shall agree to satisfy any judgment rendered against it by an Indian court, and if applicable, upheld by an appellate court in that country, where such judgment and affirmance comport with the minimal requirements of due process;
> 3. Union Carbide shall be subject to discovery under the model of the United States Federal Rules of Civil Procedure after appropriate demand by plaintiffs.

In re Union Carbide Corp. Gas Plant Disaster at Bhopal, India in December, 1984, 634 F. Supp. 842, 866-67 (S.D.N.Y. 1986).

On appeal, the Second Circuit reversed the second and third conditions imposed by the district judge, but otherwise affirmed dismissal of the consolidated action. See *In re* Union Carbide Corp. Gas Plant Disaster at Bhopal, India in Dec., 1984, 809 F.2d 195 (2d Cir. 1987). According to the international human rights agency Amnesty International, most of the victims of the Bhopal disaster — which now are estimated to include 22,000 dead and 500,000 injured — continue to await meaningful compensation, medical care, or rehabilitation assistance 20 years after the event. A settlement fund of US$470 million was established by Union Carbide with the approval of the Indian Supreme Court in 1989; however, most of the funds remained undistributed as of 2004, see Amnesty International, Clouds of Injustice: Bhopal Twenty Years On (2004), and even today controversy continues to surround the fund which has been deemed grossly inadequate by the Indian government. On June 7, 2010, an Indian court convicted eight Indian former plant employees of causing death by negligence. The seven former employees alive at the time of the conviction were each sentenced to two years in prison and fined US$2,125. See BBC News, Bhopal Trial: Eight Convicted over India Gas Disaster (June 7, 2010).

Subsequent federal cases have tended to take a similarly restrictive approach to evaluating alternative forums for inadequacy. In Aguinda v. Texaco, Inc., 303 F.3d 470 (2d Cir. 2002), several thousand Ecuadorian plaintiffs brought suit against a United States–based multinational corporation, alleging a variety of environmental harms and personal injuries arising out of the defendant's destruction of rainforest. The court of appeals affirmed the district court's dismissal under the forum non conveniens doctrine, holding that Ecuador provided an adequate alternative forum despite the fact that Ecuadorian courts were acknowledged to be more susceptible to corruption and did not provide for class action procedures, and despite the Ecuadorian government's espoused view that mass tort actions should be brought in United States courts. See also Gonzalez v. Chrysler Corp., 301 F.3d 377 (5th Cir. 2002) (Mexico provided adequate alternative forum despite its lack of strict products liability theories of recovery and its cap of $2,500 on damages for the loss of a child's life); Polanco v. H.B. Fuller Co., 941 F. Supp. 1512 (D. Minn. 1996) (acknowledging that plaintiffs' argument that Guatemalan courts have "no real respect for law and individual rights" gave the court "pause," but dismissing on forum non conveniens grounds); Rodriguez v. Shell Oil Co., 950 F. Supp. 187 (S.D. Tex. 1996) (holding that Honduras was an adequate alternative forum despite a submission by the Honduran attorney general stating that the country could not adjudicate the plaintiffs' claims due to lack of experience and resources); Delgado v. Shell Oil Co., 890 F. Supp. 1324 (S.D. Tex. 1995) (dismissing lawsuit brought on behalf of thousands of citizens of 12 foreign countries alleging personal injuries from pesticide exposure). But see Bhatnagaru v. Surrendra Overseas Ltd., 52 F.3d 1220 (3d Cir. 1995) (refusing to dismiss personal injury action in light of "extreme delay" of 15 to 20 years to resolve claims in some parts of the Indian court system).

Even if plaintiffs do secure a favorable verdict in the foreign jurisdiction after their initial suit is dismissed on forum non conveniens grounds, they may be unable to enforce the verdict domestically if U.S. courts do not view the foreign forum as adequately protective of a defendant's due process rights. See Osorio v. Dole Food Co., 665 F. Supp. 2d 1307 (S.D. Fla. 2009), *aff'd,* 635 F.3d 1277 (11th Cir. 2011) (detailing fatal shortcomings in Nicaraguan liability law and court proceedings against the defendant, which had years earlier successfully argued that toxic exposure suits filed in the United States should be dismissed in favor of litigation in Nicaragua). The plaintiffs from *Aguinda*, for instance, obtained a multibillion-dollar judgment in Ecuadorian courts against Texaco's corporate successor, Chevron, after Texaco had earlier argued against adjudication in the United States. See Simon Romero & Clifford Krauss, Ecuadoreans Plan to Pursue Chevron in Other Countries, N.Y. Times, Feb. 16, 2011, at A13. A Chevron spokesperson was quoted as saying, "We intend to resist enforcement anywhere where the plaintiffs seek to take what we perceive to be a fraudulent judgment." Id. If these defendants' allegations of infirm procedures in foreign courts are accurate, should that militate against dismissing initial claims filed in the United States on forum non conveniens grounds?

A recurring context in which foreign plaintiffs seek to adjudicate their tort claims in U.S. courts involves products liability claims against American manufacturers, particularly pharmaceutical manufacturers. See, e.g., Chang v. Baxter Healthcare Corp., 599 F.3d 728 (7th Cir. 2010); Dowling v. Richardson-Merrell, Inc., 727 F.2d 608 (6th Cir. 1984). In such cases, even when the product has been designed, manufactured, and tested in the United States by a U.S. company, courts frequently hold that the jurisdiction where marketing and distribution takes place is a more appropriate forum for adjudication, in light of the complex balancing of risks and benefits that accompanies the setting of standards by which products are evaluated for safety and defectiveness. See, e.g., Abad v. Bayer Corp., 563 F.3d 663 (7th Cir. 2009) (asserting that Argentine courts had greater competence to hear products liability actions because Argentine law applied to the suits, but U.S. courts could not know whether "Argentine courts would impose market-share liability"); Doe v. Hyland Therapeutics Div., 807 F. Supp. 1117 (S.D.N.Y. 1992) (stating that American courts are "ill-equipped to enunciate the optimal standards of safety or care" for foreign product markets); Polanco v. H.B. Fuller Co., 941 F. Supp. 1512, 1528 (D. Minn. 1996) (stating that "Guatemala's interest in setting the standards by which products manufactured there will be judged permeates" the case and counsels in favor of dismissal). In contrast, in Dorman v. Emerson Elec. Co., 789 F. Supp. 296, 298-91 (E.D. Mo. 1992), the court observed that the state of Missouri has a "significant interest" in tort litigation brought against a defendant incorporated in the state. The court noted that although British Columbia, the site of the accident at issue, also had an interest in the dispute, it was merely the interest evoked by a "simple tort suit" rather than the "broad public interest" of the state of Missouri in overseeing its corporate citizens.

Although the overwhelming majority of state courts follow the federal approach to forum non conveniens doctrine, there are some exceptions. For instance, courts in Louisiana, a civil law jurisdiction, refuse to recognize forum non conveniens as an inherent discretionary judicial power at all. See Fox v. Board of Sup'rs of Louisiana State Univ. & Agr. & Mech. College, 576 So. 2d 978 (La. 1991). A few other states hold that the forum non conveniens doctrine in their jurisdiction is more narrowly applied than, or otherwise distinct from, the federal version. In Myers v. Boeing Co, 794 P.2d 1272 (Wash. 1990), for instance, the Washington Supreme Court strongly criticized the U.S. Supreme Court's *Piper Aircraft Co.* approach as discriminatory to foreign plaintiffs:

> The Court purports to be giving lesser deference to the foreign plaintiffs' choice of forum when, in reality, it is giving lesser deference to *foreign plaintiffs*, based solely on their status as foreigners. More importantly, it is not necessarily less reasonable to assume that a foreign plaintiff's choice of forum is convenient. Why is it less reasonable to assume that a plaintiff from British Columbia, who brings suit in Washington, has chosen a less convenient forum than a plaintiff from Florida bringing the same suit? To take it one step further, why is it less reasonable to assume that a plaintiff, who is a Japanese citizen residing in Wenatchee, who brings suit in Washington, has chosen a less convenient forum than a plaintiff from Florida bringing the same suit?
>
> The Court's reference to the attractiveness of United States courts to foreigners, combined with a holding that, in application, gives less deference to foreign plaintiffs based on their status as foreigners, raises concerns about xenophobia. This alone should put us on guard.

Id. at 1281. Similarly, in Picketts v Int'l. Playtex, Inc., 576 A.2d 518, 524 (Conn. 1990), the court emphasized that in the case of foreign plaintiffs suing an in-state defendant, "the trial court must readjust the downward pressure of its thumb [on the scale in favor of plaintiffs' choice of forum], but not remove it altogether from the plaintiffs' side of the scale." The court reasoned that "[e]ven though the plaintiffs' preference has a diminished impact because the plaintiffs are themselves strangers to their chosen forum, Connecticut continues to have a responsibility to those foreign plaintiffs who properly invoke the jurisdiction of this forum, especially in the somewhat unusual situation where it is the forum resident who seeks dismissal." Id. at 524-25 (internal citations and quotations omitted). See also Ison v. E.I. DuPont de Nemours & Co., Inc., 729 A.2d 832 (Del. 1999) (observing "the strong showing a defendant must make to justify the 'drastic remedy' of dismissal, even though according less weight to the foreign plaintiff's choice of forum than that accorded a resident or other domestic plaintiff").

B. The Alien Tort Statute

Foreign plaintiffs have had some success at the federal level invoking the Alien Tort Statute (ATS), 28 U.S.C. §1350, as a vehicle for domestic adjudication of international torts, crimes, human rights violations, and other egregious behaviors perpetrated abroad. Adopted in 1789 as part of the original Judiciary Act, this statute provides simply that "[t]he district courts shall have original jurisdiction of any civil action by an alien for a tort only, committed in violation of the law of nations or a treaty of the United States." Little is known about the statute's origins or intended purpose. As Justice Souter remarked in Sosa v. Alvarez-Machain, 542 U.S. 692 (2004), one of the Supreme Court's most important pronouncements on the scope of the ATS, "'no one seems to know whence it came,' . . . and for over 170 years after its enactment it provided jurisdiction in only one case." Id. at 712 (quoting Judge Friendly in IIT v. Vencap, Ltd., 519 F.2d 1001, 1015 (2d Cir. 1975)). This period of dormancy came to a dramatic end in Filártiga v. Pena-Irala, 630 F.2d 876 (2d Cir. 1980). In that case, the court held that deliberate torture perpetrated under the color of official authority violates universally accepted norms of international law and thus gives rise to a cause of action under the ATS, assuming that personal jurisdiction, standing, venue, and other procedural requirements are satisfied.

Filártiga gave rise to a wave of ATS litigation during the 1980s and 1990s, as litigants increasingly sought to utilize the ATS in actions brought in American federal courts to enforce international human rights and environmental norms. Plaintiffs brought such suits against both governmental actors and private parties such as multinational corporations. See, e.g., Abebe-Jira v. Negewo, 72 F.3d 844 (11th Cir. 1996) (alleging torture of prisoners in Ethiopia); *In re* Estate of Ferdinand Marcos, 25 F.3d 1467 (9th Cir. 1994) (alleging torture by Ferdinand Marcos, former president of the Philippines); Tel-Oren v. Libyan Arab Republic, 726 F.2d 774 (D.C. Cir. 1984) (alleging armed attack on a civilian bus in Israel by Libyan-backed terrorists); Flores v. Southern Peru Copper Corp., 253 F. Supp. 2d 510 (S.D.N.Y. 2002) (alleging environmental pollution and personal injuries arising out of an American corporation's Peruvian mining operations).

In *Sosa*, the Supreme Court addressed the question of whether the ATS creates substantive causes of action of its own or merely provides for federal jurisdiction in the event of an independently existing cause of action. After reviewing the available historical materials regarding the adoption of the ATS, the Court concluded that "although the ATS is a jurisdictional statute creating no new causes of action, the reasonable inference from the historical materials is that the statute was intended to have practical effect the moment it became law. The jurisdictional grant is best read as having been enacted on the understanding that the common law would provide a cause of action for the modest number of international law violations with a potential for personal liability at the time." 542 U.S. at 724. Rather than limit actionable torts under the ATS to those specifically recognized by eighteenth-century common law jurisprudence, such as causes of action for "offenses against ambassadors, violations of safe conduct . . . [and] piracy," the *Sosa* majority instead held that "courts should require any ATS claim based on the present-day law of nations to rest on a norm of international character accepted by the civilized world and defined with a specificity comparable to the features of the 18th-century paradigms we have recognized." Id. at 720, 725 (internal citations omitted).

Because the *Sosa* majority declined to hold that the ATS was merely jurisdictional in nature but provided only suggestive guidelines as to its substantive scope, the lower federal courts have been forced to grapple with the import of the decision through case-by-case analyses. For instance, in Sexual Minorities Uganda v. Lively, 960 F. Supp. 2d 304 (D. Mass. 2013), an organization that advocates for the fair and equal treatment of lesbian, gay, bisexual, transgender, and intersex (LGBTI) people in Uganda brought ATS claims against a U.S. resident who was alleged to have helped foment an atmosphere of fear and repression for LGBTI individuals in that nation through his operation of "what amounts to a kind of 'Homophobia Central' in Springfield, Massachusetts." Id. at 310. The court noted that "many authorities implicitly support the principle that widespread, systematic persecution of individuals based on their sexual orientation and gender identity constitutes a crime against humanity that violates international norms." Id. at 310. The court did acknowledge that "[i]t is a somewhat closer question whether this crime constitutes what Justice Souter has termed one of the 'relatively modest set of actions alleging violations of the law of nations' for which the ATS furnishes jurisdiction," id., but went on to hold that allegations of "a systematic and widespread campaign of persecution against LGBTI people" do meet the *Sosa* standard. Id. at 319. See also Velez v. Sanchez, 693 F.3d 308 (2d Cir. 2012) (plaintiff, a 16 year-old Ecuadorian girl who was lured to the United States to work for her stepsister as a nanny and housekeeper under harsh and misleading conditions, did not adequately invoke jurisdiction of ATS; alleged exploitation was deplorable but did not rise to the level of slavery, forced labor, and trafficking within the narrow scope of ATS-eligible claims); Abdullahi v. Pfizer, Inc., 562 F.3d 163 (2d Cir 2009) (allegations that defendant drug company tested an experimental antibiotic on children in Nigeria without their consent or knowledge did invoke universally accepted norm of customary international law sufficient to fall within jurisdiction of ATS).

In addition to the substantive jurisdictional limitation of *Sosa*, other barriers to ATS litigation have been erected through recent case law. For instance, courts frequently consider whether plaintiffs should be required to exhaust their remedies in the applicable foreign jurisdiction prior to seeking relief in the United States under the ATS. See, e.g., Sarei v. Rio Tinto, PLC, 550 F.3d 822 (9th Cir. 2008) (en banc) (developing a complex framework for determining whether to impose an exhaustion requirement as a matter of judicial discretion, rather than mandatory ATS statutory interpretation). *Sarei* involved allegations that defendant mining company committed or supported the government's commitment of various war crimes, crimes against humanity, racial discrimination, and environmental torts in connection with its Papua New Guinea mining operations. The case spent over a decade in the courts before being ultimately dismissed pursuant to a recent Supreme Court decision, Kiobel v. Royal Dutch Petroleum Co., which is discussed below. See Sarei v. Rio Tinto, PLC, 722 F.3d 1109 (9th Cir. 2013).

In addition to the ATS, plaintiffs also have invoked the Torture Victim Prevention Act (TVPA), 28 U.S.C. §§1350 et seq., and the Anti-Terrorism Act (ATA), 28 U.S.C. §§2331 et seq. The TVPA creates a federal cause of action where under "color of law, of any foreign nation," an individual is subject to torture or "extra judicial killing." Unlike the ATS, the TVPA affords relief to U.S. citizens in addition to non-nationals. However, the TVPA has been interpreted not to permit suits against non-natural persons such as corporations, see Mohamad v. Palestinian Authority, 132 S. Ct. 1702 (2012), a question that remains open under the ATS, as explained below. The ATA creates a cause of action only for Americans and allows suit in U.S. courts against any foreign entity for injuries arising out of "act[s] of international terrorism." See, e.g., Wiwa v. Royal Dutch Petroleum Co., 226 F.3d 88 (2d Cir. 2000) (ATA and TVPA action against the multinational corporation Royal Dutch Petroleum/Shell for alleged participation with the Nigerian government in grave human rights violations); Rein v. Socialist People's Libyan Arab Jamahiriya, 995 F. Supp. 325 (E.D.N.Y. 1998) (examining ATA claims arising out of the 1998 bombing of Pan-Am Flight 103 over Lockerbie, Scotland). In Boim v. Holy Land Foundation for Relief and Development, 549 F.3d 685 (7th Cir. 2008), the Seventh Circuit en banc overruled an earlier panel opinion which had held that the ATA imposes "secondary liability" on those who aid and abet acts of terrorism. However, the en banc court did interpret the act's definition of international terrorism — which covers not only violent acts but also "acts dangerous to human life that are a violation of the criminal laws of the United States" — to extend to the use of charitable front organizations to channel funds to terrorist activities. See also Gill v. Arab Bank, PLC, 891 F. Supp. 2d 335, 342-43 (E.D.N.Y. 2012) (describing variety of federal court approaches to the question of ATA secondary liability).

One question noted but not addressed in *Sosa* is whether the ATS reaches conduct by private actors such as corporations. The Court observed that a split of view appears to exist among commentators over the question of corporate liability for violation of international norms. See 542 U.S. at 732 n.20. Oddly, the Court did not acknowledge that its sole prior case addressing the ATS consisted of a claim brought by corporate plaintiffs and that the Court in that case observed that the ATS "by its terms does not distinguish among classes of defendants." Argentine Republic v. Amerada Hess Shipping Corp., 488 U.S. 428, 438 (1989). Previously, case law in the lower courts had tended to accept the possibility of corporate liability. In Kadic v. Karadzic, 70 F.3d 232 (2d Cir. 1995), for instance, the court held that the ATS reaches conduct by private actors when such conduct occurs under the color of state authority or violates a norm of international law that extends to the conduct of private actors. See also Flomo v. Firestone Natural Rubber Co., 643 F.3d 1013, 1019 (7th Cir. 2011) ("If a corporation complicit in Nazi war crimes could be punished criminally for violating customary international law, as we believe it could be, then *a fortiori* if the board of directors of a corporation directs the corporation's managers to commit war crimes, engage in piracy, abuse ambassadors, or use slave labor, the corporation can be civilly liable."); Romero v. Drummond Co., 552 F.3d 1303, 1315 (11th Cir. 2008) ("The text of the Alien Tort Statute provides no express exception for corporations, see 28 U.S.C. §1350, and the law of this Circuit is that this statute grants jurisdiction from complaints of torture against corporate defendants.") (citation omitted).

However, in Kiobel v. Royal Dutch Petroleum Co., 621 F.3d 111, 120 (2d Cir. 2010), the Second Circuit held that corporations cannot be held liable for their conduct under the ATS because "customary international law has steadfastly rejected the notion of corporate liability for international crimes." In a strongly worded dissent, Judge Leval argued that the "majority's rule conflicts with two centuries of federal precedent on the ATS, and deals a blow to the efforts of international law to protect human rights." Id. at 196. The plaintiffs appealed the *Kiobel* decision to the Supreme Court and, in an unusual procedural move, the Court on its own motion asked the parties to rebrief and reargue the case, focusing on a second question of "whether and under what circumstances the ATS allows courts to recognize a cause of action for violations of the law of nations occurring" outside the United States. The Court ultimately affirmed the Second Circuit's judgment but did so based on this second question, holding that the canon of statutory interpretation that calls for a "presumption against extraterritoriality applies to claims under the ATS, and that nothing in the statute rebuts that presumption." Kiobel v. Royal Dutch Petroleum Co., 133 S. Ct. 1659, 1669, 185 L. Ed. 2d 671 (2013). The Court did not resolve the issue of corporate liability under the ATS, an avoidance that some lower courts have taken as implicitly damning the Second Circuit's unusual opinion in *Kiobel*. See In re South African Apartheid Litig., 15 F. Supp. 3d 454 (S.D.N.Y. 2014) (calling the Second Circuit *Kiobel* opinion a "stark outlier" and holding that corporations can be held liable under the ATS).

Much like its enigmatic *Sosa* decision, the Supreme Court's *Kiobel* decision left a great deal undecided for lower courts to address. Most notably, the *Kiobel* majority opinion concluded its discussion by noting that "even where the claims touch and concern the territory of the United States, they must do so with sufficient force to displace the presumption against extraterritorial application." 133 S. Ct. at 1669. Naturally, following the Supreme Court's *Kiobel* decision, ATS litigation has tended to focus narrowly on the question of whether the presumption against extraterritorial application can be overcome through a "touch and concern" showing. Compare Al Shimari v. CACI Premier Techn., Inc., 758 F.3d 516 (4th Cir. 2014) (plaintiff Iraqi citizens alleged that defendant military contractor abused and tortured plaintiffs during their detention at Abu Ghraib prison as suspected enemy combatants; such allegations did "touch and concern" the United States sufficient to establish ATS applicability), with Doe v. Drummond Co., Inc., 782 F.3d 576 (11th Cir. 2015) (heirs of Colombian citizens murdered by a paramilitary group, brought ATS action against multinational coal mining company for allegedly aiding and abetting extrajudicial killings and war crimes; allegations did not meet "touch and concern" standard).

Writing for himself and three others, Justice Breyer concurred in *Kiobel* but articulated an alternative standard for ATS applicability: "I would find jurisdiction under this statute where (1) the alleged tort occurs on American soil, (2) the defendant is an American national, or (3) the defendant's conduct substantially and adversely affects an important American national interest, and that includes a distinct interest in preventing the United States from becoming a safe harbor (free of civil as well as criminal liability) for a torturer or other common enemy of mankind." Id. at 1671. Is Justice Breyer's approach preferable to the *Kiobel* majority's "touch and concern" test?

Despite the various obstacles discussed in this section, ATS litigation continues apace. The following post-*Kiobel* decision comes from the Ninth Circuit, historically one of the friendliest courts for ATS plaintiffs. As you read the case, ask yourself how wide the ATS door remains open even in a "friendly" jurisdiction such as the Ninth Circuit.

Doe I v. Nestle USA, Inc.

766 F.3d 1013 (9th Cir. 2014)

D.W. Nelson, Senior Circuit Judge:

The plaintiffs in this case are former child slaves who were forced to harvest cocoa in the Ivory Coast. They filed claims under the Alien Tort Statute (ATS) against defendants Nestle USA, Inc., Archer Daniels Midland Company, Cargill Incorporated Company, and Cargill Cocoa, alleging that the defendants aided and abetted child slavery by providing assistance to Ivorian farmers.

The district court dismissed their complaint, finding that the plaintiffs failed to state a claim upon which relief can be granted. We reverse, vacate, and remand for further proceedings.

I. Background

The use of child slave labor in the Ivory Coast is a humanitarian tragedy. Studies by International Labour Organization, UNICEF, the Department of State, and numerous other organizations have confirmed that thousands of children are forced to work without pay in the Ivorian economy. Besides the obvious moral implications, this widespread use of child slavery contributes to poverty in the Ivory Coast, degrades its victims by treating them as commodities, and causes long-term mental and physical trauma.

The plaintiffs in this case are three victims of child slavery. They were forced to work on Ivorian cocoa plantations for up to fourteen hours per day six days a week, given only scraps of food to eat, and whipped and beaten by overseers. They were locked in small rooms at night and not permitted to leave the plantations, knowing that children who tried to escape would be beaten or tortured. Plaintiff John Doe II witnessed guards cut open the feet of children who attempted to escape, and John Doe III knew that the guards forced failed escapees to drink urine.

Though tarnished by these atrocities, the Ivory Coast remains a critical part of the international chocolate industry, producing seventy percent of the world's supply of cocoa. The defendants in this case dominate the Ivorian cocoa market. Although the defendants do not own cocoa farms themselves, they maintain and protect a steady supply of cocoa by forming exclusive buyer/seller relationships with Ivorian farms. The defendants are largely in charge of the work of buying and selling cocoa, and import most of the Ivory Coast's cocoa harvest into the United States. The defendants' involvement in the cocoa market gives them economic leverage, and along with other large multinational companies, the defendants effectively control the production of Ivorian cocoa.

To maintain their relationships with Ivorian farms, the defendants offer both financial assistance and technical farming assistance designed to support cocoa agriculture. The financial assistance includes advanced payment for cocoa and spending money for the farmers' personal use. The technical support includes equipment and training in growing techniques, fermentation techniques, farm maintenance, and appropriate labor practices. The technical support is meant to expand the farms' capacity and act as a quality control mechanism, and either the defendants or their agents visit farms several times per year as part of the defendants' training and quality control efforts.

The defendants are well aware of the child slavery problem in the Ivory Coast. They acquired this knowledge firsthand through their numerous visits to Ivorian farms. Additionally, the defendants knew of the child slave labor problems in the Ivorian cocoa sector due to the many reports issued by domestic and international organizations.

Despite their knowledge of child slavery and their control over the cocoa market, the defendants operate in the Ivory Coast "with the unilateral goal of finding the cheapest sources of cocoa." The defendants continue to supply money, equipment, and training to Ivorian farmers, knowing that these provisions will facilitate the use of forced child labor. The defendants have also lobbied against congressional efforts to curb the use of child slave labor. In 2001, the House of Representatives passed a bill that would have required United States importers and manufacturers to certify and label their products "slave free." The defendants and others in the chocolate industry rallied against the bill, urging instead the adoption of a private, voluntary enforcement mechanism. A voluntary enforcement system was eventually adopted, a result that, according to the plaintiffs, "in effect guarantee[d] the continued use of the cheapest labor available to produce [cocoa]—that of child slaves."

The plaintiffs filed a proposed class action in the United States District Court for the Central District of California, alleging that the defendants were liable under the ATS for aiding and abetting child slavery in the Ivory Coast. The district court granted the defendants' motion to dismiss in a detailed opinion, which concluded that corporations cannot be sued under the ATS, and that even if they could, the plaintiffs failed to allege the elements of a claim for aiding and abetting slave labor. The plaintiffs declined to amend their complaint, and appeal the district court's order. . . .

III. Discussion

. . . The specific norms underlying the plaintiffs' ATS claim are the norms against aiding and abetting slave labor, which the defendants allegedly violated by providing financial and non-financial assistance to cocoa farmers in the Ivory Coast. The defendants argue that this claim should be dismissed, for three reasons. First, the defendants argue that there is no specific, universal, and obligatory norm preventing corporations—as opposed to individuals—from aiding and abetting slave labor. Second, the defendants argue that the plaintiffs' complaint fails to allege the actus reus and mens rea elements of an aiding and abetting claim. Finally, the defendants argue that the plaintiffs' complaint improperly seeks extraterritorial application of federal law contrary to the Supreme Court's recent decision in Kiobel v. Royal Dutch Petroleum Co., —U.S. ——, 133 S. Ct. 1659, 185 L.Ed. 2d 671 (2013) ("*Kiobel II*"). We consider each argument in turn.

A. Corporate Liability under the ATS

The primary focus of international law, although not its exclusive focus, is the conduct of states. Kiobel v. Royal Dutch Petroleum Co., 621 F.3d 111, 165 (2d Cir. 2010) (Leval, J., concurring) ("*Kiobel I*"). Many of its prohibitions therefore only apply to state action, and an important issue in ATS litigation can be determining whether the norm asserted by the plaintiff is applicable to both state actors and private actors. . . .

We . . . established three principles about corporate ATS liability in [Sarei v. Rio Tinto, PLC, 671 F.3d 736 (9th Cir. 2011)], that we now reaffirm. First, the analysis proceeds norm-by-norm; there is no categorical rule of corporate immunity or liability. Id. at 747-48. Second, corporate liability under an ATS claim does not depend on the existence of international precedent enforcing legal norms against corporations. Id. at 760-61. Third, norms that are "universal and absolute," or applicable to "all actors," can provide the basis for an ATS claim against a corporation. Id. at 760. To determine whether a norm is universal, we consider, among other things, whether it is "limited to states" and whether its application depends on the identity of the perpetrator. Id. at 764-65.

We conclude that the prohibition against slavery is universal and may be asserted against the corporate defendants in this case. Private, non-state actors were held liable at Nuremberg for slavery offenses. The Flick Case, 6 Trials of War Criminals (T.W.C.) 1194, 1202. Moreover, the statutes of the International Criminal Tribunals for Rwanda and the former Yugoslavia are broadly phrased to condemn "persons responsible" for enslavement of civilian populations. ICTY Statute Art. 5(c), U.N. S/RES/827 (May 25, 1993); ICTR Statute Art. 3(c), U.N. S/RES/955 (Nov. 8, 1994). The prohibition against slavery applies to state actors and non-state actors alike, and there are no rules exempting acts of enslavement carried out on behalf of a corporation. Indeed, it would be contrary to both the categorical nature of the prohibition on slavery and the moral imperative underlying that prohibition to conclude that incorporation leads to legal absolution for acts of enslavement. *Kiobel I*, 621 F.3d at 155 (Leval, J., concurring) ("The majority's interpretation of international law, which accords to corporations a free pass to act in contravention of international law's norms, conflicts with the humanitarian objectives of that body of law.").

A final point of clarification is in order about the role of domestic and international law. Although international law controls the threshold question of whether an international legal norm provides the basis for an ATS claim against a corporation, there remain several issues about corporate liability which must be governed by domestic law. This division of labor is dictated by international legal principles, because international law defines norms and determines their scope, but delegates to domestic law the task of determining the civil consequences of any given violation of these norms. Thus, when questions endemic to tort litigation or civil liability arise in ATS litigation — such as damages computation, joint and several liability, and proximate causation — these issues must be governed by domestic law. Many questions that surround corporate liability fall into this category, including, most importantly, the issue of when the actions of an individual can be attributed to a corporation for purposes of tort liability. Determining when a corporation can be held liable therefore requires a court to apply customary international law to determine the nature and scope of the norm underlying the plaintiffs' claim, and domestic tort law to determine whether recovery from the corporation is permissible.

Our holding that the norm against slavery is universal and thus may be asserted against the defendants addresses only the international legal issues related to corporate liability in this case. We do not address other domestic law questions related to corporate liability, and leave them to be addressed by the district court in the first instance.

B. Aiding and Abetting Liability

We next consider whether the plaintiffs' complaint alleges the elements of a claim for aiding and abetting slavery. Customary international law — not domestic law — provides the legal standard for aiding and abetting ATS claims. When choosing between competing legal standards, we consider which one best reflects a consensus of the well-developed democracies of the world.

1. Mens Rea

The plaintiffs argue that the required mens rea for aiding and abetting is knowledge, specifically, knowledge that the aider and abetter's acts would facilitate the commission of the underlying offense. This knowledge standard dates back to the Nuremberg tribunals, and is well illustrated by the Zyklon B Case, 1 Law Reports Of Trials Of War Criminals 93 (1946). There, the defendants supplied poison gas to the Nazis knowing that it would be used to murder innocent people, and were convicted of aiding and abetting war crimes. Id. at 101. An analogous knowledge standard is applied in The Flick Case, where a defendant was convicted of aiding and abetting war crimes for donating money to the leader of the SS, knowing that it would be used to support a criminal organization. 6 T.W.C. 1216-17, 1220-21; see also The Ministries Case, 14 T.W.C. 622 (concluding that the defendant's knowledge regarding the intended use of a loan was sufficient to satisfy the mens rea requirement, but declining to find that the defendant satisfied the actus reus requirement).

As plaintiffs contend, this knowledge standard has also been embraced by contemporary international criminal tribunals. The International Criminal Tribunals for Rwanda and the former Yugoslavia consistently apply a knowledge standard. In Prosecutor v. Blagojevic, for instance, the tribunal stated that "[t]he requisite mental element of aiding and abetting is knowledge that the acts performed assist the commission of the specific crime of the principal perpetrator." No. IT-02-60-A, ¶127 (ICTY, May 9, 2007). Additionally, after conducting an extensive review of customary international law, the Appeals Chamber of the Special Court for Sierra Leone recently affirmed this knowledge standard, concluding that "an accused's knowledge of the consequence of his acts or conduct — that is, an accused's 'knowing participation' in the crimes — is a culpable mens rea standard for individual criminal liability."

However, two of our sister circuits have concluded that knowledge is insufficient and that an aiding and abetting ATS defendant must act with the purpose of facilitating the criminal act, relying on the Rome Statute of the International Criminal Court, 37 I.L.M. 999 (1998) ("Rome Statute"). See Aziz v. Alcolac, Inc., 658 F.3d 388, 399-400 (4th Cir. 2011); Presbyterian Church of Sudan v. Talisman Energy, Inc., 582 F.3d 244, 259 (2d Cir. 2009). These circuits have interpreted the Rome Statute to bar the use of a knowledge standard because it uses the term "purpose" to define aiding and abetting liability:

> [A] person shall be criminally responsible and liable for punishment for a crime within the jurisdiction of the Court if that person . . . [f]or the *purpose* of facilitating the commission of such a crime, aids, abets, or otherwise assists in its commission. . . .

Rome Statute, art. 25(3)(c) (emphasis added). Taking this text at face value, as the Second and Fourth Circuits did, it appears that the Rome Statute rejects a knowledge standard and requires the heightened mens rea of purpose, suggesting that a knowledge standard lacks the universal acceptance that *Sosa* demands.

Here, we need not decide whether a purpose or knowledge standard applies to aiding and abetting ATS claims. We conclude that the plaintiffs' allegations satisfy the more stringent purpose standard, and therefore state a claim for aiding and abetting slavery. . . .

Reading the allegations in the light most favorable to the plaintiffs, one is led to the inference that the defendants placed increased revenues before basic human welfare, and intended to pursue all options available to reduce their cost for purchasing cocoa. Driven by the goal to reduce costs in any way possible, the defendants allegedly supported the use of child slavery, the cheapest form of labor available. These allegations explain how the use of child slavery benefitted the defendants and furthered their operational goals in the Ivory Coast, and therefore, the allegations support the inference that the defendants acted with the purpose to facilitate child slavery.

The defendants' alleged plan to benefit from the use of child slave labor starkly distinguishes this case from other ATS decisions where the purpose standard was not met. . . . Here, . . . the complaint alleges that the defendants obtained a direct benefit from the commission of the violation of international law, which bolsters the allegation that the defendants acted with the purpose to support child slavery.

The defendants' control over the Ivory Coast cocoa market further supports the allegation that the defendants acted with the purpose to facilitate slavery. According to the complaint, the defendants had enough control over the Ivorian cocoa market that they could have stopped or limited the use of child slave labor by their suppliers. The defendants did not use their control to stop the use of child slavery, however, but instead offered support that facilitated it. Viewed alongside the allegation that the defendants benefitted from the use of child slavery, the defendants' failure to stop or limit child slavery supports the inference that they intended to keep that system in place. The defendants had the means to stop or limit the use of child slavery, and had they wanted the slave labor to end, they could have used their leverage in the cocoa market to stop it. Their alleged failure to do so, coupled with the cost-cutting benefit they allegedly receive from the use of child slaves, strongly supports the inference that the defendants acted with purpose.

The defendants' alleged lobbying efforts also corroborate the inference of purpose. According to the complaint, the defendants participated in lobbying efforts designed to defeat federal legislation that would have required chocolate importers and manufacturers to certify and label their chocolate as "slave free." As an alternative to the proposed legislation, the defendants, along with others from the chocolate industry, supported a voluntary mechanism through which the chocolate industry would police itself. The complaint also alleges that when the voluntary enforcement system was eventually put into practice instead of legislation, it "in effect guaranteed the continued use of the cheapest labor available to produce [cocoa] — that of child slaves."

. . . This is not to say that the purpose standard is satisfied merely because the defendants intended to profit by doing business in the Ivory Coast. Doing business with child slave owners, however morally reprehensible that may be, does not by itself demonstrate a purpose to support child slavery. Here, however, the defendants allegedly intended to support the use of child slavery as a means of reducing their production costs. In doing so, the defendants sought a legitimate goal, profit, through illegitimate means, purposefully supporting child slavery.

Thus, the allegations suggest that a myopic focus on profit over human welfare drove the defendants to act with the purpose of obtaining the cheapest cocoa possible, even if it meant facilitating child slavery. These allegations are sufficient to satisfy the mens rea required of an aiding and abetting claim under either a knowledge or purpose standard.

2. *Actus Reus*

We next consider whether the plaintiffs have alleged the actus reus elements of an aiding and abetting claim. The actus reus of aiding and abetting is providing assistance or other forms of support to the commission of a crime. As both parties agree, international law further requires that the assistance offered must be substantial. The parties dispute, however, whether international law imposes the additional requirement that the assistance must be specifically directed towards the commission of the crime. . . . [W]e decline to adopt an actus reus standard for aiding and abetting liability under the ATS. Instead, we remand to the district court with instructions to allow plaintiffs to amend their complaint in light of [two recent international criminal tribunal decisions], both of which were decided after the complaint in this case was dismissed and this appeal had been filed.

C. Extraterritorial ATS Claims

The defendants' final argument contends that the plaintiffs' ATS claim seeks an extraterritorial application of federal law that is barred by the Supreme Court's recent decision in *Kiobel II*, 133 S. Ct. at 1669. We decline to resolve the extraterritoriality issue, and instead remand to allow the plaintiffs to amend their complaint in light of *Kiobel II*. . . .

Since the presumption against extraterritoriality is a canon of statutory construction, it has no direct application to ATS claims, which, as discussed above, are claims created by federal common law, not statutory claims created by the ATS itself. In *Kiobel II*, however, the Supreme Court explained that the prudential concerns about judicial interference in foreign policy are particularly strong in ATS litigation, and concluded that "the principles underlying the presumption against extraterritoriality thus constrain courts exercising their power under the ATS." Id. [at 1664]. The Court also concluded that nothing in the text, history, and purpose of the ATS rebutted the presumption of extraterritoriality. Id. at 1669.

Turning to the specific claims asserted by the *Kiobel II* plaintiffs, the Court observed that "all the relevant conduct took place outside the United States," and that the defendants were foreign corporations whose only connection to the United States lay in their presence in this country. Id. The Court held that these claims were therefore barred, reasoning that they sought relief for violations of international law occurring outside the United States, and did not "touch and concern the territory of the United States . . . with sufficient force to displace the presumption against extraterritorial application." Id.

Kiobel II's holding makes clear that the general principles underlying the presumption against extraterritoriality apply to ATS claims, but it leaves important questions about extraterritorial ATS claims unresolved. In particular, *Kiobel II* articulates a new "touch and concern" test for determining when it is permissible for an ATS claim to seek the extraterritorial application of federal law. Id. But the opinion does not explain the nature of this test, except to say that it is not met when an ATS plaintiff asserts a cause of action against a foreign corporation based solely on foreign conduct. . . .

Rather than attempt to apply the amorphous touch and concern test on the record currently before us, we conclude that the plaintiffs should have the opportunity to amend their complaint in light of *Kiobel II*. It is common practice to allow plaintiffs to amend their pleadings to accommodate changes in the law, unless it is clear that amendment would be futile. Here, the plaintiffs seek to amend their complaint to allege that some of the activity underlying their ATS claim took place in the United States. On the record before us, we are unable to conclude that amendment would be futile, because unlike the claims at issue in *Kiobel II*, the plaintiffs contend that part of the conduct underlying their claims occurred within the United States. . . .

IV. Conclusion

The district court's order is Reversed, and we Vacate for further proceedings consistent with this opinion.

It Is So Ordered.

Rawlinson, Circuit Judge, concurring in part and dissenting in part:

. . . We all agree that the practice of engaging in child slave labor is reprehensible, indefensible, and morally abhorrent. Indeed, if that were the issue we were called upon to decide, this would be an easy case. Instead, we must decide who bears legal responsibility for the atrocities inflicted upon these Plaintiffs, forced into slave labor as children. More precisely, we must determine if the named Defendants in this case may be held legally responsible for the injuries alleged by the Plaintiffs. . . .

I. Mens Rea Requirement of the ATS

Unlike the majority, I would definitely and unequivocally decide that the purpose standard applies to the pleading of aiding and abetting liability under the ATS. In other words, Plaintiffs seeking to assert a claim against Defendants on an aiding and abetting theory of liability must allege sufficient facts to state a plausible claim for relief, i.e., that the defendants acted with the purpose of causing the injuries suffered by the Plaintiffs. . . .

Applying the proper mens rea standard of purpose, or specific intent, I strongly disagree that the allegations in Plaintiffs' Amended Complaint satisfy that standard. The contrary conclusion reached by the majority is particularly curious in light of the Plaintiffs' concession of their inability to meet the standard. Nevertheless, the majority generally relies upon allegations in the Amended Complaint as sufficient to establish that Defendants acted with the purpose to aid and abet child slavery. The majority focuses on inferences rather than on any particular allegations in the Amended Complaint that reflect the purpose mens rea. The only allegation from the Amended Complaint that is specifically referenced is the allegation that "[d]riven by the goal to reduce costs in any way possible, the defendants allegedly supported the use of child labor, the cheapest form of labor available. . . ." The majority concludes that "[r]eading the allegations in the light most favorable to the plaintiffs, one is led to the inference that the defendants placed increased revenues before basic human welfare, and intended to pursue all options available to reduce their cost for purchasing cocoa." Piling inference upon inference, the majority contends that the allegations that the defendants placed increased revenues before human welfare and acted with the intent to reduce the cost of purchasing cocoa, "support the inference that the defendants acted with the purpose to facilitate child slavery." . . .

The statement that child slavery is the cheapest form of labor available does not even implicate the Defendants. This allegation in no way raises a plausible inference that the Defendants acted with the purpose to aid and abet child slave labor. It may well be true that child slave labor is the cheapest form of labor for harvesting cocoa. But that unvarnished statement in no way supports the inferential leap that because child slave labor is the cheapest form of labor, Defendants aided and abetted the cocoa farmers who allegedly operated the child slave labor system.

To bolster the inferences discussed, the majority explains that Defendants' "use of child slavery benefitted the defendants and furthered their operational goals in the Ivory Coast . . ." However, taking advantage of a favorable existing market, while perhaps morally repugnant, does not equate to the specific intent to aid and abet child slave labor. . . .

The majority points to the fact that Defendants in this case had sufficient control over the cocoa market "that they could have stopped or limited the use of child slave labor by their suppliers." Rather than doing so, the majority concludes, Defendants "instead offered support that facilitated" child slavery. . . . Rejection of this argument is particularly appropriate in the absence of evidence that Defendants intended that the financial support be used to facilitate child slavery.

The majority also points to Defendants' lobbying efforts to "corroborate the inference of purpose." "[T]he defendants participated in lobbying efforts designed to defeat federal legislation that would have required chocolate importers and manufacturers to certify and label their chocolate as slave free." In the alternative, Defendants and others with interests in the chocolate industry advocated for the implementation of a voluntary compliance mechanism. However, exercising their right to petition the government does not reasonably support an inference that Defendants acted with the purpose to aid and abet child slavery. It is equally likely that Defendants sought to avoid additional government regulation. . . .

Plaintiffs and the majority concede that any and all actions taken by Defendants were motivated by the desire for profits rather than an intent to enslave children. This concession is fatal to the Amended Complaint as presently couched. There is absolutely no allegation that Defendants have violated any governing law or regulation in their quest for profits. And profit-seeking is the reason most corporations exist. To equate a profit-making motive with the mens rea required for ATS aiding and abetting liability would completely negate the constrained concept of ATS liability contemplated by the Supreme Court in *Sosa*.

One would hope that corporations would operate their businesses in a humanitarian and morally responsible manner. It is indeed unfortunate that many neglect to do so. However regrettable that circumstance may be, we cannot substitute the lack of humanitarianism for the pleading requirements that govern the ATS. . . . I would not conclude that the Plaintiffs have stated a claim under the ATS.

II. Extraterritorial Reach of the ATS

. . . I do not object to a remand to allow Plaintiffs to seek to further amend their Complaint in light of the Supreme Court's recent *Kiobel* decision. However, in my view, Plaintiffs face a substantial hurdle in their effort to assert a viable claim that the ATS applies to the admittedly extraterritorial child slave labor that is the basis of this case. . . .

In sum, I would affirm the district court's ruling that the Amended Complaint failed to state a claim under the ATS. In reviewing the next amended Complaint, the district court should hew closely to the guidance that the Supreme Court laid out in . . . *Sosa* and *Kiobel* that cautions federal court judges to tread lightly both when determining whether a claim has been stated under the ATS and whether the presumption against extraterritorial application of a domestic statute has been rebutted. These cases militate toward contraction rather than expansion. Therefore, I concur in a remand to allow Plaintiffs to further amend their Complaint in an effort to state a claim under the ATS. I dissent from any holding that they have adequately done so.

Other nations also have experimented with the adjudication of breaches of international law that occur beyond their territorial borders. In 1999, Belgium introduced the Act Covering the Punishment of Grave Breaches of International Humanitarian Law, which recognized the "universal competence" of the Belgian courts to address breaches of the Act's three categories of grave breaches of humanitarian law, irrespective of where geographically the breaches occurred or what nationality the alleged perpetrator or victim held. See Barnali Choudhury, Beyond the Alien Tort Claims Act: Alternative Approaches to Attributing Liability to Corporations for Extraterritorial Abuses, 26 Nw. J. Int'l L. & Bus. 43, 45-46 (2005) (describing the Act). Cf. Restatement (Third) of the Foreign Relations Law of the United States §§402, 404 (1987) (describing bases of prescriptive jurisdiction in U.S. courts to hear claims even without a territorial, national, or protective nexus to the United States). Under pressure from the United States, Belgium amended its law, such that jurisdiction under the Act only reaches Belgian citizens and long-term residents. For a review of the limited degree to which national courts have asserted "universal jurisdiction" to prosecute war crimes and other serious offenses irrespective of territorial connection, see Máximo Langer, The Diplomacy of Universal Jurisdiction: The Political Branches and the Transnational Prosecution of International Crimes, 105 Am. J. Int'l L. 1 (2011).

Courts in the United Kingdom, Canada, and Australia also have demonstrated a willingness to adjudicate claims arising out of extraterritorial conduct, particularly when brought against corporations organized or domiciled in those respective countries. See Choudhury, 26 Nw. J. Int'l L. & Bus. at 51-56. Doctrines such as forum non conveniens, however, impose similar barriers to plaintiffs in foreign courts as in the United States. Canada in particular seems to follow the restrictive approach of most U.S. courts. See, e.g., Recherches Internationales Québec v. Cambior, Inc., [1998] Q.J. No. 2554 (dismissing class action brought against Quebec corporation by 23,000 victims of a toxic spill at a gold mine in Guyana). Courts in the United Kingdom and Australia, on the other hand, seem to follow the more permissive approach of states such as Delaware, which affords greater deference to the plaintiff's chosen forum. See, e.g., Regie Nationale des Usines Renault S.A. v. Zhang (2002) 210 C.L.R. 491, 521 (observing that Australian courts provide deference to plaintiff's choice of forum unless adjudication domestically would be oppressive, prejudicial, or vexatious); Lubbe v. Cape Plc., [2000] 4 All E.R. 268 (permitting adjudication of claims by thousands of plaintiffs allegedly injured by an asbestos mining operation in South Africa in part because South Africa does not provide legal aid, contingency fee arrangements, or other mechanisms by which plaintiffs could secure adequate legal representation).

For recent scholarly commentary regarding ATS litigation, see Roger P. Alford, Human Rights After *Kiobel*: Choice of Law and the Rise of Transnational Tort Litigation, 63 Emory L.J. 1089 (2014); Fernando R. Teson, The *Kiobel* Decision: The End of an Era, 8 N.Y.U. J.L. & Liberty 161 (2013); Jide Nzelibe, Contesting Adjudication: The Partisan Divide Over Alien Tort Statute Litigation, 33 Nw. J. Int'l L. & Bus. 475 (2013).

C. Intergovernmental Liability in the Federal Context

Throughout this casebook we have seen instances in which a governmental body has defended or brought a tort suit. For instance, in City of Louisville v. Humphrey, p. 246, above, the defendant municipality faced a claim that its negligent operation of a jail facility led to the death of an inmate. In United States v. Carroll Towing Co., p. 189, above, the federal government brought suit as a plaintiff in order to recover damages for its lost cargo. And as noted above, pp. 443-444, a number of states and cities, with varying degrees of success, have turned as plaintiffs to using public nuisance litigation to challenge the marketing of tobacco products, firearms, lead paint, and even subprime mortgages. See Raymond H. Brescia, On Public Plaintiffs and Private Harms: The Standing of Municipalities in Climate Change, Firearms, and Financial Crisis Litigation, 24 Notre Dame J.L. Ethics & Pub. Pol'y 7 (2010). As perhaps the most dramatic example, prior to the advent of significant federal climate change regulation, subnational governmental bodies attempted to use the torts process to challenge certain activities, such as electricity generation or automobile production, that are known to contribute heavily to greenhouse gas emissions. See, e.g., California v. General Motors Corp., 2007 U.S. Dist. LEXIS 68547, 2007 WL 2726871 (N.D. Cal. Sept. 17, 2007) (dismissing as a non-justiciable political question California's request for monetary relief for environmental and health damages and infrastructure expenses caused by the contribution to climate change of emissions from defendant automakers vehicles).

Such cases obviously raise concerns regarding the amenability of complex policy problems to judicial resolution. In the case of expansive use of the public nuisance tort by governmental bodies, the suits also raise concerns regarding the proper division of regulatory authority between the overtly political branches and the judiciary. Before returning to the problem of climate change and suits against private parties, this section explores tort disputes arising between governmental bodies, rather than between a governmental body on one side and a private party on the other. In particular, the section explores early-twentieth-century tort litigation between states pursuant to the United States Supreme Court's original jurisdiction under §2, art. III, of the Constitution.[3] Does the fact that both sides of these tort disputes are governmental bodies alleviate some of the concerns raised regarding judicial competence and separation of powers? Does it exacerbate them?

3. Article III, §2, cl. 2, of the Constitution provides: "In all Cases . . . in which a State shall be Party, the Supreme Court shall have original Jurisdiction." In addition, Congress has provided in 28 U.S.C. §1251 that "(a) the Supreme Court shall have original and exclusive jurisdiction of: (1) All controversies between two or more States."

Missouri v. Illinois

200 U.S. 496, 26 S. Ct. 268, 50 L. Ed. 572 (1906)

MR. JUSTICE HOLMES delivered the opinion of the court:

This is a suit brought by the state of Missouri to restrain the discharge of the sewage of Chicago through an artificial channel into the Desplaines river, in the state of Illinois. That river empties into the Illinois river, and the latter empties into the Mississippi at a point about 43 miles above the city of St. Louis. It was alleged in the bill that the result of the threatened discharge would be to send 1,500 tons of poisonous filth daily into the Mississippi, to deposit great quantities of the same upon the part of the bed of the last-named river belonging to the plaintiff, and so to poison the water of that river, upon which various of the plaintiff's cities, towns, and inhabitants depended, as to make it unfit for drinking, agricultural, or manufacturing purposes. It was alleged that the defendant sanitary district was acting in pursuance of a statute of the state of Illinois, and as an agency of that state. . . . The answers deny the plaintiff's case, allege that the new plan sends the water of the Illinois river into the Mississippi much purer than it was before, that many towns and cities of the plaintiff along the Missouri and Mississippi discharge their sewage into those rivers, and that if there is any trouble the plaintiff must look nearer home for the cause.

The decision upon the demurrer discussed mainly the jurisdiction of the court, and, as leave to answer was given when the demurrer was overruled, naturally there was no very precise consideration of the principles of law to be applied if the plaintiff should prove its case. That was left to the future, with the general intimation that the nuisance must be made out upon determinate and satisfactory evidence, that it must not be doubtful, and that the danger must be shown to be real and immediate. The nuisance set forth in the bill was one which would be of international importance, — a visible change of a great river from a pure stream into a polluted and poisoned ditch. The only question presented was whether, as between the states of the Union, this court was competent to deal with a situation which, if it arose between independent sovereignties, might lead to war. Whatever differences of opinion there might be upon matters of detail, the jurisdiction and authority of this court to deal with such a case as that is not open to doubt. But the evidence now is in, the actual facts have required for their establishment the most ingenious experiments, and for their interpretation the most subtle speculations, of modern science, and therefore it becomes necessary at the present stage to consider somewhat more nicely than heretofore how the evidence in it is to be approached. . . .

In the case at bar, . . . [t]he only ground on which that state's conduct can be called in question is one which must be implied from the words of the Constitution. The Constitution extends the judicial power of the United States to controversies between two or more states, and between a state and citizens of another state, and gives this court original jurisdiction in cases in which a state shall be a party. Therefore, if one state raises a controversy with another, this court must determine whether there is any principle of law, and, if any, what, on which the plaintiff can recover. But the fact that this court must decide does not mean, of course, that it takes the place of a legislature. . . . If we suppose a case which did not fall within the power of Congress to regulate, the result of a declaration of rights by this court would be the establishment of a rule which would be irrevocable by any power except that of this court to reverse its own decision, an amendment of the Constitution, or possibly an agreement between the States, sanctioned by the legislature of the United States.

The difficulties in the way of establishing such a system of law might not be insuperable, but they would be great and new. Take the question of prescription in a case like the present. The reasons on which prescription for a public nuisance is denied or may be granted to an individual as against the sovereign power to which he is subject have no application to an independent state. See 1 Oppenheim, International Law. 293, §§242, 243. It would be contradicting a fundamental principle of human nature to allow no effect to the lapse of time, however long (Davis v. Mills, 194 U. S. 451, 457, 48 L. Ed. 1067, 1071, 24 Sup. Ct. Rep. 692), yet the fixing of a definite time usually belongs to the legislature rather than the courts. The courts did fix a time in the rule against perpetuities, but the usual course, as in the instances of statutes of limitation, the duration of patents, the age of majority, etc., is to depend upon the lawmaking power.

It is decided that a case such as is made by the bill may be a ground for relief. The purpose of the foregoing observations is not to lay a foundation for departing from that decision, but simply to illustrate the great and serious caution with which it is necessary to approach the question whether a case is proved. It may be imagined that a nuisance might be created by a state upon a navigable river like the Danube, which would amount to a casus belli for a state lower down, unless removed. If such a nuisance were created by a state upon the Mississippi, the controversy would be resolved by the more peaceful means of a suit in this court. But it does not follow that every matter which would warrant a resort to equity by one citizen against another in the same jurisdiction equally would warrant an interference by this court with the action of a state. . . .

Before this court ought to intervene, the case should be of serious magnitude, clearly and fully proved, and the principle to be applied should be one which the court is prepared deliberately to maintain against all considerations on the other side. See Kansas v. Colorado, 185 U. S. 125, 46 L. Ed. 838, 22 Sup. Ct. Rep. 552.

As to the principle to be laid down, the caution necessary is manifest. It is a question of the first magnitude whether the destiny of the great rivers is to be the sewers of the cities along their banks or to be protected against everything which threatens their purity. To decide the whole matter at one blow by an irrevocable fiat would be at least premature. If we are to judge by what the plaintiff itself permits, the discharge of sewage into the Mississippi by cities and towns is to be expected. We believe that the practice of discharging into the river is general along its banks, except where the levees of Louisiana have led to a different course. The argument for the plaintiff asserts it to be proper within certain limits. These are facts to be considered. Even in cases between individuals, some consideration is given to the practical course of events. In the black country of England parties would not be expected to stand upon extreme rights. St. Helen's Smelting Co. v. Tipping, 11 H. L. Cas. 642. See Boston Ferrule Co. v. Hills, 159 Mass. 147, 150, 20 L.R.A. 844, 34 N.E. 85. Where, as here, the plaintiff has sovereign powers, and deliberately permits discharges similar to those of which it complains, it not only offers a standard to which the defendant has the right to appeal, but, as some of those discharges are above the intake of St. Louis, it warrants the defendant in demanding the strictest proof that the plaintiff's own conduct does not produce the result, or at least so conduce to it, that courts should not be curious to apportion the blame. . . .

We assume the now-prevailing scientific explanation of typhoid fever to be correct. But when we go beyond that assumption, everything is involved in doubt. The data upon which an increase in the deaths from typhoid fever in St. Louis is alleged are disputed. The elimination of other causes is denied. The experts differ as to the time and distance within which a stream would purify itself. No case of an epidemic caused by infection at so remote a source is brought forward and the cases which are produced are controverted. The plaintiff obviously must be cautious upon this point, for, if this suit should succeed, many others would follow, and it not improbably would find itself a defendant to a bill by one or more of the states lower down upon the Mississippi. The distance which the sewage has to travel (357 miles) is not open to debate, but the time of transit, to be inferred from experiments with floats, is estimated as varying from eight to eighteen and a half days, with forty-eight hours more from intake to distribution, and when corrected by observations of bacteria is greatly prolonged by the defendants. The experiments of the defendant's experts lead them to the opinion that a typhoid bacillus could not survive the journey, while those on the other side maintain that it might live and keep its power for twenty-five days or more, and arrive at St. Louis. Upon the question at issue, whether the new discharge from Chicago hurts St. Louis, there is a categorical contradiction between the experts on the two sides. . . .

We might go more into detail, but we believe that we have said enough to explain our point of view and our opinion of the evidence as it stands. What the future may develop, of course we cannot tell. But our conclusion upon the present evidence is that the case proved falls so far below the allegations of the bill that it is not brought within the principles heretofore established in the cause.

Bill dismissed without prejudice.

In 1907, the Court revisited the question of how clearly state plaintiffs must demonstrate a threat of harm in order to invoke the Court's protective authority. In Georgia v. Tennessee Copper Company, 206 U.S. 230 (1907), the state of Georgia sought to enjoin several copper companies from "discharging noxious gas from their works in Tennessee over the plaintiff's territory," after having seen the state's appeals for relief to Tennessee authorities ignored. In an opinion written again by Justice Holmes, the Court first emphasized that the state, as "quasi-sovereign . . . has the last word as to whether its mountains shall be stripped of their forests and its inhabitants shall breathe pure air." Id. at 237. The Court then appeared to adopt a less stringent standard for demonstrating transboundary harm than suggested by Missouri v. Illinois (206 U.S. at 237-39):

> The caution with which demands of this sort, on the part of a state, for relief from injuries analogous to torts, must be examined, is dwelt upon in Missouri v. Illinois, 200 U.S. 496, 520, 521, 50 L. Ed. 572, 578, 579, 26 Sup. Ct. Rep. 268. But it is plain that some such demands must be recognized, if the grounds alleged are proved. When the states by their union made the forcible abatement of outside nuisances impossible to each, they did not thereby agree to submit to whatever might be done. They did not renounce the possibility of making reasonable demands on the ground of their still remaining quasi-sovereign interests; and the alternative to force is a suit in this court. Missouri v. Illinois, 180 U.S. 208, 241, 45 L. Ed. 497, 512, 21 Sup. Ct. Rep. 331.
>
> . . . The proof requires but a few words. It is not denied that the defendants generate in their works near the Georgia line large quantities of sulphur dioxid[e], which becomes sulphurous acid by its mixture with the air. It hardly is denied, and cannot be denied with success, that this gas often is carried by the wind great distances and over great tracts of Georgia land. On the evidence the pollution of the air and the magnitude of that pollution are not open to dispute. Without any attempt to go into details immaterial to the suit, it is proper to add that we are satisfied, by a preponderance of evidence, that the sulphurous fumes cause and threaten damage on so considerable a scale to the forests and vegetable life, if not to health, within the plaintiff state, as to make out a case within the requirements of Missouri v. Illinois, 200 U.S. 496, 50 L. Ed. 572, 26 Sup. Ct. Rep. 268. Whether Georgia, by insisting upon this claim, is doing more harm than good to her own citizens, is for her to determine. The possible disaster to those outside the state must be accepted as a consequence of her standing upon her extreme rights.

Following Missouri v. Illinois, the growth of the city of Chicago continued to cause problems for itself and neighboring states, as the city needed to divert more and more water from Lake Michigan in order to wash away the city's sewage. By 1924, the problem had become so severe that Wisconsin, Michigan, and New York sued the state of Illinois and the municipal sanitary district for exceeding their equitable entitlement to the use of the waters of Lake Michigan. The plaintiffs demonstrated that diversions by Illinois had caused significant lowering of water levels in Lakes Michigan, Huron, Erie, and Ontario, as well as in connecting waterways and the St. Lawrence River. Based on the findings of a special master appointed by the Supreme Court to assist with the dispute, the Court concluded that the plaintiff states were entitled to equitable relief. See Wisconsin v. Illinois, 278 U.S. 367 (1929). Later, the Court issued an injunction requiring Chicago to build a sewage treatment plant to enable the city to reduce its need for water from Lake Michigan. See Wisconsin v. Illinois, 281 U.S. 179 (1930); Wisconsin v. Illinois, 281 U.S. 696 (1930). When the city continued to delay implementation of the plan, the Court eventually ordered the state of Illinois to provide all funds necessary for Chicago to complete construction of the sewage treatment facility. See Wisconsin v. Illinois, 289 U.S. 395 (1933).

In New Jersey v. New York, 283 U.S. 473 (1931), the Court faced a suit by the state of New Jersey seeking relief from the city of New York's waste disposal practices (283 U.S. at 476):

> The complaint alleges that the city of New York for many years has dumped and still is dumping noxious, offensive and injurious materials — all of which are for brevity called garbage — into the ocean; that great quantities of the same moving on or near the surface of the water frequently have been and are being cast upon the beaches belonging to the state, its municipalities and its citizens, thereby creating a public nuisance and causing great and irreparable injury. It prays an injunction restraining the city from dumping garbage into the ocean or waters of the United States off the coast of New Jersey and from otherwise polluting its waters and beaches.

Relying on a special master's report detailing the extent and significance of New York's garbage dumping and the harm caused to New Jersey, the Court found that the practice constituted a public nuisance and ordered its cessation. First, however, the Court granted the defendant a period of a "reasonable time" during which New York could attempt to devise an alternative disposal plan. In the course of its analysis, the Court dispensed with New York's argument that the Court lacked jurisdiction to adjudicate harmful use of a global commons such as the ocean (283 U.S. at 482):

> Defendant contends that, as it dumps the garbage into the ocean and not within the waters of the United States or of New Jersey, this Court is without jurisdiction to grant the injunction. But the defendant is before the Court and the property of plaintiff and its citizens that is alleged to have been injured by such dumping is within the Court's territorial jurisdiction. The situs of the acts creating the nuisance, whether within or without the United States, is of no importance. Plaintiff seeks a decree in personam to prevent them in the future. The Court has jurisdiction.

Illinois v. Milwaukee

406 U.S. 91, 92 S. Ct. 1385, 31 L. Ed. 2d 712 (1972)

MR. JUSTICE DOUGLAS delivered the opinion of the Court.

This is a motion by Illinois to file a bill of complaint under our original jurisdiction against four cities of Wisconsin, the Sewerage Commission of the City of Milwaukee, and the Metropolitan Sewerage Commission of the County of Milwaukee. The cause of action alleged is pollution by the defendants of Lake Michigan, a body of interstate water. According to plaintiff, some 200 million gallons of raw or inadequately treated sewage and other waste materials are discharged daily into the lake in the Milwaukee area alone. Plaintiff alleges that it and its subdivisions prohibit and prevent such discharges, but that the defendants do not take such actions. Plaintiff asks that we abate this public nuisance.

[In Part I, the opinion interprets 28 U.S.C. §1251, which provides that "the Supreme Court shall have original and exclusive jurisdiction of . . . all controversies between two or more States," not to require the Court to assume exclusive original jurisdiction of suits involving political subdivisions of states, such as municipalities or utility districts. Part II determines that such suits fall within the federal question jurisdiction of the district courts because they invoke the federal common law of nuisance. Part III then addresses whether the growth of statutory and regulatory environmental law at the federal level alters the Court's traditional stance toward interstate tort adjudication.]

III

Congress has enacted numerous laws touching interstate waters. In 1899 it established some surveillance by the Army Corps of Engineers over industrial pollution, not including sewage, Rivers and Harbors Act of March 3, 1899, 30 Stat. 1121, a grant of power which we construed in United States v. Republic Steel Corp., 362 U.S. 482, 80 S. Ct. 884, 4 L. Ed. 2d 903, and in United States v. Standard Oil Co., 384 U.S. 224, 86 S. Ct. 1427, 16 L. Ed. 2d 492.

The 1899 Act has been reinforced and broadened by a complex of laws recently enacted. The Federal Water Pollution Control Act, 62 Stat. 1155, as amended, 33 U.S.C. s 1151, tightens control over discharges into navigable waters so as not to lower applicable water quality standards. By the National Environmental Policy Act of 1969, 83 Stat. 852, 42 U.S.C. s 4321 et seq., Congress 'authorizes and directs' that 'the policies, regulations, and public laws of the United States shall be interpreted and administered in accordance with the policies set forth in this Act' and that 'all agencies of the Federal Government shall . . . identify and develop methods and procedures . . . which will insure that presently unquantified environmental amenities and values may be given appropriate consideration in decisionmaking along with economic and technical considerations.' Sec. 102, 42 U.S.C. s 4332. Congress has evinced increasing concern with the quality of the aquatic environment as it affects the conservation and safeguarding of fish and wildlife resources. See, e.g., Fish and Wildlife Act of 1956, 70 Stat. 1119, 16 U.S.C. s 742a; the Act of Sept. 22, 1959, 73 Stat. 642, authorizing research in migratory marine game fish, 16 U.S.C. s 760e; and the Fish and Wildlife Coordination Act, 48 Stat. 401, as amended, 16 U.S.C. s 661.

Buttressed by these new and expanding policies, the Corps of Engineers has issued new Rules and Regulations governing permits for discharges or deposits into navigable waters. 36 Fed. Reg. 6564 et seq.

The Federal Water Pollution Control Act in s 1(b) declares that it is federal policy 'to recognize, preserve, and protect the primary responsibilities and rights of the States in preventing and controlling water pollution.' But the Act makes clear that it is federal, not state, law that in the end controls the pollution of interstate or navigable waters. While the States are given time to establish water quality standards, s 10(c)(1), if a State fails to do so the federal administrator promulgates one. s 10(c)(2). Section 10(a) makes pollution of interstate or navigable waters subject 'to abatement' when it 'endangers the health or welfare of any persons.' The abatement that is authorized follows a long drawn-out procedure unnecessary to relate here. It uses the conference procedure, hoping for amicable settlements. But if none is reached, the federal administrator may request the Attorney General to bring suit on behalf of the United States for abatement of the pollution. s 10(g).

The remedy sought by Illinois is not within the precise scope of remedies prescribed by Congress. Yet the remedies which Congress provides are not necessarily the only federal remedies available. 'It is not uncommon for federal courts to fashion federal law where federal rights are concerned.' Textile Workers v. Lincoln Mills, 353 U.S. 448, 457, 77 S.Ct. 912, 918, 1 L.Ed.2d 972. When we deal with air and water in their ambient or interstate aspects, there is a federal common law,[5] as Texas v. Pankey, 10 Cir., 441 F.2d 236, recently held.

The application of federal common law to abate a public nuisance in interstate or navigable waters is not inconsistent with the Water Pollution Control Act. Congress provided in s 10(b) of that Act that, save as a court may decree otherwise in an enforcement action, '(s)tate and interstate action to abate pollution of interstate or navigable waters shall be encouraged and shall not . . . be displaced by Federal enforcement action.' . . .

It may happen that new federal laws and new federal regulations may in time pre-empt the field of federal common law of nuisance. But until that comes to pass, federal courts will be empowered to appraise the equities of the suits alleging creation of a public nuisance by water pollution. While federal law governs,[9] consideration of state standards may be relevant. . . . Thus, a State with high water-quality standards may well ask that its strict standards be honored and that it not be compelled to lower itself to the more degrading standards of a neighbor. There are no fixed rules that govern; these will be equity suits in which the informed judgment of the chancellor will largely govern.

5. While the various federal environmental protection statutes will not necessarily mark the outer bounds of the federal common law, they may provide useful guidelines in fashioning such rules of decision. What we said in another connection in Textile Workers v. Lincoln Mills, 353 U.S. 448, 456-457, 77 S. Ct. 912, 918, 1 L. Ed. 2d 972, is relevant here:

> The question then is, what is the substantive law to be applied in suits under s 301(a)? We conclude that the substantive law to apply in suits under s 301(a) is federal law, which the courts must fashion from the policy of our national labor laws. The Labor Management Relations Act expressly furnishes some substantive law. It points out what the parties may or may not do in certain situations. Other problems will lie in the penumbra of express statutory mandates. Some will lack express statutory sanction but will be solved by looking at the policy of the legislation and fashioning a remedy that will effectuate that policy. The range of judicial inventiveness will be determined by the nature of the problem. Federal interpretation of the federal law will govern, not state law. But state law, if compatible with the purpose of s 301, may be resorted to in order to find the rule that will best effectuate the federal policy. Any state law applied, however, will be absorbed as federal law and will not be an independent source of private rights.

(Citations omitted.) See also Woods & Reed, The Supreme Court and Interstate Environmental Quality: Some Notes on the Wyandotte Case, 12 Ariz. L. Rev. 691, 713-714; Note, 56 Va. L. Rev. 458.

9.

> Federal common law and not the varying common law of the individual States is, we think, entitled and necessary to be recognized as a basis for dealing in uniform standard with the environmental rights of a State against improper impairment by sources outside its domain. The more would this seem to be imperative in the present era of growing concern on the part of a State about its ecological conditions and impairments of them. In the outside sources of such impairment, more conflicting disputes, increasing assertions and proliferating contentions would seem to be inevitable. Until the field has been made the subject of comprehensive legislation or authorized administrative standards, only a federal common law basis can provide an adequate means for dealing with such claims as alleged federal rights. And the logic and practicality of regarding such claims as being entitled to be asserted within the federal-question jurisdiction of s 1331(a) would seem to be self-evident.

Texas v. Pankey, 441 F.2d 236, 241-242.

We deny, without prejudice, the motion for leave to file. While this original suit normally might be the appropriate vehicle for resolving this controversy, we exercise our discretion to remit the parties to an appropriate district court whose powers are adequate to resolve the issues.

So ordered.

Motion denied.

After the Court declined to accept original jurisdiction in Illinois v. Milwaukee, the state of Illinois brought suit in federal district court. Nine years later, the case again made its way to the Supreme Court, where the defendants argued that Illinois' claim had been preempted by a major legislative overhaul of the federal water pollution scheme enacted by Congress shortly after the Supreme Court's first opinion. See Milwaukee v. Illinois, 451 U.S. 304 (1981). The Court began its analysis of this preemption argument by noting that

> [f]ederal courts, unlike state courts, are not general common-law courts and do not possess a general power to develop and apply their own rules of decision. The enactment of a federal rule in an area of national concern, and the decision whether to displace state law in doing so, is generally made not by the federal judiciary, purposefully insulated from democratic pressures, but by the people through their elected representatives in Congress. . . . When Congress has not spoken to a particular issue, however, and when there exists a significant conflict between some federal policy or interest and the use of state law, the Court has found it necessary, in a few and restricted instances to develop federal common law. Nothing in this process suggests that courts are better suited to develop national policy in areas governed by federal common law than they are in other areas, or that the usual and important concerns of an appropriate division of functions between the Congress and the federal judiciary are inapplicable. We have always recognized that federal common law is subject to the paramount authority of Congress. It is resorted to in absence of an applicable Act of Congress, and because the Court is compelled to consider federal questions which cannot be answered from federal statutes alone. Federal common law is a necessary expedient, and when Congress addresses a question previously governed by a decision rested on federal common law the need for such an unusual exercise of lawmaking by federal courts disappears.

Id. at 312-15 (citations and quotation marks omitted). Applying these standards to the newly revamped federal water pollution program, the Court "conclude[d] that, at least so far as concerns the claims of respondents, Congress has not left the formulation of appropriate federal standards to the courts through application of often vague and indeterminate nuisance concepts and maxims of equity jurisprudence, but rather has occupied the field through the establishment of a comprehensive regulatory program supervised by an expert administrative agency." Id. at 317.

Frustrated by what they perceived as a lack of legislative and regulatory progress in addressing the causes and consequences of climate change, a coalition of public and private plaintiffs sought to invoke this small and somewhat dormant body of federal common law to deem greenhouse gas emissions a public nuisance. See Connecticut v. American Elec. Power Co., 406 F. Supp. 2d 265 (S.D.N.Y. 2005). One of this casebook's authors has argued that their claims face daunting challenges on the merits, including difficulty meeting each of the basic tort elements of duty, breach, causation, and harm. See Douglas A. Kysar, What Climate Change Can Do About Tort Law, 41 Envtl. L. 1 (2011). Before those merits could be addressed, however, the plaintiffs also faced a variety of procedural and jurisdictional obstacles, including the question of whether federal common law has been displaced by existing congressional acts.

American Electric Power Co., Inc. v. Connecticut

No. 10-174, 2011 WL 2437011 (U.S. June 20, 2011)

Ginsburg, J., delivered the opinion of the Court. . . .

In Massachusetts v. EPA, 549 U.S. 497, 127 S. Ct. 1438, 167 L. Ed. 2d 248 (2007), this Court held that the Clean Air Act, 42 U.S.C. §7401 *et seq.*, authorizes federal regulation of emissions of carbon dioxide and other greenhouse gases. "[N]aturally present in the atmosphere and . . . also emitted by human activities," greenhouse gases are so named because they "trap . . . heat that would otherwise escape from the [Earth's] atmosphere, and thus form the greenhouse effect that helps keep the Earth warm enough for life." 74 Fed. Reg. 66499 (2009). *Massachusetts* held that the Environmental Protection Agency (EPA) had misread the Clean Air Act when it denied a rulemaking petition seeking controls on greenhouse gas emissions from new motor vehicles. 549 U.S., at 510-511. Greenhouse gases, we determined, qualify as "air pollutant[s]" within the meaning of the governing Clean Air Act provision, id., at 528-529 (quoting §7602(g)); they are therefore within EPA's regulatory ken. Because EPA had authority to set greenhouse gas emission standards and had offered no "reasoned explanation" for failing to do so, we concluded that the agency had not acted "in accordance with law" when it denied the requested rulemaking. *Id.*, at 534-535 (quoting §7607(d)(9)(A)). . . .

In July 2004, two groups of plaintiffs filed separate complaints in the Southern District of New York against the same five major electric power companies. The first group of plaintiffs included eight States and New York City, the second joined three nonprofit land trusts; both groups are respondents here. The defendants, now petitioners, are four private companies and the Tennessee Valley Authority, a federally owned corporation that operates fossil-fuel fired power plants in several States. According to the complaints, the defendants "are the five largest emitters of carbon dioxide in the United States." App. 57, 118. Their collective annual emissions of 650 million tons constitute 25 percent of emissions from the domestic electric power sector, 10 percent of emissions from all domestic human activities, *ibid.*, and 2.5 percent of all anthropogenic emissions worldwide, App. to Pet. for Cert. 72a.

By contributing to global warming, the plaintiffs asserted, the defendants' carbon-dioxide emissions created a "substantial and unreasonable interference with public rights," in violation of the federal common law of interstate nuisance, or, in the alternative, of state tort law. App. 103-105, 145-147. The States and New York City alleged that public lands, infrastructure, and health were at risk from climate change. App. 88-93. The trusts urged that climate change would destroy habitats for animals and rare species of trees and plants on land the trusts owned and conserved. App. 139-145. All plaintiffs sought injunctive relief requiring each defendant "to cap its carbon dioxide emissions and then reduce them by a specified percentage each year for at least a decade." App. 110, 153.

The District Court dismissed both suits as presenting non-justiciable political questions, citing Baker v. Carr, 369 U.S. 186, 82 S. Ct. 691, 7 L. Ed. 2d 663 (1962), but the Second Circuit reversed, 582 F.3d 309 (2009). . . . We granted certiorari. . . .

"There is no federal general common law," Erie R. Co. v. Tompkins, 304 U.S. 64, 78, 58 S. Ct. 817, 82 L. Ed. 1188 (1938), famously recognized. In the wake of *Erie*, however, a keener understanding developed. See generally Friendly, In Praise of *Erie* — And of the New Federal Common Law, 39 N.Y.U. L. Rev. 383 (1964). *Erie* "le[ft] to the states what ought be left to them," *id.*, at 405, and thus required "federal courts [to] follow state decisions on matters of substantive law appropriately cognizable by the states," *id.*, at 422. *Erie* also sparked "the emergence of a federal decisional law in areas of national concern." *Id.*, at 405. The "new" federal common law addresses "subjects within national legislative power where Congress has so directed" or where the basic scheme of the Constitution so demands. *Id.*, at 408, n. 119, 421-422. Environmental protection is undoubtedly an area "within national legislative power," one in which federal courts may fill in "statutory interstices," and, if necessary, even "fashion federal law." *Id.*, at 421-422. . . .

We have not yet decided whether private citizens (here, the land trusts) or political subdivisions (New York City) of a State may invoke the federal common law of nuisance to abate out-of-state pollution. Nor have we ever held that a State may sue to abate any and all manner of pollution originating outside its borders.

The defendants argue that considerations of scale and complexity distinguish global warming from the more bounded pollution giving rise to past federal nuisance suits. Greenhouse gases once emitted "become well mixed in the atmosphere," 74 Fed. Reg. 66514; emissions in New Jersey may contribute no more to flooding in New York than emissions in China. Cf. Brief for Petitioners 18-19. The plaintiffs, on the other hand, contend that an equitable remedy against the largest emitters of carbon dioxide in the United States is in order and not beyond judicial competence. See Brief for Respondents Open Space Institute et al. 32-35. And we have recognized that public nuisance law, like common law generally, adapts to changing scientific and factual circumstances. . . .

We need not address the parties' dispute in this regard. For it is an academic question whether, in the absence of the Clean Air Act and the EPA actions the Act authorizes, the plaintiffs could state a federal common law claim for curtailment of greenhouse gas emissions because of their contribution to global warming. Any such claim would be displaced by the federal legislation authorizing EPA to regulate carbon-dioxide emissions.

"[W]hen Congress addresses a question previously governed by a decision rested on federal common law," the Court has explained, "the need for such an unusual exercise of law-making by federal courts disappears." [Milwaukee v. Illinois, 451 U.S. 304, 314 (1981) (*Milwaukee II*)]. . . . The test for whether congressional legislation excludes the declaration of federal common law is simply whether the statute "speak[s] directly to [the] question" at issue. Mobil Oil Corp. v. Higginbotham, 436 U.S. 618, 625, 98 S. Ct. 2010, 56 L. Ed. 2d 581 (1978).

We hold that the Clean Air Act and the EPA actions it authorizes displace any federal common law right to seek abatement of carbon-dioxide emissions from fossil-fuel fired power plants. *Massachusetts* made plain that emissions of carbon dioxide qualify as air pollution subject to regulation under the Act. 549 U.S., at 528-529. And we think it equally plain that the Act "speaks directly" to emissions of carbon dioxide from the defendants' plants.

Section 111 of the Act directs the EPA Administrator to list "categories of stationary sources" that "in [her] judgment . . . caus[e], or contribut[e] significantly to, air pollution which may reasonably be anticipated to endanger public health or welfare." §7411(b)(1)(A). Once EPA lists a category, the agency must establish standards of performance for emission of pollutants from new or modified sources within that category.

§7411(b)(1)(B); see also §7411(a)(2). And, most relevant here, §7411(d) then requires regulation of existing sources within the same category. For existing sources, EPA issues emissions guidelines, see 40 C.F.R. §60.22, .23 (2009); in compliance with those guidelines and subject to federal oversight, the States then issue performance standards for stationary sources within their jurisdiction, §7411(d)(1).

. . . If EPA does not *set* emissions limits for a particular pollutant or source of pollution, States and private parties may petition for a rulemaking on the matter, and EPA's response will be reviewable in federal court. . . . The Act itself thus provides a means to seek limits on emissions of carbon dioxide from domestic power plants — the same relief the plaintiffs seek by invoking federal common law. We see no room for a parallel track.

The plaintiffs argue, as the Second Circuit held, that federal common law is not displaced until EPA actually exercises its regulatory authority, *i.e.*, until it sets standards governing emissions from the defendants' plants. We disagree.

The sewage discharges at issue in *Milwaukee II*, we do not overlook, were subject to effluent limits set by EPA; under the displacing statute, "[e]very point source discharge" of water pollution was "prohibited unless covered by a permit." 451 U.S., at 318-320 (emphasis deleted). As *Milwaukee II* made clear, however, the relevant question for purposes of displacement is "whether the field has been occupied, not whether it has been occupied in a particular manner." *Id.*, at 324. Of necessity, Congress selects different regulatory regimes to address different problems. Congress could hardly preemptively prohibit every discharge of carbon dioxide unless covered by a permit. After all, we each emit carbon dioxide merely by breathing.

The Clean Air Act is no less an exercise of the legislature's "considered judgment" concerning the regulation of air pollution because it permits emissions *until* EPA acts. . . . The critical point is that Congress delegated to EPA the decision whether and how to regulate carbon-dioxide emissions from power plants; the delegation is what displaces federal common law. Indeed, were EPA to decline to regulate carbon-dioxide emissions altogether at the conclusion of its ongoing §7411 rulemaking, the federal courts would have no warrant to employ the federal common law of nuisance to upset the agency's expert determination.

. . . [T]his prescribed order of decisionmaking — the first decider under the Act is the expert administrative agency, the second, federal judges — is yet another reason to resist setting emissions standards by judicial decree under federal tort law. The appropriate amount of regulation in any particular greenhouse gas–producing sector cannot be prescribed in a vacuum: as with other questions of national or international policy, informed assessment of competing interests is required. Along with the environmental benefit potentially achievable, our Nation's energy needs and the possibility of economic disruption must weigh in the balance.

The Clean Air Act entrusts such complex balancing to EPA in the first instance, in combination with state regulators. . . . It is altogether fitting that Congress designated an expert agency, here, EPA, as best suited to serve as primary regulator of greenhouse gas emissions. The expert agency is surely better equipped to do the job than individual district judges issuing ad hoc, case-by-case injunctions. Federal judges lack the scientific, economic, and technological resources an agency can utilize in coping with issues of this order. See generally Chevron U.S.A. Inc. v. Natural Resources Defense Council, Inc., 467 U.S. 837, 865-866, 104 S. Ct. 2778, 81 L. Ed. 2d 694 (1984). Judges may not commission scientific studies or convene groups of experts for advice, or issue rules under notice-and-comment procedures inviting input by any interested person, or seek the counsel of regulators in the States where the defendants are located. Rather, judges are confined by a record comprising the evidence the parties present. Moreover, federal district judges, sitting as sole adjudicators, lack authority to render precedential decisions binding other judges, even members of the same court.

Notwithstanding these disabilities, the plaintiffs propose that individual federal judges determine, in the first instance, what amount of carbon-dioxide emissions is "unreasonable," App. 103, 145, and then decide what level of reduction is "practical, feasible and economically viable," App. 58, 119. These determinations would be made for the defendants named in the two lawsuits launched by the plaintiffs. Similar suits could be mounted, counsel for the States and New York City estimated, against "thousands or hundreds or tens" of other defendants fitting the description "large contributors" to carbon-dioxide emissions. Tr. of Oral Arg. 57.

The judgments the plaintiffs would commit to federal judges, in suits that could be filed in any federal district, cannot be reconciled with the decisionmaking scheme Congress enacted. The Second Circuit erred, we hold, in ruling that federal judges may set limits on greenhouse gas emissions in face of a law empowering EPA to set the same limits. . . .

The plaintiffs also sought relief under state law, in particular, the law of each State where the defendants operate power plants. See App. 105, 147. The Second Circuit did not reach the state law claims because it held that federal common law governed. 582 F.3d, at 392; see International Paper Co. v. Ouellette, 479 U.S. 481, 488, 107 S. Ct. 805, 93 L. Ed. 2d 883 (1987) (if a case "should be resolved by reference to federal common law[,] . . . state common law [is] preempted"). In light of our holding that the Clean Air Act displaces federal common law, the availability *vel non* of a state lawsuit depends, *inter alia*, on the preemptive effect of the federal Act. *Id.*, at 489, 491, 497 (holding that the Clean Water Act does not preclude aggrieved individuals from bringing a "nuisance claim pursuant to the law of the source State"). None of the parties have briefed preemption or otherwise addressed the availability of a claim under state nuisance law. We therefore leave the matter open for consideration on remand.

For the reasons stated, we reverse the judgment of the Second Circuit and remand the case for further proceedings consistent with this opinion.

[The concurring opinion of ALITO, J., joined by THOMAS, J., is omitted.]

In a case involving transboundary air pollution problems more conventional in scope than climate change, the Fourth Circuit held in North Carolina *ex rel.* Cooper v. Tennessee Valley Authority, 615 F.3d 291 (4th Cir. 2010), that the Clean Air Act precludes both federal and state common law nuisance claims. Rather than follow the Supreme Court's holding in *Ouellette,* which preserved the common law of a source state in the water pollution context, the Fourth Circuit went out of its way to dismiss nuisance law as lacking "any manageable criteria" to guide transboundary air pollution claims. Id. at 302. In the course of its ruling, the court suggested that all tort law — federal or state — stands irrevocably in tension with a regulatory scheme such as the Clean Air Act, which reflects a "carefully created system for accommodating the need for energy production and the need for clean air." Id. at 296. Allowing common law claims to proceed would result in a "confused patchwork of standards" that might "scuttle the extensive system of anti-pollution mandates that promote clean air." Id. Other circuit courts have split on the question of Clean Air Act preemption of state common law, suggesting that the Supreme Court ultimately will have to address the issue. Compare Comer v. Murphy Oil USA, Inc.,

839 F. Supp. 2d 849 (S.D. Miss. 2012), *aff'd*, 718 F.3d 460 (5th Cir. 2013) (Clean Air Act preempted plaintiffs' state public nuisance claims), with *In re* Methyl Tertiary Butyl Ether Prods. Liab. Litig., 725 F.3d 65 (2d Cir. 2013) (Clean Air Act did not preempt jury's verdict on public nuisance claim).

Meanwhile, the Obama Administration attempted to make good on the faith in the regulatory process expressed by the *American Electric Power* court by promulgating ambitious greenhouse gas emissions rules for utilities under the Clean Air Act. The rules — dubbed the Clean Power Plan — were subject to a variety of statutory and constitutional challenges as of 2016. Representatives of some of the plaintiff parties from the *American Electric Power* litigation have insisted that if any of these court challenges to the Clean Power Plan are successful, then they will revive their climate change nuisance suit given that the Supreme Court's rationale for displacement will no longer rest on a valid premise. Does their view properly interpret the *American Electric Power* opinion?

D. Intergovernmental Liability in the International Context

Within a single nation-state, there typically exists a well-developed system for making and enforcing law. For instance, as shown in the previous section, cross-border disputes between states and their citizens in the United States may be resolved either through federal common law litigation before the Supreme Court or through recourse to standards and requirements promulgated by federal legislation and regulation. At the international level, on the other hand, the system of lawmaking is less well developed. Following the Treaty of Westphalia in the seventeenth century, the modern world has regarded nation-states as the principal, and sometimes solely, cognizable actors on the international plane. Presumptions of sovereignty and self-determination have meant that international law principles typically only bind nation-states if they consent to them, either expressly through a treaty or impliedly through customary practice or adherence to general principles of international law. Although some international law norms are taken to be universally obligatory (and are therefore called peremptory or *jus cogens* norms), the norms still must be enforced through some binding and effective legal mechanism, a practical challenge that remains a foundational problem for the international law system. In the absence of nation-state consent to adjudication before an arbitral tribunal or a standing international court such as the International Court of Justice, even peremptory norms may therefore provide a far "softer" form of law than the most mundane domestic traffic ordinance.

In this regard, one of the most important historical pronouncements on national responsibility for transboundary harm remains the 1941 decision of an international arbitration panel in a dispute involving what was at the time the largest lead and zinc smelting complex in the British Empire, the privately owned factory located at Trail, British Columbia and popularly known as the Trail Smelter. The factory's 400-foot-high stacks sent plumes of smoke down the Columbia River valley into Washington State, where the smoke allegedly caused damage to crops and forests, also privately owned. Aggrieved farmers in the United States persuaded officials in Washington, D.C., to take on their cause, and the Trail Smelter imbroglio became a prominent international dispute. The two nations referred the dispute to a joint commission in 1928, which awarded damages to the United States in 1931 in the amount of $350,000. The countries formalized this obligation in a treaty that was signed and ratified in 1935. See Convention for Settlement of Difficulties Arising from Operation of Smelter at Trail, B.C., 15 April 1935, U.S.T.S. No. 893, reprinted in 30 A.J.I.L. (Supp.)

163. The treaty also established an arbitral tribunal to further adjudicate the parties' dispute. Article III of the treaty set forth the following questions for the tribunal to decide:

> The Tribunal shall finally decide the questions, hereinafter referred to as "the Questions," set forth hereunder, namely:
>
> (1) Whether damage caused by the Trail Smelter in the State of Washington has occurred since the first day of January, 1932, and, if so, what indemnity should be paid therefor?
> (2) In the event of the answer to the first part of the preceding Question being in the affirmative, whether the Trail Smelter should be required to refrain from causing damage in the State of Washington in the future and, if so, to what extent?
> (3) In the light of the answer to the preceding Question, what measures or regime, if any, should be adopted or maintained by the Trail Smelter?
> (4) What indemnity or compensation, if any, should be paid on account of any decision or decisions rendered by the Tribunal pursuant to the next two preceding Questions?

The tribunal eventually issued two precedent-setting decisions regarding international transboundary harm, the first of which awarded further damages to the United States and issued preliminary protective measures against the Canadian factory. The second decision then finally resolved the questions posed to the tribunal under the treaty.

Trail Smelter Arbitral Tribunal

Decision Reported on March 11, 1941, to the Government of the United States of America and to the Government of the Dominion of Canada, Under the Convention Signed April 15, 1935

This Tribunal is constituted under, and its powers are derived from and limited by, the Convention between the United States of America and the Dominion of Canada signed at Ottawa, April 15, 1935, duly ratified by the two parties, and ratifications exchanged at Ottawa, August 3, 1935 (hereinafter termed "the Convention"). . . .

As between the two countries involved, each has an equal interest that if a nuisance is proved, the indemnity to damaged parties for proven damage shall be just and adequate and each has also an equal interest that unproven or unwarranted claims shall not be allowed. For, while the United States' interests may now be claimed to be injured by the operations of a Canadian corporation, it is equally possible that at some time in the future Canadian interests might be claimed to be injured by an American corporation. As has well been said: "It would not be to the advantage of the two countries concerned that industrial effort should be prevented by exaggerating the interests of the agricultural community. Equally, it would not be to the advantage of the two countries that the agricultural community should be oppressed to the interest of industry." . . .

As has been said above, the report of the International Joint Commission (1(g)) contained a definition of the word "damage" excluding "occasional damage that may be caused by SO_2 fumes being carried across the international boundary in air pockets or by reason of unusual atmospheric conditions," as far, at least, as the duty of the Smelter to reduce the presence of that gas in the air was concerned.

The correspondence between the two Governments during the interval between that report and the conclusion of the Convention shows that the problem thus raised was what parties had primarily in mind in drafting Question No. 2. Whilst Canada wished for the adoption of the report, the United States stated that it could not acquiesce in the proposal to limit consideration of damage to damage as defined in the report (letter of the Minister of the United States of America at Ottawa to the Secretary of State for External Affairs of the Dominion of Canada, January 30, 1934). The view was expressed that "so long as fumigations occur in the State of Washington with such frequency, duration and intensity as to cause injury," the conditions afforded "grounds of complaint on the part of the United States, regardless of the remedial works . . . and regardless of the effect of those works" (same letter).

The first problem which arises is whether the question should be answered on the basis of the law followed in the United States or on the basis of international law. The Tribunal, however, finds that this problem need not be solved here as the law followed in the United States in dealing with the quasi-sovereign rights of the States of the Union, in the matter of air pollution, whilst more definite, is in conformity with the general rules of international law.

Particularly in reaching its conclusions as regards this question as well as the next, the Tribunal has given consideration to the desire of the high contracting parties "to reach a solution just to all parties concerned."

As Professor Eagleton puts in (Responsibility of States in International Law, 1928, p. 80): "A State owes at all times a duty to protect other States against injurious acts by individuals from within its jurisdiction." A great number of such general pronouncements by leading authorities concerning the duty of a State to respect other States and their territory have been presented to the Tribunal. These and many others have been carefully examined. International decisions, in various matters, from the Alabama case onward, and also earlier ones, are based on the same general principle, and, indeed, this principle, as such, has not been questioned by Canada. But the real difficulty often arises rather when it comes to determine what, *pro subjectamaterie*, is deemed to constitute an injurious act. . . .

No case of air pollution dealt with by an international tribunal has been brought to the attention of the Tribunal nor does the Tribunal know of any such case. The nearest analogy is that of water pollution. But, here also, no decision of an international tribunal has been cited or has been found.

There are, however, as regards both air pollution and water pollution, certain decisions of the Supreme Court of the United States which may legitimately be taken as a guide in this field of international law, for it is reasonable to follow by analogy, in international cases, precedents established by that court in dealing with controversies between States of the Union or with other controversies concerning the quasi-sovereign rights of such States, where no contrary rule prevails in international law and no reason for rejecting such precedents can be adduced from the limitations of sovereignty inherent in the Constitution of the United States.

In the suit of the State of Missouri v. the State of Illinois (200 U.S. 496, 521) concerning the pollution, within the boundaries of Illinois, of the Illinois River, an affluent of the Mississippi flowing into the latter where it forms the boundary between that State and Missouri, an injunction was refused. "Before this court ought to intervene," said the court, "the case should be of serious magnitude, clearly and fully proved, and the principle to be applied should be one which the court is prepared deliberately to maintain against all considerations on the other side. (See Kansas v. Colorado, 185 U.S. 125.)" The court found that the practice complained of was general along the shores of the Mississippi

River at that time, that it was followed by Missouri itself and that thus a standard was set up by the defendant which the claimant was entitled to invoke.

As the claims of public health became more exacting and methods for removing impurities from the water were perfected, complaints ceased. It is significant that Missouri sided with Illinois when the other riparians of the Great Lakes' system sought to enjoin it to desist from diverting the waters of that system into that of the Illinois and Mississippi for the very purpose of disposing of the Chicago sewage.

In the more recent suit of the State of New York against the State of New Jersey (256 U.S. 296, 309), concerning the pollution of New York Bay, the injunction was also refused for lack of proof, some experts believing that the plans which were in dispute would result in the presence of "offensive odors and unsightly deposits;" other equally reliable experts testifying that they were confidently of the opinion that the waters would be sufficiently purified. The court, referring to Missouri v. Illinois, said: ". . . the burden upon the State of New York of sustaining the allegations of its bill is much greater than that imposed upon a complainant in an ordinary suit between private parties. Before this court can be moved to exercise its extraordinary power under the Constitution to control the conduct of one State at the suit of another, the threatened invasion of rights must be of serious magnitude and it must be established by clear and convincing evidence."

What the Supreme Court says there of its power under the Constitution equally applies to the extraordinary power granted this Tribunal under the Convention. What is true between States of the Union is, at least, equally true concerning the relations between the United States and the Dominion of Canada.

In another recent case concerning water pollution (283 U.S. 473), the complainant was successful. The City of New York was enjoined, at the request of the State of New Jersey, to desist, within a reasonable time limit, from the practice of disposing of sewage by dumping it into the sea, a practice which was injurious to the coastal waters of New Jersey in the vicinity of her bathing resorts.

In the matter of air pollution itself, the leading decisions are those of the Supreme Court in the State of Georgia v. Tennessee Copper Company and Ducktown Sulphur, Copper and Iron Company, Limited. Although dealing with a suit against private companies, the decisions were on questions cognate to those here at issue. Georgia stated that it had in vain sought relief from the State of Tennessee, on whose territory the smelters were located, and the court defined the nature of the suit by saying: "This is a suit by a State for an injury to it in its capacity of quasi-sovereign. In that capacity, the State has an interest independent of and behind the titles of its citizens, in all the earth and air within its domain."

On the question whether an injunction should be granted or not, the court said (206 U.S. 230):

> It (the State) has the last word as to whether its mountains shall be stripped of their forests and its inhabitants shall breathe pure air. . . . It is not lightly to be presumed to give up quasi-sovereign rights for pay and . . . if that be its choice, it may insist that an infraction of them shall be stopped. This court has not quite the same freedom to balance the harm that will be done by an injunction against that of which the plaintiff complains, that it would have in deciding between two subjects of a single political power. Without excluding the considerations that equity always takes into account . . . it is a fair and reasonable demand on the part of a sovereign that the air over its territory should not be polluted on a great scale by sulphurous acid gas, that the forests on its mountains, be they better or worse, and whatever domestic destruction they may have suffered, should not be further destroyed or

> threatened by the act of persons beyond its control, that the crops and orchards on its hills should not be endangered from the same source. . . . Whether Georgia, by insisting upon this claim, is doing more harm than good to her own citizens, is for her to determine. The possible disaster to those outside the State must be accepted as a consequence of her standing upon her extreme rights.

Later on, however, when the court actually framed an injunction, in the case of the Ducktown Company (237 U.S. 474, 477) (an agreement on the basis of an annual compensation was reached with the most important of the two smelters, the Tennessee Copper Company), they did not go beyond a decree "adequate to diminish materially the present probability of damage to its (Georgia's) citizens."

Great progress in the control of fumes has been made by science in the last few years and this progress should be taken into account.

The Tribunal, therefore, finds that the above decisions, taken as a whole, constitute an adequate basis for its conclusions, namely, that, under the principles of international law, as well as of the law of the United States, no State has the right to use or permit the use of its territory in such a manner as to cause injury by fumes in or to the territory of another or the properties or persons therein, when the case is of serious consequence and the injury is established by clear and convincing evidence.

The decisions of the Supreme Court of the United States which are the basis of these conclusions are decisions in equity and a solution inspired by them, together with the regime hereinafter prescribed, will, in the opinion of the Tribunal, be "just to all parties concerned," as long, at least, as the present conditions in the Columbia River Valley continue to prevail.

Considering the circumstances of the case, the Tribunal holds that the Dominion of Canada is responsible in international law for the conduct of the Trail Smelter. Apart from the undertakings in the Convention, it is, therefore, the duty of the Government of the Dominion of Canada to see to it that this conduct should be in conformity with the obligation of the Dominion under international law as herein determined.

The Tribunal, therefore, answers Question No. 2 as follows: (2) So long as the present conditions in the Columbia River Valley prevail, the Trail Smelter shall be required to refrain from causing any damage through fumes in the State of Washington; the damage herein referred to and its extent being such as would be recoverable under the decisions of the courts of the United States in suits between private individuals. The indemnity for such damages should be fixed in such manner as the Governments, acting under Article XI of the Convention, should agree upon. . . .

When the U.S. Congress passed amendments to the Clean Air Act in 1978, it praised the model of bilateral cooperation between Canada and the United States that was exemplified by the Trail Smelter experience and that traced back to the Boundary Waters Treaty of 1909. See 92 Stat. 990 (1978) (observing that "[t]he United States and Canada have a tradition of cooperative resolution of issues of mutual concern which is nowhere more evident than in the environmental area"). Yet in 2003, the U.S. Environmental Protection Agency (EPA) issued a unilateral administrative order to Teck Cominco Metals, Ltd., the present owner and operator of the Trail Smelter facility, directing the company to conduct a feasibility study for the clean-up and remediation of sites located in the United States that had been damaged by discharged waste from the Trail Smelter. The government of Canada swiftly protested this action and Teck Cominco objected that it was not subject to the federal hazardous waste statute under which the EPA claimed its authority to issue the order. A federal district court later sided with the EPA, holding that the federal statute could apply to Teck Cominco. See Pakootas v. Teck Cominco Metals, Ltd., 35 Envtl. L. Rep. 20,083 (E.D. Wash. 2004); see also Pakootas v. Teck Cominco Metals, Ltd., 452 F.3d 1066 (9th Cir. 2006) (upholding the district court). On June 2, 2006, however, the EPA announced that it had agreed to a settlement with Teck Cominco whereby the company agreed to conduct the site feasibility study with a broad consultative role for the Canadian government, affected states, and Indian tribes, but without direct application of the federal statute.

Reviewing this latest chapter in the now century-long Trail Smelter dispute, one commentator warned that the application of U.S. domestic law across borders to foreign corporations:

> . . . may disrupt border area industrial zones, force movement of employers (and jobs) not only from the region but from the country itself, or induce financial failure for companies unable to move. At a minimum, it leaves companies operating in our neighbors to the north and south uncertain about which environmental regime should govern their operations. Disruption of the border economies may in turn produce a loss of revenue and jobs in the U.S. portions of the border areas, as revenue declines from spending by those who had been residing and working just across the border. The lack of jobs in less developed areas may in turn lead to increased illegal immigration to the United States. Transboundary pollution must be addressed, but it is not the only transboundary problem between nations, and often not the most urgent. Nor can it be addressed without considering the sovereign rights of both nations. Unilateral application of U.S. environmental law in Canada and Mexico ignores the very reasons why the United States and its neighbors have insisted in the past that complex transboundary issues be addressed through multilateral discussions.

Gerald F. George, Environmental Enforcement Across National Borders, 21 Nat. Res. & Env. 3, 7 (2006).

The debate over unilateral versus multilateral approaches to transboundary disputes can be powerfully examined in light of the decisions of the International Court of Justice addressing complaints brought by Australia and New Zealand regarding atmospheric testing of nuclear weapons by France during the Cold War. France conducted these tests at a location in the South Pacific near enough to Australia, New Zealand, Fiji, and other nations to create a risk of fallout damage in their territories. In 1973, the court ordered France as a provisional measure to cease nuclear tests causing radioactive fallout in the Australian and New Zealand territories. It also ordered the parties to prepare written briefs addressed to the question of whether the court had jurisdiction to entertain the dispute between the various nation-states. Dissenting from the provisional measure adopted at the request of Australia, Judge Ignacio-Pinto wrote:

> In my opinion, international law is now, and will be for some time to come, a law in process of formation, and one which contains only a concept of responsibility after the fact, unlike municipal law, in which the possible range of responsibility can be determined with precision a priori. Whatever those who hold the opposite view may think, each State is free to act as it thinks fit within the limits of its sovereignty, and in the event of genuine damage or injury, if the said damage is clearly established, it owes reparation to the State having suffered that damage. . . .

> By directing the French Government to "avoid nuclear tests causing the deposit of radioactive fall-out in Australian territory," the Court certainly oversteps the limits of its powers, and appears thereby to be innovating in declaring unlawful the exercise of a right which up to now has been regarded as falling within the sovereignty of a State. The Court is not yet a supreme court as in municipal law, nor does it have legislative powers, and it has no right to hand down a decision against a State which by a formal declaration excludes its jurisdiction over disputes concerning activities connected with national defence.
>
> . . . The point is that if the Court were to adopt the contention of the Australian request it would be near to endorsing a novel conception in international law whereby States would be forbidden to engage in any risk-producing activity within the area of their own territorial sovereignty; but that would amount to granting any State the right to intervene preventively in the national affairs of other States. . . .
>
> In the present state of international law, the 'apprehension' of a State, or 'anxiety', 'the risk of atomic radiation', do not in my view suffice to substantiate some higher law imposed on all States and limiting their sovereignty as regards atmospheric nuclear tests. Those who hold the opposite view may perhaps represent the figureheads or vanguard of a system of gradual development of international law, but it is not admissible to take their wishes into account in order to modify the present state of the law.
>
> . . . Consequently, in my opinion, there is no reason to accede to the request for the indication of provisional measures. The question of the illegality of nuclear tests exceeds the competence of the Court and becomes, as I see it, a political problem. . . .

During the pendency of the proceedings at the International Court of Justice, France declared its intention to switch from atmospheric to underground testing of nuclear weapons in the South Pacific. In light of France's declaration, the court determined that it no longer had jurisdiction to hear the merits of New Zealand's complaint. Several judges issued concurring and dissenting opinions that delved more deeply into the role of international law in defining and adjudicating transboundary wrongs. Excerpts follow:

Nuclear Tests (New Zealand v. France)

International Court of Justice, December 20, 1974, General List No. 59

Separate Opinion of Judge Petrén

[W]hat is first and foremost necessary is to ask oneself whether atmospheric tests of nuclear weapons are, generally speaking, governed by norms of international law, or whether they belong to a highly political domain where the international norms of legality or illegality are still at the gestation stage. It is quite true that disputes concerning the interpretation or application of rules of international law may possess great political importance without thereby losing their inherent character of being legal disputes. It is nonetheless necessary to distinguish between disputes revolving on norms of international law and tensions between States caused by measures taken in a domain not yet governed by international law.

In that connection, I feel it may be useful to recall what has happened in the domain of human rights. In the relatively recent past, it was generally considered that the treatment given by a State to its own subjects did not come within the purview of international law. Even the most outrageous violations of human rights committed by a State towards its own nationals could not have formed the subject of an application by another State to an international judicial organ. Any such application would have been declared inadmissible and could not have given rise to any consideration of the truth of the facts alleged by the applicant State. . . . It is only an evolution subsequent to the Second World War which has made the duty of States to respect the human rights of all, including their own nationals, an obligation under international law towards all States members of the international community. . . .

We can see a similar evolution taking place today in an allied field, that of the protection of the environment. Atmospheric nuclear tests, envisaged as the bearers of a particularly serious risk of environmental pollution, are a source of acute anxiety for present-day mankind, and it is only natural that efforts should be made on the international plane to erect legal barriers against that kind of test. . . . In the present case, the Application is based upon an allegation that France's nuclear tests in the Pacific have given rise to radio-active fall-out on the territory of New Zealand. The New Zealand Government considers that its sovereignty has thereby been infringed in a manner contrary to international law. As there is no treaty link between New Zealand and France in the matter of nuclear tests, the Application presupposes the existence of a rule of customary international law whereby States are prohibited from causing, through atmospheric nuclear tests, the deposit of radio-active fall-out on the territory of other States. It is therefore the existence or non-existence of such a customary rule which has to be determined.

. . . [O]ne may ask what has been the attitude of the numerous States on whose territory radio-active fall-out from the atmospheric tests of the nuclear Powers has been deposited and continues to be deposited. Have they, generally speaking, protested to these Powers, pointing out that their tests were in breach of customary international law? I do not observe that such has been the case. The resolutions passed in the General Assembly of the United Nations cannot be regarded as equivalent to legal protests made by one State to another and concerning concrete instances. They indicate the existence of a strong current of opinion in favour of proscribing atmospheric nuclear tests. That is a political task of the highest urgency, but it is one which remains to be accomplished. Thus the claim submitted to the Court by New Zealand belongs to the political domain and is situated outside the framework of international law as it exists today.

I consider, consequently, that the Application of New Zealand was, from the very institution of proceedings, devoid of any object on which the Court could give a decision. . . .

(Signed) Sture PETRÉN.

JOINT DISSENTING OPINION OF JUDGES ONYEAMA, DILLARD, JIMENEZ DE ARECHAGA AND SIR HUMPHREY WALDOCK

. . . New Zealand's submission refers, in general terms, to nuclear tests 'that give rise to radio-active fall-out'. In making a declaration like the one requested, the Court might have had to pronounce generally on the legality of tests conducted by France in the South Pacific region, which gave rise to radio-active fall-out. The judicial declaration of illegality asked for in the submission would thus have implications not merely for future, but also for past tests, in respect of which the New Zealand Government reserved the right to hold the French Government responsible for any damage or losses. This would certainly include the tests conducted in 1973 and 1974 in disregard of the Court's interim order.

. . . New Zealand continues to ask the Court to declare that atmospheric nuclear tests are contrary to international law and is prepared to argue and develop that point. France, on its part, as recognized in the Judgment, maintains the view that 'its nuclear experiments do not contravene any subsisting provision of international law'. In announcing the cessation of the tests in 1975 the French Government, according to the Judgment, did not recognize that France was bound by any rule of international law to terminate its tests.

Consequently, the legal dispute between the Parties, far from having disappeared, still persists. A judgment by the Court on the legality of nuclear atmospheric tests in the South Pacific region would thus pronounce on a legal question in which the Parties are in conflict as to their respective rights.

. . . With regard to the right said to be inherent in New Zealand's territorial sovereignty, we think that she is justified in considering that her legal interest in the defence of that right is direct. Whether or not she can succeed in persuading the Court that the particular right which she claims falls within the scope of the principle of territorial sovereignty, she clearly has a legal interest to litigate that issue in defence of her territorial sovereignty. With regard to the rights to be free from atmospheric tests, said to be possessed by New Zealand in common with other States, the question of 'legal interest' again appears to us to be part of the general legal merits of the case. If the materials adduced by New Zealand were to convince the Court of the existence of a general rule of international law, prohibiting atmospheric nuclear tests, the Court would at the same time have to determine what is the precise character and content of that rule and, in particular, whether it confers a right on every State individually to prosecute a claim to secure respect for the rule. In short, the question of 'legal interest' cannot be separated from the substantive legal issue of the existence and scope of the alleged rule of customary international law. . . .

. . . Since we are of the opinion that the Court has jurisdiction and that the case submitted to the Court discloses no ground on which New Zealand's claims should be considered inadmissible, we consider that the Applicant had a right under the Statute and the Rules to have the case adjudicated. This right the Judgment takes away from the Applicant by a procedure and by reasoning which, to our regret, we can only consider as lacking any justification in the Statute and Rules or in the practice and jurisprudence of the Court.

(Signed) Charles D. ONYEAMA.
(Signed) Hardy C. DILLARD.
(Signed) E. JIMENEZ DE ARECHAGA.
(Signed) H. WALDOCK.

The *Trail Smelter* reports and the International Court of Justice rulings in the *Nuclear Test Cases* remain among the most important — and only — international law pronouncements on nation-state liability for transboundary harm. The sporadic and incomplete nature of international law in this regard led the International Law Commission, a body of the United Nations, to commence a project to identify an appropriate set of principles on the subject. Some 29 years later, the International Law Commission issued its Draft Principles on the Allocation of Loss in the Case of Transboundary Harm Arising Out of Hazardous Activities (2006), which apply to "transboundary damage caused by hazardous activities not prohibited by international law," and which seek to "ensure prompt and adequate compensation to victims of transboundary damage." The Draft Principles establish a strict liability standard for any transboundary damage resulting from hazardous activities. "Damage" is defined in the Draft Principles as significant damage caused to persons, property, or the environment, and includes specifically "loss of life or personal injury; loss of, or damage to, property, including property which forms part of the cultural heritage; loss or damage by impairment of the environment; the costs of reasonable measures of reinstatement of the property, or environment, including natural resources; the costs of reasonable response measures." Hazardous activity is defined as "an activity which involves a risk of causing significant harm."

With that framework established, Principle 4 of the Draft Principles then obligates nation-states in the following manner:

1. Each State should take all necessary measures to ensure that prompt and adequate compensation is available for victims of transboundary damage caused by hazardous activities located within its territory or otherwise under its jurisdiction or control.
2. These measures should include the imposition of liability on the operator or, where appropriate, other person or entity. Such liability should not require proof of fault. Any conditions, limitations or exceptions to such liability shall be consistent with draft principle 3.
3. These measures should also include the requirement on the operator or, where appropriate, other person or entity, to establish and maintain financial security such as insurance, bonds or other financial guarantees to cover claims of compensation.
4. In appropriate cases, these measures should include the requirement for the establishment of industry-wide funds at the national level.
5. In the event that the measures under the preceding paragraphs are insufficient to provide adequate compensation, the State of origin should also ensure that additional financial resources are made available.

Principle 6 also requires nation-states to "provide their domestic judicial and administrative bodies with the necessary jurisdiction and competence and ensure that these bodies have prompt, adequate and effective remedies available in the event of transboundary damage caused by hazardous activities located within their territory or otherwise under their jurisdiction or control."

Given the lack of more concrete progress on multilateral liability negotiations and the continuing problem of transboundary pollution, the American Bar Association and the Canadian Bar Association jointly prepared a Draft Treaty on a Regime of Equal Access and Remedy in Cases of Transfrontier Pollution for adoption by the United States and Canada. See Joint Bar Association Proposal for Canadian-U.S. Dispute Settlement, 74 Am. J. Int'l L. 454 (1980). Article 2 of the Draft Treaty provides:

> 2(a) The Country of origin shall ensure that any natural or legal person resident in the exposed Country, who has suffered transfrontier pollution, shall at least receive equivalent treatment to that afforded in the Country of origin, in cases of domestic pollution or the risk thereof and in comparable circumstances, to persons of equivalent condition or status in the Country of origin.
>
> (b) From a procedural standpoint, this treatment shall include but shall not be limited to the right to take part, or have resort to all administrative and judicial procedures existing within the Country of origin, in order to prevent domestic pollution, to have it abated, and/or to obtain compensation for the damage caused.

Not to be outdone, the U.S. National Conference of Commissioners on Uniform State Laws and the Uniform Law Conference of Canada also have engaged in an effort to establish principles of liability for transboundary harm. The model statute that the two associations recommend, the Uniform Transboundary Pollution Reciprocal Access Act, is intended for adoption by states and provinces of the United States and Canada in lieu of a bilateral treaty. The Uniform Act, which has been adopted by several states and provinces, provides:

> A person who suffers, or is threatened with, injury to his person or property in a reciprocating jurisdiction caused by pollution originating, or that may originate, in this jurisdiction has the same rights to relief with respect to the injury or threatened injury, and may enforce those rights in this jurisdiction as if the injury or threatened injury occurred in this jurisdiction.

Do these proposals represent a solution to the problem of transboundary harm that is preferable to the International Law Commission's more ambitious and substantive multilateral treaty approach? Is a principle of equal national treatment between resident and non-resident plaintiffs more likely to receive widespread international endorsement than a specific standard of liability?

Problem 44

Recall the facts of Problem 30 from Chapter 5, above, at pp. 477-480, concerning the challenge of responding to climate change through the tort law system. Assume that you now have been approached by leaders of an intergovernmental organization representing the interests of several small island developing nations primarily located in the Pacific Ocean. These nations recently discussed issues of particular concern to them at the United Nations–sponsored International Meeting to Review the Implementation of the Programme of Action for the Sustainable Development of Small Island Developing States, which was held in Mauritius in 2005 and was attended by 18 presidents, vice presidents and prime ministers, some 60 ministers, representatives from 15 United Nations or multilateral agencies, and nearly 2,000 delegates, civil society representatives, and journalists from 114 countries.

At this meeting, the nations adopted the Mauritius Strategy, a policy document outlining key considerations and approaches for small island developing nations as they seek to diversify and expand their economies, integrate into the world trading system, improve the health and education of their citizens, and maintain a sustainable level of environmental impact. The document emphasizes that small island developing nations "are located among the most vulnerable regions in the world in relation to the intensity and frequency of natural and environmental disasters and their increasing impact, and face disproportionately high economic, social and environmental consequences." Moreover, these nations "believe that they are already experiencing major adverse effects of climate change" and that "adaptation to adverse impacts of climate change and sea-level rise remains a major priority" for them. Because scientists anticipate rising sea levels and increases in severe weather conditions from climate change, small island nations face particular challenges and vulnerabilities. Indeed, some nations may be completely submerged in the coming decades, rendering their ancestral territories endangered. Even before that dire outcome occurs, many small island nations will become uninhabitable due to intrusion of saltwater into their scarce freshwater resources.

The small island nation leaders who have approached you seek your advice in developing litigation strategies. They are frustrated by the lack of progress in pursuing stringent climate change policies through the multilateral treaty process, which has been plagued by the failure of large greenhouse gas emitters such as the United States and China to meaningfully participate. What causes of action might these nations bring? Against what defendants? In what forum? In pursuit of what form of relief?

Appendix

Introduction to Economic Analysis of Tort Law

Richard A. Posner, Economic Analysis of Law

3-9, 11-16 (9th ed. 2014)

§1.1 Fundamental Concepts

Many lawyers still think that economics is the forbiddingly mathematized study of inflation, unemployment, business cycles, and other macroeconomic phenomena remote from the day-to-day concerns of the legal system. Actually the domain of economics is much broader. As conceived in this book, economics is the science of rational choice in a world — our world — in which resources are limited in relation to human wants. The task of economics, so defined, is to explore the implications of assuming that man is a rational maximizer of his ends in life, his satisfactions — what we shall call his "self-interest."

Rational maximization must not be confused with conscious calculation, however. Economics is not a theory about consciousness. Behavior is rational when it conforms to the model of rational choice, whatever the state of mind of the chooser. . . . And "self-interest" should not be confused with selfishness; the happiness (or for that matter the misery) of other people may be a part of one's satisfactions. To avoid this confusion, economists generally prefer to speak of "utility" than of self-interest.

Central to this book is the further assumption that a person is a rational utility maximizer in *all* areas of life, not just in his "economic" affairs, that is, not only when engaged in buying and selling in explicit markets. This idea — which is vital to economic analysis of law because so much of law concerns nonmarket behavior (such as crime, marriage and divorce, accidents, and bequests) — goes back to Jeremy Bentham in the eighteenth and early nineteenth century, but received little attention from economists until the work of Gary Becker in the 1950s and 1960s.

[The concept of man as a rational maximizer of his self-interest] implies that people respond to incentives — that if a person's surroundings change in such a way that he could increase his satisfaction by altering his behavior, he will do so. From this proposition derive four fundamental principles of economics that organize the analysis of law in this book. They are the Law of Demand; opportunity cost; the tendency of resources to gravitate toward their most valuable uses; and equilibrium.

1. The Law of Demand posits an inverse relation between price charged and quantity demanded. If the price of steak rises by 50¢ a pound, and other prices remain unchanged, a steak will now cost the consumer more, relatively, than it did before. The rational self-interested consumer will react by investigating (at least if this can be done at a low cost in time and effort) the possibility of substituting goods that he preferred less when steak was

at its old price but that are more attractive now because they are cheaper relative to steak. Many consumers will continue to buy as much steak as before; for them, other goods are poor substitutes even at somewhat lower relative prices (or the costs of searching for substitutes may exceed the benefits). But some purchasers will reduce their purchases of steak and substitute other meats (or other foods, or different products altogether), with the result that the total quantity demanded by purchasers, and so the amount produced, will decline.

. . . The Law of Demand doesn't operate just on goods with explicit prices. Unpopular teachers sometimes try to increase class enrollment by raising the average grade of the students in their courses, thereby reducing the "price" of the course to the students and so inducing them to substitute the unpopular teacher's class for another class. The convicted criminal who has served his sentence is said to have "paid his debt to society," and an economist would find the metaphor apt. Punishment is, from the criminal's standpoint (but not society's, unless the punishment takes the form of a fine), the price that society charges for a criminal offense. The economist predicts that an increase in either the severity of the punishment or the likelihood of its imposition will raise the price of crime and therefore reduce its incidence. The criminal will be encouraged to substitute other activity. Economists call nonpecuniary prices, such as disutility imposed by a prison sentence, "shadow prices."

2. The consumers in our steak example were assumed to be trying to maximize their utility (happiness, pleasure, satisfactions). The same is true of the producers of beef, though in the case of sellers (apart from nonprofits and government agencies) one usually speaks of profit maximization rather than of utility maximization. Sellers seek to maximize the difference between their costs and their sales revenues, but for the moment we are interested only in the lowest price that a rational self-interested seller would charge. That minimum is the price that the resources consumed in making (and selling) the seller's product would command in their next best useher than of utility maximization. Sellers seek out means by the cost of a good, and suggests why (subject to some exceptions that need not trouble us here) a rational seller would not sell below cost. For example, the cost of manufacturing a lawn mower is the price the manufacturer must pay for the capital and labor consumed in making it. That price must exceed the price at which the resources could have been sold to the next highest bidder, because if the manufacturer hadn't been willing to beat that price he would not have been the high bidder and would not have obtained the resources. The economic concept of cost (opportunity cost) is the second fundamental principle of economics.

A corollary of the notion of cost as alternative price is that a cost is incurred only when someone is denied the use of a resource. Since I can breathe as much air as I want without depriving anyone of any of the air he wants, no one will pay me to relinquish my air to him; therefore air is costless. . . .

The most celebrated application of the concept of opportunity cost in the economic analysis of law is the Coase Theorem. The theorem, slightly oversimplified . . . is that if transactions are costless, the initial assignment of a property right will not affect the ultimate use of the property. Suppose a farmer has the legal right to grow crops free from damage from locomotive sparks, and that it is a property right — that is, a right to exclude entry (including entry of sparks emitted by locomotives) upon his land, enforceable by an injunction or perhaps even a criminal penalty for trespass — rather than just a right to be compensated for damage. Assume that his crops are worth $100 and are flammable, that the value to the railroad of unimpeded use of its right-of-way is $120, but that at a cost of $110 the railroad can install spark arresters that will eliminate the fire hazard. On these assumptions, plus the further assumption that unless the railroad installs spark arresters its locomotives are sure to destroy the farmer's crops, the real value of the crops to the farmer is not

$100 but somewhere between $100 and $110, since at any price above $110 the railroad would install spark arresters rather than buy the farmer's property but at any price below $110 the railroad would buy the property. The farmer is better off selling his property right to the railroad at a price between $100 and $110; he will do this because the railroad will buy at a price in that range; and as a result his land will be shifted into some fire-insensitive use, just as if the railroad had owned it in the first place. If he fails to sell, his crops will be destroyed, and he will be compensated only for the lost value, $100.

Now suppose that instead of the farmer[] having the right to grow crops free from damage from locomotive sparks, the railroad has the right to the unimpeded use of its right-of-way. Because the farmer's crops are worth less than the railroad's cost of installing spark arresters, as before the locomotive will spew sparks and the farmer's land will be shifted into some fire-insensitive use. Thus, the initial assignment of property rights, whether to the railroad or to the farmer, will not affect the ultimate use to which the property will be put; in either event it will be put to its most productive use, namely a fire-insensitive use. The initial assignment of rights will affect the distribution of wealth but not the allocation of resources. Stated differently, the opportunity cost of the farmer's crops exceed their value; for the crops are an impediment to a more valuable economic activity, namely railroading with spark emission. The land is worth more to the railroad without crops on it than to the farmer with crops on it. . . .

"Equilibrium" (about which more shortly) means a stable point, that is, a point at which, unless the conditions of demand or supply change, there is no incentive for sellers to alter price or output. . . .

[3.] The significance of the concept of equilibrium is that it causes economists to think hard about the conditions that prevent resources from gravitating to their most valuable use and staying there indefinitely—conditions that, by driving a wedge between cost and price, create gluts or shortages, and in either case waste economic resources. (For example, if price is above cost, consumers may be induced to substitute products that actually cost society more to produce, but are cheaper because produced in a competitive market, where price equals rather than exceeds cost). Observation that a particular market is not in equilibrium—for example, that there are frequent gluts or shortages, firms undergoing liquidation, sudden layoffs, machinery that becomes obsolete and is junked though it's still in good working order—incites a search for economic or regulatory or even psychological reasons why the market is not in equilibrium and thus failing to allocate resources with maximum efficiency.

4. Resources tend to gravitate toward their most valuable uses if voluntary exchange—a market—is permitted. Why did the manufacturer of lawn mowers in an earlier example pay more for labor and materials than competing users of these resources? Because he thought he could use them more profitably than could competing demanders. By a process of voluntary exchange, resources are shifted to those uses in which the value to consumers, as measured by their willingness to pay, is highest. When resources are being used where their value is highest, or, equivalently, when no reallocation would increase their value, we say they are being employed efficiently. . . .

§1.2 Value, Utility, Efficiency . . .

The previous section bandied about some pretty highly charged words—value, utility, efficiency—about which we need to be more precise.

The economic *value* of a good or service is how much someone is willing to pay for it or, if he has it already, how much money he demands for parting with it. These are not always the same amounts, and this can cause difficulties, which we shall consider later. *Utility* is most commonly used in economics to distinguish an uncertain cost or benefit from a certain one. Utility (more precisely, "expected utility") in this sense is entwined with the concept of risk. Suppose you were asked whether you'd prefer to be given $1 million or a 10 percent chance of $10 million. Probably you would prefer the former, even though the expected value of the two choices is the same: $1 million (= .10 X $10 million). If so, you are risk averse. Risk aversion is a corollary of the principle of diminishing marginal utility of money, which just means that the more money you have, the less additional happiness you would get from another dollar. Suppose you had a net worth of $1 million: Would you be willing to stake it on a 50-50 bet to win $2 million? If not, it means that your first million dollars is worth more to you that a second million would be.

Risk aversion is not a universal phenomenon; gambling illustrates its opposite, risk preference. This is not because one wins big at gambling only by taking risks (for few activities are actually riskless), but because the expected value of a gamble usually is negative. Suppose you're charged $1 for a lottery ticket, and, because a million lottery tickets are sold, the probability of your winning the lottery is one in 1 million. For it to be a fair gamble the prize for winning the lottery would have to be $1 million, because the expected value of a one in a million chance of winning $1 million is $1 (= $1 million x .000001). But in fact the prize will have to be smaller, because otherwise the organizer of the lottery would have no income to cover his expenses; he would collect $1 million in ticket sales and pay out $1 million to the winner. Yet we know that many people buy lottery tickets. . . .

Economists no longer use "utility," as they once did, in the sense it bears in the philosophical theory called "utilitarianism." There "utility" bears the approximate meaning of "happiness" and society is advised to try to maximize average or total human (in some versions human plus animal) happiness. The social goal most emphasized in modern economics is not happiness or utility but the efficient allocation of resources, in a somewhat special sense. Suppose A sells a wood carving to B for $100, both parties have full information, and the transaction has no effect on anyone else. Then the allocation of resources that is brought about by the transaction is said to be Pareto superior to the allocation of resources before the transaction. A Pareto-superior transaction (or "Pareto improvement") is one that makes at least one person better off and no one worse off. In our example, it presumably made both A and B better off, and by assumption it made no one worse off. In other words, the criterion of Pareto superiority is unanimity of all affected persons.

But the conditions for Pareto superiority are rarely encountered in the real world. Most transactions (and if not a single transaction, then a series of like transactions) have effects on third parties, if only by changing the prices of other goods (as noted in the discussion of the concept of equilibrium) or by distressing observers (polygamy, an example famously discussed by John Stuart Mill in *On Liberty*). In the less austere concept of efficiency mainly used in this book — called the Kaldor-Hicks concept of efficiency, or wealth maximization — if A values the wood carving at $50 and B at $120, so that at any price between $50 and $120 the transaction creates a total benefit of $70 (at a price of $100, for example, A considers himself $50 better off and B considers himself $20 better off), it is an efficient transaction, provided that the harm (if any) done to third parties (minus any benefit to them) does not exceed $70. The transaction would not be Pareto superior unless A and B actually compensated the third parties for any harm suffered by them. The Kaldor-Hicks concept is also and suggestively called *potential* Pareto superiority: The winners *could* compensate the losers, whether or not they actually do.

The fact that the conditions for Pareto superiority are rarely satisfied in the real world, yet economists talk quite a bit about efficiency, means that the operating definition of efficiency in economics cannot be Pareto superiority. And in fact when an economist says that free trade or competition or the control of pollution or some other policy or state of the world is efficient, nine times out of ten he means Kaldor-Hicks efficient.

But what if A in our example valued the wood carving at only $70 and B at $120 not because A likes wood carvings less than B — he may like them much more — and not because there is any appealing concept of deservedness that B might invoke to validate his claim to be able to buy the wood carving, but rather because A is destitute and has to sell his wood carving in order to eat, while B, rather than being passionate about wood carvings, merely wants to diversify his enormous wealth by holding a variety of collectibles. These circumstances are not inconsistent with the sale's making both A and B better off; on the contrary, they explain *why* it makes both better off. But the circumstances undermine the moral foundations of a social system oriented to Pareto superiority, let alone potential Pareto superiority, by showing that the pattern of consumption and production is determined by the distribution of wealth. If that distribution is unjust, the pattern of economic activities derived from it will not have a strong claim to be regarded as just either. And insofar as the distribution of wealth is itself largely determined by the market, the justice of the market cannot be derived from some independent notion of the just distribution.

Furthermore, much inequality of wealth reflects sheer luck — the luck of being born in a wealthy country, the luck of being a beneficiary or casualty of unpredictable shifts in consumer demands and labor markets, the luck of inheritance, the luck of financial markets, the luck of whom you know, the luck of your parents' ability and willingness to invest in your human capital. The greater the role of luck in distribution of wealth and economic opportunities, the more difficult it is to defend the existing distribution as just in a strong sense, though it may be just in the weak sense that there is no practicable alternative.

. . . Because economics cannot tell us whether the existing distribution of income and wealth is good or bad, just or unjust, the economist cannot issue mandatory prescriptions for social change. . . .

Guido Calabresi, The Costs of Accidents

26-28, 69-72, 95-96 (1970)

Apart from the requirements of justice, I take it as axiomatic that the principal function of accident law is to reduce the sum of the costs of accidents and the costs of avoiding accidents. (Such incidental benefits as providing a respectable livelihood for a large number of judges, lawyers, and insurance agents are at best beneficent side effects.) This cost, or loss, reduction goal can be divided into three subgoals.

The first is reduction of the number and severity of accidents. This "primary" reduction of accident costs can be attempted in two basic ways. We can seek to forbid specific acts or activities thought to cause accidents, or we can make activities more expensive and thereby less attractive to the extent of the accident costs they cause. These two methods of primary reduction of accident costs are not clearly separable; a number of difficulties of definition will become apparent as we consider them in detail. But the distinction between them is useful because from it flow two very different approaches toward primary reduction of accident costs, the "general deterrence" or market method and the "specific deterrence" or collective method.

The second cost reduction subgoal is concerned with reducing neither the number of accidents nor their degree of severity. It concentrates instead on reducing the societal costs resulting from accidents. I shall attempt to show that the notion that one of the principal functions of accident law is the compensation of victims is really a rather misleading, though occasionally useful, way of stating this "secondary" accident cost reduction goal. The fact that I have termed this compensation notion secondary should in no way be taken as belittling its importance. There is no doubt that the way we provide for accident victims *after* the accident is crucially important and that the real societal costs of accidents can be reduced as significantly here as by taking measures to avoid accidents in the first place. This cost reduction subgoal is secondary only in the sense that it does not come into play until after earlier primary measures to reduce accident costs have failed. . . .

The third subgoal of accident cost reduction is rather Pickwickian but very important nonetheless. It involves reducing the costs of administering our treatment of accidents. It may be termed "tertiary" because its aim is to reduce the costs of achieving primary and secondary cost reduction. But in a very real sense this "efficiency" goal comes first. It tells us to question constantly whether an attempt to reduce accident costs, either by reducing accidents themselves or by reducing their secondary effects, costs more than it saves. By forcing us to ask this, it serves as a kind of general balance wheel to the cost reduction goal. . . .

The crucial thing about the general deterrence approach to accidents is that it does not involve an a priori collective decision as the correct number of accidents. General deterrence implies that accident costs would be treated as one of the many costs we face whenever we do anything. Since we cannot have everything we want, individually or as a society, whenever we choose one thing we give up others. General deterrence attempts to force individuals to consider accident costs in choosing among activities. The problem is getting the best combination of choices available. The general deterrence approach would let the free market or price system tally the choices.

The theoretical basis of general deterrence is not hard to find. The problem posed is simply the old one of allocation of resources which for years has been studied in the branch of economics called welfare economics; the free market solution is the one traditionally given by welfare economics. This solution presupposes certain postulates. The most important of these, and the only one we need consider now, is the notion that no one knows what is best for individuals better than they themselves do. If people want television sets, society should produce television sets; if they want licorice drops, then licorice drops should be made. The proportion of television sets to licorice drops, as well as the way in which each is made, should also be left up to individual choices because, according to the postulate, as long as individuals are adequately informed about the alternatives and as long as the cost to society of giving them what they want is reflected in the cost to the individual, the individual can decide better than anyone else what he wants. Thus, the function of the prices of various goods must be to reflect the relative costs to society of producing them, and if prices perform this function properly, the buyer will cast an informed vote in making his purchases; thus the best combination of choices available will be achieved.

The general deterrence approach treats accident costs as it does any other costs of goods and activities — such as the metal, or the time it takes, to make cars. If all activities reflect the accident costs they "cause," each individual will be able to choose for himself whether an activity is worth the accident costs it "causes." The sum of these choices is, ex hypothesis, the best combination available and will determine the degree to which accident-prone activities are engaged in (if at all), how they are engaged in, and who will engage in them. Failure to include accident costs in the prices of activities will, according to the theory, cause people to choose more accident-prone activities than they would if the prices of these activities made them pay for these accident costs, resulting in more accident costs than we want. Forbidding accident-prone activities *despite* the fact that they can "pay" their costs would, in theory, bring about an equally bad result from the resource allocation point of view. Either way, the postulate that individuals know best for themselves would be violated. . . .

For the theory to make some sense there is no need to postulate a world made up of economic men who consciously consider the relative costs of each different good and the relative pleasure derived from each. If the cost of all automobile accidents were suddenly to be paid out of a general social insurance fund, the expense of owning a car would be a good deal lower than it is now since people would no longer need to worry about buying insurance. The result would be that some people would buy more cars. Perhaps they would be teen-agers who can afford $100 for an old jalopy but who cannot afford — or whose fathers cannot afford — the insurance. Or they might be people who could only afford a second car so long as no added insurance was involved. In any event, the demand for cars would increase, and so would the number of cars produced. Indeed, the effect on car purchases would be much the same as if the government suddenly chose to pay the cost of the steel used by automobile manufacturers and to raise the money out of general taxes. In each case the objection would be the same. In each, an economist would say, resources are misallocated in that goods are produced that the consumer would not want if he had to pay the full extent of their cost to society, whether in terms of the physical components of the product or in terms of the expense of accidents associated with its production and use. . . .

I call the second approach to primary accident cost reduction specific or collective deterrence. At its extreme specific deterrence suggests that all decisions as to accident costs should be made collectively, through a political process. All the benefits and all the costs, including accident costs, of every activity would be evaluated together and a collective decision would be made regarding both how much of each activity should be allowed and the way in which each should be performed. (No one actually considers such a collective view of society either desirable or feasible, just as no one could accept a world of total general deterrence.)

General deterrence, although it cannot avoid collective valuation of accident costs, seeks to value accident costs on as individual a basis as possible. Specific deterrence would occasionally be forced to use the market, but ideally it would rely on the market only as a basis for broader collective judgments. Similarly, it might need to use the market to enforce its decisions, but it would do this only in as limited a way as possible.

In practice, specific deterrence takes a number of forms. It can be seen in a relatively pure form in decisions to bar certain acts or activities altogether. But the approach can be seen to operate even in many situations where no out-and-out bans on activities are imposed. Indeed, whenever accident costs are valued in relation to which activity causes them, a collective decision is implied, not only as to the value of the accident costs to the victim but also as to the value of the "cost-causing" activity or the way in which it was performed. In other words, activities are being collectively judged to be desirable or undesirable and are being subsidized or penalized accordingly. As we shall see, such penalties or subsidies would never be necessary in perfect specific deterrence and imply some use of the market, and hence of general deterrence notions. But they are a long way from the minimal degree of collective decisions that general deterrence, taken as a sole approach, would allow.

There are five major bases for specific deterrence as a goal of accident law. Not all of them would be accepted by everyone, but virtually everyone would accept at least one. The first is simply the antithesis of the basic postulate of general deterrence: individuals do *not* know best for themselves. The second, similar but more limited, is the notion that in deciding how many accident-causing activities we want, comparisons of nonmonetizable "costs" and "benefits" which the market cannot handle must be made. The third is that in making a decision for or against accidents we are not concerned solely with costs, however broadly defined, but must consider moral concepts. The fourth is that the inherent limitations in resource allocation theory, whether described in terms of income distribution, monopoly, or theory of the second best, require some collective decisions. The last is that general deterrence cannot efficiently reach some categories of activities and can almost never reach those very small subcategories of activities that we call acts, and that to reach these in an economically efficient way, collective action is needed.

Table of Cases

Principal cases are indicated by italics. Alphabetization is letter-by-letter (e.g., "Northfolk" precedes "North Star").

Index